POPULAR WRITING IN AMERICA

ROGER STEVENSON
NOVEMBER, 1995

POPULAR WRITING IN AMERICA

THE INTERACTION OF STYLE AND AUDIENCE

FOURTH EDITION

Donald McQuade
University of California, Berkeley

Robert Atwan
Seton Hall University

New York   Oxford
OXFORD UNIVERSITY PRESS
1988

Oxford University Press

Oxford   New York   Toronto
Delhi   Bombay   Calcutta   Madras   Karachi
Petaling Jaya   Singapore   Hong Kong   Tokyo
Nairobi   Dar es Salaam   Cape Town
Melbourne   Auckland

and associated companies in
Beirut   Berlin   Ibadan   Nicosia

LIBRARY OF CONGRESS CATALOGING-IN-PUBLICATION DATA
Popular writing in America.
1. College readers.   2. English language—Rhetoric.
3. American literature.   4. Popular literature—United States.
I. McQuade, Donald.   II. Atwan, Robert.
PE1417.P6 1988   808'.0427   87-20405
ISBN 0-19-505323-0

9 8 7 6 5 4 3 2
Printed in the United States of America
on acid-free paper

For Our Parents

PREFACE

For the fourth edition of *Popular Writing in America,* we made several changes that we trust will once again enhance the book's overall flexibility and usefulness. In response to instructors who would like to pay more attention to expository writing in class, we expanded the sections on "Press" and "Magazines" to include a generous sampling of contemporary essays and articles, featuring selections from such writers as Russell Baker, Sydney Schanberg, Calvin Trillin, Gretel Ehrlich, Anne Hollander, Noel Perrin, and Harry Crews. We have also included more selections from major contemporary nonfiction books in the "Best-Sellers" chapter. These new selections will give teachers a wide range of expository writing to work with, contemporary prose that will provide provocative topics for class discussion and practical models for student composition.

We have also responded to instructors who asked for more argumentative material by including a large cluster of selections on the death penalty and another large cluster on Bernhard Goetz, the well-known New York subway vigilante. These clusters—consisting largely of newspaper editorials—offer a variety of opinion on frequently debated issues and should help stimulate classroom discussion and argumentative essays. In addition, we have included many more discussion questions focusing on the interrelationships between a work's style, subject, and strategy and its intended audience.

As in previous editions, our choices were guided by a principle of interconnectedness that we believe is one of the most important features of the book. Virtually every selection in *Popular Writing in America* is connected either stylistically or thematically with one or more of the other selections. An expanded "Table of Linked Selections" follows the "Rhetorical Table of Contents" and will encourge students to discover the different ways the same subject can be treated by different writers or by different media (for example, how staff writers for *Time* and *Newsweek* handled the space shuttle disaster in January 1986, or how a major author like Stephen Crane used his personal experience of a disaster at sea to write both a newspaper report and a classic American short story).

We want to remind readers that our selections are not meant to serve only as models for student compositions. The selections are intended in part to generate lively and productive discussions about writing and to help students become more analytically familiar with the diversity of styles and strategies that develop within a contemporary system of communications increasingly dependent on corporate enterprise, mass audiences, interlocking media industries, and vast outlays of money. Few acts of writing—and surely student compositions are no exception—exist completely outside of competitive, socioeconomic considerations. We assume that the more conscious students are of the public and commercial pressures behind a piece of writing (pressures that can be felt *in* the writing, whether an advertisement, news item, magazine article, best-seller, or script), the more sensitive they will become to whatever particular commercial or institutional styles or "voices" they may inadvertently be endorsing in their own writing. In order to make this particular interaction of style and audience dramatically visible to students, we have added a considerable number of selections dealing with the ways in which mass-media artists and artifacts determine the shape of our consumer culture.

An awareness of how one sounds is crucial for all effective writing. "Whom or what does the writer sound like here?" and "What sort of reader does the writer imagine here?" are questions worth asking of any kind of writing, be it the work of a professional or a student, be it inspired or required. Many contemporary writers (see for example the selections from Norman Mailer, Joan Didion, and Tom Wolfe) depend on an audience critically alert to the ways in which their sentences assimilate, parody, and challenge the highly competitive languages of the mass-communication industries. The work of such writers reminds us that practical matters of style and audience remain vital topics in any writing curriculum.

In general, most of the changes we made for this edition—more newspaper editorials and feature articles, a greater range of recent magazine pieces, and more selections from best-selling nonfiction—represent our considered responses to the many instructors throughout the country who have used *Popular Writing in America* and have generously suggested specific ways they thought the book could be improved. We hope that our decisions have resulted in a stronger, more practical book—one that will be welcomed by those who have worked with the book before as well as by those who will try it for the first time.

ACKNOWLEDGMENTS

The continued success of *Popular Writing in America,* as with any book in its fourth edition, depends on the generous advice of the colleagues across the country who work with it in class each year. For this edition, we would like to thank in particular Marjorie Rush of Concordia College, who generously sent us many useful student responses to the text, and Kurt Spellmeyer of Rutgers University, who offered several suggestions that helped us in determining the general direction of this revision. Sarah Hubbard and Frank Lortscher, University of California, Berkeley, and Jane Jubilee expertly assisted us in the production of the manuscript.

We are grateful for the many helpful suggestions instructors have sent to us over the past decade. We have included as many of their recommendations as possible. In particular, we would like to thank Charles Bazerman, Richard Bonomo, Gail Bounds, Addison Bross, Douglas Butturff, Curtis Church, John Clifford, Edward P. J. Corbett, Mary Corboy, Frank D'Angelo, Kenneth O. Danz, Maury Dean, Wheeler Dixon, Kent Ekberg, Lyman Fink, Jr., Christine Freeman, David Gaines, Kate Hirsh, R. S. Hootman, Lee A. Jacobus, Ed Joyce, D. G. Kehl, Helene Keyssar, Kay Kier, Henry Knepler, Roberta Kramer, Andrea Lundsford, William Lutz, William Miller, Helen Naugle, Matthew O'Brien, Paul O'Connell, Ed Quinn, Lori Rath, Harold Schechter, Michael Schudson, Sharon Shaloo, Phillip Shew, Nancy Sommers, Charles Taylor, Victor H. Thompson, Barbara H. Traister, Patrick van den Bossche, Ruth Vande Kieft, Maureen Waters, and Harvey Wiener. William Vesterman, a long-time friend of the book, helps keep us alert to the classroom possibilities of new material. In addition, we would like to recognize the special assistance of Trudy Baltz, Richard Mikita, and Christopher Motley. Their intelligence, critical judgment, and generous encouragement continue to be felt in this fourth edition and in the Teacher's Manual that accompanies it.

We would like to acknowledge once again all those who helped us structure the original text and whose influence is still very much evident in each new edition: Paul Bertram, Anthony Cardoza, Thomas R. Edwards, Christopher Gray, the late Mark Gibbons and Betsy B. Kaufman, Ron Holland, Daniel F. Howard, Robert E. Lynch, Robert Lyons, C. F. Main, George Mandelbaum, Barbara Maxwell, Max Maxwell, John McDermott, Kevin McQuade, Charles Molesworth, Frank Moorman, Richard Poirier, Marie Ponsot, Douglas Roehm, Sandra Schor, Gary Tate, Thomas Van Laan, Ridley Whitaker, and Elissa Weaver. John Wright, Gerald Mentor, and Jean Shapiro played important roles in the success of earlier editions, and we continue to value that thoughtful assistance.

We are grateful for the cooperation of the library staffs at Columbia, Princeton, and Rutgers Universities, at Queens College, as well as at the New York Public Library and the St. Louis Public Library. John Leypoldt of the Princeton University Library was extremely helpful in producing many of the illustrations. We would like to thank Errol Somay and David Wheeler of the New York Public Library, for extraordinary research assistance. Bruce Forer, as usual, gave generously of his time and intelligence, and his efforts helped make the "Scripts" section possible.

We are indebted to the kind people at Oxford University Press who made working on this fourth edition so pleasant and productive. In particular, we would like to thank: Ed Barry, Ellie Fuchs, Fred Schneider, Wendy Keebler, Bill Sisler, Mimi Melek, and Victoria Olsen. As always, Helene Atwan and Susanne McQuade have helped in innumerable ways.

CONTENTS

PRESS   103

ON THE DEATH PENALTY   188
THE DEATH PENALTY: NINETEENTH-CENTURY VIEWS   188

THE DEATH PENALTY: TWENTIETH-CENTURY VIEWS   192

BEST-SELLERS   399

CLASSICS   531

SCRIPTS   681

RHETORICAL
TABLE OF CONTENTS

DESCRIPTION

PEOPLE

NARRATION

Advertisements

See the sections on Women, Men, Anxieties, and Eating and Drinking

EXPOSITION

DEFINITION

Advertisements

How Would You Put a Glass of Ballantine Ale into Words?   40

America   44

Without Chemicals, Life Itself Would Be Impossible   59

What's the Point of Talking   64

CLASSIFICATION

Advertisements

Separates the Men from the Boys   35

Are You Ready for an Alfa Romeo?   37

Who Ever Said the Man Who Discovers a Cure for Cancer Is Going to Be White, or Even a
   Man?   58

ARGUMENT

Advertisements

PERSUASION

Advertisements
Virtually all of them

TABLE OF
LINKED SELECTIONS

INTRODUCTION

This book grew out of our commitment to the notion—one that still might seem peculiar to many people—that *any* form of writing can be made the subject of rewarding critical attention. And because we are most interested in the written products of American culture that are continually shaping the ways we think, talk, and feel, our editorial effort has been to include as great a variety of American themes and prose styles as could be managed within a single text. Along with some traditional selections from such classic American writers as Thoreau, Twain, Crane, and Faulkner, we have brought together an assortment of material from scripts, best-sellers, popular magazines, newspapers, and advertisements. One critical principle informs our selections: we want to illustrate through historical sequences, thematic cross-references, and divergent creative intentions precisely how the most widely read forms of American writing interact with each other and with their audiences to produce that intricate network of artistic and commercial collaboration known as popular culture.

Popular Writing in America is divided into six parts. The opening section consists of some of the most successful copywriting in the history of American advertising. We have arranged the ads in clusters dealing with similar products (automobiles, cosmetics, clothing, etc.) over a number of decades both to provide a brief historical perspective on the language and rhetorical strategies of advertising and to invite speculation on changes in American culture as they are reflected in the ways our society is talked to in its advertisements. In addition, to demonstrate some of the ways advertising is thought about both inside and outside the industry, we have also included essays on the art of copywriting, several critiques of advertising, and a series of delightful letters showing a prominent American poet exercising her imagination and vocabulary in an attempt to invent a suitable name for a new automobile.

The examples of newspaper writing we include in the next chapter range from different styles of headlines through the compressed prose of teletype releases to extended forms of news coverage. Events of such historical magnitude as the Lincoln and Kennedy assassinations and the use of the atom bomb on Japan are interspersed among some of the usual kinds of news stories, feature articles, interviews, and editorials that comprise the substance of the daily American newspaper. Because we want to emphasize in this chapter the stylistic and structural consequences of writing performed under emergency conditions and against competitive deadlines—"Journalism is literature in a hurry," according to Matthew Arnold—we have weighted our selections in favor of the kinds of violence and tragedies that have inspired reporters, made history, and sold newspapers.

Magazines are eclectic by necessity. Represented are a variety of topics from some of the most popular "big" and "little" magazines published in America.

With very few exceptions, an article from a particular magazine is intended to be at least fairly typical of the kind of material and tonal quality found in that magazine around the time the article appeared. Our selections in this chapter are limited to nonfiction because much of the fiction in "Best-Sellers" and "Classics" was originally published in magazines. Consequently, an important periodical such as *Scribner's* is not represented by an article in this section but by Stephen Crane's short story that appears in "Classics."

The material reprinted in "Best-Sellers" affords the reader the opportunity to examine some of the most commercially successful prose in American publishing history. It is, for the most part, writing that the academic community has seldom paid serious attention to—selections from best-sellers are rarely made available in textbooks or anthologies. Yet, because of their massive audiences and their frequent interactions with other forms of media, best-sellers deserve to be attended to by readers interested in examining the relationship between their own verbal experiences and those of a literate public. Passages such as Tarzan's rescue of Jane in *Tarzan of the Apes* or the shooting of Don Corleone from *The Godfather* were selected not as specimens of mediocre writing—mediocre, that is, *because* they are from best-sellers—but as examples of writing that has had enormous impact on the American reading public.

The success of many of the best-selling books represented in this section depended, to a great extent, on their public's previous acceptance of similar subjects and verbal strategies in advertisements, newspapers, and magazine articles. To cite but one example, the phenomenal attention Mario Puzo's *The Godfather* received was in large measure the result of the extensive news coverage given to the felonies and frolics of underworld characters. Popular fiction, in turn, affects other forms of media, as can be seen from the account of the murder of Joey Gallo in *Time* magazine, where the report of a ritualistic gangland shooting self-consciously trades on the rendition of a similar event in *The Godfather*. Throughout the book, connections such as this one are signaled in headnotes and discussion questions in order to map out a network of thematic and stylistic interrelations.

Though our emphasis in "Classics" is on short fiction and poetry, we also include essays, excerpts from autobiographies, and other selected nonfiction from some of America's major authors. We have taken the liberty of designating the work of such contemporary writers as John Updike, Norman Mailer, Flannery O'Connor, and Joan Didion as classic because we feel that the quality of their performances and their critical alertness to the present condition of our language entitle them to be viewed in the same historical perspective as Thoreau, Twain, Crane, and Faulkner. *Classic* is a term we adopt for the sake of convenience; it is not intended to suggest writing that is antiquated, writing that is easily dissociated from popular culture because it sounds serious and elevated, but writing that has, so far, stayed around because it has stayed alive. We want to show from our selections that classic authors have not remained socially and intellectually superior to the various ordinary languages of popular culture but have tried to come to terms with those languages by appropriating them, occasionally discarding them, often shaping or extending them so that their writing can reflect the complex interplay between what we call literature and what we recognize as the accents of the life around us.

In "Scripts" we introduce popular language that is heard rather than read. Though surely the most widely responded to form of writing, radio and television scripts are seldom seen and examined by anyone other than professionals. People tend to forget that much of what they *see* in the movies or on television started first with the written word. In some cases, as in the film version of Ernest Hemingway's "Soldier's Home," what is being seen is a transcription of classic literature. Hemingway's story is included in "Classics" so that readers can examine how such adaptations are accomplished and also learn how the shaping of a text for a film audience affects the way the original material is interpreted. Episodes from such popular television series as "The Jeffersons" and "Hill Street Blues" show how writers work to create an interplay of authentic dialogue and believable characters.

It might be argued that this type of book is unnecessary because the abundance of ads, newspapers, magazines, and best-sellers makes them so available as "texts" that there is really no need to collect samples of them in a separate volume. If our texts had been chosen indiscriminately, simply to document different types of writing, that might be the case. But, quite clearly, one way the book can be used is to illustrate a verbal progression from the readily accessible language and strategies of advertising to the more obviously complicated styles of expression that characterize outstanding prose. The risk of this procedure, however, is that it may prove too schematic, may even encourage readers to regard the ads, some of the journalism and magazine articles, and most of the best-sellers as blatantly inferior forms of writing, "straw men" set up to be discarded all too easily in favor of the durable excellence of the "great works." It should be noted, therefore, that our categories and sequence were not especially designed to endorse already entrenched hierarchies by setting up fairly obvious gradations in the quality of several particular types of prose and poetry but were intended to illustrate how various kinds of writing shaped by quite different commercial purposes and intended audiences interact with and modify each other to produce what we can reasonably call a common culture.

It might also be argued that classics have no place in an anthology devoted to popular writing. Classics are among the finest holdings of an educated minority; popular writing belongs to something as repugnant as "mass culture." That is one way to look at it. Another, and one that this book is premised on, is that classics are among the best things we have to share with each other, and they ought to be encountered in all their challenging complexity as opportunities to enliven and, if necessary, toughen the questions we ask of all the other modes of expression we participate in daily. That is why we have included an excerpt from Norman Mailer's *Of a Fire on the Moon* in "Classics." Throughout his comprehensive report on the Apollo expedition, Mailer is critically aware of the ways his own prose interrelates with a variety of other, mainly competing verbal efforts. Mailer's original contract to write about the Apollo XI astronauts was with *Life*, a popular magazine. But Mailer is no ordinary reporter, and for him the moon shot was no ordinary assignment. As a writer, Mailer is so attuned to his own participation in any form of media that it was only natural that his coverage of the moon landing would inform us as much about the special tasks of modern journalism as about one of the great episodes in American history. As it stands, *Of a Fire on the Moon* is a fascinating social document incorporating the many voices of technology, science, and broadcasting that converged at that particular moment in our culture to produce the moon spectacle. Such responsiveness to the shaping influences of our verbal environment is what we want the word *classic* to suggest.

A word about the introduction to each section. A full survey outlining the history of the various forms of printed media that make up our categories would not have been practical. Also, we wanted to avoid introducing such essentially futile, if not paralyzing, questions as "Is the news truly objective?" and "Is advertising an abuse of language?" Instead, we have tried to strike an agreeable balance between saying something general about the type of material in that section and saying something specific about the verbal qualities of a particular passage. Of course, no single excerpt can typify all the writing in a chapter. Yet we have chosen to examine closely, though not at great length, those passages that we feel will conveniently clarify the relations between the distinctive features of an individual style and the kind of reader that style seems directed to. We thought that by providing models of the analytic procedure we want to encourage we would, in fact, be offering something of a consistent critical approach to what might seem a bewildering assortment of material.

Any act of composition presupposes an audience. To read a text attentively is to discover something specific about the characteristics of the people it is intended to appeal to—their interests and the ways of talking they can respond to most readily. Once we ask the question "Whom is this ad or magazine article addressed to?" we invite statements about the traits of large groups of people. Questions such as this one can be best approached not from a reader's preconceived idea of what certain groups of people in America are supposed to be like but from his or her responsiveness to the specific ways in which a society is talked to in print. Our responses to popular writing will be the more attuned to the culture we live in the more our terms can encompass the aesthetic significance of a particular work and the bearings that significance has on our shared social experiences. In the model analysis we provide in each introduction, especially in the one to "Best-Sellers," we try to show that it is only when we make an effort to measure the responses of the audience implicit in a specific passage—an audience, it should be noted, that very often *literally* appears in the work as spectators, witnesses, advertising models, and so on—against the quality of our own participation that we can assess more comprehensively the interactions between the various styles and audiences within a single society.

Popular forms of writing pose special challenges to traditional analytical methods. Popular writing is often, or so it would seem, so opaquely simple and ordinary that a standard critical vocabulary might come across as too labored or too imposing for the occasion. Yet finding an appropriate tone has always been a problem even for traditional literary criticism. It would *sound* wrong to talk about Ernest Hemingway in the highly idiosyncratic critical language of Henry James's "Prefaces" or to take the same psychological approach in a discussion of Allen Ginsberg that we would take for Emily Dickinson. Writers exist for us, unless we know them in other, more personal ways, essentially in the specific qualities of their tone and idiom. This should always be our starting point. If, for example, we try to adopt a standard analytical procedure (e.g., searching for symbols) to discuss *Tarzan of the Apes,* and our method becomes too irritatingly cumbersome, that can be an occasion for testing the critical language we are working with and for reexamining the quality of our literary responses rather than concluding that Tarzan was not worth talking about in the first place.

It should be apparent from our model of analysis in each introduction that we have made an effort to avoid using a language that relies too heavily on the terminology of traditional literary criticism, a terminology that has, for the most part, evolved from allegiances and inveterate responses to only the most highly regarded forms of literature. We certainly do not mean to disqualify any of the standard critical approaches, as we trust our "Rhetorical Table of Contents," will amply indicate, but we want instead to encourage a lively reciprocity between the academically certified terms of serious literary criticism and the ordinary languages of our popular culture. What we hope will come out of such transactions is a resilient critical language applicable to all forms of public discourse. If we cannot adjust our critical vocabularies and find interesting ways to talk about Tarzan, or advertising, or a newspaper item, then it is doubtful we have found the most spirited ways to approach even the best things in our culture.

ADVERTISING

Advertising is a business of words.
DAVID OGILVY

WE are so accustomed to signs, posters, billboards, songs, jingles, graffiti, circulars, placards, announcements, brochures, packages, commercials, and ads in newspapers and magazines that it is difficult for any of us to imagine a world without public and personal advertisements. Ads are practically inescapable; they literally surround us. Few places are remote enough to be completely free from the appeals of advertising. Suppose we picture ourselves on a secluded tropical beach experiencing a dazzling sunset. Even if we have not noticed any discarded packaging or unobtrusively placed signs, we must still recognize the alluring tropical scene itself as one continually promoted by airlines and travel agencies in newspapers, in magazines, and especially on decorative posters. Efforts to escape advertising, to "discover" landscapes removed from the intrusions of advertisements, may be merely another way of participating in the kind of world advertisements typically endorse. No place, no object, no life-style, and certainly no way of talking can be totally exempt from commercialized public notice. The world we live in is an advertised world.

The business of advertising is to invent methods of addressing massive audiences in a language designed to be easily accessible and immediately persuasive. No advertising agency wants to put out an ad that is not clear and convincing to millions of people. But the agencies, though they would agree that ads should be written to sell products, disagree when it comes down to the most effective methods of doing so. Over the years, advertising firms have developed among themselves a variety of distinctive styles based on their understanding of the different kinds of audiences they want to reach. No two agencies would handle the same product identically. To people for whom advertising is an exacting discipline and a highly competitive profession, an ad is much more than a sophisticated sales pitch, an attractive verbal and visual device to serve manufacturers. In fact, for those who examine ads critically or professionally, products may very well be no more than merely points of departure. Ads often outlive their products, and in the case of early advertisements for products that are no longer available, we cannot help but consider the advertisement independently of our responses to those products. The point of examining ads apart from their announced subjects is not that we ignore the product completely but that we try to see the product only as it is talked about and portrayed in the full context of the ad. Certainly, it is not necessary to have tried a particular product to be able to appreciate the technique and design used in its advertisement.

The emphasis of the following section is on the advertisements themselves, not the commodities they promote. To illustrate a variety of American advertising strategies and styles, we have included advertisements from the late nineteenth century to the present. Some ads have been grouped according to their products; that is, there are a number of ads regarding smoking, transportation, cosmetics, and fashions. This arrangement will allow you to observe some of the ways both advertisements and audiences have changed over the past one hundred years. Many of these ads have been selected because they represent important developments in advertising methodology. But our intentions are not exclusively historical. Other ads were chosen to display significant aspects of standard advertising procedures. We wanted to introduce advertisements that were both interesting and typical. Nearly all the ads we reprint have achieved a good deal of professional recognition. Many have been frequently singled out as examples of some of the finest copy in the history of American advertising.

A few of the early ads may strike you as unimaginative and typographically crude. They appeared in newspapers and magazines before printing innovations and marketing research radically altered advertising techniques. Yet, given their frequent inelegance, naïveté, and commandeering tones, many early ads remind us how advertisers have persistently played on certain themes despite noticeable changes in decorum, style, and methods of persuasion. Perhaps the early ads only put very bluntly the promises and claims that later on would be more politely disguised. Consider the advertisement for Madame Rowley's Toilet Mask that first appeared in 1887. This ad makes no attempt to introduce its product in a pleasing manner. The advantages of using the toilet mask are delivered in a decisively impersonal and mechanically repetitive fashion. No effort was spent on setting up an attractive backdrop or atmosphere. The only graphic detail we are allowed is the sketch of the curious toilet device in operation, appearing ingenuously at the center of an imposingly designed typographical layout.

If the advertisement for Madame Rowley's Toilet Mask makes little attempt to attract visually, neither does it try very hard to gratify its audience verbally. Even the name of the product is deliberately and unappealingly direct—no charming or engaging brand name suggests that the mask is anything more than what it announces itself to be. The copywriter uses none of the enticing and intimately sensuous language that advertisers so often turned to later when addressing women on matters of personal hygiene and beauty. Realizing that Madame Rowley's beauty apparatus was almost embarrassingly unstylish, the writer must have decided he could promote his client's product best by sounding unadornedly legalistic and scientific. While the copywriter assumes that facial beauty is desirable, he restricts his copy to "claims," "grounds," and "proofs" of the toilet mask's effectiveness, instead of extolling the advantages of a blemish-free, "cover girl" complexion. Flattering metaphors that would describe the product or its results more sensitively are avoided, apparently so as not to call into question the speaker's assertions. Only once does the idiom anticipate the language of modern cosmetic advertisements. Facial blemishes are said to "vanish from the skin, leaving it soft, clear, brilliant, and beautiful." Future copywriters would capitalize on words, such as *vanish,* that suggest magical and instantaneous remedies. Later ads for skin care would also focus more directly on the personal and social advantages of having a "soft, clear, brilliant, and beautiful" complexion. But in Madame Rowley's day, beauty in itself had not yet become an advertising commodity.

Apparently, Madame Rowley's Toilet Mask did not put the cosmetic industry out of business. As early as 1912, we find an advertisement for makeup using what has since become a familiar merchandising tactic. The claims made by Madame Rowley's copywriter stopped at a "brilliant" complexion. The ad promised women nothing more than that. But for the writer of the Pompeian Massage Cream copy, a blemish-free countenance was not all his product could supply. The Pompeian ad is one of the first ads for women to promise along with its product's "beautifying" benefits the additional advantages of marital love and social acceptance. A beautiful complexion, the ad writer suggests, means little by itself. At the heart of the Pompeian ad lies one of the most important developments in the history of advertising technique—the realization that "grounds" and "claims" restricted to the product alone will not always sell the goods. Since the Pompeian ad, copywriters have concentrated more and more on an audience's psychological needs, its attitudes and anxieties. In the Pompeian ad, the writer promotes not only an effective way to check the wrinkles and blemishes he poetically calls "Time's ravages" but also adopts an attitude toward the nature and effects of feminine appeal: "a beautiful complexion—that greatest aid to woman's power and influence." This comment, obviously made by a male copywriter, is offered after we have been told that a "Pompeian complexion" will win over any man's mother, "as it does in every other instance in social or business life." The ad inadvertently acknowledges that beauty is only skin deep, after all. Deeper than a woman's worry about facial blemishes, the copywriter intimates, is her terror of not being loved and approved.

MADAME ROWLEY'S TOILET MAS[K]

TOILET MASK

OR

FACE GLOVE.

The following are the claims made for Madame Rowley's Toilet Mask, and the grounds on which it is recommended to ladies for Beautifying, Bleaching, and Preserving the Complexion:

TOILET M[ASK]

OR

FACE GLO[VE]

First—The **Mask** is **Soft** and **Flexible** in form, and can be **Easily Applied** and **Worn** without **Discomfort** or **Inconvenience.**

Second—It is durable, and does not dissolve or come asunder, but holds its original mask shape.

Third—It has been **Analyzed** by **Eminent Scientists** and **Chemical Experts,** and pronounced **Perfectly Pure** and **Harmless.**

Fourth—With ordinary care the **Mask** will **last for years,** and its VALUABLE PROPERTIES **Never** **Become Impaired.**

Fifth—The **Mask** is protected by letters patent, and is the **only Genuine** article of the kind.

Sixth—It is **Recommended** by **Eminent Physicians** and **Scientific Men** as a SUBSTITUTE FOR INJURIOUS COSMETICS.

Seventh—The **Mask** is a **Natural Beautifier,** for **Bleaching** and **Preserving** the **Skin** and **Removing Complexional Imperfections.**

Eighth—Its use cannot be detected by the closest scr[utiny] and it may be worn with **perfect privacy,** i[f de]sired.

Ninth—The **Mask** is sold at a moderate price, and is PURCHASED BUT ONCE.

The Toilet Mask (or Face Glove) in position to the face.
TO BE WORN THREE TIMES IN THE WEEK

Tenth—Hundreds of dollars useless[ly ex]pended for cosmetics, lotions [and] like preparations, may be sav[ed by its] possessor.

Eleventh—**Ladies** in every section [of the] country are using the **Mask** [with] gratifying results.

Twelfth—It is safe, simple, cleanly [and] effective for beautifying pur[poses,] and never injures the most de[licate] skin.

Thirteenth—While it is intended [that] the **Mask** should be **Worn D**[uring] **Sleep,** it may be applied W[ith] EQUALLY GOOD RESULT[S at] **any time** to suit the conven[ience] of the wearer.

Fourteenth—The **Mask** has received the testimony of [well] known society and professional ladies, who proclaim [it to] be the greatest discovery for beautifying purposes [ever] vouchsafed to womankind.

COMPLEXION BLEMISHES

May be hidden imperfectly by cosmetics and powders, but can only be removed permanently by the Toilet Mask. By its [use] every kind of spots, impurities, roughness, etc., vanish from the skin, leaving it soft, clear, brilliant, and beautiful. [It is] harmless, costs little, and saves its user money. It prevents and removes wrinkles, and is both a complexion preserver [and] beautifier. Famous Society Ladies, actresses, belles, etc., use it.

VALUABLE ILLUSTRATED TREATISE, WITH PROOFS AND PARTICULARS.

—MAILED FREE BY—

TOILET MASK

OR

FACE GLOVE.

{Send for Descriptive Treatise.}

THE TOILET MASK COMPANY,

1164 BROADWAY,

NEW YORK.

☞ Mention this paper when you Write.

{Send for Descriptive Treatise.}

TOILET MA[SK]

OR

FACE GLOV[E]

[1887]

4

[1912]

Unlike Madame Rowley's mask, the Pompeian Massage Cream does not appear at the center of its advertisement. To be sure, the brand name (chosen to suggest the shade of red found on the walls of the "preserved" ancient city of Pompeii) has been allowed central prominence, and the illustration of the product is barely squeezed into the bottom left corner of the ad. More important than the actual cream is the rendition of the familiar dramatic situation in which a young lady is first introduced to the wary scrutiny of her suitor's mother: "Of all the moments the most trying—the son brings *her* to his mother, of all critics the most exacting." With a tone and diction borrowed from the melodramatic superlatives of soap opera and best-selling fiction, the copywriter maintains that with so much at stake a young woman cannot risk using a cosmetic that would make her look vulgar and unacceptable to such an "exacting" critic as a potential mother-in-law. The writer offers, in addition, the ultimate emotional reassurance that the massage cream "positively can not grow hair on the face." The ad leaves little doubt, then, that the "beautiful complexion" its product guarantees is not what is finally being promoted. The clear complexion, in this case, ultimately stands for something else, as it did not in the ad for Madame Rowley's Toilet Mask. Pompeian Massage Cream, not of much consequence in itself, merely personifies the real "product" of the ad—a natural, artless appearance that will ensure unqualified social approval.

Cosmetic advertisements, for the most part, avoid the slightest allusion to artificiality. Madame Rowley's Toilet Mask, which must have looked like an odd contrivance even in its own time, was nevertheless introduced as a "natural beautifier." To bring home a girl whose makeup looked artificial was, to the copywriter for Pompeian Massage Cream at least, an undeserving affront to American motherhood. In our final example of cosmetic advertising, the ad for Yardley's Next to Nature, the entire copy depends on the single notion that makeup must allow a woman to appear *natural,* to look, that is, as if she were not wearing any cosmetic at all. Though the ad does not associate its product with a comforting aura of love and matrimony, like the Pompeian ad, it still assumes that a fine complexion is not an end in itself but a means of possessing a particular kind of "look." Throughout the Next to Nature ad, the copywriter insists on the product's naturalness. The brand name itself bears, as Pompeian did not, more than a loose metaphorical relationship to the product: the name suggests not only that the cosmetic formula is literally close to nature but also that the product's use will engender an appearance that will be the next best thing to natural beauty. Since Madame Rowley's time, advertisers have discovered that probably no word of copy works as effectively as *natural.* The copywriter for Next to Nature appropriately avoids gimmicks and artificiality by adopting a casual manner of speaking and by offering a photograph of a demure and innocent-looking woman as evidence of his product's "transparent" purity. Apparently, he does not feel that he need convince us of his honesty by citing indisputable "claims" and "grounds," nor does he bank on his audience's fear of social or parental disapproval. He is confident that his readers will need no more than his own sincere tone to be persuaded that by using Next to Nature they can have "the fresh, wholesome look" of natural beauty.

These three cosmetic advertisements furnish a brief record of some of the major developments of American advertising. A glance at the ads demonstrates vividly the changes in the layout of advertisements brought about by advances in photography and graphic design. The space apportioned for illustration increases substantially. We move from the cameolike sketch of the figure in the toilet mask to the posterlike photograph of an attractive woman which dominates the Next to Nature advertisement and also conveniently eliminates the copywriter's need to write a lengthy description of what the product can do. The size of the headlines

Of all the make-ups on earth, only one is called Next to Nature.™

One of the freshest things that's happened to girls' faces since sunshine and country air: Yardley's Next to Nature Liquid Make-up.

It's made with vitamin A to moisturize, the purest of waters, and all natural colorings. They're blended into a formula so sheer, you can use it generously and still look like a natural beauty.

Try Next to Nature blushers and new Transparent Pressed Powder too.

Because when it comes to giving you the fresh, wholesome look—there's nobody on earth like Yardley.

Yardley

How to make the most of what you have.
©1973, Yardley of London, Inc.

[1973]

7

increases; the style becomes more informal. The headline for Madame Rowley's
Toilet Mask is intended to do no more than name the product explicitly. In the
Pompeian ad, however, there are actually two headlines. One simply mentions
the product by name, while the other invites a reader's response to a fictional
scene. In the Next to Nature ad, after the reader is introduced directly to the brand
name and the special quality of the product, she is then talked to marginally in a
perky and congenial voice. Few ads in Madame Rowley's day would have taken
the liberty of speaking to their readers in such a casual and ingratiating fashion.
Neither would a nineteenth-century copywriter have violated grammatical decorum by writing the kind of breezy and fragmented sentences that characterize
the brisk style of the Next to Nature copy. Quite clearly, the writing in the Next
to Nature ad is meant to sound as natural, relaxed, and sincere as the copywriter
imagines his audience would like to talk and behave. By examining these advertisements, then, we are introduced not only to three markedly different styles of
writing but also to three noticeably different attitudes toward female beauty.

Even though advertisements represent some of the most expensive and calculated acts of composition in America, the audiences they are directed to seldom
attend to them analytically. No one would deny that ads exert tremendous economic and social pressures. (See, for example, the essays by Carol Caldwell
in "Advertising" and Vance Packard in "Best-Sellers.") Yet few people, aside
from those in the advertising profession, bother to ask how or why a particular advertisement happened to be written and designed in a certain way. The
public generally reacts to advertisements exactly the way advertising agencies
would like them to—as consumers, not critics. Assuming, however, that "advertising is a business of *words*," not necessarily of products, we have included
examples of successful copy to invite you to consider more carefully *how* the
language and strategies of advertisements affect the ways we talk and think. Advertisements constitute a lively repository of American vocabulary, idiom, metaphor, and style, in short a fairly reliable index of the state of public discourse.
They create the one verbal environment in which we all participate, willingly or
unwillingly.

Often a bridesmaid but never a bride

EDNA'S case was really a pathetic one. Like every woman, her primary ambition was to marry. Most of the girls of her set were married—or about to be. Yet not one possessed more grace or charm or loveliness than she.

And as her birthdays crept gradually toward that tragic thirty-mark, marriage seemed farther from her life than ever.

She was often a bridesmaid but never a bride.

That's the insidious thing about halitosis (unpleasant breath): You, yourself, rarely know when you have it. And even your closest friends won't tell you.

Sometimes, of course, halitosis comes from some deep-seated organic disorder that requires professional advice. But usually—and fortunately—halitosis is only a local condition that yields to the regular use of Listerine as a mouth wash and gargle. It is an interesting thing that this well-known antiseptic that has been in use for years for surgical dressings, possesses these unusual properties as a breath deodorant.

It halts food fermentation in the mouth and leaves the breath sweet, fresh and clean. Not by substituting some other odor but by really removing the old one. The Listerine odor itself quickly disappears. So the systematic use of Listerine puts you on the safe and polite side.

Your druggist will supply you with Listerine. He sells lots of it. It has dozens of different uses as a safe antiseptic and has been trusted as such for a half a century. Read the interesting little booklet that comes with every bottle.
—*Lambert Pharmacal Company, Saint Louis, U. S. A.*

For HALITOSIS use LISTERINE

WOMEN

Should a gentleman offer a Tiparillo to a lab technician?

Behind that pocket of pencils beats the heart of a digital computer. This girl has already cross-indexed Tiparillo® as a cigar with a slim, elegant shape and neat, white tip.

She knows that there are two kinds. Regular Tiparillo, for a mild smoke. Or new Tiparillo M with menthol, for a cold smoke.

She knows. She's programmed.

And she's ready.

But how about you? Which Tiparillo are you going to offer? Or are you just going to stand there and stare at her pencils?

[1968]

"*Equal pay, equal recognition
and the first woman admitted
to The Club...
What more could you ask for?*"

"Old Grand-Dad."

Head of the Bourbon Family.

Old Grand-Dad
When you ask a lot more from life.

[1976]

[1978]

"...Guess who's the new Marketing V.P.?"

Peggy Ross. It's time.

Time for the Chase Advantage. Chase has helped a lot of successful people. And Chase knows you need more than just ordinary checking or savings to truly maximize your assets.

So how can Chase really help? To begin with, no bank can give you more imaginative and comprehensive banking than Chase can. With 4 different checking plans. And with a full range of credit and loan services. With 12 different savings plans—including plans that pay extra high interest without tying up your money for years, like our 6 month certificate of deposit, or our 90 day Nest Egg Account.

But most importantly, it's time for the professional and expert guidance you'll get from the world's most knowledgeable bank.

The Chase Advantage means all this and more. That's why, now it's time to put the Chase Advantage to work for you.

The Chase Advantage

CHASE

Member F.D.I.C

[1979]

"When I grow up, I'm going to be a judge, or a senator or maybe president."

Oh, no you're not little girl!

Your chances of making it into public office are very slim. Only 23 of 657 FEDERAL JUDGES are women. Only 2 of 100 SENATORS are women. No woman has ever been PRESIDENT. But you do have a 99% chance to be a NURSE. (You'll earn less than a tree-trimmer.) Or a 97% chance to be a TYPIST. (You'll earn less than the janitor.) Or a 60% chance to be a SCHOOL TEACHER. (You'll earn less than a zoo-keeper.)

Concerned mamas and daddies are asking how they can help their female children to get an equal crack at vocational training —training that opens doors to non-stereotypical, better paying jobs. Parents want their female children to get the same kind of coaching in sports and physical education as boys do.

Parents want the kind of counseling that will encourage wider career options for girls. (Most young women graduate without the science and math credits they need to exercise full options for higher education.) If your female children attend a federally supported public school in this country you can and should help them get a more equal education.

YOU CAN HELP TO CREATE A BETTER FUTURE.
Write NOW Legal Defense & Education Fund (H) 132 W. 43rd Street, N.Y., N.Y. 10036

What could have started in the park just ended with that little itch.

This was the day you thought he'd say hello. But now that he's seen that itch, just what will he say? Because even if you don't see flakes, or no one tells you, that little itch could mean dandruff.

So try Head & Shoulders. It comes in two formulas. Conditioning formula for extra manageability.

And regular formula for those who already manage beautifully. Both are great at controlling dandruff.

And, with dandruff under control, you'll say hello to soft, manageable, healthy-looking hair. And he'll say hello to you. Maybe more.

Show off your hair, not the itch of dandruff.

[1983]

[1986]

"I know she's a very important person. They always send a car around for her when the meetings are over. And it's usually a Lincoln. She's decisive and, actually, quite charming about it. Business has never been better since she took over. She even looks like a very important person."

MARY ANN RESTIVO

[1987]

One of the Yank Veterans

"We smash 'em HARD"

OWL
▾
Square-
end
6c

WHITE
OWL
▾
Invincible
Shape
7c

"Did I bayonet my first Hun? Sure! How did it feel? It *doesn't* feel! There *he* is. There *you* are. One of you has got to go. I preferred to stay.

"So when sergeant says, 'Smash 'em, boys'—we do. And we go them one better like good old Yankee Doodle Yanks. For bullets and bayonets are the only kind of lingo that a Hun can *understand!*"

* * * *

The *dependable* Yank, whose photograph appears above, first met the *dependable* Owl Cigar while boosting that *dependable* investment—the Liberty Loan.

We didn't tell him about the $2,000,000 stock of leaf that is always aging for Owl and White Owl. Nor the over 100,000,000 Owls and White Owls sold last year. We just swapped him a White Owl for a smile. And it doesn't look like the smile came hard, does it?

Why don't you, too, try an Owl or White Owl—*today?*

DEALERS:
If your distributor does not sell these dependable cigars, write us.
GENERAL CIGAR CO., INC., 119 West 40th Street, New York City

TWO DEPENDABLE CIGARS

OWL 6ȼ white OWL 7ȼ

Branded for your

Banded protection

[1918]

MEN

HOW JOE'S BODY BROUGHT HIM FAME INSTEAD OF SHAME

I Can Make YOU A New Man, Too, in Only 15 Minutes A Day!

If YOU, like Joe, have a body that others can "push around"—if you're ashamed to strip for sports or a swim—then give me just 15 minutes a day! I'll PROVE you can have a body you'll be proud of, packed with red-blooded vitality! "*Dynamic Tension*." That's the secret! That's how I changed myself from a spindle-shanked, scrawny weakling to winner of the title, "World's Most Perfectly Developed Man."

Do you want big, broad shoulders—a fine, powerful chest—biceps like steel—arms and legs rippling with muscular strength—a stomach ridged with bands of sinewy muscle—and a build you can be proud of? Then just give me the opportunity to prove that "*Dynamic Tension*" is what you need.

"Dynamic Tension" Does It!

Using "*Dynamic Tension*" only 15 minutes a day, in the privacy of your own room, you quickly begin to put on muscle, increase your chest measurements, broaden your back, fill out your arms and legs. Before you know it, this easy, NATURAL method will make you a finer specimen of REAL MANHOOD than you ever dreamed you could be! You'll be a New Man!

FREE BOOK

Send NOW for my FREE book. It tells about "*Dynamic Tension*," shows photos of men I've turned from weaklings into Atlas Champions, tells how I can do it for YOU. Don't put it off! Address me personally: Charles Atlas, Dept. 217B, 115 E. 23 St., New York 10, N. Y.

—actual photo of the man who holds the title, "The World's Most Perfectly Developed Man."

[1944]

19

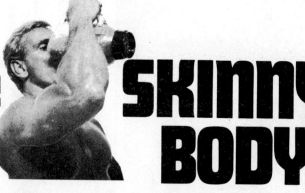

[1973]

20

CITY BOY. Paul spotted him first, just a bouncin' along, an' a grinnin' away like he know'd somethin' everybody else didn't. When he finally got to where we were a settin', Paul winked at me an' ask him real straight-faced, "You lost, city boy?"

"Not necessarily," he smiled.

Bobby ask him what it was that he was ridin', an' city boy said it was a Kawasaki. "A whut?" Bobby said. "A Kawasaki, KE175," city boy told him, real proud. Said it had some kinda new-fangled engine, an' a five-speed transmission, an' all kinds'a other fancy stuff. Said he could ride it just about anywhere he pleased, too...on the road or off—didn't make no difference. Bobby said, "I'll take my palomino any day, he don't get lost." "That's right," Paul said, "horses got brains. Know where they're goin', even if you don't."

City boy just grinned an' said, "Which way's town?"

Well, right away Paul starts ta' pointin' up the road, toward the bunkhouse. An' no sooner'n he had his finger stuck out, an' Bobby was a pointin' up t'other way.

City boy just eyed 'em both for a minute, an' then, with that same grin on his face, he started up his motor-sickle. First kick. Then he pulled out a map an' handed it over ta' Bobby an' said straight-out, "Stick it where your brains are, cowboy...and maybe you'll end up smart as your horse," An' off he rode.

Thought Paul and Bobby's faces were gonna turn redder'n their necks. Good thing that machine didn't stall.

Kawasaki
lets the good times roll.

[1976]

21

**Some people work to live.
Others live to work.**

[1981]

22

arfums Ltd. Photograph by Robert Farber

[1982]

An American Hero

aramis
cologne

The impact never fades

Aramis Inc. 1986

a r a m i s

[1986]

24

Again She Orders —
"A Chicken Salad, Please"

FOR him she is wearing her new frock. For him she is trying to look her prettiest. If only she can impress him—make him like her—just a little.

Across the table he smiles at her, proud of her prettiness, glad to notice that others admire. And she smiles back, a bit timidly, a bit self-consciously.

What wonderful poise he has! What complete self-possession! If only *she* could be so thoroughly at ease.

She pats the folds of her new frock nervously, hoping that he will not notice how embarrassed she is, how uncomfortable. He doesn't—until the waiter comes to their table and stands, with pencil poised, to take the order.

"A chicken salad, please." She hears herself give the order as in a daze. She hears him repeat the order to the waiter, in a rather surprised tone. Why *had* she ordered that again! This was the third time she had ordered chicken salad while dining with him.

He would think she didn't know how to order a dinner. Well, did she? No. She didn't know how to pronounce those French words on the menu. And she didn't know how to use the table appointment as gracefully as she would have liked; found that she couldn't create conversation—and was actually tongue-tied; was conscious of little crudities which she just knew he must be noticing. She wasn't sure of herself, she didn't *know*. And she discovered, as we all do, that there is only one way to have complete poise and ease of manner, and that is to know definitely what to do and say on every occasion.

Are You Conscious of Your Crudities?

It is not, perhaps, so serious a fault to be unable to order a correct dinner. But it is just such little things as these that betray us—that reveal our crudities to others.

Are you sure of yourself? Do you know precisely what to do and say wherever you happen to be? Or are you always hesitant and ill at ease, never quite sure that you haven't blundered?

Every day in our contact with men and women we meet little unexpected problems of conduct. Unless we are prepared to meet them, it is inevitable that we suffer embarrassment and keen humiliation.

Etiquette is the armor that protects us from these embarrassments. It makes us aware instantly of the little crudities that are robbing us of our poise and ease. It tells us how to smooth away these crudities and achieve a manner of confidence and self-possession. It eliminates doubt and uncertainty, tells us exactly what we want to know.

There is an old proverb which says "Good manners make good mixers." We all know how true this is. No one likes to associate with a person who is self-conscious and embarrassed; whose crudities are obvious to all.

Do You Make Friends Easily?

By telling you exactly what is expected of you on all occasions, by giving you a wonderful new ease and dignity of manner, the Book of Etiquette will help make you more popular—a "better mixer." This famous two-volume set of books is the recognized social authority—is a silent social secretary in half a million homes.

Let us pretend that you have received an invitation. Would you know exactly how to acknowledge it? Would you know what sort of gift to send, what to write on the card that accompanies it? Perhaps it is an invitation to a formal wedding. Would you know what to wear? Would you know what to say to the host and hostess upon arrival?

If a Dinner Follows the Wedding—

Would you know exactly how to proceed to the dining room, when to seat yourself, how

to create conversation, how to conduct yourself with ease and dignity?

Would you use a fork for your fruit salad, or a spoon? Would you cut your roll with a knife, or break it with your fingers? Would you take olives with a fork? How would you take celery—asparagus—radishes? Unless you are absolutely sure of yourself, you will be embarrassed. And embarrassment *cannot be concealed*.

Book of Etiquette Gives Lifelong Advice

Hundreds of thousands of men and women know and use the Book of Etiquette and find it increasingly helpful. Every time an occasion of importance arises—every time expert help, advice and suggestion is required—they find what they seek in the Book of Etiquette. It solves all problems, answers all questions, tells you exactly what to do, say, write and wear on every occasion.

If you want always to be sure of yourself, to have ease and poise, to avoid embarrassment and humiliation, send for the Book of Etiquette at once. Take advantage of the special bargain offer explained in the panel. Let the Book of Etiquette give you complete self-possession; let it banish the crudities that are perhaps making you self-conscious and uncomfortable when you should be thoroughly at ease.

Mail this coupon now while you are thinking of it. The Book of Etiquette will be sent to you in a plain carton with no identifying marks. Be among those who will take advantage of the special offer. Nelson Doubleday, Inc., Dept. 3911, Garden City, New York.

Don't walk when you can ride.

Presenting Another Lesson in How To Kill Yourself.

In an earlier lesson, we told you to eat, drink, be merry, and most important, to overdo it.

Now we are going to suggest that, once you've taken in all those calories, do nothing—absolutely nothing—to burn any of them off.

No matter how short the trip, don't walk when you can ride.

And if walking is out, jogging is unthinkable. Even though your doctor told you you're one of those people who could well invest in some exercise—to get your heart muscle pumping and your blood circulating.

True, you have heard it said that most children in America learn to walk by 16 months and stop walking by 16 years. But then, *you're* no child.

And, anyway, exercise is a big, fat bore.

Why Are America's Doctors Telling You This?

Well, for a long time we've been telling you how to stay alive and healthy. (In fact, about 70% of the annual budget of the American Medical Association goes to health education.) But many of you go do the opposite.

Now we figure we'll tell you how to kill yourselves. In the fervent hope that once again you'll do the exact opposite. If you do, there's every chance we'll be seeing less of you. Just for check-ups. And that's it.

Doing your bit to take care of yourself (such as exercising, but only if your doctor says it's OK) means your doctor can give everyone the best care possible. When *only* his care will do.

For a free booklet on the right kind and right amount of exercise for you, write: Box X, American Medical Association, 535 North Dearborn Street, Chicago, Illinois 60610.

America's Doctors of Medicine

(Our Best Patients Take Care of Themselves)

[1972]

26

How do you tell a kid he's been traded?

How do you explain to a .400 hitter that his Dad's been transferred to a different city? What can you say that will ease the pain of leaving his teammates behind?

Sure, there'll be another team—maybe even better—in the city he's moving to. But for awhile at least, it won't be the same.

These are the heart-tugging moments that are so often a part of moving. And United Van Lines knows how important they are to you and your family.

That's why we do our very best to take the load off your mind . . . as well as your hands. We think you should have the time you need to spend with the people you care about most.

Your nearby United agent is waiting to help. Why not give him a call today? He's listed in the Yellow Pages.

UNITED UNITED UNITED
Van Lines

SERVING 150 COUNTRIES WORLD-WIDE   United Van Lines I.C.C. No. MC 67234

[1980]

How to spell

By John Irving

International Paper asked John Irving, author of "The World According to Garp," "The Hotel New Hampshire," and "Setting Free the Bears," among other novels— and once a hopelessly bad speller himself— to teach you how to improve your spelling.

Let's begin with the bad news.

If you're a bad speller, you probably think you always will be. There are exceptions to every spelling rule, and the rules themselves are easy to forget. George Bernard Shaw demonstrated how ridiculous some spelling rules are. By following the rules, he said, we could spell <u>fish</u> this way: <u>ghoti</u>. The "f" as it sounds in enou<u>gh</u>, the "i" as it sounds in w<u>o</u>men, and the "sh" as it sounds in fi<u>ti</u>on.

With such rules to follow, no one should feel stupid for being a bad speller. But there are ways to improve. Start by acknowledging the mess that English spelling is in—but have sympathy: English spelling changed with foreign influences. Chaucer wrote "gesse," but "guess," imported earlier by the Norman invaders, finally replaced it. Most early printers in England came from Holland; they brought "ghost" and "gherkin" with them.

If you'd like to intimidate yourself—and remain a bad speller forever—just try to remember

the 13 different ways the sound "sh" can be written:

<u>sh</u>oe	suspi<u>ci</u>on
<u>s</u>ugar	nau<u>se</u>ous
o<u>ce</u>an	con<u>sci</u>ous
i<u>ss</u>ue	<u>ch</u>aperone
na<u>ti</u>on	man<u>si</u>on
<u>sch</u>ist	fu<u>chs</u>ia
p<u>sh</u>aw	

Now the good news

The good news is that 90 percent of all writing consists of 1,000 basic words. There is, also, a method to most English spelling and a great number of how-to-spell books. Remarkably, all these books propose learning the same rules! Not surprisingly, most of these books are humorless.

Just keep this in mind: If you're familiar with the words you use, you'll probably spell them correctly—and you shouldn't be writing words you're unfamiliar with anyway. USE a word—out loud, and more than once—before you try writing it, and make sure (with a new word) that you know what it means before you use it. This means you'll have to look it up in a dictionary, where you'll not only learn what it means, but you'll see how it's spelled. Choose a dictionary you enjoy browsing in, and guard it as you would a diary. You wouldn't lend a diary, would you?

A tip on looking it up

Beside every word I look up in my dictionary, I make a mark.

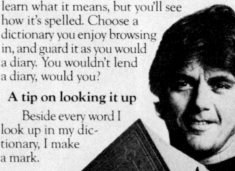

"Love your dictionary"

Beside every word I look up more than once, I write a note to myself —about WHY I looked it up. I have looked up "strictly" 14 times since 1964. I prefer to spell it with a <u>k</u>— as in "stric<u>k</u>tly." I have looked up "ubiquitous" a dozen times. I can't remember what it means.

Another good way to use your dictionary: When you have to look up a word, for any reason, learn— and learn to *spell*—a *new* word at the same time. It can be any useful word on the same page as the word you looked up. Put the date beside this new word and see how quickly, or in what way, you forget it. Eventually, you'll learn it.

Almost as important as knowing what a word means (in order to spell it) is knowing how it's pronounced. It's go<u>v</u>ernment, not goverment. It's Feb<u>ru</u>ary, not Febuary. And if you know that <u>anti</u>- means against, you should know how to spell <u>anti</u>dote and <u>anti</u>biotic and <u>anti</u>freeze. If you know that <u>ante</u>- means before, you shouldn't have trouble spelling <u>ante</u>chamber or <u>ante</u>cedent.

Some rules, exceptions, and two tricks

I don't have room to touch on <u>all</u> the rules here. It would take a book to do that. But I can share a few that help me most:

What about -<u>ary</u> or -<u>ery</u>? When a word has a primary accent on the first syllable and a secondary accent on the next-to-last syllable (sec're-tar'y), it usually ends in -<u>ary</u>. Only six important words like this end in -<u>ery</u>:

cemetery   monastery
millinery   confectionery
distillery   stationery
            (as in pape_r_)

Here's another easy rule. Only
ur words end in -_efy_. Most people
isspell them—with -_ify_, which is
ually correct. Just memorize these,
o, and use -_ify_ for all the rest.

stupefy   putrefy
liquefy   rarefy

As a former bad speller, I have
arned a few valuable tricks. Any
od how-to-spell book will teach
u more than these two, but these
o are my favorites. Of the
0,000 words in the English lanuage, the most frequently miselled is alright; just remember
at alright is all wrong. You
uldn't write alwrong, would you?
hat's how you know you should
rite all right.

The other
ck is for the
ly _worst_
ellers. I mean
ose of you who
ell so badly that you
n't get close enough to
e right way to spell a word in
der to even FIND it in the diconary. The word you're looking
r is there, of course, but you
n't find it the way you're trying
spell it. What to do is look up
synonym—another word that
eans the same thing. Chances
e good that you'll find the word
u're looking for under the definion of the synonym.

Demon words and bugbears

Everyone has a few demon
rds—they never look right, even
en they're spelled correctly.
ree of my demons are medieval,
stasy, and rhythm. I have learned
hate these words, but I have not
arned to spell them; I have to
ok them up every time.

And everyone has a spelling
le that's a bugbear—it's either too
fficult to learn or it's impossible
remember. My personal bugbear
nong the rules is the one governg whether you add -able or -ible.
an teach it to you, but I can't

remember it myself.

You add -able to a full word:
adapt, adaptable; work, workable.
You add -able to words that end in
e—just remember to drop the final
e: love, lovable. But if the word
ends in two e's, like agree, you keep
them both: agreeable.

You add -ible if the base is not
a full word that can stand on its
own: credible, tangible, horrible,
terrible. You add -ible if the root
word ends in -ns: responsible. You
add -ible if the root word ends in
-miss: permissible. You add -ible
if the root word ends in a soft c

*"This is one of the longest English words
in common use. But don't let the length of
a word frighten you. There's a rule for how
to spell this one, and you can learn it."*

(but remember to drop the final e!):
force, forcible.

Got that? I don't have it, and
I was introduced to that rule in
prep school; with that rule, I still
learn one word at a time.

Poor President Jackson

You must remember that it is
permissible for spelling to drive
you crazy. Spelling had this effect
on Andrew Jackson, who once
blew his stack while trying to write
a Presidential paper. "It's a damn
poor mind that can think of only
one way to spell a word!" the President cried.

When you have trouble, think
of poor Andrew Jackson and know
that you're not alone.

What's really important

And remember what's really
important about good writing is
not good spelling. If you spell badly
but write well, you should hold
your head up. As the poet T.S.
Eliot recommended, "Write for as
large and miscellaneous an audience as possible"—and don't be
overly concerned if you can't spell
"miscellaneous."

Also
remember
that you can
spell correctly
and write well
and still be misunderstood. Hold your
head up about that, too.

As good old G.C. Lichtenberg said, "A book is a mirror: if
an ass peers into it, you can't
expect an apostle to look out"—
whether you spell "apostle" correctly or not.

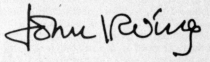

When the moment becomes more...be sure.

You don't plan it. It just happens. And when it does, be sure you have Encare® with you. It's discreet, convenient, and easy to use.

Doctors recommend Encare more than any other contraceptive suppository. Pharmacists recommend it 3 times more often than any other contraceptive suppository. But, more importantly, women trust Encare so much, it's America's leading contraceptive suppository.

Encare contains a potent, yet safe, spermicide. And, once inserted, it gently foams and forms a powerful barrier against pregnancy.

So be sure to carry Encare. Because you never know what one wonderful moment will lead to.

© 1982 Eaton-Merz Laboratories, Inc.

If your doctor has advised you against pregnancy, discuss Encare with him or her before using it. Encare is approximately as effective as vaginal foam contraceptives in actual use, without the inconvenience of an applicator.

It is essential that you insert Encare at least ten minutes before intercourse. Some Encare users experience irritation in using the product.

For best protection, follow the package instructions carefully.

The information supplied in this advertisement is based on data available as of November 1981.

Encare®

[1982]

Sexual Confidence

You can tell when someone's got it the moment they enter a room—the ability to turn people on with just the look in their eyes. And, NOW you can have it too, with the amazing bestseller, SEXUAL CONFIDENCE.

You'll learn: **How to project Sexual Charisma** • Ways to attract new mates • **How to create laughter in the bedroom, and why this will** *instantly* **triple your capacity for sexual enjoyment** • Touching techniques that help you get intimate right away • **Why "letting-go" during lovemaking will make you a** *better* **lover** • How to take a "Sexual Holiday" • **Ten techniques for ending sexual anxiety** • How to change your "sexual image" (and why people will suddenly find you far more attractive than ever before) • **Stimulating your lovemate with sensual, new kissing techniques** • A Great Lover's Vocabulary • **And so much more!**

Yes, this revolutionary, 230 page, hardcover bestseller is *fully* guaranteed to make you a better lover. In fact, within just one hour it'll have you radiating Total Sexual Confidence...because from now on you'll know exactly what your lovers want *even before they ask!* Remember, SEXUAL CONFIDENCE has been acclaimed by doctors and therapists as a breakthrough in increasing sexual pleasure. So order today. SEXUAL CONFIDENCE costs far less than a new shirt or blouse, yet it'll bring so many more wonderful people into your love life!

(To order, see coupon at right)

Shy Person's Guide To A Successful Love Life!

A brilliant psychological writer explains how you can conquer shyness literally overnight.

by P. Woodland-Smith

I am a shy person myself.

Yet I could walk into a party tonight and within five minutes be talking, laughing, dancing...even making dates with the most attractive people in the room.

I could walk into a restaurant or pub and walk out an hour later with a new acquaintance, a new friend, even a new lover.

Yet the extraordinary thing about all this is that up until recently I was so pathetically shy I often didn't go out for months at a time.

At work I did fine. Socially I was a bust. My lack of dates even became sort of a joke among my friends. Some joke.

Then about six months ago a kindly relative lent me a copy of a book called THE SHY PERSON'S GUIDE TO A HAPPIER LOVE LIFE. The rest is history. In slightly more than two weeks I was dating several new people. And today...just six months later...I have so many friends and lovers I hardly ever spend an evening home alone. My social life has blossomed to the point that it's started interfering with my work life. Sometimes I actually have to take the phone off the hook to get some of my writing done.

If only I'd known that in two short weeks I'd be able to cure myself of something that had been making me miserable every day of my life. Why, lately I've been having a ball. And I'm absolutely convinced that anyone...no matter how incurably shy they *think* they are...can do the same.

What THE SHY PERSON'S GUIDE taught me is that there are more people ready to love you than you ever dreamed possible. At work, at school, on the street, in parks, museums, restaurants, *everywhere!* All you have to do is ask. And that's precisely why THE SHY PERSON'S GUIDE can be such a help.

THE SHY PERSON'S GUIDE will show you exactly how to unleash your natural, inborn talent for charming and attracting new people. Imagine how successful you'd be with others if you weren't afraid to speak what was in your heart..to be as free and as open as you'd like.

Well, THE SHY PERSON'S GUIDE will show you scores of techniques for doing just that: For example, you will discover: **A simple, upfront way of letting someone know you're attracted to them without appearing weak or desperate**... a brilliant technique for making someone feel "special"

when they're in your company...A completely reliable way of telling if someone likes you (you'll be amazed at how many potential lovemates you've been overlooking)...**A simple way to "trick" yourself into being looser and friendlier at parties**...How to get invited to more parties and what to do once you get there (not the same old things that make you angry and frustrated with yourself the moment you get home)...AND MUCH, MUCH MORE!

The Sooner You Attack Your Shyness, The Easier It Is To Cure

Don't kid yourself into thinking that *next time* you go to a party you'll be braver, more outgoing, That's the classic shy person's trick for *staying* shy. No, if you really want to get better, really want to know the joy of laughing, dancing, meeting people who want to be with you...then send for this mind-opening bestseller today.

Alright, maybe you're thinking, *but what if THE SHY PERSON'S GUIDE doesn't work for me.* No problem. Simply return the book and the publisher will send you a complete and immediate refund. No questions asked. Even if you secretly feel the book has done you some good.

But I'm so thoroughly convinced THE SHY PERSON'S GUIDE will change your life, so incredibly *bullish* about its shyness-conquering techniques, I hate to even bring up the guarantee. That's how sure I am this amazing book will work for you.

So send for THE SHY PERSON'S GUIDE TO A HAPPIER LOVE LIFE today. And start enjoying all the love and romance you've been dreaming about. It's out there alright. And it's so darn easy to find, it'd be a crying shame not to get your share.

[1983]

The hardest thing she ever had to do was tell Roger she had herpes. But thanks to her doctor, she could also tell him it's controllable.

Whether you have a mild, intermediate or severe case of genital herpes, you should see your doctor to help gain new control over your outbreaks— especially if you haven't seen your doctor within the past year.

The medical profession now has more information than ever before about the treatment of herpes, as well as effective counselling and treatment programs that can help you reduce the frequency, duration and severity of your outbreaks.

If in the past you were told that nothing could be done for herpes, it's no longer true. Herpes *is* controllable.

Ask your doctor about these treatment programs, and whether one of them would be suitable for you.

See your doctor...there <u>is</u> help for herpes

32

[1987]

"Most Automobiles are like most Men"

"They are either all right or all wrong, but seldom one or the other for long at a time."

"That's probably why they call this a Woman's Car, it's so consistent."

"Your intuition, my dear, is perfect. That's just it. You know, I used to call the last car we had, a 'Cook Four,' because it cost more than it was worth, consumed more than it earned, and was always quitting!"

"And what do you call this?"

"Oh, the Overland is like a first-rate cook — popular with the whole family! This is the first Saturday I've had this car to myself since—"

"Heavens, Helen, you went right into that mudhole!"

"Didn't jar you, did it?"

"No, not at all! But isn't it remarkable for so light a car?"

"Yes. Harry calls it a feather bed on wheels. It's some funny new spring they've invented that lets you down easy when the going's hard. How do you like the tan velour upholstery?"

"Just love it, Helen, it is so restrained. But how about gas?"

"That's restrained, too, my dear. Harry says we're averaging twenty-five miles to the gallon."

"Twenty-five miles?"

"Sounds as incredible as a woman's age, but it's true. In fact, I've only one complaint against this Overland Sedan — it's too useful!"

"Too useful?"

"Yes, too useful. So useful that it points a moral."

"For example?"

"Well, all you ever have to do with this Overland Sedan is to step on it. And that is the fate of all useful things and all useful people. Somebody is always stepping on them!"

"Helen, you talk like a Socialist."

"It's true. This little Overland Sedan is like a household drudge — always working and never through!"

"You'd better hurry, Helen, the train's in. We'll miss Harry."

"Don't worry. He'll wait. There he is now.... oh, Harry!"

"Hello, girls! Have you room for a few bundles and may a husband presume to ride home in his wife's car?"

WILLYS-OVERLAND, INC., TOLEDO, OHIO

Sedans, Coupés, Touring Cars, Roadsters

Willys-Overland, Limited, Toronto, Canada   The John N. Willys Export Corp., New York

Overland

[1921]

AUTOMOBILES

Lemon.

This Volkswagen missed the boat.

The chrome strip on the glove compartment is blemished and must be replaced. Chances are you wouldn't have noticed it; Inspector Kurt Kroner did.

There are 3,389 men at our Wolfsburg factory with only one job: to inspect Volkswagens at each stage of production. (3000 Volkswagens are produced daily; there are more inspectors than cars.)

Every shock absorber is tested (spot checking won't do), every windshield is scanned. VWs have been rejected for surface scratches barely visible to the eye.

Final inspection is really something! VW inspectors run each car off the line onto the Funktionsprüfstand (car test stand), tote up 189 check points, gun ahead to the automatic brake stand, and say "no" to one VW out of fifty.

This preoccupation with detail means the VW lasts longer and requires less maintenance, by and large, than other cars. (It also means a used VW depreciates less than any other car.)

We pluck the lemons; you get the plums.

[1960]

Separates the men from the boys.

There are boy-type cars. And there are man-type cars. And Toronado is all man, all the way. Its styling is bold, brawny and massively male. Its handling is authoritative —thanks to the pulling power of front-wheel drive. Its ride is revolutionary, sure, unique—different from any other car.

Its engine is the strongest Rocket ever built: a bigger-than-ever, 455-cubic-inch V-8. Frankly, not everybody is cut out for a Toronado. But, then, who wants to be everybody?

Toronado.
Test drive the front-wheel-drive "youngmobile" from Oldsmobile.

GM
OF EXCELLENCE

[1969]

Which man would you vote for?

Ah yes, what could be more dazzling than watching the candidates parade about, kissing babies and flashing winning smiles.

Consider the man in the top picture.

He promises to spend your tax dollars wisely.

But see how he spends his campaign dollars.

On a very fancy convertible.

Resplendent with genuine leather seats. A big 425-horsepower engine.

And a price tag that makes it one of the most expensive convertibles you can buy.

Now consider his opponent.

He promises to spend your tax dollars wisely.

But see how he spends his campaign dollars.

On a Volkswagen Convertible.

Resplendent with a hand-fitted top.

A warranty and four free diagnostic check-ups that cover you for 24 months or 24,000 miles.*

And a price tag that makes it one of the least expensive convertibles you can buy.

So maybe this year you'll find a politician who'll do what few politicians ever do:

Keep his promises before he's elected.

*If an owner maintains and services his vehicle in accordance with the Volkswagen maintenance schedule any factory part found to be defective in material or workmanship within 24 months or 24,000 miles, whichever comes first (except normal wear and tear and service items), will be repaired or replaced by any U.S. or Canadian Volkswagen Dealer. And this will be done free of charge. See your Volkswagen dealer for details.

[1972]

Are you ready for an Alfa Romeo?

Sheila C.

Bill B.

Ray R.

"When I was a young man I dreamed that one day I would own an Alfa Romeo.

"When I was 25 I was really the perfect wife, the perfect mother and the perfect homemaker.

"I drove a great big stationwagon.

"Well, I'm no longer 25 and I'm no longer anyone's wife—my kids are grown and have kids of their own and I have a career.

"And that stationwagon is just a rusted memory.

"You know what I did? I went out and bought myself an Alfa Romeo Spider.

"It's red and it's got a convertible top and sometimes when I pass those ladies in their huge stationwagons full of kids, and dogs, and groceries I wave—and say to myself, there but for the grace of my Alfa go I."

"But then I got married and Jennifer arrived a year later; two years after that, Robert.

"My dream of owning an Alfa gave way to the reality of a mortgage, dentist's bills, and college tuition.

"But now Jennifer is married and has a Jennifer of her own, Robert Junior is through law school.

"And this 50 year old kid went out and bought himself an Alfa Romeo Spider.

"Do I love my Alfa as much as I thought I would? Well, It's a dream come true."

"I limped through college and graduate school with one crummy used car after another.

"But now that I've got a grown up job with grown up responsibility, I thought I'd treat myself to a brand new car.

"Well, at first, I thought the world had passed me by—all those cars were so boring!

"Then I discovered the Alfa Spider. First of all, it's a convertible! And most of all it's an Alfa Romeo.

"What a machine!

"Today when I leave the office after all those meetings, my hair cut short, necktie in place, I'll jump into my very own Alfa Romeo Spider.

"You know, all that college was worth it."

The Alfa Romeo Spider Veloce: $13,995. 1980 manufacturer's suggested retail price POE. Inland transportation, dealer preparation, local taxes, and optional equipment not included. For the name of your nearest Alfa Romeo Dealer, call us anytime, toll free at 800-447-4700; in Illinois call 800-322-4400.

Alfa Romeo

A CAR FOR THE LEFT SIDE OF YOUR BRAIN.

A CAR FOR THE RIGHT SIDE OF YOUR BRAIN.

The left side of your brain, recent investigations tell us, is the logical side.

It figures out that $1 + 1 = 2$. And, in a few cases, that $E = mc^2$.

On a more mundane level, it chooses the socks you wear, the cereal you eat, and the car you drive. All by means of rigorous Aristotelian logic.

However, and a big however it is, for real satisfaction, you must achieve harmony with the other side of your brain.

The right side, the poetic side, that says, "Yeah, Car X has a reputation for lasting a long time but it's so dull, who'd want to drive it that long anyway?"

The Saab Turbo looked at from all sides.

To the left side of your brain, Saab turbocharging is a technological feat that retains good gas mileage while also increasing performance.

To the right side of your brain, Saab turbocharging is what makes a Saab go like a bat out of hell.

The left side sees the safety in high performance. (Passing on a two-lane highway. Entering a freeway in the midst of high-speed traffic.)

The right side lives only for the thrills.

The left side considers that *Road & Track* magazine just named Saab "The Sports Sedan for the Eighties." By unanimous choice of its editors.

The right side eschews informed endorsements by editors who have spent a lifetime comparing cars. The right side doesn't know much about cars, but knows what it likes.

The left side scans this chart.

Wheelbase	99.1 inches
Length	187.6 inches
Width	66.5 inches
Height	55.9 inches
Fuel-tank capacity	16.6 gallons
EPA City	19 mpg*
EPA Highway	31 mpg*

The right side looks at the picture on the right.

The left side compares a Saab's comfort with that of a Mercedes. Its performance with that of a BMW. Its braking with that of an Audi.

The right side looks at the picture.

The left side looks ahead to the winter when a Saab's front-wheel drive will keep a Saab in front of traffic.

The right side looks at the picture.

The left side also considers the other seasons of the year when a Saab's front-wheel drive gives it the cornering ability of a sports car.

The right side looks again at the picture.

Getting what you need vs. getting what you want.

Needs are boring; desires are what make life worth living.

The left side of your brain is your mother telling you that a Saab is good for you. "Eat your vegetables." (In today's world, you need a car engineered like a Saab.) "Put on your raincoat." (The Saab is economical. Look at the price-value relationship.) "Do your homework." (The passive safety of the construction. The active safety of the handling.)

1982 SAAB PRICE** LIST		
900 3-Door	5-Speed	$10,400
	Automatic	10,750
900 4-Door	5-Speed	$10,700
	Automatic	11,050
900S 3-Door	5-Speed	$12,100
	Automatic	12,450
900S 4-Door	5-Speed	$12,700
	Automatic	13,050
900 Turbo 3-Door	5-Speed	$15,600
	Automatic	15,950
900 Turbo 4-Door	5-Speed	$16,260
	Automatic	16,610

All turbo models include a Sony XR70, 4-Speaker Stereo Sound System as standard equipment. The stereo can be, of course, perfectly balanced: left and right.

The right side of your brain guides your foot to the clutch, your hand to the gears, and listens for the "zzzooommm."

Together, they see the 1982 Saab Turbo as the responsible car the times demand you get. And the performance car you've always, deep down, wanted with half your mind.

*Saab 900 Turbo. Remember, use estimated mpg for comparison only. Mileage varies with speed, trip length, and weather. Actual highway mileage will probably be less. **Manufacturer's suggested retail price. Not including taxes, license, freight, dealer charges or options desired by either side of your brain.

SAAB
The most intelligent car ever built.

[1982]

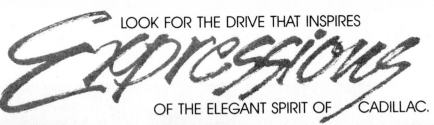

[1987]

39

ERNEST HEMINGWAY, who has been called the greatest living American writer, is also internationally famous as a deep-sea fisherman. Since publication of *The Sun Also Rises* in 1926, his novels and short stories have enriched the literature of the English language consistently, year after year. His newest book is *The Old Man and the Sea*.

EATING AND DRINKING

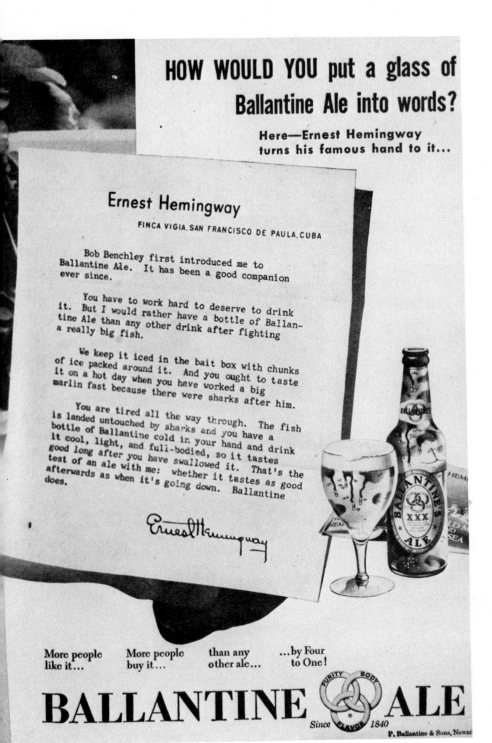

HOW WOULD YOU put a glass of Ballantine Ale into words?

Here—Ernest Hemingway
turns his famous hand to it...

Ernest Hemingway

FINCA VIGIA, SAN FRANCISCO DE PAULA, CUBA

Bob Benchley first introduced me to
Ballantine Ale. It has been a good companion
ever since.

You have to work hard to deserve to drink
it. But I would rather have a bottle of Ballantine Ale than any other drink after fighting
a really big fish.

We keep it iced in the bait box with chunks
of ice packed around it. And you ought to taste
it on a hot day when you have worked a big
marlin fast because there were sharks after him.

You are tired all the way through. The fish
is landed untouched by sharks and you have a
bottle of Ballantine cold in your hand and drink
it cool, light, and full-bodied, so it tastes
good long after you have swallowed it. That's the
test of an ale with me: whether it tastes as good
afterwards as when it's going down. Ballantine
does.

Ernest Hemingway

More people like it...   More people buy it...   than any other ale...   ...by Four to One!

BALLANTINE ALE

Since 1840

PURITY • BODY • FLAVOR

P. Ballantine & Sons, Newar

[1952]

"You're some tomato. California's written all over you.
We could make beautiful Bloody Marys together.
I'm different from those other fellows."

"I like you, Wolfschmidt.
You've got taste."

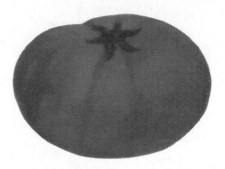

Wolfschmidt in a Bloody Mary is a tomato in triumph. Wolfschmidt has the touch of taste that marks genuine old world vodka. It heightens, accents, brings out the best in every drink.

"You sweet California doll. I appreciate you. I've got taste.
I'll bring out your inner orange. I'll make you famous. Roll over here and kiss me."

"Who was that tomato
I saw you with last week?"

Wolfschmidt in a Screwdriver is an orange in ecstasy. Wolfschmidt has the touch of taste that marks genuine old world vodka. It heightens, accents, brings out the best in every drink.

[1961]

42

Why husbands leave home:

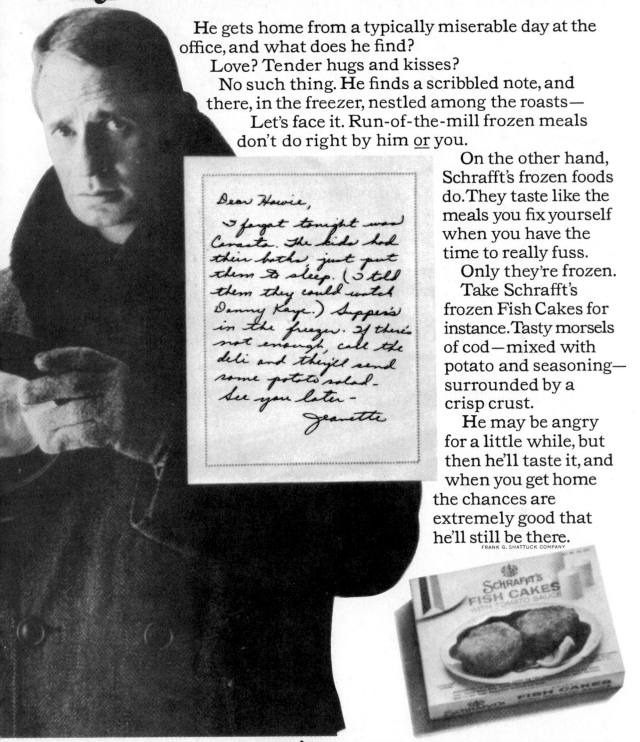

He gets home from a typically miserable day at the office, and what does he find?

Love? Tender hugs and kisses?

No such thing. He finds a scribbled note, and there, in the freezer, nestled among the roasts—

Let's face it. Run-of-the-mill frozen meals don't do right by him <u>or</u> you.

On the other hand, Schrafft's frozen foods do. They taste like the meals you fix yourself when you have the time to really fuss.

Only they're frozen.

Take Schrafft's frozen Fish Cakes for instance. Tasty morsels of cod—mixed with potato and seasoning—surrounded by a crisp crust.

He may be angry for a little while, but then he'll taste it, and when you get home the chances are extremely good that he'll still be there.

FRANK G. SHATTUCK COMPANY

HURRY-UP MEALS YOU DON'T HAVE TO MAKE EXCUSES FOR.
SCHRAFFT'S

[1966]

43

America

If you'll stop and think for just a moment, you'll find we have more of the good things in this country than anywhere else in the world.

Think of this land. From the surf at Big Sur to a Florida sunrise. And all the places in between.

The Grand Canyon... the wheat fields of Kansas... Autumn in New Hampshire...

You could go on forever. But America is more than a place of much beauty. It's a place for good times.

It's Saturday night.

It's a trip down a dirt road in a beat up old jalopy.

It's your team winning. It's a late night movie you could enjoy a thousand times.

And, yes, when you're thirsty, it's the taste of ice-cold Coca-Cola. It's the real thing.

In fact, all of the good things in this country are real. They're all around you, plainly visible. We point to many of them in our advertising. But you can discover many, many more without ever seeing a single commercial for Coke.

So have a bottle of Coke... and start looking up.

The Coca-Cola Company

[1975]

With my cooking, the army that travels on its stomach is facing a pretty bumpy road.

As far as being a rookie cook goes, I was as green as the guys who ate what I cooked.

They said my hamburgers tasted like hockey pucks.

They said my chipped beef stuck to their ribs, permanently.

And what they said about my sloppy joes could have gotten them all arrested.

I finally had to face up to it. No one could stomach my cooking. And my brilliant military career would have gone down the drain then and there if it wasn't for McCormick/Schilling.

They're the experts on spice and flavor. And they make all kinds of sauces, seasonings and gravies that can really make things taste good. Even the stuff I cook.

So, I tried their sloppy joes mix. All I had to do was brown 1,000 pounds of ground beef, mix in the McCormick/Schilling seasoning; add tomato paste and 150 gallons of water.

And in no time, I had enough to feed an army.

It was easy. And more important, it was good.

Guys were standing in line for seconds. (Before, they never stuck around for firsts).

Matter of fact, they stopped griping about my cooking long enough for me to finally get my stripes.

And I owe it all to McCormick/Schilling.

I guess you could say that when it comes to cooking, they turned me into a seasoned veteran.

My sloppy joes recipe for 6,000:

Brown 1,000 lbs. of ground beef. Mix in 1,000 packages of McCormick/Schilling Sloppy Joes Mix and blend thoroughly. Stir in 1,000 6-ounce cans of tomato paste and 1,250 cups of water. Bring to a boil. Then reduce heat and simmer 10 minutes, stirring occasionally. Spoon over hamburger buns. Makes 6,000 ½-cup servings. (To get 6 servings, divide by 1,000).

McCormick/Schilling flavor makes all the difference in the world.

McCormick/Schilling

[1976]

45

DO YOUR DINNERTIMIN'™ AT McDONALD'S.

When you're looking for a different place to have dinner, check out McDonald's. You don't have to get dressed up, there's no tipping and the kids love it.

You can relax and get down with good food that won't keep you waitin'.

Dinnertimin' or anytimin', going out is easy at McDonald's.

WE DO IT ALL FOR YOU™

McDonald's ®

[1976]

Geraldine Chaplin talks about her 'first time.'

CHAPLIN: To be perfectly blunt, it was a bit disappointing. Oh, it was good... but not at all what I had expected. In fact, I couldn't for the life of me understand why all my friends thought it was such a big deal.

INTERVIEWER: Miss Chaplin, you'd be surprised how many people feel that way. So, don't be embarrassed... just tell me what happened.

CHAPLIN: It all started at a party in Madrid. I felt a tap on my shoulder and when I turned around there stood this wonderfully attractive young man.

"Campari?" he asked.

"No," I said, "Geraldine."

He laughed and ordered a Campari and soda for me and a Campari and orange juice for himself.

INTERVIEWER: He certainly was a very assertive young man.

CHAPLIN: Yes. You see he turned out to be a cinematographer from Chile and they're like that, you know.

INTERVIEWER: Well? What was it like?

CHAPLIN: A truly bittersweet experience.

INTERVIEWER: Could you be more specific?

CHAPLIN: Yes...it was like eating a mango.

INTERVIEWER: I beg your pardon???

CHAPLIN: Well, I wasn't crazy about them the first time, either. Yet I was so intrigued by their uniqueness, I tried again... then I was a believer.

INTERVIEWER: So now you like it?

CHAPLIN: Love it. There are so many different ways to enjoy it. Once I even tried it on the rocks. But I wouldn't recommend that for beginners.

INTERVIEWER: That's great. Tell me, whatever happened to that handsome young Chilean?

CHAPLIN: We're still very close. But I'll let you in on a secret. That was his first time, too. And to this day, he still hasn't acquired a taste for it.

INTERVIEWER: That's a shame.

CHAPLIN: Yes, it is ... I guess it's because he's never had it a second time.

© 1981—Imported, prepared and bottled by Austin, Nichols & Co., Lawrenceburg, KY. 48 proof bitter liqueur

CAMPARI. THE FIRST TIME IS NEVER THE BEST.

[1981]

47

Keystone Press Agency photograph of the burning of the books, Berlin, May 10, 1933.

These are the books that Hitler burned

He had to.

These books riddle superstition and viciousness with *truth*.

These thoughts and theories built our democracies and broke the chains of bondage.

These words are more powerful than any Gestapo or thought police.

Here, in 54 superbly bound volumes, you'll find the wisdom of Shakespeare, Plato, Thomas Aquinas, Adam Smith, Tolstoy, Darwin and Freud. The truths of Homer, Augustine and many, many more.

No power-hungry madman could stand for long against these books. That's why Hitler burned them.

Now these Great Books can all be yours, 443 works by 74 immortal authors. Yours, in your own home. To enlighten you, console you, to help you guide your children.

The amazing Syntopicon

With Great Books you receive the two-volume Syntopicon, an *idea* index that took 8 years and over a million dollars to build. With the Syntopicon, you can trace every thought in the Great Books as easily as you look up words in your dictionary.

FREE OFFER...act now

Find out more about Great Books. It's free. Just mail in the attached post card for a profusely illustrated 16-page booklet—*free*. Do it today, no postage required. GREAT BOOKS, Dept. 142-J, 425 No. Michigan, Chicago, Illinois 60611.

GREAT BOOKS

54 superb volumes • 74 immortal authors • 443 works

[1966]

MEDIA

"The soaps are like Big Macs...a lot of people who won't admit it eat them up."

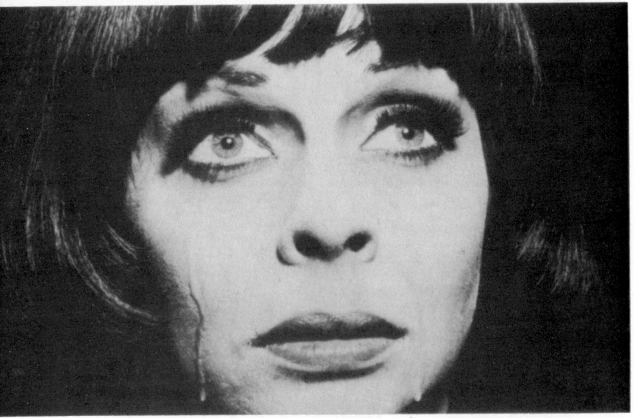

"The symbiosis between audience and show makes soap opera unique, the most powerful entertainment on or off television."

Academic amnesia, vicarious VD, hypothetical hysterectomies: the world of TV soap opera. But TIME readers are among the least avid watchers of daytime television. Why was TIME inspired to devote a cover story to TV soap opera?

Because TIME readers are also insatiably curious. TIME probed the hypnotic appeal of the soaps, found a whole subculture, discovered the iron hand behind the wet handkerchief. And in so doing, TIME demonstrates once again the rewards of analyzing seriously what seems on the surface to be egregious frivolity.

You know what TIME does. And reading it every week reminds you how well.

TIME

The Weekly Newsmagazine

[1976]

Scoop McClain?
He doesn't work here anymore.

You remember Scoop McClain—sarcastic and swaggering, a tough guy with a press card in his hat who liked pretty girls and whiskey and telling the world to go to hell. He was something else, Scoop was: a star reporter, streetwise and cynical, but with a heart of gold. He never let the facts get in the way of a good story.

Scoop graduated from the school of hard knocks. He typed with one finger, got news tips from bookies and barmaids and yelled "STOP THE PRESS!" with every fresh exposé. Murder was his specialty, but he fought City Hall, too, and saved widows from eviction. He never forgot a friend and he never told a lie—except to get a story. So here's to Scoop McClain; they don't make 'em like that anymore.

And, of course, they never did. That movie stereotype of American newspaper reporters is part of our folklore; it never had much to do with reality. But there's no question that journalism and the people who practice it have changed over the years.

Today, our reporters and editors come from universities with degrees in economics and sociology, law and public administration, literature and even medicine. Nobody specializes in murder anymore; it's labor and international affairs, politics and education, science and religion. Our exposés take more than a couple of phone calls: months of work by teams of investigators who are more likely to ask help from a computer than a bookie. Our star reporters are streetwise still—but lots smarter than Scoop ever was. They have to be.

Some of the best reporters in the country work for Knight-Ridder newspapers. We're proud of them.

Philadelphia Inquirer • Philadelphia Daily News
Detroit Free Press • Miami Herald
St. Paul Dispatch • St. Paul Pioneer Press
Charlotte Observer • Charlotte News
San Jose Mercury • San Jose News • Wichita Eagle
Wichita Beacon • Akron Beacon Journal
Long Beach Press-Telegram • Long Beach Independent
Lexington Herald • Lexington Leader
Gary Post-Tribune • Duluth News-Tribune
Duluth Herald • Macon Telegraph • Macon News
Columbus Enquirer • Columbus Ledger
Pasadena Star-News • Tallahassee Democrat
Grand Forks Herald • Journal of Commerce
Bradenton Herald • Boulder Daily Camera
Aberdeen American News • Boca Raton News

Knight-Ridder Newspapers

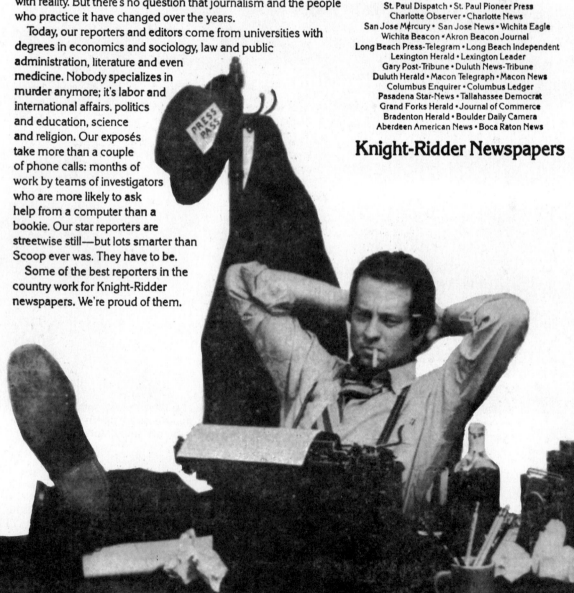

[1977]

Why teenage girls stick with their mouthwash longer than their boyfriends.

Love is different from mouthwash.

Consider: Not too many women aged 20-34 are still going steady with their first boyfriends.

Yet more than one out of every three of them still use the same mouthwash they decided to use as a teenager.

That was one of the findings of a recent major Yankelovich study. Which showed that, besides

mouthwash, girls are about equally loyal to their mascara, packaged goods, and even panty hose.

All this isn't to disparage boyfriends. But it does tend to prove what common sense and we have been saying for some time:

Long before a teenage girl is ready to settle down with the right boy, she is ready to settle down with the right product.

And the place where she does her settling down is Seventeen magazine. Where, each month, over 6,400,000 teenage girls begin lasting relationships.

If you'd like to know more about this new research, please call our Advertising Director, Bob Bunge, at (212) 759-8100.

He'll show you that, when the right one comes along, a girl knows it.

Come to think of it, maybe love isn't very different from mouthwash at all.

seventeen
Today, she's really 18-34.

[1980]

When you're ready to go out to pasture, make sure you own the pasture.

© 1982 Time Inc.

While you're racing after success, retirement's the last thing on your mind.

You're having too much fun to think about quitting.

But someday maybe you'll be ready to kick your feet up and relax on a couple hundred sweet green acres.

You want to be able to take your pick of pastures or castles or tropical isles. And that takes drive.

The nice thing is, you don't have to hide your ambition anymore.

"If you've got it, go get it." That's what society is telling you these days.

If *you're* out there on the fast track, your business reading starts with FORTUNE.

It's the horse's mouth. The authority. The one you rely on when you've just *got* to be right.

It's where you get a vital couple of steps on the competition. In management, technology, the economy, *everything*.

FORTUNE's how to make it. And keep it.

And it's where to put your advertising if you want to succeed with the fast-track people.

FORTUNE
How to succeed.

[1982]

52

SOME PEOPLE ARE SO OPPOSED TO MURDER. THEY'LL KILL ANYONE WHO COMMITS IT.

"DO YOU WANT THEM DEAD?"

There are now thirty-seven states that stand united behind the death sentence. And a total of five methods by which it's carried out. The electric chair, cyanide gas, hanging, lethal injection and firing squad.

But no matter which method is used, the result is the same. The taking of a human life.

This week, in an Eyewitness News Special Report, Roger Grimsby takes a good hard look at capital punishment.

You'll meet murderers on death row who are waiting to die. And families of their victims. Who can't wait to see them dead.

Watch "Do You Want Them Dead?" Then decide for yourself if the death penalty should become a way of life.

EYEWITNESS NEWS 6PM ⑦

[1982]

Can a girl be <u>too</u> busy? I'm taking seventeen units at Princeton, pushing on with my career during vacations and school breaks, study singing and dancing when I can, try never to lose track of my five closest chums, steal the time for Michael Jackson <u>and</u> Thomas Hardy, work for an anti-drug program for kids and, oh yes, I hang out with three horses, three cats, two birds and my dog Jack. My favorite magazine says "too busy" just means you don't want to miss any-thing...don't stop 'til you're gasping. I love that magazine. I guess you could say I'm That COSMOPOLITAN Girl.

Photographed by Francesco Scavullo

One of my most satisfying relationships is with a magazine.

COSMOPOLITAN®

A PUBLICATION OF THE HEARST CORPORATION

[1984]

54

Is this how you see our readers?

Well, look again. Our readers have evolved and so have we.

Sure our readers still wear blue collar shirts, only now they have alligators on them. They also eat more mousse than they hunt and drink as many screwdrivers as they use.

They look to MI for detailed information on how to manage their two greatest investments—their home and their car.

MI is the only magazine devoted exclusively to this market.

You won't find stories about fantasy technology or military hardware between our covers.

Last year 95% of our readers did a home improvement project. Almost 90% do their own auto maintenance. In fact, they're so involved with their home and car, they insist on being involved in every buying decision.

From power tools and tires to wall coverings and microwave ovens.

So now that you see our readers in a new light, put Mechanix Illustrated on your ad schedule. When your clients see the results they'll think you've re-invented the wheel.

For more information call Ernie Renzulli, Ad Director (212) 719-6570.

5 million home and car fanatics swear by MI

[1984]

THE NEW YORKER

See more than just this and that, now and then, here and there.

YOU'RE thumbing through it in the waiting room. You get immersed in a short story. But just as you come to the best part, the receptionist says, "You can go in now."

Or you pick it up from a coffee table when the friend you're visiting temporarily abandons you. You get absorbed in a review of a new movie. A new show. A new book. Smack in the middle, your friend comes back and announces, "Dinner is ready."

If you've arrived at a point in life where you probably ought to be enjoying The New Yorker regularly instead of seeing just this and that, now and then, here and there…

If you like the idea of keeping in closer touch with the main social, cultural, and political currents of our times…

And…if you don't mind getting the magazine at better than half price every week…why not order yourself a subscription of your own, and take more control over your life.

Run a hot tub, for example, and spend an uninterrupted hour immersing yourself in a Profile. Stretch out on the couch and catch up with what's going on in world politics. Crawl into bed early and hunker down with an update on medicine, science, law, business, the arts. *Learn how that short story ends! Find out at last whether it's worth spending money on that new movie! New show! New book!*

There's so much to savor, enjoy and learn from in The New Yorker each week. Shouldn't you be getting in on it all, instead of on just bits and pieces?

Get it for the basic rate of 62¢ a week instead of $1.75 at the newsstand. Mail card or this coupon.

By special permission of *The New Yorker.* © 1986 The New Yorker Magazine, Inc.   [1987]

Do something different around home.

You won't have 50 tons of steel parked in your driveway. But it won't be farther away than your local Army National Guard Armory. And that's important. Because you never know when you're going to need it in a hurry.

Last year, for instance, Guard tanks were called out to make war on winter. Hauling 18-wheelers out of snow drifts. Keeping roads open during the blizzards.

And like your tank crews, Guardsmen everywhere use the skills they learn in the Guard to help people in trouble.

What about you? There are a lot of ways you can help your friends and neighbors.

**Help Somebody.
Including Yourself.**

ARMY
**NATIONAL
GUARD**
The Guard belongs.

And help yourself while you're at it. The National Guard can teach you valuable career skills. Anything from communications to paramedicine to handling heavy equipment.

Skills that could very well make the difference should disaster strike your town.

It's good work. And the pay's good, too.

So do something that'll make a difference. See your nearest Army Guard recruiter. Or call us, toll free, 800-638-7600. (In Alaska, Hawaii, Puerto Rico or the Virgin Islands, consult your white pages). In Maryland call 301-728-3388.

[1978]

INSTITUTIONAL AND CORPORATE
ADVERTISING

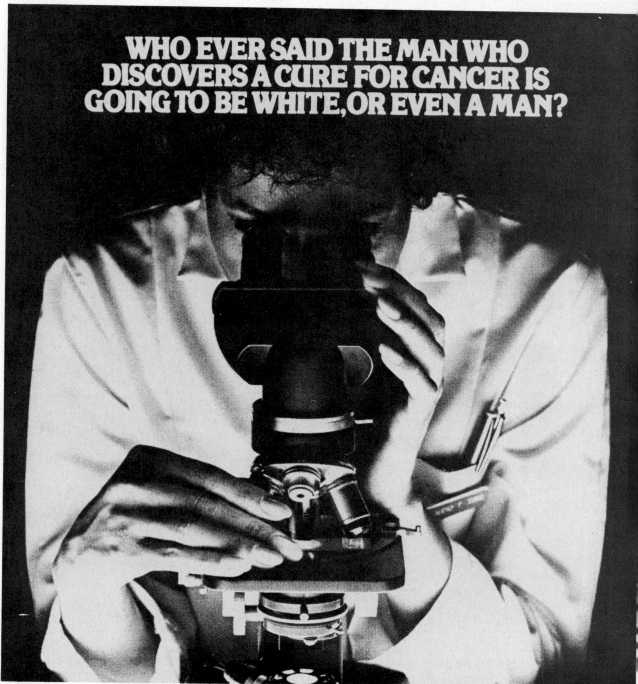

WHO EVER SAID THE MAN WHO DISCOVERS A CURE FOR CANCER IS GOING TO BE WHITE, OR EVEN A MAN?

This black woman could be America's hope...she's a United Negro College Fund graduate who could dedicate her life to finding a cure for cancer. A cure that could save thousands of lives each year. And fill every black person's heart with pride. That's why it's so important that blacks support the United Negro College Fund, 100 percent.

If she discovered the cure, in a sense, it would also be your discovery because the world would recognize it as a major black contribution.

When you give to the United Negro College Fund, you help support 41 private, predominantly black, four-year colleges and universities. Colleges that give us thousands of black graduates each year, who go on to become doctors, lawyers, accountants, engineers and scientists.

So support black education. Because black contributions help make black contributions. Send your check to the United Negro College Fund, Box Q, 500 East 62nd St., New York, N.Y. 10021. We're not asking for a handout, just a hand.

GIVE TO THE UNITED NEGRO COLLEGE FUND.
A mind is a terrible thing to waste.

[1979]

Without chemicals, life itself would be impossible.

Some people think anything "chemical" is bad and anything "natural" is good. Yet nature is chemical.

Plant life generates the oxygen we need through a chemical process called photosynthesis. When you breathe, your body absorbs that oxygen through a chemical reaction with your blood.

Life is chemical. And with chemicals, companies like Monsanto are working to help improve the quality of life.

Chemicals help you live longer. Rickets was a common childhood disease until a chemical called Vitamin D was added to milk and other foods.

Chemicals help you eat better. Chemical weed-killers have dramatically increased the supply and availability of our food. But no chemical is totally safe, all the time, everywhere. In nature or the laboratory. The real challenge is to use chemicals properly. To help make life a lot more livable. © Monsanto Company 1977

[1979]

A word to smokers
(about people who build walls)

It's no secret that there are some folks these days who are trying to build walls between smokers and nonsmokers.

The theory behind all this is that some smokers annoy nonsmokers and, of course, that can happen.

But if you want to get an idea of the ridiculous lengths that some of the wall-builders would like to go to, you have only to consider this:

In one state alone, it was estimated that the first year's cost of administering and enforcing a proposed anti-smoking law and building the physical walls required was nearly $250,000,000.

The proposal was, of course, defeated—for the plain fact is the one you have observed in your own daily life, that the overwhelming majority of smokers and nonsmokers get along very well and don't need or want to be separated.

This infuriates the wall-builders. Since they cannot have their own way in a world of free choice, they would like to eliminate that world by government fiat, by rules and regulations that would tell you where, and with whom, you may work, eat, play and shop. And the enormous burden that would place on all of us, in higher taxes and costs, does not bother them.

Certainly no one, including smokers, can properly object to the common sense rules of, for instance, banning smoking in crowded elevators, poorly ventilated spaces or, indeed, in any place where it is clearly inappropriate. And individual managers in their own interest should see to the mutual comfort of their smoking and nonsmoking patrons. It is only when the long arm, and notoriously insensitive hands, of government regulators start making these private arrangements for us that we all, smoker and nonsmoker alike, begin to lose our freedom of choice.

In the long run, the wall-builders must fail, and the walls will come tumbling down—if not to the sound of a trumpet, then at least to the slower but surer music of common decency and courtesy practiced on both sides of them.

THE TOBACCO INSTITUTE
1776 K St. N.W., Washington. D.C. 20006
Freedom of choice
is the best choice.

60

A word to nonsmokers
(about people who build walls)

The chances are that you made up your mind about smoking a long time ago — and decided it's not for you.

The chances are equally good that you know a lot of smokers — there are, after all about 60 million of them — and that you may be related to some of them, work with them, play with them, and get along with them very well.

And finally it's a pretty safe bet that you're open-minded and interested in all the various issues about smokers and nonsmokers — or you wouldn't be reading this.

And those three things make you incredibly important today.

Because they mean that yours is the voice — not the smoker's and not the anti-smoker's — that will determine how much of society's efforts should go into building walls that separate us and how much into the search for solutions that bring us together.

For one tragic result of the emphasis on building walls is the diversion of millions of dollars from scientific research on the causes and cures of diseases which, when all is said and done, still strike the nonsmoker as well as the smoker. One prominent health organization, to cite but a single instance, now spends 28¢ of every publicly-contributed dollar on "education" (much of it in anti-smoking propaganda) and only 2¢ on research.

There will always be some who want to build walls, who want to separate people from people, and up to a point, even these may serve society. The anti-smoking wall-builders have, to give them their due, helped to make us all more keenly aware of the value of courtesy and of individual freedom of choice.

But our guess, and certainly our hope, is that you are among the far greater number who know that walls are only temporary at best, and that over the long run, we can serve society's interests better by working together in mutual accommodation.

Whatever virtue walls may have, they can never move our society toward fundamental solutions. People who work together on common problems, common solutions, can.

THE TOBACCO INSTITUTE
1776 K St. N.W., Washington, D.C. 20006
Freedom of choice is the best choice.

Warning: The Surgeon General Has Determined That Cigarette Smoking Is Dangerous to Your Health.

[1979]

Really tying one on.

Getting s___ faced.

Having one more for the road.

Becoming polluted.

Drinking someone under the table.

Being plastered.

Bragging about the size
of your hangover.

Going out and getting looped.

THE BEST REASON TO RAISE THE AGE FOR BUYING ALCOHOL OFTEN GETS BURIED.

The question of raising the alcohol-purchase age to 21 has stirred emotional arguments, economic arguments, freedom-of-choice arguments.

But at Metropolitan Life, we fear the debate may have obscured the most basic argument of all. Simply stated, the lower the legal-purchase age, the more young people will die on the highways.

How do we know for sure? In states that have already increased the purchase age to 21, alcohol-related fatalities among drivers 18 to 20 have dropped as much as 21%.

If all states adopted the 21-year-old limit, it is estimated that at least 700 lives would be saved each year.

You can help save those lives. Wire or call your Senators to urge their support of the Uniform Minimum Drinking Age Act (S2719) when it is offered in the Senate. Wire or call President Reagan and let him know you want to see this bill passed.

Because if this bill gets buried, so will 700 people. One of them could be you or your child.

Metropolitan Insurance Companies

[1984]

It starts out innocently enough.

A man tunes in a football game and tunes out his wife's attempts to be heard.

A woman gets so wrapped up in her problems she barely listens as her husband talks about his own.

And before long, without even realizing how it came about, a deadly silence starts to grow between them.

The fact is, listening, like marriage, is a partnership; a shared responsibility between the person speaking and the person listening. And if the listener doesn't show genuine interest and sensitivity to what's being said, the speaker will stop talking. And the communication will fail.

Which is why we at Sperry feel it's so critical that we all become better listeners. In our homes. And in our businesses.

We've recently set up special listening programs that Sperry personnel worldwide can attend. And what we're discovering is that when people really know how to listen (and believe us, there's a lot to know) they can actually encourage

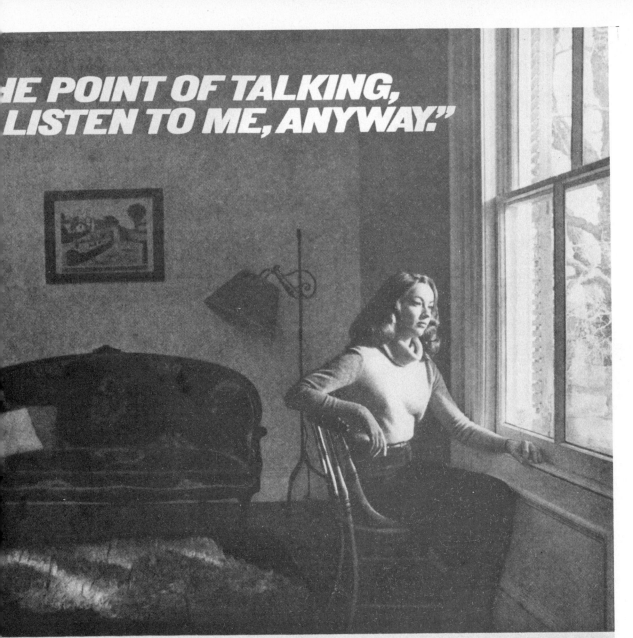

HE POINT OF TALKING,
LISTEN TO ME, ANYWAY."

the speakers to share more of their thoughts and feelings, bringing everyone closer together.

Which is of great value to us when we do business.

And perhaps even greater value when we go home.

We understand how important it is to listen.

[1982]

Funny stage they're at: George is older, but somehow he doesn't quite measure up to kid sister Shirley. "It's a stage," Dad consoles his son. "You'll outgrow it." The kids are growing up. Almost too fast. So, be sure to share those little moments, as well as the big, with faraway friends and family. Just reach out with a phone call, and they're sharing your day.

(Ⓑ) Bell System

Reach out and touch someone.

[1980]

The family is more important than the family room.

It doesn't matter which room a family chooses to gather in. It could be a favorite corner of the kitchen, or a wood panelled den. What does matter is that they choose to be together. For it is the support, the strength, the bonds and traditions of the family that give us what we all need most in life. A good home.

Home is the stage where the drama of life is played. It's the classroom where children learn right from wrong. Where old-fashioned ideals like courage and honesty, respect for oneself and others are passed down from one generation to the next.

We are concerned about the erosion of these values that should be taught at home. We see the growing problems of society—broken homes, crime, drugs, and juvenile delinquency—and are shocked by the trauma they inflict on families, especially children.

Our over-burdened schools can no longer solve these problems confronting our society. There is only one place where we can regain the values and integrity that will cure these ills. We must turn to the home—our piece of the world—the place where it all begins.

For fifty years, Ethan Allen has been dedicated to helping Americans create beautiful environments for their homes. But we know it takes more than fine quality furnishings to make a good home. It takes the love, respect and understanding of those who share it together.

Ethan Allen Galleries
A Good Home Lasts a Lifetime.

Ethan Allen Inc. A INTERCO Company

[1987]

REP. ALBERTO GUTMAN: Florida Legislator, Businessman, Husband, Member of the National Rifle Association.

"Being from a country that was once a democracy and turned communist, I really feel I know what the right to bear arms is all about. In Cuba, where I was born, the first thing the communist government did was take away everybody's firearms, leaving them defenseless and intimidated with fear. That's why our constitutional right to bear arms is so important to our country's survival.

"As a legislator I have to deal with reality. And the reality is that gun control does not work. It actually eliminates the rights of the law-abiding citizen, not the criminal. Criminals will always have guns, and they won't follow gun control laws anyway. I would like to see tougher laws on criminals as opposed to tougher laws on legitimate gun owners. We need to attack the problem of crime at its roots, instead of blaming crime on gun ownership and citizens who use them lawfully.

"It's a big responsibility that we face retaining the right to bear arms. That's why I joined the NRA. The NRA is instrumental in protecting these freedoms. It helps train and educate people, supporting legislation that benefits not only those who bear arms but all citizens of the United States. The NRA helps keep America free." **I'm the NRA.**®

The NRA's lobbying organization, the Institute for Legislative Action, is the nation's largest and most influential protector of the constitutional right to keep and bear arms. At every level of government and through local grassroots efforts, the Institute guards against infringement upon the freedoms of law-abiding gun owners. If you would like to join the NRA or want more information about our programs and benefits, write J. Warren Cassidy, Executive Vice President, P.O. Box 37484, Dept. AG-27, Washington, D.C. 20013.

Paid for by the members of the National Rifle Association of America. Copyright 1987.

69

Marianne Moore / Correspondence with the
Ford Motor Company

In the following exchange of letters, the distinguished American poet Marianne Moore (1887–1972), a professed "amateur" at the art of copywriting, tries to come up with the best name for a product that the Ford Motor Company thought would revolutionize the automobile industry.

According to Printer's Ink, *the one-time leading advertising trade publication, Ford spent more than $350 million "to create and promote the biggest and most expensive new product ever born."*

OCTOBER 19, 1955

MISS MARIANNE MOORE,
CUMBERLAND STREET,
BROOKLYN 5, NEW YORK

DEAR MISS MOORE:

This is a morning we find ourselves with a problem which, strangely enough, is more in the field of words and the fragile meaning of words than in car-making. And we just wonder whether you might be intrigued with it sufficiently to lend us a hand.

Our dilemma is a name for a rather important new series of cars.

We should like this name to be more than a label. Specifically, we should like it to have a compelling quality in itself and by itself. To convey, through association or other conjuration, some visceral feeling of elegance, fleetness, advanced features and design. A name, in short, that flashes a dramatically desirable picture in people's minds. (Another "Thunderbird" would be fine.)

Over the past few weeks this office has confected a list of three hundred-odd candidates which, it pains me to relate, are characterized by an embarrassing pedestrianism. We are miles short of our ambition. And so we are seeking the help of one who knows more about this sort of magic than we.

As to how we might go about this matter, I have no idea. But, in any event, all would depend on whether you find this overture of some challenge and interest.

Should we be so fortunate as to have piqued your fancy, we will be pleased to write more fully. And, of course, it is expected that our relations will be on a fee basis of an impeccably dignified kind.

Respectfully,
DAVID WALLACE
Special Products Division

OCTOBER 21, 1955

Let me take it under advisement, Mr. Wallace. I am complimented to be recruited in this high matter.

I have seen and admired "Thunderbird" as a Ford designation. It would be hard to match; but let me, the coming week, talk with my brother, who would bring ardor and imagination to bear on the quest.

Sincerely yours,
MARIANNE MOORE

OCTOBER 27, 1955

DEAR MR. WALLACE:

My brother thought most of the names I had considered suggesting to you for your new series too learned or too labored, but thinks I might ask if any of the following approximate the requirements:

THE FORD SILVER SWORD

This plant, of which the flower is a silver sword, I believe grows only on the Hawaiian Island Maui, on Mount Haleakala (House of the Sun); found at an altitude of from 9,500 to 10,000 feet. (The leaves—silver-white—surrounding the individual blossoms—have a pebbled texture that feels like Italian-twist backstitch allover embroidery.)

My first thought was of a bird series—the swallow species—Hirundo, or, phonetically, Aerundo. Malvina Hoffman is designing a device for the radiator of a made-to-order Cadillac, and said in her opinion the only term surpassing Thunderbird would be hurricane; and I then thought Hurricane Hirundo might be the first of a series such as Hurricane Aquila (eagle), Hurricane Accipiter (hawk), and so on. A species that takes its dinner on the wing (''swifts'').

If these suggestions are not in character with the car, perhaps you could give me a sketch of its general appearance, or hint as to some of its exciting potentialities—though my brother reminds me that such information is highly confidential.

Sincerely yours,
MARIANNE MOORE

NOVEMBER 4, 1955

DEAR MISS MOORE:

I'm delighted that your note implies that you are interested in helping us in our naming problem.

This being so, procedures in this rigorous business world dictate that we on this end at least document a formal arrangement with provision for a suitable fee or honorarium before pursuing the problem further.

One way might be for you to suggest a figure which could be considered for mutual acceptance. Once this is squared away, we will look forward to having you join us in the continuation of our fascinating search.

Sincerely,
DAVID WALLACE
Special Products Division

NOVEMBER 7, 1955

DEAR MR. WALLACE:

It is handsome of you to consider remuneration for service merely enlisted. My fancy would be inhibited, however, by acknowledgment in advance of performance. If I could be of specific assistance, we could no doubt agree on some kind of honorarium for the service rendered.

I seem to exact participation; but if you could tell me how the suggestions submitted strayed—if obviously—from the ideal, I could then perhaps proceed more nearly in keeping with the Company's objective.

Sincerely yours,
MARIANNE MOORE

NOVEMBER 11, 1955

DEAR MISS MOORE:

Our office philodendron has just benefitted from an extra measure of water as, pacing about, I have sought words to respond to your recent generous note. Let me state my quandary thus. It is unspeakably contrary to procedure to accept counsel—

They'll know you've *arrived*

when you drive up in an Edsel

Step into an Edsel and you'll learn where the excitement is this year.

Other drivers spot that classic vertical grille a block away—and never fail to take a long look at this year's most exciting car.

On the open road, your Edsel is watched eagerly for its already-famous performance.

And parked in front of your home, your Edsel always gets even more attention—because it always says a lot about you. It says you chose elegant styling, luxurious comfort and such exclusive features as Edsel's famous Teletouch Drive—only shift that puts the buttons where they belong, on the steering-wheel hub.

Your Edsel also means you made a wonderful buy. For of all medium-priced cars, this one really new car is actually priced the lowest.* See your Edsel Dealer this week.

*Based on comparison of suggested retail delivered prices of the Edsel Ranger and similarly equipped cars in the medium-price field.

Above: Edsel Citation 2-door Hardtop. Engine: the E-475, with 10.5 to one compression ratio, 345 hp, 475 ft.-lb. torque. Transmission: Automatic with Teletouch Drive. Suspension: Ball-joint with optional air suspension. Brakes: self-adjusting.

EDSEL DIVISION · FORD MOTOR COMPANY

1958 EDSEL

Of all medium-priced cars, the one that's really new is the lowest-priced, too!

[1958]

72

even needed counsel—without a firm prior agreement of conditions (and, indeed, to follow the letter of things, without a Purchase Notice in quadruplicate and three Competitive Bids). But then, seldom has the auto business had occasion to indulge in so ethereal a matter as this. So, if you will risk a mutually satisfactory outcome with us, we should like to honor your wish for a fancy unencumbered.

As to wherein your earlier suggestions may have "strayed," as you put it—they did not at all. Shipment No. 1 was fine, and we would like to luxuriate in more of same—even those your brother regarded as overlearned or labored. For us to impose an ideal on your efforts would, I fear, merely defeat our purpose. We have sought your help to get an approach quite different from our own. In short, we should like suggestions that we ourselves would not have arrived at. And, in sober fact, have not.

Now we on this end must help you by sending some tangible representation of what we are talking about. Perhaps the enclosed sketches will serve the purpose. They are not IT, but they convey the feeling. At the very least, they may give you a sense of participation should your friend Malvina Hoffman break into brisk conversation on radiator caps.

> Sincerely yours,
> DAVID WALLACE
> *Special Products Division*

NOVEMBER 13, 1955

DEAR MR. WALLACE:

The sketches. They are indeed exciting; they have quality, and the toucan tones lend tremendous allure—confirmed by the wheels. Half the magic—sustaining effects of this kind. Looked at upside down, furthermore, there is a sense of fish buoyancy. Immediately your word "impeccable" sprang to mind. Might it be a possibility? The Impeccable. In any case, the baguette lapidary glamour you have achieved certainly spurs the imagination. Car-innovation is like launching a ship—"drama."

I am by no means sure that I can help you to the right thing, but performance with elegance casts a spell. Let me do some thinking in the direction of impeccable, symmechromatic, thunderblender. . . . (The exotics, if I can shape them a little.) Dearborn might come into one.

If the sketches should be returned at once, let me know. Otherwise, let me dwell on them for a time. I am, may I say, a trusty confidante.

I thank you for realizing that under contract esprit could not flower. You owe me nothing, specific or moral.

> Sincerely,
> MARIANNE MOORE

NOVEMBER 19, 1955

Some other suggestions, Mr. Wallace, for the phenomenon:

THE RESILIENT BULLET
or Intelligent Bullet
or Bullet Cloisonné or Bullet Lavolta

(I have always had a fancy for THE INTELLIGENT WHALE—the little first Navy submarine, shaped like a sweet potato; on view in our Brooklyn Yard.)

THE FORD FABERGE

(That there is also a perfume Fabergé seems to me to do no harm, for here allusion is to the original silversmith.)

THE ARC-en-CIEL (the rainbow) ARCENCIEL?

Please do not feel that memoranda from me need acknowledgment. I am not working day and night for you; I feel that etymological hits are partially accidental.

The bullet idea has possibilities, it seems to me, in connection with Mercury (with Hermes and Hermes Trismegistus) and magic (white magic).

Sincerely,

MARIANNE MOORE

NOVEMBER 28, 1955

DEAR MR. WALLACE:

MONGOOSE CIVIQUE

ANTICIPATOR

REGNA RACER (couronne à couronne) sovereign to sovereign

AEROTERRE

Fée Rapide (Aérofée, Aéro Faire, Fée Aiglette, Magi-faire) Comme Il Faire

Tonnerre Alifère (winged thunder)

Aliforme Alifère (wing-slender, a-wing)

TURBOTORC (used as an adjective by Plymouth)

THUNDERBIRD Allié (Cousin Thunderbird)

THUNDER CRESTER

DEARBORN Diamante

MAGIGRAVURE

PASTELOGRAM

I shall be returning the sketches very soon.

M.M.

DECEMBER 6, 1955

DEAR MR. WALLACE:

Regina-rex
Taper Racer   Taper Acer
Varsity Stroke

Angelastro
Astranaut

Chaparral

Tir à l'arc (bull's eye)
Cresta Lark
Triskelion (three legs running)

Pluma Piluma (hairfine, feather-foot)

Andante con Moto (description of a good motor?)

My findings thin, so I terminate them and am returning the sketches. Two principles I have not been able to capture: 1, the topknot of the peacock and topnotcher of speed. 2, the swivel-axis (emphasized elsewhere), like the Captain's bed on the whaleship, Charles Morgan—balanced so that it levelled whatever the slant of the ship.

If I stumble on a hit, you shall have it. Anything so far has been pastime. Do not ponder appreciation, Mr. Wallace. That was embodied in the sketches.

M.M.

I cannot resist the temptation to disobey my brother and submit

TURCOTINGA (turquoise cotinga—the cotinga being a South-American finch or sparrow) solid indigo.

(I have a three-volume treatise on flowers that might produce something but the impression given should certainly be unlabored.)

DECEMBER 8, 1955

MR. WALLACE:

May I submit UTOPIAN TURTLE-TOP? Do not trouble to answer unless you like it.
MARIANNE MOORE

DECEMBER 23, 1955

MERRY CHRISTMAS TO OUR FAVORITE TURTLETOPPER.
DAVID WALLACE

DECEMBER 26, 1955

DEAR MR. WALLACE:

An aspiring turtle is certain to glory in spiral eucalyptus, white pine straight from the forest, and innumerable scarlet roses almost too tall for close inspection. Of a temperament susceptible to shock though one may be, to be treated like royalty could not but induce sensations unprecedented august.

Please know that a carfancyer's allegiance to the Ford automotive turtle—extending from the Model T Dynasty to the Wallace Utopian Dynasty—can never waver; impersonal gratitude surely becoming infinite when made personal. Gratitude to unmiserly Mr. Wallace and his idealistic associates.
MARIANNE MOORE

NOVEMBER 8, 1956

DEAR MISS MOORE:

Because you were so kind to us in our early days of looking for a suitable name, I feel a deep obligation to report on events that have ensued.

And I feel I must do so before the public announcement of same come Monday, November 19.

We have chosen a name out of the more than six thousand-odd candidates that we gathered. It fails somewhat of the resonance, gaiety, and zest we were seeking. But it has a personal dignity and meaning to many of us here. Our name, dear Miss Moore, is—Edsel.

I hope you will understand.
Cordially,
DAVID WALLACE
Special Products Division

David Ogilvy / How to Write Potent Copy 1963

David Ogilvy was born in England in 1911 and received his education at Christ Church College, Oxford. His professional experiences have been varied. At one time he served as an apprentice chef in the kitchens of the Hotel Majestic in Paris and at another time as a salesman of kitchen stoves. With the founding of Ogilvy, Benson and Mather in 1948, Ogilvy went on to become one of the leading figures and voices of American advertising. His best-known ads—those for Hathaway shirts, Schweppes tonic, and Rolls-Royce—have focused on distinctive images of Anglo-American sophistication. His most recent book, Ogilvy on Advertising, *was published in 1983.*

"How to Write Potent Copy" appeared as a chapter in Ogilvy's best-seller, Confessions of an Advertising Man.

I. HEADLINES

The headline is the most important element in most advertisements. It is the telegram which decides the reader whether to read the copy.

On the average, five times as many people read the headline as read the body copy. When you have written your headline, you have spent eighty cents out of your dollar.

If you haven't done some selling in your headline, you have wasted 80 per cent of your client's money. The wickedest of all sins is to run an advertisement *without* a headline. Such headless wonders are still to be found; I don't envy the copywriter who submits one to me.

A change of headline can make a difference of ten to one in sales. I never write fewer than sixteen headlines for a single advertisement, and I observe certain guides in writing them:

(1) The headline is the "ticket on the meat." Use it to flag down the readers who are prospects for the kind of product you are advertising. If you are selling a remedy for bladder weakness, display the words BLADDER WEAKNESS in your headline; they catch the eye of everyone who suffers from this inconvenience. If you want *mothers* to read your advertisement, display MOTHERS in your headline. And so on.

Conversely, do not say anything in your headline which is likely to *exclude* any readers who might be prospects for your product. Thus, if you are advertising a product which can be used equally well by men and women, don't slant your headline at women alone; it would frighten men away.

(2) Every headline should appeal to the reader's *self-interest*. It should promise her a benefit, as in my headline for Helena Rubinstein's Hormone Cream: HOW WOMEN OVER 35 CAN LOOK YOUNGER.

(3) Always try to inject *news* into your headlines, because the consumer is always on the lookout for new products, or new ways to use an old product, or new improvements in an old product.

The two most powerful words you can use in a headline are FREE and NEW. You can seldom use FREE, but you can almost always use NEW—if you try hard enough.

(4) Other words and phrases which work wonders are HOW TO, SUDDENLY, NOW, ANNOUNCING, INTRODUCING, IT'S HERE, JUST ARRIVED, IMPORTANT DEVELOPMENT, IMPROVEMENT, AMAZING, SENSATIONAL, REMARKABLE, REVOLUTIONARY, STARTLING, MIRACLE, MAGIC, OFFER, QUICK, EASY, WANTED, CHALLENGE, ADVICE TO, THE TRUTH ABOUT, COMPARE, BARGAIN, HURRY, LAST CHANCE.

Don't turn up your nose at these clichés. They may be shopworn, but they work.

That is why you see them turn up so often in the headlines of mail-order advertisers and others who can measure the results of their advertisements.

Headlines can be strengthened by the inclusion of *emotional* words, like DARLING, LOVE, FEAR, PROUD, FRIEND, and BABY. One of the most provocative advertisements which has come out of our agency showed a girl in a bathtub, talking to her lover on the telephone. The headline: *Darling, I'm having the most extraordinary experience . . . I'm head over heels in* DOVE.

(5) Five times as many people read the headline as read the body copy, so it is important that these glancers should at least be told what brand is being advertised. That is why you should always include the brand name in your headlines.

(6) Include your selling promise in your headline. This requires long headlines. When the New York University School of Retailing ran headline tests with the co-operation of a big department store, they found that headlines of ten words or longer, containing news and information, consistently sold more merchandise than short headlines.

Headlines containing six to twelve words pull more coupon returns than short headlines, and there is no significant difference between the readership of twelve-word headlines and the readership of three-word headlines. The best headline I ever wrote contained *eighteen* words: *At Sixty Miles an Hour the Loudest Noise in the New Rolls-Royce comes from the electric clock.*[1]

(7) People are more likely to read your body copy if your headline arouses their curiosity; so you should end your headline with a lure to read on.

(8) Some copywriters write *tricky* headlines—puns, literary allusions, and other obscurities. This is a sin.

In the average newspaper your headline has to compete for attention with 350 others. Research has shown that readers travel so fast through this jungle that they don't stop to decipher the meaning of obscure headlines. Your headline must *telegraph* what you want to say, and it must telegraph it in plain language. Don't play games with the reader.

In 1960 the *Times Literary Supplement* attacked the whimsical tradition in British advertising, calling it "self-indulgent—a kind of middle-class private joke, apparently designed to amuse the advertiser and his client." Amen.

(9) Research shows that it is dangerous to use *negatives* in headlines. If, for example, you write OUR SALT CONTAINS NO ARSENIC, many readers will miss the negative and go away with the impression that you wrote OUR SALT CONTAINS ARSENIC.

(10) Avoid *blind* headlines—the kind which mean nothing unless you read the body copy underneath them; most people *don't*.

II. BODY COPY

When you sit down to write your body copy, pretend that you are talking to the woman on your right at a dinner party. She has asked you, "I am thinking of buying a new car. Which would you recommend?" Write your copy as if you were answering that question.

(1) Don't beat about the bush—go straight to the point. Avoid analogies of the "just as, so too" variety. Dr. Gallup has demonstrated that these two-stage arguments are generally misunderstood.

(2) Avoid superlatives, generalizations, and platitudes. Be specific and factual. Be enthusiastic, friendly, and memorable. Don't be a bore. Tell the truth, but make the truth fascinating.

How long should your copy be? It depends on the product. If you are advertising chewing gum, there isn't much to tell, so make your copy short. If, on the other

---

1. When the chief engineer at the Rolls-Royce factory read this, he shook his head sadly and said, "It is time we did something about that damned clock."

The Rolls-Royce Silver Cloud—$13,550

"At 60 miles an hour the loudest noise in this new Rolls-Royce comes from the electric clock"

*What __makes__ Rolls-Royce the best car in the world? "There is really no magic about it—
it is merely patient attention to detail," says an eminent Rolls-Royce engineer.*

1. "At 60 miles an hour the loudest noise comes from the electric clock," reports the Technical Editor of THE MOTOR. The silence of the engine is uncanny. Three mufflers tune out sound frequencies — acoustically.

2. Every Rolls-Royce engine is run for seven hours at full throttle before installation, and each car is test-driven for hundreds of miles over varying road surfaces.

3. The Rolls-Royce is designed as an *owner-driven* car. It is eighteen inches shorter than the largest domestic cars.

4. The car has power steering, power brakes and automatic gear-shift. It is very easy to drive and to park. No chauffeur required.

5. There is no metal-to-metal contact between the body of the car and the chassis frame—except for the speedometer drive. The entire body is insulated and under-sealed.

6. The finished car spends a week in the final test-shop, being fine-tuned. Here it is subjected to ninety-eight separate ordeals. For example, the engineers use a *stethoscope* to listen for axle-whine.

7. The Rolls-Royce is guaranteed for *three years.* With a new network of dealers and parts-depots from

Coast to Coast, service is no longer any problem

8. The famous Rolls-Royce radiator has never been changed, except that when Sir Henry Royce died in 1933 the monogram RR was changed from red to black.

9. The coachwork is given five coats of primer paint, and hand rubbed between each coat, before *fourteen* coats of finishing paint go on.

10. By moving a switch on the steering column, you can adjust the shock-absorbers to suit road conditions. (The lack of fatigue in driving this car is remarkable.)

11. Another switch defrosts the rear window, by heating a network of 1360 invisible wires in the glass. There are two separate ventilating systems, so that you can ride in comfort with all the windows closed. Air conditioning is optional.

12. The seats are upholstered with eight hides of English leather—enough to make 128 pairs of soft shoes.

13. A picnic table, veneered in French walnut, slides out from under the dash. Two more swing out behind the front seats.

14. You can get such optional extras as an Espresso coffee-making machine, a dictating machine, a bed, hot and cold water for washing, an electric razor.

15. You can lubricate the entire chassis by simply pushing a pedal from the driver's seat. A gauge on the dash shows the level of oil in the crankcase.

16. Gasoline consumption is remarkably low and there is no need to use premium gas; a happy economy.

17. There are two separate systems of power brakes, hydraulic and mechanical. The Rolls-Royce is a very *safe* car—and also a very *lively* car. It cruises serenely at eighty-five. Top speed is in excess of 100 m.p.h.

18. Rolls-Royce engineers make periodic visits to inspect owners' motor cars and advise on service.

ROLLS-ROYCE AND BENTLEY

19. The Bentley is made by Rolls-Royce. Except for the radiators, they are identical motor cars, manufactured by the same engineers in the same works. The Bentley costs $300 less, because its radiator is simpler to make. People who feel diffident about driving a Rolls-Royce can buy a Bentley.

PRICE. The car illustrated in this advertisement, f.o.b. principal port of entry—costs **$13,550.**

If you would like the rewarding experience of driving a Rolls-Royce or Bentley, get in touch with our dealer. His name is on the bottom of this page. Rolls-Royce Inc., 10 Rockefeller Plaza, New York, N.

JET ENGINES AND THE FUTURE

Certain airlines have chosen Rolls-Royce turbo-jets for their Boeing 707's and Douglas DC8's. Rolls-Royce prop-jets are in the Vickers Viscount, the Fairchild F.27 and the Grumman Gulfstream.

Rolls-Royce engines power more than half the turbo-jet and prop-jet airliners supplied to or on order for world airlines.

Rolls-Royce now employ 42,000 people and the company's engineering experience does not stop at motor cars and jet engines. There are Rolls-Royce diesel and gasoline engines for many other applications.

The huge research and development re sources of the company are now at work on many projects for the future, including nu clear and rocket propulsion.

[1958]

hand, you are advertising a product which has a great many different qualities to recommend it, write long copy: the more you tell, the more you sell.

There is a universal belief in lay circles that people won't read long copy. Nothing could be farther from the truth. Claude Hopkins once wrote five pages of solid text for Schlitz beer. In a few months, Schlitz moved up from fifth place to first. I once wrote a page of solid text for Good Luck Margarine, with most gratifying results.

Research shows that readership falls off rapidly up to fifty words of copy, but drops very little between fifty and 500 words. In my first Rolls-Royce advertisement I used 719 words—piling one fascinating fact on another. In the last paragraph I wrote, "People who feel diffident about driving a Rolls-Royce can buy a Bentley." Judging from the number of motorists who picked up the word "diffident" and bandied it about, I concluded that the advertisement was thoroughly read. In the next one I used 1400 words.

Every advertisement should be a *complete* sales pitch for your product. It is unrealistic to assume that consumers will read a *series* of advertisements for the same product. You should shoot the works in every advertisement, on the assumption that it is the only chance you will ever have to sell your product to the reader— *now or never*.

Says Dr. Charles Edwards of the graduate School of Retailing at New York University, "The more facts you tell, the more you sell. An advertisement's chance for success invariably increases as the number of pertinent merchandise facts included in the advertisement increases."

In my first advertisement for Puerto Rico's Operation Bootstrap, I used 961 words, and persuaded Beardsley Ruml to sign them. Fourteen thousand readers clipped the coupon from this advertisement, and scores of them later established factories in Puerto Rico. The greatest professional satisfaction I have yet had is to see the prosperity in Puerto Rican communities which had lived on the edge of starvation for four hundred years before I wrote my advertisement. If I had confined myself to a few vacuous generalities, nothing would have happened.

We have even been able to get people to read long copy about gasoline. One of our Shell advertisements contained 617 words, and 22 per cent of male readers read more than half of them.

Vic Schwab tells the story of Max Hart (of Hart, Schaffner & Marx) and his advertising manager, George L. Dyer, arguing about long copy. Dyer said, "I'll bet you ten dollars I can write a newspaper page of solid type and you'd read every word of it."

Hart scoffed at the idea. "I don't have to write a line of it to prove my point," Dyer replied. "I'll only tell you the headline: THIS PAGE IS ALL ABOUT MAX HART."

Advertisers who put coupons in their advertisements *know* that short copy doesn't sell. In split-run tests, long copy invariably outsells short copy.

Do I hear someone say that no copywriter can write long advertisements unless his media department gives him big spaces to work with? This question should not arise, because the copywriter should be consulted before planning the media schedule.

> (3) You should always include testimonials in your copy. The reader finds it easier to believe the endorsement of a fellow consumer than the puffery of an anonymous copywriter. Says Jim Young, one of the best copywriters alive today, "Every type of advertiser has the same problem; namely to be believed. The mail-order man knows nothing so potent for this purpose as the testimonial, yet the general advertiser seldom uses it."

Testimonials from celebrities get remarkably high readership, and if they are honestly written they still do not seem to provoke incredulity. The better known the celebrity, the more readers you will attract. We have featured Queen Elizabeth and Winston Churchill in "Come to Britain" advertisements, and we were able to persuade Mrs. Roosevelt to make television commercials for Good Luck Margarine. When we advertised charge accounts for Sears, Roebuck, we reproduced the credit card of Ted Williams, "recently traded by Boston to Sears."

Sometimes you can cast your entire copy in the form of a testimonial. My first advertisement for Austin cars took the form of a letter from an "anonymous diplomat" who was sending his son to Groton with money he had saved driving an Austin—a well-aimed combination of snobbery and economy. Alas, a perspicacious *Time* editor guessed that I was the anonymous diplomat, and asked the headmaster of Groton to comment. Dr. Crocker was so cross that I decided to send my son to Hotchkiss.

> (4) Another profitable gambit is to give the reader helpful advice, or service. It hooks about 75 per cent more readers than copy which deals entirely with the product.

One of our Rinso advertisements told housewives how to remove stains. It was better read (Starch) and better remembered (Gallup) than any detergent advertisement in history. Unfortunately, however, it forgot to feature Rinso's main selling promise—that Rinso washes whiter; for this reason it should never have run.[2]

> (5) I have never admired the *belles lettres* school of advertising, which reached its pompous peak in Theodore F. MacManus' famous advertisement for Cadillac, "The Penalty of Leadership," and Ned Jordan's classic, "Somewhere West of Laramie." Forty years ago the business community seems to have been impressed by these pieces of purple prose, but I have always thought them absurd; they did not give the reader a single *fact*. I share Claude Hopkins' view that "fine writing is a distinct disadvantage. So is unique literary style. They take attention away from the subject."
>
> (6) Avoid bombast. Raymond Rubicam's famous slogan for Squibb, "The priceless ingredient of every product is the honor and integrity of its maker," reminds me of my father's advice: when a company boasts about its integrity, or a woman about her virtue, avoid the former and cultivate the latter.
>
> (7) Unless you have some special reason to be solemn and pretentious, write your copy in the colloquial language which your customers use in everyday conversation. I have never acquired a sufficiently good ear for vernacular American to write it, but I admire copywriters who can pull it off, as in this unpublished pearl from a dairy farmer:

> > Carnation Milk is the best in the land,
> > Here I sit with a can in my hand.
> > No tits to pull, no hay to pitch,
> > Just punch a hole in the son-of-a-bitch.

It is a mistake to use highfalutin language when you advertise to uneducated people. I once used the word OBSOLETE in a headline, only to discover that 43 per cent of housewives had no idea what it meant. In another headline, I used the word INEFFABLE, only to discover that I didn't know what it meant myself.

However, many copywriters of my vintage err on the side of underestimating the educational level of the population. Philip Hauser, head of the Sociology Department at the University of Chicago, draws attention to the changes which are taking place:

> The increasing exposure of the population to formal schooling . . .
> can be expected to effect important changes in . . . the style of advertis-

---

2. The photograph showed several different kinds of stain—lipstick, coffee, shoe-polish, blood and so forth. The blood was my own; I am the only copywriter who has ever *bled* for his client.

ing. . . . Messages aimed at the "average" American on the assumption that he has had less than a grade school education are likely to find themselves with a declining or disappearing clientele.[3]

Meanwhile, all copywriters should read Dr. Rudolph Flesch's *Art of Plain Talk*. It will persuade them to use short words, short sentences, short paragraphs, and highly *personal* copy.

Aldous Huxley, who once tried his hand at writing advertisements, concluded that "any trace of literariness in an advertisement is fatal to its success. Advertisement writers may not be lyrical, or obscure, or in any way esoteric. They must be universally intelligible. A good advertisement has this in common with drama and oratory, that it must be immediately comprehensible and directly moving." [4]

(8) Resist the temptation to write the kind of copy which wins awards. I am always gratified when I win an award, but most of the campaigns which produce *results* never win awards, because they don't draw attention to themselves.

The juries that bestow awards are never given enough information about the *results* of the advertisements they are called upon to judge. In the absence of such information, they rely on their opinions, which are always warped toward the highbrow.

(9) Good copywriters have always resisted the temptation to *entertain*. Their achievement lies in the number of new products they get off to a flying start. In a class by himself stands Claude Hopkins, who is to advertising what Escoffier is to cooking. By today's standards, Hopkins was an unscrupulous barbarian, but technically he was the supreme master. Next I would place Raymond Rubicam, George Cecil, and James Webb Young, all of whom lacked Hopkins' ruthless salesmanship, but made up for it by their honesty, by the broader range of their work, and by their ability to write civilized copy when the occasion required it. Next I would place John Caples, the mail-order specialist from whom I have learned much.

These giants wrote their advertisements for newspapers and magazines. It is still too early to identify the best writers for television.

Daniel J. Boorstin / The Rhetoric of Democracy   1974

"We are perhaps the first people in history to have a centrally organized mass-produced folk culture," writes Daniel J. Boorstin in *"The Rhetoric of Democracy,"* and *"advertising has become the heart of the folk culture and even its very prototype."* In the following essay, which first appeared in Democracy and Its Discontents *(1974) and in 1976 was featured in the advertising trade magazine* Advertising Age, *Boorstin constructs a historical context for the complex role advertising now plays in contemporary American culture.*

One of America's leading historians, Boorstin is the author of the critically acclaimed three-volume study The Americans. *He has served as director of the National Museum of History and Technology and as senior historian of the Smithsonian Institution, and was director of the Library of Congress until 1987. His most recent book is* The Discoverers *(1984).*

3. *Scientific American* (October 1962).

4. *Essays Old And New* (Harper & Brothers, 1927). Charles Lamb and Byron also wrote advertisements. So did Bernard Shaw, Hemingway, Marquand, Sherwood Anderson, and Faulkner—none of them with any degree of success.

Advertising, of course, has been part of the mainstream of American civilization, although you might not know it if you read the most respectable surveys of American history. It has been one of the enticements to the settlement of this New World, it has been a producer of the peopling of the United States, and in its modern form, in its world-wide reach, it has been one of our most characteristic products.

Never was there a more outrageous or more unscrupulous or more ill-informed advertising campaign than that by which the promoters for the American colonies brought settlers here. Brochures published in England in the seventeenth century, some even earlier, were full of hopeful overstatements, half-truths, and downright lies, along with some facts which nowadays surely would be the basis for a restraining order from the Federal Trade Commission. Gold and silver, fountains of youth, plenty of fish, venison without limit, all these were promised, and of course some of them were found. It would be interesting to speculate on how long it might have taken to settle this continent if there had not been such promotion by enterprising advertisers. How has American civilization been shaped by the fact that there was a kind of natural selection here of those people who were willing to believe advertising?

Advertising has taken the lead in promising and exploiting the new. This was a new world, and one of the advertisements for it appears on the dollar bill on the Great Seal of the United States, which reads *novus ordo seclorum,* one of the most effective advertising slogans to come out of this country. "A new order of the centuries"—belief in novelty and in the desirability of opening novelty to everybody has been important in our lives throughout our history and especially in this century. Again and again advertising has been an agency for inducing Americans to try anything and everything—from the continent itself to a new brand of soap. As one of the more literate and poetic of the advertising copywriters, James Kenneth Frazier, a Cornell graduate, wrote in 1900 in "The Doctor's Lament":

> This lean M.D. is Dr. Brown
> Who fares but ill in Spotless Town.
> The town is so confounded clean,
> It is no wonder he is lean,
> He's lost all patients now, you know,
> Because they use *Sapolio.*

The same literary talent that once was used to retail Sapolio was later used to induce people to try the Edsel or the Mustang, to experiment with Lifebuoy or Body-All, to drink Pepsi-Cola or Royal Crown Cola, or to shave with a Trac II razor.

And as expansion and novelty have become essential to our economy, advertising has played an ever-larger role: in the settling of the continent, in the expansion of the economy, and in the building of an American standard of living. Advertising has expressed the optimism, the hyperbole, and the sense of community, the sense of reaching which has been so important a feature of our civilization.

Here I wish to explore the significance of advertising, not as a force in the economy or in shaping an American standard of living, but rather as a touchstone of the ways in which we Americans have learned about all sorts of things.

The problems of advertising are of course not peculiar to advertising, for they are just one aspect of the problems of democracy. They reflect the rise of what I have called Consumption Communities and Statistical Communities, and many of the special problems of advertising have arisen from our continuously energetic effort to give everybody everything.

If we consider democracy not just as a political system, but as a set of institutions which do aim to make everything available to everybody, it would not be an overstatement to describe advertising as the characteristic rhetoric of democracy. One of the tendencies of democracy, which Plato and other antidemocrats warned against a long time ago, was the danger that rhetoric would displace or at least overshadow epistemology; that is, *the temptation to allow the problem of persuasion to overshadow the problem of knowledge.* Democratic societies tend to become more concerned with what people believe than with what is true, to become more concerned with credibility than with truth. All these problems become accentuated in a large-scale democracy like ours, which possesses all the apparatus of modern industry. And the problems are accentuated still further by universal literacy, by instantaneous communication, and by the daily plague of words and images.

In the early days it was common for advertising men to define advertisements as a kind of news. The best admen, like the best journalists, were supposed to be those who were able to make their news the most interesting and readable. This was natural enough, since the verb to "advertise" originally meant, intransitively, to take note or to consider. For a person to "advertise" meant originally, in the fourteenth and fifteenth centuries, to reflect on something, to think about something. Then it came to mean, transitively, to call the attention of another to something, to give him notice, to notify, admonish, warn or inform in a formal or impressive manner. And then, by the sixteenth century, it came to mean: to give notice of anything, to make generally known. It was not until the late eighteenth century that the word "advertising" in English came to have a specifically "advertising" connotation as we might say today, and not until the late nineteenth century that it began to have a specifically commercial connotation. By 1879 someone was saying, "Don't advertise unless you have something worth advertising." But even into the present century, newspapers continue to call themselves by the title "Advertiser"—for example, the Boston *Daily Advertiser,* which was a newspaper of long tradition and one of the most dignified papers in Boston until William Randolph Hearst took it over in 1917. Newspapers carried "Advertiser" on their mastheads, not because they sold advertisements but because they brought news.

Now, the main role of advertising in American civilization came increasingly to be that of persuading and appealing rather than that of educating and informing. By 1921, for instance, one of the more popular textbooks, Blanchard's *Essentials of Advertising,* began: "Anything employed to influence people favorably is advertising. The mission of advertising is to persuade men and women to act in a way that will be of advantage to the advertiser." This development—in a country where a shared, a rising, and a democratized standard of living was the national pride and the national hallmark—meant that advertising had become the rhetoric of democracy.

What, then, were some of the main features of modern American advertising—if we consider it as a form of rhetoric? First, and perhaps most obvious, is *repetition.* It is hard for us to realize that the use of repetition in advertising is not an ancient device but a modern one, which actually did not come into common use in American journalism until just past the middle of the nineteenth century.

The development of what came to be called "iteration copy" was a result of a struggle by a courageous man of letters and advertising pioneer, Robert Bonner, who bought the old New York *Merchant's Ledger* in 1851 and turned it into a popular journal. He then had the temerity to try to change the ways of James Gordon Bennett, who of course was one of the most successful of the American newspaper pioneers, and who was both a sensationalist and at the same time an extremely stuffy man when it came to things that he did not consider to be news. Bonner was determined to use advertisements in Bennett's wide-circulating New York *Herald* to sell his own literary product, but he found it difficult to persuade

Bennett to allow him to use any but agate type in his advertising. (Agate was the smallest type used by newspapers in that day, only barely legible to the naked eye.) Bennett would not allow advertisers to use larger type, nor would he allow them to use illustrations except stock cuts, because he thought it was undignified. He said, too, that to allow a variation in the format of ads would be undemocratic. He insisted that all advertisers use the same size type so that no one would be allowed to prevail over another simply by presenting his message in a larger, more clever, or more attention-getting form.

Finally Bonner managed to overcome Bennett's rigidity by leasing whole pages of the paper and using the tiny agate type to form larger letters across the top of the page. In this way he produced a message such as "Bring home the New York Ledger tonight." His were unimaginative messages, and when repeated all across the page they technically did not violate Bennett's agate rule. But they opened a new era and presaged a new freedom for advertisers in their use of the newspaper page. Iteration copy—the practice of presenting prosaic content in ingenious, repetitive form—became common, and nowadays of course is commonplace.

A second characteristic of American advertising which is not unrelated to this is the development of *an advertising style*. We have histories of most other kinds of style—including the style of many unread writers who are remembered today only because they have been forgotten—but we have very few accounts of the history of advertising style, which of course is one of the most important forms of our language and one of the most widely influential.

The development of advertising style was the convergence of several very respectable American traditions. One of these was the tradition of the "plain style," which the Puritans made so much of and which accounts for so much of the strength of the Puritan literature. The "plain style" was of course much influenced by the Bible and found its way into the rhetoric of American writers and speakers of great power like Abraham Lincoln. When advertising began to be self-conscious in the eary years of this century, the pioneers urged copywriters not to be too clever, and especially not to be fancy. One of the pioneers of the advertising copywriters, John Powers, said, for example, "The commonplace is the proper level for writing in business; where the first virtue is plainness, 'fine writing' is not only intellectual, it is offensive." George P. Rowell, another advertising pioneer, said, "You must write your advertisement to catch damned fools—not college professors." He was a very tactful person. And he added, "And you'll catch just as many college professors as you will of any other sort." In the 1920's, when advertising was beginning to come into its own, Claude Hopkins, whose name is known to all in the trade, said, "Brilliant writing has no place in advertising. A unique style takes attention from the subject. Any apparent effort to sell creates corresponding resistance. . . . One should be natural and simple. His language should not be conspicuous. In fishing for buyers, as in fishing for bass, one should not reveal the hook." So there developed a characteristic advertising style in which plainness, the phrase that anyone could understand, was a distinguishing mark.

At the same time, the American advertising style drew on another, and what might seem an antithetic, tradition—the tradition of hyperbole in tall talk, the language of Davy Crockett and Mike Fink. While advertising could think of itself as 99.44 percent pure, it used the language of "Toronado" and "Cutlass." As I listen to the radio in Washington, I hear a celebration of heroic qualities which would make the characteristics of Mike Fink and Davy Crockett pale, only to discover at the end of the paean that what I have been hearing is a description of the Ford dealers in the District of Columbia neighborhood. And along with the folk tradition of hyperbole and tall talk comes the rhythm of folk music. We hear that Pepsi-Cola hits the spot, that it's for the young generation—and we hear other products celebrated in music which we cannot forget and sometimes don't want to remember.

There grew somehow out of all these contradictory tendencies—combining the commonsense language of the "plain style," and the fantasy language of "tall talk"—an advertising style. This characteristic way of talking about things was especially designed to reach and catch the millions. It created a whole new world of myth. A myth, the dictionary tells us, is a notion based more on tradition or convenience than on facts; it is a received idea. Myth is not just fantasy and not just fact but exists in a limbo, in the world of the "Will to Believe," which William James has written about so eloquently and so perceptively. This is the world of the neither true nor false—of the statement that 60 percent of the physicians who expressed a choice said that our brand of aspirin would be more effective in curing a simple headache than any other leading brand.

That kind of statement exists in a penumbra. I would call this the "advertising penumbra." It is not untrue, and yet, in its connotation it is not exactly true.

Now, there is still another characteristic of advertising so obvious that we are inclined perhaps to overlook it. I call that *ubiquity*. Advertising abhors a vacuum and we discover new vacuums every day. The parable, of course, is the story of the man who thought of putting the advertisement on the other side of the cigarette package. Until then, that was wasted space and a society which aims at a democratic standard of living, at extending the benefits of consumption and all sorts of things and services to everybody, must miss no chances to reach people. The highway billboard and other outdoor advertising, bus and streetcar and subway advertising, and skywriting, radio and TV commercials—all these are of course obvious evidence that advertising abhors a vacuum.

We might reverse the old mousetrap slogan and say that anyone who can devise another place to put another mousetrap to catch a consumer will find people beating a path to his door. "Avoiding advertising will become a little harder next January," the *Wall Street Journal* reported on May 17, 1973, "when a Studio City, California, company launches a venture called StoreVision. Its product is a system of billboards that move on a track across supermarket ceilings. Some 650 supermarkets so far are set to have the system." All of which helps us understand the observation attributed to a French man of letters during his recent visit to Times Square. "What a beautiful place, if only one could not read!" Everywhere is a place to be filled, as we discover in a recent *Publishers Weekly* description of one advertising program: "The $1.95 paperback edition of Dr. Thomas A. Harris' million-copy best seller 'I'm O.K., You're O.K.' is in for full-scale promotion in July by its publisher, Avon Books. Plans range from bumper stickers to airplane streamers, from planes flying above Fire Island, the Hamptons and Malibu. In addition, the $100,000 promotion budget calls for 200,000 bookmarks, plus brochures, buttons, lipcards, floor and counter displays, and advertising in magazines and TV."

The ubiquity of advertising is of course just another effect of our uninhibited efforts to use all the media to get all sorts of information to everybody everywhere. Since the places to be filled are everywhere, the amount of advertising is not determined by the *needs* of advertising, but by the *opportunities* for advertising which become unlimited.

But the most effective advertising, in an energetic, novelty-ridden society like ours, tends to be "self-liquidating." To create a cliché you must offer something which everybody accepts. The most successful advertising therefore self-destructs because it becomes cliché. Examples of this are found in the tendency for copyrighted names of trademarks to enter the vernacular—for the proper names of products which have been made familiar by costly advertising to become common nouns, and so to apply to anybody's products. Kodak becomes a synonym for camera, Kleenex a synonym for facial tissue, when both begin with a small *k*, and Xerox (now, too, with a small *x*) is used to describe all processes of copying, and so on. These are prototypes of the problem. If you are successful enough, then you will defeat your purpose in the long run—by making the name and the message so familiar that people won't notice them, and then people will cease to distinguish your product from everybody else's.

In a sense, of course, as we will see, the whole of American civilization is an example. When this was a ''new'' world, if people succeeded in building a civilization here, the New World would survive and would reach the time—in our age—when it would cease to be new. And now we have the oldest written Constitution in use in the world. This is only a parable of which there are many more examples.

The advertising man who is successful in marketing any particular product, then—in our high-technology, well-to-do democratic society, which aims to get everything to everybody—is apt to be diluting the demand for his particular product in the very act of satisfying it. But luckily for him, he is at the very same time creating a fresh demand for his services as advertiser.

And as a consequence, there is yet another role which is assigned to American advertising. This is what I call ''erasure.'' Insofar as advertising is competitive or innovation is widespread, erasure is required in order to persuade consumers that this year's model is superior to last year's. In fact, we consumers learn that we might be risking our lives if we go out on the highway with those very devices that were last year's lifesavers but without whatever special kind of brakes or wipers or seat belt is on this year's model. This is what I mean by ''erasure''—and we see it on our advertising pages or our television screen every day. We read in the *New York Times* (May 20, 1973), for example, that ''For the price of something small and ugly, you can drive something small and beautiful''—an advertisement for the Fiat 250 Spider. Or another, perhaps more subtle example is the advertisement for shirts under a picture of Oliver Drab: ''Oliver Drab. A name to remember in fine designer shirts? No kidding. . . . Because you pay extra money for Oliver Drab. And for all the other superstars of the fashion world. Golden Vee [the name of the brand that is advertised] does not have a designer's label. But we do have designers. . . . By keeping their names *off* our label and simply saying Golden Vee, we can afford to sell our $7 to $12 shirts for just $7 to $12, which should make Golden Vee a name to remember. Golden Vee, you only pay for the shirt.''

Having mentioned two special characteristics—the self-liquidating tendency and the need for erasure—which arise from the dynamism of the American economy, I would like to try to place advertising in a larger perspective. The special role of advertising in our life gives a clue to a pervasive oddity in American civilization. A leading feature of past cultures, as anthropologists have explained, is the tendency to distinguish between ''high'' culture and ''low'' culture—between the culture of the literate and the learned on the one hand and that of the populace on the other. In other words, between the language of literature and the language of the vernacular. Some of the most useful statements of this distinction have been made by social scientists at the University of Chicago—first by the late Robert Redfield in his several pioneering books on peasant society, and then by Milton Singer in his remarkable study of Indian civilization, *When a Great Tradition Modernizes* (1972). This distinction between the great tradition and the little tradition, between the high culture and the folk culture, has begun to become a commonplace of modern anthropology.

Some of the obvious features of advertising in modern America offer us an opportunity to note the significance or insignificance of that distinction for us. Elsewhere I have tried to point out some of the peculiarities of the American attitude toward the *high* culture. There is something distinctive about the place of thought in American life, which I think is not quite what it has been in certain Old World cultures.

But what about distinctive American attitudes to *popular* culture? What is our analogue to the folk culture of other peoples? Advertising gives us some clues—to a characteristically American democratic folk culture. Folk culture is a name for the culture which ordinary people everywhere lean on. It is not the writings of Dante and Chaucer and Shakespeare and Milton, the teachings of Machiavelli and Descartes, Locke or Marx. It is, rather, the pattern of slogans, local traditions, tales, songs, dances, and ditties. And of course holiday observances. Popular culture in other civilizations has been for the most part both an area of continuity with the past, a way in which people reach back into the past and out to their community, and at the same time an area of local variations. An area of individual and amateur expression in which a person has his own way of saying, or notes his mother's way of saying or singing, or his own way of dancing, his own view of folk wisdom and the cliché.

And here is an interesting point of contrast. In other societies outside the United States, it is the *high* culture that has generally been an area of centralized, organized control. In Western Europe, for example, universities and churches have tended to be closely allied to the government. The institutions of higher learning have had a relatively limited access to the people as a whole. This was inevitable, of course, in most parts of the world, because there were so few universities. In England, for example, there were only two universities until the early nineteenth century. And there was central control over the printed matter that was used in universities or in the liturgy. The government tended to be close to the high culture, and that was easy because the high culture itself was so centralized and because literacy was relatively limited.

In our society, however, we seem to have turned all of this around. Our high culture is one of the least centralized areas of our culture. And our universities express the atomistic, diffused, chaotic, and individualistic aspect of our life. We have in this country more than twenty-five hundred colleges and universities, institutions of so-called higher learning. We have a vast population ·in these institutions, somewhere over seven million students.

But when we turn to our popular culture, what do we find? We find that in our nation of Consumption Communities and emphasis on Gross National Product (GNP) and growth rates, advertising has become the heart of the folk culture and even its very prototype. And as we have seen, American advertising shows many characteristics of the folk culture of other societies: repetition, a plain style, hyperbole and tall talk, folk verse, and folk music. Folk culture, wherever it has flourished, has tended to thrive in a limbo between fact and fantasy, and of course, depending on the spoken word and the oral tradition, it spreads easily and tends to be ubiquitous. These are all familiar characteristics of folk culture and they are ways of describing our folk culture, but how do the expressions of our peculiar folk culture come to *us?*

They no longer sprout from the earth, from the village, from the farm, or even from the neighborhood or the city. They come to us primarily from enormous centralized self-consciously *creative* (an overused word, for the overuse of which advertising agencies are in no small part responsible) organizations. They come from advertising agencies, from networks of newspapers, radio, and television, from outdoor-advertising agencies, from the copywriters for ads in the largest-circulation magazines, and so on. These "creators" of folk culture—or pseudo-folk culture—aim at the widest intelligibility and charm and appeal.

But in the United States, we must recall, the advertising folk culture (like all advertising) is also confronted with the problems of self-liquidation and erasure.

These are by-products of the expansive, energetic character of our economy. And they, too, distinguish American folk culture from folk cultures elsewhere.

Our folk culture is distinguished from others by being discontinuous, ephemeral, and self-destructive. Where does this leave the common citizen? All of us are qualified to answer.

In our society, then, those who cannot lean on the world of learning, on the high culture of the classics, on the elaborated wisdom of the books, have a new problem. The University of Chicago, for example, in the 1930's and 1940's was the center of a quest for a "common discourse." The champions of that quest, which became a kind of crusade, believed that such a discourse could be found through familiarity with the classics of great literature—and especially of Western European literature. I think they were misled; such works were not, nor are they apt to become, the common discourse of our society. Most people, even in a democracy, and a rich democracy like ours, live in a world of popular culture, our special kind of popular culture.

The characteristic folk culture of our society is a creature of advertising, and in a sense it *is* advertising. But advertising, our own popular culture, is harder to make into a source of continuity than the received wisdom and commonsense slogans and catchy songs of the vivid vernacular. The popular culture of advertising attenuates and is always dissolving before our very eyes. Among the charms, challenges, and tribulations of modern life, we must count this peculiar fluidity, this ephemeral character of that very kind of culture on which other peoples have been able to lean, the kind of culture to which they have looked for the continuity of their traditions, for their ties with the past and with the future.

We are perhaps the first people in history to have a centrally organized mass-produced folk culture. Our kind of popular culture is here today and gone tomorrow—or the day after tomorrow. Or whenever the next semiannual model appears. And insofar as folk culture becomes advertising, and advertising becomes centralized, it becomes a way of depriving people of their opportunities for individual and small-community expression. Our technology and our economy and our democratic ideals have all helped make that possible. Here we have a new test of the problem that is at least as old as Heraclitus—an everyday test of man's ability to find continuity in his experience. And here democratic man has a new opportunity to accommodate himself, if he can, to the unknown.

Carol Caldwell / You Haven't Come a Long Way, Baby: Women in Television Commercials   1977

Despite the continual efforts of feminist groups to combat sexism in the mass media, unflattering stereotypes of women still persist in advertising, especially in TV commercials targeted at housewives. Though advertisers often try to cash in on social issues (see the ad for Virginia Slims or the many ads depicting high-energy and high-heeled professional women), their message frequently contains the same old sell: more so than men, women are likely to be pictured as ideal consumers first, real people second.

In the following essay, Carol Caldwell, a former copywriter, explains why there has been so little progress in advertising's depiction of women. The article originally appeared in New Times *for June 10, 1977. "From the beginning," wrote editor Jonathan Z. Larsen in the final issue of* New Times *(January 8,*

1979), "it was our hope that there was a place out there for a medium-sized magazine that did not have to be sold on the basis of celebrities, sex, or 'service journalism,' but rather on the strength of solid reporting by the best writers we could find. . . . We were determined to make the magazine a place where journalists could practice their craft at its best. And on that score we think we were successful." But as advertisers continued to move to more readily defined markets, New Times *failed in the marketplace.*

It's the beginning of the age of television, and all around it's black and white. Millions of minuscule scan dots collide in electronic explosion to create Woman in her Immaculate Kitchen. She is Alpha, Omega, eternal and everlasting Mother Video, toasting and frying, cleansing and purifying, perfectly formed of fire and ice. Permanent-waved, magenta-lipped, demurely collared and cuffed, cone-shaped from her tightly cinched waist down through yards and yards of material that brush coquettishly mid-calf, she is Betty Furness for Westinghouse, and you can be *sure* if it's Westinghouse.

The year is 1951. On the set of CBS-TV's *Studio One*, Furness has just captured the part to become America's first full-time product spokeswoman on television. Advertising execs at Westinghouse are taking a stab at having someone other than the host sell their product; they reason (and quite correctly) that Furness, with her Brearley School cool and her Broadway glamor, is a figure thousands of women will admire and listen to. During the audition Betty alters the script supplied by the casting director. Later, she tells *Time* magazine that she ad-libbed the refrigerator routine because "it was written like men think women talk!"

1952. While John Daly, Bill Henry, and Walter Cronkite monitor Ike and Adlai at the conventions, Betty Furness opens and shuts forty-nine refrigerators, demonstrates the finer points of forty-two television sets, twenty-three dishwashers and twelve ovens for a total of four-and-a-half hours of air time. General Eisenhower is on the air approximately an hour and twenty minutes; Mr. Stevenson, fifty minutes.

1956. Bright and blondeened, twenty-eight-year-old Julia Meade is the commercial spokeswoman for Lincoln on the *Ed Sullivan Show*, for Richard Hudnut hair products on *Your Hit Parade*, for *Life* magazine on John Daly's news show. She is pulling down a hundred thousand dollars a year, which moves *Time* to comment, "Julia (34–20–34) is one of a dozen or so young women on TV who find self-effacement enormously profitable." Howard Wilson, a vice-president of Kenyon & Eckhardt, Lincoln's ad agency, hired Julia for the spots with trepidation: a woman just couldn't be convincing about such things as high torque, turbo drive, and ball-joint suspensions. His fears, it turns out, were unfounded, and Meade becomes the perky prototype for a whole slew of carefully coiffed women selling cars—selling *anything*—by means other than their technical knowledge. And so Julia Meade begat Bess Myerson, who begat Anita Bryant, who begat Carmelita Pope, who begat Florence Henderson, each wholesome, flawless, clear of eye and enunciation, in short, sixty-second reminders of everything the American woman ought to be.

Times change, however, and eventually infant TV's ideal, untouchable dozen spokeswomen were replaced by hundreds of nameless actresses who portray "the little woman" in scenarios believed, by the agencies who create them, to be honest-to-God, middle-American, slice-of-life situations. As early as 1955, this new wave of commercial realism got a pat on the back by the industry's weekly trade paper, *Advertising Age*. Procter & Gamble had just come out with a revolutionary new way to sell soap on TV: "It is very difficult for a soap commercial to emerge from the mass of suds, with every known variant on the familiar theme of the woman holding up a box of 'X' soap powder with a grisly smile pointing to a pile of clothes she has just washed. Cheer has come up with the unique approach of dramatizing an everyday washing problem from the poor woman's point of view with a sound-over technique of stream of consciousness.''

That stream of consciousness flowed unchecked until Bill Free's famous National Airlines "Fly Me" faux pas in 1971. Women activists carried signs, stormed Free's and National's offices, read proclamations, and permeated the media with protest. Free talks of this trying and critical time with a humor and stoicism that comes from a six-year perspective, and from no longer handling the account. "The women's movement was identifying itself—and our 'Fly Me' campaign was an opportunity for a public platform. We were deluged with letters and calls. I even got an absurd letter from one of the leaders of the movement (who must go unnamed) demanding that I surely planned the sexual innuendo in the word 'fly'— she meant as in men's trouser pants.'' He paused. "The ad community continues to demean women, far more subtly than in our campaign.''

There are some easy hints at why this is so: Of the seventy-five thousand people currently employed in advertising, only 16.7 percent are women in other than clerical positions—not exactly an overwhelming voice. And, while advertising executives often live in the suburbs of large cities, they just as often tend to have a low regard for anyone who isn't an urbanite. As one New York agency executive quipped, "All I really know about the Middle America I sell to everyday is that it's the place I fly over to get to L.A.''

But these notations still don't answer the question: Why have advertisers, who make their living keeping up with trends, been so slow to get on board with the women's revolution? Where was everybody the recent night David Brinkley closed the book on America's traditional homelife structure, citing the fact that a mere seven percent of our nation's homes still maintained the time-honored tradition of the everyday housewife. Mom has officially flown the coop just about everywhere, except on TV in the commercials.

At a roundtable on women's advertising sponsored by the agency trade publication *Madison Avenue*, Harriet Rex, a vice-president at J. Walter Thompson, had this comment to make: "There's always been a lag between what is and what the ad business has codified as what 'is.' '' And Rena Bartos, a senior VP at the same agency, said, "Advertising may be a mirror of society but somehow the image in that mirror is a little out of focus. It plays back a 1950s reflection in a 1970s world.''

Madison Avenue's "little woman" is hardly new, and only partially improved. When feminists cite advertising that is "acceptable," it's invariably print ads. This isn't surprising, since magazine ads are prepared for specific subscribers whose personal backgrounds and attitudes have been carefully documented by the publication and noted by the agency. Television, on the other hand, commands a much larger and subsequently less definable audience.

So it is left to the advertisers and their agencies to define who television's consuming woman might be and what type of commercial she might like. The reward is compelling: Americans heap a total $9.2 billion every year into the coffers of the nation's top three TV advertisers—Procter & Gamble, Bristol-Myers, and General Foods. Still, the women portrayed aren't always to the customers' liking, and last year agitated viewers marched en masse outside P&G headquarters in Cincinnati, suggesting in rather unladylike terms what to do with Mr. Whipple and his grocery store groupies. Inside, P&G stockholders took little heed, voting down a suggestion that their commercial portrayal of women be reconsidered.

Others in the business did listen. When the National Organization for Women sent all major advertising agencies a position paper on the role of women in commercials, no one was surprised that most of the commercials on the air didn't jibe with the NOW requirements. Several agencies, fearing intervention by the Federal

Trade Commission, prodded their own regulatory outfit to consider the matter. The National Advertising Review Board formed a panel, including Patricia Carbine, publisher of *Ms.;* Joyce Snyder, coordinator of the task force on the image of women for NOW; the vice-presidents of broadcast standards for ABC and NBC; and a number of officers of sponsoring companies. A twenty-one page directive came out in 1975, in which the panel made a number of suggestions concerning ways in which advertisers could improve their portrayal of women. Here's what came out in the wash: "Advertising must be regarded as one of the forces molding society," the study asserted. "Those who protest that advertising merely reflects society must reckon with the criticism that much of the current reflection of women in advertising is out of date." Before airing a commercial, the panel urged advertisers to run down the NARB checklist, which included the following points:

• Are sexual stereotypes perpetuated in my ads? Do they portray women as weak, silly and over-emotional?

• Are the women portrayed in my ads stupid?

• Do my ads portray women as ecstatically happy over household cleanliness or deeply depressed because of their failure to achieve near-perfection in household tasks?

• Do my ads show women as fearful of not being attractive, of not being able to keep their husbands or lovers, fearful of in-law disapproval?

• Does my copy promise unrealistic psychological rewards for using the product?

Well now, does it? With these self-regulatory commandments in mind, I spent four weeks in front of daytime TV, logging current household product commercials and trying to determine just where women stand in the advertising scheme of things. During that time, Iris dickered with Rachel and Mac's teetering marriage, Beth died, Stacy miscarried, and Jennifer killed John's wife so they could finally be together.

Now a word from our sponsors.

Ring around the collar lives. After eight long years, the little woman is still exposing hubby and the kids to this awful embarrassment. It can strike virtually anywhere—in taxis, at ballgames, even on vacation doing the limbo. Our lady of the laundry is always guilty, always lucky to have a next-door neighbor who knows about Wisk, the washday miracle, and always back in hubby's good, but wary, graces by the happy ending. The Wisk woman faces the same unspoken commercial threat that the Geritol woman faces: "My wife, I think I'll keep her . . . " *if* she keeps in line.

Jim Jordan is president of Batten, Barton, Durstine and Osborn Advertising. Eight years ago, in a fit of cosmic inspiration, he came up with "ring around the collar" for his agency's client, Lever Bros. Since then, Jordan has run check-out-counter surveys on his commercials, asking shoppers who were purchasing Wisk, "You must be buying this product because you like the commercials." The reply he got was always the same: "Why no! I hate those commercials; but why should I hold that against the product?"

Jim Jordan echoes advertising's premier axiom: "The purpose of the commercial is not the aesthetic pleasure of the viewer—it's to sell the product." And Wisk is selling like gangbusters. He doesn't believe "ring around the collar" commercials show women in an embarrassing light; and to assume that, he says, "would be giving commercials more credit than they deserve."

Perhaps. And perhaps his "ring around the collar" campaign is getting more credit than it deserves for selling Wisk. Take any commercial with a simple message, repeat it again and again, and the product, if it's good, will sell, even if the spot is mindless and annoying. It's fixing the name of the product in the consumer's mind with a quick, catchy phrase that's important.

The household slice-of-life commercial is one of the classic offenders of the

NARB checklist. (Are sexual stereotypes perpetuated? You'd best believe it. Are the women portrayed stupid? And how.) Crisco's current campaign is a flawless example of this much-imitated genre, which has been developed and designed by Procter & Gamble. In it various long-suffering husbands and condescending neighbors are put through the heartache of greasy, gobby chicken and fries, all because some unthinking corner cutter spent "a few pennies less" on that mainstay of American cookery, lard. These pound-foolish little women cause their loved ones to live through "disasters" and "catastrophes." At the cue word "catastrophe," our video crumples into wavy electronic spasms and thrusts us back to the scene of the crime: to that excruciating point in the Bicentennial picnic or the backyard cookout when Dad has to wrinkle his upper lip and take Mom aside for a little set-to about her greasy chicken. The moral, delivered by some unseen pedantic male announcer, is plain: "Ladies who've learned—buy Crisco."

These examples are, sad to say, still very much the rule for women's portrayals in thirty- and sixty-second spots. They occur with alarming regularity during the daytime hours, when stations may sell up to sixteen commercial minutes an hour. (The nighttime rate is a mere eight minutes, forty seconds per hour.) Now, you are probably not the average American who spends some six hours a day in front of the old boob tube (which, when the maximum number of commercials per hour is computed, means over an hour and a half of product propaganda). And you probably are quite sure that commercials have absolutely no effect on you. Maybe they don't. But a shaken agency copywriter told me the first word his child spoke was "McDonald's," and I've stood in a grocery line and watched while a mother, tired of her child's tears, lets him wander off and return—not with a candy bar, but with a roll of Charmin. Make no mistake about it: the cumulative effects of commercials are awesome. As the NARB study argues: "An endless procession of commercials on the same theme, all showing women using household products in the home, raises very strong implications that women have no other interests except laundry, dishes, waxing floors, and fighting dirt in any form. . . . Seeing a great many such advertisements in succession reinforces the traditional stereotype that a 'woman's place is *only* in the home.' "

There have, in the past few years, been commercials that break the homebody mold. The Fantastik spray commercial, "I'm married to a man, not a house" (which, incidentally, was written and produced by men), has reaped much praise, as has L'Oreal's "I'm worth it" campaign. "Ten years ago, it would have been, 'John thinks I'm worth it,' " says Lenore Hershey, editor of *Ladies' Home Journal. Ms.'* Pat Carbine thinks United Airlines is flying right when they address women executives, "You're the boss." She also likes the Campbell's soup "working wife" commercial, in which a man scurries around the kitchen, preparing soup for his woman, but adds, "I'm afraid they took the easy route and resorted to total role reversal—making her look good at the expense of the man."

Indeed, Lois Wyse of Wyse Advertising fears that advertisers are not only failing to talk to today's women, but they're missing men as well. The reason for this, as she sees it, is research—the extensive demographic studies done on who buys what product. Last winter Wyse told *Madison Avenue,* "About twenty years ago we were all little Ozzies and Harriets to all the people who do research, and now their idea of contemporizing is to make the Ozzies into Harriets and the Harriets into Ozzies."

Marketing research, with its charts and graphs and scientific jargon, has increased in importance over the last ten years or so, while creativity, the keystone to the Alka-Seltzer, Volkswagen, and Benson & Hedges campaigns of the sixties, has taken the backseat. Ask anybody in advertising why commercials still show the little woman bumbling around in a fearful daze, and you'll find the answer is always the same: "Because our research tells us it is so." Agencies devote hundreds of thousands of dollars to find out who's buying their client's stuff and why. And it's not just Mom up there on the charts and graphs. Marketing researchers dissect and analyze the buying habits, educational and income levels of every member of the family. They even know what we do with our leisure time, and how much God we've got.

This subjective form of research is amorphously titled life-style research, explained by the respected *Journal of Marketing* in the following brave-new-world lingo: "Life-style data—activities, interests, opinions—have proved their importance as a means of *duplicating* the consumer for the marketing researcher. . . ."And more: "Life-style attempts to answer questions like: What do women think about the job of housekeeping? Do they see themselves as homebodies or swingers? Life-style provides definitions like 'housewife role haters,' 'old fashioned homebodies' and 'active affluent urbanites.' "

But life-style research is still in its infancy and very, very expensive. The trendiest and most attainable form of research going is called focus-group research, the grassroots movement of advertising research. From lairs of hidden cameras and tape-recording devices, agency and client-types, despite the experts' warnings that focus-group samples are far too small to be projected on a national scale, eke out a vision of their consumer that almost invariably fits just the stereotype they had in mind in the first place, and proceed to advertise accordingly.

The theory, quite simply, is to get inside women's heads in order to get inside their pocketbooks. From Satellite Beach to Spokane, fact-finding specialists are retained at grand sums to commune with the natives and document their particular buying habits. For instance:

The canned-meat industry's advertising wasn't paying off in the Southeast. Focus-group researchers were called in and groups of eight women were randomly selected from Memphis neighborhoods. The women fit the product's buyer profile—in this case, all came from families with middle to lower-middle incomes. Each woman was paid ten dollars. On an assigned day each focus group would meet for a two-hour session at the suburban home of the researcher's field representative—a woman who was a veteran of several similar exercises. As the women took their seats around the dining room table, loosening up with coffee and homemade cake, the client and agency folk sat, out of sight, in the rumpus room, carefully scanning the meeting on closed-circuit monitors. This is what they heard.

MODERATOR: Do any of you ever buy canned meats?

VOICES: Oh yes. Yeah. Uh, huh.

MODERATOR: When do you buy them?

ANN: Well, my husband went to New Orleans, so I bought a lot of canned goods. The children enjoy them.

LOU: Well, I bought Vienna sausage the other day 'cause the Giant had a special on it—seventy-nine cents a can—it's usually a dollar nine, a dollar nineteen. You could only get four at a time, so I went back twice that week.

MODERATOR: Do you buy these for particular members of the family?

NORMA: If they didn't like it, I wouldn't buy it.

DELORES: Melvin loves the hot dog chili. And the baby—you can just stick a Vienna sausage in her hand and she'll go 'round happy all day.

MODERATOR: Do you read the labels on canned meats?

VOICES: Oh sure. Yes.

NORMA: The children read the labels first and called my attention to it. When I saw it had things like intestines and things like that, I didn't want to buy potted meat any more.

LOU: Fats, tissues, organs. If you read the labels on this stuff—when they say hearts . . . I don't know. I don't like hearts.

VIRGINIA: Well, psychologically you're not geared to it.

ALMA: They could lie on the label a little bit. Just don't tell us so much. (Laugh.) It would taste pretty good, but . . . yeah. I'd rather not know.

MODERATOR: What do you think ought to be on the labels?

ANNE: I think you ought to know about the chemicals.

NORMA: I love to read calories on the side of a can.

DELORES: I wonder what all's in those preservatives?

IDA: The side of this Hormel can here says that this meat is made by the same company that makes Dial soap. Says Armour-Dial.

NORMA: At least you think it's clean.

DELORES: Some preservatives do taste like soap. . . .

IDA: I wouldn't be eating that stuff with them chemicals.

ANN: Well, if you worry about that, you're going to starve to death.

VIRGINIA: You'd never eat in a restaurant if you ever got back in the kitchen.

MODERATOR: Would you buy a product because of the advertising?

VOICES: No. No. Maybe.

IDA: My children love that Libby's—the one, "Libby's, Libby's, Libby's. . . ."

NORMA: Now, if there's young kids that go to the grocery store with you, everytime they'll pick up something . . . "Libby's, Libby's, Libby's."

DELORES: Every time I see Hormel chili . . . I think about them people out at a fireside by the beach eating that chili. One of them is playing a guitar and they start singing.

VIRGINIA: Armour has a cute hot dog commercial, that's where they're all marching around, weenies, ketchup and mustard. . . .

IDA: Yeah. That's cute.

MODERATOR: Do any of you ever buy Spam?

IDA: What's Spam?

ANNE: It's chopped something. Or pressed.

LOU: It's beaver board.

MODERATOR: Beaver what?

Most researchers claim that their studies are only as good as the people who interpret them. The interpreters are usually the agency and clients who—many advertising executives will admit, but only off the record—read their own product concerns into the comments of the panelists. Quite often, complaints about daytime commercials ("They're awful!" "Ridiculous!" "Laughable!") are brushed aside. "You can formulate breakthrough approaches in order to reach this new woman," Joan Rothberg, a senior VP at Ted Bates, told *Madison Avenue,* "and yet the traditional 'Ring Around the Collar' approach wins out in terms of creating awareness and motivating people to buy the product."

One of the final research tests a commercial can go through after it's been created and storyboarded is the Burke test. One day up at my old agency, the creative director, a writer, and an art director came blazing through the halls with hats and horns, announcing at 120 decibels, "We Burked twenty-nine! We Burked twenty-nine!" Now this may sound to you as it did to me that day, as if these people were talking in tongues. What having "Burked twenty-nine" actually means is the percentage the commercial scored in recall after one viewing by a large audience. The average number on the Burke scale for the particular product my friends were testing was twenty-five—so you can understand the celebration.

Because the agencies and their clients accept Burke scores as valid, the scores become a powerful factor in what types of commercials will run. It's no accident that the Burke company is located in Cincinnati, since Cincinnati is the birthplace of Crest, Crisco, Comet, Charmin, Cheer, Bonus, Bounce, Bounty, Bold, Lava,

Lilt, Pampers, Prell, Downy, Dash, and Duz—in other words, Cincinnati is the home of the King Kong of Household Cleanliness, Procter & Gamble. From high atop magnificent offices, P&G executives control daytime television and a goodly portion of prime time, too. They are the top-dollar spender on TV, having put out $260 million last year alone in commercial time bought. They produce and have editorial control over five of the biggest soap operas on TV: *As the World Turns, Another World, Edge of Night, Guiding Light,* and *Search for Tomorrow,* which reach some forty million women every day.

Procter & Gamble is the most blatant offender in perpetuating "the little woman" commercial stereotype. Because of its monopoly on both media and marketplace (it pulls in $3.6 billion every year) and because its research is the most expensive and extensive, P&G is the recognized leader and arbiter of format and content in household product commercials—where P&G goes, others will follow.

This does not spur innovation. In one P&G agency, the creative people have two formulae they use for "concepting" a commercial: regular slice-of-life (problem in the home, solution with the wonderful product) or what the agency guys call "two C's in a K." The "K" stands for kitchen; the "C" is a four-letter word.

Once a commercial is written, tested, and approved by the client, it's got to be cast and shot. I asked Barbara Claman to talk about what agency people and their clients ask for when they're casting housewife roles. She should know: Barbara's built up one of the largest commercial casting agencies in the country. The day we talked all hell was breaking loose outside her office door. Scores of women and children had come to try out for a McDonald's commercial.

I wondered if agencies ever called for a P&G-type housewife for their commercials.

"Absolutely. She should be blond—or, if brunette, not too brunette. Pretty, but not too pretty. Midwestern in speech, middle-class looking, gentile. If they want to use blacks, they want *waspy* blacks."

"What about P&G-type husbands?"

"Same thing," Claman said. "But you'll find that the husband is getting to play the asshole more and more in American commercials."

"But do you see a change occurring? A trend in women's portrayals away from the traditional P&G type?"

"A little. I think they'd like to be a little more real. They're realizing, very slowly, that the working woman has a lot of money."

"What if they want a Rosie, a Madge or a Cora—one of the Eric Hoffer working-class philosopher-queens?"

Barbara laughed. "They'll say, 'Let's cast a ballsy one.' "

"Are you offended by the roles they want to put women in? Do you try to change their thinking on this?"

"I'm totally offended. I'm tired of seeing women hysterical over dirt spots on their glasses. I get lady producers in here all the time. We've tried to change their minds about the roles. You see how successful we've been."

Jane Green is another casting director in New York. She tells of a friend who was auditioning for a P&G spot in which the agency's creative people were trying to break out of the housewife mold. They'd called interesting faces—real people who wore real clothes. A couple of hours passed and the P&G client was obviously agitated. He turned to the agency producer: "What are you people trying to pull over on me? The woman in this commercial needs to be *my* wife, in *my* bathroom in Cincinnati—not some hip little chickie. Whom do you think we're selling to?"

One wonders. Recently an agency producer asked me and my cat Rayette to be in a kitty litter commercial. I arrived wearing blue jeans and a shirt, my usual at-home ensemble. The art director, who was wearing jeans himself, wasn't pleased:

"Where is your shirtwaist? I told the producer I wanted a *housewife* look in this commercial." I tried to explain that most women—housewives and otherwise—had left those McMullans and Villagers back at the Tri Delt house in '66. The shoot was postponed until we found something that looked more housewifey.

Some commercial trends have passed: The damsel in distress has, for the time being, retreated to her tower. (Remember the thundering White Knight? The mystical, spotless Man from Glad? Virile, barrel-chested Mr. Clean?) But others remain, the most blatantly offensive, perhaps, being those commercials using women as sex objects to entice the consumer into buying the product. Most agency people aren't allowed to comment on the scheme of things in such commercials (one slip of the tongue and that multimillion-dollar account might choose another, more circumspect agency). But Dwight Davis, VP and creative director on the Ford dealers' account with J. Walter Thompson in Detroit, says it's no secret Detroit is still the national stronghold of selling with sex. Why? The male is still the decision maker in car buying ("Our research tells us it is so"); and the auto is still an extension of the American male libido. So we've got Catherine Deneuve hawking Lincoln-Mercurys. She circles the car in her long, slinky gown and slips inside to fondle the plush interior. Catherine signs off, sprawled across the hood of the car, with a seductive grrrrr. She is, as Davis describes the phenomenon, the car advertisers' "garnish on the salad."

Commercials like this, and the little woman slice-of-life, are caricatures of themselves. That's precisely why Carol Burnett and the people at *Saturday Night Live* have so much fun with them. Even the new wave of women's commercials isn't spared. In a spoof Anne Beatts wrote for *Saturday Night,* a middle-class Mom, dressed not in a shirt-waist but a polyester pantsuit, rushes into the kitchen, crashing through a café-curtained dutch door. She starts to have a heart-to-heart with the camera: "I'm a nuclear physicist and Commissioner of Consumer Affairs." She starts to put her groceries away.

"In my spare time, I do needlepoint, read, sculpt, take riding lessons, and brush up on my knowledge of current events. Thursday's my day at the day-care center, and then there's my work with the deaf; but I still have time left over to do all my own baking and practice my backhand, even though I'm on call twenty-four hours a day as a legal aid lawyer in Family Court. . . ." Our New-Wave Mom is still running on, all the time very carefully folding the grocery bags and stuffing them into a cabinet where literally hundreds of other carefully folded bags are stacked incredibly neatly, when the omniscient announcer comes in:

"How does Ellen Sherman, Cleveland housewife, do it all? She's smart! She takes Speed. Yes, Speed—the tiny blue diet pill you don't have to be overweight to need."

If the "average" woman is true to her portrayal in commercials, we've got a pretty bitter pill to swallow. But you know, we all know, commercials don't portray real life. Nice Movies' Dick Clark, who's done spots for Coca-Cola, Toyota, and Glade, points out, most commercials are "formula answers to advertising questions—bad rip-offs of someone else's bad commercials." They are bad rip-offs of their viewers too. But, someday, some bright young advertising prodigy will begin a whole new trend of commercials that don't talk down, don't demean or debase, and still sell soap or toothpaste or cars like crazy. And then everyone will be doing it. Double your money back, guaranteed.

Why am I so sure? Because, as Brinkley so neatly points out, only seven percent of our homes have the traditional resident Mom. Because there are more women doctors, engineers, copywriters, jockeys, linesmen, you name it, than ever before. Because women are becoming more selective in their buying habits. Because, quite simply, research tells me it is so.

DISCUSSION QUESTIONS

1. Do you think Caldwell's argument about sexism in advertising is still accurate? Choose one or two recent television commercials to support your point of view.

2. Look at the ads reprinted in this section from the perspective of Caldwell's argument. Which ads conform to her contention about the role of women in advertising; which do not? How might she respond to ads you think show women in a positive manner?

Marshall Schuon / Cars and Self-Image   1983

As members of a nation on wheels, Americans have traditionally used the automobile to project themselves and advertise their individual personalities. In "Cars and Self-Image," Marshall Schuon notes how our private whims, the attitudes of our era, and the interests of the corporate automakers change the ways in which we view—and embrace—these emblems of self-importance.

Schuon, deputy editor of the New York Times *national edition, writes the consumer-oriented column "About Cars."*

I once had a fistfight with a kid named Alan. I think I won, although both Alan and my nose may dispute it. What we were fighting about was electric trains, specifically my insistence on the superior realism of American Flyer when compared to those clunky, three-rail Lionels. We were always arguing about something like that. We identified with *stuff*, and if it wasn't trains, it was comic strips, or the contention that the P-38 was a better fighter plane than the P-47. Later, in the early 1950's, it was cars, and the argument extended to all of our friends.

Back then, a sports car was an MG-TC with spindly wheels, wooden floorboards and a body made of old chewing-gum wrappers, nothing a real 17-year-old man would own. You were either a Ford guy or a Chevy guy. Plymouths didn't count, and we didn't *talk* to the guy who bought a '41 Packard. Shows how much we knew. It also shows how tightly rapt we were by the idea of a package to suit our image.

Ford had a V-8 engine. You could put dual exhausts on it. You could top it off with a whole gaggle of carburetors. You could throw in a hot cam and have something that was truly the terror of the streets. Or you could take a Jimmy truck engine, stuff it into a Chevy sedan and make a mohair monster that ate Fords for lunch. It all depended.

It still does, of course. A car says a lot about a man, and that is the real reason that dealers don't have generic automobiles on their shelves. No sensibly priced, plain-white, three-sizes-fit-all vehicles for us. What we want, whether we admit it or not, are rolling advertisements for ourselves, and the chief difficulty is in choosing the right billboard.

For myself, and for a long time after I gave up the hot-rod Fords, it was a successive line of vans and funny cars like Corvairs. And, finally, it was a Cadillac. I was wearing a cowboy hat then and, night after night, I would arrive at the newspaper I worked for, Stetson on my head, blonde on my arm and goblet of brandy in my hand. The guards in the lobby thought I was a real character. I know that because one of them told me about this bozo who was a real character. We were in the men's room and he didn't recognize me without my hat and blonde and brandy, which is what happens when you shuck the trappings.

The problem with the Cadillac, of course, was that it had to stay outside. It was just right for a man in a cowboy hat—powerful, lush and big to the point of being a crime against nature. But it wasn't any good out there in the parking lot with me in the office. I solved that by carrying the owner's manual and leaving it discreetly on the desk.

Since then, I've worked a bit on my profile, and these days I've got it down to a small Buick. I tell myself I'm more mature, less flamboyant. And I like to think it says something about increasing self-confidence. Those are nice things to think, even though I know it's only the recession.

Subtlety does have its place, however, and Mercedes-Benz has capitalized nicely on a slice of the market that demands quiet flair. "What it is," a smugly happy owner once told me, "is quality and engineering. You drive that car and it says something about you, about being smart enough to know it—and, second, being rich enough to afford it."

If money is no object, naturally, you can suit your image in the same disgusting way you can do anything when money is no object. I have a friend in the automobile business whose name is Fred. He did it by going on a diet and then buying a white Jaguar for days and a blue Ferrari for nights. He had to go on the diet because a Ferrari is a *thin* car. When you drive a Ferrari, you don't have room for an extra pack of king-size cigarettes, let alone your very own spare tire.

"The Jag is an open car, that's why it's for days," Fred says. "The Ferrari's a coupe and that's why it's for nights. But you talk about this image thing—you can pretty much typecast who will own what kind of car. If you're a pilot, for instance, you buy a Saab. Guys who are into mechanical weirdness always buy Saabs."

You can look at a guy, says Fred, and know he's an old Fiat or he's American Motors. "Take a Porsche guy," he says. "A Porsche owner is very image-conscious. He wants to be daring on the outside, but he'd never own a Ferrari because a Porsche is more practical. With a Ferrari, if you run into a repair problem, you can be in for as much as $2,000 or $3,000."

Another thing, says Fred, is the kind of man who owns a Corvette or a Pontiac Trans Am. "Those are cars people move out of," he says. "You'll see an ad that says 'Must sell my Corvette—getting married,' but you don't see it the other way, you don't see that ad for a Ferrari or a Mercedes 450 SL."

It is not just drivers who think about image though; the men who make the cars think about it too, and there have been some spectacular changes over the years in what a car is meant to say. When I was a kid, the Dodge was gray and grandfatherly. Stodgy. Nothing at all like the Dodges that were the hot ticket on the racing circuits of the late 1960's and early 1970's. And John Z. DeLorean, before garnering all his other celebrity, made a name for himself at General Motors by changing Pontiac from a dull and middle-aged widget into a wide-track screamer that was panted over by a nation's entire zit-set.

It must be admitted, however, that power and pizazz are not all things to all men. There are those, a relative few in the scheme of things, who see the positive advantage in projecting a negative image. They delight in their perversity. They don't want flashy performance or Italian good looks or a car that drips gold instead of brake fluid. They are the people who made the Volkswagen Beetle a hit, and today they are the people who joyfully fling their arms and leap into the air when they see a Toyota Tercel.

Rolls-Royce is the ultimate image car, of course, but the company has only recently tried to find out who buys its product. "You know, we've always been a sort of cottage industry,'' says Reginald Abbiss, a former BBC reporter who now employs his dulcet British tones as the Rolls spokesman in the colonies. ''We only make 60 cars a week, but we have to look ahead, and we are adopting a more aggressive approach in promotion and advertising.''

What the company is finding, he said, is that—particularly in America—a Rolls customer is saying, ''I've worked damned hard for my money, and this is a tangible result.''

Image, too, is the real reason the company continues to make the Bentley, which differs from the Rolls only in its radiator shell and costs $530 less than the $93,000 bottom-of-the-line Rolls. ''With that sort of tariff,'' says Reg Abbiss, ''the $530 obviously doesn't make any difference. What we like to believe is that the Bentley is for the man who has won the race but declines to wear the laurel.''

DISCUSSION QUESTIONS

1. Look over the automobile ads in this section. Select one ad that you believe supports Schuon's analysis. Explain why.

2. Do the advertisers themselves see a connection between an individual's car and his or her personality? How does the ad for Alfa Romeo portray such connections?

3. What about women? Have their self-images no connection to automobiles? Explain your answer. Consider the image of women in the ad for Cadillac.

Roy Blount, Jr. / A Man Who Doesn't Take His Beer Lightly
Advertising Age, April 4, 1985

Described by his peers as ''the Number One magazine writer in the country,'' Roy Blount, Jr., is a versatile stylist whose humorous treatment of a broad range of subjects has earned him a reputation as a contemporary heir of Mark Twain. Blount, however, views his work in far more modest terms: ''I am not the kind of person who feels right about calling himself a 'writer,' even. It sounds like something you would assert, falsely, in a singles bar.'' Blount is even more reluctant to call himself an author. He describes the difference in the following characteristically droll terms: ''A writer, as we know, writes; an author has written. What does an author do? Auth? Authorize? An author authors. But never in the present tense. No one says, when asked what he or she is doing, 'I'm authoring'.''

Blount's distinguished career as ''writer'' began with a one-year stint as a reporter for Georgia's Decatur-DeKalb News *and with summer internships at New York's* Morning Telegraph *and at the* New Orleans Times-Picayune—*positions he held before completing his undergraduate studies at Vanderbilt University with honors in 1963. After taking an M.A. degree at Harvard the following year, Blount returned to writing full-time and worked as a reporter, editorial writer, and columnist at the* Atlanta Journal *(1966–68) before joining* Sports Illustrated, *where he wrote for the next eight years, including service in 1974–75 as an associate editor. When asked to describe the shape of his career, Blount provided the following telegraphic summary:*

Raised in the South by Southern parents. Couldn't play third base well enough so became college journalist. Ridiculed cultural enemies. Boosted integration. Decided to write, teach. Went to Harvard Graduate School. Didn't like it. Went back to journalism. Liked it. Got a column. Ridiculed cultural enemies. Wrote limericks. Boosted integration. Wanted to write for magazines. Took writing job at Sports Illustrated. *Have seen country, met all kinds of people, heard all different kinds of talk. Like it.*

Blount has published scores of humorous articles and several noteworthy books, including Crackers *(1980),* One Fell Soup; or, I'm Just a Bug on the Windshield of Life *(1982), and* Not Exactly What I Had in Mind *(1985). Blount's humorous analysis of television commercials, and more specifically of the successful Miller Lite advertisements, originally appeared in* Advertising Age, *one of the most widely read journals in that industry.*

And now for a message that takes real courage: I can't find it in my heart to like light beer. I would rather have one heavy beer than seven light ones. I wouldn't mind having seven heavy ones. And I don't really care what brand the last four-and-a-half of them are.

The preceding message takes courage not because it implies the risk of corpulence on my part. I believe a person should live in such a way that he can carry a little corpulence. The reason it takes courage is this: I guess it rules out my appearing in a great beer commercial.

I, a living American, accept that I will never be in a great beer commercial, probably. With no less gravity would an 18th Century Viennese have said to himself, "Let's face it. You ain't ever going to hit a great lick on a clavier, probably." Great beer commercials are so good they nearly do a transcendent thing in our culture: They nearly redeem television.

I don't mean the beer commercials with actors in them. Those icky-yuppie figments of the "Tonight it's kinda special" stripe are *not beery*. Nor can I tolerate that around-the-campfire vignette in which one guy goes off into the woods to talk a grizzly bear out of a case of Stroh's. Here we have a workable concept, ruined by performances so callow that any half-grown bear, grizzly or fluffy, would chase those guys *and* their campfire all the way back to Hotchkiss.

I mean the beer commercials with real people in them: The Miller Lite ones with Bubba Smith, Boog Powell, Jim Honochick, John Madden, Marv Throneberry, Bob Uecker and all. Those commercials are the only form of television that captures what jocks are like. (Which is to say, what everybody wants to be like when he or she is drinking beer.) They may be the only form of television that captures what *people* are like.

Most of the time as we watch television what are we thinking? "Unhhhhh. Television." Or "Holy, jumping . . . Great television! But should the children be witnessing actual dismemberment?" Or "Will wonders never cease? Considering it's a television, this almost bears some relation to art or life!"

Great beer commercials, however, are fresh, full-bodied, tasty: Better than "M*A*S*H," for my money, and almost as good as "The Honeymooners." Being commercials, they are what TV is all about, and yet there is actually something genuine about them. True, the point is to sell light beer by showing heavy guys drinking it. But these guys (who have lived in such a way that they can carry a little corpulence) are being funny about drinking beer in ways that people actually are funny, or think they are, *when they are drinking beer.*

Of course these heavy guys do not take any beer into their mouths, on screen. And I know the poignance of that.

Years ago, after I wrote a book on the Steelers, I appeared in a commercial, shown in Pittsburgh, for Iron City beer. (This was back before there was light.) It wasn't a great commercial, because I was alone—didn't have Dick Butkus to bounce off of. But it was heartfelt, and it taught me how to execute "the beauty pour." The beauty pour means transferring beer from bottle to glass with so fine a touch that the suds rise just far enough above the brim; look irresistibly *heady;* but do not crest and break and come running down your arm.

The beauty pour does not, however, entail drinking any beer, aside from what you may be able to lick off your arm while the director isn't looking. I did 38 takes of my commercial and listened to 38 beers being poured unaesthetically down the toilet as I sat there feeling more and more porous and dry. Beer commercials waste more beer than Carrie Nation did.

But you can tell that the people in the Miller Lite commercials have, in their times, swallowed a few. They are not getting all misty and warm over what a wonderful institution beer is for bringing the right sort of persons together. They are getting the way people get, ideally, when they are having fun drinking beer: Rowdy without serious breakage, lightsome in a ponderous sort of way and just confused enough to be entertaining.

Why aren't more commercials, for beer or anything else, as appropriate as these? Why do so many of them involve, for instance, children beaming in ways that children never beam and exclaiming things that children never exclaim? "Gee Mom, these Hodgson-Furbinger-Reconstituted Thaw-'n-Sizzle Fish Nuggets are really *something else.*"

If only I could believe, for 30 seconds, light beer tastes like beer.

DISCUSSION QUESTIONS

1. What is Blount's principal complaint about most television advertising? To what does he attribute the success of the advertisements for Miller Lite beer? What is Blount's implied remedy for what he characterizes as "Those icky-yuppie figments of the 'Tonight it's kinda special' " beer commercials?

2. Apply Blount's standards for successful beer advertising to Ernest Hemingway's endorsement of Ballantine Ale ("How Would You Put a Glass of Ballantine Ale into Words," "Advertising"). How satisfied would Blount be with the terms Hemingway uses to talk about Ballantine Ale? About himself? Point to specific words and phrases to verify your response.

PRESS

Journalism is literature in a hurry.
MATTHEW ARNOLD

NEWS may be America's best-selling product. Despite the intense competition from radio and television broadcasts, where news is delivered instantaneously and free of charge, well over fifty-eight million Americans are still willing to pay for their daily newspaper. Serving this immense market is an industry built around twenty-three thousand daily and weekly newspapers. The industry ranges from the picturesque one-room office of a country paper, where the news is gathered, written, edited, and printed by a handful of people, to multilevel, worldwide corporate enterprises employing thousands in the strenuous business of compiling, disseminating, and even occasionally making the news. A news item, whether in a two-page rural paper or in that monstrous, practically unfinishable, several-hundred-page Sunday edition of the *New York Times,* needs to be seen, then, as something more than simply a report of current events. To be comprehended fully, the news should be considered in its largest corporate context—as the result of individual and group writing performed under the pressures of advertising revenue, available space, deadlines, audience surveys, ownership policy, editorial selection, and professional competition. The news is not only transmitted information, it is the commodity of newspapers.

The pledge "All the News That's Fit to Print" on the front page of every copy of the *New York Times* reminds us that only news deemed suitable to print has been *selected* for us by editors apparently fastidious in their taste and conscience. The *Times*'s motto, however, once prompted the following slightly cynical parody "All the News That Fits We Print." The joke here works not only at the expense of the *New York Times;* it could easily apply to any large newspaper. A simple experiment shows how relatively small is the percentage of space allotted for what is supposedly a newspaper's main product, news. If you cut out from any newspaper with a fairly large circulation all the commercial and classified advertisements; the theater, movie, radio, and television listings; the national and local gossip; the personal advice columns; the horoscope; the puzzles and games; the cartoons; the letters to the editor; the "human interest" tidbits; and the fillers, you are left with very few of what are, strictly speaking, genuine news items. In short, little of the shape and essence of a modern newspaper remains. The parody of the *Times*'s pledge is right on target. It does seem that readers of most newspapers are given only the news that fits between the spaces reserved for more profitable or entertaining pieces.

To make sure that all the news will fit—in the sense of meeting editorial standards and conforming to the physical confines of the paper—newspapers impose a strictly regulated system of reportorial procedures and conventions. A person who writes for a newspaper must not only contend with tight deadlines but must also satisfy an experienced copy editor whose job is to see to it that the report will conform to the paper's public image and fit easily into its style. The writer must also be aware that the report will compete with all other news and nonnews for prominent display in the layout of each edition. The exigencies of the newspaper business demand that the writer develop a comfortable, transferable, and conveniently alterable prose.

Any respected editor will say that clear and concise writing is encouraged. This usually means prose whittled down to short, simple sentences, the sparing use of adjectives and adverbs, a minimal reliance on synonyms, an avoidance of cumbersome syntactical relations, and brief paragraphs with few transitions. Most of the journalism reprinted in this section illustrates writing that conforms to these editorial strictures. Such standards are double-edged: they ensure the kind of writing generally considered to be most appropriate to rendering factual information quickly and precisely, and they guarantee sentences that are uniform and formulaic enough so as to be easily maneuvered into each newspaper's particular editorial requirements and emphases.

A stylistic uniformity for reporting important news stories (feature articles, editorials, and so on, are not so restricted) is enforced even further by a standardized narrative procedure reporters call the inverted pyramid. The opening of a news story conventionally contains all the significant facts—the who, what, when, where, and occasionally the why—and the story tapers off gradually (picture a pyramid upside down), delivering additional facts and embellishments in a diminishing order of importance. Editors assume that their readers will want all the major details of a story right away and that they should have the opportunity to move on to another story as soon as they feel they have absorbed enough information. Consequently, the emphasis in news writing is placed on the "lead," the opening sentences or paragraphs. In writing about a major news event, the reporter is obligated to pack in the principal facts in the first few lines. Because each succeeding sentence becomes less significant and, from an editor's point of view, increasingly dispensable, it is not unusual for reporters to let their prose slacken as their story moves farther away from the top.

By opening the story with its climax, the writer gives up the possibility of sequential development and narrative suspense so that his or her readers can focus on the most important details immediately and the editor can lop off, should he or she need space for something else, the tapered strands of the report without losing any essential points. Therefore, paragraphs in most news stories are not connected to each other within a coherent expository framework. Instead, they can be thought of as self-contained, transferable, and, occasionally, disposable units. As a result, reporters continually face a rather disconcerting problem: they must write in such a manner that enables, even encourages, their audience to stop reading after the main points have been made, and, at the same time, they must make their writing compelling enough so that their readers will want to read on.

Yet reporters contend with more than the difficulties of composition. News stories need to be covered before they can be written. Reporters are men and women often entangled in the intricacies and drawn into the pace of the events they are trying to write about. They compose stories under pressure and in a hurry. To be "on the spot" during an event of some magnitude means most often to get caught up in the uncertain movements of participants and in the prevailing mood of the occasion. The inconveniences are many and unpredictable. One famous reporter, Stephen Crane, accompanying a crew of gun runners headed for Cuba during the insurrection at the close of the last century, was shipwrecked off the coast of Florida (see "Stephen Crane's Own Story") and wound up with a tale far different from the one he had intended to write (see "The Open Boat" in "Classics"). To illustrate most dramatically the kind of difficulties encountered during a strenuous and emotionally trying reportorial assignment, we have included Tom Wicker's recollections of his efforts to cover the assassination of President Kennedy (see "The Assassination").

November 22, 1963, was for Wicker a day of great confusion and physical exhaustion. Though he was on the spot, Wicker was not close enough to the president's car to witness the shooting directly, nor did he even have the opportunity to view the principal characters afterward for more than a few moments. Covering the story of Kennedy's assassination was mainly an ordeal of getting quickly from one good news position to another and of assimilating the disparate and occasionally contradictory details of the event as rapidly as possible. The information came, as Wicker says, "in bits and pieces," and most of the time he had no way of verifying the data. The news story of the assassination was not "out there'' to be copied down leisurely, without risks of inaccuracy. It was a matter of acting on hunches, recovering quickly from wrong turns, finding reliable contacts, getting around physical and bureaucratic obstacles, and all the while trying to put as many details into as coherent a shape as conditions allowed so the story could get to press on time.

Yet the byline report printed in the *New York Times* the next day (see "Kennedy Is Killed by Sniper") conveys nothing at all of the frantic pace and exasperating confusions Wicker tells us obstructed his coverage. What Wicker went through that day—whatever public and private significances the event had for him—was not news. The conventions of newspaper reporting are exacting on one point: the reporter must not figure as a main character in his or her own story. If indeed, as Thoreau says, "It is, after all, always the first person that is speaking," we nevertheless need to work quite hard to imagine the "I" who is the eyewitness behind Wicker's writing. Not even an effort to read "between the lines" could help us reconstruct from his prose alone the tensions of Wicker's day as he hustled around Dallas for the news.

Wicker's report provides us with a fine instance of journalistic workmanship. The assassination was far too important an event for Wicker to take stylistic chances. The *Times* got what it wanted: the straightforward, informative account that is the marrow of news reporting. It saved the expressions of personal grief and the emotional record of the public sentiment appropriate to such occasions for its features and editorials. Part of Wicker's accomplishment in this byline report is his cool, professional manner—he resists the impulse to attract attention to himself as a writer privileged to have been an eyewitness to one of the most sensational news events of the twentieth century. As a narrator, Wicker is never anxious to assure his readers of his presence at the scene. He never pauses in the account to remind us that his perspectives depend on his following the day's developments through several different locations in Dallas. Wicker deliberately avoids commenting on his own emotional connection to an event that we know from his own recollection shocked and grieved him. Nor, as he writes, does he allow himself the liberty of sounding like a worried citizen reflecting on the political and social significance of Kennedy's murder. It is clear that we cannot properly read Wicker's piece as a *personal* account of the assassination. In other words, we can not respond to his writing as if it were—what most of us usually expect writing to be—the disclosure of a particular personality. If Wicker tells us anything at all about himself, it is that he has mastered the discipline of news reporting.

Wicker's prose conforms to all the rules of journalistic style outlined earlier. The writing consists, for the most part, of syntactically simple, declarative sentences. The paragraphs are brief; only one contains as many as five sentences. The first few paragraphs provide the reader with all the crucial information, and the narrative proceeds to register details in what Wicker and his editors presumably considered to be a scale of decreasing importance. Though the narrative procedure would seem to recall the inverted pryamid mentioned above, a closer look at Wicker's prose reveals a movement less narrowing than it would have been had Wicker adhered strictly to that often tyrannizing model. Instead, the narrative proceeds with a spiraling effect, moving from the center outward, moving, that is, away from its lead only to return to it repeatedly, though each time with a new angle and a diminishing emphasis.

Wicker, however, is not fully responsible for the narrative shape the story eventually took. He mentions in his retrospective analysis that he sent off to the *Times* information in "a straight narrative" he knew would be cut up by his editors as they decided on the best sequence and appropriate emphases. Although the byline officially recognizes Wicker as the author of the news release, the final report the *Times* printed was, as is usually the case in news writing, the result of a collective activity that included Wicker and several other reporters who assisted him in Dallas, along with a New York staff of rewrite, copy, and managing editors.

While he was writing his report, Wicker must have been acutely conscious of the extensive television coverage given to the assassination. In fact, Wicker tells us that he filled in a few of the gaps in his own report by drawing on some of the information provided by television. Yet, as an antidote to the bewildering discontinuities and the numbing replays of the television reports, Wicker articulated a full, dispassionate recapitulation of the Kennedy assassination, accentuating the official interconnections between people and events rather than the panorama of personalities on location. To illustrate how a journalist responded to a similar incident almost a hundred years earlier, we have included the *New York Herald*'s coverage of President Lincoln's assassination. The April 15, 1865, issue of the *Herald* furnishes us with reportorial styles that were beginning to be conditioned by the invention of the telegraph but were not yet forced into competition with radio and television networks.

Wicker's task as a reporter competing with the live transmission of news was not nearly as problematic as was Thomas O'Toole's assignment for the *Washington Post* to watch and write about the first landing on the moon in July 1969 (see " 'The Eagle Has Landed': Two Men Walk on the Moon"). Given the hermetic nature of such an electronically engineered event as Apollo XI's flight to the moon, O'Toole could not claim a better vantage point for viewing the episode than could anyone else in the world with access to a television set. If the event O'Toole reported was, as he says in his lead, "a show that will long be remembered by the worldwide television audience," then he must have seen his function as that of a television reviewer rather than a privileged eyewitness commentator. In fact, his report makes it clear that the astronauts spent a good deal of their time transforming the moon into a television studio in which they then performed and improvised before the camera. Overshadowed by television, O'Toole's report could be little more than a public transcript of conversations everyone heard and descriptions of what everyone witnessed, punctuated by hyperbolic remarks that could express only the exclamatory mood of millions. Whether viewed as a technological triumph or as a television spectacular, the moon landing came as no special blessing to the newspaper industry. Upstaged by the extensive, unprecedented television coverage, reporters like O'Toole were left with relatively little to do but gather feature stories, collate information from television broadcasts, and turn NASA press releases into intelligible prose.

Each new day does not supply newspapers with a calamity or a triumph—most days newspapers need to find their news in the ordinary occurrences of life. Though a new headline appears daily, it may be merely perfunctory. Given standard newspaper format, one event must always be given more prominence than others. In our selections, we have tried to represent a good portion of the kind of news material you would normally find in American newspapers. We have included many of the standard forms and predominant styles of journalism: headlines, the inverted pyramid of major news stories, the fictional structures of feature stories, the polemical mode of editorials, along with bylines, personal commentaries and columns, interviews, and humorous and whimsical anecdotes. Still, if the subjects for much of the writing that follows strike you as disproportionately unpleasant, that is because the newspaper business generally thrives on the purveyance of "bad news." Pick up any newspaper, and you will be likely to find some account of individual or public violence, organized crime, political scandal, skirmishes with minorities and subcultures, domestic and international conflicts, the catastrophes of floods and earthquakes and fires, and the routine disasters of modern transportation.

The material in this section is not intended as an introduction to the profession of journalism. The texts are meant to be read as examples of the often special language of the reported world. Our purpose is to invite you to consider the compositional procedures and prose styles of various kinds of reporting in order to observe how the reporter's method of writing appropriates public events in a way that makes it especially difficult for any of us to talk or to write about those events independently of the language provided by newspapers.

Staff Correspondent / Important. Assassination of President Lincoln   *New York Herald*, April 15, 1865

The following series of telegraphic dispatches and reports appeared in the New York Herald *the morning after President Lincoln's assassination.*

IMPORTANT.

·

ASSASSINATION
OF
PRESIDENT LINCOLN.

·

The President Shot at the
Theatre Last Evening.

·

SECRETARY SEWARD
DAGGERED IN HIS BED,
BUT
NOT MORTALLY WOUNDED.

·

Clarence and Frederick Seward Badly Hurt.

·

ESCAPE OF THE ASSASSINS.

·

Intense Excitement in
Washington.

·

Scene at the Deathbed of
Mr. Lincoln.

·

FIRST DISPATCH

Washington, April 14, 1865.

Assassination has been inaugurated in Washington. The bowie knife and pistol have been applied to President Lincoln and Secretary Seward. The former was shot in the throat, while at Ford's theatre to-night. Mr. Seward was badly cut about the neck, while in his bed at his residence.

SECOND DISPATCH

Washington, April 14, 1865.

An attempt was made about ten o'clock this evening to assassinate the President and Secretary Seward. The President was shot at Ford's Theatre. Result not yet known. Mr. Seward's throat was cut, and his son badly wounded.

There is intense excitement here.

DETAILS OF THE ASSASSINATION

Washington, April 14, 1865.

Washington was thrown into an intense excitement a few minutes before eleven o'clock this evening, by the announcement that the President and Secretary Seward had been assassinated and were dead.

The wildest excitement prevailed in all parts of the city. Men, women and children, old and young, rushed to and fro, and the rumors were magnified until we had nearly every member of the Cabinet killed. Some time elapsed before authentic data could be ascertained in regard to the affair.

The President and Mrs. Lincoln were at Ford's theatre, listening to the performance of *The American Cousin*, occupying a box in the second tier. At the close of the third act a person entered the box occupied by the President, and shot Mr. Lincoln in the head. The shot entered the back of his head, and came out above the temple.

The assassin then jumped from the box upon the stage and ran across to the other side, exhibiting a dagger in his hand, flourishing it in a tragical manner, shouting the same words repeated by the desperado at Mr. Seward's house, adding to it, "The South is avenged," and then escaped from the back entrance to the stage, but in his passage dropped his pistol and his hat.

Mr. Lincoln fell forward from his seat, and Mrs. Lincoln fainted.

The moment the astonished audience could realize what had happened, the President was taken and carried to Mr. Peterson's house, in Tenth Street, opposite to the theatre. Medical aid was immediately sent for, and the wound was at first supposed to be fatal, and it was announced that he could not live, but at half-past twelve he is still alive, though in a precarious condition.

As the assassin ran across the stage, Colonel J.B. Stewart, of this city, who was occupying one of the front seats in the orchestra, on the same side of the house as the box occupied by Mr. Lincoln, sprang to the stage and followed him; but he was obstructed in his passage across the stage by the fright of the actors, and reached the back door about three seconds after the assassin had passed out. Colonel Stewart got to the street just in time to see him mount his horse and ride away.

The operation shows that the whole thing was a preconcerted plan. The person who fired the pistol was a man about thirty years of age, about five feet nine, spare built, fair skin, dark hair, apparently bushy, with a large moustache. Laura Keene and the leader of the orchestra declare that they recognized him as J. Wilkes Booth the actor, and a rabid secessionist. Whoever he was, it is plainly evident that he thoroughly understood the theatre and all the approaches and modes of escape to the stage. A person not familiar with the theatre could not have possibly made his escape so well and quickly.

The alarm was sounded in every quarter. Mr. Stanton was notified, and immediately left his house.

All the other members of the Cabinet escaped attack.

Cavalrymen were sent out in all directions, and dispatches sent out to all the fortifications, and it is thought they will be captured.

About half-past ten o'clock this evening a tall, well dressed man made his appearance at Secretary Seward's residence, and applied for admission. He was refused admission by the servant, when the desperado stated that he had a prescription from the Surgeon General, and that he was ordered to deliver it in person. He was still refused, except upon the written order of the physician. This he pretended to show, and pushed by the servant and rushed up stairs to Mr. Seward's room. He was met at the door by Mr. Fred Seward, who notified him that he was master of the house, and would take charge of the medicine. After a few words had passed between them he dodged by Fred Seward and rushed to the Secretary's bed and struck him in the neck with a dagger, and also in the breast.

It was supposed at first that Mr. Seward was killed instantly, but it was found afterwards that the wound was not mortal.

Major Wm. H. Seward, Jr., paymaster, was in the room, and rushed to the defense of his father, and was badly cut in the *melee* with the assassin, but not fatally.

The desperado managed to escape from the house, and was prepared for escape by having a horse at the door. He immediately mounted his horse, and sung out the motto of the State of Virginia, *"Sic Semper Tyrannis!"* and rode cff.

Surgeon General Barnes was immediately sent for, and he examined Mr. Seward and pronounced him safe. His wounds were not fatal. The jugular vein was not cut, nor the wound in the breast deep enough to be fatal.

Washington, April 15—1 A.M.

The streets in the vicinity of Ford's Theatre are densely crowded by an anxious and excited crowd. A guard has been placed across Tenth Street and F and K Streets, and only official persons and particular friends of the President are allowed to pass.

The popular heart is deeply stirred, and the deepest indignation against leading rebels is freely expressed.

The scene at the house where the President lies in *extremis* is very affecting. Even Secretary Stanton is affected to tears.

When the news spread through the city that the President had been shot, the people, with pale faces and compressed lips, crowded every place where there was the slightest chance of obtaining information in regard to the affair.

After the President was shot, Lieutenant Rathbun, caught the assassin by the arm, who immediately struck him with a knife, and jumped from the box, as before stated.

The popular affection for Mr. Lincoln has been shown by this diabolical assassination, which will bring eternal infamy, not only upon its authors, but upon the hellish cause which they desire to avenge.

Vice President Johnson arrived at the White House, where the President lies, about one o'clock, and will remain with him to the last.

The President's family are in attendance upon him also.

As soon as intelligence could be got to the War Department, the electric telegraph and the Signal corps were put in requisition to endeavor to prevent the escape of the assassins, and all the troops around Washington are under arms.

Popular report points to a somewhat celebrated actor of known secession proclivities as the assassin; but it would be unjust to name him until some further evidence of his guilt is obtained. It is rumored that the person alluded to is in custody.

The latest advices from Secretary Seward reveals more desperate work there than at first supposed. Seward's wounds are not in themselves fatal, but, in connection with his recent injuries, and the great loss of blood he has sustained, his recovery is questionable.

It was Clarence A. Seward, instead of William H. Seward, Jr., who was wounded. Fred Seward was also badly cut, as were also three nurses, who were in attendance upon the Secretary, showing that a desperate struggle took place there. The wounds of the whole party were dressed.

One o'clock A.M.

The President is perfectly senseless, and there is not the slightest hope of his surviving. Physicians believe that he will die before morning. All of his Cabinet, except Secretary Seward, are with him. Speaker Colfax, Senator Farwell, of Maine, and many other gentlemen, are also at the house awaiting the termination.

The scene at the President's bedside is described by one who witnessed it as most affecting. He was surrounded by his Cabinet ministers, all of whom were bathed in tears, not even excepting Mr. Stanton, who, when informed by Surgeon General Barnes, that the President could not live until morning, exclaimed, "Oh, no, General; no—no;" and with an impulse, natural as it was unaffected, immediately sat down on a chair near his bedside and wept like a child.

Senator Sumner was seated on the right of the President's couch, near the head, holding the right hand of the President in his own. He was sobbing like a woman, with his head bowed down almost on the pillow of the bed on which the President was lying.

Two o'clock A.M.

The President is still alive, but there is no improvement in his condition.

DISCUSSION QUESTION

1. How does the *Herald* account differ from Wicker's report of President Kennedy's assassination? How is the president described in each? Which account do you think describes the assassination most vividly? Most informatively? With the most feeling?

Francis Pharcellus Church / Is There a Santa Claus?

New York Sun, December 31, 1897

Francis Pharcellus Church (1839–1906) was not eager to reply to the letter asking for his newspaper's official stance on the existence of Santa Claus, but papers around the world have not been at all reluctant to reprint the editorial Church finally did write. The New York Sun, *which first printed the piece, was noted at the time for its clear, colorful writing—a reputation it owed in large part to Church's prose.*

Thirty-seven years after Church wrote "Yes, Virginia, there is a Santa Claus," Heywood Broun countered with "There isn't any Santa Claus" in the New York World-Telegram. *Broun's editorial (see p. 112) responds to Church's famous letter and should be contrasted to it.*

We take pleasure in answering at once and thus prominently the communication below, expressing at the same time our great gratification that its faithful author is numbered among the friends of The Sun.

Dear Editor:
   I am 8 years old.
   Some of my little friends say there is no Santa Claus.
   Papa says "If you see it in *The Sun* it's so."
   Please tell me the truth, is there a Santa Claus?

Virginia O'Hanlon,
115 West 95th Street

Virginia, your little friends are wrong. They have been affected by the skepticism of a skeptical age. They do not believe except they see. They think that nothing can be which is not comprehensible by their little minds. All minds Virginia, whether they be men's or children's, are little. In this great universe of ours man is a mere insect, an ant, in his intellect, as compared with the boundless world about him, as measured by the intelligence capable of grasping the whole of truth and knowledge.

Yes, Virginia, there is a Santa Claus. He exists as certainly as love and generosity and devotion exist, and you know that they abound and give to your life its highest beauty and joy. Alas! How dreary would be the world if there were no Santa Claus! It would be as dreary as if there were no Virginias. There would be no childlike faith then, no poetry, no romance to make tolerable this existence. We should have no enjoyment, except in sense and sight. The eternal light with which childhood fills the world would be extinguished.

Not believe in Santa Claus! You might as well not believe in fairies! You might get your papa to hire men to watch in all the chimneys on Christmas Eve to catch Santa Claus, but even if they did not see Santa Claus coming down, what would that prove? Nobody sees Santa Claus, but that is no sign that there is no Santa Claus. The most real things in the world are those that neither children nor men can see. Did you ever see fairies dancing on the lawn? Of course not, but that's no proof that they are not there. Nobody can conceive or imagine all the wonders there are unseen and unseeable in the world.

You tear apart the baby's rattle and see what makes the noise inside but there is a veil covering the unseen world which not the strongest man, nor even the united strength of all the strongest men that ever lived, could tear apart. Only faith, fancy, poetry, love, romance, can push aside that curtain and view and picture the supernal beauty and glory beyond. Is it all real? Ah, Virginia, in all this world there is nothing else real and abiding.

No Santa Claus! Thank God he lives and he lives forever. A thousand years from now, Virginia, nay ten times ten thousand years from now, he will continue to make glad the heart of childhood.

Heywood Broun / There Isn't a Santa Claus
New York World-Telegram, December 20, 1934

> *"After we have shot Santa Claus what can be put in his place?" Heywood Broun asks at the end of his rebuttal to Francis Pharcellus Church's famous editorial, "Is There a Santa Claus?" Though seriously opposed to Church's position, Broun was not the Scrooge his question implies. Writing during the Depression, Broun was as considerate of the disappointment of the poor as Church was of the disillustionment of the innocent.*
>
> *Broun (1888–1939) was the first president of the American Newspaper Guild and a one-time candidate for Congress on the Socialist Party ticket. He was an important and influential journalist in New York throughout his distinguished career.*

Almost any day now *The Sun* will reprint the letter from a little girl about Santa Claus and what the editor said in reply. I am sorry I can't remember the names.

This annual tribute to Santa Claus has always left me cold, and I grow more chilly to the piece as the years roll on.

In the first place, the little girl showed a reasonable degree of skepticism. She was just about ready to throw off the shackles of an old myth.

The editor clamped them on again. He didn't tell her the truth. Possibly this bad precedent may account for many editorials on other subjects which have appeared from time to time in various papers.

I am all for legends and fairy stories and ancient customs. A folk story is generally true in spirit no matter how fantastic its details. It is a sort of parable built upon the accumulated wisdom of the ages.

But I have a grievance against the figure called Santa Claus. Unlike most myths, the tale of the old gentleman and his reindeer glorifies an untruth. It warps the minds of the very young with a most pernicious notion. To be sure, the average girl or boy finds out the fake about the age of 3 or 4. The child of 6 who still believes in Santa Claus I would set down as definitely backward.

But even after the literal belief is gone there lingers in the mind a yearning for some other sort of Santa Claus. Oppressed people of various kinds sometimes go from the cradle to the grave without registering any adequate protest against their lot. They are waiting for the sound of the sleigh bells. Santa Claus will come down the chimney and bestow those rights and necessities which they lack. He may be the inspired leader, or he is sent in the guise of some governmental agency or act of legislation.

Naturally, it would be folly to deny that leadership and legislation may nick deeply into many problems, and for my own part I do believe in a paternalistic government. Even so complete reliance should not be placed on any of these three factors or even on them all in combination. There isn't any Santa Claus. Groups of men and women can obtain their hopes and desires only by massing together and going out to fight and agitate for their objectives. It is far more satisfactory to pick an orange directly from the tree than to find it in the toe of your stocking.

Harsh names are hurled at those who go out telling little children that Santa Claus is a fake. These disciples of the whole truth are called cynical and crabbed and spoilsports. But man must find out sooner or later that he stands on his own feet and this information might as well come early rather than late.

If anybody intrusted a baby to my tender care I would spring the truth about Santa Claus the instant the child could walk. I'd say, "And now, fine fellow, you have achieved the art of locomotion. You can go just as far and as fast as your feet will carry you. Forget about the reindeer. They make indifferent draft animals and singularly tough steak. Let me hear no nonsense out of you about Santa Claus. You and I are rational human beings up to the extent of our ability, I hope."

I even wonder whether children do get a great deal of fun out of the old gentleman in the sleigh. No very warm memories linger in my mind. He gave me a wakeful night once a year. Always I waited with rather more fear than anticipation for the sound of his fat belly scraping down the chimney. It gave me a sense of insecurity. If Santa Claus could sneak up on me in that way so might the bogey man, or any evil witch of whom I had read in the fairy books.

As a matter of fact, it was my annual inclination to sell Santa Claus short. My invariable bet was that his gifts would be disappointing. You see, I took the story very literally. It was said that Santa Claus would be lavish and generous with only those children who were very good and had a year's record of complete compliance to all the orders of their elders. No wonder I was bearish on the entire proposition!

In childhood, as in later life, everybody hopes for more than he is likely to get—particularly if the gifts are to be dropped in his lap. The Santa Claus myth has made for more disappointment than joy, if you look over the statistics very carefully. I know of many districts in the large and crowded cities where the old gentlemen couldn't muster as much as a single vote. Of course, from my point of view, it would be better to hold the election the day after Christmas rather than the night before.

The question may be asked, "After we have shot Santa Claus what can be put in his place?" I think we don't need a single figure. How about just centering the spirit of the day around the factor of universal fellowship? Not one Santa Claus but a hundred million!

Stephen Crane / Stephen Crane's Own Story
[He Tells How the Commodore *Was Wrecked and How He Escaped]*   *New York Press,* January 7, 1897

Though Stephen Crane had not witnessed a single battle before he wrote The Red Badge of Courage *in 1895, the immense popularity of the novel helped to establish a career for him as a leading war correspondent. Crane spent most of his remaining years traveling, despite ill health, to cover the Greco-Turkish, the Boer, and the Spanish American wars.*

"Stephen Crane's Own Story" details his experiences during the wreck of the Commodore, *a cargo ship carrying guns and ammunition to Cuban insurgents. This account served as the basis for Crane's well-known short story "The Open Boat" (see "Classics").*

JACKSONVILLE, FLA., Jan. 6.—It was the afternoon of New Year's. The Commodore lay at her dock in Jacksonville and negro stevedores processioned steadily toward her with box after box of ammunition and bundle after bundle of rifles. Her hatch, like the mouth of a monster, engulfed them. It might have been the feeding time of some legendary creature of the sea. It was in broad daylight and the crowd of gleeful Cubans on the pier did not forbear to sing the strange patriotic ballads of their island.

Everything was perfectly open. The Commodore was cleared with a cargo of arms and munition for Cuba. There was none of that extreme modesty about the proceeding which had marked previous departures of the famous tug. She loaded up as placidly as if she were going to carry oranges to New York, instead of Remingtons to Cuba. Down the river, furthermore, the revenue cutter Boutwell, the old isosceles triangle that protects United States interests in the St. John's, lay at anchor, with no sign of excitement aboard her.

EXCHANGING FAREWELLS

On the decks of the Commodore there were exchanges of farewells in two languages. Many of the men who were to sail upon her had many intimates in the old Southern town, and we who had left our friends in the remote North received our first touch of melancholy on witnessing these strenuous and earnest goodbys.

It seems, however, that there was more difficulty at the custom house. The officers of the ship and the Cuban leaders were detained there until a mournful twilight settled upon the St. John's, and through a heavy fog the lights of Jacksonville blinked dimly. Then at last the Commodore swung clear of the dock, amid a tumult of goodbys. As she turned her bow toward the distant sea the Cubans ashore cheered and cheered. In response the Commodore gave three long blasts of her whistle, which even to this time impressed me with their sadness. Somehow, they sounded as wails.

Then at last we began to feel like filibusters. I don't suppose that the most stolid brain could contrive to believe that there is not a mere trifle of danger in filibustering, and so as we watched the lights of Jacksonville swing past us and heard the regular thump, thump, thump of the engines we did considerable reflecting.

But I am sure that there were no hifalutin emotions visible upon any of the faces which fronted the speeding shore. In fact, from cook's boy to captain, we were all enveloped in a gentle satisfaction and cheerfulness. But less than two miles from Jacksonville, this atrocious fog caused the pilot to ram the bow of the Commodore hard upon the mud and in this ignominious position we were compelled to stay until daybreak.

HELP FROM THE BOUTWELL

It was to all of us more than a physical calamity. We were now no longer filibusters. We were men on a ship stuck in the mud. A certain mental somersault was made once more necessary.

But word had been sent to Jacksonville to the captain of the revenue cutter Boutwell, and Captain Kilgore turned out promptly and generously fired up his old triangle, and came at full speed to our assistance. She dragged us out of the mud, and again we headed for the mouth of the river. The revenue cutter pounded along a half mile astern of us, to make sure that we did not take on board at some place along the river men for the Cuban army.

This was the early morning of New Year's Day, and the fine golden southern sunlight fell full upon the river. It flashed over the ancient Boutwell, until her white sides gleamed like pearl, and her rigging was spun into little threads of gold.

Cheers greeted the old Commodore from passing ship and from the shore. It was a cheerful, almost merry, beginning to our voyage. At Mayport, however, we changed our river pilot for a man who could take her to open sea, and again the Commodore was beached. The Boutwell was fussing around us in her venerable way, and, upon seeing our predicament, she came again to assist us, but this time, with engines reversed, the Commodore dragged herself away from the grip of the sand and again headed for the open sea.

The captain of the revenue cutter grew curious. He hailed the Commodore: ''Are you fellows going to sea to-day?''

Captain Murphy of the Commodore called back: ''Yes, sir.''

And then as the whistle of the Commodore saluted him, Captain Kilgore doffed his cap and said: ''Well, gentlemen, I hope you have a pleasant cruise,'' and this was our last word from shore.

When the Commodore came to enormous rollers that flew over the bar a certain light-heartedness departed from the ship's company.

SLEEP IMPOSSIBLE

As darkness came upon the waters, the Commodore was a broad, flaming path of blue and silver phosphorescence, and as her stout bow lunged at the great black waves she threw flashing, roaring cascades to either side. And all that was to be heard was the rhythmical and mighty pounding of the engines. Being an inexperienced filibuster, the writer had undergone considerable mental excitement since the starting of the ship, and in consequence he had not yet been to sleep and so I went to the first mate's bunk to indulge myself in all the physical delights of holding one's-self in bed. Every time the ship lurched I expected to be fired through a bulkhead, and it was neither amusing nor instructive to see in the dim light a certain accursed valise aiming itself at the top of my stomach with every lurch of the vessel.

THE COOK IS HOPEFUL

The cook was asleep on a bench in the galley. He is of a portly and noble exterior, and by means of a checker board he had himself wedged on this bench in such a manner the motion of the ship would be unable to dislodge him. He woke as I entered the galley and delivered himself of some dolorous sentiments: "God," he said in the course of his observations, "I don't feel right about this ship, somehow. It strikes me that something is going to happen to us. I don't know what it is, but the old ship is going to get it in the neck, I think."

"Well, how about the men on board of her?" said I. "Are any of us going to get out, prophet?"

"Yes," said the cook. "Sometimes I have these damned feelings come over me, and they are always right, and it seems to me, somehow, that you and I will both get out and meet again somewhere, down at Coney Island, perhaps, or some place like that."

ONE MAN HAS ENOUGH

Finding it impossible to sleep, I went back to the pilot house. An old seaman, Tom Smith, from Charleston, was then at the wheel. In the darkness I could not see Tom's face, except at those times when he leaned forward to scan the compass and the dim light from the box came upon his weatherbeaten features.

"Well, Tom," said I, "how do you like filibustering?"

He said "I think I am about through with it. I've been in a number of these expeditions and the pay is good, but I think if I ever get back safe this time I will cut it."

I sat down in the corner of the pilot house and almost went to sleep. In the meantime the captain came on duty and he was standing near me when the chief engineer rushed up the stairs and cried hurriedly to the captain that there was something wrong in the engine room. He and the captain departed swiftly.

I was drowsing there in my corner when the captain returned, and, going to the door of the little room directly back of the pilot house, he cried to the Cuban leader:

"Say, can't you get those fellows to work. I can't talk their language and I can't get them started. Come on and get them going."

HELPS IN THE FIREROOM

The Cuban leader turned to me and said: "Go help in the fireroom. They are going to bail with buckets."

The engine room, by the way, represented a scene at this time taken from the middle kitchen of hades. In the first place, it was insufferably warm, and the lights burned faintly in a way to cause mystic and grewsome shadows. There was a quantity of soapish sea water swirling and sweeping and swishing among machinery that roared and banged and clattered and steamed, and, in the second place, it was a devil of a ways down below.

Here I first came to know a certain young oiler named Billy Higgins. He was sloshing around this inferno filling buckets with water and passing them to a chain of men that extended up the ship's side. Afterward we got orders to change our point of attack on water and to operate through a little door on the windward side of the ship that led into the engine room.

NO PANIC ON BOARD

During this time there was much talk of pumps out of order and many other statements of a mechanical kind, which I did not altogether comprehend but understood to mean that there was a general and sudden ruin in the engine room.

There was no particular agitation at this time, and even later there was never a panic on board the Commodore. The party of men who worked with Higgins and me at this time were all Cubans, and we were under the direction of the Cuban leaders. Presently we were ordered again to the afterhold, and there was some hesitation about going into the abominable fireroom again, but Higgins dashed down the companion way with a bucket.

LOWERING BOATS

The heat and hard work in the fireroom affected me and I was obliged to come on deck again. Going forward, I heard as I went talk of lowering the boats. Near the corner of the galley the mate was talking with a man.

"Why don't you send up a rocket?" said this unknown man. And the mate replied: "What the hell do we want to send up a rocket for? The ship is all right."

Returning with a little rubber and cloth overcoat, I saw the first boat about to be lowered. A certain man was the first person in this first boat, and they were handing him in a valise about as large as a hotel. I had not entirely recovered from astonishment and pleasure in witnessing this noble deed when I saw another valise go to him.

HUMAN HOG APPEARS

This valise was not perhaps so large as a hotel, but it was a big valise anyhow. Afterward there went to him something which looked to me like an overcoat.

Seeing the chief engineer leaning out of his little window, I remarked to him:

"What do you think of that blank, blank, blank?"

"Oh, he's a bird," said the old chief.

It was now that was heard the order to get away the lifeboat, which was stowed on top of the deckhouse. The deckhouse was a mighty slippery place, and with each roll of the ship, the men there thought themselves likely to take headers into the deadly black sea.

Higgins was on top of the deckhouse, and, with the first mate and two colored stokers, we wrestled with that boat, which, I am willing to swear, weighed as much as a Broadway cable car. She might have been spiked to the deck. We could have pushed a little brick schoolhouse along a corduroy road as easily as we could have moved this boat. But the first mate got a tackle to her from a leeward davit, and on the deck below the captain corralled enough men to make an impression upon the boat.

We were ordered to cease hauling then, and in this lull the cook of the ship came to me and said: "What are you going to do?"

I told him of my plans, and he said:

"Well, my God, that's what I am going to do."

A WHISTLE OF DESPAIR

Now the whistle of the Commodore had been turned loose, and if there ever was a voice of despair and death, it was in the voice of this whistle. It had gained a new tone. It was as if its throat was already choked by the water, and this cry on the sea at night, with a wind blowing the spray over the ship, and the waves roaring over the bow, and swirling white along the decks, was to each of us probably a song of man's end.

It was now that the first mate showed a sign of losing his grip. To us who were trying in all stages of competence and experience to launch the lifeboat he raged in all terms of fiery satire and hammerlike abuse. But the boat moved at last and swung down toward the water.

Afterward, when I went aft, I saw the captain standing, with his arm in a sling, holding on to a stay with his one good hand and directing the launching of the boat. He gave me a five-gallon jug of water to hold, and asked me what I was going to do. I told him what I thought was about the proper thing, and he told me then that the cook had the same idea, and ordered me to go forward and be ready to launch the ten-foot dingy.

IN THE TEN-FOOT DINGY

I remember well that he turned then to swear at a colored stoker who was prowling around, done up in life preservers until he looked like a feather bed. I went forward with my five-gallon jug of water, and when the captain came we launched the dingy, and they put me over the side to fend her off from the ship with an oar.

They handed me down the water jug, and then the cook came into the boat, and we sat there in the darkness, wondering why, by all our hopes of future happiness, the captain was so long in coming over to the side and ordering us away from the doomed ship.

The captain was waiting for the other boat to go. Finally he hailed in the darkness: "Are you all right, Mr. Graines?"

The first mate answered: "All right, sir."

"Shove off, then," cried the captain.

The captain was just about to swing over the rail when a dark form came forward and a voice said: "Captain, I go with you."

The captain answered: "Yes, Billy; get in."

HIGGINS LAST TO LEAVE SHIP

It was Billy Higgins, the oiler. Billy dropped into the boat and a moment later the captain followed, bringing with him an end of about forty yards of lead line. The other end was attached to the rail of the ship.

As we swung back to leeward the captain said: "Boys, we will stay right near the ship till she goes down."

This cheerful information, of course, filled us all with glee. The line kept us headed properly into the wind, and as we rode over the monstrous waves we saw upon each rise the swaying lights of the dying Commodore.

When came the gray shade of dawn, the form of the Commodore grew slowly clear to us as our little ten-foot boat rose over each swell. She was floating with such an air of buoyancy that we laughed when we had time, and said "What a gag it would be on those other fellows if she didn't sink at all."

But later we saw men aboard of her, and later still they began to hail us.

HELPING THEIR MATES

I had forgot to mention that previously we had loosened the end of the lead line and dropped much further to leeward. The men on board were a mystery to us, of course, as we had seen all the boats leave the ship. We rowed back to the ship, but did not approach too near, because we were four men in a ten-foot boat, and we knew that the touch of a hand on our gunwale would assuredly swamp us.

The first mate cried out from the ship that the third boat had foundered alongside. He cried that they had made rafts, and wished us to tow them.

The captain said, "All right."

Their rafts were floating astern. "Jump in!" cried the captain, but there was a singular and most harrowing hesitation. There were five white men and two negroes. This scene in the gray light of morning impressed one as would a view into some place where ghosts move slowly. These seven men on the stern of the sinking Commodore were silent. Save the words of the mate to the captain there was no talk. Here was death, but here also was a most singular and indefinable kind of fortitude.

Four men, I remember, clambered over the railing and stood there watching the cold, steely sheen of the sweeping waves.

"Jump," cried the captain again.

The old chief engineer first obeyed the order. He landed on the outside raft and the captain told him how to grip the raft and he obeyed as promptly and as docilely as a scholar in riding school.

THE MATE'S MAD PLUNGE

A stoker followed him, and then the first mate threw his hands over his head and plunged into the sea. He had no life belt and for my part, even when he did this horrible thing, I somehow felt that I could see in the expression of his hands, and in the very toss of his head, as he leaped thus to death, that it was rage, rage, rage unspeakable that was in his heart at the time.

And then I saw Tom Smith, the man who was going to quit filibustering after this expedition, jump to a raft and turn his face toward us. On board the Commodore three men strode, still in silence and with their faces turned toward us. One man had his arms folded and was leaning against the deckhouse. His feet were crossed, so that the toe of his left foot pointed downward. There they stood gazing at us, and neither from the deck nor from the rafts was a voice raised. Still was there this silence.

TRIED TO TOW THE RAFTS

The colored stoker on the first raft threw us a line and we began to tow. Of course, we perfectly understood the absolute impossibility of any such thing; our dingy was within six inches of the water's edge, there was an enormous sea running, and I knew that under the circumstances a tugboat would have no light task in moving these rafts.

But we tried it, and would have continued to try it indefinitely, but that something critical came to pass. I was at an oar and so faced the rafts. The cook controlled the line. Suddenly the boat began to go backward and then we saw this negro on the first raft pulling on the line hand over hand and drawing us to him.

He had turned into a demon. He was wild—wild as a tiger. He was crouched on this raft and ready to spring. Every muscle of him seemed to be turned into an elastic spring. His eyes were almost white. His face was the face of a lost man reaching upward, and we knew that the weight of his hand on our gunwale doomed us.

THE COMMODORE SINKS

The cook let go of the line. We rowed around to see if we could not get a line from the chief engineer, and all this time, mind you, there were no shrieks, no groans, but silence, silence and silence, and then the Commodore sank.

She lurched to windward, then swung afar back, righted and dove into the sea, and the rafts were suddenly swallowed by this frightful maw of the ocean. And then by the men on the ten-foot dingy were words said that were still not words— something far beyond words.

The lighthouse of Mosquito Inlet stuck up above the horizon like the point of a pin. We turned our dingy toward the shore.

The history of life in an open boat for thirty hours would no doubt be instructive for the young, but none is to be told here and now. For my part I would prefer to tell the story at once, because from it would shine the splendid manhood of Captain Edward Murphy and of William Higgins, the oiler, but let it suffice at this time to say that when we were swamped in the surf and making the best of our way toward the shore the captain gave orders amid the wildness of the breakers as clearly as if he had been on the quarter deck of a battleship.

John Kitchell of Daytona came running down the beach, and as he ran the air was filled with clothes. If he had pulled a single lever and undressed, even as the fire horses harness, he could not seem to me to have stripped with more speed. He dashed into the water and dragged the cook. Then he went after the captain, but the captain sent him to me, and then it was that he saw Billy Higgins lying with his forehead on sand that was clear of the water, and he was dead.

Staff Corespondent / Flying Machine Soars 3 Miles in Teeth of High Wind
[First Account of the Wright Brother's Success]
                    Norfolk Virginian-Pilot, December 18, 1903

Wilbur and Orville Wright, the owners of a bicycle shop in Dayton, Ohio, where they also at one time edited a weekly newspaper, had been experimenting since their youth on designs for a workable "flying machine." Venturing to the wind-swept coast near Kitty Hawk, North Carolina, the Wright brothers set up a primitive monorail-like skid from which to launch their craft. Powered by a twelve-horse-power gasoline engine, the "monster bird hovered above the breakers" for almost a minute, traveling a distance of nearly a quarter of a mile. Surrounded by several highly publicized failures, this event, one of the major advances in twentieth-century science, went practially unnoticed. Only the Norfolk Virginian-Pilot *printed a full story of the world's first successful flight.*

FLYING MACHINE SOARS 3 MILES
IN TEETH OF HIGH WIND OVER SAND HILLS AND WAVES AT KITTY-HAWK ON CAROLINA COAST.

.

NO BALLOON ATTACHED TO AID IT.

.

The problem of aerial navigation without the use of a balloon has been solved at last.

Over the sand hills of the North Carolina coast yesterday, near Kittyhawk, two Ohio men proved that they could soar through the air in a flying machine of their own construction, with the power to steer and speed it at will.

This, too, in the face of a wind blowing at the registered velocity of twenty-one miles an hour.

Like a monster bird, the invention hovered above the breakers and circled over the rolling sand hills at the command of its navigator and, after soaring for three miles, it gracefully descended to earth again, and rested lightly upon the spot selected by the man in the car as a suitable landing place.

While the United States government has been spending thousands of dollars in an effort to make practicable the ideas of Professor Langley, of the Smithsonian Institute, Wilbur and Orville Wright, two brothers, natives of Dayton, Ohio, have, quietly, even secretly, perfected their invention and put it to a successful test.

They are not yet ready that the world should know the methods they have adopted in conquering the air, but the *Virginian-Pilot* is able to state authentically the nature of their invention, its principles and its chief dimensions.

The idea of the box kite has been adhered to strictly in the basic formation of the flying machine.

A huge framework of light timbers, thirty-three feet wide, five feet deep, and five feet across the top, forms the machine proper.

This is covered with a tough, but light canvas.

In the center, and suspended just below the bottom plane, is the small gasoline engine which furnished the motive power for the propelling and elevating wheels.

There are two six-bladed propellers, one arranged just below the center of the frame, so gauged as to exert an upward force when in motion, and the other extends horizontally to the rear from the center of the car, furnishing the forward impetus.

Protruding from the center of the car is a huge, fan-shaped rudder of canvas, stretched upon a frame of wood. This rudder is controlled by the navigator and may be moved to each side, raised, or lowered.

Wilbur Wright, the chief inventor of the machine, sat in the operator's car, and when all was ready his brother unfastened the catch which held the invention at the top of the slope.

The big box began to move slowly at first, acquiring velocity as it went, and when halfway down the hundred feet the engine was started.

The propeller in the rear immediately began to revolve at a high rate of speed, and when the end of the incline was reached the machine shot out into space without a perceptible fall.

By this time the elevating propeller was also in motion, and keeping its altitude, the machine slowly began to go higher and higher until it finally soared sixty feet above the ground.

Maintaining this height by the action of the under wheel, the navigator increased the revolutions of the rear propeller, and the forward speed of the huge affair increased until a velocity of eight miles was attained.

All this time the machine headed into a twenty-one-mile wind.

The little crowd of fisherfolk and coast guards, who have been watching the construction of the machine with unconcealed curiosity since September, were amazed.

They endeavored to race over the sand and keep up with the thing in the air, but it soon distanced them and continued its flight alone, save the man in the car.

Steadily it pursued its way, first tacking to port, then to starboard, and then driving straight ahead.

"It is a success," declared Orville Wright to the crowd on the beach after the first mile had been covered.

But the inventor waited. Not until he had accomplished three miles, putting the machine through all sorts of maneuvers en route, was he satisfied.

Then he selected a suitable place to land and, gracefully circling, drew his invention slowly to the earth, where it settled, like some big bird, in the chosen spot.

"Eureka!" he cried, as did the alchemists of old.

The success of the Wright brothers in their invention is the result of three years of hard work. Experiment after experiment has been made and failure resulted, but each experiment had its lesson, and finally, when the two reappeared at Kittyhawk last fall, they felt more confident than ever.

The spot selected for the building and perfecting of the machine is one of the most desolate upon the Atlantic seaboard. Just on the southern extremity of that coast stretch known as the graveyard of American shipping, cut off from civilization by a wide expanse of sound water and seldom in touch with the outer world save when a steamer once or twice a week touches at the little wharf to take and leave government mail, no better place could scarcely have been selected to maintain secrecy.

And this is where the failures have grown into success.

The machine which made yesterday's flight easily carried the weight of a man of 150 pounds, and is nothing like so large as the ill-fated *Buzzard* of Potomac River fame.

It is said the Wright brothers intend constructing a much larger machine, but before this they will go back to their homes for the holidays.

Wilbur Wright, the inventor, is a well-groomed man of prepossessing appearance. He is about five feet, six inches tall, weighs about 150 pounds, and is of swarthy complexion. His hair is raven-hued and straight, but a piercing pair of deep-blue eyes peer at you over a nose of extreme length and sharpness.

His brother, Orville, on the other hand, is a blond, with sandy hair and fair complexion, even features, and sparkling black eyes. He is not quite as large as Wilbur, but is of magnificent physique.

The pair have spent almost the entire fall and winter and early spring months of the past three years at Kittyhawk, working upon their invention, leaving when the weather began to grow warm and returning in the early fall to work.

Their last appearance was on September 1, and since then they have been actively engaged upon the construction of the machine which made yesterday's successful flight.

Jack Lait / Dillinger "Gets His"

International News Service, July 23, 1934

On a steamy July evening in 1934, after having seen Clark Gable and William Powell star in a popular gangster film, Manhattan Melodrama, *John Dillinger, "Public Enemy No. 1," left a run-down movie house on Chicago's East Side and walked into the waiting bullets of federal police forces. By all accounts one of the most notorious criminals of modern times, Dillinger had blazed out a legendary career for himself that had all the earmarks of best-selling detective fiction: daring bank robberies, raids on police arsenals, bloody shoot-outs, bold escapes from prison, along with disguises, blurred fingerprints, and plastic surgery to help him defy what was then described as "the greatest manhunt in contemporary criminal annals." Yet, like Joey Gallo (see "Death of a Maverick Mafioso" in "Magazines"), Dillinger eventually found the heat of the limelight deadly. Betrayed by one of the many women he supported, Dillinger finally fell victim to the facts that fed the fictions he provoked.*

Jack Lait, a hard-nosed reporter who later took over as editor of the New York Daily Mirror, *turned out his scoop for the International News Service, an*

agency set up by William Randolph Hearst in 1909 to offer news items to a
network of morning newspapers.
    "Dillinger 'Gets His' " should be compared to David Wagoner's poem on
the same subject in "Classics."

John Dillinger, ace bad man of the world, got his last night—two slugs through
his heart and one through his head. He was tough and he was shrewd, but wasn't
as tough and shrewd as the Federals, who never close a case until the end. It took
twenty-seven of them to end Dillinger's career, and their strength came out of his
weakness—a woman.

Dillinger was put on the spot by a tip-off to the local bureau of the Department
of Justice. It was a feminine voice that Melvin H. Purvis, head of the Chicago office, heard. He had waited long for it.

It was Sunday, but Uncle Sam doesn't observe any NRA* and works seven
days a week.

The voice told him that Dillinger would be at a little third-run movie house, the
Biograph, last night—that he went there every night and usually got there about
7:30. It was almost 7:30 then. Purvis sent out a call for all men within reach and
hustled all men on hand with him. They waited more than an hour. They knew
from the informer that he must come out, turn left, turn again into a dark alley
where he parked his Ford-8 coupé.

Purvis himself stood at the main exit. He had men on foot and in parked inconspicuous cars strung on both sides of the alley. He was to give the signal. He had
ascertained about when the feature film, *Manhattan Melodrama,* would end.
Tensely eying his wrist watch he stood. Then the crowd that always streams out
when the main picture finishes came. Purvis had seen Dillinger when he was
brought through from Arizona to Crown Point, Indiana, and his heart pounded as
he saw again the face that has been studied· by countless millions on the front
pages of the world.

Purvis gave the signal. Dillinger did not see him. Public Enemy No. 1 lit a cigarette, strolled a few feet to the alley with the mass of middle-class citizens going
in that direction, then wheeled left.

A Federal man, revolver in hand, stepped from behind a telegraph pole at the
mouth of the passage. "Hello, John," he said, almost whispered, his voice husky
with the intensity of the classic melodrama. Dillinger went with lightning right
hand for his gun, a .38 Colt automatic. He drew it from his trousers pocket.

But, from behind, another government agent pressed the muzzle of his service
revolver against Dillinger's back and fired twice. Both bullets went through the
bandit's heart.

He staggered, his weapon clattered to the asphalt paving, and as he went three
more shots flashed. One bullet hit the back of his head, downward, as he was falling, and came out under his eye.

Police cleared the way for the police car which was there in a few minutes. The
police were there not because they were in on the capture, but because the sight of
so many mysterious men around the theater had scared the manager into thinking
he was about to be stuck up and he had called the nearest station.

When the detectives came on the run, Purvis intercepted them and told them
what was up. They called headquarters and more police came, but with instructions to stand by and take orders from Purvis.

---

* National Recovery Administration, a New Deal Agency that, among other functions, regulated
hours of work in industry.

Dillinger's body was rushed to Alexian Brothers' hospital in a patrol wagon. There were no surgeons in it. But the policeman knew he was dead, and at the entrance of the hospital, where a kindly priest in a long cassock had come to the door to see who might be in need of help, the driver was ordered to the morgue.

I was in a taxi that caught up with the police car at the hospital, and we followed across town to the old morgue. No one bothered us, though we went fifty miles an hour.

There was no crowd then. We pulled in. Strong arms carried the limp, light form of the man who had been feared by a great government through that grim door of many minor tragedies. It lay on a rubber stretcher.

In the basement, the receiving ward of the last public hospice of the doomed, they stripped the fearsome remains.

What showed up, nude and pink, still warm, was the body of what seemed a boy, the features as though at rest and only an ugly, bleeding hole under the left eye, such as a boy might have gotten in a street fight. His arms were bruised from the fall and the bumping in the wagon.

But under the heart were two little black, bleeding holes, clean and fresh. These could not have been anything but what they were. That part of John Dillinger did not look as though it was a boy's hurt—it was the fatal finish of a cold-blooded killer and not half of what he had given Officer O'Malley in East Chicago, Indiana, in the bank robbery when he cut the policeman almost in half with a machine gun.

The marks of the garters were still on the skin of his sturdy calves, the only part of him that looked like any part of a strong man. His arms were slender, even emaciated. But his legs were powerful-looking. His feet were neat and almost womanish, after the white socks and dudish white shoes had been taken from them.

His clothes were shabby with still an attempt at smartness. The white shirt was cheap, the gray flannel trousers, and the uninitialed belt buckle were basement-counter merchandise, his maroon-and-white print tie might have cost half a dollar.

In his pockets were $7.70 and a few keys and a watch in which was the picture of a pretty female.

Two women bystanders were caught in the line of fire and wounded slightly as the Federal men blazed away. They were Miss Etta Natalsky, forty-five, and Miss Theresa Paulus, twenty-nine, both residents of the neighborhood.

Miss Natalsky was taken to the Columbus Memorial Hospital with a wound in the leg and Miss Paulus to the Grant Hospital, but her wound, also in the leg, was found to be only superficial.

The notorious desperado had resorted to facial surgery to disguise himself, and it was only by his piercing eyes—described by crime experts as "the eyes of a born killer"—that he was recognized.

In addition to the facial alterations, he had dyed his hair a jet black from its natural sandy shade, and he wore gold-rimmed glasses. Identification of the fallen man was confirmed by Purvis on the spot. Later, at the morgue, an attempt was made to identify the body from fingerprints, but the tips of the fingers had been scarred, as if with acid.

A recent wound in the chest, which had just healed, was revealed in the morgue examination. It was believed this was a memento of a recent bank robbery.

Dr. Charles D. Parker, coroner's physician, remarked on the alteration in the slain man's features. Scars which he carried on each cheek Dillinger had had smoothed out by facial surgery. Purvis, after closely examining the changed features, said:

"His nose, that originally was pronounced 'pug,' had been made nearly straight. His hair had been dyed recently."

Souvenir hunters among the excited crowds that swarmed to the scene of the shooting frantically dipped newspapers and handkerchiefs in the patch of blood left on the pavement.

Traffic became so jammed that streetcars were rerouted, police lines established, and all traffic finally blocked out of the area.

Unsatiated by their morbid milling around the death spot, the crowds a little later rushed to the morgue to view the body. Denied admittance, they battled police and shouted and yelled to get inside. More than two thousand at one time were struggling to force the doors.

I have indisputable proof that the bureau had information that Dillinger had been here for at least three days. It was the first definite location of the hunted murderer since the affray in the Little Bohemia (Wisconsin) lodge.

"We didn't have time to get him then, but we had time enough this time," Purvis said.

Evidently Purvis not only had enough time, but used it with the traditional efficiency of his department. There has always been open rancor between the Chicago police and the Federals, who have several times done them out of rewards. The Federals are not permitted to accept rewards.

But the East Chicago force—Dillinger had slaughtered three of their outfit in two raids, and the "coincidence" of their presence "when the tip came in" is obvious.

That Dillinger suspected nothing is proven by nothing as much as that the safety catch on his magazine gun was set. It was a new, high-type weapon, so powerful that its slugs would penetrate the bulletproof vests of the sort that Dillinger himself had worn in other spots. The number had been filed off. Close examination indicated it had never been fired. It was fully loaded, and a clip of extra cartridges was in a pocket.

He had no other possible instrument of offense or defense, this desperado, except a slender penknife on the other end of a thin chain that held his watch.

All his possessions lay on the marble slab beside the rubber stretcher in the basement of the morgue as the internes pawed his still warm face and body as they threw his head to this side and that, slung him over on his face, and dabbed the still-wet blood from where the bullets had bitten into him.

I wondered whether, a few brief minutes earlier, they would have had the temerity to treat John Dillinger's flesh so cavalierly.

They pointed to the scar on his shinbone, the one which had been so heavily broadcast as maiming and even killing Dillinger. It was a little bit of a thing and looked more like the result of a stone bruise than a volley from the muzzle of outraged society.

They flopped him over on the slab, quite by a clumsy accident, because the body didn't turn easily within the stretcher, what with its gangly, rubbery legs, and its thin, boneless arms. And as what was left of Dillinger clamped like a clod, face down, upon the slab which had held the clay of hoboes and who knows, a still warm but spent hand knocked off the straw hat which had fallen off his head in the alley and been trampled upon. And a good ten-cent cigar. Strangely intact.

The man who had killed him stood two feet away, smoking a cigar of the same brand. I must not mention his name. Purvis says "keep that a trade secret." With John ("Happy Jack") Hamilton and George ("Baby Face") Nelson, Dillinger's lieutenants, still at large, perhaps that is a fair enough precaution.

The Bureau of Identification men were on the job in a jiffy. They proved up the fingerprints, though they had been treated with a biting acid in an effort to obliterate the telltale. But the deltas and cores were unmistakable.

Behind the ears were well-done scars of a face-lifting job by a skillful plastic specialist. A mole on the forehead had been trimmed off rather well. His hair, by rights sandy, had been painted a muddy black with a poor grade of dye.

So had his mustache. The one identifying mark known around the globe as the Dillinger characteristic was there. And even in death he looked just like the Dillinger we all knew from the photographs. Probably the last breath of his ego.

Dillinger was a ladies' man. He didn't want to be picked up and identified by a rube sheriff. But, still, he wanted to whisper to a new sweetie in the confidences of the night:

"Baby, I can trust you—I'm John Dillinger!"

And she would look, and—he was! That mustache!

Having gone to astonishing lengths to change his inconspicuous identifying marks, with the necessary aid and advice of expert medical men, he had still refused to shave off that familiar trade-mark that every newspaper reader could see with eyes shut.

A scar on his chin had been reopened and smoothed up some, but not very convincingly. The droop at the left corner of his mouth was unmistakably intact. But the most striking facial change was in the tightening of the skin on his chin, almost completely killing his dimple, which was almost as widely known as his mustache.

Gold-rimmed eyeglasses fell off his face as he toppled over. These, one of the most amateurish of elements in disguise, did change his appearance decisively, the officers tell me.

The Federal office, as usual, issued contradictory statements and frankly admitted that certain information would not be given out.

Of the twenty-seven men who worked with Purvis, one was Captain Tim O'Neill of East Chicago, and four others were O'Neill's men. Purvis said they were there quite by chance and he had taken them in on the big adventure. A second statement also gave forth that Purvis had seen Dillinger enter as well as leave the theater.

As Dillinger emerged, walking near him were two youngish women, one of them wearing a red dress. Hundreds were leaving the house at the time, and almost any number of women would naturally have been near him. But the one with the red dress hurried up the alley, and four Federals made a formation between her and Dillinger before the first shot was fired. It is my theory that she was with Dillinger and that she was the tip-off party or in league with Purvis.

DISCUSSION QUESTIONS

1. Compare Lait's report of Dillinger's death with David Wagoner's poem "The Shooting of John Dillinger Outside the Biograph Theater, July 22, 1934" (see "Classics"). What do the titles of the two pieces suggest about their differences? How did the details of the shooting differ from news item to poem? What are the effects of those differences?

2. What can you tell about Lait's opinion of Dillinger? From what facts are you able to infer his opinion? What can you tell about Wagoner's opinion of Dillinger? How do they compare? From the style of Lait's news report and Wagoner's poem, how do they expect their respective audiences to feel about Dillinger?

George M. Mahawinney / An Invasion from the Planet Mars

Philadelphia Inquirer, November 1, 1938

> *George M. Mahawinney, a rewrite man on duty at the* Philadelphia Inquirer *the evening of the famous Orson Welles broadcast of "The War of the Worlds," was besieged by frantic telephone calls seeking information about the invasion from Mars. The* Inquirer, *close to the reputed scene of the Martian landing at Grovers Mill, near Princeton, New Jersey, became the focal point for the nation's coverage of the bizarre results of Welles's broadcast. With America's news services clamoring for reports, Mahawinney wrote the following account in less than an hour. (For an excerpt from the radio broadcast of "The War of the Worlds," See "Scripts.")*

Terror struck at the hearts of hundreds of thousands of persons in the length and breadth of the United States last night as crisp words of what they believed to be a news broadcast leaped from their radio sets—telling of catastrophe from the skies visited on this country.

Out of the heavens, they learned, objects at first believed to be meteors crashed down near Trenton, killing many.

Then out of the "meteors" came monsters, spreading destruction with torch and poison gas.

It was all just a radio dramatization, but the result, in all actuality, was nationwide hysteria.

In Philadelphia, women and children ran from their homes, screaming. In Newark, New Jersey, ambulances rushed to one neighborhood to protect residents against a gas attack. In the deep South men and women knelt in groups in the streets and prayed for deliverance.

In reality there was no danger. The broadcast was merely a Halloween program in which Orson Welles, actor-director of the Mercury Theater on the Air, related, as though he were one of the few human survivors of the catastrophe, an adaptation of H. G. Wells' *The War of the Worlds.*

In that piece of fiction men from Mars, in meteorlike space ships, come to make conquest of earth. The circumstances of the story were unbelievable enough, but the manner of its presentation was apparently convincing to hundreds of thousands of persons—despite the fact that the program was interrupted thrice for an announcement that it was fiction, and fiction only.

For the fanciful tale was broadcast casually, for all the world like a news broadcast, opening up serenely enough with a weather report.

The realism of the broadcast, especially for those who had tuned in after it had started, brought effects which none—not the directors of the Federal Radio Theater Project, which sponsored it, nor the Columbia Broadcasting Company, which carried it over a coast-to-coast chain of 151 stations, nor Station WCAU, which broadcast it locally—could foresee.

Within a few minutes newspaper offices, radio stations, and police departments everywhere were flooded with anxious telephone calls. Sobbing women sought advice on what to do; broken-voiced men wished to know where to take their families.

Station WCAU received more than four thousand calls and eventually interrupted a later program to make an elaborate explanation that death had not actually descended on New Jersey, and that monsters were not actually invading the world.

But calm did not come readily to the frightened radio listeners of the country.

The hysteria reached such proportions that the New York City Department of Health called up a newspaper and wanted advice on offering its facilities for the protection of the populace. Nurses and physicians were among the telephone callers everywhere. They were ready to offer their assistance to the injured or maimed.

Hundreds of motorists touring through New Jersey heard the broadcast over their radios and detoured to avoid the area upon which the holocaust was focused—the area in the vicinity of Trenton and Princeton.

In scores of New Jersey towns women in their homes fainted as the horror of the broadcast fell on their ears. In Palmyra some residents packed up their worldly goods and prepared to move across the river into Philadelphia.

A white-faced man raced into the Hillside, New Jersey, police station and asked for a gas mask. Police said he panted out a tale of "terrible people spraying liquid gas all over Jersey meadows."

A weeping lady stopped Motorcycle Patrolman Lawrence Treger and asked where she should go to escape the "attack."

A terrified motorist asked the patrolman the way to Route 24. "All creation's busted loose. I'm getting out of Jersey," he screamed.

"Grovers Mill, New Jersey," was mentioned as a scene of destruction. In Stockton more than a half-hundred persons abandoned Colligan's Inn after hearing the broadcast and journeyed to Groveville to view the incredible "damage." They had misheard the name of the hypothetical town of "Grovers Mill," and believed it to be Groveville.

At Princeton University, women members of the geology faculty, equipped with flashlights and hammers, started for Grovers Corners. Dozens of cars were driven to the hamlet by curious motorists. A score of university students were phoned by their parents and told to come home.

An anonymous and somewhat hysterical girl phoned the Princeton Press Club from Grovers Corners and said:

"You can't imagine the horror of it! It's hell!"

A man came into the club and said he saw the meteor strike the earth and witnessed animals jumping from the alien body.

The Trenton police and fire telephone board bore the brunt of the nation's calls, because of its geographical location close to the presumed scene of catastrophe. On that board were received calls from Wilmington, Washington, Philadelphia, Jersey City, and Newark.

North of Trenton most of New Jersey was in the midst of a bad scare.

A report spread through Newark that the city was to be the target of a "gas-bomb attack." Police headquarters were notified there was a serious gas accident in the Clinton Hills section of that city. They sent squad cars and ambulances.

They found only householders, with possessions hastily bundled, leaving their homes. The householders returned to their homes only after emphatic explanations by the police.

Fifteen persons were treated for shock in one Newark hospital.

In Jersey City one resident demanded a gas mask of police. Another telephoned to ask whether he ought to flee the area or merely keep his windows closed and hope for the best.

Many New Yorkers seized personal effects and raced out of their apartments, some jumping into their automobiles and heading for the wide-open spaces.

Samuel Tishman, a Riverside Drive resident, declared he and hundreds of others evacuated their homes, fearing "the city was being bombed."

He told of going home and receiving a frantic telephone call from a nephew.

Tishman denounced the program as "the most asinine stunt I ever heard of" and as "a pretty crumby thing to do."

The panic it caused gripped impressionable Harlemites, and one man ran into the street declaring it was the President's voice they heard, advising: "Pack up and go North, the machines are coming from Mars."

Police in the vicinity at first regarded the excitement as a joke, but they were soon hard pressed in controlling the swarms in the streets.

A man entered the Wadsworth Avenue station uptown and said he heard "planes had bombed Jersey and were headed for Times Square."

A rumor spread over Washington Heights that a war was on.

At Caldwell, New Jersey, an excited parishioner rushed into the First Baptist Church during evening services and shouted that a tremendous meteor had fallen, causing widespread death, and that north Jersey was threatened with a shower of meteors. The congregation joined in prayer for deliverance.

Reactions as strange, or stranger, occurred in other parts of the country. In San Francisco, a citizen called police, crying:

"My God, where can I volunteer my services? We've got to stop this awful thing."

In Indianapolis, Indiana, a woman ran screaming into a church.

"New York is destroyed; it's the end of the world," she cried. "You might as well go home to die."

At Brevard College, North Carolina, five boys in dormitories fainted on hearing the broadcast. In Birmingham, Alabama, men and women gathered in groups and prayed. Women wept and prayed in Memphis, Tennessee.

Throughout Atlanta was a wide-spread belief that a "planet" had struck New Jersey, killing from forty to seven thousand persons.

At Pittsburgh one man telephoned a newspaper that he had returned to his home in the middle of the broadcast and found his wife in the bathroom, clutching a bottle of poison.

"I'd rather die this way than like that," she screamed before he was able to calm her.

Another citizen telephoned a newspaper in Washington, Pennsylvania, that a group of guests in his home playing cards "fell down on their knees and prayed," and then hurried home.

At Rivesville, West Virginia, a woman interrupted the pastor's sermon at a church meeting with loud outcries that there had been "an invasion." The meeting broke up in confusion.

Two heart attacks were reported by Kansas City hospitals, and the Associated Press Bureau there received calls of inquiry from Los Angeles, Salt Lake City, Beaumont, Texas, and St. Joseph, Missouri.

Minneapolis and St. Paul police switchboards were deluged with calls from frightened people.

Weeping and hysterical women in Providence, Rhode Island, cried out for officials of the electric company there to "turn off the lights so that the city will be safe from the enemy."

In some places mass hysteria grew so great that witnesses to the "invasion" could be found.

A Boston woman telephoned a newspaper to say she could "see the fire" from her window, and that she and her neighbors were "getting out of here."

The broadcast began at eight P.M. Within a few minutes after that time it had brought such a serious reaction that New Jersey state police sent out a teletype message to its various stations and barracks, containing explanations and instructions to police officers on how to handle the hysteria.

These and other police everywhere had problems on their hands as the broadcast moved on, telling of a "bulletin from the Intercontinental Radio News Bureau" saying there had been a gas explosion in New Jersey.

"Bulletins" that came in rapidly after that told of "meteors," then corrected that statement and described the Mars monsters.

The march of the Martians was disastrous. For a while they swept everything before them, according to the pseudo-bulletins. Mere armies and navies were being wiped out in a trice.

Actually, outside the radio stations, the Martians were doing a pretty good job on the Halloween imaginations of the citizenry. The radio stations and the Columbia Broadcasting Company spent much of the remainder of the evening clearing up the situation. Again and again they explained the whole thing was nothing more than a dramatization.

In the long run, however, calm was restored in the myriad American homes which had been momentarily threatened by interplanetary invasion. Fear of the monsters from Mars eventually subsided.

There was no reason for being afraid of them, anyway. Even the bulletins of the radio broadcast explained they all soon died. They couldn't stand the earth's atmosphere and perished of pneumonia.

Dorothy Thompson / Mr. Welles and Mass Delusion

New York Herald Tribune, November 2, 1938

Dorothy Thompson (1894–1961) remained one of America's most distinguished columnists for more than a generation. Her syndicated reports, "On the Record," appeared three times a week and discussed such contemporary issues as President Roosevelt's New Deal and the emerging Nazi regime—each column marked by her commitment to journalistic candor. In "Mr. Welles and Mass Delusion," Thompson, two days after the Welles broadcast, poignantly depicts the malleability of the national psychology on the eve of another world war and reminds us of the terrifying power of mass media. (For an excerpt from the radio broadcast of "The War of the Worlds," see "Scripts.")

All unwittingly Mr. Orson Welles and the Mercury Theater on the Air have made one of the most fascinating and important demonstrations of all time. They have proved that a few effective voices, accompanied by sound effects, can so convince masses of people of a totally unreasonable, completely fantastic proposition as to create nation-wide panic.

They have demonstrated more potently than any argument, demonstrated beyond question of a doubt, the appalling dangers and enormous effectiveness of popular and theatrical demagoguery.

They have cast a brilliant and cruel light upon the failure of popular education.

They have shown up the incredible stupidity, lack of nerve and ignorance of thousands.

They have proved how easy it is to start a mass delusion.

They have uncovered the primeval fears lying under the thinnest surface of the so-called civilized man.

They have shown that man, when the victim of his own gullibility, turns to the government to protect him against his own errors of judgment.

The newspapers are correct in playing up this story over every other news event in the world. It is the story of the century.

And far from blaming Mr. Orson Welles, he ought to be given a Congressional medal and a national prize for having made the most amazing and important contribution to the social sciences. For Mr. Orson Welles and his theater have made a greater contribution to an understanding of Hitlerism, Mussolinism, Stalinism, anti-Semitism and all the other terrorisms of our times than all the words about them that have been written by reasonable men. They have made the reductio ad absurdum of mass manias. They have thrown more light on recent events in Europe leading to the Munich pact than everything that has been said on the subject by all the journalists and commentators.

Hitler managed to scare all Europe to its knees a month ago, but he at least had an army and an air force to back up his shrieking words.

But Mr. Welles scared thousands into demoralization with nothing at all.

That historic hour on the air was an act of unconscious genius, performed by the very innocence of intelligence.

Nothing whatever about the dramatization of the "War of the Worlds" was in the least credible, no matter at what point the hearer might have tuned in. The entire verisimilitude was in the names of a few specific places. Monsters were depicted of a type that nobody has ever seen, equipped with "rays" entirely fantastic; they were described as "straddling the Pulaski Skyway" and throughout the broadcast they were referred to as Martians, men from another planet.

A twist of the dial would have established for anybody that the national catastrophe was not being noted on any other station. A second of logic would have dispelled any terror. A notice that the broadcast came from a non-existent agency would have awakened skepticism.

A reference to the radio program would have established that the "War of the Worlds" was announced in advance.

The time element was obviously lunatic.

Listeners were told that "within two hours three million people have moved out of New York"—an obvious impossibility for the most disciplined army moving exactly as planned, and a double fallacy because only a few minutes before, the news of the arrival of the monster had been announced.

And of course it was not even a planned hoax. Nobody was more surprised at the result than Mr. Welles. The public was told at the beginning, at the end and during the course of the drama that it *was* a drama.

But eyewitnesses presented themselves; the report became second hand, third hand, fourth hand, and became more and more credible, so that nurses and doctors and National Guardsmen rushed to defense.

When the truth became known the reaction was also significant. The deceived were furious and of course demanded that the state protect them, demonstrating that they were incapable of relying on their own judgment.

Again there was a complete failure of logic. For if the deceived had thought about it they would realize that the greatest organizers of mass hysterias and mass delusions today are states using the radio to excite terrors, incite hatreds, inflame masses, win mass support for policies, create idolatries, abolish reason and maintain themselves in power.

The immediate moral is apparent if the whole incident is viewed in reason: no political body must ever, under any circumstances, obtain a monopoly of radio.

The second moral is that our popular and universal education is failing to train reason and logic, even in the educated.

The third is that the popularization of science has led to gullibility and new superstitions, rather than to skepticism and the really scientific attitude of mind.

The fourth is that the power of mass suggestion is the most potent force today and that the political demagogue is more powerful than all the economic forces.

For, mind you, Mr. Welles was managing an obscure program, competing with one of the most popular entertainments on the air!

The conclusion is that the radio must not be used to create mass prejudices and mass divisions and schisms, either by private individuals or by government or its agencies, or its officials, or its opponents.

If people can be frightened out of their wits by mythical men from Mars, they can be frightened into fanaticism by the fear of Reds, or convinced that America is in the hands of sixty families, or aroused to revenge against any minority, or terrorized into subservience to leadership because of any imaginable menace.

The technique of modern mass politics calling itself democracy is to create a fear—a fear of economic royalists, or of Reds, or of Jews, or of starvation, or of an outside enemy—and exploit that fear into obtaining subservience in return for protection.

I wrote in this column a short time ago that the new warfare was waged by propaganda, the outcome depending on which side could first frighten the other to death.

The British people were frightened into obedience to a policy a few weeks ago by a radio speech and by digging a few trenches in Hyde Park, and afterward led to hysterical jubilation over a catastrophic defeat for their democracy.

But Mr. Welles went all the politicians one better. He made the scare to end scares, the menace to end menaces, the unreason to end unreason, the perfect demonstration that the danger is not from Mars but from the theatrical demagogue.

Langston Hughes / Family Tree   *Chicago Defender*, ca. 1942

The author of more than sixty volumes of fiction, poetry, drama, gospel song-plays, opera lyrics, translations, and children's books, Langston Hughes has also written scores of essays and news reports. Born in Joplin, Missouri, in 1902, Hughes studied at Columbia University and later signed on as a cook's helper aboard a tramp freighter bound for Africa. He also worked as a cook in a Paris night club, as a busboy in a Washington hotel, and, after his writing had been "discovered" during the Harlem Renaissance of the late 1920s, served as a correspondent for the Baltimore Afro-American *reporting on the Spanish Civil War.*

Hughes's most popular writing features the exploits, opinions, and musings of Jesse B. Semple ("Simple"), a masterful rendition of a battered but resilient character Hughes had met in a Harlem bar in 1942. Simple tells a story (see Mark Twain's "How to Tell a Story" in "Classics") with an engaging combination of humor and irony, penetrating wit and realistic observation.

Hughes's conversations with Simple were recorded for more than two decades in the Chicago Defender, *a newspaper addressed to that city's black community, and were subsequently collected in four volumes.*

"Anybody can look at me and tell I am part Indian," said Simple.

"I see you almost every day," I said, "and I did not know it until now."

"I have Indian blood but I do not show it much," said Simple. "My uncle's cousin's great-grandma were a Cherokee. I only shows mine when I lose my temper—then my Indian blood boils. I am quick-tempered just like a Indian. If somebody does something to me, I always fights back. In fact, when I get mad, I am the toughest Negro God's got. It's my Indian blood. When I were a young man, I used to play baseball and steal bases just like Jackie. If the empire would rule me out, I would get mad and hit the empire. I had to stop playing. That Indian temper. Nowadays, though, it's mostly womens that riles me up, especially landladies, waitresses, and girl friends. To tell the truth, I believe in a woman keeping her place. Womens is beside themselves these days. They want to rule the roost.''

"You have old-fashioned ideas about sex," I said. "In fact, your line of thought is based on outmoded economics."

"What?"

"In the days when women were dependent upon men for a living, you could be the boss. But now women make their own living. Some of them make more money than you do."

"True," said Simple. "During the war they got into that habit. But boss I am still due to be."

"So you think. But you can't always put your authority into effect."

"I can try," said Simple. "I can say, 'Do this!' And if she does something else, I can raise my voice, if not my hand."

"You can be sued for raising your voice," I stated, "and arrested for raising your hand."

"And she can be annihilated when I return from being arrested," said Simple. "That's my Indian blood!"

"You must believe in a woman being a squaw."

"She better not look like no squaw," said Simple. "I want a woman to look sharp when she goes out with me. No moccasins. I wants high-heel shoes and nylons, cute legs—and short dresses. But I also do not want her to talk back to me. As I said, I am the man. *Mine* is the word, and she is due to hush."

"Indians customarily expect their women to be quiet," I said.

"I do not expect mine to be *too* quiet," said Simple. "I want 'em to sweet-talk me—'Sweet baby, this,' and 'Baby, that,' and 'Baby, you's right, darling,' when they talk to me."

"In other words, you want them both old-fashioned and modern at the same time," I said. "The convolutions of your hypothesis are sometimes beyond cognizance."

"Cog hell!" said Simple. "I just do not like no old loud back-talking chick. That's the Indian in me. My grandpa on my father's side were like that, too, an Indian. He was married five times and he really ruled his roost."

"There are a mighty lot of Indians up your family tree," I said. "Did your granddad look like one?"

"Only his nose. He was dark brownskin otherwise. In fact, he were black. And the womens! Man! They was crazy about Grandpa. Every time he walked down the street, they stuck their heads out the windows and kept 'em turned South—which was where the beer parlor was."

"So your grandpa was a drinking man, too. That must be whom you take after."

"I also am named after him," said Simple. "Grandpa's name was Jess, too. So I am Jesse B. Semple."

"What does the *B* stand for?"

"Nothing. I just put it there myself since they didn't give me no initial when I was born. I am really Jess Semple—which the kids changed around into a nickname when I were in school. In fact, they used to tease me when I were small, calling me 'Simple Simon.' But I was right handy with my fists, and after I beat the 'Simon' out of a few of them, they let me alone. But my friends still call me 'Simple.' ''

"In reality, you are Jesse Semple," I said, "colored."

"Part Indian," insisted Simple, reaching for his beer.

"Jess is certainly not an Indian name."

"No, it ain't," said Simple, "but we did have a Hiawatha in our family. She died."

"*She?*" I said. "Hiawatha was no *she.*"

"She was a *she* in our family. And she had long coal-black hair just like a Creole. You know, I started to marry a Creole one time when I was coach-boy on the L. & N. down to New Orleans. Them Louisiana girls are bee-oou-te-ful! Man, I mean!"

"Why didn't you marry her, fellow?"

"They are more dangerous than a Indian," said Simple, "also I do not want no pretty woman. First thing you know, you fall in love with her—then you got to kill somebody about her. She'll make you so jealous, you'll bust! A pretty woman will get a man in trouble. Me and my Indian blood, quick-tempered as I is. No! I do not crave a pretty woman."

"Joyce is certainly not bad-looking," I said. "You hang around her all the time."

"She is far from a Creole. Besides, she appreciates me," said Simple. "Joyce knows I got Indian blood which makes my temper bad. But we take each other as we is. I respect her and she respects me."

"That's the way it should be with the whole world," I said. "Therefore, you and Joyce are setting a fine example in these days of trials and tribulations. Everybody should take each other as they are, white, black, Indians, Creole. Then there would be no prejudice, nations would get along."

"Some folks do not see it like that," said Simple. "For instant, my landlady—and my wife. Isabel could never get along with me. That is why we are not together today."

"I'm not talking personally," I said, "so why bring in your wife?"

"Getting along *starts* with persons, don't it?" asked Simple. "You *must* include my wife. That woman got my Indian blood so riled up one day I thought I would explode."

"I still say, I'm not talking personally."

"Then stop talking," exploded Simple, "because with me it is personal. Facts, I cannot even talk about my wife if I don't get personal. That's how it is if you're part Indian—everything is personal. *Heap much personal.*"

William L. Laurence / Atomic Bombing of Nagasaki Told by Flight Member

New York Times, September 9, 1945

Science dominated the life of William L. Laurence from his early youth. When he was growing up in Lithuania, according to a biographical profile in The New Yorker, *Laurence received as a gift a book ''that speculated on the possibility of a civilization on Mars, and young [Laurence] was so impressed that he decided to go to the United States when he was old enough, because from there . . . he might most easily be able to establish contact with that planet.''*

He arrived in Hoboken, New Jersey, in 1905 and proceeded to study at Harvard and the Boston University Law School. After five years of reporting for the New York World, *Laurence went to work for the* New York Times, *where he covered some of the most momentous events in the history of twentieth-century science. The only reporter with access to the "top secret" testing and development of the atomic bomb, Laurence also prepared the War Department's press releases on the weapon.*

On August 9, 1945, Laurence flew with the mission to bomb Nagasaki, barely three days after one hundred thousand people had been killed at Hiroshima in what Time *magazine called "The Birth of an Era." Laurence's Pulitzer Prize eyewitness account is underlined by a curious aesthetic sense—one that watches this "thing of beauty" destroy a major Japanese city.*

With the atomic-bomb mission to Japan, August 9 (Delayed)—We are on our way to bomb the mainland of Japan. Our flying contingent consists of three specially designed B-29 Superforts, and two of these carry no bombs. But our lead plane is on its way with another atomic bomb, the second in three days, concentrating in its active substance an explosive energy equivalent to twenty thousand and, under favorable conditions, forty thousand tons of TNT.

We have several chosen targets. One of these is the great industrial and shipping center of Nagasaki, on the western shore of Kyushu, one of the main islands of the Japanese homeland.

I watched the assembly of this man-made meteor during the past two days and was among the small group of scientists and Army and Navy representatives privileged to be present at the ritual of its loading in the Superfort last night, against a background of threatening black skies torn open at intervals by great lightning flashes.

It is a thing of beauty to behold, this "gadget." Into its design went millions of man-hours of what is without doubt the most concentrated intellectual effort in history. Never before had so much brain power been focused on a single problem.

This atomic bomb is different from the bomb used three days ago with such devastating results on Hiroshima.

I saw the atomic substance before it was placed inside the bomb. By itself it is not at all dangerous to handle. It is only under certain conditions, produced in the bomb assembly, that it can be made to yield up its energy, and even then it gives only a small fraction of its total contents—a fraction, however, large enough to produce the greatest explosion on earth.

The briefing at midnight revealed the extreme care and the tremendous amount of preparation that had been made to take care of every detail of the mission, to make certain that the atomic bomb fully served the purpose for which it was intended. Each target in turn was shown in detailed maps and in aerial photographs. Every detail of the course was rehearsed—navigation, altitude, weather, where to land in emergencies. It came out that the Navy had submarines and rescue craft, known as Dumbos and Superdumbos, stationed at various strategic points in the vicinity of the targets, ready to rescue the fliers in case they were forced to bail out.

The briefing period ended with a moving prayer by the chaplain. [1] We then pro-

1. "Almighty God, Father of all mercies, we pray Thee to be gracious with those who fly this night. Guard and protect those of us who venture out into the darkness of Thy heaven. Uphold them on Thy wings. Keep them safe both in body and soul and bring them back to us. Give to us all the courage and strength for the hours that are ahead; give to them rewards according to their efforts. Above all else, our Father, bring peace to Thy world. May we go forward trusting in Thee and knowing we are in Thy presence now and forever. Amen." Prayer by Chaplain Downey, ending the briefing session preliminary to the bombing of Nagasaki [eds.].

ceeded to the mess hall for the traditional early-morning breakfast before departure on a bombing mission.

A convoy of trucks took us to the supply building for the special equipment carried on combat missions. This included the Mae West, a parachute, a lifeboat, an oxygen mask, a flak suit, and a survival vest. We still had a few hours before take-off time, but we all went to the flying field and stood around in little groups or sat in jeeps talking rather casually about our mission to the Empire, as the Japanese home islands are known hereabouts.

In command of our mission is Major Charles W. Sweeney, twenty-five, of 124 Hamilton Avenue, North Quincy, Massachusetts. His flagship, carrying the atomic bomb, is named *The Great Artiste,* but the name does not appear on the body of the great silver ship, with its unusually long, four-bladed, orange-tipped propellers. Instead, it carries the number 77, and someone remarks that it was "Red" Grange's winning number on the gridiron.

We took off at 3:50 this morning and headed northwest on a straight line for the Empire. The night was cloudy and threatening, with only a few stars here and there breaking through the overcast. The weather report had predicted storms ahead part of the way but clear sailing for the final and climactic stages of our odyssey.

We were about an hour away from our base when the storm broke. Our great ship took some heavy dips through the abysmal darkness around us, but it took these dips much more gracefully than a large commercial air liner, producing a sensation more in the nature of a glide than a "bump," like a great ocean liner riding the waves except that in this case the air waves were much higher and the rhythmic tempo of the glide was much faster.

I noticed a strange eerie light coming through the window high above the navigator's cabin, and as I peered through the dark all around us I saw a startling phenomenon. The whirling giant propellers had somehow become great luminous disks of blue flame. The same luminous blue flame appeared on the plexiglas windows in the nose of the ship, and on the tips of the giant wings. It looked as though we were riding the whirlwind through space on a chariot of blue fire.

It was, I surmised, a surcharge of static electricity that had accumulated on the tips of the propellers and on the di-electric material of the plastic windows. One's thoughts dwelt anxiously on the precious cargo in the invisible ship ahead of us. Was there any likelihood of danger that this heavy electric tension in the atmosphere all about us might set it off?

I expressed my fears to Captain Bock, who seems nonchalant and unperturbed at the controls. He quickly reassured me.

"It is a familiar phenomenon seen often on ships. I have seen it many times on bombing missions. It is known as St. Elmo's fire."

On we went through the night. We soon rode out the storm and our ship was once again sailing on a smooth course straight ahead, on a direct line to the Empire.

Our altimeter showed that we were traveling through space at a height of seventeen thousand feet. The thermometer registered an outside temperature of thirty-three degrees below zero Centigrade, about thirty below Fahrenheit. Inside our pressurized cabin the temperature was that of a comfortable air-conditioned room and a pressure corresponding to an altitude of eight thousand feet. Captain Bock cautioned me, however, to keep my oxygen mask handy in case of emergency. This, he explained, might mean either something going wrong with the pressure equipment inside the ship or a hole through the cabin by flak.

The first signs of dawn came shortly after five o'clock. Sergeant Curry, of Hoopeston, Illinois, who had been listening steadily on his earphones for radio reports, while maintaining a strict radio silence himself, greeted it by rising to his feet and gazing out the window.

"It's good to see the day," he told me. "I get a feeling of claustrophobia hemmed in in this cabin at night."

He is a typical American youth, looking even younger than his twenty years. It takes no mind reader to read his thoughts.

"It's a long way from Hoopeston," I find myself remarking.

"Yep," he replies, as he busies himself decoding a message from outer space.

"Think this atomic bomb will end the war?" he asks hopefully.

"There is a very good chance that this one may do the trick," I assured him, "but if not, then the next one or two surely will. Its power is such that no nation can stand up against it very long." This was not my own view. I had heard it expressed all around a few hours earlier, before we took off. To anyone who had seen this man-made fireball in action, as I had less than a month ago in the desert of New Mexico, this view did not sound overoptimistic.

By 5:50 it was really light outside. We had lost our lead ship, but Lieutenant Godfrey, our navigator, informs me that we had arranged for that contingency. We have an assembly point in the sky above the little island of Yakushima, southeast of Kyushu, at 9:10. We are to circle there and wait for the rest of our formation.

Our genial bombardier, Lieutenant Levy, comes over to invite me to take his front-row seat in the transparent nose of the ship, and I accept eagerly. From that vantage point in space, seventeen thousand feet above the Pacific, one gets a view of hundreds of miles on all sides, horizontally and vertically. At that height the vast ocean below and the sky above seem to merge into one great sphere.

I was on the inside of that firmament, riding above the giant mountains of white cumulus clouds, letting myself be suspended in infinite space. One hears the whirl of the motors behind one, but it soon becomes insignificant against the immensity all around and is before long swallowed by it. There comes a point where space also swallows time and one lives through eternal moments filled with an oppressive lone-liness, as though all life had suddenly vanished from the earth and you are the only one left, a lone survivor traveling endlessly through interplanetary space.

My mind soon returns to the mission I am on. Somewhere beyond these vast mountains of white clouds ahead of me there lies Japan, the land of our enemy. In about four hours from now one of its cities, making weapons of war for use against us, will be wiped off the map by the greatest weapon ever made by man: In one tenth of a millionth of a second, a fraction of time immeasurable by any clock, a whirlwind from the skies will pulverize thousands of its buildings and tens of thousands of its inhabitants.

But at this moment no one yet knows which one of the several cities chosen as targets is to be annihilated. The final choice lies with destiny. The winds over Japan will make the decision. If they carry heavy clouds over our primary target, that city will be saved, at least for the time being. None of its inhabitants will ever know that the wind of a benevolent destiny had passed over their heads. But that same wind will doom another city.

Our weather planes ahead of us are on their way to find out where the wind blows. Half an hour before target time we will know what the winds have decided.

Does one feel any pity or compassion for the poor devils about to die? Not when one thinks of Pearl Harbor and of the Death March on Bataan.

Captain Bock informs me that we are about to start our climb to bombing altitude.

He manipulates a few knobs on his control panel to the right of him, and I alternately watch the white clouds and ocean below me and the altimeter on the bom-bardier's panel. We reached our altitude at nine o'clock. We were then over Japanese waters, close to their mainland. Lieutenant Godfrey motioned to me to look through his radar scope. Before me was the outline of our assembly point. We shall soon meet our lead ship and proceed to the final stage of our journey.

We reached Yakushima at 9:12 and there, about four thousand feet ahead of us, was *The Great Artiste* with its precious load. I saw Lieutenant Godfrey and Sergeant Curry strap on their parachutes and I decided to do likewise.

We started circling. We saw little towns on the coastline, heedless of our presence. We kept on circling, waiting for the third ship in our formation.

It was 9:56 when we began heading for the coastline. Our weather scouts had sent us code messages, deciphered by Sergeant Curry, informing us that both the primary target as well as the secondary were clearly visible.

The winds of destiny seemed to favor certain Japanese cities that must remain nameless. We circled about them again and again and found no opening in the thick umbrella of clouds that covered them. Destiny chose Nagasaki as the ultimate target.

We had been circling for some time when we noticed black puffs of smoke coming through the white clouds directly at us. There were fifteen bursts of flak in rapid succession, all too low. Captain Bock changed his course. There soon followed eight more bursts of flak, right up to our altitude, but by this time were too far to the left.

We flew southward down the channel and at 11:33 crossed the coastline and headed straight for Nagasaki, about one hundred miles to the west. Here again we circled until we found an opening in the clouds. It was 12:01 and the goal of our mission had arrived.

We heard the prearranged signal on our radio, put on our arc welder's glasses, and watched tensely the maneuverings of the strike ship about half a mile in front of us.

"There she goes!" someone said.

Out of the belly of *The Great Artiste* what looked like a black object went downward.

Captain Bock swung around to get out of range; but even though we were turning away in the opposite direction, and despite the fact that it was broad daylight in our cabin, all of us became aware of a giant flash that broke through the dark barrier of our arc welder's lenses and flooded our cabin with intense light.

We removed our glasses after the first flash, but the light still lingered on, a bluish-green light that illuminated the entire sky all around. A tremendous blast wave struck our ship and made it tremble from nose to tail. This was followed by four more blasts in rapid succession, each resounding like the boom of cannon fire hitting our plane from all directions.

Observers in the tail of our ship saw a giant ball of fire rise as though from the bowels of the earth, belching forth enormous white smoke rings. Next they saw a giant pillar of purple fire, ten thousand feet high, shooting skyward with enormous speed.

By the time our ship had made another turn in the direction of the atomic explosion the pillar of purple fire had reached the level of our altitude. Only about forty-five seconds had passed. Awe-struck, we watched it shoot upward like a meteor coming from the earth instead of from outer space, becoming ever more alive as it climbed skyward through the white clouds. It was no longer smoke, or dust, or even a cloud of fire. It was a living thing, a new species of being, born right before our incredulous eyes.

At one stage of its evolution, covering millions of years in terms of seconds, the entity assumed the form of a giant square totem pole, with its base about three miles long, tapering off to about a mile at the top. Its bottom was brown, its center was amber, its top white. But it was a living totem pole, carved with many grotesque masks grimacing at the earth.

Then, just when it appeared as though the thing had settled down into a state of permanence, there came shooting out of the top a giant mushroom that increased the height of the pillar to a total of forty-five thousand feet. The mushroom top was even more alive than the pillar, seething and boiling in a white fury of creamy foam, sizzling upward and then descending earthward, a thousand Old Faithful geysers rolled into one.

It kept struggling in an elemental fury, like a creature in the act of breaking the bonds that held it down. In a few seconds it had freed itself from its gigantic stem and floated upward with tremendous speed, its momentum carrying it into the stratosphere to a height of about sixty thousand feet.

But no sooner did this happen when another mushroom, smaller in size than the first one, began emerging out of the pillar. It was as though the decapitated monster was growing a new head.

As the first mushroom floated off into the blue it changed its shape into a flower-like form, its giant petals curving downward, creamy white outside, rose-colored inside. It still retained that shape when we last gazed at it from a distance of about two hundred miles. The boiling pillar of many colors could also be seen at that distance, a giant mountain of jumbled rainbows, in travail. Much living substance had gone into those rainbows. The quivering top of the pillar was protruding to a great height through the white clouds, giving the appearance of a monstrous prehistoric creature with a ruff around its neck, a fleecy ruff extending in all directions, as far as the eye could see.

DISCUSSION QUESTIONS

1. How does William Laurence respond to the disastrous event he is covering? Does he include in his report his own feelings about what he is witnessing? What rhetorical devices characterize his account? What effects do these devices have on your response to his report?

2. Laurence calls the atomic bomb "a thing of beauty." Does he find any other examples of "beauty" on the mission? Explain. How does his use of detail contribute to (or detract from) the aesthetic effects he wants to convey?

3. Does Laurence have any political or moral attitudes toward the bombing? Explain. Point to specific words and phrases to verify your contention. What is the effect of the final image in Laurence's report?

Tom Wicker / Kennedy Is Killed by Sniper as He Rides in Car in Dallas   *New York Times,* November 23, 1963

Tom Wicker had a great deal of experience in journalism before he joined the Washington office of the New York Times *in 1960. Born and educated in North Carolina, Wicker worked in his home state as editor of the* Sanhill Citizen *and as managing editor of the* Robesonian. *After serving as copy editor, sports editor, and Washington correspondent for the* Winston-Salem Journal, *Wicker took on the responsibilities of the associate editorship of the* Nashville Tennessean. *After his report on the assassination of President Kennedy, Wicker moved from a featured reporter to columnist and associate editor of the* New York Times. *He has also written several novels. His most recent books include* On Press *(1978) and* Unto This Hour *(1984).*

Tom Wicker's recollections of his coverage of the tumultuous events of No-

vember 22, 1963, follow the report below. They are reprinted from Times Talk, *the monthly report circulated to members of the Times organization.*

KENNEDY IS KILLED BY SNIPER AS HE RIDES IN CAR IN DALLAS; JOHNSON SWORN IN ON PLANE.

Gov. Connally Shot;
Mrs. Kennedy Safe.

President Is Struck Down by a Rifle Shot
From Building on Motorcade Route—
Johnson, Riding Behind, Is Unhurt.

DALLAS, Nov. 22—President John Fitzgerald Kennedy was shot and killed by an assassin today.

He died of a wound in the brain caused by a rifle bullet that was fired at him as he was riding through downtown Dallas in a motorcade.

Vice President Lyndon Baines Johnson, who was riding in the third car behind Mr. Kennedy's, was sworn in as the 36th President of the United States 99 minutes after Mr. Kennedy's death.

Mr. Johnson is 55 years old; Mr. Kennedy was 46.

Shortly after the assassination, Lee H. Oswald, who once defected to the Soviet Union and who has been active in the Fair Play for Cuba Committee, was arrested by the Dallas police. Tonight he was accused of the killing.

SUSPECT CAPTURED AFTER SCUFFLE

Oswald, 24 years old, was also accused of slaying a policeman who had approached him in the street. Oswald was subdued after a scuffle with a second policeman in a nearby theater.

President Kennedy was shot at 12:30 P.M., Central Standard Time (1:30 P.M., New York time). He was pronounced dead at 1 P.M. and Mr. Johnson was sworn in at 2:39 P.M.

Mr. Johnson, who was uninjured in the shooting, took his oath in the Presidential jet plane as it stood on the runway at Love Field. The body of Mr. Kennedy was aboard. Immediately after the oath-taking, the plane took off for Washington.

Standing beside the new President as Mr. Johnson took the oath of office was Mrs. John F. Kennedy. Her stockings were spattered with her husband's blood.

Gov. John B. Connally, Jr., of Texas, who was riding in the same car with Mr. Kennedy, was severely wounded in the chest, ribs and arm. His condition was serious, but not critical.

The killer fired the rifle from a building just off the motorcade route. Mr. Kennedy, Governor Connally and Mr. Johnson had just received an enthusiastic welcome from a large crowd in downtown Dallas.

Mr. Kennedy apparently was hit by the first of what witnesses believed were three shots. He was driven at high speed to Dallas Parkland Hospital. There, in an emergency operating room, with only physicians and nurses in attendance, he died without regaining consciousness.

Mrs. Kennedy, Mrs. Connally and a Secret Service agent were in the car with Mr. Kennedy and Governor Connally. Two Secret Service agents flanked the car. Other than Mr. Connally, none of this group was injured in the shooting. Mrs. Kennedy cried, "Oh no!" immediately after her husband was struck.

Mrs. Kennedy was in the hospital near her husband when he died, but not in the operating room. When the body was taken from the hospital in a bronze coffin about 2 P.M., Mrs. Kennedy walked beside it.

Her face was sorrowful. She looked steadily at the floor. She still wore the raspberry-colored suit in which she had greeted welcoming crowds in Fort Worth and Dallas. But she had taken off the matching pillbox hat she wore earlier in the day, and her dark hair was windblown and tangled. Her hand rested lightly on her husband's coffin as it was taken to a waiting hearse.

Mrs. Kennedy climbed in beside the coffin. Then the ambulance drove to Love Field, and Mr. Kennedy's body was placed aboard the Presidential jet. Mrs. Kennedy then attended the swearing-in ceremony for Mr. Johnson.

As Mr. Kennedy's body left Parkland Hospital, a few stunned persons stood outside. Nurses and doctors, whispering among themselves, looked from the window. A larger crowd that had gathered earlier, before it was known that the President was dead, had been dispersed by Secret Service men and policemen.

PRIESTS ADMINISTER LAST RITES

Two priests administered last rites to Mr. Kennedy, a Roman Catholic. They were the Very Rev. Oscar Huber, the pastor of Holy Trinity Church in Dallas, and the Rev. James Thompson.

Mr. Johnson was sworn in as President by Federal Judge Sarah T. Hughes of the Northern District of Texas. She was appointed to the judgeship by Mr. Kennedy in October, 1961.

The ceremony, delayed about five minutes for Mrs. Kennedy's arrival, took place in the private Presidential cabin in the rear of the plane.

About 25 to 30 persons—members of the late President's staff, members of Congress who had been accompanying the President on a two-day tour of Texas cities and a few reporters—crowded into the little room.

No accurate listing of those present could be obtained. Mrs. Kennedy stood at the left of Mr. Johnson, her eyes and face showing the signs of weeping that had apparently shaken her since she left the hospital not long before.

Mrs. Johnson, wearing a beige dress, stood at her husband's right.

As Judge Hughes read the brief oath of office, her eyes, too, were red from weeping. Mr. Johnson's hands rested on a black, leatherbound Bible as Judge Hughes read and he repeated:

"I do solemnly swear that I will perform the duties of the President of the United States to the best of my ability and defend, protect and preserve the Constitution of the United States."

Those 34 words made Lyndon Baines Johnson, one-time farmboy and schoolteacher of Johnson City, the President.

JOHNSON EMBRACES MRS. KENNEDY

Mr. Johnson made no statement. He embraced Mrs. Kennedy and she held his hand for a long moment. He also embraced Mrs. Johnson and Mrs. Evelyn Lincoln, Mr. Kennedy's private secretary.

"O.K.," Mr. Johnson said. "Let's get this plane back to Washington."

At 2:46 P.M., seven minutes after he had become President, 106 minutes after Mr. Kennedy had become the fourth American President to succumb to an assassin's wounds, the white and red jet took off for Washington.

In the cabin when Mr. Johnson took the oath was Cecil Stoughton, an armed forces photographer assigned to the White House.

Mr. Kennedy's staff members appeared stunned and bewildered. Lawrence F. O'Brien, the Congressional liaison officer, and P. Kenneth O'Donnell, the appointment secretary, both long associates of Mr. Kennedy, showed evidences of weeping. None had anything to say.

Other staff members believed to be in the cabin for the swearing-in included David F. Powers, the White House receptionist; Miss Pamela Turnure, Mrs. Kennedy's press secretary; and Malcolm Kilduff, the assistant White House press secretary.

Mr. Kilduff announced the President's death, with choked voice and red-rimmed eyes, at about 1:36 P.M.

"President John F. Kennedy died at approximately 1 o'clock Central Standard Time today here in Dallas," Mr. Kilduff said at the hospital. "He died of a gunshot wound in the brain. I have no other details regarding the assassination of the President."

Mr. Kilduff also announced that Governor Connally had been hit by a bullet or bullets and that Mr. Johnson, who had not yet been sworn in, was safe in the protective custody of the Secret Service at an unannounced place, presumably the airplane at Love Field.

Mr. Kilduff indicated that the President had been shot once. Later medical reports raised the possibility that there had been two wounds. But the death was caused, as far as could be learned, by a massive wound in the brain.

Later in the afternoon, Dr. Malcolm Perry, an attending surgeon, and Dr. Kemp Clark, chief of neurosurgery at Parkland Hospital, gave more details.

Mr. Kennedy was hit by a bullet in the throat, just below the Adam's apple, they said. This wound had the appearance of a bullet's entry.

Mr. Kennedy also had a massive, gaping wound in the back and one on the right side of the head. However, the doctors said it was impossible to determine immediately whether the wounds had been caused by one bullet or two.

RESUSCITATION ATTEMPTED

Dr. Perry, the first physician to treat the President, said a number of resuscitative measures had been attempted, including oxygen, anesthesia, an indotracheal tube, a tracheotomy, blood and fluids. An electrocardiogram monitor was attached to measure Mr. Kennedy's heart beats.

Dr. Clark was summoned and arrived in a minute or two. By then, Dr. Perry said, Mr. Kennedy was "critically ill and moribund," or near death.

Dr. Clark said that on his first sight of the President, he had concluded immediately that Mr. Kennedy could not live.

"It was apparent that the President had sustained a lethal wound," he said. "A missile had gone in and out of the back of his head causing external lacerations and loss of brain tissue."

Shortly after he arrived, Dr. Clark said, "the President lost his heart action by the electrocardiogram." A closed-chest cardiograph massage was attempted, as were other emergency resuscitation measures.

Dr. Clark said these had produced "palpable pulses" for a short time, but all were "to no avail."

IN OPERATING ROOM 40 MINUTES

The President was on the emergency table at the hospital for about 40 minutes, the doctors said. At the end, perhaps eight physicians were in Operating Room No. 1, where Mr. Kennedy remained until his death. Dr. Clark said it was difficult to de-

termine the exact moment of death, but the doctors said officially that it occurred at
1 P.M.

Later, there were unofficial reports that Mr. Kennedy had been killed instantly.
The source of these reports, Dr. Tom Shires, chief surgeon at the hospital and
professor of surgery at the University of Texas Southwest Medical School, issued
this statement tonight:

"Medically, it was apparent the President was not alive when he was brought in.
There was no spontaneous respiration. He had dilated, fixed pupils. It was obvious
he had a lethal head wound.

"Technically, however, by using vigorous resuscitation, intravenous tubes and
all the usual supportive measures, we were able to raise a semblance of a heartbeat."

Dr. Shires was not present when Mr. Kennedy was being treated at Parkland Hospital. He issued his statement, however, after lengthy conferences with the doctors
who had attended the President.

Mr. Johnson remained in the hospital about 30 minutes after Mr. Kennedy died.

The details of what happened when shots first rang out, as the President's car
moved along at about 25 miles an hour, were sketchy. Secret Service agents, who
might have given more details, were unavailable to the press at first, and then returned to Washington with President Johnson.

KENNEDYS HAILED AT BREAKFAST

Mr. Kennedy had opened his day in Fort Worth, first with a speech in a parking
lot and then at a Chamber of Commerce breakfast. The breakfast appearance was a
particular triumph for Mrs. Kennedy, who entered late and was given an ovation.

Then the Presidential party, including Governor and Mrs. Connally, flew on to
Dallas, an eight-minute flight. Mr. Johnson, as is customary, flew in a separate
plane. The President and the Vice President do not travel together, out of fear of a
double tragedy.

At Love Field, Mr. and Mrs. Kennedy lingered for 10 minutes, shaking hands
with an enthusiastic group lining the fence. The group called itself "Grassroots
Democrats."

Mr. Kennedy then entered his open Lincoln convertible at the head of the motorcade. He sat in the rear seat on the right-hand side. Mrs. Kennedy, who appeared to
be enjoying one of the first political outings she had ever made with her husband, sat
at his left.

In the "jump" seat, directly ahead of Mr. Kennedy, sat Governor Connally,
with Mrs. Connally at his left in another "jump" seat. A Secret Service agent was
driving and the two others ran alongside.

Behind the President's limousine was an open sedan carrying a number of Secret
Service agents. Behind them, in an open convertible, rode Mr. and Mrs. Johnson
and Texas's senior Senator, Ralph W. Yarborough, a Democrat.

The motorcade proceeded uneventfully along a 10-mile route through downtown
Dallas, aiming for the Merchandise Mart. Mr. Kennedy was to address a group of
the city's leading citizens at a luncheon in his honor.

In downtown Dallas, crowds were thick, enthusiastic and cheering. The turnout
was somewhat unusual for this center of conservatism, where only a month ago
Adlai E. Stevenson was attacked by a rightist crowd. It was also in Dallas, during
the 1960 campaign, that Senator Lyndon B. Johnson and his wife were nearly
mobbed in the lobby of the Baker Hotel.

As the motorcade neared its end and the President's car moved out of the thick
crowds onto Stennonds Freeway near the Merchandise Mart, Mrs. Connally recalled later, "we were all very pleased with the reception in downtown Dallas."

APPROACHING 3-STREET UNDERPASS

Behind the three leading cars were a string of others carrying Texas and Dallas dignitaries, two buses of reporters, several open cars carrying photographers and other reporters, and a bus for White House staff members.

As Mrs. Connally recalled later, the President's car was almost ready to go underneath a "triple underpass" beneath three streets—Elm, Commerce and Main—when the first shot was fired.

That shot apparently struck Mr. Kennedy. Governor Connally turned in his seat at the sound and appeared immediately to be hit in the chest.

Mrs. Mary Norman of Dallas was standing at the curb and at that moment was aiming her camera at the President. She saw him slump forward, then slide down in the seat.

"My God," Mrs. Norman screamed, as she recalled it later, "he's shot!"

Mrs. Connally said that Mrs. Kennedy had reached and "grabbed" her husband. Mrs. Connally put her arms around the Governor. Mrs. Connally said that she and Mrs. Kennedy had then ducked low in the car as it sped off.

Mrs. Connally's recollections were reported by Julian Reade, an aide to the Governor.

Most reporters in the press buses were too far back to see the shootings, but they observed some quick scurrying by motor policemen accompanying the motorcade. It was noted that the President's car had picked up speed and raced away, but reporters were not aware that anything serious had occurred until they reached the Merchandise Mart two or three minutes later.

RUMORS SPREAD AT TRADE MART

Rumors of the shooting already were spreading through the luncheon crowd of hundreds, which was having the first course. No White House officials or Secret Service agents were present, but the reporters were taken quickly to Parkland Hospital on the strength of the rumors.

There they encountered Senator Yarborough, white, shaken and horrified.

The shots, he said, seemed to have come from the right and the rear of the car in which he was riding, the third in the motorcade. Another eyewitness, Mel Crouch, a Dallas television reporter, reported that as the shots rang out he saw a rifle extended and then withdrawn from a window on the "fifth or sixth floor" of the Texas Public School Book Depository. This is a leased state building on Elm Street, to the right of the motorcade route.

Senator Yarborough said there had been a slight pause between the first two shots and a longer pause between the second and third. A Secret Service man riding in the Senator's car, the Senator said, immediately ordered Mr. and Mrs. Johnson to get down below the level of the doors. They did so, and Senator Yarborough also got down.

The leading cars of the motorcade then pulled away at high speed toward Parkland Hospital, which was not far away, by the fast highway.

"We knew by the speed that something was terribly wrong," Senator Yarborough reported. When he put his head up, he said, he saw a Secret Service man in the car ahead beating his fists against the trunk deck of the car in which he was riding, apparently in frustration and anguish.

MRS. KENNEDY'S REACTION

Only White House staff members spoke with Mrs. Kennedy. A Dallas medical student, David Edwards, saw her in Parkland Hospital while she was waiting for news of her husband. He gave this description:

''The look in her eyes was like an animal that had been trapped, like a little rabbit—brave, but fear was in the eyes.''

Dr. Clark was reported to have informed Mrs. Kennedy of her husband's death.

No witnesses reported seeing or hearing any of the Secret Service agents or policemen fire back. One agent was seen to brandish a machine gun as the cars sped away. Mr. Crouch observed a policeman falling to the ground and pulling a weapon. But the events had occurred so quickly that there was apparently nothing for the men to shoot at.

Mr. Crouch said he saw two women, standing at a curb to watch the motorcade pass, fall to the ground when the shots rang out. He also saw a man snatch up his little girl and run along the road. Policemen, he said, immediately chased this man under the impression he had been involved in the shooting, but Mr. Crouch said he had been a fleeing spectator.

Mr. Kennedy's limousine—license No. GG300 under District of Columbia registry—pulled up at the emergency entrance of Parkland Hospital. Senator Yarborough said the President had been carried inside on a stretcher.

By the time reporters arrived at the hospital, the police were guarding the Presidential car closely. They would allow no one to approach it. A bucket of water stood by the car, suggesting that the back seat had been scrubbed out.

Robert Clark of the American Broadcasting Company, who had been riding near the front of the motorcade, said Mr. Kennedy was motionless when he was carried inside. There was a great amount of blood on Mr. Kennedy's suit and shirtfront and the front of his body, Mr. Clark said.

Mrs. Kennedy was leaning over her husband when the car stopped, Mr. Clark said, and walked beside the wheeled stretcher into the hospital. Mr. Connally sat with his hands holding his stomach, his head bent over. He, too, was moved into the hospital in a stretcher, with Mrs. Connally at his side.

Robert McNeill of the National Broadcasting Company, who also was in the reporters' pool car, jumped out at the scene of the shooting. He said the police had taken two eyewitnesses into custody—an 8-year-old Negro boy and a white man—for informational purposes.

Many of these reports could not be verified immediately.

EYEWITNESS DESCRIBES SHOOTING

An unidentified Dallas man, interviewed on television here, said he had been waving at the President when the shots were fired. His belief was that Mr. Kennedy had been struck twice—once, as Mrs. Norman recalled, when he slumped in his seat; again when he slid down in it.

''It seemed to just knock him down,'' the man said.

Governor Connally's condition was reported as ''satisfactory'' tonight after four hours in surgery at Parkland Hospital.

Dr. Robert R. Shaw, a thoracic surgeon, operated on the Governor to repair damage to his left chest.

Later, Dr. Shaw said Governor Connally had been hit in the back just below the shoulder blade, and that the bullet had gone completely through the Governor's chest, taking out part of the fifth rib.

After leaving the body, he said, the bullet struck the Governor's right wrist, causing a compound fracture. It then lodged in the left thigh.

The thigh wound, Dr. Shaw said, was trivial. He said the compound fracture would heal.

Dr. Shaw said it would be unwise for Governor Connally to be moved in the next 10 to 14 days. Mrs. Connally was remaining at his side tonight.

TOUR BY MRS. KENNEDY UNUSUAL

Mrs. Kennedy's presence near her husband's bedside at his death resulted from somewhat unusual circumstances. She had rarely accompanied him on his trips about the country and had almost never made political trips with him.

The tour on which Mr. Kennedy was engaged yesterday and today was only quasi-political; the only open political activity was to have been a speech tonight to a fund-raising dinner at the state capitol in Austin.

In visiting Texas, Mr. Kennedy was seeking to improve his political fortunes in a pivotal state that he barely won in 1960. He was also hoping to patch a bitter internal dispute among Texas's Democrats.

At 8:45 A.M., when Mr. Kennedy left the Texas hotel in Fort Worth, where he spent his last night, to address the parking lot crowd across the street, Mrs. Kennedy was not with him. There appeared to be some disappointment.

"Mrs. Kennedy is organizing herself," the President said good-naturedly. "It takes longer, but, of course, she looks better than we do when she does it."

Later, Mrs. Kennedy appeared late at the Chamber of Commerce breakfast in Fort Worth.

Again, Mr. Kennedy took note of her presence. "Two years ago," he said, "I introduced myself in Paris by saying that I was the man who had accompanied Mrs. Kennedy to Paris. I am getting somewhat that same sensation as I travel around Texas. Nobody wonders what Lyndon and I wear."

The speech Mr. Kennedy never delivered at the Merchandise Mart luncheon contained a passage commenting on a recent preoccupation of his, and a subject of much interest in this city, where right-wing conservatism is the rule rather than the exception.

"Voices are being heard in the land," he said, "voices preaching doctrines wholly unrelated to reality, wholly unsuited to the sixties, doctrines which apparently assume that words will suffice without weapons, that vituperation is as good as victory and that peace is a sign of weakness."

The speech went on: "At a time when the national debt is steadily being reduced in terms of its burden on our economy, they see that debt as the greatest threat to our security. At a time when we are steadily reducing the number of Federal employees serving every thousand citizens, they fear those supposed hordes of civil servants far more than the actual hordes of opposing armies.

"We cannot expect that everyone, to use the phrase of a decade ago, will 'talk sense to the American people.' But we can hope that fewer people will listen to nonsense. And the notion that this nation is headed for defeat through deficit, or that strength is but a matter of slogans, is nothing but just plain nonsense."

DISCUSSION QUESTIONS

1. What is the verb tense at the beginning of the headline for Wicker's story? What effect is created by the use of this particular verb form? Does the tense remain consistent with the verb form used in the remainder of the headline? In the text of the story?

2. Compare the headline to this story with that of the *New York Herald* on the assassination of President Lincoln. What can these examples tell you about the language of headlines in general?

3. How is the first paragraph of each story partly determined by the information presented in the headline? Contrast the leads of both news stories. Which do you find most successful? Why? Does each story adhere to the format of the inverted pyramid as described in the introduction to this section?

Tom Wicker / The Assassination   *Times Talk,* December 1963

WASHINGTON

I think I was in the first press bus. But I can't be sure. Pete Lisagor of The Chicago Daily News says he *knows* he was in the first press bus and he describes things that went on aboard it that didn't happen on the bus I was in. But I still *think* I was in the first press bus.

I cite that minor confusion as an example of the way it was in Dallas in the early afternoon of Nov. 22. At first no one knew what happened, or how, or where, much less why. Gradually, bits and pieces began to fall together and within two hours a reasonably coherent version of the story began to be possible. Even now, however, I know no reporter who was there who has a clear and orderly picture of that surrealistic afternoon; it is still a matter of bits and pieces thrown hastily into something like a whole.

It began, for most reporters, when the central fact of it was over. As our press bus eased at motorcade speed down an incline toward an underpass, there was a little confusion in the sparse crowds that at that point had been standing at the curb to see the President of the United States pass. As we came out of the underpass, I saw a motorcycle policeman drive over the curb, across an open area, a few feet up a railroad bank, dismount and start scrambling up the bank.

Jim Mathis of The Advance (Newhouse) Syndicate went to the front of our bus and looked ahead to where the President's car was supposed to be, perhaps ten cars ahead of us. He hurried back to his seat.

"The President's car just sped off," he said. "Really gunned away." (How could Mathis have seen that if there had been another bus in front of us?)

But that could have happened if someone had thrown a tomato at the President. The press bus in its stately pace rolled on to the Trade Mart, where the President was to speak. Fortunately, it was only a few minutes away.

At the Trade Mart, rumor was sweeping the hundreds of Texans already eating their lunch. It was the only rumor that I had ever *seen;* it was moving across that crowd like a wind over a wheatfield. A man eating a grapefruit seized my arm as I passed.

"Has the President been shot?" he asked.

"I don't think so," I said. "But something happened."

With the other reporters—I suppose 35 of them—I went on through the huge hall to the upstairs press room. We were hardly there when Marianne Means of Hearst Headline Service hung up a telephone, ran to a group of us and said, "The President's been shot. He's at Parkland Hospital."

One thing I learned that day; I suppose I already knew it, but that day made it plain. A reporter must trust his instinct. When Miss Means said those eight words— I never learned who told her—I knew absolutely they were true. Everyone did. We ran for the press buses.

Again, a man seized my arm—an official-looking man.

"No running in here," he said sternly. I pulled free and ran on. Doug Kiker of The Herald Tribune barreled head-on into a waiter carrying a plate of potatoes. Waiter and potatoes flew about the room. Kiker ran on. He was in his first week with The Trib, and his first Presidential trip.

I barely got aboard a moving press bus. Bob Pierrepoint of C.B.S. was aboard and he said that he now recalled having heard something that could have been shots—or firecrackers, or motorcycle backfire. We talked anxiously, unbelieving, afraid.

Fortunately again, it was only a few minutes to Parkland Hospital. There at its emergency entrance, stood the President's car, the top up, a bucket of bloody water beside it. Automatically, I took down its license number—GG300 District of Columbia.

The first eyewitness description came from Senator Ralph Yarborough, who had been riding in the third car of the motorcade with Vice President and Mrs. Johnson. Senator Yarborough is an East Texan, which is to say a Southerner, a man of quick emotion, old-fashioned rhetoric.

"Gentlemen," he said, pale, shaken, near tears. "It is a deed of horror."

The details he gave us were good and mostly—as it later proved—accurate. But he would not describe to us the appearance of the President as he was wheeled into the hospital, except to say that he was "gravely wounded." We could not doubt, then, that it was serious.

I had chosen that day to be without a notebook. I took notes on the back of my mimeographed schedule of the two-day tour of Texas we had been so near to concluding. Today, I cannot read many of the notes; on Nov. 22, they were as clear as 60-point type.

A local television reporter, Mel Crouch, told us he had seen a rifle being withdrawn from the corner fifth or sixth floor window of the Texas School Book Depository. Instinct again—Crouch sounded right, positive, though none of us knew him. We believed it and it was right.

Mac Kilduff, an assistant White House press secretary in charge of the press on that trip, and who was to acquit himself well that day, came out of the hospital. We gathered round and he told us the President was alive. It wasn't true, we later learned; but Mac thought it was true at that time, and he didn't mislead us about a possible recovery. His whole demeanor made plain what was likely to happen. He also told us—as Senator Yarborough had—that Gov. John Connally of Texas was shot, too.

Kilduff promised more details in five minutes and went back into the hospital. We were barred. Word came to us secondhand—I don't remember exactly how— from Bob Clark of A.B.C., one of the men who had been riding in the press "pool" car near the President's, that he had been lying face down in Mrs. Kennedy's lap when the car arrived at Parkland. No signs of life.

That is what I mean by instinct. That day, a reporter had none of the ordinary means or time to check and double-check matters given as fact. He had to go on what he knew of people he talked to, what he knew of human reaction, what two isolated "facts" added to in sum—above all on what he felt in his bones. I knew Clark and respected him. I took his report at face value, even at second hand. It turned out to be true. In a crisis, if a reporter can't trust his instinct for truth, he can't trust anything.

When Wayne Hawks of the White House staff appeared to say that a press room had been set up in a hospital classroom at the left rear of the building, the group of reporters began struggling across the lawn in that direction. I lingered to ask a motorcycle policeman if he had heard on his radio anything about the pursuit or capture of the assassin. He hadn't, and I followed the other reporters.

As I was passing the open convertible in which Vice President and Mrs. Johnson and Senator Yarborough had been riding in the motorcade, a voice boomed from its radio:

"The President of the United States is dead. I repeat—it has just been announced that the President of the United States is dead."

There was no authority, no word of who had announced it. But—instinct again— I believed it instantly. It sounded true. I knew it was true. I stood still a moment, then began running.

Ordinarily, I couldn't jump a tennis net if I'd just beaten Gonzales. That day, carrying a briefcase and a typewriter, I jumped a chain fence looping around the drive, not even breaking stride. Hugh Sidey of Time, a close friend of the President, was walking slowly ahead of me.

"Hugh," I said, "the President's dead. Just announced on the radio. I don't know who announced it but it sounded official to me."

Sidey stopped, looked at me, looked at the ground. I couldn't talk about it. I couldn't think about it. I couldn't do anything but run on to the press room. Then I told others what I had heard.

Sidey, I learned a few minutes later, stood where he was a minute. Then he saw two Catholic priests. He spoke to them. Yes, they told him, the President was dead. They had administered the last rites. Sidey went on to the press room and spread that word, too.

Throughout the day, every reporter on the scene seemed to me to do his best to help everyone else. Information came only in bits and pieces. Each man who picked up a bit or a piece passed it on. I know no one who held anything out. Nobody thought about an exclusive; it didn't seem important.

After perhaps 10 minutes when we milled around in the press room—my instinct was to find the new President, but no one knew where he was—Kilduff appeared red-eyed, barely in control of himself. In that hushed classroom, he made the official, the unbelievable announcement. The President was dead of a gunshot wound in the brain. Lyndon Johnson was safe, in the protective custody of the Secret Service. He would be sworn in as soon as possible.

Kilduff, composed as a man could be in those circumstances, promised more details when he could get them, then left. The search for phones began. Jack Gertz, traveling with us for A.T. & T., was frantically moving them by the dozen into the hospital, but few were ready yet.

I wandered down the hall, found a doctor's office, walked in and told him I had to use his phone. He got up without a word and left. I battled the hospital switchboard for five minutes and finally got a line to New York—Hal Faber on the other end, with Harrison Salisbury on an extension.

They knew what had happened, I said. The death had been confirmed. I proposed to write one long story, as quickly as I could, throwing in everything I could learn. On the desk, they could cut it up as they needed—throwing part into other stories, putting other facts into mine. But I would file a straight narrative without worrying about their editing needs.

Reporters always fuss at editors and always will. But Salisbury and Faber are good men to talk to in a crisis. They knew what they were doing and realized my problems. I may fuss at them again sometime, but after that day my heart won't be in it. Quickly, clearly, they told me to go ahead, gave me the moved-up deadlines, told me of plans already made to get other reporters into Dallas, but made it plain they would be hours in arriving.

Salisbury told me to use the phone and take no chances on a wire circuit being jammed or going wrong. Stop reporting and start writing in time to meet the deadline, he said. Pay anyone $50 if necessary to dictate for you.

The whole conversation probably took three minutes. Then I hung up, thinking of all there was to know, all there was I didn't know. I wandered down a corridor and ran into Sidey and Chuck Roberts of Newsweek. They'd seen a hearse pulling up at the emergency entrance and we figured they were about to move the body.

We made our way to the hearse—a Secret Service agent who knew us helped us through suspicious Dallas police lines—and the driver said his instructions were to take the body to the airport. That confirmed our hunch, but gave me, at least, another wrong one. Mr. Johnson, I declared, would fly to Washington with the body and be sworn in there.

We posted ourselves inconspicuously near the emergency entrance. Within minutes, they brought the body out in a bronze coffin.

A number of White House staff people—stunned, silent, stumbling along as if dazed—walked with it. Mrs. Kennedy walked by the coffin, her hand on it, her head down, her hat gone, her dress and stockings spattered. She got into the hearse with the coffin. The staff men crowded into cars and followed.

That was just about the only eyewitness matter that I got with my own eyes that entire afternoon.

Roberts commandeered a seat in a police car and followed, promising to "fill" Sidey and me as necessary. We made the same promise to him and went back to the press room.

There, we received an account from Julian Reade, a staff assistant, of Mrs. John Connally's recollection of the shooting. Most of his recital was helpful and it established the important fact of who was sitting in which seat in the President's car at the time of the shooting.

The doctors who had treated the President came in after Mr. Reade. They gave us copious detail, particularly as to the efforts they had made to resuscitate the President. They were less explicit about the wounds, explaining that the body had been in their hands only a short time and they had little time to examine it closely. They conceded they were unsure as to the time of death and had arbitrarily put it at 1 P.M., C.S.T.

Much of their information, as it developed later, was erroneous. Subsequent reports made it pretty clear that Mr. Kennedy probably was killed instantly. His body, as a physical mechanism, however, continued to flicker an occasional pulse and heartbeat. No doubt this justified the doctors' first account. There also was the question of national security and Mr. Johnson's swearing-in. Perhaps, too, there was a question about the Roman Catholic rites. In any case, until a later doctors' statement about 9 P.M. that night, the account we got at the hospital was official.

The doctors hardly had left before Hawks came in and told us Mr. Johnson would be sworn in immediately at the airport. We dashed for the press buses, still parked outside. Many a campaign had taught me something about press buses and I ran a little harder, got there first, and went to the wide rear seat. That is the best place on a bus to open up a typewriter and get some work done.

On the short trip to the airport, I got about 500 words on paper—leaving a blank space for the hour of Mr. Johnson's swearing-in, and putting down the mistaken assumption that the scene would be somewhere in the terminal. As we arrived at a back gate along the airstrip, we could see Air Force One, the Presidential jet, screaming down the runway and into the air.

Left behind had been Sid Davis of Westinghouse Broadcasting, one of the few reporters who had been present for the swearing-in. Roberts, who had guessed right in going to the airport when he did, had been there too and was aboard the plane on the way to Washington.

Davis climbed on the back of a shiny new car that was parked near where our bus halted. I hate to think what happened to its trunk deck. He and Roberts—true to his promise—had put together a magnificent "pool" report on the swearing-in. Davis read it off, answered questions, and gave a picture that so far as I know was complete, accurate and has not yet been added to.

I said to Kiker of The Trib: "We better go write. There'll be phones in the terminal." He agreed. Bob Manning, an ice-cool member of the White House transportation staff, agreed to get our bags off the press plane, which would return to Washington as soon as possible, and put them in a nearby telephone booth.

Kiker and I ran a half-mile to the terminal, cutting through a baggage-handling room to get there. I went immediately to a phone booth and dictated my 500-word lead, correcting it as I read, embellishing it too. Before I hung up, I got Salisbury and asked him to cut into my story whatever the wires were filing on the assassin. There was no time left to chase down the Dallas police and find out those details on my own.

Dallas Love Field has a mezzanine running around its main waiting room; it is equipped with writing desks for travelers. I took one and went to work. My recollection is that it was then about 5 P.M. New York time.

I would write two pages, run down the stairs, across the waiting room, grab a phone and dictate. Miraculously, I never had to wait for a phone booth or to get a line through. Dictating each take, I would throw in items I hadn't written, sometimes whole paragraphs. It must have been tough on the dictating room crew.

Once, while in the booth dictating, I looked up and found twitching above me the imposing mustache of Gladwin Hill. He was the first Times man in and had found me right off; I was seldom more glad to see anyone. We conferred quickly and he took off for the police station; it was a tremendous load off my mind to have that angle covered and out of my hands.

I was half through, maybe more, when I heard myself paged. It turned out to be Kiker, who had been separated from me and was working in the El Dorado room, a bottle club in the terminal. My mezzanine was quieter and a better place to work, but he had a TV going for him, so I moved in too.

The TV helped in one important respect. I took down from it an eyewitness account of one Charles Drehm, who had been waving at the President when he was shot. Instinct again: Drehm sounded positive, right, sure of what he said. And his report was the first real indication that the President probably was shot twice.

Shortly after 7 P.M., New York time, I finished. So did Kiker. Simultaneously we thought of our bags out in that remote phone booth. We ran for a taxi and urged an unwilling driver out along the dark airstrip. As we found the place, with some difficulty, an American Airlines man was walking off with the bags. He was going to ship them off to the White House, having seen the tags on them. A minute later and we'd have been stuck in Dallas without even a toothbrush.

Kiker and I went to The Dallas News. The work wasn't done—I filed a number of inserts later that night, wrote a separate story on the building from which the assassin had fired, tried to get John Herbers, Don Janson, Joe Loftus on useful angles as they drifted in. But when I left the airport, I knew the worst of it was over. The story was filed on time, good or bad, complete or incomplete, and any reporter knows how that feels. They couldn't say I missed the deadline.

It was a long taxi ride to The Dallas News. We were hungry, not having eaten since an early breakfast. It was then that I remembered John F. Kennedy's obituary. Last June, Hal Faber had sent it to me for updating. On Nov. 22, it was still lying on my desk in Washington, not updated, not rewritten, a monument to the incredibility of that afternoon in Dallas.

Thomas O'Toole / "The Eagle Has Landed":
Two Men Walk on the Moon   *Washington Post,* July 24, 1969

On July 20, 1969, Thomas O'Toole, staff writer for the Washington Post, *covered his story by watching Neil Armstrong and Buzz Aldrin participate in what President Richard Nixon called "the greatest moment in history since the Creation."*

HOUSTON, July 20—Man stepped out onto the moon tonight for the first time in his two-million-year history.

"That's one small step for man," declared pioneer astronaut Neil Armstrong at 10:56 P.M. EDT, "one giant leap for mankind."

Just after that historic moment in man's quest for his origins, Armstrong walked on the dead satellite and found the surface very powdery, littered with fine grains of black dust.

A few minutes later, Edwin (Buzz) Aldrin joined Armstrong on the lunar surface and in less than an hour they put on a show that will long be remembered by the worldwide television audience.

AMERICAN FLAG PLANTED

The two men walked easily, talked easily, even ran and jumped happily so it seemed. They picked up rocks, talked at length of what they saw, planted an American flag, saluted it, and talked by radiophone with the President in the White House, and then faced the camera and saluted Mr. Nixon.

"For every American, this has to be the proudest day of our lives," the President told the astronauts. "For one priceless moment in the whole history of man, all the people on this earth are truly one."

Seven hours earlier, at 4:17 P.M., the Eagle and its two pilots thrilled the world as they zoomed in over a rock-covered field, hovered and then slowly let down on the moon. "Houston, Tranquillity base here," Armstrong radioed. "The Eagle has landed."

At 1:10 A.M. Monday—2 hours and 14 minutes after Armstrong first stepped upon the lunar surface—the astronauts were back in their moon craft and the hatch was closed.

In describing the moon, Armstrong told Houston that it was "fine and powdery. I can kick it up loosely with my toe.

"It adheres like powdered charcoal to the boot," he went on, "but I only go in a small fraction of an inch. I can see my footprint in the moon like fine grainy particles."

Armstrong found he had such little trouble walking on the moon that he began talking almost as if he didn't want to leave it.

"It has a stark beauty all its own," Armstrong said. "It's like the desert in the Southwestern United States. It's very pretty out here."

AMAZINGLY CLEAR PICTURE

Armstrong shared his first incredible moments on the moon with the whole world, as a television camera on the outside of the wingless Eagle landing craft sent back an amazingly clear picture of his first steps on the moon.

Armstrong seemed like he was swimming along, taking big and easy steps on the airless moon despite the cumbersome white pressure-suit he wore.

"There seems to be no difficulty walking around," he said. "As we suspected, it's even easier than the one-sixth G that we did in simulations on the ground."

One of the first things he did was to scoop up a small sample of the moon with a long-handled spoon with a bag on its end like a small butterfly net.

"Looks like it's easy," Aldrin said, looking down from the Lem.

"It is," Armstrong told him. "I'm sure I could push it in farther but I can't bend down that far."

GUIDES ALDRIN DOWN LADDER

At 11:11 P.M., Aldrin started down the landing craft's ten-foot ladder to join Armstrong.

Backing down the nine-step ladder, Aldrin was guided the entire way by Armstrong, who stood at the foot of the ladder looking up at him.

"Okay," Armstrong said, "watch your 'pliss' (PLSS, for portable life support system) from underneath. Drop your pliss down. You're clear. About an inch clear on your pliss."

"Okay," Aldrin said. "You need a little arching of the back to come down."

After he stepped onto the first rung of the ladder, Aldrin went back up to the Lem's "front porch" to partially close the Lem's hatch.

"Making sure not to lock it on my way out," he said in comic fashion. "That's our home for the next couple of hours and I want to make sure we can get back in."

"Beautiful," said Aldrin when he met Armstrong on the lunar surface.

"Isn't that something," said Armstrong. "It's a magnificent sight out here."

While Armstrong watched, Aldrin went through some cautious walking experiments to see how difficult it was in his pressure suit.

"Reaching down is fairly easy," he said. "The mass of the backpack does have some effect on inertia. There's a slight tendency, I can see now, to tip backwards."

Aldrin and Armstrong then both walked around the Lem's 31-foot base, inspecting its four legs and undercarriage at the same time that they began looking over the moon's surface.

"These rocks are rather slippery," Armstrong said. "The powdery surface fills up the fine pores on the rocks, and we tend to slide over it rather easily."

While Armstrong got ready to move the television camera out about 30 feet from the Lem, Aldrin did some more experimental walking.

"If I'm about to lose my balance in one direction," said Aldrin, "recovery is quite natural and easy. You've just got to be careful leaning in the direction you want to go in."

At that, Aldrin apparently spotted an interesting rock.

"Hey, Neil," he said. "Didn't I say we'd find a purple rock?"

"Did you find a purple rock?" Armstrong asked him.

"Yep," replied Aldrin.

The next thing Armstrong did was to change lenses on the television camera, putting a telephoto lens on it for a closeup view of what was happening.

"Now we'll read the plaque for those who haven't read it before," Armstrong said, referring to a small stainless steel plaque that had been placed on one of the landing craft's legs.

"It says," Armstrong said, "Here men from the planet Earth first set foot on the moon. July 1969, A.D. We came in peace for all mankind."

"It has the crew members' signatures," Armstrong said, "and the signature of the President of the United States."

BLEAK BUT BEAUTIFUL

Armstrong next took the television camera out to a spot about 40 feet from the Lem, and placed it on a small tripod.

Incredibly clear, the picture showed a distant Lem, squatting on the bleak but beautiful lunar surface like some giant mechanical toy. It appeared to be perfectly level, not at all tilted on the rough lunar terrain.

When he got the camera mounted correctly, he walked back toward the Lem, with the camera view following him all the way.

Just after 11:30, both men removed a pole, flagstaff and a plastic American flag from one of the Lem's legs. They gently pressed the flag into the lunar surface.

After they saluted the flag, astronaut Bruce McCandless commented on the little ceremony from his perch in the Manned Spacecraft center's mission control room.

"The flag is up now," he said. "You can see the stars and stripes on the lunar surface."

At 11:48 McCandless asked both men to stand together near the flag. "The President of the United States would like to talk to you," McCandless said.

Mr. Nixon spoke to the astronauts for almost two minutes, and when he finished, the two astronauts stood erect and saluted directly at the television camera.

During most of their early time on the moon, astronaut Michael Collins not only didn't see them walking on the moon, but was behind the moon and out of radio touch in his orbiting command craft.

When he finally swung around in front of the moon again, Armstrong and Aldrin had been out almost 30 minutes.

"How's it going?" Collins asked plaintively.

"Just great," McCandless told him.

"How's the television?" he asked.

"Just beautiful," he was told.

Armstrong and Aldrin stayed out on the moon for almost two hours, with Aldrin first back into the Lem just before 1 A.M. Monday.

"Adios, Amigos," he said as he pulled himself easily back up the ladder.

Armstrong started back up the ladder a few minutes after 1 A.M. Monday. He took what seemed like the first four rungs with one huge leap upward. At 1:10 A.M., Armstrong had joined Aldrin inside the cabin. "Okay, the hatch is closed and latched," said Aldrin seconds later.

When both men had repressurized their cabin and taken off their helmets and gloves, Collins reappeared over the lunar horizon in his command craft. At once, he asked how everything had gone.

SLEEP, THEN RENDEZVOUS

"Hallelujah," he said when he was told what had happened.

All three astronauts were due to get their first sleep in almost 24 hours, a sleep that was never more richly deserved.

If nothing went wrong—and nobody was expecting anything would—Armstrong and Aldrin were due to lift back off the surface of the moon at 1:55 P.M. EDT Monday.

Burning their ascent engine full-blast for just over seven minutes, they will start a four-hour flight to rejoin Collins and the command craft 70 miles above the lunar surface.

The majestic moment of man's first steps on the moon came about six hours after Armstrong and Aldrin set their four-legged, wingless landing craft down in the moon's Sea of Tranquillity—precisely at 4:17 P.M. EDT.

"Houston, Tranquillity Base here," Armstrong announced to a breathless world. "The Eagle has landed."

"You did a beautiful job," astronaut Charles Duke said from Houston's Manned Spacecraft Center. "Be advised there's lots of smiling faces down here."

"There's two of them down here," Armstrong replied.

The landing apparently was not an easy one. It was about four miles from the target point in the southwestern edge of the Sea of Tranquillity, almost right on the lunar equator.

"We were coming down in a crater the size of a football field with lots of big rocks around and in it," Armstrong said about five minutes after landing. "We had to fly it manually over the rock field to find a place to land."

"EVERY VARIETY OF SHAPES"

A few minutes later, Aldrin gave a waiting world its first eyewitness description of the moon's surface.

"It looks like a collection of just about every variety of shapes and angularity, every variety of rock you could find," Aldrin said.

"There doesn't appear to be too much color," he went on, "except that it looks as though some of the boulders are going to have some interesting color."

Armstrong then described their landing site in a little detail.

"It's a relatively flat plain," he said, "with a lot of craters of the five- to 50-foot variety. Some small ridges 20 to 30 feet high. Thousands of little one- and two-foot craters. Some angular levees in front of us two feet in size. There is a hill in view ahead of us. It might be a half-mile or a mile away."

Armstrong then described what he said were rocks fractured by the exhaust of Eagle's rocket plume.

"Some of the surface rocks in close look like they might have a coating on them," he said. "Where they're broken, they display a very dark gray interior. It looks like it could be country basalt."

"LIKE BEING IN AN AIRPLANE"

Both men seemed to actually enjoy being in the moon's gravity, which is one-sixth that of earth's.

"It's like being in an airplane," Armstrong said. "It seems immediately natural to move around in this environment."

Armstrong and Aldrin apparently felt fine. Armstrong's heart rate went as high as 156 beats per minute at the time of landing, but dropped down into the nineties 15 minutes later.

The time leading up to the landing is difficult to describe, except to say that it was as dramatic a time as any in memory.

It all began at 3:08 P.M. EDT when Armstrong and Aldrin—flying feet first and face down—fired up their landing craft's descent engine for the first time.

Burning the engine for 27 seconds in what amounted to a braking maneuver to slow it down and start it falling, the two men were behind the moon at the time and out of radio touch with earth.

It was not until 3:47 P.M. that the men at the Manned Spacecraft Center heard that Armstrong and Aldrin were on their way down—and they heard it first from Collins, who flew from behind the moon in the command craft above and in front of the landing craft.

"Columbia, Houston," said Duke from the Center. "How did it go?"

"Listen, Babe," replied an excited Collins. "Everything's going just swimmingly. Beautiful."

Two minutes later, Duke made radio contact with Armstrong and Aldrin.

"We're standing by for your burn report," Duke said.

"The burn was on time," Aldrin told him.

"Rog, copy," Duke said. "Looks great."

At this point, the men in Mission Control bent their backs to the toughest jobs they'd ever have—following the two spacecraft at all times, to give them the guidance they would need for the Eagle's descent to the moon.

"JUST PLAY IT COOL"

Looking around the very quiet Mission Control room, flight director Gene Kranz simply said, "We're off to a good start. Just play it cool."

Flying down and westward across the moon's surface, the Eagle suddenly dropped out of radio contact with earth, but in moments was back in touch again.

"I don't know what the problem was," a totally composed Buzz Aldrin said when he came back on. "We started yawing and we're picking up a little oscillation rate now."

Still falling, the Eagle was coming up over the eastern region of the Sea of Tranquillity at an altitude of 53,000 feet and only minutes away from its second critical maneuver—the powered descent to the lunar surface.

"Five minutes to ignition," Duke radioed up. "You are go for a powered descent."

"Roger," Armstrong replied softly. "Understand."

At 4:05, Armstrong began throttling up the engine to slow the Eagle again, to drop it down toward the lunar surface.

"Light's on," he said. "Descent looks good."

Two minutes later, it was plain to everybody listening that they were indeed on their way down to the moon.

"Show an altitude of 47,000 feet," Armstrong said. "Everything looking good."

Still calm, Aldrin said he noticed a few warning lights coming on inside the spacecraft. "I'm getting some AC voltage fluctuations," he said, "and our position checks downrange show us to be a little long."

"You're looking good to us, Eagle," Duke answered. "You are go to continue powered descent. Repeat. You are go to continue powered descent."

FALLING, SLOWING APPROACH

"Altitude 27,000 feet," Aldrin read off. "This throttle down is better than the simulator."

Down they came, still falling but slowing down at the same time. At 21,000 feet, their speed had fallen to 800 miles an hour.

"You're looking great to us, Eagle," Duke said.

A minute later, it was 500 miles an hour, then it was suddenly down to less than 90 miles an hour.

"You're looking great at eight minutes. . . . You're looking great at nine minutes," Duke told them.

At this point, the two explorers began their final approach to the moon surface, coming in sideways and downwardly only 5200 feet above the moon.

When the Eagle dropped to 4200 feet Duke broke in on the radio, his voice tense and excited.

"Eagle, you are go for landing," he said.

"Roger, understand," a calm Armstrong replied. "Go for landing."

"Eagle, you're looking great," Duke said. "You're go at 1600 feet."

At that, Armstrong began to read off rapidly his altitudes and pitch angles—the angle at which the spacecraft was falling toward the lunar surface.

"Three-hundred feet," he said. "Down three and a half. A hundred feet. Three and a half down. Okay. Seventy-five feet. Looking good. Down a half."

"Sixty seconds," Duke said.

"Lights on," Armstrong replied. "Forty feet. Kicking up some dust. Great shadows.

"Four forward. Drifting to the right a little."

His voice then rose a little, as he turned off the engine for the first time and started free-falling to the moon.

"Okay, engine stop," he said. "Overdrive off. Engine arm off."

There was a pause—then the first voice came from the surface of the moon.

"Houston. Tranquillity Base here," Armstrong announced. "The Eagle has landed."

"You've got a bunch of guys about to turn blue," Duke told him. "Now we're breathing again."

"Okay, standby," Armstrong replied. "We're going to be busy for a minute."

Just then, Collins broke in from his lonesome spot 70 miles above the moon, desperately wanting in on the historic conversation.

"He has landed," Duke informed him. "Eagle has landed at Tranquillity."

"Good show," Collins said. "Fantastic."

Five minutes after touchdown, Duke told them things looked good enough for them to stay there a while.

"We thank you," Armstrong answered.

It was then that Armstrong told Houston he had to fly the spacecraft in manually to avoid a football-sized crater and a large rock field.

COULDN'T PINPOINT LOCATION

"It really was rough over the target area," he said. "It was heavily cratered and some of the large rocks may have been bigger than 10 feet around."

He then said he was not sure of his location on the moon either. "Well," he said, "the guys who said we wouldn't be able to tell exactly where we are are the winners today."

Armstrong reported that the four-legged spacecraft had landed on a level plain and appeared to be tilted at an angle no greater than 4.5 degrees.

Their first moments on the moon were truly incredible, but the entire day seemed incredible, as if the scenario for it all had been written by some bizarre science fiction writer.

"We've done everything humanly possible," Manned Spacecraft Center Director Robert C. Gilruth told one newsman, "but boy is this a tense and unreal time for me."

Preparing for the busiest and most historic day of their lives, the three crewmen hadn't even gotten to sleep until after 1 A.M.—and it was the ground that suggested they all go to bed.

"That really winds things up as far as we're concerned," astronaut Owen Garriott said in Houston. "We're ready to go to bed and get a little sleep."

COLLINS WAKES UP FIRST

"Yeah, we're about to join you," Armstrong replied.

Armstrong and Aldrin were the first to go to sleep, and then Collins finally went to sleep two hours later, at just after 3 A.M.

Four hours later, astronaut Ron Evans was manning the radio in Houston and he put in the first wake-up call.

"Apollo 11, Apollo 11," he said. "Good morning from the black team."

It was Collins who answered first, even though he'd had the least sleep. "Oh my, you guys wake up early," he said.

"You're about two minutes early on the wakeup," Evans conceded. "Looks like you were really sawing them away."

"You're right," said Collins.

Everybody got right down to business then. "Looks like the command module's in good shape," Evans told Collins. "Black team's been watching it real closely for you."

"We sure appreciate that," Collins said, "because I sure haven't."

ACTIVATES LANDING CRAFT

Just after 9:30 A.M., as the three men began their 11th orbit of the moon, Aldrin got into the Eagle for the first time—to power it up, start the oxygen flowing into the spacecraft and make sure everything was in working order. Forty-five minutes later, Armstrong joined him.

On the 13th orbit, Eagle undocked from Columbia, moving off about 40 or 50 feet from the command craft, which Collins was piloting alone.

Like most of the maneuvers they've made, this one was done behind the moon and out of contact with earth—so nobody in Houston knew for almost 45 minutes if the separation had been successful.

At 1:50 P.M., the two spacecraft came over the moon's rim.

"Eagle, we see you on the steerable," said Duke, who had just replaced Evans. "How does it look?"

"Eagle has wings," was Armstrong's simple reply.

For a while, all the astronauts did was look each other over, to make sure the two spacecraft were shipshape.

"Check that tracking light, Mike," Armstrong told Collins.

"Okay," Armstrong said next, "I'm ready to start my yaw maneuver if it suits you, Mike."

ELABORATE INSTRUMENT CHECK

Aldrin got on next, reading off what seemed like endless instrument checklists. For 15 minutes, he talked on, never once missing a word, sounding totally composed.

At 2:12 P.M., Collins fired his tiny thruster jets to increase distance between the craft.

"Thrusting," Collins said. "Everything's looking real good."

The two spacecraft were 1000 feet away from each other within moments. Collins took a radar check on the distance.

"I got a solid lock on it," he said. "It looks like point 27 miles"—about 1400 feet.

"Hey," Collins said to Armstrong when he'd looked out his window, "you're upside down."

"Somebody's upside down," Armstrong replied.

Just then, Collins asked Armstrong: "Put your tracking light on, please."

"It's on, Mike," answered Aldrin.

"Give us a mark when you're at seven-tenths of a mile," Duke said to Collins from the ground.

Moments later, Duke told Collins the big radars on the ground showed the two spacecraft seven-tenths of a mile apart.

"Rog," Collins said. "I'm oscillating between point 69 and seven-tenths."

At 2:50 P.M. Houston gave the go signal for the first maneuver, the so-called descent orbit insertion burn.

"Eagle," Duke said, "you are go for DOI."

"Roger," replied Aldrin matter-of-factly. "Go for DOI."

And while the whole world listened one of the most majestic dramas in mankind's history began to unfold.

DISCUSSION QUESTION

1. Compare Thomas O'Toole's report of the moon landing with Norman Mailer's account in "Classics." How does O'Toole's use of transcripts differ from Mailer's? Why doesn't O'Toole talk about the way the astronauts talk? Why does Mailer do this? What effect does O'Toole want the transcripts to have in his report? What role does television play in his report?

Vivian Gornick / The Next Great Moment in History Is Theirs

[*An Introduction to the Women's Liberation Movement*]

Village Voice, November 27, 1969

A persuasive introduction to the women's liberation movement, Vivian Gornick's "The Next Great Moment in History Is Theirs" is a closely reasoned, insightful commentary on the acculturated inequities that have entrapped the public and private lives of American women and a record of their continuing struggle for freedom and self-definition.

Founded in New York in 1955 by free-lance journalist Daniel Wolf, psychologist Edward Fancher, and novelist Norman Mailer, the Village Voice *was the first successful avant-garde, antiestablishment newspaper in what has come to be known as the underground press. Less expensively designed and printed than mass-circulation daily newspapers and with few of their inhibitions or restraints, the* Village Voice *of the late sixties, published weekly with a circulation well over one hundred thousand, could afford to be eclectic and extensive in its selection and coverage of contemporary events.*

A staff writer for the Voice *for several years, Gornick has also taught English at Hunter College and at the Stony Brook campus of the State University of New York. She coedited* Woman in Sexist Society *(1971), an impressive collection of feminist writings. Most recently she has written* Women in Science: Recovering the Life Within *(1983) and* Fierce Attachments: A Memoir (1987).

One evening not too long ago, at the home of a well-educated and extremely intelligent couple I know, I mentioned the women's liberation movement and was mildly astonished by the response the subject received. The man said: "Jesus, what *is* all that crap about?" The woman, a scientist who had given up 10 working years to raise her children, said: "I can understand if these women want to work and are demanding equal pay. But why on earth do they want to have children too?" To which the man rejoined: "Ah, they don't want kids. They're mostly a bunch of dykes, anyway."

Again: Having lunch with an erudite, liberal editor, trained in the humanist tradition, I was struck dumb by his reply to my mention of the women's liberation movement: "Ah shit, who the hell is oppressing them?"

And yet again: A college-educated housewife, fat and neurotic, announced with arch sweetness, "I'm sorry, I just don't *feel* oppressed."

Over and over again, in educated, thinking circles, one meets with a bizarre, almost determined, ignorance of the unrest that is growing daily and exists in formally organized bodies in nearly every major city and on dozens of campuses across America. The women of this country are gathering themselves into a sweat of civil revolt, and the general population seems totally unaware of what is happening—if, indeed, they realize *anything* is happening—or that there is a legitimate need behind what is going on. How is this possible? Why is it true? What relation is there between the peculiarly unalarmed, amused dismissal of the women's-rights movement and the movement itself? Is this relation only coincidental, only the apathetic response of a society already benumbed by civil rights and student anarchy and unable to rise to yet one more protest movement? Or is it not, in fact, precisely the key to the entire issue?

Almost invariably, when people set out to tell you there is no such thing as discrimination against women in this country, the first thing they hastily admit to is a *minor* degree of economic favoritism shown toward men. In fact, they will eagerly, almost gratefully, support the claim of economic inequity, as though that will keep the discussion within manageable bounds. Curious. But even on economic grounds or grounds of legal discrimination most people are dismally ignorant of the true proportions of the issue. They will grant that often a man will make as much as $100 more than a woman at the same job, and yes, it *is* often difficult for a woman to be hired when a man can be hired instead, but after all, that's really not so terrible.

This is closer to the facts:

Women in this country make 60 cents for every $1 a man makes.

Women do not share in the benefits of the fair employment practices laws because those laws do not specify "no discrimination on the basis of sex."

Women often rise in salary only to the point at which a man starts.

Women occupy, in great masses, the "household tasks" of industry. They are nurses but not doctors, secretaries but not executives, researchers but not writers, workers but not managers, bookkeepers but not promoters.

Women almost never occupy decision- or policy-making positions.

Women are almost non-existent in government.

Women are subject to a set of "protective" laws that restrict their working hours, do not allow them to occupy many jobs in which the carrying of weights is involved, do not allow them to enter innumerable bars, restaurants, hotels, and other public places unescorted.

Women, despite 100 years of reform, exist in the domestic and marriage laws of our country almost literally as appendages of their husbands. Did you know that rape by a husband is legal but that if a woman refuses to sleep with her husband she is subject to legal suit? Did you know that the word domicile in the law refers to the husband's domicile and that if a woman refuses to follow her husband to wherever he makes his home, legal suit can be brought against her to force her to do so? Did you know that in most states the law imposes severe legal disabilities on married women with regard to their personal and property rights? (As a feminist said to me: "The United Nations has defined servitude as necessarily involuntary, but women, ignorant of the law, put themselves into *voluntary* servitude.")

Perhaps, you will say, these observations are not so shocking. After all, women *are* weaker than men, they do need protection, what on earth is so terrible about being protected, for God's sake! And as for those laws, they're never invoked, no woman is dragged anywhere against her will, on the contrary, women's desires rule the middle-class household, and women can work at hundreds of jobs, in fact, a great deal of the wealth of the country is in their hands, and no woman ever goes hungry.

I agree. These observed facts of our national life are not so shocking. The laws and what accrues from them are not so terrible. It is what's behind the laws that is so terrible. It is not the letter of the law but the spirit determining the law that is terrible. It is not what is explicit but what is implicit in the law that is terrible. It is not the apparent condition but the actual condition of woman that is terrible.

"The woman's issue is the true barometer of social change," said a famous political theoretician. This was true 100 years ago; it is no less true today. Women and blacks were and are, traditionally and perpetually, the great "outsiders" in Western culture, and their erratic swellings of outrage parallel each other in a number of ways that are both understandable and also extraordinary. A hundred years ago a great abolitionist force wrenched this country apart and changed its history forever; many, many radical men devoted a fever of life to wrecking a system in which men were bought and sold; many radical women worked toward the same end; the abolitionist movement contained women who came out of educated and liberal 19th century families, women who considered themselves independent thinking beings. It was only when Elizabeth Cady Stanton and Lucretia Mott were not allowed to be seated at a World Anti-Slavery Conference held in the 1840s that the intellectual abolitionist women suddenly perceived that their own political existence resembled that of the blacks. They raised the issue with their radical men and were denounced furiously for introducing an insignificant and divisive issue, one which was sure to weaken the movement. Let's win this war first, they said, and then we'll see about women's rights. But the women had seen, in one swift visionary moment, to the very center of the truth about their own lives, and they knew that first was *now,* that there would never be a time when men would willingly address themselves to the question of female rights, that to strike out now for women's rights could do nothing but strengthen the issue of black civil rights because it called attention to all instances or rights denied in a nation that prided itself on rights for all.

Thus was born the original Women's Rights Movement, which became known as the Women's Suffrage Movement because the single great issue, of course, was legal political recognition. But it was never meant to begin and end with the vote, just as the abolitionist movement was never meant to begin and end with the vote. Somehow, though, that awful and passionate struggle for suffrage seemed to exhaust both the blacks and the women, especially the women, for when the vote finally came at the end of the Civil War, it was handed to black males—but not to women; the women had to go on fighting for 60 bitterly long years for suffrage. And then both blacks and women lay back panting, unable to catch their breath for generation upon generation.

The great civil rights movement for blacks in the 1950s and '60s is the second wind of that monumental first effort, necessary because the legislated political equality of the 1860s was never translated into actual equality. The reforms promised by law had never happened. The piece of paper meant nothing. Racism had never been legislated out of existence; in fact, its original virulence had remained virtually untouched, and, more important, the black in this country had never been able to shake off the slave mentality. He was born scared, he ran scared, he died scared; for 100 years after legal emancipation, he lived as though it had never happened. Blacks and whites did not regard either themselves or each other differently, and so they in no way lived differently. In the 1950s and '60s the surging force behind the renewed civil rights effort has been the desire to eradicate this condition more than any other, to enable the American black to believe in himself as a whole, independent, expressive human being capable of fulfilling and protecting himself in the very best way he knows how. Today, after more than 15 years of unremitting struggle, after a formidable array of reform laws legislated at the federal, state, and local level, after a concentration on black rights and black existence that has traumatized the nation, it is still not unfair to say that the psychology of defeat has not been lifted from black life. Still (aside from the continuance of crime, drugs, broken homes, and all the wretched rest of it), employers are able to say: "Sure, I'd love to hire one if I could find one who qualified," and while true, half the time it *is,* because black life is still marked by the "nigger mentality," the terrible inertia of spirit that accompanies the perhaps irrational but deeply felt conviction that no matter what one does, one is going to wind up a 35-year-old busboy. This "nigger mentality" characterizes black lives. It also characterizes women's lives. And it is this, and this alone, that is behind the second wave of feminism now sweeping the country and paralleling precisely, exactly as it does 100 years ago, the black rights movement. The fight for reform laws is just the beginning. What women are really after this time around is the utter eradication of the "nigger" in themselves.

Most women who feel "niggerized" have tales of overt oppression to tell. They feel they've been put down by their fathers, their brothers, their lovers, their bosses. They feel that in their families, in their sex lives, and in their jobs they have counted as nothing, they have been treated as second-class citizens, their minds have been deliberately stunted and their emotions warped. My own experience with the condition is a bit more subtle, and, without bragging, I do believe a bit closer to the true feminist point.

To begin with, let me tell a little story. Recently, I had lunch with a man I had known at school. He and his wife and I had all been friends at college; they had courted while we were in school and immediately upon graduation they got married. They were both talented art students, and it was assumed both would work in commercial art. But shortly after their marriage she became pregnant, and never did go to work. Within five years they had two children. At first I visited them often; their home was lovely, full of their mutual talent for atmosphere; the wife sparkled, the children flourished; he rose in the field of commercial art; I envied them both their self-containment, and she especially her apparently contented, settled state. But as I had remained single and life took me off in various other directions we soon began to drift apart, and when I again met the husband we had not seen each other in many years. We spoke animatedly of what we had both been doing for quite a while. Then I asked about his wife. His face rearranged itself suddenly, but I couldn't quite tell how at first. He said she was fine, but didn't sound right.

"What's wrong?" I asked. "Is she doing something you don't want her to do? Or the other way around?"

"No, no," he said hastily. "I want her to do whatever she wants to do. Anything. Anything that will make her happy. And get her off my back," he ended bluntly. I asked what he meant and he told me of his wife's restlessness of the last few years, of how sick she was of being a housewife, how useless she felt, and how she longed to go back to work.

"Well," I asked, "did you object?"

"Of course not!" he replied vigorously. "Why the hell would I do that? She's a very talented woman, her children are half grown, she's got every right in the world to go to work."

"So?" I said.

"It's *her,*" he said bewilderedly. "She doesn't seem able to just go out and get a job."

"What do you mean?" I asked. But beneath the surface of my own puzzled response I more than half knew what was coming.

"Well, she's scared, I think. She's more talented than half the people who walk into my office asking for work, but do what I will she won't get a portfolio together and make the rounds. Also, she cries a lot lately. For no reason, if you know what I mean. And then, she can't seem to get up in the morning in time to get a babysitter and get out of the house. This is a woman who was always up at 7 A.M. to feed everybody, get things going; busy, capable, doing 10 things at once.'' He shook his head as though in a true quandary. "Oh well," he ended up. "I guess it doesn't really matter any more."

"Why not?" I asked.

His eyes came up and he looked levelly at me. "She's just become pregnant again."

I listened silently, but with what internal churning! Even though the external events of our lives were quite different, I felt as though this woman had been living inside my skin all these years, so close was I to the essential nature of her experience as I perceived it listening to her husband's woebegone tale. I had wandered about the world, I had gained another degree, I had married twice, I had written, taught, edited, I had no children. And yet I knew that in some fundamental sense we were the same woman. I understood exactly—but exactly—the kind of neurotic anxiety that just beset her, and that had ultimately defeated her; it was a neurosis I shared and had recognized in almost every woman I had ever known—including Monica Vitti, having her Schiaparellied nervous breakdown, stuffing her hand into her mouth, rolling her eyes wildly, surrounded by helplessly sympathetic men who kept saying: "Just tell me what's *wrong.*"

I was raised in an immigrant home where education was worshiped. As the entire American culture was somewhat mysterious to my parents, the educational possibilities of that world were equally unknown for both the boy and the girl in our family. Therefore, I grew up in the certainty that if my brother went to college, I too could go to college; and, indeed, he did, and I in my turn did too. We both read voraciously from early childhood on, and we were both encouraged to do so. We both had precocious and outspoken opinions and neither of us was ever discouraged from uttering them. We both were exposed early to unionist radicalism and neither of us met with opposition when, separately, we experimented with youthful political organizations. And yet somewhere along the line my brother and I managed to receive an utterly different education regarding ourselves and our own expectations from life. He was taught many things but what he learned was the need to develop a kind of inner necessity. I was taught many things, but what I learned, ultimately, was that it was the prime vocation of my life to prepare myself for the love of a good man and the responsibilities of homemaking and motherhood. All the rest, the education, the books, the jobs, that was all very nice and of course, why not? I was an intelligent girl, shouldn't I learn? *make* something of myself! but oh dolly, you'll see, in the end no woman could possibly be happy without a man to love and children to raise. What's more, came the heavy implication, if I *didn't* marry I would be considered an irredeemable failure.

How did I learn this? How? I have pondered this question 1000 times. Was it really that explicit? Was it laid out in lessons strategically planned and carefully executed? Was it spooned down my throat at regular intervals? No. It wasn't. I have come finally to understand that the lessons were implicit and they took place in 100 different ways, in a continuous day-to-day exposure to an *attitude,* shared by all, about women, about what kind of creatures they were and what kind of lives they were meant to live; the lessons were administered not only by my parents but by the men and women, the boys and girls, all around me who, of course, had been made in the image of this attitude.

My mother would say to me when I was very young, as I studied at the kitchen table and she cooked: "How lucky you are to go to school! I wasn't so lucky. I had to go to work in the factory. I wanted so to be a nurse! But go be a nurse in Williamsburg in 1920! Maybe you'll be a nurse. . . ." I listened, I nodded, but somehow the message I got was that I was like her and I would one day be doing what she was now doing.

My brother was the "serious and steady" student, I the "erratic and undisciplined" one. When he studied the house was silenced; when I studied, business as usual.

When I was 14 and I came in flushed and disarrayed my mother knew I'd been with a boy. Her fingers gripped my upper arm; her face, white and intent, bent over me: What did he do to you? *Where* did he do it? I was frightened to death. What was she so upset about? What could he do to me? I learned that I was the keeper of an incomparable treasure and it had to be guarded: it was meant to be a gift for my husband. (Later that year when I read "A Rage to Live" I knew without any instruction exactly what all those elliptical sentences were about.)

When I threw some hideous temper tantrum my mother would say: "What a little female you are!" (I have since seen many little boys throw the same tantrums and have noted with interest that they are not told they are little females.)

The girls on the street would talk forever about boys, clothes, movies, fights with their mothers. The 1000 thoughts racing around in my head from the books I was reading remained secret, no one to share them with.

The boys would be gentler with the girls than with each other when we all played roughly; and our opinions were never considered seriously.

I grew up, I went to school, I came out, wandered around, went to Europe, went back to school, wandered again, taught in a desultory fashion, and at last! got married!

It was during my first marriage that I began to realize something was terribly wrong inside me, but it took me 10 years to understand that I was suffering the classic female pathology. My husband, like all the men I have known, was a good man, a man who wanted my independence for me more than I wanted it for myself. He urged me to work, to do something, anything, that would make me happy; he knew that our pleasure in each other could be heightened only if I was a functioning human being too. Yes, yes! I said, and leaned back in the rocking chair with yet another novel. Somehow, I couldn't do anything. I didn't really know where to start, what I wanted to do. Oh, I had always had a number of interests but they, through an inability on my part to stick with anything, had always been superficial; when I arrived at a difficult point in a subject, a job, an interest, I would simply drop it. Of course, what I really wanted to do was write; but that was an altogether ghastly agony and one I could never come to grips with. There seemed to be some terrible aimlessness at the very center of me, some paralyzing lack of will. My energy, which was abundant, was held in a trap of some sort; occasionally that useless energy would wake up roaring, demanding to be let out of its cage, and then I became "emotional"; I would have hysterical depressions, rage on and on about the meaninglessness of my life, force my husband into long psychoanalytic discussions about the source of my (our) trouble, end in a purging storm of tears, a determination to do "something," and six months later I was right back where I started. If my marriage had not dissolved, I am sure that I would still be in exactly that same peculiarly nightmarish position. But as it happened, the events of life forced me out into the world, and repeatedly I had to come up against myself. I found this pattern of behavior manifesting itself in 100 different circumstances; regardless of how things began, they always seemed to end in the same place. Oh, I worked, I advanced, in a sense, but only erratically and with superhuman effort. Always the battle was internal, and it was with a kind of paralyzing anxiety at the center of me that drained off my energy and retarded my capacity for intellectual concentration. It took me a long time to perceive that nearly every woman I knew exhibited the same symptoms, and when I did perceive it, became frightened. I thought, at first, that perhaps, indeed, we were all victims of some biological deficiency, that some vital ingredient had been deleted in the female of the species, that we were a physiological metaphor for human neurosis. It took me a long time to understand, with an understanding that is irrevocable, that we are the victims of culture, not biology.

Recently, I read a marvelous biography of Beatrice Webb, the English socialist. The book is full of vivid portraits, but the one that is fixed forever in my mind is that of Mrs. Webb's mother, Laurencina Potter. Laurencina Potter was a beautiful, intelligent, intellectually energetic woman of the middle 19th century. She knew 12 languages, spoke Latin and Greek better than half the classics-trained men who came to her home, and was interested in everything. Her marriage to wealthy and powerful Richard Potter was a love match, and she looked forward to a life of intellectual companionship, stimulating activity, lively participation. No sooner were they married than Richard installed her in a Victorian fortress in the country, surrounded her with servants and physical comfort, and started her off with the first of the 11 children she eventually bore. He went out into the world, bought and sold railroads, made important political connections, mingled in London society, increased his powers, and relished his life. She, meanwhile, languished. She sat in the country, staring at the four brocaded walls; her energy remained bottled up, her mind became useless, her will evaporated. The children became symbols of her enslavement and, in consequence, she was a lousy mother: neurotic, self-absorbed, increasingly colder and more withdrawn, increasingly more involved in taking her emotional temperature. She became, in short, the Victorian lady afflicted with indefinable maladies.

When I read of Laurencina's life I felt as though I was reading about the lives of most of the women I know, and it struck me that 100 years ago sexual submission was all for a woman, and today sexual fulfillment is all for a woman, and the two are one and the same.

Most of the women I know are people of superior intelligence, developed emotions, and higher education. And yet our friendships, our conversations, our lives, are not marked by intellectual substance or emotional distance or objective concern. It is only briefly and insubstantially that I ever discuss books or politics or philosophical issues or abstractions of any kind with the women I know. Mainly, we discuss and are intimate about our Emotional Lives. Endlessly, endlessly, we go on and on about our emotional ''problems'' and ''needs'' and ''relationships.'' And, of course, because we are all bright and well-educated, we bring to bear on these sessions a formidable amount of sociology and psychology, literature and history, all hoked out so that it sounds as though these are serious conversations on serious subjects, when in fact they are caricatures of seriousness right out of Jonathan Swift. Caricatures, because they have no beginning, middle, end, or point. They go nowhere, they conclude nothing, they change nothing. They are elaborate descriptions in the ongoing soap opera that is our lives. It took me a long time to understand that we were talking about nothing, and it took me an even longer and harder time, traveling down that dark, narrow road in the mind, back back to the time when I was a little girl sitting in the kitchen with my mother, to understand, at last, that the affliction was cultural not biological, that it was because we had never been taught to take ourselves seriously that I and all the women I knew had become parodies of ''taking ourselves seriously.''

The rallying cry of the black civil rights movement has always been: ''Give us back our manhood!'' What exactly does that mean? Where is black manhood? How has it been taken from blacks? And how can it be retrieved? The answer lies in one word: responsibility; therefore, they have been deprived of self-respect; therefore, they have been deprived of manhood. Women have been deprived of exactly the same thing and in every real sense have thus been deprived of womanhood. We have never been prepared to assume responsibility; we have never been prepared to make demands upon ourselves; we have never been taught to expect the development of what is best in ourselves because no one has ever expected *anything* of us—or for us. Because no one has ever had any intention of turning over any serious work to us. Both we and the blacks lost the ballgame before we ever got up to play. In order to live you've got to have nerve; and we were stripped of our nerve before we began. Black is ugly and female is inferior. These are the primary lessons of our experience, and in these ways both blacks and women have been kept, not as functioning nationals, but rather as operating objects. But a human being who remains as a child throughout his adult life is an object, not a mature specimen, and the definition of a child is: one without reponsibility.

At the very center of all human life is energy, psychic energy. It is the force of that energy that drives us, that surges continually up in us, that must repeatedly spend and renew itself in us, that must perpetually be reaching for something beyond itself in order to satisfy its own insatiable appetite. It is the imperative of that energy that has determined man's characteristic interest, problem-solving. The modern ecologist attests to that driving need by demonstrating that in a time when all the real problems are solved, man makes up new ones in order to go on solving. He must have work, work that he considers real and serious, or he will die, he will simply shrivel up and die. That is the one certain characteristic of human beings. And it is the one characteristic, above all others, that the accidentally dominant white male asserts is not necessary to more than half the members of the race, i.e., the female of the species. This assertion is, quite simply, a lie. Nothing more, nothing less. A lie. That energy is alive in every woman in the world. It lies trapped and dormant like a growing tumor, and at its center there is despair, hot, deep, wordless.

It is amazing to me that I have just written these words. To think that 100 years after Nora slammed the door, and in a civilization and a century utterly converted to the fundamental insights of that exasperating genius, Sigmund Freud, women could still be raised to believe that their basic makeup is determined not by the needs of their egos but by their peculiar child-bearing properties and their so-called unique capacity for loving. No man worth his salt does not wish to be a husband and father; yet no man is raised to be a husband and father and no man would ever conceive of those relationships as instruments of his prime function in life. Yet every woman is raised, still, to believe that the fulfillment of these relationships is her prime function in life and, what's more, her instinctive choice.

The fact is that women have no special capacities for love, and, when a culture reaches a level where its women have nothing to do but "love" (as occurred in the Victorian upper classes and as is occurring now in the American middle classes), they prove to be very bad at it. The modern American wife is not noted for her love of her husband or of her children; she is noted for her driving (or should I say driven?) domination of them. She displays an aberrated, aggressive ambition for her mate and for her offspring which can be explained only by the most vicious feelings toward the self. The reasons are obvious. The woman who must love for a living, the woman who has no self, no objective external reality to take her own measure by, no work to discipline her, no goal to provide the illusion of progress, no internal resources, no separate mental existence, is constitutionally incapable of the emotional distance that is one of the real requirements of love. She cannot separate herself from her husband and children because all the passionate and multiple needs of her being are centered on them. That's why women "take everything personally." It's all they've got to take. "Loving" must substitute for an entire range of feeling and interest. The man, who is not raised to be a husband and father specifically, and who simply loves as a single function of his existence, cannot understand her abnormal "emotionality" and concludes that this is the female nature. (Why shouldn't he? She does too.) But this is not so. It is a result of a psychology achieved by cultural attitudes that run so deep and have gone on for so long that they are mistaken for "nature" or "instinct."

A good example of what I mean are the multiple legends of our culture regarding motherhood. Let's use our heads for a moment. What on earth is holy about motherhood? I mean, why motherhood rather than fatherhood? If anything is holy, it is the consecration of sexual union. A man plants a seed in a woman; the seed matures and eventually is expelled by the woman; a child is born to both of them; each contributed the necessary parts to bring about procreation; each is responsible to and necessary to the child; to claim that the woman is more so than the man is simply not true; certainly it cannot be proven biologically or psychologically (please, no comparisons with baboons and penguins just now—I am sure I can supply 50 examples from nature to counter any assertion made on the subject); all that can be proven is that some*one* is necessary to the newborn baby; to have instilled in women the belief that their child-bearing and housewifely obligations supersede all other needs, that indeed what they fundamentally *want* and need is to be wives and mothers as distinguished from being anything else, is to have accomplished an act of trickery, an act which has deprived women of the proper forms of expression necessary to that force of energy alive in every talking creature, an act which has indeed mutilated their natural selves and deprived them of their womanhood, what*ever* that may be, deprived them of the right to say "I" and have it mean something. This understanding, grasped whole, is what underlies the current wave of feminism. It is felt by thousands of women today, it will be felt by millions tomorrow. You have only to examine briefly a fraction of the women's rights organizations already in existence to realize instantly that they form the nucleus of a genuine movement, complete with theoreticians, tacticians, agitators, manifestos, journals, and thesis papers, running the entire political spectrum from conservative reform to visionary radicalism, and powered by an emotional conviction rooted in undeniable experience, and fed by a determination that is irreversible.

One of the oldest and stablest of the feminist organizations is NOW, the National Organization for Women. It was started in 1966 by a group of professional women headed by Mrs. Betty Friedan, author of *The Feminine Mystique,* the book that was the bringer of the word in 1963 to the new feminists. NOW has more than 3000 members, chapters in major cities and on many campuses all over the country, and was read, at its inception, into the Congressional Record. It has many men in its ranks and it works, avowedly within the system, to bring about the kind of reforms that will result in what it calls a "truly equal partnership between men and women" in this country. It is a true reform organization filled with intelligent, liberal, hardworking women devoted to the idea that America is a reformist democracy and ultimately will respond to the justice of their cause. They are currently hard at work on two major issues: repeal of the abortion laws and passage of the Equal Rights Amendment (for which feminists have been fighting since 1923) which would amend the constitution to provide that "equality of rights under the law shall not be denied or abridged by the United States or by any state on account of sex." When this amendment is passed, the employment and marriage laws of more than 40 states will be affected. Also, in direct conjunction with the fight to have this amendment passed, NOW demands increased child-care facilities to be established by law on the same basis as parks, libraries, and public schools.

NOW's influence is growing by leaps and bounds. It is responsible for the passage of many pieces of legislation meant to wipe out discrimination against women, and certainly the size and number of Women's Bureaus, Women's Units, Women's Commissions springing up in government agencies and legislative bodies all over the country reflect its presence. Suddenly, there are Presidential reports and gubernatorial conferences and congressional meetings—all leaping all over each other to discuss the status of women. NOW, without a doubt, is the best established feminist group.

From NOW we move, at a shocking rate of speed, to the left. In fact, it would appear that NOW is one of the few reformist groups, that mainly the feminist groups are radical, both in structure and in aim. Some, truth to tell, strike a bizarre and puzzling note. For instance, there is WITCH (Women's International Terrorists Conspiracy From Hell), an offshoot of SDS, where members burned their bras and organized against the Miss America Pageant in a stirring demand that the commercially useful image of female beauty be wiped out. There is Valerie Solanas and her SCUM Manifesto, in which Solanas's penetrating observation on our national life was: "If the atom bomb isn't dropped, this society will hump itself to death." There is Cell 55. God know what they do.

There are the Redstockings, an interesting group that seems to have evolved from direct action into what they call "consciousness-raising." That means, essentially, that they get together in a kind of group therapy session and the women reveal their experiences and feelings to each other in an attempt to analyze the femaleness of their psychology and their circumstances, thereby increasing the invaluable weapon of self-understanding.

And finally, there are the Feminists, without a doubt the most fiercely radical and intellectually impressive of all the groups. This organization was begun a year ago by a group of defectors from NOW and various other feminist groups, in rebellion against the repetition of the hierarchical structure of power in these other groups. Their contention was: women have always been "led"; if they join the rank and file of a feminist organization they are simply being led again. It will still be someone else, even if only the officers of their own interesting group, making the decisions, doing the planning, the executing, and so on. They determined to develop a leaderless society whose guiding principle was participation by lot. And this is precisely what they have done. The organization has no officers, every woman sooner or later performs every single task necessary to the life and aims of the organization, and the organization is willing to temporarily sacrifice efficiency in order that each woman may fully develop all the skills necessary to autonomous functioning. This working individualism is guarded fiercely by a set of rigid rules regarding attendance, behavior, duties, and loyalties.

The Feminists encourage extensive theorizing on the nature and function of a leaderless society, and this has led the organization to a bold and radical view of the future they wish to work for. The group never loses sight of the fact that its primary enemy is the male-female role system which has ended in women being the oppressed and men being the oppressors. It looks forward to a time when this system will be completely eradicated. To prepare for this coming, it now denounces all the institutions which encourage the system, i.e., love, sex, and marriage. It has a quota on married women (only one-third of their number are permitted to be either married or living in a marriage-like situation). It flatly names all men as the enemy. It looks forward to a future in which the family as we know it will disappear, all births will be extra-uterine, children will be raised by communal efforts, and women once and for all will cease to be the persecuted members of the race.

Although a lot of this is hard to take in raw doses, you realize that many of these ideas represent interesting and important turns of thought. First of all, these experiments with a leaderless society are being echoed everywhere: in student radicalism, in black civil rights, in hippie communes. They are part of a great radical lusting after self-determination that is beginning to overtake this country. This is true social revolution, and I believe that feminism, in order to accomplish its aims now, does need revolution, does need a complete overthrow of an old kind of thought and the introduction of a new kind of thought. Secondly, the Feminists are right: most of what men and women now are is determined by the "roles" they play, and love *is* an institution, full of ritualized gestures and positions, and often void of any recognizable naturalness. How, under the present iron-bound social laws, can one know what is female nature and what is female role? (And that question speaks to the source of the whole female pain and confusion.) It *is* thrilling to contemplate a new world, brave or otherwise, in which men and women may free themselves of some of the crippling sexual poses that now circumscribe their lives, thus allowing them some open and equitable exchange of emotion, some release of the natural self which will be greeted with resentment from no one.

But the Feminists strike a wrong and rather hysterical note when they indicate that they don't believe there is a male or female nature, that all is role. I believe that is an utterly wrong headed notion. Not only do I believe there is a genuine male or female nature in each of us, but I believe that what is most exciting about the new world that may be coming is the promise of stripping down to that nature, of the complementary elements in those natures meeting without anxiety, of our different biological tasks being performed without profit for one at the expense of the other.

The Feminists' position is extreme and many of these pronouncements are chilling at first touch. But you quickly realize that this is the harsh, stripped-down language of revolution that is, the language of icy "honesty," of narrow but penetrating vision. (As one Feminist said sweetly, quoting her favorite author: "In order to have a revolution you must have a revolutionary theory.") And besides, you sue for thousands and hope to collect hundreds.

Many feminists, though, are appalled by the Feminists (the in-fighting in the movement is fierce), feel they are fascists, "superweak," annihilatingly single-minded, and involved in a power play no matter what they say; but then again you can find feminists who will carefully and at great length put down every single feminist group going. But there's one great thing about these chicks: if five feminists fall out with six groups, within half an hour they'll all find each other (probably somewhere on Bleecker Street), within 48 hours a new splinter faction will have announced its existence, and within two weeks the manifesto is being mailed out. It's the mark of a true movement.

Two extremely intelligent and winning feminists who are about to "emerge" as part of a new group are Shulamith Firestone, an ex-Redstocking, and Anne Koedt, an ex-Feminist, and both members of the original radical group, New York Radical Women. They feel that none of the groups now going has the capacity to build a broad mass movement among the women of this country and they intend to start one that will. Both are dedicated to social revolution and agree with many of the ideas of many of the other radical groups. Each one, in her own words, comes equipped with "impeccable revolutionary credentials." They come out of the Chicago SDS and the New York civil rights movement. Interestingly enough, like many of the radical women in this movement, they were converted to feminism because in their participation in the New Left they met with intolerable female discrimination. ("Yeah, baby, comes the revolution . . . baby, comes the revolution. . . . Meanwhile, you make the coffee and later I'll tell you where to hand out the leaflets." And when they raised the issue of women's rights with their radical young men, they were greeted with furious denunciations of introducing divisive issues! Excuse me, but haven't we been here before?)

The intention of Miss Firestone and Miss Koedt is to start a group that will be radical in aim but much looser in structure than anything they've been involved with; it will be an action group, but everyone will also be encouraged to theorize, analyze, create; it will appeal to the broad base of educated women; on the other hand, it will not sound ferocious to the timid non-militant woman. In other words . . .

I mention these two in particular, but at this moment in New York, in Cambridge, in Chicago, in New Haven, in Washington, in San Francisco, in East Podunk—yes! believe it!—there are dozens like them preparing to do the same thing. They are gathering fire and I do believe the next great moment in history is theirs. God knows, for my unborn daughter's sake, I hope so.

DISCUSSION QUESTIONS

1. Which of the advertisments reprinted in the "Advertising" section could be used to document the feminist issues discussed in Gornick's essay?

2. In what ways can Gornick's essay be used to establish an ideological context for the situations dramatized in Kate Chopin's "The Dream of an Hour" and Tillie Olsen's "I Stand Here Ironing" (see "Classics")? what attitudes toward the experiences of women do they share? In what ways do they differ?

Mike Royko / How to Kick a Machine

Chicago Daily News, November 15, 1971

Mike Royko writes a 750-word column for the Chicago Sun-Times *five times every week. He did the same for the* Chicago Daily News *for fourteen years. He has been awarded just about every major journalism prize in the business. Author of four books, one a long-time resident of the best-seller list, Royko grew up in the tough North Side of Chicago, and his columns have a streetwise slant on the social and political events of that city.*

In "How to Kick a Machine" Royko gives the "fixers, grafters, schemers, hustlers, loaders and shills" he so often writes about a breather in order to thump the malevolent inanimate objects that afflict us all.

The guy in front of me put his dime in the coffee machine. The cup dropped, the machine whirred, but nothing came out.

He muttered, then started to walk away looking dejected and embarrassed. That's the way many people react when a machine doesn't come through: as if they have been outwitted. They feel foolish.

"Aren't you going to do anything about it?" I asked.

"What's there to do?"

What a question. If he had gone in a bar and ordered a beer, and if the bartender had taken his money but not given him a beer, he'd do something. He'd yell or fight or call the police.

But he let a machine cow him.

"Kick it," I said.

"What good will that do?" he said.

"You'll feel better," I said.

He came back and got in position to kick it, but I stopped him.

"Not like that. You are going to kick it with your toe, but you can hurt yourself that way. Do it this way."

I stepped back and showed him the best way. You use the bottom of your foot, as if you're kicking in a bedroom door.

I stepped aside, and he tried it. The first time he used the ball of his foot. It was a weak effort.

"Use more of the heel," I suggested.

That did it. He gave it two good ones and the machine bounced. He has big feet.

"With feet like that," I told him, "you could knock over a sandwich machine."

He stepped back looking much more self-confident.

Somebody else who had been in line said: "I prefer pounding on it. I'll show you."

Leaning on it with his left hand, he put his forehead close to the machine, as if in deep despair. Then he pounded with his clenched fist.

"Never use the knuckles," he said, "because that hurts. Use the bottom of the fist, the way you'd pound on the table."

"Why just one fist?" someone else said. "I always use two."

He demonstrated, standing close to the machine, baring his teeth, and pounding with both fists, as if trying to break down a bedroom door with his hands.

Just then, another guy with a dime stepped up. Seeing us pounding on the machine, he asked: "Is it out of coffee?"

We told him it had shorted on a cup.

He hesitated, then said: "Sometimes it only skips one, then it works OK."

"It's your money," I told him.

He put in his dime, the cup dropped, the machine whirred, and nothing came out.

All he said was "Hmm," and started to walk away.

"Why don't you kick it?" I said.

He grimaced. "It's only a dime."

Only a dime? I don't know anyone who hasn't been cheated by a machine at least once—usually a lot more than once.

First it was the gumball machine, taking your last penny. Then it was the gum machine on the L platform. Then the peanut machine.

And now they all do it. Coffee machines, soft-drink machines, candy machines, sweet-roll machines, sandwich machines.

Only a dime? There are 200 million Americans. If each of us is taken for a dime, that adds up to $20 million.

And it has to be more, now that machines have appeared in every factory and office, depot and terminal.

I once lost an entire dollar to a dollar-changing machine. I gave it five kicks, and even that wasn't enough. For a dollar, I should have broken a chair over its intake slot.

If everyone in the country is taken for a dollar, as I suspect we all will be eventually, that's $200 million. The empty cup is a giant industry.

Putting up a note, as many people do, saying, "This machine owes me a dime," does little good. The men who service them always arrive before you get to work, or after you leave. They are ashamed to face the people they cheat.

You can put up a note saying, "Out of Coffee," which saves others from losing their dimes. But that doesn't get your dime back.

The answer is to kick and punch them. If you are old, lame, or female, bring a hammer to work with you, or an ax.

I feel better, having got this off my chest. But my foot still hurts.

Ellen Goodman / Protection from the Prying Camera

Washington Post, January 4, 1977

A widely syndicated columnist for the Boston Globe, *Ellen Goodman graduated from Radcliffe College in 1963. A 1980 recipient of the Pulitzer Prize for commentary, she has published a study on human change,* Turning Points *(1979), and two collections of her columns,* Close to Home *(1979),* At Large *(1981) and* Keeping In Touch *(1985). Goodman's writing, as illustrated by this article, is especially attuned to the daily clash of public issues and private values, trends and traditions.*

Maybe it was the year-end picture roundup that finally did it. Maybe it was the double exposure to the same vivid photographs. Or perhaps it was the memory of three amateur photographers carefully standing in the cold last fall, calculating their f-stops and exposures with light meters, trying to find the best angle, pointing their cameras at a drunk in a doorway. Or maybe it was simply my nine-year-old cousin playing Candid Camera at the family gathering.

But whatever the reason, it has finally hit me. We have become a nation of Kodachrome, Nikon, Instamatic addicts. But we haven't yet developed a clear idea of the ethics of picture-taking. We haven't yet determined the parameters of privacy in a world of flash cubes and telescopic lenses.

We "take" pictures. As psychologist Stanley Milgram puts it, "A photographer takes a picture, he does not create it or borrow it." But who has given us the right to "take" those pictures and under what circumstances?

Since the camera first became portable, we have easily and repeatedly aimed it at public people. It has always been open shooting season on them. With new technology, however, those intrusions have intensified. This year, someone with a camera committed the gross indecency of shooting an unaware Greta Garbo in the nude—and *People* printed it.

This year, again, Ron Galella "took" the image of Jacqueline Onassis and sold it as if it belonged to him. This year, we have pictures of a crumpled Wayne Hays, an indiscreet Nelson Rockefeller, and two presidential candidates in every imaginable pose from the absurd to the embarrassing.

We have accepted the idea that public people are always free targets for the camera—without even a statute of limitations for Jackie or Garbo. We have also accepted the idea that a private person becomes public by being involved in a public event. The earthquake victims of Guatemala, the lynched leftists of Thailand, the terror-stricken of Ireland—their emotions and their bodies become frozen images.

The right of the public to know, to see and to be affected is considered more important than the right of the individual to mourn, or even die, in privacy.

What happens now, however, when cameras proliferate until they are as common as television sets? What happens when the image being "taken" is that of a butcher, a baker, or a derelict, rather than a public figure? Do we all lose our right to privacy simply by stepping into view?

Should we be allowed to point cameras at each other? To regard each other as objects of art? Does the photographer or the photographed own the image?

Several years ago, *Time* photographer Steve Northup, who had covered Vietnam, and Watergate, took a group of students around Cambridge shooting pictures. He quietly insisted that they ask every pizza-maker, truck driver and beautician for permission. His attitude toward private citizens was one of careful respect for the power of "exposure." In contrast to this, the average camera bug—like the average tourist—too often goes about snapping "quaint" people, along with "quaint" scenes: See the natives smile, see the natives carrying baskets of fruit, see the native children begging, see the drunk in the doorway. As Milgram wrote, "I find it hard to understand wherein the photographer has derived the right to keep for his own purposes the image of the peasant's face."

Where do we get the right to bring other people home in a canister? Where did we lose the right to control our image?

In a study that Milgram conducted last year, a full 65 percent of the people to whom his students talked in midtown Manhattan refused to have their pictures taken, refused to be photographed. I don't think they were camera shy, in the sense of being vain. Rather they were reluctant to have their pictures "taken."

The Navahos long believed that the photographer took a piece of them away in his film. Like them, we are coming to understand the power of these frozen images. Photographs can help us to hold onto the truth of our past, to make our history and identity more real. Or they can rip something away from us as precious as the privacy which once clothed Greta Garbo.

DISCUSSION QUESTIONS

1. Compare Goodman's essay to Nora Ephron's article on a similar theme, "The Boston Photographs" in "Magazines." Which writer do you think makes a stronger case? Why?

2. Do you think that being a practicing journalist influenced Goodman's point of view? Would her response to privacy be the same if she were not a newspaperwoman? Explain how her role as a journalist affects her response to the situation she is writing about.

Susan Morse and Sandy McClure / Jet Survives Roll, Wild Dive
Detroit Free Press, April 6, 1979

The eighty passengers on board TWA flight 841 from New York to Minneapolis on April 4, 1979 assumed that the plane had hit unexpected turbulence at 39,000 feet over Michigan. Within seconds, they were locked in their seats by the centrifugal force of two complete 360-degree rollovers during a supersonic five-mile nosedive. "You couldn't move your arms," one passenger recounted. "It was like you were glued to your seat. I was just plain frightened and horrifiied." "I wasn't able to stand up," another passenger explained. "I felt I couldn't breathe. I felt that I was being smashed."

Captain Harvey ("Hoot") Gibson, the sixteen-year veteran pilot in command of the flight, told Federal Aviation Administration investigators that his Boeing 727 was hurtling toward the earth virtually out of control for nearly two minutes. "The altimeter was turning too fast to read it," Gibson reported. After several "life-saving maneuvers" had failed, he lowered the landing gear in a last-gasp effort to pull the plane out of its dive, creating enough drag to brake the plane's descent. When the wheels were lowered, Gibson recounted, "there was an incredible sound—unbelievable." As the extended wheels began to slow

*the dive, Gibson pulled back on the plane's control wheel as much as he
thought he could without creating so much stress that the plane's wings would
break off. But without the use of the altimeter and in the midst of dense clouds,
Gibson no longer was certain where the craft was. Then, he said, "we broke
through the clouds and saw the moon—it was a big spot in the windshield—and
we headed for it." Shortly after, Gibson gingerly made an emergency landing
at Detroit's Metropolitan Airport. FAA investigators declared it "a miracle that
the airliner did not disintegrate" in its 650-mph plunge toward the earth. Only
three passengers suffered minor injuries, and all but one passenger boarded another flight that evening for Minneapolis.*

*Staff reporters Susan Morse and Sandy McClure collaborated on the first de-
tailed account of TWA flight 841. Printed in the* Detroit Free Press *on April 6,
1979, their report offers a remarkably clear and concise precis of the incident,
at a time when federal investigators could only speculate about the cause of the
plane's sudden dive.*

A commercial jetliner flying at 39,000 feet apparently made a 360-degree roll over
Flint and went into a nose dive at more than the speed of sound before being
brought under control by a desperation maneuver, federal officials said Thursday.

They said it was a "miracle" the TWA jet survived and none of the 80 passengers and seven crew members were killed before the plane made an emergency
landing at Metro Airport at 10:30 p.m. Wednesday.

"I can't think of any other incident where a (commercial, passenger-carrying)
plane has done a complete 360-degree rollover and survived," said Langhorne
Bond, the highest ranking official of the Federal Aviation Administration. "The
miracle is that it held together under such extraordinary speed and circumstances."

Bond credited the crew's desperation move of lowering the landing gear to
stabilize the plane so that it could be landed after the tremendous air speed had
ripped or crushed piece after piece of its gear.

Bond said Thursday afternoon in Detroit he did not know the cause of the
incident, but the Associated Press reported that earlier, in Washington, an FAA
spokesman said there were indications the plane "suffered a loss of hydraulic
pressure in the system that controls the aircraft."

The spokesman apparently was referring to the system that moves the rudder
and ailerons in response to the wheel controlled by the pilot or co-pilot.

An investigator for the National Transportation Safety Board was sent to interview crew members Thursday in Detroit. Tapes of flight instrument data and cockpit voice recordings were flown to the board's headquarters in Washington for
analysis.

Two of three passengers who reportedly sustained bruises and minor injuries
did not require immediate treatment. The third was treated at an area hospital and
released.

Chell Roberts, 22, a junior in business administration at the University of Utah
at Salt Lake City, and his wife, Louise, 21, who is 5½ months pregnant, were
sitting in the seventh row, near the kitchen area of the plane. They were on their
way back from a three-week trip to Spain.

"At first, I thought the pilot was trying to avoid another plane," Roberts said.
"Then the plane just kept going faster. People began to scream.

"I looked around me and there was a stewardess sitting right behind me, crying.

"I thought about my family and about my wife and my little baby I thought I'd
never get to see."

Roberts said after the plane leveled out, the pilot told the passengers over the intercom, "There seems to be a small problem but we seem to have it under control."

"He told us something seemed to be bent," Roberts said, "and that that was what was causing so much vibration in the plane."

Roberts said the steward and stewardesses gathered near the plane's kitchen, which was torn apart by the force of the fall.

"They closed the curtain and had a meeting," he said, "and then they began to throw pillows, coats and other things in front of us. They told us to take off our shoes and get ready for evacuation.

"We passed over the airport (Detroit Metro) one time. The captain told us it was so people on the ground could look at the damage.

"It was awful tense. You could see blinking lights and fire trucks all over the runway," he said.

The plane involved was a Boeing 727 jet en route from New York's John F. Kennedy International Airport to Minneapolis.

An FAA spokesman said the plane, Flight 841, was cruising at about 39,000 feet over Flint at 10:01 p.m. when the pilot advised the Cleveland Air Route Traffic Control Center that "he was having a problem and requested clearance to land at Detroit Metro Airport.

The exact sequence of events in the next 29 minutes before the plane made a "hard landing" would not be clear until an investigation was completed, the FAA's Bond said Wednesday.

Bond said it appeared the flight was "very routine in clear weather" when the plane began to vibrate, yawed to the right, did a barrel roll and went into a nose dive.

In a barrel roll passengers are kept in their seats by centrifugal force.

At that point, the pilot, identified only as H. Gibson, tried to slow the descent by deploying his wing flaps, spoilers and leading-edge slats. But that did no good and some equipment was torn off or shredded by the air pressure and speed.

The pilot lowered the landing gear.

"It is clear that is the event that allowed the crew to regain control of the plane," Bond said.

Chuck Foster, associate administrator of the FAA for aviation standards, said the plane was flying about 500 miles an hour before the trouble began, but in the dive apparently exceeded 650 miles an hour—above the speed of sound at that altitude and taking into account the air temperature.

Officials claim the cabin never lost pressure, so emergency oxygen masks were not automatically released throughout the cabin.

However, in the debris-strewn cabin reporters were shown Thursday, some 12 air masks were hanging over passenger seats.

Bond theorized that the pressure exerted on the plane caused the section to bend unevenly on the inside, making some masks and some baggage racks "pop out" on one side.

There was damage to the landing gear, the gear doors, and the flaps and slats on the right wing.

All the passengers, except one who decided to drive, were flown to Minneapolis aboard a Northwest Orient airliner.

"I thought there was very little question that we were going down," said Dean Abrahamson, a professor of physics and medicine at the University of Minnesota.

After the plane landed, Abrahamson said, the passengers were given $15 vouchers each for food and drinks while airline officials arranged for them to continue their flight.

"I doubt there were too many who went for food," he said.

DISCUSSION QUESTIONS

1. Compare Susan Morse and Sandy McClure's account of TWA flight 841 with H. G. Bissinger's report on the same event. How does Bissinger's use of detail differ from that of Morse and McClure? Which specific aspects of that "miracle" flight do Morse and McClure highlight? With what effect? How, and with what effect, are these emphases changed in Bissinger's report?

2. Bissinger's report, "The Plane That Fell from the Sky," appeared more than two years after the incident. Contrast the opening paragraphs in his account with those in the report by Morse and McClure. Describe the different effects in each, and comment on the differing points of view.

H. G. Bissinger / The Plane That Fell from the Sky
St. Paul Pioneer Press, May 24, 1981

H. G. Bissinger had been working at the St. Paul Pioneer Press *for only a few months when he was assigned to report on what had happened to—and on board—TWA flight 841 as it plunged 34,000 feet in a forty-four-second super-sonic nosedive over Michigan in early April 1979. Bissinger wrote the story of that "miracle" flight, but the event, as he later reported, "stuck in my mind. I just felt that to do it as a spot news story was fine, but there was something much more there." Two years later, at his wife's urging, he decided to "see what happened to the people on this plane." The following story, recreating the event second by second, was the first of a three-part series on flight 841. "The Aftermath" described the effects of the incident on the passengers and crew; "The Investigations" recounted the official inquiries into the cause of the incident.*

Bissinger's search for passengers to interview led him to a lawyer who was representing two women passengers in a personal-injury lawsuit. The lawyer, Bissinger explained, "had gotten all the public records. . . . He had all the original information that had been compiled, the original depositions that were taken, various investigative reports, the chronology on these flight data recorders. They do it in tenth-of-a-second splits and that's how I was able to head each section down to a second." Recounting what had happened during those forty-four seconds on board TWA 841 proved more challenging than Bissinger apparently had anticipated: "It is only forty-four seconds. But forty-four seconds is unbelievable as to how many different things happen. . . . I wanted to get the sense of an entire airplane filled with the most mundane, physical questions ever raised, from people saying they are going to die, to people worrying about the leather coat that's been thrown to the floor of the airplane, to pilots erupting, yelling at each other because they can't bring the damn thing in, to stewardesses plucking glasses off people's faces. It is the event of a lifetime, and it incorporates every emotion that we will ever experience in our lives."

Bissinger has cultivated a long-standing interest in journalism, dating back to his high school years. Born in New York City and educated at the University of Pennsylvania, where he majored in English, Bissinger served as a general assignment and special projects reporter for the St. Paul Pioneer Press *from 1978 to 1981 before joining the Atlantic City bureau of the* Philadelphia Inquirer, *where he reported on subjects ranging from the courts to the casino and entertainment industries. In 1983, Bissinger moved to the home office of the* Inquirer.

*Bissinger received journalism's prestigious Livingston Award in 1982 for
"The Plane That Fell from the Sky." He also earned the distinction of being
named runner-up for that year's Pulitzer Prize in Feature Writing. According to
Bissinger, "I think this particular story shows that journalism has the potential
for character development, drama, and pacing, that journalism doesn't preclude
good, lengthy writing." In 1987, Bissinger was awarded the Pulitzer Prize for
Investigative Reporting.*

APRIL 3, 1979
9:35 A.M.
LOS ANGELES INTERNATIONAL AIRPORT

The truth was, flying commercial could be boring work. The old philosophy among
pilots, starting in the days when the DC-3 was the biggest thing going, was that
you didn't really get paid for all the times you flew without a hitch, but for the
one time out of a thousand when everything went to hell and you still brought the
airplane in. That was the test of skill, and the reason for all the other paychecks.

After 16 years of piloting for Trans World Airlines, 44-year-old Hoot Gibson
didn't find his work particularly creative. Or daring. Or exhilarating. After spending 15,709 hours of flight time in the confining cockpits of 727s, Dc-9s, and 747s
as a flight engineer, co-pilot and captain, things were bound to become as familiar
as the boring drone of a jet engine.

Gibson's excitement came when he left the lumbering commercial birds behind
and climbed alone into his own planes to do acrobatic stunts and punch in and out
of canyon crevices and clouds.

That kind of airmanship was more in line with his machismo reputation, which,
whether it was merited or not, had become the subject of shop talk in TWA
hangars and cockpits.

But whatever tidbits circulated about Hoot Gibson's lifestyle, his commercial
flying abilities were difficult to fault. In the parlance of his peers, he carried a
simple tag: he was a "good airman." He confined his colorful ways to the ground,
not the skies.

The April 3 flight package he had drawn was hardly the stuff of glamour, taking
him out of Los Angeles at 9:35 a.m. on hop-skip-and-jump tour to Phoenix, Wichita,
Kansas City, Chicago and finally Columbus, Ohio. Once there, Gibson and the
other two members of his crew, first officer Scott Kennedy and flight engineer
Gary Banks, bedded down for the night in a hotel.

The crew, which had never worked together before, got about eight hours sleep.
The next day—April 4—they left about 3 p.m. for New York's Kennedy Airport.

There was about a two-hour layover at Kennedy as they changed equipment—
to Boeing 727-100 aircraft No. N840TW—and prepared for their final hop of the
evening.

The plane was old, delivered to TWA in 1965 as part of the first batch of 727s
coming out of Boeing's suburban Seattle plant. The destination, considering TWA's
other routes, was not the kind of place a pilot would beg for—St. Paul-Minneap-
olis International on TWA Flight 841.

With all his experience, Hoot Gibson probably could make the trip—a relatively
short course over Lake Michigan and Green Bay—with his eyes closed. Any airline pilot could—just get the plane up to cruise altitude and set in the autopilot
until it was time to land.

After 15,000 hours of flying, it certainly was not the test of skill that would
make a pilot find out just how much he was really worth.

APRIL 4, 1979

6:55 P.M.

KENNEDY INTERNATIONAL AIRPORT

Just when it seemed as if there were no alternative except to stay in New York for longer than he wanted to, Bob Reber found TWA Flight 841.

The flight he hoped to get booked on—a Northwest 6 p.m. flight out of La-Guardia—was full. So Reber, 52, walked to the TWA counter at the Sheraton Hotel and the luck there was better: A seat was available on their flight to Minneapolis, leaving at 6:55 p.m.

Typically, the plane was late taking off and did not leave the JFK gate until 7:39 p.m., prompting pilot Hoot Gibson to come on the intercom and give the 82 passengers on board one of those little speeches about being held up.

Eventually, the plane took off at 8:25 p.m. Reber settled into seat 22F, a window seat in the last row of seats in the smoking section, pulled out the copy of the *New York Times* and sipped a cocktail.

The manager of data processing for Powers department stores in the Twin Cities, he stayed wide awake throughout the flight. Falling asleep on planes was a habit he had never acquired. But he thought the trip was extremely dull as airplane flights always are, with the engines humming and the funny smell of disinfectant that tried to rid the cabin of any human smell.

In the *Minneapolis Tribune* that morning, his horoscope by Jeane Dixon had at least been topical for once: "Traveling appeals, but is not favored. Try staying close to home (Cancer. June 21–July 22)." But Reber didn't pay attention to junk like that.

APRIL 4, 1979

8:45 P.M.

NEARING THE GREAT LAKES

35,000 FEET

First Officer Scott Kennedy, who had flown the 727 for all but six months of his 13 years at TWA, put the flaps up with effortless routine.

On takeoff, the flaps were extended to produce lift so the plane could get off the ground.

160 knots. Flaps up from 15 degrees to 5 degrees to increase speed.

190 knots. Flaps up from 5 degrees to 2 degrees.

200 knots. Flaps tucked in all the way.

Flight 841 was cleared by air traffic control to an altitude of 5,000 feet. Then up to 8,000, 23,000, and finally 35,000 feet at 8:45 p.m. The air was calm with a little turbulence—"smooth with a light chop" as the pilots referred to it. Nothing to get excited about.

Five minutes later, the four flight attendants on board, two men, two women, started serving the meal—hot and forgettable food served on plastic trays.

Headwinds of 110 knots were bearing down on Flight 841 as it maintained 35,000 feet altitude. Gibson didn't like that and figured the best way to beat the winds was to go below them—or above them.

At 9:24, Gibson got on the mike with the air traffic control center in Toronto and asked for clearance up to 39,000 feet to beat the winds.

"Centre TW841 like to try Flight Level 390."

"Roger, TW841 climb to maintain FL390."

"Out of 35 for 39."

At 9:38 p.m., Flight 841 reported that it was at 39,000 feet.

"Twa's 841 level 3 nine 0."

"841 roger."

The conditions at that altitude were clear and smooth. It was quiet up there, nice and quiet, the cockpit noise at a whisper compared to other altitudes.

A moonlit trail of clouds shimmered about 4,000 feet below the silver under-belly of the plane as it darted across Michigan in the black night. The clouds stretched for several miles to the shoreline of Lake Michigan, and from his seat in the cockpit, Hoot Gibson could see the on-and-off flicker of distant city lights across the mammoth lake.

At 39,000 feet, the serenity of the sky belonged to Flight 841.

APRIL 4, 1979
9:47 P.M.
NEAR SAGINAW, MICHIGAN
39,619 FEET

Dr. Peter Fehr had never particularly liked to fly. To be perfectly honest about it, Fehr used to have a horrendous fear of it, and the whole concept of motion was not something that he had ever quite gotten used to.

As a kid, when he used to go on drives with the family, the result was always the same—he got sick. And his first airplane ride, from Minneapolis to Chicago when he was interviewing to be a missionary in Africa, had left his stomach badly upset.

Fehr, an obstetrician-gynecologist, knew, of course, that it was impossible to live in the modern world without flying. So, with the help of God and large dosages of Dramamine, he had persevered. He made it to Africa as a missionary, suffering in ancient DC-3s that barely wobbled over the African swamps, making so much noise that it sounded like the metal was being sheared off.

But for the past 11 years that Fehr had lived in Minneapolis, things changed. He had been able to get on an airplane whenever it was required. For the past year, in fact, he had been flying without fear and without Dramamine.

But it still didn't take much to get unnerved. A few days earlier, when he had been on his way to New York for a convention, the woman sitting next to him, a large Italian woman, kept repeating her rosary and kissing her prayer book.

Fehr had an urge to look her straight in the eye and say, "Lady, these planes keep flying and most of 'em don't go down." A timid man, he didn't have the courage to say it. But, of course, he was right. The trip to New York was without consequence.

Fehr went to his convention at the New York Hilton, and now he was returning home on Flight 841.

The seat belt sign had gone off, dinner had been served, and the food trays picked up. It was time to relax.

Fehr and the man sitting next to him, a University of Minnesota professor, chatted for a bit.

Suddenly, without warning, the plane shuddered and began to feel as though it were sliding sideways across the sky. There was the sensation that the plane was changing speed and maybe even trying to land. But at 39,000 feet?

"We can't be in Minneapolis already?" said the professor.

Fehr knew the professor was right.

APRIL 4, 1979
9:47.57 P.M.
NEAR SAGINAW
39,046 FEET

Gary Bank's mind idled.

There wasn't much for the flight engineer to do, so he started filling out parts of his log and looked vacantly at the array of instruments and switches before him. Then he felt a high frequency vibration.

Co-pilot Kennedy was preoccupied with trying to figure out the plane's ground speed.

And Hoot Gibson, with the plane set on autopilot and flying steady, put away his charts and cleaned up the cockpit.

Then he heard a sound—a slight buzz—and saw the wheel of the airplane turning slowly to the left, about 10 degrees. The plane was turning to the right for some reason and the autopilot was trying to correct it.

The buzz continued, and now the plane was shaking slightly. And it was turning slightly, and still rolling to the right. And the autopilot was still turning the wheel to the left. But it wasn't doing a thing. The plane was still turning to the right.

Gibson watched for about 10 seconds. Then he disconnected the autopilot. The plane was still rolling to the right. Still rolling.

Gibson grabbed onto the wheel with both hands and turned it all the way to the left. Leaning back in his seat, he took his foot and punched down on the rudder pedal all the way to the left to try to bring the plane around.

It did nothing. The thing was still going to the right. Through 20 degrees. Then 30.

Speaking to his co-pilot, he said what was by now the inevitable truth.

"This airplane's going over."

It continued.

50 degrees.

60 degrees.

70 degrees.

And in that fraction of a second, Hoot Gibson felt stark terror. The plane was rolling over and going in. He knew it. That was it.

He was going to die. And take 88 other people down with him.

APRIL 4, 1979
9:48.04 P.M.
NEAR SAGINAW
36,307 FEET

The tiny 2-month-old baby in Holly Wicker's lap started gasping for breath and turning blue as the plane hurtled downward at a vertical pitch, the speed increasing.

The baby's name was Asha (it means "hope" in Hindi) and this was her first experience in the United States after coming from India. She was on her way to Minneapolis to be adopted and Holly was in charge of her.

With each foot that the plane lost, the forces of gravity (G forces) increased. The pressure was forcing Wicker back into her seat, shoving her skin backwards, almost like someone had grabbed her cheeks and was trying to pull them back to see how much they would stretch.

Wicker tried to rotate Asha onto her back and pull the baby toward her. But she couldn't—the gravity was too great—and instead Wicker leaned forward.

Out of the corner of her eye, she looked across the aisle and saw the instrument panels over the passenger's heads pop down even though they weren't supposed to—forcing down oxygen masks and light bulbs and wires.

Wicker watched the knuckles of hands turning white as passengers tried to fight gravity and reach for the masks. She watched people with their mouths open as though they were trying to scream. But there wasn't a sound, as though the gravity had frozen their cries.

Wicker bent down and gave Asha a breath. She gave another. And then another, when a searing pain ripped across her chest. She couldn't give anymore. There was nothing left. And she knew that the next breath she would take would have to be for herself—not for the tiny baby on her lap turning blue.

APRIL 4, 1979
9:48.07 P.M.
NEAR SAGINAW
34,459 FEET

The plane went into its first roll and Gibson pulled back on the control wheel to try to apply enough downward pressure to keep the passengers in their seats. With the seat belt sign off, they all could be walking around for all he knew.

He closed off the engine throttles—shutting off some of the power to the plane's engines—and started saying "Get 'em up. Get 'em up here." Kennedy thought he was talking to the plane, as pilots often do, trying to coax it back up, pleading with it.

But what Gibson wanted was for Kennedy to grab the "spoiler" handle and pull it back so the flaps on the top of the wing would pop up and help slow the plane down.

By now the plane was into a second roll—this one almost vertical. Gibson let go of the control wheel and pulled the spoiler handle up and down himself.

Nothing happened.

He tugged on the control wheel to see if he could get the plane to reduce its pitch.

It didn't matter.

The plane was in a dive.

By this time, Gary Banks had pulled his seat in between Gibson and Kennedy and tried to get a fix on their instruments. He couldn't figure out what was going on and he needed to get a look at the artificial horizon indicator—an instrument that tells a plane's position on the horizon and where it is pointing. It is divided into two colors—blue for the sky and black for the ground.

Gibson's elbow was blocking the indicator. So Banks looked over at Kennedy's panel, which has an identical set of instruments.

The indicator was black. Pure black. Not a trace of blue in there. It was like walking into a room and finding all the furniture on the ceiling. Banks couldn't believe what he was seeing. And it meant only one thing.

The plane was heading straight for the ground nose down.

He watched as Gibson and Kennedy tried to regain control. From his days as an Air Force instructor on the supersonic T-38s, where you did spiral dives on purpose just to let the student know what the plane could and couldn't do, Banks was impressed: Gibson and Kennedy were doing everything right.

But they weren't saving the plane. They weren't doing it.

Banks glanced at Gibson. He glanced to the right at Kennedy. Then he sat back in his chair and became very calm. He knew the ending now, and in a whisper he confirmed it to himself:

"It is all over. I wonder what it's gonna feel like to hit the ground."

APRIL 4, 1979
9:48.10 P.M.
NEAR SAGINAW
29,982 FEET

The increasing gravity forces pulled Peter Fehr's glasses off his face. He tried to grab them with his arms but he couldn't—gravity had glued them to the armrests. The upper part of his body went upright against his seat like a diving board.

The plane was rattling like crazy, the vibration increasing with each foot of the plunge. The noise sounded like the B-29s that went down in the World War II movies, that horrible, moaning whine that got louder and louder. And then there was another sound, the wrenching, gnarling sound of metal being torn from the right wing.

Fehr knew there was no way the pilot—*any pilot*—was going to bring the plane back up.

The passenger in the seat in front of him kept trying to coax the plane back up. It sounded like he was talking to the pilot. "Take it easy," the man whispered. "You haven't lost it yet. You can pull it out." Fehr thought the man was a fool.

He knew he was going to die.

He became calm and objective. The scene became an abstraction, with Fehr a detached observer.

In the remaining seconds left, he began to make a checklist. He reviewed his will—it was in order and his wife should be well cared for. He remembered what he had said to his four kids before he left for New York.

And it irked him now that one of his sons had taken out a loan to buy a new pair of tires for his car without coming to him. The interest rates were probably ridiculous . . . his son was probably getting gouged to death . . . it wasn't a good business deal . . . in fact, it was downright stupid . . . why did he do something like that . . . they should have talked about it beforehand . . . they really should have.

The roar of the plane grew louder.

APRIL 4, 1979
9:48.16 P.M.
NEAR SAGINAW
24,121 FEET

As the descent of the plane grew faster, Scott Kennedy's mind worked faster.

He remembered the crash of a commercial plane that had been flying at 39,000 feet and dropped into Lake Michigan.

He remembered the crash of the Pacific Southwest Airlines jet in San Diego that had happened only six months ago and left close to 150 people dead.

And then he remembered a conversation he had with the flight engineer only the night before—an insider's conversation about recovering a plane from a vertical stall.

From his experience in the Air Force, Banks knew of only one way to do it—pop the drag shoot on the tail of the plane—a parachute-type piece of equipment that was normally used to slow the aircraft down during landing. Activating it during a stall would slow the plane down enough so the pilot could get control of it back, Banks had told Kennedy.

The co-pilot watched as Gibson tried just about every maneuver there was and still the plane was screaming through the sky. He was impressed by Gibson's perseverance, his reluctance to give up.

Then Kennedy's eye was drawn to something that might help—putting the landing gear down.

He suggested that to Gibson and had his hand poised and waiting on the landing gear handle. The plane continued to plummet, the altimeter unwinding so fast that no one in the cockpit could read it.

21,000 feet.

18,000 feet.

They were getting close and Gibson could see the lights of cities spinning through the fog.

15,000 feet and dropping vertical.

"Gear down," said Gibson.

Kennedy followed the command.

For a second, the two pilots fought against each other as they worked their control wheels—Gibson pushing in to get the tail into the wind current so it would fly again, Kennedy pulling his out to keep the nose of the plane up.

The gear dropped down.

The explosion was deafening, like nothing Gibson or Kennedy or Banks had ever heard in their lives.

TWA Flight 841 continued to fall.

10,000 feet.

8,000 feet.

Gibson didn't know where he was. He couldn't read the instruments. Where the hell was the ground?

And then the plane started to fly again.

And Gibson couldn't help but feel what a damn shame it was that he was getting control back just as the plane was going to crack.

He pulled back on the control wheel as if he was trying to rein a wild mustang. The nose of the plane shot up about 50 degrees. Gibson almost looped the plane he was so desperate to avoid the Michigan farmland beneath him. He was afraid the wings might move, or snap off the plane, but he had no choice but to pull up.

The G forces were incredible—flight data showed them registering 6 at one point—meaning a person's weight was six times what it normally would be. The blood rushed downward from the brain as passengers were flattened into their seats with incredible force. Their faces were pushed sideways as though they were being held in a vise.

Gibson, the acrobatic pilot, had taken 6 Gs before and knew what they were like. Banks, as he had learned in the Air Force, tightened his stomach and tried to keep the blood from pushing down.

The nose still pointed up about 50 degrees as the plane punched through the clouds again—this time on the way up.

Banks felt a rush of panic. If Gibson pulled the nose of the plane down too fast to bring it level, the reverse force of the gravity could be enough to rip an engine off its mount.

Banks coaxed Gibson to get the wings level and gently ease the nose over. "Keep 'em level," he repeated. "Keep 'em level."

Gibson was having trouble figuring out the plane's direction. And then he saw the moon. He pinned it on the windshield, it became his compass, and he kept it in the same exact spot until he pushed the nose over and brought the plane level.

The noise and vibration in the tiny cockpit was incredible. Almost unbearable. Inside the cabin, the shaking and gravity had caused more of the overhead panels to pop open. Oxygen masks accidentally came tumbling down in some of the rows. But some of the passengers didn't realize it was an accident. They thought everyone was supposed to have a mask. And they were clawing at their closed panels with their fingers, trying to pry them open.

Gibson got on the intercom. He had to say *something*. Anything.

"We've had a slight problem, but everything seems to be under control."

APRIL 4, 1979
9:51 P.M.
NEAR SAGINAW
10,509 FEET

Even though the plane was flying again, Atul Bhatt knew something was terribly wrong. One look at the flight attendants told him that.

They were agitated, upset, one of them was crying. And he was scared to death. Once when he was 10 years old, he was riding his bicycle on the edge of a highway when he lost control and fell under a moving truck. The driver just caught a glimpse of him, and the back wheels came to a halt right next to his body.

He had missed death by a screeching second. But he had been a kid then, and the whole thing had happened so quickly.

But this wasn't happening quickly. This was taking forever. There was time—

too much time—to think again and again about what would happen. As the plane had started to plummet, the knowledge of a death that would be quick and painless had somehow been comforting.

But now the plane was going to make a crash landing, and Bhatt didn't even know where it would be. The Chicago airport maybe? Or a forest? Or a farm? It was so dark outside, he couldn't see a thing.

The fear of being paralyzed gnawed at him. Or of being maimed. Or half-burned. And Bhatt, 27, a Ph.D. candidate from India at the University of Minnesota, couldn't bear that. If the plane did crash, he wanted to die quickly. Survival at any odds, with a thousand different possible after effects, wasn't worth the risk.

But the choice wasn't his.

Bhatt was lost in his fear when an Italian woman sitting next to him, after watching his agony for a few minutes now, spoke up. "Don't be scared, young man," said the woman.

Bhatt felt a little embarrassed after that. Here he was a grown man, being admonished just like a little kid for being a coward—not even tough enough to take a bumpy little plane ride. And then he thought a little more.

And he knew in his heart exactly how he felt.

And he couldn't think of one single reason to be brave about it.

He had never been more scared in his entire life.

APRIL 4, 1979
9:55 P.M.
60 MILES FROM DETROIT, MICHIGAN
12,749 FEET

Hoot Gibson needed to find an airport. Quickly.

He checked with air traffic control about Saginaw, where the weather was overcast with light snow and three miles visibility. Then he checked Lansing. And Detroit, where the weather was a little better but certainly not perfect—overcast skies, seven miles visibility, wind at 10 knots.

Although it was the farthest away of the three choices—about 60 miles—Detroit's Metro Airport seemed to Gibson to be the most logical choice. He was familiar with the airport and it could handle a major emergency.

And he figured he could make it.

While Gibson handled the controls of the plane. Kennedy and Banks went through a series of emergency "checklists" to pinpoint what was wrong with the plane and how to try to remedy it.

The noise and vibrating inside the cockpit was still deafening. Banks and Kennedy were shouting, and they still could barely understand each other and had to rely on reading lips.

The diagnosis was not good.

One of the plane's hydraulic power systems was out, so the flaps would have to be extended by an alternate power source. A yaw damper—an electronic device on the rudder that stops a plane from weaving uncontrollably—was apparently out of commission, too.

The landing gear indicator lights inside the cockpit were red, meaning the dropped gear was unlocked and unsafe to land on. It would have to cranked down manually.

Banks' hands shook and his body shivered as he removed a plate from the floor of the cockpit and used a lever to put the main landing gear down by hand. There was no feel on the gear at all, as though it wasn't holding. And when he was through, the indicator lights still were red.

The nose landing gear was extended manually, and the indicator light showed green—the gear was down and locked into place. Once the nose gear dropped, the terrible cockpit noise stopped. Banks couldn't believe what a relief it was to have a little quiet. That noise had almost driven him crazy.

The crew then tried to use alternate power to get the flaps to extend, so the plane would slow down and be easier to land.

The flaps were barely out before the aircraft rolled sharply to the left. Gibson couldn't believe it—he figured he had lost the plane again. But he recovered, and for the rest of the trip he had to fly with the control wheel and the rudder pedal pushed all the way to the right so the plane would not roll over.

Gibson realized that his margin for error here was very small. Below about 170 knots an hour, the plane would begin to roll. Above about 210 knots an hour the same thing would happen. It gave him about 40 knots to work with, and the likelihood of a landing under the worst possible conditions.

When TWA Flight 841 came in to Detroit on runway 3L, it would be making its touchdown at almost twice the normal speed. And on landing gear that, for all Hoot Gibson knew, might not even be there.

APRIL 4, 1979
10 P.M.
NEAR DETROIT
13,000 FEET

Passenger Barbara Merrill had crashed to the floor trapped in the lavatory. Stewardess Frank Schaller, walking to the liquor cart to get someone a drink, had fallen flat in the middle of the aisle. Unable to get up, a passenger cradled her head while she clung to the cart with her left hand. Others on board had blacked out.

As the plane leveled out, Merrill, 41, crawled out of the bathroom and made it as far as the right aisle seat in the last row of the plane, Row 22.

Her ribs ached, maybe one of them was cracked. Her hip had crashed against the toilet seat when she had been thrown to the floor, and she had a cut on her knee.

Merrill's 14-year-old daughter, Susan walked to the back of the cabin to be with her mother.

She sat in seat 22E, in between her mother and Bob Reber.

Under the conditions, there couldn't have been a more reassuring figure. Reber had blacked out almost instantly after the plane had started to dive. But now he felt quite calm and not really aware that something terrible had happened—or was going to happen.

"We're gonna die!" Reber heard Mrs. Merrill repeat over and over. "We're gonna die!"

"Are we?" Mrs. Merrill's daughter asked, her mother's sense of panic becoming infectious.

Reber remained immune. "Don't worry about it," he told them. "If you get to pick your place to land, you got a 50-50 chance."

APRIL 4, 1979
10:20 P.M.
FLYING OVER DETROIT METRO AIRPORT
1,600 FEET

Gary Banks called flight attendant Mark Moscicki into the cockpit and asked him if he remembered his training for an emergency landing.

"You have 10 minutes to get the plane ready, and you get back here in eight minutes," Banks told him.

Moscicki met briefly with the three other flight attendants in the center galley. Then they went to work.

They whipped through the cabin, instructing passengers to remove their glasses, pens, high-heeled shoes, false teeth, canes, anything that was sharp and might cause injury.

They started emptying the overhead racks, distributing available pillows and blankets. One of the stewardesses threw Catherine Rascher's leather jacket on the floor, and she winced. Even in a time of fear and crises, it was hard for her to forget the coat was brand new and cost $200.

A passenger got into an argument with a flight attendant who wanted to remove his glasses. The passenger refused. The attendant persisted, and finally just plucked the glasses off the man's face.

Another passenger willingly had her glasses removed, but gave forewarning that she was blind without them. The flight attendant immediately designated the man sitting directly behind her as her guardian: The woman's life and the lives of her two children depended upon him, the man was told.

Moscicki got on the intercom and told the passengers about the plane's evacuation procedures. He showed them the impact position—hands behind the head, the body bent forward as far as it would go, a pillow to cushion the head from the seat in front.

At 1,600 feet, Gibson flew over the Detroit airport tower so ground personnel could get a look at the landing gear. Searchlights panned the underbelly of the plane. From what they could tell, the gear looked down and locked.

Peeking out the windows from the emergency position, passengers could see a mass of fire trucks sitting on the runway, waiting to see whether TWA Flight 841 would make it. The plane swooped so low that they could see the expressions on the firemen's faces.

After the fly-by, Banks opened the cockpit door to speak to the flight attendants one more time. But when he glimpsed outside, he saw everybody bent over, ready for the plane to crash.

The action was a little premature, there was still a little time left, so Banks got on the intercom and told everybody to sit easy for a moment. He said he would tell them when it was time to assume the . . . he was about to say "crash position" but then he stopped himself and just told the passengers he would let them know when it was time to get ready.

Gibson circled on the final approach to the runway.

He turned the plane downwind, his eyes glued to the strip so he wouldn't lose track of it for a second.

Suddenly, the plane started rolling to the left again.

Gibson was losing control, the plane was getting away from him again.

The crew erupted in the cockpit. After 40 minutes of fighting to keep the aircraft up, the adrenaline was running out. Now was the perfect time to screw up.

"Don't let it roll too far!" yelled Banks, on the verge of panic "Don't let it roll!"

Kennedy got on the control wheel and started working the engine throttles. He cut the power to the right engine and increased the power to the left.

Moments away from landing, TWA Flight 841 skidded level.

APRIL 4, 1979
10:30 P.M.
ON APPROACH TO DETROIT METRO AIRPORT
50 FEET

Frederick and Catherine Rascher held hands and waited.

They had been married for 43 years, had just enjoyed a wonderful trip to Spain, and were looking forward to a life of quiet retirement in St. Paul. Whatever happened now, at least, they would be together.

They turned and looked at each other as they prepared for the crash landing.

"We've had a nice life together," said Mrs. Rascher.

"It's too bad it has to end this way," said her husband.

The plane was on its approach now. Lifting his head up slightly, Frederick Rascher peeked out the window and began the final countdown.

"Forty feet . . . thirty feet . . . twenty feet . . . ten feet . . . get ready."

They bent their heads down and waited for the last time.

April 4, 1979
10:31 P.M.
Landing at Detroit Metro Airport

Gibson bore down on the runway at 170 knots. As he was coming in, the plane started again to roll to the left. The left landing gear hit the runway first—"pretty damn smooth," Gibson thought to himself—and the gear was holding.

The plane was rolling quite a bit and Gibson had to get the right gear on the runway, although he thought the gear would probably shear off on impact.

He brought the plane level and the right gear wasn't even hitting. Maybe it already had fallen off, Gibson thought.

The gear, when it had been extended during the dive, had broken its side brace. If any substantial pressure was put on it from either side, it would collapse on impact.

Using his controls, Gibson tilted the right wing down and finally the right gear hit the runway. It was there . . . and it was holding.

A burst of applause went up from the passengers as the plane touched down. Hoot Gibson was getting a sitting ovation.

Part of the right gear dragged along the runway, causing sparks as Gibson turned left toward the emergency vehicles. As soon as the plane stopped, fire engines sped up and started spraying the aircraft with foam.

Gibson felt exhausted—more exhausted perhaps than he had ever been in his entire life. He also felt relieved and surprised. From 39,000 feet until touchdown some 43 minutes later, he had been convinced that the plane was going to crash.

The only thing he hadn't figured out was where.

April 4, 1979
10:40 P.M.
On the ground at Detroit Metro Airport

Dr. Peter Fehr thought one of the passengers on board was having a heart attack.

He got an oxygen tank for her and made sure she got to a hospital. He gave medical attention to some of the other passengers. And then, once outside the plane, Peter Fehr—the cool, detached doctor—lost control. For 20 minutes he vomited and retched and his legs turned to water. Then he called home to tell his family he was safe.

* * *

Atul Bhatt looked over at the man in his row and couldn't believe what he was seeing. The plane had landed, it was probably about to blow up, there were firemen all over the place, and here was this guy whose first instinct wasn't to run for his life, or move quickly, or even to move at all. Instead he slowly took his comb out of his pocket and started combing his hair.

Bhatt had no pretentions of vanity. In his eagerness to get off the plane, he left his suit jacket on board. And when a bottle of Scotch was passed around in the shivering cold of the runway, he gladly swigged.

* * *

The passenger came up to Gary Banks as he and the other crew members were leaving the cockpit.

"Isn't it interesting?" the man said.

Interesting? What the hell was interesting about a plane that by all rights should have been a hole in the ground and left 89 people dead?

"God no!" said Banks, slightly stunned by the comment.

But the passenger wasn't finished.

"Isn't it interesting that it isn't anyone's time on this plane to die," said the man. And then he walked away.

DISCUSSION QUESTIONS

1. The event Bissinger recreated in this newspaper account had occurred more than two years before, and it is quite likely that the majority of his readers would have remembered the outcome of this widely reported story. What strategies does Bissinger use to create suspense in his account of TWA flight 841?

2. Trace the changes in point of view in this story. Discuss the advantages and disadvantages of presenting the drama of TWA flight 841 from the perspectives of both the passengers in the cabin and the crew in the cockpit.

3. Bissinger draws freely on the special terminology of aviation ("G force," "pitch," "vertical roll," etc.). Comment on his use of these technical details. How do they contribute to—or detract from—the reader's understanding and appreciation of the story Bissinger tells?

4. In an interview, Bissinger explained that "the hardest part" of preparing his account of TWA flight 841 was "not to overwrite. . . . Someone read it and commented, 'It doesn't have an adjective in it.' And I think that is true. The hardest thing was to be restrained and let the story tell itself, almost in a flat tone." What stylistic devices, in addition to his resistance to descriptive phrases, does Bissinger use to "be restrained and let the story tell itself"? Compare and contrast Bissinger's success in this respect to that of Susan Morse and Sandy McClure in "Jet Survives Roll, Wild Dive" ("Press").

ON THE DEATH PENALTY

In the following news reports and editorials, thoughtful men and women consider whether society should or should not impose the death penalty on its most violent criminals. The opinions vary, the arguments differ, but each writer takes a public stand and defends it.

The Death Penalty: Nineteenth-Century Views

On May 14, 1889, William Kemmler was convicted of murder in the first-degree and sentenced "to suffer the punishment of death, to be inflicted by the application of electricity as provided by the Code of Criminal Procedure of the State of New York." Kemmler immediately became the focal point of a legal struggle over capital punishment and, more specifically, over the use of electrocution for capital offenses.

*According to the newspaper accounts of the trial, the crime for which Kem-
mler was sentenced occurred on the night of March 28, 1889, "in the poverty-
stricken apartment in Buffalo occupied by Kemmler and Tillie Kemmler, the
woman who passed as his wife. Kemmler came home late at night, drunk and
quarrelsome. The woman was in the same condition. The quarrel that sprung up
was brought to a sudden close when Kemmler seized a hatchet and struck her
down. He was caught red-handed and expressed no penitence for the deed, remarking that his victim deserved to be killed."*

*On August 6, 1890, Kemmler was executed by electricity at the Auburn, New
York, prison. The headlines in the next day's edition of the* New York Times
*described Kemmler's execution and escalated the already-rancorous debate over
capital punishment:*

FAR WORSE THAN HANGING
Kemmler's Death Proves an Awful Spectacle
The Electric Current Had to Be Turned On Twice
Before the Deed Was Fully Accomplished

The Times *report judged Kemmler's death "a disgrace to civilization" and
characterized his life as "the bone of contention between the alleged humanitar-
ians . . . and the electric-light interests."*

Staff Correspondent / The New Execution Law; Its Constitutionality in Question; In the Case of Kemmler It Is Asserted That Killing by Electricity Is "Cruel and Unusual"

New York Times, July 10, 1889

William Kemmler, who was convicted last Spring of murder in the first degree,
was sentenced in Buffalo to be put to death for his crime. The murder was the
first that had been committed after the new electrical execution law went into
effect, and Kemmler was sentenced to be taken to Auburn Prison and there be
executed according to the provisions of the new law. W. Bourke Cockran became
interested in the case and objected to Kemmler's being executed by electricity,
claiming that the law which provided that means of death was unconstitutional, in
that the Constitution expressly provided that no criminal be put to death by means
that were "cruel or unusual."

Mr. Cockran claimed that death by electricity would be both cruel and unusual,
and asked that the question be decided before Kemmler should suffer the penalty
of his crime. Judge Day of Cuyuga County, before whom the argument was made,
thereupon appointed Tracy C. Becker, a Buffalo lawyer, as referee to take testimony in the case, which is technically known as "the case of William Kemmler
against Charles H. Durston, Warden of Auburn Prison." The hearing is being
conducted in this city in the office of Mr. Cockran, and at yesterday's session
Harold P. Brown, an electrician who has made many experiments tending to settle
the question involved and who bought the dynamos intended to be used at electrical executions, was the only witness examined.

Mr. Brown is a young man who strenuously believes that the alternating or
Westinghouse current is the deadliest current and the one which should be used
for killing criminals. Naturally the Westinghouse Company objects to the use of
its system for such a purpose, and it has been asserted and forcibly denied that
Mr. Cockran had been employed by that corporation to defeat the carrying out of

the new law. The other lawyers engaged in this case are Deputy Attorney General Poste and District Attorney Quimby of Erie County.

Mr. Brown said that in July of last year he made many experiments with electricity, using it upon animals to discover the amount of electricity necessary to be used and the method to be employed in effecting death. The experiments were also made to prove that the high-tension alternating current was dangerous and that arc-light currents could be rendered comparatively harmless. The witness explained the method by which he had put to death various animals in Edison's laboratory at Orange, N.J., in the presence of physicians, electricians, and members of the State Commission, which had been appointed to determine the best means of putting criminals to death by electricity. An alternating current with a power of 700 volts was applied to a horse weighing 1,230 pounds, and the result was fatal. The horse was killed instantly: the current was only applied for twenty-five seconds—and his death must therefore have been painless.

Mr. Brown then described minutely the killing of several other animals in the same manner, and said that, in his opinion, instantaneous and painless death could be produced in a human being by the alternating current. He then explained the apparatus which it is proposed to use in executions. The greater the number of alternations in the current, he said, the lower the amount of pressure needed to kill. With 660 alternations per minute, death would be produced by a power of 800 volts, but with alternations numbering 288 per second—the force intended to be used—160 volts—would be sufficient. The resistance offered to the electrical current by man was not greater than that offered by animals and averaged about twenty-five hundred ohms.

Mr. Cockran took the witness in hand and induced him to admit that from experiments made with electricity upon animals only an inferential knowledge was gained as to its effect upon a man, similarly applied, and that not even from fatal accidents which had occurred could it be determined absolutely just how quickly or how painlessly death had followed the coming in contact with the current. However, the witness said he could from certain results reason upon known scientific rules as to what would happen with the almost absolute surety of his deductions proving sound. This did not suit Mr. Cockran at all and he asked the witness a lot of abstruse scientific questions concerning electricity and its uses tending to test his right to testify as an expert. Witness got through with this ordeal with some credit.

Coming back to the subject of electrical executions, Mr. Cockran asked the witness how the amount of electricity to be used in killing a man would be determined upon. Mr. Brown replied that the man's "resistance" would be first ascertained by the use of an instrument called a Wheatstone bridge, and that a sufficient electrical power would be used to overcome this resistance and produce instant death. The instrument was invariably correct in its measurement of resistance? Yes, it had been ascertained to be so.

"Suppose, however," said Mr. Cockran, "that a mistake was made and an insufficient power was applied. What would be the effect upon the criminal?"

"In that case," the witness said, "the subject would be rendered unconscious and would be unable to feel any pain. The electrodes used would be kept moist, so that the flesh would not be burned."

"Is unconsciousness the inevitable result of a powerful electric shock?"

"Yes."

"Is it possible to inflict torture upon a subject without causing unconsciousness?"

"Yes, if the current were applied at a very low pressure, say 100 or 150 volts."

"At 400 volts?"

"No. I think such a pressure would result fatally."

Mr. Cockran then asked the witness something about lightning. He wanted to know whether it were possible to generate an artificial electric current which would be equal in force to a stroke of lightning, or have 100-1,000 part of its force. As far as concentrated force was concerned, the witness answered, such a thing would not be possible.

"Yet you have heard of a human being having been struck by lightning and not being killed?" asked Mr. Cockran.

"Yes," witness admitted. "I have."

Some more technical questions were asked Mr. Brown relative to his knowledge of electricity, which rather confused him and he finally said that he claimed to be an expert only in "commercial electricity," that is, as to the use and power of currents which are put to practical and daily use. The abstruse questions of electrical science, he said, which never came into the constant work of an electrician, he had never bothered himself about particularly.

The hearing was then adjourned until this morning at 11 o'clock.

A telegram was read yesterday from Elbridge T. Gerry, Chairman of the State Committee referred to, who is on a cruise on his yacht and who had been requested to attend these sessions, saying that he would be unable to attend. Mr. Cockran said that the matter was too important for Mr. Gerry to put aside merely because of his pleasure, and, at the request of all the counsel concerned, Referee Becker telegraphed again to Mr. Gerry at Newport, urgently requesting his presence.

Editorial / The Capital Punishment Question
New York Times, August 12, 1890

One effect of the first experiment with execution by electricity is a revival of discussion on the general question of capital punishment. After the cooling off of the first excitement over the execution of [William] Kemmler it becomes evident that there was nothing in it to justify any talk of going back to the punishment of hanging. Considering the fact that this was the first trial of the electrical apparatus, it was by no means a failure. The apparatus itself was not so well devised as it might have been, and the method of applying the current was probably a faulty one. Besides the novelty of the operation, the mystery and uncertainty attending its first trial, and the evident nervousness of the experts and physicians who supervised it resulted in something of a bungle, but it seems to have been demonstrated that a powerful alternating current of electricity properly applied is certain to produce instant and painless death, which was the very object sought. The greatest mischief was done by excluding the reporters of the public press and leaving them to make up their hurried accounts from vague and excited utterances of the official witnesses just from a scene which appears to have put them under a peculiar nervous strain. There were persons interested in making the experiment a failure, and they seem to have bestirred themselves to give color to the first reports allowed to reach the public and produce the impression that it was a failure.

But when the facts are sifted down it appears pretty clear that execution by electricity is altogether feasible and every way preferable to hanging. It is doubtful if a serious effort will be made, and pretty certain that a successful effort cannot be made, to induce this State to go back to the practice of choking criminals to death with a rope. That is a crude method derived from a barbarous past, and science has devised a much more effective and decent way of putting to death. The efforts of those who are determined to persist in trying to put a stop to this use of the electric current are likely to be joined with those of the mistakenly humane persons who seek the abolition of capital punishment. So far as the sentiment opposed to the death penalty is based upon horror of the means inflicting it, and the possible suffering of the victim, its force ought to be diminished by the adoption of electricity, but it is likely to be reinforced by that self-interest which regards this use of the deadly current as prejudicial to its commercial uses. But the fact cannot be denied or concealed that a powerful current of electricity directly applied to the human system so as to administer its full shock will extinguish life in an instant, and it is rather puerile to contend against the further demonstration of that indisputable fact by the use of such a current in the execution of criminals.

The old arguments on the capital punishment question are somewhat trite. The enlightened mind naturally revolts at the idea of officially putting men to death, as it revolts against the wholesale slaughter of war and as it revolts against murder or killing in any form. But it has to be admitted that the human race has not yet outgrown all its barbarism, and so long as society is in such a condition that men of brutal instincts and evil passions will kill other men so long will it be the stern duty of the State to employ the most deterrent penalties to punish and prevent that practice. There is something irrational in the sentiment that is horrified at the murder of some innocent person by a brutal ruffian and then forgets the victim and bestows its sympathy upon the murderer when it comes to the question of punishment. The putting to death of ten men who have recklessly or madly taken the lives of others should be less a subject of horror than the killing of one inoffensive person, and if it deters from one such crime it is justifiable as a matter of policy. That the death penalty does in no small measure deter from murder hardly admits of reasonable doubt. The lowest and most brutal criminals have little dread of imprisonment even for life, but they do have a dread of death. Until murder ceases in civilized society, or becomes so rare that it is safe to treat it as an aberration not to be guarded against, it will be necessary for society to protect its members by the most deterrent penalty. What is most to be deplored is not capital punishment itself, but the necessity for it, and that should disappear before the penalty is abolished. In the matter of the abolition of killing, in the words of the witty Frenchman: "Que Messieure les assassins Commencement."

The Death Penalty: Twentieth-Century Views

The following four editorials respond to the execution of John Spenkelink for murder on May 25, 1979, in Starke, Florida. Following the editorials are two front-page stories that appeared in the Atlanta Constitution *the day after the state of Florida executed Spenkelink. Bob Dart, a staff writer for the* Atlanta Constitution, *wrote one; Horace G. Davis, Jr., an editor for the* Gainesville Sun *and a witness at the execution, contributed the other as a special report.*

Public attention had been focused on capital punishment since 1977, when convicted murderer Gary Gilmore became the first person ever to be voluntarily executed in America. The "prolonged soul-searching and impassioned debate" engaged in by the editors of the Miami Herald *occurred in newspaper boardrooms throughout the nation as editors determined where their papers would stand on the issue of capital punishment.*

Editorial / Death Penalty Is Right

Miami Herald, May 23, 1979

When he signed death warrants for John Spenkelink and Willie Darden, Gov. Bob Graham fulfilled the most awesome responsibility that a state confers upon its governor. In years past, this newspaper would have said that he was wrong, that the concept of capital punishment was wrong. But today, after prolonged soul-searching and impassioned debate within our Editorial Board, we conclude that the governor was right.

Capital punishment is a question of conscience. No question pierces more thoroughly the heart of the relationship between the individual and the state. No question is as irresolvable by the usual means of proof, because the "proof" exists, finally, only in one's view of whether the state has the right to demand that those who commit heinous murder must forfeit their own lives.

To this question of conscience, which we have debated fully and fervidly, we must answer yes. The state *does* have the right—indeed, the duty—to say to the individual citizen on behalf of all other citizens: "When you murder with deliberation and malice, you shatter the bond that prevents society from becoming a jungle. And that is a transgression that society cannot condone or forgive."

Its opponents argue that capital punishment amounts to murder by the state. If one accepts that view, it therefore follows that the state, in exacting capital punishment, flouts the very sacredness of human life upon which Western civilization is premised.

We respect the wellspring of conscience from which that argument flows, but we cannot drink from it. That cup is tainted by a fundamental illogic. It cheats the victim, and weakens the civilizing bond of law, by implicitly stating that the victim's life is worth less than the life of his murderer.

Human life *is* sacred. And because it is, the society that truly values human life asserts that valuation by imposing on murderers the most extraordinary penalty possible: death. If respect for life and for society's reverence for life is to continue, the inevitability of society's maximum penalty must be clearly understood by all who would wantonly take the life of another.

That is not to say that we accept the theory that capital punishment deters heinous crime. We do not. The evidence of capital punishment's deterrent effect is tenuous at best. Moreover, the deterrence argument is both intellectually specious and irrelevant to the sole purpose of capital punishment.

If executing one murderer deters another murder, that effect is incidental. The state does not execute condemned murderers to make them object lessons for others. The state executes murderers because they have violated the cardinal rule that the people, through their Legislature and their courts, have decreed to be inviolable.

Opponents argue that capital punishment is inherently discriminatory because those condemned to death in the past were too often poor, too often black. That argument, to society's shame, is true—*as applied to the past*. But the conditions that obtained in the past, especially in the segrated South, no longer obtain. The U.S. Supreme Court rectified them in 1972 and 1976.

In those years the High Court struck down some states' death-penalty laws and upheld others' in decisions that imposed uniform standards on them all. No black man ever again will be sentenced to death by a Jim Crow judge upon conviction by a Jim Crow jury. Florida's law complies with the Supreme Court standards, which make death-penalty statutes as fair as any that man has devised.

The fundamental question, then, remains not whether capital punishment is a deterrent, not whether it is fair, but whether a civilized society can justify this ultimate sanction. And that question is, and always will be, answerable only in one's conscience.

Our answer, derived with great difficulty, comes from an institutional conscience cleared by the process of argument and thought. Our answer is yes.

Editorial / Who Gets the Chair?   *New York Times*, May 23, 1979

"There will be less brutality in our society if it is made clear we value human life." So said Governor Graham of Florida as he decreed that John Spenkelink, a drifter who murdered a fellow drifter, and Willie Jasper Darden Jr., who killed a merchant during a holdup, should be executed this morning.

Whether one or both in fact die, the Governor's dictum is not supportable. No one can say with certainty that killing deters killing. Even in symbolic terms, the Governor's words are a kind of gallows humor. What else can "less brutality" mean when used to describe the reactivation of the electric chair after a 15-year lapse? What else can "value human life" mean when a state with 132 people on Death Row, more than any other, starts to clear out the inventory? And as for "made clear," the only thing being clarified is that society values some lives more than others.

It would be easier to defend capital punishment if at least it were applied consistently—if the rich or the notable went to the chair. But that rarely happens, as is newly evident from the violence on the streets of San Francisco. A jury has found Dan White guilty only of manslaughter for gunning down a mayor and a city supervisor. Drifters, even those who get religion, get fried; former county officials, "filled with remorse," get seven years, eight months.

Why is there not more remorse about this "system" of capital punishment? One reason is that all its faces are hooded. There is a division of labor and no person or agency—be it prosecutor, jury, judge, governor, state, nation or hangman—need accept responsibility. And from all this diversity of laws, juries and defendants emerges a pattern of who among guilty murderers is condemned: they are all poor.

We abhor capital punishment because we believe it is wrong for the state so to take life; because it is applied capriciously even among the clearly guilty; because even juries make mistakes; and because we think that, far from deterring, it creates a tolerance for killing. But no argument against capital punishment is more damning than to find out who is condemned.

The way to value human life, Governor Graham, is to do so.

Editorial / The Supreme Penalty

Atlanta Constitution, May 24, 1979

It is time to ask ourselves some hard questions about capital punishment. The first and hardest: do we really believe in it?

Public opinion polls show Americans have, in recent years, reversed a previous trend against capital punishment. Now they *say*, by a considerable margin, that they favor bringing back the electric chair, the gas chamber, the noose and the firing squad. The reason for that change of heart is easy to see. Crime is now one of the half dozen overriding problems in our society. The system protecting us against criminals hasn't been working well. A get tough philosophy always looks good at such times.

Yet the last three executions scheduled in this country have won 11th-hour stays. Two in Florida this week, another in Alabama last month. The only person legally executed in this country since the mid-1960s was Gary Gilmore, and he insisted on his own execution despite a last ditch effort that might have spared him.

Why weren't all the legal questions settled one way or the other long before the 11th hour in the cases of John Spenkelink, Willie Jasper Darden and John Lewis Evans? The questions in Spenkelink's case were whether he was adequately represented and whether state prosecutors acted improperly. There is something seriously wrong with an appeals system that overlooks such questions until a few hours before a man is to be executed.

The practical effect of the death verdict today is not the removal of the condemned criminal from this world but his prolonged torture. Even if our society firmly believes in capital punishment, no one will argue that torture, psychological or otherwise, should be part of the process. Spenkelink was originally scheduled to be executed in September 1977, but an appeal saved him three days before his date with the electric chair. And a classic case, of which our society surely cannot be proud, was that of Caryl Chessman who spent 12 years on death row before finally dying in the gas chamber.

Another disturbing factor is the media circus that now surrounds the condemned man every time an execution appears imminent. The demonstrators outside the Florida prison had a perfect right to be there. The media had a perfect right to cover the demonstrations. But a stay granted under these circumstances is at least open to the suspicion that other than purely legal questions were involved. Were the judges reacting to public pressure? Or did they perhaps act out of some deep personal conviction about capital punishment itself and not merely out of consideration of abstruse legal points?

In short, does our society have whatever it takes to restore the death penalty?

If this last question is a valid one, then what *does* it take? Moral courage? Discipline? A profound sense of justice? Or, perhaps, as some would contend, a simple desire for vengeance—a revision to the "eye-for-an-eye" concept of justice?

The fastidiousness our legal system now displays in capital cases may conceal doubts about the justice of the death penalty. Whether that is true or not, the reluctance to carry out capital sentences is certainly clear. How do we explain that reluctance?

Our Judeo-Christian ethical and moral tradition has always posed a question: is killing another person ever justified? The answer in the past has always been a fairly easy "yes." It is justified in war. In defense of home and family. In protecting society. Today that "yes" is not so easy. Maybe this means that our civilization has a more sophisticated sense of right and wrong—or maybe it means simply that we are morally confused. On such questions, individuals work out their own answers. But society as a whole remains uncertain.

In a new book, *For Capital Punishment,* political scientist Walter Berns argues persuasively that justice itself requires the death penalty. In spite of the arguments that it is cruel and unusual punishment, a throwback to primitive times, an offense against human dignity or a violation of human rights, most people stubbornly continue to believe in it. Most people, Berns insists, are right. He admits that arguments favoring capital punishment—arguments claiming that it deters other criminals, for example—are not proven. But society must demand that the criminal law "be made awesome, a continual reminder of the moral order by which alone we can live as human beings."

The recent Supreme Court decision upheld the death penalty on retributive grounds, Berns writes. "In doing so, it recognized, at least implicitly, that the American people are entitled *as a people* to demand that criminals be paid back, and that the worst of them be made to pay with their lives. In doing this, it gave them the means by which they might strengthen the law that makes them a people, and not a mere aggregation of selfish individuals."

Many of those who now favor the death penalty, including the U.S. Supreme Court itself, are deeply worried about the possibility of unjustly applying it. The court ruled out the death penalty for a few years on precisely those grounds. It was determined that, in practice, capital punishment was reserved for blacks and the poor, mostly. But there are other inequities inherent in the death penalty. Spenkelink was convicted of killing a traveling companion, a petty criminal like himself, in what Spenkelink claimed was a fight over a homosexual proposition. That was murder, and the sentence was death. In California a former city official shot and killed the mayor and another official. That turned out to be manslaughter—maximum penalty eight years, but probably less than five. These terms are, of course, defined in the law, and trials are held to decide whether they apply in specific cases. Still, jurors who are called upon to decide what was in the hearts of an accused man are no wiser than the rest of us. But even if they were the wisest people on the surface of the Earth would they be able to answer such a question with the certainty required in condemning a person to death?

Editorial / With Blood on Its Hands
Milwaukee Journal, May 26, 1979

The clock has been turned back to a more barbarous time.

An American state, with the blessing of the nation's highest court, has deliberately taken the life of a man against his will. The ghastly act, if performed without official sanction, would be defined as cold blooded murder. Is the killing any less dreadful because society committed it collectively? Is the guilt less awful because it is shared? Did John Spenkelink's heinous crime require that the state, too, become a slayer?

We believe that the answer is no in each instance. Spenkelink is no less the victim of a killing than if he had been slain by a fellow criminal, and the taking of a guilty person's life is just as violent as the killing of an innocent. In short, capital punishment is too inhumane an act to have any place in a civilized society.

If a state needs to exact retribution for crimes, as we think it often must to vindicate the rule of law, imprisonment can serve the purpose. If crime is to be deterred, and we agree that it must, there are acceptable ways that do not necessitate official homicide.

The experience of Wisconsin, which decently abolished capital punishment 126 years ago, and of many other states has shown that the extreme penality isn't required in maintaining a system of law and order.

Yet a number of states, taking advantage of retrogressive Supreme Court decisions, are determined to bring back the era of executions. Hundreds of prisoners wait in death row cells.

And civilization weeps.

Horace G. Davis, Jr. / Execution Scene Stark; Death Is Undramatic

Atlanta Constitution, May 26, 1979

STARKE, FLA.—The time is 9:51 a.m. The place is a waiting room without the luxury of Muzak.

Or any luxury, for that matter. The room is austerely clinical, measuring 22 by 12 feet with tan walls, unappealing common kitchen tile on the floor, gray folding chairs.

But whoever arranged this waiting room has either a sense of humor or something special in mind. The chairs are arranged in four rows facing a plate glass window. On the other side of the window is a drawn Venetian blind.

Thirteen persons are seated on the front two rows and staring at the Venetian blind. Nine more file in to fill the third row. A huge man with a turned collar, The Rev. Tom Feamster, enters and remains standing in the fourth row. With him is a slight and bespectacled figure, Washington attorney David Kendall. He remains standing also. So do four men in khaki and four in mufti, obviously officials.

There are two doors—one to the corridor, thence to outside. The other is beside the plate glass and has 12 panes and is stenciled in paint with the number 47. When both doors close with finality, 32 persons are in that waiting room. One is a woman, a television reporter from Tampa.

The air is stuffy. Except for the odd seating, except for the snappy mufti, this could be a ghetto medical clinic. Feet shuffle, lips murmur, bodies squirm. It is a waiting room in use.

It is 9:57 a.m. Voices can be heard beyond the plate glass. Somebody jostles the Venetian blind. A man in uniform near the door with panes can view the proceedings. He looks, again and again, fascinated.

It is 9:59. A peculiar rhythmic drumming, more vibration than sound, like pounding on pipes, gently shakes the room.

It is 10:03 a.m. On the other side of the door with panes, hands tape paper over the glass. The waiting 32 shuffle, murmur, squirm.

When the Venetian blind is raised, John A. Spenkelink will be there. He will look peculiar, with shaven head, gone that shock of hair with the distinguishing white forelock swept back. He will be either standing, or sitting—but most probably sitting. He will say a few things about the unequal hand of justice. He will say a few kind things about his mom Lois who did not abandon him. He will thank the hulking Rev. Feamster, the same man who played football with Burt Reynolds at Florida State University and pulled a stint with the L.A. Rams.

He will be strapped into that sturdy three-legged oaken chair hewed with convict labor from the banks of the nearby river in 1924. His right ankle will be moistened and an electrode attached. His scalp will be moistened and a hood with electrode insert will be dropped over his face. He will be zapped with 2,500 volts and 20 amps, pulsating up and down for two minutes. He will be dead.

It is 10:11 a.m. The Venetian blind goes up.

What's this? Madame Tussaud's wax museum? A figure, and it could be John Spenkelink, is strapped bolt upright in Old Sparky only two, at the most three, feet beyond the glass. The figure is rigid, unable to move a fraction of an inch. A chin guard, maybe a football or medical jaw support, is firmly strapped around chin and mouth and seemingly cruelly fastening the head to the chairback. Perched on the head is the hood, brass nut protruding from the top, with the black face flap pulled up. The only flesh visible are the lower arms, a portion of the electrode-wrapped right leg, and four inches of face from nose to mid-forehead.

The scene is a tacky copy of Disney World's haunted mansion.

For maybe 30 seconds, this trussed and immobile figure stares into the waiting room. The eyes are wide open, they do not blink. They look neither calm nor terrified.

The figure shares the somewhat smaller room with seven men, not all readily visible. One carries a white towel, to clean up any mess? The top of the executioner's head is visible through a slit in an alcove wall. He is never identified and is getting $150 for this job. One of the men in a semi-circle around the trussed figure wears a large insulated glove. He reaches out with it and lowers the hood.

It is 10:12 a.m. There is a "thump." The waxen figure jerks, as if subjected to an explosive blast of compressed air. It does not thrash around. The right fist remains clenched. Indeed, if any motion is apparent at all in the next six minutes, it is the curved fingers of the left hand. The index finger is pointing at the chest. Is the waxen figure left-handed? Is it saying something?

The Rev. Feamster says something. He speaks loudly in that hushed room, with a voice that brooks no reply, apparently addressing the witnesses, one of them West Florida weekly newspaper publisher Tommy Green who has declared that usable organs should be removed before destruction in the drama. The Rev. Feamster says, "Gentlemen, I hope you pray in the name of God that this is just and merciful punishment, for our own souls' sake."

The convicts are drumming on the pipes again.

It is 10:14 a.m. The man with the glove unfastens the chest strap. An Oriental, supposedly the prison medical doctor, pops into view for the first time. He unbuttons the shirt of the trussed figure. He has problems loosening the undershirt from the trousers. He applies a stethoscope, murmurs something, steps back out of sight. The chest strap is left unfastened. Nothing else happens.

It is 10:16 a.m. The Oriental pops back into view, uses the stethoscope, murmurs something, steps back out of sight.

It is 10:18 a.m. The Oriental appears again, applies the stethoscope, feels the pulse, pulls back the hood slightly to examine the eyes. The jowls of the seated figure have a tinge of blue. The hands also are tinged. The Oriental nods.

The Venetian blind comes down.

Laying credence to averages, the Lord's laser struck down 5,200 Americans on Friday—all but 75 involuntarily. John Spenkelink was one of the involuntary ones.

He is different only because the laser was directed by the final early arbiter—the government—and done deliberately. He also is the first American executed involuntarily in 12 years. Waiting for their electrical trip in Florida are 131 others, one-fourth of all the condemned in the land.

He also had all the land offers—a jury trial, over five years' delay, four audiences with the U.S. Supreme Court, and a mass of tidy rule-setting paperwork in the Florida Capitol. The finest people did this to him and, in a fashion, the execution can be deemed a bequeath from Harvard. The governor who signed the warrant is a Harvard law graduate; the prison superintendent who performed so efficiently was trained at Harvard.

He had the best the state has to offer in a process which is amazingly sanitized, like the execution itself during the six-minute flash of the Venetian blind. All did their duty, and they did it well—but by shuffling and signing papers so no vote was openly taken, confronting no emotional outburst, sustaining no embarrassments. And they did it with the overwhelming approval of public sentiment, according to the Books of Gallup and Harris.

But the Rev. Feamster, the friend standing, at Spenkelink's request, in the rear of the clinical waiting room, was not reading Gallup and Harris during those six minutes. He was silently reading the fifth chapter of Matthew.

And nowhere better was contrasted the two intellectual strains underlying the raising and lowering of the Venetian blind. One is the ancient, harking back to Moses descending Mount Sinai with that terrible judgment, eye for eye, tooth for tooth, hand for hand, foot for foot, burning for burning, wound for wound, stripe for stripe. And the contrary theme, from a gentle figure also standing on a mount a thousand or two years later, declaring that the higher human achievement is overcoming the curse of vengeance—that, indeed, human perfection lies in extending mercy which others deny.

But the victor in that dispute is plain enough. Irritated with Spenkelink defense tactics back in 1973, the condemning Judge John Rudd said, "This court is not interested in philosophy."

Bob Dart / Witness Says Spenkelink Looked Scared
Atlanta Constitution, May 26, 1979

STARKE, FLA.—It was shortly after 10 a.m. Friday. The warden was called to the phone. "There are no more stays at this time," reported Florida Gov. Bob Graham. "May God be with us."

Minutes later, John Spenkelink became the first man to be executed against his will in the United States in more than a decade.

The Spenkelink deathwatch that had dragged on agonizingly for six years ended with a shocking suddenness.

Venetian blinds opened abruptly in a small room in the Florida State Prison near here, and Spenkelink, 30, could be seen through a small window. He was strapped tightly into Florida's electric chair.

"He looked at us and he looked terrified," said Kris Rebillot, one of nine reporters who witnessed the electrocution. "His eyes were opened wide. . . . He was absolutely immobile."

The haunting deep-set eyes, peering from beneath a leather deathcap, "looked to the left, looked to the right, then forward," said Wayne Ezell, another observer. "He never got too good a look at his witnesses."

There were no final words.

"In a matter of seconds, a flap was pulled down over his face," explained Miss Rebillot, a 28-year-old reporter for a Tampa television station.

Almost immediately, moving unobserved in the background, one of two hooded figures in the tiny death chamber pulled a switch.

"There was no jerking and there was no smoke and there was no hollering and screaming," said official state witness Tommy Green. "We hardly knew when it happened. It looked like (his fist) tightened, but that may have been before the juice hit him. The man was dead within fractions of a second—it was over with."

"I don't think the man ever felt anything," said Ezell, a reporter for the Tallahassee Democrat.

But state Rep. Andy Johnson, another official witness and an outspoken opponent of capital punishment, disagreed. He said it was a terrible death.

"We saw a man sizzled today, sizzled again, then sizzled again," said the Jacksonville Democrat. "The man didn't die instantly."

The first surge of electricity hit Spenkelink at 10:12 a.m., the witness agreed, then two other surges followed and by 10:18, a doctor had declared him dead.

The execution was the first in the U.S. since Gary Gilmore died before a Utah firing squad in 1977. But Gilmore had demanded death. Spenkelink, a California prison escapee who was convicted of killing another drifter in a Tallahassee motel in 1973, fought death right down to the wire. The U.S. Supreme Court refused to grant his final request for a stay only minutes before he died Friday.

So Spenkelink was the first American inmate unwillingly executed since Louis Jose Monge was put to death on June 2, 1967, in Colorado.

With more than 500 inmates now on death row in the 32 states with capital punishment laws, some anti-execution activists predict a legal "bloodbath" during the next few years.

"We're at the beginning of the end," said Joe Ingle, director of the anti-execution Southern Coalition on Prisons and Jails. "I'm trying to prepare people for a decade of executions that may claim 1,000 lives."

Spenkelink's final countdown to death began at 11:40 p.m. Thursday when a three-judge panel of the Fifth Judicial Circuit in New Orleans lifted a stay of execution granted earlier by Judge Elbert Tuttle in Atlanta. The U.S. Supreme Court earlier Thursday voted down a separate attempt at delaying the execution.

Thus, the two legal roadblocks that kept Spenkelink from going to the electric chair at 7 a.m. Wednesday were removed. His lawyers began even more last ditch maneuvering early Friday.

Meanwhile, Florida's death machinery was put in motion.

By custom, the state's executioners are anonymous, their identities known only to a few top officials. They are paid $150 plus expenses for their work. Prison officials did not explain why two hooded men were reported in the death chamber. However, there were originally two executions scheduled. Willie Darden, a convicted killer from Lakeland, was granted an indefinite stay on Tuesday. The executioner was told of the New Orleans court decision and prison officials early Friday began final preparations for the electrocution.

Spenkelink's family and close friends were summoned for a tearful, farewell "contact visit"—they were allowed to hug and touch. Lois Spenkelink, the condemned man's heavyset, white-haired mother; Carol Myers, his freckled sister; Tim Myers, his bearded brother-in-law; and Carolotta Key, his 44-year-old girlfriend, met together with Spenkelink from 3 a.m. to 5 a.m.

Then Mrs. Spenkelink, 67, sat with her only son for half an hour alone. Brief private visits with Mrs. Myers and Miss Key followed. Mrs. Myers would later complain that they were subjected to a humiliating "thorough search" by a male prison official before the visit was allowed.

After his family left, Spenkelink talked with the Rev. Tom Feamster, an Episcopal priest from nearby Keystone Heights, who had befriended the prematurely gray-haired killer.

"I gave John communion at 8 o'clock," Rev. Feamster said, adding that Spenkelink's last message was "man is what he chooses to be. He chooses that for himself."

Feamster said he watched the execution at Spenkelink's request.

"I witnessed it because John told me to witness it," he said after describing the procedure as barbaric.

"He said, 'If I can go through with it, you can, too.' "

Feamster said he left at 8:15 a.m. "so they could prepare him."

"He said he loved me. That's the last thing he said to me. And I said I loved him. We shook hands."

The death ritual then called for Spenkelink's head and right calf to be shaved, the special sponge, imported from Greece, was taken from the bucket of salt water where it had been soaking. It would be fitted into the death cap to help conduct the surge of electricity.

The final meal was foregone; Spenkelink ate no breakfast.

Wearing dark blue trousers and a white dress shirt, he was taken to the heavy oak electric chair and tightly strapped in. Prison Superintendent David Brierton had set the execution for 10 a.m.

But the appointed hour passed and Spenkelink still lived.

A prison spokesman said that executions traditionally are five to ten minutes late so that last-ditch appeals can be considered. The U.S. Supreme Court's final decision against Spenkelink was called to the prison at 9:55 a.m. A few minutes later, Brierton got the go-ahead from Graham.

Prison officials said Spenkelink was asked if he had any final words. He said ''No.''

He was bound in the chair at the chest, leg, stomach and chin, Miss Rebillot said. ''It was quieter than I expected, less gruesome. Only his eyes got to me. I was scared, but I tried to remember as much as I could.''

It was a cold, impersonal atmosphere, she said. ''It was done in such a way that it was as antiseptic as possible. One of his hands made a fist, the other was drawn up like a claw. He couldn't have slumped if he had wanted to. After the first surge, there was no movement.''

H. G. ''Buddy'' Davis, an editorial writer for the Gainesville Sun, who witnessed the electrocution, said he never even conceived the still figure trussed up in the chair as a human. ''And I'm sure that was deliberate.

''The blinds went up and we saw this wax-like figure . . . I thought he would at least say something. It was like a waxworks. . . . Just this thing sitting there.''

It ended, he recalled, with the still figure's index finger on his left hand ''pointing toward his heart.''

State Rep. Tom Woodruff another official witness, was reluctant to discuss details of the electrocution, saying only that it was ''not inhumane.''

''There was a wisp of steam from the sponge . . .'' he said. ''That's all I saw.''

DISCUSSION QUESTIONS

1. Compare and contrast the two nineteenth-century views of the death penalty. What is the substantive argument of each writer in favor of—or in opposition to—the death penalty? Which writer is more convincing? Why?

2. Compare and contrast the 1890 editorial from the *New York Times* with the one written in 1979. What is the nature of the argument in each? In what specific ways does the editorial policy of the *New York Times* seem to have changed in nearly a century? Which editorial is more convincing? Why?

3. The 1979 editorial in the *New York Times* states that it ''would be easier to defend capital punishment if it were applied consistently,'' whereas the 1979 editorial in the *Herald* claims that ''that argument, to society's shame, is true— *as applied to the past*. But conditions that obtained in the past, especially in the segregated South, no longer obtain.'' How does each paper argue its point? Which is more convincing? What makes it so? What role in the overall argument of each editorial does this point play?

4. Review the four editorials on the execution of John Spenkelink carefully. Choose two and list the points mentioned in each. Which points are common to the two editorials? Describe the different uses to which each point is put.

5. The *Atlanta Constitution* argues that the death penalty is needed because it gives the American people, in the words of Walter Berns, ''the means by which

they might strengthen the law that makes them a people, and not a mere aggregation of selfish individuals.'' The *Milwaukee Journal,* quite to the contrary, sees the death penalty as an indication of social deterioration: "The clock has been turned back to a more barbarous time.'' How does each paper support its argument? Which is more convincing? Why? What particular strategies or points can you identify to support your answer?

6. Compare the account of the Spenkelink execution written by Davis with that written by Dart. What happens to one event when reported by two people?

John J. Goldman / Beatle John Lennon Slain
Los Angeles Times, December 9, 1980

Over the past twenty years, John Goldman has covered hundreds of major breaking news stories for the L.A. Times, *including the first moon landing, the Howard Hughes/Clifford Irving hoax—and the death of John Lennon. Goldman is currently New York Bureau Chief of the* Los Angeles Times.

With a circulation of one million, the Los Angeles Times *is the third largest daily newspaper in the United States (behind the* Wall Street Journal *and the* New York Daily News). *Labeled for many years as an extremely conservative paper, the* Los Angeles Times *was infamous for its biased news coverage. In 1937, it was voted by Washington correspondents as one of America's "least fair and reliable" newspapers. But when Otis Chandler succeeded his father as publisher of the* Times *in 1960, he modernized the paper and changed its character. Now one of the West Coast's most prominent and judicious newspapers, the* Times *has dedicated itself to presenting "both sides of the political spectrum and different shades within the spectrum." Many of its writers have won Pulitzer prizes, as did the* Times *itself in 1969 for public service.*

BEATLE JOHN LENNON SLAIN

SHOT DOWN OUTSIDE NEW YORK APARTMENT

Man Termed "Screwball" Held in Death of Singer

NEW YORK—Former Beatle John Lennon, 40, who led a revolution in popular music that captured the imagination of an entire generation, was shot to death Monday night outside his exclusive Manhattan apartment house.

He was rushed to Roosevelt Hospital, less than a mile from the Dakota, the famous apartment building where he lived with his wife, Yoko Ono. Doctors pronounced him dead at the hospital.

Police announced early today that Mark David Chapman, 25, of Hawaii had been charged with murder. Chief of Detectives James Sullivan said Chapman had arrived in New York about a week ago and had been seen near the apartment building at least three times in recent days.

Sullivan said Chapman had gotten Lennon's autograph when the Lennons left the Dakota about 5 p.m. and had waited outside until they returned six hours later.

Sullivan declined to speculate on a motive for the shooting. Earlier, police had described the suspect as "a local screwball" and "a wacko."

HAD HANDGUN

Police said Lennon and his wife arrived at 10:50 p.m. in a limousine from a recording studio and had just stepped out of the car when the gunman approached them.

"Mr. Lennon?" the man said, drawing a .38-caliber handgun from under his coat.

He opened fire without waiting for an answer.

Lennon, struck in the chest, back and shoulder, staggered from the sidewalk into a small vestibule of the apartment used by the doorman.

The aghast doorman looked at the gunman.

"Do you know what you just did?" he shouted.

"I just shot John Lennon," the gunman responded, throwing down the handgun.

Lennon's wife was not injured.

Police Officer Anthony Palmer was one of the first to arrive at the Dakota. He said it was quickly apparent to him that Lennon had to be rushed to the hospital without waiting for an ambulance.

"I made the decision," Palmer said. "We had to get him out of there. . . ."

Police Officer James Moran, who was in the patrol car that took Lennon to Roosevelt Hospital, said the singer was semiconscious during the ride.

He said he asked the former Beatle if he were John Lennon and Lennon nodded, moaning.

At the hospital, a physician said Lennon was dead by the time he arrived, and efforts to resuscitate him were unsuccessful. He said there had been "a significant" loss of blood from the bullet wounds.

Palmer rode to the hospital in a squad car with Yoko Ono.

He said she was distraught and kept asking, "Tell me he's all right. . . ."

As the news spread, more than 1,000 Beatles fans gathered outside the Dakota, some of them listening to Beatles music on tape recorders.

One man walked up to the tall black iron gate that guards the impressive old building's front entrance. He placed a small bouquet of flowers between the bars and then stepped back into the crowd.

Some of the Beatles fans wept, others stood in disbelief asking each other if Lennon really was dead.

Lennon suffered seven gunshot wounds in his chest, left arm and back, "causing significant injury to major blood vessels in his chest (and) causing massive blood loss," according to Dr. Stephan Lynn, director of emergency room services at Roosevelt Hospital.

Musician, actor, songwriter, singer, author and businessman—John Lennon's 40 years of life were spent in what seemed to many a headlong revolt against and assault on the society and mores of the western world.

Yet he never accepted the role.

"I'M A HUMAN BEIN', MATE"

"I'm a human bein', mate," he said in an interview shortly after the much-publicized breakup of his first and most-successful creation—The Beatles—in 1970. "A human bein', don't never forget that. Anything else you say about me—well—it's beside the point, innit!"

The statement was accepted, studied, analyzed and finally filed with the several tons of other cryptic Lennonisms that, in their way, contributed to the mystique that surrounded the young Merseyside performer during all his adult years.

Lennon never explained. He said he had given up trying to do anything like that long before his Liverpool musical phenomenon achieved its first flash of recognition in the late 1950s.

"Make what you want of it," he said. "Anything. You will anyway, won't you. . . ."

MOP-HEADED SINGERS

Beatlemania—the near-craze that centered for more than a decade around the four mop-headed singers and instrumentalists—was a phenomenon transcending social class, age group, intellectual level or geographical location.

As acknowledged organizer-leader of the Beatles, Lennon had had a hand in writing most of the group's early musical efforts, was the author of two best-selling books of humorous verse and prose, was a prime mover in organizing their early films, such as "Hard Day's Night" and "Help!" and was credited with much of the story and dialogue for the cartoon hit, "Yellow Submarine."

But he was always ready to acknowledge that the specific style and impact of the group was a thing apart, something more than the sum of its parts or of any individual's input.

POSITIVE PHENOMENON

And in the end, even the Establishment it had caricatured and criticized came to regard the Beatles as a positive phenomenon. In 1965, all four Beatles were designated members of the Most Excellent Order of the British Empire.

"Right, mate," Lennon said. "Now to think up some real insults and we'll all be Graceful Dukes!"

John Lennon was born Oct. 9, 1940, in Liverpool, and his father, Alfred Lennon, deserted the family to seek the seafaring life when John was 3 years old.

The boy's mother, Julia Lennon (whose name later became the inspiration for one of the Beatles' most successful songs), died in an automobile accident before he was 14. However, before that, he had gone—by choice—to live with a favorite aunt, Mrs. Mary Smith.

Having shown some talent for painting while in secondary school, Lennon attended the Liverpool College of Art for two years.

But art never stood a chance compared to music, and in 1958, when he met Paul McCartney, the two young men helped each other in mastering the guitar and in developing personal musical techniques.

Billed as the Nurk Twins (a title borrowed from RAF slang), they began to offer occasional performances and, in the next year, were joined by another guitarist, George Harrison, and by drummer Pete Best. They called themselves first the Quarrymen Skiffle Group (name derived from John's old private school) and then as the Moondogs, later the Moonshiners.

Then, later, they became the Silver Beatles ("Never mind where that comes from; if you don't know, you don't want to know") and finally—perhaps, as manager Brian Epstein liked to explain, because of their four-four beat insistence—as The Beatles.

That name stuck, through experiments with washboard and banjo sounds, through cellar clubs in Liverpool and in Hamburg, Germany, where they briefly became a quintet, having been joined by bass guitarist Stuart Sutliffe (who later died of a brain ailment brought on by an injury during a mugging).

It was in Hamburg, where they frequently performed for as much as seven hours at a stretch, that they began to develop their style of easy clowning and ad-libbing —a public form they retained when they returned to Liverpool.

In October, 1961, Epstein, who ran a family record business not far from the club, received a request for a record called "My Bonnie," made by The Beatles as accompaniment for Tony Sheridan, a popular singer.

Epstein ordered 200 copies of the record, promptly sold them out and went looking for the group that had made it.

"Dead scruffy and untidy they were in those days," Epstein said. "But you could feel it, something happening when they worked, something exciting—this amazing communication with the audience, and this absolutely marvelous humor. Well, I knew they could be one of the biggest theater attractions in the world, didn't I? So what was I to do—let it pass by. . . ?"

Epstein became the Beatles' manager in January, 1962, and immediately made them shed their leather "Teddy Boy" gear and begin to dress in near-Edwardian style designed by Pierre Cardin; he had their long and shaggy hair trimmed into what was later described as "a kind of male pageboy" or "dishmop" and teamed them publicly with such name singers as Cliff Richards.

He got them bookings in nightclubs, cabarets, church halls, youth centers, ballrooms, theaters and, on Oct. 17, 1962, their first television appearance, on the British Grànada network.

He got them also a contract with Electrical and Musical Industries Ltd. (EMI), and their first hit, "Love Me Do" (written by Lennon and McCartney in an idle hour) sold 100,000 copies.

Meanwhile, the composition of the group had changed.

Pete Best had departed to be succeeded by Richard Starkey (also known as Ringo Starr).

"The rest," Epstein was fond of saying, "is musical history . . . ."

Their appearance at the London Palladium in October, 1963, established the Beatles' status as a British musical institution.

DIVORCED WIFE

"Part luck," Lennon said. "You know, there were no wars, no invasions, no state secrets opened up that particular day. The Beatles were the only good story the London comics had—so they played it up well. Luck. . . ."

Along the way, Lennon had a bobble: In 1962 he had married Cynthia Powell; they had one son, Julian. In 1968, they were divorced, and Lennon married Ono, by whom he had a son, Sean.

There were rumors of dissension within the group; stories of ego trips and business squabbles centering on the profits of the Beatles' own music-publishing firm, Apple Enterprises.

Epstein pooh-poohed the stories, managed to hold the four together for a few more successful and profitable years. And then Epstein—the Fifth Beatle—died.

And in 1970, it was all over.

The Beatles had played together for the last time.

Lennon, on his own now, wrote and recorded "The Dream Is Over" and said publicly he wanted the memory of the Beatles "off my back."

However, in an interview with Times writer Robert Hilburn two months ago, he admitted:

"I had made the physical break from The Beatles, but mentally there was still this big thing on my back about what people expected of me. It was like this invisible ghost. . . ."

Another song, "Woman Is Nigger of the World," in 1972 (which many radio stations refused to play because of its title) also was treated ironically by Lennon in the latest interview.

"I accepted intellectually what we were saying in the song," he said, "but I hadn't really accepted it in my heart."

And so, five years ago, the Lennons suddenly became, in Ono's words, "permanently unavailable" for press interviews.

Lennon learned to cook and care for his young son, and became, he said, "a house-husband in every sense."

This change, however, only gave added intensity to the rumors that it had been Ono who had been somehow responsible for the 1970 breakup of the group; for the suspicions that she interfered rather than helped in the recording studio.

Lennon also gave the lie to that in talking to Hilburn.

She had been, he said, an artistic catalyst for him—questioning, discussing and challenging. When they split up for 18 months during the early 70s (and Lennon reacted with a drunken "long weekend" in Los Angeles) he said one of his discoveries was that he needed her as much as he needed his music.

Despite their press-avoidance, the Lennons had not lived a reclusive life in their seventh-floor apartment at The Dakota for the five years since 1975.

He and the family had traveled to Japan and elsewhere; he went out regularly in New York. But he stayed away from music business and the communications media.

Then, abruptly, he began writing music again. Last summer, during a vacation with son Sean in Bermuda, he called Yoko and played her a tape he had made; she responded by writing reply songs of her own—to play them back to him a few days later.

In the end, the songs formed a man-woman dialogue and the Lennons went into a recording studio in August to record the album which they titled, "Double Fantasy," a 14-song LP released last month by Geffen Records.

The first song, released earlier, was titled "Starting Over."

The final note—the last ever—from John Lennon, came this month in an interview with Playboy Magazine writer David Sheff.

"The unknown," the interview concluded. "The unknown is what it is. And to be frightened of it is what sends everybody scurrying around chasing dreams, illusions, wars, peace, love, hate, all that—it's all illusion.

"Unknown is what it is.

"Accept that it's unknown and it's plain sailing. Everything is unknown—then you're ahead of the game. That's what it is.

"Right . . ."

Howie Evans / Joe Louis: American Folk Hero

Amsterdam News, April 18, 1981

One of the first black sportscasters to have a network radio sports show, Howie Evans was born in New York City, where he now serves as sports editor of the Amsterdam News. *A four-time varsity athlete at Maryland State, Evans coaches basketball at Fordham University and contributes regularly to numerous sports periodicals. He is currently writing a book about black athletes in America.*

The Amsterdam News, *with a circulation of more than 100,000, is a weekly newspaper directed to the black community of New York City.*

There was Daniel Boone, Davey Crockett, and Joe Louis. There was Jack Dempsey, Babe Ruth, and yes! Joe Louis. All American folk heroes. But no man has ever captured the imagination, adulation, and love of a nation, as did Joe Louis.

And now he's gone. But only in body. The spirit of Joe Louis will live forever. In his lifetime, the glory of his deeds refused to turn into ashes.

Instead they became a smouldering ember that refused to be extinguished. In the beginning, he was everything to a people that had almost forgotten how to hope.

And in the brightest moments of his being, he gave a race of people something to cherish . . . something that made him a son of every Black family in the world.

Towards the twilight years of his life, his star only grew brighter as the legend grew stronger. His was a name that didn't die as the war years of the 40's tore families apart around the world. For the record, Louis never attempted to duck his responsibilities as a citizen of this nation. The records do reveal that a very famous champ, prior to Louis, did just that in the first World War.

The 50's rushed by with a startling quickness. Almost as quick as Joe's famed, left jab. And still the man who knew no other trade than that of a pugilist, continued to expose his aging body to the fists of the "Young Turks" of his day. Joe needed money and he knew of no other way to earn it.

The 60's were a period of social turmoil, and through it all, the calm wisdom of Joe Louis acted as a buffer for the more aggressive social and political-minded reformers. A young man out of Louisville, Kentucky, took the world by storm, but never completely winning over the loyal segment of Joe Louis fans.

Joe was an American folk hero and sportswriters, fans, and other fighters constantly reminded the young man that there would always be only one Joe Louis.

With the coming of the 70's the once magnificent body that destroyed opponents with a flick of his left wrist, or a jaw-shattering right that traveled a mere six inches, began to come apart.

His life became a revolving series of traumatic episodes. But still he refused to surrender to the many ailments that ravaged his body. In his final years, Joe Louis married a wheelchair.

It was not a sight for the soft at heart. The once proud and powerful Joe Louis was confined to his second wife—an old rolling chair that he disliked so much.

Where once his mighty legs would carry him to and fro, he became dependent upon a woman who was an extension of his own life. Her strength and her faith transcended miraculously into his blood. And it was because of Martha Louis that Joe Louis was able to buy some extra time.

But life is like a clock. And in time, all clocks wind down to a final tick. Joe Louis lived every tick of his life. There were no regrets, no bitterness. And other than the countless dollars he advanced to friends and families, the monies he gave away to total strangers, Joe only wished he could have been counted out on his feet.

Around this nation, thousands upon thousands of Black children bear his name. There is a first cousin by blood of a sportswriter who bears the name . . . Joe Louis McLucas.

Certainly he must feel as if a small part of him has left his own body. His feelings are shared by all the others. There are not many man-made structures in this world that would seat all Joe Louis' in this world.

It was like that with another American folk hero. They called him Martin Luther King, Jr. There are schools, recreation centers, and for sure, thousands of Black children bearing Martin's name.

In Detroit, there is the Joe Louis Arena, once known as Cobo Arena. Who was Cobo is a question that millions of Black children around the world will never know. But as they burp their way into adulthood, the name of Joe Louis will live forever on their lips. It's that way when you become an American folk hero. Rest in peace champ.

William Blundell / The Life of the Cowboy: Drudgery and Danger

Wall Street Journal, June 10, 1981

William Blundell travels throughout the western United States reporting on commercial ventures, natural resources, and memorable people for the Wall Street Journal. *Born in New York, Blundell earned a degree from Syracuse University in 1956 before doing graduate work in journalism at the University of Kansas. During more than twenty-five years with the* Wall Street Journal, *Blundell has served as a reporter in Dallas, Los Angeles, and New York as well as page one rewrite editor and bureau chief in Los Angeles. His book-length publications include* The Innovators *and* Swindlers.

"I am in the business of introducing Americans to each other because we take each other disgracefully for granted and yet we depend on each other in an urban society to a degree that is breathtaking." Blundell's preparation for introducing his readers to "how a real cowboy [Jim Miller] lives and works in an age of cowboy hype" included "a week or more just finding the guy that I felt might be satisfactory. . . . I want an older man because I want to hear some stories. . . . I want a guy who's good because I want to show how things ought to be done. And I want a guy from traditional cattle country so I can bring in some of the flavor of the surrounding area."

Blundell's principal concern as a journalist is effective storytelling. "When I'm talking about storytelling," he explains, "I'm talking about building the dimension of time into your story. You look at the past and you also anticipate the future. You don't just deal with the present. You go for different viewpoints. . . . You always go to the action. Get down to the lowest level of where the important things in the story are happening and you detail those. You don't have other people tell us what is happening; you show them what is happening."

Blundell's advice to aspiring journalists includes some pointed remarks about the importance of firsthand experience: "One thing I am death on is the constant citation of experts which is very easy for reporters to fall into. To my way of thinking, there is no such thing as a cowboy expert. The only cowboy expert is the cowboy. And the only way you can find out and appreciate what his life is like is to work with him, and to go out with him and to be there, just hanging around. I am a tremendous believer in hanging around."

RAFTER ELEVEN RANCH, Ariz.—The lariat whirls as the man on horseback separates a calf from the herd. Suddenly, the loop snakes around the calf's rear legs and tightens. Wrapping a turn of rope around the saddle horn, the rider drags the hapless animal to his crew.

The flanker whips the calf onto its back, and the medicine man inoculates the animal. Amid blood, dust and bawling, the calf is dehorned with a coring tool, branded in an acrid cloud of smoke from burning hair and flesh, earmarked with a penknife in the ranch's unique pattern (cowboys pay more attention to earmarks in identifying cattle than to brands) and castrated. It is all over in one minute.

Jim Miller, the man in the saddle, smiles broadly as the released calf scampers back to his mother. Mr. Miller is 64 years old. Born and raised nearby, he has been working cows in Yavapai County since he was five. He will keep on until he can't throw a leg over a horse anymore. "It's all I know and I like it," he says.

The marks of his trade are stamped into his body: broken legs, a broken ankle, dislocated shoulder and elbow, a thigh torn open by a broken saddle horn. The fingers of the right hand are grotesquely broken, and he can't flex them fully. It is the roper's trademark, the digits that have been caught in the rope and crushed against the saddle horn, but Mr. Miller still wins roping competitions with that hand.

Jim Miller is a cowboy. There are still many cowboys in the West. Some wear black hats with fancy feather bands; they tear around in oversize pickups with a six-pack of Coors on the seat. These are small-town cowboys. They don't know anything about cows, and the only horses they know are under the hood.

Others become cowboys at sunset, shucking briefcases and threepiece suits for designer jeans, lizard-skin boots and silver buckles as big as headlights. Then they go to Western nightclubs to see what everyone else is wearing. They are urban cowboys, and the only bulls they know are mechanical ones.

Finally, there is a little band of men like Jim Miller. Their boots are old and cracked. They still know as second nature the ways of horse and cow, the look of sunrise over empty land—and the hazards, sheer drudgery and rock-bottom pay that go with perhaps the most overromanticized of American jobs. There are very few of these men left. "Most of the real cowboys I know," says Mr. Miller, "have been dead for a while."

HYPE AND ILLUSION

A big man with a ready laugh, he is both amused and exasperated by all the cowboy hype. "It almost makes you ashamed to be one," he says. "You've got doctors and lawyers and storekeepers runnin' around in big hats and boots." None, he intimates, would want to step into a real cowboy's place today; their image of the life is an illusion.

The typical ranch hand in this traditional cattle county, he says, is in his late teens or early 20s—so green he often doesn't know how to shoe his own horse—and must do all sorts of menial chores. Nobody can now afford the "horseback men," aristocrats of the saddle who spurned all ranch work that they couldn't do from the top of a horse except branding. Most hands are local boys who commute to work from nearby towns, as does Mr. Miller himself. With few exceptions, the bunkhouses full of "bedroll cowboys," wanderers from ranch to ranch over the West, are no more.

Some things haven't changed, though. Punching cows, says Mr. Miller, "is still the lowest-paid job for what you have to know and do." In the '30s in Yavapai County, cowboys made $45 a month plus bed and board. The standard wage now is around $500 a month without bed and board. There is Social Security and the usual state coverage for job-related injuries, but there are no pension plans, cost-of-living adjustments, medical and life-insurance packages, or anything else.

Mr. Miller is one of the elite. His salary from Fain Land & Cattle Co., the family concern that operates the ranch, is $1,150 a month, but that is because he is the cowboss. The cowboss is the master sergeant of the ranch; he leads by example, works along with his men, and is in charge of day-to-day cattle operations. At various times the cowboss, or any other top hand, has to be a geneticist, accountant, blacksmith, cook, botanist, carpenter, tinsmith, surgeon, psychologist, mechanic, nurse and a few other things beside rider and roper. "There just isn't any point in a young fellow learnin' to be a top hand when he can make so much more today doin' practically anything else," the cowboss says sadly.

Then why do some still follow the life?

* * *

It is early morning on Mr. Miller's domain, more than 50,000 acres of rolling semi-arid dun hills and mountain slopes. The cowboss and two full-time hands work this country by themselves. They are going today to 7,800-foot Mingus Mountain to collect strays missed in the recent spring roundup. Mr. Miller surveys the land critically. Here and there the grama grass is greening up, but good summer rains will be needed to get the range in condition.

There is absolutely nothing that the cowboss can do about it except pray. The land is just too big. In almost every other occupation, man seals himself off from nature in factory or office tower, struggles to bend a little patch of it to his will, or tries to wrest away its riches by force. But the cowboy knows he is only a speck on the vast plain, his works insignificant, his power to really control the land almost nil; nature herself is the only manager of the Rafter Eleven or any other ranch. So the cowboy learns to bow humbly before the perils and setbacks she brings, and to truly appreciate her gifts.

A big buck antelope squirms under a fence and springs over the plain, hoofs drumming powerfully. "Now that's one fine sight," murmurs a cowboy.

The party is not sauntering colorfully over the hills on horseback. It is bouncing over them in a pickup. The cow ponies are riding comfortably behind in a special trailer; they, too, commute to work now. Though he grew up in the days of chuckwagons, line camps, bunkhouses and the great unfenced ranges, Mr. Miller is a strong believer in modern methods. He uses an electric branding iron because it is faster, and he will even use a trailer to take small groups of cattle from place to place on the ranch rather than drive them on foot. One pound sweated off a steer costs the ranch about 67 cents.

But he and every other experienced cowman draw the line at replacing the horse. There is a strange chemistry between horse and cow, a gentling effect, that he declares irreplaceable. "Some dummies around here tried motorcycles once. Didn't work worth a damn," snorts the cowboss. No machine, he adds, can ever duplicate the instincts and balletic ability of a fine cutting horse dancing into a herd to separate steer from heifer.

At Mingus Mountain the horses go to work. There is no glamorous dashing about on the plain, only a laborious, slow plod up a mountain canyon that is rocky, steep-sided, clogged with brush. Jagged tree branches jab at the riders. It is grueling, hazardous work, but a nice piece of high country is a valuable asset to any ranch here. In winter it is actually warmer for the cattle because the cold air settles in the valley below, and the nutritious scrub oak and other bushes are available year-round and grow above snow.

In the high clearing fringed by oak, juniper and pine, 18-year-old Troy Tomerlin pauses awhile, chewing on a twig, to consider his future. He can operate a backhoe and could make almost twice as much doing that as the $500 a month he gets now. "But I don't know how I'd like diggin' septic tanks day after day," he says. "Here I can see animals, work with animals, move around a lot of country. In an office you can't see nothin' but a desk, and I don't like people lookin' over my shoulder. Jim tells us what to do, and how you do it is up to you. I like that."

Suddenly, dark clouds begin to boil up over the mountain. Last week the cowboys were pelted by hail the size of golf balls, but that is just part of the job. Lightning, however, is much feared by any mounted man caught on the open plain, and many cowboys have been killed by it. Last summer a bolt barely missed Troy and knocked him unconscious. Other cowboys have been killed or crippled when their horses fell on them and leaped back up to gallop in panic with the rider entangled in rope or stirrup. "I've had three real good friends dragged to death that way," Mr. Miller says softly.

LARIATS USED SPARINGLY

The clouds pass over harmlessly and 18 head coaxed out of the rocks and brush are driven toward the plain. Tommy Stuart, a fine rider with rodeo experience, crashes through brush again and again to divert straying animals. The men cry out to the cattle in a strangely musical series of yips, calls and growls. Tommy has to rope a balky calf, the only time anyone uses his lariat; the cowboy who does so frequently doesn't know how to drive cattle, Mr. Miller says.

The trick, he says, is to watch the way their ears are pointing and so anticipate their direction. Mr. Miller also rests cattle frequently on drives to let cows and calves "mother up" so they're more easily driven, or to calm trotty (nervous) animals. "If you don't rest them," he says, "they'll start to run, they'll get hot, then they'll get mad. Then there's no turning them. You've got to keep your cattle cool."

The fall weaning is a particularly sensitive time. Separated from their mothers until the maternal bond is broken, the calves, now sizable, are under stress that can cause pneumonia. When the animals finish days of bawling and finally lie down, the sound of a car, a dog's bark, even the cry of a night bird, may set them back on their feet and running in stampede, mowing down fences, crushing each other in the pileup of bodies. This happened to Mr. Miller twice when he was cowboss on the big Yolo ranch.

Nothing untoward happens on this drive, and the riders finally reach the plain. No chuck wagon rolls up with a bewhiskered Gabby Hayes type ready to ladle out son-of-a-bitch stew—classically, a concoction of cow brains, tongues, hearts, livers and marrow, with a handful of onions thrown in to conceal the taste. Instead everyone rumbles back to the ranch house and the cowboss himself fixes lunch for his men: steaks, beans, bread smothered in gravy, and mayonnaise jars full of iced tea.

HOW TO GET FIRED

By tradition, the cowboss looks out for his cowboys and hires and fires them himself. Besides incompetence, two things will get you fired by Jim Miller: abuse of horses and bellyaching. The latter is a breach of a cowboy code still in force. For $500 a month, the ranch expects and almost always gets total and uncomplaining loyalty to the outfit. Unionism is an utterly alien concept to cowboys; if a man doesn't like his boss, his job or anything else, he quits on the spot.

Firing is as simple. There are no hagglings over severance pay, no worries about employee lawsuits. "I just tell them, 'This is it,' and they go," says Mr. Miller.

Once, when a cowboss needed good hands, he would just drop in at the Palace Bar on Whisky Row in Prescott. This was the hiring hall and water hole, full of men who had been on the range for months and were "getting drunker'n seven hundred dollars," as Mr. Miller puts it. He doesn't go there anymore. "Now it's full of hippies and such as that, people who don't know a horse from a cow," he says. Instead, cowboys call him at home when they need work.

Lunch is over, and the men get off their rumpsprung old chairs and go out to nurse a young heifer internally damaged when calving. If they don't get her up to walk she will die.

* * *

At the offices of the Rafter Eleven, Bill Fain has been told by his computer that the cattle he soon will sell will have cost about 68 cents a pound to raise and fatten. He expects to get 67 cents for them. That's the cattle business today, says Mr. Fain, vice president of Fain Land & Cattle and the third generation of his family on this ranch. And such thin margins make men like Jim Miller particularly important.

The cowboss is considered one of the canniest judges of livestock in the area, and buys the registered bulls and replacement heifers for the ranch. It is he, more than anyone else, who maintains the quality of the herd. He coaxes an 80 percent calf crop out of the 700 mother cows here, a good ratio. He does not overburden the land, letting it rest and renew.

"Our product isn't cattle. It's grass," says Mr. Fain, "and Jimmy knows that. A lot of people can rope and ride and love the life, but there are damned few left who can do all the things he does."

Outside, cars whiz by on the road that crosses what used to be called Lonesome Valley. Some 6,000 people live there now because the Fains, trying to diversify out of an increasingly risky reliance on cattle, sold a piece of the ranch to a developer who built a town on it. The Fains developed another piece themselves.

This has made the cowboy's job harder. Cattle have been shot and cut up on the spot with chain saws by shade-tree butchers who throw the pieces in the back of a pickup and drive off, leaving head and entrails. People tear down cattle feeders for firewood, shoot holes in water tanks, breach fences to maliciously run down calves. "People and cattle don't mix," concedes Mr. Fain. "It's a sick thing," says Jim Miller, and there is icy anger in his blue eyes.

Meanwhile, the old family ranches are being sold, most of them to investors who don't know one end of a Hereford from the other and are more interested in tax shelter than running a good spread. This has driven ranchland prices so high that a young man who really wants to raise beef either can't afford to buy or has no hope of getting a return on his investment. "I really can't see much future in the cattle business," Mr. Miller says.

COUGARS AND GRASSHOPPERS

Perhaps not. But around Yavapai County the cycle of ranch life continues unchanged on the surviving family spreads. In Peeples Valley, cougars have taken 15 calves this year and lion hunter George Goswick is tracking them through the Weaver Mountains. In the pastures, mares are heavy with foals; in time, some will find their way into the gentling hands of Twister Heller, the horse breaker. On the Hays ranch, owner John Hays is stabbing a wild-eyed Hereford bull in the rump with a needle full of antibiotics and fretting about the grasshoppers that are all over the property. There is too much ranch and too many hoppers, so he must simply accept them.

At evening, Jim Miller comes home to a house and five rural acres with horse corral outside Prescott. He and his wife, Joan, have lived here 10 years; for the first 27 years of their marriage they lived on the local ranches he worked, raising four sons and two daughters, teaching all to rope and ride. None has followed in his footsteps because there isn't any money in it.

Next year, when he's 65, Mr. Miller plans to quit as cowboss at the Rafter Eleven and start collecting Social Security. But he says he will never stop working. Few men around here who have spent their lives on a horse seem able to get off. Jim's friend Tom Rigden still rides roundup and castrates calves on his ranch, though he has been blind for almost eight years.

Mr. Miller doesn't expect any trouble finding day jobs on ranches. At a time when there are so few real cowboys left, he says, there is always work for a top hand.

DISCUSSION QUESTIONS

1. William Blundell reports that he uses a six-point outline when preparing his reports for the *Wall Street Journal:* "A few of these things are of interest, and others may not be, but I always consider all six of them. (1) I deal with history. (2) I deal with scope, what I am talking about. (3) I deal with the central rea-

sons behind what is going on, political, economic, and social. (4) I deal with impacts, who's helped or hurt by this, and to what extent, and what's their emotional response to it. (5) I deal with the gathering and action of *contrary forces*. If this is going on, is somebody trying to do anything about it, and how is that working out? (6) And at the very end I will deal with the future. If this stuff keeps up, what are things going to look like five or ten years from now, in the eyes of the people who are directly involved?'' Reread ''The Life of the Cowboy'' carefully and apply Blundell's six-point outline to his profile of Jim Miller. In what specific ways does Blundell succeed at meeting the expectations of his outline in this report?

2. Consider Blundell's use of the active and passive voices in his story. Which does he use to begin his story? With what effect? When does he shift? What effect does that have? Blundell talks about the importance of structuring time in his stories. Reread his profile carefully and note when he focuses on the past, present, and future. Comment on the effectiveness of this structural device in his story. When—and with what effect—does he write in the present tense?

3. What are the conventional American stereotypes of the life of a cowboy? What are the origins of these images? How does Blundell respond to these stereotypes? Compare and contrast Blundell's treatment of such stereotypes with that of Peter Homans in ''The Western: The Legend and the Cardboard Hero'' (''Magazines''). In what ways do their analyses of the American cowboy agree? Differ?

Rushworth Kidder / On Keeping an Open Mind
Christian Science Monitor, April 7, 1982

After earning an undergraduate degree from Amherst College in 1965 and a Ph.D. from Cornell University, Rushworth Kidder began a career as a teacher and literary critic. In 1979, after ten years as an associate professor of English at Wichita State University (where he completed scholarly studies of Dylan Thomas and E. E. Cummings), Kidder abandoned his academic appointment and joined the Christian Science Monitor, *for which he has since written scores of news reports, columns, and essays. More recently, he has served as the paper's London correspondent and has traveled in and written about Central America. In the essay reprinted here, Kidder speculates about the literal and metaphysical importance of doors. He explains:*

> *I have a fairly good idea why I wrote 'On Keeping an Open Mind'; but I can't for the life of me say how long it took to compose it. All my life, I suppose—although, in the end, I spent about three hours writing. It grew out of a conversation with my wife about the door- lessness of present-day houses. . . . What it needed, clearly, was a range of solid detail upon which to anchor its more metaphysical meaning—without which it would sink into an abyss of laborious phi- losophizing which makes frightfully difficult reading. . . . Obviously, the source of detail would be the doors themselves—solid, describable things, and commonplace enough. The strategy, too, was fairly evi- dent: lest the readers doze over heavy abstractions in the opening paragraphs (and drift away into other, more lively prose), best sneak up on the main point. It's a technique I use frequently in essays, though rarely in straight journalism: Come in sideways (the opening*

sentences about the differences between my wife and me), straighten out into the ostensible topic (doors), and then, having gathered speed across that runway of detail, lift off into a discussion of its significance.

Kidder also notes that he can "never plan the lift-off. . . . That's what makes writing a process of discovery. . . . If I thought that the central part of my writing were simply the recording of ideas I had been responsible for dreaming up, I would be terrified of failure—or bored beyond words. But I've watched too many essays happen to think that. One doesn't sit down to write out what's already been thought up. One writes to open up thought."

We have few differences, my wife and I. To be sure, she pronounces the *i* in *neither* and leans toward orange instead of grapefruit juice. But we agree on most things except a certain matter of domestic architecture. For she loves modern houses and I love doors. And between the two, it seems, there is a great gulf fixed.

Contemporary architects, I have noticed, don't much care for doors. They only seem to use them where nothing else will do—at entrances, for example, or on bathrooms. So the modern house, like the American plains in the days of the bison, is a thing of great undivided spaces. The open reaches sweep from kitchen into dining area, roll on unbroken into the living room, and cascade over a step or two into the family room. Between kitchen and dining area, for example, lies a distinction as blurred as that between late winter and early spring. Standing in the midst of either, one knows it to be different from the other; but one is never just sure where the boundary is.

So at the risk of sounding positively Cenozoic in my fondness for times past, let me argue the case for doors. First, I suppose, I must explain that I grew up in a house full of them. Our kitchen alone had nine—all solidly built paneled affairs with sturdy porcelain knobs. My respect for them dates from the day our cleaning lady washed the kitchen floor at snack time and then departed. Undaunted, I mounted the hall door, feet on the knobs and hands grasping the top, and swung myself into the kitchen to the counter. Then I stepped across the stove, swung across on the broom closet door to the pantry, and availed myself of several fig newtons— with not a single toe print on her still-wet floor. The old doors, fastened like Excalibur into the rock of their spruce frames, never so much as sighed.

It was in that same kitchen that we performed a ritual twice a year. Every fall, as the north wind whistled around the back porch, we put up the black wooden storm door. And each spring the screen door reappeared. It generally had some repairs pending: for our dog, a hybrid hound whose exuberance exceeded his patience, fancied it a mere mirage. On summer days, seized by the sound of a foreign cat outside, he would boil out from under the table and rip through the doorway—whereupon the screen door would fly back in amazement with a great twanging of its spring, to slam shut again well behind his tail. Nor was his return trip any challenge. The wooden crosspieces were on the outside of the door; he would grab the one below the handle in his teeth, pull open the door until he could stick in a paw, and then flip back the door enough to wriggle through. He may have been silly but he wasn't stupid.

His partner at the water dish was a cat many years his senior, glossy and black with gold markings, like an old piano. By a kind of regal self-assurance and some very sharp claws, she had early squelched his penchant for insurrection. She was, in fact, master of the house, so much so that she called forth what may have been my finest childhood invention.

The problem she and I faced was her restlessness. I kept my bedroom door shut against the hall light and she loved to sleep at the foot of my bed. But just as I was sliding toward sleep, she would decide to go elsewhere. Moreover, she was the one with patience: she would set the timer of her meower every seven seconds and let it go off with devilish regularity until I lumbered to the door. One night amid such tumbling the invention hit me: an electric door opener. Finding a solenoid from a discarded washing machine, I fastened it to a kind of lever on the inside doorknob, and wired it back to a doorbell button beside my bed. The solenoid would yank down the lever and release the latch, whereupon a rubber band, fastened between door and baseboard, would swing the door slowly open. It worked fine, with only a couple of problems. One was the noise: for the solenoid, made to jerk great greasy washing machine gears into place, was overqualified for the job. More than once it terrified family members who, tapping like Poe's raven at my chamber door, were greeted with a great blast of buzzing magnets and crashing metal, followed by silence and the slow, mysterious opening of the door. The other problem, of course, was that the operation was irreversible. Having triumphantly let the cat out, I always had to get up to shut the door again.

I guess, in some ways, I've been shutting doors ever since. For I have great respect for them. In old New England houses they had a purpose: they kept the heat, always a scarce commodity, just where it was wanted. Only with the advent of central heating did people begin taking them down and storing them in barns—to be rediscovered by the children of a more fuel-conscious age.

But if doors had a purpose, they also had a fringe benefit. They produced privacy, quietness, the solitude that breeds deep thought. I realize that it cannot quite be proved that the tradition of academic excellence in New England is directly a function of the region's number of doors. In fact, however, few scholars could survive a doorless existence. The ability to close off the intrusive and the distracting—to shut out all the bustle of the senses—is the first prerequisite to deep thought.

Or so I used to think. Recently, however, I have felt a change coming on. Maybe it stems from my job: my desk now sits in the middle of a newsroom, surrounded by phones and conversations. The people I most admire know how to write in the midst of 50 different noises, all of them intriguing. They have taught me a great lesson: that there are ways, if the physical door is lacking, to shut the mental door.

I'm not a master of that discipline. I still find within myself too much of the dog, bolting after every cat that passes on the far side of the screen door of my mind. But I have at least seen the promise—that concentration is a habit of thought and not an accident of place, and that a warm and open sociableness brings as much benefit as a cloistered solitude.

I'm not about to shift my pronunciation of *neither*. But I'm getting more interested in modern houses.

DISCUSSION QUESTIONS

1. Outline the structure of Rushworth Kidder's essay. Into what large units does he organize it? Comment on the effectiveness of his use of transitions to connect the different parts of his essay.

2. When asked to account for the origins of his essays, Kidder explained: ''A lot of my essays go back to childhood and pick up examples from the past. Quite often they will start with a paradox, some kind of contradiction that strikes me as odd, that I would like to resolve.'' Apply Kidder's explanation to

the beginning of "On Keeping an Open Mind." In what specific ways does this statement seem to apply to his essay?

3. How would you describe the sound of the speaker's voice in this essay? Point to specific words and phrases to verify your conclusion. Given Kidder's diction and phrasing, who do you imagine would be the primary audience for this essay?

4. Consider Kidder's use of simile and metaphor. Comment on the effects of such phrases as "The old doors, fastened like Excalibur into the rock of their spruce frames . . ." and "tapping like Poe's raven at my chamber door." What does Kidder's use of metaphor contribute to the overall effect of his essay?

Manuela Hoelterhoff / Walt's Wonderful World Turns Out to Be Flat   *Wall Street Journal*, July 2, 1982

Born in Hamburg, West Germany, in 1948, Manuela Hoelterhoff served as editor in chief of Art & Auction *magazine and is currently the arts editor for the* Wall Street Journal. *She has published articles and essays for* Art Forum, Art News, Dial, *and* Horizon *and was awarded the 1982 Pulitzer Prize for criticism. Employing a lively and provocative style, Hoelterhoff writes on a broad range of subjects, including opera, architecture, television, and travel. "Walt's Wonderful World Turns Out to Be Flat," which appeared in the Leisure and the Arts section of the* Wall Street Journal, *reveals one critic's less than enchanted musings on the Magic Kingdom.*

The Wall Street Journal, *the most prestigious business and financial newspaper in the world, was started by an enterprising young stock-market reporter, Charles H. Dow, in 1889. Over the years, the paper has enlarged its concept of business news to include a daily quotient of social and cultural phenomena, sometimes only peripherally related to the American economy.*

DISNEY WORLD, FLA.—Another happy, sunny day. I am having breakfast on Main Street, USA, the long shoplined street that leads to Cinderella's Castle—the heart of Walt Disney World's Magic Kingdom. Music fills the air. Friendly birds pick crumbs off the restaurant's balustrade. And here's a gaily decked out pony pulling smiling visitors in a festooned wagon.

By day's end, about 35,000 adults and children (adults outnumber kids four to one) will have strolled up Main Street. By year's end, the admirers of Donald, Dumbo, Mickey and Pluto are expected to reach 13.2 million, making Disney World even more popular than the older Disneyland in Anaheim, Calif. Since Disney World opened ten-and-a-half years ago, it has clocked over 131 million visitors. In fact, my travel guide says this is the most popular vacation spot on this planet. That is why I came here and why I am wearing this attractive hat. As the large 36-year-old child who accompanied me said: "Opera isn't everything, kid. You got to learn about America and talk to the people."

Over there at an adjacent table is a middle-aged couple forking in pancakes. His shortsleeved shirt reveals a tattoo; her print slack ensemble is as happily colored as a flower bed. We chat about their trip and she tells me that he is a construction worker and she a bookkeeper. They are celebrating their 25th anniversary here in

Disney. Good choice? I ask. "Oh, God, yes," she says. "We're so amazed. It's better, it's more than we imagined. Everything is so clean." They were hoping to spend their next vacation here.

Their satisfaction was echoed in varying decibel levels by virtually everyone I spoke to during my four-day stay. "We wouldn't change anything," said a retired couple from Mississippi. "I've been here 11 times; it's an uplifting place," said a young lawyer from Ohio. And a Vermont-based doctor and his wife sang a duet of praise of which one stanza focused on the place's cheerfulness and another on its efficiency.

This joyous ensemble of voices is offered for reasons of balance. I did not have a great time, I ate food no self-respecting mouse would eat, stayed in a hotel that could have been designed by the Moscow corps of engineers and suffered through entertainment by smiling, uniformed young people who looked like they had their hair arranged at a lobotomy clinic. Somehow the plastic heart of Disney didn't beat for me.

Still, I have to give Walt credit for standing in the swamplands surrounding Orlando and envisioning a drained, jillion-dollar amusement/vacation spot presided over by a castle and courtly mouse. Walt's world is simply immense. You need to be Peter Pan to cover its 27,400 acres. As our guide kept telling us: Disney World is much, much more than just the Magic Kingdom with its rides, attractions and restaurants. It's hotels, golf courses, a heap of shops and such other components of the perfect vacation as horsebackriding, boating and swimming. The entire fiefdom is laced together by a battalion of buses and a monorail that zooms above your head and right through the Contemporary Resort Hotel (my happy home).

Anyway, you're thinking, this all sounds neat enough, nobody promised you Paris, poisonous food is at every streetcorner, so what if people smile a lot and what really is your problem, you Fair Isle-sweater-wearing snob? Well, let me offer some highlights of Disney and its parameters, and if it seems really good and you act quickly, you can probably still book a room in the Contemporary sometime next year. The waiting list here is longer than at the George V in Paris.

The Magic Kingdom is divided into various areas bearing such names as Tomorrowland, Adventureland and Frontierland. In Adventureland we stop at an attraction called the Enchanted Tiki Birds, which has a long line of mostly adults waiting to get into "the sunshine pavilion." While we wait, two robot (or, in Disney jargon, AudioAnimatronic) parrots entertain us with a story that starts "many birdbaths ago." One of the many sunny young folks who keep things running smoothly in the kingdom pops out dressed in a disgusting orange outfit. "Aloha!" he shouts. The people stare at him. "I said, 'Aloha,' " he yells smiling madly. "Aloha!" the audience shouts back, making up in volume what it had lacked in spontaneity. "Everyone raise his arm and wave goodbye!" he commands. And everyone raises his arm and waves goodbye.

Any minute, we figured, he's going to have them saluting and clicking their sandals.

We decided to break ranks and headed for Tomorrowland, where we bobbed about in the air sitting in something called sky jets and had some lunch at the Space Port shop. So many choices. We picked Splashdown Peach Punch over a Cosmic Cooler and settled for a Satellite sandwich. In Disney, language lovers will quickly note, Mickey Mouse and Donald Duck worked wonders with alliteration and little rhymes, though it must be said that Walt was no Whitman.

Fortified, we took in a short movie introducing EPCOT (the acronym for Experimental Prototype Community of Tomorrow), a new 600-acre attraction scheduled to open this fall. "Relax and enjoy," says the smooth-voiced narrator as a tenorino begins to croon: "Dreams of the future, lalala, the world belongs to the dreamer, the dreamer inside you.'' The future apparently includes homes that look like aquariums and people cavorting with dolphins dressed up in pretty outfits. The level of the narration is such that it could be understood by an Audio-Animatronic audience.

In contrast, there is nothing futuristic or fantastical about the next stop, our hotel, except for that monorail speeding through its innards. That was a terrific design idea. And when the hotel opened, the decor had other 21st century touches. But visitors apparently felt uncomfortable with the unfamiliar and the rooms were redecorated. As I dial to a religious program on the TV, I sit on a purple-green bedspread surrounded by swimming-pool-blue plastic furniture, enormous lamps with tumor-like bases and textured green and beige walls. I look out over a parking lot and carefully planted vegetation that is pure Middle America—boring trees and dinky little flowers. I may be in tropical Florida, but there isn't a palm tree in sight. The beach behind the parking lot is as dully laid out as the golf course.

Once outside the fun and games of the Magic Kingdom, the rest of Disney World looks like a condo village. Which is a large part, I would argue, of its attraction. Many Americans spend most of their life preparing for a retirement community and Disney provides a good prelude with its own security force and hassle-free, clean living. Unlike in Europe, you don't have to deal with funny languages, funny-colored money or funny food. And there's no garbage. Never. The smallest scrap of litter is instantly sucked underground, and rushed via pipes to the most fabulous compactor in the universe. The place is obsessively antiseptic. When the Disney characters dance and ride up Main Street in the parade scheduled for every afternoon, a special squad equipped with scoopers follows the ponies.

There's nothing left to chance here, nothing at all. The instant you arrive, you are watched over and taken care of. This place has crowd control down to a science. Mazes set up in front of the popular attractions like ''20,000 Leagues Under the Sea,'' which features plastic-looking, half-submerged submarines paddling past plastic monsters, keep the people-flow smooth and constant. Even though it took us 30 minutes to meet the mermaid, we had the impression our sub was just around the corner. The only time I saw the system break down was in front of the Haunted Mansion. ''Disney World is your land'' as the song frequently heard hereabouts goes. But not if you're fat. One unhappy girl got stuck in the turnstile and had to be pushed back out. Like Cinderella's step-sisters, no matter how hard she tried, she just wouldn't fit.

Evenings, too, were crammed with events. One night we dined at the Papeete Bay Verandah restaurant in the Polynesian Village hotel, *the* place if you aren't at the Contemporary. An overamplified and oversimplified combo entertained us as we sipped a Chi-Chi, particularly popular, the menu points out, in Pago Pago, and stared at prawns blown up with breading to look like chicken legs.

But the unquestioned highlight was the Hoop-Dee-Doo Revue at Pioneer Hall in the camping area. ''Enthusiastic performers sing, dance and joke up a storm until your mouth is as sore from laughing as your stomach is from ingesting all the food,'' promises my guide book. I couldn't have said it better. As we sat down, the hearty sextet appeared singing ''Hoop-dee-doo, hoop-dee-doo.'' Then they beat pans and washboards and established friendly rapport with the eating audience. With Robert, for instance, of Virile Beach (could have been Floral Beach, those washboards get noisy). And Chris. Let's hear it for Chris from Daytona Beach! He's 29 today! Let's hear it for Chris! People waved their napkins in Chris's direction. ''Hoop-dee-doo'' sang the ensemble, jumping up and down.

Our meal—greasy ribs and chicken—arrived in little buckets. When we were done staring again, the hearty sextet reappeared and rubbed their bellies as they sang: ''Mom's in the kitchen fixing up a special dessert just for *you*.'' Out came globs of possibly strawberry shortcake and then more jokes like ''You got a wooden head; that's better than a cedar chest. Think about that for a while.'' Everybody did and whooped and hollered.

Was nothing nice in Disney? Oh, all right. We had a scary time on the roller coaster ride through darkness on Space Mountain; I always enjoy carousels and Disney has one with handsome horses. And I had a fine meal at the Empress Room aboard a riverboat anchored by the shopping complex, probably the only restaurant on the premises that doesn't microwave toast.

The next day, we left Disney World for Cypress Gardens, one of the many attractions beckoning in the Orlando area and bearing names like Sea World, Wet 'n Wild, Gatorland, Circus World, Monkey Jungle. And so on. The landscape is flat and straggled-out. The big thing seems to be gas stations with restaurants attached, chicken salad bars and shacks selling hot boiled peanuts. ''Yahoo,'' says my pal. ''Wouldn't mind trying a bag of them hot boiled peanuts.'' We buy a bag. They are soggy and awful. Our proximity to Cypress Gardens is periodically announced by signs for 12 million flowers and the chief attraction, dramatic ducks. (You're in Luck; A Banjo-Playing Duck.)

The gardens are much, much more than just a botanical garden. A water ski show is going on in the stadium. ''He hit a wet spot!'' exclaims the announcer as a performer disappears into the water. The audience jeers. A child in a carriage leans over and dribbles on my foot. ''I wish you'd stop calling America a land of morons,'' says my friend. ''It's not fitting for a foreigner.'' We pass 12 million flowers and don't miss a one, thanks to helpful signs like: ''Look up! Don't miss the orchid.'' Look has little eyes painted into the o's. ''Don't miss the scenic waterfall coming up on your right,'' warns another sign. ''Have you forgotten to load your camera?'' wonders a third. ''Is America turning into a land of morons?'' wonders my companion.

We are too early for the gator show (watch them make pocketbooks right in front of your eyes?). But Bill the Wackie-Quackie man is setting up the duck follies and we sit down just in time to see a duck waddle out onto a tiny stage, and peck at a tiny piano with its beak. ''Waddaya call a rich duck?'' asks Bill the Wackie-Quackie man of the audience. ''A Ritzy Quacker!'' he shouts. ''Argh, argh'' laughs the man in front of us, tugging at his visor cap. Liberace Duck leaves, followed by Kentucky Ducky playing ''The Ballad of the Mallard.'' The Valeducktorian is introduced to a pleased audience as we fly to our car.

We press on to Circus World, which seems to have suffered an unexplained evacuation prior to our arrival. It doesn't seem to affect the place, which looks designed and run by a computer. A sound system keeps churning out electronic organ grinder music, the rides dip and turn even though there is no one waiting to get on. Holding pre-wrapped cotton candy we stand for a few horrible minutes on the deserted Avenue of Spins and Grins before peering into the concrete Big Top. An announcer is introducing what he calls ''our ponderous pachyderms.'' The beasts do headstands in a ring without sawdust in front of a listless little crowd. The memories of my childhood circuses are stronger than any scent in the wind.

What's it all add up to? The only message I can offer after a few days down here in Central Florida is that America is getting cutified at a far more rapid rate than many of us may be aware of. In gritty New York this mania for babble, alliteration, dumb rhymes—and understandably, sanitation—had largely escaped me. Very few of the places I visited in Disney or its environs seemed to be expecting any functioning adults or intelligent children. They were expecting cartoon characters. And the visitors behave accordingly. At Cypress Gardens, a number of able oldsters very happily tucked themselves into wheel-barrow-shaped wheelchairs. At Sea World, a theme park offering large fish in large tanks, adults obligingly stuffed kids into dolphin-shaped carriages.

In fact, it was at Sea World that I had a brief encounter with insanity. There I was holding a snack bought at Snacks 'n Suds, wandering past Fountain Fantasy on my way to Hawaiian Punch Village. Shamu, I thought. Got to find Shamu, the much-praised killer whale. So I fluttered about, finally coming to this big pool with a dark half-submerged hulk at one end. It was very still, not showing an inch of killer tail. Then it moved and I thought, this can't be real, it's a plastic submarine. Shamu? Submarine? I just couldn't tell anymore. It was time to go.

And quicker than you could say Mickey Mouse, we were in the friendly skies having another indescribable meal. Hoop-de-doo, we sang. Hoop-de-doo.

Rheta Grimsley Johnson / A Good and Peaceful Reputation
Memphis Commercial Appeal, November 1, 1982

Rheta Grimsley Johnson was born in Colquitt, Georgia, grew up in Montgomery, Alabama, and graduated from Auburn University in 1975 with a degree in journalism. After founding a weekly newspaper on St. Simons Island, Georgia, Johnson worked for various newspapers in Alabama and for UPI (United Press International) before joining the Memphis Commercial Appeal *in 1980. She covers Mississippi for the* Commercial Appeal *from an office in Jackson. At the time she wrote the following commentary, she had never traveled farther north than Washington, D.C. "I love the South. It's all I've ever known."*

"A Good and Peaceful Reputation" grew out of Johnson's coverage of the trial of Jimmy Lancaster, accused and convicted of murdering a black deputy sheriff.

> *Something about the Jimmy Lancaster trial had been bothering me for months when I finally sat down and wrote 'A Good and Peaceful Reputation.' . . . It had been, from the beginning, a story that eluded print. Oh, I had reported dutifully the strategies of the prosecution and defense and described in some detail the crowded, racially-divided courtroom. With every day's story, though, there came the feeling I'd managed to ignore as much truth as I imparted. I had covered the seventh game of the World Series and omitted the score.*

> *Johnson explained that "there had been a crowd of people [at the trial] who simply did not believe killing a black man was enough to blot a solid citizen's reputation. . . . The South is full of people who are wise and good and kind in most respects but wear bigotry like a scar on their humanity. That fact wasn't news.*

> *" 'I killed, but I'm not a killer,' Lancaster told that jury. . . . The jury didn't buy it. Intimidated as the jurors were by their white friends and neighbors and bosses seated in that courtroom, they remembered their oath. That was news, and news that begged for commentary."*

It seemed like a family reunion. Like a ritual gathering deep in the country where there are no secrets or pretenses and the black sheep break bread and belch loudly with the rest of the clan. The children run barefoot and unchecked and old men spit wherever they please as acceptance prevails.

That's sort of the way it was. Relatives huddled around a prodigal son who grudgingly put in an appearance.

The women wore tentative smiles with their Dacron summer finery and carried patent leather bags on arms the Mississippi sun had mottled.

The men held back to avoid the endless hugging and to clear their throats. Then, those not desperate for a smoke moved in with handshakes and conspiratorial winks and whispered reassurances for their white friend and neighbor who had shot and killed a black deputy sheriff.

It was a somber, special occasion. A funeral where everyone got to speak to the corpse.

At each brief recess, the crowded courtroom seemed to shift forward as a high tide of women lapped around defendant Jimmy Lancaster of Van Vleet. He smiled a weak smile summoned from somewhere in his uncomplicated past and allowed himself to be pressed and pitied. He knew his role.

Lancaster periodically fingered his wide, polyester lapels to find and fasten the missing galluses. The suit was a strange new uniform for the jail-paled, lanky welder who liked to hunt and keep to himself. He held his head stiffly erect, as if his shirt collar pinched and there was no polite way to loosen it. He had the self-conscious look of someone posing for a Polaroid.

His supporters might not comprehend the seriousness of the offense; months in jail had almost convinced Lancaster. Still, here with a forgiving family and well-wishers cooing over him, even Lancaster must have found new hope.

If the district attorney wanted to avoid the case and the considerable controversy it generated, he didn't let on, leading the prosecution with the barely-bridled ferocity of a Baptist preacher. He made the most of bloody clothing and color photographs of the victim; there was nothing half-hearted or cavalier in his manner.

The black man's law enforcement ties made it more respectable to aggressively prosecute a white man for the murder, but it still wasn't politic.

And the state's confidence was mostly superficial. They had a dead deputy and the man who said he shot him eight times in self-defense. But they had only one black on a Chickasaw County jury that came from and would return to a largely segregated society.

Lancaster told his story. Robert Kirby had come to the front door of his home early one morning, ringing the doorbell and then waiting. When he answered the door and asked what the deputy wanted, Kirby for apparent reason shot up from his hip, through the bottom of his holster and the glass storm door.

Only grazed, Lancaster told how he grabbed a rifle and started firing at the fleeing deputy. For a better aim, he dropped one gun and went for his powerful 7mm hunting rifle that had a scope.

At least eight rounds later—after he saw Kirby's body bounce from the impact of bullets—Lancaster said he felt a little sick and went back inside.

The district attorney pulled an undamaged holster from Kirby's stained clothing to refute the Lancaster story. The defendant was slightly injured by flying glass from his own shots through the storm door, not one of Kirby's bullets, he said.

Kirby was trying to do his job.

He was trying to deliver an assault warrant filed against Lancaster by his wife who had the day before provoked a beating.

A parade of character witnesses attested to Lancaster's good and peaceful reputation. A Methodist minister, a farmer, a shop foreman and an elderly, former justice court judge all took Lancaster's part. One such witness was the employer of a white juror. In the audience, reporters could hear other testaments to Lancaster's worth. "He deserves a medal," one man said, sniffing at no one in particular.

Robert Kirby couldn't demand justice. That was in the hands of a white district attorney who must worry about re-election. It was in the purview of a white judge. It was up to a mostly white jury whose friends sat on the white side of a distinctly black and white courtroom.

Dick Gregory wasn't there. There were no banners or rallies or network television cameras. There was a crowd, but it was composed of local folks who waited for a verdict.

The widow of the slain deputy waited, too, across a narrow aisle from Lancaster's supporters. Her husband had been brash enough to interrupt a white family's feuding. And he'd gotten himself shot.

After the trial, Robert Kirby's widow went home alone. The friends of Jimmy Lancaster disbanded.

The jurors went back to the homes in towns where not much changes, and progress must be diluted and served up in small doses. They had been drafted to serve justice and now were coming home from a war with their own consciences.

They had looked down the barrel of Lancaster's rifle and seen the moment of one man's death and another man's madness. The oath they'd taken to uphold that truth mattered more than peer pressure or the politics of race. It mattered more than some unspoken allegiance to a past pockmarked by prejudice. They had been color-blinded by the truth.

In Mississippi, there are two men serving life sentences for killing blacks. One of them is Jimmy Lancaster.

DISCUSSION QUESTIONS

1. Reread the opening paragraphs of Rheta Grimsley Johnson's report on Jimmy Lancaster's trial. What stylistic devices does she use to establish a mood for her report? What, for example, are the effects of such phrases as "like a family reunion," "Like a ritual gathering," "black sheep break bread and belch loudly," and "the rest of the clan"? What are the implications of the notion that "old men spit wherever they please"?

2. Johnson presents the first dramatic piece of information at the end of the fourth paragraph: "their white friend and neighbor . . . had shot and killed a black deputy sheriff." What are the advantages (and the disadvantages) of Johnson's delay in presenting this information? Comment on the importance of the fact that Johnson wrote her commentary after news stories of the event had been published.

3. Johnson's ending may strike many readers as surprising. Review her essay carefully, and discuss the strategies she uses to heighten the sense of surprise in her final paragraph.

Ann Landers / Love or Infatuation?

San Diego Union Tribune, May 25, 1983

Esther Pauline Lederer was born on July 4, 1918, in Sioux City, Iowa. In 1955, the Chicago Sun-Times *was looking for a replacement for Ruth Crowley, who had written popular articles under the name of Ann Landers until her death earlier that year. Esther Lederer was chosen to fill this position and has gone on to make "Ann Landers" a household word.*

"Ann Landers" is one of the most widely read advice columns today and appears in more than nine hundred newspapers across the country. Landers re-

ceives almost one thousand letters daily asking for advice on every imaginable topic. In addition to her frank, down-to-earth, and sometimes wisecracking advice, Landers's column also provides a kind of open forum where people can speak to each other through their letters.

DEAR ANN LANDERS: When I was in high school, I clipped your column that described the difference between love and infatuation. I looked at it often, and it saved me from making some foolish mistakes.

I'm a graduate student now and find myself in need of some solid emotional grounding. I wish I had that column. Will you hunt it up and run it again?

—STARRY-EYED IN KANSAS

DEAR STARRY: It's one of the most requested columns of all. Thanks for asking.

LOVE OR INFATUATION?

Infatuation is instant desire. It is one set of glands calling to another. Love is friendship that has caught fire. It takes root and grows—one day at a time.

Infatuation is marked by a feeling of insecurity. You are excited and eager, but not genuinely happy. There are nagging doubts, unanswered questions, little bits and pieces about your beloved that you would just as soon not examine too closely. They might spoil the dream.

Love is quiet understanding and the mature acceptance of imperfection. It is real. It gives you strength and grows beyond you—to bolster your beloved. You are warmed by his presence, even when he is away. Miles do not separate you. You want him nearer. But near or far, you know he is yours and you can wait.

Infatuation says, "We must get married right away. I can't risk losing him."

Love says, "Be patient. Don't panic. He is yours. Plan your future with confidence."

Infatuation has an element of sexual excitement. If you are honest, you will admit it is difficult to be in one another's company unless you are sure it will end in intimacy. Love is the maturation of friendship. You must be friends before you can be lovers.

Infatuation lacks confidence. When he's away, you wonder if he's cheating. Sometimes you even check.

Love means trust. You are calm, secure and unthreatened. He feels that trust, and it makes him even more trustworthy.

Infatuation might lead you to do things you'll regret later, but love never will.

Love is an upper. It makes you look up. It makes you think up. It makes you a better person than you were before.

DEAR ANN LANDERS: Tonight I came across a shocking figure. Are you aware, Ann, that one in five Americans can't read?

When I receive thank-you notes from my teenage nieces and nephews, I am appalled at their poor grammar, spelling and penmanship. How do they get into high school when their literary skills are clearly inadequate? What can be done about this?

—MORRISTOWN, N.J.

DEAR N.J.: Many high school graduates can't read or spell or put together a grammatically correct sentence because too many teachers promote poor students to get rid of them. Shocking, isn't it?

We need higher standards, better pay for teachers, remedial classes and tutors for those who have fallen behind. If we don't get serious about this problem soon, this country will find itself in big trouble.

DEAR ANN: I cheered when I read the letter from the clergyman who was displeased with parents who let their kids cry and talk and disrupt the congregation while he was trying to deliver a sermon he had worked on all week. I hope our pastor read it and changes his tune.

Our church has an average attendance of 225. We have two nurseries—one for babies and one for toddlers and older. A couple behind us chose to bring their 2-month-old infant into the church. The child cried *loud* throughout the service. Several people gave the parents long, hard looks. We even turned around and stared a couple of times. They ignored all signs of displeasure.

Two weeks later the pastor said he had something on his mind and proceeded to give us a scorching lecture on "tolerance." He said he had worked hard and long to get a certain couple to join the congregation and because we had the audacity to give them dirty looks when their baby cried they resigned their membership. He ended by saying, "I can talk louder than any baby can cry! Don't ever let this happen again!"

The tone of his voice was like that of a parent reprimanding a child. We felt insulted. May we have your opinion?

—JUST PEW

DEAR PEW: I don't wish to speak unkindly of a servant of the Lord, but I think your pastor has cornflakes where his brains belong. To chew out his congregation because they resented having their Sunday sermon ruined by a crying baby (whose parents could easily have taken him to the nursery) was childish. I hope someone will send him a clipping of the next letter.

DEAR ANN LANDERS: Recently my husband and I attended a church play. Before the performance began, the minister appeared on the stage and said, "Crying babies and disruptive children, like good intentions, should be carried out immediately. Thank you for your cooperation."

He received a big round of applause. Please print this so other clergymen can take a page from his book.

—STILL SMILING IN OKLAHOMA CITY

DEAR OKLAHOMA: So am I. Thanks for sharing.

DEAR ANN LANDERS: This letter is for the millions of women who are being beaten by their husbands and boyfriends. You are not alone. Professionals estimate that 70 percent of all emergency room assault cases are battered wives. We, the battered women, come from every economic and intellectual segment of society. Some folks believe we enjoy getting knocked around and that we provoke the attacks. What an absurd notion! No one needs to provoke a wife-beater.

Why does she stay? Because she doesn't realize that there is a place she can go. Battered women, hear me! You have a right to live in peace! You have the right to share your feelings and not be isolated and terrified. There are shelters all over the United States for you and your children. They will take you in with no money. Write to the National Coalition Against Domestic Violence, P.O. Box 31015, Santa Barbara, Calif. 93105 for more information and make plans now to change your life.

—ALIVE AND WELL IN AUSTIN, TEXAS

DEAR TEX: Bless you for all the women you helped today.

Byron Lutz / Type of Vehicle You Drive Reveals Your Personality

National Enquirer, May 24, 1983

The National Enquirer, *with a circulation of more than three million, is a weekly tabloid sold principally at supermarkets and newsstands. Specializing in what it calls "attention-grabbing" articles and photos, the paper often features celebrity profiles, scandals, the occult, medical "breakthroughs," curiosities, adventure tales, and items offering some special angle on whatever happens to be in the news.*

The following two brief articles, by Byron Lutz and Arline Brecker respectively, represent a popular approach to individual psychology, one that frequently finds its way into the mass media. (See Marshall Schuon's "Cars and Self-Image" in "Advertising" for a more sophisticated version of Lutz's article.)

The kind of vehicle you drive reveals your personality, say behavior experts.

"Surveys have shown a direct relationship between automobiles and personality," said California psychologist Dr. Stephen Brown.

Here are the personality traits revealed by different kinds of "wheels," according to Dr. Brown and New York psychiatrist Dr. Emory Breitner.

Subcompact: These drivers like to be in control, and it's easy to be in control of a tiny subcompact. They're frugal, pragmatic people who are in a hurry. Subcompact owners don't want to be bogged down by a big car—with payments to match.

Mid-size or Compact: Reserved and conservative, these drivers rarely make moves without considerable thought. They're sensitive and emotional—but never foolish. They don't gamble, they check things out, work hard and are honest to a fault. These drivers like to blend in, not make waves.

Full-size: The drivers of these giants like to do everything in a big way. They're ambitious, desire money and material goods—and are literally driven to success.

They like big homes—and if they throw a party, they want it to be an all-out affair with people singing, eating and having a ball. They aim for important jobs, and can't stand a cramped office or a tiny car that cramps their style.

Station Wagon: Family comes first for these people. They're good neighbors, very friendly, enjoy children and animals, and will always try to help you out if you have a problem. Image isn't important. They just want to use their station wagon to enjoy life.

Jeep: These drivers are trailblazers who love adventure. They enjoy striking out on their own, and don't mind questioning authority. They're practical, energetic survivors who like to win under tough conditions, and work best when they can make their own rules.

Convertible: The top's up one day, and down the next. These drivers are exactly like their car—changing from day to day. Convertible owners are impulsive, quick-witted and restless. But they're excellent at communicating ideas and love to shine on short-term projects—jobs where they can see instant results. They love art, music and creative activities.

Pickup Truck: These people are ready to tackle any job. They have a determined, fighting spirit, and a do-it-yourself attitude that makes them self-sufficient. They're forceful, opinionated, and like to pitch right in and get a job done.

Sportscar Hardtop: The cars are fast and fashionable—so are the drivers. They're impatient, quick-paced and flashy. They like to have a lot of irons in the fire, and if a job falls through, they have another lined up and are ready to move quickly.

Hatchback: This car is a cross between a station wagon, economy car and sports car—and the people who drive them are practical, but dreamers at the same time. They're neat, discriminating and good organizers, as the practical, smart hatchback layout suggests.

Van: These drivers love to be comfortable and feel at home no matter where they are. They're romantic and idealistic, and can't stand quarreling and friction. Van drivers love peace. And as their vehicles are big enough to haul things they enjoy collecting.

Arline Brecker / Puzzles You Enjoy Most Reveal Your Personality
National Enquirer, May 31, 1983

The type of puzzle you enjoy reveals your personality, says a psychologist.

Here's what you're really like if you take pleasure in solving the following kinds of puzzles, according to Dr. Herbert Hoffman, director of the Hillside Psychological Guidance Center, Queens Village, N.Y.

Crossword: "You are well-read, work hard at keeping informed and have an excellent memory," said Dr. Hoffman, a former associate professor of education and psychology at City University of New York. "If someone asks you a question that you can't answer, you will look it up."

Rubik's Cube: You have the enviable ability to put thoughts into action. You have a high tolerance for frustration, so you stick with a task no matter how unpleasant or monotonous it is.

Anagram: "If you enjoy these puzzles, which consist of scrambled words, you frequently plunge headlong into knotty situations," said Dr. Hoffman. "But you can be depended on to get at the truth and straighten things out."

Word Find: You're well-organized, hard-driving and ambitious. When you make an important decision, you stand by it. And you can't be talked into doing anything against your better judgment.

Take-Aparts or Put-Togethers: If you like Chinese rings, intertwined nails or locking blocks, you're a person who responds best to touch. You're a "hugger" and "kisser" who prefers expressing affection physically. And you take a "hands on" approach to problems.

Jigsaw Puzzles: When it comes to problem-solving, you're not afraid to try something new. "For example," said Dr. Hoffman, "when faced with the problem of taking a group of visiting relatives sight-seeing, you'd rent a van rather than arrange for cars to transport them."

Cryptograms: You're a private person, not likely to divulge personal affairs. You don't like to borrow, and prefer to think your own way out of a problem.

Connect-the-Dots: You're a disciplined, highly responsible individual. Said Dr. Hoffman: "When faced with problems, you adopt a logical, step-by-step approach."

James Kindall / A Visitation of Evil

Kansas City Star, September 25, 1983

Perspiration rather than inspiration seems to lie at the heart of James Kindall's work as a writer: "I have been known in the past to pull all-nighters and be all red-eyed and rumpled and look like a bad imitation of Bela Lugosi by morning. That relates to something of my philosophy of writing. The result is in direct proportion to the effort made. So if I've wrung myself out, that will be reflected in the text." Kindall followed his usual preparation for writing when working on "A Visitation of Evil," his dramatic account of "a madman . . . loose on a bloodlust rampage" in a tranquil Kansas town. That preparation included efforts to "soak up" the ambience of the setting for his stories: "I talk to as many people as I can, both on a formal and informal basis. I eat the food, I chat with the people in the restaurant, I go to a bar or two at night and talk to the patrons over a beer. I go to the local pool hall. I talk to the kids who are cruising the square. I'll even go to the town library and look up the history of the town."

When commenting on "A Visitation of Evil," Kindall explained: "I hope the ellipsis—what isn't said—is conveyed in the text, that a lot more could have been said. This gives the story an overall tone of truth. I went to the town library and probably had another hundred inches of town history that I discarded. But overall it was helpful to this piece and necessary." Those local details help highlight, as he notes, "the stark contrast of that rural tapestry and the violence that was committed there."

With the exception of a year's military service in Munich, West Germany, Kindall has spent most of his life in Missouri. Born in Springfield, Kindall graduated from Southwest Missouri State University before earning a master's degree in journalism from the University of Missouri. He began writing for the Kansas City Star in 1974 and served first as a reporter and consumer affairs writer before shifting to the Star's Sunday magazine as a feature writer.

Jeff Heinrich is staring. The 18-year-old senior has just finished track practice and his blond hair is plastered into dark wetness. Nearby at Everett Shepherd Park, kids are thrashing in a white concrete pool built by the CCC in the 1930s, and a half block away people are gathering for a barbecue during Farm-City Days, summer's last hurrah for the 7,000-strong town of Iola, Kan.

Jeff is staring toward the dike at the park's edge, an elongated grassy mound restraining the Neosho River, recently subdued into scummy stillness by hot weather. The dike and other obscure spots near the city have taken on grisly significance for townspeople lately.

It was last summer that Jeff, running a final lap along the mound at the head of his cross-country team, saw several boys scramble over the top yelling about someone in the river. Veering off for the tree-lined bank, he spotted a figure doubled over in the water, a young man beaten so badly that life was a feeble pulse in his body.

The discovery was the beginning of a horror of revelations.

In a 24-hour period, three bodies would be discovered in Allen County. Bodies slain and discarded like worthless mannequins. Bodies savaged in acts of animal brutality that would have shocked a callous metropolis, let alone a close-knit community.

The events that unfolded from that point were a paradigm of a small town's worst nightmare. Somewhere a madman was loose on a bloodlust rampage. No one was safe.

At the episode's conclusion, Nathaniel ''Yorkie'' Smith, the 37-year-old son of an Iola railroad worker, was sentenced to seven consecutive life sentences for the crimes. A convicted murderer who had been out of jail three months at the time of the killings, he will be eligible for parole again. In 105 years.

A year has passed now since Iola's visitation of evil. That such malevolence could settle upon a community in the rural heartland seemed a crushing refutation to its lifestyle, its structure. It was a weekend many still wonder about. And all would like to forget.

Jeff's eyes glaze as he looks into the distance. He shakes his head and issues a statement containing more wonder than opinion.

''Huh,'' he grunts. ''This was supposed to be a nice place to live.''

*   *   *

It was hot in Iola on Aug. 20, 1982. The partly cloudy skies that appeared could not blunt the heat that had settled in for the duration of the weeklong Allen County Fair held annually at the city park west of town.

The fair was a break in the somnolent community pace. About 109 miles southwest of Kansas City, Iola is stocked with the requisite number of herd-wide streets, churches and porch-front homes. A chamber of commerce pamphlet a few years back described its attractions. ''Iola lives in harmony,'' it said. ''We have no racial friction. Our crime is infrequent. Our youth are constructive members of the community. This isn't a claim to perfection—just a reminder that small-town living is remote indeed from big-city problems.''

An obscure sort of notoriety was made by the municipality at one time.

A natural-gas boom town of 20,000 people at the turn of the century, Iola was filled with entrepreneurs rushing to the city to tap the supposedly inexhaustible resource. During the period, the square was caparisoned with lighted gas tubing. A huge gas ''gun'' periodically shot a flame into the air 50 feet long and 20 feet wide.

Depletion of the supply a few years later set back city growth and began a recovery resulting in a comfortable, slow-moving environment with industry that is, if not bustling, then at least ongoing.

The earthen flavor of the countryside is never far removed. After a rain, the air is atomized with the perfume of wet fields. At darkness, cicadas begin a nightly resonance while an aged moon rises over crop-land like a large ivory cueball.

On such evenings, teens cruise the square taunting the night. Boys draped over parked cars flash grins halfway between innocence and sensuality. Girls pass on parade with a Lolita-like coyness that thickens the air with excitement.

The area's infrequent crime usually is relegated to vandalism or theft of oil-well equipment and farm machinery. The good guy-bad guy battle is cyclic, with most of the participants known. Burglars steal, are arrested, serve time, leave prison, steal again, are arrested and so on.

Before last summer, the last serious outbreak of violence had occurred 12 years earlier, when the bodies of two women were discovered the same day in apparently unrelated incidents. One was a 28-year-old waitress killed in what appeared to be a robbery attempt; the other a ninth-grader discovered in a ditch, her death still unsolved.

The summer of 1982 had been uneventful, with a few exceptions.

A Moran, Kan., couple lost a race with the stork and their 7-pound boy was born in their car in front of the Allen County Courthouse. The cornerstone of the Methodist Episcopal Church in nearby Neosho falls was purloined by vandals.

Iola jerked to attention briefly when an ABC-TV truck pulled into town to film part of a coast-to-coast bike race. The chance for national exposure evaporated when the crew discovered its subject had sped through the city on another route.

Advent of the county fair that year did not prompt undue concern for Allen County Sheriff Ron Moore. A former grocery-man with a bulldog build and a quiet country manner, Moore had initiated normal security in the form of a few patrolling deputies for the fete.

Only one thing had troubled him the previous couple of weeks, a worry revealed to the public Aug. 16 when *The Iola Register* noted that Tom Walsh, a freckle-faced, red-haired youngster whose father ran the local 7-Eleven store, had been missing for two weeks.

Runaways were occasionally reported to the sheriff's office; this was nothing new. But Tom had taken no belongings for such an adventure, his parents reported. Two school ID cards had been found on a dirt road outside of town. The sheriff and a deputy walked the area without finding anything; Sheriff Moore felt uneasy about the incident.

*   *   *

The events that began Aug. 20 came in a sanguinary rush.

The sheriff was in his weekly meeting with the county commissioners when his secretary entered about 9 a.m. with a message. The undersheriff had been notified about a youth apparently beaten and found sitting in the river. Signs indicated more than a routine call.

The boy had been pistol-whipped with a mercilessness hard to believe. His face was lacerated, his jaw and skull fractured, the tip of his tongue bitten off, possibly by his own teeth during a blow to his head. His right eye was protruding from its socket.

The department's investigator, Steve Junkerman, was sent to the county hospital to talk to the youth, identified as 15-year-old Gerald Short of Gas, Kan. Edging a few inches from the boy's face to take his mumbled statement, Steve Junkerman heard Gerald say he had been assaulted and beaten by a black man wearing a ski mask.

Before he coughed up blood and the interview ended, Gerald said he had not been alone when he was attacked. And he did not know what had happened to his friend Steven Mangus.

*   *   *

Friday morning began placidly for George Jones, a road grader for the county. His assignment was smoothing a crooked section of country road about three miles west of town. An initial swing earlier had been past a small, blue-green body of water in a quarry, and he was "closing" the road, sweeping the gravel back over its surface, on a return sweep about 1 p.m. when he spotted something.

Normally Jones looked into ditches or across fields as he drove, checking to see if anything had fallen out of cars or off trucks. It was a natural thing to do, a way to pass the time.

What he saw lying on the quarry rampway was something he still has nightmares about. Stopping the grader, he climbed over the wire fence to make sure, then climbed shakily back into the cab to radio the county maintenance department.

He had found something discarded, all right. The body of a 17-year-old boy.

*   *   *

Steve Junkerman, a burly former Ohio policeman who had joined the sheriff's department as investigator three months before, was sleepy from working the previous night when he received the sheriff's call that morning. Events following were eye-openers.

The seriousness of the assault was something he quickly realized after talking to Gerald at the hospital. Returning to examine the crime scene, he began talking to people at the fair who might have seen anything connected with the crime while Moore and others searched high weeds on horseback for the youth's friend.

Junkerman found out that Gerald Short and Steve Mangus had shown animals at the fair the evening before and planned on staying in the pen area for the night, a common practice at stock shows. The two were drinking beer in the park when they were approached by the assailant. Gerald's clothing was found on the river bank, including his empty billfold.

A boat was brought in by authorities to begin dragging the river. At 1:30 p.m., a call came in that ended that search. A county maintenance man wanted the sheriff at his work site a few miles west of town; he wouldn't say why.

Steve Junkerman and the rest guessed what it meant.

*   *   *

As they drove to the quarry site, the speculation was confirmed. The body of Steve Mangus, a slender, blond-haired youth also from Gas, was found lying face down at the quarry's shallow end. Two bullet holes were visible in his shirt and one in the top of his head.

Agents from the Kansas Bureau of Investigation had arrived by this time. Photos were taken, the area diagrammed. A gaff, hooks and a magnet were brought in to search the quarry. No one knew what might turn up.

The incidents of the morning were grim enough, but a call that afternoon began to stretch credulity.

An abandoned red Maverick had been found in a car wash in town. A man wanting to wash his truck had been irked to find it sitting driverless in the bay he needed to use. Looking closer, he had seen a purse emptied on the front seat. He also had noticed the car was spattered with blood inside and out.

Arriving at the scene, investigators learned the car belonged to a Mrs. Adeline Fisk, a reclusive 59-year-old housecleaner who lived by herself in a farm house outside of town. Smears and splashes of blood could be seen on the left fender, door and windshield, as if someone had been placed against the side of the car and bludgeoned. A palm print of blood was found on the hood. Patches of hair and blood were inside.

A prim, gray-haired widow who began work each day at 3:30 a.m. for a retired man in town, Mrs. Fisk had not been seen at his residence that morning. At the man's house, authorities found break-in marks on the screen door. A pot of morning coffee, most of which she usually drank herself, had been made. This time, the pot was full.

The investigator and his team figured out something else as they continued their search.

Mrs. Fisk lived west of town. The route she would have taken that morning could have gone past a now significant spot. Perhaps she had driven by at just the wrong time. The wrong time to be passing the turnoff to an abandoned rock quarry.

*   *   *

The towing of the Fisk car that afternoon set in motion an unorthodox search from an unlikely quarter.

One of the tow truck operators, 21-year-old Mike Hedman, was acquainted with Mrs. Fisk. He decided, along with his brother, Jim, and a co-worker who also knew the woman, to canvass the area. Perhaps the woman was lying injured in a ditch somewhere, he thought. Anyway, driving around a few country roads to check couldn't hurt.

The three met after supper and headed for a site near the quarry homicide scene. Turning down a road at random, they noticed it had been recently graded, the gravel piled on one side but not re-spread. Driving slowly, they saw a spot where tire marks crossed the ridge. Distinct tire marks.

Mike Hedman and his co-worker who had towed in the car remembered something about the Fisk auto, something that clicked. The front wheels of the car had been mounted with regular tires, the back with snow tires. The tracks that crossed the gravel mound matched that pattern.

Another thing came to mind. Sunflowers had been trapped in the door of the bloodied vehicle. The field they looked out upon contained sunflowers.

Mike Hedman and his brother got out and walked fewer than 50 feet before spotting something. It was a pair of boots along with a pair of men's underwear.

Stooping down to examine the articles, the two saw a form lying beneath a grove of small trees a few feet away. A figure wearing a dress and no shoes.

There was no need to check; Mike Hedman knew instantly she was dead. And that Adeline Fisk had been found.

*   *   *

As unnerving as the discovery was, the boots and underwear spotted near the Fisk corpse brought a realization that more dark finds probably were on the horizon. Odds were that at least one more body was to be found.

The three searchers who discovered the body of Mrs. Fisk hadn't actually expected to find anything on their jaunt the day before and were shocked by the sighting. But maybe there was other evidence to be found connected with the killings, they thought. It couldn't hurt to try again.

Gathering Saturday morning, the three repeated their drive in the direction of the quarry and began a slow patrol. Close by the quarry on the other side of the road they were hit by a "deadly dead" smell. Their best guess was that a possum or some other varmint had been hit and was decomposing in the woods.

The spot, a wooded area sloping into a small valley, was full of poison ivy. Mike Hedman caught it easily. His brother, less susceptible, slipped carefully through the brush to the source of the smell.

All three had trouble grasping the reality of what was there. Once more, within a half hour after beginning their search, the three had found something they didn't really want to find at all. Jim scrambled back up the hill.

"We've found another one," he said. It was Tom Walsh.

*   *   *

Small-town normality in Iola was devastated by news of the killings. Homicide is different in an environment where everyone knows everyone else. The municipality's reaction was archetypal, fear translated into paranoia coupled with a circling of community wagons.

Initially, misinformation was coordinated with more misinformation. News spread through the peer group of Mangus and Short, for instance.

"At first when they found Gerald everyone said Steve had beaten him up and what a rotten thing to do," says a high school girl who knew both boys. "Then later when they found Steven's body, everyone started saying, 'Oh, Steve was my best friend.' "

Restaurants and friends brought food into the sheriff's department for the swelling band of laymen working day and night. Gun displays and deadbolt locks at hardware stores were cleaned out. Chairs were placed in front of doors at night. Streets emptied at dusk. The ceaseless town-square circling by local teens for once was halted.

The last day of the county fair on Saturday drew a handful of people. Media members from outlying cities descended on the town, sticking microphones in the faces of blinking townspeople or chasing down friends of the victims.

Cars entering and leaving the city were spot-checked and occupants interviewed by police. Kansas Gov. John Carlin announced a $5,000 reward for information leading to a conviction in the crime and local residents chipped in a few thousand more.

Everyone wanted to help; no one knew exactly what to do. When a 4-year-old wandered away from her farm home a few weeks later, neighbors and townsmen poured out as volunteer searchers. She was found safe later that day.

Suggestions for suspects and motives were rained on the sheriff's department. Rumors richocheted like bullets. The mayor's teen-age daughter left town to visit relatives and was immediately rumored missing or dead. "Is it true," a sheriff's department caller asked, "that you found five more bodies?"

Pressure for answers built quickly. What sort of monster was loose in the community? Would he strike again? Why hadn't anyone been jailed yet?

"People wanted an arrest on Monday," said Bob Johnson, city editor of *The Iola Register*. "When they didn't get one on Monday, they wanted one on Tuesday."

Suspects were hauled in from all quarters. Two transient crews of black painters who had been in the area were interviewed, one crew pursued to their next worksite in Emporia.

Phone tips, many from unidentified callers who feared retribution, made the phone a constant background noise. A black man who lived at the edge of town reportedly had been seen by a tipster throwing his suitcase in a car occupied by two other blacks and fleeing town. Tracing the man down, authorities found he had fled, all right. On his vacation.

Among those called in for questioning was a thickset maintenance worker whose appearance surprised Sheriff Moore. His name was Nathaniel "Yorkie" Smith. Both authorities and people in town knew of Smith. His reputation for bursts of brutal mayhem was well earned.

In jail for much of his 37 years, Smith first had shocked Iola by assaulting a couple in their car on Easter Sunday in 1965. After ordering the driver out of the car, Smith shot him twice, then beat him with the barrel of a rifle. The woman also was beaten. A rifle was found at Smith's home with the barrel bent and the stock cracked. Later he pleaded guilty to the violence and served six years in prison.

Released for two years, he returned to prison in 1974 after stabbing and killing a Kansas City, Kan., man during an argument over a marijuana deal. While incarcerated, he also was convicted by the penitentiary disciplinary board of aggravated sexual assault on a prisoner.

Sheriff Moore was startled to see Smith brought into the department that weekend because parole officials had notified him not long before that Smith, then serving time at the Kansas State Penitentiary at Lansing, wanted to come back to Iola if paroled. The sheriff had sent the paperwork back recommending against the request. He did not learn until later that Smith had been released anyway.

Smith returned to his hometown in May and had remained mostly unnoticed. No evidence was found at first to link him to the crime that August. Initially, he refused to be photographed and fingerprinted when called in. After consulting with his parole officer, he returned and cooperated. Afterward, he was released.

Public outcry continued in the weeks of investigation following. No weapon had been found. No hard evidence pointed to one person. But coincidence finally did.

A burglar in adjoining Wilson County was arrested by sheriffs deputies there in November. Confessing to his crimes in a tape-recorded session, he at one point asked authorities to turn off the machine. What he said next he did not want on tape: It might have something to do with the Iola killings.

He and a friend had burglarized an oil equipment business in Allen County last Aug. 20, the man said. Cutting through back roads in the early morning, they came across a riderless motorcycle parked on the road and decided to steal it, too.

Going to pick it up, they discovered the motor was still hot. Realizing the owner probably was in the area, they jumped in their truck and drove away.

It would have been about 3 a.m., the man said. The area was near a rock quarry.

Authorities slowly started to assemble the puzzle. The observation also fit with another piece of information taken earlier from an anonymous tipster. The man, who met with the sheriff outside of town to give him the information, had seen an Iola resident late on the night of the homicides riding a motorcycle. The man was Yorkie Smith.

*   *   *

When Smith was indicted in April of this year the move came as no surprise to some townspeople. It was more anticlimax.

Speculation about the identity of the killer had centered on Smith for some time. City editor Johnson remembers his son coming home the first day of school and asking if Yorkie had been arrested yet. Why? his father asked. Well, everyone at school knew he had done it, the boy said.

"They wouldn't have needed a trial here," Johnson says. "All they would have had to do was find a jury and send them out."

Both events during the trial and testimony itself kept interest high.

Much of the prosecution's case was based on ballistics tests. Bullets from a gun lent to Smith by a girlfriend were recovered from a hillside along with other bullets from the same weapon fired by Yorkie into a tree. The tree was cut down, sectioned and taken to a hospital to be fluoroscoped. The .22-caliber slugs matched those in the bodies of the victims.

Another large chunk of circumstantial evidence was provided when Smith's brother, Roger, testified that he had seen Yorkie in Iola with a pistol and riding a stolen motorcycle the night of the slayings. He also said he had been wearing goggles, gloves, a hunting vest and an Army poncho with the hood pulled over his head, a description matching what Gerald Short said his assailant had been wearing.

The viciousness of the attacks, as well as Smith's past deeds, were factors in the trial.

Smith's victim in the 1974 killing in Kansas City had been shot once, stabbed in the chest and his throat slashed with a butcher knife. An anthropology professor who examined the body of the Walsh boy testified that he had counted 188 knife marks, some of the blows delivered with such force that the bones were splintered.

A physician at the trial showed slides proving that Steve Mangus had been shot five times, Mrs. Fisk three. The shots were fired at point-blank range.

But by far the most damaging testimony came from the beaten boy, Gerald Short.

Wearing a patch over the eye he lost in the assault, he described the evening in a wavering voice, testimony that might serve as a recital of restless youth in rural America. At the beginning of the evening, Gerald said, he met his friend Steve in town, then the two of them joined their girlfriends and played video games. After dropping the girls off (they were sisters), the friends, along with an acquaintance who had a car, bought a case of beer with a fake ID and cruised to nearby Humboldt.

More beer was bought; the boys later were dropped off by the park. By early morning, they were sitting in a large playground barrel, the kind that rolls as you walk inside, drinking the last of their beer and deep in discussion, Gerald said. They would make some money from the sale of their sheep, the two knew. Should they take their girlfriends out to eat at a nice restaurant?

A man approached from the darkness. The time was about 1:30 a.m., past the city's curfew, and Gerald though it was a cop. Instead, he saw a stocky man with high cheekbones and goggles who was wearing lace-up boots like a paratrooper. He ordered them out of the barrel with a gun.

''You. Get over here,'' he said to Gerald.

Warning them not to look back or he would kill them, he took shoelaces from Steve's tennis shoes and tied the wrists of the two boys together. When Gerald looked over, Steve was crying.

The two were repeatedly asked if they had any money, then led over the dike and molested. The boys pleaded with him not to hurt them. They had some beer; he could have all he wanted, they said.

At one point, Gerald thought his friend had been shot and he would be next. Things appeared to go in slow motion from then on, he said. He felt himself being hit with a metal object and heard Steve say, hey, leave him alone. Then blackness.

Was the man who did this in the courtroom? Gerald Short pointed his finger at Nathaniel ''Yorkie'' Smith.

*   *   *

Visitors to Iola today would be hard put to find remnants of the visitation of evil from that period. There is no plaque, no sculpture. The paper has returned to stories about soybeans, dead dogs and vandalism. Crowds once more swelled the Allen County Fair this year.

A parade held on a sweltering afternoon at the culmination of Farm-City Days produced an hour of local floats, clowning Shriners, clomping horse clubs and armadas of massive farm machinery churning forward on a street as hot as metal.

''Watch the pompon girls. You might be one some day,'' a mother says.

Repugnance with the incident coupled with the injustice of its location have made the subject a topic not many are easy with, one residents seem to view with the embarrassment of a person who feels guilty while having committed no crime.

''A thing like this could happen anywhere,'' says Mike Hedman. ''It doesn't really matter what size town it is.''

Results of the trial have left bitterness.

Smith's defense attorney complained repeatedly during the trial about material withheld by the prosecution. As a result of those allegations, the judge asked the county Bar Association to investigate the handling of the case by the prosecutor. He also asked the Kansas attorney general to find out why Smith was released by the Kansas Adult Authority.

''The State of Kansas decided early on in this case, 'We've got Yorkie,' '' the defense attorney said in his closing statement. '' 'He's a bad guy. He just got out of prison. Why do we need to look for anyone but him?' ''.

The jury deliberated only four hours before delivering the convictions, ''hardly time to read and vote on the 16 charges,'' an observer said.

The presumption of guilt and the fast jury conviction, despite the matrix of the prosecution's evidence, are things about which a few in town have wondered. And how the swirling force of evil that weekend came to collide randomly with innocence is something everyone still ponders.

Was Gerald Short left for dead? Or was the killer interrupted before he could finish his deed? How did Mrs. Fisk fit in? What did she see? Did she even realize its importance at the time?

''You know,'' says Steve Junkerman, echoing the thoughts of others, ''there are a lot of things I'm going to be wondering about all my life.''

DISCUSSION QUESTIONS

1. What are the effects of Kindall's decision to present his readers with a sense of Iola's "teens cruising the square and taunting the night"? In what specific ways do such moments add to—or detract from—the overall effect of the story?

2. Reread Kindall's report, concentrating on his use of verbs. How emotionally charged are his verb choices? What are the effects of his verb choices? Consider Kindall's use of the present tense in the opening section of his story. When— and with what effect—does he shift to the past tense?

3. What strategies does Kindall use to draw his readers closer to his account of "a madman . . . loose on a bloodlust rampage"? What, for example, are the effects of a sentence such as "What he saw lying on the quarry rampway was something he still has nightmares about"?

4. Compare and contrast Kindall's account on the "bloodlust rampage" in Iola, Kansas, with H. G. Bissinger's narrative of the dramatic events aboard TWA flight 841 ("Press"). Which writer establishes a greater distance between himself and the events he recounts? Point to specifice words and phrases to verify your response.

Joe Nawrozski / A Family Stops a Thug

Baltimore News American, December 7, 1983

Joe Nawrozski has a fondness for writing about people who fight back. "I think as a writer that people like to read these things," Nawrozski explains. "We're so caught up with the violence and the sadness that too often surround us. People like to cheer inside. If I can initiate some of those cheers, all the better." In the following news report, Nawrozski recounts—and celebrates—the collective efforts of a family who have been "living peacefully for 25 years in Pikesville" [Maryland] to "go to war" against an intruder who tries to disrupt that tranquility.

The recipient of several journalism awards and a two-time nominee for the Pulitzer Prize, Nawrozski has been writing professionally—and for the News American *in Baltimore—since he graduated from high school. After attending Johns Hopkins University and the University of Baltimore, Nawrozski served as an army combat correspondent in Vietnam and has remained active in support groups for Vietnam veterans. In addition to crime reports, Nawrozski has written for the sports pages and has edited his colleagues during a stint at the* News American *rewrite desk. "I'm a fast writer and I'm an easy writer," he noted in an interview. "There are people that sit around and wring their hands and smoke four packs of cirgarettes and beat their heads against the VDT. I sit down. I clear my head. And I write. But that's after thorough study of what I have to write about. Sometimes you might miss a fact or too hurriedly put together a sentence. I do go back and reread the story two or three times to look for changes. . . . I just believe in the discipline of doing it and doing it and doing it."*

After living peacefully for 25 years in Pikesville, Mary and Irving Berman Tuesday night had to go to war.

And they won. Boy, how they won. Just ask James Matthew Carter.

The Bermans, both 55, of the 4100 block of Raleigh Road, returned to their split-level home about 10 p.m. after doing some Christmas shopping. Nothing unusual. Sidney, 56, Irving's brother, was watching television upstairs, and Vincent Dicrescenzo, 61, Mary's brother, was downstairs.

As Mary was about to close the front door, something happened. As she tells it:

"I'm trying to slam the door shut and I feel somebody pushing from the outside. . . . . I thought it was company or something."

The next thing Mary Berman saw was a foot slip inside, then a hand holding a gun.

"I said to myself 'Well.' I grabbed the gun. I kept holding the gun and just screamed as loudly as I could. He got just inside and I kept fighting him, pushing him to the door," she said.

Meanwhile, her brother—hearing the screams—though Mary had fallen down the steps and ran to the front hallway. Irving and Sidney were also running toward the ruckus.

"It seemed like all three of them hit this bum at once. That's when his friend outside ran. But we got the gun away and Vince sat on him. He's 200 pounds and I kept his legs down," Mary said.

Irving and Sidney helped immobilize the man, whom Baltimore County police identified as Carter.

"And do you know what this guy was saying to us?" Mary said. "He said that he made a mistake, that he was in the wrong house."

He certainly was.

After police arrived and arrested Carter, 19, of the 3400 block of St. Ambrose Avenue, the tally was taken.

Vince had been bitten on the forearm and went to the hospital for stitches.

Sidney received a minor injury to his leg.

Mary and Irving came away physically unscathed.

And Carter? Besides being in the county jail charged with assault with intent to rob, he is nursing a head injury and a cut lower lip.

Now, because Mary and her family fear the second man who never made it inside might attempt a return, she said Irving and Sidney and Vince are going to get guns and learn how to use them.

Actually, Mary said, the intruder was lucky the family's black Labrador, Oliver, barking madly, couldn't get out of the basement.

"Yes," Mary said today. "He's fortunate Oliver didn't get to him, too."

DISCUSSION QUESTIONS

1. Consider carefully the narrative voice that speaks to us in this news story. What is the effect of Nawrozski's colloquial expressions ("Boy, how they won"), his seemingly casual syntax, and his use of the central characters' first names? What would be the effect of recasting this story in the more conventional syntax and tone of newspaper stories?

2. Identify and comment on the effects of the comic elements in Nawrozski's story. Who, finally, are the comic figures in this story? James Matthew Carter? Mary and Irving Berman? Sidney Berman? Vincent Dicrescenzo? All of these people? None of them? Explain and verify your response by pointing to specific words and phrases.

3. Reread this news story, paying special attention to what you can reasonably infer about contemporary American values from what you've read. More generally, what inferences can you draw about the state of contemporary American culture from the details reported in Nawrozski's story?

4. Consider the two advertisements espousing different positions on the issue of gun control (''Advertising''). Given that Nawrozski reports that Irving and Sidney Berman, as well as Vincent Dicrescenzo, ''are going to get guns and learn how to use them,'' how might you expect them to respond to Mrs. James Brady's plea to ban handguns? What might you imagine to be the basis of their argument for arming themselves? How would you imagine Mrs. Brady would respond to each of the points they might make?

ON BERNHARD GOETZ

"Depending on one's perspective," columnist Elizabeth Mehren wrote in the San Francisco Chronicle, *"he is either a saint or a sociopath. In either case, subway shooter Bernhard Goetz, by all accounts the most reluctant of celebrities, has vaulted from subject of instant controversy to object of overnight industry." Even before the thirty-seven-year-old electronics specialist was indicted on illegal-weapons charges in early 1985 (later to be expanded to include criminal assault and attempted homicide), "Thugbuster" T-shirts with such slogans as "Acquit Bernhard Goetz" or "Goetz Four, Crooks Zero" quickly became the latest fad in New Yorkers' conversations and in Manhattan tourist shops.*

The December 22, 1984 incident in which Goetz shot four black teenagers who he said had accosted him for money aboard a New York subway ignited angry public debates on racism and vigilantism. The nation watched a new morality play unfold in the daily newspapers and on network and local newscasts. Labeled a felon by some, a hero by others, Goetz instantly became the target of a media blitz and the focal point of national controversy; his actions were alternately seen as a test of the nation's judicial system and a confirmation of its citizens' rights of self-protection. In a press conference two weeks after the subway shooting, President Ronald Reagan "crystallized" several of the issues for the American public. Asked for his views on citizens who use deadly force to defend themselves against attack, Reagan, alluding to the Goetz incident, observed: "In general, I think we can all understand the frustration of people who are constantly threatened by crime and feel that law and order is not particularly protecting them." "On the other hand," the president continued, "I think we all realize there is a breakdown of civilization if people start taking the law into their own hands. So while we may feel understanding or sympathy for someone who was tested beyond his control—his ability to control himself—at the same time we have to abide by the law and stand for law and order."

After a tumultuous seven-week trial, Goetz was acquitted on June 16, 1987 by a jury of twelve of the thirteen charges listed in the indictment against him. After thirty hours of deliberations, the twelve jurors convicted Goetz only of illegal possession of a handgun, the .38-caliber pistol he used to shoot the four youths. Jurors said they discounted Goetz's own videotaped confession of the shooting, particularly his account of how he walked over to one of the youths on the subway seat and fired another round, saying, "You seem to be all right, here's another." "We couldn't accept what we saw on that videotape," said one juror. "The man was near hysteria."

Jurors reported that the defense arguments were not as important to them as understanding and sympathy for the fear Goetz felt when he believed he would be robbed and beaten. "He was a sad, frightened man," another juror noted. "I ride the trains. I know what it is in New York." Rejecting the prosecutor's argument that Goetz was seeking vengeance for two previous muggings, the jurors reasoned that Goetz "was trapped on the train" and "fired in self-defense." According to news reports, the jurors also "insisted that the verdict was not meant to condone vigilante violence in a city beset with racial tensions and rising crime."

The crime of illegal possession of a handgun carries a maximum penalty of seven years in prison, but Goetz's lawyers reportedly said that "he is unlikely to be sent to prison as a first offender."

Robert D. McFadden / A Gunman Wounds 4 on IRT Train, Then Escapes   *New York Times,* December 23, 1984

Robert McFadden began writing for the New York Times *soon after his graduation from the University of Wisconsion in 1960, where he had majored in journalism. The coauthor of* No Hiding Place, *a 1981 account of the Iranian hostage crisis, McFadden has earned numerous awards for his writing, including the Newspaper Guild of New York's "Page One Award" (1978) and, most recently, the New York Press Club's "By-Line Award" (1987).*

A middle-aged man with a silver-colored pistol strode into a subway car rolling through lower Manhattan yesterday and shot four young men he had apparently singled out from among the passengers, the Transit Authority police reported.

As the victims collapsed, all bleeding profusely from wounds of the upper body, a dozen other passengers, screaming and sobbing, fell on the floor or herded into the next car. The train, a No. 2 Seventh Avenue IRT express, halted just north of the Chambers Street station at about 1:45 P.M.

Then, in a bizarre twist to what transit authorities called one of the worst crimes of the year in the subways, the gunman discussed the shootings briefly with a conductor, according to investigators, one of whom described a colloquy.

GUNMAN DESCRIBED AS "CALM"

"Are you a cop?" the conductor was said to have asked as he approached the man, who had shoved the gun into his waistband and was bending over and saying something to a victim.

"No," the gunman replied. "They tried to rip me off."

The gunman, who was described as "calm, cool and collected," then noticed two trembling women lying on the floor and, along with the conductor, helped them up.

As the women fled into the next car, the conductor, whose name was not released, turned again to the assailant.

"Give me the gun," he urged.

But the gunman turned without responding and stepped through the door at the end of the car. The conductor tried to grab him, the police said, but he leaped to the tracks from between cars and vanished in the dark tunnel.

As ambulances rushed the victims to Bellevue and St. Vincent's Hospitals, police officers searched the tunnels and the nearby area, but nothing was found.

Subway service through the area was disrupted for two hours as power was turned off to allow the search. Trains, crowded yesterday with shoppers, resumed normal runs at 4:11 P.M.

The motive for the shootings was unclear, but transit officials said they apparently stemmed from an earlier confrontation aboard the train.

"He picked out these four guys and shot every one of them," said Capt. John Kelly of the Transit Authority police. "He knew what he was doing. He was not just shooting indiscriminately. He was either harassed or robbed by these guys earlier on the train."

The police said two of the wounded young men, interviewed later in the hospitals, denied robbing or harassing the man who shot them.

Witnesses said the victims, all teenagers from the Bronx, were behaving boisterously just before the shootings. Three of them have arrest records, and three were carrying long screwdrivers in their jackets, the police said.

At Bellevue Hospital, two victims were listed in serious condition. They were identified as Barry Allen, 18 years old, of 1372 Washington Avenue, and James Ranseur, 18, of 3673 Third Avenue. One had been shot in the chest and the other in the back.

At St. Vincent's Hospital, 19-year-old Darryl Cabey, of 423 East 168th Street, was in critical condition; a bullet had passed through his spinal cord and left lung, a spokesman said. Troy Canty, 19, of 1372 Washington Avenue, was in critical condition with a wound in the left side of the chest above the heart.

The police said the shootings erupted at 1:44 P.M. on the sixth car of an eight-car southbound No. 2 train, an express that begins its run in the northern reaches of the Bronx and ends at New Lots Avenue in the East New York section of Brooklyn.

GUNMAN WAS NEATLY DRESSED

As the train neared the Chambers Street station, two blocks west of City Hall, the gunman, moving between cars, entered from the rear.

He was described as a thin, blond, clean-shaven white man about 6 feet tall and weighing about 155 pounds. The city police said he appeared to be about 30, but the transit police said he was about 45. Witnesses said he was neatly dressed in a light blue jacket and gray sweater, and was wearing clear, gold-rimmed spectacles.

His gun was described by transit officials as silver-colored and of high velocity, perhaps a .357 Magnum. Some bullets passed through the victims and dented the walls of the subway car, Captain Kelly said.

The victims, all friends, were seated in the rear of the car near the door where the gunman entered, three on one side and one on the other, witnesses said. There were at least a dozen other people in the car, including an off-duty Transit Authority porter.

NUMBER OF SHOTS UNCLEAR

They said that the gunman paid no attention to others in the car, but singled out the four and, apparently without conversation, opened fire. The number of shots was unclear.

"He could have shot 10 others, but he picked out these four," Captain Kelly said.

As the victims collapsed and other passengers fled, the conductor riding in the fifth car, just ahead, looked in and saw what had happened.

The train was halted—either by the conductor pulling an emergency cord or by the motorman he alerted—seven or eight car lengths north of the Chambers Street station. Fleeing passengers "ran into the car with panic-stricken faces—I've never seen such faces," said David Kriegel, who was riding in the car just ahead.

For reasons that were not explained, the conductor walked back and approached the assailant, who by then had placed his gun into his waistband and was bending down, saying something to one of the victims. The conductor and the gunman then spoke briefly.

"Apparently, this individual tells the conductor that he was harassed or robbed or whatever by the four, earlier in the ride uptown," Captain Kelly said, who said the conductor seemed not to feel afraid of the assailant.

NOTIFIES POLICE

As the motorman notified transit police with his radio, the gunman stepped between the cars, jumped to the tracks and ran north toward the Franklin Street station.

Transit police officers were on the scene within minutes. One of the first was Officer Joel Scollo, who dashed through the train looking for the assailant. "I went into the last car and there were about 40 people in there huddled on the floor," he recalled.

Shortly afterward, the train was moved into the station, the doors were opened and frightened passengers fled. The police later found only three witnesses and urged others to contact detectives at 477-7447.

The police searched the tunnel with flashlights for more than an hour, but found no trace of the assailant. Power on the Seventh Avenue line was cut at 2:12 P.M., the Transit Authority said.

While there have been homicides and other violent crimes on city subways this year, John Cunningham, a Transit Authority spokesman, said he could recall no single crime involving more violence in 1984.

Editorial / On New York's Subway

Washington Post, December 28, 1984

> *As the most prominent morning daily in the nation's capital, the* Washington Post *has a wide readership among and considerable impact on political leaders and government workers—both in Washington and across the country. The* Post *vies with the* New York Times *for the unofficial title of the nation's newspaper of record.*

New York has a new folk hero, the slim, bespectacled young man who was reading a newspaper and minding his own business on a Manhattan subway train early last Saturday afternoon when four young men began to hassle him. According to witnesses, the four, armed with sharpened screwdrivers, approached the rider and "asked" him for money. He stood up, calmly drew a silver revolver from his belt and shot all four. Then he helped a few women to their feet, told the conductor he was not a policeman and disappeared into the subway tunnels. Of the four, all are in the hospital, one paralyzed by the gunman's bullet.

The event has provoked an enormous public response. A columnist speculates that the gunman had seen the current Charles Bronson movie "Death Wish." A hot line set up to receive tips about the man with the gun was deluged by thousands of calls supporting him. Mayor Koch has promised an all-out effort to solve the case, but the joke on the streets is that he just wants to find the gunman before the Republicans nominate him for mayor.

It's easy to understand why New Yorkers are responding in this spirit. Their subway, once a fast, efficient, cheap, 24-hour-a-day transit network that other American cities envied, has fallen on hard times. Much of the equipment is old and constantly breaking down. The cars and the stations are filthy, covered with graffiti and littered with trash. There are thousands of fires in the system each year, most started in refuse strewn on the tracks. But the most frightening element is the crime. The four young men involved in Saturday's incident all had arrest records and appeared to be typical of the toughs who roam the trains, even in midday, terrorizing and robbing passengers.

This is the heart of it. The mayor has put more than 3,000 uniformed police officers on the trains and stations, and Gov. Cuomo has counseled calm. "A very firm, even tough criminal justice system," says the governor, is the way to fight crime. He's right, of course, but such a system is not in place. When people feel they are not adequately protected, the force of the argument that they should not take their defense into their own hands diminishes.

The subway riders of New York had been sorely provoked. An episode of do-it-yourself law enforcement has undeniable implications of spreading violence and chaos, but it reflects directly upon those in official positions, like the mayor and the governor, who had failed to provide the protection that the citizenry has every right to demand.

Editorial / The Vigilante of the Subways

San Francisco Chronicle, December 28, 1984

> *The* San Francisco Chronicle *is the most widely read newspaper in the Bay Area and that city's only morning daily. The* Chronicle *combines a large staff of reporters and a strong, clear editorial policy to extend its readership throughout northern California.*

Most New Yorkers, black and white, ride their subway system with an acute sense of apprehension. And most of them seem to be hailing as a hero a bespectacled blond man who shot down four black youths in sneakers who began hassling him on a downtown express.

The hardened riders on the crime-ridden New York transit system are flooding police and newspaper switchboards with praise for the fugitive gunman who took matters into his own hands to avoid a $5 robbery. His teenaged tormentors had arrest records and were armed with sharpened heavy-duty screwdrivers.

An indication of the widespread support for the white gunman came this week when the Congress of Racial Equality, a civil rights group, hired a top lawyer to defend the vigilante if he is caught.

Support for the fugitive has extended beyond New York. Certainly for other Americans who face the potential for mugging every day it is easy to understand the anger and frustration that led the mysterious subway vigilante to carry a gun and to use it.

Despite this understanding, however, some thoughtful voices have been raised to strip away any halo of heroism the gunman may be wearing. Mayor Edward Koch condemned the shooting as bloodthirsty. Governor Mario Cuomo said, "The vigilante spirit is dangerous and it's wrong. In the long run that's what produces the slaughter of innocent people."

These New York officials are correct. This anonymous gunman on the No. 2 Express should be apprehended and swiftly brought to trial. Only then will justice prevail.

Abe Mellinkoff / Latest from the Subway Super Bowl Wars
San Francisco Chronicle, January 4, 1985

A Phi Beta Kappa graduate of Stanford University in 1932 with a degree in political science, Abe Mellinkoff has written for the San Francisco Chronicle *since 1935. He says, "The one thing to remember about journalism is that there are always limits. You have to do the best you can with whatever time and space you have." Such constraints have not prevented Mellinkoff from earning many awards for his reporting and commentary during his more than a half-century in journalism.*

The New York Subway Super Bowl lines up this way: Bernhard Hugo Goetz and his pistol vs. four young punks, with criminal records and armed with sharpened screwdrivers. It was a no-contest contest. The four are in the hospital, seriously wounded.

And there is no need to worry abut Goetz's future. Any number of hungry lawyers, hungry for publicity, will appear to defend him as a public service.

That sacrifice may not be necessary. Countless New Yorkers are stepping forward with offers of money to help finance Goetz's defense.

Both the shooting and the public reaction to it are understandable. The punks were trying to float a non-voluntary loan for five dollars from a fellow passenger in a subway car. He had the money but pulled his gun instead.

Passengers built on the order of 49er stars aren't approached. I'm sure that Ronnie Lott and Keith Fahnhorst could ride that subway for a year and never loan anybody anything.

Others are not that fortunate. On an average day, forty felonies of one kind or another are committed on the New York subway. Only a small percentage end in arrests and an even smaller number result in jail sentences.

Shooting mass transit passengers is clearly against the law. And from a purely selfish point of view, I wouldn't want the practice to spread, say, to the Muni and especially not to the crowded 30 Line, mine.

Still, I wouldn't like to see anything severe—even like thirty days in jail—be meted out to Goetz. Whether he intended it or not, he is carrying on his rather narrow shoulders the frustration of millions of more or less law-abiding citizens. Our rights have been unbelievably extended. We can dash off to court to right any slight infringement against us.

But through all progress in our individual rights, we still find vast areas of our chosen city closed to us at night by the fear of attack. That it is not done by legislation from City Hall doesn't make it any less unbearable. That it is done by the usurped power of criminals makes it only worse.

Sydney H. Schanberg / Support Your Local Shooter

New York Times, January 5, 1985

Sydney Schanberg began his distinguished career in journalism with the New York Times *in 1959. After serving as bureau chief in Albany, New York (1967– 69), and New Delhi, India (1969–73), Schanberg became the Southeast Asia correspondent from 1973 to 1975. Among his most notable reports is the fall of Phnom Penh, which served as the basis for the Academy Award-winning film* The Killing Fields. *He is the recipient of numerous awards for excellence in journalism.*

Bernhard Hugo Goetz, the accused subway shooter, has become an overnight household celebrity—to the point where the Australian newspaper in this city is close to abandoning Mayor Koch and backing the shooter instead.

This sad and frightened and confused man was not likely seeking this starring role when, on Dec. 22, he allegedly pulled a revolver from his waistband and shot and wounded four black youths who were apparently harassing him for money on an IRT train. But, by his choice or not, he has become the pivot of what is being wrongly shaped as an ideological debate.

Conservative commentators have attacked any expression of concern about the dangers of vigilantism as the soft-headed mewlings of bleeding-heart liberals. One such spokesman for the right wrote in the Australian paper: "Far from being a manifestation of 'insanity' or 'madness,' the universal rejoicing in New York over the gunman's success is a sign of moral health."

If by "moral health" he meant it is healthy to be angry about crime, then I agree. The trouble is, he went on to draw a parallel with the Revolutionary War and to praise subway revengers as the "direct descendants of rebellious forebears who took up arms and shot down British troops. . . ."

The sympathy with Bernhard Goetz that has been voiced by people of all persuasions and classes in this city is not hard to understand, but talk about taking up arms is. New Yorkers are angry about lawlessness and anarchy in the subways, and that's why we are hearing people say these days: "I can't really blame the guy."

There's nothing ideological or alarming in this popular identification with Bernhard Goetz's fears. What's alarming is the ideological hint that maybe the rest of us ought to imitate his behavior. Wonderful. We all buy .38-caliber revolvers and descend into the subways to shoot the next person who menaces or harasses or bothers us—or even asks us for money. The ensuing mayhem would make the present anarchy on the subways look like a Girl Scout slumber party. Those youths whom Bernhard Goetz apparently shot may indeed have menaced him—or at least seemed meancing to him—but mowing them down by frontier justice is not the way to use our fears and our anger.

These emotions should be directed toward strengthening a law-enforcement system that we all agree is not working very well. The police and the District Attorney, in arresting and bringing charges against Bernhard Goetz, are acting correctly and doing the right thing, whether or not they feel any sympathy for this troubled man's frustrations.

They are defending an incompetent system because there is no other sane choice. Our choice is either to try to make it more competent by legal public action, such as organizing to put pressure on elected officials, or to throw it overboard and start a reign of every-man-for-himself in the subways.

This city already has stunning evidence of what happens when the public rules of order are no longer much enforced and private rules are substituted. Thus we have the rampant running of red lights, littering on virtually every street and antisocial behavior on the subways. We need less of this destructive individualism, not more.

What I don't fathom in those who seek to frame the reaction to this event as a vindication of right over left is why the conservatives, who are the vanguard of all law-and-order campaigns, now seem to be the first in favor of wild private justice when police and prosecutors and courts are in difficulty.

The subways are uncivilized, there's no doubt about that. But how would they become more civilized if riders stocked up arms and ammo?

And what about the potential racial overtones—which some commentators are quick to deny. Listen to what a very reasoned and very reasonable black friend wrote to me: "To me, his act of violence is more fearful than that of the criminal element because it may provoke an escalation of violence underground. Who's to say that the next 'vigilante' will be sane, will be able to distinguish between black males—since we all look alike—or will not simply start shooting everyone in sight because he can't shoot straight."

We all know that a lot of the crime on the subways is commited by black and Hispanic youths. What will happen to law-abiding blacks and Hispanics, who are the bulk of the subway ridership, if tribal justice is encouraged?

Those who are using this episode to score ideological points are playing with dangerous tinder and are doing nothing to improve the state of public safety.

Russell Baker / Waiting for Wyatt

New York Times, January 5, 1985

The winner of two Pulitzer Prizes (one in 1979 for distinguished commentary, the other in 1982 for Growing Up, *the autobiography of his childhood), Russell Baker remains one of America's most widely read and respected humorists and satirists. After several years of service as a reporter and London bureau chief for the* Baltimore Sun, *Baker joined the Washington bureau of the* New York Times. *In 1962, Baker resigned his reportorial duties ("I just got bored. I had done enough reporting") and began his celebrated column, "Observer."*

I never knew Abilene on Saturday night, or Dodge City, or Tombstone in the old days, but the old-timers still talked about those places when I first came to New York.

"I'll tell you this, young feller—" That was the way they talked, only with a Bronx accent. "I'll tell you this, young feller, anybody who could survive Dodge and Tombstone and Abilene on a Satiddy night, he jest naturally ain't gonna have one bit of trouble surviving the New York subway."

I thought of those words the first time I walked down those mean steps and put token to turnstile. As I did so, four men jumped over the other turnstiles, thus breaking the social contract under which all riders had agreed to pay equally for underground travel.

My instinct was to seize the rebellious louts and compel them to pay for their rides, but I remembered the old-timers, who had said:

"The way sensible folks survived Dodge and Tombstone and Abilene of a Satiddy night was jest pretend nothing the least bit unusual was goin' on. Then eventually, of course, Wyatt Earp, he'd come a-ridin' into town and pretty soon the place would be so safe that everybody'd feel like they was in St. Patricks' Cathedral."

Remembering the wisdom of the old-timers, I let the turnstile-jumpers go free, thus—so I have since been assured—saving my life.

With the passing years I saw it was easy to save my life in the subway. The old-timers had been right when they told me:

"You see, son, if a feller wanted to survive Tombstone and Dodge and Abilene of a Satiddy night, he had to know things like where the line of fire would be, so's he could stay out of it until Wyatt Earp could eventually come along and make everything as safe as Macy's on Monday morning. Same rule applies for subways."

And it did. That's why, when everybody used to push everybody else off the platform in front of oncoming trains, I was never killed by a train. I was back in the middle of the platform hunkered down behind the trash can where the pushers couldn't find me.

That's why the man with the hatchet who used to come out of the subway doors splitting skulls of people on the platform never managed to brain me. Behind the trash can, I was out of the line of hatchet.

The years passed. Loved ones pleaded with me: "Stay out of those barbaric subways." I knew it was offensive to them to have a regular subway rider in the house, constantly reeking of the overflowed-toilet smell which makes it so easy to distinguish the subway rider from humanity.

Still, I would not be moved. "A man's got to do what a man's got to do," I told them.

A few God-fearing people—farepayers, schoolmarms, parsons—had to keep a toehold underground until Wyatt Earp arrived to restore civilization.

More years passed, working their evil change upon my youth. Light bulbs were going out all over the subways. Subway doors that had once opened partly now opened scarcely at all; when they did, the menacing figure that slithered in and gave each passenger a glance so villainous as to chill the most felonious blood was—yes, that figure was mine.

How had this foul distortion of human nature been wrought from the charming, romantic youth who had once listened with delight to the old-timers talking about Tombstone and Dodge and Abilene on Satiddy night? Years of subway riding had done it.

I had realized that Wyatt Earp was never going to come, at least in my lifetime. That Mayor Koch and Governor Cuomo were never going to come either. Why should they come? Up, up, up in the sunlit world of limousines, up in the bird-filled blue with their helicopters, why should they venture into the ruins of civilization?

And so I had turned myself into a creature of such menacing appearance that other subway riders scurried for other cars when they saw me.

Then—a horror! Two weeks ago, another subway rider shot four teenagers because they looked menacing. And the subway riders of New York still applaud.

They want more shooting. I must get rid quickly of my menacing look, but I cannot. Cultivated so long, it will not come off.

Ed Koch, Mario Cuomo, send me your limousines. Better yet, get hold of Wyatt Earp fast.

Art Buchwald / Vigilantes: Doing the Best They Can

Washington Post, January 8, 1985

Art Buchwald's career as a humorist and satirist spans his service as managing editor and frequent contributor to Wampus, *the University of Southern California's humor magazine, to his current syndication in more than five hundred-fifty newspapers worldwide. The author of nearly thirty books, Buchwald has used Washington as a base since 1962 for his humorous and caustic commentary on contemporary American political and social foibles.*

After noting the positive reaction of citizens to the shooting of four thugs by a vigilante in the New York City subway, a bunch of us in Washington decided to form our own vigilante organization to see that justice was served in the nation's capital.

There are tough gun laws in the District of Columbia so we drove over to Virginia where you can buy anything you want, from a .22 Saturday night special snub-nosed revolver to an Uzi semiautomatic machine gun.

I chose a .38 Smith & Wesson because it fits snugly under my coat and reminds me of the old westerns when the good guys constantly drove the bad guys out of town.

Our vigilante group didn't have long to wait. Schneider had been mugged the night before and he said he could identify the guys who did it. We went with him to a Georgetown bar and he pointed them out to us.

"Are you sure they're the ones?" I asked him.

"Of course I'm sure," he said. "The big guy is wearing a raincoat just like the one I owned."

That was good enough for us. So we took the three men out of the bar and shot them.

The police were furious that we had done their jobs for them. But the public was delighted and we became folk heroes overnight.

The next time we went out was when a 7-Eleven in the neighborhood was held up.

The clerk in the store said the stickup man wore a Halloween mask, but he had a hunch it was a taxi driver who lived down the street.

We routed the cabbie out of bed and brought him down for identification. "The clerk said, "It could be him."

"Wait a minute," Pester said. "We have to be certain because as vigilantes we don't want to hurt an innocent man. You said the guy was wearing a Halloween mask. What kind of mask was it?"

"It was a Darth Vader mask."

We sent Pittman to get a mask at the costume shop. Then we put it on the cab driver.

The clerk said excitedly, "That's the guy."

"You're sure?"

The clerk replied, "I never forget a face."

So we took the cabbie out in the alley and broke his legs.

After that we were dubbed "The Magnificent 7-Eleven" and more people were rooting for us than for the Redskins.

The liberal press wrote bleeding-heart editorials accusing us of being nothing more than hooligans, and the mayor went on television to condemn us. It didn't matter, because the criminals were now more afraid of us than they were of the police.

Christmas night Alvin told us, "I just got a tip that there's a bunch of drug dealers holed up in a house in Northwest Washington. Let's burn it down to teach all the drug dealers in town a lesson."

We hopped in our van with 10 gallons of gasoline and drove to the address the tipster gave Alvin. We threw the liquid all over the house and set it on fire. A father and mother and three children came pouring out of the front door. The father screamed, "What the hell are you doing?"

"Teaching you drug dealers a lesson."

"I'm not a drug dealer! I'm a postman."

"Is this your address?" Alvin asked, showing him the one the tipster had written down.

The postman looked at it and said, "No, you dumb SOBs. That's in *Southwest* Washington, not Northwest. You guys burned down the wrong house!"

"Don't get all shook up, pal," I said. "Even vigilantes make a mistake once in a while."

Kenneth B. Clark / In Cities, Who Is the Real Mugger?
New York Times, January 14, 1985

Kenneth B. Clark is Distinguished Professor Emeritus of Psychology at City College of the City University of New York. Born in 1914 in the Panama Canal Zone, Clark attended Howard University before completing a Ph.D. at Columbia University in 1940. Clark's studies of the psychological effects of racism were cited by the U.S. Supreme Court in its landmark desegregation decision in 1954. The founder of HARYOU (Harlem Youth Opportunities Unlimited), Clark has been awarded numerous honorary degrees and citations for his community service as well as for his articulation and advocacy of minority-related public issues.

Bernhard Hugo Goetz has become a folk hero. Respectable citizens have identified with his shooting of four teenagers who "harassed" him on the subway and asked him for $5. In so dealing with these potential "muggers," Mr. Goetz personified and aroused the general and pervasive fears, anger and sense of personal powerlessness of a large segment of the public faced with rising urban crime. The outrage over lawlessness in our cities has masked the lawless act of an individual. But this incident cannot be understood in isolation.

The overwhelming support given to Mr. Goetz and the related rejection of his victims must be seen as grave symptoms of larger and systemic social problems.

In our cities, fear of crime is valid. Almost everyone, without regard to race, becomes anxious about the possibility of being mugged when approached by a group of seemingly aimless teenagers. The media cover the more sensational incidents, dramatizing the victims as well as the criminals and muggers. There are outraged cries for retaliation and punishment, demands for a more severe criminal-justice system and more prisons, suggestions that outraged citizens protect themselves by whatever means necessary. The muggers are perceived as animals or, at best, as "creatures" who must be caged or destroyed. They are not seen as socially distorted humans.

But this ignores some significant problems. For a variety of complex reasons, our society does not ask itself, "How do so many young people become mindlessly antisocial and, at times, self-destructive?" A painfully disturbing answer to this core question is that "mugged communities," "mugged neighborhoods" and, probably most important, "mugged schools" spawn urban "muggers."

Given this fact, a more severe criminal-justice system, more prisons and more citizen shootings will not solve the problem of urban crime.

These are selective forms of anger directed toward the visible "muggers." The educationally rejected and despised "muggers"—the pool of the unemployed and unemployable from which they come—will increase in numbers, defiance and venom. Not able to express their frustrations in words, their indignation takes the form of more crime. They now riot as individuals rather than as a mob. Having been robbed of the minimum self-esteem essential to their humanity, they have nothing to lose. No one offers them financial support for their lawless behavior as was offered to Mr. Goetz. They reject the values of a hypocritical society that demands that they act passively human even as their humanity is being systematically destroyed.

These rejected, dehumanized "muggers" are the products of the silent "respectables" who make a hero of one who fights the fire of urban deterioration and crime by firing a gun. The "respectables" do not express outrage at the pervasive community, economic and educational muggings in our society. They are indignant only at the inevitable criminality that comes out of the degradation of humans. They seek to protect themselves from increasing violent crimes while they remain silent about the crimes of deteriorating neighborhoods, job discrimination and criminally inferior education.

As the victims of these pervasive social muggings are punished and rejected, their numbers increase, their defiance deepens, their dehumanization hardens. Their bitterness and aggression are matched only by public acceptance of the cruelties, insensitivites and the lawlessness of the "respectables."

There is no question that society must be protected from those who assault, rob or otherwise violate others. These forms of lawless behavior must be punished. But they cannot be punished constructively by the lawlessness of another individual. Frustration, fear and outrage afflict both the rejected and the "respectables." This common predicament blurs the boundaries between the lawful and the lawless. As a society adjusts to, or rewards, its accepted cruelties and continues to deny their consequences, it makes heroes of lawless "respectables" and in so doing develops a selective form of moral indignation and outrage as a basis for the anomaly of a civilization without a conscience.

Phil McCombs / The Vigilante Mystique

Washington Post, January 17, 1985

Born in Ogdensburg, New York, in 1944, Phil McCombs graduated from Yale University in 1966 before earning an M.A. degree from the Johns Hopkins School of Advanced International Studies in 1968. After two years of service in the army, McCombs joined the staff of the Washington Post *as a reporter. The recipient of several awards for distinguished journalism, McCombs is also the coauthor of* The Typhoon Shipments *(1974).*

Bernhard Hugo Goetz apparently didn't plan on being a hero.

But what the New York "subway vigilante" did last Dec. 22 tapped into a fantasy that resonates deeply in the American soul: lone justice, an individual battling evil. It is a fantasy to be found in the superhero comic books, in the exploits of the Lone Ranger and Dirty Harry, in the world of the private detective from Sam Spade to Mike Hammer. At 37, Goetz belongs to a generation that grew up watching Richard Boone play a TV gunslinger whose calling card said, "Have Gun, Will Travel. Wire Paladin, San Francisco," and saw Charles Bronson avenge the murder of his wife by shooting street thugs in the movie "Death Wish."

The New York Daily News found that citizens approved of Goetz's shooting the four youths who approached him on the subway, 49 to 31 percent. Roy Innis, the head of the Congress of Racial Equality, called it "the greatest contribution to crime reduction in the last 25 to 30 years." Journalists dubbed Goetz the " 'Death Wish' Vigilante" after the 1974 film.

Wire Goetz, New York. The Ultimate Neighborhood Watch.

"The reason this guy is being responded to so favorably," says the director of American studies at Georgetown University, Ronald Johnson, "is rooted [in] frustration with safety in the streets. . . . This guy stood up and exercised his right to respond, to protect himself."

Adds University of Maryland criminologist Lawrence Sherman: "He's a new role model. There in fact could be a lot more individual acts of violence as a result."

The Goetz case comes to Washington today as a Senate judiciary panel headed by Arlen Specter (R-Pa.) opens hearings to look into issues it raises.

According to a spokesman, Specter sees the Goetz incident as " 'the kind of thing that happens when law and order break down.' He wants to know if law and order has failed in the New York City subway system" and, if so, what can be done about it. Scheduled witnesses include Goetz's chief defense lawyer, Joseph Kelner; James B. Meehan, chief of the New York City transit police; Curtis Sliwa, head of the Guardian Angels, a New York-based citizen-patrol group; and academic experts on justice and vigilantism.

Kelner himself has been beaten unconscious by a mugger. Goetz reportedly told a friend he hired Kelner because the attorney could understand his feelings.

"Mr. Goetz is not a vigilante," says Kelner. ". . . The truth and the facts are that he acted reasonably and understandably in a life-threatening situation. . . . He did not take the law into his own hands."

From an academic and historical point of view, Goetz doesn't fall within the American vigilante tradition of group action outside the law. Classic vigilantism, says University of Oregon historian Richard Maxwell Brown, was a phenomenon of the frontier, where established citizens usually led "committees of vigilance," as they were called. President Andrew Jackson once advised settlers to punish a murderer by lynching, and Theodore Roosevelt, when he was a rancher, sought unsuccessfully to join a vigilante movement.

Brown, scheduled to testify in today's Senate hearings, is an expert on vigilantism. He contributed to the 1969 report of the National Commission on the Causes and Prevention of Violence, and his widely respected book "Strain of Violence:

Historical Studies of American Violence and Vigilantism'' examines the phenomenon in depth.

According to Brown, the 19th-century vigilante groups often followed quasi-legal procedures. They were intellectually defended on grounds of the need for self-preservation, the right of popular sovereignty—and plain economics. In 1858, vigilantes in northern Indiana paraded under a banner that said, ''No expense to the County.'' Brown concluded that, to an extent, the early vigilante movement was ''a positive facet of the American experience.''

Vigilantism in this form is rare these days. One possible modern example was the 1982 shooting of the town bully in Skidmore, Mo. Some 20 to 40 people surrounded him in his pickup truck in broad daylight. Someone shot him dead and reportedly almost everyone saw it, but no one talked. Local authorities and the FBI were unable to crack the case.

After about 1890, something more sinister—what Brown calls ''neovigilantism''—began spreading. Groups worked outside the law for their own political ends. The victims tended to be Catholics, Jews, immigrants, blacks, political radicals and others. Three distinct Ku Klux Klan movements targeted blacks. By the 1960s, Brown testified, ''a new wave of vigilantism is a real prospect today.''

It didn't happen. ''It is a mystery to me, the restraint that people had,'' says Brown of the modern period.

Instead, community patrols and Neighborhood Watch programs, working within the law while fueled by what Brown calls a ''vigilante impulse,'' proliferated. The Guardian Angels, which began in New York, have by now spread to many cities across the country and in Canada. The modern groups have tended to work with the police. There have, though, been exceptions; where there have been racial tensions, groups have organized along racial lines to defend turf.

Brown thinks that respect for the rule of law has become ingrained in American life. No longer do public leaders condone vigilantism. New York Mayor Edward I. Koch decried vigilantism in the wake of public support for Goetz, and President Reagan said, ''There is a breakdown of civilization if people start taking the law in their own hands.''

In many ways, Goetz is a typical crime victim. After a 1981 beating by muggers in a New York subway station, he reportedly became frightened and preoccupied, outraged that police detained him six hours while releasing one of his attackers in three; and further outraged at being turned down for a pistol permit. The facts aren't all in, but apparently Goetz felt threatened when the four youths riding the IRT asked for $5. After shooting and wounding them (one remained in a coma yesterday), he fled, later turning himself in to face a charge of attempted murder—and a hero's welcome in the city, where a Daily News poll found that 7 percent of all residents have been mugged in a subway.

Millions of Americans are frustrated victims of crime. The 1982 report of the President's Task Force on Victims of Crime concluded, ''Somewhere along the way, the system began to serve lawyers and judges and defendants, treating the victim with institutionalized disinterest.''

Bernhard Goetz, it seems, wasn't going to take it anymore.

Brown, the vigilantism expert, sees Goetz as ''an isolated incident, but maybe I'm all wrong. . . . What might put it in a vigilante context is this: It's been reported that in his apartment house there was a group he was very active in, he was very concerned about security. That's a little bit like these community patrols, which are in the vigilante tradition.''

The University of Maryland's Sherman points out that Goetz may fit another quasi-vigilante tradition in America: the small storekeeper who ''has been held up many times [and who] keeps a gun illegally and shoots at armed robbers.''

Though the gun may be illegal, and the storekeeper may go beyond the strict legal definition of self-defense in shooting back, Sherman says, convictions of such storekeepers are rare.

"With maturation, we learn to deal more thoughtfully with our strong emotions, but that doesn't always take place," says Dr. Stephen M. Sonnenberg, a psychoanalyst and scholar-in-residence at the Washington School of Psychiatry. ". . . An act of vigilantism is not simply an act of the id. It involves all of the psychic systems. It involves a moral judgment, a decision, cognition. . . .

"If you look at what happened in New York, you can at least speculate. The man was attacked and made a conscious decision to carry a weapon. Before he left the train he [reportedly] helped a couple of people up. We don't think of this as simply a violent outburst. We see this person was apparently thinking something through . . ."

Another psychiatrist, Dr. Judd Marmor, says that when people feel deeply frustrated, "[their] anger is really at the authority figures who are not protecting them. That's why a lot of people are sympathetic. . . . They share the feelings of frustration, and they're pleased when someone acts out their anger."

Promoting this kind of response, says Marmor, is an "ethical climate of our time [that] affects our attitudes toward violence and retribution toward those who offend us. . . . The pervading morale of our country today is we're not going to let people push us around. That comes from the top down. It's part of the prevailing ethic of our political climate today."

As for Goetz himself, Marmor, a past president of the American Psychiatric Association, speculated that "he must have felt frustrated and decided somewhere along the way if Daddy wasn't going to take care of him he was going to have to take care of himself."

There hasn't been anything quite like the popular response to the Goetz phenomenon in recent memory, but some experts on social behavior believe his popularity rests on a delicate balance.

"He was one shot away from not being a vigilante," says Albert Record, associate dean of the School of Criminal Justice at Rutgers University. "If the bullet had gone through one of those four and hit a child or an elderly woman, how would people feel then? [They'd say,] 'He's not a vigilante, he's a kook.' "

"The danger of vigilante justice," warns Georgetown's Johnson, "is that it can incorporate a new evil. Look at the whole suppression and oppression of blacks. At the time, you would have had a good argument from the man in the street that they [the KKK] were simply . . . protecting their women from rape."

Since Goetz is white and his attackers black, Dane Archer, a professor of sociology at the University of California at Santa Cruz, raises this question: "What if the races were reversed? Presumably the public reaction would have been very different. There would have been much less support" for a black vigilante. In Archer's view, race may have played a role in the widespread public "presumption that the young men are guilty and [Goetz] was merely acting in self-defense."

Similarly, Alvin F. Poussaint, professor of psychiatry at Harvard Medical School, says, "There would be much more questioning about Goetz's behavior if those were white kids. The public is rather callous about this. They have no sympathy for that young black kid who is paralyzed from the waist down. . . . I think there's been an attempt to make these kids subhuman in order to justify what Goetz did. . . . The punishment doesn't fit the crime at all."

Support for Goetz among blacks is only slightly less than white support, according to the Daily News poll (49 percent versus 52 percent). But Poussaint says, "I think that some of the black people are getting sucked into supporting Goetz and not appreciating the racist elements that may be in the white public response to it. . . . Would Goetz have gotten on a subway and felt that white kids would attack him?''

Many experts find the public support for Goetz the most fascinating aspect of the entire affair.

''What's interesting is so many people approve of it, it means there is a problem,'' says Tom Plaut of the behavioral sciences research branch of the National Institute of Mental health.

In 1964, in a case that horrified the nation, New Yorker Kitty Genovese, screaming for help, was murdered within earshot of dozens of her neighbors. The distance from Kitty Genovese to Bernhard Goetz is two decades, but Plaut wonders if anything has really changed. ''I was raised in New York,'' he said. ''I was in New York two weeks ago, and the graffiti on the subway. . . . The obscenities don't bother me, but it indicates something amiss in the social fabric. Every square inch, the whole thing is so defaced. It's as though it's a place nobody cared about, an alien world.''

Plaut, in his fifties now, rode the subways to school. Now, he says, no one would ''rush to the help of someone who is attacked,'' and a person might feel justified in strong defense measures.

Remnants of America's frontier psychology remain, Plaut says, ''Look at the strength of the gun lobby and the National Rifle Association. It's not basically the hunters that are the strength of the NRA. It's that hunters and nonhunters think they may have to defend themselves, [that they] can't count on society to defend them.''

Indeed, each month the NRA magazines present examples of successful self-defense culled from papers around the country: ''A burglar trying to enter the home of a Kansas City, Kan., woman was scared off twice within several hours by police who responded to the resident's complaints,'' says a recent item. ''He gained entry on the third attempt, but the woman, who had armed herself with a handgun, shot and killed him.''

''It's self-defense,'' says NRA spokeswoman Denise Tray Rosson. ''We believe that every citizen has the right to be armed to protect their life and property. Vigilantism goes to an extreme. . . . We don't support the notion of private citizens taking the law into their own hands in going out and looking for criminals, [but] people do feel strongly about their right to pursue happiness without being threatened by criminals and thugs.''

Assistant U.S. Attorney General Lois Haight Herrington, who chaired the recent task force on victims of crime, says she sees no connection between programs like Neighborhood Watch and vigilantism. ''I hate to see these two things linked,'' she says. ''It puts a pejorative connotation on a very positive contribution of citizens.''

She also speaks of the importance of citizen involvement in the criminal justice system. The latest figures from the Bureau of Justice Statistics show that only 48 of every 100 violent crimes are reported; in only eight are there convictions; in only two are the criminals incarcerated.

To a large extent, the conviction and incarceration rates are low because victims ''are treated so badly'' in the legal process and drop out, she says.

Sociologist Donald Black, a lecturer at Harvard Law School, has an interesting twist on it all. His research shows that many crimes in America—including murders, robberies, and many forms of vandalism—are on close examination forms of what Black calls ''self-help justice.'' That is, folks getting even with one another through criminal acts carried out ''in the name of justice.''

''Conventional legal scholars like to say law replaced self-help, in the Middle Ages,'' says Black. ''That's grossly mistaken. Self-help continues on a large scale in our society and . . . when processed by legal authorities, is usually treated quite leniently.''

Black thinks Americans may have developed ''an overdependence on law,'' expecting authorities to take care of everything for them. He once suggested, in an article, cutting police protection in order to stimulate a self-help mentality among citizens.

''Goetz said, 'The hell with it. If I have to go to jail to protect myself, I'm going to do it.' ''

After the Goetz case broke, Georgetown sociology professor William F. Mc-Donald began thinking about the ''Oresteia,'' Aeschylus' trilogy of 458 B.C. tracing the cycle of vengeance that haunted the House of Atreus: Agamemnon sacrificed his daughter, then was slain in retribution by his wife, Clytemnestra. She was killed by Agamemnon's son Orestes and his sister, Electra. And, in turn, Orestes was to be hounded endlessly by the Furies. Orestes appealed to the Olympian god Apollo, and the goddess Athena then conducted a trial before 12 citizens, casting the deciding vote that freed Orestes.

''Let no man live uncurbed by law, nor curbed by tyranny,'' Athena charged the jury. In the end, institutionalized human and divine justice combined to stop the cycle of bloodletting.

''I had been thinking of the vigilante movement all weekend, watching 'Agronsky and Company,' '' says McDonald. ''It seemed to me their time frame and their perspective on the issue was too small. You're talking about the institution of human justice . . . and living with the system, which has horrible flaws to it.''

McDonald added a personal note:

''Two weeks ago I was robbed by the police in Mexico City. I felt vulnerable, a tremendous sense of loss. It sort of hung in with me. . . . It shakes you up. . . . I went away feeling sort of de-balled, less a man.''

Afterward, he felt edgy, hostile; the other day, a salesman was rude and McDonald somehow ''couldn't muster the civility'' to let it pass.

''We had a nasty tiff.''

William Safire / Vigilante   *New York Times,* February 10, 1985

The former chief speechwriter for President Nixon, William Safire joined the New York Times *as a syndicated columnist in 1973. His twice-weekly column, ''Essay,'' and his ''On Language'' essay for the* Times's *Sunday magazine section have earned him a wide readership and a reputation as one of America's most astute voices of conservatism. His columns are now reprinted in more than five hundred newspapers. The author of nearly a dozen books, including* On Language *(1980), Safire is also the recipient of the 1978 Pulitzer Prize for distinguished commentary. Safire observes that he tries ''not to write for the history books but for that morning's paper. If I am angry or moved, why not let it show?''*

Is calling someone a *vigilante* an insult or a compliment? Is the philosophy of the vigilante called *vigilantism* or *vigilante-ism?*

These questions are posed by the issue raised in the New York subway shooting of four teen-agers by Bernhard H. Goetz, who felt menaced when accosted by them. His act was hailed by many people who feel threatened by hoodlums and was denounced by many who adhere to the rule of law even when it falls short. Mr. Goetz was indicted by a grand jury for criminal possession of a gun; only the linguistic case will be considered in this space.

Vigilante is a noun in English that comes from the Spanish noun for *watchman;* the Spanish adjective *vigilante* means "watchful, wide-awake," same as the English adjective *vigilant.* The origin of the English noun is in the Vigilance Committees organized in the South in the 1820's and 30's to intimidate blacks and abolitionists. "The slave States," said the abolition leader William Lloyd Garrison in 1835, ". . . have organized Vigilance Committees and Lynch Clubs." The assumption of control of law by citizens not empowered by law was applied more generally as well: "The prevalence of crime in San Francisco," wrote The Whig Almanac in 1851, "led to the formation of a voluntary association . . . called the Vigilance Committee."

At first, these committees—their members were called *vigilantes,* starting just after the Civil War—were usually considered praiseworthy. Abolitionists called some of their own Underground Railroad organizations by that name, refusing to concede the word to their opponents; the Republican clubs formed to support Lincoln were called "Wide-Awakes." After the war, as the nation expanded westward, "vigilance committee" was the name given to the citizenry that combined to combat lawlessness before the law arrived, or that took charge when the lawmen failed.

But from the start, another meaning grew. "We hate what are called vigilant men; they are a set of suspicious, mean spirited mortals, that dislike fun," wrote The Missouri Intelligencer in 1821. Abolitionists equated vigilance with lynching: "As gross a violation of justice," wrote Horace Greeley's New York Tribune in 1858, "as vigilance committee or lynching mob was ever guilty of."

Thus, the word comes into modern times with competing senses: good (providing law where there is none) and (taking the law into your own hands). When used today in a historical sense, the word looks back at the frontier's rough justice, rather than at the South's repression of blacks, and is usually a compliment. But when applied to modern-day activities, the word *vigilante*—and especially the *-ism* that grows out of it—is usually used to suggest that outdated and unnecessary methods are being employed, and is pejorative.

On National Public Radio, most newscasters sasy *vigilantism,* though I've heard several say *vigilante-ism;* NBC and CBS agree on *vigilantism.* Which is correct?

I prefer *vigilante-ism,* pronouncing the final *e* in *vigilante.* This *-ism* does not refer merely to "being vigilant"; it has to do with "being a vigilante." Because the *-ism* flows from the noun *vigilante* rather than the adjective *vigilant,* we should logically say *vigilante-ism.*

You think it looks awkward with the hyphen and is hard to say? If you prefer *vigilantism,* then maybe you would like *McCarthism.* Of course not; its *McCarthyism* and *vigilante-ism.* (Next time I hear an announcer drop the *e,* I'm gonna let him have it.)

Bill Mandel / Everybody Get a Gun!

San Francisco Examiner, March 10, 1985

Bill Mandel worked as the principal television critic for the San Francisco Examiner *for several years before shifting in 1981 to writing a daily column. His
incisive commentary on people, places, and national phenomena has earned him
a wide readership in the Bay Area.*

Since when is it front-page news when a transient shoots a street person on Market
Street? Since Bernhard Goetz, that's when.

Dan White, who killed Mayor George Moscone and Supervisor Harvey Milk,
is famous for the Twinkie Defense. Now New York subway vigilante Goetz will
go down in history for sparking his own form of jurisprudence. Goetz (and the
public reaction to what he did) has wrought a complete change in urban law
enforcement.

In the years Before Goetz (B.G.), defense of one's life was the only justification for shooting someone else in a public place. And even then, you had to prove
it in court.

Now, in the months immediately A.G., we have something new: Did the victim
"have it coming"? If so, and if the news media and the cops sustain the interpretation, the shooter may avoid legal penalties and become a mini-folk hero.

Here is another example of how New York has seized the initiative from California. In the old days, fads swept from West Coast to East Coast. Now it takes
a New Yorker to bring back the Wild, Wild West.

The Goetz Effect was at work this week in the Market Street killing of a Franklin Levi Clingenpeel, described as a street person, by Tony C. Thomas, a 68-year-
old retired gardener and resident of a Tenderloin transient hotel. Authorities were
unable to identify Clingenpeel for 24 hours after his death.

"Unknown killed by nobody" is hardly the stuff of banner headlines, but we
are living in inflamed times. The immediate question about the shooting concerned
its degree of vigilantism. Did the victim "have it coming"? Had he been Goetzed?

The Examiner's front-page headlines on Tuesday traced that concern. The first
edition's headline merely announced the killing, but each successive edition zoomed
in on the real issue. By the four-star final, the sub-headline said, "Market Street
suspect was no Goetz, cops say."

The story's account of the shooting first presented Thomas' version. In it Clingenpeel came face-to-face with him on the street, called him the worst thing our
language provides and added, "Watch where you're going."

"Screw you," Thomas quoted himself in reply.

Clingenpeel then balled up his fists, at which point, Thomas said, he drew a
.357 Magnum from under his sweater and fired. One witness said Thomas pumped
two extra rounds into his victim while he lay on Market Street's rough brick
sidewalk.

"He had it coming," Thomas reportedly told police, invoking the Goetz defense.

However, a witness said the victim had never blocked Thomas' path, had not
sworn at him and had not raised his fists.

This was the hinge on which the story swung—B.G., blocking someone's path,
swearing, even balling up fists were not justification for pumping four .357 slugs

into the offender. Now, A.G., the question of whether the victim cursed or blocked Thomas' path is vital, the main issue explored by news accounts.

If this logic continues, someday soon we'll have killers pleading for instant, Goetz-style self-defense street verdicts because the victim offended them by wearing brown shoes with a blue suit or by wearing a bare midriff with too much tummy hanging out.

Actually, the more interesting San Francisco shooting of the week never made it off Tuesday's back pages. It happened in the foggy netherworld of the Great Highway and Skyline Boulevard, and involved another modern kill-or-be-killed issue: driving.

Joseph Singer, 83, was out for a drive with his wife in their '76 Chevy. Robert Brigaerts, 37, following in his '77 Mercury, was apparently displeased with the speed Singer was driving.

After Brigaerts could not coax more speed out of Singer by honking his horn and tail-gating, he reportedly pulled around the Singers and slammed on his brakes, forcing the 83-year-old to stop. So far this is an incident we can visualize easily— an old man in his s—l—o—w car and an impatient jerk trying to be a complete windhole in an area of The City not known for the swift pace of life.

Brigaerts reportedly got out of his car and walked toward the Singers. Frightened, Singer pointed a starter's pistol at Brigaerts, who got back in his car. The Singers drove away. Moments later, Brigaerts pulled up to the left side of the Chevy and allegedly shot out two windows in the Singers' car with a .38.

This is frightening. Not because people will come to shots over driving hassles—that's old news. But, until recently, it would seem unlikely that two motorists chosen at random would both be armed.

The fact that both drivers had guns (even though Singer's was non-lethal) is less surprising than the fact that the story was buried back by the classified ads.

If there's a lesson to be learned from this, it's that carrying a starter's pistol to scare off bad guys isn't enough anymore. Now the guy you're trying to scare probably has a real gun in his glove compartment.

The Constitution provides the right to bear arms in aid of a citizen militia. What we've got now are one-person citizen militias cruising the streets looking for someone, anyone, who's got it coming.

DISCUSSION QUESTIONS

1. Reread Robert McFadden's news report on the shooting of four black youths on a New York City subway train. McFadden's report was among the earliest to be written about the incident. What details does McFadden seem to emphasize in his story? Compare and contrast the details in this account with the additional details provided in the subsequent editorials and columns written about the shooting. How well does McFadden's report stand up under the light of the details either provided by Goetz in his confession or discovered later by the police?

2. Compare and contrast the editorials on the subway shootings published in the *Washington Post* and the *San Francisco Chronicle*. List the points made in each argument. Which editorial do you find more convincing? Explain.

3. Comment on the effectivenss of Abe Mellinkoff's use of the metaphor of the Super Bowl to discuss the subway shootings. How would you characterize his diction and tone in this column? Do they add to or detract from the effectiveness of his essay? Explain. Outline the nature of Mellinkoff's argument. What

is his attitude toward the judicial system? What recommendations are implicit in what he says about the court system?

4. Compare and contrast the nature of Mellinkoff's argument with that of Sydney Schanberg in "Support Your Local Shooter." Which do you find more convincing? Why? Compare and contrast the points of view presented in Shanberg's and Mellinkoff's columns. Which column do you think uses irony more effectively? Point to specific words and phrases to verify your response.

5. Consider the strategies used by Russell Baker and Art Buchwald to treat the subway shootings from irreverent points of view. Which column do you judge the more humorous? What aspects of composition underscore the humorous effects in each? Point to specific passages to confirm each point you make. What serious points, if any, are made in the Baker and Buchwald columns? What images of contemporary America emerge from each column?

6. What is the overriding point made in Kenneth Clark's essay "In Cities, Who Is the Real Mugger?"? What concept of heroism does Clark respond to in his essay? How does that notion of a "folk hero" agree or differ with Phil McCombs's treatment of the cultural implications of the public's depicting Goetz as a "hero"? How does McCombs account for Goetz's extraordinary popularity? What is McCombs's attitude toward the public recognition and celebration accorded Goetz in the aftermath of his shooting of four youths on the subway?

7. What, in McCombs's judgment, does the Goetz incident tell us about contemporary American values? About the state of American culture? How has the Goetz incident "tapped into a fantasy that resonates deeply in the American soul"? What specific evidence does McCombs cite to validate this contention? How convincing do you find his analysis? Why?

8. Compare and contrast McCombs's sense of Goetz as a "vigilante" with William Safire's essay on the subject. How does each define the term? Which writer makes a more convincing case on this point? Point to specific passages to verify each point you make. In what specific respects are the emphases in each column different? Comment on the overall effectiveness of each essay.

9. Compare and contrast the structure, diction, and tone of Bill Mandel's column on the Goetz incident with those of Mellinkoff in "Latest from the Subway Super Bowl Wars." For what larger purpose does Mandel invoke the Goetz story? What what effect? Comment on the effectiveness of Mandel's argument.

Jonathan Freedman / Abolish American Apartheid
San Diego Union Tribune, May 9, 1985

Jonathan Freedman followed a rather circuitous path toward a career in journalism:

> *I call it more of a careen than a career. I always wanted to write. I read that Jack Kerouac went to Columbia University, so I went to Columbia and majored in English. I won the Cornell Woolrich Writing Fellowship, named after the detective writer. When I graduated in 1972, I took the $2500 prize and traveled down the Pan American Highway. I ran out of cash in Rio. I met a girl, who said, "Do you speak English? I think I know where you can get a job." She took me*

*over to the Associated Press where by luck there was a fine bureau
chief who went to Columbia Journalism School. He hired me, although I had never written a newspaper story.*

*After a few years with the A.P. in Rio de Janeiro and São Paulo, Freedman
worked for five years as a free-lancer, writing both fiction and nonfiction and
publishing columns in leading American newspapers. The author of a volume of
short fiction (*The Man Who'd Bounce the World, *1979), Freedman signed on
as an editorial writer at the* San Diego Union Tribune *in 1981. His writing
earned him the distinction of being named a Pulitzer Prize finalist in 1983 and
1984.*

People tell me that they can recognize my editorials. . . . [The editorial page] speaks with voices . . . not with bylines. The joke here is
that my editorials are so long that no one will ever read them. But I
think that sometimes a very long editorial will get more people to read
all the way through, because there's enough room to involve the readers and not repulse them with shorthand.

They live in polluted squatter camps. They toil in factories by day, but at night
they are hunted like animals. They produce the crops, but they are not permitted
to own the land. They serve in homes but sleep in shacks. They have no rights,
no representation in government, no freedom of speech in a land which is a democracy. If they are passive and do their work, they are tolerated by the white
elite. But if they protest, they are fired and returned to their homelands. Periodically the owners of the land become appalled by the squatters and bulldoze the
camps. Their children, born far from their homelands, are strangers in the new
land and strangers in their fathers' land. Generations live in a separate society,
serving the main society, but denied its rights and privileges.

These victims of apartheid are not thousands of miles away in South Africa,
but here in America—in San Diego. We call them illegal aliens, but their status
and their living conditions are not that different from the blacks of Soweto.

Americans are justly incensed by the horrors of apartheid in South Africa. But
students protesting against apartheid at the University of California at San Diego
are blind to the system of illegal alien farm labor in San Diego County. Concerned
Americans raising money to boycott South Africa are unaware that the waiters and
busboys serving them at fund-raisers are illegal aliens. The joggers who eat fresh
strawberries at the roadside avert their heads from the field workers stooping in
the sun, who live in the squatter camps of California.

South African apartheid is evil, a system which dooms that land to despair and
bloodshed. But South Africa is at least honest about its separate and unequal
society. America is not. An estimated 6 million to 12 million illegal aliens live in
this country, picking our crops, working in our sweatshops, an invisible minority.

Yes, many are better off economically than their brothers in their distant villages. So also the blacks in Soweto are better off than those in the impoverished
homelands. But the illegal aliens are not free. They live in constant fear of being
caught in the wrong place and deported. They cannot, in many places, go to a
bus station or eat in a restaurant without being detected and deported.

And yet they are working for the benefit of employers who know they are
illegal, know they have no rights, and exploit them.

Many Americans want to disinvest from firms doing business with South Africa. But we do not disinvest from farms and factories and restaurants and hotels
that hire illegal aliens in America. We maintain a system by which it is legal to

hire illegal aliens but illegal for them to work here, a system equal in hypocrisy to the pass laws of South Africa.

Americans look the other way when dealing with their own system of apartheid. And Congress, by its repeated deadlock, has ratified the system of illegal immigration and illegal labor. Some sing of the virtues of illegal labor for the United States economy. They resemble the Afrikaaner apologists for apartheid who turn up at newspapers, arguing the justice of their system, or their predecessors in the American South, the gentlemanly apologists for that benign, Bible-recognized institution, slavery.

Apartheid is racist wherever it exists. It is inhuman in South Africa and inhuman in southern California. It destroys the moral fabric of our society and leaves a legacy of discrimination and suffering.

But we are blind to it. We point our finger at the South Africans and feel self-satisfied at our enlightened society. While the waiters bring us fresh strawberries picked by illegal aliens living in ravines and hootches. Here. Today.

We have no direct power to halt apartheid in South Africa. But we can and must stop illegal immigration and exploitation here. We must make it illegal for employers to hire illegal aliens. We must offer amnesty to aliens, to bring them out of hiding. We must abolish apartheid in America.

DISCUSSION QUESTIONS

1. Comment on the effectiveness of Freedman's strategy to delay identifying the "they" until the second paragraph of his editorial. What are the impications of Freedman's use of the phrase "Illegal aliens" in paragraph two? Freedman repeats this phrase several times in his commentary. What are the effects of doing so?

2. Freedman does not focus on his announced subject—apartheid—until the third paragraph. What would be the effects of Freedman's having chosen to open his essay when a direct and immediate discussion of what he sees as the ironies of students in San Diego protesting against apartheid in South Africa?

3. Comment on how Freedman handles the issue of hypocrisy both in South Africa and in the United States. What is the consequence of his decision to shift from "they" early in the essay to "we" toward the end? Whom does Freedman include in this "we"? With what effect?

Alice Kahn / The Real Thing   *East Bay Express*, October 4, 1985

Born in Chicago in 1943, Alice Kahn was educated in that city's public schools, an experience she recalls with a humorous barb: "Studies have shown that for each year a child spends in the Chicago public schools, their IQ drops 3 points." A graduate of Columbia University's School of General Studies, where she majored in writing, Kahn moved to San Francisco and taught high school English for three years. In 1969, she changed careers and began work as a nurse, continuing with that profession until 1986.

Kahn began writing health articles in the 1970s and published essays in various professional journals in nursing. In the early 1980s, she shifted the focus of her writing to humor, publishing delightfully outrageous essays for Berkeley's celebrated East Bay Express. *More recently, Kahn has published a column in the* San Jose Mercury-News *and the* San Francisco Chronicle, *for which she now has a twice-weekly assignment.*

Her humorous essays on the contemporary cultural, political, and medical scenes have appealed to a wide readership, both locally in northern California and nationally. In 1985, she published her first volume of collected essays, Multiple Sarcasm, *followed in 1987 by* My Life as a Gal: Memoirs, Essays, and Outright Silliness, *from which the following essay is drawn.*

Nothing gets my dander up faster than the phrase "real Chicago pizza." I mean, what is real? What is Chicago? What is pizza? (And what, for that matter, is dander?)

It's time somebody warned innocent Californians of the danger of this hoax. Otherwise they will continue to allow their taste buds to be molested by these counterfeits while assuming there's no need to go to Chicago for research. Why risk experiencing bad weather and being machine-gunned by some gangster if you can get the real thing here at home?

Many places in the area offer what purports to be "real Chicago pizza," but I've yet to find it. The worst offender is the so-called Uno's franchise chain—an insult to any of us who spent our youth waiting for hours on the windiest corner in the windy city for quintessential Chicago pizza. This pizza consisted of a fresh crust covered with herbs and tomatoes buried under enough mozzarella so that you could stretch the cheese from one end of Wrigley Field to the other without breaking the strand. This was brought to your table in a cast-iron skillet, sizzling hot, so that, unless you had a Studs Terkel–like Chicago chatterbox keeping you from it, you inevitably bit into it too soon and burned your mouth. This, then, is a major point. If you walk out with your oral mucosa unscathed—it's not the real thing.

What you get at these franchises instead of this lethal meltdown is a pile of stale mush on a cardboard crust in a fake iron skillet. It's not real. It's mozzarella Memorex.

I'm not saying you can't get good pizza in California. You can get wonderful gourmet pizza at Chez Panisse and all its imitators. This is brick-oven, top-ingredient, innovative combo pie—very tasty. For my money, it's one of the best additions yet to California cuisine. If you feel you must be more experimental, get a side order of nasturtiums.

You can also get real New York junk pizza. But California/New York junk pizza will never recall Tony's on Broadway and 105th in Manhattan. I went to Tony's in the winter of 1963. Each time I walked into the place, Tony would say, "Hey, Natalie Wood, what you want?" I put on a quick twenty pounds falling for the Natalie Wood line. But had he said, "Hey, Anna Magnani," would I have kept coming back?

But what I am looking for when I hear "real Chicago pizza" is something that will transport me back in time, back to a certain graystone apartment house on a grimly real west side of Chicago in the winter of 1956. It was there in that sacred shrine, which I would memorialize with a plaque if I could, that I first took the mozzarella sacrament.

On that deadend street in the city without a heart, I was born-again Sicilian in the kitchen of my best friend Palma Zaccagnini. Even if the miracle of the oregano had never taken place, Palma was a great best friend. She looked and acted like Madonna, and she was tops in school at math. You could hang around with her, pick up the boyfriend discards, and learn exponentiation at the same time.

She taught me the art of flirting, self-defense, eyelining, and the highly developed Catholic science of guilt elimination. She taught me to dance the Chicken to the Coasters' "Searchin' (Gonna Find Her)," although—let the record show—she was a Pat Boone fan. But I never guessed that, through Palma, I would be exposed to the archetypal pizza pie.

When I visited her home the first time, I was surprised by how poor the Zaccagninis were. It wasn't just the three-room flat practically right on the new freeway. It wasn't just that she shared the bedroom with her big sisters, Mary Beth and Natalie, while her parents shared the living room with her little brothers, Peter and Paul. It was the dinner I had there that seemed particularly impoverished. They served canned Franco-American spaghetti and a loaf of Wonder Bread. (Years later I heard that Palma married the owner of a funeral home, and I pray it means she's come into some Mafia money and can afford fresh pasta.)

The second time I was over, the family, which was generous the way poor families frequently are, asked me to stay again. I was picky about my food and hesitated. But I loved how much they laughed together, so I decided to risk the Franco-American again. Unbeknown to me the grandmother from Sicily was staying there. (Where they put her, God only knows—on top of the fridge?) As we were seated around the kitchen table, a toothless white-haired woman, Our Lady of the Deep Pan, placed what appeared to me to be a piece of cake on my plate. It was thick, dry, slightly crunchy bread dough with a light tomatoey icing, graced with oregano, anointed with oil, and topped with a halo of mozzarella. Real Chicago pizza. *Marone,* it was good.

When Californians talk about "real Chicago pizza," they are obviously not thinking of Mama Zaccagnini. They are thinking of Mama Celeste. In order to come up with a reasonable facsimile, I was forced to learn to make pizza. Forced is perhaps too strong a word. Obviously, nobody put an Uzi to my head. Nevertheless, I think I have come up with a good alternative and am going to share. Before you finish the next ink-stained paragraph, you, my drooling reader, can begin your novitiate.

REAL CHICAGO PIZZA

1. Take one numbers runner and place in cement boots. Drive to Lake Michigan (optional step for those seeking surreal Chicago pizza).

2. Place checkered tablecloth and Chianti bottle with candle on table. Attach neon sign saying TONY's to outside window.

3. Place Julius LaRosa 78 on record player (alternative: Rosemary Clooney singing, "Come on-a My House").

4. Swear and gesture wildly. Begin dough.

THE DOUGH

1. (You can use any white bread dough, but here's mine.) Place one cup luke-hot water in a warmed bowl. Add one package or tablespoon yeast and dissolve. FADE TO SHELF.

2. Add one tablespoon sugar, one tablespoon oil, and a half-tablespoon salt. Mix.

3. Add flour to get right consistency. Right consistency is that of a baby's tushy. Should take three or so cups. Go by look and feel, not measurement (this is art, not life).

4. With oily hands and a floury board, knead.

5. Place kneaded tushy in well-oiled bowl in warm spot and let rise (about thirty minutes).

6. When risen, spank down, and with oily hands, spread in oily cast-iron skillet or any other receptacle you like. Cookie sheet is fine. Silver vase is weird. (If crust seems too big, break off some and shape into *La Pietà*.) Bake.

THE TOPPINGS

1. Easiest is to fingerpaint about a half can of tomato paste across the top, but you can also slave over homemade special sauce for days. You can also just drizzle olive oil (we don't need virgin—this is the '80s) and add fresh tomato slices.

2. Add shitload of minced garlic and best oregano you can get. Crush oregano between your bare fingers. Add fresh basil if desired (or sweet william, for that matter).

3. Now add whatever your little heart desires: sautéed mushrooms, peppers, onions, zucchini, best sausages (which are not kosher no matter what you pay for them), or some other disgusting things some people like on their pizza. Kind of shove this stuff into the dough.

4. Top with fresh-grated parmesan and *lots* of sliced okay-quality (not top) mozzarella.

5. Let rise for doughier-than-thou effect or stick soon in really hot oven, up there in 475-degree city. Watch and pray. You may need to bake ten minutes before adding cheese. Take out when cheese starts to brown. If dough is too soft, sue me (and cook without cheese first next time or let dough rise longer).

6. Dig in and burn roof of mouth.

That, give or take a few failures, and a few curses aimed my way, should take you there—Zaccagnini fields forever. If it doesn't work out and you see me walking down the street—walk on by. If you like it, you take my hand, kiss, and say, "Thank you, Godmother."

David Finkel / Joy Griffith's Killing: Act of Love or Murder?

St. Petersburg Times, November 17, 1985

Born in Reading, Pennsylvania, David Finkel spent his youth in Pennsylvania, Maryland, New Jersey, and Florida. He graduated from the University of Florida with a bachelor of science degree in 1977 and began working for a magazine called Urology Times *(where he was acclaimed "the most prolific writer in the history of the magazine") before joining the staff of the* Tallahassee Democrat, *assigned to the crime beat. He moved to the* St. Petersburg Times *in 1981 and writes general assignment stories, several of which have won awards from Florida press associations.*

Finkel describes himself as a classic procrastinator: "I put off writing as long as I can. If I didn't have a deadline, I'd probably never write a story. . . . If I had six months, I'd probably begin writing at five months and twenty-nine days." He describes his writing principally as a matter of revision: "I don't write and then go through and change everything. I edit as I go along. So it's all revision. I get into these silly arguments with myself: 'Is it time for a simple sentence or a compound one? How's the rhythm going? If I have the reader at this point, does he have the same reading rhythm that I have in mind?

> *. . . . I almost always go through the whole thing again, not for major changes at that point but mostly simplifying.''*

MIAMI—He was a distraught man that day, a man who sang lullabies and wept. With one hand, he held a gun. With the other, he stroked the smooth face of his daughter, a 3-year-old existing in limbo between life and death.

An hour before, he had given her what he thought was a fatal overdose of Valium. But here she was still breathing, her tiny chest rising and falling rhythmically, if ever so slightly.

She was in a crib at Miami Children's Hospital, lying on her back. She had been there for eight months, since the day she nearly suffocated. He leaned over the crib railing and looked at her eyes. They were open. They stared ahead, mirrored no emotions, saw nothing. It was the same for her other senses. The damage to her brain was total and irreversible, and because of it, she couldn't hear his weeping, and she couldn't feel his last touch goodbye before he aimed the gun at her heart.

He shot her twice. He dropped the gun. He prayed that her suffering was over. He fell into a nurse's arms, cried and said he wanted to die. He said, ''Maybe I should get the electric chair to make things even. I killed my daughter. I shot her twice. But I'm glad she has gone to heaven.''

* * *

On Tuesday morning in a Miami courtroom, almost five months after the death of his daughter Joy, Charles Griffith is scheduled to go on trial for murder. The defense, says Griffith's attorney, Mark Krasnow, will be mercy. ''It was an act of love,'' Krasnow says, ''not an act of malice.''

The case is troubling to everyone involved. Even the prosecutor, Abe Laeser, says he feels sympathy for Griffith. Nonetheless, the state has charged Griffith with first-degree murder because, Laeser says, ''It's offensive to assume you can actively execute someone because you think it's a merciful act.''

To Floridians, that line of thinking will probably sound familiar; in a highly publicized trial earlier this year, 76-year-old Roswell Gilbert was convicted of murdering his wife, Emily, who was dying of Alzheimer's disease. He, too, contended it was mercy rather than murder.

There are obvious similarities between the two cases. Both victims lived in South Florida, both were ill, both were loved, both were shot. But it is the differences that make Griffith's case especially pathetic.

While Roswell Gilbert was a successful engineer who at least had a long and fulfilling life to look back on, Griffith was adrift in depression and loneliness. And while Emily Gilbert was a dying old woman, Joy Griffith never had the chance to bloom.

She was, by all accounts, the center of her father's life. ''Believe me, he worshiped her,'' says his father, Leroy Griffith. He took photographs constantly. He taped some of them to a wall in the place he worked, the projection booth of an X-rated theater owned by his father.

After her illness and death, the photos came down, but not before he wrote on the back of one of them in red pen, the one that showed her lying comatose and open-eyed in the hospital crib, ''Our Father who art in heaven—why would You do this?''

The question referred to her accident. From the moment he shot her, he has taken responsibility for pulling the trigger. But the accident he never could understand.

It was a freakish thing. Joy was at her grandparents' house along with her mother, Becky. She went into the living room to watch TV. She began climbing onto her grandfather's recliner, poking her head through the space between the chair and the footrest. Somehow, as she tried to wiggle through, the footrest folded in a bit, closing on her neck. She began choking. She tried to get free, but the more she struggled, the tighter the chair folded up. She went a minute without breathing. Two minutes. . . .

Becky, in the kitchen, heard the TV go on and began fixing Joy's lunch. Five minutes went by, perhaps eight. She walked out to the living room.

There was Joy, wedged in the chair, motionless, bluish in color, hanging unconscious.

"Had she not been found for another two minutes, she probably would have been dead at the scene," says Dr. Charles Wetli, assistant Dade County medical examiner. As it was, the lack of oxygen ruined her beyond repair. Much of her brain, and many of her nerves, were dead. It would take paramedics 40 minutes just to get her heart beating regularly.

"She was in what you call a chronic, persistent, vegetative state—virtually no hope of recovery," says Dr. Robert Cullen, the neurologist who treated her at Miami Children's Hospital. "The best they could hope for was that she would remain blind, spastic, perhaps off the respirator. . . . Basically, this girl had only one route, and that was to eventually die."

* * *

At the time of the accident, Griffith and his wife were still getting along, still talking. Estrangement, then accusations, and finally divorce would come later. But up until that moment—considering how idiosyncratic their life together was anyway—everything was fine.

They met in Miami in the late 1970s. To be sure, they had their differences. She was the daughter of Cuban immigrants; he was born in a traveling circus. She grew up in Miami; he was raised by his mother in North Carolina. She lived in a modest home; he dropped out of high school in 11th grade, left his mother behind, and moved into the estate his father had bought from running a string of porno theaters.

They also had their peculiar traits. He drank a six-pack of beer every day; she dabbled occasionally in a secretive, magic-filled religion called Santeria. They met when they both applied for the same job: training 33 poodles for a circus act.

Seven months later, they were married. And three years after that, on April 4, 1982, Joy was born.

They didn't have much money. They lived rent-free in one of Leroy Griffith's apartments. The apartment itself wasn't bad—at least it had air conditioning—but the neighborhood was. It was toward the southern end of Miami Beach, next to one of the Griffith theaters. The streets were filled with drunks, transients, and destitute refugees from the Mariel boatlift.

A few times, Griffith got into trouble. There were some arrests for burglaries and drugs, minor stuff. He got probation and drifted along. He went to computer school. He tried a few other dead ends. Always, he ended up back at the Gayety, one of his father's theaters.

Once, it had been a burlesque house. Now it was nonstop films. He got paid $100 or so a week for running the projector, and whenever things got really tight, his father would give him money, often folding a $100 bill into one of Joy's hands and having her present it to him.

The family survived. Joy turned 1, learned to walk, turned 2, started talking. Every morning, they would hang out in the apartment or at the beach. Then Griffith would kiss his wife and baby goodbye and head off to the theater. He would enter through a side door marked "Peep Show." He would climb the flight of steps leading past his father's office, go into the projection booth, thread up the first film, and settle in for a long day.

Sometimes he would read, sometimes he'd talk to his aunt who ran the box office, sometimes he'd look at the photographs of Joy taped to the wall: Joy sitting on a bench, Joy with a dog, Joy with some kittens. She always smiled. Her hair was getting long.

* * *

The day of her accident—Oct. 24, 1984—he was at the theater. Becky called, hysterical, and said Joy wasn't breathing, that the paramedics were there. But he didn't know how bad it was until he got to the hospital. Her heart was beating, but a respirator was breathing for her. Her color had come back, but she was lifeless.

He wouldn't leave. Both he and Becky stayed day and night, alternating shifts. For the first six months, Joy was never alone.

He would dab lemon juice on her lips. He would run a cloth under cool water, lay it on her leg, and say, "Joy, this is cold." He would put filters over a flashlight, aim it toward her eyes, and say, "Joy, this is red."

He would say, "This is Daddy. If you can hear me, move your toes."

"If you love me, blink your eyes."

He swore her toes moved and her eyes blinked. But the doctors told him that was impossible, that any movements were nothing more than reflexive.

She would sleep with her eyes open. She couldn't swallow. She was fed through a tube into her stomach. For the first few months, a bolt was inserted into her head to monitor any swelling in her brain. She was kept from further deterioration only through incredible medical wizardry:

Nystatin in her mouth to fight off infection. Lacri-Lube in her eyes when they got too dry. Tylenol as a suppository to control her temperature.

And an entire medicine cabinet fed into her through the gastronomy tube:

Pedialyte for nourishment, Colace for constipation, Phenobarbital to control seizures, Backtrim to control infection, Valium to relax her muscles and more.

How long can she live like this? Griffith once asked. They told him possibly only a few years, possibly until she was 50.

Nurses were in with her constantly. There was always a tube to check, a drug to introduce. When they rolled her over or were readying an injection, Griffith would yell at them, "Tell her what you're doing!" More than a few times, he could be heard shouting, "If you won't say anything, get out of here."

Stories began circulating about him. One nurse said he showed up reeking of liquor, another said he offered her marijuana, another said he threatened to hit her.

He and Becky began fighting, first about how much the nurses should be doing to Joy, then about everything. Becky filed for divorce and got a doctor's order limiting what kind of contact Griffith could have with Joy. She came to the hospital during the day. He came at night.

The only thing it seemed they could agree on was that they would never sign an agreement called a no-code, which would allow doctors to let Joy live or die on her own—no respirator, no heart massage, no help.

Then that changed. On her third birthday, Griffith came in dressed like a clown. He painted his hair orange and his face white and put on a red rubber nose. He thought she'd notice. He lifted her out of the crib, held her and sang to her, but she was stiff in his arms. He asked her to blink, but she didn't. He started to cry, put her back in the crib and left the room.

After that, she seemed to get worse. She got pneumonia and couldn't get rid of it. She began having seizures. She no longer moved her toes.

Griffith told doctors he would agree to a no-code.

But Becky wouldn't.

So on June 28, Griffith came to the hospital with a gun. It was tucked in a pocket along with some Valium.

A neighbor of his, Jeffrey Metcalf, told lawyers that Griffith had talked for a month about ways to "discontinue his child's pain."

"He thought about suffocation, but that was why she was in the hospital, so he didn't want to do it that way," Metcalf said.

*   *   *

He got to the hospital around 8 p.m. Becky was there. Joy was in her arms. He took her and cradled her. Becky left, and he started to cry. A nurse, Geraldine Goskey, got him some tissues. He thanked her and kept crying.

Around 9 p.m., he laid Joy back in her crib. He combed her hair. He caressed her.

He kissed her on the forehead.

He kissed her face.

Just before 10 p.m., when Goskey walked by the crib to check on Joy, Griffith put his hand on her, drew her close, and said, "Ma'am. I've got a gun."

He showed her the gun, a 32-caliber revolver. He told her he had crushed up 100 milligrams of Valium and fed it to Joy through her gastronomy tube. Scared, Goskey began to cry. Another nurse saw her and told the supervisor, Mary Leali. Leali walked over to the crib. She didn't know what was going on.

"Is she sleeping?" she asked.

"Not yet," she says Griffith answered.

"He was weepy-eyed," she said later. "He said, 'I don't want her to live like that any more. I don't want her to suffer any more.' And then he started in on God. 'If there's a God, why is He doing this? If there's a God, I want her to go where He is.' "

They stood there, against the side of the crib, watching Joy. After a while, Goskey moved off to feed another baby in the room.

Eleven o'clock came and went.

Leali said to him, "The nurses are going to wonder what I'm doing standing at this bedside for this length of time. Now why don't you take that gun, put it in your pocket, walk out that door, and no one will know anything."

She says he stood there awhile. "Then he ordered me to go call the police.

"So I did an about-face, prayed, and walked out the door."

Goskey was still in there. She was listening, but not looking, when he brought the gun close to Joy's heart and fired.

"I hear a shot," she said. "I turn around. I smell smoke. He has the gun in his right hand. He's standing over his child, right at the crib, near her chest area. He moves up again, closer, bends down a little bit. . . . Bang! I saw it, and I heard it."

He straightened up. Goskey stood absolutely still. He turned toward her. She looked at his face. "It looked very sad, very depressed." She watched as he knelt, put the gun on the floor, and pushed it away from him. She heard people running down the hall. He did, too.

He yelled, "Don't touch my baby! Don't come near my baby! Don't let them hurt my baby!"

They ran into the room, toward the crib. "Leave my baby alone," he screamed. "She's not going to suffer anymore. You're not going to cut her anymore."

They surrounded the crib, realized nothing could be done. They covered the body with a white blanket while a nurse held onto Griffith, who sagged in her arms.

"I shot my little girl," he said. "I killed my baby. I'm not an animal. Don't treat me like an animal."

* * *

His lawyer, Mark Krasnow, says he will attempt three paths of defense.

The first will be temporary insanity, an insanity that took root the day of the accident.

"Doing what he did certainly indicates that he has a mental problem," Krasnow said in court documents, "and if he did not have a mental problem before he did it, he sure had one after he did it, after he saw his baby die due to his own act."

The second will be that Griffith couldn't have killed his daughter because she was already brain dead, the standard of death in Florida.

"It's an interesting argument," says Laeser, the prosecutor, but "it has nothing to do with the case. She was never brain dead, and I've got the EEGs to prove it."

The third is the main one, the trouble one, the one based on emotions rather than legalities—the notion of mercy.

Even Laeser is bothered by this one. He has children. He had a father-in-law who lapsed into a fatal coma. "I'm sympathetic to him. I realize it was obviously very difficult for him during those several months," he says.

But he adds, "I don't have a legal question on it. I think the evidence is absolutely consistent with first-degree murder."

So starting Tuesday, unless a last-minute plea bargain can be worked out, the question of mercy will be put before a jury of 12, some of whom will be parents, some of whom may have confronted their own tragedies, some of whom will no doubt look over at Griffith and wonder how in the world he was able to pull the trigger. Twice.

For Griffith, it will be the first time he has been out of jail in quite a while. After he killed Joy, he was arrested, declared a suicide risk, stripped naked, and put in an isolation cell. Sedated, he slept on the concrete floor, woke up shivering, slept some more. Two days later, he was allowed to put on a suit and visit the funeral home for a viewing. Then it was back to the jail, where he has been since.

He has remained there in seclusion. He is in a cell decorated with 12 photographs of Joy, plus a drawing of her done by another inmate in exchange for three packs of cigarettes.

In a brief interview last week, he said, "I don't care what happens. They can't do anything to hurt me any more than I already hurt. The important thing is she's in heaven, she can move and talk and laugh."

He said a psychiatrist suggested he take down the photographs of Joy, but he hadn't.

He said he watches TV during the day and dreams at night that he is in the hospital, running down a corridor, Joy in his arms, doctors in pursuit.

"She's always in mind," he said.

He said that after Joy's burial, he called the cemetery and bought the grave site next to hers.

Says his father, who is helping him pay for it, "He must be thinking, 'If there's a heaven, and she's there, where am I going to go?' "

DISCUSSION QUESTIONS

1. David Finkel compares and contrasts the decision of Charles Griffith with that of Roswell Gilbert, another resident of Florida tried for killing a loved one. Where do Finkel's sympathies lie in creating a broader context for Griffith's

story? What additional strategies does Finkel use to elicit the reader's sympathies?

2. Comment on the structure of Finkel's story. According to what principle of organization is the story controlled? Does it proceed, for example, in terms of chronology? What techniques does Finkel use to create unity for his narrative?

3. Comment on the effectiveness of the scene in which the nurses watch helplessly as Griffith waits for his daughter to die. What stylistic strategies does Finkel use to intensify the impact of these moments? What is the effect of Finkel's decision to close the story with Griffith speaking?

William F. Buckley, Jr. / With All Deliberate Speed: What's So Bad about Writing Fast?

New York Times Book Review, February 9, 1986

Considered by many to be one of America's finest debators for and defenders of political conservatism, William F. Buckley, Jr., currently writes a syndicated column that appears three times a week in more than three hundred newspapers. He is the founder and editor of the National Review, *an influential fortnightly magazine, and also the host of a television interview show called "Firing Line." Several of his spy novels have enjoyed long runs on the best-seller lists.*

As much and as frequently as Buckley writes, he admits, "I do not like to write, for the simple reason that writing is extremely hard work, and I do not 'like' extremely hard work."

If, during spring term at Yale University in 1949 you wandered diagonally across the campus noticing here and there an undergraduate with impacted sleeplessness under his eyes and coarse yellow touches of fear on his cheeks, you were looking at members of a masochistic set who had enrolled in a course called Daily Themes. No Carthusian novitiate embarked on a bout of mortification of the flesh suffered more than the students of Daily Themes, whose single assignment, in addition to attending two lectures per week, was to write a 500-to-600-word piece of descriptive prose every day, and to submit it before midnight (into a large box outside a classroom). Sundays were the only exception (this was before the Warren Court outlawed Sunday).

For anyone graduated from Daily Themes who went on to write, in journalism or in fiction or wherever, the notion that a burden of 500 words per day is the stuff of nightmares is laughable. But caution: 500 words a day is what Graham Greene writes, and Nabokov wrote 180 words per day, devoting to their composition (he told me) four or five hours. But at that rate, Graham Greene and Nabokov couldn't qualify for a job as reporters on The New York Times. Theirs is high-quality stuff, to speak lightly of great writing. But Georges Simenon is also considered a great writer, at least by those who elected him to the French Academy, and he writes books in a week or so. Dr. Johnson wrote "Rasselas," his philosophical romance, in nine days. And Trollope . . . we'll save Trollope.

I am fired up on the subject because, to use a familiar formulation, they have been kicking me around a lot; it has got out that I write fast, which is qualifiedly true. In this august journal, on Jan. 5, Morton Kondracke of Newsweek took it all the way: "He [me—W.F.B.] reportedly knocks out his column in 20 minutes flat—three times a week for 260 newspapers. That is too little time for serious contemplation of difficult subjects."

Now that is a declaration of war, and I respond massively.

To begin with: it is axiomatic, in cognitive science, that there is no necessary correlation between profundity of thought and length of time spent on thought. J.F.K. is reported to have spent 15 hours per day for six days before deciding exactly how to respond to the missile crisis, but it can still be argued that his initial impulse on being informed that the Soviet Union had deployed nuclear missiles in Cuba (bomb the hell out of them?) might have been the strategically sounder course. This is not an argument against deliberation, merely against the suggestion that to think longer (endlessly?) about a subject is necessarily to probe it more fruitfully.

Mr. Kondracke, for reasons that would require more than 20 minutes to fathom, refers to composing columns in 20 minutes "flat." Does he mean to suggest that I have a stopwatch which rings on the 20th minute? Or did he perhaps mean to say that I have been known to write a column in 20 minutes? Very different. He then goes on, in quite another connection, to cite "one of the best columns" in my new book—without thinking to ask: How long did it take him to write that particular column?

The chronological criterion, you see, is without validity. Every few years, I bring out a collection of previously published work, and this of course requires me to reread everything I have done in order to make that season's selections. It transpires that it is impossible to distinguish a column written very quickly from a column written very slowly. Perhaps that is because none is written very slowly. A column that requires two hours to write is one which was interrupted by phone calls or the need to check a fact. I write fast—but not, I'd maintain, remarkably fast. If Mr. Kondracke thinks it intellectually risky to write 750 words in 20 minutes, what must he think about people who speak 750 words in five minutes, as he often does on television?

The subject comes up now so regularly in reviews of my work that I did a little methodical research on my upcoming novel. I began my writing (in Switzerland, removed from routine interruption) at about 5 P.M., and wrote usually for two hours. I did that for 45 working days (the stretch was interrupted by a week in the United States, catching up on editorial and television obligations). I then devoted the first 10 days in July to revising the manuscript. On these days I worked on the manuscript an average of six hours per day, including retyping. We have now a grand total: 90 plus 60, or 150 hours. My novels are about 70,000 words, so that averaged out to roughly 500 words per hour.

Anthony Trollope rose at 5 every morning, drank his tea, performed his toilette and looked at the work done the preceding day. He would then begin to write at 6. He set himself the task of writing 250 words every 15 minutes for three and one-half hours. Indeed it is somewhere recorded that if he had not, at the end of 15 minutes, written the required 250 words he would simply "speed up" the next quarter-hour, because he was most emphatic in his insistence on his personally imposed daily quota: 3,500 words.

Now the advantages Trollope enjoys over me are enumerable and nonenumerable. I write only about the former, and oddly enough they are negative advantages. He needed to write by hand, having no alternative. I use a word processor. Before beginning this article, I tested my speed on this instrument and discovered that I type more slowly than I had imagined. Still, it comes out at 80 words per minute. So that if Trollope had had a Kaypro or an I.B.M., he'd have written, in three and one-half hours at my typing speed, not 3,500 words but 16,800 words per day.

Ah, you say, but could anyone think that fast? The answer is, sure people can think that fast. How did you suppose extemporaneous speeches get made? Erle Stanley Gardner dictated his detective novels nonstop to a series of secretaries, having previously pasted about in his studio 3-by-5 cards reminding him at exactly what hour the dog barked, the telephone rang, the murderer coughed. He knew where he was going, the plot was framed in his mind, and it became now only an act of extrusion. Margaret Coit wrote in her biography of John C. Calhoun that his memorable speeches were composed not in his study but while he was outdoors, plowing the fields on his plantation. He would return then to his study and write out what he had framed in his mind. His writing was an act of transcription. I own the holograph of Albert Jay Nock's marvelous book on Jefferson, and there are fewer corrections on an average page than I write into a typical column. Clearly Nock knew exactly what he wished to say and how to say it; prodigious rewriting was, accordingly, unnecessary.

Having said this, I acknowledge that I do not know exactly what I am going to say, or exactly how I am going to say it. And in my novels, I can say flatly, as Mr. Kondracke would have me say it, that I really do not have any idea where they are going—which ought not to surprise anyone familiar with the nonstop exigencies of soap opera writing or of comic strip writing or, for that matter, of regular Sunday sermons. It is not necessary to know how your protagonist will get out of a jam into which you put him. It requires only that you have confidence that you will be able to get him out of that jam. When you begin to write a column on, let us say, the reaction of Western Europe to President Reagan's call for a boycott of Libya it is not necessary that you should know *exactly* how you will say what you will end up saying. You are, while writing, drawing on huge reserves: of opinion, prejudice, priorities, presumptions, data, ironies, drama, histrionics. And these reserves you enhance during practically the entire course of the day, and it doesn't matter all that much if a particular hour is not devoted to considering problems of foreign policy. You can spend an hour playing the piano and develop your capacity to think, even to create; and certainly you can grasp more keenly, while doing so, your feel for priorities.

The matter of music flushes out an interesting point: Why is it that critics who find it arresting that a column can be written in 20 minutes, a book in 150 hours, do not appear to find it remarkable that a typical graduate of Julliard can memorize a prelude and fugue from "The Well-Tempered Clavier" in an hour or two? It would take me six months to memorize one of those *numeros*. And mind, we're not talking here about the "Guinness Book of World Records" types. Isaac Asimov belongs in "Guinness," and perhaps Erle Stanley Gardner, but surely not an author who averages a mere 500 words per hour, or who occasionally writes a column at one-third his typing speed.

There are phenomenal memories in the world. Claudio Arrau is said to hold in his memory music for 40 recitals, two and a half hours each. *That* is phenomenal. Ralph Kirkpatrick, the late harpsichordist, actually told me that he had not played the "Goldberg" Variations for 20 years before playing it to a full house in New Haven in the spring of 1950. *That* is phenomenal. Winston Churchill is said to have memorized all of "Paradise Lost" in a week, and throughout his life he is reported to have been able to memorize his speeches after a couple of readings. (I have a speech I have delivered 50 times, and could not recite one paragraph of it by heart.)

So cut it out, Kondracke. I am, I fully grant, a phenomenon, but not because of any speed in composition. I asked myself the other day, Who else, on so many issues, has been so right so much of the time? I couldn't think of anyone. And I devoted to the exercise 20 minutes. Flat.

MAGAZINES

I'm obsessed by Time Magazine.
I read it every week.
Its cover stares at me every time I slink past the corner
    candystore.

ALLEN GINSBERG, "AMERICA"

FROM an early exposé of child labor violations to an analysis of television violence, the following selection of American magazine writing illustrates a variety of prose styles and compositional procedures adopted by writers to address many different levels of reading interest and aptitude.

No magazine is addressed to everyone. Though all magazines are eager to increase their circulation, they nevertheless operate with a fairly limited market in mind. A magazine's image is often as firmly established as the brand image devised by advertisers to ensure a commercially reliable consumer identification with a product. "What Sort of Man Reads *Playboy?*" is, according to that magazine's advertisement, a question easily answered, if not by the details of the photograph in the ad, then certainly by the language describing what the "typical" *Playboy* reader is like. Depending on the issue you look at, he may be "urbane," "stylish," "his own man," "literate," "free-wheeling," "an individualist." "Can a Girl Be Too Busy" and "Is This How You See Our Readers?" (see "Advertising") offer further instances, though playfully exaggerated, of a magazine's personification of its public image through characters and voices that supposedly convey the life-style, or desired life-style, of its readers.

Regardless of the ways a magazine goes about promoting its public identity, the type of audience it wants to attract can be seen in the total environment created by such material as the magazine's fiction and nonfiction, advertisements, editorial commentary, paper quality, and overall physical design. An article in *The New Yorker*, for example, is forced to compete for its readers' attention with glossy scenes of high fashion, mixed drinks, and the allure of exotic places. Yet not all magazines imagine or address their readers in quite such fashionable terms. An article appearing in *Good Housekeeping, Harper's, Psychology Today*, or *Scientific American* does not usually take its tone from the modish world that forms the context of magazines such as *The New Yorker, Playboy, Cosmopolitan, Vogue*, and *Esquire.* For example, advertisements for precision instruments, various types of machinery, automobiles, and corporate accountability, along with mathematical games, puzzles, and instructions for home experiments, surround the technical articles published in *Scientific American.* The readers of a magazine like *Good Housekeeping* are expected to be particularly attentive to products, services, and expertise that promise to improve a family's immediate domestic environment.

The ideal reader for a given magazine—the reader as housewife, playboy, academic, outdoorsman—is a vague entity, invented by the magazine more for simple identification than realistic description. No one is *just* a housewife or an academic, even assuming that we know exactly who or what these categories stand for in the first place. Naturally, labels like these suggest different associations to different people. For example, the audiences imagined by Hugh Hefner for *Playboy* and by Lew Dietz in "The Myth of the Boss Bear" for *True* may both be comprised of adventurous males, but they certainly are men who find their sport in different environments. The risks and failure detailed by Dietz in his personal adventure in the outdoors would not be nearly as alluring to the self-described "urban male" readers of *Playboy* who, as one recent ad put it, "enjoy mixing up cocktails and an *hors d'oeuvre* or two, putting a little mood on the phonograph and inviting in a female acquaintance for a quiet discussion on Picasso, Nietzsche, jazz, or sex." To contend, then, that the audience for Hefner's and Dietz's articles are both male and to let it go at that is like arguing that the reader of an article in an issue of *TV Guide* can be described solely as someone who has the ability to watch television.

Some affinity surely exists between the readership a magazine commercially promotes and the individual reader a particular article within that magazine assumes. But to characterize more accurately the audience addressed by a particular article, we need to go beyond the conveniently stereotyped reader presupposed by the magazine's title or its public image. For instance, *Everybody's,* a popular magazine first published nationwide in 1903, certainly could not appeal to everyone in America. Like any other magazine, it selected articles that approximated most closely the style of talk and the strategies of persuasion it felt its readers were most accustomed to. For a number of years, *Everybody's* played a prominent role in helping to develop the mode of American journalism that Theodore Roosevelt scornfully christened "muckraking." Along with other leading newspapers and periodicals, *Everybody's* featured a number of successful articles devoted to exposing public scandals and attacking vice and corruption in business and politics. Its readers were assumed to be civic-minded, generally well-informed people concerned with what they felt was a growing network of moral irresponsibility on the part of public administrators and industrial leaders.

William Hard's article "De Kid Wot Works at Night," which appeared in the January 1908 issue of *Everybody's,* was directed to readers already aware of the abuses of child labor and the insidious corruption of urban life through their reading of some of the very newspapers that Hard's young subjects worked so energetically to sell. The boys Hard investigated earned their living out on the streets at night, where they were sadly vulnerable to the sundry temptations of a big city after dark. Hard argued seriously for legislative reform:

> Mr. J. J. Sloan, when he was superintendent of the John Worthy School (which is the local municipal juvenile reformatory), reported that the newsboys committed to his care were, on the average, one-third below the stature and one-third below the strength of average ordinary boys of the same age. In the face of testimony of this kind, which could be duplicated from every city in the United States, it seems absurd to talk about the educative influence of the street. That it has a certain educative influence is undeniable, but it is equally undeniable that the boys who are exposed to this influence should be prevented, by proper legislation, from exposing themselves to it for too many hours a day and should especially be prevented from exposing themselves to it for even a single hour after seven o'clock in the evening.

The facts are certainly unpleasant, and Hard is confident that his readers will be persuaded by the weight of professional testimony and their own natural sympathy for the plight of such unfortunate children.

Yet Hard himself seems not always convinced that his newsboys and messengers are the hopeless victims of a ruthless economic system. It is precisely after seven o'clock in the evening that the children he is writing about come to life. The following description portrays "Jelly," the newsboy Hard chooses as his representative "case," and his little sister in ways not nearly so pathetic as engaging:

> At half past ten he went to an elevated railway station to meet his little sister. She was ten years old. She had dressed herself for the part. From her ragged and scanty wardrobe she had chosen her most ragged and her scantiest clothes.
>
> Accompanied by his sister, "Jelly" then went to a flower shop and bought a bundle of carnations at closing prices. With these carnations he took his sister to the entrance of the Grand Opera House. There she sold the whole bundle to the people coming out from the performance.

Her appearance was picturesque and pitiful. Her net profit from the sale of her flowers was usually about thirty-five cents.

Life on the street surely has its "undeniable educative influence." If roaming the streets at night stunted Jelly's growth, it certainly did not cripple his resourcefulness and imagination.

Hard's attitude toward the life-style of Jelly and his associates is ambivalent. The reader of the article is asked to acknowledge the seriousness of the terrible conditions surrounding the lives of impoverished children in the city and, at the same time, to recognize that such circumstances do not always culminate in the melodramatic ruination of their victims. Hard transforms Jelly into an entrepreneur responsive to the fluctuations in the flower market—he buys carnations at "closing prices." Jelly also knows how to profit from the "ragged and scanty wardrobe"of his little sister. She, too, willingly participates in the act, choosing only those clothes that will show her poverty to best advantage. Hard's diction ("dressed . . . for the part," "most ragged," "scantiest," "picturesque") alerts the reader to the theatricality implicit in the attempts of these children to earn a living.

It should be clear from the language of the passage that Hard does not think of Jelly and his sister simply as "pitiful" figures. In fact, the word *pitiful* works not so much to move his readers to compassion for the abject condition of the children as much as to describe the self-conscious ways the children display themselves before a fashionable urban audience. From a sociological standpoint, Jelly and his sister may very well be pitiful, but they are also *acting* pitiful, and the awareness of that distinction is what makes it so difficult for Hard to write a disinterested report wholly committed to immediate legislative reform. Hard's predicament in this article is that the corruption he is striving to eliminate as a reformer sustains the very set of characters he finds, as a writer, so appealing in their verbal energy and playful perseverance.

The attractiveness of the kids who work at night and Hard's reluctance to render them merely in sociological terms prompt him to fictionalize their lives, treating them more like characters in a short story than as subjects to be documented. He takes us beyond the limits of factual observation by vividly imagining many details of the newsboys' behavior in situations that must have been annoyingly inaccessible to him. Whatever *Everybody's* public image and vested interests, Hard's article presupposes a reader attuned to both the need for legislative action and the nuances of parody. Like Gay Talese's example of "new journalism" which also appears in this section, Hard's piece exists in a territory somewhere between the reportorial prose of newspapers and the inventions of fiction.

With the exception of highly specialized journals and periodicals, most magazines, despite their commercial or artistic differences, want their articles to be both informative and entertaining, responding to those timely topics the renowned American novelist and magazine editor William Dean Howells once termed "contemporarnics." Pick up any popular magazine and you will be sure to come across essays offering information about some subject that is a topic of current public interest. Sex, celebrities, success, catastrophes, scandals, the bizarre—it would be difficult to find a magazine that does not contain a single article with a contemporary slant on one of these perennial subjects. Precisely how these subjects will be rendered in prose most often depends on the vigorous interplay between an author's style and purpose and whatever specific compositional standards or general tone the magazine encourages or requires.

Jack London / The Story of an Eyewitness
[An Account of the San Francisco Earthquake]

Collier's Weekly, May 1906

> *Jack London (1876–1916), a native of San Francisco, happened to be working near the city when the earthquake struck on the evening of April 16, 1906. An internationally prominent novelist, reporter, and social critic, London telegraphed the following vivid eyewitness account of the disaster to* Collier's Weekly, *for which he was paid twenty-five cents a word. London's dramatic report, which appeared in an issue devoted entirely to photographs and articles on the earthquake, was perfectly suited to* Collier's *characteristically hard-hitting journalism. With a weekly circulation of more than one million,* Collier's *was the country's leading public affairs magazine and an important precursor of modern photojournalism.*

The earthquake shook down in San Francisco hundreds of thousands of dollars' worth of walls and chimneys. But the conflagration that followed burned up hundreds of millions of dollars' worth of property. There is no estimating within hundreds of millions the actual damage wrought. Not in history has a modern imperial city been so completely destroyed. San Francisco is gone! Nothing remains of it but memories and a fringe of dwelling houses on its outskirts. Its industrial section is wiped out. Its social and residential section is wiped out. The factories and warehouses, the great stores and newspaper buildings, the hotels and the palaces of the nabobs, are all gone. Remains only the fringe of dwelling houses on the outskirts of what was once San Francisco.

Within an hour after the earthquake shock the smoke of San Francisco's burning was a lurid tower visible a hundred miles away. And for three days and nights this lurid tower swayed in the sky, reddening the sun, darkening the day, and filling the land with smoke.

On Wednesday morning at a quarter past five came the earthquake. A minute later the flames were leaping upward. In a dozen different quarters south of Market Street, in the working-class ghetto, and in the factories, fires started. There was no opposing the flames. There was no organization, no communication. All the cunning adjustments of a twentieth-century city had been smashed by the earthquake. The streets were humped into ridges and depressions and piled with debris of fallen walls. The steel rails were twisted into perpendicular and horizontal angles. The telephone and telegraph systems were disrupted. And the great water mains had burst. All the shrewd contrivances and safeguards of man had been thrown out of gear by thirty seconds' twitching of the earth crust.

By Wednesday afternoon, inside of twelve hours, half the heart of the city was gone. At that time I watched the vast conflagration from out on the bay. It was dead calm. Not a flicker of wind stirred. Yet from every side wind was pouring in upon the city. East, west, north, and south, strong winds were blowing upon the doomed city. The heated air rising made an enormous suck. Thus did the fire of itself build its own colossal chimney through the atmosphere. Day and night, this dead calm continued, and yet, near to the flames, the wind was often half a gale, so mighty was the suck.

The edict which prevented chaos was the following proclamation by Mayor E. E. Schmitz:

"The Federal Troops, the members of the Regular Police Force, and all Special Police Officers have been authorized to KILL any and all persons found engaged in looting or in the commission of any other crime.

"I have directed all the Gas and Electric Lighting Companies not to turn on gas or electricity until I order them to do so; you may therefore expect the city to remain in darkness for an indefinite time.

"I request all citizens to remain at home from darkness until daylight of every night until order is restored.

"I warn all citizens of the danger of fire from damaged or destroyed chimneys, broken or leaking gas pipes or fixtures, or any like cause."

Wednesday night saw the destruction of the very heart of the city. Dynamite was lavishly used, and many of San Francisco's proudest structures were crumbled by man himself into ruins, but there was no withstanding the onrush of the flames. Time and again successful stands were made by the fire fighters, and every time the flames flanked around on either side, or came up from the rear, and turned to defeat the hard-won victory.

An enumeration of the buildings destroyed would be a directory of San Francisco. An enumeration of the buildings undestroyed would be a line and several addresses. An enumeration of the deeds of heroism would stock a library and bankrupt the Carnegie medal fund. An enumeration of the dead—will never be made. All vestiges of them were destroyed by the flames. The number of the victims of the earthquake will never be known. South of Market Street, where the loss of life was particularly heavy, was the first to catch fire.

Remarkable as it may seem, Wednesday night, while the whole city crashed and roared into ruin, was a quiet night. There were no crowds. There was no shouting and yelling. There was no hysteria, no disorder. I passed Wednesday night in the part of the advancing flames, and in all those terrible hours I saw not one woman who wept, not one man who was excited, not one person who was in the slightest degree panic-stricken.

Before the flames, throughout the night, fled tens of thousands of homeless ones. Some were wrapped in blankets. Others carried bundles of bedding and dear household treasures. Sometimes a whole family was harnessed to a carriage or delivery wagon that was weighted down with their possessions. Baby buggies, toy wagons, and gocarts were used as trucks, while every other person was dragging a trunk. Yet everybody was gracious. The most perfect courtesy obtained. Never in all San Francisco's history were her people so kind and courteous as on this night of terror.

All the night these tens of thousands fled before the flames. Many of them, the poor people from the labor ghetto, had fled all day as well. They had left their homes burdened with possessions. Now and again they lightened up, flinging out upon the street clothing and treasures they had dragged for miles.

They held on longest to their trunks, and over these trunks many a strong man broke his heart that night. The hills of San Francisco are steep, and up these hills, mile after mile, were the trunks dragged. Everywhere were trunks, with across them lying their exhausted owners, men and women. Before the march of the flames were flung picket lines of soldiers. And a block at a time, as the flames advanced, these pickets retreated. One of their tasks was to keep the trunk pullers moving. The exhausted creatures, stirred on by the menace of bayonets, would arise and struggle up the steep pavements, pausing from weakness every five or ten feet.

Often after surmounting a heart-breaking hill, they would find another wall of flame advancing upon them at right angles and be compelled to change anew the line of their retreat. In the end, completely played out, after toiling for a dozen hours like giants, thousands of them were compelled to abandon their trunks. Here the shopkeepers and soft members of the middle class were at a disadvantage. But the workingmen dug holes in vacant lots and back yards and buried their trunks.

At nine o'clock Wednesday evening I walked down through miles and miles of magnificent buildings and towering skyscrapers. Here was no fire. All was in perfect order. The police patrolled the streets. Every building had its watchman at the door. And yet it was doomed, all of it. There was no water. The dynamite was giving out. And at right angles two different conflagrations were sweeping down upon it.

At one o'clock in the morning I walked down through the same section. Everything still stood intact. There was no fire. And yet there was a change. A rain of ashes was falling. The watchmen at the doors were gone. The police had been withdrawn. There were no firemen, no fire engines, no men fighting with dynamite. The district had been absolutely abandoned. I stood at the corner of Kearney and Market, in the very innermost heart of San Francisco. Kearney Street was deserted. Half a dozen blocks away it was burning on both sides. The street was a wall of flame. And against this wall of flame, silhouetted sharply, were two United States cavalrymen sitting on their horses, calmly watching. That was all. Not another person was in sight. In the intact heart of the city two troopers sat on their horses and watched.

Surrender was complete. There was no water. The sewers had long since been pumped dry. There was no dynamite. Another fire had broken out further uptown, and now from three sides conflagrations were sweeping down. The fourth side had been burned earlier in the day. In that direction stood the tottering walls of the Examiner Building, the burned-out Call Building, the smoldering ruins of the Grand Hotel, and the gutted, devastated, dynamited Palace Hotel.

The following will illustrate the sweep of the flames and the inability of men to calculate their spread. At eight o'clock Wednesday evening I passed through Union Square. It was packed with refugees. Thousands of them had gone to bed on the grass. Government tents had been set up, supper was being cooked, and the refugees were lining up for free meals.

At half-past one in the morning three sides of Union Square were in flames. The fourth side, where stood the great St. Francis Hotel, was still holding out. An hour later, ignited from top and sides, the St. Francis was flaming heavenward. Union Square, heaped high with mountains of trunks, was deserted. Troops, refugees, and all had retreated.

It was at Union Square that I saw a man offering a thousand dollars for a team of horses. He was in charge of a truck piled high with trunks from some hotel. It had been hauled here into what was considered safety, and the horses had been taken out. The flames were on three sides of the square, and there were no horses.

Also, at this time, standing beside the truck, I urged a man to seek safety in flight. He was all but hemmed in by several conflagrations. He was an old man and he was on crutches. Said he: "Today is my birthday. Last night I was worth thirty thousand dollars. I bought five bottles of wine, some delicate fish, and other things for my birthday dinner. I have had no dinner, and all I own are these crutches."

I convinced him of his danger and started him limping on his way. An hour later, from a distance, I saw the truckload of trunks burning merrily in the middle of the street.

On Thursday morning, at a quarter past five, just twenty-four hours after the earthquake, I sat on the steps of a small residence of Nob Hill. With me sat Japanese, Italians, Chinese, and Negroes—a bit of the cosmopolitan flotsam of the wreck of the city. All about were the palaces of the nabob pioneers of Forty-nine. To the east and south, at right angles, were advancing two mighty walls of flame.

I went inside with the owner of the house on the steps of which I sat. He was cool and cheerful and hospitable. "Yesterday morning," he said, "I was worth six hundred thousand dollars. This morning this house is all I have left. It will go in fifteen minutes." He pointed to a large cabinet. "That is my wife's collection of china. This rug upon which we stand is a present. It cost fifteen hundred dollars. Try that piano. Listen to its tone. There are few like it. There are no horses. The flames will be here in fifteen minutes.''

Outside, the old Mark Hopkins residence, a palace, was just catching fire. The troops were falling back and driving refugees before them. From every side came the roaring of flames, the crashing of walls, and the detonations of dynamite.

I passed out of the house. Day was trying to dawn through the smoke pall. A sickly light was creeping over the face of things. Once only the sun broke through the smoke pall, blood-red, and showing quarter its usual size. The smoke pall itself, viewed from beneath, was a rose color that pulsed and fluttered with lavender shades. Then it turned to mauve and yellow and dun. There was no sun. And so dawned the second day on stricken San Francisco.

An hour later I was creeping past the shattered dome of the City Hall. Than it there was no better exhibit of the destructive force of the earthquake. Most of the stones had been shaken from the great dome, leaving standing the naked framework of steel. Market Street was piled high with the wreckage, and across the wreckage lay the overthrown pillars of the City Hall shattered into short crosswise sections.

This section of the city, with the exception of the Mint and the Post Office, was already a waste of smoking ruins. Here and there through the smoke, creeping warily under the shadows of tottering walls, emerged occasional men and women. It was like the meeting of the handful of survivors after the day of the end of the world.

On Mission Street lay a dozen steers, in a neat row stretching across the street, just as they had been struck down by the flying ruins of the earthquake. The fire had passed through afterward and roasted them. The human dead had been carried away before the fire came. At another place on Mission Street I saw a milk wagon. A steel telegraph pole had smashed down sheer through the driver's seat and crushed the front wheels. The milk cans lay scattered around.

All day Thursday and all Thursday night, all day Friday and Friday night, the flames still raged.

Friday night saw the flames finally conquered, though not until Russian Hill and Telegraph Hill had been swept and three quarters of a mile of wharves and docks had been licked up.

The great stand of the fire fighters was made Thursday night on Van Ness Avenue. Had they failed here, the comparatively few remaining houses of the city would have been swept.

Here were the magnificent residences of the second generation of San Francisco nabobs, and these, in a solid zone, were dynamited down across the path of the fire. Here and there the flames leaped the zone, but these fires were beaten out, principally by the use of wet blankets and rugs.

San Francisco, at the present time, is like the crater of a volcano, around which are camped tens of thousands of refugees. At the Presidio alone are at least twenty thousand. All the surrounding cities and towns are jammed with the homeless ones, where they are being cared for by the relief committees. The refugees were carried free by the railroads to any point they wished to go, and it is estimated that over one hundred thousand people have left the peninsula on which San Francisco stood. The government has the situation in hand, and thanks to the immediate relief given by the whole United States, there is not the slightest possibility of a famine. The bankers and businessmen have already set about making preparations to rebuild San Francisco.

DISCUSSION QUESTIONS

1. Having read London's essay carefully, work back over it once more and note the significant words and phrases that are repeated. What is the purpose of such

repetition? Examine the development of London's sentences. Do they work primarily through logic? Emotion? Accumulation of detail? How does this strategy seem best suited to London's occasion and audience?

2. What terms does London use to measure the disastrous effects of the San Francisco earthquake? Does he see the event from a personal or an objective point of view? Does he use, for example, aesthetic, economic, sociological, or psychological language to define his response?

3. Contrast London's point of view and the effects that perspective elicits from his audience with the eyewitness report of another disaster written by William L. Laurence (see ''Press'').

William Hard / De Kid Wot Works at Night

Everybody's Magazine, January 1908

Everybody's Magazine *(1899–1929) was a leading advocate of social, economic, and political reform in the early years of the twentieth century. When William Hard's article appeared, the magazine had more than a half-million readers. Although the self-consciously melodramatic and playful tone of Hard's prose may have surprised an audience accustomed to a more earnest style of social crusading, Hard's article nevertheless accomplished its goal by helping to instigate child labor reform legislation in Illinois.*

When the shades of night look as if they were about to fall; when the atmosphere of Chicago begins to change from the dull gray of unaided local nature to the brilliant white of artificial illumination; when the Loop District, the central crater of the volcano, is filling up rapidly with large numbers of straps [trolley cars] which have been brought downtown from outlying carbarns for the convenience of those who have had enough and who now wish to withdraw; when the sound of the time clock being gladly and brutally punched is heard through every door and window—
    When all these things are happening, and, besides—
    When all the fat men in the city get to the streetcars first, and all the lean and energetic and profane men have to climb over them to the inner seats; when the salesladies in the department stores throw the night-covers over bargain ormolu clocks just as you pant up to the counter; when the man who has just bought a suburban house stops at the wholesale meat market and carries home a left-over steak in order to have the laugh on the high-priced suburban butcher; when you are sorry your office is on the fifth floor because there are so many people on the eleventh floor and the elevator goes by you without stopping, while you scowl through the glass partition—
    When all these things are happening, and, besides—
    When the clocks in the towers of the railway stations are turned three minutes ahead so that you will be sure to be on time and so that you will also be sure to drop into your seat with fractured lungs; when the policeman blows his whistle to make the streetcar stop, and the motorman sounds his gong to make the pedestrian stop, and both the motorman and the pedestrian look timorously but longingly at the area of death just in front of the fender; when the streets are full and the straps are full, and the shoes of the motor-cars of the elevated trains are throwing yellow sparks on the shoulders of innocent bystanders; when the reporters, coming back to their of-

fices from their afternoon assignments, are turning about in their doorways to watch the concentrated agony of an American home-going and are thanking God that they go home at the more convenient hour of 1 A.M.—

When all these things are happening, and when, in short, it is between five and six o'clock in the afternoon, the night newsboy and the night messenger boy turn another page in the book of experience and begin to devote themselves once more to the thronging, picturesque, incoherent characters of the night life of a big American city.

Then it is, at just about five o'clock, that the night messenger boy opens the door of his office by pushing against it with his back, turns around and walks sidewise across the floor, throws himself down obliquely on his long, smooth bench, slides a foot or two on the polished surface, comes to a stop against the body of the next boy, and begins to wait for the telegrams, letters and parcels that will keep him engaged till one o'clock the next morning and that may lead his footsteps either to the heavily curtained drawing rooms of disorderly houses in the Red Light district or to the wet planks of the wharves on the Calumet River twelve miles away, where he will curl up under the stars and sleep till the delayed boat arrives from Duluth.

Then it is that the night messenger boy's friend and ally, the night newsboy, gets downtown from school, after having said good-by to his usually mythical "widowed mother," and after having assumed the usually imaginary burden of the support of a "bereaved family." Then it is, at about five o'clock, that he approaches his favorite corner, grins at the man who owns the corner news stand, receives "ten *Choinals,* ten *Murrikins,* ten *Snoozes,* and five *Posts*"; goes away twenty feet, turns around, watches the corner-man to see if he has marked the papers down in his notebook, hopes that he hasn't marked them down, thinks that perhaps he has forgotten just how many there were, wonders if he couldn't persuade him that he didn't give him any *"Murrikins,"* calculates the amount of his profit if he should be able to sell the *"Murrikins"* without having to pay the corner-man for them, turns to the street, dodges a frenzied automobile, worms his way into a hand-packed street-car (which is the only receptacle never convicted by the city government of containing short measure), disappears at the car door, comes to the surface in the middle of the aisle, and hands a *News* to a regular customer.

From the time when the arc lamps sputter out bravely against the evening darkness to the time when they chatter and flicker themselves into extinction before the cold, reproving rays of the early morning sun, what does the street-boy do? What does he see? What films in the moving picture of a big American city are unrolled before his eyes? These are questions that are important to every American city, to every mission superintendent, to every desk sergeant, to every penitentiary warden, to every father, to every mother.

Night, in these modern times, is like the United States Constitution. It is an admirable institution, but it doesn't know what is happening beneath it. Night comes down on Chicago and spreads its wings as largely and as comfortably now as when the *Tribune* building was a sand dune. You stand on Madison Street and look upward, through the glare of the arc lamps, and you see old Mother Night still brooding about you, calmly, imperturbably, quite unconscious of the fact that her mischievous children have lined her feathers with electricity, kerosene, acetylene, coal gas, water gas, and every other species of unlawful, unnatural illuminating substance. She still spreads her wings, simply, grandly, with the cosmic unconcern of a hen that doesn't know she is hatching out ducks instead of chickens; and in the morning she rises from her nest and flutters away westward, feeling quite sure that she has fulfilled her duty in an ancient, regular and irreproachable manner.

She would be quite maternally surprised if she could know what her newsboys and messenger boys are doing while she (good, proper mother!) is nodding her head beautifully among the stars.

I do not mean by this remark to disparage the newsboy. He occupies in Chicago a legal position superior to that of the president of a railway company. The president of a railway company is only an employee. He receives a weekly, a monthly, or at least a yearly salary. The newsboy does not receive a salary. He is not an employee. He is a merchant. He buys his papers and then resells them. He occupies the same legal position as Marshall Field & Co. Therefore he does not fall within the scope of the child-labor law. Therefore no rascally paternalistic factory inspector may vex him in his pursuit of an independent commercial career.

At about five o'clock he strikes his bargain with the corner-man. The corner-man owns the corner. It is a strange and interesting system, lying totally without the pale of recognized law. Theoretically, Dick Kelly, having read the Fourteenth Amendment to the Constitution of the United States, and having become conscious of his rights, might try to set up a news stand at the southwest corner of Wabash and Madison. Practically, the Constitution does not follow the flag as far as that corner. Mr. Kelly's news stand would last a wonderfully short time. The only person who can have a news stand at the corner of Wabash and Madison is Mr. Heffner.

Mr. Heffner is the recognized owner, holder, occupant, possessor, etc., of some eighty square feet of sidewalk at that point, and his sovereignty extends halfway down the block to the next corner southward, and halfway down the other block to the next corner westward. When Mr. Heffner has been in business long enough he will deed, convey and transfer his rights to some other man for anywhere between $5 and $1,500.

These rights consist exclusively of the fact that the newspapers recognize the corner-man as their only agent at that particular spot. When the corner-man wishes to transfer his corner to somebody else, he must see that the newspapers are satisfied with his choice of a successor.

The newsboy deals, generally speaking, with the corner-man. The corner-man pays the *Daily News* sixty cents for every hundred copies. He then hands out these hundred copies in "bunches" of, say, ten or fifteen or twenty to the newsboys who come to him for supplies. Each newsboy receives, as a commission, a certain number of cents for every hundred copies that he can manage to sell. This commission varies from five to twenty cents. The profit of the corner-man varies therefore with the commission that he pays the newsboy. The public pays one hundred cents for one hundred copies of the *News*. The *News* itself gets sixty cents; the newsboy gets from five to twenty cents, the corner-man gets what is left, namely, from thirty-five down to twenty cents in net profit.

On the basis of this net profit, plus the gross profit on his own sales made directly by himself to his customers, there is more than one corner-man in Chicago who owns suburban property and who could live on the income from his real-estate investments.

From five o'clock, therefore, on to about half past six, the newsboy flips streetcars and yells "turrible murdur" on commission. But pretty soon the corner-man wants to go home. He then sells outright all the papers left on the stand. . . .

The best specimen of the finished type of newsboy, within my knowledge, is an Italian boy named "Jelly." His father's surname is Cella, but his own name has been "Jelly" ever since he can remember.

"Jelly" was born on the great, sprawly West Side. His father worked during the summer, digging excavations for sewers and gas mains. His mother worked during the winter, making buttonholes in coats, vests, and pants. Neither parent worked during the whole year.

This domestic situation was overlooked by the Hull House investigators. In their report on newsboys they found that the number of paper-selling orphans had been grossly overestimated by popular imagination. Out of 1,000 newsboys in their final tabulation, there were 803 who had both parents living. There were 74 who had only a father living. There were 97 who had only a mother living. There were only 26, out of the whole 1,000, who had neither a father nor a mother to care for them.

But "Jelly" occupied a peculiar position. He had both parents living and yet, from the standpoint of economics, he was a half-orphan, since neither parent worked all the year.

At the age of ten, therefore, "Jelly" began selling papers. His uncle had a news stand on a big important corner not far from "Jelly's" house on the West Side. At the age of ten "Jelly" was selling papers from five to eight in the morning and from five to eight in the evening. He was therefore inclined to go to sleep at his desk when he was receiving his lesson in mental arithmetic in the public school where he was an unwilling attendant. Nevertheless, he showed an extraordinary aptitude for mental arithmetic a few hours later when he was handing out change to customers on his uncle's corner.

"Jelly" was a pretty good truant in those days. There was no money to be made by going to school and it looked like a waste of time. His acquaintance among truant officers came to be broad and thorough. He was dragged back to school an indefinite number of times. Yet, with the curious limitations of a newsboy's superficially profound knowledge of human nature, he has confided to me the fact that every truant officer gets $1 for every boy that he returns to the principal of his school.

Besides being a pretty good truant, "Jelly" became also a pretty good fighter.

His very first fight won him the undying gratitude of his uncle.

It happened that at that time the struggle between the circulation departments of the evening newspapers was particularly keen. "Jelly's" uncle allowed himself, unwisely, to be drawn into it. The local circulation experts of the *News* and the *American* noticed that on the news stand kept by "Jelly's" uncle the *Journal* was displayed with excessive prominence and the *News* and the *American* were concealed down below. It was currently reported in the neighborhood that "Jelly's" uncle was receiving $10 a week from the *Journal* for behaving in the manner aforesaid.

In about twenty-four hours the corner owned by "Jelly's" uncle bore a tumultuous aspect. The *News* and the *American* had established a rival stand on the other side of the street. This stand was in charge of a man named Gazzolo. Incidentally, it happened that a man named Gazzolo had beaten and killed a man named Cella in the vicinity of Naples some five years before.

Gazzolo's news stand had confronted Cella's, frowning at it from across the street, for about a week, when it began to be guarded by some six or seven broad-chested persons in sweaters. Meanwhile Cella's news stand had also acquired a few sweaters inhabited by capable young men of a combative disposition.

On the afternoon of the eighth day the sweatered agents of the *News* and the *American* advanced across the street and engaged the willing agents of the *Journal* in a face-to-face and then hand-to-hand combat.

At least three murders have happened in Chicago since that time in similar encounters. "Nigger" Clark, an agent of the *News*, was killed on the South Side, and the Higgins brothers were killed on the Ashland Block corner in the downtown district itself, within view of the worldwide commerce transacted in the heart of Chicago. And a Chicago publisher has told me that these three open murders, recognized by everybody as circulation-department murders, must be supplemented by at least six or seven other clandestine murders before the full story of the homicidal rivalry between the agents of Chicago afternoon newspapers is told.

It was amateur murder before the *American* arrived. Then circulation agents began to be enlisted from the ranks of the pupils in the boxing schools, and since that time the circulation situation has become increasingly pugnacious, until today it has reached the State Attorney's office and has come back to the street in the form of indictments and prosecutions.

Typical of this warfare was the fray that followed when the sweatered agents of the *News* and the *American* came across the street and fell rudely upon the news stand of "Jelly's" uncle.

"Jelly's" uncle had his shoulder-blade broken, but "Jelly" himself, being young and agile, escaped from his pursuers and was instantly and miraculously filled with a beautiful idea.

The agents of the *News* and the *American*, coming across the street to attack "Jelly's" uncle, had left Gazzolo's corner unprotected. "Jelly" traversed the cedar blocks of the street and reached Gazzolo in an ecstatic moment when he was surveying the assault on Cella's shoulder-blade with absorbing glee. Just about one-tenth of a second later Mr. Gazzolo was pierced in the region of the abdomen by the largest blade of a small and blunt pocket-knife in the unhesitating right hand of Mr. Cella's nephew, "Jelly."

It was a slight wound, but in consideration of his thoughtfulness in promptly perceiving Mr. Gazzolo's unprotected situation and in immediately running across the street in order to take advantage of it, "Jelly" was transferred by his uncle to a position of independent responsibility. He was put in charge of a news stand just outside an elevated railway station on the South Side.

Nevertheless, even after this honorable promotion, "Jelly's" father continued to take all his money away from him when he came home at night. And the elder Cella did not desist from this practice till his son had been advanced to the supereminent honor of selling papers in the downtown district.

This final transfer happened to "Jelly" when he was fifteen. He still retained his stand on the South Side, selling papers there from five to ten in the morning, but he also came downtown and sold papers at a stand within the Loop from five to nine at night. His uncle had prospered and had been able to invest $1,000 in a downtown corner, which was on the point of being abandoned by a fellow Italian who desired to return to the hills just south of Naples.

Thereafter, till he was sixteen years old, "Jelly" led a full and earnest life. He rose at four; he reached his South Side stand by five; he sold papers there till ten; he reached the downtown district by eleven; he inspected the five-cent theaters and the penny arcades and the alley restaurants till five in the afternoon; he sold papers for his uncle on commission till half past six; he bought his uncle's left-over papers at half past six and sold them on his own account till nine; and then, before going home at ten in order to get his five hours of sleep, he spent a happy sixty minutes reinspecting the five-cent theaters and the penny arcades and dodging Mr. Julius F. Wengierski.

Mr. Wengierski is a probation officer of the Juvenile Court. At that time he was making nightly tours through the downtown district talking to the children on the streets and trying to induce them to go home. He made a special study of some fifty cases, looking into the home circumstances of each child and gathering notes on the reasons why the child was at work. He was assisted by the agents of a reputable and conscientious charitable society.

In only two instances, out of the whole fifty, was the boy's family in need of the actual necessaries of life. In one instance the boy's father was the owner of his house and lot and was earning $5 a day. He also had several hundred dollars in the bank. In only a few instances did the family, as a family, make any considerable gain, for the purposes of household expenses, from the child's labor.

Some fathers, it is true (notably the one who owned his house and lot), used the child selfishly and cruelly as a worker who required no wages and whose total earnings could be appropriated as soon as he came home. It was the same system as that to which "Jelly" had been subjected from ten to fifteen. But these cases were exceptional.

One of the boys was working in order to get the money for the installment payments on a violin, and another was working in order to pay for lessons on a violin of which he was already the complete and enthusiastic owner.

One little girl was selling late editions in the saloons on Van Buren Street in order to have white shoes for her first communion. Another little girl needed shoes of the same color for Easter. Still a third was working in order that after a while she might have clothes just as good as those of the girl who lived next door.

In at least ten of Mr. Wengierski's cases, the reason for earning money on the street at night was the penny arcade and the five-cent theater. The passion for these amusements among children is intense. They will, some of them, work until they have a nickel, expend it on a moving-picture performance, and then start in and work again until they have another nickel to be spent for the same purpose at another "theatorium."

The earnings of these children, according to the Hull House investigation, which is the only authoritative investigation on record, vary from ten cents a day when the children are five years old up to ninety cents a day when they are sixteen. This is the average, but of course there are many children who make less and many who, because of superior skill, make more. Among these latter is "Jelly."

"Jelly's" high average, which used to reach almost $2 a day, was due partly to his own personal power and partly to the fact that on Saturday night he employed the services of his little sister.

Saturday night was "Jelly's" big time. On other nights he went home by ten o'clock. He had to get up by four and it was necessary for even him to take some sleep. But on Saturday night he gave himself up with almost complete abandon to the opportunities of the street.

On that night he used to close up his stand by eight o'clock and then go down to the river and sell his few remaining papers to the passengers on the lake boats. "Last chanst ter git yer *Murrikin!*" "Only one *Choinal* left! De only *Choinal* on de dock!" "Buy a *Post,* mister! Youse won't be able ter sleep ter-night on de boat! De only paper fer only two cents!" "Here's yer *Noose!* Only one cent! No more *Nooses* till youse comes back! Last chanst! Dey will cost yer ten cents apiece on de boat!" "Git yer *Murrikin.* No papers sold on de boat!" "Git yer *Post.* Dey charges yer five cents w'en youse gits 'em on de boat!"

Slightly contradictory those statements of his used to be, but they attained their object. They sold the papers. And as soon as the boats had swung away from their moorings "Jelly" would come back to the region of the five-cent theaters and the penny arcades and resume his nocturnal inquiries into the state of cheap art.

At half past ten he went to an elevated railway station to meet his little sister. She was ten years old. She had dressed herself for the part. From her ragged and scanty wardrobe she had chosen her most ragged and her scantiest clothes.

Accompanied by his sister, "Jelly" then went to a flower shop and bought a bundle of carnations at closing prices. With these carnations he took his sister to the entrance of the Grand Opera House. There she sold the whole bundle to the people coming out from the performance. Her appearance was picturesque and pitiful. Her net profit from the sale of her flowers was usually about thirty-five cents.

As soon as the flowers were sold and the people had gone away, "Jelly" took his sister back to the elevated station. There he counted the money she had made and put it in his pocket. He then handed her out a nickel for carfare and, in addition, a supplementary nickel for herself. "Jelly" was being rapidly Americanized. If he had remained exactly like his father, he would have surrendered only the nickel for carfare.

It was time now to go to the office of the *American* and get the early morning Sunday editions. "Jelly" began selling these editions at about twelve o'clock. He sold them to stragglers in the downtown streets till two. It was then exactly twenty-two hours since he had left his bed. He began to feel a little bit sleepy. He therefore went down to the river and slept on a dock, next to an old berry crate, till four. At four he rose and took the elevated train to the South Side. There he reached his own news stand and opened it up at about five o'clock. This was his Saturday, Saturday-night, and Sunday-morning routine for a long time. On the other nights "Jelly" slept five hours. On Saturday nights he found that two hours was quite enough. And his ability to get along without sleep is characteristic of newsboys and messenger boys rather than exceptional among them.

The reason why "Jelly" used to dodge Mr. Wengierski is now explainable. To begin with, his opinion of all probation officers is unfavorable. He classes them with truant officers. They are not "on the level." They discriminate between different classes of boys. "Jelly" was once accosted by a probation officer at about ten o'clock at night on Clark Street. He gave this probation officer a good tip about a lot of boys who were staying out nights attending services in the old First Methodist Church. These boys had been seen by "Jelly" going home as late as half past ten. The probation officer took no action in their case while at the same time he advised "Jelly" to stop selling papers at an early hour.

Incidents like this had convinced "Jelly" that probation officers were certainly not on the level and were possibly "on the make." But in Mr. Wengierski's case he had an additional reason. Mr. Wengierski was looking for boys of fourteen and under, and, while "Jelly" was entitled by age to escape Mr. Wengierski's notice, he was not so entitled by size. He was sixteen, but he looked not more than thirteen. The street had given him a certain superficial knowledge, but it had dwarfed his body just as surely as it had dwarfed his mind.

Mr. J. J. Sloan, when he was superintendent of the John Worthy School (which is the local municipal juvenile reformatory), reported that the newsboys committed to his care were, on the average, one-third below the stature and one-third below the strength of average ordinary boys of the same age. In the face of testimony of this kind, which could be duplicated from every city in the United States, it seems absurd to talk about the educative influence of the street. That it has a certain educative influence is undeniable, but it is equally undeniable that the boys who are exposed to this influence should be prevented, by proper legislation, from exposing themselves to it too many hours a day and should especially be prevented from exposing themselves to it for even a single hour after seven o'clock in the evening.

"Jelly" has now become a messenger boy and has been given a new name by his new associates. He will some day go back to the newspaper business because there is more money in it, and "Jelly" is fundamentally commercial. But there seems to be, after all, a certain struggling, unruly bubble of romanticism in his nature and it had to rise to the surface and explode.

"Jelly" first thought of the messenger service when he was attending a five-cent theater. "Jelly" went in. The fleeting pictures on the screen at the farther end of the room were telling a story that filled him with swelling interest. A messenger boy is run over by an automobile. He is taken to the hospital. He regains consciousness in his bed. He remembers his message. He calls for a portable telephone. He phones the message to the young man to whom it was addressed. The young man comes at once to the hospital. The young woman who had sent the message also comes. She wants to find out what has happened to the message. The young man and the young woman meet at the bedside of the messenger boy. They fall into each other's arms and the messenger boy sinks back on his pillow and dies. And it is a mighty good story even if the rough points are not rubbed off.

"Jelly" determined at once to be a messenger boy, without delay. [. . .]

Peter Homans / The Western: The Legend and the Cardboard Hero

Look, March 13, 1962

One way to look at the heroes and heroines of popular culture is to see them as reflections of age-old myths. This is the perspective Peter Homans adopts in the following essay, which originally appeared in Look *magazine on March 13, 1962. By analyzing all of the characteristic elements of the typical Western, Homans demonstrates what all Westerns have in common.*

Peter Homans was born in New York in 1930 and has earned degrees at Princeton and the University of Chicago. He is the author of Theology after Freud: An Interpretive Inquiry *(1970) and has written on popular culture, psychology, and theology.*

Along with Life *and the* Saturday Evening Post, Look *was one of the giant-circulation general magazines that died as a weekly in the 1970s. "The power of* Look," *the magazine's publisher once said, "is that it spans the whole universe of interests. It is a platform of all Americans to turn to, to learn about the basic issues, the real gut issues of the day. . . . It is information and entertainment for the whole family."*

He is the Law West of Tombstone, he is The Virginian at High Noon. He is Frontier Marshal, Knight of the Range, Rider of the Purple Sage. He Has Gun, Will Travel, and his name is Matt Dillon, Destry, Shane.

He is the hero of every Western that ever thundered out of the movies or TV screen, this Galahad with a Colt .45 who stalks injustice on the dusty streets of Dodge. Or Carson City. Or Virginia City.

Once he accomplishes his mission, he vanishes into the mists, as do all true heroes of all true legends. But where Hercules goes to Olympus and King Arthur to Avalon, this galoot rides Old Paint into the sunset.

With few variations, the movies have been telling this story for more than half a century. There have, in fact, been Western movies as long as there have been movies; the first American narrative film was a Western, *The Great Train Robbery*, made in 1903. Without the Westerns, it would be hard to imagine television today. Far outstripping the rowdy little boys who were its first enraptured audience, the Western has gone round the globe to become the youngest of the world's mythologies.

For each of us, even the word "Western" brings to mind an ordered sequence of character, event and detail. There may, of course, be variations within the pattern—but the basic outline remains constant. Details often vary, especially between movie and television Westerns, because the latter are essentially continued stories. Nonetheless, from the endless number of Westerns we have all seen, a basic concept emerges:

The Western takes place in a desolate, abandoned land. The desert, as a place without life, is indispensable. The story would not be credible were it set in a jungle, a fertile lowland or an arctic wasteland. We are dealing with a form of existence deprived of vitality.

This desert effect is contradicted by the presence of a town. Among the slapped-together buildings with false fronts, lined awkwardly along a road forever thick with dust, only three stand out—the saloon, the bank and the marshal's office (the hero's dwelling).

286

The saloon is the most important building in the Western. It is the only place in the story where people can be seen together time after time. It thereby functions as a meetinghouse, social center, church. More important, it is the setting for the climax of the story, the gunfight. No matter where the fight ends, it starts in the saloon.

The bank is a hastily constructed, fragile affair. Its only protection consists of a sniveling, timid clerk, with a mustache and a green eyeshade, who is only too glad to hand over the loot. Has there ever been a Western in which a robber wondered whether he could pull off his robbery?

The marshal's office appears less regularly. Most noticeable is the absence of any evidence of domesticity. We rarely see a bed, a place for clothes or any indication that a person actually makes his home here. There is not even a mirror. The overall atmosphere is that of austerity, which, we are led to suspect, is in some way related to our hero's virtue, and not to his finances.

The town as a whole has no business or industry. People have money, but we rarely see them make it. Homelife is conspicuous by its absence. There are no families, children, dogs. The closest thing to a home is a hotel, and this is rarely separated from the saloon.

One of the most interesting people in the town is the "derelict professional." He was originally trained in one of the usual Eastern professions (law, medicine, letters, ministry), but since his arrival in the West, he has become corrupted by drink, gambling, sex or violence. The point is that the traditional mentors of society (counselor, healer, teacher, shepherd) cannot exist in an uncorrupted state under the pressure of Western life. Somewhat similar is the "nonviolent Easterner." He often appears as a well-dressed business man, or as a very recent graduate of Harvard. In the course of the plot's development, this character is either humiliated or killed. The East, we soon note, is incapable of action when action is most needed.

The "good girl" is another supporting type in the cast of characters. Pale and without appetite, she, too, is from the East and is classically represented as the new schoolmarm. The "bad girl" is alone in the world and usually works for her living in the saloon as a waitress or dancer. Both girls have their eye on the hero.

The bartender observes the action, but rarely becomes involved in it. "The boys," those bearded, grimy people who are always "just there" drinking and gambling in the saloon, function as an audience. No hero ever shot it out with his adversary without these people watching.

Then we come to the principals. We meet the hero in the opening phase of the action. He is, above all, a transcendent figure, originating beyond the town. He rides into the town from nowhere; even if he is the marshal, his identity is disassociated from the people he must save. We know nothing of any past activities, relationships, future plans or ambitions. There are no friends, relatives, family, mistresses—not even a dog or cat—and even with his horse, he has a strangely formal relationship.

At first, the hero is lax to the point of laziness. Take his hat, for example. It sits exactly where it was placed—no effort has been made to align it. With feet propped up on the porch rail, frame balanced on a chair or stool tilted back on its rear legs, hat pushed slightly over the eyes, hands clasped over the buckle of his gun belt, he is a study in contrived indolence. Now he has time on his hands, but he knows his time is coming, and so do we.

The hero indicates no desire for women. He appears somewhat bored with the whole business. He never blushes, or betrays any enthusiasm. His monosyllabic stammer and brevity of speech clearly indicate an intended indifference.

In the drinking scenes, we are likely to see the hero equipped with the traditional shot glass and bottle. We seldom see him pay for more than one drink. He gulps his drink, rarely enjoys it and is impatient to be off. In the gambling scenes, his poker face veils any inner feelings of greed, enthusiasm or apprehension. We note, however, that he always wins or refuses to play. Similarly, he is utterly unimpressed by and indifferent to money.

There are hundreds of variations of the villain, but each is unshaven, darkly clothed and from the West. Like the hero, he is from beyond the town. He is inclined to cheat at cards, get drunk, lust after women who do not return the compliment, rob banks and, finally, shoot people he does not care for, especially heroes.

The impact of this evil one on the town is electric, suddenly animating it with vitality and purpose. Indeed, it is evil, rather than good, that actually gives meaning to the lives of these people. Nevertheless, they all know (as we do) that they are of themselves ultimately powerless to meet this evil. What is required is the hero—a transcendent power originating from beyond the town.

Notice what has happened to this power. Gone are the hero's indolence and lack of intention. Now, he is infused with vitality, direction and seriousness, in order to confront this ultimate threat. Once the radical shift has been accomplished, the hero (like the audience) is ready for the final conflict.

While the fight can take many forms (fistfight, fight with knives or whips, even a scowling match in which the hero successfully glares down the evil one), the classic and most popular form is the encounter with six-guns. It is a built-up and drawn-out affair, always allowing enough time for an audience to gather. The two men must adhere to an elaborate and well-defined casuistry as to who draws first, when it is proper to draw, etc. Although the hero's presence makes the fight possible—i.e., he insists on obstructing the evil one in some way; it is the latter who invariably attacks first. Were the hero ever to draw first, the story would no longer be a Western. With the destruction of the evil one, the action phase is completed.

In the closing phase, the town and its hero return to their preaction ways. One more event must take place, however, before the story can conclude. The hero must renounce any further involvement with the town. Traditionally, the hero marries the heroine and settles down. The Western hero always refuses—at least on television. He cannot identify himself with the situation he has influenced. When this has been made clear, the story is over.

The Western is, as most people by this time are willing to acknowledge, a popular myth that sets forth certain meanings about what is good and bad, right and wrong. Evil, according to the myth, is the failure to resist temptation. Temptation consists of five activities: drinking, gambling, moneymaking, sex and violence. In the drinking scenes, the hero is offered not one drink, but a whole bottle. He has at his disposal the opportunity for unlimited indulgence and its consequent loss of self-control. Gambling is a situation over which one has rather limited control—one loses, but the hero does not lose. He wins, thereby remaining in control. Wealth is not seized, although it is available to him through the unguarded bank. And both good girl and bad girl seek out the hero, to no avail—he remains a hero.

We perceive in the evil one a terrible power, which he has acquired at a great price; he has forfeited the control and resistance that sustain and make the hero what he is. The villain is the embodiment of the failure to resist temptation; he is the failure of denial. This is the real meaning of evil in the myth of the Western, and it is this that makes the evil one truly evil. He threatens the hero's resistance; each taunt and baiting gesture is a lure to the forfeiture of control and leads to the one temptation that the hero cannot afford to resist: the temptation to destroy temptation.

But why must the hero wait to be attacked? Why must he refrain from drawing first? The circumstances are contrived in order to make the violent destruction of the evil one appear just and virtuous. This process whereby desire is at once indulged and veiled is the "inner dynamic." It is the key to the Western, explaining not only the climax of the story, but everything else uniquely characteristic of it. What is required is that temptation be indulged while providing the appearance of having been resisted. Each of the minor-temptation episodes—drink, cards, moneymaking and sex—takes its unique shape from this need and is a climaxless Western in itself.

The derelict professional is derelict, and the nonviolent Easterner is weak, precisely because they have failed to resist temptation in the manner characteristic of the hero. Because these two types originate in the East, they have something in common with the good girl. Everything Eastern in the Western is weak, emotional, feminine. This covers family life, intellectual life, professional life. Only by becoming Westernized can the East be redeemed. The Western therefore is more a myth about the East than it is about the West; it is a secret and bitter parody of Eastern ways.

In summary, then, the Western is a myth in which evil appears as a series of temptations to be resisted by the hero. When faced with the embodiment of these temptations, he destroys the threat. But the story is so structured that the responsibility for the act falls upon the adversary, permitting the hero to destroy while appearing to save.

The Western bears a significant relationship to puritanism, in which it is the proper task of the will to rule and contain the spontaneous, vital aspects of life. Whenever vitality becomes too pressing, and the dominion of the will becomes threatened, the self must find some other mode of control. The puritan will seek a situation that allows him to express vitality while appearing to resist it. The Western provides just this opportunity, for the entire myth is shaped by the inner dynamic of apparent control and veiled expression. Indeed, in the gunfight, the hero's heightened gravity and dedicated exclusion of all other loyalties present a study in puritan virtue, while the evil one presents nothing more or less than the old New England Protestant devil—strangely costumed, to be sure—the traditional tempter whose horrid lures never allow the good puritan a moment's peace. In the gunfight, there are deliverance and redemption.

Here, then, is the real meaning of the Western: It is a puritan morality tale in which the savior-hero redeems the community from the temptations of the devil. Tall in the saddle, he rides straight from Plymouth Rock to a dusty frontier town, and though he be the fastest gun this side of Laramie, his Colt .45 is on the side of the angels.

DISCUSSION QUESTIONS

1. Read Homans's essay in connection with Gretel Ehrlich's "The Solace of Open Spaces." How are the images of the West in each essay similar? How are they different?

2. Could Homans's analysis be applied to other popular forms? For example, how might someone using Homans's method of interpretation read Edgar Rice Burroughs's *Tarzan of the Apes* or Chuck Yeager's recollection of breaking the sound barrier (see "Best-Sellers")?

Gay Talese / The Bridge

Esquire, December 1964

A 1953 graduate of the University of Alabama, Gay Talese worked as a staff writer on the New York Times *for ten years and as a contributing editor to* Esquire. *Talese has written articles for the* Saturday Evening Post, Show *magazine,* Life, *and* Reader's Digest. *Two of his fictionalized studies have made the best-seller lists:* The Kingdom and the Power *(1969), a history of the New York* Times *enterprise, and* Honor Thy Father *(1971), an intimate, inside view of an Italian-American family. Both books are written in a mode of reporting that fuses the techniques of fiction with the craft of nonfiction. His most recent work is* Thy Neighbor's Wife *(1980). In an introduction to a collection of his reporting,* Fame and Obscurity, *Talese describes his approach to journalism:*

> *The new journalism, though often reading like fiction, is not like fiction. It is, or should be, as reliable as the most reliable reportage although it seeks a larger truth than is possible through the mere compilation of verifiable facts, the use of direct quotations, and adherence to the rigid organizational style of the older form. The new journalism allows, demands in fact, a more imaginative approach to reporting, and it permits the writer to inject himself into the narrative if he wishes, as many writers do, or to assume the role of a detached observer, as others do, including myself.*
>
> *I try to follow my subjects unobtrusively while observing them in revealing situations, noting their reactions and the reactions of others to them. I attempt to absorb the whole scene, the dialogue and mood, the tension, drama, conflict, and then I try to write it all from the point of view of the persons I am writing about, even revealing whenever possible what these individuals are* thinking *during those moments that I am describing. This latter insight is not obtainable, of course, without the full cooperation of the subject, but if the writer enjoys the confidence and trust of his subjects it is possible, through interviews, by asking the right question at the right time, to learn and to report what goes on within other people's minds.*

The title Fame and Obscurity *also helps describe one of the characteristic features of modern journalism. Celebrities and the oddly insignificant are equally attractive to reporters: the famous because the reporter can then publicize the obscurities behind official appearances, and the anonymous so the reporter can then bestow on the truly obscure the status of celebrities.*

They drive into town in big cars, and live in furnished rooms, and drink whiskey with beer chasers, and chase women they will soon forget. They linger only a little while, only until they have built the bridge; then they are off again to another town, another bridge, linking everything but their lives.

They possess none of the foundation of their bridges. They are part circus, part gypsy—graceful in the air, restless on the ground; it is as if the wide-open road below lacks for them the clear direction of an eight-inch beam stretching across the sky six hundred feet above the sea.

When there are no bridges to be built, they will build skyscrapers, or highways, or power dams, or anything that promises a challenge—and overtime. They will go anywhere, will drive a thousand miles all day and night to be part of a new building boom. They find boom towns irresistible. That is why they are called "the boomers."

In appearance, boomers usually are big men, or if not always big, always strong, and their skin is ruddy from all the sun and wind. Some who heat rivets have charred complexions; some who drive rivets are hard of hearing; some who catch rivets in small metal cones have blisters and body burns marking each miss; some who do welding see flashes at night while they sleep. Those who connect steel have deep scars along their shins from climbing columns. Many boomers have mangled hands and fingers sliced off by slipped steel. Most have taken falls and broken a limb or two. All have seen death.

They are cocky men, men of great pride, and at night they brag and build bridges in bars, and sometimes when they are turning to leave, the bartender will yell after them, "Hey, you guys, how's about clearing some steel out of here?"

Stray women are drawn to them, like them because they have money and no wives within miles—they liked them well enough to have floated a bordello boat beneath one bridge near St. Louis, and to have used upturned hardhats for flower-pots in the red-light district of Paducah.

On weekends some boomers drive hundreds of miles to visit their families, are tender and tolerant, and will deny to the heavens any suggestion that they raise hell on the job—except they'll admit it in whispers, half proud, half ashamed, fearful the wives will hear and then any semblance of marital stability will be shattered.

Like most men, the boomer wants it both ways.

Occasionally his family will follow him, living in small hotels or trailer courts, but it is no life for a wife and child.

The boomer's child might live in forty states and attend a dozen high schools before he graduates, *if* he graduates, and though the father swears he wants no boomer for a son, he usually gets one. He gets one, possibly, because he really wanted one, and maybe that is why boomers brag so much at home on weekends, creating a wondrous world with whiskey words, a world no son can resist because this world seems to have everything: adventure, big cars, big money—sometimes $350 or $450 a week—and gambling on rainy days when the bridge is slippery, and booming around the country with Indians who are sure-footed as spiders, with Newfoundlanders as shifty as the sea they come from, with roaming Rebel riveters escaping the poverty of their small Southern towns, all of them building something big and permanent, something that can be revisited years later and pointed to and said of: "See that bridge over there, son—well one day, when I was younger, I drove twelve hundred rivets into that goddamned thing."

They tell their sons the good parts, forgetting the bad, hardly ever describing how men sometimes freeze with fear on high steel and clutch to beams with closed eyes, or admitting that when they climb down they need three drinks to settle their nerves; no, they dwell on the glory, the overtime, not the weeks of unemployment; they recall how they helped build the Golden Gate and Empire State, and how their fathers before them worked on the Williamsburg Bridge in 1902, lifting steel beams with derricks pulled by horses.

They make their world sound as if it were an extension of the Wild West, which in a way it is, with boomers today still regarding themselves as pioneering men, the last of America's unhenpecked heroes, but there are probably only a thousand of them left who are footloose enough to go anywhere to build anything. And when they arrive at the newest boom town, they hold brief reunions in bars, and talk about old times, old faces: about Cicero Mike, who once drove a Capone whiskey truck during Prohibition and recently fell to his death off a bridge near Chicago; and Indian Al Deal, who kept three women happy out West and came to the bridge each morning in a fancy silk shirt; and about Riphorn Red, who used to paste twenty-dollar bills along the sides of his suitcase and who went berserk one night in a cemetery. And there was the Nutley Kid, who smoked long Indian cigars and chewed snuff and used toilet water and, at lunch, would drink milk and beer—without taking out the snuff. And there was Ice Water Charley, who on freezing wintry days up on the bridge would send apprentice boys all the way down to fetch hot water, but by the time they'd climbed back up, the water was cold, and he would spit it out, screaming angrily, *"Ice water, ice water!"* and send them all the way down for more. And there was that one-legged lecher, Whitey Howard, who, on a rail bridge one day, did not hear the train coming, and so he had to jump the tracks at the last second, holding on to the edge, during which time his wooden leg fell off, and Whitey spent the rest of his life bragging about how he lost his left leg twice.

Sometimes they go on and on this way, drinking and reminiscing about the undramatic little things involving people known only to boomers, people seen only at a distance by the rest of the world, and then they'll start a card game, the first of hundreds to be played in this boom town while the bridge is being built—a bridge many boomers will never cross. For before the bridge is finished, maybe six months before it is opened to traffic, some boomers get itchy and want to move elsewhere. The challenge is dying. So is the overtime. And they begin to wonder: "Where next?" This is what they were asking one another in the early spring of 1957, but some boomers already had the answer: New York.

New York was planning a number of bridges. Several projects were scheduled upstate, and New York City alone, between 1958 and 1964, planned to spend nearly $600,000,000 for, among other things, the double-decking of the George Washington Bridge, the construction of the Throgs Neck Bridge across Long Island Sound—and, finally, in what might be the most challenging task of a boomer's lifetime, the construction of the world's largest suspension span, the Verrazano-Narrows Bridge.

The Verrazano-Narrows, linking Brooklyn and Staten Island (over the futile objections of thousands of citizens in both boroughs), would possess a 4,260-foot center span that would surpass San Francisco's Golden Gate by 60 feet, and would be 460 feet longer than the Mackinac Bridge in upper Michigan, just below Canada.

It was the Mackinac Bridge, slicing down between Lake Huron and Lake Michigan and connecting the cities of St. Ignace and Mackinaw City, that had attracted the boomers between the years 1954 and 1957. And though they would now abandon it for New York, not being able to resist the big movement eastward, there were a few boomers who actually were sorry to be leaving Michigan, for in their history of hell-raising there never had been a more bombastic little boom town than the once tranquil St. Ignace.

Before the boomers had infiltrated it, St. Ignace was a rather sober city of about 2,500 residents, who went hunting in winter, fishing in summer, ran small shops that catered to tourists, helped run the ferryboats across five miles of water to Mackinaw City, and gave the local police very little trouble. The land had been inhabited first by peaceful Indians, then by French bushrangers, then by missionaries and fur traders, and in 1954 it was still clean and uncorrupt, still with one hotel, called the Nicolet—named after a white man, Jean Nicolet, who in 1634 is said to have paddled in a canoe through the Straits of Mackinac and discovered Lake Michigan.

So it was the Nicolet Hotel, and principally its bar, that became the boomers' headquarters, and soon the place was a smoky scene of nightly parties and brawls, and there were girls down from Canada and up from Detroit, and there were crap games along the floor—and if St. Ignace had not been such a friendly city, all the boomers might have gone to jail and the bridge might never have been finished.

But the people of St. Ignace were pleased with the big new bridge going up. They could see how hard the men worked on it and they did not want to spoil their little fun at night. The merchants, of course, were favorably disposed because, suddenly, in this small Michigan town by the sea, the sidewalks were enhanced by six hundred or seven hundred men, each earning between $300 and $500 a week—and some spending it as fast as they were making it.

The local police did not want to seem inhospitable, either, and so they did not raid the poker or crap games. The only raid in memory was led by some Michigan state troopers; and when they broke in, they discovered gambling among the boomers another state trooper. The only person arrested was the boomer who had been winning the most. And since his earnings were confiscated, he was unable to pay the $100 fine and therefore had to go to jail. Later that night, however, he got a poker game going in his cell, won $100, and bought his way out of jail. He was on the bridge promptly for work the next morning.

It is perhaps a slight exaggeration to suggest that, excepting state troopers, everybody else in St. Ignace either fawned upon or quietly tolerated boomers. For there were some families who forbade their daughters to date boomers, with some success, and there were young local men in town who despised boomers, although this attitude may be attributed as much to their envy of boomers' big cars and money as to the fact that comparatively few boomers were teetotalers or celibates. On the other hand, it would be equally misleading to assume that there were not some boomers who were quiet, modest men—maybe as many as six or seven— one of them being, for instance, a big quiet Kentuckian named Ace Cowan (whose wife was with him in Michigan), and another being Johnny Atkins, who once at the Nicolet drank a dozen double Martinis without causing a fuss or seeming drunk, and then floated quietly, happily out into the night.

And there was also Jack Kelly, the tall 235-pound son of a Philadelphia sailmaker, who, despite years of work on noisy bridges and despite getting hit on the head by so much falling hardware that he had fifty-two stitches in his scalp, remained ever mild. And finally there was another admired man on the Mackinac—the superintendent, Art "Drag-Up" Drilling, a veteran boomer from Arkansas who went West to work on the Golden Gate and Oakland Bay bridges in the thirties, and who was called "Drag-Up" because he always said, though never in threat, that he'd sooner drag-up and leave town than work under a superintendent who knew less about bridges than he.

So he went from town to town, bridge to bridge, never really satisfied until he became the top bridgeman—as he did on the Mackinac, and as he hoped to do in 1962 on the Verrazano-Narrows Bridge.

In the course of his travels, however, Drag-Up Drilling sired a son named John. And while John Drilling inherited much of his father's soft Southern charm and easy manner, these qualities actually belied the devil beneath. For John Drilling, who was only nineteen years old when he first joined the gang on the Mackinac, worked as hard as any to leave the boomer's mark on St. Ignace.

John Drilling had been born in Oakland in 1937 while his father was finishing on the Bay bridge there. And in the next nineteen years he followed his father, living in forty-one states, attending two dozen schools, charming the girls—marrying one, and living with her for four months. There was nothing raw nor rude in his manner. He was always extremely genteel and clean-cut in appearance, but, like many boomers' offspring, he was afflicted with what old bridgemen call "rambling fever."

This made him challenging to some women, and frustrating to others, yet intriguing to most. On his first week in St. Ignace, while stopped at a gas station, he noticed a carload of girls nearby and, exuding all the shy and bumbling uncertainty of a new boy in town, addressed himself politely to the prettiest girl in the car—a Swedish beauty, a very healthy girl whose boy friend had just been drafted—and thus began an unforgettable romance that would last until the next one.

Having saved a few thousand dollars from working on the Mackinac, he became, very briefly, a student at the University of Arkansas and also bought a $2,700 Impala. One night in Ola, Ark., he cracked up the car and might have gotten into legal difficulty had not his date that evening been the judge's daughter.

John Drilling seemed to have a charmed life. Of all the bridge builders who worked on the Mackinac, and who would later come East to work on the Verrazano-Narrows Bridge, young John Drilling seemed the luckiest—with the possible exception of his close friend, Robert Anderson.

Anderson was luckier mainly because he had lived longer, done more, survived more; and he never lost his sunny disposition or incurable optimism. He was thirty-four years old when he came to the Mackinac. He had been married to one girl for a dozen years, to another for two weeks. He had been in auto accidents, been hit by falling tools, taken falls—once toppling forty-two feet—but his only visible injury was two missing inside fingers on his left hand, and he never lost its full use.

One day on the north tower of the Mackinac, the section of catwalk upon which Anderson was standing snapped loose, and suddenly it came sliding down like a rollercoaster, with Anderson clinging to it as it bumped and raced down the cables, down 1,800 feet all the way to near the bottom where the cables slope gently and straighten out before the anchorage. Anderson quietly got off and began the long climb up again. Fortunately for him, the Mackinac was designed by David B. Steinman, who preferred long, tapering backspans; had the bridge been designed by O. H. Ammann, who favored shorter, chunkier backspans, such as the type he was then creating for the Verrazano-Narrows Bridge, Bob Anderson would have had a steeper, more abrupt ride down, and might have gone smashing into the anchorage and been killed. But Anderson was lucky that way.

Off the bridge, Anderson had a boomer's luck with women. All the moving around he had done during his youth as a boomer's son, all the shifting from town to town and the enforced flexibility required of such living, gave him a casual air of detachment, an ability to be at home anywhere. Once, in Mexico, he made his home in a whorehouse. The prostitutes down there liked him very much, fought over him, admired his gentle manners and the fact that he treated them all like ladies. Finally the madam invited him in as a full-time house guest and each night Anderson would dine with them, and in the morning he stood in line with them awaiting his turn in the shower.

Though he stands six feet and is broad-shouldered and erect, Bob Anderson is not a particularly handsome fellow; but he has bright alert eyes, and a round, friendly, usually smiling face, and he is very disarming, a sort of Tom Jones of the bridge business—smooth and swift, somewhat gallant, addicted to good times and hot-blooded women, and yet never slick or tricky.

He is also fairly lucky at gambling, having learned a bit back in Oklahoma from his uncle Manuel, a guitar-playing rogue who once won a whole carnival playing poker. Anderson avoids crap games, although one evening at the Nicolet, when a crap game got started on the floor of the men's room and he'd been invited to join, he did.

"Oh, I was drunk that night," he said, in his slow Southwestern drawl, to a friend some days later. "I was so drunk I could hardly see. But I jes' kept rolling them dice, and all I was seeing was sevens and elevens, sevens and elevens, *Jee-sus Kee-rist,* all night long it went like that, and I kept winning and drinking and winning some more. Finally lots of other folks came jamming in, hearing all the noise and all, in this men's toilet room there's some women and tourists who also came in—jes' watching me roll those sevens and elevens.

"Next morning I woke up with a helluva hangover, but on my bureau I seen this pile of money. And when I felt inside my pockets they were stuffed with bills, crumpled up like dried leaves. And when I counted it all, it came to more than one thousand dollars. And that day on the bridge, there was guys coming up to me and saying, 'Here, Bob, here's the fifty I borrowed last night,' or, 'Here's the hundred,' and I didn't even remember they borrowed it. Jee-sus Kee-rist, what a night!"

When Bob Anderson finally left the Mackinac job and St. Ignace, he had managed to save five thousand dollars, and, not knowing what else to do with it, he bought a round-trip airplane ticket and went flying off to Tangier, Paris and Switzerland—"whoring and drinking," as he put it—and then, flat broke, except for his return ticket, he went back to St. Ignace and married a lean, lovely brunette he'd been unable to forget.

And not long after that, he packed his things and his new wife, and along with dozens of other boomers—with John Drilling and Drag-Up, with Ace Cowan and Jack Kelly and other veterans of the Mackinac and the Nicolet—he began the long road trip eastward to try his luck in New York. [. . .]

DISCUSSION QUESTIONS

1. Compare Talese's account of the boomers with Hard's description of newsboys. Which writer maintains more distance between himself and the working groups? How is that distance expressed in style and tone?

2. Describe the differences in each writer's use of details. Which writer tries harder to give the impression of journalistic objectivity? How are details used in each case to convey a sense of closely knit working communities? Which community do you feel is described more satisfactorily? Explain.

3. Would the working people described by Talese and Hard be included as part of each writer's imagined audience? Describe the distinctions (if any) you think exist between the audience and subjects of each work. Which writer's style is more suited to the language spoken by his subjects? Do you think the smaller the stylistic margin the more honest the appraisal? Explain.

Time **Staff / Death of a Maverick Mafioso**
[*On the Shooting of Joey Gallo*]   *Time,* April 1972

For many years, the slogan of Time *magazine was "curt, concise, complete." Founded in 1923 by Henry Luce and Briton Hadden,* Time, the Weekly News Magazine, *was intended to appeal to the growing number of American college graduates. Its title was meant to suggest both the scope of the magazine's coverage of current events and its sensitivity to the limited time which "busy men are able to spend on simply keeping informed." Luce and Hadden rejected the conventional format of objective news reporting and promoted instead a highly idiosyncratic, self-consciously lively narrative and a somewhat subjective, though corporate, journalistic style.*

Joey Gallo's murder received national attention. Inevitable were the comparisons with Mario Puzo's The Godfather *(see "Best-Sellers") to show how ruthlessly life imitates art.*

The scene could have been lifted right out of that movie. First, a night of champagne and laughter at Manhattan's Copacabana as Mobster Joseph ("Crazy Joe") Gallo, one of New York's most feared Mafiosi, celebrated his 43rd birthday. Then on to a predawn Italian breakfast at a gleaming new restaurant in the city's Little Italy area. Seated at his left at a rear table in Umbertos Clam House was his brawny bodyguard, Pete ("The Greek") Diopioulis; at Gallo's right, his sister Carmella. Across the table sat Gallo's darkly attractive bride of just three weeks, Sina, 29, and her daughter Lisa, 10. Quietly, a lone gunman stepped through a rear door and strode toward the table.

Both Gallo and Diopioulis were carelessly facing the wall instead of the door. The triggerman opened fire with a .38-caliber revolver. Women screamed. Joey and Pete were hit instantly. The Greek drew his own gun, began shooting back. So did one Gallo ally, seated at the front clam bar. Within 90 seconds, 20 shots ripped through the restaurant. Tables crashed over, hurling hot sauce and ketchup across the blue-tiled floor to mix with the blood of the wounded. The gunman whirled, ran out the same rear door and into a waiting car.

Gallo, wounded in a buttock, an elbow and his back, staggered toward the front of the café. He lurched through a front door and collapsed, bleeding, on the street. Carmella's screams attracted officers in a passing police car. They rushed Gallo to a hospital, but he died before reaching it.

MUSCLING

That melodramatic end to the short, brutal life of Joey Gallo surprised no one in New York's increasingly fratricidal underworld. There had been a contract out on his life ever since Mafia Boss Joe Colombo had been shot at an Italian Day rally in New York last June (TIME cover, July 12). Police do not believe that Gallo plotted that murder attempt, but friends of Colombo, who remains unable to talk or walk, thought he had. Gallo had been counted among the walking dead ever since he also aroused the anger of the biggest boss of them all, aging Carlo Gambino. Told to stop muscling into Gambino's operations, including the lucrative narcotics traffic in East Harlem, the cocky Gallo hurled the ultimate Mafia insult at Gambino: he spat at him.

If that act seemed foolhardy, it was nevertheless typical of Gallo, who never had the sense to play by the rigid rules of the brotherhood. He grew up with his brothers Larry and Albert in Brooklyn's Bath Beach, where mobsters often dumped their victims. One of his neighbors recalled Joey as "the kind of guy who wanted to grow up to be George Raft. He would stand on the corner when he was 15, flipping a half-dollar, and practice talking without moving his lips."

Joey first witnessed a gang murder in his early teens. After the victim was hauled away, he studied the scene, counted the bullet holes and took notes on how the killing must have been done. He began packing a pistol about the same time. Later, he affected the black shirt and white tie of Killer Richard Widmark in the movie *Kiss of Death.* He saw the movie so many times he knew all its lines. He spent hours in front of a mirror, trying to look as tough as Widmark—and he succeeded. He had a mercurial temper and acted out his movie fantasies as the cruelest of the Gallo brothers.

By the time Joey was 21, he was in trouble with the law, and a court-appointed psychiatrist found him insane. Other mobsters started calling him "Crazy Joe" but never to his face. He was too mean. Joey took pleasure in breaking the arm of one of his clients who was sluggish about paying protection money. He punctured an enemy with ice picks. He had gained his status by serving as one member (Colombo was another) of a five-man execution squad of Mafia Boss Joe Profaci in the late '50s. Police claim they had scored 40 hits. By then he and his brothers had carved out a chunk of the Brooklyn rackets; they turned against Profaci, touching off a gang war in which nine mobsters died and three disappeared.

Over the years, Gallo developed a wise-guy kind of humor that led some naive acquaintances to consider him a sort of folk hero. He was summoned to Robert Kennedy's office in 1959 when Kennedy was counsel to a Senate rackets investigating committee, looked at the rug and said, "Hey, this would be a great spot for a crap game." He once told a courtroom: "The cops say I've been picked up 15, maybe 17 times. That's junk. It was 150 times. I been worked over for nothing until my hat sits on my head like it belongs on a midget." Someone in 1961 overheard him trying to shake down a Brooklyn restaurant owner for a share of the profits. The proprietor asked for time to think about it. "Sure," said Gallo, "take three months in the hospital on me."

That quip cost Gallo nine years for extortion. In Attica state prison, Gallo earned a reputation as a civil rights leader of sorts. He helped lead an inmate drive to force white prison barbers to cut the hair of blacks; he had his own hair cut by a black barber to show his lack of prejudice. Actually, his motive seemed to be to recruit black toughs for his gang. When he got out of prison in March of 1971, he began hiring blacks as "button men" (musclemen)—pricking the ethnic sensibilities of other Mafiosi. He had openly toured Little Italy with four black henchmen a few days before he was hit. Some officials think that may have hastened execution of the contract.

HEARTY HOOD

Gallo's defiance of Mafia tradition did not mark him as particularly savvy. Neither did his open claim that he was about to write his memoirs. Other gangsters do not appreciate such literature. There was, for example, a $100,000 contract—for his death, not his papers—out on Joseph Valachi, who wrote in detail of his life with the Mob (he died of natural causes in prison). But Author Marta Curro, the wife of Actor Jerry Orbach, eagerly agreed to help write the book because she had discovered that Joey was "a great person, brilliant, absolutely charming."

It was at the Orbach apartment that Gallo married Sina Essary, a dental assistant he had met eleven years ago, before he went to jail. He and his first wife Jeffie Lee were divorced a few months ago. Joey and Sina, whose young daughter opened in the Broadway play *Voices* last week, soon became a part of the theatergoing, nightclubbing celebrity set. Crazy Joe, the killer, had become Pal Joey, the hearty hood. That, too, did not go down well with various godfathers.

SCRIPTS

Gallo kept telling his new found friends that he had gone straight. He told Celebrity Columnist Earl Wilson: "I'll never go back there—I think there is nothing out there for me but death." Police insist that Gallo was gulling others; that he actually was as much involved in the rackets as ever.

The truth seems to be that Gallo was leading a schizophrenic life in those last days: a steel-tough gunman in racket circles; a philosophic, warm conversationalist outside the Mob. Whether he was really at home in both roles, or just a good actor, he was clearly convincing. Actress Joan Hackett found him fascinating well before she knew of his Mafia connections. "I liked him completely apart from any grotesque glamorization of the underworld," she recalls. "I thought his attempt to leave that life was genuine. He was the brightest person I've ever known." But Gallo also conceded that "I'll never make it in the straight world."

With the slaying of two other lesser mobsters in New York last week, full gang warfare seemed imminent. The new image of Mafiosi as soft-spoken, smart-dressing businessmen, who shun such crudities as murder and torture as old-fashioned, seemed to be fading. Perhaps the Mob was taking those gory movie scripts about itself too seriously. At any rate, it was exposing the cruelty and ruthlessness of racketeering. Off-screen, murder is brutally final. Indeed, Gallo did not like parts of the *The Godfather*. He told a friend that he thought the death scenes seemed "too flashy."

Lew Dietz / The Myth of the Boss Bear   *True*, May 1973

> *Edited for an adult male audience interested in reading about adventure, mysteries, sports, military feats, "masculine" personalities, and the outdoors,* True *prefers its nonfiction articles to be anecdotal, carefully documented, and written "with a strong punch." When compared with William Faulkner's* The Bear (*see* "Classics"), *written some thirty years earlier, the following essay reminds us of how "factual" accounts often depend on the expectations we derive from fiction and myth.*

The northern Maine wilds were cloaked by a thick haze on my arrival, and when I flew out a week later there was a mountain-hugging fog. Within that span there was rain, more fog—and a bear called Lonesome George. Actually there were nine black bears sighted that week in June and one brought to earth with a bullet from a .284 Winchester. But only Lonesome George mattered to the hunters of Yankee-tu-laidi.

It was Glenn Wilcox who had dubbed the animal Lonesome George and Wilcox who had had the only confrontation with this seemingly immortal beast, a meeting that had left the bear with an altered forefoot. Mostly the animal was called simply The Bear, as though there were no other of its species in this remote and all but inaccessible region north of the Allagash.

Yankee-tu-laidi is the stream which flashes through this ridged country like a bright scepter. Local woodsmen suggest that the name might be a corruption of *touradie,* the French word for lake trout, but the origin is obscure. It's a fine, gamy hunk of territory, primarily because it is all but impossible to get into, and the hunters of Yankee-tu-laidi would like to keep it that way.

The day's hunting was over when I arrived. I tossed my sleeping bag into the loft, the only vacant nook in the gear-cluttered camp. John, the cook by tacit agreement—his stew was no more than tolerable but he was fastidiously clean—was stirring up the potluck. When a bottle started its rounds, I heard about The Bear.

Buzz Barry, a portly and imperturbable fellow with the dark soulful eyes of an Italian opera tenor, put it simply. "Glenn swears he's bigger than Joey's bear. And you saw Joey's bear."

I'd hunted with Barry and his Yankee-tu-laidi irregulars for a number of years. I knew about Joey Wilcox's bear. The spring before, Joey had come upon this King Kong of bears just a mile up the ridge from camp. The bear was shaking its great head as though bewildered by some awesome experience. It was only after Joey had dropped the bear at close range that he gained a clue to the nature of the drama. The dead bear showed evidence of having been bested in a brawl. Joey's bear went close to 400 pounds dressed, which meant a live weight of nearly 500, a big one, considering that the average mature black bear weighs around 300 pounds.

So what about the bear that was the winner and still champion? It was, as Buzz Barry put it, something to think about.

Barry was my host. Since he had the only camp lease in this 200 square miles of bear country, he might well have been elected top dog by expedient acclamation, like the sandlot kid with the only ball in town. Barry, however, had earned his stripes. He and his hunting partner, Glenn Wilcox, had pioneered bear hunting in this shaggy corner of Maine. In the course of five years, the pair had accounted for many bears and they'd got them the hard way, mostly before the state elevated the black bear to the status of game animal and established a limit of one in a season which extends from June 1 to December 31.

There was no further talk about The Bear that night. What else was there to say? These were Maine men who found ease and joy in the fraternity of hunting. They hunted for the challenge and the love of it, as had their fathers and grandfathers before them. And the ease in the camp was an ease that exists among men who have hunted long years together.

Five other men had come primarily to fish. Buzz Barry, Bob York and the Wilcox brothers were the bear hunters. For these four there was a special feeling about a bear hunt, something about the quest as warming and full-bodied as good bourbon. Until recent years few Maine hunters set out specifically for a bear. Bears were trapped, shot over bait or killed at a camp dump. And each fall a few were shot by deer hunters who came upon them accidentally. Maine has a good supply of bears and they seem to be on the increase. But the fellow who thinks he can walk into the woods any fine day and dispatch a bear has neglected to take this crafty animal into his calculation.

There are woodsmen who have spent a good part of their lives in Maine bear country and have never seen a live bear. A truly wild bear has ears like a lynx and the nose of a truffle hound. And although its eyes are no better than a deer's, a bear can identify a motionless man for what he is at 100 yards. A bear seldom waits to learn more.

The hunters had been in camp two days and, as was their custom, they had devoted the time to scouting the country in an attempt to learn how the bears were moving and where they were feeding. The first few months after leaving their winter dens, bears feed primarily on grass, sedges and herbs. These items, along with grubs and other insects, constitute their diet until the berries ripen in late July. The scouts reported encouraging bear signs but no great concentration in any one section. Our best bet, Buzz Barry thought, would be to hunt the overgrown woods, roads and grassy openings.

I was to hunt with him in his rig the next morning. Wheels are not a prerequisite to hunting bears in that big country but they do help, for while a deer is satisfied to live within a few square miles of territory, the "home" range of a mature black bear in Maine is possibly 700 square miles; a sow with cubs as much as 300. June is the peak of the bear's rut season, at which time both the sows and boars are apt to roam a bit more than normal. Eight years earlier, Barry decided that since there was no all-terrain vehicle available to meet the demanding requirements of Maine bear hunting, he would have to build his own rig.

Essentially his woods buggy is a dune buggy adapted to offer more low-gear pulling power and increased clearance. Bus transaxles solved both these problems. They reduced gear ratios and increased undercarriage clearance. And since there was no worry about making gear ratios too high, the hunters were able to go to over-sized tires for better traction. Reducing tire pressures to six pounds forward and eight in the rear offered additional traction and eased the punishing ride. The year before, I'd made the 30-mile buggy ride into Yankee-tu-laidi and can say that the trip would have made a hairy episode for *Mission Impossible*.

Buzz Barry and I set out shortly after sunup, leaving word of our itinerary and expected return time—an obvious precaution. Machines can break down under the punishing paces they are put through. There is no sleep or drink at the camp until all vehicles are accounted for.

Barry wanted to look over the Landry "road" (the quotes are used advisedly). At one point some busy beaver had created a daunting water hazard. As we broke a few holes in the damn to lower the water, I thought about a dialogue Teddy Roosevelt reported after he and his Maine guide had managed to get a wagon through to a camp on Munsungan Lake in mud season. "How," Teddy asked his guide, "do you Maine folks tell a road from a river?" "No beaver dams on the roads," was the guide's ready answer. Which goes to show that even a Maine guide can be wrong sometimes.

It was a dark day with a threat of rain, which was good, Buzz said, because it would make for soft going. Also it would give the hunter something closer to an even break. A bear can smell a man a country mile away. In wet weather a man can smell a bear, not a country mile perhaps, but a good 50 yards if the wind is right. I'd come to know a bear's rank, amonic scent, much like a skunk's, but less penetrating. Once you've smelled a bear, you'll never forget it.

A mile or so beyond the beaver flowage, we came upon fresh bear scats (in spring, a fresh bear dropping is green, turning brown and then black as it ages). Encouraged, we parked the buggy by a swollen brook. The still hunt on foot began.

Barry went ahead 30 paces or so and I took up the rear as we followed the twisting, grass-choked old-haul road. At each turn, my friend would ease to the outside of the trail and peer ahead before exposing himself. You spot a bear at an opening or you don't spot him at all. And if the bear sees you before you see the bear—well, it's good-bye Charlie.

"The bear has one flaw in his defenses. You might call it a character weakness," Barry said earlier. "A bear is a glutton. A bear's not apt to look up between nips when he's feeding, the way a deer does. If you sight a bear and the wind is right, you can stalk him. It takes patience, though. The biggest bear I ever shot took three hours of stalking.

"Matter of fact, there's one other advantage the bear hunter has. In the spring woods there is nothing in the world blacker than a black bear. You may mistake something in the woods for a bear, but you never mistake a bear for anything else. For one thing, a bear in the spring is seldom still; it moves frequently."

The Maine hunter is essentially a still hunter. He prefers to hunt alone or with a seasoned partner of long-standing. There is an incomparable excitement to a still hunt in gamy country. The hunter becomes a part of the natural realm. He tries to match eyes for eyes, ears for ears and cunning for cunning with his quarry. The fact that his rifle is an equalizer makes still-hunting no less a humbling experience.

We saw no sign of The Bear that day nor did we sight a bear of any stripe. The brothers Glenn and Joey Wilcox had arrived in camp when we trundled in. Glenn, plump as Friar Tuck; Joey, a mild apologetic fellow, make an unlikely looking pair of bear hunters. All the same, you'll have to search a long way to find anyone to match their knowledge of bears and their love of the hunt.

"The bears have begun to grub," Joey said. "They're doing a bit of frogging, too. Saw where a sow and her two cubs crossed the trail this morning below Dodge City."

"Dodge City" was a whimsy certainly, but an in-group place-name as well. This decaying cluster of old logging buildings had a story. A bear had broken into the hovel looking for forgotten oats and had been waylaid while attempting to escape through a window frame. There was "Pole Bridge" and "Mary's Tits," a pair of low knobs where Buzz had made that long stalk; "Trail 49," where one spring they had counted 49 bear scats on a two-mile stretch. And there was "Joey's Bend," that turn above the camp where Joey and his great bear had had their confrontation.

"Been a few bears working on the Loop Trail," Glenn said. "Small ones, yearlings, I'd guess.

Four bears had been sighted that day, only one large enough to be considered respectable. No one, not even Glenn Wilcox, mentioned The Bear, though he was the fiercest of all to get the animal dead to rights. I had the feeling that no one wished to hear the very real possibility that this grizzled lord of Yankee-tu-laidi had renounced his kingdom and departed. Only George, one of the fishermen who delighted in ribbing Lester, a pal, made a glancing reference to the subject.

"Lester and I come upon a bear flop near Fall Brook that two men could have shook hands across. I asked Lester to taste it for freshness, but he declined."

That night we feasted on a mess of fresh-caught brook trout. When the Coleman lamps were lit, Glenn decided it was high time he confessed that a bear had once driven him to water. This was early in his bear-hunting career before he'd learned to forgo mixing it up with a she-bear and her cubs. That afternoon he'd squeezed a shot off at a smallish bear. As he'd stepped into the brush to see what damage he'd done, he'd heard a low growl.

"There was that big sow, ears back, teeth bared, coming right for me. There wasn't time to do much more than shoot from the hip. A howl told me I'd creased her, but she came right on. I tried to take a hasty side step, but I wasn't quite fast enough. She caught me on the shoulder as she went by and sent me flying.

"It was just then that I remembered I'd fired the last round in my clip. As I frisked myself for my spare clip, I had a sinking feeling—I'd left my spare clip in my buggy. As that bear was preparing for a fresh charge, I took off for a beaver pond some 50 paces away. I hardly think my boots ever touched the ground."

For a good two hours Wilcox remained in that beaver pond up to his belly button, empty rifle held over his head. Twice he tried to go ashore and each time was driven back. Finally, with night coming on, he made a run for it.

That next morning Buzz Barry and I saw our first bear. Our plot was to leave the buggy at the beginning of Trail 29 and still-hunt the six miles back to camp on the Ridge Road. We were a mile or so from the trail when we spotted a bear down on its hunkers, feeding on grass.

Buzz eased the buggy to a halt. Stepping out, he slid a cartridge into his magazine. What he carried that day was his light carbine, figuring it would be right for that brushy terrain on the ridge. The bear was just under 200 yards away. My old .303 was under a tarp and little help in the situation. Since the bear had sighted us by then, there was no chance for a stalk. We simply stood there and watched the animal wander across the road and pass from view. Buzz estimated that the bear would have gone around 200 pounds, hardly respectable.

So soft was the going that day that we were able to come to within a few yards of deer; and rounding one twist in the trail we were met by a great bull moose which regarded us with lofty disdain and shuffled off in its own good time.

We saw a fair assortment of bear scats, but they weren't fresh enough to excite what Buzz called his turdometer, an instrument allegedly calibrated to degrees of freshness of bear droppings.

We did see where bears had been working earlier that spring. Here and there the bark of young balsams had been peeled back at their bases by sow bears to offer the treat of resin to their cubs. And we saw where bears had dismembered rotted trees seeking grubs in past seasons. I had my eye out for a bear tree, or what Maine woodsmen call a bear "marking post." When a boss bear feels an urge to express its machismo, it will commonly scribe a set of claw marks on a tree at the fullest extent of its reach for any lesser bear to try to match. Presumably an aspirant failing to meet the test moves on.

Back at camp that afternoon we learned that several yearling bears had been sighted on the back side of Haffey Mountain. Since cubs are dropped in midwinter, a "yearling" bear is nearly a year-and-a-half old in June. This is when the sow bear, ready for her biennial mating, drives off her youngsters to fend for themselves. Freshly out of custody and not yet seasoned to danger, these young bears are sighted more frequently than fully mature animals.

Barry wasn't interested in a yearling, but figured that if young bears were feeding in that area, bigger bears might be lurking not too far off. So Haffey Mountain was our destination as we headed out that next morning.

We were no more than three miles from camp when we saw a wolf. What made the sighting special was that wolves are officially extinct in Maine. Only in very recent years have there been reports of canids variously identified as wild dogs, coy-dogs, coyotes and wolves. We had a good, if brief, view of that animal as it crossed no more than 25 yards in front of us. Its coat was gray, tinged with red. We estimated its weight at something over 70 pounds, heavier than any coyote. It was similar in size and conformation to the wolf-coyote hybrids I'd seen in East Texas.

As we slogged into Haffey Mountain, it struck me that for these men the machines were every bit as much a challenge as the game. In this operation it's not enough to be a good hunter, you'd better be a damn good Yankee mechanic as well. There were few days that week when at least one buggy didn't come in under jury-rig. The year before, a fuel pump had given out 20 miles from base. No problem. The gas tank had been unbolted and we rode home with one man holding the tank over the engine and feeding gas directly into the carburetor.

We did some hard traveling that day. We saw game aplenty, but the closest we came to a bear was a set of fresh droppings no more than three hours old. . . .

There was a bear hanging from a tree at the camp when we got in that night, however. Bob York had come upon it that afternoon near the Pole Bridge. By general agreement, it was a two-year-old that would go around 200 pounds.

Time was running out for most of the hunters. A hunt seldom falls into the classical pattern of beginning, middle and final climax. But there is usually a discernible form to a hunting week. The first days are characterized by dalliance and casual exploration, the savoring of a release from structured life. Then as the hunters get down to the prime business of the hunt, the tempo picks up. The last days of the hunt there is a further quickening. Logic, industry, experience having failed, hunters fall back upon hunches.

Buzz Barry aired his that night as we prepared to hit the sack. "We might try that piece west of Joey's Turn," he said. "No one's been in there this spring."

Glenn grunted. "Nothing in there but bog, puckerbrush and blowdowns. What makes you think . . ."

"I'm half Irish," Buzz said. "I'm listening to the Irish in me. I say if he's still around, he's got to be there. We've covered just about every other place."

Expectancy is an emotion that can be as tangible as heat. Barry said little as we climbed out of the buggy and began to still-hunt up the trail above Joey's Turn that next morning, but I was aware of his leashed excitement. We eased along for a good 20 minutes without seeing any encouraging sign. We were up among the blowdowns when the first fresh bear scats began to show up.

Suddenly Buzz Barry motioned and I moved up abreast him. His eyes were luminous. "My computer's working," he said.

He grinned at my perplexity. "You've hunted long enough to know what I mean. Call it a hunter's sixth sense. Everything is right. The sign, the weather, the time of day, the wind direction and the look of the terrain. Unconsciously, you feed all this data into your computer. Right now, it comes out bear.''

We moved on, climbing up over a steep washout. The rain that had been with us off and on all week began to fall in a fine mist. I could hear the rush of a swollen brook. The croak of a young raven was as sharp as drumfire in the stillness. Then I, too, felt the nerve-twanging feeling of something impending.

We saw The Bear that morning. It was no more than a snatch vision. The great black shape was there and then it was gone, so quickly that I was not at all certain that my eyes hadn't been tricked by imagination.

Ahead, Barry had lowered his half-raised rifle. I waited a full minute, then slid up beside him. Together we stepped into the trees. It was only then that I was sure. The smell of bear was astringent and as real as a solid right to the midsection. Abruptly the wind changed, and there was only the smell of the dank woods.

The hunters were lunching when we stepped into camp. Something in our faces or in our silent deliberation as we stacked our rifles compelled their eyes toward us. I was aware of tension in the room.

Finally Glenn Wilcox snapped, ''Well, let's have it.''

Barry said, ''He was too smart for us. We didn't even get a shot.''

The hunters stirred and ease came back into the room.

''There'll be another year,'' someone said. ''Good old Lonesome George.''

And in that moment I learned something about the hunters of Yankee-tu-laidi. To a man they prefer the myth to a dead bear. Its passing would have removed something irreplaceable; without say-so, the myth—the symbol of a wilderness they knew—was doomed.

Now at least there would be another year.

DISCUSSION QUESTIONS

1. Compare ''The Myth of the Boss Bear'' with William Faulkner's rendition of an equally ''unsuccessful'' bear hunt (see ''Classics''). What are the different expectations made by each writer concerning his audience's knowledge of hunting? The wilderness? Bears? Myths? Other writers? Other literature on the same subject? Which writer spends more time talking about the technical details of a hunting expedition? Why is such information introduced?

2. Characterize Dietz's use of such similes and metaphors as ''as real as a solid right to the midsection,'' ''the dark soulful eyes of an Italian opera tenor,'' ''King Kong of bears.'' Compare them with Faulkner's figurative language (for example, ''like pygmies about the ankles of a drowsing elephant,'' ''a flavor like brass in the sudden run of saliva in his mouth'').

Nora Ephron / The Boston Photographs

Esquire, November 1975

Reporter, free-lance journalist, magazine contributor, columnist, editor, and author of Wallflower at the Orgy *(1970),* Crazy Salad *(1975),* Scribble, Scribble *(1978) and* Heartburn *(1983), Nora Ephron has become well known for her pert prose style and perspicacious eye. In ''The Boston Photographs,'' Ephron examines the outrage so many people felt toward the papers that printed*

the photos of a woman and child falling from a burning building and explains
why they deserved to be printed in papers all over the country. (For further
discussion of this issue, see Ellen Goodman in "Press.")

"I made all kinds of pictures because I thought it would be a good rescue shot over the ladder . . . never dreamed it would be anything else. . . . I kept having to move around because of the light set. The sky was bright and they were in deep shadow. I was making pictures with a motor drive and he, the fire fighter, was reaching up and, I don't know, everything started falling. I followed the girl down taking pictures . . . I made three or four frames. I realized what was going on and I completely turned around, because I didn't want to see her hit."

You probably saw the photographs. In most newspapers, there were three of them. The first showed some people on a fire escape—a fireman, a woman and a child. The fireman had a nice strong jaw and looked very brave. The woman was holding the child. Smoke was pouring from the building behind them. A rescue ladder was approaching, just a few feet away, and the fireman had one arm around the woman and one arm reaching out toward the ladder. The second picture showed the fire escape slipping off the building. The child had fallen on the escape and seemed about to slide off the edge. The woman was grasping desperately at the legs of the fireman, who had managed to grab the ladder. The third picture showed the woman and child in midair, falling to the ground. Their arms and legs were outstretched, horribly distended. A potted plant was falling too. The caption said that the woman, Diana Bryant, nineteen, died in the fall. The child landed on the woman's body and lived.

The pictures were taken by Stanley Forman, thirty, of the *Boston Herald American*. He used a motor-driven Nikon F set at 1/250, f 5.6–8. Because of the motor, the camera can click off three frames a second. More than four hundred newspapers in the United States alone carried the photographs; the tear sheets from overseas are still coming in. The *New York Times* ran them on the first page of its second section; a paper in south Georgia gave them nineteen columns; the *Chicago Tribune*, the *Washington Post* and the *Washington Star* filled almost half their front pages, the *Star* under a somewhat redundant headline that read: SENSATIONAL PHOTOS OF RESCUE ATTEMPT THAT FAILED.

The photographs are indeed sensational. They are pictures of death in action, of that split second when luck runs out, and it is impossible to look at them without feeling their extraordinary impact and remembering, in an almost subconscious way, the morbid fantasy of falling, falling off a building, falling to one's death. Beyond that, the pictures are classics, old-fashioned but perfect examples of photojournalism at its most spectacular. They're throwbacks, really, fire pictures, 1930s tabloid shots; at the same time they're technically superb and thoroughly modern—the sequence could not have been taken at all until the development of the motor-driven camera some sixteen years ago.

Most newspaper editors anticipate some reader reaction to photographs like Forman's; even so, the response around the country was enormous, and almost all of it was negative. I have read hundreds of the letters that were printed in letters-to-the-editor sections, and they repeat the same points. "Invading the privacy of death." "Cheap sensationalism." "I thought I was reading the *National Enquirer*." "Assigning the agony of a human being in terror of imminent death to the status of a side-show act." "A tawdry way to sell newspapers." The *Seattle Times* received sixty letters and calls; its managing editor even got a couple of them at home. A reader wrote the *Philadelphia Inquirer: "Jaws* and *Towering Inferno* are playing downtown; don't take business away from people who pay good money to advertise in your own paper." Another reader wrote the *Chicago Sun-*

Copyright Boston Herald American, Stanley J. Forman, Boston Newspaper Division of the Hearst Corporation.

Times: "I shall try to hide my disappointment that Miss Bryant wasn't wearing a skirt when she fell to her death. You could have had some award-winning photographs of her underpants as her skirt billowed over her head, you voyeurs." Several newspaper editors wrote columns defending the pictures: Thomas Keevil of the *Costa Mesa* (California) *Daily Pilot* printed a ballot for readers to vote on whether they would have printed the pictures; Marshall L. Stone of Maine's *Bangor Daily News*, which refused to print the famous assassination picture of the Vietcong prisoner in Saigon, claimed that the Boston pictures showed the dangers of fire escapes and raised questions about slumlords. (The burning building was a five-story brick apartment house on Marlborough Street in the Back Bay section of Boston.)

For the last five years, the *Washington Post* has employed various journalists as ombudsmen, whose job is to monitor the paper on behalf of the public. The *Post*'s curren: ombudsman is Charles Seib, former managing editor of the *Washington Star;* the day the Boston photographs appeared, the paper received over seventy calls in protest. As Seib later wrote in a column about the pictures, it was "the largest reaction to a published item that I have experienced in eight months as the *Post*'s ombudsman. . . .

"In the *Post*'s newsroom, on the other hand, I found no doubts, no second thoughts . . . the question was not whether they should be printed but how they should be displayed. When I talked to editors . . . they used words like 'interesting' and 'riveting' and 'gripping' to describe them. The pictures told something about life in the ghetto, they said (although the neighborhood where the tragedy occurred is not a ghetto, I am told). They dramatized the need to check on the safety of fire escapes. They dramatically conveyed something that had happened, and that is the business we're in. They were news. . . .

"Was publication of that [third] picture a bow to the same taste for the morbidly sensational that makes gold mines of disaster movies? Most papers will not print the picture of a dead body except in the most unusual circumstances. Does the fact that the final picture was taken a millisecond before the young woman died make a difference? Most papers will not print a picture of a bare female breast. Is that a more inappropriate subject for display than the picture of a human being's last agonized instant of life?" Seib offered no answers to the questions he raised, but he went on to say that although as an editor he would probably have run the pictures, as a reader he was revolted by them.

In conclusion, Seib wrote: "Any editor who decided to print those pictures without giving at least a moment's thought to what purpose they served and what their effect was likely to be on the reader should ask another question: Have I become so preoccupied with manufacturing a product according to professional traditions and standards that I have forgotten about the consumer, the reader?"

It should be clear that the phone calls and letters and Seib's own reaction were occasioned by one factor alone: the death of the woman. Obviously, had she survived the fall, no one would have protested; the pictures would have had a completely different impact. Equally obviously, had the child died as well—or instead—Seib would undoubtedly have received ten times the phone calls he did. In each case, the pictures would have been exactly the same—only the captions, and thus the responses, would have been different.

But the questions Seib raises are worth discussing—though not exactly for the reasons he mentions. For it may be that the real lesson of the Boston photographs is not the danger that editors will be forgetful of reader reaction, but that they will continue to censor pictures of death precisely because of that reaction. The protests Seib fielded were really a variation on an old theme—and we saw plenty of it during the Nixon-Agnew years—the "Why doesn't the press print the good news?" argument. In this case, of course, the objections were all dressed up and cleverly disguised as righteous indignation about the privacy of death. This is a form of puritanism that is often justifiable; just as often it is merely puritanical.

Seib takes it for granted that the widespread though fairly recent newspaper policy against printing pictures of dead bodies is a sound one; I don't know that it makes any sense at all. I recognize that printing pictures of corpses raises all sorts of problems about taste and titillation and sensationalism; the fact is, however, that people die. Death happens to be one of life's main events. And it is irresponsible—and more than that, inaccurate—for newspapers to fail to show it, or to show it only when an astonishing set of photos comes in over the Associated Press wire. Most papers covering fatal automobile accidents will print pictures of mangled cars. But the significance of fatal automobile accidents is not that a great deal of steel is twisted but that people die. Why not show it? That's what accidents are about. Throughout the Vietnam war, editors were reluctant to print atrocity pictures. Why *not* print them? That's what that war was about. Murder victims are almost never photographed; they are granted their privacy. But their relatives are relentlessly pictured on their way in and out of hospitals and morgues and funerals.

I'm not advocating that newspapers print these things in order to teach their readers a lesson. The *Post* editors justified their printing of the Boston pictures with several arguments in that direction; every one of them is irrelevant. The pictures don't show anything about slum life; the incident could have happened anywhere, and it did. It is extremely unlikely that anyone who saw them rushed out and had his fire escape strengthened. And the pictures were not news—at least they were not national news. It is not news in Washington, or New York, or Los Angeles that a woman was killed in a Boston fire. The only newsworthy thing about the pictures is that they were taken. They deserve to be printed because they are great pictures, breathtaking pictures of something that happened. That they disturb readers is exactly as it should be: that's why photojournalism is often more powerful than written journalism.

Annie Dillard / Death of a Moth   *Harper's*, May 1976

In the midst of a recent resurgence of nostalgia for the outdoors, Annie Dillard has distinguished herself by the clarity of her vision, the tenacity of her refusal to sentimentalize nature, and the forcefulness of her prose. Born Annie Doak in Pittsburgh in 1945, she took B.A. and M.A. degrees at Hollins College in Virginia's Roanoke Valley. A contributing editor to Harper's *magazine and a columnist for the Wilderness Society, Dillard has also written strikingly original essays for such publications as the* Christian Science Monitor, Atlantic Monthly, Travel and Leisure, Cosmopolitan, Sports Illustrated, Prose, *and* American Scholar. *Many of these essays, refashioned from precise observations entered in notebooks during leisurely walks in the countryside, were collected as* Pilgrim at Tinker Creek, *which received the 1974 Pulitzer Prize for nonfiction.*

"If there are any faults to find here," wrote a critic for the New York Times Book Review *about Dillard's journal* Holy the Firm *(1977), "let others find them. This is a rare and precious book." Included in her three-day journal written in a one-room house overlooking Puget Sound is the following essay, "Death of a Moth," which first appeared in* Harper's *magazine.*

Harper's, *one of the oldest (1850) magazines in America, characterizes itself as addressed to "well-educated, socially concerned, widely read men and women who are active in community and political affairs."*

I live alone with two cats, who sleep on my legs. There is a yellow one, and a black one whose name is Small. In the morning I joke to the black one, Do you remember last night? Do you remember? I throw them both out before breakfast, so I can eat.

There is a spider, too, in the bathroom, of uncertain lineage, bulbous at the abdomen and drab, whose six-inch mess of web works, works somehow, works miraculously, to keep her alive and me amazed. The web is in a corner behind the toilet, connecting tile wall to tile wall. The house is new, the bathroom immaculate, save for the spider, her web, and the sixteen or so corpses she's tossed to the floor.

The corpses appear to be mostly sow bugs, those little armadillo creatures who live to travel flat out in houses, and die round. In addition to sow-bug husks, hollow and sipped empty of color, there are what seem to be two or three wingless moth bodies, one new flake of earwig, and three spider carcasses crinkled and clenched.

I wonder on what fool's errand an earwig, or a moth, or a sow bug, would visit that clean corner of the house behind the toilet; I have not noticed any blind parades of sow bugs blundering into corners. Yet they do hazard there, at a rate of more than one a week, and the spider thrives. Yesterday she was working on the earwig, mouth on gut; today he's on the floor. It must take a certain genius to throw things away from there, to find a straight line through that sticky tangle to the floor.

Today the earwig shines darkly, and gleams, what there is of him: a dorsal curve of thorax and abdomen, and a smooth pair of pincers by which I knew his name. Next week, if the other bodies are any indication, he'll be shrunk and gray, webbed to the floor with dust. The sow bugs beside him are curled and empty, fragile, a breath away from brittle fluff. The spiders lie on their sides, translucent and ragged, their legs drying in knots. The moths stagger against each other, headless, in a confusion of arcing strips of chitin like peeling varnish, like a jumble of buttresses for cathedral vaults, like nothing resembling moths, so that I would hesitate to call them moths, except that I have had some experience with the figure Moth reduced to a nub.

Two summers ago I was camped alone in the Blue Ridge Mountains of Virginia. I had hauled myself and gear up there to read, among other things, *The Day on Fire,* by James Ullman, a novel about Rimbaud that had made me want to be a writer when I was sixteen; I was hoping it would do it again. So I read every day sitting under a tree by my tent, while warblers sang in the leaves overhead and bristle worms trailed their inches over the twiggy dirt at my feet; and I read every night by candlelight, while barred owls called in the forest and pale moths seeking mates massed round my head in the clearing, where my light made a ring.

Moths kept flying into the candle. They would hiss and recoil, reeling upside down in the shadows among my cooking pans. Or they would singe their wings and fall, and their hot wings, as if melted, would stick to the first thing they touched—a pan, a lid, a spoon—so that the snagged moths could struggle only in tiny arcs, unable to flutter free. These I could release by a quick flip with a stick; in the morning I would find my cooking stuff decorated with torn flecks of moth wings, ghostly triangles of shiny dust here and there on the aluminum. So I read, and boiled water, and replenished candles, and read on.

One night a moth flew into the candle, was caught, burnt dry, and held. I must have been staring at the candle, or maybe I looked up when a shadow crossed my page; at any rate, I saw it all. A golden female moth, a biggish one with a two-inch wingspread, flapped into the fire, dropped abdomen into the wet wax, stuck, flamed, and frazzled in a second. Her moving wings ignited like tissue paper, like angels' wings, enlarging the circle of light in the clearing and creating out of the darkness the sudden blue sleeves of my sweater, the green leaves of jewelweed by my side, the ragged red trunk of a pine; at once the light contracted again and the moth's wings vanished in a fine, foul smoke. At the same time, her six legs clawed, curled, blackened, and ceased, disappearing utterly. And her head jerked in spasms, making a spattering noise; her antennae crisped and burnt away and her heaving mouthparts cracked like pistol fire. When it was all over, her head was, so far as I could determine, gone, gone the long way of her wings and legs. Her head was a hole lost to time. All that was left was the glowing horn shell of her abdomen and thorax—a fraying, partially collapsed gold tube jammed upright in the candle's round pool.

And then this moth-essence, this spectacular skeleton, began to act as a wick. She kept burning. The wax rose in the moth's body from her soaking abdomen to her thorax to the shattered hole where her head should have been, and widened into flame, a saffron-yellow flame that robed her to the ground like an immolating monk. That candle had two wicks, two winding flames of identical light, side by side. The moth's head was fire. She burned for two hours, until I blew her out.

She burned for two hours without changing, without swaying or kneeling—only glowing within, like a building fire glimpsed through silhouetted walls, like a hollow saint, like a flame-faced virgin gone to God, while I read by her light, kindled, while Rimbaud in Paris burnt out his brain in a thousand poems, while night pooled wetly at my feet.

So. That is why I think those hollow shreds on the bathroom floor are moths. I believe I know what moths look like, in any state.

I have three candles here on the table which I disentangle from the plants and light when visitors come. The cats avoid them, although Small's tail caught fire once; I rubbed it out before she noticed. I don't mind living alone. I like eating alone and reading. I don't mind sleeping alone. The only time I mind being alone is when something is funny; then, when I am laughing at something funny, I wish someone were around. Sometimes I think it is pretty funny that I sleep alone.

N. Scott Momaday / A First American Views His Land
National Geographic, July 1976

The National Geographic *magazine was founded in 1888 under the auspices of the National Geographic Society as a professional journal devoted to technical essays on exploration and earth sciences. As the society invested more and more heavily in expeditions that would capture the popular imagination, the editors decided to alter the magazine's contents in the hope of attracting a larger, nonspecialized audience. Over the years, the* National Geographic *has become a popular forum for travel, adventure, anthropology, and geographical research. Its consistently high standard of color photography has been a major factor in the magazine's enormous circulation, now more than nine million.*

N. Scott Momaday's "A First American Views His Land" clearly fulfills the National Geographic's *announced criteria for publication:*

> *First person narratives, making it easy for the reader to share the author's experience and observations. Writing should include plenty of human-interest incident, authentic direct quotation, and a bit of humor where appropriate. Accuracy is fundamental. Contemporary problems such as those of pollution and ecology are treated on a factual basis. The magazine is especially seeking short American place pieces with a strong regional "people" flavor.*

Born in Lawton, Oklahoma, in 1934, Momaday received his B.A. from the University of New Mexico, his M.A. and Ph.D. from Stanford. A professor of English at Stanford, Momaday won the Pulitzer Prize for fiction in 1969 for his novel House of Dawn. *He regularly contributes articles, fiction, and poetry to numerous periodicals and frequently reviews work on American Indian culture.*

The poem woven into the selection printed below is drawn from his book, The
Gourd Dancer *(1976).*

> *First Man*
> *behold:*
> *the earth*
> *glitters*
> *with leaves;*
> *the sky*
> *glistens*
> *with rain.*
> *Pollen*
> *is borne*
> *on winds*
> *that low*
> *and lean*
> *upon*
> *mountains.*
> *Cedars*
> *blacken*
> *the slopes—*
> *and pines.*

One hundred centuries ago. There is a wide, irregular landscape in what is now
northern New Mexico. The sun is a dull white disk, low in the south; it is a perfect mystery, a deity whose coming and going are inexorable. The gray sky is
curdled, and it bears very close upon the earth. A cold wind runs along the
ground, dips and spins, flaking drift from a pond in the bottom of a ravine.
Beyond the wind the silence is acute. A man crouches in the ravine, in the darkness there, scarcely visible. He moves not a muscle; only the wind lifts a lock of
his hair and lays it back along his neck. He wears skins and carries a spear. These
things in particular mark his human intelligence and distinguish him as the lord of
the universe. And for him the universe is especially *this* landscape; for him the
landscape is an element like the air. The vast, virgin wilderness is by and large his
whole context. For him there is no possibility of existence elsewhere.

Directly there is a blowing, a rumble of breath deeper than the wind, above
him, where some of the hard clay of the bank is broken off and the clods roll
down into the water. At the same time there appears on the skyline the massive
head of a long-horned bison, then the hump, then the whole beast, huge and black
on the sky, standing to a height of seven feet at the hump, with horns that extend
six feet across the shaggy crown. For a moment it is poised there; then it lumbers
obliquely down the bank to the pond. Still the man does not move, though the
beast is now only a few steps upwind. There is no sign of what is about to happen;
the beast meanders; the man is frozen in repose.

Then the scene explodes. In one and the same instant the man springs to his feet
and bolts forward, his arm cocked and the spear held high, and the huge animal
lunges in panic, bellowing, its whole weight thrown violently into the bank, its
hooves churning and chipping earth into the air, its eyes gone wide and wild and
white. There is a moment in which its awful, frenzied motion is wasted, and it is
mired and helpless in its fear, and the man hurls the spear with his whole strength,
and the point is driven into the deep, vital flesh, and the bison in its agony stag-
gers and crashes down and dies.

This ancient drama of the hunt is enacted again and again in the landscape. The
man is preeminently a predator, the most dangerous of all. He hunts in order to

survive; his very existence is simply, squarely established upon that basis. But he hunts also because he can, because he has the means; he has the ultimate weapon of his age, and his prey is plentiful. His relationship to the land has not yet become a moral equation.

But in time he will come to understand that there is an intimate, vital link between the earth and himself, a link that implies an intricate network of rights and responsibilities. In some unimagined future he will understand that he has the ability to devastate and perhaps destroy his environment. That moment will be one of extreme crisis in his evolution.

The weapon is deadly and efficient. The hunter has taken great care in its manufacture, especially in the shaping of the flint point, which is an extraordinary thing. A larger flake has been removed from each face, a groove that extends from the base nearly to the tip. Several hundred pounds of pressure, expertly applied, were required to make these grooves. The hunter then is an artisan, and he must know how to use rudimentary tools. His skill, manifest in the manufacture of this artifact, is unsurpassed for its time and purpose. By means of this weapon is the Paleo-Indian hunter eminently able to exploit his environment.

Thousands of years later, about the time that Columbus begins his first voyage to the New World, another man, in the region of the Great Lakes, stands in the forest shade on the edge of a sunlit brake. In a while a deer enters into the pool of light. Silently the man fits an arrow to a bow, draws aim, and shoots. The arrow zips across the distance and strikes home. The deer leaps and falls dead.

But this latter-day man, unlike his ancient predecessor, is only incidentally a hunter; he is also a fisherman, a husbandman, even a physician. He fells trees and builds canoes; he grows corn, squash, and beans, and he gathers fruits and nuts; he uses hundreds of species of wild plants for food, medicine, teas, and dyes. Instead of one animal, or two or three, he hunts many, none to extinction as the Paleo-Indian may have done. He has fitted himself far more precisely into the patterns of the wilderness than did his ancient predecessor. He lives on the land; he takes his living from it; but he does not destroy it. This distinction supports the fundamental ethic that we call conservation today. In principle, if not yet in name, this man is a conservationist.

These two hunting sketches are far less important in themselves than is that long distance between them, that whole possibility within the dimension of time. I believe that in that interim there grew up in the mind of man an idea of the land as sacred.

> *At dawn*
> *eagles*
> *lie and*
> *hover*
> *above*
> *the plain*
> *where light*
> *gathers*
> *in pools.*
> *Grasses*
> *shimmer*
> *and shine.*
> *Shadows*
> *withdraw*
> *and lie*
> *away*
> *like smoke.*

"The earth is our mother. The sky is our father." This concept of nature, which is at the center of the Native American world view, is familiar to us all. But it may well be that we do not understand entirely what that concept is in its ethical and philosophical implications.

I tell my students that the American Indian has a unique investment in the American landscape. It is an investment that represents perhaps thirty thousand years of habitation. That tenure has to be worth something in itself—a great deal, in fact. The Indian has been here a long time; he is at home here. That simple and obvious truth is one of the most important realities of the Indian world, and it is integral in the Indian mind and spirit.

How does such a concept evolve? Where does it begin? Perhaps it begins with the recognition of beauty, the realization that the physical world *is* beautiful. We don't know much about the ancient hunter's sensibilities. It isn't likely that he had leisure in his life for the elaboration of an aesthetic ideal. And yet the weapon he made was beautiful as well as functional. It has been suggested that much of the minute chipping along the edges of his weapon served no purpose but that of aesthetic satisfaction.

A good deal more is known concerning that man of the central forests. He made beautiful boxes and dishes out of elm and birch bark, for example. His canoes were marvelous, delicate works of art. And this aesthetic perception was a principle of the whole Indian world of his time, as indeed it is of our time. The contemporary Native American is a man whose strong aesthetic perceptions are clearly evident in his arts and crafts, in his religious ceremonies, and in the stories and songs of his rich oral tradition. This, in view of the pressures that have been brought to bear upon the Indian world and the drastic changes that have been effected in its landscape, is a blessing and an irony.

Consider for example the Navajos of the Four Corners area. In recent years an extensive coal-mining operation has mutilated some of their most sacred land. A large power plant in that same region spews a contamination into the sky that is visible for many miles. And yet, as much as any people of whom I have heard, the Navajos perceive and celebrate the beauty of the physical world.

There is a Navajo ceremonial song that celebrates the sounds that are made in the natural world, the particular voices that beautify the earth:

> *Voice above,*
> *Voice of thunder,*
> *Speak from the*
> *dark of clouds;*
> *Voice below,*
> *Grasshopper voice,*
> *Speak from the*
> *green of plants;*
> *So may the earth*
> *be beautiful.*

There is in the motion and meaning of this song a comprehension of the world that is peculiarly native, I believe, that is integral in the Native American mentality. Consider: The singer stands at the center of the natural world, at the source of its sound, of its motion, of its life. Nothing of that world is inaccessible to him or lost upon him. His song is filled with reverence, with wonder and delight, and with confidence as well. He knows something about himself and about the things around him—and he knows that he knows. I am interested in what he sees and hears; I am interested in the range and force of his perception. Our immediate impression may be that his perception is narrow and deep—vertical. After all, "voice above . . . voice below," he sings. But is it vertical only? At each level of his expression there is an extension of his awareness across the whole landscape. The voice above is the voice of thunder, and thunder rolls. Moreover, it issues from the impalpable dark clouds and runs upon their horizontal range. It is a sound that integrates the whole of the atmosphere. And even so, the voice below, that of the grasshopper, issues from the broad plain and multiplicity of plants. And of course the singer is mindful of much more than thunder and insects; we are given in his song the wide angle of his vision and his hearing—and we are given the testimony of his dignity, his trust, and his deep belief.

This comprehension of the earth and air is surely a matter of morality, for it brings into account not only man's instinctive reaction to his environment but the full realization of his humanity as well, the achievement of his intellectual and spiritual development as an individual and as a race.

In my own experience I have seen numerous examples of this regard for nature. My grandfather Mammedaty was a farmer in his mature years; his grandfather was a buffalo hunter. It was not easy for Mammedaty to be a farmer; he was a Kiowa, and the Kiowas never had an agrarian tradition. Yet he had to make his living, and the old, beloved life of roaming the plains and hunting the buffalo was gone forever. Even so, as much as any man before him, he fitted his mind and will and spirit to the land; there was nothing else. He could not have conceived of living apart from the land.

In *The Way to Rainy Mountain* I set down a small narrative that belongs in the oral tradition of my family. It indicates something essential about the Native American attitude toward the land:

"East of my grandmother's house, south of the pecan grove, there is buried a woman in a beautiful dress. Mammedaty used to know where she is buried, but now no one knows. If you stand on the front porch of the house and look eastward towards Carnegie, you know that the woman is buried somewhere within the range of your vision. But her grave is unmarked. She was buried in a cabinet, and she wore a beautiful dress. How beautiful it was! It was one of those fine buckskin dresses, and it was decorated with elk's teeth and beadwork. That dress is still there, under the ground."

It seems to me that this statement is primarily a declaration of love for the land, in which the several elements—the woman, the dress, and this plain—are at last become one reality, one expression of the beautiful in nature. Moreover, it seems to me a peculiarly Native American expression in this sense: that the concentration of things that are explicitly remembered—the general landscape, the simple, almost abstract nature of the burial, above all the beautiful dress, which is wholly singular in kind (as well as in its function within the narrative)—is especially Indian in character. The things that are *not* explicitly remembered—the woman's name, the exact location of her grave—are the things that matter least in the special view of the storyteller. What matters here is the translation of the woman into the landscape, a translation particularly signified by means of the beautiful and distinctive dress, an *Indian* dress.

When I was a boy, I lived for several years at Jemez Pueblo, New Mexico. The Pueblo Indians are perhaps more obviously invested in the land than are other people. Their whole life is predicated upon a thorough perception of the physical world and its myriad aspects. When I first went there to live, the cacique, or chief, of the Pueblos was a venerable old man with long, gray hair and bright, deep-set eyes. He was entirely dignified and imposing—and rather formidable in the eyes of a boy. He excited my imagination a good deal. I was told that this old man kept the calendar of the tribe, that each morning he stood on a certain spot of ground near the center of the town and watched to see where the sun appeared on the skyline. By means of this solar calendar did he know and announce to his people when it was time to plant, to harvest, to perform this or that ceremony. This image of him in my mind's eye—the old man gazing each morning after the ranging sun—came to represent for me the epitome of that real harmony between man and the land that signifies the Indian world.

One day when I was riding my horse along the Jemez River, I looked up to see a long caravan of wagons and people on horseback and on foot. Men, women, and children were crossing the river ahead of me, moving out to the west, where most of the cultivated fields were, the farmland of the town. It was a wonderful sight to see, this long procession, and I was immediately deeply curious. I wanted to investigate, but it was not in me to do so at once, for that racial reserve, that sense of propriety that is deep-seated in Native American culture, stayed me, held me up. Then I saw someone coming toward me on horseback, galloping. It was a friend of mine, a boy of my own age. "Come on," he said. "Come with us." "Where are you going?" I asked casually. But he would not tell me. He simply laughed and urged me to come along, and of course I was very glad to do so. It was a bright spring morning, and I had a good horse under me, and the prospect of adventure was delicious. We moved far out across the eroded plain to the farthest fields at the foot of a great red mesa, and there we planted two large fields of corn. And afterward, on the edge of the fields, we sat on blankets and ate a feast in the shade of a cottonwood grove. Later I learned it was the cacique's fields we planted. And this is an ancient tradition at Jemez. The people of the town plant and tend and harvest the cacique's fields, and in the winter the hunters give to him a portion of the meat that they bring home from the mountains. It is as if the cacique is himself the translation of man, every man, into the landscape.

I have not forgotten that day, nor shall I forget it. I remember the warm earth of the fields, the smooth texture of seeds in my hands, and the brown water moving slowly and irresistibly among the rows. Above all I remember the spirit in which the procession was made, the work was done, and the feasting was enjoyed. It was a spirit of communion, of the life of each man in relation to the life of the planet and of the infinite distance and silence in which it moves. We made, in concert, an appropriate expression of that spirit.

One afternoon an old Kiowa woman talked to me, telling me of the place in Oklahoma in which she had lived for a hundred years. It was the place in which my grandparents, too, lived; and it is the place where I was born. And she told me of a time even further back, when the Kiowas came down from the north and centered their culture in the red earth of the southern plains. She told wonderful stories, and as I listened, I began to feel more and more sure that her voice proceeded from the land itself. I asked her many things concerning the Kiowas, for I wanted to understand all that I could of my heritage. I told the old woman that I had come there to learn from her and from people like her, those in whom the old ways were preserved. And she said simply: "It is good that you have come here." I believe that her word "good" meant many things; for one thing it meant *right,* or *appropriate.* And indeed it was appropriate that she should speak of the land. She was eminently qualified to do so. She had a great reverence for the land, and an ancient perception of it, a perception that it acquired only in the course of many generations.

It is this notion of the appropriate, along with that of the beautiful, that forms the Native American perspective on the land. In a sense these considerations are indivisible; Native American oral tradition is rich with songs and tales that celebrate natural beauty, the beauty of the natural world. What is more appropriate to our world than that which is beautiful:

> *At noon*
> *turtles*
> *enter*
> *slowly*
> *into*
> *the warm*
> *dark loam.*

Bees hold
the swarm.
Meadows
recede
through planes
of heat
and pure
distance.

Very old in the Native American world view is the conviction that the earth is vital, that there is a spiritual dimension to it, a dimension in which man rightly exists. It follows logically that there are ethical imperatives in this matter. I think: Inasmuch as I am in the land, it is appropriate that I should affirm myself in the spirit of the land. I shall celebrate my life in the world and the world in my life. In the natural order man invests himself in the landscape and at the same time incorporates the landscape into his own most fundamental experience. This trust is sacred.

The process of investment and appropriation is, I believe, preeminently a function of the imagination. It is accomplished by means of an act of the imagination that is especially ethical in kind. We are what we imagine ourselves to be. The Native American is someone who thinks of himself, imagines himself in a particular way. By virtue of his experience his idea of himself comprehends his relationship to the land.

And the quality of this imagining is determined as well by racial and cultural experience. The Native American's attitudes toward this landscape have been formulated over a long period of time, a span that reaches back to the end of the Ice Age. The land, *this* land, is secure in his racial memory.

In our society as a whole we conceive of the land in terms of ownership and use. It is a lifeless medium of exchange; it has for most of us, I suspect, no more spirituality than has an automobile, say, or a refrigerator. And our laws confirm us in this view, for we can buy and sell the land, we can exclude each other from it, and in the context of ownership we can use it as we will. Ownership implies use, and use implies consumption.

But this way of thinking of the land is alien to the Indian. His cultural intelligence is opposed to these concepts; indeed, for him they are all but inconceivable quantities. This fundamental distinction is easier to understand with respect to ownership than to use, perhaps. For obviously the Indian does use, and has always used, the land and the available resources in it. The point is that *use* does not indicate in any real way his idea of the land. "Use" is neither his word nor his idea. As an Indian I think: "You say that I *use* the land, and I reply, yes, it is true; but it is not the first truth. The first truth is that I *love* the land; I see that it is beautiful; I delight in it; I am alive in it."

In the long course of his journey from Asia and in the realization of himself in the New World, the Indian has assumed a deep ethical regard for the earth and sky, a reverence for the natural world that is antipodal to that strange tenet of modern civilization that seemingly has it that man must destroy his environnment. It is this ancient ethic of the Native American that must shape our efforts to preserve the earth and the life upon and within it.

At dusk
the gray
foxes
stiffen
in cold;
blackbirds

are fixed
in white
branches.
Rivers
follow
the moon,
the long
white track
of the
full moon.

Toni Morrison / Cinderella's Stepsisters   *Ms.*, September 1979

Born in Lorain, Ohio, in 1931, Toni Morrison has emerged over the past de-
cade as one of the most admired and accomplished voices in black American lit-
erature. After receiving a master's degree in English from Cornell University in
1955, Morrison taught for a number of years until she was hired as a senior
editor at Random House in 1968. Since then, she has also taught classes in
black literature and techniques of fiction at Yale and Bard colleges, although
writing remains her primary occupation. Her novels include The Bluest Eye
(1970), Sula *(1973),* Song of Solomon *(1977), which won that year's National*
Book Award, and Tar Baby *(1981).*

Instead of dealing with the conflict between races, Morrison's work focuses
on the difficulties among people from various backgrounds within the black
community. Combining elements of harsh reality with mythic images and fairy
tales, her novels show how men and women attempt to hold on to love, beauty,
and a belief in miracles in a world "where we are all of us, in some measure,
victims of something." In the following article, adapted from a speech delivered
at Barnard College, Morrison uses the Cinderella story as a metaphor for ex-
horting her fellow sisters to a greater vigilance on each other's behalf.

Cofounded by Gloria Steinem in 1972, Ms. *is a monthly magazine featuring*
articles on politics and contemporary social developments, particularly those
that most directly affect the women's movement.

Let me begin by taking you back a little. Back before the days at college. To
nursery school, probably, to a once-upon-a-time time when you first heard, or read,
or, I suspect, even saw "Cinderella." Because it is Cinderella that I want to talk
about; because it is Cinderella who causes me a feeling of urgency. What is unsettling about that fairy tale is that it is essentially the story of household—a world,
if you please—of women gathered together and held together in order to abuse
another woman. There is, of course, a rather vague absent father and a nick-of-
time prince with a foot fetish. But neither has much personality. And there are the
surrogate "mothers," of course (god- and step-), who contribute both to Cinderella's grief and to her release and happiness. But it is her stepsisters who interest
me. How crippling it must have been for those young girls to grow up with a
mother, to watch and imitate that mother, enslaving another girl.

I am curious about their fortunes after the story ends. For contrary to recent
adaptations, the stepsisters were not ugly, clumsy, stupid girls with outsize feet.
The Grimm collection describes them as "beautiful and fair in appearance." When
we are introduced to them they are beautiful, elegant, women of status, and clearly

women of power. Having watched and participated in the violent dominion of another woman, will they be any less cruel when it comes their turn to enslave other children, or even when they are required to take care of their own mother?

It is not a wholly medieval problem. It is quite a contemporary one: feminine power when directed at other women has historically been wielded in what has been described as a "masculine" manner. Soon you will be in a position to do the very same thing. Whatever your background—rich or poor—whatever the history of education in your family—five generations or one—you have taken advantage of what has been available to you at Barnard and you will therefore have both the economic and social status of the stepsisters *and* you will have their power.

I want not to *ask* you but to *tell* you not to participate in the oppression of your sisters. Mothers who abuse their children are women, and another woman, not an agency, has to be willing to stay their hands. Mothers who set fire to school buses are women, and another woman, not an agency, has to tell them to stay their hands. Women who stop the promotion of other women in careers are women, and another woman must come to the victim's aid. Social and welfare workers who humiliate their clients may be women, and other women colleagues have to deflect their anger.

I am alarmed by the violence that women do to each other: professional violence, competitive violence, emotional violence. I am alarmed by the willingness of women to enslave other women. I am alarmed by a growing absence of decency on the killing floor of professional women's worlds. You are the women who will take your place in the world where *you* can decide who shall flourish and who shall wither; you will make distinctions between the deserving poor and the undeserving poor; where you can yourself determine which life is expendable and which is indispensable. Since you will have the power to do it, you may also be persuaded that you have the right to do it. As educated women the distinction between the two is first-order business.

I am suggesting that we pay as much attention to our nurturing sensibilities as to our ambition. You are moving in the direction of freedom and the function of freedom is to free somebody else. You are moving toward self-fulfillment, and the consequences of that fulfillment should be to discover that there is something just as important as you are and that just-as-important thing may be Cinderella—or your stepsister.

In your rainbow journey toward the realization of personal goals, don't make choices based only on your security and your safety. Nothing is safe. That is not to say that anything ever was, or that anything worth achieving ever should be. Things of value seldom are. It is not safe to have a child. It is not safe to challenge the status quo. It is not safe to choose work that has not been done before. Or to do old work in a new way. There will always be someone there to stop you. But in pursuing your highest ambitions, don't let your personal safety diminish the safety of your stepsister. In wielding the power that is deservedly yours, don't permit it to enslave your stepsisters. Let your might and your power emanate from that place in you that is nurturing and caring.

Women's rights is not only an abstraction, a cause; it is also a personal affair. It is not only about "us"; it is also about me and you. Just the two of us.

Jay Cocks / The Last Day in the Life   *Time*, December 22, 1980

The untimely death of a cultural hero often shocks the world into reevaluating its dreams, its ideals, and its youth. When John Lennon, founder of the Beatles, rebel, pacifist, and family man, was assassinated on December 8, 1980, an entire generation lost one of its most brilliant and beloved leaders. The response to his murder came from all across the world and from a diversity of voices. Yet one factor unified all of these reactions—an expression of grief and amazement at the truly unimaginable. The following is an example of one reporter's assessment of a complex life, tragically cut short.

Jay Cocks is a contributing editor to Time *magazine.*

Just a voice out of the American night. "Mr. Lennon." He started to turn around. There is no knowing whether John Lennon saw, for what would have been the second time that day, the young man in the black raincoat stepping out of the shadows. The first shot hit him that fast, through the chest. There were at least three others.

Not that night, or the next day, but a little later, after the terror ebbed and the grief could be managed, Lennon's wife, Yoko Ono, took their five-year-old son Sean to the spot in the apartment courtyard where she had seen his father murdered. She had already shown Sean a newspaper with his father's picture on the front page. She tried to do what everyone else has done since that Monday night. She tried to explain.

Like everyone else, too, the boy asked simple questions to which there would never be simple or satisfactory answers. If, as was being said, the man liked his father so much, why did he shoot him? His mother explained: "He was probably a confused person." Not good enough. Better to know, Sean Lennon said, if he was confused or really meant to kill. His mother said that was up to the courts to decide, and Sean wanted to know which courts she was talking about: tennis or basketball? Then Sean cried, and he also said, "Now Daddy is part of God. I guess when you die you become much more bigger because you're part of everything."

Sean did not really know or understand about the Beatles, or what his father was to the world. But Sean will surely know, soon enough, that his father did not have to die to become part of everything. Given the special burden and grace of his great gift, he already was. Not just for his wife or son but for more people than anyone could ever begin to number, the killing of John Lennon was a death in the family.

For all the official records, the death would be called murder. For everyone who cherished the sustaining myth of the Beatles—which is to say, for much of an entire generation that is passing, as Lennon was, at age 40, into middle age, and coming suddenly up against its own mortality—the murder was something else. It was an assassination, a ritual slaying of something that could hardly be named. Hope, perhaps; or idealism. Or time. Not only lost, but suddenly dislocated, fractured.

The outpouring of grief, wonder and shared devastation that followed Lennon's death had the same breadth and intensity as the reaction to the killing of a world figure: some bold and popular politician, like John or Robert Kennedy, or a spiritual leader, like Martin Luther King Jr. But Lennon was a creature of poetic political metaphor, and his spiritual consciousness was directed inward, as a way of nurturing and widening his creative force. That was what made the impact, and the difference—the shock of his imagination, the penetrating and pervasive traces of his genius—and it was the loss of all that, in so abrupt and awful a way, that was mourned last week, all over the world. The last *Day in the Life,* "I read the news today, oh boy . . ."

Sorrow was expressed, sympathies extended by everyone from Presidents and Presidents-elect, Prime Ministers and Governors and mayors to hundreds of fans who gathered at the arched entryway to the Lennons' Manhattan apartment building, the Dakota, crying and praying, singing and decorating the tall iron gates with wreaths and single flowers and memorial banners. CHRISTMAS IN HEAVEN, read one. Another recalled the magical invocation of a childhood memory that became one of his finest songs: *Strawberry Fields Forever.*

Ringo Starr flew to New York to see Yoko. George Harrison, "shattered and stunned," went into retreat at his home in Oxfordshire, England. Paul McCartney, whom Lennon plainly loved and just as plainly hated like the brother he never had, said, "I can't tell you how much it hurts to lose him. His death is a bitter, cruel blow—I really loved the guy." Having no wish to contribute to the hysteria that always follows the grief at such public mournings, McCartney, who has hired two bodyguards to protect himself and his family, said he would stay home in Sussex, England, even if there was a funeral. There was not. Lennon's body was cremated in a suburban New York cemetery, and Ono issued a statement inviting everyone "to participate from wherever you are" in a ten-minute silent vigil on Sunday afternoon.

Before that, it had been a week of tributes. Radio stations from New Orleans to Boston cleared the air ways for Lennon and Beatles retrospectives. In Los Angeles, more than 2,000 people joined in a candlelight vigil at Century City; in Washington, D.C., several hundred crowded the steps of the Lincoln Memorial in a "silent tribute" that recalled the sit-ins of the '60s. Record stores all over the country reported sellouts on the new Lennon-Ono album, *Double Fantasy,* their first record in five years, as well as the back stock of Lennon's previous records.

Some reaction was tragic. A teen-age girl in Florida and a man of 30 in Utah killed themselves, leaving notes that spoke of depression over Lennon's death. On Thursday, Ono said, "This is not the end of an era. The '80s are still going to be a beautiful time, and John believed in it."

All the brutal and finally confounding facts of the killing were examined like runes and held up to the light like talismans, small shards of some awful psychic puzzle. A pudgy Georgia-born ex-security guard from Hawaii named Mark David Chapman fired his shots at Lennon from what the police call "combat stance": in a stiff crouch, one hand wrapped around the butt of his newly purchased revolver, the other around his wrist to steady it. As Lennon took six staggering steps, Chapman, 25, simply stood still, and then went with the arresting officers like a model citizen who had been unfairly rousted on a traffic bust. Chapman's personal history showed, in retrospect, many ominous byways, but immediately after the shooting, he offered no explanations. And no regrets.

Chapman arrived in New York three days before the killing, checked into a Y.M.C.A. nine blocks from Lennon's apartment, and started hanging out in front of the building, waiting for Lennon like any other fan. There were usually fans at the gates of the Dakota, a grand, gloomy, high-maintenance Gothic fortress overlooking the west side of Central Park, because the building houses several celebrities: Lauren Bacall, Roberta Flack, Leonard Bernstein. Fans of the Beatles and Lennon lovers accounted for the largest portion of the curious. Two unidentified women told an ABC television reporter that they had fallen into conversation with Chapman outside the Dakota. Said one, "He just seemed like a really nice, genuine, honest person who was there because he admired John." Others, like WPLJ

Disc Jockey Carol Miller, who lives near the Dakota, had noticed Chapman and thought "he looked strange. He was older than the kids who hung around there." When Miller first heard that Lennon had been shot, Chapman's face flashed in her mind.

On Saturday night, Chapman hailed a cab and told Driver Mark Snyder to take him to Greenwich Village. On the way he boasted that he had just dropped off the tapes of an album John Lennon and Paul McCartney made that day. He said that he was the recording engineer and that they had played for three hours.

On Monday afternoon Chapman spotted Lennon and asked him to autograph an album. Lennon hastily scribbled his name and climbed into a waiting car to take him to a recording studio. Did Chapman feel slighted by Lennon? Possibly. But the night before he had suddenly checked out of the Y and moved into the cushier Sheraton Center hotel and bought himself a big meal. It was as if he were rewarding himself in advance for some proud accomplishment. Now on Monday, only hours after getting Lennon's autograph, Chapman was waiting again, this time in the shadows of the entryway, with a gun. When the police grabbed him after the shooting, they found he still had the autographed album with him. He also had a paperback copy of J.D. Salinger's *The Catcher in the Rye*.

Lennon was no stranger to threats on his life. As early as 1964, at the first Beatles concert in France, Lennon got a note backstage that read, "I am going to shoot you at 9 tonight." He had only lately become accustomed to the freewheeling anarchy of New York street life: "I can go out this door now and go into a restaurant . . . Do you want to know how great that is?" he told the BBC. But friends remember him as being guarded both in public and around the few people he and Ono met during the long years of self-willed isolation that were only ending with the completion of the new album. "John was always wary," says his friend, Actor Peter Boyle. "Maybe partly because he was extraordinarily tuned in. He'd pick up on people, and they'd pick up on him."

Lennon also shared with many other rockers a kind of operational fatalism, a sense that doing your best, whether on record or in concert, required laying yourself open, making yourself vulnerable. It was not only the pressures and excesses of the rock-'n'-roll life that moved the Who's Peter Townshend to remark, "Rock is going to kill me somehow." And it was not just the death of Elvis Presley that Lennon had in mind when he said to friends in 1978, "If you stay in this business long enough, it'll get you."

Rock, Lennon knew as well as anyone, is the applied art of big risk and big feelings. The songs he and Paul McCartney wrote for the Beatles, separately and together, brought more people up against the joy and boldness of rock music than anything else ever has. It wasn't just that Aaron Copland and Leonard Bernstein were taking the Beatles as seriously—and a good deal more affectionately—than Stockhausen. The worldwide appeal of the Beatles had to do with their perceived innocence, their restless idealism that stayed a step or two ahead of the times and once in a while turned, bowed low, gave the times a razz and dared them to catch up. The slow songs were heart stoppers, the fast ones adrenaline rushes of wit, low-down love and high, fabulous adventure. The songs became, all together, an orchestration of a generation's best hopes and fondest dreams.

The songs Lennon wrote later on his own—*Imagine* and *Whatever Gets You Thru the Night, Instant Karma* and *Give Peace a Chance* and the gentle and unapologetic *Watching the Wheels* from the new album, or the gorgeous seasonal anthem, *Happy Xmas (War Is Over)*, which he recorded with Ono in 1972—kept the standard high and his conscience fine-tuned. The political songs were all personal, the intimate songs all singular in their fierce insistence on making public all issues of the heart, on working some common moral out of private pain. Rock music is still benefitting from lessons that Lennon fought hard for, then passed along. All his music seemed to be torn from that small, stormy interior where, as Robert Frost once wrote, "work is play for mortal stakes."

Despite the universality of interest in his death, Lennon remained chiefly the property—one might even be tempted to say prisoner—of his own generation. Some—those who regarded the Beatles as a benign cultural curiosity, and Lennon as some overmoneyed songwriter with a penchant for political pronouncements and personal excess—wondered what all the fuss was about and could not quite understand why some of the junior staff at the office would suddenly break into tears in the middle of the day. "A garden-variety Nobel prizewinner would not get this kind of treatment," said a teacher in Oxford, England. Across the Atlantic, in schools and on college campuses, those from other generations showed almost as great a sense of puzzlement, even distance, as of loss. Gretchen Steininger, 16, a junior at Evergreen Park High School in suburban Chicago, said, "I recognize the end of an era—my mom's."

So a little reminder was in order, a small history lesson, and there was no one better to lead the class than Bruce Springsteen. Lennon had lately become warmly admiring of Springsteen, especially his hit single *Hungry Heart*. Springsteen could probably have let Lennon's death pass unremarked, and few in the audience at his Philadelphia concert last Tuesday would have been troubled. But instead of ripping right into the first song, Springsteen simply said, "If it wasn't for John Lennon, a lot of us would be some place much different tonight. It's a hard world that asks you to live with a lot of things that are unlivable. And it's hard to come out here and play tonight, but there's nothing else to do."

Then Bruce and the E Street Band tore into Springsteen's own anthem, *Born to Run*, making it clear that playing was the best thing to do. Guitarist Steve Van Zandt let the tears roll down his face, and Organist Danny Federici hit the board so hard he broke a key. By the second verse, the song turned into a challenge the audience was happy to accept: "I wanna know love is wild, I wanna know love is real," Springsteen yelled, and they yelled back. By the end, it sounded like redemption. John Lennon knew that sound too. He could use it like a chord change because he had been chasing it most of his life.

John Lennon grew up on Penny Lane, and after a time he moved to a house outside Liverpool, hard by a boys' reformatory. There was another house in the neighborhood where John and his pals would go to a party and sell lemonade bottles for a penny. The house was called Strawberry Fields. His boyhood was neither as roughly working-class as early Beatles p.r. indicated, nor quite as benign as the magical association of those place names might suggest. But John's adolescence in the suburbs, the garden outside the back door and the warm ministrations of his Auntie Mimi did not diminish either the pain or the sense of separateness that was already stirring.

His father, a seaman named Alfred, left home shortly after John was born, and his mother Julia sent him to her sister Mimi because, it was said, she could not support her child. John was 4½ when he was farmed out to the suburbs. All the sorrow, rage and confusion of this early boyhood were taken up again and again in songs like *Julia* and *Mother*. These early years were not an unhealed wound for Lennon, but more nearly a root, a deep psychic wellspring from which he could draw reserves of hard truth.

Reserves of another sort gave him trouble even early on. "In one way, I was always hip," Lennon remarked recently in *Playboy*, during an interview that could stand as lively proof that some of the best Lennon/Ono art was their life. "I was hip in kindergarten. I was different from the others . . . There was something wrong with me, I thought, because I seemed to see things other people didn't see. I was always seeing things in a hallucinatory way." Lennon's songs made peace with those hallucinations and expanded them—whether with psychedelics, psychiatry or a sort of domestic mysticism—while keeping them always within reach, as a man might keep a flashlight on a nightstand in case he had to get up in the dark.

Lennon was already well into his teens, living 15 minutes away from his mother but seldom seeing her, when rock 'n' roll grabbed hold of him and never let loose. All the raw glories of Elvis Presley, Little Richard, Chuck Berry and Jerry Lee Lewis shook him to his shoes. He responded with the rowdiness of spirit and emotional restlessness that already set him apart from his peers and caused their parents concern. Paul McCartney's father warned his son to steer clear of John, which amounted to an open if inadvertent invitation to friendship.

By his 16th year, John had formed his first band, the Quarrymen, and Paul McCartney had enlisted as guitar player. John and Paul began to write songs together almost as soon as they had finished tuning up, and they played any gig the band could get. By the end of 1956, though he had his first group and a best friend, Lennon suffered a lasting wound. His mother was killed in an accident while she stood waiting for a bus. As he said, "I lost her twice."

Two years later, George Harrison had joined the Quarrymen, and the band was actually earning some money. They had their own fans, and a growing reputation that took them to club dates in the gritty seaport of Hamburg, West Germany, where they eventually changed their name to the Beatles and got a double dose of the seamier side of rock life. Lennon, who like the rest of the boys favored black leather jackets, pegged pants and stomper boots, was sending long and passionate mash notes back home to Cynthia Powell. "Sexiest letters this side of Henry Miller," he observed.

He was also a student at the Liverpool College of Art while the Quarrymen were still gigging around. "I knew John would always be a bohemian," Aunt Mimi recalled. "But I wanted him to have some sort of job. Here he was nearly 21 years old, touting round stupid halls for £3 a night. Where was the point in that?"

Well, the point was the music, a peak-velocity transplant of American rock, with its original blistering spirit not only restored but exalted. There was some concern for the future, however. A Liverpool record-store owner named Brian Epstein thought he might be able to lend a hand there. He signed on as the group's manager in 1961. By the end of the following year, the boys got their first record contract and their first producer, George Martin, who remained aboard for the crazy cruise that came to be called Beatlemania. There was one final change of personnel: Drummer Pete Best was replaced by a gentleman named Richard Starkey, who favored quantities of heavy jewelry, most of it worn on the digits, and who went by the name of Ringo Starr.

It took just a month for the second Beatles single, *Please Please Me,* to reach the top of the English charts. That was in January of 1963. By the end of that year, they had released *She Loves You* and appeared live on a BBC variety show in front of thousands of screaming fans in the audience and unverifiable millions of new converts and dazed parents sitting at home in front of the telly. *I Want to Hold Your Hand* came out in the U.S. in the first week of 1964, and it seemed then for a while that both sides of the Atlantic were up for grabs. Beatles forever.

Some history becomes myth, some myth goes down in history, some statistics boggle the mind: the Beatles have sold, all over the world, upwards of 200 million records. They made history so quickly, and so seismically, that their chronology can be given like a code, or an association game in which words, phrases, snatches of lyrics, names, can stand for whole years. Even the skeptical on either side of the Beatles generation will be startled to see how easily they can play along. Start off with an easy one. Yeah, yeah, yeah. Now you're off . . . Ed Sullivan. Jelly babies. Plaza Hotel. Moptops. Arthur and *A Hard Day's Night*. The Maharishi and M.B.E.s. *Sergeant Pepper*. LSD. Apple. "More popular than Jesus." Shea Stadium. White Album. *Yesterday*. "I'd love to turn you on." Jane, Pattie, Cynthia. Linda. Yoko. "Paul is dead." Abbey Road. *Let It Be*.

The history and the resonance of those fragments are so strong that even out of chronological sequence they form their own associations, like a Joseph Cornell collage. Some of the colors may be psychedelic, but the shadings are the pastel of memory, the patina made of remembered melody. Lennon, the only wedded Beatle—he had married Cynthia in 1962 and had a son, Julian—had early been typed as the most restless, outspoken and creative of the group, even though he led, outwardly, the most settled life. There was paradox in this popular portrait, just as there was considerable tension in Lennon's belief that the well-noted contradictions were true. There were both beauty and ambition in his music, and a full measure of turmoil too. He was experimenting with drugs and working up some of the material that would eventually find its way into *Sergeant Pepper's Lonely Hearts Club Band,* when he walked into a London gallery in 1966 and there, among ladders, spyglasses, nail boards, banners and other props of her art, met Yoko Ono.

The daughter of a well-to-do Japanese banker, Ono, now 47, was born in Tokyo. She had lived in San Francisco before World War II, foraged for food back home during it, and afterward returned to the States, where she attended Sarah Lawrence College and became interested in the far-flung reaches of the avant-garde. Her first husband was a Japanese musician. The marriage so offended Ono's mother that she never reconciled with her daughter. She worked on concerts for John Cage, became associated with other artists such as La Monte Young and Charlotte Moorman, the topless cellist whose staging of and participation in art "events" came a little later to be called happenings. Ono married again, a conceptual artist named Tony Cox, and they had a daughter, Kyoko. Ono once brought the baby onstage during a concert as "an uncontrollable instrument." Eventually, Cox and Kyoko went to Japan, and Ono to England. Her artworks, or happenings, began to show a sense of humor that was both self-mocking and affirmative, and when John Lennon climbed a ladder to look through a telescope at that London gallery, what he saw was no distant landscape but a simple YES.

The other Beatles were not delighted to have Ono around. Besides whatever personal antagonisms or random jealousies might have existed, one suspects now, Paul, George and Ringo may have considered her dedicated avant-gardism somewhat inimical to the best popular instincts of their music. For her part, she felt she was under heavy surveillance. "I sort of went to bed with this guy that I liked and suddenly the next morning I see these three in-laws standing there," she recalled recently. John, separated from Cynthia, fell in love with Yoko and her ideas. Some of her conceptual art had the same intellectual playfulness as his lyrics, and Lennon became a collaborator in many of her projects. They made films—of flies crawling, of dozens of bare bums. They made records, including the notorious *Two Virgins,* for which they posed naked, front and back. Shock! Scandal! Grim predictions for the future!

In fact, there was already a fair amount of dissension among the members of the band: McCartney wanted to get out more and play for the folks, Lennon wanted to work in the recording studio, like an artist with a canvas. The ideological pressures and upheavals of the decade made the four Beatles stand out in even sharper contrast to each other. John became much more political, George more spiritual, Paul seemingly more larky, and Ringo more social. In the more than two years between *Sergeant Pepper* and *Abbey Road*, Lennon and McCartney wrote, separately and still (but more tenuously) together, some of their greatest songs *(Penny*

Lane, All You Need Is Love, and *Strawberry Fields Forever).* But if the turmoil had an immediate, productive side, it also took an inevitable toll. In 1969, after the completion of *Abbey Road,* John told the boys he was leaving.

Next year, McCartney went his own way and that, one would have thought, was that. End of Beatles, end of era. But the Beatles would never go away because their music endured; it became part of a common heritage, a shared gift. No matter how many times they were played in elevators or gas stations, Beatles songs were too vibrant ever to qualify as "standards." That these were *Beatles* songs, not the single expression of an individual, needs to be remembered amid all the Lennon eulogies, which call him the strong creative force of the group.

In the process of riding out all the massive changes of the '60s and bringing about a few on their own, the Beatles also trashed an elementary law of geometry: this was one whole that was greater than the sum of its parts. Lennon was unfairly used as a means to put McCartney in his place, although Lennon had taken pains lately to redefine details of his collaboration with Paul, and to make sure credit was distributed accurately. The melodic range of the music ran from marching band to rhythm and blues, from tonal stunt flying to atonal acrobatics, once in a while all in the same song. The Beatles sang ballads that could almost be Elizabethan, rockers that still sound as if they come from the distant future, and it was hard to peg all that invention to any single source. Lennon joked about walking into a restaurant and being saluted by the band with a rendition of *Yesterday,* a pure McCartney effort. Many radio and video memorials to Lennon included *Let It Be,* another Beatles tune that was all McCartney.

If it was hard to keep the credits straight with all the Beatles, it was harder still for them to keep their friendly equilibrium. McCartney, married to Linda Eastman and staying close to the hearthside, released a series of albums that were roundly drubbed as corny, until he broke through splendidly in 1973 with *Band on the Run.* Lennon, married to Ono and living in New York, released a great solo record, *Plastic Ono Band,* then threw himself headlong into uncertainty. He and Ono lived in a series of elaborate post-hippie crash pads, became obsessed not only with artistic experimentation but with radical political flamboyance. Lennon's subsequent albums remained achingly personal, but turned increasingly random, unfocused. They were indignant and assaultive, adrift.

When he and Ono separated for a time in the early '70s, Lennon went on an 18-month bender of drink, drugs and general looniness. "We were all drinking too much and tearing up houses," recalls one of his cronies at the time, Drummer Jim Keltner. "No one drank like he did. He had broken up with Ono and was with another woman at the time. Suddenly, he just started screaming out Ono's name. That separation from her almost killed him." Being treated as some sort of witchy parasite was no treat for the estranged Mrs. Lennon either, and when they both finally reconciled, they changed their lives in unexpected ways.

Lennon released one more record—a collection of rock oldies—then settled back with Ono in the Dakota to raise their son Sean, who was born on Oct. 9, 1975, the day of his father's birthday. Said Lennon: "We're like twins." Occasionally, John and Ono would go public, often to fight the ultimately unsuccessful attempts of the Nixon Justice Department to deport Lennon on an old marijuana conviction in England. Mostly, however, they stayed at home, rearing Sean, redecorating the 25 rooms in their four Dakota apartments (art deco and artifacts of ancient Egypt, including a sarcophagus in the living room; but clouds painted on the ceiling of a downstairs office), expanding their financial holdings (Lennon left an estate estimated at $235 million), buying property and Holstein cows.

The Holsteins were selected because they were meant to yield nourishment, not be slaughtered for it. Ono took care of all the details, and Lennon did not know about the sale of one of the cows until he read an item in the paper. He was even more pleased than surprised. "Only Yoko," he said admiringly, "could sell a cow for $250,000."

Ono could do a lot more than that. The banker's daughter set herself to mastering the mysteries of commercial law and deal making just as, earlier, she had wrestled with the exotic exigencies of John Cage. She met the attorneys and the accountants; she supervised the buying up of property in Palm Beach, Fla., Cold Spring Harbor, an exclusive enclave on Long Island, and in upstate New York. When the Lennons decided to make another album earlier this year, it was Ono who called Record Executive David Geffen and worked out the deal.

The Lennons may have been taking a step or two aside from art, living quietly, but they were not hermits. They were collecting themselves, looking for a center, a core. It seemed hard to understand, but shouldn't have been. Ono sat behind the desk and John stayed home with the little boy. Julian, Lennon's other, older son, was now a teen-ager who lived in Britain with his mother, but wore leather jackets and jeans, like his Dad back in the days of the Quarrymen, and talked of becoming a rocker. John did not see Julian often, and said recently, "I don't remember seeing him as a child." But Lennon suggested that he had lately wanted to know Julian better, and one of the most haunted faces in last week's gallery of grief was Julian's, enduring the same pain that had afflicted his father at almost the same age some 25 years before. He, like John, had lost a parent twice.

John gloried in playing parent to Sean, and liked to call himself a househusband. What upset traditionalists was the fact that he obviously reveled in his domestic role. This role reversal was seen by the man raised by an aunt and three of her sisters as no threat at all. He insisted—indeed, proved—that he was putting nothing at risk, not his manhood and not his artistry.

Double Fantasy, the new record, demonstrated that. Ono's contributions are especially accessible and congenial after years of punk and New Wave conditioning. John's songs, simple, direct and melodic, were celebrations of love and domesticity that asked for, and required, no apology. It was not a great record, like *Plastic Ono Band*, but it might have been the start of another time of greatness.

The subjects of *Double Fantasy*, released last month, were supposedly not the stuff of rock, but John Lennon never bound himself to tradition. "My life revolves around Sean," he told some radio interviewers from San Francisco on the afternoon of the day he was killed. "Now I have more reason to stay healthy and bright . . . And I want to be with my best friend. My best friend's me wife. If I couldn't have worked with her, I wouldn't have bothered . . . I consider that my work won't be finished until I'm dead and buried, and I hope that's a long, long time." As he spoke those words, Mark David Chapman waited for him out on the street.

Lennon's death was not like Elvis Presley's. Presley seemed, at the end, trapped, defeated and hopeless. Lennon could have gone that way too, could have destroyed himself. But he did something harder. He lived. And, for all the fame and finance, that seemed to be what he took the most pride in.

"He beat the rock-'n'-roll life," Steve Van Zandt said the day after Lennon died. "Beat the drugs, beat the fame, beat the damage. He was the only guy who beat it all." That was the victory Mark Chapman took from John Lennon, who had an abundance of what everyone wants and wanted only what so many others have, and take for granted. A home and family. Some still center of love. A life. One minute more.

DISCUSSION QUESTIONS

1. Compare *Time* magazine's account of John Lennon's murder with the *Los Angeles Times* report in "Press." In what basic ways do the two accounts differ? How do these differences reflect the differences between a daily newspaper and a weekly news magazine?

2. Examine the openings of both selections. Comment on their differences in tone and diction. How can you account for these differences? What can the *Time* magazine writer assume that the newspaper reporter cannot?

3. How is the difference in assumptions about audience reflected in the way each article is titled? What does the *Time* magazine title allude to?

Calvin Trillin / The Mystery of Walter Bopp
The New Yorker, May 11, 1981

"Reporters love murders," writes Calvin Trillin, who has been traveling around the United States since 1967 tracking down stories for his "U.S. Journal" series which appears regularly in The New Yorker. *But Trillin draws a distinction between newspaper reporting and the pieces he writes for the magazine:*

> *A magazine like* The New Yorker *does not have the record-keeping function that a newspaper has. If a federal judge is assassinated in Texas or twelve people are killed by floods in the West,* The New Yorker *is not responsible for registering the event for the record. By the same token, it can . . . record the death of a single unimportant person without feeling the need to justify its interest the way a newspaper might ("The Iowa murder is part of a growing national trend toward vaguely disreputable people in small towns killing each other").*

Trillin, a nationally syndicated columnist, has been on the staff of The New Yorker *since 1963 and is the author of such books on crime, cuisine, and American culture as* U.S. Journal, American Fried, Alice Let's Eat, Floater, *and* Third Helpings. *His humor columns for* The Nation *magazine have been collected in* Uncivil Liberties. *His latest collection is* If You Don't Have Anything Nice to Say.

What happened to Walter Bopp is a mystery. In fact, the more that is known about what happened to him, the more mysterious it becomes. The first incident did not seem mysterious at all. In the fall of 1979, Walter Bopp, a vigorous man in his late seventies, was attacked and presumably robbed in downtown Tucson— right in front of the business he and his wife had founded in 1934 as the first health-food store in the city. The incident did not make the newspapers. Tucson is one of those middle-sized Sun Belt cities that are becoming accustomed to the routine muggings and burglaries which a few years ago were associated with the huge old industrial cities of the Northeast. It is no longer unusual for residents of Tucson to own a sophisticated burglar-alarm system or a gun or even, as Walter Bopp did, an attack dog. The second incident—a house fire last spring which the fire department blamed on an electrical short circuit—would probably have gone unreported as well except that when firemen reached the cellar they found, to their understandable dismay, a supply of dynamite and blasting caps that, according to a department spokesman, could have caused a large enough explosion to obliterate Bopp's house, all the firemen in it, and a couple of neighboring houses. The mystery of why someone would store dynamite in his basement seemed to be cleared up when Bopp explained that it was from a nonproducing mine he had operated near Arivaca—a tiny gold- and silver-mining town about an hour in the direction of the Mexican border. Last December, though, Bopp was involved in an incident that was not simply mysterious to itself but suffused the previous incidents with mystery. On a Saturday morning, someone phoned Bopp's second store, on East Speedway Boulevard, and informed a clerk that the proprietor had met with an accident and could be found in the back storeroom. Walter Bopp had been bound with tape and badly beaten the night before. He had serious facial bruises and several broken ribs and a broken pelvis. His attack dog had been killed by having its belly slit open. His pickup truck had been driven to the downtown store and then set on fire. Both stores had been gone through, but no money was missing.

Bopp claimed that all the incidents were related—that the fire had been caused by arson rather than a short circuit, that the mugging a year earlier had been not a simple mugging but an act of terrorism. He even implied that he knew who was to blame—but that was as far as he would go in helping police identify his tormentors. He wouldn't say who and he wouldn't say why. "It's the same people," he was quoted as telling his interrogators. "I don't want to say anything more." Two weeks later, just after Bopp was released from the hospital, it was reported that someone had backed a truck up to his Speedway store and was presumably loading something into it while colleagues stood by with what looked like machine guns or automatic rifles. The police arrived too late, and if Walter Bopp knew who might be removing what from his store he wasn't saying. He still hadn't said in January, when he reentered the hospital and, a day or two later, died of a pulmonary embolism. All of which set a lot of people in Tucson thinking about what in the world might have happened to Walter Bopp.

"I didn't think he had an enemy in the world," one of Walter Bopp's employees had told the *Arizona Daily Star* after the December beating. That is, of course, a remark often made when a respectable citizen meets with what is obviously not random violence. To the casual customer of Bopp Health Food, Walter Bopp probably did appear to be a particularly unlikely candidate for vicious assault—a robust, rosy-cheeked old vegetarian whose knowledge of herbal remedies led some of his customers to refer to him as Dr. Bopp. A Swiss immigrant who retained a slight accent, Bopp was known as a man who worked hard and lived frugally. A lot of people in Tucson had seen him on the back of his pickup truck loading or unloading stock; nobody in Tucson had ever seen him in a necktie. Who would want to terrorize a simple purveyor of wheat germ and herbal tea?

It wasn't long, of course, before it became known that Bopp had interests beyond health food. The *Star* reported in January that he had been in disagreements with several people about land near Arivaca. It also reported that he had been in "supernatural" activities. Then two young reporters for the *Tucson Citizen,* Dan Huff and Shawn Hubler, poked around in Walter Bopp's life and found people who referred to him not as Dr. Bopp but as Dr. Jekyll and Mr. Hyde. Bopp, the *Citizen* reporters discovered, had indeed been capable of great kindness. He had also been, they wrote, a "tight-lipped, sometimes hateful man who believed in witches and who once said that Lyndon Johnson, Lady Bird and Robert McNamara turned into animals and slithered over White House fences at night." It was known in Tucson that Bopp had divorced his wife a few years earlier, after forty-seven years of marriage, but the *Citizen* piece revealed that he was thought to have done so under advice from a psychic. (Most of Bopp's acquaintances—he didn't seem to have any close friends—were unaware that he had remarried until the newspapers carried the name of a second wife as his survivor.) It also revealed that Bopp had strong racist views about Mexicans and blacks. The kindly Dr. Bopp, Huff and Hubler were told, had been a contentious man who never admitted he was wrong and never let loose of a grudge.

Newspaper reports indicating that there were areas in Bopp's life which could indeed have produced an enemy or two did not clear up the mystery, of course; they simply made it more complicated. Had Walter Bopp been terrorized because of a dispute over a silver claim? Could he had discovered something in Arivaca that someone else wanted to know? Was it possible that he have found himself among the sort of cultists who beat up elderly vegetarians? What were Bopp's tormentors after? Gold? Silver? Information? His store? What could have been secret or private enough to restrain Walter Bopp from helping police find the people who had left him bound and beaten on the floor of his storeroom?

From the start, of course, there were ways of explaining what happened to Walter Bopp that did not require knowledge of his ventures into mining or racial theory or the supernatural. Who leans on respectable businessmen? "They were obviously hit men," a clerk at Bopp's store said after the December beating. Tucson happens to have a substantial and well-publicized colony of the sort of citizens who are photographed by the F.B.I. at funerals, and a lot of speculation naturally centered on the possibility that Bopp had run afoul of the mob. Did Walter Bopp have something the mob wanted? Were mobsters trying to persuade him to do something they wanted? It was also possible, of course, that Walter Bopp had simply wandered into some private dispute over pride or sex or vengeance. People in Tucson developed a stunning variety of theories to account for what happened to him: he was a loan shark, he was a bagman, he was a drug dealer, he was an arms dealer, he was a rich miser. "I know he was sitting on a lot of gold," a bartender at the Poco Loco, a tavern next door to Bopp's Speedway store, said not long ago. "He had been buying gold that'd be worth a million dollars in today's market. I think that's why he was dusted."

Walter Bopp arrived in America in the twenties and, doing farm work, made his way across the country to California. Just before the crash of 1929, he sent for his childhood sweetheart—a young Englishwoman who had been at a Swiss school in Bopp's village. Apparently, whatever money he had saved was lost in a get-rich-quick real-estate scheme; at the beginning of the Depression he was working as a dishwasher. What brought him to Tucson in the early thirties was a job as a salad chef at the Pioneer Hotel. When Bopp Health Food opened in 1934, in a tiny downtown storefront, Bopp's wife, Mae, used to say that the cash register was worth more than the stock. Bopp let his wife mind the store for a couple of years while he held on to his salad-chef job. Then they both began working—working without taking vacations or weekends, as far as anyone in Tucson remembers—to build what was for a dozen years the only health-food business in Tucson.

Health food was hardly a national fad in the thirties. "It was not just unfashionable," someone who got into the business a decade or so later said recently. "It was practically clandestine." Tucson, though, did have more than its share of potential customers. In those days, doctors used to send patients to the Arizona desert on the theory that the dry air would alleviate suffering from allergies or asthma or arthritis or emphysema—or simply on the theory that it might be a soothing climate for someone whose disease seemed beyond the reach of conventional medicine. Some of the desperately ill looked for remedies in nutrition, and

Walter Bopp was their adviser. He also developed a trade supplying grain and cereal in bulk to ranchers. As a businessman, Walter Bopp was Old World—thrifty, hardworking, cautious, impervious to suggestions about merchandising techniques. He didn't hold much with spring sales or regular salary increases. The original store remained the same size, in a part of downtown that gradually became characterized by cheap furniture stores and pawnshops. Bopp didn't open a second store until the sixties—on East Speedway Boulevard, a wide street that for miles seems to be one run-on strip-shopping development. The Speedway store was modern when Bopp built it, but hardly modern compared with the flashy health-food chains that blossomed when the business began to attract people who saw health food as a market rather than a cause. Walter Bopp plugged away—grumbling about the insincere people who had come into the business, moving supplies from one store to the other in his pickup truck, working late into the night on his order forms. The block he had chosen on Speedway turned out to be even less uplifting that the old block downtown. After a while, Bopp found himself with the Poco Loco on one side and on the other a place called the Empress Theatre, which offered hard-core films, "adult books and novelties," and a "hot-tub spa." Bopp complained belligerently about tavern and porn-store customers jamming the parking spaces in front of his shop and using the small parking lot he had for his own customers. "An American businessman might have just moved," someone who knew him at that time said recently. "But he was very set in his ways."

Bopp's ways were strange from the start. Mae Bopp—a diminutive, well-spoken woman who seemed almost timid, particularly in his presence—worked constantly in the store, but the Bopps were otherwise not seen together. He seemed to live mainly in the back of the downtown store. He was kind to some employees and cold to others. He fired at least two clerks in the belief that they were witches who were trying to hex him. ("He was good to me until then," one of them has said. "He was a sweet old man.") To a lot of people, he seemed secretive and aloof. His feelings against Jews were even more vitriolic than his feelings against blacks and Mexicans. Some people who knew Bopp for years were unaware of his racial views; some were treated to them in intense, sotto-voce lectures in a back corner of the store. "He was very intelligent," one of his former employees said recently. "He knew herbs very well. He was the first one to help you if you went to him with a problem. He had so many good ways—it's too bad he got mixed up in all that weird stuff. He said some weird things about Jewish people. Once, he told me that a customer was a witch and I shouldn't look her in the eye. He'd start talking real mysterious, real low. He told me she would come to my bedroom in the form of a vampire, and I should get a silver cross to ward her off. I don't believe in witches, but, I'll tell you, when he got through with me I wished I had a silver cross."

Among his other views, Bopp had a strong belief that the economic system—or perhaps all of society—would come crashing down one day, in an even more disastrous way than it had come crashing down in 1929. At that point, of course, stocks and real estate and even paper money would not be worth having. The only wealth would be in gold and silver. There is reason to believe that Walter Bopp did indeed have some gold or silver stashed somewhere. Gold and silver would allow him to survive the economic disaster. According to someone who used to work for Bopp, the silver would have an even more important use: "He figured he could use the silver against Satan. Evil spirits are afraid of silver."

As a young man in southern California, Bopp had shopped around in what must have been the Western world's most extensive display of yogis and mystics and cults, eventually settling on a Hindu offshoot called the Benares League. His belief in the occult may have intensified as he grew older. He seemed more certain

of the forces allied against him. He told an acquaintance that he had paid to have
a counter-hex placed on someone who was trying to hex him. The woman he
married a few months before his death is said to be a soothsayer or a psychic—
the same one who advised him during the dissolution of his previous marriage. A
former employee of Bopp's was told by the police that the closest Bopp would
come to identifying his assailants was to say that he had been done in by the Evil
Force. A lot of people who knew Bopp remain convinced that his death had
something to do with his otherworldly beliefs. ("It must have been that damn cult
thing.") But what? A hex does not in fact cause a vicious beating. The secrets of
the afterlife are not ordinarily sought by torturing a man of spiritual powers until
he tells. How can Bopp's silence be explained? Could Walter Bopp—confused,
increasingly obsessed with the otherworldly, slipping toward paranoia—have mistaken a couple of thugs after gold for the Evil Force?

The most romantic notions of what might have happened to Walter Bopp have
to do with mining, which has been part of the folklore of southern Arizona for
much longer than the mob has. A lot of people in Tucson who may do something
else for a living prospect as a sort of sideline—somewhere between a hobby and
a disease—and for at least thirty years Walter Bopp was one of them. Some of
them still dream of the big strike—a lode of silver that has somehow been missed
by all the holes poked into the desert all of these years, the fabulous lost mines
that the Jesuits are said to have left when they were expelled from Arizona in the
eighteenth century. Some people in Tucson theorized that Walter Bopp might have
hit such a strike, but the mining people around Arivaca find that notion amusing.
From what they say, Bopp must have been one of the most consistently unsuccessful miners in the state.

"I don't think he ever shipped a pound of ore out of here," someone familiar
with mining in Arivaca said recently. Occasionally, Bopp would show up at the
assay office with a test bore that looked mildly promising, but, as far as anyone
knows, he never followed it up. Bopp was not simply a weekend prospector with
a pan or a pickaxe. He filed dozens of claims and did dozens of test bores. ("He
sank holes all over this country.") Just outside of Arivaca, he kept a couple of
miners working for a dozen years to sink two shafts deep into the ground. There
are people in Arivaca who believe that Bopp was almost willfully unsuccessful—
ignoring promising samples, choosing the least likely place to drill. His method
of finding gold or silver was what prospectors call "witchin' it"—trying to divine
it, the way a dowser divines water. It is not uncommon for prospectors—even
prospectors who don't believe in witches—to try to witch gold or silver, and
apparently just about all of them do better at it than Walter Bopp did.

People around Arivaca remember Bopp as a contentious man—quick to assert
his rights, quick to take an argument to court. It is possible, of course, that he
got into a dispute with someone over a claim or had some mine information someone else wanted or let one of the arguments miners are always having with ranchers in southern Arizona get out of hand. Nobody who knows much about mining
thinks that explains what happened to him. They don't think that Bopp got into a
dispute of great seriousness, and they don't think what happened to him is characteristic of the way such a dispute would be settled. That doesn't mean that they
think there was nothing mysterious about Walter Bopp's mining operations. They
wonder where he got all of the money he spent for what miners call "holes in the
ground." A lot of them figure he was using someone else's money. Whose? What
does that have to do with what happened to Walter Bopp?

The police have been to Arivaca and they have visited one of the people Bopp
suspected of witchcraft, but they are apparently not taken with some of the more

ornate theories about the fate of Walter Bopp. Detectives, in the accepted manner, appear to have concentrated their attention on those closest to Walter Bopp and on those who might profit from his death and on anyone who both knew him and seems capable of having terrorized him. (One of Bopp's Speedway neighbors, for example, was once charged with extortion and, in plea bargaining, pleaded guilty to aggravated assault.) It has been five months now since Walter Bopp was attacked, and there is some feeling in Tucson that the police have shifted their energies to other matters. The mystery may always be a mystery.

Among people familiar with the case, of course, the speculation continues. Someone has called Dan Huff at the *Citizen* with an involved story based on Bopp's being connected with Swiss banking houses. Someone else reported having seen Bopp at a Klan recruiting meeting. The various aspects of Bopp's life can be put together in any number of combinations: Bopp owed the mob money he had borrowed to pour into holes in the ground around Arivaca; Bopp met some hippie cultists in the desert—where hippies still seem to exist, as if preserved by the dry climate—and made the mistake of telling them that he had a fortune in gold; Bopp's views on race led him into contact with some people whose viciousness went beyond sotto-voce lectures; Bopp was using mob money for mining; Bopp was using Swiss banking money for mining; Bopp was using Fascist money for mining.

It is said around Tucson that Bopp's widow intends to reopen the health-food stores, but it is also said that the East Speedway store has been sold to the porno operation next door. Both stores are locked, with ornamental grilles protecting their windows. At the Speedway store, the grille is festooned with signs saying that parking is for customers of Bopp Health Food only. In the window, among the displays of sweet orange-spice tea and the Naturade jojoba hair-treatment formula, is a handwritten note that says, "Closed due to death in family."

POSTSCRIPT

A solution was offered for the killing that had been the basis for the greatest variety of speculation—the mysterious death of Walter Bopp. About a year after I left Tucson, three men were charged with Bopp's murder. According to the police, Bopp had indeed been a hoarder of silver—silver accumulated over years of thrifty living rather than silver witched from the Southern Arizona desert—and had died because of it. Authorities said that at least two hundred thousand dollars' worth of silver bars and jewelry had been stolen from Bopp, and that the men who tortured him in the back of his store were trying to find out where to get more. Some of the mystery of why he remained silent about the identity of his attackers may been been cleared up by the fact that one of the three accused men was Jerry Gilligan—a son of Bopp's second wife, the soothsayer. Gilligan was still at large a year later when the other two men charged in the case pleaded guilty to second-degree murder.

DISCUSSION QUESTIONS

    1. "What I was interested in," Calvin Trillin says of his crime series, "was writing about America." In what sense is "The Mystery of Walter Bopp" about America? Why do you think Trillin selected this particular crime to write about? How important is the location to Trillin?

    2. The "Postscript" appeared in Trillin's introduction to a collection of his murder pieces, *Killings* (1984). Do you think this additional information clears up the "mystery" of Walter Bopp? Explain.

Gretel Ehrlich / The Solace of Open Spaces   *Atlantic*, May 1981

One of the most prevalent topics of contemporary nonfiction is outdoor life—
essays and articles on natural history, the wilderness, the environment, ranch-
ing and farming, camping, and travel. The writers who work best with this
theme, such as Annie Dillard, Barry Lopez, Edward Hoagland, Edward Abbey,
and Gretel Ehrlich, are writers who have learned to see nature in both its ordi-
nary details and its breathtaking surprises. They are also writers who have
masterfully combined two kinds of composition: the subjectively personal and
the objectively descriptive.

Gretel Ehrlich's essays have appeared in Harper's, Atlantic, Time, *the* New
York Times, New Age Journal, *and* Antaeus. *She is the author of* Wyoming
Stories *and* The Solace of Open Spaces. *She lives with her husband on a ranch*
in Shell, Wyoming.

The Atlantic *is one of the oldest literary magazines in the country. Estab-*
lished in 1857, it regularly publishes fiction, poetry, and essays as well as seri-
ous articles devoted to education, science, politics, the arts, and general cul-
ture.

It's May and I've just awakened from a nap, curled against sagebrush the way my
dog taught me to sleep—sheltered from wind. A front is pulling the huge sky over
me, and from the dark a hailstone has hit me on the head. I'm trailing a band of
two thousand sheep across a stretch of Wyoming badlands, a fifty-mile trip that
takes five days because sheep shade up in hot sun and won't budge until it's cool.
Bunched together now, and excited into a run by the storm, they drift across dry
land, tumbling into draws like water and surge out again onto the rugged, choppy
plateaus that are the building blocks of this state.

The name Wyoming comes from an Indian word meaning "at the great plains,"
but the plains are really valleys, great arid valleys, sixteen hundred square miles,
with the horizon bending up on all sides into mountain ranges. This gives the
vastness a sheltering look.

Winter lasts six months here. Prevailing winds spill snowdrifts to the east, and
new storms from the northwest replenish them. This white bulk is sometimes
dizzying, even nauseating, to look at. At twenty, thirty, and forty degrees below
zero, not only does your car not work, but neither do your mind and body. The
landscape hardens into a dungeon of space. During the winter, while I was riding
to find a new calf, my jeans froze to the saddle, and in the silence that such cold
creates I felt like the first person on earth, or the last.

Today the sun is out—only a few clouds billowing. In the east, where the sheep
have started off without me, the benchland tilts up in a series of eroded red-
earthed mesas, planed flat on top by a million years of water; behind them, a bold
line of muscular scarps rears up ten thousand feet to become the Big Horn Mountains. A tidal pattern is engraved into the ground, as if left by the sea that once
covered this state. Canyons curve down like galaxies to meet the oncoming rush
of flat land.

To live and work in this kind of open country, with its hundred-mile views, is
to lose the distinction between background and foreground. When I asked an older
ranch hand to describe Wyoming's openness, he said, "It's all a bunch of nothing—wind and rattlesnakes—and so much of it you can't tell where you're going
or where you've been and it don't make much difference." John, a sheepman I

know, is tall and handsome and has an explosive temperament. He had a perfect intuition about people and sheep. They call him "Highpockets," because he's so long-legged; his graceful stride matches the distances he has to cover. He says, "Open space hasn't affected me at all. It's all the people moving in on it." The huge ranch he was born on takes up much of one county and spreads into another state; to put 100,000 miles on his pickup in three years and never leave home is not unusual. A friend of mine has an aunt who ranched on Powder River and didn't go off her place for eleven years. When her husband died, she quickly moved to town, bought a car, and drove around the States to see what she'd been missing.

Most people tell me they've simply driven through Wyoming, as if there were nothing to stop for. Or else they've skied in Jackson Hole, a place Wyomingites acknowledge uncomfortably because its green beauty and chic affluence are mismatched with the rest of the state. Most of Wyoming has a "lean-to" look. Instead of big, roomy barns and Victorian houses, there are dugouts, low sheds, log cabins, sheep camps, and fence lines that look like driftwood blown haphazardly into place. People here still feel pride because they live in such a harsh place, part of the glamorous cowboy past, and they are determined not to be the victims of a mining-dominated future.

Most characteristic of the state's landscape is what a developer euphemistically describes as "indigenous growth right up to your front door"—a reference to waterless stands of salt sage, snakes, jack rabbits, deerflies, red dust, a brief respite of wildflowers, dry washes, and no trees. In the Great Plains the vistas look like music, like Kyries of grass, but Wyoming seems to be the doing of a mad architect—tumbled and twisted, ribboned with faded, deathbed colors, thrust up and pulled down as if the place had been startled out of a deep sleep and thrown into a pure light.

I came here four years ago. I had not planned to stay, but I couldn't make myself leave. John, the sheepman, put me to work immediately. It was spring, and shearing time. For fourteen days of fourteen hours each, we moved thousands of sheep through sorting corrals to be sheared, branded, and deloused. I suspect that my original motive for coming here was to "lose myself" in new and unpopulated territory. Instead of producing the numbness I thought I wanted, life on the sheep ranch woke me up. The vitality of the people I was working with flushed out what had become a hallucinatory rawness inside me. I threw away my clothes and bought new ones; I cut my hair. The arid country was a clean slate. Its absolute indifference steadied me.

Sagebrush covers 58,000 square miles of Wyoming. The biggest city has a population of fifty thousand, and there are only five settlements that could be called cities in the whole state. The rest are towns, scattered across the expanse with as much as sixty miles between them, their populations two thousand, fifty, or ten. They are fugitive-looking, perched on a barren, windblown bench, or tagged onto a river or a railroad, or laid out straight in a farming valley with implement stores and a block-long Mormon church. In the eastern part of the state, which slides down into the Great Plains, the new mining settlements are boomtowns, trailer cities, metal knots on flat land.

Despite the desolate look, there's a coziness to living in this state. There are so few people (only 470,000) that ranchers who buy and sell cattle know one another statewide; the kids who choose to go to college usually go to the state's one university, in Laramie; hired hands work their way around Wyoming in a lifetime of hirings and firings. And despite the physical separation, people stay in touch, often driving two or three hours to another ranch for dinner.

Seventy-five years ago, when travel was by buckboard or horseback, cowboys

who were temporarily out of work rode the grub line—drifting from ranch to
ranch, mending fences or milking cows, and receiving in exchange a bed and
meals. Gossip and messages traveled this slow circuit with them, creating an intimacy between ranchers who were three and four weeks' ride apart. One old-time
couple I know, whose turn-of-the-century homestead was used by an outlaw gang
as a relay station for stolen horses, recall that if you were traveling, desperado or
not, any lighted ranch house was a welcome sign. Even now, for someone who
lives in a remote spot, arriving at a ranch or coming to town for supplies is cause
for celebration. To emerge from isolation can be disorienting. Everything looks
bright, new, vivid. After I had been herding sheep for only three days, the sound
of the camp tender's pickup flustered me. Longing for human company, I felt a
foolish grin take over my face; yet I had to resist an urgent temptation to run and
hide.

Things happen suddenly in Wyoming, the change of seasons and weather; for
people, the violent swings in and out of isolation. But good-naturedness is con-
comitant with severity. Friendliness is a tradition. Strangers passing on the road
wave hello. A common sight is two pickups stopped side by side far out on a
range, on a dirt track winding through the sage. The drivers will share a cigarette,
uncap their thermos bottles, and pass a battered cup, steaming with coffee, between windows. These meetings summon up the details of several generations,
because, in Wyoming, private histories are largely public knowledge.

Because ranch work is a physical and, these days, economic strain, being "at
home on the range" is a matter of vigor, self-reliance, and common sense. A
person's life is not a series of dramatic events for which he or she is applauded
or exiled but a slow accumulation of days, seasons, years, fleshed out by the
generational weight of one's family and anchored by a land-bound sense of place.

In most parts of Wyoming, the human population is visibly outnumbered by the
animal. Not far from my town of fifty, I rode into a narrow valley and startled a
herd of two hundred elk. Eagles look like small people as they eat car-killed deer
by the road. Antelope, moving in small, graceful bands, travel at sixty miles an
hour, their mouths open as if drinking in the space.

The solitude in which westerners live makes them quiet. They telegraph thoughts
and feelings by the way they tilt their heads and listen; pulling their Stetsons into
a steep dive over their eyes, or pigeon-toeing one boot over the other, they lean
against a fence with a fat wedge of Copenhagen beneath their lower lips and take
in the whole scene. These detached looks of quiet amusement are sometimes cynical, but they can also come from a dry-eyed humility as lucid as the air is clear.

Conversation goes on in what sounds like a private code; a few phrases imply
a complex of meanings. Asking directions, you get a curious list of details. While
trailing sheep I was told to "ride up that that kinda upturned rock, follow the pink
wash, turn left at the dump, and then you'll see the water hole." One friend told
his wife on roundup to "turn at the salt lick and the dead cow," which turned out
to be a scattering of bones and no salt lick at all.

Sentence structure is shortened to the skin and bones of a thought. Descriptive
words are dropped, even verbs; a cowboy looking over a corral full of horses will
say to a wrangler, "Which one needs rode?" People hold back their thoughts in
what seems to be a dumbfounded silence, then erupt with an excoriating, percep-
tive remark. Language, so compressed, becomes metaphorical. A rancher ended
a relationship with one remark: "You're a bad check," meaning bouncing in and
out was intolerable, and even coming back would be no good.

What's behind this laconic style is shyness. There is no vocabulary for the
subject of feelings. It's not a hangdog shyness, or anything coy—always there's
a robust spirit in evidence behind the restraint, as if the earth-dredging wind that

pulls across Wyoming had carried its people's voices away but everything else in them had shouldered confidently into the breeze.

I've spent hours riding to sheep camp at dawn in a pickup when nothing was said; eaten meals in the cookhouse when the only words spoken were a mumbled "Thank you, ma'am" at the end of dinner. The silence is profound. Instead of talking, we seem to share one eye. Keenly observed, the world is transformed. The landscape is engorged with detail, every movement on it chillingly sharp. The air between people is charged. Days unfold, bathed in their own music. Nights become hallucinatory; dreams, prescient.

Spring weather is capricious and mean. It snows, then blisters with heat. There have been tornadoes. They lay their elephant trunks out in the sage until they find houses, then slurp everything up and leave. I've noticed that melting snowbanks hiss and rot, viperous, then drip into calm pools where ducklings hatch and livestock, being trailed to summer range, drink. With the ice cover gone, rivers churn a milkshake brown, taking culverts and small bridges with them. Water in such an arid place (the average annual rainfall where I live is less than eight inches) is like blood. It festoons drab land with green veins; a line of cottonwoods following a stream; a strip of alfalfa; and, on ditch banks, wild asparagus growing.

I've moved to a small cattle ranch owned by friends. It's at the foot of the Big Horn Mountains. A few weeks ago, I helped them deliver a calf who was stuck halfway out of his mother's body. By the time he was freed, we could see a heartbeat, but he was straining against a swollen tongue for air. Mary and I held him upside down by his back feet, while Stan, on his hands and knees in the blood, gave the calf mouth-to-mouth resuscitation. I have a vague memory of being pneumonia-choked as a child, my mother giving me her air, which may account for my romance with this wind-swept state.

If anything is endemic to Wyoming, it is wind. This big room of space is swept out daily, leaving a bone yard of fossils, agates, and carcasses in every stage of decay. Though it was water that initially shaped the state, wind is the meticulous gardener, raising dust and pruning the sage.

I try to imagine a world in which I could ride my horse across uncharted land. There is no wilderness left; wildness, yes, but true wilderness has been gone on this continent since the time of Lewis and Clark's overland journey.

Two hundred years ago, the Crow, Shoshone, Arapaho, Cheyenne, and Sioux roamed the intermountain West, orchestrating their movements according to hunger, season, and warfare. Once they acquired horses, they traversed the spines of all the big Wyoming ranges—the Absarokas, the Wind Rivers, the Tetons, the Big Horns—and wintered on the unprotected plains that fan out from them. Space was life. The world was their home.

What was life-giving to Native Americans was often nightmarish to sodbusters who had arrived encumbered with families and ethnic pasts to be transplanted in nearly uninhabitable land. The great distances, the shortage of water and trees, and the loneliness created unexpected hardships for them. In her book *O Pioneers!*, Willa Cather gives a settler's version of the bleak landscape:

> The little town behind them had vanished as if it had never been, had fallen behind the swell of the prairie, and the stern frozen country received them into its bosom. The homesteads were few and far apart; here and there a windmill gaunt against the sky, a sod house crouching in a hollow.

The emptiness of the West was for others a geography of possibility. Men and women who amassed great chunks of land and struggled to preserve unfenced empires were, despite their self-serving motives, unwitting geographers. They understood the lay of the land. But by the 1850s the Oregon and Mormon trials sported bumper-to-bumper traffic. Wealthy landowners, many of them aristocratic absentee landlords, known as remittance men because they were paid to come West and get out of their families' hair, overstocked the range with more than a million head of cattle. By 1885 the feed and water were desperately short, and the winter of 1886 laid out the gaunt bodies of dead animals so closely together that when the thaw came, one rancher from Kaycee claimed to have walked on cowhide all the way to Crazy Woman Creek, twenty miles away.

Territorial Wyoming was a boy's world. The land was generous with everything but water. At first there was room enough, food enough, for everyone. And, as with all beginnings, an expansive mood set in. The young cowboys, drifters, shopkeepers, schoolteachers, were heroic, lawless, generous, rowdy, and tenacious. The individualism and optimism generated during those times have endured.

John Tisdale rode north with the trail herds from Texas. He was a college-educated man with enough money to buy a small outfit near the Powder River. While driving home from the town of Buffalo with a buckboard full of Christmas toys for his family and a winter's supply of food, he was shot in the back by an agent of the cattle barons who resented the encroachment of small-time stockmen like him. The wealthy cattlemen tried to control all the public grazing land by restricting membership in the Wyoming Stock Growers Association, as if it were a country club. They ostracized from roundups and brandings cowboys and ranchers who were not members, then denounced them as rustlers. Tisdale's death, the second such cold-blooded murder, kicked off the Johnson County cattle war, which was no simple good-guy-bad-guy shoot-out but a complicated class struggle between landed gentry and less affluent settlers—a shocking reminder that the West was not an egalitarian sanctuary after all.

Fencing ultimately enforced boundaries, but barbed wire abrogated space. It was stretched across the beautiful valleys, into the mountains, over desert badlands, through buffalo grass. The "anything is possible" fever—the lure of any new place—was constricted. The integrity of the land as a geographical body, and the freedom to ride anywhere on it, were lost.

I punched cows with a young man named Martin, who is the great-grandson of John Tisdale. His inheritance is not the open land that Tisdale knew and prematurely lost but a rage against restraint.

Wyoming tips down as you head northeast; the highest ground—the Laramie Plains—is on the Colorado border. Up where I live, the Big Horn River leaks into difficult, arid terrain. In the basin where it's dammed, sandhill cranes gather and, with delicate legwork, slice through the stilled water. I was driving by with a rancher one morning when he commented that cranes are "old-fashioned." When I asked why, he said, "Because they mate for life." Then he looked at me with a twinkle in his eyes, as if to say he really did believe in such things but also understood why we break our own rules.

In all this open space, values crystalize quickly. People are strong on scruples but tenderhearted about quirky behavior. A friend and I found one ranch hand, who's "not quite right in the head," sitting in front of the badly decayed carcass of a cow, shaking his finger and saying, "Now, I don't want you to do this ever again!" when I asked what was wrong with him, I was told, "He's goofier than hell, just like the rest of us." Perhaps because the West is historically new, conventional morality is still felt to be less important than rock-bottom truths. Though there's always a lot of teasing and sparring, people are blunt with one another, sometimes even cruel, believing honesty is stronger medicine than sympathy, which may console but often conceals.

The formality that goes hand in hand with the rowdiness is known as the Western Code. It's a list of practical do's and don'ts, faithfully observed. A friend, Cliff, who runs a trap-line in the winter, cut off half his foot while chopping a hole in the ice. Alone, he dragged himself to his pickup and headed for town, stopping to open the ranch gate as he left, and getting out to close it again, thus losing, in his observance of rules, precious time and blood. Later, he commented, "How would it look, them having to come to the hospital to tell me their cows had gotten out?"

Accustomed to emergencies, my friends doctor each other from the vet's bag with relish. When one old-timer suffered a heart attack in hunting camp, his partner quickly stirred up a brew of red horse liniment and hot water and made the half-conscious victim drink it, then tied him onto a horse and led him twenty miles to town. He regained consciousness and lived.

The roominess of the state has affected political attitudes as well. Ranchers keep up with world politics and the convulsions of the economy but are basically isolationists. Being used to running their own small empires of land and livestock, they're suspicious of big government. It's a "don't fence me in" holdover from a century ago. They still want the elbow room their grandfathers had, so they're strongly conservative, but with a populist twist.

Summer is the season when we get our "cowboy tans"—on the lower parts of our faces and on three fourths of our arms. Excessive heat, in the nineties and higher, sends us outside with the mosquitoes. In winter we're tucked inside our houses, and the white wasteland outside appears to be expanding, but in summer all the greenery abridges space. Summer is a go-ahead season. Every living thing is off the block and in the race: battalions of bugs in flight and biting; bats swinging around my log cabin as if the bases were loaded and someone had hit a home run. Some of summer's high-speed growth is ominous: larkspur, death camas, and green greasewood can kill sheep—an ironic idea, dying in this desert from eating what is too verdant. With sixteen hours of daylight, farmers and ranchers irrigate feverishly. There are first, second, and third cuttings of hay, some crews averaging only four hours of sleep a night for weeks. And, like the cowboys who in summer ride the night rodeo circuit, night-hawks make daredevil dives at dusk with an eerie whirring sound like a plane going down on the shimmering horizon.

In the town where I live, they've had to board up the dance-hall windows because there have been so many fights. There's so little to do except work that people wind up in a state of idle agitation that becomes fatalistic, as if there were nothing to be done about all this untapped energy. So the dark side to the grandeur of these spaces is the small-mindedness that seals people in. Men become hermits; women go mad. Cabin fever explodes into suicides, or into grudges and lifelong family feuds. Two sisters in my area inherited a ranch but found they couldn't get along. They fenced the place in half. When one's cows got up and mixed with the other's, the women went at each other with shovels. They ended up in the same hospital room but never spoke a word to each other for the rest of their lives.

After the brief lushness of summer, the sun moves south. The range grass is brown. Livestock is trailed back down from the mountains. Water holes begin to frost over at night. Last fall Martin asked me to accompany him on a pack trip. With five horses, we followed a river into the mountains behind the tiny Wyoming town of Meeteetse. Groves of aspen, red and orange, gave off a light that made us look toasted. Our hunting camp was so high that clouds skidded across our foreheads, then slowed to sail out across the warm valleys. Except for a bull moose who wandered into our camp and mistook our black gelding for a rival, we shot at nothing.

One of our evening entertainments was to watch the night sky. My dog, a dingo bred to herd sheep, also came on the trip. He is so used to the silence and empty skies that when an airplane flies over he always looks up and eyes the distant intruder quizzically. The sky, lately, seems to be much more crowded than it used to be. Satellites make their silent passes in the dark with great regularity. We counted eighteen in one hour's viewing. How odd to think that while they circumnavigated the planet, Martin and I had moved only six miles into our local wilderness and had seen no other human for the two weeks we stayed there.

At night, by moonlight, the land is whittled to slivers—a ridge, a river, a strip of grassland stretching to the mountains, then the huge sky. One morning a full moon was setting in the west just as the sun was rising. I felt precariously balanced between the two as I loped across a meadow. For a moment, I could believe that the stars, which were still visible, work like cooper's bands, holding together everything above Wyoming.

Space has a spiritual equivalent and can heal what is divided and burdensome in us. My grandchildren will probably use space shuttles for a honeymoon trip or to recover from heart attacks, but closer to home we might also learn how to carry space inside ourselves in the effortless way we carry our skins. Space represents sanity, not a life purified, dull, or "spaced out" but one that might accommodate intelligently any idea or situation.

From the clayey soil of northern Wyoming is mined bentonite, which is used as a filler in candy, gum, and lipstick. We Americans are great on fillers, as if what we have, what we are, is not enough. We have a cultural tendency toward denial, but, being affluent, we strangle ourselves with what we can buy. We have only to look at the houses we build to see how we build *against* space, the way we drink against pain and loneliness. We fill up space as if it were a pie shell, with things whose opacity further obstructs our ability to see what is already there.

DISCUSSION QUESTIONS

1. Compare "The Solace of Open Spaces" to N. Scott Momaday's "A First American Views His Land" in this section and Barry Lopez's "The Arctic Hunters" in "Best-Sellers." Explain how each writer responds to landscape. What differences and similarities can you find among the selections?

2. Read Peter Homans's "The Western: The Legend and the Cardboard Hero" in this section in connection with Ehrlich's essay. Does Ehrlich endorse or reject the cowboy myth? Explain.

Stephen King / Now You Take "Bambi" or "Snow White"— *That's* Scary!   *TV Guide*, June 13, 1981

Before the commercial success of Carrie *in 1973, Stephen King had worked as a schoolteacher and a gas-station attendant and even pressed sheets in an industrial laundry. Author of a succession of best-selling novels, including* Salem's Lot *(1975),* The Shining *(1977),* The Stand *(1978),* The Dead Zone *(1979),*

Firestarter *(1980),* Cujo *(1981), and* Christine *(1983), King has more than forty million copies of his books in print and is the first author in literary history to have three books simultaneously on the* New York Times *hard- and soft-cover best-seller list.*

Few contemporary writers can match King's gift for combining essentially normal—almost mundane—descriptions of everyday life with disturbingly believable depictions of paranormal events. His characters gain our sympathy because their surroundings, cluttered with cereal boxes, battered household appliances, popular rock-and-roll songs, and other elements of our modern society, seem so familiar.

TV Guide has the largest weekly circulation of any magazine in the world. It publishes, along with local and cable television listings, articles about TV celebrities and programs.

Read the story synopsis below and ask yourself if it would make the sort of film you'd want your kids watching on the Friday- or Saturday-night movie:

A good but rather weak man discovers that, because of inflation, recession and his second wife's fondness for overusing his credit cards, the family is tottering on the brink of financial ruin. In fact, they can expect to see the repossession men coming for the car, the almost new recreational vehicle and the two color TVs any day; and a pink warning-of-foreclosure notice has already arrived from the bank that holds the mortgage on their house.

The wife's solution is simple but chilling: kill the two children, make it look like an accident and collect the insurance. She browbeats her husband into going along with this homicidal scheme. A wilderness trip is arranged, and while wifey stays in camp, the father leads his two children deep into the Great Smoky wilderness. In the end, he finds he cannot kill them in cold blood; he simply leaves them to wander around until, presumably, they will die of hunger and exposure.

The two children spend a horrifying three days and two nights in the wilderness. Near the end of their endurance, they stumble upon a back-country cabin and go to it, hoping for rescue. The woman who lives alone there turns out to be a cannibal. She cages the two children and prepares to roast them in her oven as she has roasted and eaten other wanderers before them. The boy manages to get free. He creeps up behind the woman as she stokes her oven and pushes her in, where she burns to death in her own fire.

You're probably shaking your head no, even if you have already recognized the origin of this bloody little tale (and if you didn't, ask your kids: they probably will) as "Hansel and Gretel," a so-called "fairy tale" that most kids are exposed to even before they start kindergarten. In addition to this story, with its grim and terrifying images of child abandonment, children lost in the woods and imprisoned by an evil woman, cannibalism and justifiable homicide, small children are routinely exposed to tales of mass murder and mutilation ("Bluebeard"), the eating of a loved one by a monster ("Little Red Riding-Hood"), treachery and deceit ("Snow White") and even the specter of a little boy who must face a black-hooded, ax-wielding headsman ("The 500 Hats of Bartholomew Cubbins," by Dr. Seuss).

I'm sometimes asked what I allow my kids to watch on the tube, for two reasons: first, my three children, at 10, 8 and 4, are still young enough to be in the age group that opponents of TV violence and horror consider to be particularly impressionable and at risk; and second, my seven novels have been popularly classified as "horror stories." People tend to think those two facts contradictory. But . . . I'm not sure that they are.

Three of my books have been made into films, and at this writing, two of them have been shown on TV. In the case of "Salem's Lot," a made-for-TV movie, there was never a question of allowing my kids to watch it on its first run on CBS; it began at 9 o'clock in our time zone, and all three children go to bed earlier than that. Even on a weekend, and even for the oldest, an 11 o'clock bedtime is just not negotiable. A previous TV GUIDE article about children and frightening programs mentioned a 3-year-old who watched "Lot" and consequently suffered night terrors. I have no wish to question any responsible parent's judgment—all parents raise their children in different ways—but it did strike me as passingly odd that a 3-year-old should have been allowed to stay up that late to get scared.

But in my case, the hours of the telecast were not really a factor, because we have one of those neat little time-machines, a videocassette recorder. I taped the program and, after viewing it myself, decided my children could watch it if they wanted to. My daughter had no interest; she's more involved with stories of brave dogs and loyal horses these days. My two sons, Joe, 8, and Owen, then 3, did watch. Neither of them seemed to have any problems either while watching it or in the middle of the night—when those problems most likely turn up.

I also have a tape of "Carrie," a theatrical film first shown on TV about two and a half years ago. I elected to keep this one on what my kids call "the high shelf" (where I put the tapes that are forbidden to them), because I felt that its depiction of children turning against other children, the lead character's horrifying embarrassment at a school dance and her later act of matricide would upset them. "Lot," on the contrary, is a story that the children accepted as a fairy tale in modern dress.

Other tapes on my "high shelf" include "Night of the Living Dead" (cannibalism), "The Brood" (David Cronenberg's film of intergenerational breakdown and homicidal "children of rage" who are set free to murder and rampage) and "The Exorcist." They are all up there for the same reason: they contain elements that I think might freak the kids out.

Not that it's possible to keep kids away from everything on TV (or in the movies, for that matter) that will freak them out; the movies that terrorized my own nights most thoroughly as a kid were not those through which Frankenstein's monster or the Wolfman lurched and growled, but the Disney cartoons. I watched Bambi's mother shot and Bambi running frantically to escape being burned up in a forest fire. I watched, appalled, dismayed and sweaty with fear, as Snow White bit into the poisoned apple while the old crone giggled in evil ecstasy. I was similarly terrified by the walking brooms in "Fantasia" and the big, bad wolf who chased the fleeing pigs from house to house with such grim and homicidal intensity. More recently, Owen, who just turned 4, crawled into bed with my wife and me, "Cruella DeVille is in my room," he said. Cruella DeVille is, of course, the villainess of "101 Dalmatians," and I suppose Owen had decided that a woman who would want to turn puppies into dogskin coats might also be interested in little boys. All these films would certainly get G-ratings if they were produced today, and frightening excerpts of them have been shown on TV during "the children's hour."

Do I believe that all violent or horrifying programming should be banned from network TV? No, I do not. Do I believe it should be telecast only in the later evening hours, TV's version of the "high shelf"? Yes, I do. Do I believe that children should be forbidden all violent or horrifying programs? No, I do not. Like their elders, children have a right to experience the entire spectrum of drama, from such warm and mostly unthreatening programs as *Little House on the Prairie* and *The Waltons* to scarier fare. It's been suggested again and again that such entertainment offers us a catharsis—a chance to enter for a little while a scary and yet controllable world where we can express our fears, aggressions and possibly even hostilities. Surely no one would suggest that children do not have their own fears and hostilities to face and overcome; those dark feelings are the basis of many of the fairy tales children love best.

Do I think a child's intake of violent or horrifying programs should be limited? Yes, I do, and that's why I have a high shelf. But the pressure groups who want to see all horror (and anything smacking of sex, for that matter) arbitrarily removed from television make me both uneasy and angry. The element of Big Brotherism inherent in such an idea causes the unease; the idea of a bunch of people I don't even know presuming to dictate what is best for my children causes the anger. I feel that deciding such things myself is my right—and my responsibility.

Responsibility is the bottom line, I guess. If you are going to have that magic window in your living room, you have to take a certain amount of responsibility for what it will show kids when they push the ON button. And when your children ask to stay up to watch something like "The Shining" (when it is shown on cable TV this month), here are some ideas on how you might go about executing your responsibility to your children—from a guy who's got kids of his own and who also wears a fright wig from time to time.

If it's a movie you've seen yourself, you should have no problem. It is not possible to know *everything* that will frighten a child—particularly a small one—but there are certain plot elements that can be very upsetting. These include physical mutilation, the death of an animal the child perceives as "good," the murder of a parent, a parent's treachery, blood in great quantities, drowning, being locked in a tight place and endings that offer no hope—and no catharsis.

If it's a movie you haven't seen, check the listings carefully for the elements listed above, or for things you know upset your children in particular (if, for instance, you have a child who was once lost and was badly shaken by the experience, you may want to skip even such a mild film as "Mountain Family Robinson").

If you're not getting a clear fix on the program from the listings, call the station. They'll be happy to help you; in fact, the station managers I queried said they fall all over themselves trying to help parents who request such information, but usually end up fielding complaints from adults who couldn't be bothered to call until after the offending program.

If the listing is marked *Meant for mature audiences only,* don't automatically give up. What may not be suitable for some families (or for some younger children) may be perfectly OK for your children.

If you do elect to let your children watch a frightening TV program, discuss it with them afterward. Ask them what frightened them and why. Ask them what made them feel good, and why. In most cases, you'll find that kids handle frightening make-believe situations quite well; most of them can be as tough as they need to be. And "talking it through" gives a parent a better idea of where his or her child's private fear button is located—which means a better understanding of the child and the child's mind.

If you think it's too scary, don't let them watch it. Period. The end. Remind yourself that you are bigger than they are, if that's what it takes. Too much frightening programming is no good for anyone, child or adult.

Most of all, try remembering that television spreads out the most incredible smorgasbord of entertainment in the history of the world, and it does so *every day.* Your child wants to taste a little of everything, even as you do yourself. But it would be wrong to let him or her eat only one single dish, particularly one as troublesome and as potentially dangerous as this one. Parenting presumes high shelves of all kinds, and that applies to some TV programs as well as to dangerous medicines or household cleaners.

One last word: when the scary program comes and you've decided that your children may watch, try to watch *with* them. Most children have to walk through their own real-life version of Hansel and Gretel's "dark wood" from time to time, as we did ourselves. The tale of terror can be a dress rehearsal for those dark times.

But if we remember our own scary childhood experiences, we'll probably remember that it was easier to walk through that dark wood with a friend.

Bob Greene / Fifteen   *Esquire*, August 1982

When asked which of his columns he thought were his favorites, Bob Greene responded, "The ones I like are the ones that people don't remember, just the little stories I find while traveling around the country that don't get a whole lot of letters or a whole lot of response; the kind of column where I'll go into a town and meet someone who has a small story to tell, but whose story might never have appeared in the newspaper otherwise."

Born in 1947, Greene became a professional writer by the age of twenty-three, reporting for the Chicago Sun-Times. *Later, as a syndicated columnist and contributing correspondent to ABC-TV's "Nightline" as well as the author of the "American Beat" column for* Esquire, *Greene had earned much critical acclaim as a writer dedicated to the human-interest story. In the following piece, Greene investigates—with a writer's knack for detail—the cruising habits of two bored fifteen-year-old boys whose only source of entertainment is the local shopping mall.*

Esquire *first appeared in October 1933, during the middle of the Depression. Developed as a men's fashion and literary quarterly dedicated to "The Art of Living and The New Leisure," the magazine was an immediate commercial success, thanks in large part to contributions by Ernest Hemingway, Dashiell Hammett, John Dos Passos, and Ring Lardner, among others. Now a monthly,* Esquire *has a circulation of 750,000 and continues to publish talented contemporary writers.*

"This would be excellent, to go in the ocean with this thing," says Dave Gembutis, fifteen.

He is looking at a $170 Sea Cruiser raft.

"Great," says his companion, Dan Holmes, also fifteen.

This is at Herman's World of Sporting Goods, in the middle of the Woodfield Mall in Schaumburg, Illinois.

The two of them keep staring at the raft. It is unlikely that they will purchase it. For one thing, Dan has only twenty dollars in his pocket, Dave five dollars. For another thing—ocean voyages aside—neither of them is even old enough to drive. Dave's older sister, Kim, has dropped them off at the mall. They will be taking the bus home.

Fifteen. What a weird age to be male. Most of us have forgotten about it, or have idealized it. But when you are fifteen . . . well, things tend to be less than perfect.

You can't drive. You are only a freshman in high school. The girls your age look older than you and go out with upperclassmen who have cars. You probably don't shave. You have nothing to do on the weekends.

So how do you spend your time? In 1982, most likely at a mall. Woodfield is an enclosed shopping center sprawling over 2.25 million square feet in northern Illinois. There are 230 stores at Woodfield, and on a given Saturday those stores are cruised in and out of by thousands of teenagers killing time. Today two of those teenagers are Dave Gembutis and Dan Holmes.

Dave is wearing a purple Rolling Meadows High School Mustangs Windbreaker over a gray M*A*S*H T-shirt, jeans, and Nike running shoes. He has a red plastic spoon in his mouth, and will keep it there for most of the afternoon. Dan is wearing a white Ohio State Buckeyes T-shirt, jeans, and Nike running shoes.

We are in the Video Forum store. Paul Simon and Art Garfunkel are singing "Wake Up Little Susie" from their Central Park concert on four television screens. Dave and Dan have already been wandering around Woodfield for an hour.

"There's not too much to do at my house," Dan says to me.

"Here we can at least look around," Dave says. "At home I don't know what we'd do."

"Play catch or something," Dan says. "Here there's lots of things to see."

"See some girls or something, start talking," Dave says.

I ask them how they would start a conversation with girls they had never met.

"Ask them what school they're from," Dan says. "Then if they say Arlington Heights High School or something, you can say, 'Oh, I know somebody from there.'"

I ask them how important meeting girls is to their lives.

"About forty-five percent," Dan says.

"About half your life," Dave says.

"Half is girls," Dan says. "Half is going out for sports."

An hour later, Dave and Dan have yet to meet any girls. They have seen a girl from their own class at Rolling Meadows High, but she is walking with an older boy, holding his hand. Now we are in the Woodfield McDonald's. Dave is eating a McRib sandwich, a small fries, and a small Coke. Dan is eating a cheeseburger, a small fries, and a medium root beer.

In here, the dilemma is obvious. The McDonald's is filled with girls who are precisely as old as Dave and Dan. The girls are wearing eye shadow, are fully developed, and generally look as if they could be dating the Green Bay Packers. Dave and Dan, on the other hand . . . well, when you're a fifteen-year-old boy, you look like a fifteen-year-old boy.

"They go with the older guys who have the cars," Dan says.

"It makes them more popular," Dave says.

"My ex-girlfriend is seeing a junior," Dan says.

I ask him what happened.

"Well, I was in Florida over spring vacation," he says. "And when I got back I heard that she was at Cinderella Rockefella one night, and she was dancing with this guy, and she liked him, and he drove her home and stuff."

"She two-timed him," Dave says.

"The guy's on the basketball team," Dan says.

I ask Dan what he did about it.

"I broke up with her," he says, as if I had asked the stupidest question in the world.

I ask him how he did it.

"Well, she was at her locker," he says. "She was working the combination. And I said, 'Hey, Linda, I want to break up.' And she was opening her locker door and she just nodded her head yes. And I said, 'I hear you had a good time while I was gone, but I had a better time in Florida.' "

I ask him if he feels bad about it.

"Well, I feel bad," he says. "But a lot of guys told me, 'I heard you broke up with her. Way to be.' "

"It's too bad the Puppy Palace isn't open," Dan says.

"They're remodeling," Dave says.

We are walking around the upper level of Woodfield. I ask them why they would want to go to the Puppy Palace.

"The dogs are real cute and you feel sorry for them," Dan says.

We are in a fast-food restaurant called the Orange Bowl. Dave is eating a frozen concoction called an O-Joy. They still have not met any girls.

"I feel like I'd be wasting my time if I sat at home," Dan says. "If it's Friday or Saturday and you sit home, it's considered . . . low."

"Coming to the mall is about all there is," Dave says. "Until we can drive."

"Then I'll cruise," Dan says. "Look for action a little farther away from my house, instead of just riding my bike around."

"When you're sixteen, you can do anything," Dave says. "You can go all the way across town."

"When you have to ride your bike . . ." Dan says. "When it rains, it ruins everything."

In the J.C. Penney store, the Penney Fashion Carnival is under way. Wally the Clown is handing out favors to children, but Dave and Dan are watching the young female models parade onto a stage in bathing suits.

"Just looking is enough for me," Dan says.

Dave suggests that they head out back into the mall and pick out some girls to wave to. I ask why.

"Well, see, even if they don't wave back, you might see them later in the day," Dan says. "And then they might remember that you waved at them, and you can meet them."

We are at the Cookie Factory. These guys eat approximately every twenty minutes.

It is clear that Dan is attracted to the girl behind the counter. He walks up, and his voice is slower and about half an octave lower than before.

The tone of voice is going to have to carry the day, because the words are not all that romantic:

"Can I have a chocolate-chip cookie?"

The girl does not even look up as she wraps the cookie in tissue paper.

Dan persists. The voice might be Clark Gable's:

"What do they cost?"

The girl is still looking down.

"Forty-seven," she says and takes his money, still looking away, and we move on.

Dave and Dan tell me that there are lots of girls at Woodfield's indoor ice-skating rink. It costs money to get inside, but they lead me to an exit door, and when a woman walks out we slip into the rink. It is chilly in here, but only three people are on the ice.

"It's not time for open skating yet," Dan says. "This is all private lessons."

"Not much in here," Dave says.

We sit on benches. I ask them if they wish they were older.

"Well," Dan says, "when you get there, you look back and you remember. Like I'm glad that I'm not in the fourth or fifth grade now. But I'm glad I'm not twenty-five, either."

"Once in a while I'm sorry I'm not twenty-one," Dave says. "There's not much you can do when you're fifteen. This summer I'm going to caddy and try to save some money."

"Yeah," Dan says. "I want to save up for a dirt bike."

"Right now, being fifteen is starting to bother me a little bit," Dave says. "Like when you have to get your parents to drive you to Homecoming with a girl."

I ask him how that works.

"Well, your mom is in the front seat driving," he says. "And you're in the back seat with your date."

I ask him how he feels about that.

"It's embarrassing," he says. "Your date understands that there's nothing you can do about it, but it's still embarrassing."

Dave says he wants to go to Pet World.

"I think they closed it down," Dan says, but we head in that direction anyway.

I ask them what the difference is between Pet World and the Puppy Palace.

"They've got snakes and fish and another assortment of dogs," Dan says. "But not as much as the Puppy Palace."

When we arrive, Pet World is, indeed, boarded up.

We are on the upper level of the mall. Dave and Dan have spotted two girls sitting on a bench directly below them, on the mall's main level.

"Whistle," Dan says. Dave whistles, but the girls keep talking.

"Dave, wave to them and see if they look," Dan says.

"They aren't looking," Dave says.

"There's another one over there," Dan says.

"Where?" Dave says.

"Oh, that's a mother," Dan says. "She's got her kid with her."

They return their attention to the two downstairs.

Dan calls to them: "Would you girls get the dollar I just dropped?"

The girls look up.

"Just kidding," Dan says.

The girls resume their conversation.

"I think they're laughing." Dan says.

"What are you going to do when the dumb girls won't respond," Dave says.

"At least we tried," Dan says.

I ask him what response would have satisfied him.

"The way we would have known that we succeeded," he says, "they'd have looked up here and started laughing."

The boys keep staring at the two girls.

"Ask her to look up," Dan says. "Ask her what school they go to."

"I did," Dave says. "I did."

The two boys lean over the railing.

"Bye, girls," Dave yells.

"See you later," Dan yells.

The girls do not look up.

"Too hard," Dan says. "Some girls are stuck on themselves, if you know what I mean by that."

We go to a store called the Foot Locker, where all the salespeople are dressed in striped referee's shirts.

"Dave!" Dan says. "Look at this! Seventy bucks!" He holds up a pair of New Balance running shoes. Both boys shake their heads.

We move on to a store called Passage to China. A huge stuffed tiger is placed by the doorway. There is a PLEASE DO NOT TOUCH sign attached to it. Dan rubs his hand over the tiger's back. "This would look so great in my room," he says.

We head over to Alan's TV and Stereo. Two salesmen ask the boys if they are interested in buying anything, so they go back outside and look at the store's window. A color television set is tuned to a baseball game between the Chicago Cubs and the Pittsburgh Pirates.

They watch for five minutes. The sound is muted, so they cannot hear the announcers.

"I wish they'd show the score," Dave says.

They watch for five minutes more.

"Hey, Dave," Dan says. "You want to go home?"

"I guess so," Dave says.

They do. We wave goodbye. I watch them walk out of the mall toward the bus stop. I wish them girls, dirt bikes, puppies, and happiness.

Darryl Pinckney / Step and Fetch It: The Darker Side of the Sitcoms
Vanity Fair, March 1983

One of the most elegant magazines of the 1920s and 1930s, Vanity Fair *specialized in articles about the world of fashion, art, music, theater, literature, and the high life of international celebrities. Perhaps more than any other periodical, it brought the European avant-garde to the attention of the American public—even the magazine's advertising reflected the influence of cubism and surrealism. Though suited to the flamboyant mood of the 1920s,* Vanity Fair *struck the wrong chord during the Depression, and it was merged with* Vogue *in 1936.*

In 1983, Vanity Fair *was revived. Its unabashed blend of serious art and literature with high-fashion celebrity spreads made it seem as though* The New Yorker *had joined forces with* People *magazine. The new* Vanity Fair *has struggled through several editorial changes, and though it has published many excellent writers it has still not discovered the most agreeable balance of the talented with the trendy.*

The following essay on the role of blacks in television comedy appeared in Vanity Fair's *first issue (March 1983). Darryl Pinckney contributes criticism to the* New York Review of Books *and is the author of a novel,* High Cotton.

I remember Rochester. Not quite valet, not quite butler, not really factotum—it is hard to say what he was. Rochester performed his vague duties faithfully, through years of radio, film, and then 343 television episodes of *The Jack Benny Show.* Perhaps he was a kind of chorus, commenting on developments and sometimes fanning the flickering plot himself; or maybe he was confidant and straight man, rushing to Mr. Benny's side to catch another quip, lunging toward the door, elbows tucked close to rib cage, eyes bright as headlights, to intercept some wacky news. He was a thoughtless, soothing caricature of "the Negro"—benign, in his place. He kept his place from 1937 to 1965.

The "real" Rochester, Eddie Anderson, died in 1977, having outlived the show and the boss if not the cultural mood in which the name Rochester became synonymous with shameless, unsavory Uncle Tom antics. Television producers are very careful now about domestic employees—not to mention blacks—and progress is measured by the distance from the old, offensive images. When Robert Guillaume played the part of the butler, Benson, on the comedy series *Soap*, he demonstrated that the stereotype was not so much in the role as in the style brought to the job. He was sardonic, sane, well dressed, and he talked back. Guillaume went on to star in his own show, *Benson*. Eventually Benson was promoted from governor's housekeeper to state budget director. Not bad—and not as funny either.

Why not? Isn't his upward course retribution for all those years of Rochester? Affirmative action has infiltrated the prime-time hours, and though I busily note the number of blacks in each frame, their importance and the jobs they're given, I can't quite give up my sympathy for the underdog, for the underside of life.

Who remembers Ethel Waters in *Beulah*—and who dares? The show first aired in 1950. Miss Waters played the title role for two years, and the part of her crazy, luckless friend was played by none other than the great Butterfly McQueen. Together they turned a New York attorney's home into a tidewater plantation. *Beulah* surfaced one last time in 1952, with another veteran of the kitchen range as the star, Louise Beavers. The show has since been withdrawn from syndication—to spare our feelings, one assumes.

These actresses, the old guard, played similar roles in films. They lived out the professional lives then permitted black actresses, but often they infused their portrayals of maids with a weird subversiveness. In *She Done Him Wrong*, Louise Beavers's hands are so well manicured as she toils over Mae West's cast-off blouses that they signal to the audience that she's not really busting anybody's suds. And what about the repertoire of facial expressions Hattie McDaniel used on that sad girl in *Alice Adams?* It's indecent, even dangerous, to admit a certain late-night nostalgia for those grainy black-and-white masochistic moments of cinema from the 1930s and '40s, but—as a wise woman once told me—don't forget that masochists are the proudest people on earth. Only the brave risk asking Beulah for the peeled grape. Equality as irony is hip, complicated, and far beyond the range of television, with its smug, scaled-down narratives.

Situation comedies bring us a self-congratulatory view of the American home, a place confident and leisured enough to permit humor and mild skepticism about prevailing ideas. (More recently, this definition has been expanded to include the workplace, which is another version of home and family.) As our need for reassurance and escapism increases, so does the number of sitcoms on the air—and these days part of the American myth is that blacks too have a fair share of the harmony and prosperity.

"Serious" television is another matter, reserved for pious resolutions of troublesome themes. Remember Barney, the electronics wizard of the Impossible Missions Force; Mannix's "girl Friday," Peggy; the sandwich-chomping captain so tolerant of Starsky, of Hutch; Lieutenant Uhura of the starship *Enterprise*—they were so skilled and presentable. Remember all those black cops, square or cool, upholding law, sticking by order, in wide-angle action shots, always rigidly self-conscious, everyone on his best behavior.

Headline entertainers, with their variety series, are also on their best behavior, being stars. There have been so many because black entertainers at this level are, oddly enough, seen as neutral. *The Leslie Uggams Show, The Barbara McNair Show, The Melba Moore-Clifton Davis Show, Ben Vereen—Comin' at Ya, The Gladys Knight & the Pips Show, The Jacksons*, to mention only a few, suggest a quest for the proper vehicle and leave memories of tires sputtering in the mud. (Richard Pryor, whose weekly show ran only from September to October of 1977, could not conform to this requirement of neutrality, and was canned.) Blacks were looking out from the tube into the dens of America as early as 1949—all singing and dancing. Blacks had no public or private concerns suitable for dramatization.

Not until recently did the images of the new day—sitcoms featuring "ordinary" black people—begin to appear on the screen. Television was rather sluggish to reflect the change in society. Seasons of *Leave It to Beaver, F Troop,* and *Mr. Ed* hardly jibed with the unsettling realization that there were a lot of black people who lived in this country, at least according to the evening news.

The thaw began in 1965 with *I Spy.* Bill Cosby portrayed a trainer-masseur opposite Robert Culp's tennis pro, but—not to worry—they were both really undercover agents. The show seldom touched on the issue of race. It ended in 1968, and the next year Cosby was back, in, yes, *The Bill Cosby Show.* He played the part of a coach, Chet Kincaid, whose business was to be helpful to everyone—students, parents, brother. Cosby is seen as something of a trailblazer as a black in television. His first series brought him three Emmys, and though later shows were not as memorable, it scarcely mattered to someone who could project his own personality through whatever role he assumed. Cosby is trusted when he feeds a multiracial group of kids pudding, and he is applauded when he is in a foul mood while hosting *The Tonight Show.*

Trustworthy characters were all the rage in the late '60s. The aim was to reassure everyone, black and white, that blacks were good Americans. The most upright citizen of them all was created in *Julia,* starring Diahann Carroll, whose performance was remarkable for excluding even the slightest nuance. That was 1968, post-Moynihan Report days, and if Julia Baker was a single parent, she was so by the grace of God. Her husband, an air force captain, had been killed in Vietnam. She, a registered nurse employed at Astro Space Industries (a vague but equal-opportunity-sounding place), was left to bring up a docile young son, Corey, who, the TV mags said, got chubby from rehearsing so many after-school-snack scenes. Julia, the attentive mother, sat on a kitchen stool and explained life while Corey munched away in a daze. At such times, with his high whine echoing her polite colorless hum, they seemed like robots off duty.

Julia's boss, Dr. Chegley, was warmhearted and wise, in the Marcus Welby manner. He and Julia decorously stared down department store clerks who got the wrong idea about their relationship. But the viewing audience learned that the clerks were shocked not because they were an interracial couple but because they were a May–December one. Oh, how we misjudge our enemies. *Julia* was put to sleep in 1971.

If black women on television are not stunning, they are cast as oracular, Bible-backed mamas. In 1974 *That's My Mama* had Clifton Davis unraveling the messes stirred up by Theresa Merritt. *What's Happening!!'s* goofy teenagers were rewarded or punished by large-girthed Mabel King. These mothers are essential—black family life is a touchy point. One situation comedy that never caught on, *Baby, I'm Back,* involved a father who returns after an absence of seven years and sets out to prove that he has matured enough to take on the anxieties of a happy home life. The nuclear family surrounds a black leading character on television these days like a steel casing.

Television's hymn to the nuclear family was *Good Times,* featuring the Evanses, slapping five and playing the dozens in the Chicago projects. One of those Norman Lear spin-offs, the series starred John Amos and Esther Rolle. As the strong, loving father with a terrible temper who threw things and slammed the refrigerator door in frustration with the job market and his lack of education, Amos stormed and bellowed his way through episode after episode like an inner-city Kunta Kinte.

Esther Rolle was the pious mama, consulting the serene face of a blond Jesus in times of trouble, lifting her eyes in an attitude of thanksgiving, stretching dollars, wielding the spatula over a frying pan, trying to reason with her hotheaded (and hot-blooded: he says ''Have mercy'' when things get cozy) husband, and keeping the children on the right path. The children (portrayed by woefully bad actors) were made to stand for rather sentimental notions of the rising tide, their hearts set on growing up to be doctors, artists, and Supreme Court justices.

The teleplays never failed to include some moral tag about the ceaseless struggle to make it. Authenticity was also important to *Good Times:* a parade of types were assembled from the popular picture of the American ghetto—corrupt aldermen, outrageously dressed loan sharks, prissy social workers, harmless winos, long-lost fathers, child-abusing young mothers, teens hooked on smack, and a slightly fast divorced neighbor with a heart of gold, Willona, played by Ja'net DuBois. The totemic accessories of popular black culture were trotted out and explained on cue: the dancing, the pork chops, the wakes, the preaching style, the welfare bureaucracy, the guns.

Think of the early comedies, programs such as *The Honeymooners* or *The Life of Riley.* The husbands were bus drivers or plant workers. Since then, life has been upgraded, everyone on television has a better job, and blacks have shared in the boom. We even have a remake of *The Odd Couple* with black actors playing the successful; urban characters. On *Barney Miller* Ron Glass played a dapper detective first class; *WKRP in Cincinnati* had a black deejay; the high-society boarding school of *Facts of Life* boasts among its student body one sweet-looking black girl.

Ron Glass was too chilled out to do more than raise an eyebrow when some visitor to the precinct would blurt out an ill-advised remark. WKRP was a liberal, flaky station. Even so, the with-it young manager worried in one episode that his sister was seeing too much of the black deejay, Venus Flytrap—and at the wrong hours. Of course, Venus and the sister were *just friends,* but if they had been more than that, they boldly proclaimed, well, tain't nobody's bizness. The safety exit.

The girl who integrates the school on *Facts of Life,* Tootie; restless and agreeable, seems born to the Andover life. In one segment she was visiting her young aunt, a gorgeous newscaster, as black women newscasters tend to be. Much to the surprise of a classmate who came along for the weekend, Tootie's aunt was married to a white, hunky coach. (Coaches seem the preferred type for interracial plots. Everyone knows that sports breed mutual respect. Check out *The White Shadow.*) Television seldom presents a black man with a white woman unless Desdemona is a fallen woman and the Moor a pimp. No ''Perdition catch my soul but I do love thee''—but then *Othello* is not a comedy. Nowhere is this taboo more strictly heeded than on that fatuous program *The Love Boat.* The black bartender, Ted Lange, has to wait for someone foxy like Debbie Allen to save enough money to take the tedious cruise before he can lose his heart. He never, never ogles a white woman.

The family show that hit big was *The Jeffersons,* a spin-off from *All in the Family.* It began its ascent into the hearts of America in 1975. George Jefferson, played by Sherman Hemsley, and Louise, his wife, played by gravel-voiced Isabel Sanford, had been neighbors of the Bunkers in Queens. ''We're movin' on up,'' the theme song goes, ''to the East Side, to a deluxe apartment in the sky.'' There's something off about this move: George's chain of dry-cleaning stores has made him more money than Ford has earned building sedans. He prospers, never lays off anyone; this is a miracle suitable to the fantasies of Ronald Reagan. ''We finally got a piece of the pie!''

George is short, blustering, and opinionated, and is offset (naturally) by his patient, honest, and devoted wife. The doorman wheedles George for tips. One neighbor, Mr. Bentley, a dotty Englishman with the U.N., is no longer with the show. Perhaps he moved on down to a refurbished brownstone. The Jeffersons have friends upstairs: Tom and Helen Willis. He is a plump senior vice-president in publishing, and white. She is a thin fancy dresser with a degree in journalism, and black. George makes wisecracks about their marriage every week. The Will-ises have two children. One is white-looking, a son, who was accused at one point of trying to pass. He hasn't been seen since. Perhaps he is in Paris, snorting and whooping it up nightly in one of the Bains Douches. The other child, Jenny, is the black-looking one, though George refers to her as "the zebra."

In the beginning, the story lines of *The Jeffersons* revolved around what all that money was doing to them. Louise often warned George not to forget where he came from. George argued that there was no point in being rich if he had to act poor. Of course, George in the end saw the light—as if remembering humble origins were a brake on greedy impulses. That plot couldn't last: through the seasons they had to get used to the money. Louise has a new hairdo; the practical bun is out, bring on the curls. They have a lot of glad rags—unfortunate pantsuits and garish three-piece suits—and this one realistic detail is perhaps inadvertent.

Marla Gibbs plays the Jeffersons' black maid, Florence. Her snide comments are exquisitely timed. "I might as well be working for white folks," she said when too much was demanded of her. Florence is diffident about her duties. "Doorbell, Florence!" "Well, answer it!" In one show, Florence appeared in a costume straight out of *Gone with the Wind* and so overwhelmed "Massa Jefferson" with her let-me-shine-yo-shoes-and-sew-dat-dere-button-O-Lawd-I-done-made-you-mad act that George had to apologize.

The character of Florence raises an odd question: Why is "the help" so funny? For one thing, comedy is more plausible at the bottom. Blacks on television must work and have a family, like all good Americans. and yet there remains the con-tradiction that the lingering stereotypes seem less foolish than the new stereotype of success and satisfaction. Shirley Hemphill was wonderful when she played the waitress on *What's Happening!!* and disappointing when she starred in her own show as the philanthropic owner of a multimillion-dollar conglomerate. Esther Rolle held her own as Florida, maid to the suburban feminist Maude. The gifted Nell Carter, who stars in the series *Gimme a Break,* has combined perfectly the images of the family retainer and the new professional. The ambiguity of her status is her freedom. Not only does she cook and mend for a widowed police chief and his adolescent daughters, she gives her advice and her consent in all their affairs.

Redd Foxx was the last nigger on television. In *Sanford and Son,* Fred Sanford was crafty, lazy, nasty-looking, and nasty-sounding. He steadfastly resisted self-improvement, and his attitude toward the larger world recalled the tradition of hu-mor in which the lowly outwitted the masters. There is more satiric potential in such parts, more opportunity for putdowns and unexpected reversals. And black actors in these comic roles live through their subversion of Mammy and Rochester and even Buckwheat.

Ishmael Reed has a phrase—"crazy dada nigger"—and that is what Buckwheat was, in school, at the birthday party, in the clubhouse with the gang of *The Little Rascals.* He has been reborn, in homogenized form, in the precocious Gary Cole-man of *Diff'rent Strokes.* He is a complete anachronism. He pouts ("Whatchu talkin' 'bout, Willis"), his eyes bug out of his fuzzy round head, he mugs it up. Where did he learn that? Coleman plays one of two brothers taken from Harlem and adopted by a Park Avenue executive. He is a domesticated black child, suit-able for import from the black side of town to the land of opportunity, and he has dragged with him the baggage of the minstrel style. (And Amos and Andy are back on the air—in the form of Laverne and Shirley, who are missing only the blackface.)

It is not only in the subversion of the old sterotypes that black television man-ages to be funny. Great comic moments on the tube have not always been part of the regular programming. I once passed a bar in Boston and saw economist Thomas

Sowell on the screen. The clientele roared as Sowell applied the principles of Milton Friedman to people who didn't have two quarters to rub together. Who can forget Sammy Davis, Jr., Mr. Goodvibes, scurrying across the stage to hug Richard Nixon? This incident was so bizarre that black tourists in Las Vegas snubbed Sammy in the elevators. Black Republicans haven't been cool since Reconstruction. Did Pearl Bailey's ratings suffer when she chatted away on her show about the chair Nixon gave her from the White House and her designation as "ambassador of love"? The lesson of fame is that the famous can get away with everything. Miss Bailey appeared at the opening of the World Series a few years back in a slick wig and a stunning fur, moaning "The Star-Spangled Banner." Which is funnier, Eldridge Cleaver then or now? Scare me, black man—and then be my pal (this is the secret of *Rocky*'s success). No matter—even Eartha Kitt is a patriot these days. "How I Got Over" can be heard on your way to the bank as well as in Baptist churches. But that is the message of blacks on television: all will be well, forgiven, forgotten.

That demand for positive images, for relevance—was it a just but doomed cause, given the medium? Think of the graceful, poised Princess Elizabeth of Toro on *To Tell the Truth* a few years ago, or Harry Belafonte's daughter floating through a recent episode of *Trapper John, M.D.*, more chic than Italian *Vogue*. Is that what we mean by "positive" in a culture that communicates in images? The riveting questions about blacks in American society are addressed in film, not TV, in the leagues of footage from *The Birth of a Nation* to *Superfly* to *48 HRS*. Trying to decode television takes one to the Formica counters of the banal, where megabucks act as a sponge. Everything can be turned into a commodity, and in this way social issues are reduced. The status quo, or what is ambiguously called traditional values, is easily digestible, suitable to the demands of glut, or rapid programming. Have some *Soul Train* and shut up. The profusion of nice, clean-cut professionals represents a cultural payoff. Is the soggy narcissism of *Fame* really the future? There were no blacks in Mayberry, there were none in Fernwood, and that was as true to life as anything.

DISCUSSION QUESTIONS

1. Read the episode of "The Jeffersons" in "Scripts." How is Pinckney's general analysis of the show supported by "The Black Out"? Do you think the characters on "The Jeffersons" reflect a "positive" image of black people, or do you think Pinckney's objections to the show are basically correct? Explain.

2. What precisely does Pinckney mean by "positive images" of blacks? Does his approval of Redd Foxx's role in "Sanford and Son" endorse or reject the "demand for positive images"? Explain.

Anne Hollander / Dressed to Thrill

New Republic, January 28, 1985

Fashion styles have always been closely linked to sexual identity. In the following essay, art historian Anne Hollander examines the connections between contemporary styles of dress and our society's redefinition of sexual roles. Hol-

*lander, who was born in Cleveland, Ohio, in 1930, is an independent scholar
and writer living in New York City. She is the author of* Seeing Through
Clothes, *a study of the representation of clothing in art. Her essays and reviews
on art, culture, and film have appeared in a wide variety of magazines.*

Founded in 1914, New Republic *can be said to retain its original editorial
purpose as a magazine that exists "less to inform or entertain its readers than
to start little insurrections in the realm of their convictions."*

When Quentin Bell applied Veblen's principles of Conspicuous Consumption and
Conspicuous Waste to fashion, he added another—Conspicuous Outrage. This one
now clearly leads the other two. In this decade we want the latest trends in appearance to strain our sense of the suitable and give us a real jolt. The old social
systems that generated a need for conspicuous display have modified enough to
dull the chic of straight extravagance: the chic of shock has continuous vitality.
Dramatically perverse sexual signals are always powerful elements in the modern
fashionable vocabulary; and the most sensational component among present trends
is something referred to as androgyny. Many modish women's clothes imitate
what Robert Taylor wore in 1940 publicity stills, and Michael Jackson's startling
feminine beauty challenges public responses from every store window, as well as
in many living replicas.

The mode in appearance mirrors collective fantasy, not fundamental aims and
beliefs. We are not all really longing for two sexes in a single body, and the true
hermaphrodite still counts as a monster. We are seeing a complete and free inter-
change of physical characteristics across the sexual divide. There are no silky false
moustaches or dashing fake goatees finely crafted of imported sable for the discriminating woman, or luxuriant jaw-length sideburns of the softest bristle sold
with moisturizing glue and a designer applicator. Although the new ideal feminine
torso has strong square shoulders, flat hips, and no belly at all, the corresponding
ideal male body is certainly not displaying the beauties of a soft round stomach,
flaring hips, full thighs, and delicately sloping shoulders. On the new woman's
ideally athletic shape, breasts may be large or not—a flat chest is not required;
and below the belt in back, the buttocks may sharply protrude. But no space
remains in front to house a safely cushioned uterus and ovaries, or even well-
upholstered labia: under the lower half of the new, high-cut minimal swimsuits,
there is room only for a clitoris. Meanwhile the thrilling style of male beauty
embodied by Michael Jackson runs chiefly to unprecedented surface adornment—
cosmetics and sequins, jewels and elaborate hair, all the old privileges once granted
to women, to give them every erotic advantage in the sex wars of the past.

The point about all this is clearly not androgyny at all, but the idea of detachable pleasure. Each sex is not trying to take up the fundamental qualities of the
other sex, but rather of the other sexuality—the erotic dimension, which can transcend biology and its attendant social assumptions and institutions. Eroticism is
being shown to float free of sexual function. Virility is displayed as a capacity for
feeling and generating excitement, not for felling trees or enemies and generating
children. Femininity has abandoned the old gestures of passivity to take on main
force: ravishing female models now stare purposefully into the viewer's eyes instead of flashing provocative glances or gazing remotely away. Erotic attractiveness appears ready to exert its strength in unforeseeable and formerly forbidden
ways and places. Recognition is now being given to sexual desire for objects of
all kinds once considered unsuitable—some of them inanimate, judging from the
seductiveness of most advertising photography.

Homosexual desire is now an acknowledged aspect of common life, deserving
of truthful representation in popular culture, not just in coterie vehicles of expres-

sion. The aging parents of youthful characters in movie and television dramas are no longer rendered as mentally stuffy and physically withered, but as stunningly attractive sexual things—legitimate and nonridiculous rivals for the lustful attentions of the young. The curved flanks of travel irons and food processors in Bloomingdale's catalogue make as strong an appeal to erotic desire as the satiny behinds and moist lips of the makeup and underwear models. So do the unfolding petals of lettuces and the rosy flesh of cut tomatoes on TV food commercials. In this general eroticization of the material world, visual culture is openly acknowledging that lust is by nature wayward.

To register as attractive under current assumptions, a female body may now show its affinities not only with delicious objects but with attractive male bodies, without having to relinquish any feminine erotic resources. Male beauty may be enhanced by feminine usages that increase rather than diminish it masculine effect. Men and women may both wear clothes loosely fashioned by designers like Gianni Versace or Issey Miyake to render all bodies attractive whatever their structure, like the drapery of antiquity. In such clothes, sexuality is expressed obliquely in a fluid fabric envelope that follows bodily movement and also forms a graceful counterpoint to the nonchalant postures of modern repose. The aim of such dress is to emphasize the sexiness of a rather generalized sensuality, not of male or female characteristics; and our present sense of personal appearance, like our sense of all material display, shows that we are more interested in generalized sensuality than in anything else. In our multiform culture, it seems to serve as an equalizer.

In fashion, however, pervasive eroticism is still frequently being represented as the perpetual overthrow of all the restrictive categories left over from the last century, a sort of ongoing revolution. We are still pretending to congratulate ourselves on what a long way we have come. The lush men and strong girls now on view in the media may be continuing a long-range trend that began between the World Wars; but there have been significant interruptions and an important shift of tone. Then, too, men had smooth faces, thick, wavy hair and full, pouting lips, and women often wore pants, had shingled hair, and athletic torsos. But the important point in those days was to be as anti-Victorian as possible. The rigid and bearded Victorian male was being eased out of his tight carapace and distancing whiskers; the whole ladylike panoply was being simplified so that the actual woman became apparent to the eye and touch. Much of our present female mannishness and feminized manhood is a nostalgic reference to the effects fashionable for men and women in those pioneering days, rather than a new revolutionary expression of the same authentic kind.

There is obviously more to it all now than there was between the wars. We have already gone through some fake Victorian revivals, both unself-conscious in the 1950s and self-conscious in the sixties and seventies, and lately our sense of all style has become slightly corrupt. Apart from the sexiness of sex, we have discovered the stylishness of style and the fashionableness of fashion. Evolving conventions of dress and sudden revolts from them have both become stylistically forced; there have been heavy quotation marks around almost all conspicuous modes of clothing in the last fifteen or twenty years, as there were not in more hopeful days. Life is now recognized to have a grotesque and inflated media dimension by which ordinary experience is measured, and all fashion has taken to looking over its own shoulder. Our contemporary revolutionary modes are mostly theatrical costumes, since we have now learned to assume that appearances are detachable and interchangeable and only have provisional meanings.

Many of the more extreme new sartorial phenomena display such uncooked incoherence that they fail to represent any main trend in twentieth-century taste except a certain perverse taste for garbage—which is similarly fragmented and inexpressive, even though it can always be sifted and categorized. We have become obsessed with picking over the past instead of plowing it under, where it can do some good. Perversity has moreover been fostered in fashion by its relentless presentation as a form of ongoing public entertainment. The need for constant impact naturally causes originality to get confused with the capacity to cause a sensation; and sensations can always be created, just as in all show business, by the crudest of allusions.

In the twenties, the revolutionary new fashions were much more important but much less brutally intrusive. Photos from the twenties, thirties, and even the very early forties, show the young Tyrone Power and Robert Taylor smiling with scintillating confidence, caressed by soft focus and glittering highlights, and wearing the full-cut, casual topcoats with the collar up that we see in today's ads for women, then as now opened to show the fully-draped trousers, loose sweaters, and long, broad jackets of that time. Then it was an alluringly modern and feminized version of male beauty, freshly suggesting pleasure without violence or loss of decorum, a high level of civilization without any forbidding and tyrannical stiffness or antiquated formality. At the same time, women's fashions were stressing an articulated female shape that sought to be perceived as clearly as the male. Both were the first modern styles to take up the flavor of general physical ease, in timely and pertinent defiance of the social restrictions and symbolic sexual distinctions made by dress in the preceding time. Now, however, those same easy men's clothes are being worn by women; and the honest old figure of freedom seems to be dressed up in the spirit of pastiche. We did come a long way for a while, but then we stopped and went on the stage.

Strong and separate sexual definition in the old Victorian manner tried to forbid the generally erotic and foster the romantic. Against such a background even slightly blurring the definition automatically did the opposite; and so when Victorian women dared adopt any partial assortment of male dress they were always extremely disturbing. They called attention to those aspects of female sexuality that develop in sharp contrast to both female biology and romantic rhetoric. Consequently, when female fashion underwent its great changes early in this century, such aspects were deliberately and vehemently emphasized by a new mobility and quasi-masculine leanness. Women with no plump extensions at all but with obvious and movable legs suddenly made their appearance, occasionally even in trousers. They indicated a mettlesome eagerness for action, even unencumbered amorous action, and great lack of interest in sitting still receiving homage or rocking the cradle. Meanwhile when men adopted the casual suits of modern leisure, they began to suggest a certain new readiness to sit and talk, to listen and laugh at themselves, to dally and tarry rather than couple briskly and straightway depart for work or battle. Men and women visibly desired to rewrite the rules about how the two sexes should express their interest in sex; and the liberated modern ideal was crystallized.

But a sexual ideal of maturity and enlightened savoir faire also informed that period of our imaginative history. In the fantasy of the thirties, manifested in the films of Claudette Colbert, for example, or Gable and Lombard, adult men and women ideally pursued pleasure without sacrificing reason, humor, or courtesy— even in those dramas devoted to the ridiculous. The sexes were still regarded as fundamentally different kinds of being, although the style of their sexuality was reconceived. The aim of amorous life was still to take on the challenging dialectic of the sexes, which alone could yield the fullest kind of sexual pleasure. Erotic feeling was inseparable from dramatic situation.

By those same thirties, modern adult clothing was also a fully developed stylistic achievement. It duly continued to refine, until it finally became unbearably mannered in the first half of the sixties. The famous ensuing sartorial revolution, though perfectly authentic, was also the first to occur in front of the camera—always in the mirror, as it were. And somehow the subsequent two decades have seen a great fragmentation both of fashion and of sexuality.

Extreme imagery, much of it androgynous like Boy George's looks, or the many punk styles and all the raunchier fashion photos, has become quite commonplace; but it has also become progressively remote from most common practice. It offers appearances that we may label "fashion," but that we really know to be media inventions created especially to stun, provoke, and dismay us. At the same time, some very conventional outrageous effects have been revived in the realm of accessible fashion, where there is always room for them. Ordinary outrageousness and perverse daring in dress are the signs of licensed play, never the signal of serious action. They are licitly engaged in by the basically powerless, including clowns and children and other innocuous performers, who are always allowed to make extreme emotional claims that may stir up strong personal responses but have no serious public importance. Women's fashion constantly made use of outrage in this way during the centuries of female powerlessness, and selective borrowing from men was one of its most effective motifs.

After the sixties and before the present menswear mode, the masculine components in women's fashions still made girls look either excitingly shocking or touchingly pathetic. The various neat tuxedos made famous by Yves St. Laurent, for example, were intended to give a woman the look of a depraved youth, a sort of tempting Dorian Gray. The *Annie Hall* clothes swamped the woman in oversized male garments, so that she looked at first like a small child being funny in adult gear, and then like a fragile girl wrapped in a strong man's coat, a combined emblem of bruised innocence and clownishness. These are both familiar "outrageous" devices culled particularly from the theatrical past.

Long before modern fashion took it up, the conventionally outrageous theme of an attractive feminine woman in breeches proved an invariably stimulating refinement in the long history of racy popular art, both for the stage and in print. The most important erotic aim of this theme was never to make a woman actually seem to be a man—looking butch has never been generally attractive—but to make a girl assume the unsettling beauty that dwells in the sexual uncertainty of an adolescent boy. It is an obviously clever move for modern fashionable women to combine the old show-businesslike excitement of the suggestive trousered female with the cultivated self-possession of early twentieth-century menswear—itself already a feminized male style. It suits, especially in the present disintegrated erotic climate that has rendered the purer forms of outrageousness somewhat passé.

Such uses of men's clothes have nothing to do with an impulse toward androgyny. They instead invoke all the old tension between the sexes; and complete drag, whichever sex wears it, also insists on sexual polarity. Most drag for men veers toward the exaggerated accountrements of the standard siren; and on the current screen, *Tootsie* and *Yentl* are both demonstrating how different and how divided the sexes are.

While the extreme phenomena are getting all the attention, however, we are acting out quite another forbidden fantasy in our ordinary lives. The really androgynous realm in personal appearance is that of active sports clothing. The unprecedented appeal of running gear and gym clothes and all the other garb associated with strenuous physical effort seems to be offering an alternative in sexual expression. Beyond the simple pleasures of physical fitness, and the right-minded satisfactions of banishing class difference that were first expressed in the blue-jeans revolution of the sixties, this version of pastoral suggests a new erotic appeal in the perceived androgyny of childhood. The short shorts and other ingenuous bright play clothes in primary colors that now clothe bodies of all sizes and sexes are giving a startling kindergarten cast to everybody's public looks, especially in summer.

The real excitement of androgynous appearance is again revealed as associated only with extreme youth—apparently the more extreme the better. The natural androgyny of old age has acquired no appeal. The tendency of male and female bodies to resemble each other in late maturity is still conventionally ridiculous and deplorable; sportswear on old women looks crisp and convenient, not sexually attractive. But the fresh, unfinished androgyny of the nursery is evidently a newly expanded arena for sexual fantasy.

In the unisex look of the ordinary clothing that has become increasingly common in the past two decades, there has been a submerged but unmistakable element of child-worship. This note has been struck at a great distance from the slick and expensive ambiguities of high fashion that include couture children's clothes aping the vagaries of current adult chic. It resonates instead in the everyday sexual ambiguity of rough duck or corduroy pants, flannel shirts, T-shirts, sweaters, and sneakers. Any subway car or supermarket is full of people dressed this way. The guises for this fantasy have extended past play clothes to children's underwear, the little knitted shirts and briefs that everyone wears at the age of five. One ubiquitous ad for these even showed a shirtee sliding up to expose an adult breast, to emphasize the sexiness of the fashion; but the breast has been prudently canceled in publicly displayed versions.

Our erotic obsession with children has overt and easily deplored expressions in the media, where steamy twelve-year-old fashion models star in ads and twelve-year-old prostitutes figure in dramas and news stories. The high-fashion modes for children also have the flavor of forced eroticism. Child abuse and kiddy porn are now publicly discussed concerns, ventilated in the righteous spirit of reform; and yet unconscious custom reflects the same preoccupation with the sexual condition of childhood. The androgynous sportswear that was formerly the acceptable everyday dress only of children is now everyone's leisure clothing; its new currency must have more than one meaning.

On the surface, of course, it invokes the straight appeal of the physical life, the rural life, and perhaps even especially the taxing life of the dedicated athlete, which used to include sexual abstinence along with the chance of glory. The world may wish to look as if it were constantly in training to win, or equipped to explore; but there is another condition it is also less obviously longing for—freedom from the strain of fully adult sexuality. These styles of clothing signal a retreat into the unfinished, undefined sexuality of childhood that we are now finding so erotic, and that carries no difficult social or personal responsibilities.

From 1925 to 1965, four-year-old girls and boys could tumble in the sandbox in identical cotton overalls or knitted suits, innocently aping the clothes of skiers, railroadmen, or miners, while their mom wore a dress, hat, and stockings, and their dad a suit, hat, and tie—the modern dress of sexual maturity, also worn by Gable, Lombard, and all the young and glittering Hollywood company. Now the whole family wears sweat suits and overalls and goes bareheaded. Such gear is also designed to encourage the game of dressing up like all the non-amorous and ultraphysical heroes of modern folklore—forest rangers and cowboys, spacemen and frogmen, pilots and motorcyclists, migrant workers and terrorists—that is constantly urged on children. The great masquerade party of the late sixties ostensibly came to an end; but it had irreversibly given to ordinary grownups the right to wear fancy costumes for fun that was formerly a child's privilege. The traditional dress of the separate adult sexes is reserved for public appearances, and in general it is now socially correct to express impatience with it. "Informal" is the only proper style in middle-class social life; and for private leisure, when impulse governs choices, kids' clothes are the leading one. Apparently the erotic androgynous child is the new forbidden creature of unconscious fantasy, not only the infantile fashion model or rock star but the ordinary kid, who has exciting sexual potential hidden under its unsexed dress-up play clothes.

Fashions of the remote past dealt straightforwardly with the sexuality of children by dressing them just like ordinary adults, suitably different according to sex. But in Romantic times, children were perceived to exist in a special condition much purer and closer to beneficent nature than their elders, requiring clothes that kept them visibly separate from the complex corruptions of adult society, including full-scale erotic awareness. The habit of putting children in fancy dress began then, too, especially boys. They were dressed as wee, chubby, and harmless soldiers and sailors, or Turks and Romans, to emphasize their innocence by contrast. Children's clothes still differed according to sex—girls had sweet little chemises and sashes instead of fancy costumes—but their overriding common flavor was one of artlessness.

Later on the Victorians overdid it, and loaded their children with clothing, but it was still two-sexed and distinctively designed for them. Finally the enlightened twentieth century invented the use of mock sportswear for the wiggly little bodies of both boys and girls. Nevertheless, the costumes now suitable for children on display still tend toward the Victorian, with a good deal of nostalgic velvet and lace. In line with Romantic views of women, some feminine styles also used to feature infantine suggestions drawn from little girls' costumes: the last was the tiny baby dress worn with big shoes and big hair in the later sixties, just before the eruption of the women's movement. But only since then has a whole generation of adults felt like dressing up in mock rough gear, like androgynous children at play, to form a race of apparently presexual but unmistakably erotic beings.

Once again, very pointedly, the clothes for the role are male. Our modern sense of artlessness seems to prefer the masculine brand; and when we dress our little boys and girls alike to blur their sexuality—or ourselves in imitation of them— that means we dress the girls like the boys, in the manifold costumes celebrating nonsexual physical prowess. At leisure, both men and women prefer to suggest versions of Adam alone in Eden before he knew he had a sex, innocently wearing his primal sweat suit made only of native worth and honor.

The Romantic sense of the child as naturally privileged and instinctively good like Adam seems to stay with us. But we have lately added the belief in a child's potential depravity, which may go unpaid for and unpunished just because of all children's categorical innocence. Perhaps this society abuses its children, and also aggressively dresses them in lipstick and sequins, for the same reason it imitates them—from a helpless envy of what they get away with. The everyday androgynous costume is the suit of diminished erotic responsibility and exemption from adult sexual risk. What it clothes is the child's license to make demands and receive gratification with no risk of dishonor—to be erotic, but to pose as unsexual and therefore unaccountable.

Even more forbidden and outrageous than the sexual child is its near relation, the erotic angel. While the ordinary world is routinely dressing itself and its kids in unisex jeans, it is simultaneously conjuring up mercurial apparitions who offer an enchanting counterpoint to life's mundane transactions. In the rock star form, they embody the opposing fantasy face of the troublesome domestic child or adolescent: the angelic visitor who needs to obey no earthly rules. Funny little E.T. was only one version. The type includes all those supremely compelling creatures who may shine while they stomp and whirl and scream and hum and never suffer the slightest humiliation.

A child, however ideologized, is always real and problematic, but an angel has a fine mythic remoteness however palpable he seems. The opposing kind of androgyny invests him: he exists not before but beyond human sexual life, and he comes as a powerful messenger from spheres where there is no taking or giving in marriage, but where extreme kinds of joy are said to be infinite. Our rock-video beings cultivate the unhuman look of ultimate synthesis: they aim to transcend sexual conflict by becoming fearsome angels, universally stimulating creatures fit for real existence only out of this world. Like all angels, they profoundly excite; but they don't excite desire, even though they do make the air crackle with promise and menace. Their job is to bring the message and then leave, having somehow transformed the world. Michael Jackson reportedly leads a life both angelic and artificially childlike, and he makes his appearances in epiphanic style. David Bowie still appears to be the man who fell to earth, not someone born here. Grace Jones also seems to come from altogether elsewhere. Such idols only function in the sphere of unattainability. While they flourish they remain sojourners, leading lives of vivid otherness in what seems a sexual no man's land.

Angels were in fact once firmly male and uncompromisingly austere. The disturbing sensuality they acquired in the art of later centuries, like that of the luscious angel in Leonardo's *Virgin of the Rocks,* always reads as a feminization— and from this one must conclude that adding feminine elements to the male is what produces androgyny's most intense effects. Almost all our androgynous stars are in fact males in feminized trim; their muscular and crop-haired female counterparts, such as Annie Lennox, are less numerous and have a more limited appeal. The meaning in all our androgyny, both modish and ordinary, still seems to be the same: the male is the primary sex, straightforward, simple, and active. He can be improved and embellished, however, and have and give a better time if he allows himself to be modified by the complexities of female influence.

The process does not work the other way. Elegant women in fashionable menswear expound the same thought, not its opposite: traditional jackets and trousers are austerely beautiful, but they are patently enhanced by high heels, flowing scarves, cosmetics, and earrings. Lisa Lyon, the body builder, has been photographed by Robert Mapplethorpe to show that her excessively developed muscles do not make her mannish but instead have been feminized to go with, not against, her flowered hats and lipstick. Ordinary women wearing men's active gear while wheeling strollers on the street or carrying bags across the parking lot are subduing and adapting harsh male dress to flexible female life and giving it some new scope. Common androgynous costume is always some kind of suit or jumpsuit, or pants, shirt and jacket, not some kind of dress, bodice and skirt, or gown. A hat may go with it, or perhaps a hood or scarf, but not a coif or veil. A few real female skirts (not kilts or Greek evzone skirts) are now being very occasionally and sensationally tried out by some highly visible men—daring designers, media performers and their imitators, fashion models and theirs—but all kinds of pants are being worn by all kinds of women all the time. We can read the message: the male is the first sex, now at last prepared to consider the other one anew, with much fanfare. It is still a case of female sexuality enlightening the straight male world—still the arrival of Eve and all her subsequent business in and beyond the garden—that is being celebrated. The "androgynous" mode for both sexes suggests that the female has come on the scene to educate the male about the imaginative pleasures of sex, signified chiefly by the pleasures of adornment. About its difficulties, summed up by that glaringly absent round belly, she is naturally keeping quiet.

Meanwhile the more glittering versions of modish androgyny continue to reflect what we adore in fantasy. Many of us seem to feel that the most erotic condition of all could not be that of any man or woman, or of any child, or of a human being with two sexes, but that of a very young and effeminate male angel—a new version of art history's lascivious *putto*. Such a being may give and take a guiltless delight, wield limitless sexual power without sexual politics, feel all the pleasures of sex with none of the personal risks, can never grow up, never get wise, and never be old. It is a futureless vision, undoubtedly appropriate to a nuclear age; but if any of us manages to survive, the soft round belly will surely again have its day.

In the meantime, as we approach the end of the century and the millennium, the impulse toward a certain fusion in the habits of the sexes may have a more hopeful meaning. After a hundred years of underground struggle, trousers are no longer male dress sometimes worn by women. They have been successfully feminized so as to become authentic costume for both sexes, and to regain the authoritative bisexual status the gown once had in the early Middle Ages. This development is clearly not a quick trend but a true change, generations in the making. Male skirts have yet to prove themselves; but men have in fact succeeded in making long-term capital out of the short-lived and now forgotten Peacock Revolution of the late sixties. Whole new ranges of rich color, interesting pattern, texture, and unusual cut have become generally acceptable in male dress since then, and so has a variety of jewelry. The sort of fashionable experiment once associated only with women has become a standard male option. Some new agreement between the sexes may actually be forming, signaled by all these persistent visual projections; but just what that accord will turn out to be it is not safe to predict, nor whether it will continue to civilize us further or only perplex us more.

DISCUSSION QUESTIONS

1. Hollander mentions "the seductiveness of most advertising photography." From the "Advertising" section, select several ads that illustrate her ideas about contemporary fashion and sex roles. Do the ads support her point about androgyny? Explain.

2. In "The Unromantic Generation," in this section, Bruce Weber also offers an analysis of contemporary culture. Can you find any resemblances between his and Hollander's procedures? What connections can you find between Weber's views of this generation and Hollander's views about its style of clothing?

Perri Klass / "Who Knows This Patient?"   *Discover,* June 1985

Perri Klass, who was born in Trinidad in 1958, graduated from Harvard Medical School in 1986 and is currently an intern in pediatrics. She has written fiction and has recently published a collection of essays, A Not Entirely Benign Procedure. *She regularly contributes personal essays to* Discover *and other magazines. She has also published a novel,* Recombinations *(1985), and a collection of short stories,* I Am Having an Adventure *(1986).*

Founded in 1980, Discover *is a popular monthly devoted to science writing for a nonscientific community. The magazine has featured many fine medical essayists, including Lewis Thomas and Gerald Weissmann.*

"Code call, 5 south. Code call, 5 south." All day the hospital loudspeaker system has been paging one doctor or another, frequently in tones too muffled to be intelligible (was that Dr. Joe Sung or Dr. Johnson?), relaying messages that suggest small hospital dramas of one kind or another ("Patrick Mark Watson, please return immediately to your floor"). All day long people have been listening with a low level of attention, tuned in just enough to catch their own names.

Then "Code call, 5 south, Code call, 5 south." The operator's voice is the same. No bells ring, no lights flash. But everyone is off and running, pounding down the hall, stethoscopes streaming in the breeze, the resident and the intern running as fast as they can, while you, the medical student, as usual are trailing a tiny bit (just where is 5 south anyway, and what would I do if I got there?). A code call means someone has stopped breathing, someone's heart has stopped, someone is dying, come at once.

There's a certain element of competition in the way resident and interns react to a code; you can't "run" the code unless you're one of the early arrivals; if you get there too late, there may well be no role for you. So it's down the stairs two at a time, and you emerge panting on 5 south, where you easily locate the room by the crowd of early arrivals massed outside.

The senior medical resident present is running the code, calling out orders. One intern is doing CPR, compressing the patient's chest as he counts, "One-one-thousand, two-one-thousand, three-one-thousand . . ." Another intern is desperately trying to get an IV line started in the patient's arm, while a junior resident is working on putting one into the jugular vein. A respiratory specialist is getting ready to put a breathing tube down the patient's throat. A nurse is taking an electrocardiogram, another is holding an oxygen mask on the patient's face, and others are filling syringes with medicines. Everyone seems purposeful and assured, and although there's a definite air of crisis in the room, there's also a certain calm.

As you stand on the sidelines, you attempt to convey by your demeanor two somewhat conflicting messages: I'm very happy to be of use in any way possible, and, please don't give me any responsibility, because I'm terrified. You're a third-year medical student. Most likely, exactly two years ago all these interns were third-year medical students. The residents are another year or two along, but that's all. You aren't watching people who've invested whole careers in learning how to handle this kind of emergency. You're going to be in their shoes in just two years.

When I first started work in the hospital, one of the lectures given to the medical students was about codes. We sat there, remembering all the stories we had been told—"So, they sent this med student to take a patient to x-ray, and they got stuck in the elevator and the patient coded right there"—and inventing even worse stories for ourselves. O.K., said the head of our training program, I'm going to teach you how to run a code. Some of us exchanged glances. *Run* a code? Well, said our teacher, what you do, in order to take control of a code, is stride forcefully into the room, bang on the table, and say fiercely, "Who knows this patient?" Good point—in the chaos of a code it's easy to find yourself caring for a patient without any idea of why that patient is in the hospital in the first place, let alone details like a history of heart attacks or bad lung disease. Anyway, after you've established your authority with that first question, you buttress it by banging on the table again and yelling "How many amps of bicarb has this patient gotten?" We all laughed—it wasn't serious, we weren't expected to run codes. And then, like many of my fellow students, I carefully wrote down, "Who knows this patient? How many amps of bicarb has this patient gotten?"

There are various terrors tied up with the change from medical student to doctor, but the worst is probably this terror of responsibility. In just a couple of years—before the next presidential election, say, or before Brooke Shields graduates from Princeton—there will be a life-and-death situation, and you'll be the one making the decisions. And this very dramatic terror serves as a focus for all the vaguer terrors about the other kinds of responsibility in your future, all the small decisions you'll make, all the advice you'll give.

So you stand there, at the code, and imagine yourself as the intern trying to start the IV line. After all, you know how to start an IV. That could easily be you, kneeling at the side of the bed, feverishly swabbing the arm once again with alcohol, searching for a vein. And all you can think is: What if I failed to start it, what if the patient couldn't get the drugs she needed because I never got the IV in?

"Let's give her another amp of bicarb, please," says the senior resident running the code.

Well, by stretching your imagination you can see yourself trying to start the IV, but you certainly can't imagine that you will ever, in a million years, be the one in charge. How can that resident stand there so calmly, even remember to say please? How can she be sure she's saying the right things? If it were you, you'd be thumbing desperately through the little spiral-bound outline-of-absolutely-everything you carry in the bulging pocket of your white coat, looking up "code," or "cardiac arrest," or "respiratory failure," or "death."

I remember the first time I saw an intern pull out a similar book and look up what to do. I'd been proceeding miserably along, sure that I was the only one in any way uncertain of my medical knowledge. I watched the intern matter-of-factly look up the instructions for his particular problem, and I felt a tremendous wave of relief—well, if you're allowed to look things up, maybe I might be able to do this too some day. And then I realized that the intern had hurried off to follow the instructions, that he was actually going to *give* the recommended drugs in the dosages he'd just checked, and it suddenly seemed strange and frightening all over again. There's a tremendous gap between looking up what to do so you can say something intelligent when a senior person asks what the right thing to do is, and looking it up so you can then go and do it.

Anyway, the intern has gotten the IV started in the patient's arm. You feel a personal triumph, after identifying yourself so strongly with the attempt. You wait for some congratulations, some recognition, and in fact the senior resident in charge finds a second to say "Good work." The intern now devotes himself to getting a sample of arterial blood to be analyzed for oxygen content; he's unable to get it from the wrist arteries and has to go for a femoral stick, putting a needle into the major artery in the groin. This is something else you know how to do, and once again you're grateful that you aren't doing it.

The code isn't going well. The patient has been given all the right drugs, the CPR has continued without letup, she finally has a breathing tube in, electric shock to her heart has been tried. She doesn't seem to be responding. You're standing next to the bed of someone you don't know, and she's dying.

The intern gets the arterial blood sample. It looks ominously dark, not the bright red it should be. Finally, there's something you can do; the syringe full of blood is put into a cup of ice, and you take it and run down several flights of stairs to the lab, where you puff out that this is a sample from a code. And then you stand there while the technician puts some blood into a machine that will read out the amount of oxygen and carbon dioxide in it. The numbers appear on the meter, and they don't look good. You scribble them down on a piece of paper. The lab will call the patient's floor with the results, of course, but you run back up the stairs and get there before anybody has called.

"Blood gas results," you announce.

"Yes?" The senior resident gives you her full attention. You read the numbers off your slip of paper. The resident reflects for a second, then shakes her head. "They're the same as they were half an hour ago. This woman has essentially been getting no oxygen for half an hour, so in all good conscience I don't think we can continue trying to start her heart up. Her brain will be gone."

There's a pause in the room. Then, slowly, people begin to undo what they've been doing. The electrocardiogram electrodes are removed. The chest compressions stop. All the bustle around the patient's bed quiets down, until just two nurses are left, wiping the patient clean of blood, removing all the various tubes, so that her relatives will see her resting in peace.

"Thank you all," says the senior resident. "Good job."

And as you drift out of the room, you're thinking that you still don't understand how you'll ever make the jump, the assumption of responsibility. After all, it was you who carried those lab values upstairs, you who read aloud the numbers that made the resident decide to stop the code, and that already seems to you a tremendous and terrifying responsibility. And then as you wander down the hall, you catch yourself murmuring under your breath, "Who knows this patient?"

DISCUSSION QUESTIONS

1. Klass is concerned primarily with portraying the "terror of responsibility" associated with becoming a doctor. What is the nature of that responsibility? What are some of the ways in which Klass manifests that responsibility in this essay? How is that responsibility contrasted to the world of the medical student?

2. The effectiveness of this essay depends in part on Klass's ability to make the reader identify with her. What are some of the techniques she uses to achieve this end? Comment on the effectiveness of each strategy.

3. Klass also identifies vicariously with the various interns and residents involved in the emergency case. Describe the role this plays in the medical student's learning process. Throughout the essay, Klass emphasizes her inability to imagine herself in a position of authority. In this respect, what is the significance of the last sentence? Of the essay's title? How does the title relate to both the world of the medical student and the issue of responsibility for death?

4. What does Klass mean when she says that the "dramatic terror" of assuming responsibility for death "serves as a focus for all the vaguer terrors about the winds of responsibility in your future"? What are those "vaguer terrors"?

5. In what way does the author feel responsible for the death of the patient in this particular case? Do you think her feeling is justified? Why might Klass have chosen to end her essay with her "involvement"?

Noel Perrin / The Old State Fair   *Smithsonian,* September 1985

One of America's best-known essayists, Noel Perrin has been writing about rural life for more than twenty-five years. Perrin was born in New York City in 1927 and was educated at Williams College, Duke University, and Cambridge University, where he received a M.Litt. He served as a first lieutenant in Korea and was awarded a Bronze Star. His books include A Passport Secretly Green,

Vermont: In All Weather, *and the series of essays,* First, Second, *and* Third
Person Plural. *He teaches English at Dartmouth College and manages a
hundred-acre dairy farm in Vermont.*

Established in 1970, Smithsonian *magazine is published monthly for associate
members of the Smithsonian Institution—85 percent of whom have a college education. The magazine describes itself as "a broadly based special interest
magazine concerned with natural and hard sciences, history, American culture,
and environmental issues."*

Last year about 13 million people attended professional football games and 23
million went to symphony concerts. Nearly 130 million, however, went to state,
regional and county fairs. There was a day in North Carolina when the North
Carolina State Fair was the fourth largest city in the state. There were numerous
days when the ascending order of size in Ohio went: Dayton, Akron, Ohio State
Fair, Toledo.

The Kansas State Fair is not one of the giants. Even on a good day there may
be no more than 50,000 people on the grounds. But it is one of the most thoroughly American—as befits the fair of our central state, the one that occupies the
geographical heart of the country.

Consider. State fairs began basically as cattle and sheep shows. The fairgrounds
in Hutchinson, Kansas, swarms with cows and sheep. Long ago they added entertainment. On one day at last year's Kansas fair I counted 172 different modes of
entertainment, from car races to 4-H fashion shows to avant-garde theater. Right
now foreign exhibits are in fashion at many state fairs. In Hutchinson I saw not
only Governor Carlin of Kansas but also Governor He (you pronounce it Huh)
Zhukang of Henan Province, China. He was there with a delegation of 30 Chinese
officials to open the fair's first foreign trade exhibit. To all this Kansas adds a
down-home quality that sometimes gets lost at bigger fairs—even at some its own
size.

The Kansas fair runs for ten days in early September—nine regular days and
one extra tacked on the front. That's called Preview Day and admission to the
grounds is free so as to encourage people to pour in and get the fair off to a lively
start. The other nine days you pay $2.50 to enter. I chose to arrive on Preview
Day because I like to see things begin. Within two hours I knew I was in luck.
Coming from rural New England where there are lots of small, local fairs and a
mere handful of big ones, I had evolved three criteria for judging the down-
homeness—you might even say the authenticity—of a fair.

One is food. All fairs sell large quantities of junk food. In fact, fairs probably
invented junk food. They were supplying an eager public with cotton candy and
fried dough long before fast-food chains were dreamt of. But the best fairs also
have plenty of good home-made food. Quite often it's church food. You can tell
when a fair has gone commercial by the decline in the number of booths selling
home-made baked goods, by the disappearance of suppers put on by local groups.

Another is the proportion of volunteer workers. No fair worth its salt can be
staffed entirely by volunteers because a good fair needs a midway, and a midway
that involves much more than throwing darts at balloons needs to be operated by
professional carnival workers. Who else has access to Ferris wheels and Tilt-A-
Whirls? But when the booths *and* the rides come to be operated by bored carnies,
you know that the fair has ceased to command the loyalty of its community.

The third is the ratio of participants to spectators; the higher the ratio, the more
genuine the fair. A tribal ceremony would be the ultimate in genuineness, since
the entire tribe participates and no one is merely a spectator. That never happens
at an American fair, but some come close. The month before going to Kansas I'd

been to the fair in Chelsea, Vermont, a special, fancy one celebrating the 200th anniversary of the town. The immense parade down the main (and almost only) street in Chelsea had so many of the townspeople in it that there were barely a couple of hundred left to watch. Even I, though not from Chelsea, was there as a participant: I was one of the float judges.

By all three criteria, the Kansas fair is authentic. When I reached Hutchinson later in the day than I'd meant to, I checked into a local motel and went right over to the fairgrounds to check things out—and to get something to eat.

Strolling in through Gate 12, the first thing I passed was a cluster of gigantic horse trailers. One of the main events of the first regular fair day is the draft-horse pull, and the participants were beginning to arrive. Men and women in cowboy hats were unloading enormous Belgian horses, pulling out hay bales, checking harnesses. There were more draft horses than I had ever seen in one place before.

Next I passed the Sheep and Swine Barn, already filled. Then a building devoted entirely to rabbits. Soon—I have a sure instinct for food—I came to a cluster of eating places. Some were commercial, but the three that caught my eye were all church. In a small white building, an all-male contingent from Our Lady of Guadalupe was busy serving tacos and frijoles to a mixed crowd of Kansas farmer-types and teenage couples. Fifty yards away, side by side, were the larger eating places run by the Central Christian School (of Hutchinson) and by the United Methodist Church (of South Hutchinson).

I know Methodist food intimately. Vermont is well supplied with Methodists, and I have been to numerous suppers put on by them—have even worked in the kitchen at a few. One can nearly always count on a good meal. Even at times of peak demand—say, during fall-foliage season, when many supper organizers get overwhelmed by the sheer volume of tourists and take to serving pie with a crust made from mix, or actually going to a store and *buying* the dinner rolls—even then, Vermont Methodists go right on making the crust from scratch and kneading the bread dough. It was the work of an instant to decide to sample the Methodist cuisine of Kansas.

When I went inside, I found myself in a large white rectangular space. There were six tables, each holding 16 people, and a serving line at the back. Five of the tables were full and there were only a few places left at the sixth, even though it was now past dinnertime. I asked the people in front of me in line what I ought to get. "Chicken with noodles and raisin cream pie, don't you think, Fred?" the wife answered. So I did. Delicious, both. Real crust on the pie, and real cream, too. It would pass muster in Union Village, Vermont.

Sitting there eating my chicken and noodles, I had plenty of time to look around—at the Bible quotations on the walls, the printed graces up and down the red-checked tablecloth, the sign that said "God deserves our best." I also noticed another, more secular sign. This one noted that at the 1983 fair, the women of the church had baked 2,045 pies. Wow! That's roughly 2,000 pies more than I'm used to—that's down-home food on a truly gargantuan scale. (I never said the Kansas fair was small; it's only small compared with giants like the Texas State Fair, which on some days is as large as Trenton, New Jersey, and Wilmington, Delaware, and Charleston, South Carolina, combined.)

When I finished the last crumb of my pie, I slid out past a remarkably thin farmer who had three pieces, all different, laid out in front of his noodles. Then I ambled back to the Sheep and Swine Barn. The midway was going full tilt—a cacophony of music and recorded spiels. I was tempted to try a roller-coaster or maybe even look in on one of the two freak shows and see the lobster people. But I raise a few sheep and pigs myself, and state fairs did begin with animals, 144 years ago. I decided to start there.

By now it was 9 P.M. Pigs like their sleep. What you'd have seen on the swine side of that huge barn were hundreds of recumbent pigs. They were sleeping two to a pen and quite often one pig would have an affectionate trotter resting on the other pig. Occasionally a small group of people would walk through, quietly commenting on a handsome Duroc or Berkshire. It was sort of like night rounds at an old-fashioned hospital, where there are wards.

By contrast, the sheep side of the barn was all noise and activity. The exhibiting of farm animals has changed a lot since the first state fair, held in Syracuse, New York, in 1841. (There was an attempt to start a New Jersey state fair as early as the 17th century, and George Washington tried his hand at encouraging them in 1796. But the New York State Fair—it's still at Syracuse—is generally agreed to be the true beginning.)

Of course farmers groomed their animals back then—and there were plenty to groom. On one train alone, 25 carloads of livestock arrived in Syracuse in 1841. But what was then amateur beauty treatment has now become professional. All over the sheep side of the barn were slender metal stands, each with a fancy head-grip at the top. To each stand was tied a reluctant sheep, its head held high. Owners busily trimmed their coats with electric shears and gave them sponge baths. Hundreds of other sheep watched, most wearing canvas overcoats—not because it's cold in Kansas in September, but to keep them clean. Almost every sheep steadily baaed. In the distance you could hear five kinds of midway music. The pigs slept through it all.

"THAT'S HIS WIFE—SHE'S PLAYING THE CRITTER"

From there I went next door to the Horse Arena, empty as yet of draft horses. Instead there was one lone cowboy out in the arena and maybe 50 people in the stands watching him. In front of him a blonde young woman in a red shirt darted from side to side and as she darted, he wheeled his horse. I had to ask one of the spectators what was going on.

"He's practicing for the Open Championship Cutting," my neighbor said. When I still looked blank, he explained that there were five different competitions in which a rider's job was to separate one cow from a herd. "That's his wife," he went on; "she's playing the critter." As I later learned, there are a total of 308 horse competitions at the fair. A far cry from the first New York State Fair, which featured a plowing contest.

Leaving the cowboy still wheeling, I followed the noise from this now mostly dark side of the fair over to the brilliant midway. I was still too full of dinner to be tempted by the homemade cake and candy being sold by teenage members of the Apostolic Faith Tabernacle. I did ride the Ferris wheel, from whose top I could see into the main grandstand, where close to 8,000 people were listening to a concert by the Beach Boys. I tried a couple of other rides. I proved too squeamish to go in and see the lobster people, though I listened entranced to the recorded spiel out front: "They're reeel! They're a-lahv! Ten thousand dollars reward if they're not reeel and not a-lahv! They have claws instead of hands. They have flippers instead of feet. Fahv generations of their kind have baffled medical science." I also talked to a young carnival worker from Texas, who advised me to be sure to have some Methodist food the next day. He said he himself began to think about chicken and noodles when he was still three fairs away.

As I see it, state fairs have passed through four stages in their history, and I'd already had glimpses of all four in Kansas. In the first stage, a very brief one, fairs were entirely for farmers and they were almost wholly educational. You went there to learn how to plow better, or to look at new farm machinery, or maybe to win a small cash prize for your cattle or carrots. You still do if you're a farmer or a 4-H kid. There were three carrot prizes awarded at the Kansas fair—nothing to make a person rich, being $3 for best carrots, then $2 and $1, but still prizes. There were also 778 sheep prizes, mostly in the $4 to $18 range, six turnip prizes, 27 hay prizes, 92 apple prizes, and so on.

But there is a certain lack of drama to carrots or even (unless you're a farmer) to a display of new farm machinery. Fair organizers quickly discovered that it's hard to draw really big crowds unless you add a bit of frivolity to your educational enterprise. Since state fairs were cropping up all over in the mid-19th century, there were lots of organizers around to make the discovery. So along the way they added two more elements: politicians and fast horses. The politicians, of course, came to make speeches, just like Governors Carlin and He in Kansas in 1984. Daniel Webster and Henry Clay were both star attractions in the late 1840s. A generation later. President Grant canceled appearances two years running at my own state fair in Vermont, causing a local journalist to write somewhat bitterly, "It is a settled fact that public men do not always keep their promises."

The horses originally came to be put through their paces in exhibitions of fancy riding and "trials of speed." A top attraction at the Iowa fair in 1854 was the competition for "boldest and most graceful female equestrian." Prize: a gold watch. Educational value for farmers: zero. Interest: intense. The crowd got so excited that when judges gave the watch to what it considered the wrong girl, there was a near-riot. The spectators collected a purse of $165 (read $5,000) for their candidate—and gave her a college scholarship as well.

It is hard to bet on exhibitions of fancy riding, however; the horses began to race for money. What ensued was probably the most corrupt period in the history of state fairs. The education of farmers was never quite forgotten and politicians kept coming to speak but horse races dominated most fairs in the late 19th century. Many of the races were fixed and sometimes the people who fixed them also ran the fair. In Minnesota in the 1880s the state fair was accused of becoming a private enterprise run for the benefit of the Twin-City Jockey Club. When farmers complained and asked for more attention to carrots and sheep, the gamblers in Minneapolis and St. Paul could hardly contain their laughter. "Let 'em have a fair run on Sunday-school lines," said a Jockey Club official. "There won't be enough people there to trample down the grass."

He was wrong. The wrath of farmers and the concerted efforts of farm magazines did eventually restore the fairs to respectability, though it took a generation. (As late as 1902, novelist William Dean Howells went to an eastern fair, which he carefully didn't name, and was aghast. "There was not one honest start in all the races at that fair," he wrote indignantly.)

But when the gambling died, the crowds remained. What kept them coming was a wonderful French invention called the Midway Plaisance. It first appeared in America in 1893. The original elements, all but one, were direct borrowings from abroad: the balloon rides, the belly dancers, the first primitive roller-coaster. To these the organizers of the World's Columbian Exposition in Chicago added one local attraction that has since become almost the symbol of American fairs. George Ferris built the first Ferris wheel, and it was an instant success (SMITHSONIAN, July 1983).

By the turn of the century many state fairs had a midway and had assumed the form later immortalized by the movie *State Fair,* starring Jeanne Crain and the state of Iowa. They have that form still, though there have been some major additions.

I got up early, and over the next two days I indulged in a kind of orgy of fairgoing. One morning was really early: I arrived at 4 A.M. to catch the predawn action at the Milking Parlor. (Not much of a crowd. People mostly watch the afternoon milking.) Some hours later I had an outstanding pancake breakfast at a stand run by the First Congregational Church of Hutchinson. Then I spent a long time in the giant farm-exhibit building known as the Pride of Kansas, visiting with judges of hay and corn and with members of the all-female support group for the Kansas cattle business known as the CowBelles. I stuffed myself with tacos at Our Lady of Guadalupe. I watched a performance of Complex Improvisational Theater and another of the State Fair Promenaders. I rode Dodgem cars.

And I ate and ate. For lunch one day I bought a porkburger at the stand run by the Kansas Pork Producers Council and topped it off with a corn dog from one of the dozen or so commercial corn dog stands. Then I had a jaffle (a wafflelike tart). After that I waddled off to watch a set of stock-car races, regretting that I wouldn't be there the day they were going to have a demolition derby featuring farm combines.

AFTER THE BEACH BOYS, TRUCKLOADS OF TRASH

I also kept meeting more participants. I got to know a Kansas sheep farmer named Chuck Woodard, who keeps almost a hundred times as many sheep as I do, and who was head chef at a lamb barbecue the sheep exhibitors put on. I went back to the Methodists one afternoon to sample some more kinds of pie and got to know Lyle Case, head of the 200 or so volunteers who run the cafeteria, 16 or 18 to a shift, four shifts a day for ten days. I even had a chance to meet a couple of the 60 prisoners from the Kansas State Industrial Reformatory who volunteer to clean up the fairgrounds each morning (ten dumptruck loads alone from the grandstand after the Beach Boys concert).

But two events stand out. One represents the still-vital rural past of state fairs, the other their urban, show-biz present. One full morning I spent in the packed stands of the Horse Arena, watching the draft-horse pull. About 1,500 other people were also watching: teenage girls in pink T-shirts as well as farmers in Stetsons and dark blue overalls. Nineteen teams competed. What each had to do was pull a sort of sled loaded with 50-pound salt blocks. To start things even, each began by pulling its own weight, so that out in the arena a group of men threw on a few salt blocks or pulled off a few as a team backed up to the sled.

All 19 pulled their own weight with ease and none needed the full three tries allowed to get the sled the required ten feet forward. After the first round, the handlers added 1,000 pounds, then 500. Every team managed that, too. Meanwhile, the audience was getting a sense of the drivers: whether he (or in one case she) could *talk* the horses into lunging their hardest or had to use a whip; whether after a pull he dashingly rode the whiffletree on around the arena like a Roman charioteer whose chariot had happened to disintegrate, or just clutched the reins and ran alongside.

By 11:36 the load was up to own-weight plus 3,000 pounds and there were only three teams left. At this moment a series of events occurred that sums up one whole aspect of state fairs. One of the remaining teams got so excited trying and failing to pull 3.1 tons of salt that when the horses were unhitched they kept right on lunging. They very nearly crashed into the stands.

There was no panic, but there *was* a moment's confusion—and the busy salt handlers forgot to add three blocks for the next team. This was hard luck for Gene Boyd of Redfield, not to mention Pat and Duke, his horses. When you get up to several tons, there's a rule that if a team doesn't pull five or six feet on the first lunge, there's no way they'll make it to ten because that first heave takes so much out of the horses. Three blocks light, Pat and Duke got eight feet, six inches on their first lunge. But it's disqualified and they must start over. This time they make a scant three feet.

"Hard luck, Gene," the announcer calls—and for the first time the crowd mutters a little. The announcer, who's been calling the horse pull for 25 years, stops dead. He looks around. ''All right,'' he says. ''It's partly my fault. But Gene's a good sport and I know he's going to accept my judgment.'' Gene says nothing. Certainly he doesn't throw his racket down. He brings Pat and Duke around for the third pull. He clucks to them—they give a mighty heave and pull the remaining seven feet. At one minute to 12 Gene has won the pulling contest and a purse of $210. Good guys sometimes finish first at the Kansas State Fair.

The other event that stands out was a concert. It differed in almost every way from the horse pull. That was daytime; this is at night—the warm Kansas night, full of locusts singing and young couples courting. That was a local thing and inexpensive; this is national and rather pricey. That was low tech; this is high.

On the fair's third night, I joined 3,700 other people in the main grandstand to listen to country music. George Strait and his Texans were the warm-up; Loretta Lynn and the Coalminers were the main show. For an afternoon performance plus this, Strait picked up $9,000. Lynn got $25,000, plus 70 percent of the gate over $65,000—netting her just under $10,000 more.

The grandstand faces due east. A huge moon was rising as we took our seats. It was tinged with red, said to be caused by prairie fires to the north. Big as that moon looked, though, it was not nearly as big as the loudspeaker in front of my section of the stand. That was something out of science fiction. A stupendous rectangular boxlike thing, it hovered 20 feet up in the air, supported by a giant metal arm. It seemed to have six speakers in it. It easily produced more noise than a supersonic jet taking off.

Almost stunned with sound as I was, I didn't particularly enjoy the concert—though the accompanying light show had its moments. I did enjoy the eager response of the mostly young crowd in the stands. They were prepared to love every song, to shout and scream and stamp and whistle. And it is that kind of audience enthusiasm that has sustained state fairs at times when it looked as if they might fade away.

Take 1952, for example. The place was Ohio. The Ohio fair, today the biggest in the country, had done badly. Despite the livestock, the Ferris wheels, the racing, the food, it lost $58,000 that year, and there was talk of closing it. Instead, the manager introduced the fourth stage to his state: he hired a big name to draw the crowds. When the fair opened in 1953, a native of Ohio named Roy Rogers was on hand, fresh from Hollywood. Twice a day he did a show. The crowds picked up instantly and the fair made money.

Other managers were watching. A few years later, the Wisconsin fair paid Rogers $234,000 for a ten-day appearance. Same happy effect. Soon it struck fair managers that almost any big-time performer would do—it didn't have to be Roy Rogers. It also struck them that it would be better to have ten different celebrities during a ten-day fair instead of recycling the same one day after day. The state fair as it now exists had come into being.

What will be next? Somewhere, another stage is waiting to happen. There are signs that it has already begun—in a return to more purely agricultural activities and lower-cost entertainment. But what form it will actually take I do not care to predict. Predictions made at or about state fairs are too apt to be wrong. Horace Greeley was one of the attractions of the 1865 Minnesota fair; he gave a speech in which he freely made predictions. One was that Minnesota farmers would soon be able to control rainfall by firing heavy artillery into the air. It hasn't happened yet. Another was that there would never be any decent apple pie in the state: ''I should like to live in Minnesota but for one thing. You will never be able to raise apples here.'' Returning in 1871, he found his remark painted on a huge banner. Under it was an exhibit of a hundred varieties of Minnesota-grown apples.

One prediction does seem safe, though. State fairs will be around for some time to come. Last year the Ohio fair drew three and a half million people and the Texas fair three million. Even a "small" fair like Kansas drew 340,000. State fairs will be around, and they will embody most of the best and a little of the worst in American history.

John Waters / Why I Love the *National Enquirer*
Rolling Stone, October 10, 1985

Self-proclaimed celebrity freak John Waters has himself become a celebrity—at least in his home town of Baltimore, where the mayor recently instituted a "John Waters Day." Waters, who regularly contributes essays and reviews to Rolling Stone, American Film, *and* The National Lampoon, *is perhaps best known as the filmmaker of such tasteless classics as* Pink Flamingoes *and* Polyester. *A connoisseur of the trashy and tacky, Waters is the author of two books, appropriately titled* Shock Value *and* Crackpot.

A thick, tabloid-sized biweekly, Rolling Stone *was launched by Jann Wenner as a sixteen-page San Francisco counterculture magazine in 1967 on a $7,500 loan. "Rock and roll is more than just music," ran a full-page ad for the magazine in the* New York Times *in 1967, "it is the energy center of the new culture and youth revolution." Since then the "new culture" and its celebrities have occupied an increasing number of* Rolling Stone's *pages.*

The best thing about subscribing to the *National Enquirer* is that it arrives in the mailbox the same day as *The New York Review of Books*. How well rounded I feel. Happily snatching this national institution from the slot, I wonder if the mailman thinks I'm a slob for getting it. To hell with him, I figure, as I scan the headlines, hoping they'll top "Barry Manilow: I've Got a Big Nose—and I Like It!" Riding the elevator up to my apartment, I feel so lucky to be a subscriber. After all, the *Enquirer* boasts the largest circulation of any paper in the country, and it's one of the few chances I have to participate in something so genuinely mainstream. For once, I feel normal. Like millions of others, I, too, love the *National Enquirer*.

I'm secretly jealous of every celebrity hounded by this great tabloid, since only the really big stars need be worried. Coverage in the *National Enquirer* proves you're hot; it's the only true barometer of fame in America. Every day I feel depressed that no *paparazzi* jump out from behind a bush when I go across the street to get cigarettes. Being featured in the *Enquirer* has been a lifelong dream of mine; even a date with Suzanne Somers might be worth it.

Think how exciting it must be to have eight-hour shifts of reporters camped outside your building, hoping to get a shot of whomever you might be sleeping with. Or bartenders or waiters being bribed to reveal even the most mundane details of your life. Aren't stars impressed that *anyone*—much less fifteen million readers—cares that they prefer a tuna sandwich to salami?

Does the *Enquirer* really hurt celebrities? I doubt it, not in the way *Confidential* did in the 1950s or even Louella Parsons or Hedda Hopper did before that. What the *Enquirer* does is *embarrass*, but at least it picks on the living and gives them a chance to fight back. Although some agents reportedly make deals to "lay off my clients" in return for dirt about others, nobody is really safe. Joan Rivers is always shouting, "Grow up, read the *Enquirer*," but the editors disregarded this apple polishing and published one of the most unflattering, horse-faced photos of her imaginable. Letting bygones be bygones, Liberace was smart enough not to hold a grudge in a no-win situation. He gave the *Enquirer* an interview even though it had supposedly ruined his career by publishing details from the "gayi-mony" lawsuit filed by his former bodyguard. Mr. Showmanship said the scandal actually brought him new fans.

I'm convinced that typical *Enquirer* readers move their lips while they read, are physically unattractive, badly dressed, lonely and overweight. Especially over-weight. Since the paper treats everyone except its readers badly, it's OK to be a behemoth as long as you're a nobody. Witness the "Fattest Couple" contests, in which roly-poly closet celebs compete for a measly $200 prize by sending hideous snapshots of themselves for publication. Or the endless pages of advertising for suspicious weight-loss schemes. But if you're fat *and* famous, beware; the *En-quirer's* most vitriolic copy will be aimed your way. The first headline I clipped for my collection of fat exposés was "167 Pounds! That's a Lotta Liz." I guess the then-chubby Liz had hopped on the scale in some hotel suite and a telephoto lens zoomed in on the exact reading. Or what about wonderful Anita Ekberg, featured in "then and now" shots, naturally looking beautiful in her early career, but now hugely overweight, wrapped in a blanket, with no makeup, clutching a carrot from her garden in what she, mistakenly, assumed was the privacy of her own backyard. The headline read, "Anita Ekberg . . . What a Waist!" My all-time favorite, however, was "Whale of a Gal! That's Tubby Tina Onassis." Lis-ten to the copy accompanying the eye-popping photos of Tina at the height of her career as the Fatty You Love to Hate Because She's So Rich. If there were a Pulitzer for trash, this writer would deserve the award: "Fat cat Christina Onassis is worth a ton of money, and she's turning into a whopper herself. Tubby Tina, dubbed 'Thunder Thighs' by the European press, is so fat she has to be helped out of her helicopter. The roly-poly 31-year-old heiress waddles away from her chopper—no doubt to get herself a square meal."

Even though the *Enquirer* no longer has staff photographers, it remains one of the top-paying purchasers of celebrity *paparazzi* shots. A front-page photo can fetch more then $2,000, and even "floaters" (pictures of cute animals, babies) can bring $400. No photo credit is ever given, but the money is so good, no one complains. "Ugly shots" are always welcome. Take the extremely unflattering photo of Robert Redford in the glare of the sun, with this screaming headline: "It Really IS Robert Redford." The caption read, "Redford's wrinkles are overcom-ing his dimples in this startlingly unretouched photo of the 47-year-old superstar, who's finally showing his age—and then some."

High fashion seems to be especially hated, by both editors and readers. The most outlandish outfits are featured with the prices prominently displayed and such copy as "So stiff and binding the model can't even sit down" or "This is going too far!" The skirts-for-men look is treated with terror. If one of the aliens the *Enquirer* so lovingly depicts ever were to read the paper, he'd assume that every man in America was contemplating whether to slip on a mini the next time he attended the Super Bowl. As much as high fashion is loathed, the paper's photo files of celebrities' outfits must be voluminous. Even Jackie herself might have laughed when they ran the headline "Oh No, Jackie O! She's Wearing the Same Outfit After 4 Years," with the pictures to prove it.

The *Enquirer's* readers love death, and so do I. Who wouldn't buy its biggest-selling issue, the one with the photo of Elvis in his coffin on the cover? And how exciting to read about, and actually see, Michael Washington, a black man with his shirt open to the waist, who is now the proud owner of white hunk Jon-Erik Hexum's heart. Beating inside of him yet! And Baby Fae. God, what a controversy ("Baboon-Heart Baby Shocker"), what a *star*—just look at the innocent little darling. Look directly under that photo at the shot of the hideous baby baboon. How interesting to see the nice coverage her parents received in the *Enquirer* until they sold their exclusive story to *People* instead. Like a jilted lover, the editors responded: "Her Mother Is Wanted for Jumping Bail; Her Father Is a Drug Abuser Who Beat Her Mother." Bad taste has never been so naked. Or cheap. A mere 65¢ for all this? What a deal!

Being sick is also a big story. From nursing homes all over this great nation, shut-ins cry out for details. A gravely ill Peter Lawford or David Niven becomes a pinup for the terminally sick. Under oxygen tents, beside respirators and in chemotherapy clinics, they want to know! Arthritis news is heralded almost weekly, even "2 Million Gout Sufferers" are not ignored. And the Betty Ford clinic; why, it must be the most glamorous place on earth! "Devastating Problems have Taken Toll on Liza," shrieks the caption of a shocking photo taken before she checked in. And never fear, the *Enquirer* delivers what any self-respecting substance abuser wants to find out: "Treatment at Famed Drug & Alcohol Clinic Is a Living Nightmare—*Enquirer* Reporter Goes Undercover at Betty Ford Center." If only Liz Taylor had checked into *my* hospital, patients fantasize. Now that would be heaven on earth!

Even the lonely have a voice. My all-time favorite self-help piece in this civic-minded publication was "Want to Enrich Your Life? Just Go to a Coffee Shop—Here's How to Meet Interesting People." Its detailed plan for making new friends included: "(1) Always sit at the counter—never at a table. (2) Make sure that you're neatly dressed—people won't want to chat with a slob. (3) Strike up a conversation. Start by talking about the weather. (4) Greet the waitress with a smile . . . people would rather talk to someone who is smiling than to a grouch." The author of this profound advice, one Dr. Frank Caprio, warned, "Not all conversations over a cup of coffee will lead to something, but even if they don't, you can learn something that will enrich your life from everyone you meet." I wondered if the Dean sisters, two Baltimore spinsters whose sad lives were featured in the *Baltimore Sun,* had read this piece. Reportedly, they were so lonely that they kissed the furniture in their apartment, waved out their window to oncoming traffic and hung out in doughnut shops saying hi to strangers until they got so desperate they held hands and jumped off a bridge together.

Sometimes the *Enquirer* tackles a real social issue: "Expert Claims Cabbage Patch Dolls Can Be Possessed by the Devil" was one howler scoop. The accompanying photo showed "famed psychic researcher Ed Warren" holding up a crucifix at a Cabbage Patch doll levitating over its crib. And you think these stories don't influence people? My cleaning lady, Rosa, who is so filled with great tales that Studs Terkel should marry her, recently confided her fear of Cabbage Patch dolls to me: "I heard about this woman who had one, and the doll tore up her china closet. The lady came downstairs, and her glasses were all broke. The dog started speaking in tongues and told her it was because she didn't wrap up the doll at Christmas."

"Oh, Rosa, you don't believe that," I said.

"Not really," she said, "but I'm leery of them. There's something about them, just like the devil. I don't want to be in the same room with a Cabbage Patch. My little grandson has one named Lester, and I tell him, 'Don't you be bringing Lester over here.' He just looks at me and laughs, but my son tells me, 'You're right, Mama, I don't like those dolls either.' "

After a top-selling issue treated the death of Grace Kelly with the same seriousness one would expect for the outbreak of nuclear war, the *Enquirer* began running updates on the attempt by a priest in Italy to have Grace canonized a saint. It was hinted that there were actual witnesses to miracles she had performed. I imagined Saint Grace at the premiere of *Rear Window,* stepping out of her limousine, the hem of her mink coat accidentally brushing across the face of a kneeling blind fan who is instantly cured of her affliction.

I also admire the *Enquirer*'s gall when it ruins entire overhyped TV shows by revealing much-anticipated plot twists months in advance. Plots from "Dynasty" and the final episode of "M*A*S*H" were sneaked to the *Enquirer* by well-placed spies on the set and splashed across the front page. Being an espionage agent for the *Enquirer* is probably more lucrative than working for the Russians. Maybe the editors are doing a political service by keeping people in this line of work busy with ridiculous secrets that could hardly topple foreign governments. They're also keeping big-time do-gooders such as Billy Graham, Art Linkletter and Lorne Greene out of trouble by publishing their folksy little advice columns on how to have happy little lives. The irony of these hypocrites' allowing themselves to be connected with the most despised scandal sheet in the professional Hollywood community, just because of its giant circulation, still amazes me. I must admit, however, that the New York subway-vigilante case was better handled by the *New York Post.* The *Enquirer* tried to convince you that the real-life Charles Bronson, Bernhard Goetz, had given them an exclusive interview, even though he refused. "Subway Vigilante—His Own Story," the headline screamed, despite the fact that the only sources in the article were police snitches. Two of his victims did take the bait, for a reported $300 each, but later bitched to *The Washington Post.* "The *Enquirer* robbed me," one said angrily. "My lawyer said I could have gotten at least $1,000."

I became sick of this whole story quickly. At first, the Archie Bunker outpouring of sympathy for Goetz got on my nerves, but then I started thinking, "Well, I don't blame him. I feel like shooting four or five people every time I step out of the house." Once, on a plane, I was deeply offended by a passenger seated near me who was guilty of the ultimate fashion violation—wearing summer white *after* Labor Day and before Memorial Day. Trying to be liberal, I hoped he was connecting later to some flight to the Caribbean, but his booming, drunken conversation soon convinced me this was not the case. Did he deserve to die for his hideous outfit? Would the readers of *Women's Wear Daily* and *GQ* have rallied wildly to my defense if I had blown him away?

When the parody the *Irrational Inquirer* was released in 1983, I was delighted at how funny it was. How difficult it must have been to parody a parody. Their joke headlines could almost have been the real thing: "I Died and Went to Heck"; "It's Hinckley's Baby,' Sobs Jodie"; "Dr. Tarnower's Diet Tips from Beyond the Grave."

But even more insane and ludicrous is the *Enquirer*'s bad stepchild, the one they never talk about, the rag put out apparently to utilize the old *Enquirer*'s black-and-white press—the *Weekly World News.* Closer in spirit to the old "I Ate My Baby" *Enquirer* before it got upscale enough to be sold in the supermarket, this fanatical, right-wing prime example of hepatitis-yellow journalism seems to be popular with illiterates and, not surprisingly, shock-loving hard-core punks and New Wavers. They even had Divine on the cover because irate viewers had complained to the BBC that she was "disgusting." The *News'* editorial policy can be best summed up by one of its stories: "Russkies Vow . . . We'd Blast Santa Out of Our Skies!" Whatever the rage in the other tabloids, they'll go further: "Ape Gives Birth to Human Baby" or "Vigilante Kills 27 Muggers." Sometimes their stories cheer me up considerably: "Good News for Smokers—It's Good for You."

Perhaps the most irresponsibly berserk columnist in the country, Ed Anger, is given space for his fanatical tirades each week in his column, "My America." He's beyond belief. His homophobia is legend—"Treat AIDS spreading sickos like the killers they are," he wrote once. "Is there any guarantee that the guy that used the water fountain in the park ahead of your little boy is not a gay with

AIDS?'' How about ''Junk food made our country great: You never saw The Duke [John Wayne] strolling around munching a pita bread sandwich stuffed with alfalfa sprouts and sipping tea . . . If all Americans looked as washed out and wimpy as those broccoli Bruces, the Russkies would be dropping down on us and taking over right now.'' And best of all: ''I'm madder than a doctor with a broken golf club at all this bellyaching about violence on TV when there's something even worse on the tube. I'm talking about the disgusting sex that's in most of today's top programs.'' Confirming everything I expected, an inside source of mine says Ed Anger is one Rafe Klinger, an ''off-the-wall'' guy who believes none of the stuff he cranks out.

The *News* ''*TViews*'' column has such heads as ''David Letterman's Show Is Like Garbage—It Stinks.'' And their Ann Landers–type advice column, ''Dear Dotti,'' can really dish out the hard-boiled advice—it's good to spank your children, and ''the vast majority of kids between 13 and 18 are rotten—so rotten that their parents can barely tolerate them.'' But ultimately, the *Weekly World News* gets old quickly; its shock style becomes numbing, the celebrity gossip old hat and lifted from other papers I've already read, and I go back to the *Enquirer* for its, by comparison, class act.

Of course, the *Enquirer* isn't perfect. Its story format—with that opening punch— always promises more than it delivers, the ''in mind'' inner-thought quotes are pushed too far to be credible, and its self-congratulatory ''You Read It Here First'' pieces are a little pompous. The predictions every year leave me cold, and I'm sick of Princess Caroline—she's not even *American,* for God's sake. And the clip-out coupons to send to parole boards to demand that none of the Manson Family ever be released is my idea of poor taste.

But if only some of the more high-minded periodicals would follow the *Enquirer*'s example, maybe they'd pick up some much-needed circulation. Each publication has its own set of stars, and why are they immune? ''Is Mr. Rogers' Marriage Falling Apart?'' Readers of *Weekly Reader* would like to know. Wouldn't *The New York Review of Books* be a little spicier if they ran ''Oriana Fallaci Is a Big Grouch'' or ''Isak Dinesen and Karen Carpenter—The Untold Link'' or even ''Gore Vidal Is Nellie.'' Couldn't the *Columbia Journalism Review* run stories such as ''Helen Thomas Wears Same Outfit Every Day'' or ''Exclusive: Nora Ephron Nude!'' What if the gay *Advocate* published ''John Rechy Is Straight'' or ''Ronald Firbank Didn't Have to Die.'' And in the *National Review:* ''Tricky Dicky and Rose Mary Woods—320 Whopping Pounds Together on the Scale.'' Or *Film Comment:* ''Prediction: Jean-Luc Godard Will Remake 'Ice Castles.' '' Wouldn't this be fair game? If you don't want to be in the papers, be a plumber; I guarantee no one will be interested in your private life. But if you're in the public spotlight in any way, watch out!

''Does Nancy Kissinger Have Big Feet and Love It?''

''Has Jeane Kirkpatrick Ever Had Sex on a UFO?''

''Is Margaret Thatcher Having an Affair with Eddie Murphy?''

Who wants to know? *I* want to know.

DISCUSSION QUESTIONS

1. How would you describe Waters's attitude in this essay? In what sense does he ''love'' the *National Enquirer?* What does he love about it? Why does he mention right from the start that he also subscribes to the *New York Review of Books?* Do you think he would have written an essay titled ''Why I Love the *New York Review of Books''?*

2. Read the selections from the *National Enquirer* in the ''Press'' section. Do you find that they support Waters's claims about the paper? Explain why or why not.

THE SPACE SHUTTLE DISASTER

The explosion of the space shuttle Challenger *shortly after takeoff on January 28, 1986, was one of the leading news stories of that year. Both* Time *and* Newsweek *prepared lengthy articles on the event, and both ran identical covers with photographs of the fiery explosion. The magazines prefaced their reports with the following brief reflective essays by senior staff writers Lance Morrow* (Time) *and Jerry Adler* (Newsweek).*

Thomas J. C. Martyn, the first foreign news editor of Time *magazine, started* News-Week *in early 1933 as a simpler, less interpretive digest of the week's major events than* Time *had been in its first ten years. Although a merger with* Today *magazine in 1937 changed its title to* Newsweek, The Magazine of News Significance, *the periodical remained uncompetitive with* Time *until it was taken over by the* Washington Post *in the early 1960s. Ever since, the two magazines have competed fiercely at the newsstand and for subscriptions. For additional information on* Time *magazine, see p. 295.*

Lance Morrow / A Nation Mourns   *Time*, February 10, 1986

The eye accepted what the mind could not: a sudden burst of white and yellow fire, then white trails streaming up and out from the fireball to form a twisted Y against a pure heaven, and the metal turning to rags, dragging white ribbons into the ocean. A terrible beauty exploded like a primal event of physics—the birth of a universe; the death of a star; a fierce, enigmatic violence out of the blue. The mind recoiled in sheer surprise. Then it filled with horror.

One thought first of the teacher and her children—her own and her students. One wanted to snatch them away from the sight and rescind the thing they had seen. But the moment was irrevocable. Over and over, the bright extinction played on the television screen, almost ghoulishly repeated until it had sunk into the collective memory. And there it will abide, abetted by the weird metaphysics of videotape, which permits the endless repetition of a brute finality.

In last week's grief, some people rebelled, a little brusquely, and asked whether the nation would be pitched into such mourning if, say, a 747 went down with 300 Americans. Chuck Yeager, protohero of the space age, observed, "I don't see any difference, except for the public exposure of the shuttle, between this accident and one involving a military or a commercial airplane."

That had the machismo of matter-of-factness. It is true that the tragedy played itself out to maximum dramatic effect: the shuttle, now boringly routine, lifting off and then annihilating itself in full view of the world. It is true that television pitched itself fervently into what has become its sacramental role in national tragedies—first wounding with its vivid repetitions of the event, then consoling, grieving, reconciling, administering the anchor's unctions. It is true that Christa McAuliffe, a teacher representing all the right things in America, rode as a nonprofessional, an innocent, into space, and her death therefore seemed doubly poignant and unfair.

But the loss of the shuttle was a more profound event than that suggests. It inflicted upon Americans the purest pain that they have collectively felt in years. It was a pain uncontaminated by the anger and hatred and hungering for revenge that come in the aftermath of terrorist killings, for example. It was pain uncomplicated by the divisions, political, racial, moral, that usually beset American tragedies (Viet Nam and Watergate, to name two). The shuttle crew, spectacularly democratic (male, female, black, white, Japanese American, Catholic, Jewish, Protestant), was the best of us, Americans thought, doing the best of things Americans do. The mission seemed symbolically immaculate, the farthest reach of a perfectly American ambition to cross frontiers. And it simply vanished in the air.

Jerry Adler / We Mourn Seven Heroes

Newsweek, February 10, 1986

Long after the wind had swept the last traces of Shuttle Mission 51-L from the skies, the mission clocks all around the launch site kept counting up the seconds since liftoff, as if holding out hope that it had all been a mistake, and the orbiter might at any minute pop up on a radar screen halfway around the globe, the pilot laconically apologizing for a glitch in the downlink. The machinery, like the nation itself, seemed unprepared to cope with a mission that went up and didn't come back down. As the cameras gaped at the roiling cloud where three contrails converged, terminals at mission control were displaying mute electronic puzzlement, the computers frozen in contemplation of those last bits of data that had escaped the doomed ship, as if they, like us, were reluctant to believe the evidence of their senses.

So swift, so sudden was the catastrophe that it appeared to elude even the computers' comprehension, yet on another level it was a disaster that could be grasped by a six-year-old, or almost so: on being told that the astronauts had been blown up over the ocean, one second grader in an Idaho school hopefully asked his teacher: "Can they swim?" The nation's schoolchildren, of course, were linked to this flight by the ebullient presence of Christa McAuliffe, who was to achieve immortality by going where no social-studies teacher had dared go before, and teach two lessons when she got there. It seemed natural—to one Brooklyn youngster, anyway—to ask how long it would be before children themselves went up into space: to which the answer is, a lot longer than it was a week ago.

If the disaster was a humiliating failure of rocket technology, it was at best an equivocal success of technology for the dissemination and amplification of grief. There was something at once dreadful and compelling in watching the footage of the families assembled in the spectator's gallery at Cape Canaveral, trying to spot on individual faces the exact moment when excitement turned to doubt, doubt to shock and horror. Ronald Reagan, who has had much practice in the role of chief national mourner, spoke movingly and well that same afternoon; yet even as his somber words sounded across a darkening land, an unruly horde was descending with lights and cameras on Concord, N.H., in hopes of illuminating an authentic tear from a genuine member of the same community as Christa McAuliffe. Some there thought they should be allowed to grieve in peace, but the organs of mourning, once brought to full sepulchral voice, are not so easily muffled; by the weekend we knew everything of interest about the lives, families and careers of the seven. Except why they died.

Why did they die? We won't know for sure, even after we answer the related, but separate, question of why Challenger blew up barely a minute into its 10th flight at 11:39 last Tuesday morning. A weld, a bolt, an icicle—somewhere in the volumes of data NASA has impounded is the clue to the anomaly that brought

hydrogen and oxygen into catastrophic contact. Precautions will be ordered and
the shuttle will fly again; if it flies long enough, it will probably have another
accident. "We always knew there would be a day like this," former astronaut,
now senator, John Glenn said last week—a fine time to tell us, one might say,
but a point worth keeping in mind.

One is tempted to say that they died because, as long as there are frontiers to
cross, there will be men and women to whom the challenge is worth the risk of
their lives. A noble generalization—although presumably the weighing of risk was
different for the professional pilots who flew the shuttle than for Christa Mc-
Auliffe, teacher and the mother of two young children. This much, though, we
can say of them all: that they died in the service of their country, and in the cause
of professions they believed in; and that having died, they can live forever in our
memories, poised in the clear blue sky almost 10 miles up and climbing, in that
perfect instant before holocaust.

DISCUSSION QUESTIONS

1. Both of the essays on the shuttle disaster are five paragraphs long, and both
respond to the same event. Can you find other similarities in style and approach?

2. Which essay strikes you as more emotional? Which seems more interested in
the technical details of the disaster? How are these emphases reflected in the
words and images of each writer?

Laurence Shames / Yikes! Business Superstars!

Playboy, August 1986

*Over the past several years, a new type of cultural hero has emerged in Amer-
ica: the successful, dynamic executive. In ads and commercials, he (sometimes
she) is often portrayed as having it all—money, youth, health, looks, athletic
ability. In the following essay, Laurence Shames takes a close look at this new
breed of "overachievers" and offers some reasons for this "rampant business
mythologizing." Shames, who was born in Newark, New Jersey, in 1951, graduated from New York University in 1972 and is the author of* The Big Time:
The Harvard Business School's Most Successful Class and How It Shaped
America. *A free-lance writer and a former contributing editor to* Esquire,
*Shames has published articles on sports, ethics, and contemporary culture in a
wide variety of magazines.*

*Playboy was founded by Hugh Hefner in 1953. From its inception, Hefner
intended it to "entertain and inform a literate, urban, male audience."*

Business is not rock 'n' roll. Nor is it guerrilla warfare, Roller Derby, cowboys
and Indians or the Friday-night fights.

Businessmen and businesswomen are not gladiators. Nor are they conquista-
dors, *ninjas,* test pilots, Olympic pole vaulters or movie stars.

Business is . . . well . . . *business*—that necessary but generally routine set
of activities that most of us perform in order to pay our rent, buy eggs and cheese

and stay out of trouble between breakfast and happy hour. And business people—which is to say, *most* people—tend to be regular folks, with the standard mixture of brains and limitations, daydreams and terrors, quirks, pettinesses, humor and dread. Free enterprise—the construct itself and the people who keep it going—is actual size.

Now, I realize that all of that is pretty elementary, even self-evident. And I say it only because there seems to be a movement afoot to deny it, to inject America's sagging business fortunes with the silicone of myth, so that mere functions are portrayed as high adventures, the gray processes of commerce are passed off as invigorating guests and business success—an equivocal goal that has historically held its share of squalor, bitterness and suicides, as well as the recent Wall Streeters' trinity of bimbos, limos and lines—is held up as a grail. From King Arthur to the ale man, our communal legends are being conscripted into the service of the business rah-rahs. We've got number crunchers out there talking about *the right stuff:* the accountant as astronaut. We've got ad execs talking about swinging from the heels for the new dog-food launch; the middle manager as cleanup man in the batting order of industry.

What is going on is a national campaign to kid ourselves into thinking that business is more dramatic, more heroic and just plain more interesting than it almost always is; and, as usual, the media are in the vanguard of the bamboozling. Looked at a magazine rack lately? Maybe you've seen a glossy rag called *Manhattan, inc.,* the fashion magazine about money, whose stock in trade is the celebrity tycoon, preferably under 40, and which fawns so cravenly on business overachievers that last year it saw fit to devote nine pages to Donald Trump's utterly inscrutable views on world peace. For the silver-haired set, there's *M,* which addresses itself to the sticky problem of satisfying people's medieval hankering for aristocracy in a country whose first premise is that there shall be no aristocracy. The *M* solution harks back to Calvin: 55-year-old C.E.O.s, having proved their preferred status in the eyes of Providence by their obvious successes in large-scale commerce, can then be offered up as exalted role models as they hold forth on the pleasures of polo or comment sagely on the sad decline of big-game hunting in postcolonial Africa.

The imagery, too, of business and the businessman has undergone a radical jazzing up of late. It used to be that an executive portrait consisted of the head and shoulders of some Episcopalian sitting at his desk, with his hands folded, a pen set in front of him and a globe alongside, and looking as if he'd rather undergo a tax audit than crack a smile. These days, C.E.O. pictures look a lot like album covers. Business bigs are being photographed—literally—sitting in the lotus position, standing on their heads and wearing clown costumes. By the deft use of strobes, enterpreneurs in crew-neck sweaters and beat-up moccasins are made to look as if they're spinning off an aura of cosmic energy. *American Photographer* pegged the trend perfectly by comparing the new executive-snapshot style to—you guessed it—the rock-'n'-roll portraiture poineered by Annie Leibovitz and showcased in *Rolling Stone* back when people looked there, rather than in *Fortune,* for fan-zine gossip and close-ups of celebs, preferably with their shirts off.

Nor is business' grab for drama and immediacy limited to the print medium. Consider *The Wall Street Journal Report,* a breathless business-news spot now carried on 85 radio stations nationwide. The *W.S.J.R.* announcer comes on sounding as if he's introducing an episode of *The Untouchables,* then proceeds to intone some stunningly meaningless factoid, such as that inventories of durable goods increased by one tenth of one percent last month, equalizing the decrease of the month before, so we're all back where we started from. This information is of use to no one; but, of course, that's not the point. The point is that a fix has been provided to America's burgeoning ranks of business junkies. Millions of people—

not by working, not by getting anything accomplished, but merely by tuning in—have been reassured that they are plugged in to the fast-paced, adrenaline-laced, roller-coaster world of business and that they are part of the hyped-up, sexed-up crusade that is American enterprise today. They feel like they belong.

The irony of all this is that we Americans, as a breed, pride ourselves on being ferociously independent, on defining our own goals and going merrily to hell by our own self-chosen paths; we fancy ourselves immune to, and above, herd psychology. Let's face it—even as the Japanese ace us out in business, we secretly despise them, with their company songs, their blind loyalties, their fanatical teamwork. Sure, they get results—but at the unforgivable cost of surrendering their individuality and abdicating their sacred eccentricities in favor of the all-compelling myths of the company and the national objective. But think about it: Is our own recent mythologizing of business fundamentally any different? Our legends, too, are designed to motivate, to steer ambitions onto acceptable tracks, to subjugate individual choices to some irresistible vision of "success" as defined by someone else. So, OK, here in America, we don't sing company songs. We tap our feet to the patter of the business cheerleaders and call it rock 'n' roll.

And we lie a lot.

We sexualize business by making it sound like a series of titillating, high-stakes gambles, a tightrope act performed without a net; when, in fact, as John Kenneth Galbraith asserted in his 1958 classic, *The Affluent Society,* "modern business enterprise can be understood only as a comprehensive effort to *reduce* risk." The businessman who *really* comports himself as a high roller is neither typical nor smart.

We rationalize business by portraying it not as a scramble after wealth but as the passport to life's civilized pleasures, when, in fact, it most often becomes such a draining and narrowing vocation that civilization's pleasures, once you get past cellular phones in German cars, end up scudding by unsavored. "More attention needs to be accorded," opined a recent column in *The New York Times,* "to what the executive gives up . . . of [his] one certain life" in return for his salary and perks. Amen—though, of course, bringing that kind of humanistic perspective to bear on the trade-offs demanded by a fast-track career would constitute what the business rah-rahs call a disincentive.

And, finally, we glamorize business by making it one of those fantasylands in which we live vicariously. Barbara Howar, who, as East Coast correspondent for TV's *Entertainment Tonight,* knows about celebrity obsession, recently observed that "shopgirls from Bloomingdale's read *The Forbes Four Hundred* as avidly as a corporate vice-president." Why? They have about as much chance of entering those circles as they do of looking as lissome as the models in *Vogue.* But business, like *haute couture,* seems to have become one of those things that, by a truly sublime illogic, make us feel good by making us feel bad about what we're not.

The question that remains, however, is why this rampant business mythologizing should be going on right now. Part of the answer, no doubt, lies in the adventure vacuum that otherwise pertains in this well-behaved and inglorious decade. After the local, intellectual and, yes, *moral* ferment of the Sixties and Seventies, the current historical moment . . . well, you can give it the benefit of the doubt and call it a period of regrouping and redirecting of national energies, or you can just say it's as dull as shit. It is the sort of dead spot in time during which the self-concerned have always consolidated their grains and nothing much else happens. Which is not to say that business is bad or that businessmen are villains—*that*'s just another version of the business myth, another strained and bogus way of lending resonance to what is, finally, a value-neutral game.

But there's the rub: *Value-neutral* doesn't satisfy us. We are, in spite of ourselves, idealists. We call ourselves pragmatic, and we think we mean it as a compliment; yet even in our most mundane doings, we yearn to cloak our ambitions in grandeur; we spin myths around ourselves the way a worm bedecks its tiny self in silk. And this would seem to be especially true of us baby boomers—who are both the central subject and the central target of the business cheerleaders, not to say the majority of the cheerleaders themselves. We boomers, with a cockiness that came from our sheer stampeding numbers, always knew that a very special destiny awaited us, and we tried on and outgrew alternative rhetorics the way a tall kid outgrows pants. The buzz words came and went; what was constant was the belief that we would live lives different from those that had been lived before.

Except that it hasn't quite turned out that way, has it? Most of us have settled into lives *exactly* like those that have been lived before: lives in business in a culture that's *about* business. So now the mythology is undergoing an ingenious twist: Having largely given up our dreams of being unconventional, we must contrive to make the conventional itself appear exalted. And that's what the business rah-rahs are trying to sell us.

A while back, a piece called "A Wall Street Rocker" ran in the "About Men" column of the *New York Times Magazine*. It was written by a 32-year-old fellow named Jim Fusilli, identified as "a corporate-relations associate for Dow Jones & Company." Fusilli came across as a damn nice guy, and his story just about broke my heart. It was about the frustration and ambivalence of trying to hold together a rock band when half the players were wearing suits and filling what are piously called positions of responsibility in the business world. What it was really about was the death throes not of adolescence but of the naïve faith that, even as prospering adults, we would have the prerogative of cranking the volume up, crushing the microphone in our hot fists and singing the damn song any way we pleased. Well, we haven't. But we're with you in your yearning, Jimbo—millions of us. We wish you success on the job and joy with the music. But, for Christ's sake, don't let the business rah-rahs befuddle you, even for a single beat, into mixing up the two.

DISCUSSION QUESTIONS

1. Select examples of the new imagery of business from the "Advertising" section. How do these ads support Shames's claim about superstars? Look, for example, at the ad for "Aramis."

2. Compare Shames's essay with the excerpt from Lee Iacocca's autobiography in "Best-Sellers." Do you think Iacocca presents himself as a business superstar in Shames's sense of the word? Explain.

Elting E. Morison / Positively the Last Word on Baseball
American Heritage, August/September 1986

Baseball is the only American sport that truly reveals our national character, argues Elting E. Morison in the following essay. Killian Professor of Humanities, Emeritus, at the Massachusetts Institute of Technology, Morison is the au-

thor of Men, Machines and Modern Times *and* From Know-How to Nowhere.
A contributing editor to American Heritage, *he is also the editor of* The Letters
of Theodore Roosevelt *(8 vols.)*.

American Heritage *was established in 1954. Its articles cover all areas of the
American past, and they tend to deal as much with culture and social institutions as with historical events. According to its editors, the magazine looks for
"historical articles intended for intelligent lay readers rather than professional
historians."*

The other day I met a professor who said he was having some luck with a course
called Physics and Sport. By following the action of a blocking back in the I
formation, for instance, he found he could give students a feeling for how force
becomes the product of mass times acceleration without their quite realizing that
they were taking in serious information. It certainly seemed an improvement over
those earlier ventures in "Physics for Poets," which turned out simply to double
the degree of difficulty for your average scholar. Also, the more I thought about
it, it seemed to offer a useful way to get across other kinds of subject matter—
history, for example.

Following the lead suggested above, I began to feel it might be possible to
recover much of the essential information about this country's past through a course
on baseball. My project has not been carried forward to so satisfying a culmination as a syllabus and teachers' guide. That is for others to do. But I have some
suggestions and observations that might help them with their work.

Because "relevance" is now so large a consideration in the learning process, I
suggest that it would be useful to begin with an examination of how deeply the
technical terms of the game permeate our language: "Pinch-hit for," "threw me
a curve ball," "out in left field," "caught in a squeeze play," "never got to first
base," "has two strikes against him," "just a ball-park figure," "fouled out,"
"touched all bases," "it's a whole new ball game." The list could be continued
almost indefinitely.

Why is baseball's terminology so dominant an influence in the language? Does
it suggest that the situations that develop as the game is played are comparable to
the patterns of our daily work? Does the sport imitate the fundamentals of the
national life or is the national life shaped to an extent by the character of the
sport? In any case, here is an opportunity to reflect on the meaning of what I think
I heard Reggie Jackson say in his spot on a national network in the last World
Series: "The country is as American as baseball."

It is not only the common usage of baseball's technical terms. Over and over
again, the observations of those associated with the game have been used to give
a frame for our ordinary experience or a clearer focus for some of our national
characteristics; that is, they have entered the culture. Consider these few examples: Yogi's "I can't think and bat at the same time," which puts our continuing
difficulties in finding the right relation between theory and practice as nicely as
possible; Dizzy's jaunty "Me and Paul can do it all," which sharply defines the
assumption, so significant in our past, that the impossible only takes a little longer;
Branch Rickey's opinion (made, I think, while reviewing the success of his farm
system) that "luck is the residue of design," which implies that while for some it
may be better to be lucky than good, for those who are bound to rise it's best to
get your ducks in a row by cool and clear-eyed calculation. Then there is Leo
Durocher's "Nice guys finish last," that bleak and generally accepted assessment
of the qualities required to make room for yourself at the top of a competitive
society. Finally, there is Yogi's "It ain't over 'til it's over." This central finding

could not be derived from any other major team sport, where the duration of the exercise is determined by the artificial means of the clock.

So much for relevance. It must be clear by now that as the game goes, so goes the Union. Now what about the game itself? Let us start at the beginning.

Everyone knows the story of Abner Doubleday. One summer 150 years ago in Cooperstown, New York, he established the controlling conditions for play. He laid out a space that, in accordance with the national tendency to gild (or in recent times to chrome-plate) our artifacts, we think of as a precious stone—though it is in fact, and more appropriately for our national game, square. Within this configuration he worked out certain ratios among time, distance, and speed that provided a settled context for the coherent and constructive development of actions and intents. Put simply, on the basis of some experience and much logical deduction, he put together in a summer season a frame of government for the ordering of some human affairs.

Not everyone, to be sure, accepts the story of Abner Doubleday. This very magazine, for instance, three years ago printed an article cleverly designed to demonstrate that the man was somewhere else as the game was slowly evolving. Even while preparing this account, I received a learned paper from the president of Yale, one of the leading revisionists on this subject. With the aid of a good many literary allusions and a direct citation to a Princeton student's use of the phrase ''baste ball'' in 1786, he concludes that something like the present game was played ''before the birth of the Republic.''

For various reasons I reject this view, though I do believe that when it is laid against the orthodox account the comparison can provide an interesting classroom exercise in the difficulties of obtaining correct historical inferences from limited and conflicting evidence—which is the name of our game. In large part I accept the authorized version because it feels right. At various times in our history we have had to look for appropriate ways to organize human activity. What we do then is seek a logical containing structure, devise rules to ensure sensible action within it, and get it all down on paper ahead of time.

For instance, fifty years before Cooperstown, men met at Philadelphia to create a new order of things. Interpreting experience in the rational temper of their century, fortified with the power of deductive thought, they produced in a short season a frame of government that has, ever since, enabled men to live together in a coherent and constructive way. From the Mayflower Compact to the covenant for a League of Nations put forward in Paris eighty years after Cooperstown, this instinct for prefabricated structures goes very deep with us, and on the whole has served us well. As Gladstone said, our Constitution is the ''most wonderful work ever struck off at a given time by the brain and purpose of man.''

As with other ideas we have thought up and that have served us well, we tend to believe our way of doing things has made us Number One and should serve as an appealing standard for all others to repair to. This has sometimes—as the League of Nations proved—made for difficulties, and in any case there are other ways of going at things. As Gladstone also remarked, the British Constitution, another very useful frame of government, was a ''most subtle organism which proceeded from progressive history.''

A study of the difference between a wonderful work devised in a moment of time (our Constitution) and a most subtle organism evolving through the ages (the British Constitution) should get us to the heart of our peculiar national character. It can be done in terms of political theory or social history, but a far more telling classroom instruction can be achieved through a comparison of baseball with the game of soccer. At the time Abner Doubleday was drawing up his neat program for controlling the play of the future American game, soccer in England was a "chaos" of odd manuevers with a "blown bladder." There were no written rules. A decade later some were prepared but soon mislaid and within a twelvemonth looked upon as lost. So the order of play, exactly like the British Constitution, went on "broadening down from precedent to precedent." When, in the 1860s, these precedents seemed settled enough to print up in a "code of laws" for soccer, they contained an "offside rule" so complicated no one could interpret it. For half a century, therefore, it was applied to accord with the views of the spectators who roared the loudest. By such mutations soccer has become a "most subtle organism" that has to be seen to be believed.

In the contrast between these two games—soccer with its messy origins and confusing flows of movement, baseball's preprogrammed geometry and ordered action—there is food for further thought. First it should be pointed out that our national sport, like our Constitution, has stood the test of time. The major modifications in each that are required by changing conditions have been relatively few, and some of these, such as the Eighteenth Amendment and the Designated Hitter, have only gone to prove that the founding fathers got it right the first time.

That baseball "works" for us is therefore obvious; that it does not work for almost anybody else is also clear. In disconcerting fact, it is that other game of illogical design and flimsy structure that exerts an almost universal attraction. The competition for soccer's World Cup actually takes place all around the globe and often brings together for the final contest such unlikely and disparate countries as Uruguay and Poland. What we like to think of as baseball's World Series has not yet been conducted outside our own borders and only last November was played out between two cities located in the same state.

Such a condition of things should pose interesting questions for students who live in a land that seeks to be the managing partner for other lands. If we haven't yet made the world safe for our national game beyond our continental limits, how can we hope, or should we even try, to transport the rules for our way of life to an unpersuaded world? To put it baldly and probably a little too specifically, if most humans have never made an effort to understand the infield fly rule, what makes us think we can make them believe in something like Amendment XIV, Section 4, of the Constitution, which reads in part: "The validity of the public debt . . . shall not be questioned." Especially at a time like this.

Or take a different kind of question for those with a more philosophical turn of mind: Does a wonderful work that perfectly fitted the time in which it was struck off have a better chance of useful survival in a future that looks increasingly untidy than a subtle organism that for centuries has accommodated itself to the confusions of evolving history?

From such speculations we can turn back to the game itself. It is often said to be a sport of inches, but in fact it is subject to an infinite variety of nice measurements. It is therefore primarily a game of numbers—three strikes, three outs, four balls, ninety feet, nine innings set the fundamental structure. Batting averages, slugging averages, fielding averages, RBIs, ERAs report the nature of the action often to three decimal points. And you can go from these gross averages to the most esoteric particulars of performance—he hits .312 with men on base and .278 when the bases are empty; he averages six strikeouts a game played in the sun and eleven under the lights.

From all the accumulated figures, a man can tell in absolute terms how he is doing; where he stands in relation to his teammates; where he is placed among those who are now playing his position or have ever played it since they began to keep records. Probably in no other walk of life is the contribution of the single member to his community so accurately calculated and the errors he has made along the way so surely defined and carefully added up. And probably in no other walk of life is the essential truth of an endeavor so precisely quantified and the quantifiable truth so near the whole truth. They can even pin down an unearned run.

For those who live in a society where it is difficult to place oneself, to know how high is really up, where position is neither determined nor defined by birth or class distinctions, such measured evidence of what you've got, where you fit, and who the other fellow is must have its subtle, strong attractions.

The advantages of such clean calculations are not restricted to the individual case; the accumulated data in the immense data bank can be directly applied to the control of the individuals acting together—that is, to the conduct of the game. When, for instance, you know that a man on first base with one out has a 14 percent chance to score, you have a hard and ordering fact to work with. Or when there is a man on second, first base unoccupied, two outs, a man at the plate who is hitting .327 to be followed by a batter now hitting .234 and mostly singles—in that situation it is reassuring to know that you can control the developing action simply by playing the percentages, that is, in this case, by ordering your pitcher to walk the man at bat.

Enough has been said to establish the point that baseball is a game of numbers and mathematical expressions. The same can be said for the society in which the game is played. I once heard the great Yale philosopher F. S. C. Northrop assert that we had our very origins in mathematics. The Declaration of Independence, he claimed in a pyrotechnic hour, could not have been written had Thomas Jefferson not studied the calculus at the College of William and Mary. The line of argument need not detain us here; Northrop's conclusion that from the outset we have sought to define and resolve issues through numerical means seems unassailable.

A few years after the Declaration, we dealt in the Constitution with one aspect of our racial difficulties by the calculation that one black man added up to three-fifths of a white person. For many years we distinguished between slavery and freedom by drawing a line at 39°43'. Later we subsumed a wide range of important political and social differences in the ratio of 16 to 1 for the coinage of silver and gold. Right now we take the percentage points marking the change in the growth of our Gross National Product during the last quarter as a reliable figure for our current state of grace.

The fact is that from 54°40' to the forty-niners and the Fourteen Points, our political life has been shot through with numbers. Which may be taken as an accurate reflection of the way we go at all things both great and small. The whole westward course of Empire was set within the pattern of the 640-acre section. By his calculations of time and motion, Frederick Winslow Taylor altered the entire character of our industrial development and life. And when it became necessary to describe the attributes of a really high society, we settled on the "Four Hundred." In a fuller and more careful survey of all the historical evidence, it can be made to seem small wonder that the nation is as American as baseball.

In any good standard history textbook, notice is taken of the fact that while most citizens hold public office, fight, and grow or make things, some write, draw, and compose. This notice is taken in a paragraph that, in listing names and principal works, suggests not much more than that these people were alive at the time. There has always been some difficulty in explaining how abstract expressions of music, static interpretations in paint or bronze, and the distillations of poetry connect with the statements on the bottom line. In any study of baseball these difficulties diminish because the game itself is an—and quite possibly *the*—American art form.

As with the ballet in Russia and perhaps the opera in Italy, in baseball the artistic word is made lively flesh, which also makes it easier to understand. But there is a lot more to it than that. Start with the lovely sight—that glistening greensward, exquisitely cared for and marked out with such exactitude from the tawdry urban sprawl surrounding it. In such a setting it may even be a diamond at that. But in any case it demonstrates that a form so precisely faithful to the function can, by knowing hands, be turned into something beautiful without the need for deprecating explanation or embarrassment. Then those uniforms—spotless, sophisticatedly simple, cut perfectly to fit the purpose. And then the exhibition itself; those instantaneous responses neatly accumulated into resolving interaction—fast enough to take the breath away, slow enough to take it all in. The form of baseball is determined by precise configuration, exact measurement, and satisfying ratios among different kinds of known quantities. Within this immaculate conception each can play his identifiable individual part and all can work together in amazing grace—even in the most routine transactions, like a putout at first or a double play.

Edna St. Vincent Millay held that Euclid alone had looked on Beauty bare. But anyone sitting in the bleachers on any given day can see the possibility of beauty (albeit appropriately clad) in the collective action within that nice geometry.

If it were only a lovely sight it would be no more than an aesthete's pastime. If it were only a game, "winning," as Vince Lombardi said, would be "the only thing." But those who give their lives to it have a far larger point to make. Any legitimate art form, in paring away the muddle of reality, leaves the clean lines of an ideal state so the possibility of doing better with life is postulated and confirmed. The design for a more perfect union that baseball presents must have a continuing fascination for a people who have lived in a rational constitutional scheme, who believe in a government of well-defined laws and who like to fool around with numbers.

This concludes my effort to suggest that modern students may find in baseball the key to the storehouse where the historical treasures of the great Republic are contained. And perhaps, if I were wise, I would conclude at this point. But my love of the game—and my concern for the relevance of any instruction and my foreboding sense of the kind of future we may try to figure out—lead me to a few more comments that have not so much to do with the past as with the years to come.

I have suggested that baseball has served as some sort of ideal expression that our better selves could aspire to, a kind of model to work toward even though it could never really be. The fact is that in the past it could be no more than that. We had not accumulated enough percentages and numbers to put our very lives in so nice a framework. But in recent days we have reached enough exact assessments, assigned enough integers to known quantities, and worked out enough statistical probabilities to think of controlling experience through useful equations and ingenious numeracy, as it is now sometimes called. The power in all these new findings—as students know far better than their teachers—is marvelously multiplied by the computers.

In such conditions it may be useful to study baseball not as an ideal expression but as a kind of manual or handbook for the successful management of a numbers game. It is, I think, the only team sport in which it is possible to play a flawless exhibition and, because the nature of the flawlessness is clearly stated in mathematical terms, to know that you have done so. These occasions, called "perfect games," are rare, but they do occur—eleven times in the last eighty-five years. The definition of perfection is no runs, no hits, no walks, no errors. That is, you know you've got it exactly right only when absolutely nothing happens.

It would be quite possible to increase the incidence of these games by altering the structure of the play—reducing the allotment of strikes for the batter, shortening the distance between bases and so forth. But those in authority have realized that if they carried the numbers to their logical conclusions, all they would get was more zeros. They have resisted this temptation to push the game across the line of semiaridity.

From the beginning they have operated on a different premise; perfection, like Beauty bare or only winning, is an *ignis fatuus* for those in search of decent principles of human organization. In an obviously flawed world one can do no more than create conditions that enable people to do the best they can. And it must be recognized that the best is really never very good.

The finest hitters in the game are successful one time in three; the good infielder makes an error one game in four; a pitcher who wins twelve games and loses ten finds a place in the rotation; and all the daily play is stained with foul balls, wild pitches, dropped flies, and getting caught off base.

The achievement of baseball—what makes it the prototype for future organizations—is that while accepting all this ineptitude and untidiness, it provides a scheme where men at work can, with satisfaction to their selves, produce results that are almost always interesting and more often than not exhilarating. The beauty of this scheme derives from the way the precision of the structure, the logic of the rules, and the claims of the human potential are brought into invigorating consonance. I would cite the three determining principles on which this scheme is built: First, the fundamental dimensions of the composition are keyed to the known and measurable quantities in human potential—how fast a man can run, the speed of the ball he throws, how far he can hit a ball and all that. Second, since it is known that the human best is not very good—or at least very predictable—carefully calculated routine opportunities for a man to show the stuff that is in him are ingeniously created within the settled total composition. For a single simplified instance, the controlling context of three strikes and four balls is found to give a batter a reasonable amount of room to prove his truth by his endeavor (getting a hit), especially since the context is enlarged by the fact that a foul ball is never counted as a third strike unless it is a foul tip caught by the catcher. That such arrangements to give appropriate accommodation to the needs of the human potential have been worked out so firmly, so clearly, and in such detail is one of the primary·sources of strength in the total composition.

And finally, in that composition a place is made for those things in the human condition that no one can figure out. There is the two-week slump that sets in when a man unconsciously changes his batting stance or when there is trouble at home. There is the shining moment, the little miracle of Coogan's Bluff, when Bobby Thomson's homer turns a whole season around. And there is the demonstration every day that those "intangibles" Stinky Stanky had can be used by anyone to upend the controlling influence of the percentages.

Now what, in the fewest possible words, does all this prove? Briefly, it appears that all our students will be going out to shape a society that will be increasingly organized by the skilled manipulation of the numbers, by the enlarging capacity of the brain for quantitative thinking, and probably, in time, by the sharpness of artificial intelligence. The record shows (and as Casey Stengel used to say, "You can look it up") that baseball has had more experience and success with ordering a society such as ours than any other agency. And the record further indicates that the way to make the programs fit and the statistical probabilities appropriately apply and the numbers fall into the right place is to start with what the players are like—insofar as you can tell. As Casey Stengel also almost certainly said, "You

hafta know your players and what they can't do before you start your thinkin'.''
If you can get that point across in an introductory course to enough students, it is
even possible that we might have a whole new ball game.

DISCUSSION QUESTIONS

1. Morison sees baseball as a working model for American life. List all the
similarities he finds between the game and our culture. Can you think of any
additional similarities?

2. Use Morison's analysis of baseball and the national character as a way of
reading Ernest Laurence Thayer's famous poem, "Casey at the Bat" (in "Best-
Sellers"). Which elements of the poem conform most closely to Morison's
interpretation of baseball?

Harry Crews / The Mythic Mule   *Southern Magazine*, October 1986

*Southern Magazine was launched in 1986 by editors and writers from Little
Rock, Arkansas, who thought the South needed a general magazine to serve the
interests of the entire region. As one of the founding editors, Linton Weeks, put
it: "The South deserves a provocative, entertaining magazine that not only celebrates its quirky quintessence, but meets regional controversies head on, probes
the paradoxes of what it means to be Southern today, and treats our homeland
with a critical eye and a gentle hand."*

*"The Mythic Mule" appeared in the magazine's premiere issue. A Southerner
who writes out of a powerful sense of place, Harry Crews was born the son of a
farmer in Bacon County, Georgia. A graduate of the University of Florida,
Crews served in the Marine Corps between 1953 and 1956. He is the author of
a number of books, including* The Gospel Singer, This Thing Don't Lead to
Heaven, Karate Is a Thing of the Spirit, Car, A Childhood: The Biography of a
Place, Blood and Guts, Florida Frenzy, *and* Two. *He is a Professor of English
at the University of Florida.*

Anybody who traces his blood back three generations in the South owes the mule
the same debt I owe. This is true even of Southerners who never lived on farms.
Maybe the city folk never plowed them or rode them, or smelled them, or tended
their hurts, but nonetheless, the cane mules of Louisiana produced the sugar they
ate, the cotton mules of Alabama put clothes on their backs, and draft mules
snaked the logs that built their houses and hauled the dirt that made their roads.

Consider that as recent as 50 years ago there were better than 4 million mules
in the deep South. Why mules instead of horses? For starters, horses have no
stamina in front of a plow. A good mule will do 12 hours in the harness in front
of a turn plow, and he'll do it on 30 ears of corn and two bats of hay. Even if a
horse could do the work, he could not do it on that amount of rough food, and he
would never recover enough in one night to be able to go back to the plow the
next morning. A mule needs little water, little food, tolerates extremes of weather,
and requires very little time to recover after intense labor.

The mule is without question the most successful and productive mutant man has ever produced, and his history is a long and noble one. Mules were doing faithful labor in the Holy Land before the time of King David, replacing the donkey as the royal beast. We read about him in the Bible in II Samuel (13:29): "Then all the king's sons arose, and every man gat him up upon his mule and fled." The great traveler Marco Polo was much taken by the Turkoman mules he found in Central Asia. And while everyone who knows anything about the history of the Arctic exploration is familiar with the tragedy of Robert Falcon Scott and his party, almost no one knows that when the sleds of the relief expedition reached Scott's tent they were drawn by mules.

But it is not for his long history or the work he has done around the world that I come now to celebrate the mule. Rather, I celebrate the mule because he made the South, helped my people make and shape themselves, and, finally, is a necessary part of my fondest memories.

Where I come from, Bacon County, Georgia, horses were playthings that few people could afford; mules put grits on the table and bought the baby's shoes. From a farmer's point of view, though, one of the best things about a mule is the care he takes about where he puts his feet. He will walk all day long beside cotton that is eight inches high and never step on a hill of it. A horse will step all over it. A horse just doesn't give a damn. If a mule steps on your foot, you can be sure he meant to do it. There are no such guarantees with a horse.

With the exception of his land, the Southerner owned nothing he prized more than his mules. But, obviously, the land was no good without mules to work it. And they were never cheap. In the depth of the Depression, when my daddy would walk five miles before sunup and work all day for another man for 50 cents, a good mule might cost $200. And because they did cost so much, a farmer had to be careful not to get beaten in a trade. I was privileged on many Saturdays of my childhood to watch and listen while farmers bought and sold and traded mules. The Saturdays were all special and memorable in a way that few other days have been in my life.

I never learned to drive a car until I was 21 years old because we never had anything on the farm with a motor in it. Wagons pulled by mules were the only way we had of going long distances. On one Saturday a month throughout the year, we got up before daylight for the long ride to Alma, the county seat of Bacon County. If my mother or grandmother were along, they sat in ladder-back chairs in the bed of the wagon. The children lay on the floor wrapped in quilts if it was winter, or sat on the tailgate with their feet dangling just above the dirt road if it was warm weather. A good mule will walk four miles an hour, and so we would get to town at mid-morning and go directly to the great dirt square, which would be filling up with dozens of wagons and mules standing easy in their halters. We would take the mule out of his harness and water him and leave the 15 ears of corn we had brought for him to eat in a foot tub.

The dusty air would be heavy with the pleasant smell of mule dung and mule sweat. The whole square was alive with the ragged sound of mules braying and stamping. Farmers were everywhere in small groups, talking and chewing, and bonneted women stood together trading recipes and news of children. After I got to be 8 or 9 years old, I was free for the day until all of us met back at the wagon in late afternoon. Sometimes I would have as much as a dime to spend on penny candy, but better than the taste of the candy was finding a telephone in a store and standing beside it until somebody used it. I never talked on one myself until I was almost grown, but I knew what a phone was, knew that a man's voice could be carried on a wire all the way across town. No film or play I have ever watched since has been as wonderful as the telephones I watched as a boy in Alma, Georgia. (I can hear voices beginning to mutter that Crews is singing a sad song for the bad good old days, wishing he was back barefoot again traveling in wagons and struck dumb by the mystery of telephones. I am singing no such song and I would be a fool if I were. What I am talking about here is a hard time in the shaping of the South, a necessary experience that made us the unique people we are. And, moreover, I am saying that the shaping and the experience could not have been shared by a beast more faithful and steadfast than the mule.)

At some point in the middle of the day I would wander over to The Alma Mule Company, or, as it was universally called, the mule barn. There was such a mule barn in every settlement of any size in the South. My uncle, Major Eason, owned the one in Alma. He was a big, gruff, gray-haired man in high boots, and he was always good for an R.C. Cola or a Dr Pepper and a sack of boiled or parched peanuts. With the peanuts in one hand and the drink in the other, I was free to wander among the men talking mules. They stood about or squatted on their haunches drawing little designs in the dirt and chewing tobacco or rolling cigarettes from cans of Prince Albert. And everywhere there were mules, mules in stables or running loose in the lot or being led about on halters through the bright air heavy with the smell of corn or hay. There were never any women at the mule barn. This was the place of fathers and brothers and uncles, a quintessentially male world, and for that very reason a place that was almost unbearably pleasant for a young boy who, although he did not know it, was learning the ways of manhood. There was a certain amount of kidding and joking and storytelling, but undergirding it all was the bedrock seriousness of trading mules.

In the same way that today the first thing a man trading for a car does is kick a tire, the first thing—and probably the last—that a man trading for a mule did was look in the mule's mouth. He was looking to see how old the animal was. A mule is born with a full set of teeth. When he is 2 years old he sheds two front teeth. They grow back rapidly, and the next year, around spring, he sheds again, one tooth on each side of where he shed before. Now he is 3 years old. Every year he sheds again, until he is 5 years old, the last year he sheds. After that, the depth of the little trenches in the top of his teeth determine the mule's age. Each year that passes, the trenches in the teeth are not quite as deep as they were the year before. And at about the age of 10 a mule is mostly smooth-mouthed, that is, the trenches have been entirely worn away from eating corn and salt and the sand that is invariably in hay. Past the age of 10 a mule starts to get buck-toothed, and a farmer can tell within a year how old he is by the angle of his front teeth.

After a mule is smooth-mouthed, the trenches can be put back in his teeth using a electric drill bit about as big as a match, or by using a hand file. The trenches are then stained with a substance that has as its base the juice of green walnut hulls. Every once in a while there would be some heated argument over whether or not a mule's teeth had been worked on, whether they had been altered or not. There would be a commotion, a flurry of movement, and the shouting of angry voices around a mule with a twist on his upper lip where men were examining his mouth.

"He's drilled, by damn. He's been drilled."

"Naw, he ain't. You'd rather climb a tree and tell a lie than stand on flat ground and tell the truth."

"If I'm lying, I'm flying. I can see, cain't I?"

"You eyes just gone bad on you. My grandma can see better than you can, and that poor old lady's been dead 20 year and more."

If the question of deception came up in the Alma mule barn, Major Eason was always the final arbiter. His reputation for honesty and his experience with mules was such that his decision was never questioned. If he found that the trenches had been put back in a mule's mouth, he would hunker down on his heels and have the mule led away from him so he could see how the mule tracked, see how smooth the action of his hindquarters was. Then he would look at the color of the mule's gums and tongue, inspect his hide and the configuration of his hooves. And if the mule had been misrepresented, he never hesitated to say so.

He would back off and examine the end of his cigarette for a minute and say, "It ain't ever been a trader that ain't been beat, and this mule beat me. He's 10 year old if he's a day."

And I would stand there and watch it all, not even understanding what I was learning. But there are worse ways for a boy to come to an understanding of what it is to be a man whose word is good, to be a man who will admit a mistake when he's made it, and who will instantly set it right.

But a boy could witness more at the mule barn than men trading honestly with one another. Major Eason had a donkey, rather unimaginatively named Jack, who infrequently stood at stud. The mules were only passing through The Alma Mule Company, but Jack lived there, and he was kept in a certain style. His stable was big and airy and always had good straw on the floor, a trough of fresh water, and a large salt block. He was bigger than most donkeys I've ever seen, and he had unusually long, finely-shaped legs and small hooves. Because of Jack's configuration, men throughout the county though that he sired a particularly fine mule, and mares were sometimes brought to him from great distances. The relative scarcity of mares, though, meant that Jack did not work very often.

But he did work on occasion, and on occasion I was there to see it. The fascination with the event had nothing to do with sex. As a boy who had spent his life on the farm, I was used to seeing animals couple, and it seemed as natural and right as breathing. The fascination was with Jack's manner. A donkey is in some danger of looking absurd beside a beautiful mare that may be three times bigger than he is. But not Jack. No king ever approached his queen's couch with greater dignity or delicacy than Jack approached a mare. She would be backed down into a shallow hole, and Jack would approach in a little prance that was at once finely measured—almost mincing—and utterly confident. He would raise his great head and, with his upper lip extended, breathing like a bellows, he would test and taste the air about the mare. And she, nervous, a little beside herself, would turn to look at him over her withers with nostrils flaring, flanks trembling, ready to bolt. But he would soothe her, calm her, and caress her with the gentlest little nips along her ribs with his great, strong teeth.

Although unable to articulate it at the time, even a boy could be struck by the mystery and beauty and essential rightness of the moment when life is created. And I am a better man for having been that boy who was privileged to witness that moment.

After a day in town staring at things that were wondrous strange to my country eyes, after the inevitable visit to uncle Major Eason's barn to listen to the talk of men, it was time to put the harness back on the mule and take the long, slow trip back to the farm curled on a quilt in the bed of the wagon sucking on a penny sugar-candy and dreaming of all that I had seen and heard. The wagon would be variously filled with sacks of grits and meal ground from the corn we had shucked, shelled, and brought with us, and filled too with the new smell of patterned cloth my mama would have traded for the eggs her hens had laid, and all the other marvelous booty of the trip to town.

As tired as I was, it would be my job to take care of the mule when we got home. I would take the traces loose from the singletree and hang them on the hames, walk the mule out of the shaves of the wagon, and lead him to the barn. After I hung the hames and collar on a wooden peg, I would take a currycomb down from another peg and curry the mule, combing away the sweated dust of the road before I watered and fed him and put him in the stable.

I'd be lying if I told you I would want to unharness and curry and water and feed a mule after a long trip today, but I would also be lying if I told you my life has not been diminished—diminished in a way too personal to name—by the mule having gone forever out of the South and out of my life.

Bruce Weber / The Unromantic Generation

New York Times Magazine, April 5, 1987

Today's young people face a world that differs in many respects from that of the previous generation. An increasing divorce rate, the fear of sexually transmitted diseases, the nuclear arms race, grim economic predictions, housing shortages, and altered sex roles have all helped shape attitudes that appear self-centered, cynical, careerist, unromantic. For the following article, Bruce Weber interviewed sixty people between the ages of twenty-two and twenty-six in order to discover how they viewed themselves, their careers, and their society.

An editor of the New York Times Magazine, *Weber has also edited an anthology of American short stories,* Look Who's Talking. *The* New York Times Magazine, *one of America's most influential magazines, appears weekly and, besides its regular columns, features timely articles on international, national, and local issues and personalities.*

Here is a contemporary love story.

Twenty-four-year-old Clark Wolfsberger, a native of St. Louis, and Kim Wright, 25, who is from Chicago (they are shown on the cover), live in Dallas. They've been going together since they met as students at Southern Methodist University three years ago. They are an attractive pair, trim and athletic, she dark and lissome, he broad-shouldered and square-jawed. They have jobs they took immediately after graduating—Clark works at Talent Sports International, a sports marketing and management company; Kim is an assistant account executive at Tracy-Locke, a large advertising agency—and they are in love.

"We're very compatible," she says.

"We don't need much time together to confirm our relationship," he says.

When they speak about the future, they hit the two-career family notes that are conventional now in the generations ahead of them. "At 30, I'll probably be married and planning a family," says Kim. "I'll stay in advertising. I'll be a late parent."

"By 30, I'll definitely be married; either that or water-skiing naked in Monaco," Clark says, and laughs. "No, I'll be married. Well-established in my line of work. Have the home, have the dog. Maybe not a kid yet, but eventually. I'm definitely in favor of kids."

In the month I spent last winter visiting several cities around the country, interviewing recent college graduates about marriage, relationships, modern romance, I heard a lot of this, life equations already written, doubt banished. I undertook the trip because of the impression so many of us have; that in one wavelike rush to business school and Wall Street, young Americans have succumbed to a culture of immediate gratification and gone deep-down elitist on us. I set out to test the image with an informal survey meant to take the emotional temperature of a generation, not far behind my own, that *seems* so cynical, so full of such "material" girls and boys.

The 60 or so people I interviewed, between the ages of 22 and 26, were a diverse group. They spoke in distinct voices, testifying to a range of political and social views. Graduate students, lawyers, teachers, entertainers, business people, they are pursuing a variety of interests. What they have in common is that they graduated from college, are living in or around an urban center and are heterosexual, mirrors of myself when I graduated from college in 1975. And yet as I moved from place to place, beginning with acquaintances of my friends and then randomly pursuing an expanding network of names and phone numbers, another quality emerged to the degree that I'd call it characteristic: they are planners. It was the one thing that surprised me, this looking ahead with certainty. They have priorities. I'd ask about love; they'd give me a graph.

This isn't how I remember it. Twelve years ago, who knew? I was three years away from my first full-time paycheck, six from anything resembling the job I have now. It was all sort of desultory and hopeful, a time of dabbling and waiting around for some event that would sprout a future. Frankly, I had it in mind that meeting a woman would do it.

My cultural prototype was Benjamin Braddock, the character played by Dustin Hoffman in Mike Nichols's 1967 film "The Graduate," who, returning home after his college triumphs finds the prospect of life after campus daunting in the extreme, and so plunges into inertia. His refrain "I'm just a little worried about my future," served me nicely as a sort of wryly understated mantra.

What hauls Benjamin from his torpor is love. Wisely or not, he responds to a force beyond logic and turns the world upside down for Elaine Robinson. And though in the end their future together is undermined, the message of the movie is that love is meant to triumph, that its passion and promise, however naïve, is its strength, and that if we are lucky it will seize us and transform our lives.

Today I'm still single and, chastened by that, I suppose, a little more rational about what to expect from love. Setting out on my trip, I felt as if I'd be plumbing a little of my past. But the people I spoke with reminded me more of the way I am now than the way I was then. I returned thinking that young people are older than they used to be, "The Graduate" is out of date, and for young people just out of college today, the belief that love is all you need no longer obtains.

"Kim's a great girl; I love her," Clark Wolfsberger says. "But she's very career-oriented. I am, too, and with our schedules the way they are, we haven't put any restrictions on each other. I think that's healthy."

"He might want to go back to St. Louis," Kim Wright says. "I want to go back to Chicago. If it works out, great. If not, that's fine, too. I can handle it either way."

They are not heartless, soulless, cold or unimaginative. They *are* self-preoccupied, but that's a quality, it seems to me, for which youthful generations have always been known. What distinguishes this generation from mine, I think, is that they're aware of it. News-conscious, media-smart, they are sophisticated in a way I was not.

They have come of age, of course, at a time when American social traditions barely survive. Since 1975, there have been more than a million divorces annually, and it is well publicized that nearly half of all marriages now end in divorce. Yet the era of condoned casual promiscuity and sexual experimentation—itself once an undermining of the nation's social fabric—now seems to be drawing to a close with the ever-spreading plague of sexually transmitted disease.

The achievements of feminist activism—particularly the infusion of women into the work force—have altered the expectations that the sexes have for each other and themselves.

And finally, the new college graduates have been weaned on scarifying forecasts of economic gloom. They feel housing problems already; according to *American Demographics* magazine, the proportion of young people living at home with their parents was higher in 1985 than in the last three censuses. They're aware, too, of predictions that however affluent they are themselves, they're probably better off than their children will be.

With all this in mind, today's graduates seem keenly aware that the future is bereft of conventional expectations, that what's ahead is more chaotic than mysterious. I've come to think it ironic that in a youth-minded culture such as ours, one that ostensibly grants greater freedom of choice to young people than it ever has before, those I spoke with seem largely restrained. Concerned with, if not consumed by, narrowing the options down, getting on track, they are aiming already at a distant comfort and security. I spoke, on my travels, with several college counselors and administrators, and they concur that the immediate concerns of today's graduates are more practical than those of their predecessors. "I talk to them about sex," says Gail Short Hanson, dean of students at George Washington University, in Washington. "I talk about careers. And marriage, with women, because of the balancing act they have to perform these days. But love? I can't remember the last conversation I had about love."

Career-minded, fiercely self-reliant, they responded to me, a single man with a good job, with an odd combination of comradeliness and respect. When the interviews were over, I fielded a lot of questions about what it's like to work at The New York Times. How did I get my job? Occasionally, someone would ask about my love life. Considering the subject of our discussions, I was surprised it happened so rarely. When it did, I told them I'd come reasonably close to marriage once, but it didn't work out. Nobody asked me why. Nobody asked if I was lonely.

Micah Materre, 25, recently completed an internship at CBS News in Chicago and is looking for a job in broadcast journalism. Like many of the young people I talked to, she is farsighted in her romantic outlook: "I went out with a guy last fall. He had a good job as a stockbroker. He was nice to me. But then he started telling me about his family. And there were problems. And I thought, 'What happens if I fall in love and we get married? What then?' "

It may be a memory lapse, but I don't recall thinking about marriage much at all until I fell in love. I was 29; late, that's agreed. But the point is that for me (and for my generation as a whole, I believe, though you hate to make a statement like that), marriage loomed only as an outgrowth of happenstance; you met a person. Today's graduates, however, seem uneasy with that kind of serendipity. All of the married couples I spoke with are delighted to be married, but they do say their friends questioned their judgment. "I heard a lot of reasons why I shouldn't do it," one recent bride told me. "Finally, I just said to myself, 'I feel happier than I've ever felt. Why should I give this up just because I'm young?' "

Most of them too young to remember the assassination of *either* Kennedy, they are old enough to have romantic pasts, to have experienced the trauma of failure in love. What surprised me was how easily so many of them accepted it; it seems a little early to be resigned to the idea that things fall apart. In each interview, I asked about past involvements. Were you ever serious about anyone? Any marital close calls? And virtually everyone had a story. But I heard very little about heartbreak or lingering grief. Instead, with an almost uniform equanimity, they spoke of maturity gained, lessons learned. It isn't disillusionment exactly, and they *are* too young to be weary; rather, it sounds like determination.

Twenty-five-year-old Peter Mundy of San Francisco, for example, says that until six months ago he'd had a series of steady girlfriends. "I'm down on romance," he says. "There's too much pain, too much pressure. There are so many variables, and you can't tell until you're in the middle of it whether it'll be positive. It's only in retrospect that you can see how things went wrong. In the meantime, you end up neglecting other things.''

The prevalent notion is that chemistry is untrustworthy; partners need to be up to snuff according to pretty rigorous standards. Ellen Lubin, 26, of Los Angeles, for example, has just gotten engaged to the man she has been living with for two years. When she met him, she says: ''I wasn't that attracted to him right away. But there were things about him that made me say, 'This is what I want in a man.' He's bright. He's a go-getter. He was making tons of money at the age of 25. He's well-connected. He was like my mentor in coming to deal with life in the city.''

At the end of ''The Graduate,'' Benjamin Braddock kidnaps his lady love at the altar, an instant after she has sealed her vows to someone else, and they manage to make their escape because Benjamin bolts the church door from the outside with a cross. That was the 1960's, vehement times. When I graduated, we were less obstreperous. Sacraments we could take or leave. And marriage wasn't much of an issue. If we put it off, it wasn't for the sake of symbolism so much as that it didn't seem necessary. In the last few years, I've been to a number of weddings among my contemporaries, people in their 30's, and that impression of us is still with me. What we did was drift toward marriage, arriving at it eventually, and with some surprise. Some of us are still drifting.

Today's graduates have forged a new attitude entirely. In spite of the high divorce rate, many of those I spoke with have marriage in mind. Overwhelmingly, they see it as not only desirable, but inevitable. Because of the odds, they approach it with wariness and pragmatism. More cautious than their parents (for American men in 1985, the median age at the time of their first marriage was 25.5, the highest since the turn of the century; it was 23.3 for women, a record), they are methodical in comparison with me.

Perhaps that explains why I find the way they speak about marriage so unromantic. Men and women tend to couch their views in different terms, but they seem to share the perception that marriage is necessarily restricting. Nonetheless they trust in its rewards, whatever they are. Overall, it doesn't represent the kind of commitment that seems viable without adequate preparation.

''I've been dating someone for a year and a half,'' says Tom Grossman, a 24-year-old graduate of the University of Texas. ''We don't talk about marriage, and frankly I don't think it'll occur.'' Currently area sales manager in San Antonio for the John H. Harland Company, a check-printing concern, Grossman says he has professional success in mind first. ''I want to be really well-off financially, and I don't want that struggle to interfere with the marriage. There are too many other stress factors involved. I want to be able to enjoy myself right away. And I never want to look back and think that if I hadn't gotten married, I could have accomplished more.''

Many young women say they responded with some alarm to last year's *Newsweek* report on the controversial demographic study conducted at Harvard, which concluded that once past 30, a woman faces rapidly dwindling chances of marrying. At a time when women graduates often feel it incumbent on them to pursue careers, they worry that the possibility of ''having it all'' is, in fact, remote.

Janie Russell, 25, graduated from the University of North Carolina in 1983, left a serious boyfriend behind and moved to Los Angeles to pursue a career in the film industry. Working now as a director of production services at New Visions Inc., like many other young women she believes the independence fostered by a career is necessary, not only for her own self-esteem but as a foundation for a future partnership. ''I look forward to marriage,'' she says. ''But this is a very selfish time for me. I have to have my career. I have to say to myself, 'I did this on my own.' It makes me feel more interesting than I would otherwise. Of course, what may happen is that I'll look up one day and say, 'O.K., husband, where are you?' And he won't be there.''

About halfway through my trip I stopped interviewing married couples because they tended to say similar things. They consider themselves the lucky ones. As 24-year-old Adam Cooper put it, at dinner with his wife, Melanee, also 24, in their Chicago apartment: ''The grass is not greener on the other side.''

I came away thinking it is as true as ever: All happy families are the same. But the couples I spoke with seemed to me part of a generation other than their own, older even than mine. Calling the Coopers to arrange an interview, I was invited for ''a good, home-cooked meal.''

The next day, I met Micah Materre, who expressed the prevailing contemporary stance as well as anyone. Outgoing and self-possessed, she gave me a long list of qualities she's looking for in a man: good looks, sense of humor, old-fashioned values, but also professional success, financial promise and a solid family background. ''Why not?'' she said. ''I deserve the best.'' But as I was folding up my notebook, she added a plaintive note: ''I'll get married, won't I? It's the American way, right?''

Very early on in my sexual experience I was flattered by a woman who told me she ordinarily wouldn't go to bed with men who were under 26. ''Until then,'' she said, ''all they're doing when they're with you is congratulating themselves.'' For whatever reason, she never returned my calls after that night. Not an untypical encounter, all in all. Congratulations to both of us.

We were a lusty, if callow, bunch, not least because we thought we could afford to be. Encouraged by the expansive social mores spawned by the sexual revolution, fortified by the advent of a widespread availability of birth control and fundamentally unaware of germs, we interpreted sex, for our convenience, as pure pleasure shared by ''consenting parties.'' If it feels good, do it. Remember that?

It is an attitude that the current generation inherited and put into practice at an early age. Asked about her circle of friends in Los Angeles, Lesley Bracker, 23, puts it nonchalantly: ''Oh, yeah, we were all sexually active as teen-agers. When we were younger, it was considered O.K. to sleep around.''

Now, however, they are reconsidering. In general, on this topic, I found them shy. They hesitate to speak openly about their sex lives, are prone to euphemism (''I'm not exactly out there, you know, mingling''), and say they worry about promiscuity only because they have friends who still practice it. According to Laura Kavesh and Cheryl Lavin, who write a column about single life, ''Tales from the Front,'' for the *Chicago Tribune* that is syndicated in some 60 other papers around the country, a letter from a reader about the virtues of virginity generated more supportive mail than anything that has appeared in the column in its two years of existence. I'm not about to say there's a new celibacy among the young, but my impression is that even if they've having twice as much sex as they say they're having, it's not as much as you would think.

The AIDS scare, of course, is of primary relevance. ''I talk about AIDS on first dates,'' says Jill Rotenberg, 25, publishing manager of a rare-book company in San Francisco. ''I talk about it all the time. I've spoken with the guy I'm dating about taking an AIDS test. Neither one of us is thrilled about condoms. But we use them. The first time we had sex, I was the one who had one in my wallet.''

Not everyone is so vehement. But seriously or jokingly, in earnest tête-à-tête or idly at dinner parties, they all talk about it. To some, the new concern is merely a source of disappointment. Several of the young people I spoke with express the sense of having been robbed. It's tough to find sex when you want it, tougher than it used to be, is the lament of many, mostly men. As it was put to me at one point, "I wish I'd been born 10 years earlier."

Jill Rotenberg says she feels betrayed: "I've had one long relationship in my life. He was my first lover, and for a long time my only one. So I feel I've had an untainted past. Now I feel I'm being punished anyway, even though I've been a good girl."

"I feel like I'm over the hurdle," says Douglas Ertman, 22, of San Francisco, who got engaged last summer. "I'm really lucky to know that I'll have one sexual partner forever."

Most agree that the solution is monogamy, at least on a temporary basis. "It's a coupled-up society," says Alan Forman, 26, a law student at George Washington University who, for the last several months, has been in a monogamous relationship. "Now more than ever. A lot of people I know are feeling the pressure to get hooked up with somebody."

I ask Forman and his girlfriend, 24-year-old Debra Golden, about their future together. They say they don't know ("I'm too insecure to make a decision like that," she says), and I get the sense they never talk about it. Then she turns to him, genuinely curious. "Say you break up with me and go to New York next year," she says.

"I don't know," he says. "If I meet someone and I like her, what do I have to do, ask her to take a blood test?"

A decade ago, one of the privileges that my contemporaries and I inferred from our sexual freedom was more or less to deny that there might be, in the sexual act, an innately implied emotional exchange. It's no longer feasible, however, to explain away sex as frivolity, inconsequential gratification. And that has complicated things for all of us, of course, whatever age, single or not.

But for young people, it's an issue, like marriage, that has been raised early: What does sex mean, if it doesn't mean nothing?

It's clearly a struggle for them. In one of my first interviews, 25-year-old Karl Wright of Chicago told me: "Maybe there's a silver lining in all this. Maybe AIDS will bring back romance." The more I think about that, the more chilling it gets.

Beverly Caro, a 25-year-old associate in the Dallas law firm of Gardere & Wynne, graduated from Drake University, in Des Moines, in 1983, and attended law school there as well. Her office high above the street looks out on the city's jungle of futuristic skyscrapers. She had offers from firms in Denver and her hometown of Kansas City, Mo., she says, but chose to come to Dallas because "I see upward mobility here; that's what I was looking for."

Ms. Caro has an attractive, thoughtful manner and a soft voice, but like many of her contemporaries, given the chance to discuss her personal goals, she speaks with a certitude that borders on defiance. Currently, she sees two men "somewhat regularly," she says. "I'd like to have a companion. A friend, I guess. But finding a man is not a top priority. I want to travel. I want to establish myself in the community. I don't see any drastic changes in my life by the time I turn 30. Except that I'll be a property owner."

During my interviews, the theme of getting on track and staying there surfaced again and again. I came to think of it as the currency of self-definition. As a generation, they are not a particularly well-polled group, but certain figures bear out my impression.

According to annual surveys of 300,000 college freshmen conducted by the Higher Education Research Institute at the Graduate School of Education of the University of California at Los Angeles, young people today, by the time they *enter* college, are more inclined to express concrete life objectives than they've been for many years. Of those surveyed last fall, 73.2 percent cited being "very well off financially" as an essential or very important objective. That's up from 63.3 percent in 1980, 49.5 percent in 1975. Other objectives that the survey shows have risen in importance include "obtain recognition from colleagues for contributions to my special field"; "have administrative responsibility for the work of others"; "be successful in my own business"; and "raise a family." At the same time, the percentage of freshmen who consider it important to "develop a meaningful philosophy of life" has declined from 64.2 percent in 1975 to 40.6 percent last year.

Many of the people I spoke to feel the pressure of peer scrutiny. A status thing has evolved, to which many seem to have regretfully succumbed. Several expressed a weariness with meeting someone new and having to present themselves by their credentials. Yet, overwhelmingly, asked what they're looking for in a romantic partner, they responded first with phrases such as "an educated professional" and "someone with direction." They've conceded, more or less consciously, that unenlightened and exclusionary as it is, it's very uncool not to know what you want and not to be already chasing it.

"Seems like everyone in our generation has to be out there achieving," says Scott Birnbaum, 25, who is the chief accountant for TIC United Corp., a holding company in Dallas.

Birnbaum graduated from the University of Texas in 1984, where, he says, "For me, the whole career-oriented thing kicked in." A native Texan with a broad drawl, he lives in the Greenville section of the city, an area populated largely by young singles. His apartment is comfortably roomy, not terribly well appointed. He shakes his head amiably as he points to the television set propped on a beer cooler. "What do I need furniture for?" he says. "Most of my time is taken up going to work."

Confident in himself professionally, Birnbaum was one of very few interviewees who spoke frankly about the personal cost of career success. Many speculated that they'll be worried if, in their 30's, they haven't begun to settle their love lives; this was more true of women than men. But Birnbaum confesses a desire to marry now. "It's kind of lonely being single," he says. "I'd hate to find myself successful at 30 without a family. Maybe once I'm married and have children, that might make being successful career-wise less important."

The problem, he goes on, is the collective outlook he's part and parcel of. "Here's how we think," he says. "Get to this point, move on. Get to that point, move on. Acquire, acquire. Career, career. We're all afraid to slow down for fear of missing out on something. That extends to your social life as well. You go out on a date and you're thinking, 'Hell, is there someone better for me?' I know how terrible that sounds but it seems to be my problem. Most of my peers are in the same position. Men and women. I tell you, it's tough out there right now."

When I returned to New York, I called Alex de Gramont, whom I'd been saving to interview last. I've known Alex for a long time, since he was a gawky and curious high school student and I was his teacher. Handsome now, gentle-looking, he's a literary sort, prone to attractive gloom and a certain lack of perspective. He once told me that his paradigm of a romantic, his role model, was Heathcliff, the mad, doomed passion-monger from Emily Brontë's "Wuthering Heights."

A year out of Wesleyan University in Middletown, Conn., Alex has reasons to be hopeful. His book-length senior thesis about Albert Camus has been accepted for publication, and on the strength of it, he has applied to four graduate programs in comparative lieterature. But he's unenthuastic, and he has applied to law schools, too. In the meantime, he is living with his parents in New Jersey.

He tells me that last summer he went to West Germany in pursuit of a woman he'd met when he was in college. He expected to live there with her, but he was back in this country in a couple of weeks. "Camus has a line," Alex says, " 'Love can burn or love can last. It can't do both.' " Like Benjamin Braddock, Alex is a little worried about his future.

Dustin Hoffman is 49. I'm 33. Both of us are doing pretty well. Alex, at 23, confesses to considerable unease. "Every minute I'm not accomplishing something, I feel is wasted," he says, sort of miserably. "I feel a lot of pressure to decide what to do with my life. I'm a romantic, but these are very unromantic times."

DISCUSSION QUESTIONS

1. Who does Weber include in the "unromantic generation"? Is he a member himself? What types of people does he interview? Do any types seem to be missing? How representative do you find his sample? Explain.

2. Read Weber's article in connection with Laurence Shames's "Yikes! Business Superstars!" Where do you think the "unromantic generation" stands with respect to contemporary business values?

BEST-SELLERS

I concluded at length that the People were the best Judges of my Merit; for they buy my Works . . .

BENJAMIN FRANKLIN

F EW scenes in best-selling fiction can compare with the one from *Tarzan of the Apes* (1914) in which Tarzan, the son of a shipwrecked British aristocrat, raised from infancy by a tribe of apes in the African jungle, rescues Jane, the comely daughter of an American professor, from the evil clutches of the cruel and capricious ape-king Terkoz:

> Jane—her lithe, young form flattened against the trunk of a great tree, her hands tight pressed against her rising and falling bosom, and her eyes wide with mingled horror, fascination, fear, and admiration— watched the primordial ape battle with the primeval man for possession of a woman—for her.
>
> As the great muscles of the man's back and shoulders knotted beneath the tension of his efforts, and the huge biceps and forearm held at bay those mighty tusks, the veil of centuries of civilization and culture was swept from the blurred vision of the Baltimore girl.

Passion, violence, vengeance, and a melodramatic rescue—the passage is a paradigm of popular fiction.

After killing Terkoz, Tarzan carries off the reluctantly yielding Jane "deeper and deeper into the savage fastness of the untamed forest" to the security of his bower of bliss. What does he do when they get there?

> Tarzan had long since reached a decision as to what his future procedure should be. He had had time to recollect all that he had read of the ways of men and women in the books at the cabin. He would act as he imagined the men in the books would have acted were they in his place.

Apparently, even a situation so geographically and imaginatively far-fetched as that depicting an ape-man entertaining a captivating young woman from Baltimore cannot be entirely free from the guidance, if not the directions, of literature. In a moment obviously more threatening for him than any of his daily adventures in the uncharted jungle, Tarzan can offer no instinctive, spontaneous response. Instead, the "natural" man rescues himself by ponderously turning to the lessons of fiction. Though Tarzan does not tell us what books he had in his cabin library, he will undoubtedly model his future social behavior on the same late-nineteenth-century popular romances from which his creator, Edgar Rice Burroughs, derived his literary style.

Burroughs, like most best-selling novelists, knew what a reading public wanted. In the Tarzan books he satisfied a contemporary interest in imperialistic adventures and a psychological need for violent, bestial conflicts. A large part of his continuing success is attributable also to his grasp of a fundamental mythic element—that the popular masculine ideal of the twentieth century would be a sensitive brute, a natural aristocrat, a killer with a tender heart. As a type of masculine hero, Tarzan is intended to be not only alluringly primitive (a "woodland demi-god") but also the kind of man that heroines of American fiction have conventionally desired—a cultivated gentleman, preferably a foreign aristocrat.

The image—with variations, of course—dominates twentieth-century popular fiction and advertising. Michael Rossi, the hero of Grace Metalious's *Peyton Place* (1956), is "a massive boned man with muscles that seemed to quiver every time he moved. . . . His arms, beneath sleeves rolled above the elbow, were knotted powerfully, and the buttons of his work shirts always seemed about to pop off under the strain of trying to cover his chest." Though built like Tarzan, Michael Rossi is not going to wrestle wild beasts. Instead, he arrives in Peyton Place a stranger about to take on the job of headmaster at the local high school, for he "had a mind as analytical as a mathematician's and as curious as a philosopher's."

Styles and idioms may change (though in these passages it may not seem so), but a successful formula for fiction is hard to let go of.

Not all best-sellers, of course, are so masculinely aggressive, though even a predominately sentimental book like Harriet Beecher Stowe's *Uncle Tom's Cabin* (1852) contains its whip-wielding Simon Legree. Moreover, *Tarzan of the Apes* and *Peyton Place,* for all their self-conscious primitivsm and casual disregard for "centuries of civilization and culture," never really stray very far from the unassailable proprieties and the cozy gentility to which their authors and readers finally subscribe. At the end of *Peyton Place,* Michael Rossi is a vigorous, comfortable, middle-aged married man. And the final scene in *Tarzan of the Apes* finds an educated, love-lorn "demi-god" in conversation at a train station in Wisconsin: " 'I am Monsieur Tarzan,' said the ape-man."

One reason readers respond so positively to a best-selling novel is that it invariably reaffirms in easily accessible language its audience's attitudes, values, and collective fantasies and identifies reassuringly with its anxieties. Novels such as *Tarzan of the Apes* and *Peyton Place* become best-sellers, then, because, along with excursions into fantasy, they return to what are essentially nonnegotiable domestic standards. In that sense they resemble many other American best-sellers that have insisted on the inviolability of family bonds. Consider, for instance, the best-seller by Mario Puzo, *The Godfather* (1969), in which a world of official corruption, blurred loyalties, and misdirected justice is contrasted with a closely knit patriarchal "family" carrying out its obligations and vendettas in a style that ensures the dignity and personal honor of all its members. Another best-seller, *Uncle Tom's Cabin,* fiercely opposes the institution of slavery, not entirely on political or legal grounds but because it mercilessly breaks up the home by separating children from their parents, husbands from their wives.

Best-selling nonfiction also corroborates its readers' collective values. Many very successful volumes of nonfiction have taken the form of ready-reference compilations of practical advice. Dale Carnegie's *How to Win Friends and Influence People* (1936), Wilfred Funk and Norman Lewis's *Thirty Days to a More Powerful Vocabulary* (1942), and Benjamin Spock's *The Common Sense Book of Baby Care* (1946) exemplify the kinds of self-improvement and "how-to-do-it" books that offer their readers guidance that will presumably help them deal successfully with their feelings of ineptitude, confusion, and inferiority and reaffirm their yearnings for an uncomplicated life. Most best-sellers offer their characters, and vicariously their readers, a way out of public and private dilemmas by providing them with the possibilities of wealth, sexual gratification, justice or vengeance, romance and adventure, a hard-won optimistic philosophy, or a return to traditional loyalties and uncomplicated codes of behavior.

Like advertisements, newspapers, and magazines, best-sellers are frequently written in response to the pressures of contemporary events, issues, and tastes. They capitalize on the public's interests. Some best-selling authors "hit on" or invent something (practical advice for self-improvement, a timely exposé, or an extraordinary private eye) that many people want to read about. Others design their books to attract readers predisposed to certain kinds of material by news coverage and magazine articles. Stowe, a dedicated abolitionist, recognized that the much debated issue of slavery, or, more precisely, the Fugitive Slave Law, was a suitable subject for fiction and wrote what became America's first major best-selling novel. The enormous popularity of Puzo's *The Godfather,* one of the fastest-selling novels in the history of American publishing, can be partly explained by pointing to a reading public fascinated by the news coverage of the personalities, stratagems, and violence of organized crime.

Yet books like *Uncle Tom's Cabin* and *The Godfather* did not become best-sellers merely because of their responsiveness to newsworthy public events. If readers were interested only in the events or issues detailed in these books, they could have satisfied that need more easily and less expensively by reading newspapers and magazines. But these best-sellers, like many of the others included here, offer readers something more than reportage or polemics; they combine an awareness of topical subjects with the conventions and techniques of fiction. Readers can feel that they are learning about the management of the slave trade in the South or the operations of organized crime while at the same time being entertained by the invented characters, situations, and plots that give factual information the shape of fiction.

The excerpts from best-sellers appearing in this section are meant to characterize the kinds of writing that millions of readers have found and still find informative, entertaining, or both.[1] Perhaps the best way to read the following passages is to imagine yourself in a role opposite that of an editor who examines a piece of writing to try to decide whether it will be commercially successful. Instead, you have material that has been demonstrably successful, and you want to try to account for that success. What is it about the *writing* that has made it so popular? To what extent is the book's success attributable to the quality of its prose? To the types of characters rendered? To the kinds of themes dramatized? To the information proposed? To the particular psychological, social, or political issues involved? These and similar questions can, of course, be asked about any literary work, popular or unpopular, significant or insignificant. But because a best-seller attracts such a large audience, the answers to questions about its compositional strategies and its overall verbal performance suggest a great deal about the nature of popular writing and the characteristics of the people who read it.

You are being invited to look closely at the following selections from what might be called a socio-aesthetic point of view. That is, you are being asked to infer from the distinctive features of the author's prose the kind of people he or she expects will attend to his or her writing. By doing so, you will establish the identity of the book's "ideal reader"—the type of person you imagine the writer would feel most comfortable talking to. You will have also constructed a criterion against which you can measure your own response to the work. Whatever your final judgment about the relative worth of the material you have read, your criticism will be more attuned to the particular verbal characteristics of the work the more carefully you can determine how *you,* as the reader and individual you imagine yourself to be, are taken into account by the author's act of writing.

The audience presupposed by the author's style can become, if the book is a best-seller, the critical justification of his or her creative efforts. Mickey Spillane, author of the extraordinarily successful Mike Hammer detective novels, made this point clear when asked in an interview what he thought of the literary criticism of his fiction: "The public is the only critic. And the only *literature* is what the public reads. The first printing of my last book was more than two million copies—that's the kind of opinion that interests me." This tough talk is characteristic of Spillane's literary manner. It is a style he worked out before he became a celebrity, so his assurance is not necessarily the result of his having sold more than seventy-five million copies of his novels. In fact, the Spillane we hear speaking as a professional writer in the interview quoted above is most likely being playfully imitative of the Spillane who talks to us in the guise of his detective-narrator, Mike Hammer, in the following passage from *I, the Jury* (1947):

---

1. Margaret Mitchell's *Gone with the Wind,* one of America's most important best-selling novels, has been omitted because the author's estate refuses to allow the book to be excerpted.

> I said no more. I just sat there and glowered at the wall. Someday I'd trig-
> ger the bastard that shot Jack. In my time I've done it plenty of times. No
> sentiment. That went out with the first. After the war I've been almost
> anxious to get to some of the rats that make up the section of humanity
> that prey on people. People. How incredibly stupid they could be some-
> times. A trial by law for a killer. A loophole in the phrasing that lets a kil-
> ler crawl out. But in the end the people have their justice. They get it
> through guys like me once in a while. They crack down on society and I
> crack down on them. I shoot them like the mad dogs they are and society
> drags me to court to explain the whys and wherefores of the extermi-
> nation. They investigate my past, check my fingerprints and throw a
> million questions my way. The papers make me look like a kill-crazy
> shamus, but they don't bear down too hard because Pat Chambers [Ham-
> mer's police detective friend] keeps them off my neck. Besides, I do my
> best to help the boys out and they know it. And I'm usually good for a
> story when I wind up a case.

In this angry interior monologue, Hammer does not talk to himself any differently from the way he talks to anyone else in the novel. This is his characteristic voice: tough, vindictive, self-assured. It is the voice of a man (rarely do
women talk like this in fiction) who refuses to mince his words, who thinks that
a more complicated way of talking would invariably associate him with the legalistic language that permits those loopholes through which killers are allowed
to escape justice.

The language in this passage carries with it an authority that would gratify those
readers who feel that their own lives are helplessly trapped in bureaucratic laby-
rinths and compromising civilities and who consequently seldom, if ever, have the
occasion to talk to anybody the way Mike Hammer does. If Hammer recognizes in this passage that he is forced occasionally to make concessions to the
police, the courts, and the press, he does so without compromising his role as a
self-appointed arbiter of social justice. He does so also without ever having to modify unwillingly his deliberately aggressive, hard-boiled tone to suit the different
types of characters he is obliged to confront. Hammer's is a voice that never interrupts itself to reconsider what it has said. It is a language without hesitations or unnecessary qualifications.

Hammer's style disassociates him from the official language of law enforcement,
a language traditionally dependent on a complicated system of qualifications and
constraints. By taking the law into his own hands, Hammer essentially transforms
the law into his own language. If, as the self-assertion of the title indicates, Hammer *is* the jury, then he symbolically embodies the "People," whose expectations
of justice he considers it is his mission in life to fulfill. The overwhelming public
approval that Spillane confidently refers to as the most legitimate criticism of his
fiction has been anticipated in the public approbation he has allowed his most
successful character to take for granted.

It is not unusual for best-selling authors to find a confirmation of their talent
in sales figures. Stowe, an author whose literary intentions differ radically from
Spillane's and who would have been offended even by his idiom, acknowledged
her enthusiasm for the public's approval of America's first major best-selling
novel in terms Spillane would surely understand. Writing in the third person for
an introduction to one of the many editions of *Uncle Tom's Cabin,* she remarks:

> The despondency of the author as to the question whether anybody would
> read or attend to her appeal was soon dispelled. Ten thousand copies
> were sold in a few days, and over three hundred thousand within a year;
> and eight power-presses, running day and night, were barely able to keep
> pace with the demand for it. It was read everywhere, apparently, and by
> everybody; and she soon began to hear echoes of sympathy all over the

land. The indignation, the pity, the distress, that had long weighed upon her soul seemed to pass off from her into the readers of the book.

It would be difficult to find a more apt description of the merger of writer and reader in the collective enterprise that makes a book a best-seller.

Harriet Beecher Stowe / *Uncle Tom's Cabin*   1852

The daughter of a New England Congregational pastor, Harriet Beecher Stowe (1811–96) moved to Cincinnati when her father was appointed head of the Lane Theological Seminary. She began writing sketches for magazines, but after her marriage to Calvin Ellis Stowe, a professor of biblical literature at her father's seminary, she abandoned the idea of a literary career. At the time, Lane Theological Seminary was a center of antislavery sentiment. In this environment, and also through occasional visits to the slave state of Kentucky, Stowe gradually formed the abolitionist opinions that were given full expression in Uncle Tom's Cabin. *After a successful serialization in a Washington, D.C., antislavery weekly,* The National Era, *the novel was brought out in two volumes in 1852. It was a momentous publishing event: three hundred thousand copies were sold in the first year, and by 1856 the sales in England alone were well over a million. Translations were worldwide. Stowe, then living in Brunswick, Maine, where her husband had a teaching position at Bowdoin, found herself the most famous literary figure in America and an international celebrity. Though she continued to write (averaging nearly a book a year for the next thirty years), none of her later novels ever attained the success of her first.*

SELECT INCIDENT OF LAWFUL TRADE

> *"In Ramah there was a voice heard,—weeping, and lamentation, and great mourning; Rachel weeping for her children, and would not be comforted."*
>
> —Jeremiah, 31:15

Mr. Haley and Tom jogged onward in their wagon, each, for a time, absorbed in his own reflections. Now, the reflections of two men sitting side by side are a curious thing,—seated on the same seat, having the same eyes, ears, hands and organs of all sorts, and having pass before their eyes the same objects,—it is wonderful what a variety we shall find in these same reflections!

As, for example, Mr. Haley: he thought first of Tom's length, and breadth, and height, and what he would sell for, if he was kept fat and in good case till he got him into market. He thought of how he should make out his gang; he thought of the respective market value of certain supposititious men and women and children who were to compose it, and other kindred topics of the business; then he thought of himself, and how humane he was, that whereas other men chained their "niggers" hand and foot both, he only put fetters on the feet, and left Tom the use of his hands, as long as he behaved well; and he sighed to think how ungrateful human nature was, so that there was even room to doubt whether Tom appreciated his mercies. He had been taken in so by "niggers" whom he had favored; but still he was astonished to consider how good-natured he yet remained!

As to Tom, he was thinking over some words of an unfashionable old book, which kept running through his head, again and again, as follows: "We have here no continuing city, but we seek one to come; wherefore God himself is not ashamed to be called our God; for he hath prepared for us a city.'' These words of an ancient volume, got up principally by ''ignorant and unlearned men,'' have, through all time, kept up, somehow, a strange sort of power over the minds of poor, simple fellows, like Tom. They stir up the soul from its depths, and rouse, as with trumpet call, courage, energy, and enthusiasm, where before was only the blackness of despair.

Mr. Haley pulled out of his pocket sundry newspapers, and began looking over their advertisements, with absorbed interest. He was not a remarkably fluent reader, and was in the habit of reading in a sort of recitative half-aloud, by way of calling in his ears to verify the deductions of his eyes. In this tone he slowly recited the following paragraph:

''EXECUTOR'S SALE,—NEGROES!—*Agreeably to order of court, will be sold, on Tuesday, February 20, before the Court-house door, in the town of Washington, Kentucky, the following negroes: Hagar, aged 60; John, aged 30; Ben, aged 21; Saul, aged 25; Albert, aged 14. Sold for the benefit of the creditors and heirs of the estate of Jesse Blutchford, Esq.*

SAMUEL MORRIS,
THOMAS FLINT,
Executors''

''This yer I must look at,'' said he to Tom, for want of somebody else to talk to.

''Ye see, I'm going to get up a prime gang to take down with ye, Tom; it'll make it sociable and pleasant like,—good company will, ye know. We must drive right to Washington first and foremost, and then I'll clap you into jail, while I does the business.''

Tom received this agreeable intelligence quite meekly; simply wondering, in his own heart, how many of these doomed men had wives and children, and whether they would feel as he did about leaving them. It is to be confessed, too, that the naïve, off-hand information that he was to be thrown into jail by no means produced an agreeable impression on a poor fellow who had always prided himself on a strictly honest and upright course of life. Yes, Tom, we must confess it, was rather proud of his honesty, poor fellow,—not having very much else to be proud of;—if he had belonged to some of the higher walks of society, he, perhaps, would never have been reduced to such straits. However, the day wore on, and the evening saw Haley and Tom comfortably accommodated in Washington,—the one in a tavern, and the other in a jail.

About eleven o'clock the next day, a mixed throng was gathered around the court-house steps,—smoking, chewing, spitting, swearing, and conversing, according to their respective tastes and turns,—waiting for the auction to commence. The men and women to be sold sat in a group apart, talking in a low tone to each other. The woman who had been advertised by the name of Hagar was a regular African in feature and figure. She might have been sixty, but was older than that by hard work and disease, was partially blind, and somewhat crippled with rheumatism. By her side stood her only remaining son, Albert, a bright-looking little fellow of fourteen years. The boy was the only survivor of a large family, who had been successively sold away from her to a southern market. The mother held on to him with both her shaking hands, and eyed with intense trepidation every one who walked up to examine him.

''Don't be feared, Aunt Hagar,'' said the oldest of the men, ''I spoke to Mas'r Thomas 'bout it, and he thought he might manage to sell you in a lot both together.''

''Dey needn't call me worn out yet,'' said she, lifting her shaking hands. ''I can cook yet, and scrub, and scour,—I'm wuth a buying, if I come cheap;—tell em dat ar,—you *tell* em,'' she added, earnestly.

Haley here forced his way into the group, walked up to the old man, pulled his mouth open and looked in, felt of his teeth, made him stand and straighten himself, bend his back, and perform various evolutions to show his muscles; and then passed on to the next, and put him through the same trial. Walking up last to the boy, he felt of his arms, straightened his hands, and looked at his fingers, and made him jump, to show his agility.

"He an't gwine to be sold widout me!" said the old woman, with passionate eagerness; "he and I goes in a lot together; I 's rail strong yet, Mas'r and can do heaps o' work,—heaps on it, Mas'r."

"On plantation?" said Haley, with a contemptuous glance. "Likely story!" and, as if satisfied with his examination, he walked out and looked, and stood with his hands in his pocket, his cigar in his mouth, and his hat cocked on one side, ready for action.

"What think of 'em?" said a man who had been following Haley's examination, as if to make up his own mind from it.

"Wal," said Haley, spitting, "I shall put in, I think, for the youngerly ones and the boy."

"They want to sell the boy and the old woman together," said the man.

"Find it a tight pull;—why, she's an old rack o'bones,—not worth her salt."

"You wouldn't then?" said the man.

"Anybody 'd be a fool 't would. She's half blind, crooked with rheumatis, and foolish to boot."

"Some buys up these yer old critturs, and ses there's a sight more wear in 'em than a body 'd think," said the man, reflectively.

"No go, 't all," said Haley; "wouldn't take her for a present,—fact,—I've *seen,* now."

"Wal, 't is kinder pity, now, not to buy her with her son,—her heart seems so sot on him,—s'pose they fling her in cheap."

"Them that's got money to spend that ar way, it's all well enough. I shall bid off on that ar boy for a plantation-hand;—wouldn't be bothered with her, no way,—not if they'd give her to me," said Haley.

"'She'll take on desp't," said the man.

"Nat'lly, she will," said the trader, coolly.

The conversation was here interrupted by a busy hum in the audience; and the auctioneer, a short, bustling, important fellow, elbowed his way into the crowd. The old woman drew in her breath, and caught instinctively at her son.

"Keep close to yer mammy, Albert,—close,—dey'll put us up togedder," she said.

"O, mammy, I'm feard they won't," said the boy.

"Dey must, child; I can't live, no ways, if they don't," said the old creature, vehemently.

The stentorian tones of the auctioneer, calling out to clear the way, now announced that the sale was about to commence. A place was cleared, and the bidding began. The different men on the list were soon knocked off at prices which showed a pretty brisk demand in the market; two of them fell to Haley.

"Come, now, young un," said the auctioneer, giving the boy a touch with his hammer, "be up and show your springs, now."

"Put us two up togedder, togedder,—do please, Mas'r," said the old woman, holding fast to her boy.

"Be off," said the man, gruffly, pushing her hands away; "you come last. Now, darkey, spring;" and, with the word, he pushed the boy toward the block, while a deep, heavy groan rose behind him. The boy paused, and looked back; but there was no time to stay, and dashing the tears from his large, bright eyes, he was up in a moment.

His fine figure, alert limbs, and bright face, raised an instant competition, and half a dozen bids simultaneously met the ear of the auctioneer. Anxious, half-frightened, he looked from side to side, as he heard the clatter of contending bids,—now here, now there,—till the hammer fell. Haley had got him. He was pushed from the block toward his new master, but stopped one moment, and looked back, when his poor old mother, trembling in every limb, held out her shaking hands toward him.

"Buy me too, Mas'r, for de dear Lord's sake!—buy me,—I shall die if you don't!"

"You'll die if I do, that's the kink of it," said Haley,—"no!" And he turned on his heel.

The bidding for the poor old creature was summary. The man who had addressed Haley, and who seemed not destitute of compassion, bought her for a trifle, and the spectators began to disperse.

The poor victims of the sale, who had been brought up in one place together for years, gathered round the despairing old mother, whose agony was pitiful to see.

"Couldn't dey leave me one? Mas'r allers said I should have one,—he did," she repeated over and over, in heart-broken tones.

"Trust in the Lord, Aunt Hagar," said the oldest of the men, sorrowfully.

"What good will it do?" said she, sobbing passionately.

"Mother, mother,—don't! don't!" said the boy. "They say you's got a good master."

"I don't care—I don't care. O, Albert! oh, my boy! you's my last baby. Lord, how ken I?"

"Come, take her off, can't some of ye?" said Haley, dryly; "don't do no good for her to go on that ar way."

The old men of the company, partly by persuasion and partly by force, loosed the poor creature's last despairing hold, and, as they led her off to her new master's wagon, strove to comfort her.

"Now!" said Haley, pushing his three purchases together, and producing a bundle of handcuffs, which he proceeded to put on their wrists; and fastening each handcuff to a long chain, he drove them before him to the jail.

A few days saw Haley, with his possessions, safely deposited on one of the Ohio boats. It was the commencement of his gang, to be augmented, as the boat moved on, by various other merchandise of the same kind, which he, or his agent, had stored for him in various points along shore.

The La Belle Rivière, as brave and beautiful a boat as ever walked the waters of her namesake river, was floating gayly down the stream, under a brilliant sky, the stripes and stars of free America waving and fluttering over head; the guards crowded with well-dressed ladies and gentlemen walking and enjoying the delightful day. All was full of life, buoyant and rejoicing;—all but Haley's gang, who were stored, with other freight, on the lower deck, and who, somehow, did not seem to appreciate their various privileges, as they sat in a knot, talking to each other in low tones.

"Boys," said Haley, coming up, briskly, "I hope you keep up good heart, and are cheerful. Now, no sulks, ye see; keep stiff upper lip, boys; do well by me, and I'll do well by you."

The boys addressed responded the invariable "Yes, Mas'r," for ages the watchword of poor Africa; but it's to be owned they did not look particularly cheerful; they had their various little prejudices in favor of wives, mothers, sisters, and children, seen for the last time,—and though "they that wasted them required of them mirth," it was not instantly forthcoming.

"I've got a wife," spoke out the article enumerated as "John, aged thirty," and he laid his chained hand on Tom's knee,—"and she don't know a word about this, poor girl!"

"Where does she live?" said Tom.

"In a tavern a piece down here," said John; "I wish, now, I *could* see her once more in this world," he added.

Poor John! It *was* rather natural; and the tears that fell, as he spoke, came as naturally as if he had been a white man. Tom drew a long breath from a sore heart, and tried, in his poor way, to comfort him.

And over head, in the cabin, sat fathers and mothers, husbands and wives; and merry, dancing children moved round among them, like so many little butterflies, and everything was going on quite easy and comfortable.

"O, mamma," said a boy, who had just come up from below, "there's a negro trader on board, and he's brought four or five slaves down there."

"Poor creatures!" said the mother, in a tone between grief and indignation.

"What's that?" said another lady.

"Some poor slaves below," said the mother.

"And they've got chains on," said the boy.

"What a shame to our country that such sights are to be seen!" said another lady.

"O, there's a great deal to be said on both sides of the subject," said a genteel woman, who sat at her state-room door sewing, while her little girl and boy were playing round her. "I've been south, and I must say I think the negroes are better off than they would be to be free."

"In some respects, some of them are well off, I grant," said the lady to whose remark she had answered. "The most dreadful part of slavery, to my mind, is its outrages on the feelings and affections,—the separating of families, for example."

"That *is* a bad thing, certainly," said the other lady, holding up a baby's dress she had just completed, and looking intently on its trimmings; "but then, I fancy, it don't occur often."

"O, it does," said the first lady, eagerly; "I've lived many years in Kentucky and Virginia both, and I've seen enough to make any one's heart sick. Suppose, ma'am, your two children, there, should be taken from you, and sold?"

"We can't reason from our feelings to those of this class of persons," said the other lady, sorting out some worsteds on her lap.

"Indeed, ma'am, you can know nothing of them, if you say so," answered the first lady, warmly. "I was born and brought up among them. I know they *do* feel, just as keenly,—even more so, perhaps,—as we do."

The lady said "Indeed!" yawned, and looked out the cabin window, and finally repeated, for a finale, the remark with which she had begun,—"After all, I think they are better off than they would be to be free."

"It's undoubtedly the intention of Providence that the African race should be servants,—kept in a low condition," said a grave-looking gentleman in black, a clergyman, seated by the cabin door. " 'Cursed be Canaan; a servant of servants shall he be,' the Scripture says."

"I say, stranger, is that ar what that text means?" said a tall man, standing by.

"Undoubtedly. It pleased Providence, for some inscrutable reason, to doom the race to bondage, ages ago; and we must not set up our opinion against that."

"Well, then, we'll all go ahead and buy up niggers," said the man, "if that's the way of Providence,—won't we, Squire?" said he, turning to Haley, who had been standing, with his hands in his pockets, by the stove and intently listening to the conversation.

"Yes," continued the tall man, "we must all be resigned to the decrees of Providence. Niggers must be sold, and trucked round, and kept under; it's what they's made for. 'Pears like this yer view 's quite refreshing, ain't it, stranger?" said he to Haley.

"I never thought on 't," said Haley. "I couldn't have said as much, myself; I ha'nt no larning. I took up the trade just to make a living; if 'tan't right, I calculated to 'pent on 't in time, *ye* know."

"And now you'll save yerself the trouble, won't ye?" said the tall man. "See what 't is, now, to know scripture. If ye'd only studied yer Bible, like this yer good man, ye might have know'd it before, and saved ye a heap o' trouble. Ye could jist have said, 'Cussed be'—what's his name?—'and 't would all have come right.' " And the stranger, who was no other than the honest drover whom we introduced to our readers in the Kentucky tavern, sat down, and began smoking, with a curious smile on his long, dry face.

A tall, slender young man, with a face expressive of great feeling and intelligence, here broke in, and repeated the words, " 'All things whatsoever ye would that men should do unto you, do ye even so unto them.' I suppose," he added, "*that* is scripture, as much as 'Cursed be Canaan.' "

"Wal, it seems quite *as* plain a text, stranger," said John the drover, "to poor fellows like us, now;" and John smoked on like a volcano.

The young man paused, looked as if he was going to say more, when suddenly the boat stopped, and the company made the usual steamboat rush, to see where they were landing.

"Both them ar chaps parsons?" said John to one of the men, as they were going out.

The man nodded.

As the boat stopped, a black woman came running wildly up the plank, darted into the crowd, flew up to where the slave gang sat, and threw her arms round that unfortunate piece of merchandise before enumerated—"John, aged thirty," and with sobs and tears bemoaned him as her husband.

But what needs tell the story, told too oft,—every day told,—of heart-strings rent and broken,—the weak broken and torn for the profit and convenience of the strong! It needs not to be told;—every day is telling it,—telling it, too, in the ear of One who is not deaf, though he be long silent.

The young man who had spoken for the cause of humanity and God before stood with folded arms, looking on this scene. He turned, and Haley was standing at his side. "My friend," he said, speaking with thick utterance, "how can you, how dare you, carry on a trade like this? Look at those poor creatures! Here I am, rejoicing in my heart that I am going home to my wife and child; and the same bell which is a signal to carry me onward towards them will part this poor man and his wife forever. Depend upon it, God will bring you into judgment for this."

The trader turned away in silence.

"I say, now," said the drover, touching his elbow, "there's differences in parsons, an't there? 'Cussed be Cannan' don't seem to go down with this 'un, does it?"

Haley gave an uneasy growl.

"And that ar an't the worst on 't," said John; "mabbee it won't go down with the Lord, neither, when ye come to settle with Him, one o' these days, as all on us must, I reckon."

Haley walked reflectively to the other end of the boat.

"If I make pretty handsomely on one or two next gangs," he thought, "I reckon I'll stop off this yer; it's really getting dangerous." And he took out his pocketbook, and began adding over his accounts,—a process which many gentlemen besides Mr. Haley have found a specific for an uneasy conscience.

The boat swept proudly away from the shore, and all went on merrily, as before. Men talked, and loafed, and read, and smoked. Women sewed, and children played, and the boat passed on her way.

One day, when she lay to for a while at a small town in Kentucky, Haley went up into the place on a little matter of business.

Tom, whose fetters did not prevent his taking a moderate circuit, had drawn near the side of the boat, and stood listlessly gazing over the railing. After a time, he saw the trader returning, with an alert step, in company with a colored woman, bearing in her arms a young child. She was dressed quite respectably, and a colored man followed her, bringing along a small trunk. The woman came cheerfully onward, talking, as she came, with the man who bore her trunk, and so passed up the plank into the boat. The bell rung, the steamer whizzed, the engine groaned and coughed, and away swept the boat down the river.

The woman walked forward among the boxes and bales of the lower deck, and, sitting down, busied herself with chirruping to her baby.

Haley made a turn or two about the boat, and then, coming up, seated himself near her, and began saying something to her in an indifferent undertone.

Tom soon noticed a heavy cloud passing over the woman's brow; and that she answered rapidly, and with great vehemence.

"I don't believe it,—I won't believe it!" he heard her say. "You're jist a foolin with me."

"If you won't believe it, look here!" said the man, drawing out a paper; "this yer 's the bill of sale, and there's your master's name to it; and I paid down good solid cash for it, too, I can tell you,—so, now!"

"I don't believe Mas'r would cheat me so; it can't be true!" said the woman, with increasing agitation.

"You can ask any of these men here, that can read writing. Here!" he said, to a man that was passing by, "jist read this yer, won't you! This yer gal won't believe me, when I tell her what 't is."

"Why, it's a bill of sale, signed by John Fosdick," said the man, "making over to you the girl Lucy and her child. It's all straight enough, for aught I see."

The woman's passionate exclamations collected a crowd around her, and the trader briefly explained to them the cause of the agitation.

"He told me that I was going down to Louisville, to hire out as cook to the same tavern where my husband works,—that's what Mas'r told me, his own self; and I can't believe he'd lie to me," said the woman.

"But he has sold you, my poor woman, there's no doubt about it," said a good-natured looking man, who had been examining the papers; "he has done it, and no mistake."

"Then it's no account talking," said the woman, suddenly growing quite calm; and, clasping her child tighter in her arms, she sat down on her box, turned her back round, and gazed listlessly into the river.

"Going to take it easy, after all!" said the trader. "Gal's got grit, I see."

The woman looked calm, as the boat went on; and a beautiful soft summer breeze passed like a compassionate spirit over her head,—the gentle breeze, that never inquires whether the brow is dusky or fair that it fans. And she saw sunshine sparkling on the water, in golden ripples, and heard gay voices, full of ease and pleasure, talking around her everywhere; but her heart lay as if a great stone had fallen on it. Her baby raised himself up against her, and stroked her cheeks with his little hands; and, springing up and down, crowing and chatting, seemed determined to arouse her. She strained him suddenly and tightly in her arms, and slowly one tear after another fell on his wondering, unconscious face; and gradually she seemed, and little by little, to grow calmer, and busied herself with tending and nursing him.

The child, a boy of ten months, was uncommonly large and strong of his age, and very vigorous in his limbs. Never, for a moment, still, he kept his mother constantly busy in holding him, and guarding his springing activity.

"That's a fine chap!" said a man, suddenly stopping opposite to him, with his hands in his pockets. "How old is he?"

"Ten months and a half," said the mother.

The man whistled to the boy, and offered him part of a stick of candy, which he eagerly grabbed at, and very soon had it in a baby's general depository, to wit, his mouth.

"Rum fellow!" said the man. "Knows what's what!" and he whistled, and walked on. When he had got to the other side of the boat, he came across Haley, who was smoking on top of a pile of boxes.

The stranger produced a match, and lighted a cigar, saying, as he did so,

"Decentish kind o' wench you've got round there, stranger."

"Why, I reckon she *is* tol'able fair," said Haley, blowing the smoke out of his mouth.

"Taking her down south?" said the man.

Haley nodded, and smoked on.

"Plantation hand?" said the man.

"Wal," said Haley, "I'm fillin' out an order for a plantation, and I think I shall put her in. They told me she was a good cook; and they can use her for that, or set her at the cotton-picking. She's got the right fingers for that; I looked at 'em. Sell well, either way;" and Haley resumed his cigar.

"They won't want the young 'un on the plantation," said the man.

"I shall sell him, first chance I find," said Haley, lighting another cigar.

"S'pose you'd be selling him tol'able cheap," said the stranger, mounting the pile of boxes, and sitting down comfortably.

"Don't know 'bout that," said Haley; "he's a pretty smart young 'un,—straight, fat, strong; flesh as hard as a brick!"

"Very true, but then there's the bother and expense of raisin'."

"Nonsense!" said Haley; "they is raised as easy as any kind of critter there is going; they an't a bit more trouble than pups. This yer chap will be running all around, in a month."

"I've got a good place for raisin', and I thought of takin' in a little more stock," said the man. "One cook lost a young 'un last week,—got drownded in a wash-tub while she was a hangin' out clothes,—and I reckon it would be well enough to set her to raisin' this yer."

Haley and the stranger smoked a while in silence, neither seeming willing to broach the test question of the interview. At last the man resumed:

"You wouldn't think of wantin' more than ten dollars for that ar chap, seeing you *must* get him off yer hand, any how?"

Haley shook his head, and spit impressively.

"That won't do, no ways," he said, and began his smoking again.

"Well, stranger, what will you take?"

"Well, now," said Haley, "I *could* raise that ar chap myself, or get him raised; he's oncommon likely and healthy, and he'd fetch a hundred dollars, six months hence; and, in a year or two, he'd bring two hundred, if I had him in the right spot;—so I shan't take a cent less nor fifty for him now."

"O, stranger! that's rediculous, altogether," said the man.

"Fact!" said Haley, with a decisive nod of his head.

"I'll give thirty for him," said the stranger, "but not a cent more."

"Now, I'll tell ye what I will do," said Haley, spitting again, with renewed decision. "I'll split the difference, and say forty-five; and that's the most I will do."

"Well, agreed!" said the man, after an interval.

"Done!" said Haley, "Where do you land?"

"At Louisville," said the man.

"Louisville," said Haley. "Very fair, we get there about dusk. Chap will be asleep,—all fair,—get him off quietly, and no screaming,—happens beautiful,—I like to do everything quietly,—I hates all kind of agitation and fluster.'' And so, after a transfer of certain bills had passed from the man's pocket-book to the trader's, he resumed his cigar.

It was a bright, tranquil evening when the boat stopped at the wharf at Louisville. The woman had been sitting with her baby in her arms, now wrapped in a heavy sleep. When she heard the name of the place called out, she hastily laid the child down in a little cradle formed by the hollow among the boxes, first carefully spreading under it her cloak; and then she sprung to the side of the boat, in hopes that, among the various hotel-waiters who thronged the wharf, she might see her husband. In this hope, she pressed forward to the front rails, and, stretching far over them, strained her eyes intently on the moving heads on the shore, and the crowd pressed in between her and the child.

''Now's your time,'' said Haley, taking the sleeping child up, and handing him to the stranger. ''Don't wake him up, and set him to crying, now; it would make a devil of a fuss with the gal.'' The man took the bundle carefully, and was soon lost in the crowd that went up the wharf.

When the boat, creaking, and groaning, and puffing, had loosed from the wharf, and was beginning slowly to strain herself along, the woman returned to her old seat. The trader was sitting there,—the child was gone!

''Why, why,—where?'' she began, in bewildered surprise.

''Lucy,'' said the trader, ''your child's gone; you may as well know it first as last. You see, I know'd you couldn't take him down south; and I got a chance to sell him to a first-rate family, that'll raise him better than you can.''

The trader had arrived at that stage of Christian and political perfection which has been recommended by some preachers and politicians of the north, lately, in which he had completely overcome every humane weakness and prejudice. His heart was exactly where yours, sir, and mine could be brought, with proper effort and cultivation. The wild look of anguish and utter despair that the woman cast on him might have disturbed one less practised; but he was used to it. He had seen that same look hundreds of time. You can get used to such things, too, my friend; and it is the great object of recent efforts to make our whole northern community used to them, for the glory of the Union. So the trader only regarded the mortal anguish which he saw working in those dark features, those clenched hands, and suffocating breathings, as necessary incidents of the trade, and merely calculated whether she was going to scream, and get up a commotion on the boat; for, like other supporters of our peculiar institution, he decidedly disliked agitation.

But the woman did not scream. The shot had passed too straight and direct through the heart, for cry or tear.

Dizzily she sat down. Her slack hands fell lifeless by her side. Her eyes looked straight forward, but she saw nothing. All the noise and hum of the boat, the groaning of the machinery, mingled dreamily to her bewildered ear; and the poor, dumb-stricken heart had neither cry nor tear to show for its utter misery. She was quite calm.

The trader, who, considering his advantages, was almost as humane as some of our politicians, seemed to feel called on to administer such consolation as the case admitted of.

''I know this yer comes kinder hard, at first, Lucy,'' said he; ''but such a smart, sensible gal as you are, won't give way to it. You see it's *necessary*, and can't be helped!''

''O! don't, Mas'r, don't!'' said the woman, with a voice like one that is smothering.

''You're a smart wench, Lucy,'' he persisted; ''I mean to do well by ye, and get ye a nice place down river; and you'll soon get another husband,—such a likely gal as you—''

"O! Mas'r, if you *only* won't talk to me now," said the woman, in a voice of such quick and living anguish that the trader felt that there was something at present in the case beyond his style of operation. He got up, and the woman turned away, and buried her head in her cloak.

The trader walked up and down for a time, and occasionally stopped and looked at her.

"Takes it hard, rather," he soliloquized, "but quiet, tho';—let her sweat a while; she'll come right, by and by!"

Tom had watched the whole transaction from first to last, and had a perfect understanding of its results. To him, it looked like something unutterably horrible and cruel, because, poor, ignorant black soul! he had not learned to generalize, and to take enlarged views. If he had only been instructed by certain ministers of Christianity, he might have thought better of it, and seen in it an every-day incident of a lawful trade; a trade which is the vital support of an institution which an American divine [1] tells us has *"no evils but such as are inseparable from any other relations in social and domestic life."* But Tom, as we see, being a poor, ignorant fellow, whose reading had been confined entirely to the New Testament, could not comfort and solace himself with views like these. His very soul bled within him for what seemed to him the *wrongs* of the poor suffering thing that lay like a crushed reed on the boxes; the feeling, living, bleeding, yet immortal *thing,* which American state law coolly classes with the bundles, and bales, and boxes, among which she is lying.

Tom drew near, and tried to say something; but she only groaned. Honestly, and with tears running down his own cheeks, he spoke of a heart of love in the skies, of a pitying Jesus, and an eternal home; but the ear was deaf with anguish, and the palsied heart could not feel.

Night came on,—night calm, unmoved, and glorious, shining down with her innumerable and solemn angel eyes, twinkling, beautiful, but silent. There was no speech nor language, no pitying voice or helping hand, from that distant sky. One after another, the voices of business or pleasure died away; all on the boat were sleeping, and the ripples at the prow were plainly heard. Tom stretched himself out on a box, and there, as he lay, he heard, ever and anon, a smothered sob or cry from the prostrate creature,—"O! what shall I do? O Lord! O good Lord, do help me!" and so, ever and anon, until the murmur died away in silence.

At midnight, Tom waked, with a sudden start. Something black passed quickly by him to the side of the boat, and he heard a splash in the water. No one else saw or heard anything. He raised his head,—the woman's place was vacant! He got up, and sought about him in vain. The poor bleeding heart was still, at last, and the river rippled and dimpled just as brightly as if it had not closed above it.

Patience! patience! ye whose hearts swell indignant at wrongs like these. Not one throb of anguish, not one tear of the oppressed, is forgotten by the Man of Sorrows, the Lord of Glory. In his patient, generous bosom he bears the anguish of a world. Bear thou, like him, in patience, and labor in love; for sure as he is God, "the year of his redeemed *shall* come."

The trader waked up bright and early, and came out to see to his live stock. It was now his turn to look about in perplexity.

"Where alive is that gal?" he said to Tom.

Tom, who had learned the wisdom of keeping counsel, did not feel called upon to state his observations and suspicions, but said he did not know.

"She surely couldn't have got off in the night at any of the landings, for I was awake, and on the look-out, whenever the boat stopped. I never trust these yer things to other folks."

---

1. Dr. Joel Parker of Philadelphia.

This speech was addressed to Tom quite confidentially, as if it was something that would be specially interesting to him. Tom made no answer.

The trader searched the boat from stem to stern, among boxes, bales and barrels, around the machinery, by the chimneys, in vain.

"Now, I say, Tom, be fair about this yer," he said, when, after a fruitless search, he came where Tom was standing. "You know something about it, now. Don't tell me,—I know you do. I saw the gal stretched out here about ten o'clock, and ag'in at twelve, and ag'in between one and two; and then at four she was gone, and you was a sleeping right there all the time. Now, you know something,—you can't help it."

"Well, Mas'r," said Tom, "towards morning something brushed by me, and I kinder half woke; and then I hearn a great splash, and then I clare woke up, and the gal was gone. That's all I know on 't."

The trader was not shocked nor amazed; because, as we said before, he was used to a great many things that you are not used to. Even the awful presence of Death struck no solemn chill upon him. He had seen Death many times,—met him in the way of trade, and got acquainted with him,—and he only thought of him as a hard customer, that embarrassed his property operations very unfairly; and so he only swore that the gal was a baggage, and that he was devilish unlucky, and that, if things went on in this way, he should not make a cent on the trip. In short, he seemed to consider himself an ill-used man, decidedly; but there was no help for it, as the woman had escaped into a state which *never will* give up a fugitive,—not even at the demand of the whole glorious Union. The trader, therefore, sat discontentedly down, with his little account-book, and put down the missing body and soul under the head of *losses!*

"He's a shocking creature, isn't he,—this trader? so unfeeling! It's dreadful, really!"

"O, but nobody thinks anything of these traders! They are universally despised,—never received into any decent society."

But who, sir makes the trader? Who is most to blame? the enlightened, cultivated, intelligent man, who supports the system of which the trader is the inevitable result, or the poor trader himself? You make the public statement that calls for his trade, that debauches and depraves him, till he feels no shame in it; and in what are you better than he?

Are you educated and he ignorant, you high and he low, you refined and he coarse, you talented and he simple?

In the day of a future Judgment, these very considerations may make it more tolerable for him than for you.

In concluding these little incidents of lawful trade, we must beg the world not to think that American legislators are entirely destitute of humanity, as might, perhaps, be unfairly inferred from the great efforts made in our national body to protect and perpetuate this species of traffic.

Who does not know how our great men are outdoing themselves, in declaiming against the *foreign* slave-trade. There are a perfect host of Clarksons and Wilberforces risen up among us on that subject, most edifying to hear and behold. Trading negroes from Africa, dear reader, is so horrid! It is not to be thought of! But trading them from Kentucky,—that's quite another thing!

Ernest Laurence Thayer / Casey at the Bat 1888

Ernest Laurence Thayer (1863–1940) published the humorous poem "Casey at the Bat" in June 3, 1888, San Francisco Examiner, using the pseudonym "Phin." The poem became famous when a well-known entertainer of the time, DeWolf Hopper, made it part of his vaudeville act. So compellingly does "Casey at the Bat" document the drama and idiom of the game that poet-critic Louis Untermeyer has called it "the acknowledged classic of baseball, its anthem and theme song."

The outlook wasn't brilliant for the Mudville nine that day:
The score stood four to two with but one inning more to play.
And then when Cooney died at first, and Barrows did the same,
A sickly silence fell upon the patrons of the game.

A straggling few got up to go in deep despair. The rest 5
Clung to that hope which springs eternal in the human breast;
They thought if only Casey could but get a whack at that—
We'd put up even money now with Casey at the bat.

But Flynn preceded Casey, as did also Jimmy Blake,
And the former was a lulu and the latter was a cake; 10
So upon that stricken multitude grim melancholy sat,
For there seemed but little chance of Casey's getting to the bat..

But Flynn let drive a single, to the wonderment of all,
And Blake, the much despis-ed, tore the cover off the ball;
And when the dust had lifted, and the men saw what had occurred, 15
There was Jimmy safe at second and Flynn a-hugging third.

Then from 5,000 throats and more there rose a lusty yell;
It rumbled through the valley, it rattled in the dell;
It knocked upon the mountain and recoiled upon the flat,
For Casey, mighty Casey, was advancing to the bat. 20

There was ease in Casey's manner as he stepped into his place;
There was pride in Casey's bearing and a smile on Casey's face.
And when, responding to the cheers, he lightly doffed his hat,
No stranger in the crowd could doubt 'twas Casey at the bat.

Ten thousand eyes were on him as he rubbed his hands with dirt; 25
Five thousand tongues applauded when he wiped them on his shirt.
Then while the writhing pitcher ground the ball into his hip,
Defiance gleamed in Casey's eye, a sneer curled Casey's lip.

And now the leather-covered sphere came hurtling through the air,
And Casey stood a-watching it in haughty grandeur there. 30
Close by the sturdy batsman the ball unheeded sped—
"That ain't my style," said Casey. "Strike one," the umpire said.

From the benches back with people, there went up a muffled roar,
Like the beating of the storm-waves on a stern and distant shore.
"Kill him! Kill the umpire!" shouted some one on the stand;   35
And it's likely they'd have killed him had not Casey raised his hand.

With a smile of Christian charity great Casey's visage shone;
He stilled the rising tumult; he bade the game go on;
He signaled to the pitcher, and once more the spheroid flew;
But Casey still ignored it, and the umpire said, "Strike two."   40

"Fraud!" cried the maddened thousands, and echo answered fraud;
But one scornful look from Casey and the audience was awed.
They saw his face grow stern and cold, they saw his muscles strain,
And they knew that Casey wouldn't let that ball go by again.

The sneer is gone from Casey's lip, his teeth are clenched in hate;   45
He pounds with cruel violence his bat upon the plate.
And now the pitcher holds the ball, and now he lets it go,
And now the air is shattered by the force of Casey's blow.

Oh, somewhere in this favored land the sun is shining bright;
The band is playing somewhere, and somewhere hearts are light,   50
And somewhere men are laughing, and somewhere children shout;
But there is no joy in Mudville—mighty Casey has struck out.

Edgar Rice Burroughs / *Tarzan of the Apes*
[Tarzan Meets Jane; or Girl Goes Ape]   1914

> *A one-time soldier, policeman, cowboy, Sears Roebuck department store man-*
> *ager, advertising copywriter, gold miner, salesman, and business failure, Edgar*
> *Rice Burroughs (1875–1950) began one of the most successful writing careers in*
> *the history of popular literature with the publication of* Tarzan of the Apes. *The*
> *first of a series of twenty-six novels,* Tarzan of the Apes *initially appeared in the*
> All Story *magazine for October 1912 and, when no publisher would touch it, was*
> *serialized in the* New York Evening World. *The newspaper serialization*
> *triggered a demand for the story in book form, and* Tarzan of the Apes *was finally*
> *published in 1914.*
>
> *Tarzan provided exactly the kind of material the new movie industry was looking*
> *for. The first Tarzan film was released in 1918, and the series remained popular*
> *until the 1960s. Burroughs's fantasies posed a challenge to "realism" that Holly-*
> *wood must have delighted in, as the following description of the technical efforts*
> *that went into producing Tarzan's barbaric yawp so perfectly demonstrates:*
>
> > *M-G-M spared no expense on the Tarzan yell. Miles of sound track of*
> > *human, animal and instrument sounds were tested in collecting the*
> > *ingredients of an unearthly howl. The cry of a mother camel robbed of*
> > *her young was used until still more mournful sounds were found. A*
> > *combination of five different sound tracks is used today for the Tarzan*
> > *yell. There are: 1. Sound track of Weissmuller yelling amplified. 2.*
> > *Track of hyena howl, run backward and volume diminished. 3. Soprano*
> > *note sung by Lorraine Bridges, recording on sound track at reduced*

speed; then rerecorded at varying speeds to give a "flutter" in sound. 4. Growl of dog, recorded very faintly. 5. Raspy note of violin G-string, recorded very faintly. In the experimental stage the five sound tracks were played over five different loud speakers. From time to time the speed of each sound track was varied and the volume amplified or diminished. When the orchestration of the yell was perfected, the five loudspeakers were played simultaneously and the blended sounds recorded on the master sound track. By constant practice Weissmuller is now able to let loose an almost perfect imitation of the sound track.

From the time Tarzan left the tribe of great anthropoids in which he had been raised, it was torn by continual strife and discord. Terkoz proved a cruel and capricious king, so that, one by one, many of the older and weaker apes, upon whom he was particularly prone to vent his brutish nature, took their families and sought the quiet and safety of the far interior.

But at last those who remained were driven to desperation by the continued truculence of Terkoz, and it so happened that one of them recalled the parting admonition of Tarzan:

"If you have a chief who is cruel, do not do as the other apes do, and attempt, any one of you, to pit yourself against him alone. But, instead, let two or three or four of you attack him together. Then, if you will do this, no chief will dare to be other than he should be, for four of you can kill any chief who may ever be over you."

And the ape who recalled this wise counsel repeated it to several of his fellows, so that when Terkoz returned to the tribe that day he found a warm reception awaiting him.

There were no formalities. As Terkoz reached the group, five huge, hairy beasts sprang upon him.

At heart he was an arrant coward, which is the way with bullies among apes as well as among men; so he did not remain to fight and die, but tore himself away from them as quickly as he could and fled into the sheltering boughs of the forest.

Two more attempts he made to rejoin the tribe, but on each occasion he was set upon and driven away. At last he gave it up, and turned, foaming with rage and hatred, into the jungle.

For several days he wandered aimlessly, nursing his spite and looking for some weak thing on which to vent his pent anger.

It was in this state of mind that the horrible, man-like beast, swinging from tree to tree, came suddenly upon two women in the jungle.

He was right above them when he discovered them. The first intimation Jane Porter had of his presence was when the great hairy body dropped to the earth beside her, and she saw the awful face and the snarling, hideous mouth thrust within a foot of her.

One piercing scream escaped her lips as the brute hand clutched her arm. Then she was dragged toward those awful fangs which yawned at her throat. But ere they touched that fair skin another mood claimed the anthropoid.

The tribe had kept his women. He must find others to replace them. This hairless white ape would be the first of his new household, and so he threw her roughly across his broad, hairy shoulders and leaped back into the trees, bearing Jane away.

Esmeralda's scream of terror had mingled once with that of Jane, and then, as was Esmeralda's manner under stress of emergency which required presence of mind, she swooned.

But Jane did not once lose consciousness. It is true that that awful face, pressing close to hers, and the stench of the foul breath beating upon her nostrils, paralyzed her with terror; but her brain was clear, and she comprehended all that transpired.

With what seemed to her marvelous rapidity the brute bore her through the forest, but still she did not cry out or struggle. The sudden advent of the ape had confused her to such an extent that she thought now that he was bearing her toward the beach.

For this reason she conserved her energies and her voice until she could see that they had approached near enough to the camp to attract the succor she craved.

She could not have known it, but she was being borne farther and farther into the impenetrable jungle.

The scream that had brought Clayton and the two older men stumbling through the undergrowth had led Tarzan of the Apes straight to where Esmeralda lay, but it was not Esmeralda in whom his interest centered, though pausing over her he saw that she was unhurt.

For a moment he scrutinized the ground below and the trees above, until the ape that was in him by virtue of training and environment, combined with the intelligence that was his by right of birth, told his wondrous woodcraft the whole story as plainly as though he had seen the thing happen with his own eyes.

And then he was gone again into the swaying trees, following the high-flung spoor which no other human eye could have detected, much less translated.

At boughs' ends, where the anthropoid swings from one tree to another, there is most to mark the trail, but least to point the direction of the quarry; for there the pressure is downward always, toward the small end of the branch, whether the ape be leaving or entering a tree. Nearer the center of the tree, where the signs of passage are fainter, the direction is plainly marked.

Here, on this branch, a caterpillar has been crushed by the fugitive's great foot, and Tarzan knows instinctively where that same foot would touch in the next stride. Here he looks to find a tiny particle of the demolished larva, ofttimes not more than a speck of moisture.

Again, a minute bit of bark has been upturned by the scraping hand, and the direction of the break indicates the direction of the passage. Or some great limb, or the stem of the tree itself has been brushed by the hairy body, and a tiny shred of hair tells him by the direction from which it is wedged beneath the bark that he is on the right trail.

Nor does he need to check his speed to catch these seemingly faint records of the fleeing beast.

To Tarzan they stand out boldly against all the myriad other scars and bruises and signs upon the leafy way. But strongest of all is the scent, for Tarzan is pursuing up the wind, and his trained nostrils are as sensitive as a hound's.

There are those who believe that the lower orders are specially endowed by nature with better olfactory nerves than man, but it is merely a matter of development.

Man's survival does not hinge so greatly upon the perfection of his senses. His power to reason has relieved them of many of their duties, and so they have, to some extent, atrophied, as have the muscles which move the ears and scalp, merely from disuse.

The muscles are there, about the ears and beneath the scalp, and so are the nerves which transmit sensations to the brain, but they are under-developed because they are not needed.

Not so with Tarzan of the Apes. From early infancy his survival had depended upon acuteness of eyesight, hearing, smell, touch, and taste far more than upon the more slowly developed organ of reason.

The least developed of all in Tarzan was the sense of taste, for he could eat luscious fruits, or raw flesh, long buried with almost equal appreciation; but in that he differed but slightly from more civilized epicures.

Almost silently the ape-man sped on in the track of Terkoz and his prey, but the sound of his approach reached the ears of the fleeing beast and spurred it on to greater speed.

Three miles were covered before Tarzan overtook them, and then Terkoz, seeing that further flight was futile, dropped to the ground in a small open glade, that he might turn and fight for his prize or be free to escape unhampered if he saw that the pursuer was more than a match for him.

He still grasped Jane in one great arm as Tarzan bounded like a leopard into the arena which nature had provided for this primeval-like battle.

When Terkoz saw that it was Tarzan who pursued him, he jumped to the conclusion that this was Tarzan's woman, since they were of the same kind—white and hairless—and so he rejoiced at this opportunity for double revenge upon his hated enemy.

To Jane the strange apparition of this god-like man was as wine to sick nerves.

From the description which Clayton and her father and Mr. Philander had given her, she knew that it must be the same wonderful creature who had saved them, and she saw in him only a protector and a friend.

But as Terkoz pushed her roughly aside to meet Tarzan's charge, and she saw the great proportions of the ape and the mighty muscles and the fierce fangs, her heart quailed. How could any vanquish such a mighty antagonist?

Like two charging bulls they came together, and like two wolves sought each other's throat. Against the long canines of the ape was pitted the thin blade of the man's knife.

Jane—her lithe, young form flattened against the trunk of a great tree, her hands tight pressed against her rising and falling bosom, and her eyes wide with mingled horror, fascination, fear, and admiration—watched the primordial ape battle with the primeval man for possession of a woman—for her.

As the great muscles of the man's back and shoulders knotted beneath the tension of his efforts, and the huge biceps and forearm held at bay those mighty tusks, the veil of centuries of civilization and culture was swept from the blurred vision of the Baltimore girl.

When the long knife drank deep a dozen times of Terkoz' heart's blood, and the great carcass rolled lifeless upon the ground, it was a primeval woman who sprang forward with outstretched arms toward the primeval man who had fought for her and won her.

And Tarzan?

He did what no red-blooded man needs lessons in doing. He took his woman in his arms and smothered her upturned, panting lips with kisses.

For a moment Jane lay there with half-closed eyes. For a moment—the first in her young life—she knew the meaning of love.

But as suddenly as the veil had been withdrawn it dropped again, and an outraged conscience suffused her face with its scarlet mantle, and a mortified woman thrust Tarzan of the Apes from her and buried her face in her hands.

Tarzan had been surprised when he had found the girl he had learned to love after a vague and abstract manner a willing prisoner in his arms. Now he was surprised that she repulsed him.

He came close to her once more and took hold of her arm. She turned upon him like a tigress, striking his great breast with her tiny hands.

Tarzan could not understand it.

A moment ago and it had been his intention to hasten Jane back to her people, but that little moment was lost now in the dim and distant past of things which were but can never be again, and with it the good intention had gone to join the impossible.

Since then Tarzan of the Apes had felt a warm, lithe form close pressed to his. Hot, sweet breath against his cheek and mouth had fanned a new flame to life within his breast, and perfect lips had clung to his in burning kisses that had seared a deep brand into his soul—a brand which marked a new Tarzan.

Again he laid his hand upon her arm. Again she repulsed him. And then Tarzan of the Apes did just what his first ancestor would have done.

He took his woman in his arms and carried her into the jungle. . . .

When Jane realized that she was being borne away a captive by the strange forest creature who had rescued her from the clutches of the ape she struggled desperately to escape, but the strong arms that held her as easily as though she had been but a day-old babe only pressed a little more tightly.

So presently she gave up the futile effort and lay quietly, looking through half-closed lids at the face of the man who strode easily through the tangled undergrowth with her.

The face above her was one of extraordinary beauty.

A perfect type of the strongly masculine, unmarred by dissipation, or brutal or degrading passions. For, though Tarzan of the Apes was a killer of men and of beasts, he killed as the hunter kills, dispassionately, except on those rare occasions when he had killed for hate—though not the brooding, malevolent hate which marks the features of its own with hideous lines.

When Tarzan killed he more often smiled than scowled, and smiles are the foundation of beauty.

One thing the girl had noticed particularly when she had seen Tarzan rushing upon Terkoz—the vivid scarlet band upon his forehead, from above the left eye to the scalp; but now as she scanned his features she noticed that it was gone, and only a thin white line marked the spot where it had been.

As she lay more quietly in his arms Tarzan slightly relaxed his grip upon her.

Once he looked down into her eyes and smiled, and the girl had to close her own to shut out the vision of that handsome, winning face.

Presently Tarzan took to the trees, and Jane, wondering that she felt no fear, began to realize that in many respects she had never felt more secure in her whole life than now as she lay in the arms of this strong, wild creature, being borne, God alone knew where or to what fate, deeper and deeper into the savage fastness of the untamed forest.

When, with closed eyes, she commenced to speculate upon the future, and terrifying fears were conjured by a vivid imagination, she had but to raise her lids and look upon that noble face so close to hers to dissipate the last remnant of apprehension.

No, he could never harm her; of that she was convinced when she translated the fine features and the frank, brave eyes above her into the chivalry which they proclaimed.

On and on they went through what seemed to Jane a solid mass of verdure, yet ever there appeared to open before this forest god a passage, as by magic, which closed behind them as they passed.

Scarce a branch scraped against her, yet above and below, before and behind, the view presented naught but a solid mass of inextricably interwoven branches and creepers.

As Tarzan moved steadily onward his mind was occupied with many strange and new thoughts. Here was a problem the like of which he had never encountered, and he felt rather than reasoned that he must meet it as a man and not as an ape.

The free movement through the middle terrace, which was the route he had followed for the most part, had helped to cool the ardor of the first fierce passion of his new found love.

Now he discovered himself speculating upon the fate which would have fallen to the girl had he not rescued her from Terkoz.

He knew why the ape had not killed her, and he commenced to compare his intentions with those of Terkoz.

True, it was the order of the jungle for the male to take his mate by force; but could Tarzan be guided by the laws of the beasts? Was not Tarzan a Man? But what did men do? He was puzzled; for he did not know.

He wished that he might ask the girl, and then it came to him that she had already answered him in the futile struggle she had made to escape and to repulse him.

But now they had come to their destination, and Tarzan of the Apes with Jane in his strong arms, swung lightly to the turf of the arena where the great apes held their councils and danced the wild orgy of the Dum-Dum.

Though they had come many miles, it was still but midafternoon, and the amphitheater was bathed in the half light which filtered through the maze of encircling foliage.

The green turf looked soft and cool and inviting. The myriad noises of the jungle seemed far distant and hushed to a mere echo of blurred sounds, rising and falling like the surf upon a remote shore.

A feeling of dreamy peacefulness stole over Jane as she sank down upon the grass where Tarzan had placed her, and as she looked up at his great figure towering above her, there was added a strange sense of perfect security.

As she watched him from beneath half-closed lids, Tarzan crossed the little circular clearing toward the trees upon the further side. She noted the graceful majesty of his carriage, the perfect symmetry of his magnificent figure and the poise of his well-shaped head upon his broad shoulders.

What a perfect creature! There could be naught of cruelty or baseness beneath that godlike exterior. Never, she thought had such a man strode the earth since God created the first in his own image.

With a bound Tarzan sprang into the trees and disappeared. Jane wondered where he had gone. Had he left her there to her fate in the lonely jungle?

She glanced nervously about. Every vine and bush seemed but the lurking-place of some huge and horrible beast waiting to bury gleaming fangs into her soft flesh. Every sound she magnified into the stealthy creeping of a sinuous and malignant body.

How different now that he had left her!

For a few minutes that seemed hours to the frightened girl, she sat with tense nerves waiting for the spring of the crouching thing that was to end her misery of apprehension.

She almost prayed for the cruel teeth that would give her unconsciousness and surcease from the agony of fear.

She heard a sudden, slight sound behind her. With a cry she sprang to her feet and turned to face her end.

There stood Tarzan, his arms filled with ripe and luscious fruit.

Jane reeled and would have fallen, had not Tarzan, dropping his burden, caught her in his arms. She did not lose consciousness, but she clung tightly to him, shuddering and trembling like a frightened deer.

Tarzan of the Apes stroked her soft hair and tried to comfort and quiet her as Kala had him, when, as a little ape, he had been frightened by Sabor, the lioness, or Histah, the snake.

Once he pressed his lips lightly upon her forehead, and she did not move, but closed her eyes and sighed.

She could not analyze her feelings, nor did she wish to attempt it. She was satisfied to feel the safety of those strong arms, and to leave her future to fate; for the last few hours had taught her to trust this strange wild creature of the forest as she would have trusted but few of the men of her acquaintance.

As she thought of the strangeness of it, there commenced to dawn upon her the realization that she had, possibly, learned something else which she had never really known before—love. She wondered and then she smiled.

And still smiling, she pushed Tarzan gently away; and looking at him with a half-smiling, half-quizzical expression that made her face wholly entrancing, she pointed to the fruit upon the ground, and seated herself upon the edge of the earthen drum of the anthropoids, for hunger was asserting itself.

Tarzan quickly gathered up the fruit, and, bringing it, laid it at her feet; and then he, too, sat upon the drum beside her, and with his knife opened and prepared the various fruits for her meal.

Together and in silence they ate, occasionally stealing sly glances at one another, until finally Jane broke into a merry laugh in which Tarzan joined.

"I wish you spoke English," said the girl.

Tarzan shook his head, and an expression of wistful and pathetic longing sobered his laughing eyes.

Then Jane tried speaking to him in French, and then in German; but she had to laugh at her own blundering attempt at the latter tongue.

"Anyway," she said to him in English, "you understand my German as well as they did in Berlin."

Tarzan had long since reached a decision as to what his future procedure should be. He had had time to recollect all that he had read of the ways of men and women in the books at the cabin. He would act as he imagined the men in the books would have acted were they in his place.

Again he rose and went into the trees, but first he tried to explain by means of signs that he would return shortly, and he did so well that Jane understood and was not afraid when he had gone.

Only a feeling of loneliness came over her and she watched the point where he had disappeared, with longing eyes, awaiting his return. As before, she was appraised of his presence by a soft sound behind her, and turned to see him coming across the turf with a great armful of branches.

Then he went back again into the jungle and in a few minutes reappeared with a quantity of soft grasses and ferns. Two more trips he made until he had quite a pile of material at hand.

Then he spread the ferns and grasses upon the ground in a soft flat bed, and above it leaned many branches together so that they met a few feet over its center. Upon these he spread layers of huge leaves of the great elephant's ear, and with more branches and more leaves he closed one end of the little shelter he had built.

Then they sat down together again upon the edge of the drum and tried to talk by signs.

The magnificent diamond locket which hung about Tarzan's neck, had been a source of much wonderment to Jane. She pointed to it now, and Tarzan removed it and handed the pretty bauble to her.

She saw that it was the work of a skilled artisan and that the diamonds were of great brilliancy and superbly set, but the cutting of them denoted that they were of a former day.

She noticed too that the locket opened, and, pressing the hidden clasp, she saw the two halves spring apart to reveal in either section an ivory miniature.

One was of a beautiful woman and the other might have been a likeness of the man who sat beside her, except for a subtle difference of expression that was scarcely definable.

She looked up at Tarzan to find him leaning toward her gazing on the miniatures with an expression of astonishment. He reached out his hand for the locket and took it away from her, examining the likenesses within with unmistakable signs of surprise and new interest. His manner clearly denoted that he had never before seen them, nor imagined that the locket opened.

This fact caused Jane to indulge in further speculation, and it taxed her imagination to picture how this beautiful ornament came into the possession of a wild and savage creature of the unexplored jungles of Africa.

Still more wonderful was how it contained the likeness of one who might be a brother, or, more likely, the father of this woodland demi-god who was even ignorant of the fact that the locket opened.

Tarzan was still gazing with fixity at the two faces. Presently he removed the quiver from his shoulder, and emptying the arrows upon the ground reached into the bottom of the bag-like receptacle and drew forth a flat object wrapped in many soft leaves and tied with bits of long grass.

Carefully he unwrapped it, removing layer after layer of leaves until at length he held a photograph in his hand.

Pointing to the miniature of the man within the locket he handed the photograph to Jane, holding the open locket beside it.

The photograph only served to puzzle the girl still more, for it was evidently another likeness of the same man whose picture rested in the locket beside that of the beautiful young woman.

Tarzan was looking at her with an expression of puzzled bewilderment in his eyes as she glanced up at him. He seemed to be framing a question with his lips.

The girl pointed to the photograph and then to the miniature and then to him, as though to indicate that she thought the likenesses were of him, but he only shook his head, and then shrugging his great shoulders, he took the photograph from her and having carefully rewrapped it, placed it again in the bottom of his quiver.

For a few moments he sat in silence, his eyes bent upon the ground, while Jane held the little locket in her hand, turning it over and over in an endeavor to find some further clue that might lead to the identity of its original owner.

At length a simple explanation occurred to her.

The locket had belonged to Lord Greystoke, and the likenesses were of himself and Lady Alice.

This wild creature had simply found it in the cabin by the beach. How stupid of her not to have thought of that solution before.

But to account for the strange likeness between Lord Greystoke and this forest god—that was quite beyond her, and it is not strange that she could not imagine that this naked savage was indeed an English nobleman.

At length Tarzan looked up to watch the girl as she examined the locket. He could not fathom the meaning of the faces within, but he could read the interest and fascination upon the face of the live young creature by his side.

She noticed that he was watching her and thinking that he wished his ornament again she held it out to him. He took it from her and taking the chain in his two hands he placed it about her neck, smiling at her expression of surprise at his unexpected gift.

Jane shook her head vehemently and would have removed the golden links from about her throat, but Tarzan would not let her. Taking her hands in his, when she insisted upon it, he held them tightly to prevent her.

At last she desisted and with a little laugh raised the locket to her lips.

Tarzan did not know precisely what she meant, but he guessed correctly that it was her way of acknowledging the gift, and so he rose, and taking the locket in his hand, stooped gravely like some courtier of old, and pressed his lips upon it where hers had rested.

It was a stately and gallant little compliment performed with the grace and dignity of utter unconsciousness of self. It was the hall-mark of his aristocratic birth, the natural out-cropping of many generations of fine breeding, an hereditary instinct of graciousness which a lifetime of uncouth and savage training and environment could not eradicate.

It was growing dark now, and so they ate again of the fruit which was both food and drink for them; then Tarzan rose, and leading Jane to the little bower he had erected, motioned her to go within.

For the first time in hours a feeling of fear swept over her, and Tarzan felt her draw away as though shrinking from him.

Contact with this girl for half a day had left a very different Tarzan from the one on whom the morning's sun had risen.

Now, in every fiber of his being, heredity spoke louder than training.

He had not in one swift transition become a polished gentleman from a savage ape-man, but at last the instincts of the former predominated, and over all was the desire to please the woman he loved, and to appear well in her eyes.

So Tarzan of the Apes did the only thing he knew to assure Jane of her safety. He removed his hunting knife from its sheath and handed it to her hilt first, again motioning her into the bower.

The girl understood, and taking the long knife she entered and lay down upon the soft grasses while Tarzan of the Apes stretched himself upon the ground across the entrance.

And thus the rising sun found them in the morning.

When Jane awoke, she did not at first recall the strange events of the preceding day, and so she wondered at her odd surroundings—the little leafy bower, the soft grasses of her bed, the unfamiliar prospect from the opening at her feet.

Slowly the circumstances of her position crept one by one into her mind. And then a great wonderment arose in her heart—a mighty wave of thankfulness and gratitude that though she had been in such terrible danger, yet she was unharmed.

She moved to the entrance of the shelter to look for Tarzan. He was gone; but this time no fear assailed her for she knew that he would return.

In the grass at the entrance to her bower she saw the imprint of his body where he had lain all night to guard her. She knew that the fact that he had been there was all that had permitted her to sleep in such peaceful security.

With him near, who could entertain fear? She wondered if there was another man on earth with whom a girl could feel so safe in the heart of this savage African jungle. Even the lions and panthers had no fears for her now.

She looked up to see his lithe form drop softly from a near-by tree. As he caught her eyes upon him his face lighted with that frank and radiant smile that had won her confidence the day before.

As he approached her Jane's heart beat faster and her eyes brightened as they had never done before at the approach of any man.

He had again been gathering fruit and this he laid at the entrance of her bower. Once more they sat down together to eat.

Jane commenced to wonder what his plans were. Would he take her back to the beach or would he keep her here? Suddenly she realized that the matter did not seem to give her much concern. Could it be that she did not care!

She began to comprehend, also, that she was entirely contented sitting here by the side of this smiling giant eating delicious fruit in a sylvan paradise far within the remote depths of an African jungle—that she was contented and very happy.

She could not understand it. Her reason told her that she should be torn by wild anxieties, weighted by dread fears, cast down by gloomy forebodings; but instead, her heart was singing and she was smiling into the answering face of the man beside her.

When they had finished their breakfast Tarzan went to her bower and recovered his knife. The girl had entirely forgotten it. She realized that it was because she had forgotten the fear that prompted her to accept it.

Motioning her to follow, Tarzan walked toward the trees at the edge of the arena, and taking her in one strong arm swung to the branches above.

The girl knew that he was taking her back to her people, and she could not understand the sudden feeling of loneliness and sorrow which crept over her.

For hours they swung slowly along.

Tarzan of the Apes did not hurry. He tried to draw out the sweet pleasure of that journey with those dear arms about his neck as long as possible, and so he went far south of the direct route to the beach.

Several times they halted for brief rests, which Tarzan did not need, and at noon they stopped for an hour at a little brook, where they quenched their thirst, and ate.

So it was nearly sunset when they came to the clearing, and Tarzan, dropping to the ground beside a great tree, parted the tall jungle grass and pointed out the little cabin to her.

She took him by the hand to lead him to it, that she might tell her father that this man had saved her from death and worse than death, that he had watched over her as carefully as a mother might have done.

But again the timidity of the wild thing in the face of human habitation swept over Tarzan of the Apes. He drew back, shaking his head.

The girl came close to him, looking up with pleading eyes. Somehow she could not bear the thought of his going back into the terrible jungle alone.

Still he shook his head, and finally he drew her to him very gently and stooped to kiss her, but first he looked into her eyes and waited to learn if she were pleased, or if she would repulse him.

Just an instant the girl hesitated, and then she realized the truth, and throwing her arms about his neck she drew his face to hers and kissed him—unashamed.

"I love you—I love you," she murmured.

From far in the distance came the faint sound of many guns. Tarzan and Jane raised their heads.

From the cabin came Mr. Philander and Esmeralda.

From where Tarzan and the girl stood they could not see the two vessels lying at anchor in the harbor.

Tarzan pointed toward the sounds, touched his breast and pointed again. She understood. He was going, and something told her that it was because he thought her people were in danger.

Again he kissed her.

"Come back to me," she whispered. "I shall wait for you—always."

Dale Carnegie / *How to Win Friends and Influence People*   1936

> *One of the most successful nonfiction books in the history of American publishing,* How to Win Friends and Influence People *was the culmination of Dale Carnegie's experiences in training thousands of business and professional people in the art of public speaking and the techniques of "handling people." A compilation of popular psychology, etiquette rules, and after-dinner speech anecdotes,* How to Win Friends and Influence People *suggests that the fuzzy areas of social relationships and human discourse can be gotten through effectively and profitably with elocutionary acumen, a little shrewdness, and the application of proper procedures.*

FUNDAMENTAL TECHNIQUES IN HANDLING PEOPLE

CHAPTER 1: "IF YOU WANT TO GATHER HONEY,
DON'T KICK OVER THE BEEHIVE"

On May 7, 1931, New York City witnessed the most sensational man-hunt the old town had ever known. After weeks of search, "Two Gun" Crowley—the killer, the gunman who didn't smoke or drink—was at bay, trapped in his sweetheart's apartment on West End Avenue.

One hundred and fifty policemen and detectives laid siege to his top-floor hideaway. Chopping holes in the roof, they tried to smoke out Crowley, the "cop killer," with tear gas. Then they mounted their machine guns on surrounding buildings, and for more than an hour one of New York's fine residential sections reverberated with the crack of pistol fire and the rat-tat-tat of machine guns. Crowley, crouching behind an overstuffed chair, fired incessantly at the police. Ten thousand excited people watched the battle. Nothing like it had ever been seen before on the sidewalks of New York.

When Crowley was captured, Police Commissioner Mulrooney declared that the two-gun desperado was one of the most dangerous criminals ever encountered in the history of New York. "He will kill," said the Commissioner, "at the drop of a feather."

But how did "Two Gun" Crowley regard himself? We know, because while the police were firing into his apartment, he wrote a letter addressed "To whom it may concern." And, as he wrote, the blood flowing from his wounds left a crimson trail on the paper. In this letter Crowley said: "Under my coat is a weary heart, but a kind one—one that would do nobody any harm."

A short time before this, Crowley had been having a necking party on a country road out on Long Island. Suddenly a policeman walked up to the parked car and said: "Let me see your license."

Without saying a word, Crowley drew his gun, and cut the policeman down with a shower of lead. As the dying officer fell, Crowley leaped out of the car, grabbed the officer's revolver, and fired another bullet into the prostrate body. And that was the killer who said: "Under my coat is a weary heart, but a kind one—one that would do nobody any harm."

Crowley was sentenced to the electric chair. When he arrived at the death house at Sing Sing, did he say, "This is what I get for killing people?" No, he said: "This is what I get for defending myself."

The point of the story is this: "Two Gun" Crowley didn't blame himself for anything.

Is that an unusual attitude among criminals? If you think so, listen to this:

"I have spent the best years of my life giving people the lighter pleasures, helping them have a good time, and all I get is abuse, the existence of a hunted man."

That's Al Capone speaking. Yes, America's erstwhile Public Enemy Number One—the most sinister gang leader who ever shot up Chicago. Capone doesn't condemn himself. He actually regards himself as a public benefactor—an unappreciated and misunderstood public benefactor.

And so did Dutch Schultz before he crumpled up under gangster bullets in Newark. Dutch Schultz, one of New York's most notorious rats, said in a newspaper interview that he was a public benefactor. And he believed it.

I have had some interesting correspondence with Warden Lawes of Sing Sing on this subject, and he declares that "few of the criminals in Sing Sing regard themselves as bad men. They are just as human as you and I. So they rationalize, they explain. They can tell you why they had to crack a safe or be quick on the trigger finger. Most of them attempt by a form of reasoning, fallacious or logical, to justify their anti-social acts even to themselves, consequently stoutly maintaining that they should never have been imprisoned at all."

If Al Capone, "Two Gun" Crowley, Dutch Schultz, the desperate men behind prison walls don't blame themselves for anything—what about the people with whom you and I come in contact?

The late John Wanamaker once confessed: "I learned thirty years ago that it is foolish to scold. I have enough trouble overcoming my own limitations without fretting over the fact that God has not seen fit to distribute evenly the gift of intelligence.''

Wanamaker learned this lesson early; but I personally had to blunder through this old world for a third of a century before it even began to dawn upon me that ninety-nine times out of a hundred, no man ever criticizes himself for anything, no matter how wrong he may be.

Criticism is futile because it puts a man on the defensive, and usually makes him strive to justify himself. Criticism is dangerous, because it wounds a man's precious pride, hurts his sense of importance, and arouses his resentment.

The German army won't let a soldier file a complaint and make a criticism immediately after a thing has happened. He has to sleep on his grudge first and cool off. If he files his complaint immediately, he is punished. By the eternals, there ought to be a law like that in civil life too—a law for whining parents and nagging wives and scolding employers and the whole obnoxious parade of fault-finders.

You will find examples of the futility of criticism bristling on a thousand pages of history. Take, for example, the famous quarrel between Theodore Roosevelt and President Taft—a quarrel that split the Republican Party, put Woodrow Wilson in the White House, and wrote bold, luminous lines across the World War and altered the flow of history. Let's review the facts quickly: When Theodore Roosevelt stepped out of the White House in 1908, he made Taft president, and then went off to Africa to shoot lions. When he returned, he exploded. He denounced Taft for his conservatism, tried to secure the nomination for a third term himself, formed the Bull Moose Party, and all but demolished the G.O.P. In the election that followed, William Howard Taft and the Republican Party carried only two states—Vermont and Utah. The most disastrous defeat the old party had ever known.

Theodore Roosevelt blamed Taft; but did President Taft blame himself? Of course not. With tears in his eyes, Taft said: "I don't see how I could have done any differently from what I have."

Who was to blame? Roosevelt or Taft? Frankly, I don't know, and I don't care. The point I am trying to make is that all of Theodore Roosevelt's criticism didn't persuade Taft that he was wrong. It merely made Taft strive to justify himself and to reiterate with tears in his eyes: "I don't see how I could have done any differently from what I have."

Or, take the Teapot Dome Oil scandal. Remember it? It kept the newspapers ringing with indignation for years. It rocked the nation! Nothing like it had ever happened before in American public life within the memory of living men. Here are the bare facts of the scandal: Albert Fall, Secretary of the Interior in Harding's cabinet, was entrusted with the leasing of government oil reserves at Elk Hill and Teapot Dome—oil reserves that had been set aside for the future use of the Navy. Did Secretary Fall permit competitive bidding? No sir. He handed the fat, juicy contract outright to his friend, Edward L. Doheny. And what did Doheny do? He gave Secretary Fall what he was pleased to call a "loan" of one hundred thousand dollars. Then, in a high-handed manner, Secretary Fall ordered United States Marines into the district to drive off competitors whose adjacent wells were sapping oil out of the Elk Hill reserves. These competitors, driven off their ground at the ends of guns and bayonets, rushed into court—and blew the lid off the hundred million dollar Teapot Dome scandal. A stench arose so vile that it ruined the Harding administration, nauseated an entire nation, threatened to wreck the Republican Party, and put Albert B. Fall behind prison bars.

Fall was condemned viciously—condemned as few men in public life have ever been. Did he repent? Never! Years later Herbert Hoover intimated in a public speech that President Harding's death had been due to mental anxiety and worry because a friend had betrayed him. When Mrs. Fall heard that, she sprang from her chair, she wept, she shook her fists at fate, and screamed: "What! Harding betrayed by Fall? No! My husband never betrayed anyone. This whole house full of gold would not tempt my husband to do wrong. He is the one who has been betrayed and led to the slaughter and crucified."

There you are; human nature in action, the wrong-doer blaming everybody but himself. We are all like that. So when you and I are tempted to criticize someone tomorrow, let's remember Al Capone, "Two Gun" Crowley, and Albert Fall. Let's realize that criticisms are like homing pigeons. They always return home. Let's realize that the person we are going to correct and condemn will probably justify himself, and condemn us in return; or, like the gentle Taft, he will say: "I don't see how I could have done any differently from what I have."

On Saturday morning, April 15, 1865, Abraham Lincoln lay dying in a hall bedroom of a cheap lodging house directly across the street from Ford's Theatre, where Booth had shot him. Lincoln's long body lay stretched diagonally across a sagging bed that was too short for him. A cheap reproduction of Rosa Bonheur's famous painting, "The Horse Fair," hung above the bed, and a dismal gas jet flickered yellow light.

As Lincoln lay dying, Secretary of War Stanton said, "There lies the most perfect ruler of men that the world has ever seen."

What was the secret of Lincoln's success in dealing with men? I studied the life of Abraham Lincoln for ten years, and devoted all of three years to writing and rewriting a book entitled *Lincoln the Unknown*. I believe I have made as detailed and exhaustive a study of Lincoln's personality and home life as it is possible for any human being to make. I made a special study of Lincoln's method of dealing with men. Did he indulge in criticism? Oh, yes. As a young man in the Pigeon Creek Valley of Indiana, he not only criticized but he wrote letters and poems ridiculing people and dropped these letters on the country roads where they were sure to be found. One of these letters aroused resentments that burned for a lifetime.

Even after Lincoln had become a practicing lawyer in Springfield, Illinois, he attacked his opponents openly in letters published in the newspapers. But he did this just once too often.

In the autumn of 1842, he ridiculed a vain, pugnacious Irish politician by the name of James Shields. Lincoln lampooned him through an anonymous letter published in the *Springfield Journal*. The town roared with laughter. Shields, sensitive and proud, boiled with indignation. He found out who wrote the letter, leaped on his horse, started after Lincoln, and challenged him to fight a duel. Lincoln didn't want to fight. He was opposed to dueling; but he couldn't get out of it and save his honor. He was given the choice of weapons. Since he had very long arms, he chose cavalry broad swords, took lessons in sword fighting from a West Point graduate; and, on the appointed day, he and Shields met on a sand bar in the Mississippi River, prepared to fight to the death; but, at the last minute, their seconds interrupted and stopped the duel.

That was the most lurid personal incident in Lincoln's life. It taught him an invaluable lesson in the art of dealing with people. Never again did he write an insulting letter. Never again did he ridicule anyone. And from that time on, he almost never criticized anybody for anything.

Time after time, during the Civil War, Lincoln put a new general at the head of the Army of the Potomac, and each one in turn—McClellan, Pope, Burnside, Hooker, Meade—blundered tragically, and drove Lincoln to pacing the floor in despair. Half the nation savagely condemned these incompetent generals, but Lincoln, "with malice towards none, with charity for all," held his peace. One of his favorite quotations was "Judge not, that ye be not judged."

And when Mrs. Lincoln and others spoke harshly of the Southern people, Lincoln replied: "Don't criticize them; they are just what we would be under similar circumstances."

Yet, if any man ever had occasion to criticize, surely it was Lincoln. Let's take just one illustration:

The Battle of Gettysburg was fought during the first three days of July, 1863. During the night of July 4, Lee began to retreat southward while storm clouds deluged the country with rain. When Lee reached the Potomac with his defeated army, he found a swollen, impassable river in front of him, and a victorious Union army behind him. Lee was in a trap. He couldn't escape. Lincoln saw that. Here was a golden, heaven-sent opportunity—the opportunity to capture Lee's army and end the war immediately. So, with a surge of high hope, Lincoln ordered Meade not to call a council of war but to attack Lee immediately. Lincoln telegraphed his orders and then sent a special messenger to Meade demanding immediate action.

And what did General Meade do? He did the very opposite of what he was told to do. He called a council of war in direct violation of Lincoln's orders. He hesitated. He procrastinated. He telegraphed all manner of excuses. He refused point blank to attack Lee. Finally the waters receded and Lee escaped over the Potomac with his forces.

Lincoln was furious. "What does this mean?" Lincoln cried to his son Robert. "Great God! What does this mean? We had them within our grasp, and had only to stretch forth our hands and they were ours; yet nothing that I could say or do could make the army move. Under the circumstances, almost any general could have defeated Lee. If I had gone up there, I could have whipped him myself."

In bitter disappointment, Lincoln sat down and wrote Meade this letter. And remember, at this period of his life he was extremely conservative and restrained in his phraseology. So this letter coming from Lincoln in 1863 was tantamount to the severest rebuke.

"My dear General,

"I do not believe you appreciate the magnitude of the misfortune involved in Lee's escape. He was within our easy grasp, and to have closed upon him would, in connection with our other late successes, have ended the war. As it is, the war will be prolonged indefinitely. If you could not safely attack Lee last Monday, how can you possibly do so south of the river, when you can take with you very few—no more than two-thirds of the force you then had in hand? It would be unreasonable to expect and I do not expect that you can now effect much. Your golden opportunity is gone, and I am distressed immeasurably because of it."

What do you suppose Meade did when he read that letter?

Meade never saw that letter. Lincoln never mailed it. It was found among Lincoln's papers after his death.

My guess is—and this is only a guess—that after writing that letter, Lincoln looked out of the window and said to himself, "Just a minute. Maybe I ought not to be so hasty. It is easy enough for me to sit here in the quiet of the White House and order Meade to attack; but if I had been up at Gettysburg, and if I had seen as much blood as Meade has seen during the last week, and if my ears had been pierced with the screams and shrieks of the wounded and dying, maybe I wouldn't be so anxious to attack either. If I had Meade's timid temperament, perhaps I would have done just what he has done. Anyhow, it is water under the bridge now. If I send this letter, it will relieve my feelings but it will make Meade try to justify himself. It will make him condemn me. It will arouse hard feelings, impair all his further usefulness as a commander, and perhaps force him to resign from the army."

So, as I have already said, Lincoln put the letter aside, for he had learned by bitter experience that sharp criticisms and rebukes almost invariably end in futility.

Theodore Roosevelt said that when he, as President, was confronted with some perplexing problem, he used to lean back and look up at a large painting of Lincoln that hung above his desk in the White House and ask himself, "What would Lincoln do if he were in my shoes? How would he solve this problem?"

The next time we are tempted to give somebody "hail Columbia," let's pull a five-dollar bill out of our pocket, look at Lincoln's picture on the bill, and ask, "How would Lincoln handle this problem if he had it?"

Do you know someone you would like to change and regulate and improve? Good! That is fine. I am all in favor of it. But why not begin on yourself? From a purely selfish standpoint, that is a lot more profitable than trying to improve others—yes, and a lot less dangerous.

"When a man's fight begins within himself," said Browning, "he is worth something." It will probably take from now until Christmas to perfect yourself. You can then have a nice long rest over the holidays and devote the New Year to regulating and criticizing other people.

But perfect yourself first.

"Don't complain about the snow on your neighbor's roof," said Confucius, "when your own doorstep is unclean."

When I was still young and trying hard to impress people, I wrote a foolish letter to Richard Harding Davis, an author who once loomed large on the literary horizon of America. I was preparing a magazine article about authors; and I asked Davis to tell me about his method of work. A few weeks earlier, I had received a letter from someone with this notation at the bottom: "Dictated but not read." I was quite impressed. I felt the writer must be very big and busy and important. I wasn't the slightest bit busy; but I was eager to make an impression on Richard Harding Davis so I ended my short note with the words: "Dictated but not read."

He never troubled to answer the letter. He simply returned it to me with this scribbled across the bottom: "Your bad manners are exceeded only by your bad manners." True, I had blundered, and perhaps I deserved his rebuke. But, being human, I resented it. I resented it so sharply that when I read of the death of Richard Harding Davis ten years later, the one thought that still persisted in my mind—I am ashamed to admit—was the hurt he had given me.

If you and I want to stir up a resentment tomorrow that may rankle across the decades and endure until death, just let us indulge in a little stinging criticism—no matter how certain we are that it is justified.

When dealing with people, let us remember we are not dealing with creatures of logic. We are dealing with creatures of emotion, creatures bristling with prejudices and motivated by pride and vanity.

And criticism is a dangerous spark—a spark that is liable to cause an explosion in the powder magazine of pride—an explosion that sometimes hastens death. For example, General Leonard Wood was criticized and not allowed to go with the army to France. That blow to his pride probably shortened his life.

Bitter criticism caused the sensitive Thomas Hardy, one of the finest novelists that ever enriched English literature, to give up the writing of fiction forever. Criticism drove Thomas Chatterton, the English poet, to suicide.

Benjamin Franklin, tactless in his youth, became so diplomatic, so adroit at handling people that he was made American Ambassador to France. The secret of his success? "I will speak ill of no man," he said, ". . . and speak all the good I know of everybody."

Any fool can criticize, condemn, and complain—and most fools do.

But it takes character and self-control to be understanding and forgiving.

"A great man shows his greatness," said Carlyle, "by the way he treats little men."

Instead of condemning people, let's try to understand them. Let's try to figure out why they do what they do. That's a lot more profitable and intriguing than criticism; and it breeds sympathy, tolerance, and kindness. "To know all is to forgive all."

As Dr. Johnson said: "God Himself, sir, does not propose to judge man until the end of his days."

Why should you and I?

DISCUSSION QUESTIONS

1. Discuss whether Carnegie's prose style is an implementation of his contention that "When dealing with people, let us remember we are not dealing with creatures of logic. We are dealing with creatures of emotion, creatures bristling with prejudices and motivated by pride and vanity." How does Carnegie try to convince his audience of the benefits to be gained by refraining from personal criticism?

2. Compare the sense of an audience implicit in *How to Win Friends and Influence People* with the audience imagined for Funk and Lewis's *Thirty Days to a More Powerful Vocabulary*. What characteristics are common to the audiences anticipated by these writers? What distinctions can you make between these audiences? Show how the writers's particular ways of talking are indicative of the readers they imagine for their prose. How does the fact that these writers achieved a great deal of success affect the voices they adopt when addressing their readers?

Wilfred Funk and Norman Lewis / *Thirty Days to a More Powerful Vocabulary*   1942

Written in 1942 by Wilfred Funk, lexicographer, publisher, and author, and Norman Lewis, instructor in English at the City College of New York and New York University, Thirty Days to a More Powerful Vocabulary *has been one of the most widely used "how-to-do-it" books published in this country. As an introductory pep talk, "Give Us 15 Minutes a Day" started millions of students and adults off on a self-improvement regimen that promised nothing less than success and personal fulfillment when the exercises were completed.*

FIRST DAY: GIVE US 15 MINUTES A DAY

Your boss has a bigger vocabulary than you have.

That's one good reason why he's your boss.

This discovery has been made in the word laboratories of the world. Not by theoretical English professors, but by practical, hard-headed scholars who have been searching for the secrets of success.

After a host of experiments and years of testing they have found out:

That if your vocabulary is limited your chances of success are limited.

That one of the easiest and quickest ways to get ahead is by consciously building up your knowledge of words.

That the vocabulary of the average person almost stops growing by the middle
twenties.

And that from then on it is necessary to have an intelligent plan if progress is to
be made. No haphazard hit-or-miss methods will do.

It has long since been satisfactorily established that a high executive does not
have a large vocabulary merely because of the opportunities of his position. That
would be putting the cart before the horse. Quite the reverse is true. His skill in
words was a tremendous help in getting him his job.

Dr. Johnson O'Connor of the Human Engineering Laboratory of Boston and of
the Stevens Institute of Technology in Hoboken, New Jersey, gave a vocabulary test
to 100 young men who were studying to be industrial executives.

Five years later those who had passed in the upper ten per cent *all,* without exception, had executive positions, while *not a single young man of the lower twenty-five
per cent had become an executive.*

You see, there are certain factors in success that can be measured as scientifically
as the contents of a test-tube, and it has been discovered that the most common characteristic of outstanding success is "an extensive knowledge of the exact meaning
of English words."

The extent of your vocabulary indicates the degree of your intelligence. Your
brain power will increase as you learn to know more words. Here's the proof.

Two classes in a high school were selected for an experiment. Their ages and
their environment were the same. Each class represented an identical cross-section
of the community. One, the control class, took the normal courses. The other class
was given special vocabulary training. At the end of the period the marks of the latter class surpassed those of the control group, not only in English, but in every subject, including mathematics and the sciences.

Similarly it has been found by Professor Lewis M. Terman, of Stanford University, that a vocabulary test is as accurate a measure of intelligence as any three units
of the standard and accepted Stanford-Binet I. Q. tests.

The study of words is not merely something that has to do with literature. Words
are your tools of thought. *You can't even think at all without them.* Try it. If you are
planning to go down town this afternoon you will find that you are saying to yourself: "I think I will go down town this afternoon." You can't make such a simple
decision as this without using words.

Without words you could make no decisions and form no judgments whatsoever.
A pianist may have the most beautiful tunes in his head, but if he had only five keys
on his piano he would never get more than a fraction of these tunes out.

Your words are *your* keys for *your* thoughts. And the more words you have at
your command the deeper, clearer and more accurate will be your thinking.

A command of English will not only improve the processes of your mind. It will
give you assurance; build your self-confidence; lend color to your personality;
increase your popularity. Your words are your personality. Your vocabulary is you.

Your words are all that we, your friends, have to know and judge you by. You
have no other medium for telling us your thoughts—for convincing us, persuading
us, giving us orders.

Words are explosive. Phrases are packed with TNT. A simple word can destroy a
friendship, land a large order. The proper phrases in the mouths of clerks have
quadrupled the sales of a department store. The wrong words used by a campaign
orator have lost an election. For instance, on one occasion the four unfortunate
words, "Rum, Romanism and Rebellion" used in a Republican campaign speech
threw the Catholic vote and the presidential victory to Grover Cleveland. Wars are
won by words. Soldiers fight for a phrase. "Make the world safe for Democracy."
"All out for England." "V for Victory." The "Remember the Maine" of Spanish
war days has now been changed to "Remember Pearl Harbor."

Words have changed the direction of history. Words can also change the direction of your life. They have often raised a man from mediocrity to success.

If you consciously increase your vocabulary you will unconsciously raise yourself to a more important station in life, and the new and higher position you have won will, in turn, give you a better opportunity for further enriching your vocabulary. It is a beautiful and successful cycle.

It is because of this intimate connection between words and life itself that we have organized this small volume in a new way. We have not given you mere lists of unrelated words to learn. We háve grouped the words around various departments of your life.

This book is planned to enlist your active cooperation. The authors wish you to read it with a pencil in your hand, for you will often be asked to make certain notations, to write answers to particular questions. The more you use your pencil, the more deeply you will become involved, and the deeper your involvement the more this book will help you. We shall occasionally ask you to use your voice as well as your pencil—to say things out loud. You see, we really want you to keep up a running conversation with us.

It's fun. And it's so easy. And we've made it like a game. We have filled these pages with a collection of devices that we hope will be stimulating. Here are things to challenge you and your friends. Try these tests on your acquaintances. They will enjoy them and it may encourage them to wider explorations in this exciting field of speech. There are entertaining verbal calisthenics here, colorful facts about language, and many excursions among the words that keep our speech the rich, flexible, lively means of communication that it is.

Come to this book every day. Put the volume by your bedside, if you like. A short time spent on these pages before you turn the lights out each night is better than an irregular hour now and then. If you can find the time to learn only two or three words a day—we will still promise you that at the end of thirty days you will have found a new interest. Give us *fifteen minutes a day*, and we will guarantee, at the end of a month, when you have turned over the last page of this book, that your words and your reading and your conversation and your life will all have a new and deeper meaning for you.

For words can make you great!

Ogden Nash / Kindly Unhitch That Star, Buddy   1945

Few writers, especially in the twentieth century, have been able to earn a living exclusively by writing poetry. Ogden Nash is one who has. The Pocket Book of Ogden Nash *(1935) ranks among the top ten poetry best-sellers of the last eighty years, and nearly every volume of his poetry from* Free Wheeling *(1931) to* Boy Is a Boy *(1960) has found a highly receptive audience.*

Nash (1902–71) is a master of what is usually termed "light verse"—poetry that is witty, humorous, often sophisticated, and not without a slight sting of satire. Nash brought to light verse an exceptionally playful imagination, one that enjoyed challenging the conventions of language and poetry without surrendering a stroke of technical virtuosity. Like the Depression film comedies that were popular just around the time his first volumes began to appear, Nash's verse succeeded in striking a fine balance between tough talk and innocence, urbanity and absurdity.

The following poem, which takes its lead from Ralph Waldo Emerson's advice

that we "hitch our wagon to a star," appeared in Many Long Years Ago (*1945*).
For another poetic version of this distinctively American theme, see Emily Dickinson's "Success Is Counted Sweetest" in "Classics."

I hardly suppose I know anybody who wouldn't rather be a success than a failure,
Just as I suppose every piece of crabgrass in the garden would much rather be an azalea,
And in celestial circles all the run-of-the-mill angels would rather be archangels or at least cherubim and seraphim,
And in the legal world all the little process-servers hope to grow up into great big bailiffim and sheriffim.
Indeed, everybody wants to be a wow,
But not everybody knows exactly how.
Some people think they will eventually wear diamonds instead of rhinestones
Only by everlastingly keeping their noses to their ghrine-stones,
And other people think they will be able to put in more time at Palm Beach and the Ritz
By not paying too much attention to attendance at the office but rather in being brilliant by starts and fits.
Some people after a full day's work sit up all night getting a college education by correspondence,
While others seem to think they'll get just as far by devoting their evenings to the study of the difference in temperament between brunettance and blondance.
In short, the world is filled with people trying to achieve success,
And half of them think they'll get it by saying No and half of them by saying Yes,
And if all the ones who say No said Yes, and vice versa, such is the fate of humanity that ninety-nine per cent of them still wouldn't be any better off than they were before,
Which perhaps is just as well because if everybody was a success nobody could be contemptuous of anybody else and everybody would start in all over again trying to be a bigger success than everybody else so they would have somebody to be contemptuous of and so on forevermore,
Because when people start hitching their wagons to a star,
That's the way they are.

Mickey Spillane / *I, the Jury*
[Mike Hammer Plots Revenge]   1947

Born in 1918 in Brooklyn, the son of an Irish bartender, Mickey Spillane grew up in what he calls a "very tough neighborhood in Elizabeth, New Jersey." He attended Kansas State College, worked summers as captain of lifeguards at Breezy Point, New York, and supplemented his income by writing comic books. In 1935, Spillane began selling stories to detective magazines, and after flying fighter missions in World War II, he worked as a trampoline artist for the Ringling Brothers Circus. Since his first novel, I, the Jury, *published in 1947, Spillane's books have had extraordinary sales. At one time seven of his novels were included in a list of the top ten best-selling fiction works of the last fifty years. Many of the*

novels have been turned into movies, a few with Spillane playing the role of
Mike Hammer.

CHAPTER ONE

I shook the rain from my hat and walked into the room. Nobody said a word. They stepped back politely and I could feel their eyes on me. Pat Chambers was standing by the door to the bedroom trying to steady Myrna. The girl's body was racking with dry sobs. I walked over and put my arms around her.

"Take it easy, kid," I told her. "Come on over here and lie down." I led her to a studio couch that was against the far wall and sat her down. She was in pretty bad shape. One of the uniformed cops put a pillow down for her and she stretched out.

Pat motioned me over to him and pointed to the bedroom. "In there, Mike," he said.

In there. The words hit me hard. In there was my best friend lying on the floor dead. The body. Now I could call it that. Yesterday it was Jack Williams, the guy that shared the same mud bed with me through two years of warfare in the stinking slime of the jungle. Jack, the guy who said he'd give his right arm for a friend and did when he stopped a bastard of a Jap from slitting me in two. He caught the bayonet in the biceps and they amputated his arm.

Pat didn't say a word. He let me uncover the body and feel the cold face. For the first time in my life I felt like crying. "Where did he get it, Pat?"

"In the stomach. Better not look at it. The killer carved the nose off a forty-five and gave it to him low."

I threw back the sheet anyway and a curse caught in my throat. Jack was in shorts, his one hand still clutching his belly in agony. The bullet went in clean, but where it came out left a hole big enough to cram a fist into.

Very gently I pulled the sheet back and stood up. It wasn't a complicated setup. A trail of blood led from the table beside the bed to where Jack's artificial arm lay. Under him the throw rug was ruffled and twisted. He had tried to drag himself along with his one arm, but never reached what he was after.

His police positive, still in the holster, was looped over the back of the chair. That was what he wanted. With a slug in his gut he never gave up.

I pointed to the rocker, overbalanced under the weight of the .38. "Did you move the chair, Pat?"

"No, why?"

"It doesn't belong there. Don't you see?"

Pat looked puzzled. "What are you getting at?"

"That chair was over there by the bed. I've been here often enough to remember that much. After the killer shot Jack, he pulled himself toward the chair. But the killer didn't leave after the shooting. He stood here and watched him grovel on the floor in agony. Jack was after that gun, but he never reached it. He could have if the killer didn't move it. The trigger-happy bastard must have stood by the door laughing while Jack tried to make his last play. He kept pulling the chair back, inch by inch, until Jack gave up. Tormenting a guy who's been through all sorts of hell. Laughing. This was no ordinary murder, Pat. It's as cold-blooded and as deliberate as I ever saw one. I'm going to get the one that did this."

"You dealing yourself in, Mike?"

"I'm in. What did you expect?"

"You're going to have to go easy."

"Uh-uh. Fast, Pat. From now on it's a race. I want the killer for myself. We'll work together as usual, but in the homestretch, I'm going to pull the trigger."

"No, Mike, it can't be that way. You know it."

"Okay, Pat," I told him. "You have a job to do, but so have I. Jack was about the best friend I ever had. We lived together and fought together. And by Christ, I'm not letting the killer go through the tedious process of the law. You know what happens, damn it. They get the best lawyer there is and screw up the whole thing and wind up a hero! The dead can't speak for themselves. They can't tell what happened. How could Jack tell a jury what it was like to have his insides ripped out by a dumdum? Nobody in the box would know how it felt to be dying or have your own killer laugh in your face. One arm. Hell, what does that mean? So he has the Purple Heart. But did they ever try dragging themselves across a floor to a gun with that one arm, their insides filling up with blood, so goddamn mad to be shot they'd do anything to reach the killer. No, damn it. A jury is cold and impartial like they're supposed to be, while some snotty lawyer makes them pour tears as he tells how his client was insane at the moment or had to shoot in self-defense. Swell. The law is fine. But this time I'm the law and I'm not going to be cold and impartial. I'm going to remember all those things."

I reached out and grabbed the lapels of his coat. "And something more, Pat. I want you to hear every word I say. I want you to tell it to everyone you know. And when you tell it, tell it strong, because I mean every word of it. There are ten thousand mugs that hate me and you know it. They hate me because if they mess with me I shoot their damn heads off. I've done it and I'll do it again."

There was so much hate welled up inside me I was ready to blow up, but I turned and looked down at what was once Jack. Right then I felt like saying a prayer, but I was too mad.

"Jack, you're dead now. You can't hear me any more. Maybe you can. I hope so. I want you to hear what I'm about to say. You've known me a long time, Jack. My word is good just as long as I live. I'm going to get the louse that killed you. He won't sit in the chair. He won't hang. He will die exactly as you died, with a .45 slug in the gut, just a little below the belly button. No matter who it is, Jack, I'll get the one. Remember, no matter who it is, I promise."

When I looked up, Pat was staring at me strangely. He shook his head. I knew what he was thinking. "Mike, lay off. For God's sake don't go off half-cocked about this. I know you too well. You'll start shooting up anyone connected with this and get in a jam you'll never get out of."

"I'm over it now, Pat. Don't get excited. From now on I'm after one thing, the killer. You're a cop, Pat. You're tied down by rules and regulations. There's someone over you. I'm alone. I can slap someone in the puss and they can't do a damn thing. No one can kick me out of my job. Maybe there's nobody to put up a huge fuss if I get gunned down, but then I still have a private cop's license with the privilege to pack a rod, and they're afraid of me. I hate hard, Pat. When I latch on to the one behind this they're going to wish they hadn't started it. Some day, before long, I'm going to have my rod in my mitt and the killer in front of me. I'm going to watch the killer's face. I'm going to plunk one right in his gut, and when he's dying on the floor I may kick his teeth out.

"You couldn't do that. You have to follow the book because you're a Captain of Homicide. Maybe the killer will wind up in the chair. You'd be satisfied, but I wouldn't. It's too easy. That killer is going down like Jack did."

There was nothing more to say. I could see by the set of Pat's jaw that he wasn't going to try to talk me out of it. All he could do was to try to beat me to him and take it from there. We walked out of the room together. The coroner's men had arrived and were ready to carry the body away.

I didn't want Myrna to see that. I sat down on the couch beside her and let her sob on my shoulder. That way I managed to shield her from the sight of her fiancé being carted off in a wicker basket. She was a good kid. Four years ago, when Jack was on the force, he had grabbed her as she was about to do a Dutch over the Brooklyn

Bridge. She was a wreck then. Dope had eaten her nerve ends raw. But he had taken her to his house and paid for a full treatment until she was normal. For the both of them it had been a love that blossomed into a beautiful thing. If it weren't for the war they would have been married long ago.

When Jack came back with one arm it had made no difference. He no longer was a cop, but his heart was with the force. She had loved him before and she still loved him. Jack wanted her to give up her job, but Myrna persuaded him to let her hold it until he really got settled. It was tough for a man with one arm to find employment, but he had many friends.

Before long he was part of the investigating staff of an insurance company. It had to be police work. For Jack there was nothing else. Then they were happy. Then they were going to be married. Now this.

Pat tapped me on the shoulder. "There's a car waiting downstairs to take her home."

I rose and took her by the hand. "Come on, kid. There's no more you can do. Let's go."

She didn't say a word, but stood up silently and let a cop steer her out the door. I turned to Pat. "Where do we start?" I asked him.

"Well, I'll give you as much as I know. See what you can add to it. You and Jack were great buddies. It might be that you can add something that will make some sense."

Inwardly I wondered. Jack was such a straight guy that he never made an enemy. Even while on the force. Since he'd gotten back, his work with the insurance company was pretty routine. But maybe an angle there, though.

"Jack threw a party last night," Pat went on. "Not much of an affair."

"I know," I cut in, "he called me and asked me over, but I was pretty well knocked out. I hit the sack early. Just a group of old friends he knew before the army."

"Yeah. We got their names from Myrna. The boys are checking on them now."

"Who found the body?" I asked.

"Myrna did. She and Jack were driving out to the country today to pick a building site for their cottage. She got here at eight A.M. or a little after. When Jack didn't answer, she got worried. His arm had been giving him trouble lately and she thought it might have been that. She called the super. He knew her and let her in. When she screamed the super came running back and called us. Right after I got the story about the party from her, she broke down completely. Then I called you."

"What time did the shooting occur?"

"The coroner places it about five hours before I got here. That would make it about three fifteen. When I get an autopsy report we may be able to narrow it down even further."

"Anyone hear a shot?"

"Nope. It probably was a silenced gun."

"Even with a muffler, a .45 makes a good-sized noise."

"I know, but there was a party going on down the hall. Not loud enough to cause complaints, but enough to cover up any racket that might have been made here."

"What about those that were here?" Pat reached in his pocket and pulled out a pad. He ripped a leaf loose and handed it to me.

"Here's a list Myrna gave me. She was the first to arrive. Got here at eight thirty last night. She acted as hostess, meeting the others at the door. The last one came about eleven. They spent the evening doing some light drinking and dancing, then left as a group about one."

I looked at the names Pat gave me. A few of them I knew well enough, while a couple of the others were people of whom Jack had spoken, but I had never met.

"Where did they go after the party, Pat?"

"They took two cars. The one Myrna went in belonged to Hal Kines. They drove straight up to Westchester, dropping Myrna off on the way. I haven't heard from any of the others yet."

Both of us were silent for a moment, then Pat asked, "What about a motive, Mike?"

I shook my head. "I don't see any yet. But I will. He wasn't killed for nothing. I'll bet this much, whatever it was, was big. There's a lot here that's screwy. You got anything?"

"Nothing more than I gave you, Mike. I was hoping you could supply some answers."

I grinned at him, but I wasn't trying to be funny. "Not yet. Not yet. They'll come though. And I'll relay them on to you, but by that time I'll be working on the next step."

"The cops aren't exactly dumb, you know. We can get our own answers."

"Not like I can. That's why you buzzed me so fast. You can figure things out as quickly as I can, but you haven't got the ways and means of doing the dirty work. That's where I come in. You'll be right behind me every inch of the way, but when the pinch comes I'll get shoved aside and you slap the cuffs on. That is, if you can shove me aside. I don't think you can."

"Okay, Mike, call it your own way. I want you in all right. But I want the killer, too. Don't forget that. I'll be trying to beat you to him. We have every scientific facility at our disposal and a lot of men to do the leg work. We're not short in brains, either," he reminded me.

"Don't worry, I don't underrate the cops. But cops can't break a guy's arm to make him talk, and they can't shove his teeth in with the muzzle of a .45 to remind him that you aren't fooling. I do my own leg work, and there are a lot of guys who will tell me what I want to know because they know what I'll do to them if they don't. My staff is strictly ex officio, but very practical."

That ended the conversation. We walked out into the hall where Pat put a patrolman on the door to make sure things stayed as they were. We took the self-operated elevator down four flights to the lobby and I waited while Pat gave a brief report to some reporters.

My car stood at the curb behind the squad car. I shook hands with Pat and climbed into my jalopy and headed for the Hackard Building, where I held down a two-room suite to use for operation.

CHAPTER TWO

The office was locked when I got there. I kicked on the door a few times and Velda clicked the lock back. When she saw who it was she said, "Oh, it's you."

"What do you mean—'Oh, it's you'! Surely you remember me, Mike Hammer, your boss."

"Poo! You haven't been here in so long I can't tell you from another bill collector." I closed the door and followed her into my sanctum sanctorum. She had million-dollar legs, that girl, and she didn't mind showing them off. For a secretary she was an awful distraction. She kept her coal-black hair long in a page-boy cut and wore tight-fitting dresses that made me think of the curves in the Pennsylvania Highway every time I looked at her. Don't get the idea that she was easy, though. I've seen her give a few punks the brush off the hard way. When it came to quick action she could whip off a shoe and crack a skull before you could bat an eye.

Not only that, but she had a private op's ticket and on occasions when she went out with me on a case, packed a flat .32 automatic—and she wasn't afraid to use it. In the three years she worked for me I never made a pass at her. Not that I didn't want to, but it would be striking too close to home.

Velda picked up her pad and sat down. I plunked myself in the old swivel chair, then swung around facing the window. Velda threw a thick packet on my desk.

"Here's all the information I could get on those that were at the party last night." I looked at her sharply.

"How did you know about Jack? Pat only called my home." Velda wrinkled that pretty face of hers up into a cute grin.

"You forget that I have an in with a few reporters. Tom Dugan from the *Chronicle* remembered that you and Jack had been good friends. He called here to see what he could get and wound up by giving me all the info he had—and I didn't have to sex him, either." She put that in as an afterthought. "Most of the gang at the party were listed in your files. Nothing sensational. I got a little data from Tom who had more personal dealings with a few of them. Mostly character studies and some society reports. Evidently they were people whom Jack had met in the past and liked. You've even spoken about several yourself."

I tore open the package and glanced at a sheaf of photos. "Who are these?" Velda looked over my shoulder and pointed them out.

"Top one is Hal Kines, a med student from a university upstate. He's about twenty-three, tall, and looks like a crew man. At least that's the way he cuts his hair." She flipped the page over. "These two are the Bellemy twins. Age, twenty-nine, unmarried. In the market for husbands. Live off the fatta the land with dough their father left them. A half interest in some textile mills someplace down South."

"Yeah," I cut in, "I know them. Good lookers, but not very bright. I met them at Jack's place once and again at a dinner party."

She pointed to the next one. A newspaper shot of a middle-aged guy with a broken nose. George Kalecki. I knew him pretty well. In the roaring twenties he was a bootlegger. He came out of the crash with a million dollars, paid up his income tax, and went society. He fooled a lot of people but he didn't fool me. He still had his finger in a lot of games just to keep in practice. Nothing you could pin on him though. He kept a staff of lawyers on their toes to keep him clean and they were doing a good job. "What about him?" I asked her.

"You know more than I do. Hal Kines is staying with him. They live about a mile above Myrna in Westchester." I nodded. I remembered Jack talking about him. He had met George through Hal. The kid had been a friend of George ever since the older man had met him through some mutual acquaintance. George was the guy that was putting him through college, but why, I wasn't sure.

The next shot was one of Myrna with a complete history of her that Jack had given me. Included was a medical record from the hospital when he had made her go cold turkey, which is dope-addict talk for an all-out cure. They cut them off from the stuff completely. It either kills them or cures them. In Myrna's case, she made it. But she made Jack promise that he would never try to get any information from her about where she got the stuff. The way he fell for the girl, he was ready to do anything she asked, and so far as he was concerned, the matter was completely dropped.

I flipped through the medical record. Name, Myrna Devlin. Attempted suicide while under the influence of heroin. Brought to emergency ward of General Hospital by Detective Jack Williams. Admitted 3-15-40. Treatment complete 9-21-40. No information available on patient's source of narcotics. Released into custody of Detective Jack Williams 9-30-40. Following this was a page of medical details which I skipped.

"Here's one you'll like, chum," Velda grinned at me. She pulled out a full-length photo of a gorgeous blonde. My heart jumped when I saw it. The picture was taken at a beach, and she stood there tall and languid-looking in a white bathing suit. Long solid legs. A little heavier than the movie experts consider good form, but the kind that make you drool to look at. Under the suit I could see the muscles of her stomach. Incredibly wide shoulders for a woman, framing breasts that jutted out, seeking freedom from the restraining fabric of the suit. Her hair looked white in the picture, but I could tell that it was a natural blonde. Lovely, lovely yellow hair. But her face was what got me. I thought Velda was a good looker, but this one was even lovelier. I felt like whistling.

"Who is she?"

"Maybe I shouldn't tell you. That leer on your face could get you into trouble, but it's all there. Name's Charlotte Manning. She's a female psychiatrist with offices on Park Avenue, and very successful. I understand she caters to a pretty ritzy clientele."

I glanced at the number and made up my mind that right here was something that made this business a pleasurable one. I didn't say that to Velda. Maybe I'm being conceited, but I've always had the impression that she had designs on me. Of course she never mentioned it, but whenever I showed up late in the office with lipstick on my shirt collar, I couldn't get two words out of her for a week.

I stacked the sheaf back on my desk and swung around in the chair. Velda was leaning forward ready to take notes. "Want to add anything, Mike?"

"Don't think so. At least not now. There's too much to think about first. Nothing seems to make sense."

"Well, what about motive? Could Jack have had any enemies that caught up with him?"

"Nope. None I know of. He was square. He always gave a guy a break if he deserved it. Then, too, he never was wrapped up in anything big."

"Did he own anything of any importance?"

"Not a thing. The place was completely untouched. He had a few hundred dollars in his wallet that was lying on the dresser. The killing was done by a sadist. He tried to reach his gun, but the killer pulled the chair it hung on back slowly, making him crawl after it with a slug in his gut, trying to keep his insides from falling out with his hand."

"Mike, please."

I said no more. I just sat there and glowered at the wall. Someday I'd trigger the bastard that shot Jack. In my time I've done it plenty of times. No sentiment. That went out with the first. After the war I've been almost anxious to get to some of the rats that make up the section of humanity that prey on people. People. How incredibly stupid they could be sometimes. A trial by law for a killer. A loophole in the phrasing that lets a killer crawl out. But in the end the people have their justice. They get it through guys like me once in a while. They crack down on society and I crack down on them. I shoot them like the mad dogs they are and society drags me to court to explain the whys and wherefores of the extermination. They investigate my past, check my fingerprints and throw a million questions my way. The papers make me look like a kill-crazy shamus, but they don't bear down too hard because Pat Chambers keeps them off my neck. Besides, I do my best to help the boys out and they know it. And I'm usually good for a story when I wind up a case.

Velda came back into the office with the afternoon edition of the sheets. The kill was spread all over the front page, followed by a four-column layout of what details were available. Velda was reading over my shoulder and I heard her gasp.

"Did you come in for a blasting! Look." She was pointing to the last paragraph. There was my tie-up with the case, but what she was referring to was the word-for-word statement that I had made to Jack. My promise. My word to a dead friend that I would kill this murderer as he had killed him. I rolled the paper into a ball and threw it viciously at the wall.

"The louse! I'll break his filthy neck for printing that. I meant what I said when I made that promise. It's sacred to me, and they make a joke out of it. Pat did that. And I thought he was a friend. Give me the phone."

Velda grabbed my arm. "Take it easy. Suppose he did. After all, Pat's still a cop. Maybe he saw a chance of throwing the killer your way. If the punk knows you're after him for keeps he's liable not to take it standing still and make a play for you. Then you'll have him."

"Thanks, kid," I told her, "but your mind's too clean. I think you got the first part right, but your guess on the last part smells. Pat doesn't want me to have any part of him because he knows the case is ended right there. If he can get the killer to me you can bet your grandmother's uplift bra that he'll have a tail on me all the way with someone ready to step in when the shooting starts."

"I don't know about that, Mike. Pat knows you're too smart not to recognize when you're being tailed. I wouldn't think he'd do that."

"Oh, no? He isn't dumb by any means. I'll bet you a sandwich against a marriage license he's got a flatfoot downstairs covering every exit in the place ready to pick me up when I leave. Sure, I'll shake them, but it won't stop there. A couple of experts will take up where they leave off."

Velda's eyes were glowing like a couple of hot brands. "Are you serious about that? About the bet, I mean?"

I nodded. "Dead serious. Want to go downstairs with me and take a look?" She grinned and grabbed her coat. I pulled on my battered felt and we left the office, but not before I had taken a second glance at the office address of Charlotte Manning.

Pete, the elevator operator, gave me a toothy grin when we stepped into the car. "Evening, Mr. Hammer," he said.

I gave him an easy jab in the short ribs and said, "What's new with you?"

"Nothing much, 'cepting I don't get to sit down much on the job anymore." I had to grin. Velda had lost the bet already. That little piece of simple repartee between Pete and myself was a code system we had rigged up years ago. His answer meant that I was going to have company when I left the building. It cost me a fin a week but it was worth it. Pete could spot a flatfoot faster than I can. He should. He had been a pickpocket until a long stretch up the river gave him a turn of mind.

For a change I decided to use the front entrance. I looked around for my tail but there was none to be seen. For a split second my heart leaped into my throat. I was afraid Pete had gotten his signals crossed. Velda was a spotter, too, and the smile she was wearing as we crossed the empty lobby was a thing to see. She clamped onto my arm ready to march me to the nearest justice of the peace.

But when I went through the revolving doors her grin passed as fast as mine appeared. Our tail was walking in front of us. Velda said a word that nice girls don't usually use, and you see scratched in the cement by some evil-minded guttersnipe.

This one was smart. We never saw where he came from. He walked a lot faster than we did, swinging a newspaper from his hand against his leg. Probably, he spotted us through the windows behind the palm, then seeing what exit we were going to use, walked around the corner and came past us as we left. If we had gone the other way, undoubtedly there was another ready to pick us up.

But this one had forgotten to take his gun off his hip and stow it under his shoulder, and guns make a bump look the size of a pumpkin when you're used to looking for them.

When I reached the garage he was nowhere to be seen. There were a lot of doors he could have ducked behind. I didn't waste time looking for him. I backed the car out and Velda crawled in beside me. "Where to now?" she asked.

"The automat, where you're going to buy me a sandwich."

Grace Metalious / *Peyton Place*
[Michael Rossi Comes to Peyton Place]   1956

*One of the greatest-selling novels in American publishing history was written by a
New Hampshire housewife with little formal education and no literary background
or cultural advantages. Born in Manchester, New Hampshire, in 1924, Grace
Marie Antoinette Jeanne d'Arc de Repentigny was the daughter of parents who had
not much more to give her than her fancy name. At seventeen she married George
Metalious, a mill worker, who later put himself through college to become a schoolteacher only to lose his job as a result of the public scandal caused by his wife's
novel. What is perhaps most remarkable about* Peyton Place, *for all its faults of
gracelessness and composition, is not that the book became a best-seller so unexpectedly and rapidly, but that a generally uneducated young woman, with three
small children and very little money, had the literary ambition and steady application needed to write publishable fiction.*

*Metalious was a tough-talking, hard-working, hard-drinking woman. Like
many authors of best-sellers, she was often defensive about her work. "If I'm a
lousy writer," she once said, "a hell of a lot of people have got lousy taste."
She died at the age of thirty-nine of a severe liver ailment.*

A few days later, Michael Rossi stepped off the train in front of the Peyton Place
railroad station. No other passenger got off with him. He paused on the empty platform and looked around thoroughly, for it was a habit with him to fix a firm picture
of a new place in his mind so that it could never be erased nor forgotten. He stood
still, feeling the two heavy suitcases that he carried pulling at his arm muscles, and
reflected that there wasn't much to see, nor to hear, for that matter. It was shortly
after seven o'clock in the evening, but it might have been midnight or four in the
morning for all the activity going on. Behind him there was nothing but the two
curving railroad tracks and from a distance came the long-drawn-out wail of the
train as it made the pull across the wide Connecticut River. And it was cold.

For April, thought Rossi, shrugging uncomfortably under his topcoat, it was
damned cold.

Straight ahead of him stood the railroad station, a shabby wooden building with a
severely pitched roof and several thin, Gothic-looking windows that gave it the air
of a broken-down church. Nailed to the front of the building, at the far left of the
front door, was a blue and white enameled sign. PEYTON PLACE, it read. POP. 3675.

Thirty-six seventy-five, thought Rossi, pushing open the railroad station's narrow
door. Sounds like the price of a cheap suit.

The inside of the building was lit by several dim electric light bulbs suspended
from fixtures which obviously had once burned gas, and there were rows of benches
constructed of the most hideous wood obtainable, golden oak. No one was sitting on
them. The brown, roughly plastered walls were trimmed with the same yellow
wood and the floor was made of black and white marble. There was an iron-barred
cage set into one wall and from behind this a straight, thin man with a pinched-look-
ing nose, steel-rimmed glasses and a string tie stared at Rossi.

"Is there a place where I can check these?" asked the new principal, indicating
the two bags at his feet.

"Next room," said the man in the cage.

"Thank you," said Rossi and made his way through a narrow archway into
another, smaller room. It was a replica of the main room, complete with golden

oak, marble and converted gas fixtures, but with the addition of two more doors. These were clearly labeled. MEN, said one. WOMEN, said the other. Against one wall there was a row of pale gray metal lockers, and to Rossi, these looked almost friendly. They were the only things in the station even faintly resembling anything he had ever seen in his life.

"Ah," he murmured, "shades of Grand Central," and bent to push his suitcases into one of the lockers. He deposited his dime, withdrew his key and noticed that his was the only locker in use.

Busy town, he thought, and walked back to the main room. His footsteps rang disquietingly on the scrubbed marble floor.

Leslie Harrington had instructed Rossi to call him at his home as soon as he got off the train, but Rossi by-passed the solitary telephone booth in the railroad station. He wanted to look at the town alone first, to see it through no one's eyes but his own. Besides, he had decided the night that Harrington had called long-distance that the chairman of the Peyton Place School Board sounded like a man puffed up with his own importance, and must therefore be a pain in the ass.

"Say, Dad," began Rossi, addressing the man in the cage.

"Name's Rhodes," said the old man.

"Mr. Rhodes," began Rossi again, "could you tell me how I can get into town from here? I noticed a distressing lack of taxicabs outside."

"Be damned peculiar if I couldn't."

"If you couldn't what?"

"Tell you how to get uptown. Been living here for over sixty years."

"That's interesting."

"You're Mr. Rossi, eh?"

"Admitted."

"Ain't you goin' to call up Leslie Harrington?"

"Later. I'd like to get a cup of coffee first. Listen, isn't there a cab to be had anywhere around here?"

"No."

Michael Rossi controlled a laugh. It was beginning to look as if everything he had ever heard about these sullen New Englanders was true. The old man in the cage gave the impression that he had been sucking lemons for years. Certainly sourness had not been one of the traits in that little Pittsburgh secretary who claimed to be from Boston, but she said herself that she was East Boston Irish, and therefore not reliably representative of New England.

"Do you mind, then, telling me how I can walk into town from here, Mr. Rhodes?" asked Rossi.

"Not at all," said the stationmaster, and Rossi noticed that he pronounced the three words as one: Notatall. "Just go out this front door, walk around the depot to the street and keep on walking for two blocks. That will bring you to Elm Street."

"Elm Street? Is that the main street?"

"Yes."

"I had the idea that the main streets of all small New England towns were named Main Street."

"Perhaps," said Mr. Rhodes, who prided himself, when annoyed, on enunciating his syllables, "it is true that the main streets of all *other* small towns are named Main Street. Not, however, in Peyton Place. Here the main street is called Elm Street."

Period. Paragraph, thought Rossi. Next question. "Peyton Place is an odd name," he said. "How did anyone come to pick that one?"

Mr. Rhodes drew back his hand and started to close the wooden panel that backed the iron bars of his cage.

"I am closing now, Mr. Rossi," he said. "And I suggest that you be on your way if you want to obtain a cup of coffee. Hyde's Diner closes in half an hour."

"Thank you," said Rossi to the wooden panel which was suddenly between him and Mr. Rhodes.

Friendly bastard, he thought, as he left the station and began to walk up the street labeled Depot.

Michael Rossi was a massively boned man with muscles that seemed to quiver every time he moved. In the steel mills of Pittsburgh he had looked, so one smitten secretary had told him, like a color illustration of a steelworker. His arms, beneath sleeves rolled above the elbow, were knotted powerfully, and the buttons of his work shirts always seemed about to pop off under the strain of trying to cover his chest. He was six feet four inches tall, weighed two hundred and twelve pounds, stripped, and looked like anything but a schoolteacher. In fact, the friendly secretary in Pittsburgh had told him that in his dark blue suit, white shirt and dark tie, he looked like a steelworker disguised as a schoolteacher, a fact which would not inspire trust in the heart of any New Englander.

Michael Rossi was a handsome man, in a dark-skinned, black-haired, obviously sexual way, and both men and women were apt to credit him more with attractiveness than intellect. This was a mistake, for Rossi had a mind as analytical as a mathematician's and as curious as a philosopher's. It was his curiosity which had prompted him to give up teaching for a year to go to work in Pittsburgh. He had learned more about economics, labor and capital in that one year than he had learned in ten years of reading books. He was thirty-six years old and totally lacking in regret over the fact that he had never stayed in one job long enough to "get ahead," as the Pittsburgh secretary put it. He was honest, completely lacking in diplomacy, and the victim of a vicious temper which tended to loosen a tongue that had learned to speak on the lower East Side of New York City.

Rossi was halfway through the second block on Depot Street, leading to Elm, when Parker Rhodes, at the wheel of an old sedan, passed him. The stationmaster looked out of the window on the driver's side of his car and looked straight through Peyton Place's new headmaster.

Sonofabitch, thought Rossi. Real friendly sonofabitch to offer me a lift in his junk heap of a car.

Then he smiled and wondered why Mr. Rhodes had been so sensitive on the subject of his town's name. He would ask around and see if everyone in this godforsaken place reacted the same way to his question. He had reached the corner of Elm Street and paused to look about him. On the corner stood a white, cupola-topped house with stiff lace curtains at the windows. Silhouetted against the light inside, he could see two women sitting at a table with what was obviously a checkerboard between them. The women were big, saggy bosomed and white haired, and Rossi thought that they looked like a pair who had worked too long at the same girls' school.

I wonder who they are? he asked himself, as he looked in at the Page Girls. Maybe they're the town's two Lizzies.

Reluctantly, he turned away from the white house and made his way west on Elm Street. When he had walked three blocks, he came to a small, clean-looking and well-lighted restaurant. *Hyde's Diner* said a polite neon sign, and Rossi opened the door and went in. The place was empty except for one old man sitting at the far end of the counter, and another man who came out of the kitchen at the sound of the door opening.

"Good evening, sir," said Corey Hyde.

"Good evening," said Rossi. "Coffee, please, and a piece of pie. Any kind."

"Apple, sir?"

"Any kind is O.K."

"Well, we have pumpkin, too."

"Apple is fine."

"I think there's a piece of cherry left, also."

"Apple," said Rossi, "will be fine."

"You're Mr. Rossi, aren't you?"

"Yes."

"Glad to meet you, Mr. Rossi. My name is Hyde. Corey Hyde."

"How do you do?"

"Quite well, as a rule," said Corey Hyde. "I'll keep on doing quite well, as long as no one starts up another restaurant."

"Look, could I have my coffee now?"

"Certainly. Certainly, Mr. Rossi."

The old man at the end of the counter sipped his coffee from a spoon and looked surreptitiously at the newcomer to town. Rossi wondered if the old man could be the village idiot.

"Here you are, Mr. Rossi," said Corey Hyde. "The best apple pie in Peyton Place."

"Thank you."

Rossi stirred sugar into his coffee and sampled the pie. It was excellent.

"Peyton Place," he said Corey Hyde, "is the oddest name for a town I've ever heard. Who is it named for?"

"Oh, I don't know," said Corey, making unnecessary circular motions with a cloth on his immaculate counter. "There's plenty of towns have funny names. Take that Baton Rouge, Louisiana. I had a kid took French over to the high school. Told me Baton Rouge means Red Stick. Now ain't that a helluva name for a town? Red Stick, Louisiana. And what about that Des Moines, Iowa? What a crazy name that is."

"True," said Rossi. "But for whom is Peyton Place named, or for what?"

"Some feller that built a castle up here back before the Civil War. Feller by the name of Samuel Peyton," said Corey reluctantly.

"A castle!" exclaimed Rossi.

"Yep. A real, true, honest-to-God castle, transported over here from England, every stick and stone of it."

"Who was this Peyton?" asked Rossi. "An exiled duke?"

"Nah," said Corey Hyde. "Just a feller with money to burn. Excuse me, Mr. Rossi. I got things to do in the kitchen."

The old man at the end of the counter chuckled. "Fact of the matter, Mr. Rossi," said Clayton Frazier in a loud voice, "is that this town was named for a friggin' nigger. That's what ails Corey. He's delicate like, and just don't want to spit it right out."

While Michael Rossi sipped his coffee and enjoyed his pie and conversation with Clayton Frazier, Parker Rhodes arrived at his home on Laurel Street. He parked his ancient sedan and entered the house where, without first removing his coat and hat, he went directly to the telephone.

"Hello," he said, as soon as the party he had called answered. "That you, Leslie? Well, he's here, Leslie. Got off the seven o'clock, checked his suitcases and walked uptown. He's sitting down at Hyde's right now. What's that? No, he can't get his bags out of the depot until morning, you know that. What? Well, goddamn it, he didn't ask me, that's why. He didn't ask for information about when he could get them out. He just wanted to know where he could check his bags, so I told him. What'd you say, Leslie? No, I did not tell him that no one has used those lockers since they were installed five years ago. What? Well, goddamn it, he didn't ask me, that's why. Yes. Yes, he is, Leslie. *Real* dark, and big. Sweet Jesus, he's as big

as the side of a barn. Yes. Down at Hyde's. Said he wanted a cup of coffee.''

If Michael Rossi had overheard this conversation, he would have noticed again
that Rhodes pronounced his last three words as one: Kupakawfee. But at the moment, Rossi was looking at the tall, silver-haired man who had just walked through
Hyde's front door.

My God! thought Rossi, awed. This guy looks like a walking ad for a Planter's
Punch. A goddamned Kentucky colonel in this place!

''Evenin', Doc,'' said Corey Hyde, who had put his head out of the kitchen at the
sound of the door, looking, thought Rossi, rather like a tired turtle poking his head
out of his shell.

''Evenin', Corey,'' and Rossi knew as soon as the man spoke, that this was no
fugitive Kentucky colonel but a native.

''Welcome to Peyton Place, Mr. Rossi,'' said the white-haired native. ''It's nice
to have you with us. My name is Swain. Matthew Swain.''

''Evenin', Doc,'' said Clayton Frazier. ''I just been tellin' Mr. Rossi here some
of our local legends.''

''Make you want to jump on the next train out, Mr. Rossi?'' asked the doctor.

''No, sir,'' said Rossi, thinking that there was, after all, one goddamned face in
this godforsaken town that looked human.

''I hope you'll enjoy living here,'' said the doctor. ''Maybe you'll let me show
you the town after you get settled a little.''

''Thank you, sir. I'd enjoy that,'' said Rossi.

''Here comes Leslie Harrington,'' said Clayton Frazier.

The figure outside the glass door of the restaurant was clearly visible to those inside. The doctor turned to look.

''It's Leslie, all right,'' he said. ''Come to fetch you home, Mr. Rossi.''

Harrington strode into the restaurant, a smile like one made of molded ice cream
on his face.

''Ah, Mr. Rossi,'' he cried jovially, extending his hand. ''It is indeed a pleasure
to welcome you to Peyton Place.''

He was thinking, Oh, Christ, he's worse and more of it than I'd feared.

''Hello, Mr. Harrington,'' said Rossi, barely touching the extended hand.
''Made any long-distance calls lately?''

The smile on Harrington's face threatened to melt and run together, but he
rescued it just in time.

''Ha, ha, ha,'' he laughed. ''No, Mr. Rossi, I haven't had much time for tele-
phoning these days. I've been too busy looking for a suitable apartment for our new
headmaster.''

''I trust you were successful,'' said Rossi.

''Yes. Yes, I was, as a matter of fact. Well, come along. I'll take you over in my
car.''

''As soon as I finish my coffee,'' said Rossi.

''Certainly, certainly,'' said Harrington. ''Oh, hello, Matt. 'Lo, Clayton.''

''Coffee, Mr. Harrington?'' asked Corey Hyde.

''No, thanks,'' said Harrington.

When Rossi had finished, everyone said good night carefully, all the way around,
and he and Harrington left the restaurant. As soon as the door had closed behind
them, Dr. Swain began to laugh.

''Goddamn it,'' he roared, ''I'll bet my sweet young arse that Leslie has met his
match this time!''

''There's one schoolteacher that Leslie ain't gonna shove around,'' observed
Clayton Frazier.

Corey Hyde, who owed money at the bank where Leslie Harrington was a trustee, smiled uncertainly.

"The textile racket must be pretty good," said Rossi, as he opened the door of Leslie Harrington's new Packard.

"Can't complain," said Harrington. "Can't complain," and the mill-owner shook himself angrily at this sudden tendency to repeat all his words.

Rossi stopped in the act of getting into the car. A woman was walking toward them, and as she stepped under the street light on the corner, Rossi got a quick glimpse of blond hair and a swirl of dark coat.

"Who's that?" he demanded.

Leslie Harrington peered through the darkness. As the figure drew nearer, he smiled.

"That's Constance MacKenzie," he said. "Maybe you two will have a lot in common. She used to live in New York. Nice woman; good looking, too. Widow."

"Introduce me," said Rossi, drawing himself up to his full height.

"Certainly. Certainly, be glad to. Oh, Connie!"

"Yes, Leslie?"

The woman's voice was rich and husky, and Rossi fought down the urge to straighten the knot in his tie.

"Connie," said Harrington, "I'd like you to meet our new headmaster, Mr. Rossi. Mr. Rossi, Constance MacKenzie."

Constance extended her hand and while he held it, she gazed at him full in the eyes.

"How do you do?" she said at last, and Michael Rossi was puzzled, for something very much like relief showed through her voice.

"I'm glad to know you, Mrs. MacKenzie," said Rossi, and he thought, Very glad to know you, baby. I want to know you a lot better, on a bed, for instance, with that blond hair spread out on a pillow.

Vance Packard / *The Hidden Persuaders*   1957

With the publication of The Hidden Persuaders, *Vance Packard, a former columnist for the* Boston Daily Record *and a staff writer for* American Magazine *and* Collier's, *became the most widely read analyst of America's shopping habits. Based on motivational research and the techniques of depth psychology, Packard's findings served as a popular exposé of the manipulations of Madison Avenue. In "Babes in Consumerland," he focuses on how the goods are packaged and positioned in supermarkets to ensure impulse buying.*

BABES IN CONSUMERLAND

> *"You have to have a carton that attracts and hypnotizes this woman, like waving a flashlight in front of her eyes."*
> —Gerald Stahl, executive vice-president, Package Designers Council

For some years the DuPont company has been surveying the shopping habits of American housewives in the new jungle called the supermarket. The results have been so exciting in the opportunities they suggest to marketers that hundreds of leading food companies and ad agencies have requested copies. Husbands fretting over the high cost of feeding their families would find the results exciting, too, in a dismaying sort of way.

The opening statement of the 1954 report exclaimed enthusiastically in display type: "Today's shopper in the supermarket is more and more guided by the buying philosophy—'If somehow your product catches my eye—and for some reason it looks especially good—I WANT IT.' " That conclusion was based on studying the shopping habits of 5,338 shoppers in 250 supermarkets.

DuPont's investigators have found that the mid-century shopper doesn't bother to make a list or at least not a complete list of what she needs to buy. In fact less than one shopper in five has a complete list, but still the wives always manage to fill up their carts, often while exclaiming, according to DuPont: "I certainly never intended to get that much!" Why doesn't the wife need a list? DuPont gives this blunt answer: "Because seven out of ten of today's purchases are decided in the store, where the shoppers buy on impulse!!!"

The proportion of impulse buying of groceries has grown almost every year for nearly two decades, and DuPont notes that this rise in impulse buying has coincided with the growth in self-service shopping. Other studies show that in groceries where there are clerks to wait on customers there is about half as much impulse buying as in self-service stores. If a wife has to face a clerk she thinks out beforehand what she needs.

The impulse buying of pungent-odored food such as cheese, eye-appealing items like pickles or fruit salad in glass jars, and candy, cake, snack spreads, and other "self-gratifying items" runs even higher than average, 90 per cent of all purchases. Other investigators have in general confirmed the DuPont figures on impulse buying. The Folding Paper Box Association found that two-thirds of all purchases were completely or partially on impulse; the *Progressive Grocer* put the impulse figure about where DuPont does: seven out of ten purchases. And *Printer's Ink* observed with barely restrained happiness that the shopping list had become obsolescent if not obsolete.

One motivational analyst who became curious to know why there had been such a great rise in impulse buying at supermarkets was James Vicary. He suspected that some special psychology must be going on inside the women as they shopped in supermarkets. His suspicion was that perhaps they underwent an increase in tension when confronted with so many possibilities that they were forced into making quick purchases. He set out to find out if this was true. The best way to detect what was going on inside the shopper was a galvanometer or lie detector. That obviously was impractical. The next best thing was to use a hidden motion-picture camera and record the eye-blink rate of the women as they shopped. How fast a person blinks his eyes is a pretty good index of his state of inner tension. The average person, according to Mr. Vicary, normally blinks his eyes about thirty-two times a minute. If he is tense he blinks them more frequently, under extreme tension up to fifty or sixty times a minute. If he is notably relaxed on the other hand his eye-blink rate may drop to a subnormal twenty or less.

Mr. Vicary set up his cameras and started following the ladies as they entered the store. The results were startling, even to him. Their eye-blink rate, instead of going up to indicate mounting tension, went down and down, to a very subnormal fourteen blinks a minute. The ladies fell into what Mr. Vicary calls a hypnoidal trance, a light kind of trance that, he explains, is the first stage of hypnosis. Mr. Vicary has decided that the main cause of the trance is that the supermarket is packed with products that in former years would have been items that only kings and queens could afford, and here in this fairyland they were available. Mr. Vicary theorizes: "Just in this generation, anyone can be a king or queen and go through these stores where the products say 'Buy me, buy me.' "

Interestingly many of these women were in such a trance that they passed by neighbors and old friends without noticing or greeting them. Some had a sort of glassy stare. They were so entranced as they wandered about the store plucking things off shelves at random that they would bump into boxes without seeing them and did not even notice the camera although in some cases their face would pass within a foot and a half of the spot where the hidden camera was clicking away. When the wives had filled their carts (or satisfied themselves) and started toward the check-out counter their eye-blink rate would start rising up to a slightly subnormal twenty-five blinks per minute. Then, at the sound of the cash-register bell and the voice of the clerk asking for money, the eye-blink rate would race up past normal to a high abnormal of forty-five blinks per minute. In many cases it turned out that the women did not have enough money to pay for all the nice things they had put in the cart.

In this beckoning field of impulse buying psychologists have teamed up with merchandising experts to persuade the wife to buy products she may not particularly need or even want until she happens to see it invitingly presented. The 60,000,000 American women who go into supermarkets every week are getting "help" in their purchases and "splurchases" from psychologists and psychiatrists hired by the food merchandisers. On May 18, 1956, *The New York Times* printed a remarkable interview with a young man named Gerald Stahl, executive vice-president of the Package Designers Council. He stated: "Psychiatrists say that people have so much to choose from that they want help—they will like the package that hypnotizes them into picking it." He urged food packers to put more hypnosis into their package designing, so that the housewife will stick out her hand for it rather than one of many rivals.

Mr. Stahl has found that it takes the average woman exactly twenty seconds to cover an aisle in a supermarket if she doesn't tarry; so a good package design should hypnotize the woman like a flashlight waved in front of her eyes. Some colors such as red and yellow are helpful in creating hypnotic effects. Just putting the name and maker of the product on the box is old-fashioned and, he says, has absolutely no effect on the mid-century woman. She can't read anything, really, until she has picked the box up in her hands. To get the woman to reach and get the package in her hands designers, he explained, are now using "symbols that have a dreamlike quality." To cite examples of dreamlike quality, he mentioned the mouth-watering frosted cakes that decorate the packages of cake mixes, sizzling steaks, mushrooms frying in butter. The idea is to sell the sizzle rather than the meat. Such illustrations make the woman's imagination leap ahead to the end product. By 1956 package designers had even produced a box that, when the entranced shopper picked it up and began fingering it, would give a soft sales talk, or stress the brand name. The talk is on a strip that starts broadcasting when a shopper's finger rubs it.

The package people understandably believe that it is the package that makes or breaks the impulse sale, and some more objective experts agree. A buyer for a food chain told of his experience in watching women shopping. The typical shopper, he found, "picks up one, two, or three items, she puts them back on the shelf, then she picks up one and keeps it. I ask her why she keeps it. She says, 'I like the package.' " (This was a buyer for Bohack.)

The Color Research Institute, which specializes in designing deep-impact packages, won't even send a package out into the field for testing until it has been given ocular or eye-movement tests to show how the consumer's eye will travel over the package on the shelf. This is a gauge of the attention-holding power of the design.

According to some psychologists a woman's eye is most quickly attracted to items wrapped in red; a man's eye to items wrapped in blue. Students in this field have speculated on the woman's high vulnerability to red. One package designer, Frank Gianninoto, has developed an interesting theory. He has concluded that a majority of women shoppers leave their glasses at home or will never wear glasses in public if they can avoid it so that a package to be successful must stand out "from the blurred confusion."

Other merchandisers, I should add, have concluded that in the supermarket jungle the all-important fact in impulse buying is shelf position. Many sharp merchandisers see to it that their "splurge" items (on which their profit margin is highest) tend to be at eye level.

Most of the modern supermarkets, by the mid-fifties, were laid out in a carefully calculated manner so that the high-profit impulse items would be most surely noticed. In many stores they were on the first or only aisle the shopper could enter. Among the best tempters, apparently, are those items in glass jars where the contents can be seen, or where the food is actually out in the open, to be savored and seen. Offering free pickles and cubes of cheese on toothpicks has proved to be reliable as a sales booster. An Indiana supermarket operator nationally recognized for his advanced psychological techniques told me he once sold a half ton of cheese in a few hours, just by getting an enormous half-ton wheel of cheese and inviting customers to nibble slivers and cut off their own chunks for purchase. They could have their chunk free if they could guess its weight within an ounce. The mere massiveness of the cheese, he believes, was a powerful influence in making the sales. "People like to see a lot of merchandise," he explained. "When there are only three or four cans of an item on a shelf, they just won't move." People don't want the last package. A test by *The Progressive Grocer* showed that customers buy 22 per cent more if the shelves are kept full. The urge to conformity, it seems, is profound with many of us.

People also are stimulated to be impulsive, evidently, if they are offered a little extravagance. A California supermarket found that putting a pat of butter on top of each of its better steaks caused sales to soar 15 per cent. The Jewel Tea Company set up "splurge counters" in many of its supermarkets after it was found that women in a just-for-the-heck-of-it mood will spend just as freely on food delicacies as they will on a new hat. The Coca-Cola Company made the interesting discovery that customers in a supermarket who paused to refresh themselves at a soft-drink counter tended to spend substantially more. The Coke people put this to work in a test where they offered customers free drinks. About 80 per cent accepted the Cokes and spent on an average $2.44 more than the store's average customer had been spending.

Apparently the only people who are more prone to splurging when they get in a supermarket than housewives are the wives' husbands and children. Supermarket operators are pretty well agreed that men are easy marks for all sorts of impulse items and cite cases they've seen of husbands who are sent to the store for a loaf of bread and depart with both their arms loaded with their favorite snack items. Shrewd supermarket operators have put the superior impulsiveness of little children to work in promoting sales. The Indiana supermarket operator I mentioned has a dozen little wire carts that small children can push about the store while their mothers are shopping with big carts. People think these tiny carts are very cute; and the operator thinks they are very profitable. The small children go zipping up and down the aisles imitating their mothers in impulse buying, only more so. They reach out, hypnotically I assume, and grab boxes of cookies, candies, dog food, and everything else that delights or interests them. Complications arise, of course, when mother and child come out of their trances and together reach the check-out counter. The store operator related thus what happens: "There is usually a wrangle when the mother sees all the things the child has in his basket and she tries to make him take the stuff back. The child will take back items he doesn't particularly care about such as coffee but will usually bawl and kick before surrendering cookies, candy, ice cream, or soft drinks, so they usually stay for the family."

All these factors of sly persuasion may account for the fact that whereas in past years the average American family spent about 23 per cent of its income for food it now spends nearly 30 per cent. The Indiana operator I mentioned estimates that any supermarket shopper could, by showing a little old-fashioned thoughtfulness and preplanning, save 25 per cent easily on her family's food costs.

The exploration of impulse buying on a systematic basis began spreading in the mid-fifties to many other kinds of products not available in food stores. Liquor stores began organizing racks so that women could browse and pick up impulse items. This idea was pioneered on New York's own "ad alley," Madison Avenue, and spread to other parts of the country. Department and specialty stores started having counters simply labeled, "Why Not?" to promote the carefree, impulsive purchasing of new items most people had never tried before. One store merchandiser was quoted as saying: "Just give people an excuse to try what you are selling and you'll make an extra sale."

One of the most daring ventures into impulse selling was that launched by a Chicago insurance firm, Childs and Wood, which speculated that perhaps even insurance could be sold as an impulse item. So it set up a counter to sell insurance to passers-by at the department store Carson Pirie Scott and Company. Women who happened to be in that area, perhaps to shop for fur coats or a bridal gown, could buy insurance (life, automobile, household, fire, theft, jewelry, hospital) from an assortment of firms. The experiment was successful and instituted on a permanent basis. Auto, household, and fire insurance were reported to be the most popular impulse items.

Social scientists at the Survey Research Center at the University of Michigan made studies of the way people make their decisions to buy relatively expensive durable items such as TV sets, refrigerators, washing machines, items that are usually postponable. It concluded: "We did *not* find that all or most purchases of large household goods are made after careful consideration or deliberation . . . that much planning went into the purchasing . . . nor much seeking of information. About a quarter of these purchases of large household goods were found to lack practically all features of careful deliberation."

In a study that was made on the purchasing of homes in New London, Connecticut,[1] investigators were amazed that even with this, the most important purchase a family is likely to make in the year if not the decade, the shopping was lethargic and casual. On an average the people surveyed looked at less than a half-dozen houses before making a decision; 10 per cent of the home buyers looked at only one house before deciding; 19 per cent looked at only two houses before choosing one of them.

Dr. Warren Bilkey, of the University of Connecticut, and one of the nation's authorities on consumer behavior, systematically followed a large (sixty-three) group of families for more than a year as they wrestled with various major purchasing decisions. He learned that he could chart after each visit the intensity of two opposing factors, "desire" and "resistance." When one finally overwhelmed the other, the decision, pro or con, was made. He found that these people making major decisions, unlike the ladies in the supermarket, did build up a state of tension within themselves. The longer they pondered the decision, the higher the tension. He found that very often the people became so upset by the indecision that they often threw up their hands and decided to make the purchase just to find relief from their state of tension.

---

1. Ruby T. Norris, "Processes and Objectives in the New London Area," *Consumer Behavior,* ed. Lincoln Clark (New York: New York University Press, 1954), pp. 25–29.

DISCUSSION QUESTIONS

1. What are the sources of Packard's data on consumerism? Does personal observation play any role in the development of his argument? Explain how his attitudes toward the data are different from the attitudes of those who supply the data. What means does Packard use to suggest these differences?

2. What is the effect of calling the supermarket a "new jungle"? One source Packard cites calls it a "fairyland." Which metaphor seems closest to the data that Packard is using? Which image do you agree with?

3. What image of women is conveyed by the title of Packard's essay? Compare his attitude toward women with the images of women in the "Advertising" section.

Mario Puzo / *The Godfather*
[The Shooting of Don Corleone]   1969

> *Mario Puzo was born in New York City and educated at City College, Columbia, and the New School for Social Research. In two novels before* The Godfather— The Dark Arena *(1955) and* The Passionate Pilgrim *(1965)—both of which he claims are better books, Puzo explored generational conflicts and the New York Italian community. Puzo disclaims any Mafia connections:*
>
>> *I'm ashamed to admit that I wrote* The Godfather *entirely from research. I never met a real honest-to-god gangster. I knew the gambling world pretty good, but that's all. After the book became "famous," I was introduced to a few gentlemen related to the material. They were flattering. They refused to believe that I had never been in the rackets. They refused to believe that I had never had the confidence of a Don. But all of them loved the book.*

That evening, Hagen went to the Don's house to prepare him for the important meeting the next day with Virgil Sollozzo. The Don had summoned his eldest son to attend, and Sonny Corleone, his heavy Cupid-shaped face drawn with fatigue, was sipping at a glass of water. He must still be humping that maid of honor, Hagen thought. Another worry.

Don Corleone settled into an armchair puffing his Di Nobili cigar. Hagen kept a box of them in his room. He had tried to get the Don to switch to Havanas but the Don claimed they hurt his throat.

"Do we know everything necessary for us to know?" the Don asked.

Hagen opened the folder that held his notes. The notes were in no way incriminating, merely cryptic reminders to make sure he touched on every important detail. "Sollozzo is coming to us for help," Hagen said. "He will ask the family to put up at least a million dollars and to promise some sort of immunity from the law. For that we get a piece of the action, nobody knows how much. Sollozzo is vouched for by the Tattaglia family and they may have a piece of the action. The action is narcotics. Sollozzo has the contacts in Turkey, where they grow the poppy. From there he ships to Sicily. No trouble. In Sicily he has the plant to process into heroin. He has safety-valve operations to bring it down to morphine and bring it up to heroin if necessary. But it would seem that the processing plant in Sicily is protected in every way. The only hitch is bringing it into this country, and then distribution. Also initial capital. A million dollars cash doesn't grow on trees.'' Hagen saw Don Corleone grimace. The old man hated unnecessary flourishes in business matters. He went on hastily.

"They call Sollozzo the Turk. Two reasons. He's spent a lot of time in Turkey and is supposed to have a Turkish wife and kids. Second. He's supposed to be very quick with the knife, or was, when he was young. Only in matters of business, though, and with some sort of reasonable complaint. A very competent man and his own boss. He has a record, he's done two terms in prison, one in Italy, one in the United States, and he's known to the authorities as a narcotics man. This could be a plus for us. It means that he'll never get immunity to testify, since he's considered the top and, of course, because of his record. Also he has an American wife and three children and he is a good family man. He'll stand still for any rap as long as he knows that they will be well taken care of for living money.''

The Don puffed on his cigar and said, "Santino, what do you think?''

Hagen knew what Sonny would say. Sonny was chafing at being under the Don's thumb. He wanted a big operation of his own. Something like this would be perfect.

Sonny took a long slug of scotch. "There's a lot of money in that white powder,'' he said. "But it could be dangerous. Some people could wind up in jail for twenty years. I'd say that if we kept out of the operations end, just stuck to protection and financing, it might be a good idea.''

Hagen looked at Sonny approvingly. He had played his cards well. He had stuck to the obvious, much the best course for him.

The Don puffed on his cigar. "And you, Tom, what do you think?''

Hagen composed himself to be absolutely honest. He had already come to the conclusion that the Don would refuse Sollozzo's proposition. But what was worse, Hagen was convinced that for one of the few times in his experience, the Don had not thought things through. He was not looking far enough ahead.

"Go ahead, Tom," the Don said encouragingly. "Not even a Sicilian *Consigliori* always agrees with the boss.'' They all laughed.

"I think you should say yes," Hagen said. "You know all the obvious reasons. But the most important one is this. There is more money potential in narcotics than in any other business. If we don't get into it, somebody else will, maybe the Tattaglia family. With the revenue they earn they can amass more and more police and political power. Their family will become stronger than ours. Eventually they will come after us to take away what we have. It's just like countries. If they arm, we have to arm. If they become stronger economically, they become a threat to us. Now we have the gambling and we have the unions and right now they are the best things to have. But I think narcotics is the coming thing. I think we have to have a piece of that action or we risk everything we have. Not now, but maybe ten years from now.''

The Don seemed enormously impressed. He puffed on his cigar and murmured, "That's the most important thing of course.'' He sighed and got to his feet. "What time do I have to meet this infidel tomorrow?''

Hagen said hopefully, "He'll be here at ten in the morning.'' Maybe the Don would go for it.

"I'll want you both here with me," the Don said. He rose, stretching, and took his son by the arm. "Santino, get some sleep tonight, you look like the devil himself. Take care of yourself, you won't be young forever.''

Sonny, encouraged by this sign of fatherly concern, asked the question Hagen did not dare to ask. "Pop, what's your answer going to be?''

Don Corleone smiled. "How do I know until I hear the percentages and other details? Besides I have to have time to think over the advice given here tonight. After all, I'm not a man who does things rashly.'' As he went out the door he said casually to Hagen, "Do you have in your notes that the Turk made his living from prostitution before the war? As the Tattaglia family does now. Write that down before you forget.'' There was just a touch of derision in the Don's voice and Hagen flushed. He had deliberately not mentioned it, legitimately so since it really had no bearing, but he had feared it might prejudice the Don's decision. He was notoriously straitlaced in matters of sex.

Virgil ''the Turk'' Sollozzo was a powerfully built, medium-sized man of dark complexion who could have been taken for a true Turk. He had a scimitar of a nose and cruel black eyes. He also had an impressive dignity.

Sonny Corleone met him at the door and brought him into the office where Hagen and the Don waited. Hagen thought he had never seen a more dangerous-looking man except for Luca Brasi.

There were polite handshakings all around. If the Don ever asks me if this man has balls, I would have to answer yes, Hagen thought. He had never seen such force in one man, not even the Don. In fact the Don appeared at his worst. He was being a little too simple, a little too peasantlike in his greeting.

Sollozzo came to the point immediately. The business was narcotics. Everything was set up. Certain poppy fields in Turkey had pledged him certain amounts every year. He had a protected plant in France to convert into morphine. He had an absolutely secure plant in Sicily to process into heroin. Smuggling into both countries was as positively safe as such matters could be. Entry into the United States would entail about five percent losses since the FBI itself was incorruptible, as they both knew. But the profits would be enormous, the risk nonexistent.

''Then why do you come to me?'' the Don asked politely. ''How have I deserved your generosity?''

Sollozzo's dark face remained impassive. ''I need two million dollars cash,'' he said. ''Equally important, I need a man who has powerful friends in the important places. Some of my couriers will be caught over the years. That is inevitable. They will all have clean records, that I promise. So it will be logical for judges to give light sentences. I need a friend who can guarantee that when my people get in trouble they won't spend more than a year or two in jail. Then they won't talk. But if they get ten and twenty years, who knows? In this world there are many weak individuals. They may talk, they may jeopardize more important people. Legal protection is a must. I hear, Don Corleone, that you have as many judges in your pocket as a bootblack has pieces of silver.''

Don Corleone didn't bother to acknowledge the compliment. ''What percentage for my family?'' he asked.

Sollozzo's eyes gleamed. ''Fifty percent.'' He paused and then said in a voice that was almost a caress, ''In the first year your share would be three or four million dollars. Then it would go up.''

Don Corleone said, ''And what is the percentage of the Tattaglia family?''

For the first time Sollozzo seemed to be nervous. ''They will receive something from my share. I need some help in the operations.''

''So,'' Don Corleone said, ''I receive fifty percent merely for finance and legal protection. I have no worries about operations, is that what you tell me?''

Sollozzo nodded. ''If you think two million dollars in cash is 'merely finance,' I congratulate you, Don Corleone.''

The Don said quietly, ''I consented to see you out of my respect for the Tattaglias and because I've heard you are a serious man to be treated also with respect. I must say no to you but I must give you my reasons. The profits in your business are huge but so are the risks. Your operation, if I were part of it, could damage my other interests. It's true I have many, many friends in politics, but they would not be so friendly if my business were narcotics instead of gambling. They think gambling is something like liquor, a harmless vice, and they think narcotics a dirty business.

No, don't protest. I'm telling you their thoughts, not mine. How a man makes his living is not my concern. And what I am telling you is that this business of yours is too risky. All the members of my family have lived well the last ten years, without danger, without harm. I can't endanger them or their livelihoods out of greed.''

The only sign of Sollozzo's disappointment was a quick flickering of his eyes around the room, as if he hoped Hagen or Sonny would speak in his support. Then he said, ''Are you worried about security for your two million?''

The Don smiled coldly. ''No,'' he said.

Sollozzo tried again. ''The Tattaglia family will guarantee your investment also.''

It was then that Sonny Corleone made an unforgivable error in judgment and procedure. He said eagerly, ''The Tattaglia family guarantees the return of our investment without any percentage from us?''

Hagen was horrified at this break. He saw the Don turn cold, malevolent eyes on his eldest son, who froze in uncomprehending dismay. Sollozzo's eyes flickered again but this time with satisfaction. He had discovered a chink in the Don's fortress. When the Don spoke his voice held a dismissal. ''Young people are greedy,'' he said. ''And today they have no manners. They interrupt their elders. They meddle. But I have a sentimental weakness for my children and I have spoiled them. As you see. Signor Sollozzo, my no is final. Let me say that I myself wish you good fortune in your business. It has no conflict with my own. I'm sorry that I had to disappoint you.''

Sollozzo bowed, shook the Don's hand and let Hagen take him to his car outside. There was no expression on his face when he said good-bye to Hagen.

Back in the room, Don Corleone asked Hagen, ''What did you think of that man?''

''He's a Sicilian,'' Hagen said dryly.

The Don nodded his head thoughtfully. Then he turned to his son and said gently, ''Santino, never let anyone outside the family know what you are thinking. Never let them know what you have under your fingernails. I think your brain is going soft from all that comedy you play with that young girl. Stop it and pay attention to business. Now get out of my sight.''

Hagen saw the surprise on Sonny's face, then anger at his father's reproach. Did he really think the Don would be ignorant of his conquest, Hagen wondered. And did he really not know what a dangerous mistake he had made this morning? If that were true, Hagen would never wish to be the *Consigliori* to the Don of Santino Corleone.

Don Corleone waited until Sonny had left the room. Then he sank back into his leather armchair and motioned brusquely for a drink. Hagen poured him a glass of anisette. The Don looked up at him. ''Send Luca Brasi to see me,'' he said.

Three months later, Hagen hurried through the paper work in his city office hoping to leave early enough for some Christmas shopping for his wife and children. He was interrupted by a phone call from a Johnny Fontane bubbling with high spirits. The picture had been shot, the rushes, whatever the hell they were, Hagen thought, were fabulous. He was sending the Don a present for Christmas that would knock his eyes out, he'd bring it himself but there were some little things to be done in the movie. He would have to stay out on the Coast. Hagen tried to conceal his impatience. Johnny Fontane's charm had always been lost on him. But his interest was aroused. ''What is it?'' he asked. Johnny Fontane chuckled and said, ''I can't tell, that's the best part of a Christmas present.'' Hagen immediately lost all interest and finally managed, politely, to hang up.

Ten minutes later his secretary told him that Connie Corleone was on the phone and wanted to speak to him. Hagen sighed. As a young girl Connie had been nice, as a married woman she was a nuisance. She made complaints about her husband. She kept going home to visit her mother for two or three days. And Carlo Rizzi was turning out to be a real loser. He had been fixed up with a nice little business and was running it into the ground. He was also drinking, whoring around, gambling and beating his wife up occasionally. Connie hadn't told her family about that but she had told Hagen. He wondered what new tale of woe she had for him now.

But the Christmas spirit seemed to have cheered her up. She just wanted to ask Hagen what her father would really like for Christmas. And Sonny and Fred and Mike. She already knew what she would get her mother. Hagen made some suggestions, all of which she rejected as silly. Finally she let him go.

When the phone rang again, Hagen threw his papers back into the basket. The hell with it. He'd leave. It never occurred to him to refuse to take the call, however. When his secretary told him it was Michael Corleone he picked up the phone with pleasure. He had always liked Mike.

"Tom," Michael Corleone said, "I'm driving down to the city with Kay tomorrow. There's something important I want to tell the old man before Christmas. Will he be home tomorrow night?"

"Sure," Hagen said. "He's not going out of town until after Christmas. Anything I can do for you?"

Michael was as closemouthed as his father. "No," he said. "I guess I'll see you Christmas, everybody is going to be out at Long Beach, right?"

"Right," Hagen said. He was amused when Mike hung up on him without any small talk.

He told his secretary to call his wife and tell her he would be home a little late but to have some supper for him. Outside the building he walked briskly downtown toward Macy's. Someone stepped in his way. To his surprise he saw it was Sollozzo.

Sollozzo took him by the arm and said quietly, "Don't be frightened. I just want to talk to you." A car parked at the curb suddenly had its door open. Sollozzo said urgently, "Get in, I want to talk to you."

Hagen pulled his arm loose. He was still not alarmed, just irritated. "I haven't got time," he said. At that moment two men came up behind him. Hagen felt a sudden weakness in his legs. Sollozzo said softly, "Get in the car. If I wanted to kill you you'd be dead now. Trust me."

Without a shred of trust Hagen got into the car.

Michael Corleone had lied to Hagen. He was already in New York, and he had called from a room in the Hotel Pennsylvania less than ten blocks away. When he hung up the phone, Kay Adams put out her cigarette and said, "Mike, what a good fibber you are."

Michael sat down beside her on the bed. "All for you, honey; if I told my family we were in town we'd have to go there right away. Then we couldn't go out to dinner, we couldn't go to the theater, and we couldn't sleep together tonight. Not in my father's house, not when we're not married." He put his arms around her and kissed her gently on the lips. Her mouth was sweet and he gently pulled her down on the bed. She closed her eyes, waiting for him to make love to her and Michael felt an enormous happiness. He had spent the war years fighting in the Pacific, and on those bloody islands he had dreamed of a girl like Kay Adams. Of a beauty like hers. A fair and fragile body, milky-skinned and electrified by passion. She opened her eyes and then pulled his head down to kiss him. They made love until it was time for dinner and the theater.

After dinner they walked past the brightly lit department stores full of holiday shoppers and Michael said to her, "What shall I get you for Christmas?"

She pressed against him. "Just you," she said. "Do you think your father will approve of me?"

Michael said gently, "That's not really the question. Will your parents approve of me?"

Kay shrugged. "I don't care," she said.

Michael said, "I even thought of changing my name, legally, but if something happened, that wouldn't really help. You sure you want to be a Corleone?" He said it only half-jokingly.

"Yes," she said without smiling. They pressed against each other. They had decided to get married during Christmas week, a quiet civil ceremony at City Hall with just two friends as witnesses. But Michael had insisted he must tell his father. He had explained that his father would not object in any way as long as it was not done in secrecy. Kay was doubtful. She said she could not tell her parents until after the marriage. "Of course they'll think I'm pregnant," she said. Michael grinned. "So will my parents," he said.

What neither of them mentioned was the fact that Michael would have to cut his close ties with his family. They both understood that Michael had already done so to some extent and yet they both felt guilty about this fact. They planned to finish college, seeing each other weekends and living together during summer vacations. It seemed like a happy life.

The play was a musical called *Carousel* and its sentimental story of a braggart thief made them smile at each other with amusement. When they came out of the theater it had turned cold. Kay snuggled up to him and said, "After we're married, will you beat me and then steal a star for a present?"

Michael laughed. "I'm going to be a mathematics professor," he said. Then he asked, "Do you want something to eat before we go to the hotel?"

Kay shook her head. She looked up at him meaningfully. As always he was touched by her eagerness to make love. He smiled down at her, and they kissed in the cold street. Michael felt hungry, and he decided to order sandwiches sent up to the room.

In the hotel lobby Michael pushed Kay toward the newsstand and said, "Get the papers while I get the key." He had to wait in a small line; the hotel was still short of help despite the end of the war. Michael got his room key and looked around impatiently for Kay. She was standing by the newsstand, staring down at a newspaper she held in her hand. He walked toward her. She looked up at him. Her eyes were filled with tears. "Oh, Mike," she said, "oh, Mike." He took the paper from her hands. The first thing he saw was a photo of his father lying in the street, his head in a pool of blood. A man was sitting on the curb weeping like a child. It was his brother Freddie. Michael Corleone felt his body turning to ice. There was no grief, no fear, just cold rage. He said to Kay, "Go up to the room." But he had to take her by the arm and lead her into the elevator. They rode up together in silence. In their room, Michael sat down on the bed and opened the paper. The headlines said, VITO CORLEONE SHOT. ALLEGED RACKET CHIEF CRITICALLY WOUNDED. OPERATED ON UNDER HEAVY POLICE GUARD. BLOODY MOB WAR FEARED.

Michael felt the weakness in his legs. He said to Kay, "He's not dead, the bastards didn't kill him." He read the story again. His father had been shot at five in the afternoon. That meant that while he had been making love to Kay, having dinner, enjoying the theater, his father was near death. Michael felt sick with guilt.

Kay said, "Shall we go down to the hospital now?"

Michael shook his head. "Let me call the house first. The people who did this are crazy and now that the old man's still alive they'll be desperate. Who the hell knows what they'll pull next."

Both phones in the Long Beach house were busy and it was almost twenty minutes before Michael could get through. He heard Sonny's voice saying, "Yeah."

"Sonny, it's me," Michael said.

He could hear the relief in Sonny's voice. "Jesus, kid, you had us worried. Where the hell are you? I've sent people to that hick town of yours to see what happened."

"How's the old man?" Michael said. "How bad is he hurt?"

"Pretty bad," Sonny said. "They shot him five times. But he's tough." Sonny's voice was proud. "The doctors said he'll pull through. Listen, kid, I'm busy, I can't talk, where are you?"

"In New York," Michael said. "Didn't Tom tell you I was coming down?"

Sonny's voice dropped a little. "They've snatched Tom. That's why I was worried about you. His wife is here. She don't know and neither do the cops. I don't want them to know. The bastards who pulled this must be crazy. I want you to get out here right away and keep your mouth shut. OK?"

"OK," Mike said, "do you know who did it?"

"Sure," Sonny said. "And as soon as Luca Brasi checks in they're gonna be dead meat. We still have all the horses."

"I'll be out in an hour," Mike said. "In a cab." He hung up. The papers had been on the streets for over three hours. There must have been radio news reports. It was almost impossible that Luca hadn't heard the news. Thoughtfully Michael pondered the question. Where was Luca Brasi? It was the same question that Hagen was asking himself at that moment. It was the same question that was worrying Sonny Corleone out in Long Beach.

At a quarter to five that afternoon, Don Corleone had finished checking the papers the office manager of his olive oil company had prepared for him. He put on his jacket and rapped his knuckles on his son Freddie's head to make him take his nose out of the afternoon newspaper. "Tell Gatto to get the car from the lot," he said. "I'll be ready to go home in a few minutes."

Freddie grunted. "I'll have to get it myself. Paulie called in sick this morning. Got a cold again."

Don Corleone looked thoughtful for a moment. "That's the third time this month. I think maybe you'd better get a healthier fellow for this job. Tell Tom."

Fred protested. "Paulie's a good kid. If he says he's sick, he's sick. I don't mind getting the car." He left the office. Don Corleone watched out the window as his son crossed Ninth Avenue to the parking lot. He stopped to call Hagen's office but there was no answer. He called the house at Long Beach but again there was no answer. Irritated, he looked out the window. His car was parked at the curb in front of his building. Freddie was leaning against the fender, arms folded, watching the throng of Christmas shoppers. Don Corleone put on his jacket. The office manager helped him with his overcoat. Don Corleone grunted his thanks and went out the door and started down the two flights of steps.

Out in the street the early winter light was failing. Freddie leaned casually against the fender of the heavy Buick. When he saw his father come out of the building Freddie went out into the street to the driver's side of the car and got in. Don Corleone was about to get in on the sidewalk side of the car when he hesitated and then turned back to the long open fruit stand near the corner. This had been his habit lately, he loved the big out-of-season fruits, yellow peaches and oranges, that glowed in their green boxes. The proprietor sprang to serve him. Don Corleone did not handle the fruit. He pointed. The fruit man disputed his decisions only once, to show him that one of his choices had a rotten underside. Don Corleone took the paper bag in his left hand and paid the man with a five-dollar bill. He took his change and, as he turned to go back to the waiting car, two men stepped from around the corner. Don Corleone knew immediately what was to happen.

The two men wore black overcoats and black hats pulled low to prevent identification by witnesses. They had not expected Don Corleone's alert reaction. He dropped the bag of fruit and darted toward the parked car with startling quickness for a man of his bulk. At the same time he shouted, "Fredo, Fredo." It was only then that the two men drew their guns and fired.

The first bullet caught Don Corleone in the back. He felt the hammer shock of its impact but made his body move toward the car. The next two bullets hit him in the buttocks and sent him sprawling in the middle of the street. Meanwhile the two gunmen, careful not to slip on the rolling fruit, started to follow in order to finish him off. At that moment, perhaps no more than five seconds after the Don's call to his son, Frederico Corleone appeared out of his car, looming over it. The gunmen fired two more hasty shots at the Don lying in the gutter. One hit him in the fleshy part of his arm and the second hit him in the calf of his right leg. Though these wounds were the least serious they bled profusely, forming small pools of blood beside his body. But by this time Don Corleone had lost consciousness.

Freddie had heard his father shout, calling him by his childhood name, and then he had heard the first two loud reports. By the time he got out of the car he was in shock, he had not even drawn his gun. The two assassins could easily have shot him down. But they too panicked. They must have known the son was armed, and besides too much time had passed. They disappeared around the corner, leaving Freddie alone in the street with his father's bleeding body. Many of the people thronging the avenue had flung themselves into doorways or on the ground, others had huddled together in small groups.

Freddie still had not drawn his weapon. He seemed stunned. He stared down at his father's body lying face down on the tarred street, lying now in what seemed to him a blackish lake of blood. Freddie went into physical shock. People eddied out again and someone, seeing him start to sag, led him to the curbstone and made him sit down on it. A crowd gathered around Don Corleone's body, a circle that shattered when the first police car sirened a path through them. Directly behind the police was the *Daily News* radio car and even before it stopped a photographer jumped out to snap pictures of the bleeding Don Corleone. A few moments later an ambulance arrived. The photographer turned his attention to Freddie Corleone, who was now weeping openly, and this was a curiously comical sight, because of his tough, Cupid-featured face, heavy nose and thick mouth smeared with snot. Detectives were spreading through the crowd and more police cars were coming up. One detective knelt beside Freddie, questioning him, but Freddie was too deep in shock to answer. The detective reached inside Freddie's coat and lifted his wallet. He looked at the identification inside and whistled to his partner. In just a few seconds Freddie had been cut off from the crowd by a flock of plainclothesmen. The first detective found Freddie's gun in its shoulder holster and took it. Then they lifted Freddie off his feet and shoved him into an unmarked car. As that car pulled away it was followed by the *Daily News* radio car. The photographer was still snapping pictures of everybody and everything.

DISCUSSION QUESTIONS

1. How does Puzo go about making Don Corleone an attractive figure? For example, compare the characterization of Don Corleone to that of Sollozzo the Turk. In what ways are the Don's criminal activities given a kind of legitimacy?

In this sense, how do Don Corleone's activities compare with those of Joey Gallo (see "Magazines")?

2. What is the literary effect of having Don Corleone's shooting first reported in the newspapers? How do the newspapers determine Puzo's description of the shooting? Compare his description with the account of Joey Gallo's death in "Magazines."

Woody Allen / *Getting Even*   1971

"Comic Genius—Woody Allen Comes of Age," read the cover of Time *magazine in the spring of 1979 after the release of his critically acclaimed film* Manhattan. *Certainly Allen has come a long way from age fifteen when he was paid $25 a week to write jokes on a wholesale basis—50 each day after school for two years, or 25,000 jokes. A succession of television writing jobs, stand-up comedian gigs, short stories for the* New Yorker, *and more than a dozen movies brought Allen to his present popular acclaim.*

In Spring Bulletin *Allen employs a serious, informative (or expository) style, typical of college catalogues ("The poetry of William Butler Yeats is analyzed . . ."), which he continually undercuts with absurdities (". . . against a backdrop of proper dental care"). Even in the course heading—"Yeats and Hygiene, A Comparative Study"—he juxtaposes the everyday with the absurd. As funny as Allen's material can be, there is usually an undercurrent of anxiety about the difficult moral choices of life and the inevitability of death.*

SPRING BULLETIN

The number of college bulletins and adult-education come-ons that keep turning up in my mailbox convinces me that I must be on a special mailing list for dropouts. Not that I'm complaining; there is something about a list of extension courses that piques my interest with a fascination hitherto reserved for a catalogue of Hong Kong honeymoon accessories, sent to me once by mistake. Each time I read through the latest bulletin of extension courses, I make immediate plans to drop everything and return to school. (I was ejected from college many years ago, the victim of unproved accusations not unlike those once attached to Yellow Kid Weil.) So far, however, I am still an uneducated, unextended adult, and I have fallen into the habit of browsing through an imaginary, handsomely printed course bulletin that is more or less typical of them all:

SUMMER SESSION

Economic Theory: A systematic application and critical evaluation of the basic analytic concepts of economic theory, with an emphasis on money and why it's good. Fixed coefficient production functions, cost and supply curves, and nonconvexity comprise the first semester, with the second semester concentrating on spending, making change, and keeping a neat wallet. The Federal Reserve System is analyzed, and advanced students are coached in the proper method of filling out a deposit slip. Other topics include: Inflation and Depression—how to dress for each. Loans, interest, welching.

History of European Civilization: Ever since the discovery of a fossilized eohippus in the men's washroom at Siddon's Cafeteria in East Rutherford, New Jersey, it has been suspected that at one time Europe and America were connected by a strip of land that later sank or became East Rutherford, New Jersey, or both. This throws a new perspective on the formation of European society and enables historians to conjecture about why it sprang up in an area that would have made a much better Asia. Also studied in the course is the decision to hold the Renaissance in Italy.

Introduction to Psychology: The theory of human behavior. Why some men are called "lovely individuals" and why there are others you just want to pinch. Is there a split between mind and body, and, if so, which is better to have? Aggression and rebellion are discussed. (Students particularly interested in these aspects of psychology are advised to take one of these Winter Term courses: Introduction to Hostility; Intermediate Hostility; Advanced Hatred; Theoretical Foundations of Loathing.) Special consideration is given to a study of consciousness as opposed to unconsciousness, with many helpful hints on how to remain conscious.

Psychopathology: Aimed at understanding obsessions and phobias, including the fear of being suddenly captured and stuffed with crabmeat, reluctance to return a volleyball serve, and the inability to say the word "mackinaw" in the presence of women. The compulsion to seek out the company of beavers is analyzed.

Philosophy I: Everyone from Plato to Camus is read, and the following topics are covered:
  Ethics: The categorical imperative, and six ways to make it work for you.
  Aesthetics: Is art the mirror of life, or what?
  Metaphysics: What happens to the soul after death? How does it manage?
  Epistemology: Is knowledge knowable? If not, how do we know this?
  The Absurd: Why existence is often considered silly, particularly for men who wear brown-and-white shoes. Manyness and oneness are studied as they relate to otherness. (Students achieving oneness will move ahead to twoness.)

Philosophy XXIX-B: Introduction to God. Confrontation with the Creator of the universe through informal lectures and field trips.

The New Mathematics: Standard mathematics has recently been rendered obsolete by the discovery that for years we have been writing the numeral five backward. This has led to a reëvaluation of counting as a method of getting from one to ten. Students are taught advanced concepts of Boolean Algebra, and formerly unsolvable equations are dealt with by threats of reprisals.

Fundamental Astronomy: A detailed study of the universe and its care and cleaning. The sun, which is made of gas, can explode at any moment, sending our entire planetary system hurtling to destruction; students are advised what the average citizen can do in such a case. They are also taught to identify various constellations, such as the Big Dipper, Cygnus the Swan, Sagittarius the Archer, and the twelve stars that form Lumides the Pants Salesman.

Modern Biology: How the body functions, and where it can usually be found. Blood is analyzed, and it is learned why it is the best possible thing to have coursing through one's veins. A frog is dissected by students and its digestive tract is compared with man's, with the frog giving a good account of itself except on curries.

Rapid Reading: This course will increase reading speed a little each day until the end of the term, by which time the student will be required to read *The Brothers Karamozov* in fifteen minutes. The method is to scan the page and eliminate everything except pronouns from one's field of vision. Soon the pronouns are eliminated. Gradually the student is encouraged to nap. A frog is dissected. Spring comes. People marry and die. Pinkerton does not return.

Musicology III: The Recorder. The student is taught how to play "Yankee Doodle" on this end-blown wooden flute, and progresses rapidly to the Brandenburg Concertos. Then slowly back to "Yankee Doodle."

Music Appreciation: In order to "hear" a great piece of music correctly, one must: (1) know the birthplace of the composer, (2) be able to tell a rondo from a scherzo, and back it up with action. Attitude is important. Smiling is bad form unless the composer has intended the music to be funny, as in *Till Eulenspiegel,* which abounds in musical jokes (although the trombone has the best lines). The ear, too, must be trained, for it is our most easily deceived organ and can be made to think it is a nose by bad placement of stereo speakers. Other topics include: The four-bar rest and its potential as a political weapon. The Gregorian Chant: Which monks kept the beat.

Writing for the Stage: All drama is conflict. Character development is also very important. Also what they say. Students learn that long, dull speeches are not so effective, while short, "funny" ones seem to go over well. Simplified audience psychology is explored: Why is a play about a lovable old character named Gramps often not as interesting in the theatre as staring at the back of someone's head and trying to make him turn around? Interesting aspects of stage history are also examined. For example, before the invention of italics, stage directions were often mistaken for dialogue, and great actors frequently found themselves saying, "John rises, crosses left." This naturally led to embarrassment and, on some occasions, dreadful notices. The phenomenon is analyzed in detail, and students are guided in avoiding mistakes. Required text: A. F. Shulte's *Shakespeare: Was He Four Women?*

Introduction to Social Work: A course designed to instruct the social worker who is interested in going out "in the field." Topics covered include: how to organize street gangs into basketball teams, and vice versa; playgrounds as a means of preventing juvenile crime, and how to get potentially homicidal cases to try the sliding pond; discrimination; the broken home; what to do if you are hit with a bicycle chain.

Yeats and Hygiene, A Comparative Study: The poetry of William Butler Yeats is analyzed against a background of proper dental care. (Course open to a limited number of students.)

Alex Haley / *Roots*
[What Are Slaves?]   1976

A former magazine writer and Coast Guard chief journalist, Alex Haley had a modest reputation until the publication of his mammoth worth, Roots: The Saga of an American Family, *first condensed in* Reader's Digest *in 1974 and then*

published in its entirety by Doubleday in 1976. Twelve years in the making,
Roots *won for Haley international fame and personal fortune. An eight-part
ABC television dramatization of* Roots *drew 130 million viewers. The last episode attracted 80 million alone, making it one of the most popular television
programs ever aired.*

*Kunta Kinte, Haley's African ancestor, born in Gambia in 1750 and carried
to America as a slave in 1767, is the most vividly portrayed character in* Roots.
*His story fills more than half of the book's 688 pages. In the following selec-
tion, young Kunta Kinte and his brother, Lamin, learn from their father,
Omoro, the meaning of slavery.*

"What are slaves?" Lamin asked Kunta one afternoon. Kunta grunted and fell
silent. Walking on, seemingly lost in thought, he was wondering what Lamin had
overheard to prompt that question. Kunta knew that those who were taken by
toubob became slaves, and he had overheard grown-ups talking about slaves who
were owned by people in Juffure. But the fact was that he really didn't know what
slaves *were*. As had happened so many other times, Lamin's question embarrassed
him into finding out more.

The next day, when Omoro was getting ready to go out after some palm wood
to build Binta a new food storehouse, Kunta asked to join his father; he loved to
go off anywhere with Omoro. But neither spoke this day until they had almost
reached the dark, cool palm grove.

Then Kunta asked abruptly, "Fa, what are slaves?"

Omoro just grunted at first, saying nothing, and for several minutes moved
about in the grove, inspecting the trunks of different palms.

"Slaves aren't always easy to tell from those who aren't slaves," he said finally. Between blows of his bush ax against the palm he had selected, he told
Kunta that slaves' huts were roofed with nyantang jongo and free people's huts
with nyantang foro, which Kunta knew was the best quality of thatching grass.

"But one should never speak of slaves in the presence of slaves," said Omoro,
looking very stern. Kunta didn't understand why, but he nodded as if he did.

When the palm tree fell, Omoro began chopping away its thick, tough fronds.
As Kunta plucked off for himself some of the ripened fruits, he sensed his father's
mood of willingness to talk today. He thought happily how now he would be able
to explain to Lamin all about slaves.

"Why are some people slaves and others not?" he asked.

Omoro said that people became slaves in different ways. Some were born of
slave mothers—and he named a few of those who lived in Juffure, people whom
Kunta knew well. Some of them were the parents of some of his own kafo mates.
Others, said Omoro, had once faced starvation during their home villages' hungry
season, and they had come to Juffure and begged to become the slaves of someone
who agreed to feed and provide for them. Still others—and he named some of Juffure's older people—had once been enemies and been captured as prisoners.
"They become slaves, being not brave enough to die rather than be taken," said
Omoro.

He had begun chopping the trunk of the palm into sections of a size that a
strong man could carry. Though all he had named were slaves, he said, they were
all respected people, as Kunta well knew. "Their rights are guaranteed by the
laws of our forefathers," said Omoro, and he explained that all masters had to
provide their slaves with food, clothing, a house, a farm plot to work on half
shares, and also a wife or husband.

"Only those who permit themselves to be are despised," he told Kunta—those
who had been made slaves because they were convicted murderers, thieves, or

other criminals. These were the only slaves whom a master could beat or otherwise punish as he felt they deserved.

"Do slaves have to remain slaves always?" asked Kunta.

"No, many slaves buy their freedom with what they save from farming on half share with their masters." Omoro named some in Juffure who had done this. He named others who had won their freedom by marrying into the family that owned them.

To help him carry the heavy sections of palm, Omoro made a stout sling out of green vines, and as he worked, he said that some slaves, in fact, prospered beyond their masters. Some had even taken slaves for themselves, and some had become very famous persons.

"Sundiata was one!" exclaimed Kunta. Many times, he had heard the grandmothers and the griots speaking of the great forefather slave general whose army had conquered so many enemies.

Omoro grunted and nodded, clearly pleased that Kunta knew this, for Omoro also had learned much of Sundiata when he was Kunta's age. Testing his son, Omoro asked, "And who was Sundiata's mother?"

"Sogolon, the Buffalo Woman!" said Kunta proudly.

Omoro smiled, and hoisting onto his strong shoulders two heavy sections of the palm pole within the vine sling, he began walking. Eating his palm fruits, Kunta followed, and nearly all the way back to the village, Omoro told him how the great Mandinka Empire had been won by the crippled, brilliant slave general whose army had begun with runaway slaves found in swamps and other hiding places.

"You will learn much more of him when you are in manhood training," said Omoro—and the very thought of that time sent a fear through Kunta, but also a thrill of anticipation.

Omoro said that Sundiata had run away from his hated master, as most slaves did who didn't like their masters. He said that except for convicted criminals, no slaves could be sold unless the slaves approved of the intended master.

"Grandmother Nyo Boto also is a slave," said Omoro, and Kunta almost swallowed a mouthful of palm fruit. He couldn't comprehend this. Pictures flashed across his mind of beloved old Nyo Boto squatting before the door of her hut, tending the village's twelve or fifteen naked babies while weaving baskets of wigs, and giving the sharp side of her tongue to any passing adult—even the elders, if she felt like it. "That one is nobody's slave," he thought.

The next afternoon, after he had delivered his goats to their pens, Kunta took Lamin home by a way that avoided their usual playmates, and soon they squatted silently before the hut of Nyo Boto. Within a few moments the old lady appeared in her doorway, having sensed that she had visitors. And with but a glance at Kunta, who had always been one of her very favorite children, she knew that something special was on his mind. Inviting the boys inside her hut, she set about the brewing of some hot herb tea for them.

"How are your papa and mama?" she asked.

"Fine. Thank you for asking," said Kunta politely. "And you are well, Grandmother?"

"I'm quite fine, indeed," she replied.

Kunta's next words didn't come until the tea had been set before him. Then he blurted, "Why are you a slave, Grandmother?"

Nyo Boto looked sharply at Kunta and Lamin. Now it was she who didn't speak for a few moments. "I will tell you," she said finally.

"In my home village one night, very far from here and many rains ago, when I was a young woman and wife," Nyo Boto said, she had awakened in terror as flaming grass roofs came crashing down among her screaming neighbors. Snatching up her own two babies, a boy and a girl, whose father had recently died in a tribal war, she rushed out among the others—and awaiting them were armed white slave raiders with their black slatee helpers. In a furious battle, all who didn't escape were roughly herded together, and those who were too badly injured or too old or too young to travel were murdered before the others' eyes. Nyo Boto began to sob, "—including my own two babies and my aged mother."

As Lamin and Kunta clutched each other's hands, she told them how the terrified prisoners, bound neck-to-neck with thongs, were beaten and driven across the hot, hard inland country for many days. And every day, more and more of the prisoners fell beneath the whips that lashed their backs to make them walk faster. After a few days, yet more began to fall of hunger and exhaustion. Some struggled on, but those who couldn't were left for the wild animals to get. The long line of prisoners passed other villages that had been burned and ruined, where the skulls and bones of people and animals lay among the burned-out shells of thatch and mud that had once been family huts. Fewer than half of those who had begun the trip reached the village of Juffure, four days from the nearest place on the Kambi Bolongo where slaves were sold.

"It was here that one young prisoner was sold for a bag of corn," said the old woman. "That was me. And this was how I came to be called Nyo Boto," which Kunta knew meant "bag of corn." The man who bought her for his own slave died before very long, she said, "and I have lived here ever since."

Lamin was wriggling in excitement at the story, and Kunta felt somehow ever greater love and appreciation than he had before for old Nyo Boto, who now sat smiling tenderly at the two boys, whose father and mother, like them, she had once dandled on her knee.

"Omoro, your papa, was of the first kafo when I came to Juffure," said Nyo Boto, looking directly at Kunta. "Yaisa, his mother, who was your grandmother, was my very good friend. Do you remember her?" Kunta said that he did and added proudly that he had told his little brother all about their grandma.

"That is good!" said Nyo Boto. "Now I must get back to work. Run along, now."

Thanking her for the tea, Kunta and Lamin left and walked slowly back to Binta's hut, each deep in his own private thoughts.

The next afternoon, when Kunta returned from his goatherding, he found Lamin filled with questions about Nyo Boto's story. Had any such fire ever burned in Juffure? he wanted to know. Well, he had never heard of any, said Kunta, and the village showed no signs of it. Had Kunta ever seen one of those white people? "Of course not!" he exclaimed. But he said that their father had spoken of a time when he and his brothers had seen the toubob and their ships at a point along the river.

Kunta quickly changed the subject, for he knew very little about toubob, and he wanted to think about them for himself. He wished that he could *see* one of them—from a safe distance, of course, since everything he'd ever heard about them made it plain that people were better off who never got too close to them.

Only recently a girl out gathering herbs—and before her two grown men out hunting—had disappeared, and everyone was certain that toubob had stolen them away. He remembered, of course, how when drums of other villages warned that toubob had either taken somebody or was known to be near, the men would arm themselves and mount a double guard while the frightened women quickly gathered all of the children and hid in the bush far from the village—sometimes for several days—until the toubob was felt to be gone.

Kunta recalled once when he was out with his goats in the quiet of the bush, sitting under his favorite shade tree. He had happened to look upward and there, to his astonishment, in the tree overhead, were twenty or thirty monkeys huddled along the thickly leaved branches as still as statues, with their long tails hanging down. Kunta had always thought of monkeys rushing noisily about, and he couldn't forget how quietly they had been watching his every move. He wished that now *he* might sit in a tree and watch some toubob on the ground below him.

The goats were being driven homeward the afternoon after Lamin had asked him about toubob when Kunta raised the subject among his fellow goatherds—and in no time they were telling about the things they had heard. One boy, Demba Conteh, said that a very brave uncle had once gone close enough to *smell* some toubob, and they had a peculiar stink. All of the boys had heard that toubob took people away to eat them. But some had heard that the toubob claimed the stolen people were not eaten, only put to work on huge farms. Sitafa Silla spat out his grandfather's answer to that: "White man's lie!"

The next chance he had, Kunta asked Omoro, "Papa, will you tell me how you and your brothers saw the toubob at the river?" Quickly, he added, "The matter needs to be told correctly to Lamin." It seemed to Kunta that his father nearly smiled, but Omoro only grunted, evidently not feeling like talking at that moment. But a few days later, Omoro casually invited both Kunta and Lamin to go with him out beyond the village to collect some roots he needed. It was the naked Lamin's first walk anywhere with his father, and he was overjoyed. Knowing that Kunta's influence had brought this about, he held tightly onto the tail of his big brother's dundiko.

Omoro told his sons that after their manhood training, his two older brothers Janneh and Saloum had left Juffure, and the passing of time brought news of them as well-known travelers in strange and distant places. Their first return home came when drumtalk all the way from Juffure told them of the birth of Omoro's first son. They spent sleepless days and nights on the trail to attend the naming ceremony. And gone from home so long, the brothers joyously embraced some of their kafo mates of boyhood. But those few sadly told of others gone and lost—some in burned villages, some killed by fearsome firesticks, some kidnaped, some missing while farming, hunting, or traveling—and all because of toubob.

Omoro said that his brothers had then angrily asked him to join them on a trip to see what the toubob were doing, to see what might be done. So the three brothers trekked for three days along the banks of the Kamby Bolongo, keeping carefully concealed in the bush, until they found what they were looking for. About twenty great toubob canoes were moored in the river, each big enough that its insides might hold all the people of Juffure, each with a huge white cloth tied by ropes to a treelike pole as tall as ten men. Nearby was an island, and on the island was a fortress.

Many toubob were moving about, and black helpers were with them, both on the fortress and in small canoes. The small canoes were taking such things as dried indigo, cotton, beeswax, and hides to the big canoes. More terrible than he could describe, however, said Omoro, were the beatings and other cruelties they saw being dealt out to those who had been captured for the toubob to take away.

For several moments, Omoro was quiet, and Kunta sensed that he was pondering something else to tell him. Finally he spoke: "Not as many of our people are being taken away now as then." When Kunta was a baby, he said, the King of Barra, who ruled this part of The Gambia, had ordered that there would be no more burning of villages and the capturing or killing of all their people. And soon it did stop, after the soldiers of some angry kings had burned the big canoes down to the water, killing all the toubob on board.

"Now," said Omoro, "nineteen guns are fired in salute to the King of Barra by every toubob canoe entering the Kamby Bolongo." He said that the King's personal agents now supplied most of the people whom the toubob took away—usually criminals or debtors, or anyone convicted for suspicion of plotting against the king—often for little more than whispering. More people seemed to get convicted of crimes, said Omoro, whenever toubob ships sailed in the Kamby Bolongo looking for slaves to buy.

"But even a king cannot stop the stealings of some people from their villages," Omoro continued. "You have known some of those lost from our village, three from among us just within the past few moons, as you know, and you have heard the drumtalk from other villages." He looked hard at his sons, and spoke slowly. "The things I'm going to tell you now, you must hear with more than your ears— for not to do what I say can mean your being stolen away forever!" Kunta and Lamin listened with rising fright. "Never be alone when you can help it," said Omoro. "Never be out at night when you can help it. And day or night, when you're alone, keep away from any high weeds or bush if you can avoid it."

For the rest of their lives, "even when you have come to be men," said their father, they must be on guard for toubob. "He often shoots his firesticks, which can be heard far off. And wherever you see much smoke away from any villages, it is probably his cooking fires, which are too big. You should closely inspect his signs to learn which way the toubob went. Having much heavier footsteps than we do, he leaves signs you will recognize as not ours: he breaks twigs and grasses. And when you get close where he has been, you will find that his scent remains there. It's like a wet chicken smells. And many say a toubob sends forth a nervousness that we can feel. If you feel that, become quiet, for often he can be detected at some distance."

But it's not enough to know the toubob, said Omoro. "Many of our own people work for him. They are slatee *traitors*. But without knowing them, there is no way to recognize them. In the bush, therefore, trust *no* one you don't know."

Kunta and Lamin sat frozen with fear. "You cannot be told these things strongly enough," said their father. "You must know what your uncles and I saw happening to those who had been stolen. It is the difference between slaves among ourselves and those whom toubob takes away to be slaves for him." He said that they saw stolen people chained inside long, stout, heavily guarded bamboo pens along the shore of the river. When small canoes brought important-acting toubob from the big canoes, the stolen people were dragged outside their pens onto the sand.

"Their heads had been shaved, and they had been greased until they shined all over. First they were made to squat and jump up and down," said Omoro. "And then, when the toubob had seen enough of that, they ordered the stolen people's mouths forced open for their teeth and their throats to be looked at."

Swiftly, Omoro's finger touched Kunta's crotch, and as Kunta jumped, Omoro said, "Then the men's foto was pulled and looked at. Even the women's private parts were inspected." And the toubob finally made the people squat again and stuck burning hot irons against their backs and shoulders. Then, screaming and struggling, the people were shipped toward the water, where small canoes waited to take them out to the big canoes.

"My brothers and I watched many fall onto their bellies, clawing and eating the sand, as if to get one last hold and bite of their own home," said Omoro. "But they were dragged and beaten on." Even in the small canoes out in the water, he told Kunta and Lamin, some kept fighting against the whips and the clubs until they jumped into the water among terrible long fish with gray backs and white bellies and curved mouths full of thrashing teeth that reddened the water with their blood.

Kunta and Lamin had huddled close to each other, each gripping the other's hands. "It's better that you know these things than that your mother and I kill the white cock one day for you." Omoro looked at his sons. "Do you know what that means?"

Kunta managed to nod, and found his voice. "When someone is missing, Fa?" He had seen families frantically chanting to Allah as they squatted around a white cock bleeding and flapping with its throat slit.

"Yes," said Omoro. "If the white cock dies on its breast, hope remains. But when a white cock flaps to death on its back, then *no* hope remains, and the whole village joins the family in crying to Allah."

"Fa—" Lamin's voice, squeaky with fear, startled Kunta, "where do the big canoes take the stolen people?"

"The elders say to Jong Sang Doo," said Omoro, "a land where slaves are sold to huge cannibals called toubabo koomi, who eat us. No man knows any more about it."

Benjamin Spock / *The Common Sense Book of Baby Care*

1976

Pediatrician, psychiatrist, former columnist for Ladies' Home Journal *and* Redbook, *and Vietnam antiwar activist, Dr. Benjamin Spock became America's most influential authority on child care soon after the publication of* The Common Sense Book of Baby Care *in 1945. The book was meant to counter some of the absurd notions promulgated by Spock's predecessors, including Dr. John B. Watson who had asserted in his widely distributed text,* Psychological Care of Infant and Child *(1928): "Never, never kiss your child. Never hold it on your lap. Never rock its carriage." Spock's reassuring "common sense," evident in the selection reprinted below, encourages a more relaxed approach to the difficulties of parenthood. Millions of Americans have been raised according to Spocks' principles. The book has enjoyed greater total sales than any other work except the Bible and Shakespeare's plays.*

The following selection on gun play—showing Spock's change of mind on the subject—is taken from the 1976 edition of his best-selling book.

SHOULD CHILDREN PLAY WITH GUNS?

Is gun play good or bad for children? For many years I emphasized its harmlessness. When thoughtful parents expressed doubt about letting their children have pistols and other warlike toys, because they didn't want to encourage them in the slightest degree to become delinquents or militarists, I would explain how little connection there was. In the course of growing up, children have a natural tendency to bring their aggressiveness more and more under control provided their parents encourage this. One- to 2-year-olds, when they're angry with another child, may bite the child's arm without hesitation. But by 3 or 4 they have already learned that crude aggression is not right. However, they like to pretend to shoot a pretend bad buy. They may pretend to shoot their mother or father, but grinning to assure them that the gun and the hostility aren't to be taken seriously.

In the 6- to 12-year-old period, children will play an earnest game of war, but it has lots of rules. There may be arguments and roughhousing, but real fights are relatively infrequent. At this age children don't shoot at their mother or father, even in fun. It's not that the parents have turned stricter; the children's own conscience has. They say, "Step on a crack; break your mother's back," which means that even the thought of wishing harm to their parents now makes them uncomfortable. In adolescence, aggressive feelings become much stronger, but well-brought-up children sublimate them into athletics and other competition or into kidding their pals.

In other words, I'd explain that playing at war is a natural step in the disciplining of the aggression of young children; that most clergymen and pacifists probably did the same thing; that an idealistic parent doesn't really need to worry about producing a scoundrel; that the aggressive delinquent was not distorted in personality by being allowed to play bandit at 5 or 10, he was neglected and abused in his first couple of years, when his character was beginning to take shape; that he was doomed before he had any toys worthy of the name.

But nowadays I'd give parents much more encouragement in their inclination to guide their child away from violence. A number of occurrences have convinced me of the importance of this.

One of the first things that made me change my mind, several years ago, was an observation that an experienced nursery school teacher told me about. Her children were crudely bopping each other much more than previously, without provocation. When she remonstrated with them, they would protest, "But that's what the Three Stooges do." (This was a children's TV program full of violence and buffoonery which had recently been introduced and which immediately became very popular.) This attitude of the children showed me that watching violence can lower a child's standards of behavior. Recent psychological experiments have shown that being shown brutality on film stimulates cruelty in adults, too.

What further shocked me into reconsidering my point of view was the assassination of President Kennedy, and the fact that some schoolchildren cheered about this. (I didn't so much blame the children as I blamed the kind of parents who will say about a President they dislike, "I'd shoot him if I got the chance!")

These incidents made me think of other evidences that Americans have often been tolerant of harshness, lawlessness, and violence. We were ruthless in dealing with the Indians. In some frontier areas we slipped into the tradition of vigilante justice. We were hard on the later waves of immigrants. At times we've denied justice to groups with different religions or political views. We have crime rates way above those of other, comparable nations. A great proportion of our adult as well as our child population has been endlessly fascinated with dramas of Western violence and with brutal crime stories, in movies and on television. We have had a shameful history of racist lynchings and murders, as well as regular abuse and humiliation. In recent years it has been realized that infants and small children are being brought to hospitals with severe injuries caused by gross parental brutality.

Of course, some of these phenomena are characteristic of only a small percentage of the population. Even the others that apply to a majority of people don't necessarily mean that we Americans on the average have more aggressiveness inside us than the people of other nations. I think rather that the aggressiveness we have is less controlled, from childhood on.

To me it seems very clear that in order to have a more stable and civilized national life we should bring up the next generation of Americans with a greater respect for law and for other people's rights and sensibilities than in the past. There are many ways in which we could and should teach these attitudes. One simple opportunity we could utilize in the first half of childhood is to show our disapproval of lawlessness and violence in television programs and in children's gun play.

I also believe that the survival of the world now depends on a much greater awareness of the need to avoid war and to actively seek peaceful agreements. There are enough nuclear arms to utterly destroy all civilization. One international incident in which belligerence or brinkmanship was carried a small step too far could escalate into annihilation within a few hours. This terrifying situation demands a much greater stability and self-restraint on the part of national leaders and citizens than they have ever shown in the past. We owe it to our children to prepare them very deliberately for this awesome responsibility. I see little evidence that this is being done now.

When we let people grow up feeling that cruelty is all right provided they know it is make-believe, or provided they sufficiently disapprove of certain individuals or groups, or provided the cruelty is in the service of their country (whether the country is right or wrong), we make it easier for them to go berserk when the provocation comes.

But can we imagine actually depriving American children of their guns or of watching their favorite Western or crime programs? I think we should consider it—to at least a partial degree.

I believe that parents should firmly stop children's war play or any other kind of play that degenerates into deliberate cruelty or meanness. (By this I don't mean they should interfere in every little quarrel or tussle.)

If I had a 3- or 4-year-old son who asked me to buy him a gun, I'd tell him— with a friendly smile, not a scowl—that I don't want to give him a gun for even pretend shooting because there is too much meanness and killing in the world, that we must all learn how to get along in a friendly way together. I'd ask him if he didn't want some other present instead.

If I saw him, soon afterward, using a stick for a pistol in order to join a gang that was merrily going "bang-bang" at each other, I wouldn't rush out to remind him of my views. I'd let him have the fun of participating as long as there was no cruelty. If his uncle gave him a pistol or a soldier's helmet for his birthday, I myself wouldn't have the nerve to take it away from him. If when he was 7 or 8 he decided he wanted to spend his own money for battle equipment, I wouldn't forbid him. I'd remind him that I myself don't want to buy war toys or give them as presents; but from now on he will be playing more and more away from home and making more of his own decisions; he can make this decision for himself. I wouldn't give this talk in such a disapproving manner that he wouldn't dare decide against my policy. I would feel I'd made my point and that he had been inwardly influenced by my viewpoint as much as I could influence him. Even if he should buy weapons then, he would be likely to end up—in adolescence and adulthood— as thoughtful about the problems of peace as if I'd prohibited his buying them, perhaps more so.

One reason I keep backing away from a flat prohibition is that it would have its heaviest effect on the individuals who need it least. If all the parents of America became convinced and agreed on a toy-weapons ban on the first of next month, this would be ideal from my point of view. But this isn't going to happen for a long time, unless one nuclear missile goes off by accident and shocks the world into a banning of all weapons, real and pretend. A small percentage of parents— those most thoughtful and conscientious—will be the first ones who will want to dissuade their children from war toys; but their children will be most apt to be the sensitive, responsible children anyway. So I think it's carrying the issue unneces- sarily far for those of us who are particularly concerned about peace and kindli- ness to insist that our young children demonstrate a total commitment to our cause while all their friends are gun toters. (It might be practical in a neighborhood where a majority of parents had the same conviction.) The main ideal is that children should grow up with a fond attitude toward all humanity. That will come about basically from the general atmosphere of our families. It will be strengthened by the attitude that we teach specifically toward other nations and groups. The elim- ination of war play would have some additional influence, but not as much as the two previous factors.

I feel less inclined to compromise on brutality on television and in movies. The sight of a real human face being apparently smashed by a fist has a lot more impact on children than what they imagine when they are making up their own stories. I believe that parents should flatly forbid programs that go in for violence. I don't think they are good for adults either. Young children can only partly distinguish between dramas and reality. Parents can explain, "It isn't right for people to hurt each other or kill each other and I don't want you to watch them do it."

Even if children cheat and watch such a program in secret, they'll know very well that their parents disapprove, and this will protect them to a degree from the coarsening effect of the scenes.

Studs Terkel / *American Dreams: Lost & Found*   1980

Studs Terkel has held nearly as many jobs as the people he has tape-recorded for his ongoing oral history of everyday working America. Before, during, and after earning advanced degrees in literature and law at the University of Chicago, Terkel worked as a government statistician, news commentator, sportscaster, disc jockey, jazz critic, host of music festivals, playwright, stage and radio actor (he played the gangster on the popular thirties soap operas "Ma Perkins" and "Road to Life"), and talk-show host. Born in New York City in 1912, he moved to Chicago at eleven and has been associated ever since with both the city's blue-collar workers and its celebrities. His identification with working-class Chicago was perhaps further enhanced when he borrowed the nickname of the protagonist of James T. Farrell's celebrated trilogy of the Prohibition and Depression eras, Studs Lonigan.

Wielding a portable tape recorder to capture what he calls "the man of inchoate thought," Terkel has turned out three impressive volumes of best-selling nonfiction. Division Street, America *(1966) records the bitterness and anguish that flared in urban America during the sixties.* Hard Times: An Oral History of the Great Depression *(1970) is a "memory book" of the "hard facts," the still smoldering sense of guilt and failure, and the "small triumphs" of both the rich and the poor who survived that protracted decade.*

Working: People Talk about What They Do All Day and How They Feel about What They Do *(1974), a tape-recorded exploration of the collective consciousness of American workers, was drawn from 133 interviews conducted over three years, almost exclusively with nonprofessional, seemingly anonymous Americans, most of whom repeatedly startled Terkel with what he has characterized as a search for "daily meaning as well as daily bread, for recognition as well as cash, for astonishment rather than torpor; in short, for a sort of life rather than a Monday through Friday sort of dying."*

The following two selections are taken from American Dreams: Lost & Found *(1980).*

Miss U.S.A., EMMA KNIGHT

Miss U.S.A., 1973. She is twenty-nine.

I wince when I'm called a former beauty queen or Miss U.S.A. I keep thinking they're talking about someone else. There are certain images that come to mind when people talk about beauty queens. It's mostly what's known as t and a, tits and ass. No talent. For many girls who enter the contest, it's part of the American Dream. It was never mine.

You used to sit around the TV and watch Miss America and it was exciting, we thought, glamorous. Fun, we thought. But by the time I was eight or nine, I didn't feel comfortable. Soon I'm hitting my adolescence, like fourteen, but I'm not doing any dating and I'm feeling awkward and ugly. I'm much taller than most of the people in my class. I don't feel I can compete the way I see girls competing for guys. I was very much of a loner. I felt intimidated by the amount of competition females were supposed to go through with each other. I didn't like being told by *Seventeen* magazine: Subvert your interests if you have a crush on a guy, get interested in what he's interested in. If you play cards, be sure not to beat him. I was very bad at these social games.

After I went to the University of Colorado for three and a half years, I had it. This was 1968 through '71. I came home for the summer. An agent met me and wanted me to audition for commercials, modeling, acting jobs. Okay. I started auditioning and winning some.

I did things actors do when they're starting out. You pass out literature at conventions, you do print ads, you pound the pavements, you send out your resumés. I had come to a model agency one cold day, and an agent came out and said: "I want you to enter a beauty contest." I said: "No, uh-uh, never, never, never. I'll lose, how humiliating." She said: "I want some girls to represent the agency, might do you good." So I filled out the application blank: hobbies, measurements, blah, blah, blah. I got a letter: "Congratulations. You have been accepted as an entrant into the Miss Illinois-Universe contest." Now what do I do? I'm stuck.

You have to have a sponsor. Or you're gonna have to pay several hundred dollars. So I called up the lady who was running it. Terribly sorry, I can't do this. I don't have the money. She calls back a couple of days later: "We found you a sponsor, it's a lumber company."

It was in Decatur. There were sixty-some contestants from all over the place. I went as a lumberjack: blue jeans, hiking boots, a flannel shirt, a pair of suspenders, and carrying an axe. You come out first in your costume and you introduce yourself and say your astrological sign or whatever it is they want you to say. You're wearing a banner that has the sponsor's name on it. Then you come out and do your pirouettes in your one-piece bathing suit, and the judges look at you a lot. Then you come out in your evening gown and pirouette around for a while. That's the first night.

The second night, they're gonna pick fifteen people. In between, you had judges' interviews. For three minutes, they ask you anything they want. Can you answer questions? How do you handle yourself? Your poise, personality, blah, blah, blah. They're called personality judges.

I thought: This will soon be over, get on a plane tomorrow, and no one will be the wiser. Except that my name got called as one of the fifteen. You have to go through the whole thing all over again.

I'm thinking: I don't have a prayer. I'd come to feel a certain kind of distance, except that they called my name. I was the winner, Miss Illinois. All I could do was laugh. I'm twenty-two, standing up there in a borrowed evening gown, thinking: What am I doing here? This is like Tom Sawyer becomes an altar boy.

I was considered old for a beauty queen, which is a little horrifying when you're twenty-two. That's very much part of the beauty queen syndrome: the young, untouched, unthinking human being.

I had to go to this room and sign the Miss Illinois-Universe contract right away. Miss Universe, Incorporated, is the full name of the company. It's owned by Kaiser-Roth, Incorporated, which was bought out by Gulf & Western. Big business.

I'm sitting there with my glass of champagne and I'm reading over this contract. They said: "Oh, you don't have to read it." And I said: "I never sign anything that I don't read." They're all waiting to take pictures, and I'm sitting there reading this long document. So I signed it and the phone rang and the guy was from a Chicago paper and said: "Tell me, is it Miss or Ms.?" I said: "It's Ms." He said: "You're kidding." I said: "No, I'm not." He wrote an article the next day saying something like it finally happened: a beauty queen, a feminist. I thought I was a feminist before I was a beauty queen, why should I stop now?

Then I got into the publicity and training and interviews. It was a throwback to another time where crossed ankles and white gloves and teacups were present. I was taught how to walk around with a book on my head, how to sit daintily, how to pose in a bathing suit, and how to frizz my hair. They wanted curly hair, which I hate.

One day the trainer asked me to shake hands. I shook hands. She said: "That's wrong. When you shake hands with a man, you always shake hands ring up." I said: "Like the pope? Where my hand is up, like he's gonna kiss it?" Right. I thought: Holy mackerel! It was a very long February and March and April and May.

I won the Miss U.S.A. pageant. I started to laugh. They tell me I'm the only beauty queen in history that didn't cry when she won. It was on network television. I said to myself: "You're kidding." Bob Barker, the host, said: "No, I'm not kidding." I didn't know what else to say at that moment. In the press releases, they call it the great American Dream. There she is, Miss America, your ideal. Well, not my ideal, kid.

The minute you're crowned, you become their property and subject to whatever they tell you. They wake you up at seven o'clock next morning and make you put on a negligee and serve you breakfast in bed, so that all the New York papers can come in and take your picture sitting in bed, while you're absolutely bleary-eyed from the night before. They put on the Kaiser-Roth negligee, hand you the tray, you take three bites. The photographers leave, you whip off the negligee, they take the breakfast away, and that's it. I never did get any breakfast that day. (Laughs.)

You immediately start making personal appearances. The Jaycees or the chamber of commerce says: "I want to book Miss U.S.A. for our Christmas Day parade." They pay, whatever it is, seven hundred fifty dollars a day, first-class air fare, round trip, expenses, so forth. If the United Fund calls and wants me to give a five-minute pitch on queens at a luncheon, they still have to pay a fee. Doesn't matter that it's a charity. It's one hundred percent to Miss Universe, Incorporated. You get your salary. That's your prize money for the year. I got fifteen thousand dollars, which is all taxed in New York. Maybe out of a check of three thousand dollars, I'd get fifteen hundred dollars.

From the day I won Miss U.S.A. to the day I left for Universe, almost two months, I got a day and a half off. I made about two hundred fifty appearances that year. Maybe three hundred. Parades, shopping centers, and things. Snip ribbons. What else do you do at a shopping center? Model clothes. The nice thing I got to do was public speaking. They said: "You want a ghost writer?" I said: "Hell, no, I know how to talk." I wrote my own speeches. They don't trust girls to go out and talk because most of them can't.

One of the big execs from General Motors asked me to do a speech in Washington, D.C., on the consumer and the energy crisis. It was the fiftieth anniversary of the National Management Association. The White House, for some reason, sent me some stuff on it. I read it over, it was nonsense. So I stood up and said: "The reason we have an energy crisis is because we are, industrially and personally, pigs. We have a short-term view of the resources available to us; and unless we wake up to what we're doing to our air and our water, we'll have a dearth, not just a crisis." Oh, they weren't real pleased. (Laughs.)

What I resent most is that a lot of people didn't expect me to live this version of the American Dream for myself. I was supposed to live it their way.

When it came out in a newspaper interview that I said Nixon should resign, that he was a crook, oh dear, the fur flew. They got very upset until I got an invitation to the White House. They wanted to shut me up. The Miss Universe corporation had been trying to establish some sort of liaison with the White House for several years. I make anti-Nixon speeches and get this invitation.

I figured they're either gonna take me down to the basement and beat me up with a rubber hose or they're gonna offer me a cabinet post. They had a list of fifteen or so people I was supposed to meet. I've never seen such a bunch of people with raw nerve endings. I was dying to bring a tape recorder but thought if you mention the word "Sony" in the Nixon White House, you're in trouble. They'd have cardiac arrest. But I'm gonna bring along a pad and paper. They were patronizing. And when one of 'em got me in his office and talked about all the journalists and television people being liberals, I brought up blacklisting, *Red Channels,* and the TV industry. He changed the subject.

Miss Universe took place in Athens, Greece. The junta was still in power. I saw a heck of a lot of jeeps and troops and machine guns. The Americans were supposed to keep a low profile. I had never been a great fan of the Greek junta, but I knew darn well I was gonna have to keep my mouth shut. I was still representing the United States, for better or for worse. Miss Philippines won. I ran second.

At the end of the year, you're run absolutely ragged. That final evening, they usually have several queens from past years come back. Before they crown the new Miss U.S.A., the current one is supposed to take what they call the farewell walk. They call over the PA: Time for the old queen's walk. I'm now twenty-three and I'm an old queen. And they have this idiot farewell speech playing over the airwaves as the old queen takes the walk. And you're sitting on the throne for about thirty seconds, then you come down and they announce the name of the new one and you put the crown on her head. And then you're out.

As the new one is crowned, the reporters and photographers rush on the stage. I've seen photographers shove the girl who has just given her reign up thirty seconds before, shove her physically. I was gone by that time. I had jumped off the stage in my evening gown. It is very difficult for girls who are terrified of this ending. All of a sudden (snaps fingers), you're out. Nobody gives a damn about the old one.

Miss U.S.A. and remnants thereof is the crown stored in the attic in my parents' home. I don't even know where the banners are. It wasn't me the fans of Miss U.S.A. thought was pretty. What they think is pretty is the banner and crown. If I could put the banner and crown on that lamp, I swear to God ten men would come in and ask it for a date. I'll think about committing an axe murder if I'm not called anything but a former beauty queen. I can't stand it any more.

Several times during my year as what's-her-face I had seen the movie *The Sting.* There's a gesture the characters use which means the con is on: they rub their nose. In my last fleeting moments as Miss U.S.A, as they were playing that silly farewell speech and I walked down the aisle and stood by the throne, I looked right into the camera and rubbed my finger across my nose. The next day, the pageant people spent all their time telling people that I hadn't done it. I spent the time telling them that, of course, I had. I simply meant: the con is on. (Laughs.)

Miss U.S.A. is in the same graveyard that Emma Knight the twelve-year-old is. Where the sixteen-year-old is. All the past selves. There comes a time when you have to bury those selves because you've grown into another one. You don't keep exhuming the corpses.

If I could sit down with every young girl in America for the next fifty years, I could tell them what I liked about the pageant, I could tell them what I hated. It wouldn't make any difference. There're always gonna be girls who want to enter the beauty pageant. That's the fantasy: the American Dream.

THE TRAIN, CLARENCE SPENCER

We're on a day coach of the train bound for Washington, D.C. August 25, 1963.
It is on the eve of the march, led by Martin Luther King. The hour is late. Most
of the passengers are asleep or trying to. He is wide awake. He is seventy.

It's something like a dream, children. I'm just proud to ride this train down there, whether I march or not. I'm so proud just to be *in* it. It means something I wanted ever since I've been big enough to think about things. That's my freedom, making me feel that I'm a man, like all the rest of the men. I've had this feeling ever since I was about ten years old.

I was born and raised in the state of Louisiana. I did all kinds of work. I followed saw mills. I followed the levee camps, railroads, sugar farms, picked cotton. And I all the time wondered *why* in the world is it that some human being thinks he's so much more than the other. I can't never *see* that. I just can't *see* it. I don't *understand* it. I speak to you, you hear me, you understands me. You work like I work, eats like I eats, sleeps like I sleeps. Yet and still, how come? Why is it that they have to take the back seat for everything? So this trip is something like a dream to me.

I would put it thisaway. If you was down and out and you was longing for a thing and somebody would come and punch you out in a way that you could find it, you would feel like a different man, wouldn't you? That's the way I'm feelin'. I feel like I'm headed into something, that I would live to see some of the beneficial out of it. Maybe a day or two days. But I would enjoy those two days or one day better than I have enjoyed the whole seventy years which I've lived. Just to see myself as a man. Never mind the blackness, because that doesn't mean anything. I'm still a man.

When this thing started out, I said to my wife: "This I wants to be *in*. I don't want to see it on the television or hear it on the radio. I want to be *in* it. I crave to get into that light." I sit at home one day, and I read a portion of the Scripture in the Bible. I think it's the third chapter of the Lamentations of Jeremiah. This writer went on to say: He have led me and brought me in the darkness and not to light. I would like to get out of that darkness and into the light. That's what I'm working for.

I have fought it from years past up until now, and I'm still meanin' to be in it. In 1918, when I was in the service, I thought I was playing my part in the war, dignifiably. If I can take that, looks to me now I can take it anywheres else. Wouldn't it be that way to you? So this train can't get me down to Washington fast enough for me. Even if I don't be in the parade, just to stand somewhere and see this great bunch of people who have rosed up and some of the white people who have come with us. Let us live together. We can do so.

A man doesn't have to hunt another'n if he doesn't want to. If you says a thing I doesn't like, I can tell you about it. If he treats me wrong, I'm gonna speak to him like he's a man, not like he's an animal. Let him know he had did me wrong. Not anything he says, I must say yes. Every time you speak, it doesn't have to be right because you're speaking. Maybe you say something that I can see even deeper than you can. And lots of times it's the other way.

I got that letter in 1925 from Ku Kluck Klan for no reason at all, not for what I did to this man. They used to have a little magazine out, they call it *True Story*. He bought one and the guy that wrote the magazine, he had a story about a little colored boy and a crocodile was runnin' him. He was runnin' down the road barefooted and like they used to put the colored people in pictures with the hair all standin' up on the head. Let's make a loblolly out of him, you recall it. This man said to me: "Spencer, you from Dixie? I see where the crocodile run behind the little colored boy in the South." I said: "How come a crocodile will run a colored and won't run a white? A dumb beast doesn't know the difference.'' Did you know that liked to cause a killin' scrape over nothin'? We got to arguin' and arguin' over that. He threatened to kill me and wrote me that Ku Kluck Klan letter, and he got a rope and hung it to a post and it hung down where they were gonna put it around my neck.

When you don't do a person nothing, just try to straighten them out in their silly own doings and then he wanta talk about hangin', that's pretty bad, isn't it? You got the feelin' and you just can't get over it. That thing will wear you for a long, long time to come.

That's why I'm on this train. This train don't carry no liars, this train. That's a good old song.

This train is bound for glory . . .

. . . this train. That's right. We know it. Our people can compose those old songs. Like in the South, we had old blues songs. Things got tough, you couldn't hardly find a job, like back in the thirties. ''I'm gonna leave here walkin', baby, that I may get a ride.'' Get a ride, someway, somehow. That's the way we are fightin' in this. Someway, some means, somehow, we're gonna win it. We haven't got anything to fight with but what's right. This government have been run a long time with justice for *some* people, *not* all the people.

The thing that hurts so bad, we have built this country. My daddy was a slave, my daddy was. We have worked. We have built the railroads. We have built good roads. We have cut the ditches, we have cleaned up the ground. They tell me we've worked three hundred sixty-five years for nothin', and we have worked hundred two, hundred three years for a damned little bit of anything. You know a fella should be tired now, don't you? He should be really tired and wore out with it. But I'm proud to be in this. I'm kind of overjoyed.

Ray Bradbury / *The Stories of Ray Bradbury*   1980

Futuria Fantasia was the title of the mimeographed quarterly Ray Bradbury began while a high-school student in Waukegan, Illinois. He sold his first story at the age of twenty-one and wrote full-time thereafter. Bradbury estimates that he has written more than a thousand short stories, mostly fantasy and science fiction. Many of his stories have appeared in The New Yorker, Harper's, Mademoiselle, Playboy, *and other popular magazines; many more have appeared in science-fiction magazines and collections. For several years he also wrote for ''The Twilight Zone'' and ''Alfred Hitchcock Presents.'' His work is represented in more than 150 anthologies.*

Bradbury describes his life as a writer much as he does his stories: ''Exactly one half terror, exactly one half exhilaration.'' In the selection below, we can clearly see Bradbury's terror and exhilaration with the idea of, even momentarily, stepping out of the limits of time.

A SOUND OF THUNDER

The sign on the wall seemed to quaver under a film of sliding warm water. Eckels felt his eyelids blink over his stare, and the sign burned in this momentary darkness:

TIME SAFARI, INC.
SAFARIS TO ANY YEAR IN THE PAST.
YOU NAME THE ANIMAL.
WE TAKE YOU THERE.
YOU SHOOT IT.

A warm phlegm gathered in Eckels' throat; he swallowed and pushed it down. The muscles around his mouth formed a smile as he put his hand slowly out upon the air, and in that hand waved a check for ten thousand dollars at the man behind the desk.

"Does this safari guarantee I come back alive?"

"We guarantee nothing," said the official, "except the dinosaurs." He turned. "This is Mr. Travis, your Safari Guide in the Past. He'll tell you what and where to shoot. If he says no shooting, no shooting. If you disobey instructions, there's a stiff penalty of another ten thousand dollars, plus possible government action, on your return."

Eckels glanced across the vast office at a mass and tangle, a snaking and humming of wires and steel boxes, at an aurora that flickered now orange, now silver, now blue. There was a sound like a gigantic bonfire burning all of Time, all the years and all the parchment calendars, all the hours piled high and set aflame.

A touch of the hand and this burning would, on the instant, beautifully reverse itself. Eckels remembered the wording in the advertisements to the letter. Out of chars and ashes, out of dust and coals, like golden salamanders, the old years, the green years, might leap; roses sweeten the air, white hair turn Irish-black, wrinkles vanish; all, everything fly back to seed, flee death, rush down to their beginnings, suns rise in western skies and set in glorious easts, moons eat themselves opposite to the custom, all and everything cupping one in another like Chinese boxes, rabbits into hats, all and everything returning to the fresh death, the seed death, the green death, to the time before the beginning. A touch of a hand might do it, the merest touch of a hand.

"Hell and damn," Eckels breathed, the light of the Machine on his thin face. "A real Time Machine." He shook his head. "Makes you think. If the election had gone badly yesterday, I might be here now running away from the results. Thank God Keith won. He'll make a fine President of the United States."

"Yes," said the man behind the desk. "We're lucky. If Deutscher had gotten in, we'd have the worst kind of dictatorship. There's an anti-everything man for you, a militarist, anti-Christ, anti-human, anti-intellectual. People called us up, you know, joking but not joking. Said if Deutscher became President they wanted to go live in 1492. Of course it's not our business to conduct Escapes, but to form Safaris. Anyway, Keith's President now. All you got to worry about is—"

"Shooting my dinosaur." Eckels finished it for him.

"A *Tyrannosaurus rex*. The Thunder Lizard, the damndest monster in history. Sign this release. Anything happens to you, we're not responsible. Those dinosaurs are hungry."

Eckels flushed angrily. "Trying to scare me!"

"Frankly, yes. We don't want anyone going who'll panic at the first shot. Six Safari leaders were killed last year, and a dozen hunters. We're here to give you the damndest thrill a *real* hunter ever asked for. Traveling you back sixty million years to bag the biggest damned game in all Time. Your personal check's still there. Tear it up."

Mr. Eckels looked at the check for a long time. His fingers twitched.

"Good luck," said the man behind the desk. "Mr. Travis, he's all yours."

They moved silently across the room, taking their guns with them, toward the Machine, toward the silver metal and the roaring light.

First a day and then a night and then a day and then a night, then it was day-night-day-night-day. A week, a month, a year, a decade. A.D. 2055. A.D. 2019. 1999! 1957! Gone! the Machine roared.

They put on their oxygen helmets and tested the intercoms.

Eckels swayed on the padded seat, his face pale, his jaw stiff. He felt the trembling in his arms and he looked down and found his hands tight on the new rifle. There were four other men in the Machine. Travis, the Safari leader, his assistant, Lesperance, and two other hunters, Billings and Kramer. They sat looking at each other, and the years blazed around them.

"Can these guns get a dinosaur cold?" Eckels felt his mouth saying.

"If you hit them right," said Travis on the helmet radio. "Some dinosaurs have two brains, one in the head, another far down the spinal column. We stay away from those. That's stretching luck. Put your first two shots into the eyes, if you can, blind them, and go back into the brain."

The Machine howled. Time was a film run backward. Suns fled and ten million moons fled after them. "Good God," said Eckels. "Every hunter that ever lived would envy us today. This makes Africa seem like Illinois."

The Machine slowed; its scream fell to a murmur. The Machine stopped.

The sun stopped in the sky.

The fog that had enveloped the Machine blew away and they were in an old time, a very old time indeed, three hunters and two Safari Heads with their blue metal guns across their knees.

"Christ isn't born yet," said Travis. "Moses has not gone to the mountain to talk with God. The Pyramids are still in the earth, waiting to be cut out and put up. *Remember* that. Alexander, Caesar, Napoleon, Hitler—none of them exists."

The men nodded.

"That"—Mr. Travis pointed—"is the jungle of sixty million two thousand and fifty-five years before President Keith."

He indicated a metal path that struck off into green wilderness, over steaming swamp, among giant ferns and palms.

"And that," he said, "is the Path, laid by Time Safari for your use. It floats six inches above the earth. Doesn't touch so much as one grass blade, flower, or tree. It's an anti-gravity metal. Its purpose is to keep you from touching this world of the past in any way. Stay on the Path. Don't go off it. I repeat. *Don't go off.* For *any* reason! If you fall off, there's a penalty. And don't shoot any animal we don't okay."

"Why?" asked Eckels.

They sat in the ancient wilderness. Far birds' cries blew on a wind, and the smell of tar and an old salt sea, moist grasses, and flowers the color of blood.

"We don't want to change the Future. We don't belong here in the Past. The government doesn't *like* us here. We have to pay big graft to keep our franchise. A Time Machine is damn finicky business. Not knowing it, we might kill an important animal, a small bird, a roach, a flower even, thus destroying an important link in a growing species."

"That's not clear," said Eckels.

"All right," Travis continued, "say we accidentally kill one mouse here. That means all the future families of this one particular mouse are destroyed, right?"

"Right."

"And all the families of the families of the families of that one mouse! With a stamp of your foot, you annihilate first one, then a dozen, then a thousand, a million, a *billion* possible mice!"

"So they're dead," said Eckels. "So what?"

"So what?" Travis snorted quietly. "Well, what about the foxes that'll need those mice to survive? For want of ten mice, a fox dies. For want of ten foxes, a lion starves. For want of a lion, all manner of insects, vultures, infinite billions of life forms are thrown into chaos and destruction. Eventually it all boils down to this: fifty-nine million years later, a cave man, one of a dozen on the *entire world,* goes hunting wild boar or saber-tooth tiger for food. But you, friend, have *stepped* on all the tigers in that region. By stepping on *one* single mouse. So the cave man starves. And the cave man, please note, is not just *any* expendable man, no! He is an *entire future nation.* From his loins would have sprung ten sons. From *their* loins one hundred sons, and thus onward to a civilization. Destroy this one man, and you destroy a race, a people, an entire history of life. It is comparable to slaying some of Adam's grandchildren. The stamp of your foot, on one mouse, could start an earthquake, the effects of which could shake our Earth and destinies down through Time, to their very foundations. With the death of that one cave man, a billion others yet unborn are throttled in the womb. Perhaps Rome never rises on its seven hills. Perhaps Europe is forever a dark forest, and only Asia waxes healthy and teeming. Step on a mouse and you crush the Pyramids. Step on a mouse and you leave your print, like a Grand Canyon, across Eternity. Queen Elizabeth might never be born, Washington might not cross the Delaware, there might never be a United States at all. So be careful. Stay on the Path. *Never* step off!''

"I see," said Eckels. "Then it wouldn't pay for us even to touch the *grass?*"

"Correct. Crushing certain plants could add up infinitesimally. A little error here would multiply in sixty million years, all out of proportion. Or course maybe our theory is wrong. Maybe Time *can't* be changed by us. Or maybe it can be changed only in little subtle ways. A dead mouse here makes an insect imbalance there, a population disproportion later, a bad harvest further on, a depression, mass starvation, and, finally, a change in *social* temperament in far-flung countries. Something much more subtle, like that. Perhaps only a soft breath, a whisper, a hair, pollen on the air, such a slight, slight change that unless you looked close you wouldn't see it. Who knows? Who really can say he knows? We don't know. We're guessing. But until we do know for certain whether our messing around in Time *can* make a big roar or a little rustle in History, we're being damned careful. This Machine, this Path, your clothing and bodies, were sterilized, as you know, before the journey. We wear these oxygen helmets so we can't introduce our bacteria into an ancient atmosphere."

"How do we know which animals to shoot?"

"They're marked with red paint," said Travis. "Today, before our journey, we sent Lesperance here back with the Machine. He came to this particular era and followed certain animals."

"Studying them?"

"Right," said Lesperance. "I track them through their entire existence, noting which of them lives longest. Not long. How many times they mate. Not often. Life's short. When I find one that's going to die when a tree falls on him, or one that drowns in a tar pit, I note the exact hour, minute, and second. I shoot a paint bomb. It leaves a red patch on his hide. We can't miss it. Then I correlate our arrival in the Past so that we meet the Monster not more than two minutes before he would have died anyway. This way, we kill only animals with no future, that are never going to mate again. You see how *careful* we are?"

"But if you came back this morning in Time," said Eckels eagerly, "you must've bumped into *us,* our Safari! How did it turn out? Was it successful? Did all of us get through—alive?"

Travis and Lesperance gave each other a look.

"That'd be a paradox," said the latter. "Time doesn't permit that sort of mess— a man meeting himself. When such occasions threaten, Time steps aside. Like an airplane hitting an air pocket. You felt the Machine jump just before we stopped?

That was us passing ourselves on the way back to the Future. We saw nothing. There's no way of telling *if* this expedition was a success, *if* we got our Monster, or whether all of us—meaning *you*, Mr. Eckels—got out alive.''

Eckels smiled palely.

"Cut that," said Travis sharply. "Everyone on his feet!"

They were ready to leave the Machine.

The jungle was high and the jungle was broad and the jungle was the entire world forever and forever. Sounds like music and sounds like flying tents filled the sky, and those were pterodactyls soaring with cavernous gray wings, gigantic bats out of a delirium and a night fever. Eckels, balanced on the narrow Path, aimed his rifle playfully.

"Stop that!" said Travis. "Don't even aim for fun, damn it! If your gun should go off—"

Eckels flushed. "Where's our *Tyrannosaurus?*"

Lesperance checked his wristwatch. "Up ahead. We'll bisect his trail in sixty seconds. Look for the red paint, for Christ's sake. Don't shoot till we give the word. Stay on the Path. *Stay on the Path!*"

They moved forward in the wind of morning.

"Strange," murmured Eckels. "Up ahead, sixty million years, Election Day over. Keith made President. Everyone celebrating. And here we are, a million years lost, and they don't exist. The things we worried about for months, a lifetime, not even born or thought about yet."

"Safety catches off, everyone!" ordered Travis. "You, first shot, Eckels. Second, Billings. Third, Kramer."

"I've hunted tiger, wild boar, buffalo, elephant, but Jesus, this is *it*," said Eckels. "I'm shaking like a kid."

"Ah," said Travis.

Everyone stopped.

Travis raised his hand. "Ahead," he whispered. "In the mist. There he is. There's His Royal Majesty now."

The jungle was wide and full of twitterings, rustlings, murmurs, and sighs.

Suddenly it all ceased, as if someone had shut a door.

Silence.

A sound of thunder.

Out of the mist, one hundred yards away, came *Tyrannosaurus rex*.

"Jesus God," whispered Eckels.

"Shh!"

It came on great oiled, resilient, striding legs. It towered thirty feet above half of the trees, a great evil god, folding its delicate watchmaker's claws close to its oily reptilian chest. Each lower leg was a piston, a thousand pounds of white bone, sunk in thick ropes of muscle, sheathed over in a gleam of pebbled skin like the mail of a terrible warrior. Each thigh was a ton of meat, ivory, and steel mesh. And from the great breathing cage of the upper body, those two delicate arms dangled out front, arms with hands which might pick up and examine men like toys, while the snake neck coiled. And the head itself, a ton of sculptured stone, lifted easily upon the sky. Its mouth gaped, exposing a fence of teeth like daggers. Its eyes rolled, ostrich eggs, empty of all expression save hunger. It closed its mouth in a death grin. It ran, its pelvic bones crushing aside trees and bushes, its taloned feet clawing damp earth, leaving prints six inches deep wherever it settled its weight. It ran with a gliding ballet step, far too poised and balanced for its ten tons. It moved into a sunlit arena warily, its beautifully reptile hands feeling the air.

"My God!" Eckels twitched his mouth. "It could reach up and grab the Moon."

"Shh!" Travis jerked angrily. "He hasn't seen us yet."

"It can't be killed." Eckels pronounced this verdict quietly, as if there could be no argument. He had weighed the evidence and this was his considered opinion. The rifle in his hands seemed a cap gun. "We were fools to come. This is impossible."

"Shut up!" hissed Travis.

"Nightmare."

"Turn around," commanded Travis. "Walk quietly to the Machine. We'll remit one-half your fee."

"I didn't realize it would be this *big*," said Eckels. "I miscalculated, that's all. And now I want out."

"It *sees* us!"

"There's the red paint on its chest!"

The Thunder Lizard raised itself. Its armored flesh glittered like a thousand green coins. The coins, crusted with slime, steamed. In the slime, tiny insects wriggled, so that the entire body seemed to twitch and undulate, even while the Monster itself did not move. It exhaled. The stink of raw flesh blew down the wilderness.

"Get me out of here," said Eckels. "It was never like this before. I was always sure I'd come through alive. I had good guides, good safaris, and safety. This time, I figured wrong. I've met my match and admit it. This is too much for me to get hold of."

"Don't run," said Lesperance. "Turn around. Hide in the Machine."

"Yes." Eckels seemed to be numb. He looked at his feet as if trying to make them move. He gave a grunt of helplessness.

"Eckels!"

He took a few steps, blinking, shuffling.

"Not *that* way!"

The Monster, at the first motion, lunged forward with a terrible scream. It covered one hundred yards in four seconds. The rifles jerked up and blazed fire. A windstorm from the beast's mouth engulfed them in the stench of slime and old blood. The Monster roared, teeth glittering with sun.

Eckels, not looking back, walked blindly to the edge of the Path, his gun limp in his arms, stepped off the Path, and walked, not knowing it, in the jungle. His feet sank into green moss. His legs moved him, and he felt alone and remote from the events behind.

The rifles cracked again. Their sound was lost in shriek and lizard thunder. The great lever of the reptile's tail swung up, lashed sideways. Trees exploded in clouds of leaf and branch. The Monster twitched its jeweler's hands down to fondle at the men, to twist them in half, to crush them like berries, to cram them into its teeth and its screaming throat. Its boulder-stone eyes leveled with the men. They saw themselves mirrored. They fired at the metallic eyelids and the blazing black iris.

Like a stone idol, like a mountain avalanche, *Tyrannosaurus* fell. Thundering, it clutched trees, pulled them with it. It wrenched and tore the metal Path. The men flung themselves back and away. The body hit, ten tons of cold flesh and stone. The guns fired. The Monster lashed its armored tail, twitched its snake jaws, and lay still. A fount of blood spurted from its throat. Somewhere inside, a sac of fluids burst. Sickening gushes drenched the hunters. They stood, red and glistening.

The thunder faded.

The jungle was silent. After the avalanche, a green peace. After the nightmare, morning.

Billings and Kramer sat on the pathway and threw up. Travis and Lesperance stood with smoking rifles, cursing steadily.

In the Time Machine, on his face, Eckels lay shivering. He had found his way back to the Path, climbed into the Machine.

Travis came walking, glanced at Eckels, took cotton gauze from a metal box, and returned to the others, who were sitting on the Path.

"Clean up."

They wiped the blood from their helmets. They began to curse too. The Monster lay, a hill of solid flesh. Within, you could hear the sighs and murmurs as the furthest chambers of it died, the organs malfunctioning, liquids running a final instant from pocket to sac to spleen, everything shutting off, closing up forever. It was like standing by a wrecked locomotive or a steam shovel at quitting time, all valves being released or levered tight. Bones cracked; the tonnage of its own flesh, off-balance, dead weight, snapped the delicate forearms, caught underneath. The meat settled, quivering.

Another cracking sound. Overhead, a gigantic tree branch broke from its heavy mooring, fell. It crashed upon the dead beast with finality.

"There." Lesperance checked his watch. "Right on time. That's the giant tree that was scheduled to fall and kill this animal originally." He glanced at the two hunters. "You want the trophy picture?"

"What?"

"We can't take a trophy back to the Future. The body has to stay right here where it would have died originally, so the insects, birds, and bacteria can get at it, as they were intended to. Everything in balance. The body stays. But we *can* take a picture of you standing near it."

The two men tried to think, but gave up, shaking their heads.

They let themselves be led along the metal Path. They sank wearily into the Machine cushions. They gazed back at the ruined Monster, the stagnating mound, where already strange reptilian birds and golden insects were busy at the steaming armor.

A sound on the floor of the Time Machine stiffened them. Eckels sat there, shivering.

"I'm sorry," he said at last.

"Get up!" cried Travis.

Eckels got up.

"Go out on that Path alone," said Travis. He had his rifle pointed. "You're not coming back in the Machine. We're leaving you here!"

Lesperance seized Travis's arm. "Wait—"

"Stay out of this!" Travis shook his hand away. "This son of a bitch nearly killed us. But it isn't *that* so much. Hell, no. It's his *shoes!* Look at them! He ran off the Path. My God, that *ruins* us! Christ knows how much we'll forfeit! Tens of thousands of dollars of insurance! We guarantee no one leaves the Path. He left it. Oh, the damn fool! I'll have to report to the government. They might revoke our license to travel. God knows *what* he's done to Time, to History!"

"Take it easy, all he did was kick up some dirt."

"How do we *know?*" cried Travis. "We don't know anything! It's all a damn mystery! Get out there, Eckels!"

Eckels fumbled his shirt. "I'll pay anything. A hundred thousand dollars!"

Travis glared at Eckels' checkbook and spat. "Go out there. The Monster's next to the Path. Stick your arms up to your elbows in his mouth. Then you can come back with us."

"That's unreasonable!"

"The Monster's dead, you yellow bastard. The bullets! The bullets can't be left behind. They don't belong in the Past; they might change something. Here's my knife. Dig them out!''

The jungle was alive again, full of the old tremorings and bird cries. Eckels turned slowly to regard that primeval garbage dump, that hill of nightmares and terror. After a long time, like a sleepwalker, he shuffled out along the Path.

He returned, shuddering, five minutes later, his arms soaked and red to the elbows. He held out his hands. Each held a number of steel bullets. Then he fell. He lay where he fell, not moving.

"You didn't have to make him do that," said Lesperance.

"Didn't I? It's too early to tell." Travis nudged the still body. "He'll live. Next time he won't go hunting game like this. Okay." He jerked his thumb wearily at Lesperance. "Switch on. Let's go home."

1492.   1776.   1812.

They cleaned their hands and faces. They changed their caking shirts and pants. Eckels was up and around again, not speaking. Travis glared at him for a full ten minutes.

"Don't look at me," cried Eckels. "I haven't done anything."

"Who can tell?"

"Just ran off the Path, that's all, a little mud on my shoes—what do you want me to do—get down and pray?"

"We might need it. I'm warning you. Eckels, I might kill you yet. I've got my gun ready."

"I'm innocent. I've done nothing!"

1999.   2000.   2055.

The Machine stopped.

"Get out," said Travis.

The room was there as they had left it. But not the same as they had left it. The same man sat behind the same desk. But the same man did not quite sit behind the same desk.

Travis looked around swiftly. "Everything okay here?" he snapped.

"Fine. Welcome home!"

Travis did not relax. He seemed to be looking at the very atoms of the air itself, at the way the sun poured through the one high window.

"Okay, Eckels, get out. Don't ever come back."

Eckels could not move.

"You heard me," said Travis. "What're you *staring* at?"

Eckels stood smelling of the air, and there was a thing to the air, a chemical taint so subtle, so slight, that only a faint cry of his subliminal senses warned him it was there. The colors, white, gray, blue, orange, in the wall, in the furniture, in the sky beyond the window, were . . . were . . . And there was a *feel*. His flesh twitched. His hands twitched. He stood drinking the oddness with the pores of his body. Somewhere, someone must have been screaming one of those whistles that only a dog can hear. His body screamed silence in return. Beyond this room, beyond this wall, beyond this man who was not quite the same man seated at this desk that was not quite the same desk . . . lay an entire world of streets and people. What sort of world it was now, there was no telling. He could feel them moving there, beyond the walls, almost, like so many chess pieces blown in a dry wind. . . .

But the immediate thing was the sign painted on the office wall, the same sign he had read earlier today on first entering.

Somehow, the sign had changed:

TYME SEFARI INC.
SEFARIS TU ANY YEER EN THE PAST.
YU NAIM THE ANIMALL.
WEE TAEK YU THAIR.
YU SHOOT ITT.

Eckels felt himself fall into a chair. He fumbled crazily at the thick slime on his boots. He held up a clod of dirt, trembling. "No, it *can't* be. Not a *little* thing like that. No!"

Embedded in the mud, glistening green and gold and black, was a butterfly, very beautiful, and very dead.

"Not a little thing like *that!* Not a butterfly!" cried Eckels.

It fell to the floor, an exquisite thing, a small thing that could upset balances and knock down a line of small dominoes and then big dominoes and then gigantic dominoes, all down the years across Time. Eckels' mind whirled. It *couldn't* change things. Killing one butterfly couldn't be *that* important! Could it?

His face was cold. His mouth trembled, asking: "Who—who won the presidential election yesterday?"

The man behind the desk laughed. "You joking? You know damn well. Deutscher, of course! Who else? Not that damn weakling Keith. We got an iron man now, a man with guts, by God!" The official stopped. "What's wrong?"

Eckels moaned. He dropped to his knees. He scrabbled at the golden butterfly with shaking fingers. "Can't we," he pleaded to the world, to himself, to the officials, to the Machine, "can't we take it *back,* can't we *make* it alive again? Can't we start over? Can't we—"

He did not move. Eyes shut, he waited, shivering. He heard Travis breathe loud in the room; he heard Travis shift his rifle, click the safety catch, and raise the weapon.

There was a sound of thunder.

William Least Heat Moon / *Blue Highways*   1982

One of the most enduring traditions in American culture is the literature of the open road. From Walt Whitman and Henry David Thoreau to John Steinbeck and Jack Kerouac, American writers have eloquently expressed our collective fascination with wandering through the nation's landscape and meeting its people. The most recent—and deservedly celebrated—contribution to this literary tradition is William Least Heat Moon's Blue Highways *(1982), a finely crafted narrative and cultural commentary on a fourteen-thousand-mile trek across the nation on rural back roads, those colored blue on our maps.*

The author, whose legal name is William Trogdon, derives his pseudonym from his Osage Indian blood. Released from his job teaching English at a small college in Missouri and separated from his wife (whom he calls simply "The Cherokee") at the age of thirty-eight, Heat Moon decided that if he couldn't make things go right he could at least go. He felt "a nearly desperate sense of isolation and a growing suspicion that I had lived in an alien land." Setting out in the small van he named "Ghost Dancer" and accompanied by volumes of Whitman and Nietzsche, Heat Moon drove America's back roads in search of "places where change did not mean ruin and where time and men and deeds connected." Citing Daniel Boone, who "moved at the sight of smoke from a new neighbor's chimney,'' Heat Moon kept ''moving from the sight of my own.''

Heat Moon writes evocatively of the land, the weather, and the dazzling array of American originals he meets along the way: Kentuckians rebuilding log cabins, a Brooklyn cop turned Trappist monk in Georgia, the boys in the barbershop in Dime Box, Texas, the drinkers in a roadside brothel in Nevada. And in each instance, Heat Moon's copious note taking allows these characters to tell their own stories in their own words.

In a recent interview, Heat Moon noted, ''If writing isn't a process of discovery, then I can't imagine why anyone would write.'' In the following selection, he takes us to a seemingly nondescript town in eastern Tennessee. And in presenting the characters and stories of Nameless, Tennessee, Heat Moon helps us recognize the inadequacy of the generalizations we turn to when we describe who we are as Americans and where we are headed.

NAMELESS, TENNESSEE

Had it not been raining hard that morning on the Livingston square, I never would have learned of Nameless, Tennessee. Waiting for the rain to ease, I lay on my bunk and read the atlas to pass time rather than to see where I might go. In Kentucky were towns with fine names like Boreing, Bear Wallow, Decoy, Subtle, Mud Lick, Mummie, Neon; Belcher was just down the road from Mouthcard, and Minnie only ten miles from Mousie.

I looked at Tennessee. Turtletown eight miles from Ducktown. And also: Peavine, Wheel, Milky Way, Love Joy, Dull, Weakly, Fly, Spot, Miser Station, Only, McBurg, Peeled Chestnut, Clouds, Topsy, Isoline. And the best of all, Nameless. The logic! I was heading east, and Nameless lay forty-five miles west. I decided to go anyway.

The rain stopped, but things looked saturated, even bricks. In Gainesboro, a hill town with a square of businesses around the Jackson County Courthouse, I stopped for directions and breakfast. There is one almost infallible way to find honest food at just prices in blue-highway America: count the wall calendars in a cafe.

> No calendar: Same as an interstate pit stop.
> One calendar: Preprocessed food assembled in New Jersey.
> Two calendars: Only if fish trophies present.
> Three calendars: Can't miss on the farm-boy breakfasts.
> Four calendars: Try the ho-made pie too.
> Five calendars: Keep it under your hat, or they'll franchise.

One time I found a six-calendar cafe in the Ozarks, which served fried chicken, peach pie, and chocolate malts, that left me searching for another ever since. I've never seen a seven-calendar place. But old-time travelers—road men in a day when cars had running boards and lunchroom windows said AIR COOLED in blue letters with icicles dripping from the tops—those travelers have told me the golden legends of seven-calendar cafes.

To the rider of back roads, nothing shows the tone, the voice of a small town more quickly than the breakfast grill or the five-thirty tavern. Much of what the people do and believe and share is evident then. The City Cafe in Gainesboro had three calendars that I could see from the walk. Inside were no interstate refugees with full bladders and empty tanks, no wild-eyed children just released from the glassy cell of a stationwagon backseat, no longhaul truckers talking in CB numbers. There were only townspeople wearing overalls, or catalog-order suits with five-and-dime ties, or uniforms. That is, here were farmers and mill hands, bank clerks, the dry goods merchant, a policeman, and chiropractor's receptionist. Because it was Saturday, there were also mothers and children.

I ordered my standard on-the-road breakfast: two eggs up, hashbrowns, tomato juice. The waitress, whose pale, almost translucent skin shifted hue in the gray light like a thin slice of mother of pearl, brought the food. Next to the eggs was a biscuit with a little yellow Smiley button stuck in it. She said, "You from the North?"

"I guess I am." A Missourian gets used to Southerners thinking him a Yankee, a Northerner considering him a cracker, a Westerner sneering at his effete Easternness, and the Easterner taking him for a cowhand.

"So whata you doin' in the mountains?"

"Talking to people. Taking some pictures. Looking mostly."

"Lookin' for what?"

"A three-calendar cafe that serves Smiley buttons on the biscuits."

"You needed a smile. Tell me really."

"I don't know. Actually, I'm looking for some jam to put on this biscuit now that you've brought one."

She came back with grape jelly. In a land of quince jelly, apple butter, apricot jam, blueberry preserves, pear conserves, and lemon marmalade, you always get grape jelly.

"Whata you lookin' for?"

Like anyone else, I'm embarrassed to eat in front of a watcher, particularly if I'm getting interviewed. "Why don't you have a cup of coffee?"

"Cain't right now. You gonna tell me?"

"I don't know how to describe it to you. Call it harmony."

She waited for something more. "Is that it?" Someone called her to the kitchen. I had managed almost to finish by the time she came back. She sat on the edge of the booth. "I started out in life not likin' anything, but then it grew on me. Maybe that'll happen to you." She watched me spread the jelly. "Saw your van." She watched me eat the biscuit. "You sleep in there?" I told her I did. "I'd love to do that, but I'd be scared spitless."

"I don't mind being scared spitless. Sometimes."

"I'd love to take off cross country. I like to look at different license plates. But I'd take a dog. You carry a dog?"

"No dogs, no cats, no budgie birds. It's a one-man campaign to show Americans a person can travel alone without a pet."

"Cain't travel without a dog!"

"I like to do things the hard way."

"Shoot! I'd take me a dog to talk to. And for protection."

"It isn't traveling to cross the country and talk to your pug instead of people along the way. Besides, being alone on the road makes you ready to meet someone when you stop. You get sociable traveling alone."

She looked out toward the van again. "Time I get the nerve to take a trip, gas'll cost five dollars a gallon."

"Could be. My rig might go the way of the steamboat." I remembered why I'd come to Gainesboro. "You know the way to Nameless?"

"Nameless? I've heard of Nameless. Better ask the amlance driver in the corner booth." She pinned the Smiley on my jacket. "Maybe I'll see you on the road somewhere. His name's Bob, by the way."

"The ambulance driver?"

"The Smiley. I always name my Smileys—otherwise they all look alike. I'd talk to him before you go."

"The Smiley?"

"The amlance driver."

And so I went looking for Nameless, Tennessee, with a Smiley button named Bob.

"I don't know if I got directions for where you're goin'," the ambulance driver said. "I *think* there's a Nameless down the Shepardsville Road."

"When I get to Shepardsville, will I have gone too far?"

"Ain't no Shepardsville."

"How will I know when I'm there?"

"Cain't say for certain."

"What's Nameless look like?"

"Don't recollect."

"Is the road paved?"

"It's possible."

Those were the directions. I was looking for an unnumbered road named after a nonexistent town that would take me to a place called Nameless that nobody was sure existed.

Clumps of wild garlic lined the county highway that I hoped was the Shepardsville Road. It scrimmaged with the mountain as it tried to stay on top of the ridges; the hillsides were so steep and thick with oak, I felt as if I were following a trail through the misty treetops. Chickens, doing more work with their necks than legs, ran across the road, and, with a battering of wings, half leapt and half flew into the lower branches of oaks. A vicious pair of mixed-breed German shepherds raced along trying to eat the tires. After miles, I decided I'd missed the town—assuming there truly *was* a Nameless, Tennessee. It wouldn't be the first time I'd qualified for the Ponce de Leon Believe Anything Award.

I stopped beside a big man loading tools in a pickup. "I may be lost."

"Where'd you lose the right road?"

"I don't know. Somewhere around nineteen sixty-five."

"Highway fifty-six, you mean?"

"I came down fifty-six. I think I should've turned at the last junction."

"Only thing down that road's stumps and huckleberries, and the berries ain't there in March. Where you tryin' to get to?"

"Nameless. If there is such a place."

"You might not know Thurmond Watts, but he's got him a store down the road. That's Nameless at his store. Still there all right, but I might not vouch you that tomorrow." He came up to the van. "In my Army days, I wrote Nameless, Tennessee, for my place of birth on all the papers, even though I lived on this end of the ridge. All these ridges and hollers got names of their own. That's Steam Mill Holler over yonder. Named after the steam engine in the gristmill. Miller had him just one arm but done a good business."

"What business you in?"

"I've always farmed, but I work in Cookeville now in a heatin' element factory. Bad back made me go to town to work." He pointed to a wooden building not much bigger than his truck. By the slanting porch, a faded Double Cola sign said J M WHEELER STORE. "That used to be my business. That's me—Madison Wheeler. Feller came by one day. From Detroit. He wanted to buy the sign because he carried my name too. But I didn't sell. Want to keep my name up." He gave a cigarette a good slow smoking. "Had a decent business for five years, but too much of it was in credit. Then them supermarkets down in Cookeville opened, and I was buyin' higher than they was sellin'. With these hard roads now, everybody gets out of the hollers to shop or work. Don't stay up in here anymore. This tar road under my shoes done my business in, and it's likely to do Nameless in."

"Do you wish it was still the old way?"

"I got no debts now. I got two boys raised, and they never been in trouble. I got a brick house and some corn and tobacco and a few Hampshire hogs and Here-fords. A good bull. Bull's pumpin' better blood than I do. Real generous man in town let me put my cow in with his stud. I couldna paid the fee on that specimen otherwise.'' He took another long, meditative pull on his filtertip. ''If you're sat-isfied, that's all they are to it. I'll tell you, people from all over the nation—Flor-ida, Mississippi—are comin' in here to retire because it's good country. But our young ones don't stay on. Not much way to make a livin' in here anymore. Take me. I been beatin' on these stumps all my life, tryin' to farm these hills. They don't give much up to you. Fightin' rocks and briars all the time. One of the first things I recollect is swingin' a briar blade—filed out of an old saw it was. Now they come in with them crawlers and push out a pasture in a day. Still, it's a grudgin' land—like the gourd. Got to hard cuss gourd seed, they say, to get it up out of the ground.''

The whole time, my rig sat in the middle of the right lane while we stood talk-ing next to it and wiped at the mist. No one else came or went. Wheeler said, ''Factory work's easier on the back, and I don't mind it, understand, but a man becomes what he does. Got to watch that. That's why I keep at farmin', although the crops haven't ever throve. It's the doin' that's important.'' He looked up sud-denly. ''My apologies. I didn't ask what you do that gets you into these hollers.''

I told him. I'd been gone only six days, but my account of the trip already had taken on some polish.

He nodded. ''Satisfaction is doin' what's important to yourself. A man ought to honor other people, but he's got to honor what he believes in too.''

As I started the engine, Wheeler said, ''If you get back this way, stop in and see me. Always got beans and taters and a little piece of meat.''

Down along the ridge, I wondered why it's always those who live on little who are the ones to ask you to dinner.

Nameless, Tennessee, was a town of maybe ninety people if you pushed it, a dozen houses along the road, a couple of barns, same number of churches, a gen-eral merchandise store selling Fire Chief gasoline, and a community center with a lighted volleyball court. Behind the center was an open-roof, rusting metal privy with PAINT ME on the door; in the hollow of a nearby oak lay a full pint of Jack Daniel's Black Label. From the houses, the odor of coal smoke.

Next to a red tobacco barn stood the general merchandise with a poster of Sen-ator Albert Gore, Jr., smiling from the window. I knocked. The door opened part-way. A tall, thin man said, ''Closed up. For good,'' and started to shut the door.

''Don't want to buy anything. Just a question for Mr. Thurmond Watts.''

The man peered through the slight opening. He looked me over. ''What ques-tion would that be?''

''If this is Nameless, Tennessee, could he tell me how it got that name?''

The man turned back into the store and called out, ''Miss Ginny! Somebody here wants to know how Nameless come to be Nameless.''

Miss Ginny edged to the door and looked me and my truck over. Clearly, she didn't approve. She said, ''You know as well as I do, Thurmond. Don't keep him on the stoop in the damp to tell him.'' Miss Ginny, I found out, was Mrs. Virginia Watts, Thurmond's wife.

I stepped in and they both began telling the story, adding a detail here, the other correcting a fact there, both smiling at the foolishness of it all. It seems the hilltop settlement went for years without a name. Then one day the Post Office Depart-ment told the people if they wanted mail up on the mountain they would have to give the place a name you could properly address a letter to. The community met; there were only a handful, but they commenced debating. Some wanted patriotic names, some names from nature, one man recommended in all seriousness his own name. They couldn't agree, and they ran out of names to argue about. Finally, a fellow tired of the talk; he didn't like the mail he received anyway. "Forget the durn Post Office," he said. "This here's a nameless place if I ever seen one, so leave it be." And that's just what they did.

Watts pointed out the window. "We used to have signs on the road, but the Halloween boys keep tearin' them down."

"You think Nameless is a funny name," Miss Ginny said. "I see it plain in your eyes. Well, you take yourself up north a piece to Difficult or Defeated or Shake Rag. Now them are silly names."

The old store, lighted only by three fifty-watt bulbs, smelled of coal oil and baking bread. In the middle of the rectangular room, where the oak floor sagged a little, stood an iron stove. To the right was a wooden table with an unfinished game of checkers and a stool made from an apple-tree stump. On shelves around the walls sat earthen jugs with corncob stoppers, a few canned goods, and some of the two thousand old clocks and clockworks Thurmond Watts owned. Only one was ticking; the others he just looked at. I asked how long he'd been in the store.

"Thirty-five years, but we closed the first day of the year. We're hopin' to sell it to a churchly couple. Upright people. No athians."

"Did you build this store?"

"I built this one, but it's the third general store on the ground. I fear it'll be the last. I take no pleasure in that. Once you could come in here for a gallon of paint, a pickle, a pair of shoes, and a can of corn."

"Or horehound candy," Miss Ginny said. "Or corsets and salves. We had cough syrups and all that for the body. In season, we'd buy and sell blackberries and walnuts and chestnuts, before the blight got them. And outside, Thurmond milled corn and sharpened plows. Even shoed a horse sometimes."

"We could fix up a horse or a man or a baby," Watts said.

"Thurmond, tell him we had a doctor on the ridge in them days."

"We had a doctor on the ridge in them days. As good as any doctor alivin'. He'd cut a crooked toenail or deliver a woman. Dead these last years."

"I got some bad ham meat one day," Miss Ginny said, "and took to vomitin'. All day, all night. Hangin' on the drop edge of yonder. I said to Thurmond, 'Thurmond, unless you want shut of me, call the doctor.' "

"I studied on it," Watts said.

"You never did. You got him right now. He come over and put three drops of iodeen in half a glass of well water. I drank it down and the vomitin' stopped with the last swallow. Would you think iodeen could do that?"

"He put Miss Ginny on one teaspoon of spirits of ammonia in well water for her nerves. Ain't nothin' works better for her to this day."

"Calms me like the hand of the Lord."

Hilda, the Wattses' daughter, came out of the backroom. "I remember him," she said. "I was just a baby. Y'all were talkin' to him, and he lifted me up on the counter and gave me a stick of Juicy Fruit and a piece of cheese."

"Knew the old medicines," Watts said. "Only drugstore he needed was a good kitchen cabinet. None of them antee-beeotics that hit you worsen your ailment. Forgotten lore now, the old medicines, because they ain't profit in iodeen."

Miss Ginny started back to the side room where she and her sister Marilyn were taking apart a duck-down mattress to make bolsters. She stopped at the window for another look at Ghost Dancing. "How do you sleep in that thing? Ain't you all cramped and cold?"

"How does the clam sleep in his shell?" Watts said in my defense.

"Thurmond, get the boy a piece of buttermilk pie afore he goes on."

"Hilda, get him some buttermilk pie." He looked at me. "You like good music?" I said I did. He cranked up an old Edison phonograph, the kind with the big morning-glory blossom for a speaker, and put on a wax cylinder. "This will be 'My Mother's Prayer,' " he said.

While I ate buttermilk pie, Watts served as disc jockey of Nameless, Tennessee. "Here's 'Mountain Rose.' " It was one of those moments that you know at the time will stay with you to the grave: the sweet pie, the gaunt man playing the old music, the coals in the stove glowing orange, the scent of kerosene and hot bread. "Here's 'Evening Rhapsody.' " The music was so heavily romantic we both laughed. I thought: It is for this I have come.

Feathered over and giggling, Miss Ginny stepped from the side room. She knew she was a sight. "Thurmond, give him some lunch. Still looks hungry."

Hilda pulled food off the woodstove in the backroom: home-butchered and canned whole-hog sausage, home-canned June apples, turnip greens, cole slaw, potatoes, stuffing, hot cornbread. All delicious.

Watts and Hilda sat and talked while I ate. "Wish you would join me."

"We've ate," Watts said. "Cain't beat a woodstove for flavorful cookin'."

He told me he was raised in a one-hundred-fifty-year-old cabin still standing in one of the hollows. "How many's left," he said, "that grew up in a log cabin? I ain't the last surely, but I must be climbin' on the list."

Hilda cleared the table. "You Watts ladies know how to cook."

"She's in nursin' school at Tennessee Tech. I went over for one of them football games last year there at Coevul." To say *Cookeville,* you let the word collapse in upon itself so that it comes out "Coevul."

"Do you like football?" I asked.

"Don't know. I was so high up in that stadium, I never opened my eyes."

Watts went to the back and returned with a fat spiral notebook that he set on the table. His expression had changed. "Miss Ginny's *Deathbook.*"

The thing startled me. Was it something I was supposed to sign? He opened it but said nothing. There were scads of names written in a tidy hand over pages incised to crinkliness by a ballpoint. Chronologically, the names had piled up: wives, grandparents, a stillborn infant, relatives, friends close and distant. Names, names. After each, the date of *the* unknown finally known and transcribed. The last entry bore yesterday's date.

"She's wrote out twenty years' worth. Ever day she listens to the hospital report on the radio and puts the names in. Folks come by to check a date. Or they just turn through the books. Read them like a scrapbook."

Hilda said, "Like Saint Peter at the gates inscribin' the names."

Watts took my arm. "Come along." He led me to the fruit cellar under the store. As we went down, he said, "Always take a newborn baby upstairs afore you take him downstairs, otherwise you'll incline him downwards."

The cellar was dry and full of cobwebs and jar after jar of home-canned food, the bottles organized as a shopkeeper would: sausage, pumpkin, sweet pickles, tomatoes, corn relish, blackberries, peppers, squash, jellies. He held a hand out toward the dusty bottles. "Our tomorrows."

Upstairs again, he said, "Hope to sell the store to the right folk. I see now, though, it'll be somebody offen the ridge. I've studied on it, and maybe it's the end of our place." He stirred the coals. "This store could give a comfortable livin', but not likely get you rich. But just gettin' by is dice rollin' to people nowadays. I never did see my day guaranteed."

When it was time to go, Watts said, "If you find anyone along your way wants a good store—on the road to Cordell Hull Lake—tell them about us."

I said I would. Miss Ginny and Hilda and Marilyn came out to say goodbye. It was cold and drizzling again. "Weather to give a man the weary dismals," Watts grumbled. "Where you headed from here?"

"I don't know."

"Cain't get lost then."

Miss Ginny looked again at my rig. It had worried her from the first as it had my mother. "I hope you don't get yourself kilt in that durn thing gallivantin' around the country."

"Come back when the hills dry off," Watts said. "We'll go lookin' for some of them round rocks all sparkly inside."

I thought a moment. "Geodes?"

"Them's the ones. The county's properly full of them."

Lee Iacocca / From *Iacocca: An Autobiography* 1985

The son of poor Italian immigrants, Lee Iacocca grew up in Allentown, Pennsylvania, attended public schools there, and graduated with an engineering degree from Lehigh University. "The Depression turned me into a materialist. Years later, when I graduated from college, my attitude was: 'Don't bother me with philosophy. I want to make ten thousand a year by the time I'm twenty-five, and then I want to be a millionaire.' I wasn't interested in a snob degree. I was after the bucks."

In 1946, Iacocca began working for the Ford Motor Company as a student engineer. He rose within the ranks of the company with remarkable speed, becoming its president in 1970, only to be fired eight years later. He assumed the leadership of Chrysler and led it not only out of bankruptcy but also, through strong management and extraordinarily effective marketing, to a position of fiscal solvency, enabling the company to repay its $1.2 billion federal loan far earlier than most in Washington had anticipated.

In the following chapters from Iacocca, *written with the assistance of William Novak, a journalist, lecturer, and author of several nonfiction books, Iacocca recounts the circumstances that catapulted him into the national spotlight and offers his detailed recommendations for "making America great again." Asked to explain why he wrote the book, Iacocca reported:*

> *Certainly not to become famous. The television ads for Chrysler have already made me more famous than I ever wanted to be. And I didn't write it to get rich. I already have every material thing a person could need. That's why I'm donating every penny I earn from this book to diabetes research. And I didn't write this book to get back at Henry Ford for firing me. I've already done that the old-fashioned American way—by fighting it out in the marketplace. The truth is that I wrote this book to set the record straight (and to keep my mind straight), to tell the story of my life at Ford and Chrysler the way it really happened. While I was working on it and reliving my life, I kept thinking of all those young people I meet whenever I speak at universities and business schools. If this book can give them a realistic picture of the excitement and challenge of big business in America today and some idea of what is worth fighting for, then all of this hard work will have been worth something.*

PROLOGUE

You're about to read the story of a man who's had more than his share of successes. But along the way, there were some pretty bad times, too. In fact, when

I look back on my thirty-eight years in the auto industry, the day I remember most vividly had nothing at all to do with new cars and promotions and profits.

I began my life as the son of immigrants, and I worked my way up to the presidency of the Ford Motor Company. When I finally got there, I was on top of the world. But then fate said to me: "Wait. We're not finished with you. Now you're going to find out what it feels like to get kicked off Mt. Everest!"

On July 13, 1978, I was fired. I had been president of Ford for eight years and a Ford employee for thirty-two. I had never worked anywhere else. And now, suddenly, I was out of a job. It was gut-wrenching.

Officially, my term of employment was to end in three months. But under the terms of my "resignation," at the end of that period I was to be given the use of an office until I found a new job.

On October 15, my final day at the office, and just incidentally my fifty-fourth birthday, my driver drove me to World Headquarters in Dearborn for the last time. Before I left the house, I kissed my wife, Mary, and my two daughters, Kathi and Lia. My family had suffered tremendously during my final, turbulent months at Ford, and that filled me with rage. Perhaps I was responsible for my own fate. But what about Mary and the girls? Why did they have to go through this? They were the innocent victims of the despot whose name was on the building.

Even today, their pain is what stays with me. It's like the lioness and her cubs. If the hunter knows what's good for him, he'll leave the little ones alone. Henry Ford made my kids suffer, and for that I'll never forgive him.

The next day I got into my car and headed out to my new office. It was in an obscure warehouse on Telegraph Road, only a few miles from Ford's World Headquarters. But for me, it was like visiting another planet.

I wasn't exactly sure where the office was, and it took me a few minutes to find the right building. When I finally got there, I didn't even know where to park.

As it turned out, there were plenty of people around to show me. Someone had alerted the media that the newly deposed president of Ford would be coming to work here this morning, and a small crowd had gathered to meet me. A TV reporter shoved a microphone in my face and asked: "How do you feel, coming to this warehouse after eight years at the top?"

I couldn't bring myself to answer him. What could I say? When I was safely out of camera range, I muttered the truth. "I feel like shit," I said.

My new office was little more than a cubicle with a small desk and a telephone. My secretary, Dorothy Carr, was already there, with tears in her eyes. Without a word, she pointed to the cracked linoleum floor and the two plastic coffee cups on the desk.

Only yesterday, she and I had been working in the lap of luxury. The office of the president was the size of a grand hotel suite. I had my own bathroom. I even had my own living quarters. As a senior Ford executive, I was served by white-coated waiters who were on call all day. I once brought some relatives from Italy to see where I worked, and they thought they had died and gone to heaven.

Today, however, I could have been a million miles away. A few minutes after I arrived, the depot manager stopped by to pay a courtesy call. He offered to get me a cup of coffee from the machine in the hall. It was a kind gesture, but the incongruity of my being there made us both feel awkward.

For me, this was Siberia. It was exile to the farthest corner of the kingdom. I was so stunned that it took me a few minutes before I realized I had no reason to stay. I had a telephone at home, and somebody could bring me the mail. I left that place before ten o'clock and never went back.

This final humiliation was much worse than being fired. It was enough to make me want to kill—I wasn't quite sure who, Henry Ford or myself. Murder or suicide were never real possibilities, but I did start to drink a little more—and shake a lot more. I really felt I was coming apart at the seams.

As you go through life, there are thousands of little forks in the road, and there are a few really big forks—those moments of reckoning, moments of truth. This was mine as I wondered what to do. Should I pack it all in and retire? I was fifty-four years old. I had already accomplished a great deal. I was financially secure. I could afford to play golf for the rest of my life.

But that just didn't feel right. I knew I had to pick up the pieces and carry on.

There are times in everyone's life when something constructive is born out of adversity. There are times when things seem so bad that you've got to grab your fate by the shoulders and shake it. I'm convinced it was that morning at the warehouse that pushed me to take on the presidency of Chrysler only a couple of weeks later.

The private pain I could have endured. But the deliberate public humiliation was too much for me. I was full of anger, and I had a simple choice: I could turn that anger against myself, with disastrous results. Or I could take some of that energy and try to do something productive.

"Don't get mad," Mary reminded me. "Get even." In times of great stress and adversity, it's always best to keep busy, to plow your anger and your energy into something positive.

As it turned out, I went from the frying pan into the fire. A year after I signed up, Chrysler came within a whisker of bankruptcy. There were many days at Chrysler when I wondered how I had got myself into this mess. Being fired at Ford was bad enough. But going down with the ship at Chrysler was more than I deserved.

Fortunately, Chrysler recovered from its brush with death. Today I'm a hero. But strangely enough, it's all because of that moment of truth at the warehouse. With determination, with luck, and with help from lots of good people, I was able to rise up from the ashes.

Now let me tell you my story.

MAKING AMERICA GREAT AGAIN

These days, *everybody's* talking about the national deficit. But because we almost lost Chrysler a few years ago, I had the dubious honor of starting to worry about this problem a little earlier than most people. We were being killed by high interest rates, and it was clear that as long as the government was using up more than 50 percent of the nation's credit, interest rates could never come down very much.

So back in the summer of 1982, I wrote a piece for *Newsweek* where I proposed a simple way of cutting the national deficit in half. At the time, the deficit was only—*only!*—$120 billion. My plan involved cutting $30 billion from government spending while raising another $30 billion in revenues.

I had already learned firsthand that Chrysler was alive only because of the combined efforts of management, labor, the banks, the supplier, and the government. And so I wondered: why couldn't the principle of "equality of sacrifice" be applied to the federal deficit as well?

My plan was simple. First I would cut 5 percent a year out of the defense budget. That would come to $15 billion, and it could be done without affecting a single hardware program.

Then we'd call in the Democrats and say to them: "Okay, boys, I want you to match this $15 billion cut with an equal cut in the social programs you've put in over the past forty years."

Then comes the hard part. Once we've cut $30 billion in spending, we match it dollar for dollar on the revenue side. First, we raise $15 billion with a surtax on imported oil, designed to help OPEC keep their oil prices at $34 a barrel. Then we add a fifteen-cent tax to gas at the pump, which raises another $15 billion.

Even with these new taxes, American gas and oil would still be cheaper than anywhere else outside the Arab world. And in addition to all that revenue, we'd finally be creating an energy policy. The next time OPEC struck, we'd be ready for them.

Taken together, these "four 15s" would cut the deficit by $60 billion a year. The beauty of this program is that it spreads the sacrifice equally among all our people——Republicans and Democrats, business as well as labor.

When I came up with this plan, I went to every CEO I knew on Wall Street and asked them: "What would happen if the President went on TV and announced that he was cutting the federal deficit in half?" They all agreed that this announcement would trigger the biggest investment binge in our history. It would restore our credibility as a country. It would prove that we knew what we were doing.

Needless to say, we didn't do it. But it's not as if nobody was listening. Thousands of *Newsweek* readers wrote to tell me they liked my plan. I even got a call from the White House asking me to come and see the President.

When I walked into the Oval Office, President Reagan greeted me with the *Newsweek* article in his hand. "Lee," he said, "I like what you've written here. And I'm worried about the size of the deficit, too. But Richard Wirthlin, my pollster, tells me that a gas tax is the most unpopular thing I could do."

"Wait a minute," I thought. "Are we running this country by the polls? Is that what leadership is all about?"

The President wanted to talk about the defense budget. "We spent too little under Carter," he told me. "We've got to spend a lot more for our national security. You don't understand the whole picture."

"That's true," I replied. "I don't understand it all. And I don't want to be presumptuous. But the defense budget is now more than $300 billion. I'm a businessman. Believe me, I can cut 5 percent out of *anything* and you'll never know I did it. In fact, I've been doing that all my life."

Well, we didn't cut the deficit in August 1982. And now it's grown to over $200 billion. As I write these words in the spring of 1984, we're still wringing our hands about what to do.

Unfortunately, the budget deficit is only the tip of the iceberg. If anyone doubts that we've lost some of our economic greatness, let's consider the following questions:

Why does the country that produced Walter Chrysler, Alfred Sloan, and the original Henry Ford have so much trouble making and selling cars competitively?

Why does the country of Andrew Carnegie have so much trouble competing in steel?

Why does the country of Thomas Edison have to import most of its phonographs, radios, television sets, videorecorders, and other forms of consumer electronics?

Why does the country of John D. Rockefeller have oil problems?

Why does the country of Eli Whitney have to import so many of its machine tools?

Why does the country of Robert Fulton and the Wright brothers face such heavy competition in transportation equipment?

What became of the industrial machine that was once the envy and the hope of the rest of the world?

How, in less than forty years, did we manage to dismantle the "arsenal of democracy'' and wind up with an economy that is flabby in so many critical areas?

Our loss of leadership did not come about overnight. The gradual erosion of our strength and power began in those halcyon years following World War II. But in no period of our history has America showed more vulnerability than in this past decade.

First, we woke up one morning and discovered that something called OPEC had the power to bring America to its knees. Like Pavlov, who rang a bell to achieve his desired results, OPEC rang its bell and we responded. And now, more than ten years later, we still have no real program to respond to this monumental economic danger.

Second, in the name of free trade, we're sitting by and watching Japan systematically capture our industrial and technological base. By combining the skills and efficiencies of their culture with a whole host of unfair economic advantages, Japan appears capable of looting our markets with impunity.

In Washington this is known as laissez-faire economics, and they love it. In Tokyo they call it *Veni, Vidi, Vici* economics, and believe me, they love it even more. The Japanese have come, they've seen, and they are conquering. And our dependence on Japan will continue to grow until we establish some practical limits to their enjoyment of our markets.

Third, the Soviet Union has caught us in overall nuclear capability. America no longer has a decisive military edge. We've now defined a program to regain the edge, but its dominance of the national agenda has been so total that I'm beginning to wonder what all these new weapons are going to *protect*. Without a strong, vital industrial infrastructure, we're a nation bristling with missiles that surround a land of empty factories, unemployed workers, and decaying cities. Where is the wisdom in this policy?

Finally, at some point in our recent past America lost sight of its true source of power and greatness. From a nation whose strength has always flowed from investments in the production and consumption of goods, we have somehow turned into a nation enamored with investing in paper.

And so our biggest companies are pouring huge sums of money into buying up the stock of other companies. Where is all this capital ending up? In new factories? In new production equipment? In product innovation?

Some of it is, but not very much. Most of that money is ending up in banks and other financial institutions who are turning around and lending it out to countries such as Poland, Mexico, and Argentina. That doesn't help America much. But at least when these countries went broke and the banks cried wolf, they accomplished what Chrysler, International Harvester, and the housing industry could never have done: they persuaded the Federal Reserve to back off of tight money.

Each month, some new type of financial instrument is created for the express purpose of absorbing consumer purchasing power and enriching the brokerage houses. Looking back on this period of deep-discount this and zero-coupon that, I can't help but think that never before in history has so much capital produced so little of lasting value.

Right now, our biggest industrial employers are in autos, steel, electronics, aircraft, and textiles. If we want to save millions of jobs, we've got to preserve these industries. They're the ones that create markets for the service sector as well as for high technology. They're also critical to our national interest. Can we really maintain the backbone of our defense system without strong steel, machine tool, and auto industries?

Without a strong industrial base, we can kiss our national security good-bye. We can also bid farewell to the majority of our high value-added jobs. Take away America's $10 to $15-an-hour industrial jobs and you undercut our whole economy. Oops—there goes the middle class!

So we've got to make some basic decisions. Unless we act soon, we're going to lose both steel and autos to Japan by the year 2000. And worst of all, we will have given them up without a fight.

Some people seem to think that this defeat is inevitable. They believe we should even hasten along the process by abandoning our industrial base and concentrating instead on high technology.

Now, I don't for a moment dispute the importance of high technology in America's industrial future. But high tech alone won't save us. It's important to our economy precisely because so many other segments of American industry are its customers.

Especially the auto industry. We're the ones who use all the robots. We've got more computer-aided design and manufacturing facilities than anyone. We're using computers to get better fuel economy, to clean up emissions, and to get precision and quality in the way we build our cars.

Not many people know that IBM's three biggest customers (excluding defense) are GM, Ford, and Chrysler. There can't be a Silicon Valley without a Detroit. If somebody is producing silicon chips, somebody else has to *use* them. And we do. There's now at least one computer on board every car we build. Some of our more exotic models have as many as five!

You can't sell your silicon chips in a brown paper bag down at the hardware store. They've got to have a use. And America's basic industries are the users. Close us down and you close down your market. Close down autos and you close down steel and rubber—and then you've lost about one of every seven jobs in the country.

Where would that leave us? We'd have a country of people who serve hamburgers to each other and silicon chips to the rest of the world.

Don't get me wrong: high technology is critical to our economic future. But as important as it is; high tech will never employ the number of people that our basic industries do today. That's a lesson we should have learned from the demise of the textile industry. Between 1957 and 1975, 674,000 textile workers were laid off in New England. But despite that region's booming high-tech industries, only 18,000 of those workers—about 3 percent—found work in the computer industry.

Nearly five times as many ended up in lower-wage retail trade and service jobs. In other words, if you lost your job in a textile mill in Massachusetts, you were five times as likely to end up working at K-Mart or McDonald's than at Digital Equipment or Wang. You just can't take a forty-year-old pipefitter from Detroit or Pittsburgh or Newark, put a white coat on him, and expect him to program computers in Silicon Valley.

So the answer isn't to promote high technology at the expense of our basic industries. The answer is to promote *both* of them together. There's room for all of us in the cornucopia, but we need a concerted national effort to make it happen.

In other words, our country needs a rational industrial policy.

These days, "industrial policy" is a loaded term. It's like yelling "fire!" in a crowded theater. A lot of people panic whenever they hear the phrase.

Don't they want America to be strong and healthy? Sure they do. But they want it to happen without any planning. They want America to be great *by accident.*

The ideologues argue that industrial policy would mark the end of the free-enterprise system as we know it. Well, our wonderful free-enterprise system now includes a $200 billion deficit, a spending program that's out of control, and a trade deficit of $100 billion. The plain truth is that the marketplace isn't always efficient. We live in a complex world. Every now and then the pump has to be primed.

Unlike some people who talk about industrial policy, I don't mean that the government should be picking winners and losers. The government has proved again and again that it's not smart enough to do that.

And I don't want the government interfering in the operations of my company—or any other company, for that matter. Believe me, the existing regulations are bad enough.

As I see it, industrial policy means restructuring and revitalizing our so-called sunset industries—the older industries that are in trouble. Government must become more active in helping American industry meet the challenge of foreign competition and a changing world.

Almost everyone admires the Japanese, with their clear vision of the future; the cooperation among their government, banks, and labor; and the way they lead from their strengths. But whenever somebody suggests that *we* ought to follow their lead, the image suddenly shifts to the Soviets and their five-year plans.

But government planning doesn't have to mean socialism. All it means is having a game plan, an objective. It means coordinating all the pieces of economic policy instead of setting it piecemeal, in dark rooms, by people who have only their own vested interests at heart.

Is planning un-American? We do a great deal of planning at Chrysler. So does every other successful corporation. Football teams plan. Universities plan. Unions plan. Banks plan. Governments all over the world plan—except for ours.

We're not going to make progress until we give up the ridiculous idea that any planning on a national level represents an attack on the capitalist system. Because of this fear, we're the only advanced country in the world without an industrial policy.

Actually, that's not entirely true. America already *has* an industrial policy, and it's a bad one. Nobody who's familiar with Washington can claim that the government would somehow violate free enterprise if it helped American industry. Washington is Subsidy City! And each subsidy adds up to an industrial policy.

Let's start with federal loan guarantees. (I'm an expert in this area.) Chrysler wasn't the first. Before we came along, there were $409 billion in guaranteed loans. Now the figure is up to $500 billion and still climbing. That's industrial policy.

Then there's defense. Eisenhower warned us about this one when he talked about the military-industrial complex. That complex has us spending over $300 billion a year. It's the only protected industry we have left in this country. It's the only industry where, by law, the Japanese are not allowed to compete.

That's why when we at Chrysler sold our tank division to General Dynamics, a lot of people asked: "Why don't you sell the car business and keep the tanks? The tanks are making you $60 million a year guaranteed and protected!"

Then there's NASA and the space program. That's industrial policy, too. The moon shot is what sent our computer industry into high gear.

Or what about the International Monetary Fund? It bails out foreign countries that have borrowed beyond their means and can't keep up the payments. Not long ago Paul Volcker gave Mexico another $1 billion to keep its credit intact and to relieve some big U.S. banks that lent them the money in the first place. Volcker made his loan overnight, without a hearing. But in order to get $1.2 billion to save Chrysler—an American company—we had to tie up Congress for weeks. What kind of industrial policy is that?

In the past, the U.S. government has made loans to Poland at 8 percent while we ask Polish Americans to buy houses at 14 percent. If the Democrats can't make hay out of that, they *deserve* to lose.

And what about tax policy? The auto industry in the aggregate pays 50 percent of its income in taxes. The banking industry pays only 2 percent. That's another form of industrial policy.

So we *do* have an industrial policy—or more accurately, *hundreds* of industrial policies. The only problem is that they're all over the lot and do little if anything for our basic industries.

Is industrial policy some kind of radical new idea? Not at all. We had an industrial policy in America even before we had a nation. Back in 1643, Massachusetts granted a new smelting company exclusive iron-producing privileges for twenty-one years to encourage this developing industry.

More recently, in the nineteenth century, our industrial policy included extensive government support for our railroads, the Erie Canal, and even our universities.

In the twentieth century, we've seen government support for our highways, for synthetic rubber, modern jet travel, the moon shot, integrated-circuit industries, high technology, and much more.

Over the past few decades we've had a phenomenally successful industrial policy—in agriculture. Three percent of our population not only feeds the rest of us—they feed much of the rest of the world to boot. Now, *that's* productivity!

How did that happen? Well, there's more going on here than good climate, rich soil, and hardworking farmers. We had all those things fifty years ago, and all we got were dust bowls and disasters.

The difference lies in a wide range of government-sponsored projects. There are federal research grants; county agents to educate people; state experimental farms; rural electrification and irrigation projects such as the TVA: crop insurance; export credits; price supports; acreage controls; and now Payment in Kind—which pays farmers *not* to grow certain crops. That program alone now comes to over $20 billion a year.

With all of that government help (or, some would say, interference) we've created a miracle. Our agricultural industrial policy has made us the envy of the world.

Now, if we've got an agricultural-industrial policy and a military-industrial policy, why the hell can't we have an *industrial*-industrial policy?

I guess my attitude toward an industrial policy is the same as Abraham Lincoln's when somebody told him that Ulysses S. Grant got drunk a lot. Lincoln said: "Find out what kind of whiskey he drinks and send it to my other generals."

Here's my six-point program that could form the basis for a new industrial policy.

First, we should provide for energy independence by 1990 by taxing foreign energy, both at the port and at the pump, in order to restore the conservation ethic and rekindle investments in alternate sources of energy. We must not be lulled by the current depressed demand. OPEC will always act in its own interest, and that interest will always be served best by high prices and tight supplies. The American people are willing to pay a price for energy independence. They know it can't be achieved without a sacrifice.

Second, we should provide for specific limits to Japan's market share for certain critical industries. We should declare a state of economic emergency for those industries and unilaterally set aside the restrictive GATT provisions during this period. We don't have to apologize for taking this common-sense approach to trade with Japan. At this point in our history, we can't afford a trading partner who insists on the right to sell but who refuses to buy.

Third, as a nation, we've got to face reality on the costs and funding mechanisms for federal entitlement programs. They're studying this to death in Washington because it's a political hot potato. But the answer has always been right in front of our noses: we can't continue to pay out more than we take in, and that will mean some very painful adjustments.

Fourth, America needs more engineers, scientists, and technicians. On a per-capita basis, Japan graduates about four times as many engineers as we do. (But we graduate fifteen times as many lawyers!) Special education grants and loans should be provided for high-technology fields of study. The Soviets and the Japanese are both dedicated to building up their technological competence—and we are not keeping up.

Fifth, we need new incentives to increase research and development efforts in the private sector and to accelerate factory modernization and productivity in critical industries. One approach is to offer investment tax credits for R&D and twelve-month depreciation write-offs for productivity-related investments.

Finally, we need to establish a long-term program for rebuilding America's arteries of commerce—our roadways, bridges, railroads, and water systems. Our infrastructure, which is vital to any strengthening and expansion of our industrial power, is deteriorating at an alarming rate. Something must be done. Such a program could be partially funded by the OPEC energy tax. It would also provide a major buffer from the future employment dislocation that will inevitably result from productivity gains and industrial automation.

To put all these programs into practice, we should set up a Critical Industries Commission—a forum where government, labor, and management could get together to find a way out of the mess we're in. We have to learn how to talk to each other before we can take joint action.

This tripartite coalition would recommend specific measures to strengthen our vital industries and to restore and enhance their competitiveness in international markets.

Let me make clear that I am *not* proposing a welfare system for every company that gets into trouble. *We need a program that kicks in only when troubled American companies have agreed to equality of sacrifice among management, labor, suppliers, and financial backers.* It worked for Chrysler, and it can work for the rest of America.

When an industry or a company comes looking for help, as I did five years ago in Washington, the commission should ask on behalf of the taxpayers, who are going to take the risk, "What's in it for us?" What's in it for the people? In other words, "What are management and labor bringing to the party?"

I've lived through this, and it's simple. It's management agreeing to do something *before* the government does *anything*—such as loan guarantees, or import restraints, or investment tax credits, or R&D help. Management might have to agree to plow back its earnings into job-creating investments—in *this* country. It might have to agree to profit sharing with its employees. It might even have to agree to keeping a lid on prices.

As for the unions, they would have to come out of the dark ages. They'd have to agree to changes in the many work rules that hamper productivity—such as having 114 job classifications in assembly plants where about 6 would do fine. They might even have to agree to restraints on the runaway medical costs that are now built into our system.

If neither management nor labor is going to make sacrifices, then the meeting's over. You can't expect to get government help if you're not willing to get your own house in order. In other words, there's no free lunch. Whoever applies for assistance will have to understand that there are strings attached.

If all of this sounds a little like a Marshall Plan for America, that's exactly what it is. If America could rebuild Western Europe after World War II, if we could create the International Monetary Fund and a dozen international development banks to help rebuild the world, we ought to be able to rebuild our own country today. If the World Bank—which is a profit-making institution—can successfully help out underdeveloped countries, why couldn't a new national development bank do as well in helping out troubled American industries?

Maybe what we need is an *American* Monetary Fund. What's so terrible about a $5 billion national development bank to get our basic industries competitive again?

Early in 1984, the Kissinger Commission requested $8 billion for the economic development of Central America. Now, I always thought that Central America meant places like Michigan, Ohio, and Indiana. (Shows you how simple-minded I am!) What about *our* Central America? How can we spend $8 billion to strengthen the economies of other countries while neglecting ailing industries in our own backyard?

Some people say that an industrial policy is nothing more than lemon socialism. If it is, I'll take a crateful—because unless we act fast, our industrial heartland is going to turn into an industrial wasteland.

Any realistic industrial policy for America will have to include a monetary and fiscal policy.

We can't have a stable, healthy economy with high interest rates—or with interest rates that fluctuate every ten minutes. High interest rates are man-made disasters. And what man makes, man can unmake.

I look back on October 6, 1979, as a day of infamy in this country. That's when Paul Volcker and the Federal Reserve Board let the prime rate float. That's when the monetarists said, ''The only way to break inflation is by controlling the supply of money—and to hell with interest rates.''

As we all learned the hard way, that decision unleashed a tidal wave of economic destruction. There's got to be a better way to control inflation than to break it on the backs of the workers in the auto and housing industries. When future historians look back on our way of curing inflation and all the pain the cure caused, they'll probably compare it to bloodletting in the Middle Ages!

Detroit got hit first. We suffered the longest car-sales depression in fifty years. The housing industry came next. After that, almost everybody else in the country got hit.

Before the prime rate came unglued, interest rates had gone as high as 12 percent only once in our entire history, and that was during the Civil War. But now, once they hit 12 percent, they kept on going. At one point they reached as high as 22 percent. That's legalized usury. Some states have laws that kick in at 25 percent, suggesting criminal intent. The Mafia calls it vigorish.

But as tough as 20 percent interest rates are, what's even worse is the yo-yo effect. From October 6, 1979, to October 1982, rates went up (or down) eighty-six times, which comes out to once every 13.8 days. How can you plan anything on that?

When interest rates are high, consumers divert a lot of money into short-term securities. But making money on money isn't productive. It doesn't create any jobs. And those of us who *do* create jobs, who invest in productivity and want to expand and are willing to pay our fair share of taxes, end up downstream waiting for a few measly drops of credit to get through so we can put a few more people back to work.

High interest rates encourage the big boys to play their new game of making money on money. When money is expensive, investment in research and development is risky. When rates are high, it's cheaper to buy a company than to build one.

Of the ten largest corporate mergers in U.S. history, nine have taken place during the Reagan administration. One of the biggest involved U.S. Steel. While protected by trigger prices (which cost us $100 more per car to buy American steel), U.S. Steel paid $4.3 billion to buy Marathon Oil. Most of that money was borrowed. It should have been used to buy modern basic oxygen furnaces and continuous casters to compete with the Japanese.

When the steel workers saw what was going on, they were so mad they demanded that any wage concessions they made be plowed back into the steel business. It's almost unbelievable that American management should have to be lectured to by the workers on just how our system works.

Or what about DuPont buying Conoco for $7.5 billion, and in the process tripling its debt to $4 billion? It costs DuPont $600 million a year in interest just to service that debt. Wouldn't we all be better off if DuPont used that money to develop the kind of new and inventive products that made them world-famous?

And what about Bendix, United Technologies, and Martin Marietta borrowing $5.6 billion to fund their corporate cannibalism—without creating a single new job in the process? That three-ring circus ended only when Allied threw a tent over it all and put a stop to the whole thing.

Think of this: in the decade between 1972 and 1982, the total number of employees in America's five hundred largest industrial companies actually declined. All the new jobs—well over ten million—came from two other sources. One was small business. The other, I'm sorry to say, was government—which may be the only real growth industry left.

Why don't we pass a law that says when you borrow money to buy somebody else and cannibalize him, the interest payments on those loans are not deductible? That would get the excesses out of the system pretty fast.

Right now, if you want to buy up a competitor, generally you can't. That would violate the antitrust laws. But if you want to buy a company that does something else entirely, that's okay.

Where's the sense in that? Why should a guy who's been in the steel business suddenly become an oil man? It's a completely different world. It will take him years to learn about it. And most important, it's not productive.

If we lowered interest rates and ended this merger madness, we could get the money changers out of the temple of the national economy. We could get back to doing business the American way, by reinvesting and competing instead of buying each other up. And by creating more jobs so more people could participate in our economic growth. Welfare costs for local, state, and federal governments would come down. Capital would begin to accumulate. Plants would expand again.

As everyone knows, the way to lower interest rates is to make big cuts in the federal deficit. It's time somebody took away the government's charge card. Today Washington uses more than half of all the available credit (54 percent to be exact) to finance the national debt.

Despite all of President Reagan's campaign promises, the national debt is out of control. Back in 1835, the federal debt was a mere $38,000. In 1981, it broke $100 billion for the first time in history. Today it's about $200 billion. And, over the next five years it's expected to total over $1 *trillion!*

We picked up a deficit that big once before—during the period from 1776 through 1981. Think of it. It took us 206 years, with eight wars, two major depressions, a dozen recessions, two space programs, the opening of the West, and the terms of thirty-nine presidents to do that. Now we're going to duplicate that record in just five years while we're at peace—and during a so-called economic recovery.

To put it another way, there are sixty-one million families in this country and we're going to put all of them in hock for $3,000 a year *without their permission.* It's like Uncle Sam is using your credit card without asking. As a result, we're mortgaging the futures of our kids and our grandchildren. Since most of them can't vote yet, they've given us their proxy. And we're not using it very well. In my book, the boys in Washington—all of them—get an F on the budget.

We have to attack the budget deficit and our other economic problems before they completely overwhelm us. Of course, to solve big problems we have to be willing to do unpopular things. As a child of the Great Depression, I've always been a great fan of F.D.R. He did a lot for this country, even though the ideologues were fighting him every step of the way. He melted the pot. He included the excluded. He had the audacity to take people off the street corners where they were selling apples and put them to work.

Above all, he was pragmatic. When he was confronted by big problems, he *did* something—and that always takes more courage than doing nothing. Roosevelt did not attack the problems of the Depression with charts and graphs, with Laffer curves, or with Harvard Business School theories. He took concrete action. He was always willing to try something new. And if that didn't work, he was willing to try something else.

We need a little more of that spirit in Washington today. Our problems are huge and they're complicated. But there *are* solutions. They aren't always easy, and they aren't always comfortable. But they do exist.

The great issues facing us today are not Republican issues or Democratic issues. The political parties can debate the means, but both parties must embrace the end objective, which is to make America great again.

Can we succeed in this undertaking? Someone once said that in great undertakings there is glory even in failure. So we must try, and if we do, I believe that we'll make it.

We are, after all, a resourceful people in a nation that has been blessed with abundance. With direction, leadership, and the support of the American people, we can't miss. I'm convinced that this country can once again be that bright and shining symbol of power and freedom—challenged by none and envied by all.

DISCUSSION QUESTIONS

1. What is the effect of Iacocca's decision to begin the prologue to his autobiography with a report on the day he was fired from his position as president of the Ford Motor Company? How does he reinforce this effect in the paragraphs that follow? What relationship do the anecdotes reported in the prologue establish between Iacocca and his readers? Point to specific words and phrases to verify your response.

2. Characterize the sound of Iacocca's voice in the prologue. Do the same for his diction. What are the effects of choosing such clichés as "I went from the frying pan into the fire," Chrysler's coming "within a whisker" of bankruptcy, and his recognition that "going down with the ship was more than I deserved"? What overall image of himself does Iacocca project in the prologue?

3. Outline the nature of Iacocca's argument in "Making America Great Again." What do you regard to be the strongest points he makes in his plan to make this country "once again be that bright and shining symbol of power and feedom—challenged by none and envied by all"? What in your judgment are the weakest aspects of Iacocca's argument? Assume that Iacocca had the opportunity—and the desire—to revise this chapter. What specific suggestions would you make for strengthening his plan for "making American great again"?

4. Based on your reading of these passages from *Iacocca*, what inferences can you draw about Iacocca's conception of the American hero? What are the specific qualities he recommends that the American people look for in thier leaders? Compare and contrast Iacocca's vision of the American hero with that of Chuck Yeager (''Best-Sellers''). In what ways are their conceptions of the American hero similar? How are they different?

Tracy Kidder / *House* [Carpenters]   1985

The construction of a new house—from the selection of a site to the moment the owners move in—can be immensely rich in human drama. Through the spring and fall of 1983, Tracy Kidder followed every facet of house building, recording in detail the efforts of an architect and a crew of carpenters (Apple Corps) as they constructed a luxurious house for a family in Amherst, Massachusetts. In the passage below, Kidder portrays the background and attitudes of one of Apple Corps's skilled carpenters, Richard Gougeon, who lives in Ashfield, Massachusetts, a rural town northwest of Amherst.

Born in New York City in 1945, Kidder graduated from Harvard University, served in Vietnam, and studied writing at the University of Iowa. A contributing editor to The Atlantic, *Kidder is the author of* The Road to Yuma City *and* The Soul of a New Machine, *a book about the computer industry which won both the Pulitzer Prize and the American Book Award for nonfiction in 1982. An enormous best-seller—the book was on the* New York Times *best-seller list for twenty-six weeks—*House *was selected by the* Times *as one of the best books of 1985.*

Just after dawn, Ashfield's Boy Scout leader, Richard Gougeon, stands at the picture window and looks north out of his living room. His house rests on a hillside just down the Hawley Road from the part of Ashfield that someone long ago described as Little Switzerland. Richard says, ''Right here, it drops right off. You can see for a *long* ways. A lot of mornings you can see out over the fog in the valleys, and the hills look like little islands out there.'' The air is clear this morning. There's the ridge up in Heath where blueberries grow by the truckload, and the radio mast, still faintly blinking, that's WRSI in Greenfield, the station he'll probably listen to at work today. Richard's window is a geographer's station. The views are even better from the hill above his house, part of the twenty acres of field and woods he bought five years ago, to add to his houselot. ''My father never owned any land when I was growing up. I had to *own* land. *Had* to. I wasn't going to be a whole person till I *owned* land, and two acres just wasn't enough. Lindy felt the same way,'' Richard has explained. Up on his high meadow the intricate landscape of hills and valleys is laid out as clearly as on a map. Richard has the sort of lofty and expansive views from which the world makes perfect sense. Once, while walking down the meadow toward his house, he suddenly stopped, raised his arms as if to embrace the mountain view, and cried, ''I'm king!''

Feeling a little strapped for cash and ready for work, Richard launches himself on the morning. He wears jeans, a checkered woolen shirt, a wide leather belt, brown boots. His clothes have the clean, gently worn, well-oiled look of old, cared-for-wood-working machines. He clowns when he walks to the kitchen, dragging his heels, making as much noise as possible, and saying to no one in particular, "I put on three pounds over the weekend. Must be my fat's all turning to muscle. Yup. I'm just a stout little French-Canadian."

This spring, as Richard likes to explain, he made syrup from his own maple trees. At breakfast, he enacts the fantasy of local self-sufficiency. Most things on the table come from Ashfield: the apples in the pancakes from the trees outside his back door, the bacon from a neighbor's pig, the cream from the top of the jug that he and Lindy get filled at the one remaining dairy farm in Apple Valley.

Lindy is about as tall as Richard, and plump, but like him, sturdy rather than stout. She has brown hair and astonished-looking eyes. She talks rapidly, sometimes loudly—maybe from long competition with Richard—and she is given to wry smiles. "I always preferred Edgar Allan Poe to *Cinderella,*" she says. She has a fiery side. Richard says, "It's a good thing Lindy wasn't a man. There'd be a lot of beat-up people around. We joke about that a lot. She knows it."

Lindy wasn't always a good cook. "She made pork chops the consistency of my shoe. I didn't even know what it was," says Richard of the first meal she ever made for him. Richard was in the Navy then and they were living in Okinawa. "When we were there I decided that was what I wanted," says Lindy. "To live on a farm, have kids and animals, and cook a lot. I got good at cooking." She made some meals for Richard's friends. They praised the food. Her cooking thrived on praise. The pastries Richard brings to work in his lunch basket are known in Apple Corps's idiom as "Lindy cakes," and Richard is envied for them.

Lindy planned to go to college when their last child left diapers. When that time arrived, she thought she might not risk college after all. Richard talked her into it. She told him not to expect too much. She went to a local community college and got preposterously good grades. Richard was always telling his partners how Lindy had gotten 104 on her latest exam. She would soon be accepted, with a scholarship, at Smith College, and Richard would say, "This is a dream come true. I always wanted to go out with a Smithie."

Richard reads, but with difficulty. His dyslexia has never been professionally diagnosed, but clearly his long, enduring puzzlement with reading was the cause of his childhood travail in school. When they were first married, Lindy says, they used to fight about her reading. She always loved reading books, and she thinks that Richard envied her then. Many years later, however, it was Richard who urged her to go to college. Lindy knows that encouraging her must have cost Richard something.

"He was very worried last winter," she says, "I studied with a very bright man in my class. Richard wasn't exactly jealous, but he said to me, 'I thought this would happen.' "

Lindy says, "He worried ever since I started college that I would meet somebody smarter."

Lindy was a proud, shy, rather lonely girl. Of Lindy as he found her, Richard says, "Her idea of a big time, even in high school, was readin' a book." She kept to herself mostly. Richard was a mannerly boy, the sort whom old folks like. "I was a pretty reasonable kid, I guess. All's I ever got was one speeding ticket. We'd swear and cuss, me and my friends, when we got alone. Maybe get some hard cider and drink it at the Mohawk Drive-In. I didn't even know what marijuana was, until I joined the navy." His bedroom in the house trailer in Buckland, where he spent most of his childhood, was very small. You had to back into it, and it was always tidy and his clothes were always decent, but he never had friends over to his house to play, because there really wasn't room. Besides, he always worked, before and after his daily humiliation at school, so he didn't have a great deal of time for friends. He was eighteen, a senior in trade school, and he owned a '56 Chevy and a box of tools. He did odd jobs after school specializing in the repair of bulkheads for cellar stairs and of screen doors. He was fixing one of those at a restaurant outside Shelburne Falls, and Lindy's mother, who worked there, asked him if he would make a rabbit hutch for her little daughter. He agreed and then he put it off. "I was no better then than I am now." Finally, he made the cage, went to deliver it, expecting to find a twelve-year-old waiting, and instead found Lindy, who was sixteen. "I thought she was neat, you know. I *liked her*. I liked her a lot right then." He found her after school a few days later and showed her how to shift the gears in his Chevy. In Shelburne Falls in those days, girls went out on dates with curlers in their hair, all the apparatus done up in scarves. "Probably girls were doing that in the fifties everywhere else. In Shelburne Falls we were doing it in the sixties," Lindy says. Richard liked to pull the pins out of her curlers. He was more like a brother than a boyfriend. Usually they would go on long drives, north into Vermont and New Hampshire, in the '56 Chevy. Gas was cheap. Richard could afford that kind of date. In the car they could talk about themselves without any risk of feeling foolish. "He always said that I helped him a lot just by liking him," says Lindy. "I was somebody outside of his home to talk to. He helped me, too. I didn't think much of myself, either."

When Richard met Lindy, rabbit hutch in his arms, he stuttered. He did not just have trouble reading. He could hardly speak. By the time they were married, after Lindy graduated from high school, Richard's stutter had vanished, never to return in force. They were small-town kids. Innocents, Richard says. He knew little of the birds and bees, as he put it, and they had never traveled far from home. Then Richard got drafted, joined the Navy, and as the old promise went, they saw the world.

Richard took care of airplanes the three years they lived on Okinawa. He flew as a crewman in the planes for which he had responsibility, and he saw a lot of Asia from the air. Then he was assigned to an aircraft carrier bound for the coast of Vietnam. Lindy went home. Richard, meanwhile, was chosen to look after the airplane that transported the admiral of the Seventh Fleet. It was Richard's job to ensure that the admiral's plane was safe for flying. One of Richard's partners says, "What a perfect choice for that job! Richard taking care of the admiral's plane. It almost restores your faith in the military."

Lindy says, "They knew they could count on Richard. Richard would do the job."

As a boy, Richard often accompanied his father on the various missions undertaken by Gougeon's Nite Owl Service. He'd help his father grease trucks. He'd hand him tools and watch him repair machines. It made Richard feel very proud when he overheard a hilltown tradesman describe his father as an artist with the welding rod. Out of all those late nights, Richard remembers one with special clarity. It was perhaps one o'clock in the morning. His father had worked for hours remaking a set of old-fashioned babbitt bearings. A tricky piece of work— you had to pour the bearings molten and everything had to be just the right temperature. This time, it didn't work. Richard's father leaned on one knee, took a cigar from his breast pocket, fired up the cigar with his propane torch, and grinned at Richard. He said to Richard that he guessed they'd have to do that one over again. Richard cannot remember his father losing his temper over a job. He says, "My father has a real good way about him. He has a tremendous amount of patience. A *tremendous* amount." To his father, Richard pays his homage: "He always worked nights. I remember always wanting to go with him."

When Richard's Boy Scout troop pitches its summer camp, on the top of Peter Hill in Ashfield, they run the American flag up a tree. The boys learn woodcraft, mainly, and manners in the woods. Richard does not care for military protocol. They do perform the prescribed flag ceremony, though, and, three fingers raised, promise to be trustworthy, loyal, helpful, friendly, courteous, kind, obedient,

cheerful, thrifty, brave, and reverent. The words seem renewed when they're ut-
tered in the woods, without spectators, by a dozen boys and by Richard, who
speaks softly for once and stands straight-backed and unusually straight-faced during the ceremony.

Richard began to have misgivings about the Catholic Church while flying repeatedly over remote villages in the Philippines. Grass huts surrounding marble
churches—from the air that seemed to be the pattern. "Why?" says Richard.
"They should've put the people in marble houses and the church in a hut, because
you can pray to God as well in a grass hut as anywhere. That's what I was always
told. It started me off it." Richard says he worried for a long time about his
inability to believe what he'd been taught in church and about the thought that he
would be consigned to hell for his lapse in faith, or as he puts it, become "burnt
French fries." Then, he says, he grew tired of worrying. "I figured there was
nothing I could do about it, so I decided to forget about it."

Richard left Buckland in 1967, when he returned four years later, he was, like
Rip Van Winkle, astonished at the sights. Skirts had risen six inches above the
knee. Long hair and drugs were everywhere. He shunned the local antiwar protests, because he disliked some of the protesters. "Some of them were into drugs
terrible. I'm not going to go down and march with them. Go down and protest
against the war and then go up and sell a trunkload of drugs to the high school
kids. I *wanted* to demonstrate, though." He felt lost, but most especially over the
changes in himself. For most of four years he had flown every few days to some
exotic, distant place, such as Hong Kong or Bangkok or Saigon. Suddenly, as it
seemed to him, he was deposited back in Shelbourne Falls, in a little town beside
the Deerfield River, and he was bored, among other things. "I was owly. I'd fight
with Lindy and take off through the woods for half a day."

When Richard came home from Vietnam, he accepted food stamps for a time,
but to do so made him sick at heart. So he went to work picking apples. This was
a favorite short-term occupation for many youths about his age. Many of them
looked like hippies to Richard. He remembers being asked again and again. "Hey,
man, what are you working so hard for, man?" He was out to become a fast
apple picker, in fact. "I was the fastest apple picker in the valley," he says. "I'd
pick seven boxes a day. Some of these guys wouldn't even pick half a box."

Lindy wanted to buy a house. She had found one that they might be able to
afford, for $15,000, on the main street of Shelburne Falls. The idea frightened
Richard—to buy a real house without a real job. And it frightened Lindy, too, but
she reasoned that at the worst they'd simply have to sell the place. She told
Richard, "We're going to try." For a short time between trade school and the
Navy, Richard had worked for a local building contractor. Richard went to him
and got his old job back. Then he went to the bank. He had a job. They lent him
the money.

According to Richard, he and his classmates at the trade school were all misfits,
"the kids they couldn't do anything else with." They were of two different sorts,
however: ones who caused trouble and ones who merely had trouble. He was one
of the latter. The troublemakers were kept inside in the shops, where they could
be watched. The well-behaved, such as Richard, got to build real houses. He
helped to build three while in school. To get a passing grade in English, something he had never before accomplished, Richard found he merely had to keep
quiet in class. He actually got an A on one English paper, his only A in an
academic subject. He entitled that paper "How to Frame a Roof." The explanation was lucid, the teacher felt.

The first contractor Richard went to work for was a seasoned builder, an able
craftsman who was thrifty both with money and with words. "When he picked

up your handsaw and it wasn't sharp, there was a lot of snuffing and snorting. Same thing with your block plane.'' Richard learned the trade mainly by watching. Once in a while, his boss complimented him on a piece of work. ''And he wasn't much for compliments either. Gradually, Richard came to feel accomplished. After a couple of years, he went to his boss and asked for a raise. His boss offered him ten cents an hour more. ''I didn't understand him. I thought he was saying, 'You're fired.' It hurt.'' Richard gave that builder two weeks' notice, and went to work for a younger and more congenial contractor. He and this builder worked together, putting up new houses and repairing old ones in a hurry. This second builder worked very quickly, and he taunted Richard when Richard started taking pains and fell behind. Much later on, Richard realized that a game had been played on him. His boss had tricked him into competing for speed. The memory amuses Richard. He still worries, though, about some of the work he did. ''Jeez, I did some things I didn't like. Cut the board and nail it on. Still, I didn't do . . . I've seen some terrible things that carpenters do. I do remember that first stairway we did, though. Oh, it was terrible. I still have nightmares of how that came out.''

Meanwhile, in the evenings, he fixed up the old house in Shelburne Falls. Then he and Lindy sold it and with that money made the down payment on two acres of land in Apple Valley and on the materials for a new house. They chose Ashfield and Apply Valley first of all because the spot looked beautiful to them and the land was inexpensive. They had ties to Ashfield, too. Richard's mother grew up on a farm within the town's borders, and Lindy is a direct descendant of a Captain John Phillips, a member of the little band of land-hungry Yankees who trekked up through the forest from Deerfield sometime around 1740 and started to build the town.

Not long after Richard had built his house in Apple Valley, he got his invitation to join the brand-new local building company, which until then had been made up exclusively of college-educated carpenters. Apple Corps—funny name, good pay.

In superficial ways, Richard ten years later hardly resembles the short-haired, clean-shaven fellow who looked uncomfortable and very ''straight'' to Jim on first encounter. In his black beard, Richard manages to look both humorous and diabolical. His hair, now tipped with gray, curls out from under his various caps, and he sometimes lets it grow long enough to cover his ears before he looks up a barber. (''I look quite crisp,'' says Richard after a haircut. ''I look very business-like.'') His politics are unpredictable. He belongs to the National Rifle Association, and he holds opinions such as this: ''Communism works great for some countries. It's a lot better than having one fat guy sit up on the hill and eat everything.''

Richard's partner Alex Ghiselin, who went to Dartmouth, showed up for work with a wicker lunch basket. ''Classy,'' Richard thought, and he got a wicker lunch basket, too. Lindy says, ''I don't think Apple Corps would have survived without Richard. And he's needed them, too. Sharing responsibility and having someone to talk to, working with others as an equal, not always working for somebody else. He's got a lot more confidence now. The other day someone at school asked me what my husband does and I said he's part of a collective. I don't think I should *call* it that, but that's what it is.'' She laughs. ''Richard's never been narrow-minded. No one could mistake Richard for a redneck. And I think Apple Corps has helped to keep him that way. We grew up in small towns. They're mill towns and they're poor towns. I don't think we feel better than the people we grew up with, but we have very little in common with the world we grew up in. I don't want to be part of that world, or the world of the type of people Richard sometimes works for, though in our attitudes and taste, I guess we're a lot more like the people he works for. It sounds like I'm a terrible snob, but I look back and think how terrible it would be if we'd never had a chance to see another world outside of our hometowns. What makes Richard different from a lot of the people we grew up with is more than what he has. It's more than he dreams.''

Richard would like to have the time to learn the craft of furniture making and to master fully the art of shooting with a bow. He goes hunting every fall, and afterward Jim always says, ''Richard's deer is still intact.'' Richard would like to get a deer some day. He would like to own a Corvette. Often, in the middle of work, he stops and pictures himself in the wilderness: ''What I love is shooting my muzzle loader. When I'm shooting, I fantasize I'm a French-Canadian fur trapper in the 1850s. In the Rocky Mountains. A coonskin cap. A short French-Canadian. I'd fit right in.'' He goes back to work. A little later, ''Next summer I might take a month off and go across the country. I'll have my truck painted, get all new tires, new brakes, be all set. This was supposed to be the year. But Lindy's got to get through college. Same old story. No money.'' He grins and swaggers: ''No. I'm going to work in the summer. June, July, and August. Do a couple of kitchens and bathrooms in the winter. But September to January first I'm going to have to hunt. Take in the turkey season in four states.''

Richard's dreams sit lightly on him. They do not have the force of complaints. He counts his blessings with more feeling than he expends in wishing for other ones. On the April morning in his thirty-sixth year when Richard selects the cap with the Jonsered chain saw company's logo and sets out from Apple Valley, fortified with pancakes, to work on the new house down in Amherst, he feels that he has more than he could have reasonably hoped for out of life: a good job that takes him outdoors and is not repetitive, neither a boss nor the difficulties of being the only boss, a house and land of his own in the country, the praise of many former customers, a Lindy cake in his lunch basket. The only thing Richard really has his heart set on in the near, realistic future, is a new paint job for his truck. Richard often says—it is like a favorite grace—''I'm real pleased with where I am in life, compared to how I started out.''

DISCUSSION QUESTIONS

1. Why do you think Kidder went into so much detail about the life of one of the house's carpenters? What is Kidder's purpose? What does he want his readers to understand about the construction of a house?

2. Compare Kidder's account of the carpenters with Gay Talese's descriptions of construction workers in ''The Bridge'' (see ''Magazines''). What similarities can you see between the approach each writer takes toward his subject? How does a knowledge of the occupation enhance our understanding of the product, whether it be a bridge or a house?

Garrison Keillor / *Lake Wobegon Days*   1985

''Smart doesn't count for so much'' in Lake Wobegon, the imaginary small town in Minnesota invented by Garrison Keillor in 1974 as the setting of his weekly monologue for his popular radio show, ''A Prairie Home Companion.'' Lake Wobegon is the quintessence of the American small town, just as Keillor's comic style contains the essence of American humor—the tall tale, the exagger-

ated regionalism, the deadpan understatement. "Sumus Quod Sumus" means "We are what we are"; it is the town's motto.

Born in Anoka, Minnesota, in 1942, Keillor graduated from the University of Minnesota in 1966. His first book, Happy to Be Here, *was also a best-seller.*

SUMUS QUOD SUMUS

Why isn't my town on the map?—Well, back before cartographers had the benefit of an aerial view, when teams of surveyors tramped from one town to the next, mistakes were made. Sometimes those towns were farther apart than they should have been. Many maps were drawn by French explorers in the bows of canoes bucking heavy rapids, including Sieur Marine de St. Croix, who was dizzy and nauseated when he penciled in the river that bears his name. He was miles off in some places, but since the river formed the Minnesota-Wisconsin border, revision was politically impossible and the mistakes were inked in, though it left thousands of people sitting high and dry on the other side.

A worse mistake was made by the Coleman Survey of 1866, which omitted fifty square miles of central Minnesota (including Lake Wobegon), an error that lives on in the F.A.A.'s Coleman Course Correction, a sudden lurch felt by airline passengers as they descend into Minnesota air space on flights from New York or Boston.

Why the state jobbed out the survey to drunks is a puzzle. The Coleman outfit, headed by Lieutenant Michael Coleman, had been attached to Grant's army, which they misdirected time and again so that Grant's flanks kept running head-on into Lee's rear until Union officers learned to make "right face" a 120-degree turn. Governor Marshall, however, regarded the 1866 survey as preliminary—"It will provide us a good general idea of the State, a foundation upon which we can build in the future," he said—though of course it turned out to be the final word.

The map was drawn by four teams of surveyors under the direction of Finian Coleman, Michael having left for the Nebraska gold rush, who placed them at the four corners of the state and aimed them inward. The southwest and northwest contingents moved fast over level ground, while the eastern teams got bogged down in the woods, so that, when they met a little west of Lake Wobegon, the four quadrants didn't fit within the boundaries legislated by Congress in 1851. Nevertheless, Finian mailed them to St. Paul, leaving the legislature to wrestle with the discrepancy.

The legislature simply reproportioned the state by eliminating the overlap in the middle, the little quadrangle that is Mist County. "The soil of that region is unsuited to agriculture, and we doubt that its absence would be much noticed," Speaker of the House Randolph remarked.

In 1933, a legislative interim commission proposed that the state recover the lost county by collapsing the square mileage of several large lakes. The area could be removed from the centers of the lakes, elongating them slightly so as not to lose valuable shoreline. Opposition was spearheaded by the Bureau of Fisheries, which pointed out the walleye breeding grounds to be lost; and the State Map Amendment was attached as a rider to a bill requiring the instruction of evolution in all secondary schools and was defeated by voice vote.

Proponents of map change, or "accurates" as they were called, were chastised by their opponents, the so-called "moderates," who denied the existence of Mist County on the one hand—"Where is it?" a moderate cried one day on the Senate floor in St. Paul. "Can you show me one scintilla of evidence that it exists?"—and, on the other hand, denounced the county as a threat to property owners everywhere. "If this county is allowed to rear its head, then no boundary is sacred, no deed is certain," the moderates said. "We might as well reopen negotiations with the Indians."

Wobegonians took the defeat of inclusion with their usual calm. "We felt that we were a part of Minnesota by virtue of the fact that when we drove more than a few miles in any direction, we were in Minnesota," Hjalmar Ingqvist says. "It didn't matter what anyone said."

In 1980, Governor Al Quie became the first governor to set foot in Mist County, slipping quietly away from his duties to attend a ceremony dedicating a plaque attached to the Statue of the Unknown Norwegian. "We don't know where he is. He was here, then he disappeared," his aides told reporters, all the time the Governor was enjoying a hearty meatball lunch in the company of fellow Lutherans. In his brief remarks, he saluted Lake Wobegon for its patience in anonymity. "Seldom has a town made such a sacrifice in remaining unrecognized so long," he said, though other speakers were quick to assure him that it had been no sacrifice, really, but a true pleasure.

"Here in 1867 the first Norwegian settlers knelt to thank God for bringing them to this place," the plaque read, "and though noting immediately the rockiness of the soil, remained, sowing seeds of Christian love."

What's special about this town, it's pretty much like a lot of towns, isn't it? There is a perfectly good answer to that question, it only takes a moment to think of it.

For one thing, the Statue of the Unknown Norweigan. If other towns have one, we don't know about it. Sculpted by a man named O'Connell or O'Connor in 1896, the granite youth stands in a small plot at a jog in the road where a surveyor knocked off for lunch years ago and looks down Main Street to the lake. A proud figure, his back is erect, his feet are on the ground on account of no money remained for a pedestal, and his eyes—well, his eyes are a matter of question. Probably the artist meant him to exude confidence in the New World, but his eyes are set a little deep so that dark shadows appear in the late afternoon and by sunset he looks worried. His confident smile turns into a forced grin. In the morning, he is stepping forward, his right hand extended in greeting, but as the day wears on, he hesitates, and finally he appears to be about to turn back. The right hand seems to say, Wait here. I think I forgot something.

Nevertheless, he is a landmark and an asset, so it was a shame when the tornado of 1947 did damage to him. That tornado skipped in from the northeast; it blew away one house except for a dresser mirror that wasn't so much as cracked—amazing; it's in the historical society now, and people still bring their relatives to look at it. It also picked up a brand-new Chevy pickup and set it down a quarter-mile away. *On a road. In the right-hand lane.* In town, it took the roof off the Lutheran church, where nobody was, and missed the Bijou, which was packed for *Shame,* starring Cliff DeCarlo. And it blew a stalk of quackgrass about six inches into the Unknown Norweigan, in an unusual place, a place where you wouldn't expect to find grass in a person, a part of the body where you've been told to insert nothing bigger than your finger in a washcloth.

Bud, our municipal employee, pulled it out, of course, but the root was imbedded in the granite, so it keeps growing out. Bud has considered using a pre-emergent herbicide on him but is afraid it will leave a stain on the side of his head, so, when he mows, simply reaches up to the Unknown's right ear and snips off the blade with his fingernails. It's not so noticeable, really; you have to look for it to see it.

The plaque that wouldn've been on the pedestal the town couldn't afford was bolted to a brick and set in the ground until Bud dug it out because it was dinging up his mower blade. Now in the historical society museum in the basement of the town hall, it sits next to the Lake Wobegon runestone, which proves that Viking explorers were here in 1381. Unearthed by a Professor Oftedahl or Ostenwald around 1921 alongside County Road 2, where the professor, motoring from Chicago to Seattle, had stopped to bury garbage, the small black stone is covered with Viking runic characters which read (translated by him): "8 of [us] stopped & stayed awhile to visit & have [coffee] & a short nap. Sorry [you] weren't here. Well, that's about [it] for now."

Every Columbus Day, the runestone is carried up to the school and put on a card-table in the lunchroom for the children to see, so they can know their true heritage. It saddens Norwegians that America still honors this Italian, who arrived late in the New World and by accident, who wasn't even interested in New Worlds but only in spices. Out on a spin in search of curry powder and hot peppers—a man on a voyage to the grocery—he stumbled onto the land of heroic Vikings and proceeded to get the credit for it. And then to name it *America* after Amerigo Vespucci, an Italian who never saw the New World but only sat in Italy and drew incredibly inaccurate maps of it. By rights, it should be called Erica, after Eric the Red, who did the work five hundred years earlier. The United States of Erica. Erica the Beautiful. The Erican League.

Not many children come to see the runestone where it spends the rest of the year. The museum is a locked door in the town hall, down the hall and to the left by the washroom. Viola Tordahl the clerk has the key and isn't happy to be bothered for it. "I don't know why I ever agreed to do it. You know, they don't pay me a red cent for this," she says as she digs around in a junk drawer for it.

The museum is in the basement. The light switch is halfway down the steps, to your left. The steps are concrete, narrow and steep. It's going to be very interesting, you think, to look at these many objects from olden days, and then when you put your hand on the switch, you feel something crawl on it. Not a fly. You brush the spider off, and then you smell the must from below, like bilgewater, and hear a slight movement as if a man sitting quietly in the dark for several hours had just risen slowly and the chair scraped a quarter-inch. He sighs a faint sigh, licks his upper lip, and shifts the axe from his left to his right hand so he can scratch his nose. He is left-handed, evidently. No need to find out any more about him. You turn off the light and shut the door.

What's so special about this town is not the food, though Ralph's Pretty Good Grocery has got in a case of fresh cod. Frozen, but it's fresher than what's been in his freezer for months. In the grocery business, you have to throw out stuff sometimes, but Ralph is Norwegian and it goes against his principles. People bend down and peer into the meat case. "Give me a pork loin," they say. "One of those in the back, one of the pink ones." "These in front are better," he says. "They're more aged. You get better flavor." But they want a pink one, so Ralph takes out a pink one, bites his tongue. This is the problem with being in retail; you can't say what you think.

More and more people are sneaking off to the Higgledy-Piggledy in St. Cloud, where you find two acres of food, a meat counter a block long with huge walloping roasts and steaks big enough to choke a cow, and exotic fish lying on crushed ice. Once Ralph went to his brother Benny's for dinner and Martha put baked swordfish on the table. Ralph's face burned. His own sister-in-law! "It's delicious," said Mrs. Ralph. "Yeah," Ralph said, "if it wasn't for the mercury poisoning, I'd take swordfish every day of the week." Cod, he pointed out, is farther down in the food chain, and doesn't collect the mercury that the big fish do. Forks paused in midair. He would have gone on to describe the effects of mercury on the body, how it lodges in the brain, wiping the slate clean until you wind up in bed attached to tubes and can't remember your own Zip Code, but his wife contacted him on his ankle. Later, she said, "You had no business saying that."

"I'll have no business, period," he said, "if people don't wake up."

"Well, it's a free country, and she has a perfect right to go shop where she wants to."

"Sure she does, and she can go live there, too."

When the Thanatopsis Club hit its centennial in 1982 and Mrs. Hallberg wrote to the White Huse and asked for an essay from the President on small-town life, she got one, two paragraphs that extolled Lake Wobegon as a model of free enterprise and individualsim, which was displayed in the library under glass, although the truth is that Lake Wobegon survives to the extent that it does on a form of voluntary socialism with elements of Deism, fatalism, and nepotism. Free enterprise runs on self-interest.* This is socialism, and it runs on loyalty. You need a toaster, you buy it at Co-op Hardware even though you can get a deluxe model with all the toaster attachments for less money at K-Mart in St. Cloud. You buy it at Co-op because you know Otto. Glasses you will find at Clifford's which also sells shoes and ties and some gloves. (It is trying to be the department store it used to be when it was The Mercantile, which it is still called by most people because the old sign is so clear on the brick facade, clearer than the "Clifford's" in the window.) Though you might rather shop for glasses in a strange place where they'll encourage your vanity, though Clifford's selection of frames is clearly based on Scripture ("Take no thought for what you shall wear. . . .") and you might put a hideous piece of junk on your face and Clifford would say, "I think you'll like those" as if you're a person who looks like you don't care what you look like—nevertheless you should think twice before you get the Calvin Klein glasses from Vanity Vision in the St. Cloud Mall. Calvin Klein isn't going to come with the Rescue Squad and he isn't going to teach your children about redemption by grace. You couldn't find Calvin Klein to save your life.

If people were to live by comparison shopping, the town would go bust. It cannot compete with other places item by item. Nothing in town is quite as good as it appears to be somewhere else. If you live there, you have to take it as a whole. That's loyalty.

This is why Judy Ingqvist does not sing "Holy City" on Sunday morning, although everyone says she sounds great on "Holy City"—it's not her wish to sound great, though she is the leading soprano; it's her wish that all the sopranos sound at least okay. So she sings quietly. One Sunday when the Ingqvists went to the Black Hills on vacation, a young, white-knuckled seminarian filled in; he gave a forty-five minute sermon and had a lot of sermon left over when finally three deacons cleared their throats simultaneously. They sounded like German shepherds barking, and their barks meant that the congregation now knew that he was bright and he had nothing more to prove to them. The young man looked on the sermon as free enterprise.* You work like hell on it and come up a winner. He wanted to give it all the best what was in him, of which he had more than he needed. He was opening a Higgledy-Piggledy of theology, and the barks were meant to remind him where he was: in Lake Wobegon, where smart doesn't count

---

*The smoke machine at the Sidetrack Tap, if you whack it about two inches below the Camels, will pay off a couple packs for free, and some enterprising patrons find it in their interest to use this knowledge. Past a certain age, you're not supposed to do this sort of thing anymore. You're supposed to grow up. Unfortuantely, that is just the age when many people start to smoke.

*He is no longer in the ministry. He is vice-president for sales at Devotional Systems, Inc., maker of quadraphonic sanctuary speakers for higher fidelity sermons, home devotional programs on floppy disks, and individual biofeedback systems in the pews. Two wires with electrodes hang from each hymnal rack, which the faithful press to their temples as they pray, attempting to bring the needle on the biometer into the reverence zone. For some reason, prayer doesn't accomplish that so well as, say, thinking about food, but DSI is working on it and thinks this may be a breakthrough in the worship of the future.

for so much. A minister has to be able to read a clock. At noon, it's time to go home and turn up the pot roast and get the peas out of the freezer. Everybody gets their pot roast at Ralph's. It's not the tenderest meat in the Ninth Federal Reserve District, but after you bake it for four hours until it falls apart in shreds, what's the difference?

So what's special about this town is not smarts either. It counted zero when you worked for Bud on the road crew, as I did one summer. He said, "Don't get smart with me," and he meant it. One week I was wrestling with great ideas in dimly-lit college classrooms, the next I was home shoveling gravel in the sun, just another worker. I'd studied the workers in humanities class, spent a whole week on the labor movement as it related to ideals of American individualism, and I thought it was pretty funny to sing "Soldiarity Forever" while patching potholes, but he didn't, he told me to quit smarting off. Work was serious business, and everybody was supposed to do it—*hard* work, unless of course you thought you were too good for it, in which case to hell with you. Bud's wife kept telling him to retire, he said, but he wasn't going to; all the geezers he'd known who decided to take it easy were flat on their backs a few months later with all their friends commenting on how natural they looked. Bud believed that when you feel bad, you get out of bed and put your boots on. "A little hard work never killed anybody," he told us, I suppose, about fifteen thousand times. Lean on your shovel for one second to straighten your back, and there was Bud to remind you. It would have been satisfying to choke him on the spot. We had the tar right there, just throw the old coot in and cook him and use him for fill. But he was so strong he might have taken the whole bunch of us. Once he said to me, "Here, take the other end of this." It was the hoist for the backhoe. I lifted my end, and right then I went from a 34- to a 36-inch sleeve. I thought my back was going to break. "Heavy?" he said. *Nooo.* "Want to set her down?" *Nooo. That's okay.* "Well, better set her down, cause this is where she goes." *Okay.* All my bones had been reset, making me a slightly curved person. "Next time try lifting with your legs," he said.

People who visit Lake Wobegon come to see somebody, otherwise they missed the turn on the highway and are lost. *Ausländers,* the Germans call them. They don't come for Toast 'n Jelly Days, or the Germans' quadrennial Gesuffa Days, or Krazy Daze, or the Feast Day of St. Francis, or the three-day Mist County Fair with its exciting Death Leap from the top of the grandstand to the arms of the haystack for only ten cents. What's special about here isn't special enough to draw a major crowd, though Flag Day—you could drive a long way on June 14 to find another like it.

Flag Day, as we know it, was the idea of Herman Hochstetter, Rollie's dad, who ran the dry goods store and ran Armistice Day, the Fourth of July, and Flag Day. For the Fourth, he organized a double-loop parade around the block which allowed people to take turns marching and watching. On Armistice Day, everyone stepped outside at 11 A.M. and stood in silence for two minutes as Our Lady's bell tolled eleven times.

Flag Day was his favorite. For a modest price, he would install a bracket on your house to hold a pole to hang your flag on, or he would drill a hole in the sidewalk in front of your store with his drill gun powered by a .22 shell. *Bam!* And in went the flag. On patriotic days, flags flew all over; there were flags on the tall poles, flags on the short, flags in the brackets on the pillars and the porches, and if you were flagless you could expect to hear from Herman. His hairy arm around your shoulder, his poochlike face close to yours, he would say how proud he was that so many people were proud of their country, leaving you to see the obvious, that you were a gap in the ranks.

In June 1944, the day after D-Day, a salesman from Fisher Hat called on Herman and offered a good deal on red and blue baseball caps. "Do you have white also?" Herman asked. The salesman thought that white caps could be had for the same wonderful price. Herman ordered two hundred red, two hundred white, and one hundred blue. By the end of the year, he still had four hundred and eighty-six caps. The inspiration of the Living Flag was born from that overstock.

On June 14, 1945, a month after V-E Day, a good crowd assembled in front of the Central Building in response to Herman's ad in the paper:

> Honor "AMERICA" June 14 AT 4 p.m. Be proud of "Our Land & People". Be part of the "LIVING FLAG". Don't let it be said that Lake Wobegon was "Too Busy". Be on time. 4 p.m. "Sharp".

His wife Louise handed out the caps, and Herman stood on a stepladder and told people where to stand. He lined up the reds and whites into stripes, then got the blues into their square. Mr. Hanson climbed up on the roof of the Central Building and took a photograph, they sang the national anthem, and then the Living Flag dispersed. The photograph appeared in the paper the next week. Herman kept the caps.

In the flush of victory, people were happy to do as told and stand in place, but in 1946 and 1947, dissension cropped up in the ranks: people complained about the heat and about Herman—what gave *him* the idea he could order *them* around? "People! Please! I need your attention! You blue people, keep your hats on! Please! Stripe No. 4, you're sagging! You reds, you're up here! We got too many white people, we need more red ones! Let's do this without talking, people! I can't get you straight if you keep moving around! Some of you are not paying attention! Everybody shut up! Please!"

One cause of resentment was the fact that none of them got to see the Flag they were in; the picture in the paper was black and white. Only Herman and Mr. Hanson got to see the real Flag, and some boys too short to be needed down below. People wanted a chance to go up to the roof and witness the spectacle for themselves.

"How can you go up there if you're supposed to be down here?" Herman siad. "You go up there to look, you got nothing to look at. Isn't it enough to know that you're doing your part?"

On Flag Day, 1949, just as Herman said, "That's it! Hold it now!" one of the reds made a break for it—dashed up four flights of stairs to the roof and leaned over and had a long look. Even with the hole he left behind, it was a magnificent sight. The Living Flag filled the street below. A perfect Flag! The reds so brilliant! He couldn't take his eyes off it. "Get down here! We need a picture!" Herman yelled up to him. "How does it look?" people yelled up to him. "Unbelievable! I can't describe it!" he said.

So then everyone had to have a look. "No!" Herman siad, but they took a vote and it was unanimous. One by one, members of the Living Flag went up to the roof and admired it. It *was* marvelous! It brought tears to the eyes, it made one reflect on this great country and on Lake Wobegon's place in it. One wanted to stand up there all afternoon and just drink it in. So, as the first hour passed, and only forty of the five hundred had been to the top, the others got more and more restless. "Hurry up! Quite dawdling! *You've* seen it! Get down here and give someone else a chance!" Herman sent people up in groups of four, and then ten, but after two hours, the Living Flag became the Sitting Flag and then began to erode, as the members who had had a look thought about heading home to supper, which infuriated the ones who hadn't. "Ten more minutes!" Herman cried, but ten minutes became twenty and thirty, and people snuck off and the Flag that remained for the last viewer was a Flag shot through by cannon fire.

In 1950, the Sons of Knute took over Flag Day. Herman gave them the boxes of caps. Since then, the Knutes have achieved several good Flags, though most years the attendance was poor. You need at least four hundred to make a good one. Some years the Knutes made a "no-look" rule, other years they held a lottery. One year they experimented with a large mirror held by two men over the edge of the roof, but when people leaned back and looked up, the Flag disappeared, of course.

DISCUSSION QUESTIONS

1. Why does Garrison Keillor spend the first part of his story on "maps"? What is he making fun of? What is the relation of maps to reality?

2. In what way is the story about maps at the beginning of the essay similar to the story about "Flag Day" at the end? What do these stories tell us about human accuracy? The "Flag Day" incident almost reads like a parable. How do you interpret its larger meaning?

3. Compare Keillor's humorous attitude toward his imaginary hometown with Mark Twain's attitude toward his real hometown in "Old Times on the Mississippi" (see "Classics").

Chuck Yeager / *Yeager: An Autobiography*
[Against the Wall]   1985

General Chuck Yeager—the first man to fly faster than the speed of sound, "the greatest test pilot of them all," the World War II fighter pilot who shot down a Messerschmidt jet with a propeller-driven plane, the American hero of postwar aviation whose life defined "the right stuff." "The secret of my success," Yeager explained, "is that I always manged to live to fly another day."

Yeager joined the Air Force at eighteen, fresh out of high school and driven by a passion for flying. By the age of twenty-two, his heroic exploits as a fighter pilot in World War II had earned him considerable recognition not only in the military but also in reports circulated on the home front. He had established an enviable record of "kills" in dogfights over Europe, and he had escaped from occupied France after being shot down in combat. He continued to fly, resisting orders authorizing him to return home.

In 1947, Yeager captured worldwide recognition as the first test pilot to smash the sound barrier, flying a supersonic Bell X-1 despite cracked ribs from a riding accident a few days before. Yeager helped establish what has been called the "Golden Age of Aviation," when test pilots either set records or were killed in thunderous explosions. Yeager's years as America's premier test pilot ended in 1954, when he left Edwards Air Force Base for a series of assignments around the world—commanding a fighter squadron in Europe, flying tactical bombers in Southeast Asia, and supervising military defense in the Pakistan-India war.

Written with the assistance of Leo Janos, an award-winning former Time *cor-*

respondent who covered the Apollo space missions, Yeager: An Autobiography *offered the American public a portrait of a rugged individual, an American hero of monumental proportions.* Yeager *became an instant best-seller on its publication in 1985. The following excerpts recapture the events that create legends.*

FIRST POWERED FLIGHT: AUGUST 29, 1947

Shivering, you bang your gloved hands together and strap on your oxygen mask inside the coldest airplane ever flown. You're being cold-soaked from the hundreds of gallons of liquid oxygen (LOX) fuel stored in the compartment directly behind you at minus 296 degress. No heater, no defroster; you'll just have to grit your teeth for the next fifteen minutes until you land and feel that wonderful hot desert sun. But that cold saps your strength: it's like trying to work and concentrate inside a frozen food locker.

That cold will take you on the ride of your life. You watched the X-1 get its 7:00 A.M. feeding in a swirling cloud of vapor fog, saw the frost form under its orange belly. That was an eerie sight; you're carrying six hundred gallons of LOX and water alcohol on board that can blow up at the flick of an igniter switch and scatter your pieces over several counties. But if all goes well, the beast will chug-a-lug a ton of fuel a minute.

Anyone with brain cells would have to wonder what in hell he was doing in such a situation—strapped inside a live bomb that's about to be dropped out of a bomb bay. But risks are the spice of life, and this is the kind of moment that a test pilot lives for. The butterflies are fluttering, but you feed off fear as if it's a high-energy candy bar. It keeps you alert and focused.

You accept risk as part of every new challenge; it comes with the territory. So you learn all you can about the ship and its systems, practice flying it on ground runs and glide flights, plan for any possible contingency, until the odds against you seem more friendly. You like the X-1; she's a sound airplane, but she's also an experimental machine, and you're a researcher on an experimental flight. You know you can be hammered by something unexpected, but you count on your experience, concentration, and instincts to pull you through. And luck. Without luck . . .

You can't watch yourself fly. But you know when you're in sync with the machine, so plugged into its instruments and controls that your mind and your hand become the heart of its operating system. You can make that airplane talk, and like a good horse, the machine knows when it's in competent hands. You know what you can get away with. And you can be wrong only once. You smile reading newspaper stories about a pilot in a disabled plane that maneuvered to miss a schoolyard before he hit the ground. That's crap. In an emergency situation, a pilot thinks only about one thing—survival. You battle to survive right down to the ground; you think about nothing else. Your concentration is riveted on what to try next. You don't say anything on the radio, and you aren't even aware that a schoolyard exists. That's exactly how it is.

There are at least a dozen different ways that the X-1 can kill you, so your concentration is total during the preflight check procedures. You load up nitrogen gas pressures in the manifolds—your life's blood because the nitrogen gas runs all the internal systems as well as the flaps and landing gear. Then you bleed off the liquid oxygen manifold and shut it down. All's in order.

Half an hour ago, we taxied out to takeoff in the mother ship. Because of the possibility of crashing with so much volatile fuel, they closed down the base until we were safely off the ground. That's the only acknowledgement from the base commander that we even exist. There's no interest in our flights because practically nobody at Muroc gives us any chance for success. Those bastards think they have it all figured. They call our flights ''Slick Goodlin's Revenge.'' The word is that he knew when to get out in one piece by quitting over money.

One minute to drop. Ridley flashes the word from the copilot's seat in the mother ship. We're at 25,000 feet as the B-29 noses over and starts its shallow dive. Major Cardenas, the driver, starts counting backwards from ten.

C-r-r-ack. The bomb shackle release jolts you up from your seat, and as you sail out of the dark bomb bay the sun explodes in brightness. You're looking into the sky. *Wrong!* You should be dropped level. The dive speed was too slow, and they dropped you in a nose-up stall. You blink to get your vision, fighting the stall with your control wheel, dropping toward the basement like an elevator whose cable snapped. You're three thousand pounds heavier than in those glide flights. Down goes that nose and you pick up speed. You level out about a thousand feet below the mother ship and reach for that rocket igniter switch.

The moment of truth: if you are gonna be blown up, this is likely to be when. You light the first chamber.

Whoosh. Slammed back in your seat, a tremendous kick in the butt. Nose up and hold on. Barely a sound; you can hear your breathing in the oxygen mask— you're outracing the noise behind you—and for the first time in a powered airplane you can hear the air beating against the windshield as the distant dot that is Hoover's high chase P-80 grows ever bigger. You pass him like he's standing still, and he reports seeing diamond-shaped shock waves leaping out of your fiery exhaust. Climbing faster than you can even think, but using only one of four rocket chambers, you turn it off and light another. We're streaking up at .7 Mach; this beast's power is awesome. You've never known such a feeling of speed while pointing up in the sky. At 45,000 feet, where morning resembles the beginning of dusk, you turn on the last of the four chambers. God, what a ride! And you still have nearly half your fuel left.

Until this moment, you obeyed the flight plan to the letter: firing only one chamber at a time, to closely monitor the chamber pressures; if you use two or more, there's too much to watch. If you fire all four, you may accelerate too rapidly, be forced to raise your nose to slow down, and get yourself into a high-speed stall.

Now the flight plan calls for you to jettison remaining fuel and glide down to land. But you're bug-eyed, thrilled to your toes, and the fighter jock takes over from the cautious test pilot. Screw it! You're up there in the dark part of the sky in the most fabulous flying machine ever built, and you're just not ready to go home. The moment calls for a nice slow roll, and you lower your wing, pulling a couple of Gs until you're hanging upside down in zero Gs and the engine quits. As soon as the X-1 rights itself it starts again, but you've been stupid. At zero Gs the fuel couldn't feed the engine, and you might have been blown up. But the X-1 is forgiving—this time.

You know what you're supposed to do, but you know what you're gonna do. You turn off the engine, but instead of jettisoning the remaining fuel, you roll over and dive for Muroc Air Base. We blister down, shit-heavy, .8 Mach in front of the needle, a dive-glide faster than most jets at full power. You're thinking, ''Let's show those bastards the real X-1.''

Below 10,000 feet is the danger zone, the limit for jettisoning fuel with enough maneuver time to glide down to a safe landing. But we're below 5,000, lined up with Muroc's main runway. And we're still in a dive.

We whistle down that main runway, only 300 feet off the ground, until we are parallel with the control tower. You hit the main rocket switch. The four chambers blow a thirty-foot lick of flame. Christ, the impact nearly knocks you back into last week. That nose is pointed so straught up that you can't see the blue sky out the windshield. We are no longer an airplane: we're a skyrocket. You're not flying. You're holding on to the tiger's tail. Straight up, you're going .75 Mach! In one minute the fuel is gone. By then you're at 35,000 feet, traveling at .85 Mach. You're so excited, scared, and thrilled that you can't say a word until the next day.

But others said plenty. The NACA team thought I was a wild man. Dick Frost chewed me out for doing that slow roll. Even Jack Ridley shook his head. He said, "Any spectators down there knew damned well that wasn't Slick rattling those dishes. Okay, son, you got it all out of your system, but now you're gonna hang tough." Colonel Boyd fired a rocket of his own. "Reply by endorsement about why you exceeded .82 Mach in violation of my direct orders." I asked Ridley to write my reply. "Bullshit," he said. "You did it. You explain it."

I wrote back: "The airplane felt so good and flew so well that I felt certain we would have no trouble going slightly above the agreed speed. The violation of your direct orders was due to the excited state of the undersigned and will not be repeated."

A few days later, the old man called me. "Damn it, I expect you to stick to the program and do what you are supposed to. Don't get overeager and cocky. Do you want to jeopardize the first Air Corps research project?"

"No, sir."

"Well, then obey the goddamn rules."

From then on I did. But on that first powered flight I wanted to answer those who said we were doomed in the attmept to go faster than sound. My message was, "Stick it where the sun don't shine."

Going out to .85 Mach put the program out on a limb because it carried us beyond the limits of what was then known about high-speed aerodynamics. Wind tunnels could only measure up to .85 Mach, and as Walt Williams of NACA was quick to point out to me, "From now on, Chuck, you'll be flying in the realm of the unknown." Ridley and I called it "the Ughknown."

Whatever happened, I figured I was better off than the British test pilots who had attempted supersonic flights in high-powered dives. If they got into trouble, that was it—especially in a tailless airplane like *The Swallow*. All my attempts would be made in climbs—the power of the rocket over the jet—and that way, if I encountered a problem, I could quickly slow down. But the price of rocket power was flying with volatile fuel. Running four chambers, my fuel lasted only two and a half minutes; it lasted five minutes on two chambers and ten mintues on one. Each minute of climbing we got lighter and faster, so that by the time we had climbed up and over at 45,000 feet, we were at max speed.

Who would decide the max speed of a particular flight? This was an Air Corps research project, but the seventeen NACA engineers and technicians used their expertise to try to control these missions. They were there as advisers, with high-speed wind tunnels experience, and were performing the data reduction collected on the X-1 flights, so they tried to dictate the speed in our flight plans. Ridley, Frost, and I always wanted to go faster than they did. They would recommend a Mach number, then the three of us would sit down and decide whether or not we wanted to stick with their recommendation. They were so conservative that it would've taken me six months to get to the barrier.

I wanted to be careful, but I also wanted to get it over with. Colonel Boyd sided with NACA caution, going up only two-hundredths of a Mach on each consecutive flight. Once I flew back with Hoover to see if I could get the old man to agree to speed things up. We met in the evening at his home. But Bob led off by trying to explain why he had been forced to crash-land a P-80 a few days before. I could tell the old man wasn't buying Bob's explanations; those thick eyebrows were bunching up. But ol' Hoover pushed on, becoming emotional to the point where he accidentally spat a capped tooth onto the old man's lap. I decided to have my say at another time.

So I flew in small increments of speed. On October 5, I made my sixth powered flight and experienced shock-wave buffeting for the first time as I reached .86 Mach. It felt like I was driving on bad shock absorbers over uneven paving stones. The right wing suddenly got heavy and began to drop, and when I tried to correct it my controls were sluggish. I increased my speed to .88 Mach to see what would happen. I saw my aileron vibrating with shock waves, and only with effort could I hold my wing level.

The X-1 was built with a high tail to avoid air turbulence off the wings; the tail was also thinner than the wings, so that shock waves would not form simultaneously on both surfaces. Thus far, the shock waves and buffeting had been manageable, and because the ship was stressed for eighteen Gs, I never was concerned about being shaken apart. Also, I was only flying twice a week, to give NACA time to reduce all the flight data and analyze it. Special sensing devices pinpointed the exact location of shock waves on any part of the airframe. The data revealed that the airplane was functioning exactly as its designers planned.

But on my very next flight we got knocked on our fannies. I was flying at .94 Mach at 40,000 feet, experiencing the usual buffeting, when I pulled back on the control wheel, and Christ, nothing happened! The airplane continued flying with the same attitude and in the same direction.

The control wheel felt as if the cables had snapped. I didn't know what in hell was happening. I turned off the engine and slowed down. I jettisoned my fuel and landed feeling certain that I had taken my last ride in the X-1. Flying at .94, I lost my pitch control. My elevator ceased to function. At the speed of sound, the ship's nose was predicted to go either up or down, and without pitch control, I was in a helluva bind.

I told Ridley I thought we had had it. There was no way I was going faster than .94 Mach without an elevator. He looked sick. So did Dick Frost and the NACA team. We called Colonel Boyd at Wright, and he flew out immediately to confer with us. Meanwhile, NACA analyzed the telemetry data from the flight and found that at .94 Mach, a shock wave was slammed right at the hinge point of the elevator on the tail, negating my controls. Colonel Boyd just shook his head. "Well," he said, "it looks to me like we've reached the end of the line." Everyone seemed to agree except for Jack Ridley.

He sat at a corner of the conference table scribbling little notes and equations. He said, "Well, maybe Chuck can fly without using the elevator. Maybe he can get by using only the horizontal stabilizer." The stabilizer was the winglike structure on the tail that stabilized pitch control. Bell's engineers had purposely built into them an extra control authority because they had anticipated elevator ineffectiveness caused by shock waves. This extra authority was a trim switch in the cockpit that would allow a small air motor to pivot the stabilizer up or down, creating a moving tail that could act as an auxiliary elevator by lowering or raising the airplane's nose. We were leery about trying it while flying at high speeds; instead, we set the trim on the ground and left it alone.

Jack thought we should spend a day ground testing the hell out of that system, learn everything there was to know about it, then flight test it. No one disagreed. There was no other alternative except to call the whole thing quits, but Jack got a lot of "what if" questions that spelled out all the risks. What if the motor got stuck in a trim up or trim down position? Answer: Yeager would have a problem. What if the turbulent airflow at high speed Mach overwhelmed the motor and kept the tail from pivoting? Answer: Yeager would be no worse off than he was during the previous mission. Yeah, but what if that turbulent air ripped off that damned tail as it was pivoting? Answer: Yeager better have paid-up insurance. We were dealing with the Ughknown.

Before returning to Wright, Colonel Boyd approved our ground tests. We were to report the results to him, and then he'd decide whether to proceed with a flight test. Then the old man took me aside. "Listen," he said, "I don't want you to be railroaded into this deal by Ridley or anyone else. If you don't feel comfortable with the risks, I want you to tell me so. I'll respect your decision. Please don't play the hero, Chuck. It makes no sense getting you hurt or killed."

I told him, "Colonel Boyd, it's my ass on the line. I want us to succeed but I'm not going to get splattered doing it."

So, Ridley and I ground tested that stabilizer system every which way but loose. It worked fine, and provided just enough control (about a quarter of a degree change in the angle of incidence) so that we both felt I could get by without using the airplane's elevator. "It may not be much," Ridley said, "and it may feel ragged to you up there, but it will keep you flying." I agreed. But would the system work at high Mach speed? Only one way to find out. Colonel Boyd gave us the go ahead.

No X-1 flight was ever routine. But when I was dropped to repeat the same flight profile that had lost my elevator effectiveness, I admit to being unusually grim. I flew as alert and precisely as I knew how. If the damned Ughknown swallowed me up, there wasn't much I could do about it, but I concentrated on that trim switch. At the slightest indication that something wasn't right, I would break the record for backing off.

Pushing the switch forward opened a solenoid that allowed high-pressure nitrogen gas through the top motor to the stabilizer, changing its angle of attack and stabilizing its upward pitch. If I pulled back, that would start the bottom motor, turning it in the opposite direction. I could just beep it and supposedly make pitch changes. I let the airplane accelerate up to .85 Mach before testing the trim switch. I pulled back on the switch, moving the leading edge of the stabilizer down one degree, and her nose rose, I retrimmed it back to where it was, and we leveled out. I climbed and accelerated up to .9 Mach and made the same chance, achieving the same result. I retrimmed it and let it go out to .94 Mach, where I had lost my elevator effectiveness, made the same trim change, again raising the nose, just as I had done at the lower Mach numbers. Ridley was right: the stabilizer gave me just enough pitch control to keep me safe. I felt we could probably make it through without the elevator.

I had her out to .96 at 43,000 feet and was about to turn off the engine and begin jettisoning the remaining fuel, when the windshield began to frost. Because of the intense cabin cold, fogging was a continual problem, but I was usually able to wipe it away. This time, though, a solid layer of frost quickly formed. I even took off my gloves and used my fingernails, which only gave me frostbite. That windshield was lousy anyway, configured to the bullet-shaped fuselage and affording limited visibility. It was hard to see out during landings, but I had never expected to fly the X-1 on instruments. I radioed Dick Frost, flying low chase, and told him the problem. "Okay, pard," he said, "I'll talk you in. You must've done a lot of sweating in that cockpit to ice the damned windshield." I told him, "Not as much as I'm gonna do having you talk me in. You better talk good, Frost." He laughed. "I know. A dumb bastard like you probably can't read instruments."

The X-1 wasn't the Space Shuttle. There were no on-board computers to line you up and bring you down. The pilot was the computer. Under normal flight conditions, I'd descend to 5,000 feet above the lakebed and fly over the point where I wanted to touch down, then turn and line up downwind, lowering my landing gear at around 250 mph. The X-1 stalled around 190 mph, so I held my glide speed to around 220 and touched down at around 190. The ship rolled out about three miles if I didn't apply the brakes. Rogers Day Lake gave me an eight-mile runway, but that didn't make the landing untricky. Coming in nose-high, you couldn't see the ground at all. You had to feel for it. I was sensitive to ground effect, and felt the differences as we lowered down. There was also that depth perception problem, and a lot of pilots bent airplanes porpoising in, or flaring high then cracking off their landing gears. My advantage was that I had landed on these lakebeds hundreds of times. Even so, the X-1 was not an easy-landing airplane. At the point of touchdown, you had to discipline yourself to do nothing but allow the ship to settle in by itself. Otherwise you'd slam it on its weak landing gear.

So, landing blind was not something you'd ever want to be forced to do. I had survived the Ughknown only to be kicked in the butt by the Unexpected. But that was a test pilot's life, one damned thing after another. Frost was a superb pilot, who knew the X-1's systems and characteristics even better than I did. I had plenty of experience flying on instruments, and in a hairy deal like this, experience really counted. Between the two of us we made it look deceptively easy, although we both knew that it wasn't exactly a routine procedure. Frost told me to turn left ten degrees, and I followed by using my magnetic compass, monitoring my rate of turn by the needle and ball. I watched the airspeed and rate of descent, so I knew how fast I was coming down from that and the feel of the ground effect. I followed his directions moving left or right to line up on the lakebed, which was also five miles wide, allowing him to fly right on my wing and touch down with me.

He greased me right in, but my body sweat added another layer of frost to the windshield. "Pard," Dick teased, "that's the only time you haven't bounced her down. Better let me hold your hand from now on."

Before my next flight, Jack Russell, my crew chief, applied a coating of Drene Shampoo to the windshield. For some unknown reason it worked as an effective antifrost device, and we continued using it even after the government purchased a special chemical that cost eighteen bucks a bottle.

Despite the frosted windshield, I now had renewed confidence in the X-1. We had licked the elevator problem, and Ridley and I phoned Colonel Boyd and told him we thought we could safely continue the flights. He told us to press on. This was on Thursday afternoon. The next scheduled flight would be on Tuesday. So we sat down with the NACA team to discuss a flight plan. I had gone up to .955 Mach, and they suggested a speed of .97 Mach for the next mission. What we didn't know until the flight data was reduced several days later, was that I had actually flown .988 Mach while testing the stabilizer. In fact, there was a fairly good possibility that I had attained supersonic speed.

Instrumentation revealed that a shock wave was interfering with the airspeed gauge on the wing.. But we wouldn't learn about this until after my next flight.

All I cared about was that the stabilizer was still in one piece and so was I. We were all exhuasted from a long, draining week, and quit early on Friday to start the weekend. I had promised Glennis that I would take her to Elly Anderson's, in Auburn, for a change of scene and to get her away from the kids. As cautiously as we were proceeding on these X-1 flights, I figured that my attempt to break the barrier was a week or two away. So I looked forward to a relaxed few days off. But when I got home, I found Glennis lying down, feeling sick. We canceled the babysitter and called Elly. By Sunday she was feeling better, so we went over to Pancho's place for dinner. On the way over, I said to Glennis, "Hey, how about riding horses after we eat?" She was raised around horses and was a beautiful rider.

Pancho's place was a dude ranch, so after dinner we walked over to the corral and had them saddle up a couple of horses. It was a pretty night and we rode for about an hour through the Joshua trees. We decided to race back. Unfortunately there was no moon, otherwise I would have seen that the gate we had gone out of was now closed. I only saw the gate when I was practically on top of it. I was slightly in the lead, and I tried to veer my horse and miss it, but it was too late. We hit the gate and I tumbled through the air. The horse got cut and I was knocked silly. The next thing I remember was Glennis kneeling over me, asking me if I was okay. I was woozy, and she helped me stand up. It took a lot to straighten up, feeling like I had a spear in my side.

Glennis knew immediately. "You broke a rib," she said. She was all for driving straight to the base hospital. I said, no, the flight surgeon will ground me. "Well, you can't fly with broken ribs," she argued. I told her, "If I can't, I won't. If I can, I will."

Monday morning, I struggled out of bed. My shoulder was sore, and I ached generally from bumps and bruises, but my ribs near to killed me. The pain took my breath away. Glennis drove me over to Rosemond, where a local doctor confirmed I had two cracked ribs, and taped me up. He told me to take it easy. The tape job really helped. The pain was at least manageable and I was able to drive myself to the base that afternoon.

I was really low. I felt we were on top of these flights now, and I wanted to get them over with. And as much as I was hurting, I could only imagine what the old man would say if I was grounded for falling off a horse. So, I sat down with Jack Ridley and told him my troubles. I said, "If this were the first flight, I wouldn't even think about trying it with these busted sumbitches. But, hell, I know every move I've got to make, and most of the major switches are right on the control wheel column."

He said, "True, but how in hell are you gonna be able to lock the cockpit door? That takes some lifting and shoving." So we walked into the hangar to see what we were up against.

We looked at the door and talked it over. Jack said, "Let's see if we can get a stick or something that you can use in your left hand to raise the handle up on the door to lock it. Get it up at least far enough where you get both hands on it and get a grip on it." We looked around the hangar and found a broom. Jack sawed off a ten-inch piece of broomstick, and it fit right into the door handle. Then I crawled into the X-1 and we tried it out. He held the door against the frame, and by using that broomstick to raise the door handle, I found I could manage to lock it. We tried it two or three times, and it worked. But finally, Ridley said, "Jesus, son, how are you gonna get down that ladder?"

I said, "One rung at a time. Either that or you can piggyback me."

Jack respected my judgment. "As long as you really think you can hack it," he said. We left that piece of broomstick in the X-1 cockpit.

NINTH POWERED FLIGHT: OCTOBER 14, 1947

Glennis drove me to the base at six in the morning. She wasn't happy with my decision to fly, but she knew that Jack would never let me take off if he felt I would get into trouble. Hoover and Jack Russell, the X-1 crew chief, heard I was dumped off a horse at Pancho's, but thought the only damage was to my ego, and hit me with some "Hi-Ho Silver" crap, as well as a carrot, a pair of glasses, and a rope in a brown paper bag—my bucking bronco survival kit.

Around eight, I climbed aboard the mother ship. The flight plan called for me to reach .97 Mach. The way I felt that day, .97 would be enough. On that first rocket ride I had a tiger by the tail; but by this ninth flight, I felt I was in the driver's seat. I knew that airplane inside and out. I didn't think it would turn against me. Hell, there wasn't much I could do to hurt it; it was built to withstand three times as much stress as I could survive. I didn't think the sound barrier would destroy her, either. But the only way to prove it was to do it.

That moving tail really bolstered my morale, and I wanted to get to that sound barrier. I suppose there were advantages in creeping up on Mach 1, but my vote was to stop screwing around before we had some stupid accident that could cost us not only a mission, but the entire project. If this mission was successful, I was planning to really push for a sound barrier attempt on the very next flight.

Going down that damned ladder hurt. Jack was right behind me. As usual, I slid feet-first into the cabin. I picked up the broom handle and waited while Ridley pushed the door against the frame, then I slipped it into the door handle and raised it up into lock position. It worked perfectly. Then I settled in to go over my checklist. Bob Cardenas, the B-29 driver, asked if I was ready.

"Hell, yes," I said. "Let's get it over with."

He dropped the X-1 at 20,000 feet, but his dive speed was once again too slow and the X-1 started to stall. I fought it with the control wheel for about five hundred feet, and finally got her nose down. The moment we picked up speed I fired all four rocket chambers in rapid sequence. We climbed at .88 Mach and began to buffet, so I flipped the stabilizer switch and changed the setting two degrees. We smoothed right out, and at 36,000 feet, I turned off two rocket chambers. At 40,000 feet, we were still climbing at a speed of .92 Mach. Leveling off at 42,000 feet, I had thirty percent of my fuel, so I turned on rocket chamber three and immediately reached .96 Mach. I noticed that the faster I got, the smoother the ride.

Suddenly the Mach needle began to fluctuate. It went up to .965 Mach—then tipped right off the scale. I thought I was seeing things! We were flying supersonic! And it was as smooth as a baby's bottom: Grandma could be sitting up there sipping lemonade. I kept the speed off the scale for about twenty seconds, then raised the nose to slow down.

I was thunderstruck. After all the anxiety, breaking the sound barrier turned out to be a perfectly paved speedway. I radioed Jack in the B-29. "Hey, Ridley, that Machmeter is acting screwy. It just went off the scale on me."

"Fluctuated off?"

"Yeah, at point nine-six-five."

"Son, you is imagining things."

"Must be. I'm still wearing my ears and nothing else fell off, neither."

The guys in the NACA tracking van interrupted to report that they heard what sounded like a distant rumble of thunder: my sonic boom! The first one by an airplane ever heard on earth. The X-1 was supposedly capable of reaching nearly twice the speed of sound, but the Machmeter aboard only registered to 1.0 Mach, which showed how much confidence they had; I estimated I had reached 1.05 Mach. (Later data showed it was 1.07 Mach—700 mph.)

And that was it. I sat up there feeling kind of numb, but elated. After all the anticipation to achieve this moment, it really was a let-down. It took a damned instrument meter to tell me what I'd done. There should've been a bump on the road, something to let you know you had just punched a nice clean hole through that sonic barrier. The Ughknown was a poke through Jello. Later on, I realized that this mission had to end in a let-down, because the real barrier wasn't in the sky, but in our knowledge and experience of supersonic flight.

I landed tired, but relieved to have hacked the program. There is always strain in research flying. It's the same as flying in combat, where you never can be sure of the outcome. You try not to think about possible disasters, but fear is churning around inside whether you think of it consciously or not. I thought now that I'd reached the top of the mountain, the remainder of these X-1 experimental flights would be downhill. But having sailed me safely through the sonic barrier, the

X-1 had plenty of white-knuckle flights in store over the next year. The real hero in the flight test business is a pilot who manages to survive.

And so I was a hero this day. As usual, the fire trucks raced out to where the ship had rolled to a stop on the lakebed. As usual, I hitched a ride back to the hangar with the fire chief. That warm desert sun really felt wonderful. My ribs ached.

DISCUSSION QUESTIONS

1. Read the passage on Chuck Yeager from Tom Wolfe's book *The Right Stuff* ("Classics"). In what specific ways do Wolfe's and Yeager's accounts of Yeager's testing of the Bell X-1 agree? How do they differ? Which version do you prefer? Why?

2. Compare and contrast the distinctive qualities of Yeager's personality that emerge from his autobiography with H. G. Bissinger's characterization of Harvey ("Hoot") Gibson, the pilot in command of TWA flight 841 in "The Plane That Fell from the Sky" ("Press"). What traits do they seem to share? In what specific ways can they be said to be quite different—in temperament, in action, in attitudes?

3. Make a list of the attributes that distinguish Yeager's identity from that of his peers. Then read the selections from Lee Iacocca's autobiography reprinted in "Best-Sellers." What traits do these public figures share? In what ways are they different? In philosophy, values, behavior? How does each define the term *hero?* What are the broader cultural implications of their respective definitions of heroism?

4. Compare and contrast Yeager's and Iacocca's conception of an American hero with the image presented in the advertisement for Aramis cologne ("Advertising"). What specific details in this ad do you think Yeager and Iacocca would find appealing? Which aspects of this image of "An American Hero" do you think they would find unattractive? Why? In what ways does this ad challenge Yeager's and Iacocca's images of the heroic contemporary male?

Barry Lopez / *Arctic Dreams* [The Arctic Hunters]   1986

The Arctic has long beckoned American writers: Edgar Allan Poe wrote a novel about an imaginary voyage to the region; Jack London set many of his stories there; and John McPhee explored it recently in one of his most successful books, Coming into the Country. *In* Arctic Dreams, *Barry Lopez investigates how our fascination with the region is intimately linked to the wonders of its landscape. The following section of his best-selling book examines the connections between the Arctic landscape and the spiritual nature of the Eskimo hunting culture.*

Lopez was born in Port Chester, New York, in 1945. After receiving his B.A. and M.A. in English from Notre Dame, he studied folklore and anthropology at the University of Oregon. He began writing full-time in 1970 and is the author of several books, including Of Wolves and Men, Winter Count, *and a recent collection of essays,* Crossing Open Ground. *He has published essays and stories in a wide variety of periodicals.* Arctic Dreams *won an American Book Award in 1986.*

There is a small village in the central Brooks Range today called Anaktuvuk Pass. The Eskimos there are called Nunamiut, a group that until recently subsisted largely on caribou, Dall sheep, and moose. Originally nomadic, they spent winters in the Brooks Range and summers with relatives on the Beaufort Sea coast, trading caribou skins for sealskins and blubber. Their initial experience with modern trade goods was with such things as Russian tobacco in the eighteenth century, which they obtained from Eskimos living around the mouth of the Colville River, who had traded for it with Bering Sea Eskimos. After 1850 American whalers brought in large quantities of flour, tea, coffee, sugar, and tobacco, as well as guns, ammunition, and alcohol to the northwest coast of Alaska. The Nunamiut were less directly involved in this trade than their coastal relations, but they were profoundly affected nevertheless. The caribou herds they depended on were decimated to feed the whaling crews, and the Nunamiut were forced to abandon their life in the mountains. They shifted away from an economy based on hunting toward one based on trade. A few found seasonal employment on the coast, and most began trapping for furs in earnest.

A change came over the Nunamiut in the 1930s when the market for fur collapsed and the trading posts were closed, distant effects of economic depression in the United States. In 1934 a handful of families, knowing the caribou population had recovered and was again migrating through the mountains, sought to return to an earlier, more satisfying way of life. They set up a camp that first year at the junction of the Anaktuvuk and Colville rivers. For a few years they continued to travel regularly to the coast, where they fished and hunted seals, but in 1939, after this short period of readjustment, they returned to their homeland in the Brooks Range.

Ten years later the promise of trade goods to be brought into the mountains by airplane and the services of a temporary teacher in the summer induced several bands of Nunamiut to gather at a place called Tulugak Lake. In 1951 this group of sixty-five people moved a few miles farther south and a United States post office was established at Anaktuvuk Pass at the skin tent of a hunter named Homer Mekiana. A permanent school was built in 1961, by which time many of the Nunamiut were staying in or near the village year-round. Today about 180 people live there. There is a village store; satellites provide both telephone and television service; and there is a new school with sauna baths and a swimming pool, built with royalty money from Alaskan oil discoveries.

This story has been repeated many times in the same sequence across the Arctic in the past fifty years. Nomadic hunters are consolidated in one place for purposes of trade; radical changes are made in the native way of life in order to adapt to a trade-based or cash-based economy; some make strenuous efforts to return to a semblance of the older way of life; and, finally, large segments of the native language are lost, and the deep erosion of social, religious, political, and dietary customs occurs under intense pressure from missionaries, bureaucrats, and outside entrepreneurs. Hunting expertise, the ability of a man and a woman to keep a family going, the kind of knowledge of life that grew from patience and determination—such attributes were not as highly regarded by the interlopers, who sought to instill other virutes: promptness personal cleanliness, self-improvement, and a high degree of orderliness and scheduling in daily life.*

---

*It is easy to impugn the worth of such nebulous virtues, and to find among the interlopers venal and self-aggrandizing people. But it disparages Eskimos to see them as helpless in this situation. Most Eskimos are not opposed to changing their way of life, but they want the timing and the direction of change to be of their own choosing. "There is no insistence," a man once told me, "on living as hard a life as possible." In passing, it should be noted that many people have offered genuine assistance to Eskimos. One frequently hears praise in the Canadian Arctic, for example, for Catholic missionaries, because of their long-term commitment to a single village, their practice of learning to speak the language and to hunt, and their emphasis on good schooling.

Among those in the outside culture whom the Nunamiut have counted as friends in modern times are several anthropologists and biologists who recognized a repository of knowledge in the Nunamiut, particularly about the natural history of the local landscape, and who honored them for it. Some of the Nunamiut men and women who have led balanced and dignified lives through all the changes they have had to face have become symbols of unpretentious wisdom to visiting scientists. The situation, of course, is not unique to Anaktuvuk Pass. Many scientists comment in their papers and books and in private conversation about the character of their Eskimo companions. They admire their humble intelligence, their honesty, and their humor. They find it invigorating to be in the presence of people who, when they do speak, make so few generalized or abstract statements, who focus instead on the practical, the specific, the concrete.

I visited Anaktuvuk Pass in 1978 with a friend, a wolf biologist who had made a temporary home there and who was warmly regarded for his tact, his penchant for listening, and his help during an epidemic of flu in the village. We spent several days watching wolves and caribou in nearby valleys and visiting at several homes. The men talked a lot about hunting. The evenings were full of stories. There were moments of silence when someone said something very true, peals of laughter when a man told a story expertly at his own expense. One afternoon we left and traveled far to the west to the headwaters of the Utukok River.

The Alaska Department of Fish and Game had a small field camp on the Utukok, at the edge of a gravel-bar landing strip. Among the biologists there were men and women studying caribou, moose, tundra grizzly, wolverine, and, now that my companion had arrived, wolves. The country around the Utukok and the headwaters of the Kokolik River is a wild and serene landscape in summer. Parts of the Western Arctic caribou herd are drifting over the hills, returning from the calving grounds. The sun is always shining, somewhere in the sky. For a week or more we had very fine, clear weather. Golden eagles circled high over the tundra, hunting. Snowy owls regarded us from a distance from their tussock perches. Short-eared owls, a gyrfalcon. Familiar faces.

A few days after we arrived, my companion and I went south six or seven miles and established a camp from which we could watch a distant wolf den. In that open, rolling country without trees, I had the feeling, sometimes, that nothing was hidden. It was during those days that I went for walks along Ilingnorak Ridge and started visiting ground-nesting birds, and developed the habit of bowing to them out of regard for what was wonderful and mysterious in their lives.

The individual animals we watched tested their surroundings, tried things they had not done before, or that possibly no animal like them had ever done before—revealing their capacity for the new. The preservation of this capacity to adapt is one of the central mysteries of evolution.

We watched wolves hunting caribou, and owls hunting lemmings. Arctic ground squirrel eating *irok,* the mountain sorrel. I thought a great deal about hunting. In 1949, Robert Flaherty told an amazing story, which Edmund Carpenter was later successful in getting published, It was about a man named Comock. In 1902, when he and his family were facing starvation, Comock decided to travel over the sea ice to an island he knew about, where he expected they would be able to find food (a small island off Cape Wolstenholme, at the northern tip of Quebec's Ungava Peninsula). On the journey across, they lost nearly all their belongings—all of Comock's knives, spears, and harpoons, all their skins, their stone lamps, and most of their dogs—when the sea ice suddenly opened one night underneath their camp. They were without hunting implements, without a stone lamp to melt water to drink, without food or extra clothing. Comock had left only one sled, several dogs, his snow knife, with which he could cut snow blocks to build a snow house, and stones to make sparks for a fire.

They ate their dogs. The dogs they kept ate the other dogs, which were killed for them. Comock got his family to the island. He fashioned, from inappropriate materials, new hunting weapons. He created shelter and warmth. He hunted successfully. He reconstructed his entire material culture, almost from scratch, by improvising and, where necessary, inventing. He survived. His family survived. His dogs survived and multiplied.

Over the years they carefully collected rare bits of driftwood and bone until Comock had enough to build the frame for an umiak. They saved bearded-seal skins, from which Comock's wife made a waterproof hull. And one summer day they sailed away, back toward Ungava Peninsula. Robert Flaherty, exploring along the coast, spotted Comock and his family and dogs approaching across the water. When they came close, Flaherty, recognizing the form of an umiak and the cut of Eskimo clothing but, seeing that the materials were strange and improvised, asked the Eskimo who he was. He said his name was Comock. "Where in the world have you come from?" asked Flaherty. "From far away, from big island, from far over there," answered Comock, pointing. Then he smiled and made a joke about how poor the umiak must appear, and his family burst into laughter.

I think of this story because at its heart is the industry and competence, the determination and inventiveness of a human family. And because it is about people who lived resolutely in the heart of every moment they found themselves in, disastrous and sublime.

During those days I spent on Ilingnorak Ridge, I did not know what I know now about hunting; but I had begun to sense the outline of what I would learn in the years ahead with Eskimos and from being introduced, by various people, to situations I could not have easily found my way to alone. The insights I felt during those days had to do with the nature of hunting, with the movement of human beings over the land, and with fear. The thoughts grew out of watching the animals.

The evidence is good that among all northern aboriginal hunting peoples, the hunter saw himself bound up in a sacred relationship with the larger animals he hunted. The relationship was full of responsibilities—to the animals, to himself, and to his family. Among the great and, at this point, perhaps tragic lapses in the study of aboriginal hunting peoples is a lack of comprehension about the role women played in hunting. We can presume, I think, that in the same way the hunter felt bound to the animals he hunted, he felt the contract incomplete and somehow even inappropriate if his wife was not part of it. In no hunting society could a man hunt successfully alone. He depended upon his wife for obvious reasons—for the preparation of food and clothing, companionship, humor, subtle encouragement—and for things we can only speculate about, things of a religious nature, bearing on the mutual obligations and courtesies with which he approached the animals he hunted.

Hunting in my experience—and by hunting I simply mean being out on the land—is a state of mind. All of one's faculties are brought to bear in an effort to become fully incorporated into the landscape. It is more than listening for animals or watching for hoofprints or a shift in the weather. It is more than an analysis of what one *senses*. To hunt means to have the land around you like clothing. To engage in a wordless dialogue with it, one so absorbing that you cease to talk with your human companions. It means to release yourself from rational images of what something "means" and to be concerned only that it "is." And then to recognize that things exist only insofar as they can be related to other things. These relationships—fresh drops of moisture on top of rocks at a river crossing and a raven's distant voice—become patterns. The patterns are always in motion. Suddenly the pattern—which includes physical hunger, a memory of your family, and memories of the valley you are walking through, these particular plants and smells—takes in the caribou. There is a caribou standing in front of you. The release of the arrow or bullet is like a word spoken out loud. It occurs at the periphery of your concentration.

The mind we know in dreaming, a nonrational, nonlinear comprehension of events in which slips in time and space are normal, is, I believe, the conscious working mind of an aboriginal hunter. It is a frame of mind that redefines patience, endurance, and expectation.

The focus of a hunter in a hunting society was not killing animals but attending to the myriad relationships he understood bound him into the world he occupied with them. He tended to those duties carefully because he perceived in them everything he understood about survival. This does not mean, certainly, that every man did this, or that good men did not starve. Or that shamans whose duty it was to intercede with the forces that empowered these relationships weren't occasionally thinking of personal gain or subterfuge. It only means that most men understood how to behave.

A fundamental difference between our culture and Eskimo culture, which can be felt even today in certain situations, is that we have irrevocably separated ourselves from the world that animals occupy. We have turned all animals and elements of the natural world into objects. We manipulate them to serve the complicated ends of our destiny. Eskimos do not grasp this separation easily, and have difficulty imagining themselves entirely removed from the world of animals. For many of them, to make this separation is analogous to cutting oneself off from light or water. It is hard to imagine how to do it.

A second difference is that, because we have objectified animals, we are able to treat them impersonally. This means not only the animals that live around us but animals that live in distant lands. For Eskimos, most relationships with animals are local and personal. The animals one encounters are part of one's community, and one has obligations to them. A most confusing aspect of Western culture for Eskimos to grasp is our depersonalization of relationships with the human and animal members of our communities. And it is compounded, rather than simplified, by their attempting to learn how to objectify animals.

Eskimos do not maintain this intimacy with nature without paying a certain price. When I have thought about the ways in which they differ from people in my own culture, I have realized that they are more afraid than we are. On a day-to-day basis, they have more fear. Not of being dumped into cold water from an umiak, not a debilitating fear. They are afraid because they accept fully what is violent and tragic in nature. It is a fear tied to their knowledge that sudden, cataclysmic events are as much a part of life, of really living, as are the moments when one pauses to look at something beautiful. A Central Eskimo shaman named Aua, queried by Knud Rasmussen about Eskimo beliefs, answered, "We do not believe. We fear."

To extend these thoughts, it is wrong to think of hunting cultures like the Eskimo's as living in perfect harmony or balance with nature. Their regard for animals and their attentiveness to nuance in the landscape were not rigorous or complete enough to approach an idealized harmony. No one knew that much. No one would say they knew that much. They faced nature with fear, with *ilira* (nervous awe) and *kappia* (apprehension). And with enthusiasm. They accepted hunting as a way of life—its violence, too, though they did not seek that out. They were unsentimental, so much so that most outsiders thought them cruel, especially in their treatment of dogs. Nor were they innocent. There is murder and warfare and tribal vendetta in their history; and today, in the same villages I walked out of to hunt, are families shattered by alcohol, drugs, and ambition. While one cannot dismiss culpability in these things, any more than one can hold to romantic notions about hunting, it is good to recall what a *struggle* it is to live with dignity and understanding, with perspicacity or grace, in circumstances far better than these. And it is helpful to imagine how the forces of life must be construed by people who live in a world where swift and fatal violence, like *ivu,* the suddenly leaping shore ice, is inherent in the land. The land, in a certain, very real way, compels the minds of the people.

A good reason to travel with Eskimo hunters in modern times is that, beyond nettlesome details—foods that are not to one's liking, a loss of intellectual conversation, a consistent lack of formal planning—in spite of these things, one feels the constant presence of people who know something about surviving. At their best they are resilient, practical, and enthusiastic. They pay close attention in realms where they feel a capacity for understanding. They have a quality of *nuannaarpoq,* of taking extravagant pleasure in being alive; and they delight in finding it in other people. Facing as we do our various Armageddons, they are a good people to know.

In the time I was in the field with Eskimos I wondered at the basis for my admiration. I admired an awareness in the men of providing for others, and the soft tone of voice they used around bloodshed. I never thought I could understand, from their point of view, that moment of preternaturally heightened awareness, and the peril inherent in taking a life; but I accepted it out of respect for their seriousness toward it. In moments when I felt perplexed, that I was dealing with an order outside my own, I discovered and put to use a part of my own culture's wisdom, the formal divisions of Western philosophy—metaphysics, epistemology, ethics, aesthetics, and logic—which pose, in order, the following questions. What is real? What can we understand? How should we behave? What is beautiful? What are the patterns we can rely upon?

As I traveled, I would say to myself, What do my companions see where I see death? Is the sunlight beautiful to them, the way it sparkles on the water? Which for the Eskimo hunter are the patterns to be trusted? The patterns, I know, could be different from ones I imagined were before us. There could be other, remarkably different insights.

Those days on Ilingnorak Ridge, when I saw tundra grizzly tearing up the earth looking for ground squirrels, and watched wolves hunting, and horned lark sitting so resolutely on her nest, and caribou crossing the river and shaking off the spray like diamonds before the evening sun, I was satisfied only to watch. This was the great drift and pause of life. These were the arrangements that made the land ring with integrity. Somewhere downriver, I remembered, a scientist named Edward Sable had paused on a trek in 1947 to stare at a Folsom spear point, a perfectly fluted object of black chert resting on a sandstone ledge. People, moving over the land.

DISCUSSION QUESTIONS

1. In what ways do the Eskimo hunters differ from hunters in our culture? Why are these differences critical to our understanding of the Eskimo? How are these differences related to the Eskimo's sense of the land?

2. Lopez is asking us to see connections between the landscape and our imagination. What are some of these connections? Compare his view of the land with that of N. Scott Momaday and Gretel Ehrlich (see ''Magazines''). What do all of these writers have in common?

CLASSICS

Literature is news that stays news.

EZRA POUND

IN its popular sense, *classic* means something that remains in style. The word often comes up in talk about a particular cut of clothing, the movements of dancers and athletes, someone's features, the lines of a building or an automobile, and even the preparation of food. *Classic,* in such instances, describes certain qualities of craftsmanship, performance, or appearance that remain constant despite changes in fashion, taste, doctrine, or government. Unlike most of the ads, best-sellers, articles, and journalism you have read in previous sections of this book, the prose and poetry reprinted in the following pages represent the work of many writers who have been read continuously over the years, writers who have remained in style. A classic is durable; it is writing that stays in print.

Why do some works preserve a lively reputation for generations while others are forgotten by the end of a season? Surely it is not because the writers of what eventually become classics attend to different subjects than do the authors of even those best-sellers whose popularity does not endure very much beyond their arrival in paperback at local bookstores. Adventure and romance, love and death, individual freedom and social order, innocence and experience, success and failure are, for example, often themes of classics and best-sellers as well as, for that matter, most journalism and advertising. If what makes a work a classic is not simply the author's choice of material—all material is, strictly speaking, in the public domain—then the best place to find the reason for a work's continuing success is in the quality of its writing.

In general, our selections from American classics will provide you with more complicated uses of language than most of the other forms of writing you have encountered in earlier sections of this book. It should be added, however, that the authors of classics are not necessarily hostile to those other, less complicated forms of writing. If anything, they are probably more willing to incorporate the multiplicity of styles and voices surrounding them than are writers who must, because of a greater commercial investment, appeal to quite specific audiences. Journalists, for example, may be reluctant to record the interferences and intrusions they may have encountered in their attempted news coverage. (They have copy editors to satisfy and only a limited amount of newspaper space for their stories.) So too, authors of best-sellers may not want to, may not know how to, or may not even dare to risk unsettling their readers with sudden shifts in tone or point of view or subtle maneuvers into irony or parody.

From the philosophical manner of Henry David Thoreau to the Beat poetics of Allen Ginsberg, the writing collected here is meant to suggest the variety and complexity of classic American literature. It is literature whose authors, for the most part, have been receptive, at times competitively responsive, to whatever environment of language they chose to work in. Mark Twain, who told many good stories in his own lifetime, makes it clear that telling a story well is a performance of tone and nuance that ought to rival the most successful forms of contemporary entertainment. Twain wants his audience to delight, as he does, in the art of mimicry and parody. "How to Tell a Story" is much more than an enjoyable training manual for delivering effective jokes; it is also a fine critical statement reminding us that the art of reading well is also the art of listening attentively. John Updike in "A & P," James Thurber in "The Secret Life of Walter Mitty," Tillie Olsen in "I Stand Here Ironing," and Allen Ginsberg in "A Supermarket in California" expect (as Twain does) their audiences to be fully attuned to the ways their styles embody the nonliterary idioms and intonations of American advertising, popular music, and film.

Along with Mark Twain, such writers as Stephen Crane, Ernest Hemingway, and Norman Mailer are competitively aware of how the techniques and verbal formulations of journalism can be exploited and even parodied in their own efforts to render events distinctively. Having been reporters themselves, they have experienced firsthand the advantages and limitations of writing the kind of prose that newspapers consistently promote. For example, a comparison of Mailer's account with the newspaper report of the astronauts' walk on the moon will demonstrate what a major novelist considers to be the obligations of a literary consciousness contending with an event that is surrounded, if not dominated, by the machinery of news coverage. In Crane's "The Open Boat," we can observe how a writer transforms the raw data of a journalist scoop (see "Stephen Crane's Own Story" in "Press") into the complex arrangements of classic fiction.

It should be clear from the following selections that the writers of classics use language in the most demanding and selective ways possible. Theirs is a prose that requires its audience to have attained a more highly developed reading aptitude than that needed to respond to much of the writing appearing earlier in this book. A classic expects its readers to be more than simply literate. Readers of classics are obliged to engage in difficult, sometimes highly complicated verbal experiences and, at the same time, are encouraged in the act of reading to refer these verbal experiences to a wide network of accumulated literary responses. In fact, the writers of classic prose (whether it be fiction or nonfiction) very often imagine for themselves readers who take delight in having such demands made on them.

Few authors are more exacting in the demands their writing makes on their audience than William Faulkner. Take, for example, the following passage from *The Bear,* in which Faulkner describes the culmination of young Ike McCaslin's nearly obsessive, increasingly solitary search for the elusive, indomitable bear, Old Ben:

> Then he saw the bear. It did not emerge, appear: it was just there, immobile, fixed in the green and windless noon's hot dappling, not as big as he had dreamed it but as big as he had expected, bigger, dimensionless against the dappled obscurity, looking at him. Then it moved. It crossed the glade without haste, walking for an instant into the sun's full glare and out of it, and stopped again and looked back at him across one shoulder. Then it was gone. It didn't walk into the woods. It faded, sank back into the wilderness without motion as he had watched a fish, a huge old bass, sink back into the dark depths of its pool and vanish without even any movement of its fins.

Faulkner allows Ike his long-awaited confrontation with the bear only after the boy has willingly surrendered himself to the woods by relinquishing his gun, watch, and compass. Bereft of weapon and instruments, those "tainted" items of civilization, Ike can *know* the wilderness in ways that permit him to go further than even his mastery of the technique of woodmanship could take him. When Ike finally encounters Old Ben, it is because he has entered into a new relation with the woods, one that has superseded the boundaries set up by the rules and rituals of hunting and tracking.

As a factual account of a hunting incident, this passage is rather unremarkable, surely anticlimactic. Nothing much seems to happen. The boy sees the bear. The bear sees the boy. The bear disappears into the woods. There is no kill, no breathtaking capture or escape. Furthermore, the reader is given few of the details that might be anticipated in such an encounter. Nothing is told of the bear's size, color, or smell; there is none of the usual metaphorical approximations hunters like to make of an animal's brute power. What is perhaps even more surprising, the reader is told nothing at all about the boy's emotional response to the one moment he has trained and waited for through so many hunting seasons.

If the reader cannot easily picture this episode within the frame of a glossy photograph from *Field and Stream* or *True,* it is because Faulkner's writing resists the kind of imagination that would want to reduce the scene to one more clearly and conventionally focused. The total effect produced by the blurring of the bear and woods, the amorphous presence of the boy, the uncertainty of movement, and the confusing shifts of sunlight and shadow is not the result of a verbal or pictorial incompetence but, on the contrary, is the consequence of a deliberate and complex effort of intelligence. Faulkner's style demands that the reader participate in that complexity. The reliance on negatives ("It did not emerge . . . not as big . . . It didn't walk"), the sudden modification of syntax ("but as big as he had expected, bigger, dimensionless"), the struggle to find adequate verbs or adjectives ("emerge, appear . . . immobile, fixed . . . faded, sank"), the process of expansion ("a fish, a huge old bass"), and the apparently reluctant concessions to narrative sequence ("Then he saw the bear . . . Then it moved . . . Then it was gone.") force the reader into suspending temporarily his expectations of the dimensions of an experience and the conduct of sentences. The style, in effect, compels the reader to experience a dislocation and conversion analogous to those that made Ike McCaslin's initiation into the wilderness possible.

A writer's style attests to the quality of his perceptions. Though Faulkner's verbal expansiveness in *The Bear* may seem difficult, even discouragingly so, the demands he makes on his readers are not necessarily any greater than those of writers like Thoreau, Crane, Wright, or Hemingway whose difficulties may seem, at first, much less apparent. The writing in "Soldier's Home" certainly looks easy, but that does not mean the tale is a simple one. Hemingway's stylistic reticence, his self-conscious artistic control, is the consequence of a literary acuity that is perhaps only slightly less remarkable than Faulkner's. If the styles of writers like Hemingway and Faulkner are based on perceptions that happen to be intricate, even unsettling, that is only because each writer struggles to master in his own way the countless verbal options at his disposal. Such writing presupposes an energetic reader, one who is willing to work almost as hard at reading as the author worked at writing. The readers imagined by the writers of the selections that follow would not be intimidated by the kind of rigorous training that, according to Thoreau, they must undergo if they are to read proficiently:

> To read well, that is, to read books in a true spirit, is a noble exercise, and one that will task the reader more than any exercise which the customs of the day esteem. It requires a training such as the athletes underwent, the steady intention almost of the whole life to this object. Books must be read as deliberately and reservedly as they were written. ("Reading," from *Walden.*)

Thoreau's metaphor is an appropriate one. By comparing the exertion of reading to the exercise of athletics, Thoreau converts what is ordinarily regarded as an idle occasion into a tough and invigorating practice. To read well is to do something more than just be a spectator to what Robert Frost terms "the feat of words."

Throughout his literary career, Nathaniel Hawthorne (1804–64) was acutely conscious of his Puritan ancestors, one of whom presided at the infamous Salem witchcraft trials. After graduating from Bowdoin College in 1825, Hawthorne spent the next twelve years in relative seclusion at his home in Salem, researching and brooding over the chronicles and annals of New England local history that were to supply him with material for the sketches and tales he published continually in the popular periodicals of the day. In 1836, Hawthorne went to Boston, where he edited the American Magazine of Useful and Entertaining Knowledge. *Three years later he was offered a political appointment in the Boston Custom House, where he was able to support himself for a number of years while writing short stories and his first novel,* The Scarlet Letter (1850).*

First published in the New England Magazine *for May, 1835, "Wakefield" was later included in* Twice-Told Tales (1837).

In some old magazine or newspaper I recollect a story, told as truth, of a man—let us call him Wakefield—who absented himself for a long time from his wife. The fact, thus abstractedly stated, is not very uncommon, nor—without a proper distinction of circumstances—to be condemned either as naughty or nonsensical. Howbeit, this, though far from the most aggravated, is perhaps the strangest, instance on record, of marital delinquency; and, moreover, as remarkable a freak as may be found in the whole list of human oddities. The wedded couple lived in London. The man, under pretence of going a journey, took lodgings in the next street to his own house, and there, unheard of by his wife or friends, and without the shadow of a reason for such self-banishment, dwelt upwards of twenty years. During that period, he beheld his home every day, and frequently the forlorn Mrs. Wakefield. And after so great a gap in his matrimonial felicity—when his death was reckoned certain, his estate settled, his name dismissed from memory, and his wife, long, long ago, resigned to her autumnal widowhood—he entered the door one evening, quietly, as from a day's absence, and became a loving spouse till death.

This outline is all that I remember. But the incident, though of the purest originality, unexampled, and probably never to be repeated, is one, I think, which appeals to the generous sympathies of mankind. We know, each for himself, that none of us would perpetrate such a folly, yet feel as if some other might. To my own contemplations, at least, it has often recurred, always exciting wonder, but with a sense that the story must be true, and a conception of its hero's character. Whenever any subject so forcibly affects the mind, time is well spent in thinking of it. If the reader choose, let him do his own meditation; or if he prefer to ramble with me through the twenty years of Wakefield's vagary, I bid him welcome; trusting that there will be a pervading spirit and a moral, even should we fail to find them, done up neatly, and condensed into the final sentence. Thought has always its efficacy, and every striking incident its moral.

What sort of a man was Wakefield? We are free to shape out our own idea, and call it by his name. He was now in the meridian of life; his matrimonial affections, never violent, were sobered into a calm, habitual sentiment; of all husbands, he was likely to be the most constant, because a certain sluggishness would keep his heart at rest, wherever it might be placed. He was intellectual, but not actively so; his mind occupied itself in long and lazy musings, that ended to no purpose, or had not vigor to attain it; his thoughts were seldom so energetic as to seize hold of words. Imagination, in the proper meaning of the term, made no part of Wakefield's gifts. With a cold but not depraved nor wandering heart, and a mind never feverish with riotous thoughts, nor perplexed with originality, who could have anticipated that our friend would entitle himself to a foremost place among the doers of eccentric deeds? Had his acquaintances been asked, who was the man in London the surest to perform nothing today which should be remembered on the morrow, they would have thought of Wakefield. Only the wife of his bosom might have hesitated. She, without having analyzed his character, was partly aware of a quiet selfishness, that had rusted into his inactive mind; of a peculiar sort of vanity, the most uneasy attribute about him; of a disposition to craft, which had seldom produced more positive effects than the keeping of petty secrets, hardly worth revealing; and, lastly, of what she called a little strangeness, sometimes, in the good man. This latter quality is indefinable, and perhaps non-existent.

Let us now imagine Wakefield bidding adieu to his wife. It is the dusk of an October evening. His equipment is a drab great-coat, a hat covered with an oilcloth, top-boots, an umbrella in one hand and a small port-manteau in the other. He has informed Mrs. Wakefield that he is to take the night coach into the country. She would fain inquire the length of his journey, its object, and the probable time of his return; but, indulgent to his harmless love of mystery, interrogates him only by a look. He tells her not to expect him positively by the return coach, nor to be alarmed should he tarry three or four days; but, at all events, to look for him at supper on Friday evening. Wakefield himself, be it considered, has no suspicion of what is before him. He holds out his hand, she gives her own, and meets his parting kiss in the matter-of-course way of a ten years' matrimony; and forth goes the middle-aged Mr. Wakefield, almost resolved to perplex his good lady by a whole week's absence. After the door has closed behind him, she perceives it thrust partly open, and a vision of her husband's face, through the aperture, smiling on her, and gone in a moment. For the time, this little incident is dismissed without a thought. But, long afterwards, when she has been more years a widow than a wife, that smile recurs, and flickers across all her reminiscences of Wakefield's visage. In her many musings, she surrounds the original smile with a multitude of fantasies, which make it strange and awful: as, for instance, if she imagines him in a coffin, that parting look is frozen on his pale features; or, if she dreams of him in heaven, still his blessed spirit wears a quiet and crafty smile. Yet, for its sake, when all others have given him up for dead, she sometimes doubts whether she is a widow.

But our business is with the husband. We must hurry after him along the street, ere he lose his individuality, and melt into the great mass of London life. It would be vain searching for him there. Let us follow close at his heels, therefore, until, after several superfluous turns and doublings, we find him comfortably established by the fireside of a small apartment, previously bespoken. He is in the next street to his own, and at his journey's end. He can scarcely trust his good fortune, in having got thither unperceived—recollecting that, at one time, he was delayed by the throng, in the very focus of a lighted lantern; and, again, there were footsteps that seemed to tread behind his own, distinct from the multitudinous tramp around him; and, anon, he heard a voice shouting afar, and fancied that it called his name. Doubtless, a dozen busybodies had been watching him, and told his wife the whole affair. Poor Wakefield! Little knowest thou thine own insignificance in this great world! No mortal eye but mine has traced thee. Go quietly to thy bed, foolish man; and, on the morrow, if thou wilt be wise, get thee home to good Mrs. Wakefield, and tell her the truth. Remove not thyself, even for a little week, from thy place in her chaste bosom. Were she, for a single moment, to deem thee dead, or lost, or lastingly divided from her, thou wouldst be woefully conscious of a change in thy true wife forever after. It is perilous to make a chasm in human affections; not that they gape so long and wide—but so quickly close again!

Almost repenting of his frolic, or whatever it may be termed, Wakefield lies down betimes, and starting from his first nap, spreads forth his arms into the wide and solitary waste of the unaccustomed bed. ''No,''—thinks he, gathering the bedclothes about him—''I will not sleep alone another night.''

In the morning he rises earlier than usual, and sets himself to consider what he really means to do. Such are his loose and rambling modes of thought that he has taken this very singular step with the consciousness of a purpose, indeed, but without being able to define it sufficiently for his own contemplation. The vagueness of the project, and the convulsive effort with which he plunges into the execution of it, are equally characteristic of a feeble-minded man. Wakefield sifts his ideas, however, as minutely as he may, and finds himself curious to know the progress of matters at home—how his exemplary wife will endure her widowhood of a week; and, briefly, how the little sphere of creatures and circumstances, in which he was a central object, will be affected by his removal. A morbid vanity, therefore, lies nearest the bottom of the affair. But, how is he to attain his ends? Not, certainly, by keeping close in this comfortable lodging, where, though he slept and awoke in the next street to his home, he is as effectually abroad as if the stage-coach had been whirling him away all night. Yet, should he reappear, the whole project is knocked in the head. His poor brains being hopelessly puzzled with this dilemma, he at length ventures out, partly resolving to cross the head of the street, and send one hasty glance towards his forsaken domicile. Habit—for he is a man of habits—takes him by the hand, and guides him, wholly unaware, to his own door, where, just at the critical moment, he is aroused by the scraping of his foot upon the step. Wakefield! whither are you going?

At that instant his fate was turning on the pivot. Little dreaming of the doom to which his first backward step devotes him, he hurries away, breathless with agitation hitherto unfelt, and hardly dares turn his head at the distant corner. Can it be that nobody caught sight of him? Will not the whole household—the decent Mrs. Wakefield, the smart maid servant, and the dirty little footboy—raise a hue and cry, through London streets, in pursuit of their fugitive lord and master? Wonderful escape! He gathers courage to pause and look homeward, but is perplexed with a sense of change about the familiar edifice, such as affects us all, when, after a separation of months or years, we again see some hill or lake, or work of art, with which we were friends of old. In ordinary cases, this indescribable impression is caused by the comparison and contrast between our imperfect reminiscences and the reality. In Wakefield, the magic of a single night has wrought a similar transformation, because, in that brief period, a great moral change has been effected. But this is a secret from himself. Before leaving the spot, he catches a far and momentary glimpse of his wife, passing athwart the front window, with her face turned towards the head of the street. The crafty nincompoop takes to his heels, scared with the idea that, among a thousand such atoms of mortality, her eye must have detected him. Right glad is his heart, though his brain be somewhat dizzy, when he finds himself by the coal fire of his lodgings.

So much for the commencement of this long whimwham. After the initial conception, and the stirring up of the man's sluggish temperament to put it in practice, the whole matter evolves itself in a natural train. We may suppose him, as the result of deep deliberation, buying a new wig, of reddish hair, and selecting sundry garments, in a fashion unlike his customary suit of brown, from a Jew's old-clothes bag. It is accomplished. Wakefield is another man. The new system being now established, a retrograde movement to the old would be almost as difficult as the step that placed him in his unparalleled position. Furthermore, he is rendered obstinate by a sulkiness occasionally incident to his temper, and brought on at present by the inadequate sensation which he conceives to have been produced in the bosom of Mrs. Wakefield. He will not go back until she be frightened half to death. Well; twice or thrice has she passed before his sight, each time with a heavier step, a paler cheek, and more anxious brow; and in the third week of his non-appearance he detects a portent of evil entering the house, in the guise of an apothecary. Next day the knocker is muffled. Towards nightfall comes the chariot of a physician, and deposits its big-wigged and solemn burden at Wakefield's door, whence, after a quarter of an hour's visit, he emerges, perchance the herald of a funeral. Dear woman! Will she die? By this time, Wakefield is excited to something like energy of feeling, but still lingers away from his wife's bedside, pleading with his conscience that she must not be disturbed at such a juncture. If aught else restrains him, he does not know it. In the course of a few weeks she gradually recovers; the crisis is over; her heart is sad, perhaps, but quiet; and, let him return soon or late, it will never be feverish for him again. Such ideas glimmer through the midst of Wakefield's mind, and render him indistinctly conscious that an almost impassable gulf divides his hired apartment from his former home. "It is but in the next street!" he sometimes says. Fool! it is in another world. Hitherto, he has put off his return from one particular day to another; henceforward, he leaves the precise time undetermined. Not tomorrow—probably next week—pretty soon. Poor man! The dead have nearly as much chance of revisiting their earthly homes as the self-banished Wakefield.

Would that I had a folio to write, instead of an article of a dozen pages! Then might I exemplify how an influence beyond our control lays its strong hand on every deed which we do, and weaves its consequences into an iron tissue of necessity. Wakefield is spell-bound. We must leave him, for ten years or so, to haunt around his house, without once crossing the threshold, and to be faithful to his wife, with all the affection of which his heart is capable, while he is slowly fading out of hers. Long since, it must be remarked, he had lost the perception of singularity in his conduct.

Now for a scene! Amid the throng of a London street we distinguish a man, now waxing elderly, with few characteristics to attract careless observers, yet bearing, in his whole aspect, the handwriting of no common fate, for such as have the skill to read it. He is meagre; his low and narrow forehead is deeply wrinkled; his eyes, small and lustreless, sometimes wander apprehensively about him, but oftener seem to look inward. He bends his head, and moves with an indescribable obliquity of gait, as if unwilling to display his full front to the world. Watch him long enough to see what we have described, and you will allow that circumstances—which often produce remarkable men from nature's ordinary handiwork—have produced one such here. Next, leaving him to sidle along the footwalk, cast your eyes in the opposite direction, where a portly female, considerably in the wane of life, with a prayer-book in her hand, is proceeding to yonder church. She has the placid mien of settled widowhood. Her regrets have either died away, or have become so essential to her heart, that they would be poorly exchanged for joy. Just as the lean man and well-conditioned woman are passing, a slight obstruction occurs, and brings these two figures directly in contact. Their hands touch; the pressure of the crowd forces her bosom against his shoulder; they stand, face to face, staring into each other's eyes. After a ten years' separation, thus Wakefield meets his wife!

The throng eddies away, and carries them asunder. The sober widow, resuming her former pace, proceeds to church, but pauses in the portal, and throws a perplexed glance along the street. She passes in, however, opening her prayer-book as she goes. And the man! with so wild a face that busy and selfish London stands to gaze after him, he hurries to his lodgings, bolts the door, and throws himself upon the bed. The latent feelings of years break out; his feeble mind acquires a brief energy from their strength; all the miserable strangeness of his life is revealed to him at a glance: and he cries out, passionately, "Wakefield! Wakefield! You are mad!"

Perhaps he was so. The singularity of his situation must have so moulded him to himself, that, considered in regard to his fellow-creatures and the business of life, he could not be said to possess his right mind. He had contrived, or rather he had happened, to dissever himself from the world—to vanish—to give up his place and privileges with living men, without being admitted among the dead. The life of a hermit is nowise parallel to his. He was in the bustle of the city, as of old; but the crowd swept by and saw him not; he was, we may figuratively say, always beside his wife and at his hearth, yet must never feel the warmth of the one nor the affection of the other. It was Wakefield's unprecedented fate to retain his original share of human sympathies, and to be still involved in human interests, while he had lost his reciprocal influence on them. It would be a most curious speculation to trace out the effect of such circumstances on his heart and intellect, separately, and in unison. Yet, changed as he was, he would seldom be conscious of it, but deem himself the same man as ever; glimpses of the truth, indeed, would come, but only for the moment; and still he would keep saying, "I shall soon go back!"—nor reflect that he had been saying so for twenty years.

I conceive, also, that these twenty years would appear, in the retrospect, scarcely longer than the week to which Wakefield had at first limited his absence. He would look on the affair as no more than an interlude in the main business of his life. When, after a little while more, he should deem it time to reënter his parlor, his wife would clap her hands for joy, on beholding the middle-aged Mr. Wakefield. Alas, what a mistake! Would Time but await the close of our favorite follies, we should be young men, all of us, and till Doomsday.

One evening, in the twentieth year since he vanished, Wakefield is taking his customary walk towards the dwelling which he still calls his own. It is a gusty night of autumn, with frequent showers that patter down upon the pavement, and are gone before a man can put up his umbrella. Pausing near the house, Wakefield discerns, through the parlor windows of the second floor, the red glow and the glimmer and fitful flash of a comfortable fire. On the ceiling appears a grotesque shadow of good Mrs. Wakefield. The cap, the nose and chin, and the broad waist, form an admirable caricature, which dances, moreover, with the up-flickering and down-sinking blaze, almost too merrily for the shade of an elderly widow. At this instant a shower chances to fall, and is driven, by the unmannerly gust, full into Wakefield's face and bosom. He is quite penetrated with its autumnal chill. Shall he stand, wet and shivering here, when his own hearth has a good fire to warm him, and his own wife will run to fetch the gray coat and small-clothes, which, doubtless, she has kept carefully in the closet of their bed chamber? No! Wakefield is no such fool. He ascends the steps—heavily!—for twenty years have stiffened his legs since he came down—but he knows it not. Stay, Wakefield! Would you go to the sole home that is left you? Then step into your grave! The door opens. As he passes in, we have a parting glimpse of his visage, and recognize the crafty smile, which was the precursor of the little joke that he has ever since been playing off at his wife's expense. How unmercifully has he quizzed the poor woman! Well, a good night's rest to Wakefield!

This happy event—supposing it to be such—could only have occurred at an unpremeditated moment. We will not follow our friend across the threshold. He has left us much food for thought, a portion of which shall lend its wisdom to a moral, and be shaped into a figure. Amid the seeming confusion of our mysterious world, individuals are so nicely adjusted to a system, and systems to one another and to a whole, that, by stepping aside for a moment, a man exposes himself to a fearful risk of losing his place forever. Like Wakefield, he may become, as it were, the Outcast of the Universe.

*Although Henry David Thoreau participated very deeply in American political
and cultural life, his name has become synonymous with the archetypal voluntary
exile who rejects a crass, materialistic world in favor of a rugged, self-reliant outdoor existence and a career as an amateur naturalist. The image is partly
true: Thoreau consistently endorses a simple, independent, organic life. But it is
important to remember that Thoreau was also an outspoken abolitionist, a defender of John Brown even after the bloody raid on Harper's Ferry, and a conscientious dissenter who devised a highly influential philosophy of civil disobedi-
ence.*

*Born in Concord, Massachusetts, son of a pencil manufacturer, Thoreau grad-
uated from Harvard having mastered Greek in 1837. He was also a master of
many trades, though all his life he worked only sporadically—at chores, at surveying, at tutoring, at his father's shop, at lecturing, at odd jobs. He never
made a good living, although he apparently lived a good life. Only two of his
books were published in his lifetime:* A Week on the Concord and Merrimack
Rivers *(1849) and* Walden *(1854). He never married; he left parties early; he
seldom traveled beyond Concord. He died of tuberculosis, a disappointment to
his family and friends, when he was forty-four.*

*At a time in American history when thousands voluntarily exiled themselves in
tiny cabins on the slopes of western mountains to search for gold, Thoreau
searched for a different kind of wealth along the gentle edges of a small Massachusetts pond. The book he wrote describing his twenty-six-month retreat has
long been considered a classic account of a peculiarly American consciousness.
The following section, "Where I Lived, and What I Lived For," is an excerpt from
the second chapter of* Walden.

WHERE I LIVED, AND WHAT I LIVED FOR

I went to the woods because I wished to live deliberately, to front only the essential facts of life, and see if I could not learn what it had to teach, and not, when
I came to die, discover that I had not lived. I did not wish to live what was not
life, living is so dear; nor did I wish to practise resignation, unless it was quite
necessary. I wanted to live deep and suck out all the marrow of life, to live so
sturdily and Spartan-like as to put to rout all that was not life, to cut a broad swath
and shave close, to drive life into a corner, and reduce it to its lowest terms, and,
if it proved to be mean, why then to get the whole and genuine meanness of it,
and publish its meanness to the world; or if it were sublime, to know it by experience, and be able to give a true account of it in my next excursion. For most men,
it appears to me, are in a strange uncertainty about it, whether it is of the devil or
of God, and have *somewhat hastily* concluded that it is the chief end of man here
to "glorify God and enjoy him forever."

Still we live meanly, like ants; though the fable tells us that we were long ago
changed into men; like pygmies we fight with cranes; it is error upon error, and
clout upon clout, and our best virtue has for its occasion a superfluous and evitable
wretchedness. Our life is frittered away by detail. An honest man has hardly need
to count more than his ten fingers, or in extreme cases he may add his ten toes,
and lump the rest. Simplicity, simplicity, simplicity! I say, let your affairs be as
two or three, and not a hundred or a thousand; instead of a million count half a

dozen, and keep your accounts on your thumb-nail. In the midst of this chopping sea of civilized life, such are the clouds and storms and quicksands and thousand-and-one items to be allowed for, that a man has to live, if he would not founder and go to the bottom and not make his port at all, by dead reckoning, and he must be a great calculator indeed who succeeds. Simplify, simplify. Instead of three meals a day, if it be necessary eat but one; instead of a hundred dishes, five; and reduce other things in proportion. Our life is like a German Confederacy, made up of petty states, with its boundary forever fluctuating, so that even a German cannot tell you how it is bounded at any moment. The nation itself, with all its so-called internal improvements, which, by the way, are all external and superficial, is just such an unwieldy and overgrown establishment, cluttered with furniture and tripped up by its own traps, ruined by luxury and heedless expense, by want of calculation and a worthy aim, as the million households in the land· and the only cure for it, as for them, is in a rigid economy, a stern and more than Spartan simplicity of life and elevation of purpose. It lives too fast. Men think that it is essential that the *Nation* have commerce, and export ice, and talk through a telegraph, and ride thirty miles an hour, without a doubt, whether *they* do or not; but whether we should live like baboons or like men, is a little uncertain. If we do not get out sleepers, and forge rails, and devote days and nights to the work, but go to tinkering upon our *lives* to improve *them,* who will build railroads? And if railroads are not built, how shall we get to Heaven in season? But if we stay at home and mind our business, who will want railroads? We do not ride on the railroad; it rides upon us. Did you ever think what those sleepers are that underlie the railroad? Each one is a man, an Irishman, or a Yankee man. The rails are laid on them, and they are covered with sand, and the cars run smoothly over them. They are sound sleepers, I assure you. And every few years a new lot is laid down and run over; so that, if some have the pleasure of riding on a rail, others have the misfortune to be ridden upon. And when they run over a man that is walking in his sleep, a supernumerary sleeper in the wrong position, and wake him up, they suddenly stop the cars, and make a hue and cry about it as if this were an exception. I am glad to know that it takes a gang of men for every five miles to keep the sleepers down and level in their beds as it is, for this is a sign that they may sometime get up again.

Why should we live with such hurry and waste of life? We are determined to be starved before we are hungry. Men say that a stitch in time saves nine, and so they take a thousand stitches to-day to save nine tomorrow. As for *work,* we haven't any of any consequence. We have the Saint Vitus' dance, and cannot possibly keep our heads still. If I should only give a few pulls at the parish bell-rope, as for a fire, that is, without setting the bell, there is hardly a man on his farm in the outskirts of Concord, notwithstanding that press of engagements which was his excuse so many times this morning, nor a boy, nor a woman, I might almost say, but would forsake all and follow that sound, not mainly to save property from the flames, but, if we will confess the truth, much more to see it burn, since burn it must, and we, be it known, did not set it on fire,—or to see it put out, and have a hand in it, if that is done as handsomely; yes, even if it were the parish church itself. Hardly a man takes a half-hour's nap after dinner, but when he wakes he holds up his head and asks, "What's the news?" as if the rest of mankind had stood his sentinels. Some give directions to be waked every half-hour, doubtless for no other purpose; and then, to pay for it, they tell what they have dreamed. After a night's sleep the news is as indispensable as the breakfast. "Pray tell me anything new that has happened to a man anywhere on this globe,"—and he reads it over his coffee and rolls, that a man has had his eyes gouged out this morning on the Wachito River; never dreaming the while that he lives in the dark unfathomed mammoth cave of this world, and has but the rudiment of an eye himself.

For my part, I could easily do without the post-office. I think that there are very few important communications made through it. To speak critically, I never received more than one or two letters in my life—I wrote this some years ago—that were worth the postage. The penny-post is, commonly, an institution through which you seriously offer a man that penny for his thoughts which is so often safely offered in jest. And I am sure that I never read any memorable news in a newspaper. If we read of one man robbed, or murdered, or killed by accident, or one house burned, or one vessel wrecked, or one steamboat blown up, or one cow run over on the Western Railroad, or one mad dog killed, or one lot of grasshoppers in the winter,—we never need read of another. One is enough. If you are acquainted with the principle, what do you care for a myriad instances and applications? To a philosopher all *news*, as it is called, is gossip and they who edit and read it are old women over their tea. Yet not a few are greedy after this gossip. There was such a rush, as I hear, the other day at one of the offices to learn the foreign news by the last arrival, that several large squares of plate glass belonging to the establishment were broken by the pressure,—news which I seriously think a ready wit might write a twelvemonth, or twelve years, beforehand with sufficient accuracy. As for Spain, for instance, if you know how to throw in Don Carlos and the Infanta, and Don Pedro and Seville and Granada, from time to time in the right proportions,—they may have changed the names a little since I saw the papers,—and serve up a bull-fight when other entertainments fail, it will be true to the letter, and give us as good an idea of the exact state or ruin of things in Spain as the most succinct and lucid reports under this head in the newspapers: and as for England, almost the last significant scrap of news from that quarter was the revolution of 1649; and if you have learned the history of her crops for an average year, you never need attend to that thing again, unless your speculations are of a merely pecuniary character. If one may judge who rarely looks into the newspapers, nothing new does ever happen in foreign parts, a French revolution not excepted.

What news! how much more important to know what that is which was never old! "Kieou-he-yu (great dignitary of the state of Wei) sent a man to Khoung-tseu to know his news. Khoung-tseu caused the messenger to be seated near him, and questioned him in these terms: What is your master doing? The messenger answered with respect: My master desires to diminish the number of his faults, but he cannot come to the end of them. The messenger being gone, the philosopher remarked: What a worthy messenger! What a worthy messenger!'' The preacher, instead of vexing the ears of drowsy farmers on their day of rest at the end of the week,—for Sunday is the fit conclusion of an ill-spent week, and not the fresh and brave beginning of a new one,—with this one other draggle-tail of a sermon, should shout with thundering voice, "Pause! Avast! Why so seeming fast, but deadly slow?''

Shams and delusions are esteemed for soundest truths, while reality is fabulous. If men would steadily observe realities only, and not allow themselves to be deluded, life, to compare it with such things as we know, would be like a fairy tale and the Arabian Nights' Entertainments. If we respected only what is inevitable and has a right to be, music and poetry would resound along the streets. When we are unhurried and wise, we perceive that only great and worthy things have any permanent and absolute existence, that petty fears and petty pleasures are but the shadow of the reality. This is always exhilarating and sublime. By closing the eyes and slumbering, and consenting to be deceived by shows, men establish and confirm their daily life of routine and habit everywhere, which still is built on purely illusory foundations. Children, who play life, discern its true law and relations more clearly than men, who fail to live it worthily, but who think that they are wiser by experience, that is, by failure. I have read in a Hindoo book, that "there was a king's son, who, being expelled in infancy from his native city, was brought up by a forester, and, growing up to maturity in that state, imagined himself to belong to the barbarous race with which he lived. One of his father's ministers having discovered him, revealed to him what he was, and the misconception of his character was removed, and he knew himself to be a prince. So soul," continues the Hindoo philosopher, "from the circumstances in which it is placed, mistakes its own character, until the truth is revealed to it by some holy teacher, and then it knows itself to be *Brahme*." I perceive that we inhabitants of New England live this mean life that we do because our vision does not penetrate the surface of things. We think that this *is* which *appears* to be. If a man should walk through this town and see only the reality, where, think you, would the "Mill-dam" go to? If he should give us an account of the realities he beheld there, we should not recognize the place in his description. Look at a meeting-house, or a court-house, or a jail, or a shop, or a dwelling-house, and say what that thing really is before a true gaze, and they would all go to pieces in your account of them Men esteem truth remote, in the outskirts of the system, behind the farthest star, before Adam and after the last man. In eternity there is indeed something true and sublime. But all these times and places and occasions are now and here. God himself culminates in the present moment, and will never be more divine in the lapse of all the ages. And we are enabled to apprehend at all what is sublime and noble only by the perpetual instilling and drenching of the reality that surrounds us. The universe constantly and obediently answers to our conceptions; whether we travel fast or slow, the track is laid for us. Let us spend our lives in conceiving then. The poet or the artist never yet had so fair and noble a design but some of his posterity at least could accomplish it.

Let us spend one day as deliberately as Nature, and not be thrown off the track by every nutshell and mosquito's wing that falls on the rails. Let us rise early and fast, or break fast, gently and without perturbation; let company come and let company go, let the bells ring and the children cry,—determined to make a day of it. Why should we knock under and go with the stream? Let us not be upset and overwhelmed in that terrible rapid and whirlpool called a dinner, situated in the meridian shallows. Weather this danger and you are safe, for the rest of the way is down hill. With unrelaxed nerves, with morning vigor, sail by it, looking another way, tied to the mast like Ulysses. If the engine whistles, let it whistle till it is hoarse for its pains. If the bell rings, why should we run? We will consider what kind of music they are like. Let us settle ourselves, and work and wedge our feet downward through the mud and slush of opinion, and prejudice, and tradition, and delusion, and appearance, that alluvion which covers the globe, through Paris and London, through New York and Boston and Concord, through Church and State, through poetry and philosophy and religion, till we come to a hard bottom and rocks in place, which we can call *reality,* and say, This is, and no mistake; and then begin, having a *point d'appui,* below freshet and frost and fire, a place where you might found a wall or a state, or set a lamp-post safely, or perhaps a gauge, not a Nilometer, that future ages might know how deep a freshet of shams and appearances had gathered from time to time. If you stand right fronting and face to face to a fact, you will see the sun glimmer on both its surfaces, as if it were a cimeter, and feel its sweet edge dividing you through the heart and marrow, and so you will happily conclude your mortal career. Be it life or death we crave only reality. If we are really dying, let us hear the rattle in our throats and feel cold in the extremities; if we are alive, let us go about our business.

Time is but the stream I go a-fishing in. I drink at it; but while I drink I see the sandy bottom and detect how shallow it is. Its thin current slides away, but eternity remains. I would drink deeper; fish in the sky, whose bottom is pebbly with stars. I cannot count one. I know not the first letter of the alphabet. I have always been regretting that I was not as wise as the day I was born. The intellect is a cleaver; it discerns and rifts its way into the secret of things. I do not wish to be any more busy with my hands than is necessary. My head is hands and feet. I feel all my best faculties concentrated in it. My instinct tells me that my head is an organ for burrowing, as some creatures use their snout and fore paws, and with it I would mine and burrow my way through these hills. I think that the richest vein is somewhere hereabouts; so by the divining-rod and thin rising vapors I judge; and here I will begin to mine.

DISCUSSION QUESTIONS

1. Compare Thoreau's description of nature with N. Scott Momaday's "A First American Views His Land" (see "Magazines"). What perspective does each writer adopt in order to describe the natural world? What attitude does each express toward nature?

2. Which author attends more carefully to details in describing nature? Which uses the most figurative language? To what effect? Does each writer draw on the same kinds of experience? Explain.

3. In which description of nature does the personal life of the speaker play the most prominent role? Explain. Which writer goes to the natural world to seek adventure? To search for self-improvement? To enjoy an idyllic experience?

4. What are the reasons for each writer's excursion into the natural world? Do you find any of these unconvincing? For which writer is nature most associated with political controversy?

Emily Dickinson / Success Is Counted Sweetest   ca. 1859

Born in Amherst, Massachusetts, in 1830, Emily Dickinson remained within the confines of her father's house in that small conservative village for most of her life. Her poems are marked by an acute awareness of psychological states and physical sensations as much as by their brilliant images and melodic blending of assonant and dissonant sounds. Only seven of Dickinson's many poems appeared in print before she died in 1886.

Success is counted sweetest
By those who ne'er succeed.
To comprehend a nectar
Requires sorest need.

Not one of all the purple Host   5
Who took the Flag to-day
Can tell the definition,
So clear, of Victory,

As he defeated—dying—
On whose forbidden ear   10
The distant strains of triumph
Burst agonized and clear!

Emily Dickinson / I Like to See It Lap the Miles   ca. 1862

I like to see it lap the Miles—
And lick the Valleys up—
And stop to feed itself at Tanks
And then—prodigious step

Around a Pile of Mountains—
And supercilious peer
In Shanties—by the sides of Roads—
And then a Quarry pare

To fit its Ribs
And crawl between   10
Complaining all the while
In horrid—hooting stanza—
Then chase itself down Hill—

And neigh like Boanerges[1]—
Then—punctual as a Star
Stop—docile and omnipotent
At its own stable door—

Emily Dickinson / Because I Could Not Stop for Death   ca. 1863

Because I could not stop for Death—
He kindly stopped for me—
The Carriage held but just Ourselves—
And Immortality.

We slowly drove—He knew no haste
And I had put away
My labor and my leisure too,
For His Civility—

We passed the School, where Children strove
At Recess—in the Ring—   10
We passed the Fields of Gazing Grain—
We passed the Setting Sun—

Or rather—He passed Us—
The Dews drew quivering and chill—
For only Gossamer, my Gown—
My Tippet—only Tulle—

We paused before a House that seemed
A Swelling of the Ground—

1. In Hebrew, "sons of thunder," used to describe loud-voiced ministers and orators.

The Roof was scarcely visible—
The Cornice—in the Ground—   20

Since then—'tis Centuries—and yet
Feels shorter than the Day
I first surmised the Horses' Heads
Were toward Eternity—

Mark Twain / *Old Times on the Mississippi*   1875

> *Samuel Langhorne Clemens (Mark Twain), like many prominent American nov-*
> *elists, began his writing career as a journalist. He was born along the Missis-*
> *sippi River in Florida, Missouri, in 1835, and throughout his life that great*
> *river remained a vital presence. After briefly working on the Mississippi as a*
> *riverboat pilot and mining for silver in Nevada, Twain felt his energies would*
> *be better spent writing for newspapers. He learned early how to combine skill-*
> *fully the official prose of news reporting with the folksy language of tall tales,*
> *and his work in this humorous vein began to attract literary attention. He trav-*
> *eled to Hawaii, then to the Middle East, and later turned these experiences into*
> *parodies of the then popular conventional guidebooks. In 1876 he wrote* The
> Adventures of Tom Sawyer, *a best-selling nostalgic glance at his Missouri boy-*
> *hood, and in 1885 he brought out his masterpiece.* The Adventures of Huckle-
> berry Finn, *the book Ernest Hemingway claimed marked the origins of "all*
> *modern American literature."*
>
> *Twain's later career, though productive, was interrupted by a series of futile*
> *business ventures (he invested heavily in an aborted typesetting invention) and*
> *personal tragedies. The tone of much of his later work hinges on his own pessi-*
> *mistic answers to the question posed in one of his final essays, "What Is Man?"*
>
> Old Times on the Mississippi *was originally written as a series for* The At-
> lantic Monthly *and ran through seven installments in 1875.*
>
> *In "How to Tell a Story" (1897), Twain, by then a distinguished novelist and*
> *man of letters, explains why effective narrative styles need to be rooted in an*
> *oral tradition.*

When I was a boy, there was but one permanent ambition among my comrades in
our village[1] on the west bank of the Mississippi River. That was, to be a steamboatman. We had transient ambitions of other sorts, but they were only transient.
When a circus came and went, it left us all burning to become clowns; the first
negro minstrel show that came to our section left us all suffering to try that kind
of life; now and then we had a hope that if we lived and were good, God would
permit us to be pirates. These ambitions faded out, each in its turn; but the ambitions to be a steamboatman always remained.

Once a day a cheap, gaudy packet arrived upward from St. Louis, and another
downward from Keokuk. Before these events had transpired, the day was glorious
with expectancy; after they had transpired, the day was a dead and empty thing.
Not only the boys, but the whole village, felt this. After all these years I can
picture that old time to myself now, just as it was then: the white town drowsing

---

1. Hannibal, Missouri.

in the sunshine of a summer's morning; the streets empty, or pretty nearly so; one or two clerks sitting in front of the Water Street stores, with their splint-bottomed chairs tilted back against the wall, chins on breasts, hats slouched over their faces, asleep—with shingle-shavings enough around to show what broke them down; a sow and a litter of pigs loafing along the sidewalk, doing a good business in water-melon rinds and seeds; two or three lonely little freight piles scattered about the "levee"; a pile of "skids" on the slope of the stone-paved wharf, and the fragrant town drunkard asleep in the shadow of them; two or three wood flats at the head of the wharf, but nobody to listen to the peaceful lapping of the wavelets against them; the great Mississippi, the majestic, the magnificent Mississippi, rolling its mile-wide tide along, shining in the sun; the dense forest away on the other side; the "point" above the town, and the "point" below, bounding the river-glimpse and turning it into a sort of sea, and withal a very still and brilliant and lonely one. Presently a film of dark smoke appears above one of those remote "points"; instantly a negro drayman, famous for his quick eye and prodigious voice, lifts up the cry, "S-t-e-a-m-boat a-comin!" and the scene changes! The town drunkard stirs, the clerks wake up, a furious clatter of drays follows, every house and store pours out a human contribution, and all in a twinkling the dead town is alive and moving. Drays, carts, men, boys, all go hurrying from many quarters to a com-mon centre, the wharf. Assembled there, the people fasten their eyes upon the coming boat as upon a wonder they are seeing for the first time. And the boat *is* rather a handsome sight, too. She is long and sharp and trim and pretty; she has two tall, fancy-topped chimneys, with a gilded device of some kind swung be-tween them; a fanciful pilot-house, all glass and "gingerbread," perched on top of the "texas" deck behind them; the paddle-boxes are gorgeous with a picture or with gilded rays above the boat's name; the boiler deck, the hurricane deck, and the texas deck are fenced and ornamented with clean white railings; there is a flag gallantly flying from the jack-staff; the furnace doors are open and the fires glaring bravely; the upper decks are black with passengers; the captain stands by the big bell, calm, imposing, the envy of all; great volumes of the blackest smoke are rolling and tumbling out of the chimneys—a husbanded grandeur created with a bit of pitch pine just before arriving at a town; the crew are grouped on the forecastle; the broad stage is run far out over the port bow, and an envied deck-hand stands picturesquely on the end of it with a coil of rope in his hand; the pent steam is screaming through the gauge-cocks; the captain lifts his hand, a bell rings, the wheels stop; then they turn back, churning the water to foam, and the steamer is at rest. Then such a scramble as there is to get aboard, and to get ashore, and to take in freight and to discharge freight, all at once and the same time; and such a yelling and cursing as the mates facilitate it all with! Ten minutes later the steamer is under way again, with no flag on the jack-staff and no black smoke issuing from the chimneys. After ten more minutes the town is dead again, and the town drunkard asleep by the skids once more.

My father was a justice of the peace, and I supposed he possessed the power of life and death over all men and could hang anybody that offended him. This was distinction enough for me as a general thing; but the desire to be a steam-boatman kept intruding, nevertheless. I first wanted to be a cabin-boy, so that I could come out with a white apron on and shake a table-cloth over the side, where all my old comrades could see me; later I thought I would rather be the deck-hand who stood on the end of the stageplank with the coil of rope in his hand, because he was particularly conspicuous. But these were only daydreams—they were too heavenly to be contemplated as real possibilities. By and by one of our boys went away. He was not heard of for a long time. At last he turned up as apprentice engineer or "striker" on a steamboat. This thing shook the bottom out of all my Sunday-school teachings. That boy had been notoriously worldly, and I just the reverse; yet he was exalted to this eminence, and I left in obscurity and misery. There was nothing generous about this fellow in his greatness. He would always manage to have a rusty bolt to scrub while his boat tarried at our town, and he would sit on the inside guard and scrub it, where we could all see him and envy him and loathe him. And whenever his boat was laid up he would come home and swell around the town in his blackest and greasiest clothes, so that nobody could help remembering that he was a steamboatman; and he used all sorts of steamboat technicalities in his talk, as if he were so used to them that he forgot common people could not understand them. He would speak of the "labboard" side of a horse in an easy, natural way that would make one wish he was dead. And he was always talking about "St. Looy" like an old citizen; he would refer casually to occasions when he "was coming down Fourth Street," or when he was "passing by the Planter's House," or when there was a fire and he took a turn on the brakes of "the old Big Missouri"; and then he would go on and lie about how many towns the size of ours were burned down there that day. Two or three of the boys had long been persons of consideration among us because they had been to St. Louis once and had a vague general knowledge of its wonders, but the day of their glory was over now. They lapsed into a humble silence, and learned to disappear when the ruthless "cub"-engineer approached. This fellow had money, too, and hair oil. Also an ignorant silver watch and a showy brass watch chain. He wore a leather belt and used no suspenders. If ever a youth was cordially admired and hated by his comrades, this one was. No girl could withstand his charms. He "cut out" every boy in the village. When his boat blew up at last, it diffused a tranquil contentment among us such as we had not known for months. But when he came home the next week, alive, renowned, and appeared in church all battered up and bandaged, a shining hero, stared at and wondered over by everybody, it seemed to us that the partiality of Providence for an undeserving reptile had reached a point where it was open to criticism.

This creature's career could produce but one result, and it speedily followed. Boy after boy managed to get on the river. The minister's son became an engineer. The doctor's and the postmaster's sons became "mud clerks"; the wholesale liquor dealer's son became a bar-keeper on a boat; four sons of the chief merchant, and two sons of the county judge, became pilots. Pilot was the grandest position of all. The pilot, even in those days of trivial wages, had a princely salary—from a hundred and fifty to two hundred and fifty dollars a month, and no board to pay. Two months of his wages would pay a preacher's salary for a year. Now some of us were left disconsolate. We could not get on the river—at least four parents would not let us.

So by and by I ran away. I said I never would come home again till I was a pilot and could come in glory. But somehow I could not manage it. I went meekly aboard a few of the boats that lay packed together like sardines at the long St. Louis wharf, and very humbly inquired for the pilots, but got only a cold shoulder and short words from mates and clerks. I had to make the best of this sort of treatment for the time being, but I had comforting daydreams of a future when I should be a great and honored pilot, with plenty of money, and could kill some of these mates and clerks and pay for them.

Months afterward the hope within me struggled to a reluctant death, and I found myself without an ambition. But I was ashamed to go home. I was in Cincinnati, and I set to work to map out a new career. I had been reading about the recent exploration of the river Amazon by an expedition sent out by our government. It was said that the expedition, owing to difficulties, had not thoroughly explored a part of the country lying about the head-waters, some four thousand miles from the mouth of the river. It was only about fifteen hundred miles from Cincinnati to New Orleans, where I could doubtless get a ship. I had thirty dollars left; I would go and complete the exploration of the Amazon. This was all the thought I gave to the subject. I never was great in matters of detail. I packed my valise, and took passage on an ancient tub called the Paul Jones, for New Orleans. For the sum of sixteen dollars I had the scarred and tarnished splendors of "her" main saloon principally to myself, for she was not a creature to attract the eye of wiser travelers.

When we presently got under way and went poking down the broad Ohio, I became a new being, and the subject of my own admiration. I was a traveler! A word never had tasted so good in my mouth before. I had an exultant sense of being bound for mysterious lands and distant climes which I never have felt in so uplifting a degree since. I was in such a glorified condition that all ignoble feelings departed out of me, and I was able to look down and pity the untraveled with a compassion that had hardly a trace of contempt in it. Still, when we stopped at villages and wood-yards, I could not help lolling carelessly upon the railings of the boiler deck to enjoy the envy of the country boys on the bank. If they did not seem to discover me, I presently sneezed to attract their attention, or moved to a position where they could not help seeing me. And as soon as I knew they saw me I gaped and stretched, and gave other signs of being mightily bored with traveling.

I kept my hat off all the time, and stayed where the wind and the sun could strike me, because I wanted to get the bronzed and weather-beaten look of an old traveler. Before the second day was half gone, I experienced a joy which filled me with the purest gratitude; for I saw that the skin had begun to blister and peel off my face and neck. I wished that the boys and girls at home could see me now.

We reached Louisville in time—at least the neighborhood of it. We stuck hard and fast on the rocks in the middle of the river and lay there four days. I was now beginning to feel a strong sense of being a part of the boat's family, a sort of infant son to the captain and younger brother to the officers. There is no estimating the pride I took in this grandeur, or the affection that began to swell and grow in me for those people. I could not know how the lordly steamboatman scorns that sort of presumption in a mere landsman. I particularly longed to acquire the least trifle to notice from the big stormy mate, and I was on the alert for an opportunity to do him a service to that end. It came at last. The riotous powwow of setting a spar was going on down on the forecastle, and I went down there and stood around in the way—or mostly skipping out of it—till the mate suddenly roared a general order for somebody to bring him a capstan bar. I sprang to his side and said: "Tell me where it is—I'll fetch it!"

If a rag-picker had offered to do a diplomatic service for the Emperor of Russia, the monarch could not have been more astounded than the mate was. He even stopped swearing. He stood and stared down at me. It took him ten seconds to scrape his disjointed remains together again. Then he said impressively: "Well, if this don't beat hell!" and turned to his work with the air of a man who had been confronted with a problem too abstruse for solution.

I crept away, and courted solitude for the rest of the day. I did not go to dinner; I stayed away from supper until everybody else had finished. I did not feel so much like a member of the boat's family now as before. However, my spirits returned, in installments, as we pursued our way down the river. I was sorry I hated the mate so, because it was not in (young) human nature not to admire him. He was huge and muscular, his face was bearded and whiskered all over; he had a red woman and a blue woman tattooed on his right arm,—one on each side of a blue anchor with a red rope to it; and in the matter of profanity he was perfect. When he was getting out cargo at a landing, I was always where I could see and hear. He felt all the sublimity of his great position, and made the world feel it, too. When he gave even the simplest order, he discharged it like a blast of lightning, and sent a long, reverberating peal of profanity thundering after it. I could not help contrasting the way in which the average landsman would give an order, with the mate's way of doing it. If the landsman should wish the gangplank moved a foot farther forward, he would probably say: "James, or William, one of you push that plank forward, please;" but put the mate in his place, and he would roar out: "Here, now, start that gang-plank for'ard! Lively, now! *What*'re you about! Snatch it! *snatch* it! There! there! Aft again! aft again! Don't you hear me? Dash it to dash! are you going to *sleep* over it! *'Vast* heaving. 'Vast heaving, I tell you! Going to heave it clear astern? WHERE're you going with that barrel! *for'ard* with it 'fore I make you swallow it, you dash-dash-dash-*dashed* split between a tired mud-turtle and a crippled hearse-horse!"

I wished I could talk like that.

When the soreness of my adventure with the mate had somewhat worn off, I began timidly to make up to the humblest official connected with the boat—the night watchman. He snubbed my advances at first, but I presently ventured to offer him a new chalk pipe, and that softened him. So he allowed me to sit with him by the big bell on the hurricane deck, and in time he melted into conversation. He could not well have helped it, I hung with such homage on his words and so plainly showed that I felt honored by his notice. He told me the names of dim capes and shadowy islands as we glided by them in the solemnity of the night, under the winking stars, and by and by got to talking about himself. He seemed oversentimental for a man whose salary was six dollars a week—or rather he might have seemed so to an older person than I. But I drank in his words hungrily, and with a faith that might have moved mountains if it had been applied judiciously. What was it to me that he was soiled and seedy and fragrant with gin? What was it to me that his grammar was bad, his construction worse, and his profanity so void of art that it was an element of weakness rather than strength in his conversation? He was a wronged man, a man who had seen trouble, and that was enough for me. As he mellowed into his plaintive history his tears dripped upon the lantern in his lap, and I cried, too, from sympathy. He said he was the son of an English nobleman—either an earl or an alderman, he could not remember which, but believed he was both; his father, the nobleman, loved him, but his mother hated him from the cradle; and so while he was still a little boy he was sent to "one of them old, ancient colleges"—he couldn't remember which; and by and by his father died and his mother seized the property and "shook" him, as he phrased it. After his mother shook him, members of the nobility with whom he was acquainted used their influence to get him the position of "loblolly-boy in a ship"; and from that point my watchman threw off all trammels of date and locality and branched out into a narrative that bristled all along with incredible adventures; a narrative that was so reeking with bloodshed and so crammed with hair-breadth escapes and the most engaging and unconscious personal villainies, that I sat speechless, enjoying, shuddering, wondering, worshiping.

It was a sore blight to find out afterwards that he was a low, vulgar, ignorant, sentimental, half-witted humbug, an untraveled native of the wilds of Illinois, who had absorbed wildcat literature and appropriated its marvels, until in time he had woven odds and ends of the mess into this yarn, and then gone on telling it to fledgelings like me, until he had come to believe it himself.

I do not claim that I can tell a story as it ought to be told. I only claim to know how a story ought to be told, for I have been almost daily in the company of the most expert story-tellers for many years.

There are several kinds of stories, but only one difficult kind—the humorous. I will talk mainly about that one. The humorous story is American, the comic story is English, the witty story is French. The humorous story depends for its effect upon the *manner* of the telling; the comic story and the witty story upon the *matter*.

The humorous story may be spun out to great length, and may wander around as much as it pleases, and arrive nowhere in particular; but the comic and witty stories must be brief and end with a point. The humorous story bubbles gently along, the others burst.

The humorous story is strictly a work of art—high and delicate art—and only an artist can tell it; but no art is necessary in telling the comic and the witty story; anybody can do it. The art of telling a humorous story—understand, I mean by word of mouth, not print—was created in America, and has remained at home.

The humorous story is told gravely; the teller does his best to conceal the fact that he even dimly suspects that there is anything funny about it; but the teller of the comic story tells you beforehand that it is one of the funniest things he has ever heard, then tells it with eager delight, and is the first person to laugh when he gets through. And sometimes, if he has had good success, he is so glad and happy that he will repeat the ''nub'' of it and glance around from face to face, collecting applause, and then repeat it again. It is a pathetic thing to see.

Very often, of course, the rambling and disjointed humorous story finishes with a nub, point, snapper, or whatever you like to call it. Then the listener must be alert, for in many cases the teller will divert attention from that nub by dropping it in a carefully casual and indifferent way, with the pretense that he does not know it is a nub.

Artemus Ward used that trick a good deal; then when the belated audience presently caught the joke he would look up with innocent surprise, as if wondering what they had found to laugh at. Dan Setchell used it before him, Nye and Riley and others use it to-day.

But the teller of the comic story does not slur the nub; he shouts it at you—every time. And when he prints it, in England, France, Germany, and Italy, he italicizes it, puts some whooping exclamation-points after it and sometimes explains it in a parenthesis. All of which is very depressing, and makes one want to renounce joking and lead a better life.

Let me set down an instance of the comic method, using an anecdote which has been popular all over the world for twelve or fifteen hundred years. The teller tells it in this way:

The Wounded Soldier

In the course of a certain battle a soldier whose leg had been shot off appealed to another soldier who was hurrying by to carry him to the rear, informing him at the same time of the loss which he had sustained; whereupon the generous son of Mars, shouldering the unfortunate, proceeded to carry out his desire. The bullets and cannon-balls were flying in all directions, and presently one of the latter took the wounded man's head off—without, however, his deliverer being aware of it. In no long time he was hailed by an officer, who said:

"Where are you going with that carcass?"

"To the rear, sir—he's lost his leg!"

"His leg, forsooth?" responded the astonished officer, "you mean his head, you booby."

Whereupon the soldier dispossessed himself of his burden, and stood looking down upon it in great perplexity. At length he said:

"It is true, sir, just as you have said." Then after a pause he added. *"But he* TOLD *me* IT WAS HIS LEG ! ! ! ! !"

Here the narrator bursts into explosion after explosion of thunderous horse-laughter, repeating that nub from time to time through his gaspings and shriekings and suffocatings.

It takes only a minute and a half to tell that in its comic-story form; and isn't worth the telling, after all. Put into the humorous-story form it takes ten minutes, and is about the funniest thing I have ever listened to—as James Whitcomb Riley tells it.

He tells it in the character of a dull-witted old farmer who has just heard it for the first time, thinks it is unspeakably funny, and is trying to repeat it to a neighbor. But he can't remember it; so he gets all mixed up and wanders helplessly round and round, putting in tedious details that don't belong in the tale and only retard it; taking them out conscientiously and putting in others that are just as useless; making minor mistakes now and then and stopping to correct them and explain how he came to make them; remembering things which he forgot to put in in their proper place and going back to put them in there; stopping his narrative a good while in order to try to recall the name of the soldier that was hurt, and finally remembering that the soldier's name was not mentioned, and remarking placidly that the name is of no real importance, anyway—better, of course if one knew it, but not essential, after all—and so on, and so on, and so on.

The teller is innocent and happy and pleased with himself, and has to stop every little while to hold himself in and keep from laughing outright; and does hold in, but his body quakes in a jelly-like way with interior chuckles; and at the end of the ten minutes the audience have laughed until they are exhausted, and the tears are running down their faces.

The simplicity and innocence and sincerity and unconsciousness of the old farmer are perfectly simulated, and the result is a performance which is thoroughly charming and delicious. This is art—and fine and beautiful, and only a master can compass it; but a machine could tell the other story.

To string incongruities and absurdities together in a wandering and sometimes purposeless way, and seem innocently unaware that they are absurdities, is the basis of the American art, if my position is correct. Another feature is the slurring of the point. A third is the dropping of a studied remark apparently without knowing it, as if one were thinking aloud. The fourth and last is the pause.

Artemus Ward dealt in numbers three and four a good deal. He would begin to tell with great animation something which he seemed to think was wonderful; then lose confidence, and after an apparently absent-minded pause add an incongruous remark in a soliloquizing way; and that was the remark intended to explode the mine—and it did.

For instance, he would say eagerly, excitedly, "I once knew a man in New Zealand who hadn't a tooth in his head"—here his animation would die out; a silent, reflective pause would follow, then he would say dreamily, and as if to himself, "and yet that man could beat a drum better than any man I ever saw."

The pause is an exceedingly important feature in any kind of story, and a frequently recurring feature, too. It is a dainty thing, and delicate, and also uncertain and treacherous; for it must be exactly the right length—no more and no less—or it fails of its purpose and makes trouble. If the pause is too short the impressive point is passed, and the audience have had time to divine that a surprise is intended—and then you can't surprise them, of course.

On the platform I used to tell a negro ghost story that had a pause in front of the snapper on the end, and that pause was the most important thing in the whole story. If I got it the right length precisely, I could spring the finishing ejaculation with effect enough to make some impressible girl deliver a startled little yelp and jump out of her seat—and that was what I was after. This story was called "The Golden Arm," and was told in this fashion. You can practise with it yourself—and mind you look out for the pause and get it right.

The Golden Arm

Once 'pon a time dey wuz a monsus mean man, en he live 'way out in de prairie all 'lone by hisself, 'cep'n he had a wife. En bimeby she died, en he tuck en toted her way out dah in de prairie en buried her. Well, she had a golden arm—all solid gold, fum de shoulder down. He wuz pow'ful mean—pow'ful; en dat night he couldn't sleep, caze he want dat golden arm so bad.

When it come midnight he couldn't stan' it no mo'; so he git up, he did, en tuck his lantern en shoved out thoo de storm en dug her up en got de golden arm; en he bent his head down 'gin de win', en plowed en plowed en plowed thoo de snow. Den all on a sudden he stop (make a considerable pause here, and look startled, and take a listening attitude) en say: "My *lan'*, what's dat?"

En he listen—en listen—en de win' say (set your teeth together and imitate the wailing and wheezing singsong of the wind), "Bzzz-z-zzz"—en den, way back yonder whah de grave is, he hear a *voice!*—he hear a voice all mix' up in de win'—can't hardly tell 'em 'part—"Bzzz—zzz—W-h-o—g-o-t—m-y—g-o-l-d-e-n arm?" (You must begin to shiver violently now.)

En he begin to shiver en shake, en say, "Oh, my! *Oh,* my lan'!" en de win' blow de lantern out, en de snow en sleet blow in his face en mos' choke him, en he start a-plowin' knee-deep towards home mos' dead, he so sk'yerd—en pooty soon he hear de voice agin, en (pause) it 'us comin' *after* him! "Bzzz—zzz—zzz—W-h-o—g-o-t—m-y—g-o-l-d-e-n—*arm?*"

When he git to de pasture he hear it agin—closter now, en a-*comin'!*—a-comin' back dah in de dark en de storm—(repeat the wind and the voice). When he git to de house he rush up-stairs en jump in de bed en kiver up, head and years, en lay dah shiverin' en shakin'—en den way out dah he hear it *agin!*—en a-*comin'!* En bimeby he hear (pause—awed, listening attitude)—pat—pat—pat—*hit's a-comin upstairs!* Den he hear de latch, en he *know* it's in de room!

Den pooty soon he know it's a-*stannin' by de bed!* (Pause.) Den—he know it's a-*bendin' down over him*—en he cain't skasely git his breath! Den—den—he seem to feel someth'n' *c-o-l-d*, right down 'most agin his head! (Pause.)

Den de voice say, *right at his year*—"W-h-o—g-o-t—m-y—g-o-l-d-e-n arm?" (You must wail it out very plaintively and accusingly; then you stare steddily and impressively into the face of the farthest-gone auditor—a girl, preferably—and let that awe-inspiring pause begin to build itself in the deep hush. When it has reached exactly the right length, jump suddenly at that girl and yell, "*You've* got it!")

If you've got the *pause* right, she'll fetch a dear little yelp and spring right out of her shoes. But you *must* get the pause right; and you will find it the most troublesome and aggravating and uncertain thing you ever undertook.

DISCUSSION QUESTIONS

1. How does Twain's advice about the proper methods of storytelling help you read the opening chapter of *Old Times on the Mississippi?* Does Twain put into practice his oral techniques for telling a story? Identify a few elements of his

narrative style that are directly related to his methods of oral pacing and delivery.

2. Do you think Twain glamorizes the occupation of riverboat pilot? Compare his treatment of an occupation with those of Gay Talese (in ''Magazines'') and Tracy Kidder (in ''Best-Sellers'').

Walt Whitman / A Noiseless Patient Spider   1881

For most of his life, Walt Whitman (1819–92) lived in neighborly relation to poverty. He worked as an apprentice in a printing shop, as a journalist for New York City and Long Island newspapers, as editor of the Brooklyn Eagle, *as a teacher, as a building contractor, and as a clerk in the Bureau of Indian Affairs until the sullied reputation of his collection of poems,* Leaves of Grass, *provoked his hurried dismissal.*

Said to have been set in type by Whitman himself and published at his own expense, Leaves of Grass *attracted little critical attention and sold few copies when first published in 1855. Of all the editors and writers to whom Whitman sent copies, Ralph Waldo Emerson responded most readily and enthusiastically: ''I find in it the most extraordinary piece of wit and wisdom that America has yet contributed.'' But Emerson was well ahead of his time in appreciating Whitman's verse. Its seeming formlessness, boasts, sexual overtones, and ''vulgar'' language stirred much controversy in the decades that followed. Several generations of critics characterized his work as ''the poetry of barbarism'' and admonished audiences that this was poetry ''not to be read aloud to mixed audiences.'' The poet John Greenleaf Whittier went further. He condemned the poems as ''loose, lurid, and impious'' and tossed his copy into a fire.*

After service in Washington during the Civil War, Whitman suffered a paralytic stroke in 1873 and moved to his brother's home in Camden, New Jersey, where he spent his remaining years revising Leaves of Grass.

In Leaves of Grass, *an unprecedented mixture of a radically new poetic consciousness, commonplace subject matter, and distinctively colloquial rhythms, Whitman aspired to create nothing less than an epic of American democracy. But while his ambition to be known as ''the bard of democracy'' was never fully endorsed during his lifetime, Whitman's vision and innovative verse have cut a deepening course through which much of twentieth-century poetry has passed.*

''A Noiseless Patient Spider'' was written in 1868 and included in the ''Whispers of Heavenly Death'' section of Leaves of Grass *in 1881. ''To a Locomotive in Winter'' was written in 1876 and included in the ''From Noon to Starry Night'' section of the 1881 edition. These poems offer a sample of both Whitman's attitudes toward nature and technology and his single-handed attempt to introduce a new style and idiom into American literature. They also demonstrate Whitman's belief that the process of reading should be:*

a half-sleep, but . . . an exercise, a gymnast's struggle; that the reader is to do something for himself, must be on the alert, must . . . construct indeed the poem, argument, history, metaphysical essay—the text furnishing the hints, the clue, the start or frame-work.

A noiseless patient spider,
I mark'd where on a little promontory it stood isolated,
Mark'd how to explore the vacant vast surrounding,
It launch'd forth filament, filament, filament, out of itself,
Ever unreeling them, ever tirelessly speeding them.

And you O my soul where you stand,
Surrounded, detached, in measureless oceans of space,
Ceaselessly musing, venturing, throwing, seeking the spheres to connect them,
Till the bridge you will need be form'd, till the ductile anchor hold,
Till the gossamer thread you fling catch somewhere, O my soul.   10

Walt Whitman / To a Locomotive in Winter   1881

Thee for my recitative;
Thee in the driving storm even as now, the snow, the winter-day declining,
Thee in thy panoply, thy measur'd dual throbbing and thy beat convulsive,
Thy black cylindric body, golden brass and silvery steel,
Thy ponderous side-bars, parallel and connecting rods, gyrating, shuttling at thy sides,
Thy metrical, now swelling pant and roar, now tapering in the distance,
Thy great protruding head-light fix'd in front,
Thy long, pale, floating vapor-pennants, tinged with delicate purple,
The dense and murky clouds out-belching from thy smoke-stack,
Thy knitted frame, thy springs and valves, the tremulous twinkle of thy wheels,   10
Thy train of cars behind, obedient, merrily following,
Through gale or calm, now swift, now slack, yet steadily careering;
Type of the modern—emblem of motion and power—pulse of the continent,
For once come serve the Muse and merge in verse, even as here I see thee,
With storm and buffeting gusts of wind and falling snow,
By day thy warning ringing bell to sound its notes,
By night thy silent signal lamps to swing.

Fierce-throated beauty!
Roll through my chant with all thy lawless music, thy swinging lamps at night,
Thy madly-whistled laughter, echoing, rumbling like an earthquake, rousing all,   20
Law of thyself complete, thine own track firmly holding,
(No sweetness debonair of tearful harp or glib piano thine,)
Thy trills of shrieks by rocks and hills return'd,
Launch'd o'er the prairies wide, across the lakes,
To the free skies unpent and glad and strong.

Kate Chopin / The Dream of an Hour   1894

Born Katherine O'Flaherty in St. Louis in 1851 to a wealthy Irish father and a Creole mother, Kate Chopin was raised in French, Southern, Catholic, aristocratic circumstances. After studies at a convent school, she entered and was soon bored with the fashionable social circle of St. Louis: "I am invited to a ball and I go.—I dance with people I despise; amuse myself with men whose only talent lies

in their feet.'' At nineteen, she married a Creole cotton broker and moved first to
New Orleans and then to the bayou country that forms a backdrop for many of
her stories. A year after her husband died of swamp fever in 1883, Chopin
returned to St. Louis with her six children and began composing short fiction,
novels, and children's books. Writing in the midst of her children's activities,
she obviously enjoyed the spontaneity such circumstances imposed:

> *I am completely at the mercy of unconscious selection. To such an ex-*
> *tent is this true, that what is called the polishing up process always*
> *proved disastrous to my work, and I avoid it, preferring the integrity of*
> *crudities to artificialities.*

"The Dream of an Hour'' appeared originally in Vogue *magazine in 1894.*
Chopin's stories were frequently published in such leading periodicals as
Atlantic Monthly, Harper's, *and* Century *and were subsequently collected in*
Bayou Folk *(1894) and* A Night in Acadia *(1897). Demoralized by the severe*
criticism that attended the publication of her third novel, The Awakening, *a tale*
of extramarital and interracial love, she wrote little more before her death in
1904.

Knowing that Mrs. Mallard was afflicted with a heart trouble, great care was taken
to break to her as gently as possible the news of her husband's death.

It was her sister Josephine who told her, in broken sentences; veiled hints that
revealed in half concealing. Her husband's friend Richards was there, too, near
her. It was he who had been in the newspaper office when intelligence of the
railroad disaster was received, with Brently Mallard's name leading the list of
"killed." He had only taken the time to assure himself of its truth by a second
telegram, and had hastened to forestall any less careful, less tender friend in bearing the sad message.

She did not hear the story as many women have heard the same, with a paralyzed inability to accept its significance. She wept at once, with sudden, wild
abandonment, in her sister's arms. When the storm of grief had spent itself she
went away to her room alone. She would have no one follow her.

There stood, facing the open window, a comfortable, roomy armchair. Into this
she sank, pressed down by a physical exhaustion that haunted her body and
seemed to reach into her soul.

She could see in the open square before her house the tops of trees that were all
aquiver with the new spring life. The delicious breath of rain was in the air. In the
street below a peddler was crying his wares. The notes of a distant song which
some one was singing reached her faintly, and countless sparrows were twittering
in the eaves.

There were patches of blue sky showing here and there through the clouds that
had met and piled one above the other in the west facing her window.

She sat with her head thrown back upon the cushion of the chair, quite motionless, except when a sob came up into her throat and shook her, as a child who has
cried itself to sleep continues to sob in its dreams.

She was young, with a fair, calm face, whose lines bespoke repression and even
a certain strength. But now there was a dull stare in her eyes, whose gaze was
fixed away off yonder on one of those patches of blue sky. It was not a glance of
reflection, but rather indicated a suspension of intelligent thought.

There was something coming to her and she was waiting for it, fearfully. What
was it? She did not know; it was too subtle and elusive to name. But she felt it,
creeping out of the sky, reaching toward her through the sounds, the scents, the
color that filled the air.

Now her bosom rose and fell tumultuously. She was beginning to recognize this thing that was approaching to possess her, and she was striving to beat it back with her will—as powerless as her two white slender hands would have been.

When she abandoned herself a little whispered word escaped her slightly parted lips. She said it over and over under her breath: "free, free, free!" The vacant stare and the look of terror that had followed it went from her eyes. They stayed keen and bright. Her pulses beat fast, and the coursing blood warmed and relaxed every inch of her body.

She did not stop to ask if it were or were not a monstrous joy that held her: A clear and exalted perception enabled her to dismiss the suggestion as trivial.

She knew that she would weep again when she saw the kind, tender hands folded in death; the face that had never looked save with love upon her, fixed and gray and dead. But she saw beyond that bitter moment a long procession of years to come that would belong to her absolutely. And she opened and spread her arms out to them in welcome.

There would be no one to live for her during those coming years; she would live for herself. There would be no powerful will bending hers in that blind persistence with which men and women believe they have a right to impose a private will upon a fellow-creature. A kind intention or a cruel intention made the act seem no less a crime as she looked upon it in that brief moment of illumination.

And yet she had loved him—sometimes. Often she had not. What did it matter! What could love, the unsolved mystery, count for in face of this possession of self-assertion which she suddenly recognized as the strongest impulse of her being!

"Free! Body and soul free!" she kept whispering.

Josephine was kneeling before the closed door with her lips to the keyhole, imploring for admission. "Louise, open the door! I beg; open the door—you will make yourself ill. What are you doing, Louise? For heaven's sake open the door."

"Go away. I am not making myself ill." No; she was drinking in a very elixir of life through that open window.

Her fancy was running riot along those days ahead of her. Spring days, and summer days, and all sorts of days that would be her own. She breathed a quick prayer that life might be long. It was only yesterday she had thought with a shudder that life might be long.

She arose at length and opened the door to her sister's importunities. There was a feverish triumph in her eyes, and she carried herself unwittingly like a goddess of Victory. She clasped her sister's waist, and together they descended the stairs. Richards stood waiting for them at the bottom.

Some one was opening the front door with a latchkey. It was Brently Mallard who entered, a little travel-stained, composedly carrying his grip-sack and umbrella. He had been far from the scene of accident, and did not even know there had been one. He stood amazed at Josephine's piercing cry; at Richards' quick motion to screen him from the view of his wife.

But Richards was too late.

When the doctors came they said she had died of heart disease—of joy that kills.

DISCUSSION QUESTION

1. Robert Frost often argued that poetry exists "for griefs, not grievances." Do you think this distinction is applicable to Chopin's "The Dream of an Hour"? Explain. Locate other stories and essays in this collection to which this distinction may be applied.

"The Open Boat," written a few months after his report on the sinking of the Commodore *for the* New York Press *on January 7, 1897 (see "Stephen Crane's Own Story" in "Press"), was Crane's second attempt to fictionalize his near disaster at sea. According to a fellow journalist, Crane was so worried about accuracy that he wanted the captain of the wrecked vessel, Edward Murphy, to go over the manuscript. "Listen, Ed. I want to have this* right, *from your point of view. How does it sound so far?" "You've got it, Steve," said the other man. "That is just how it happened, and how it felt." Long regarded as a masterpiece of naturalistic fiction, "The Open Boat" is an early attempt by a major American writer to give literary certification to the ironic, jocularly resilient speech of average men trapped in difficult circumstances. (See, for example, the transcripts of the astronaut's conversations in "Press.") In his efforts to combine the crafts of journalism and literature, Crane helped to set a new tone for fiction, one that could express, as he puts it in "The Open Boat," "humour, contempt, tragedy, all in one."*

A TALE INTENDED TO BE AFTER THE FACT: BEING THE EXPERIENCE OF FOUR MEN FROM THE SUNK STEAMER COMMODORE

I

None of them knew the colour of the sky. Their eyes glanced level, and were fastened upon the waves that swept toward them. These waves were of the hue of slate, save for the tops, which were of foaming white, and all of the men knew the colours of the sea. The horizon narrowed and widened, and dipped and rose, and at all times its edge was jagged with waves that seemed thrust up in points like rocks.

Many a man ought to have a bathtub larger than the boat which here rode upon the sea. These waves were most wrongfully and barbarously abrupt and tall, and each froth-top was a problem in small-boat navigation.

The cook squatted in the bottom, and looked with both eyes at the six inches of gunwale which separated him from the ocean. His sleeves were rolled over his fat forearms, and the two flaps of his unbuttoned vest dangled as he bent to bail out the boat. Often he said, "Gawd! that was a narrow clip." As he remarked it he invariably gazed eastward over the broken sea.

The oiler, steering with one of the two oars in the boat, sometimes raised himself suddenly to keep clear of water that swirled in over the stern. It was a thin little oar, and it seemed often ready to snap.

The correspondent, pulling at the other oar, watched the waves and wondered why he was there.

The injured captain, lying in the bow, was at this time buried in that profound dejection and indifference which comes, temporarily at least, to even the bravest and most enduring when, willy-nilly, the firm fails, the army loses, the ship goes down. The mind of the master of a vessel is rooted deep in the timbers of her, though he command for a day or a decade; and this captain had on him the stern impression of a scene in the greys of dawn of seven turned faces, and later a stump of a topmast with a white ball on it, that slashed to and fro at the waves, went low and lower, and down. Thereafter there was something strange in his voice. Although steady, it was deep with mourning, and of a quality beyond oration or tears.

"Keep 'er a little more south, Billie," said he.

"A little more south, sir," said the oiler in the stern.

A seat in his boat was not unlike a seat upon a bucking broncho, and by the same token a broncho is not much smaller. The craft pranced and reared and plunged like an animal. As each wave came, and she rose for it, she seemed like a horse making at a fence outrageously high. The manner of her scramble over these walls of water is a mystic thing, and, moreover, at the top of them were ordinarily these problems in white water, the foam racing down from the summit of each wave requiring a new leap, and a leap from the air. Then, after scornfully bumping a crest, she would slide and race and splash down a long incline, and arrive bobbing and nodding in front of the next menace.

A singular disadvantage of the sea lies in the fact that after successfully surmounting one wave you discover that there is another behind it just as important and just as nervously anxious to do something effective in the way of swamping boats. In a ten-foot dinghy one can get an idea of the resources of the sea in the line of waves that is not probable to the average experience which is never at sea in a dinghy. As each slaty wall of water approached, it shut all else from the view of the men in the boat, and it was not difficult to imagine that this particular wave was the final outburst of the ocean, the last effort of the grim water. There was a terrible grace in the move of the waves, and they came in silence, save for the snarling of the crests.

In the wan light the faces of the men must have been grey. Their eyes must have glinted in strange ways as they gazed steadily astern. Viewed from a balcony, the whole thing would doubtless have been weirdly picturesque. But the men in the boat had no time to see it, and if they had had leisure, there were other things to occupy their minds. The sun swung steadily up the sky, and they knew it was broad day because the colour of the sea changed from slate to emerald green streaked with amber lights, and the foam was like tumbling snow. The process of the breaking day was unknown to them. They were aware only of this effect upon the colour of the waves that rolled toward them.

In disjointed sentences the cook and the correspondent argued as to the difference between a life-saving station and a house of refuge. The cook had said: "There's a house of refuge just north of the Mosquito Inlet Light, and as soon as they see us they'll come off in their boat and pick us up."

"As soon as who see us?" said the correspondent.

"The crew," said the cook.

"Houses of refuge don't have crews," said the correspondent. "As I understand them, they are only places where clothes and grub are stored for the benefit of shipwrecked people. They don't carry crews."

"Oh, yes, they do," said the cook.

"No, they don't," said the correspondent.

"Well, we're not there yet, anyhow," said the oiler, in the stern.

"Well," said the cook, "perhaps it's not a house of refuge that I'm thinking of as being near Mosquito Inlet Light; perhaps it's a life-saving station."

"We're not there yet," said the oiler in the stern.

II

As the boat bounced from the top of each wave the wind tore through the hair of the hatless men, and as the craft plopped her stern down again the spray slashed past them. The crest of each of these waves was a hill, from the top of which the men surveyed for a moment a broad tumultuous expanse, shining and wind-riven. It was probably splendid, it was probably glorious, this play of the free sea, wild with lights of emerald and white and amber.

"Bully good thing it's an on-shore wind," said the cook. "If not, where would we be? Wouldn't have a show."

"That's right," said the correspondent.

The busy oiler nodded his assent.

Then the captain, in the bow, chuckled in a way that expressed humour, contempt, tragedy, all in one. "Do you think we've got much of a show now, boys?" said he.

Whereupon the three were silent, save for a trifle of hemming and hawing. To express any particular optimism at this time they felt to be childish and stupid, but they all doubtless possessed this sense of the situation in their minds. A young man thinks doggedly at such times. On the other hand, the ethics of their condition was decidedly against any open suggestion of hopelessness. So they were silent.

"Oh, well," said the captain, soothing his children, "we'll get ashore all right."

But there was that in his tone which made them think; so the oiler quoth, "Yes! if this wind holds."

The cook was bailing. "Yes! if we don't catch hell in the surf."

Canton-flannel gulls flew near and far. Sometimes they sat down on the sea, near patches of brown seaweed that rolled over the waves with a movement like carpets on a line in a gale. The birds sat comfortably in groups, and they were envied by some in the dinghy, for the wrath of the sea was no more to them than it was to a covey of prairie chickens a thousand miles inland. Often they came very close and stared at the men with black bead-like eyes. At these times they were uncanny and sinister in their unblinking scrutiny, and the men hooted angrily at them, telling them to be gone. One came, and evidently decided to alight on the top of the captain's head. The bird flew parallel to the boat and did not circle, but made short sidelong jumps in the air in chicken-fashion. His black eyes were wistfully fixed upon the captain's head. "Ugly brute," said the oiler to the bird. "You look as if you were made with a jackknife." The cook and the correspondent swore darkly at the creature. The captain naturally wished to knock it away with the end of the heavy painter, but he did not dare do it, because anything resembling an emphatic gesture would have capsized this freighted boat; and so, with his open hand, the captain gently and carefully waved the gull away. After it had been discouraged from the pursuit the captain breathed easier on account of his hair, and others breathed easier because the bird struck their minds at this time as being somehow gruesome and ominous.

In the meantime the oiler and the correspondent rowed. And also they rowed. They sat together in the same seat, and each rowed an oar. Then the oiler took both oars; then the correspondent took both oars; then the oiler: then the correspondent. They rowed and they rowed. The very ticklish part of the business was when the time came for the reclining one in the stern to take his turn at the oars. By the very last star of truth, it is easier to steal eggs from under a hen than it was to change seats in the dinghy. First the man in the stern slid his hand along the thwart and moved with care, as if he were of Sevres. Then the man in the rowing-seat slid his hand along the other thwart. It was all done with the most extraordinary care. As the two sidled past each other, the whole party kept watchful eyes on the coming wave, and the captain cried: "Look out, now! Steady, there!"

The brown mats of seaweed that appeared from time to time were like islands, bits of earth. They were travelling, apparently, neither one way nor the other. They were, to all intents, stationary. They informed the men in the boat that it was making progress slowly toward the land.

The captain, rearing cautiously in the bow after the dinghy soared on a great swell, said that he had seen the lighthouse at Mosquito Inlet. Presently the cook remarked that he had seen it. The correspondent was at the oars then, and for some reason he too wished to look at the lighthouse; but his back was toward the far shore, and the waves were important, and for some time he could not seize an opportunity to turn his head. But at last there came a wave more gentle than the others, and when at the crest of it he swiftly scoured the western horizon.

"See it?" said the captain.

"No," said the correspondent, slowly; "I didn't see anything."

"Look again," said the captain. He pointed. "It's exactly in that direction."

At the top of another wave the correspondent did as he was bid, and this time his eyes chanced on a small, still thing on the edge of the swaying horizon. It was precisely like the point of a pin. It took an anxious eye to find a lighthouse so tiny.

"Think we'll make it, Captain?"

"If this wind holds and the boat don't swamp, we can't do much else," said the captain.

The little boat, lifted by each towering sea and splashed viciously by the crests, made progress that in the absence of seaweed was not apparent to those in her. She seemed just a wee thing wallowing, miraculously top up, at the mercy of five oceans. Occasionally a great spread of water, like white flames, swarmed into her.

"Bail her, cook," said the captain, serenely.

"All right, Captain," said the cheerful cook.

III

It would be difficult to describe the subtle brotherhood of men that was here established on the seas. No one said that it was so. No one mentioned it. But it dwelt in the boat, and each man felt it warm him. They were a captain, an oiler, a cook, and a correspondent, and they were friends—friends in a more curiously iron-bound degree than may be common. The hurt captain, lying against the water-jar in the bow, spoke always in a low voice and calmly; but he could never command a more ready and swiftly obedient crew than the motley three of the dinghy. It was more than a mere recognition of what was best for the common safety. There was surely in it a quality that was personal and heart-felt. And after this devotion to the commander of the boat, there was this comradeship, that the correspondent, for instance, who had been taught to be cynical of men, knew even at the time was the best experience of his life. But no one said that it was so. No one mentioned it.

"I wish we had a sail," remarked the captain. "We might try my overcoat on the end of an oar, and give you two boys a chance to rest." So the cook and the correspondent held the mast and spread wide the overcoat; the oiler steered; and the little boat made good way with her new rig. Sometimes the oiler had to scull sharply to keep a sea from breaking into the boat, but otherwise sailing was a success.

Meanwhile the lighthouse had been growing slowly larger. It had now almost assumed colour, and appeared like a little grey shadow on the sky. The man at the oars could not be prevented from turning his head rather often to try for a glimpse of this little grey shadow.

At last, from the top of each wave, the men in the tossing boat could see land. Even as the lighthouse was an upright shadow on the sky, this land seemed but a long black shadow on the sea. It certainly was thinner than paper. "We must be about opposite New Smyrna," said the cook, who had coasted this shore often in schooners. "Captain, by the way, I believe they abandoned that life-saving station there about a year ago."

"Did they?" said the captain.

The wind slowly died away. The cook and the correspondent were not now obliged to slave in order to hold high the oar. But the waves continued their old impetuous swooping at the dinghy, and the little craft, no longer under way, struggled woundily over them. The oiler or the correspondent took the oars again.

Shipwrecks are apropos of nothing. If men could only train for them and have them occur when the men had reached pink condition, there would be less drowning at sea. Of the four in the dinghy none had slept any time worth mentioning for two days and two nights previous to embarking in the dinghy, and in the excitement of clambering about the deck of a foundering ship they had also forgotten to eat heartily.

For these reasons, and for others, neither the oiler nor the correspondent was fond of rowing at this time. The correspondent wondered ingenuously how in the name of all that was sane could there be people who thought it amusing to row a boat. It was not an amusement; it was a diabolical punishment, and even a genius of mental aberrations could never conclude that it was anything but a horror to the muscles and a crime against the back. He mentioned to the boat in general how the amusement of rowing struck him, and the weary-faced oiler smiled in full sympathy. Previously to the foundering, by the way, the oiler had worked a double watch in the engine-room of the ship.

"Take her easy now, boys," said the captain. "Don't spend yourselves. If we have to run a surf you'll need all your strength, because we'll sure have to swim for it. Take your time."

Slowly the land arose from the sea. From a black line it became a line of black and a line of white—trees and sand. Finally the captain said that he could make out a house on the shore. "That's the house of refuge, sure," said the cook. "They'll see us before long, and come out after us."

The distant lighthouse reared high. "The keeper ought to be able to make us out now, if he's looking through a glass," said the captain. "He'll notify the life-saving people."

"None of those other boats could have got ashore to give word of this wreck," said the oiler, in a low voice, "else the life-boat would be out hunting us."

Slowly and beautifully the land loomed out of the sea. The wind came again. It had veered from the north-east to the south-east. Finally a new sound struck the ears of the men in the boat. It was the low thunder of the surf on the shore. "We'll never be able to make the lighthouse now," said the captain. "Swing her head a little more north, Billie."

"A little more north, sir," said the oiler.

Whereupon the little boat turned her nose once more down the wind, and all but the oarsman watched the shore grow. Under the influence of this expansion doubt and direful apprehension were leaving the minds of the men. The management of the boat was still most absorbing, but it could not prevent a quiet cheerfulness. In an hour, perhaps, they would be ashore.

Their backbones had become thoroughly used to balancing in the boat, and they now rode this wild colt of a dinghy like circus men. The correspondent thought that he had been drenched to the skin, but happening to feel in the top pocket of his coat, he found therein eight cigars. Four of them were soaked with sea-water; four were perfectly scatheless. After a search, somebody produced three dry matches; and thereupon the four waifs rode impudently in their little boat and, with an assurance of an impending rescue shining in their eyes, puffed at the big cigars, and judged well and ill of all men. Everybody took a drink of water.

IV

"Cook," remarked the captain, "there don't seem to be any signs of life about your house of refuge."

"No," replied the cook. "Funny they don't see us!"

A broad stretch of lowly coast lay before the eyes of the men. It was of low dunes topped with dark vegetation. The roar of the surf was plain, and sometimes they could see the white lip of a wave as it spun up the beach. A tiny house was blocked out black upon the sky. Southward, the slim lighthouse lifted its little grey length.

Tide, wind, and waves were swinging the dinghy northward. "Funny they don't see us," said the men.

The surf's roar was here dulled, but its tone was nevertheless thunderous and mighty. As the boat swam over the great rollers the men sat listening to this roar. "We'll swamp sure," said everybody.

It is fair to say here that there was not a life-saving station within twenty miles in either direction; but the men did not know this fact, and in consequence they made dark and opprobrious remarks concerning the eyesight of the nation's life-savers. Four scowling men sat in the dinghy and surpassed records in the invention of epithets.

"Funny they don't see us."

The light-heartedness of a former time had completely faded. To their sharpened minds it was easy to conjure pictures of all kinds of incompetency and blindness and, indeed, cowardice. There was the shore of the populous land, and it was bitter and bitter to them that from it came no sign.

"Well," said the captain, ultimately, "I suppose we'll have to make a try for ourselves. If we stay out here too long, we'll none of us have strength left to swim after the boat swamps."

And so the oiler, who was at the oars, turned the boat straight for the shore. There was a sudden tightening of muscles. There was some thinking.

"If we don't all get ashore," said the captain—"if we don't all get ashore, I suppose you fellows know where to send news of my finish?"

They then briefly exchanged some addresses and admonitions. As for the reflections of the men, there was a great deal of rage in them. Perchance they might be formulated thus: "If I am going to be drowned—if I am going to be drowned—if I am going to be drowned, why, in the name of the seven mad gods who rule the sea, was I allowed to come thus far and contemplate sand and trees? Was I brought here merely to have my nose dragged away as I was about to nibble the sacred cheese of life? It is preposterous. If this old ninny-woman, Fate, cannot do better than this, she should be deprived of the management of men's fortunes. She is an old hen who knows not her intention. If she has decided to drown me, why did she not do it in the beginning and save me all this trouble? The whole affair is absurd.—But no; she cannot mean to drown me. She dare not drown me. She cannot drown me. Not after all this work." Afterward the man might have had an impulse to shake his fist at the clouds. "Just you drown me, now, and then hear what I call you!"

The billows that came at this time were more formidable. They seemed always just about to break and roll over the little boat in a turmoil of foam. There was a preparatory and long growl in the speech of them. No mind unused to the sea would have concluded that the dinghy could ascend these sheer heights in time. The shore was still afar. The oiler was a wily surfman. "Boys," he said swiftly, "she won't live three minutes more, and we're too far out to swim. Shall I take her to sea again, Captain?"

"Yes; go ahead!" said the captain.

This oiler, by a series of quick miracles and fast and steady oarsmanship, turned the boat in the middle of the surf and took her safely to sea again.

There was a considerable silence as the boat bumped over the furrowed sea to deeper water. Then somebody in gloom spoke: "Well, anyhow, they must have seen us from the shore by now."

The gulls went in slanting flight up the wind toward the grey, desolate east. A squall, marked by dingy clouds and clouds brick-red like smoke from a burning building, appeared from the south-east.

"What do you think of those life-saving people? Ain't they peaches?"

"Funny they haven't seen us."

"Maybe they think we're out here for sport! Maybe they think we're fishin'. Maybe they think we're damned fools."

It was a long afternoon. A changed tide tried to force them southward, but wind and wave said northward. Far ahead, where coast-line, sea, and sky formed their mighty angle, there were little dots which seemed to indicate a city on the shore.

"St. Augustine?"

The captain shook his head. "Too near Mosquito Inlet."

And the oiler rowed, and then the correspondent rowed; then the oiler rowed. It was a weary business. The human back can become the seat of more aches and pains than are registered in books for the composite anatomy of a regiment. It is a limited area, but it can become the theatre of innumerable muscular conflicts, tangles, wrenches, knots, and other comforts.

"Did you ever like to row, Billie?" asked the correspondent.

"No," said the oiler; "hang it!"

When one exchanged the rowing-seat for a place in the bottom of the boat, he suffered a bodily depression that caused him to be careless of everything save an obligation to wiggle one finger. There was cold sea-water swashing to and fro in the boat, and he lay in it. His head, pillowed on a thwart, was within an inch of the swirl of a wave-crest, and sometimes a particularly obstreperous sea came inboard and drenched him once more. But these matters did not annoy him. It is almost certain that if the boat had capsized he would have tumbled comfortably out upon the ocean as if he felt sure that it was a great soft mattress.

"Look! There's a man on the shore!"

"Where?"

"There! See 'im? See 'im?"

"Yes, sure! He's walking along."

"Now he's stopped. Look! He's facing us!"

"He's waving at us!"

"So he is! By thunder!"

"Ah, now we're all right! Now we're all right! There'll be a boat out here for us in half an hour."

"He's going on. He's running. He's going up to that house there."

The remote beach seemed lower than the sea, and it required a searching glance to discern the little black figure. The captain saw a floating stick, and they rowed to it. A bath towel was by some weird chance in the boat, and, tying this on the stick, the captain waved it. The oarsman did not dare turn his head, so he was obliged to ask questions.

"What's he doing now?"

"He's standing still again. He's looking, I think.—There he goes again—toward the house.—Now he's stopped again."

"Is he waving at us?"

"No, not now; he was, though."

"Look! There comes another man!"

"He's running."

"Look at him go, would you!"

"Why, he's on a bicycle. Now he's met the other man. They're both waving at us. Look!"

"There comes something up the beach."

"What the devil is that thing?"

"Why, it looks like a boat."

"Why, certainly, it's a boat."

"No; it's on wheels."

"Yes, so it is. Well, that must be the life-boat. They drag them along shore on a wagon."

"That's the life-boat, sure."

"No, by God, it's—it's an omnibus."

"I tell you it's a life-boat."

"It is not! It's an omnibus. I can see it plain. See? One of these big hotel omnibuses."

"By thunder, you're right. It's an omnibus, sure as fate. What do you suppose they are doing with an omnibus? Maybe they are going around collecting the life-crew, hey?"

"That's it, likely. Look! There's a fellow waving a little black flag. He's standing on the steps of the omnibus. There come those other two fellows. Now they're all talking together. Look at the fellow with the flag. Maybe he ain't waving it!"

"That ain't a flag, is it? That's his coat. Why, certainly, that's his coat."

"So it is; it's his coat. He's taken it off and is waving it around his head. But would you look at him swing it!"

"Oh, say, there isn't any life-saving station there. That's just a winter-resort hotel omnibus that has brought over some of the boarders to see us drown."

"What's that idiot with the coat mean? What's he signalling, anyhow?"

"It looks as if he were trying to tell us to go north. There must be a life-saving station up there."

"No; he thinks we're fishing. Just giving us a merry hand. See? Ah, there, Willie!"

"Well, I wish I could make something out of those signals. What do you suppose he means?"

"He don't mean anything; he's just playing."

"Well, if he'd just signal us to try the surf again, or to go to sea and wait, or go north, or go south, or go to hell, there would be some reason in it. But look at him! He just stands there and keeps his coat revolving like a wheel. The ass!"

"There come more people."

"Now there's quite a mob. Look! Isn't that a boat?"

"Where? Oh, I see where you mean. No, that's no boat."

"That fellow is still waving his coat."

"He must think we like to see him do that. Why don't he quit it? It don't mean anything."

"I don't know. I think he is trying to make us go north. It must be that there's a life-saving station there somewhere."

"Say, he ain't tired yet. Look at 'im wave!"

"Wonder how long he can keep that up. He's been revolving his coat ever since he caught sight of us. He's an idiot. Why aren't they getting men to bring a boat out? A fishing-boat—one of those big yawls—could come out here all right. Why don't he do something?"

"Oh, it's all right now."

"They'll have a boat out here for us in less than no time, now that they've seen us."

A faint yellow tone came into the sky over the low land. The shadows on the sea slowly deepened. The wind bore coldness with it, and the men began to shiver.

"Holy smoke!" said one, allowing his voice to express his impious mood, "if we keep on monkeying out here! If we've got to flounder out here all night!"

"Oh, we'll never have to stay here all night! Don't you worry. They've seen us now, and it won't be long before they'll come chasing out after us."

The shore grew dusky. The man waving a coat blended gradually into this gloom, and it swallowed in the same manner the omnibus and the group of people. The spray, when it dashed uproariously over the side, made the voyagers shrink and swear like men who were being branded.

"I'd like to catch the chump who waved the coat. I feel like socking him one, just for luck."

"Why? What did he do?"

"Oh, nothing, but then he seemed so damned cheerful."

In the meantime the oiler rowed, and then the correspondent rowed, and then the oiler rowed. Grey-faced and bowed forward, they mechanically, turn by turn, plied the leaden oars. The form of the lighthouse had vanished from the southern horizon, but finally a pale star appeared, just lifting from the sea. The streaked saffron in the west passed before the all-merging darkness, and the sea to the east was black. The land had vanished, and was expressed only by the low and drear thunder of the surf.

"If I am going to be drowned—if I am going to be drowned—if I am going to be drowned, why, in the name of the seven mad gods who rule the sea, was I allowed to come thus far and contemplate sand and trees? Was I brought here merely to have my nose dragged away as I was about to nibble the sacred cheese of life?"

The patient captain, drooped over the water-jar, was sometimes obliged to speak to the oarsman.

"Keep her head up! Keep her head up!"

"Keep her head up, sir." The voices were weary and low.

This was surely a quiet evening. All save the oarsman lay heavily and listlessly in the boat's bottom. As for him, his eyes were just capable of noting the tall black waves that swept forward in a most sinister silence, save for an occasional subdued growl of a crest.

The cook's head was on a thwart, and he looked without interest at the water under his nose. He was deep in other scenes. Finally he spoke. "Billie," he murmured, dreamfully, "what kind of pie do you like best?"

v

"Pie!" said the oiler and the correspondent, agitatedly. "Don't talk about those things, blast you!"

"Well," said the cook, "I was just thinking about ham sandwiches and—"

A night on the sea in an open boat is a long night. As darkness settled finally, the shine of the light, lifting from the sea in the south, changed to full gold. On the northern horizon a new light appeared, a small bluish gleam on the edge of the waters. These two lights were the furniture of the world. Otherwise there was nothing but waves.

Two men huddled in the stern, and distances were so magnificent in the dinghy that the rower was enabled to keep his feet partly warm by thrusting them under his companions. Their legs indeed extended far under the rowing-seat until they touched the feet of the captain forward. Sometimes, despite the efforts of the tired oarsman, a wave came piling into the boat, an icy wave of the night, and the chilling water soaked them anew. They would twist their bodies for a moment and groan, and sleep the dead sleep once more, while the water in the boat gurgled about them as the craft rocked.

The plan of the oiler and the correspondent was for one to row until he lost the ability, and then arouse the other from his sea-water couch in the bottom of the boat.

The oiler plied the oars until his head drooped forward and the overpowering sleep blinded him; and he rowed yet afterward. Then he touched a man in the bottom of the boat, and called his name. "Will you spell me for a little while?" he said, meekly.

"Sure, Billie," said the correspondent, awaking and dragging himself to a sitting position. They exchanged places carefully, and the oiler, cuddling down in the sea-water at the cook's side, seemed to go to sleep instantly.

The particular violence of the sea had ceased. The waves came without snarling. The obligation of the man at the oars was to keep the boat headed so that the tilt of the rollers would not capsize her, and to preserve her from filling when the crests rushed past. The black waves were silent and hard to be seen in the darkness. Often one was almost upon the boat before the oarsman was aware.

In a low voice the correspondent addressed the captain. He was not sure that the captain was awake, although this iron man seemed to be always awake. "Captain, shall I keep her making for that light north, sir?"

The same steady voice answered him. "Yes. Keep it about two points off the port bow."

The cook had tied a life-belt around himself in order to get even the warmth which this clumsy cork contrivance could donate, and he seemed almost stove-like when a rower, whose teeth invariably chattered wildly as soon as he ceased his labour, dropped down to sleep.

The correspondent, as he rowed, looked down at the two men sleeping underfoot. The cook's arm was around the oiler's shoulders, and, with their fragmentary clothing and haggard faces, they were the babes of the sea—a grotesque rendering of the old babes in the wood.

Later he must have grown stupid at his work, for suddenly there was a growling of water, and a crest came with a roar and a swash into the boat, and it was a wonder that it did not set the cook afloat in his life-belt. The cook continued to sleep, but the oiler sat up, blinking his eyes and shaking with the new cold.

"Oh, I'm awful sorry, Billie," said the correspondent, contritely.

"That's all right, old boy," said the oiler, and lay down again and was asleep.

Presently it seemed that even the captain dozed, and the correspondent thought that he was the one man afloat on all the oceans. The wind had a voice as it came over the waves, and it was sadder than the end.

There was a long, loud swishing astern of the boat, and a gleaming trail of phosphorescence, like blue flame, was furrowed on the black waters. It might have been made by a monstrous knife.

Then there came a stillness, while the correspondent breathed with open mouth and looked at the sea.

Suddenly there was another swish and another long flash of bluish light, and this time it was alongside the boat, and might almost been reached with an oar. The correspondent saw an enormous fin speed like a shadow through the water, hurling the crystalline spray and leaving the long glowing trail.

The correspondent looked over his shoulder at the captain. His face was hidden, and he seemed to be asleep. He looked at the babes of the sea. They certainly were asleep. So, being bereft of sympathy, he leaned a little way to one side and swore softly into the sea.

But the thing did not then leave the vicinity of the boat. Ahead or astern, on one side or the other, at intervals long or short, fled the long sparkling streak, and there was to be heard the *whirroo* of the dark fin. The speed and power of the thing was greatly to be admired. It cut the water like a gigantic and keen projectile.

The presence of this biding thing did not affect the man with the same horror that it would if he had been a picnicker. He simply looked at the sea dully and swore in an undertone.

Nevertheless, it is true that he did not wish to be alone with the thing. He wished one of his companions to awake by chance and keep him company with it. But the captain hung motionless over the water-jar, and the oiler and the cook in the bottom of the boat were plunged in slumber.

VI

"If I am going to be drowned—if I am going to be drowned—if I am going to be drowned, why, in the name of the seven mad gods who rule the sea, was I allowed to come thus far and contemplate sand and trees?"

During this dismal night, it may be remarked that a man would conclude that it was really the intention of the seven mad gods to drown him, despite the abominable injustice of it. For it was certainly an abominable injustice to drown a man who had worked so hard, so hard. The man felt it would be a crime most unnatural. Other people had drowned at sea since galleys swarmed with painted sails, but still—

When it occurs to a man that nature does not regard him as important, and that she feels she would not maim the universe by disposing of him, he at first wishes to throw bricks at the temple, and he hates deeply the fact that there are no bricks and no temples. Any visible expression of nature would surely be pelleted with his jeers.

Then, if there be no tangible thing to hoot, he feels, perhaps, the desire to confront a personification and indulge in pleas, bowed to one knee, and with hands supplicant, saying, "Yes, but I love myself."

A high cold star on a winter's night is the word he feels that she says to him. Thereafter he knows the pathos of his situation.

The men in the dinghy had not discussed these matters, but each had, no doubt, reflected upon them in silence and according to his mind. There was seldom any expression upon their faces save the general one of complete weariness. Speech was devoted to the business of the boat.

To chime the notes of his emotion, a verse mysteriously entered the correspondent's head. He had even forgotten that he had forgotten this verse, but it suddenly was in mind.

> A soldier of the Legion lay dying in Algiers;
> There was lack of woman's nursing, there was dearth of woman's tears;
> But a comrade stood beside him, and he took that comrade's hand,
> And he said, "I never more shall see my own, my native land."

In his childhood the correspondent had been made acquainted with the fact that a soldier of the Legion lay dying in Algiers, but he had never regarded the fact as important. Myriads of his school-fellows had informed him of the soldier's plight, but the dinning had naturally ended by making him perfectly indifferent. He had never considered it his affair that a soldier of the Legion lay dying in Algiers, nor had it appeared to him as a matter for sorrow. It was less to him than the breaking of a pencil's point.

Now, however, it quaintly came to him as a human, living thing. It was no longer merely a picture of a few throes in the breast of a poet, meanwhile drinking tea and warming his feet at the grate; it was an actuality—stern, mournful, and fine.

The correspondent plainly saw the soldier. He lay on the sand with his feet out straight and still. While his pale left hand was upon his chest in an attempt to thwart the going of his life, the blood came between his fingers. In the far Algerian distance, a city of low square forms was set against a sky that was faint with the last sunset hues. The correspondent, plying the oars and dreaming of the slow and slower movements of the lips of the soldier, was moved by a profound and perfectly impersonal comprehension. He was sorry for the soldier of the Legion who lay dying in Algiers.

The thing which had followed the boat and waited had evidently grown bored at the delay. There was no longer to be heard the slash of the cutwater, and there was no longer the flame of the long trail. The light in the north still glimmered, but it was apparently no nearer to the boat. Sometimes the boom of the surf rang in the correspondent's ears, and he turned the craft seaward then and rowed harder. Southward, some one had evidently built a watch-fire on the beach. It was too low and too far to be seen, but it made a shimmering, roseate reflection upon the bluff in back of it, and this could be discerned from the boat. The wind came stronger, and sometimes a wave suddenly raged out like a mountain cat, and there was to be seen the sheen and sparkle of a broken crest.

The captain, in the bow, moved on his water-jar and sat erect. "Pretty long night," he observed to the correspondent. He looked at the shore. "Those life-saving people take their time."

"Did you see that shark playing around?"

"Yes, I saw him. He was a big fellow, all right."

"Wish I had known you were awake."

Later the correspondent spoke into the bottom of the boat. "Billie!" There was a slow and gradual disentanglement. "Billie, will you spell me?"

"Sure," said the oiler.

As soon as the correspondent touched the cold, comfortable sea-water in the bottom of the boat and had huddled close to the cook's life-belt he was deep in sleep, despite the fact that his teeth played all the popular airs. This sleep was so good to him that it was but a moment before he heard a voice call his name in a tone that demonstrated the last stages of exhaustion. "Will you spell me?"

"Sure, Billie."

The light in the north had mysteriously vanished, but the correspondent took his course from the wide-awake captain.

Later in the night they took the boat farther out to sea, and the captain directed the cook to take one oar at the stern and keep the boat facing the seas. He was to call out if he should hear the thunder of the surf. This plan enabled the oiler and the correspondent to get respite together. "We'll give those boys a chance to get into shape again," said the captain. They curled down and, after a few preliminary chatterings and trembles, slept once more the dead sleep. Neither knew they had bequeathed to the cook the company of another shark, or perhaps the same shark.

As the boat caroused on the waves, spray occasionally bumped over the side and gave them a fresh soaking, but this had no power to break their repose. The ominous slash of the wind and the water affected them as it would have affected mummies.

"Boys," said the cook, with the notes of every reluctance in his voice, "she's drifted in pretty close. I guess one of you had better take her to sea again." The correspondent, aroused, heard the crash of the toppled crests.

As he was rowing, the captain gave him some whisky-and-water, and this steadied the chills out of him. "If I ever get ashore and anybody shows me even a photograph of an oar—"

At last there was a short conversation.

"Billie!—Billie, will you spell me?"

"Sure," said the oiler.

VII

When the correspondent again opened his eyes, the sea and the sky were each of the grey hue of the dawning. Later, carmine and gold was painted upon the waters. The morning appeared finally, in its splendour, with a sky of pure blue, and the sunlight flamed on the tips of the waves.

On the distant dunes were set many little black cottages, and a tall white windmill reared above them. No man, nor dog, nor bicycle appeared on the beach. The cottages might have formed a deserted village.

The voyagers scanned the shore. A conference was held in the boat. "Well," said the captain, "if no help is coming, we might better try a run through the surf right away. If we stay out here much longer we will be too weak to do anything for ourselves at all." The others silently acquiesced in this reasoning. The boat was headed for the beach. The correspondent wondered if none ever ascended the tall wind-tower, and if then they never looked seaward. This tower was a giant, standing with its back to the plight of the ants. It represented in a degree, to the correspondent, the serenity of nature amid the struggles of the individual—nature in the wind, and nature in the vision of men. She did not seem cruel to him then, nor beneficent, nor treacherous, nor wise. But she was indifferent, flatly indifferent. It is, perhaps, plausible that a man in this situation, impressed with the unconcern of the universe, should see the innumerable flaws of his life, and have them taste wickedly in his mind, and wish for another chance. A distinction between right and wrong seems absurdly clear to him, then, in this new ignorance of the grave-edge, and he understands that if he were given another opportunity he would mend his conduct and his words, and be better and brighter during an introduction or at a tea.

"Now, boys," said the captain, "she is going to swamp sure. All we can do is to work her in as far as possible, and then when she swamps, pile out and scramble for the beach. Keep cool now, and don't jump until she swamps sure."

The oiler took the oars. Over his shoulders he scanned the surf. "Captain," he said, "I think I'd better bring her about and keep her head-on to the seas and back her in."

"All right, Billie," said the captain. "Back her in." The oiler swung the boat then, and, seated in the stern, the cook and the correspondent were obliged to look over their shoulders to contemplate the lonely and indifferent shore.

The monstrous inshore rollers heaved the boat high until the men were again enabled to see the white sheets of water scudding up the slanted beach. "We won't get in very close," said the captain. Each time a man could wrest his attention from the rollers, he turned his glance toward the shore, and in the expression of the eyes during this contemplation there was a singular quality. The correspondent, observing the others, knew that they were not afraid, but the full meaning of their glances was shrouded.

As for himself, he was too tired to grapple fundamentally with the fact. He tried to coerce his mind into thinking of it, but the mind was dominated at this time by the muscles, and the muscles said they did not care. It merely occurred to him that if he should drown it would be a shame.

There were no hurried words, no pallor, no plain agitation. The men simply looked at the shore. "Now, remember to get well clear of the boat when you jump," said the captain.

Seaward the crest of a roller suddenly fell with a thunderous crash, and the long white comber came roaring down upon the boat.

"Steady now," said the captain. The men were silent. They turned their eyes from the shore to the comber and waited. The boat slid up the incline, leaped at the furious top, bounced over it, and swung down the long back of the wave. Some water had been shipped, and the cook bailed it out.

But the next crest crashed also. The tumbling, boiling flood of white water caught the boat and whirled it almost perpendicular. Water swarmed in from all sides. The correspondent had his hands on the gunwale at this time, and when the water entered at that place he swiftly withdrew his fingers, as if he objected to wetting them.

The little boat, drunken with this weight of water, reeled and snuggled deeper into the sea.

"Bail her out, cook! Bail her out!" said the captain.

"All right, Captain," said the cook.

"Now, boys, the next one will do for us sure," said the oiler. "Mind to jump clear of the boat."

The third wave moved forward, huge, furious, implacable. It fairly swallowed the dinghy, and almost simultaneously the men tumbled into the sea. A piece of life-belt had lain in the bottom of the boat, and as the correspondent went overboard he held this to his chest with his left hand.

The January water was icy, and he reflected immediately that it was colder than he had expected to find it off the coast of Florida. This appeared to his dazed mind as a fact important enough to be noted at the time. The coldness of the water was sad; it was tragic. This fact was somehow mixed and confused with his opinion of his own situation, so that it seemed almost a proper reason for tears. The water was cold.

When he came to the surface he was conscious of little but the noisy water. Afterward he saw his companions in the sea. The oiler was ahead in the race. He was swimming strongly and rapidly. Off to the correspondent's left, the cook's great white and corked back bulged out of the water; and in the rear the captain was hanging with his one good hand to the keel of the overturned dinghy.

There is a certain immovable quality to a shore, and the correspondent wondered at it amid the confusion of the sea.

It seemed also very attractive; but the correspondent knew that it was a long journey, and he paddled leisurely. The piece of life-preserver lay under him, and sometimes he whirled down the incline of a wave as if he were on a hand-sled.

But finally he arrived at a place in the sea where travel was beset with difficulty. He did not pause swimming to inquire what manner of current had caught him, but there his progress ceased. The shore was set before him like a bit of scenery on a stage, and he looked at it and understood with his eyes each detail of it.

As the cook passed, much farther to the left, the captain was calling to him, "Turn over on your back, cook! Turn over on your back and use the oar."

"All right, sir." The cook turned on his back, and, paddling with an oar, went ahead as if he were a canoe.

Presently the boat also passed to the left of the correspondent, with the captain clinging with one hand to the keel. He would have appeared like a man raising himself to look over a board fence if it were not for the extraordinary gymnastics of the boat. The correspondent marvelled that the captain could still hold to it.

They passed on nearer to shore—the oiler, the cook, the captain—and following them went the water-jar, bouncing gaily over the seas.

The correspondent remained in the grip of this strange new enemy—a current. The shore, with its white slope of sand and its green bluff topped with little silent cottages, was spread like a picture before him. It was very near to him then, but he was impressed as one who, in a gallery, looks at a scene from Brittany or Holland.

He thought: "I am going to drown? Can it be possible? Can it be possible? Can it be possible?" Perhaps an individual must consider his own death to be the final phenomenon of nature.

But later a wave perhaps whirled him out of this small deadly current, for he found suddenly that he could again make progress toward the shore. Later still he was aware that the captain, clinging with one hand to the keel of the dinghy, had his face turned away from the shore and toward him, and was calling his name. "Come to the boat! Come to the boat!"

In his struggle to reach the captain and the boat, he reflected that when one gets properly wearied drowning must really be a comfortable arrangement—a cessation of hostilities accompanied by a large degree of relief; and he was glad of it, for the main thing in his mind for some moments had been horror of the temporary agony. He did not wish to be hurt.

Presently he saw a man running along the shore. He was undressing with most remarkable speed. Coat, trousers, shirt, everything flew magically off him.

"Come to the boat!" called the captain.

"All right, Captain." As the correspondent paddled, he saw the captain let himself down to bottom and leave the boat. Then the correspondent performed his one little marvel of the voyage. A large wave caught him and flung him with ease and supreme speed completely over the boat and far beyond it. It struck him even then as an event in gymnastics and a true miracle of the sea. An overturned boat in the surf is not a plaything to a swimming man.

The correspondent arrived in water that reached only to his waist, but his condition did not enable him to stand for more than a moment. Each wave knocked him into a heap, and the undertow pulled at him.

Then he saw the man who had been running and undressing, and undressing and running, come bounding into the water. He dragged ashore the cook, and then waded toward the captain; but the captain waved him away and sent him to the correspondent. He was naked—naked as a tree in winter; but a halo was about his head, and he shone like a saint. He gave a strong pull, and a long drag, and a bully heave at the correspondent's hand. The correspondent, schooled in the minor formulae, said, "Thanks, old man." But suddenly the man cried, "What's that?" He pointed a swift finger. The correspondent said, "Go."

In the shallows, face downward, lay the oiler. His forehead touched sand that was periodically, between each wave, clear of the sea.

The correspondent did not know all that transpired afterward. When he achieved safe ground he fell, striking the sand with each particular part of his body. It was as if he had dropped from a roof, but the thud was grateful to him.

It seemed that instantly the beach was populated with men with blankets, clothes, and flasks, and women with coffee-pots and all the remedies sacred to their minds. The welcome of the land to the men from the sea was warm and generous; but a still and dripping shape was carried slowly up the beach, and the land's welcome for it could only be the different and sinister hospitality of the grave.

When it came night, the white waves paced to and fro in the moonlight, and the wind brought the sound of the great sea's voice to the men on the shore, and they felt that they could then be interpreters.

DISCUSSION QUESTIONS

1. How does the fictionalized tale "The Open Boat" differ from the newspaper report of the same event in "Stephen Crane's Own Story"? Have any incidents been changed or added? Has anything been distorted? Explain how Crane's role as a participant and writer changes as he turns from journalism to fiction.

2. How do Crane's tone and imagery change as he imagines a different form and audience for his writing? Point to specific examples.

Jack London / To Build a Fire   1908

One of America's most prolific and popular authors, Jack London was born in San Francisco in 1876. By the age of fourteen he had dropped out of school to take on risky jobs and hang around the Oakland saloons. His adventures did not interfere with his love of reading and thirst for knowledge, however, and for a time London studied at the University of California, Berkeley. In 1897, London joined the Klondike gold rush and lived for nearly a year on the Alaskan frontier. He found no gold but instead found the subjects for many stories and novels. His first collection of short stories, The Son of the Wolf, *appeared in 1900, and three years later London published his best-selling novel,* The Call of the Wild. *Over the next several years London wrote some of his most important novels—*The Sea Wolf *(1904),* White Fang *(1906), and the autobiographical* Martin Eden *(1909). London, who ran unsuccessfully in two Oakland mayoral elections as a Socialist, also wrote much social criticism. He died of an overdose of morphine in 1916.*

For more information on London, see "Magazines."

Day had broken cold and gray, exceedingly cold and gray, when the man turned aside from the main Yukon trail and climbed the high earth-bank, where a dim and little-travelled trail led eastward through the fat spruce timberland. It was a steep bank, and he paused for breath at the top, excusing the act to himself by looking at his watch. It was nine o'clock. There was no sun nor hint of sun, though there was not a cloud in the sky. It was a clear day, and yet there seemed an intangible pall over the face of things, a subtle gloom that made the day dark, and that was due to the absence of sun. This fact did not worry the man. He was used to the lack of sun. It had been days since he had seen the sun, and he knew that a few more days must pass before that cheerful orb, due south, would just peep above the sky line and dip immediately from view.

The man flung a look back along the way he had come. The Yukon lay a mile wide and hidden under three feet of ice. On top of this ice were as many feet of snow. It was all pure white, rolling in gentle undulations where the ice jams of the freeze-up had formed. North and south, as far as the eye could see, it was unbroken white, save for a dark hairline that curved and twisted from around the spruce-covered island to the south, and that curved and twisted away into the north, where it disappeared behind another spruce-covered island. This dark hair-line was the trail—the main trail—that led south five hundred miles to the Chil-coot Pass, Dyea, and salt water; and that led north seventy miles to Dawson, and still on to the north a thousand miles to Nulato, and finally to St. Michael, on Bering Sea, a thousand miles and half a thousand more.

But all this—the mysterious, far-reaching hairline trail, the absence of sun from the sky, the tremendous cold, and the strangeness and weirdness of it all—made no impression on the man. It was not because he was long used to it. He was a newcomer in the land, a *chechaquo,* and this was his first winter. The trouble with him was that he was without imagination. He was quick and alert in the things of life, but only in the things, and not in the significances. Fifty degrees below zero meant eighty-odd degrees of frost. Such fact impressed him as being cold and uncomfortable, and that was all. It did not lead him to meditate upon his frailty as a creature of temperature, and upon man's frailty in general, able only to live within certain narrow limits of heat and cold; and from there on it did not lead him to the conjectural field of immortality and man's place in the universe. Fifty degrees below zero stood for a bite of frost that hurt and that must be guarded against by the use of mittens, ear flaps, warm moccasins, and thick socks. Fifty degrees below zero was to him just precisely fifty degrees below zero. That there should be anything more to it than that was a thought that never entered his head.

As he turned to go on, he spat speculatively. There was a sharp, explosive crackle that startled him. He spat again. And again, in the air, before it could fall to the snow, the spittle crackled. He knew that at fifty below spittle crackled on the snow, but this spittle had crackled in the air. Undoubtedly it was colder than fifty below—how much colder he did not know. But the temperature did not matter. He was bound for the old claim on the left fork of Henderson Creek, where the boys were already. They had come over across the divide from the Indian Creek country, while he had come the roundabout way to take a look at the possibilities of getting out logs in the spring from the islands in the Yukon. He would be in to camp by six o'clock; a bit after dark, it was true, but the boys would be there, a fire would be going, and a hot supper would be ready. As for lunch, he pressed his hand against the protruding bundle under his jacket. It was also under his shirt, wrapped up in a handkerchief and lying against the naked skin. It was the only way to keep the biscuits from freezing. He smiled agreeably to himself as he thought of those biscuits, each cut open and sopped in bacon grease, and each enclosing a generous slice of fried bacon.

He plunged in among the big spruce trees. The trail was faint. A foot of snow had fallen since the last sled had passed over, and he was glad he was without a sled, travelling light. In fact, he carried nothing but the lunch wrapped in the handkerchief. He was surprised, however, at the cold. It certainly was cold, he concluded, as he rubbed his numb nose and cheekbones with his mittened hand. He was a warm-whiskered man, but the hair on his face did not protect the high cheekbones and the eager nose that thrust itself aggressively into the frosty air.

At the man's heels trotted a dog, a big native husky, the proper wolf dog, gray-coated and without any visible or temperamental difference from its brother, the wild wolf. The animal was depressed by the tremendous cold. It knew that it was no time for travelling. Its instinct told it a truer tale than was told to the man by the man's judgment. In reality, it was not merely colder than fifty below zero; it was colder than sixty below, than seventy below. It was seventy-five below zero. Since the freezing point is thirty-two above zero, it meant that one hundred and seven degrees of frost obtained. The dog did not know anything about thermometers. Possibly in its brain there was no sharp consciousness of a condition of very cold such as was in the man's brain. But the brute had its instinct. It experienced a vague but menacing apprehension that subdued it and made it slink along at the man's heels, and that made it question eagerly every unwonted movement of the man as if expecting him to go into camp or to seek shelter somewhere and build a fire. The dog had learned fire, and it wanted fire, or else to burrow under the snow and cuddle its warmth away from the air.

The frozen moisture of its breathing had settled on its fur in a fine powder of frost, and especially were its jowls, muzzle, and eyelashes whitened by its crystalled breath. The man's red beard and mustache were likewise frosted, but more solidly, the deposit taking the form of ice and increasing with every warm, moist breath he exhaled. Also, the man was chewing tobacco, and the muzzle of ice held his lips so rigidly that he was unable to clear his chin when he expelled the juice. The result was that a crystal beard of the color and solidity of amber was increasing its length on his chin. If he fell down it would shatter itself, like glass, into brittle fragments. But he did not mind the appendage. It was the penalty all tobacco chewers paid in that country, and he had been out before in two cold snaps. They had not been so cold as this, he knew, but by the spirit thermometer at Sixty Mile he knew they had been registered at fifty below and at fifty-five.

He held on through the level stretch of woods for several miles, crossed a wide flat of nigger heads, and dropped down a bank to the frozen bed of a small stream. This was Henderson Creek, and he knew he was ten miles from the forks. He looked at his watch. It was ten o'clock. He was making four miles an hour, and he calculated that he would arrive at the forks at half-past twelve. He decided to celebrate that event by eating his lunch there.

The dog dropped in again at his heels, with a tail drooping discouragement, as the man swung along the creek bed. The furrow of the old sled trail was plainly visible, but a dozen inches of snow covered the marks of the last runners. In a month no man had come up or down that silent creek. The man held steadily on. He was not much given to thinking, and just then particularly he had nothing to think about save that he would eat lunch at the forks and that at six o'clock he would be in camp with the boys. There was nobody to talk to; and, had there been, speech would have been impossible because of the ice muzzle on his mouth. So he continued monotonously to chew tobacco and to increase the length of his amber beard.

Once in a while the thought reinterated itself that it was very cold and that he had never experienced such cold. As he walked along he rubbed his cheekbones and nose with the back of his mittened hand. He did this automatically, now and again changing hands. But, rub as he would, the instant he stopped his cheekbones went numb, and the following instant the end of his nose went numb. He was sure to frost his cheeks; he knew that, and experienced a pang of regret that he had not devised a nose strap of the sort Bud wore in cold snaps. Such a strap passed across the cheeks, as well, and saved them. But it didn't matter much, after all. What were frosted cheeks? A bit painful, that was all; they were never serious.

Empty as the man's mind was of thoughts, he was keenly observant, and he noticed the changes in the creek, the curves and bends and timber jams, and always he sharply noted where he placed his feet. Once, coming around a bend, he shied abruptly, like a startled horse, curved away from the place where he had been walking, and retreated several paces back along the trail. The creek he knew was frozen clear to the bottom—no creek could contain water in that arctic winter—but he knew also that there were springs that bubbled out from the hillsides and ran along under the snow and on top the ice of the creek. He knew that the coldest snaps never froze these springs, and he knew likewise their danger. They were traps. They hid pools of water under the snow that might be three inches deep, or three feet. Sometimes a skin of ice half an inch thick covered them, and in turn was covered by the snow. Sometimes there were alternate layers of water and ice skin, so that when one broke through he kept on breaking through for a while, sometimes wetting himself to the waist.

That was why he had shied in such panic. He had felt the give under his feet and heard the crackle of a snow-hidden ice skin. And to get his feet wet in such a temperature meant trouble and danger. At the very least it meant delay, for he would be forced to stop and build a fire, and under its protection to bare his feet while he dried his socks and moccasins. He stood and studied the creek bed and its banks, and decided that the flow of water came from the right. He reflected awhile, rubbing his nose and cheeks, then skirted to the left, stepping gingerly and testing the footing for each step. Once clear of the danger, he took a fresh chew of tobacco and swung along at his four-mile gait.

In the course of the next two hours he came upon several similar traps. Usually the snow above the hidden pools had a sunken, candied appearance that advertised the danger. Once again, however, he had a close call; and once, suspecting danger, he compelled the dog to go on in front. The dog did not want to go. It hung back until the man shoved it toward, and then it went quickly across the white, unbroken surface. Suddenly it broke through, floundered to one side, and got away to firmer footing. It had wet its forefeet and legs, and almost immediately the water that clung to it turned to ice. It made quick efforts to lick the ice off its legs, then dropped down in the snow and began to bite out the ice that had formed between the toes. This was matter of instinct. To permit the ice to remain would mean sore feet. It did not know this. It merely obeyed the mysterious prompting that arose from the deep crypts of its being. But the man knew, having achieved a judgment on the subject, and he removed the mitten from his right hand and helped tear out the ice particles. He did not expose his fingers more than a minute, and was astonished at the swift numbness that smote them. It certainly was cold. He pulled on the mitten hastily, and beat the hand savagely across the chest.

At twelve o'clock the day was at its brightest. Yet the sun was too far south on its winter journey to clear the horizon. The bulge of the earth intervened between it and Henderson Creek, where the man walked under a clear sky at noon and cast no shadow. At half-past twelve, to the minute, he arrived at the forks of the creek. He was pleased at the speed he had made. If he kept it up, he would certainly be with the boys by six. He unbuttoned his jacket and shirt and drew forth his lunch. The action consumed no more than a quarter of a minute, yet in that brief moment the numbness laid hold of the exposed fingers. He did not put the mitten on, but, instead, struck the fingers a dozen sharp smashes against his leg. Then he sat down on a snow-covered log to eat. The sting that followed upon the striking of his fingers against his leg ceased so quickly that he was startled. He had had no chance to take a bit of biscuit. He struck the fingers repeatedly and returned them to the mitten, baring the other hand for the purpose of eating. He tried to take a mouthful, but the ice muzzle prevented. He had forgotten to build a fire and thaw out. He chuckled at his foolishness, and as he chuckled he noted the numbness creeping into the exposed fingers. Also, he noted that the stinging which had first come to his toes when he sat down was already passing away. He wondered whether the toes were warm or numb. He moved them inside the moccasins and decided that they were numb.

He pulled the mitten on hurriedly and stood up. He was a bit frightened. He stamped up and down until the stinging returned into the feet. It certainly was cold, was his thought. That man from Sulphur Creek had spoken the truth when telling how cold it sometimes got in the country. And he had laughed at him at the time! That showed one must not be too sure of things. There was no mistake about it, it was cold. He strode up and down, stamping his feet and threshing his arms, until reassured by the returning warmth. Then he got out matches and proceeded to make a fire. From the undergrowth, where high water of the previous spring had lodged a supply of seasoned twigs, he got his firewood. Working carefully from a small beginning, he soon had a roaring fire, over which he thawed the ice from his face and in the protection of which he ate his biscuits. For the moment the cold of space was outwitted. The dog took satisfaction in the fire, stretching out close enough for warmth and far enough away to escape being singed.

When the man had finished, he filled his pipe and took his comfortable time over a smoke. Then he pulled on his mittens, settled the ear flaps of his cap firmly about his ears, and took the creek trail up the left fork. The dog was disappointed and yearned back toward the fire. This man did not know cold. Possibly all the generations of his ancestry had been ignorant of cold, of real cold, of cold one hundred and seven degrees below freezing point. But the dog knew; all its ancestry knew, and it had inherited the knowledge. And it knew that it was not good to walk abroad in such fearful cold. It was the time to lie snug in a hole in the snow and wait for a curtain of cloud to be drawn across the face of outer space whence this cold came. On the other hand, there was no keen intimacy between the dog and the man. The one was the toil slave of the other, and the only caresses it had ever received were the caresses of the whip lash and of harsh and menacing throat sounds that threatened the whip lash. So the dog made no effort to communicate its apprehension to the man. It was not concerned in the welfare of the man; it was for its own sake that it yearned back toward the fire. But the man whistled, and spoke to it with the sound of whip lashes, and the dog swung in at the man's heels and followed after.

The man took a chew of tobacco and proceeded to start a new amber beard. Also, his moist breath quickly powdered with white his mustache, eyebrows, and lashes. There did not seem to be so many springs on the left fork of the Henderson, and for half an hour the man saw no signs of any. And then it happened. At a place where there were no signs, where the soft, unbroken snow seemed to advertise solidity beneath, the man broke through. It was not deep. He wet himself halfway to the knees before he foundered out to the firm crust.

He was angry, and cursed his luck aloud. He had hoped to get into camp with the boys at six o'clock, and this would delay him an hour, for he would have to build a fire and dry out his footgear. This was imperative at that low temperature—he knew that much; and he turned aside to the bank, which he climbed. On top, tangled in the underbrush about the trunks of several small spruce trees, was a highwater deposit of dry firewood—sticks and twigs, principally, but also larger portions of seasoned branches and fine, dry, last year's grasses. He threw down several large pieces on top of the snow. This served for a foundation and prevented the young flame from drowning itself in the snow it otherwise would melt. The flame he got by touching a match to a small shred of birch bark that he took from his pocket. This burned even more readily than paper. Placing it on the foundation, he fed the young flame with wisps of dry grass and with the tiniest dry twigs.

He worked slowly and carefully, keenly aware of his danger. Gradually, as the flame grew stronger, he increased the size of the twigs with which he fed it. He squatted in the snow, pulling the twigs out from their entanglement in the brush and feeding directly to the flame. He knew there must be no failure. When it is seventy-five below zero, a man must not fail in his first attempt to build a fire— that is, if his feet are wet. If his feet are dry, and he fails, he can run along the trail for half a mile and restore his circulation. But the circulation of wet and freezing feet cannot be restored by running when it is seventy-five below. No matter how fast he runs, the wet feet will freeze the harder. All this the man knew. The old-timer on Sulphur Creek had told him about it the previous fall, and now he was appreciating the advice. Already all sensation had gone out of his feet. To build the fire he had been forced to remove his mittens, and the fingers had quickly gone numb. His pace of four miles an hour had kept his heart pumping blood to the surface of his body and to all the extremities. But the instant he stopped, the action of the pump eased down. The cold of space smote the unprotected tip of the planet, and he, being on that unprotected tip, received the full force of the blow. The blood of his body recoiled before it. The blood was alive, like the dog, and like the dog it wanted to hide away and cover itself up from the fearful cold. So long as he walked four miles an hour, he pumped that blood, willy-nilly, to the surface; but now it ebbed away and sank down into the recesses of his body. The extremities were the first to feel its absence. His wet feet froze the faster, and his exposed fingers numbed the faster, though they had not yet begun to freeze. Nose and cheeks were already freezing, while the skin of all his body chilled as it lost its blood.

But he was safe. Toes and nose and cheeks would be only touched by the frost, for the fire was beginning to burn with strength. He was feeding it with twigs the size of his finger. In another minute he would be able to feed it with branches the size of his wrist, and then he could remove his wet footgear, and, while it dried, he could keep his naked feet warm by the fire, rubbing them at first, of course, with snow. The fire was a success. He was safe. He remembered the advice of the old-timer on Sulphur Creek, and smiled. The old-timer had been very serious in laying down the law that no man must travel alone in the Klondike after fifty below. Well, here he was; he had had the accident, he was alone; and he had saved himself. Those old-timers were rather womanish, some of them, he thought. All a man had to do was to keep his head, and he was all right. Any man who was a man could travel alone. But it was surprising, the rapidity with which his cheeks and nose were freezing. And he had not thought his fingers could go lifeless in so short a time. Lifeless they were, for he could scarcely make them move together to grip a twig, and they seemed remote from his body and from him. When he touched a twig, he had to look and see whether or not he had hold of it. The wires were pretty well down between him and his finger ends.

All of which counted for little. There was the fire, snapping and crackling and promising life with every dancing flame. He started to untie his moccasins. They were coated with ice; the thick German socks were like sheaths of iron halfway to the knees; and the moccasin strings were like rods of steel all twisted and knotted as by some conflagration. For a moment he tugged with his numb fingers, then, realizing the folly of it, he drew his sheath knife.

But before he could cut the strings, it happened. It was his own fault or, rather, his mistake. He should not have built the fire under the spruce tree. He should have built it in the open. But it had been easier to pull the twigs from the brush and drop them directly on the fire. Now the tree under which he had done this carried a weight of snow on its boughs. No wind had blown for weeks, and each bough was fully freighted. Each time he had pulled a twig he had communicated a slight agitation to the tree—an imperceptible agitation, so far as he was concerned, but an agitation sufficient to bring about the disaster. High up in the tree one bough capsized its load of snow. This fell on the boughs beneath, capsizing them. This process continued, spreading out and involving the whole tree. It grew like an avalanche, and it descended without warning upon the man and the fire, and the fire was blotted out! Where it had burned was a mantle of fresh and disordered snow.

The man was shocked. It was as though he had just heard his own sentence of death. For a moment he sat and stared at the spot where the fire had been. Then he grew very calm. Perhaps the old-timer on Sulphur Creek was right. If he had only had a trail mate he would have been in no danger now. The trail mate could have built the fire. Well, it was up to him to build the fire over again, and this second time there must be no failure. Even if he succeeded, he would most likely lose some toes. His feet must be badly frozen by now, and there would be some time before the second fire was ready.

Such were his thoughts, but he did not sit and think them. He was busy all the time they were passing through his mind. He made a new foundation for a fire, this time in the open, where no treacherous tree could blot it out. Next he gathered dry grasses and tiny twigs from the highwater flotsam. He could not bring his fingers together to pull them out, but he was able to gather them by the handful. In this way he got many rotten twigs and bits of green moss that were undesirable, but it was the best he could do. He worked methodically, even collecting an armful of the larger branches to be used later when the fire gathered strength. And all the while the dog sat and watched him, a certain yearning wistfulness in its eyes, for it looked upon him as the fire provider, and the fire was slow in coming.

When all was ready, the man reached in his pocket for a second piece of birch bark. He knew the bark was there, and though he could not feel it with his fingers, he could hear its crisp rustling as he fumbled for it. Try as he would, he could not clutch hold of it. And all the time, in his consciousness, was the knowledge that each instant his feet were freezing. This thought tended to put him in a panic, but he fought against it and kept calm. He pulled on his mittens with his teeth, and threshed his arms back and forth, beating his hands with all his might against his sides. He did this sitting down, and he stood up to do it; and all the while the dog sat in the snow, its wolf brush of a tail curled around warmly over its forefeet, its sharp wolf ears pricked forward intently as it watched the man. And the man, as he beat and threshed with his arms and hands, felt a great surge of envy as he regarded the creature that was warm and secure in its natural covering.

After a time he was aware of the first faraway signals of sensation in his beaten fingers. The faint tingling grew stronger till it evolved into a stinging ache that was excruciating, but which the man hailed with satisfaction. He stripped the mitten from his right hand and fetched forth the birch bark. The exposed fingers were quickly going numb again. Next he brought out his bunch of sulphur matches. But the tremendous cold had already driven the life out of his fingers. In his effort to separate one match from the others, the whole bunch fell in the snow. He tried to pick it out of the snow, but failed. The dead fingers could neither touch nor clutch. He was very careful. He drove the thought of his freezing feet, and nose, and cheeks, out of his mind, devoting his whole soul to the matches. He watched, using the sense of vision in place of that of touch, and when he saw his fingers on each side the bunch, he closed them—that is, he willed to close them, for the wires were down, and the fingers did not obey. He pulled the mitten on the right hand, and beat it fiercely against his knee. Then, with both mittened hands, he scooped the bunch of matches, along with much snow, into his lap. Yet he was no better off.

After some manipulation he managed to get the bunch between the heels of his mittened hands. In this fashion he carried it to his mouth. The ice crackled and snapped when by a violent effort he opened his mouth. He drew the lower jaw in, curled the upper lip out of the way, and scraped the bunch with his upper teeth in order to separate a match. He succeeded in getting one, which he dropped on his lap. He was no better off. He could not pick it up. Then he devised a way. He picked it up in his teeth and scratched it on his leg. Twenty times he scratched before he succeeded in lighting it. As it flamed he held it with his teeth to the birch bark. But the burning brimstone went up his nostrils and into his lungs, causing him to cough spasmodically. The match fell into the snow and went out.

The old-timer on Sulphur Creek was right, he thought in the moment of controlled despair that ensued: after fifty below, a man should travel with a partner. He beat his hands, but failed in exciting any sensation. Suddenly he bared both hands, removing the mittens with his teeth. He caught the whole bunch between the heels of his hands. His arm muscles not being frozen enabled him to press the hand heels tightly against the matches. Then he scratched the bunch along his leg. It flared into flame, seventy sulphur matches at once! There was no wind to blow them out. He kept his head to one side to escape the strangling fumes, and held the blazing bunch to the birch bark. As he so held it, he became aware of sensation in his hand. His flesh was burning. He could smell it. Deep down below the surface he could feel it. The sensation developed into pain that grew acute. And still he endured it, holding the flame of the matches clumsily to the bark that would not light readily because his own burning hands were in the way, absorbing most of the flame.

At last, when he could endure no more, he jerked his hands apart. The blazing matches fell sizzling into the snow, but the birch bark was alight. He began laying dry grasses and the tiniest twigs on the flame. He could not pick and choose, for he had to lift the fuel between the heels of his hands. Small pieces of rotten wood and green moss clung to the twigs, and he bit them off as well as he could with his teeth. He cherished the flame carefully and awkwardly. It meant life, and it must not perish. The withdrawal of blood from the surface of his body now made him begin to shiver, and he grew more awkward. A large piece of green moss fell squarely on the little fire. He tried to poke it out with his fingers, but his shivering frame made him poke too far, and he disrupted the nucleus of the little fire, the burning grasses and tiny twigs separating and scattering. He tried to poke them together again, but in spite of the tenseness of the effort, his shivering got away with him, and the twigs were hopelessly scattered. Each twig gushed a puff of smoke and went out. The fire provider had failed. As he looked apathetically about him, his eyes chanced on the dog, sitting across the ruins of the fire from him, in the snow, making restless, hunching movements, slightly lifting one forefoot and then the other, shifting its weight back and forth on them with wistful eagerness.

The sight of the dog put a wild idea into his head. He remembered the tale of the man, caught in a blizzard, who killed a steer and crawled inside the carcass, and so was saved. He would kill the dog and bury his hands in the warm body until the numbness went out of them. Then he could build another fire. He spoke to the dog, calling it to him; but in his voice was a strange note of fear that frightened the animal, who had never known the man to speak in such way before. Something was the matter, and its suspicious nature sensed danger—it knew not what danger, but somewhere, somehow, in its brain arose an apprehension of the man. It flattened its ears down at the sound of the man's voice, and its restless, hunching movements and the liftings and shiftings of its forefeet became more pronounced; but it would not come to the man. He got on his hands and knees and crawled toward the dog. This unusual posture again excited suspicion, and the animal sidled mincingly away.

The man sat up in the snow for a moment and struggled for calmness. Then he pulled on is mittens, by means of his teeth, and got upon his feet. He glanced down at first in order to assure himself that he was really standing up, for the absence of sensation in his feet left him unrelated to the earth. His erect position in itself started to drive the webs of suspicion from the dog's mind; and when he spoke peremptorily, with the sound of whip lashes in his voice, the dog rendered its customary allegiance and came to him. As it came within reaching distance, the man lost his control. His arms flashed out to the dog, and he experienced genuine surprise when he discovered that his hands could not clutch, that there was neither bend nor feeling in the fingers. He had forgotten for the moment that they were frozen and that they were freezing more and more. All this happened quickly, and before the animal could get away, he encircled its body with his arms. He sat down in the snow, and in this fashion held the dog, while it snarled and whined and struggled.

But it was all he could do, hold its body encircled in his arms and sit there. He realized that he could not kill the dog. There was no way to do it. With his helpless hands he could neither draw nor hold his sheath knife nor throttle the animal. He released it, and it plunged wildly away, with tail between its legs, and still snarling. It halted forty feet away and surveyed him curiously, with ears sharply pricked forward.

The man looked down at his hands in order to locate them, and found them hanging on the ends of his arms. It struck him as curious that one should have to use his eyes in order to find out where his hands were. He began threshing his arms back and forth, beating the mittened hands against his sides. He did this for five minutes, violently, and his heart pumped enough blood up to the surface to put a stop to his shivering. But no sensation was aroused in the hands. He had an impression that they hung like weights on the ends of his arms, but when he tried to run the impression down, he could not find it.

A certain fear of death, dull and oppressive, came to him. This fear quickly became poignant as he realized that it was no longer a mere matter of freezing his fingers and toes, or of losing his hands and feet, but that it was a matter of life and death with the chances against him. This threw him into a panic, and he turned and ran up the creek bed along the old, dim trail. The dog joined in behind and kept up with him. He ran blindly, without intention, in fear such as he had never known in his life. Slowly as he plowed and floundered through the snow, he began to see things again—the banks of the creek, the old timber jams, the leafless aspens, and the sky. The running made him feel better. He did not shiver. Maybe, if he ran on, his feet would thaw out; and, anyway, if he ran far enough, he would reach camp and the boys. Without doubt he would lose some fingers and toes and some of his face; but the boys would take care of him, and save the rest of him when he got there. And at the same time there was another thought in his mind that said he would never get to the camp and the boys; that it was too many miles away, that the freezing had too great a start on him, and that he would soon be stiff and dead. This thought he kept in the background and refused to consider. Sometimes it pushed itself forward and demanded to be heard, but he thrust it back and strove to think of other things.

It struck him as curious that he could run at all on feet so frozen that he could not feel them when they struck the earth and took the weight of his body. He seemed to himself to skim along above the surface, and to have no connection with the earth. Somewhere he had once seen a winged Mercury, and he wondered if Mercury felt as he felt when skimming over the earth.

His theory of running until he reached camp and the boys had one flaw in it: he lacked the endurance. Several times he stumbled, and finally he tottered, crumpled up, and fell. When he tried to rise, he failed. He must sit and rest, he decided, and next time he would merely walk and keep on going. As he sat and regained his breath, he noted that he was feeling quite warm and comfortable. He was not shivering, and it even seemed that a warm glow had come to his chest and trunk. And yet, when he touched his nose or cheeks, there was no sensation. Running would not thaw them out. Nor would it thaw out his hands and feet. Then the thought came to him that the frozen portions of his body must be extending. He tried to keep this thought down, to forget it, to think of something else; he was aware of the panicky feeling that it caused, and he was afraid of the panic. But the thought asserted itself, and persisted, until it produced a vision of his body totally frozen. This was too much, and he made another wild run along the trail. Once he slowed down to a walk, but the thought of the freezing extending itself made him run again.

And all the time the dog ran with him, at his heels. When he fell down a second time, it curled its tail over its forefeet and sat in front of him, facing him, curiously eager and intent. The warmth and security of the animal angered him, and he cursed it till it flattened down its ears appeasingly. This time the shivering came more quickly upon the man. He was losing in his battle with the frost. It was creeping into his body from all sides. The thought of it drove him on, but he ran no more than a hundred feet, when he staggered and pitched headlong. It was his last panic. When he had recovered his breath and control, he sat up and entertained in his mind the conception of meeting death with dignity. However, the conception did not come to him in such terms. His idea of it was that he had been making a fool of himself, running around like a chicken with its head cut off—such was the simile that occurred to him. Well, he was bound to freeze anyway, and he might as well take it decently. With this new-found peace of mind came the first glimmerings of drowsiness. A good idea, he thought, to sleep off to death. It was like taking an anesthetic. Freezing was not so bad as people thought. There were lots worse ways to die.

He pictured the boys finding his body next day. Sudddenly he found himself with them, coming along the trail and looking for himself. And, still with them, he came around a turn in the trail and found himself lying in the snow. He did not belong with himself any more, for even then he was out of himself, standing with the boys and looking at himself in the snow. It certainly was cold, was his thought. When he got back to the States he could tell the folks what real cold was. He drifted on from this to a vision of the old-timer on Sulphur Creek. He could see him quite clearly, warm and comfortable, and smoking a pipe.

"You were right, old hoss; you were right," the man mumbled to the old-timer of Sulphur Creek.

Then the man drowsed off into what seemed to him the most comfortable and satisfying sleep he had ever known. The dog sat facing him and waiting. The brief day drew to a close in a long, slow twilight. There were no signs of a fire to be made, and, besides, never in the dog's experience had it known a man to sit like that in the snow and make no fire. As the twilight drew on, its eager yearning for the fire mastered it, and with a great lifting and shifting of forefeet, it whined softly, then flattened its ears down in anticipation of being chidden by the man. But the man remained silent. Later the dog whined loudly. And still later it crept close to the man and caught the scent of death. This made the animal bristle and back away. A little longer it delayed, howling under the stars that leaped and danced and shone brightly in the cold sky. Then it turned and trotted up the trail in the direction of the camp it knew, where were the other food providers and fire providers.

DISCUSSION QUESTIONS

1. Though London's Yukon stories are often full of action and suspense, they are nevertheless meant to convey a moral significance beyond narrative. How would you describe the philosophy of this story?

2. Compare "To Build a Fire" with Barry Lopez's "Arctic Hunters" (in "Best-Sellers"). Though their purposes are different, each writer is dealing in his own way with the relationship of landscape to human imagination. What similarities in the handling of this theme can you detect in both writers? What differences can you find?

Robert Frost / Design   1922

"There are tones of voice that mean more than words," wrote Robert Frost (1874–1963) in a letter:

> *Sentences may be so constructed as definitely to indicate these tones. Only when we are making sentences so shaped are we really writing. And that is flat. A sentence must convey a meaning by tone of voice and it must be the particular meaning the writer intended. The reader must have no choice in the matter. The tone of voice and its meaning must be in black and white on the page.*

Frost wanted to direct readers away from the conventional notion of syntax as a grammatical arrangement toward a new definition of a sentence as a cluster of sounds, "because to me a sentence is not interesting merely in conveying a meaning in words. It must do something more; it must convey a meaning by sound." But more often than not, it was the "meaning in words" that most of his large audience attended to, and more often than that to the image of Frost projected by the mass media: a kindly and wise old man, rugged in appearance yet homely and whimsical in the way he talked publicly. To the average citizen, Frost was the American representative of poetry. Yet his public image even to-day induces his readers to concentrate almost exclusively on paraphrasing the thought, the "meaning in words," of his poetry without paying adequate attention to the ways in which that thought comes into existence through the dynamics of voice, through the "meaning by sound."

Frost's poem "Design" first appeared in American Poetry *in 1922. "The Gift Outright" was first published in the* Virginia Quarterly Review *in 1942. The poem was also read by Frost at John F. Kennedy's inauguration in 1961.*

I found a dimpled spider, fat and white,
On a white heal-all,[1] holding up a moth

---

1. Plant thought to have medicinal value.

Like a white piece of rigid satin cloth—
Assorted characters of death and blight
Mixed ready to begin the morning right,
Like the ingredients of a witches' broth—
A snow-drop spider, a flower like a froth,
And dead wings carried like a paper kite.

What had that flower to do with being white,
The wayside blue and innocent heal-all?   10
What brought the kindred spider to that height,
Then steered the white moth thither in the night?
What but design of darkness to appall?—
If design govern in a thing so small.

The Gift Outright   1942

The land was ours before we were the land's.
She was our land more than a hundred years
Before we were her people. She was ours
In Massachusetts, in Virginia,
But we were England's, still colonials,
Possessing what we still were unpossessed by,
Possessed by what we now no more possessed.
Something we were withholding made us weak
Until we found out that it was ourselves
We were withholding from our land of living,   10
And forthwith found salvation in surrender.
Such as we were we gave ourselves outright
(The deed of gift was many deeds of war)
To the land vaguely realizing westward,
But still unstoried, artless, unenhanced,
Such as she was, such as she would become.

Ernest Hemingway / Soldier's Home   1925

Ernest Hemingway (1899–1961) was first employed as a reporter for the Kansas
City Star *in 1917. After serving in a Red Cross ambulance unit on the Italian
front during World War I, Hemingway wrote for the* Toronto Star Weekly *and
later worked briefly for a Chicago advertising firm. He gradually turned to
free-lance journalism and published a good deal of short fiction characterized by
a lean, understated prose style that he later partially attributed to the constraints of having to write cablegrams. With the encouragement of Sherwood
Anderson and the promise of a job as foreign correspondent for the* Toronto
Daily Star, *Hemingway left for Paris in 1921. There he met Gertrude Stein and
gravitated toward her corps of literary expatriates.*

*"Soldier's Home," the tale of a young man returning from World War I to
the routines of his hometown and family, was collected in Hemingway's first
major volume of short stories,* In Our Time *(1925). For a film adaptation of this
story, see "Scripts."*

Krebs went to the war from a Methodist college in Kansas. There is a picture which shows him among his fraternity brothers, all of them wearing exactly the same height and style collar. He enlisted in the Marines in 1917 and did not return to the United States until the second division returned from the Rhine in the summer of 1919.

There is a picture which shows him on the Rhine with two German girls and another corporal. Krebs and the corporal look too big for their uniforms. The German girls are not beautiful. The Rhine does not show in the picture.

By the time Krebs returned to his home town in Oklahoma the greeting of heroes was over. He came back much too late. The men from the town who had been drafted had all been welcomed elaborately on their return. There had been a great deal of hysteria. Now the reaction had set in. People seemed to think it was rather ridiculous for Krebs to be getting back so late, years after the war was over.

At first Krebs, who had been at Belleau Wood, Soissons, the Champagne, St. Mihiel and in the Argonne did not want to talk about the war at all. Later he felt the need to talk but no one wanted to hear about it. His town had heard too many atrocity stories to be thrilled by actualities. Krebs found that to be listened to at all he had to lie, and after he had done this twice he, too, had a reaction against the war and against talking about it. A distaste for everything that had happened to him in the war set in because of the lies he had told. All of the times that had been able to make him feel cool and clear inside himself when he thought of them; the times so long back when he had done the one thing, the only thing for a man to do, easily and naturally, when he might have done something else, now lost their cool, valuable quality and then were lost themselves.

His lies were quite unimportant lies and consisted in attributing to himself things other men had seen, done or heard of, and stating as facts certain apocryphal incidents familiar to all soldiers. Even his lies were not sensational at the pool room. His acquaintances, who had heard detailed accounts of German women found chained to machine guns in the Argonne forest and who could not comprehend, or were barred by their patriotism from interest in, any German machine gunners who were not chained, were not thrilled by his stories.

Krebs acquired the nausea in regard to experience that is the result of untruth or exaggeration, and when he occasionally met another man who had really been a soldier and they talked a few minutes in the dressing room at a dance he fell into the easy pose of the old soldier among other soldiers: that he had been badly, sickeningly frightened all the time. In this way he lost everything.

During this time, it was late summer, he was sleeping late in bed, getting up to walk down town to the library to get a book, eating lunch at home, reading on the front porch until he became bored and then walking down through the town to spend the hottest hours of the day in the cool dark of the pool room. He loved to play pool.

In the evening he practised on his clarinet, strolled down town, read and went to bed. He was still a hero to his two young sisters. His mother would have given him breakfast in bed if he had wanted it. She often came in when he was in bed and asked him to tell her about the war, but her attention always wandered. His father was non-committal.

Before Krebs went away to the war he had never been allowed to drive the family motor car. His father was in the real estate business and always wanted the car to be at his command when he required it to take clients out into the country to show them a piece of farm property. The car always stood outside the First National Bank building where his father had an office on the second floor. Now, after the war, it was still the same car.

Nothing was changed in the town except that the young girls had grown up. But they lived in such a complicated world of already defined alliances and shifting feuds that Krebs did not feel the energy or the courage to break into it. He liked to look at them, though. There were so many good-looking young girls. Most of them had their hair cut short. When he went away only little girls wore their hair like that or girls that were fast. They all wore sweaters and shirt waists with round Dutch collars. It was a pattern. He liked to look at them from the front porch as they walked on the other side of the street. He liked to watch them walking under the shade of the trees. He liked the round Dutch collars above their sweaters. He liked their silk stockings and flat shoes. He liked their bobbed hair and the way they walked.

When he was in town their appeal to him was not very strong. He did not like them when he saw them in the Greek's ice cream parlor. He did not want them themselves really. They were too complicated. There was something else. Vaguely he wanted a girl but he did not want to have to work to get her. He would have liked to have a girl but he did not want to have to spend a long time getting her. He did not want to get into the intrigue and the politics. He did not want to have to do any courting. He did not want to tell any more lies. It wasn't worth it.

He did not want any consequences. He did not want any consequences ever again. He wanted to live along without consequences. Besides he did not really need a girl. The army had taught him that. It was all right to pose as though you had to have a girl. Nearly everybody did that. But it wasn't true. You did not need a girl. That was the funny thing. First a fellow boasted how girls mean nothing to him, that he never thought of them, that they could not touch him. Then a fellow boasted that he could not get along without girls, that he had to have them all the time, that he could not go to sleep without them.

That was all a lie. It was all a lie both ways. You did not need a girl unless you thought about them. He learned that in the army. Then sooner or later you always got one. When you were really ripe for a girl you always got one. You did not have to think about it. Sooner or later it would come. He had learned that in the army.

Now he would have liked a girl if she had come to him and not wanted to talk. But here at home it was all too complicated. He knew he could never get through it all again. It was not worth the trouble. That was the thing about French girls and German girls. There was not all this talking. You couldn't talk much and you did not need to talk. It was simple and you were friends. He thought about France and then he began to think about Germany. On the whole he had liked Germany better. He did not want to leave Germany. He did not want to come home. Still, he had come home. He sat on the front porch.

He liked the girls that were walking along the other side of the street. He liked the look of them much better than the French girls or the German girls. But the world they were in was not the world he was in. He would like to have one of them. But it was not worth it. They were such a nice pattern. He liked the pattern. It was exciting. But he would not go through all the talking. He did not want one badly enough. He liked to look at them all, though. It was not worth it. Not now when things were getting good again.

He sat there on the porch reading a book on the war. It was a history and he was reading about all the engagements he had been in. It was the most interesting reading he had ever done. He wished there were more maps. He looked forward with a good feeling to reading all the really good histories when they would come out with good detail maps. Now he was really learning about the war. He had been a good soldier. That made a difference.

One morning after he had been home about a month his mother came into his bedroom and sat on the bed. She smoothed her apron.

"I had a talk with your father last night, Harold," she said, "and he is willing for you to take the car out in the evenings."

"Yeah?" said Krebs, who was not fully awake. "Take the car out? Yeah?"

"Yes. Your father has felt for some time that you should be able to take the car out in the evenings whenever you wished but we only talked it over last night."

"I'll bet you made him," Krebs said.

"No. It was your father's suggestion that we talk the matter over."

"Yeah. I'll bet you made him," Krebs sat up in bed.

"Will you come down to breakfast, Harold?" his mother said.

"As soon as I get my clothes on," Krebs said.

His mother went out of the room and he could hear her frying something downstairs while he washed, shaved and dressed to go down into the dining-room for breakfast. While he was eating breakfast his sister brought in the mail.

"Well, Hare," she said. "You old sleepy-head. What do you ever get up for?"

Krebs looked at her. He liked her. She was his best sister.

"Have you got the paper?" he asked.

She handed him *The Kansas City Star* and he shucked off its brown wrapper and opened it to the sporting page. He folded *The Star* open and propped it against the water pitcher with his cereal dish to steady it, so he could read while he ate.

"Harold," his mother stood in the kitchen doorway, "Harold, please don't muss up the paper. Your father can't read his *Star* if it's been mussed."

"I won't muss it," Krebs said.

His sister sat down at the table and watched him while he read.

"We're playing indoor over at school this afternoon," she said. "I'm going to pitch."

"Good," said Krebs. "How's the old wing?"

"I can pitch better than lots of the boys. I tell them all you taught me. The other girls aren't much good."

"Yeah?" said Krebs.

"I tell them all you're my beau. Aren't you my beau, Hare?"

"You bet."

"Couldn't your brother really be your beau just because he's your brother?"

"I don't know."

"Sure you know. Couldn't you be my beau, Hare, if I was old enough and if you wanted to?"

"Sure. You're my girl now."

"Am I really your girl?"

"Sure."

"Do you love me?"

"Uh, huh."

"Will you love me always?"

"Sure."

"Will you come over and watch me play indoor?"

"Maybe."

"Aw, Hare, you don't love me. If you loved me, you'd want to come over and watch me play indoor."

Kreb's mother came into the dining-room from the kitchen. She carried a plate with two fried eggs and some crisp bacon on it and a plate of buckwheat cakes.

"You run along, Helen," she said. "I want to talk to Harold."

She put the eggs and bacon down in front of him and brought in a jug of maple syrup for the buckwheat cakes. Then she sat down across the table from Krebs.

"I wish you'd put down the paper a minute, Harold," she said.

Krebs took down the paper and folded it.

"Have you decided what you are going to do yet, Harold?" his mother said, taking off her glasses.

"No," said Krebs.

"Don't you think it's about time?" His mother did not say this in a mean way. She seemed worried.

"I hadn't thought about it," Krebs said.

"God has some work for every one to do," his mother said. "There can be no idle hands in His Kingdom."

"I'm not in His Kingdom," Krebs said.

"We are all of us in His Kingdom."

Krebs felt embarrassed and resentful as always.

"I've worried about you so much, Harold," his mother went on. "I know the temptations you must have been exposed to. I know how weak men are. I know what your own dear grandfather, my own father, told us about the Civil War and I have prayed for you. I pray for you all day long, Harold."

Krebs looked at the bacon fat hardening on his plate.

"Your father is worried, too," his mother went on. "He thinks you have lost your ambition, that you haven't got a definite aim in life. Charley Simmons, who is just your age, has a good job and is going to be married. The boys are all settling down; they're all determined to get somewhere; you can see that boys like Charley Simmons are on their way to being really a credit to the community."

Krebs said nothing.

"Don't look that way, Harold," his mother said. "You know we love you and I want to tell you for your own good how matters stand. Your father does not want to hamper your freedom. He thinks you should be allowed to drive the car. If you want to take some of the nice girls out riding with you, we are only too pleased. We want you to enjoy yourself. But you are going to have to settle down to work, Harold. Your father doesn't care what you start in at. All work is honorable as he says. But you've got to make a start at something. He asked me to speak to you this morning and then you can stop in and see him at his office."

"Is that all?" Krebs said.

"Yes. Don't you love your mother, dear boy?"

"No," Krebs said.

His mother looked at him across the table. Her eyes were shiny. She started crying.

"I don't love anybody," Krebs said.

It wasn't any good. He couldn't tell her, he couldn't make her see it. It was silly to have said it. He had only hurt her. He went over and took hold of her arm. She was crying with her head in her hands.

"I didn't mean it," he said. "I was just angry at something. I didn't mean I didn't love you."

His mother went on crying. Krebs put his arm on her shoulder.

"Can't you believe me, mother?"

His mother shook her head.

"Please, please, mother. Please believe me."

"All right," his mother said chokily. She looked up at him. "I believe you, Harold."

Krebs kissed her hair. She put her face up to him.

"I'm your mother," she said. "I held you next to my heart when you were a tiny baby."

Krebs felt sick and vaguely nauseated.

"I know, Mummy," he said. "I'll try and be a good boy for you."

"Would you kneel and pray with me, Harold?" his mother asked.

They knelt down beside the dining-room table and Krebs's mother prayed.

"Now, you pray, Harold," she said.

"I can't," Krebs said.

"Try, Harold."

"I can't."

"Do you want me to pray for you?"

"Yes."

So his mother prayed for him and then they stood up and Krebs kissed his mother and went out of the house. He had tried so to keep his life from being complicated. Still, none of it had touched him. He had felt sorry for his mother and she had made him lie. He would go to Kansas City and get a job and she would feel all right about it. There would be one more scene maybe before he got away. He would not go down to his father's office. He would miss that one. He wanted his life to go smoothly. It had just gotten going that way. Well, that was all over now, anyway. He would go over to the schoolyard and watch Helen play indoor baseball.

William Carlos Williams / The Use of Force   1933

Five minutes, ten minutes, can always be found. I had my typewriter in my office desk. All I needed to do was pull up the leaf to which it was fastened and I was ready to go. I worked at top speed. If a patient came in at the door while I was in the middle of a sentence, bang would go the machine—I was a physician. When the patient left, up would come the machine. My head developed a technique: something growing inside me demanded reaping. It had to be attended to. Finally, after eleven at night, when the last patient had been put to bed, I could always find time to bang out ten or twelve pages. In fact, I couldn't rest until I had freed my mind from the obsessions which had been tormenting me all day. Cleansed of that torment, having scribbled, I could rest.

As the above passage from his Autobiography *makes clear, William Carlos Williams worked hard all his life at two demanding careers. A busy pediatrician in a densely populated northern New Jersey area, Williams also attained a reputation as one of the leading figures in modern American poetry. In his best work he succeeds in giving literary form to the discordant, brittle, nonliterary idioms of an industrial civilization.*

Born in Rutherford, New Jersey, in 1883, Williams received a medical education at the University of Pennsylvania, where he became acquainted with the poet and critic Ezra Pound. After a year's study abroad, Williams returned to his home town to discipline himself in the arts of healing and writing. His first book of poems, published at his own expense in 1909, was followed by nearly forty volumes of poetry, short stories, novels, plays, history, biography, and criticism, in which he consistently demonstrates a special fondness for local subjects and his native grounds. His most ambitious effort, an epic of a modern industrial city, Paterson, *received the National Book Award in 1949. Williams died in Rutherford in 1963.*

"The Use of Force" documents in unsentimental terms an encounter between a determined physician and the seriously ill child of a poor, backward family–the kind of people Williams cared for all his life. It originally appeared in Blast, *a short-lived American literary magazine that, according to Williams, was started by an unemployed "tool designer living precariously over a garage in Brooklyn."*

They were new patients to me, all I had was the name, Olson. Please come down as soon as you can, my daughter is very sick.

When I arrived I was met by the mother, a big startled-looking woman, very clean and apologetic who merely said, Is this the doctor? and let me in. In the back, she added. You must excuse us, doctor, we have her in the kitchen where it is warm. It is very damp here sometimes.

The child was fully dressed and sitting on her father's lap near the kitchen table. He tried to get up, but I motioned for him not to bother, took off my overcoat and started to look things over. I could see that they were all very nervous, eyeing me up and down distrustfully. As often, in such cases, they weren't telling me more than they had to, it was up to me to tell them; that's why they were spending three dollars on me.

The child was fairly eating me up with her cold, steady eyes, and no expression to her face whatever. She did not move and seemed, inwardly, quiet; an unusually attractive little thing, and as strong as a heifer in appearance. But her face was flushed, she was breathing rapidly, and I realized that she had a high fever. She had magnificent blond hair, in profusion. One of those picture children often reproduced in advertising leaflets and the photogravure sections of the Sunday papers.

She's had a fever for three days, began the father and we don't know what it comes from. My wife has given her things, you know, like people do, but it don't do no good. And there's been a lot of sickness around. So we tho't you'd better look her over and tell us what is the matter.

As doctors often do I took a trial shot at it as a point of departure. Has she had a sore throat?

Both parents answered me together, No . . . No, she says her throat don't hurt her.

Does your throat hurt you? added the mother to the child. But the little girl's expression didn't change nor did she move her eyes from my face.

Have you looked?

I tried to, said the mother, but I couldn't see.

As it happens we had been having a number of cases of diphtheria in the school to which this child went during that month and we were all, quite apparently, thinking of that, though no one had as yet spoken of the thing.

Well, I said, suppose we take a look at the throat first. I smiled in my best professional manner and asking for the child's first name I said, come on, Mathilda, open your mouth and let's take a look at your throat.

Nothing doing.

Aw, come on, I coaxed, just open your mouth wide and let me take a look. Look, I said opening both hands wide, I haven't anything in my hands. Just open up and let me see.

Such a nice man, put in the mother. Look how kind he is to you. Come on, do what he tells you to. He won't hurt you.

At that I ground my teeth in disgust. If only they wouldn't use the word "hurt" I might be able to get someplace. But I did not allow myself to be hurried or disturbed but speaking quietly and slowly I approached the child again.

As I moved my chair a little nearer suddenly with one cat-like movement both her hands clawed instinctively for my eyes and she almost reached them too. In fact she knocked my glasses flying and they fell, though unbroken, several feet away from me on the kitchen floor.

Both the mother and father almost turned themselves inside out in embarrassment and apology. You bad girl, said the mother, taking her and shaking her by one arm. Look what you've done. The nice man . . .

For heaven's sake, I broke in. Don't call me a nice man to her. I'm here to look at her throat on the chance that she might have diphtheria and possibly die of it. But that's nothing to her. Look here, I said to the child, we're going to look at your throat. You're old enough to understand what I'm saying. Will you open it now by yourself or shall we have to open it for you?

Not a move. Even her expression hadn't changed. Her breaths however were coming faster and faster. Then the battle began. I had to do it. I had to have a throat culture for her own protection. But first I told the parents that it was entirely up to them. I explained the danger but said that I would not insist on a throat examination so long as they would take the responsibility.

If you don't do what the doctor says you'll have to go to the hospital, the mother admonished her severely.

Oh yeah? I had to smile to myself. After all, I had already fallen in love with the savage brat, the parents were contemptible to me. In the ensuing struggle they grew more and more abject, crushed, exhausted while she surely rose to magnificent heights of insane fury of effort bred of her terror of me.

The father tried his best, and he was a big man but the fact that she was his daughter, his shame at her behavior and his dread of hurting her made him release her just at the critical moment several times when I had almost achieved success, till I wanted to kill him. But his dread also that she might have diphtheria made him tell me to go on, go on though he himself was almost fainting, while the mother moved back and forth behind us raising and lowering her hands in an agony of apprehension.

Put her in front of you on your lap, I ordered, and hold both her wrists.

But as soon as he did the child let out a scream. Don't, you're hurting me. Let go of my hands. Let them go I tell you. Then she shrieked terrifyingly, hysterically. Stop it! Stop it! You're killing me!

Do you think she can stand it, doctor! said the mother.

You get out, said the husband to his wife. Do you want her to die of diphtheria? Come on now, hold her, I said.

Then I grasped the child's head with my left hand and tried to get the wooden tongue depressor between her teeth. She fought, with clenched teeth, desperately! But now I also had grown furious—at a child. I tried to hold myself down but I couldn't. I know how to expose a throat for inspection. And I did my best. When finally I got the wooden spatula behind the last teeth and just the point of it into the mouth cavity, she opened up for an instant but before I could see anything she came down again and gripping the wooden blade between her molars she reduced it to splinters before I could get it out again.

Aren't you ashamed, the mother yelled at her. Aren't you ashamed to act like that in front of the doctor?

Get me a smooth-handled spoon of some sort, I told the mother. We're going through with this. The child's mouth was already bleeding. Her tongue was cut and she was screaming in wild hysterical shrieks. Perhaps I should have desisted and come back in an hour or more. No doubt it would have been better. But I have seen at least two children lying dead in bed of neglect in such cases, and feeling that I must get a diagnosis, now or never I went at it again. But the worst of it was that I too had got beyond reason. I could have torn the child apart in my own fury and enjoyed it. It was a pleasure to attack her. My face was burning with it.

The damned little brat must be protected against her own idiocy, one says to one's self at such times. Others must be protected against her. It is social necessity. And all these things are true. But a blind fury, a feeling of adult shame, bred of a longing for muscular release are the operatives. One goes on to the end.

In a final unreasoning assault I overpowered the child's neck and jaws. I forced the heavy silver spoon back on her teeth and down her throat till she gagged. And there it was—both tonsils covered with membrane. She had fought valiantly to keep me from knowing her secret. She had been hiding that sore throat for three days at least and lying to her parents in order to escape just such an outcome as this.

Now truly she *was* furious. She had been on the defensive before but now she attacked. Tried to get off her father's lap and fly at me while tears of defeat blinded her eyes.

William Faulkner / *The Bear*   1942

Sole owner, proprietor, historian, and inventor of the most turbulent 2,400 square miles in America, Yoknapatawpha County, Mississippi, William Faulkner (1897–1962) remains the most powerful American novelist of the first half of the twentieth century. The major portion of his life was spent in Oxford, Mississippi, except for a brief period during World War I with the British Flying Corps in Canada, a job in a bookstore in New York City, a stint writing sketches for the New Orleans Time-Picayune, *and an occasional acquiescence to the lure of Hollywood. We have reprinted the opening section of* The Bear, *a novella in five parts, which originally appeared (also excerpted) in the* Saturday Evening Post *in 1942 with the caption "Boy Meets Bear after Years of Stalking."*

PART I

There was a man and a dog too this time. Two beasts, counting Old Ben, the bear, and two men, counting Boon Hogganbeck, in whom some of the same blood ran which ran in Sam Fathers, even though Boon's was a plebeian strain of it and only Sam and Old Ben and the mongrel Lion were taintless and incorruptible.

He was sixteen. For six years now he had been a man's hunter. For six years now he had heard the best of all talking. It was of the wilderness, the big woods, bigger and older than any recorded document:—of white man fatuous enough to believe he had bought any fragment of it, of Indian ruthless enough to pretend that any fragment of it had been his to convey; bigger than Major de Spain and the scrap he pretended to, knowing better; older than old Thomas Sutpen of whom Major de Spain had had it and who knew better; older even than old Ikkemotubbe, the Chickasaw chief, of whom old Sutpen had had it and who knew better in his turn. It was of the men, not white nor black nor red but men, hunters, with the will and hardihood to endure and the humility and skill to survive, and the dogs and the bear and deer juxtaposed and reliefed against it, ordered and compelled by and within the wilderness in the ancient and unremitting contest according to the ancient and immitigable rules which voided all regrets and brooked no quarter;—the best game of all, the best of all breathing and forever the best of all listening, the voices quiet and weighty and deliberate for retrospection and recollection and èxactitude among the concrete trophies—the racked guns and the heads and skins—in the libraries of town houses or the offices of plantation houses or (and best of all) in the camps themselves where the intact and still-warm meat yet hung, the men who had slain it sitting before the burning logs on hearths when there were houses and hearths or about the smoky blazing of piled wood in front of stretched tarpaulins when there were not. There was always a bottle present, so that it would seem to him that those fine fierce instants of heart and brain and courage and wiliness and speed were concentrated and distilled into that brown liquor which not women, not boys and children, but only hunters drank, drinking not of the blood they spilled but some condensation of the wild immortal spirit, drinking it moderately, humbly even, not with the pagan's base and baseless hope of acquiring thereby the virtues of cunning and strength and speed but in salute to them. Thus it seemed to him on this December morning not only natural but actually fitting that this should have begun with whisky.

He realised later that it had begun long before that. It had already begun on that day when he first wrote his age in two ciphers and his cousin McCaslin brought him for the first time to the camp, the big woods, to earn for himself from the wilderness the name and state of hunter provided he in his turn were humble and enduring enough. He had already inherited then, without ever having seen it, the big old bear with one trap-ruined foot that in an area almost a hundred miles square had earned for himself a name, a definite designation like a living man:—the long legend of corn-cribs broken down and rifled, of shoats and grown pigs and even calves carried bodily into the woods and devoured and traps and deadfalls overthrown and dogs mangled and slain and shotgun and even rifle shots delivered at point-blank range yet with no more effect than so many peas blown through a tube by a child—a corridor of wreckage and destruction beginning back before the boy was born, through which sped, not fast but rather with the ruthless and irresistible deliberation of a locomotive, the shaggy tremendous shape. It ran in his knowledge before he ever saw it. It loomed and towered in his dreams before he even saw the unaxed woods where it left its crooked print, shaggy, tremendous, red-eyed, not malevolent but just big, too big for the dogs which tried to bay it, for the horses which tried to ride it down, for the men and the bullets they fired into it; too big for the very country which was its constricting scope. It was as if the boy had already divined what his senses and intellect had not encompassed yet: that doomed wilderness whose edges were being constantly and punily gnawed at by men with plows and axes who feared it because it was wilderness, men myriad and nameless even to one another in the land where the old bear had earned a name, and through which ran not even a mortal beast but an anachronism indomitable and invincible out of an old dead time, a phantom, epitome and apotheosis of the old wild life which the little puny humans swarmed and hacked at in a fury of abhorrence and fear like pygmies about the ankles of a drowsing elephant;—the old bear, solitary, indomitable, and alone; widowered childless and absolved of mortality—old Priam reft of his old wife and outlived all his sons.

· Still a child, with three years then two years then one year yet before he too could make one of them, each November he would watch the wagon containing the dogs and the bedding and food and guns and his cousin McCaslin and Tennie's Jim and Sam Fathers too until Sam moved to the camp to live, depart for the Big Bottom, the big woods. To him, they were going not to hunt bear and deer but to keep yearly rendezvous with the bear which they did not even intend to kill. Two weeks later they would return, with no trophy, no skin. He had not expected it. He had not even feared that it might be in the wagon this time with the other skins and heads. He did not even tell himself that in three years or two years or one year more he would be present and that it might even be his gun. He believed that only after he had served his apprenticeship in the woods which would prove him worthy to be a hunter, would he even be permitted to distinguish the crooked print, and that even then for two November weeks he would merely make another minor one, along with his cousin and Major de Spain and General Compson and Walter Ewell and Boon and the dogs which feared to bay it and the shotguns and rifles which failed even to bleed it, in the yearly pageant-rite of the old bear's furious immortality.

His day came at last. In the surrey with his cousin and Major de Spain and General Compson he saw the wilderness through a slow drizzle of November rain just above the ice point as it seemed to him later he always saw it or at least always remembered it—the tall and endless wall of dense November woods under the dissolving afternoon and the year's death, sombre, impenetrable (he could not even discern yet how, at what point they could possibly hope to enter it even though he knew that Sam Fathers was waiting there with the wagon), the surrey moving through the skeleton stalks of cotton and corn in the last of open country, the last trace of man's puny gnawing at the immemorial flank, until, dwarfed by that perspective into an almost ridiculous diminishment, the surrey itself seemed to have ceased to move (this too to be completed later, years later, after he had grown to a man and had seen the sea) as a solitary small boat hangs in lonely immobility, merely tossing up and down, in the infinite waste of the ocean while the water and then the apparently impenetrable land which it nears without appreciable progress, swings slowly and opens the widening inlet which is the anchorage. He entered it. Sam was waiting, wrapped in a quilt on the wagon seat behind the patient and steaming mules. He entered his novitiate to the true wilderness with Sam beside him as he had begun his apprenticeship in miniature to manhood after the rabbits and such with Sam beside him, the two of them wrapped in the damp, warm, negro-rank quilt while the wilderness closed behind his entrance as it had opened momentarily to accept him, opening before his advancement as it closed behind his progress, no fixed path the wagon followed but a channel nonexistent ten yards ahead of it and ceasing to exist ten yards after it had passed, the wagon progressing not by its own volition but by attrition of their intact yet fluid circumambience, drowsing, earless, almost lightless.

It seemed to him that at the age of ten he was witnessing his own birth. It was not even strange to him. He had experienced it all before, and not merely in dreams. He saw the camp—a paintless six-room bungalow set on piles above the spring highwater—and he knew already how it was going to look. He helped in the rapid orderly disorder of their establishment in it and even his motions were familiar to him, foreknown. Then for two weeks he ate the coarse, rapid food—the shapeless sour bread, the wild strange meat, venison and bear and turkey and coon which he had never tasted before—which men ate, cooked by men who were hunters first and cooks afterward; he slept in harsh sheetless blankets as hunters slept. Each morning the gray of dawn found him and Sam Fathers on the stand, the crossing, which had been allotted him. It was the poorest one, the most barren. He had expected that; he had not dared yet to hope even to himself that he would even hear the running dogs this first time. But he did hear them. It was on the third morning—a murmur, sourceless, almost indistinguishable, yet he knew what it was although he had never before heard that many dogs running at once, the murmur swelling into separate and distinct voices until he could call the five dogs which his cousin owned from among the others. "Now," Sam said, "slant your gun up a little and draw back the hammers and then stand still."

But it was not for him, not yet. The humility was there; he had learned that. And he could learn the patience. He was only ten, only one week. The instant had passed. It seemed to him that he could actually see the deer, the buck, smoke-colored, elongated with speed, vanished, the woods, the gray solitude still ringing even when the voices of the dogs had died away; from far away across the sombre woods and the gray half-liquid morning there came two shots. "Now let your hammers down," Sam said.

He did so. "You knew it too," he said.

"Yes," Sam said. "I want you to learn how to do when you didn't shoot. It's after the chance for the bear or the deer has done already come and gone that men and dogs get killed."

"Anyway, it wasn't him," the boy said. "It wasn't even a bear. It was just a deer."

"Yes," Sam said, "it was just a deer."

Then one morning, it was in the second week, he heard the dogs again. This time before Sam even spoke he readied the too-long, too-heavy, man-size gun as Sam had taught him, even though this time he knew the dogs and the deer were coming less close than ever, hardly within hearing even. They didn't sound like any running dogs he had ever heard before even. Then he found that Sam, who had taught him first of all to cock the gun and take position where he could see best in all directions and then never to move again, had himself moved up beside him. "There," he said. "Listen." The boy listened, to no ringing chorus strong and fast on a free scent but a moiling yapping an octave too high and with something more than indecision and even abjectness in it which he could not yet recognise, reluctant, not even moving very fast, taking a long time to pass out of hearing, leaving even then in the air that echo of thin and almost human hysteria, abject, almost humanly grieving, with this time nothing ahead of it, no sense of a fleeing unseen smoke-colored shape. He could hear Sam breathing at his shoulder. He saw the arched curve of the old man's inhaling nostrils.

"It's Old Ben!" he cried, whispering.

Sam didn't move save for the slow gradual turning of his head as the voices faded on and the faint steady rapid arch and collapse of his nostrils. "Hah," he said. "Not even running. Walking."

"But up here!" the boy cried. "Way up here!"

"He do it every year," Sam said. "Once. Ash and Boon say he comes up here to run the other little bears away. Tell them to get to hell out of here and stay out until the hunters are gone. Maybe." The boy no longer heard anything at all, yet still Sam's head continued to turn gradually and steadily until the back of it was toward him. Then it turned back and looked down at him—the same face, grave, familiar, expressionless until it smiled, the same old man's eyes from which as he watched there faded slowly a quality darkly and fiercely lambent, passionate and proud. "He dont care no more for bears than he does for dogs or men neither. He come to see who's here, who's new in camp this year, whether he can shoot or not, can stay or not. Whether we got the dog yet that can bay and hold him until a man gets there with a gun. Because he's the head bear. He's the man." It faded, was gone; again they were the eyes as he had known them all his life. "He'll let them follow him to the river. Then he'll send them home. We might as well go too; see how they look when they get back to camp."

The dogs were there first, ten of them huddled back under the kitchen, himself and Sam squatting to peer back into the obscurity where they crouched, quiet, the eyes rolling and luminous, vanishing, and no sound, only that effluvium which the boy could not quite place yet, of something more than dog, stronger than dog and not just animal, just beast even. Because there had been nothing in front of the abject and painful yapping except the solitude, the wilderness, so that when the eleventh hound got back about mid-afternoon and he and Tennie's Jim held the passive and still trembling bitch while Sam daubed her tattered ear and raked shoulder with turpentine and axle-grease, it was still no living creature but only the wilderness which, leaning for a moment, had patted lightly once her temerity. "Just like a man," Sam said. "Just like folks. Put off as long as she could having to be brave, knowing all the time that sooner or later she would have to be brave once so she could keep on calling herself a dog, and knowing beforehand what was going to happen when she done it."

He did not know just when Sam left. He only knew that he was gone. For the next three mornings he rose and ate breakfast and Sam was not waiting for him. He went to his stand alone; he found it without help now and stood on it as Sam had taught him. On the third morning he heard the dogs again, running strong and free on a true scent again, and he readied the gun as he had learned to do and heard the hunt sweep past on since he was not ready yet, had not deserved other yet in just one short period of two weeks as compared to all the long life which he had already dedicated to the wilderness with patience and humility; he heard the shot again, one shot, the single clapping report of Walter Ewell's rifle. By now he could not only find his stand and then return to camp without guidance, by using the compass his cousin had given him he reached Walter waiting beside the buck and the moiling of dogs over the cast entrails before any of the others except Major de Spain and Tennie's Jim on the horses, even before Uncle Ash arrived with the one-eyed wagon-mule which did not mind the smell of blood or even, so they said, of bear.

It was not Uncle Ash on the mule. It was Sam, returned. And Sam was waiting when he finished his dinner and, himself on the one-eyed mule and Sam on the other one of the wagon team, they rode for more than three hours through the rapid shortening sunless afternoon, following no path, no trail even that he could discern, into a section of country he had never seen before. Then he understood why Sam had made him ride the one-eyed mule which would not spook at the smell of blood, of wild animals. The other one, the sound one, stopped short and tried to whirl and bolt even as Sam got down, jerking and wrenching at the rein while Sam held it, coaxing it forward with his voice since he did not dare risk hitching it, drawing it forward while the boy dismounted from the marred one which would stand. Then, standing beside Sam in the thick great gloom of ancient woods and the winter's dying afternoon, he looked quietly down at the rotted log scored and gutted with claw-marks and, in the wet earth beside it, the print of the enormous warped two-toed foot. Now he knew what he had heard in the hounds' voices in the woods that morning and what he had smelled when he peered under the kitchen where they huddled. It was in him too, a little different because they were brute beasts and he was not, but only a little different—an eagerness, passive; an abjectness, a sense of his own fragility and impotence against the timeless woods, yet without doubt or dread; a flavor like brass in the sudden run of saliva in his mouth, a hard sharp constriction either in his brain or his stomach, he could not tell which and it did not matter; he knew only that for the first time he realised that the bear which had run in his listening and loomed in his dreams since before he could remember and which therefore must have existed in the listening and the dreams of his cousin and Major de Spain and even old General Compson before they began to remember in their turn, was a mortal animal and that they had departed for the camp each November with no actual intention of slaying it, not because it could not be slain but because so far they had no actual hope of being able to. "It will be tomorrow," he said.

"You mean we will try tomorrow," Sam said. "We aint got the dog yet."

"We've got eleven," he said. "They ran him Monday."

"And you heard them," Sam said. "Saw them too. We aint got the dog yet. It wont take but one. But he aint there. Maybe he aint nowhere. The only other way will be for him to run by accident over somebody that had a gun and knowed how to shoot it."

"That wouldn't be me," the boy said. "It would be Walter or Major or——"

"It might," Sam said. "You watch close tomorrow. Because he's smart. That's how come he has lived this long. If he gets hemmed up and has got to pick out somebody to run over, he will pick out you."

"How?" he said. "How will he know. . . ." He ceased. "You mean he already knows me, that I aint never been to the big bottom before, aint had time to find out yet whether I . . ." He ceased again, staring at Sam; he said humbly, not even amazed: "It was me he was watching. I don't reckon he did need to come but once."

"You watch tomorrow," Sam said. "I reckon we better start back. It'll be long after dark now before we get to camp."

The next morning they started three hours earlier than they had ever done. Even Uncle Ash went, the cook, who called himself by profession a camp cook and who did little else save cook for Major de Spain's hunting and camping parties, yet who had been marked by the wilderness from simple juxtaposition to it until he responded as they all did, even the boy who until two weeks ago had never even seen the wilderness, to a hound's ripped ear and shoulder and the print of a crooked foot in a patch of wet earth. They rode. It was too far to walk: the boy and Sam and Uncle Ash in the wagon with the dogs, his cousin and Major de Spain and General Compson and Boon and Walter and Tennie's Jim riding double on the horses; again the first gray light found him, as on that first morning two weeks ago, on the stand where Sam had placed and left him. With the gun which was too big for him, the breech-loader which did not even belong to him but to Major de Spain and which he had fired only once, at a stump on the first day to learn the recoil and how to reload it with the paper shells, he stood against a big gum tree beside a little bayou whose black still water crept without motion out of a cane-brake, across a small clearing and into the cane again, where, invisible, a bird, the big woodpecker called Lord-to-God by negroes, clattered at a dead trunk. It was a stand like any other stand, dissimilar only in incidentals to the one where he had stood each morning for two weeks; a territory new to him yet no less familiar than that other one which after two weeks he had come to believe he knew a little—the same solitude, the same loneliness through which frail and timorous man had merely passed without altering it, leaving no mark nor scar, which looked exactly as it must have looked when the first ancestor of Sam Fathers' Chickasaw predecessors crept into it and looked about him, club or stone axe or bone arrow drawn and ready, different only because, squatting at the edge of the kitchen, he had smelled the dogs huddled and cringing beneath it and saw the raked ear and side of the bitch that, as Sam had said, had to be brave once in order to keep on calling herself a dog, and saw yesterday in the earth beside the gutted log, the print of the living foot. He heard no dogs at all. He never did certainly hear them. He only heard the drumming of the woodpecker stop short off, and knew that the bear was looking at him. He never saw it. He did not know whether it was facing him from the cane or behind him. He did not move, holding the useless gun which he knew now he would never fire at it now or ever, tasting in his saliva that taint of brass which he had smelled in the huddled dogs when he peered under the kitchen.

Then it was gone. As abruptly as it had stopped, the woodpecker's dry hammering set up again, and after a while he believed he even heard the dogs—a murmur, scarce a sound even, which he had probably been hearing for a time, perhaps a minute or two, before he remarked it, drifting into hearing and then out again, dying away. They came nowhere near him. If it was dogs he heard, he could not have sworn to it; if it was a bear they ran, it was another bear. It was Sam himself who emerged from the cane and crossed the bayou, the injured bitch following at heel as a bird dog is taught to walk. She came and crouched against his leg, trembling. ''I didn't see him,'' he said. ''I didn't, Sam.''

''I know it,'' Sam said. ''He done the looking. You didn't hear him neither, did you?''

''No,'' the boy said. ''I—''

''He's smart,'' Sam said. ''Too smart.'' Again the boy saw in his eyes that quality of dark and brooding lambence as Sam looked down at the bitch trembling faintly and steadily against the boy's leg. From her raked shoulder a few drops of fresh blood clung like bright berries. ''Too big. We aint got the dog yet. But maybe some day.''

Because there would be a next time, after and after. He was only ten. It seemed to him that he could see them, the two of them, shadowy in the limbo from which time emerged and became time: the old bear absolved of mortality and himself who shared a little of it. Because he recognised now what he had smelled in the huddled dogs and tasted in his own saliva, recognised fear as a boy, a youth, recognises the existence of love and passion and experience which is his heritage but not yet his patrimony, from entering by chance the presence or perhaps even merely the bedroom of a woman who has loved and been loved by many men. *So I will have to see him,* he thought, without dread or even hope. *I will have to look at him.* So it was in June of the next summer. They were at the camp again, celebrating Major de Spain's and General Compson's birthdays. Although the one had been born in September and the other in the depth of winter and almost thirty years earlier, each June the two of them and McCaslin and Boon and Walter Ewell (and the boy too from now on) spent two weeks at the camp, fishing and shooting squirrels and turkey and running coons and wildcats with the dogs at night. That is, Boon and the negroes (and the boy too now) fished and shot squirrels and ran the coons and cats, because the proven hunters, not only Major de Spain and old General Compson (who spent those two weeks sitting in a rocking chair before a tremendous iron pot of Brunswick stew, stirring and tasting, with Uncle Ash to quarrel with about how he was making it and Tennie's Jim to pour whisky into the tin dipper from which he drank it) but even McCaslin and Walter Ewell who were still young enough, scorned such other than shooting the wild gobblers with pistols for wagers or to test their marksmanship.

That is, his cousin McCaslin and the others thought he was hunting squirrels. Until the third evening he believed that Sam Fathers thought so too. Each morning he would leave the camp right after breakfast. He had his own gun now, a new breech-loader, a Christmas gift; he would own and shoot it for almost seventy years, through two new pairs of barrels and locks and one new stock, until all that remained of the original gun was the silver-inlaid trigger-guard with his and Mc-Caslin's engraved names and the date in 1878. He found the tree beside the little bayou where he had stood that morning. Using the compass he ranged from that point; he was teaching himself to be better than a fair woodsman without even knowing he was doing it. On the third day he even found the gutted log where he had first seen the print. It was almost completely crumbled now, healing with unbelievable speed, a passionate and almost visible relinquishment, back into the earth from which the tree had grown. He ranged the summer woods now, green with gloom, if anything actually dimmer than they had been in November's gray dissolution, where even at noon the sun fell only in windless dappling upon the earth which never completely dried and which crawled with snakes—moccasins and water-snakes and rattlers, themselves the color of the dappled gloom so that he would not always see them until they moved; returning to camp later and later and later, first day, second day, passing in the twilight of the third evening the little log pen enclosing the log barn where Sam was putting up the stock for the night. "You aint looked right yet," Sam said.

He stopped. For a moment he didn't answer. Then he said peacefully, in a peaceful rushing burst, as when a boy's miniature dam in a little brook gives way: "All right. Yes. But how? I went to the bayou. I even found that log again. I——"

"I reckon that was all right. Likely he's been watching you. You never saw his foot?"

"I . . ." the boy said. "I didn't . . . I never thought . . ."

"It's the gun," Sam said. He stood beside the fence, motionless, the old man, son of a negro slave and a Chickasaw chief, in the battered and faded overalls and the frayed five-cent straw hat which had been the badge of the negro's slavery and was now the regalia of his freedom. The camp—the clearing, the house, the barn and its tiny lot with which Major de Spain in his turn had scratched punily and evanescently at the wilderness—faded in the dusk, back into the immemorial darkness of the woods. *The gun,* the boy thought. *The gun.* "You will have to choose," Sam said.

He left the next morning before light, without breakfast, long before Uncle Ash would wake in his quilts on the kitchen floor and start the fire. He had only the compass and a stick for the snakes. He could go almost a mile before he would need to see the compass. He sat on a log, the invisible compass in his hand, while the secret night-sounds which had ceased at his movements, scurried again and then fell still for good and the owls ceased and gave over to the waking day birds and there was light in the gray wet woods and he could see the compass. He went fast yet still quietly, becoming steadily better and better as a woodsman without yet having time to realise it; he jumped a doe and a fawn, walked them out of the bed, close enough to see them—the crash of undergrowth, the white scut, the fawn scudding along behind her, faster than he had known it could have run. He was hunting right, upwind, as Sam had taught him, but that didn't matter now. He had left the gun; by his own will and relinquishment he had accepted not a gambit, not a choice, but a condition in which not only the bear's heretofore inviolable anonymity but all the ancient rules and balances of hunter and hunted had been abrogated. He would not even be afraid, not even in the moment when the fear would take him completely: blood, skin, bowels, bones, memory from the long time before it even became his memory—all save that thin clear quenchless lucidity which alone differed him from this bear and from all the other bears and bucks he would follow during almost seventy years, to which Sam had said: ''Be scared. You cant help that. But dont be afraid. Aint nothing in the woods going to hurt you if you dont corner it or it dont smell that you are afraid. A bear or a deer has got to be scared of a coward the same as a brave man has got to be.''

By noon he was far beyond the crossing on the little bayou, farther into the new and alien country than he had ever been, travelling now not only by the compass but by the old, heavy, biscuit-thick silver watch which had been his father's. He had left the camp nine hours ago; nine hours from now, dark would already have been an hour old. He stopped, for the first time since had had risen from the log when he could see the compass face at last, and looked about, mopping his sweating face on his sleeve. He had already relinquished, of his will, because of his need, in humility and peace and without regret, yet apparently that had not been enough, the leaving of the gun was not enough. He stood for a moment—a child, alien and lost in the green and soaring gloom of the markless wilderness. Then he relinquished completely to it. It was the watch and the compass. He was still tainted. He removed the linked chain of the one and the looped thong of the other from his overalls and hung them on a bush and leaned the stick beside them and entered it.

When he realised he was lost, he did as Sam had coached and drilled him: made a cast to cross his backtrack. He had not been going very fast for the last two or three hours, and he had gone even less fast since he left the compass and watch on the bush. So he went slower still now, since the tree could not be very far; in fact, he found it before he really expected to and turned and went to it. But there was no bush beneath it, no compass nor watch, so he did next as Sam had coached and drilled him: made this next circle in the opposite direction and much larger, so that the pattern of the two of them would bisect his track somewhere but crossing no trace nor mark anywhere of his feet or any feet, and now he was going faster though still not panicked, his heart beating a little more rapidly but strong and steady enough, and this time it was not even the tree because there was a down log beside it which he had never seen before and beyond the log a little swamp, a seepage of moisture somewhere between earth and water, and he did what Sam had coached and drilled him as the next and the last, seeing as he sat down on the log the crooked print, the warped indentation in the wet ground which while he looked at it continued to fill with water until it was level full and the water began to overflow and the sides of the print began to dissolve away. Even as he looked up he saw the next one, and, moving, the one beyond it; moving, not hurrying, running, but merely keeping pace with them as they appeared before him as though they were being shaped out of thin air just one constant pace short of where he would lose them forever and be lost forever himself, tireless, eager, without doubt or dread, panting a little above the strong rapid little hammer of his heart, emerging suddenly into a little glade and the wilderness coalesced. It rushed, soundless, and solidified—the tree, the bush, the compass and the watch glinting where a ray of sunlight touched them. Then he saw the bear. It did not emerge, appear: it was just there, immobile, fixed in the green and windless noon's hot dappling, not as big as he had dreamed it but as big as he had expected, bigger, dimensionless against the dappled obscurity, looking at him. Then it moved. It crossed the glade without haste, walking for an instant into the sun's full glare and out of it, and stopped again and looked back at him across one shoulder. Then it was gone. It didn't walk into the woods. It faded, sank back into the wilderness without motion as he had watched a fish, a huge old bass, sink back into the dark depths of its pool and vanish without even any movement of its fins.

James Thurber / The Secret Life of Walter Mitty   1942

One of America's outstanding humorists, James Thurber (1894–1961) was born in Columbus, Ohio, and graduated from Ohio State University. He edited his college's humor magazine and after World War I worked as a reporter for several newspapers. In 1927, he began an association with The New Yorker *as a writer and cartoonist. One of his great themes, as the following classic short story reveals, is the extraordinary persistence of fantasy and illusion in what appear to be quite ordinary, even humdrum, human lives.*

Thurber's many books include a parody of sex manuals he wrote with his New Yorker colleague, E. B. White, Is Sex Necessary? *(1929),* The Owl in the Attic and Other Perplexities *(1931),* Fables for Our Time and Famous Poems Illustrated *(1940),* Men, Women, and Dogs *(1943), and* Thurber Country *(1953). One of his best loved books is his comic autobiography,* My Life and Hard Times *(1933).*

"We're going through!" The Commander's voice was like thin ice breaking. He wore his full-dress uniform, with the heavily braided white cap pulled down rakishly over one cold gray eye. "We can't make it, sir. It's spoiling for a hurricane, if you ask me." "I'm not asking you, Lieutenant Berg," said the Commander. "Throw on the power lights! Rev her up to 8,500! We're going through!" The pounding of the cylinders increased: ta-pocketa-pocketa-pocketa-*pocketa-pocketa*. The Commander stared at the ice forming on the pilot window. He walked over and twisted a row of complicated dials. "Switch on No. 8 auxiliary!" he shouted. "Switch on No. 8 auxiliary!" repeated Lieutenant Berg. "Full strength in No. 3 turret!" The crew, bending to their various tasks in the huge, hurtling eight-engined Navy hydroplane, looked at each other and grinned. "The Old Man'll get us through," they said to one another. "The Old Man ain't afraid of Hell!" . . .

"Not so fast! You're driving too fast!" said Mrs. Mitty. "What are you driving so fast for?"

"Hmm?" said Walter Mitty. He looked at his wife, in the seat beside him, with shocked astonishment. She seemed grossly unfamiliar, like a strange woman who had yelled at him in a crowd. "You were up to fifty-five," she said. "You know I don't like to go more than forty. You were up to fifty-five." Walter Mitty drove on toward Waterbury in silence, the roaring of the SN202 through the worst storm in twenty years of Navy flying fading in the remote, intimate airways of his mind.

"You're tensed up again," said Mrs. Mitty. "It's one of your days. I wish you'd let Dr. Renshaw look you over."

Walter Mitty stopped the car in front of the building where his wife went to have her hair done. "Remember to get those overshoes while I'm having my hair done," she said. "I don't need overshoes," said Mitty. She put her mirror back into her bag. "We've been all through that," she said, getting out of the car. "You're not a young man any longer." He raced the engine a little. "Why don't you wear your gloves? Have you lost your gloves?" Walter Mitty reached in a pocket and brought out the gloves. He put them on, but after she had turned and gone into the building and he had driven on to a red light, he took them off again. "Pick it up, brother!" snapped a cop as the light changed, and Mitty hastily pulled on his gloves and lurched ahead. He drove around the streets aimlessly for a time, and then he drove past the hospital on his way to the parking lot.

. . . "It's the millionaire banker, Wellington McMillan," said the pretty nurse. "Yes?" said Walter Mitty, removing his gloves slowly. "Who has the case?" "Dr. Renshaw and Dr. Benbow, but there are two specialists here, Dr. Remington from New York and Mr. Pritchard-Mitford from London. He flew over." A door opened down a long, cool corridor and Dr. Renshaw came out. He looked distraught and haggard. "Hello, Mitty," he said. "We're having the devil's own time with McMillan, the millionaire banker and close personal friend of Roosevelt. Obstreosis of the ductal tract. Tertiary. Wish you'd take a look at him." "Glad to," said Mitty.

In the operating room there were whispered introductions: "Dr. Remington, Dr. Mitty. Mr. Pritchard-Mitford, Dr. Mitty." "I've read your book on streptothricosis," said Pritchard-Mitford, shaking hands. "A brilliant performance, sir." "Thank you," said Walter Mitty. "Didn't know you were in the States, Mitty," grumbled Remington. "Coals to Newcastle, bringing Mitford and me up here for a tertiary." "You are very kind," said Mitty. A huge, complicated machine, connected to the operating table, with many tubes and wires, began at this moment to go pocketa-pocketa-pocketa. "The new anesthetizer is giving way!" shouted an interne. "There is no one in the East who knows how to fix it!" "Quiet, man!" said Mitty, in a low, cool voice. He sprang to the machine, which was now going pocketa-pocketa-queep-pocketa-queep. He began fingering delicately a row of glistening dials. "Give me a fountain pen!" he snapped. Someone handed him a fountain pen. He pulled a faulty piston out of the machine and inserted the pen in its place. "That will hold for ten minutes," he said. "Get on with the operation." A nurse hurried over and whispered to Renshaw, and Mitty saw the man turn pale. "Coreopsis has set in," said Renshaw nervously. "If you would take over, Mitty?" Mitty looked at him and at the craven figure of Benbow, who drank, and at the grave, uncertain faces of the two great specialists. "If you wish," he said. They slipped a white gown on him; he adjusted a mask and drew on thin gloves; nurses handed him shining . . .

"Back it up, Mac! Look out for that Buick!" Walter Mitty jammed on the brakes. "Wrong lane, Mac," said the parking-lot attendant, looking at Mitty closely. "Gee. Yeh," muttered Mitty. He began cautiously to back out of the lane marked "Exit Only." "Leave her sit there," said the attendant. "I'll put her away." Mitty got out of the car. "Hey, better leave the key." "Oh," said Mitty, handing the man the ignition key. The attendant vaulted into the car, backed it up with insolent skill, and put it where it belonged.

They're so damn cocky, thought Walter Mitty, walking along Main Street; they think they know everything. Once he had tried to take his chains off, outside New Milford, and he had got them wound around the axles. A man had had to come out in a wrecking car and unwind them, a young, grinning garageman. Since then Mrs. Mitty always made him drive to a garage to have the chains taken off. The next time, he thought, I'll wear my right arm in a sling; they won't grin at me then. I'll have my right arm in a sling and they'll see I couldn't possibly take the chains off myself. He kicked at the slush on the sidewalk. "Overshoes," he said to himself, and he began looking for a shoe store.

When he came out into the street again, with the overshoes in a box under his arm, Walter Mitty began to wonder what the other thing was his wife had told him to get. She had told him, twice, before they set out from their house for Waterbury. In a way he hated these weekly trips to town—he was always getting something wrong. Kleenex, he thought, Squibb's, razor blades? No. Toothpaste, toothbrush, bicarbonate, carborundum, initiative and referendum? He gave it up. But she would remember it. "Where's the what's-its-name?" she would ask. "Don't tell me you forgot the what's-its-name." A newsboy went by shouting something about the Waterbury trial.

. . . "Perhaps this will refresh your memory." The District Attorney suddenly thrust a heavy automatic at the quiet figure on the witness stand. "Have you ever seen this before?" Walter Mitty took the gun and examined it expertly. "This is my Webley-Vickers 50.80," he said calmly. An excited buzz ran around the courtroom. The Judge rapped for order. "You are a crack shot with any sort of firearms, I believe?" said the District Attorney, insinuatingly. "Objection!" shouted Mitty's attorney. "We have shown that the defendant could not have fired the shot. We have shown that he wore his right arm in a sling on the night of the fourteenth of July." Walter Mitty raised his hand briefly and the bickering attorneys were stilled. "With any known make of gun," he said evenly, "I could have killed Gregory Fitzhurst at three hundred feet *with my left hand.*" Pandemonium broke loose in the courtroom. A woman's scream rose above the bedlam and suddenly a lovely, dark-haired girl was in Walter Mitty's arms. The District Attorney struck at her savagely. Without rising from his chair, Mitty let the man have it on the point of the chin. "You miserable cur!" . . .

"Puppy biscuit," said Walter Mitty. He stopped walking and the buildings of Waterbury rose up out of the misty courtroom and surrounded him again. A woman who was passing laughed. "He said 'Puppy biscuit,' " she said to her companion. "That man said 'Puppy biscuit' to himself." Walter Mitty hurried on. He went into an A. & P., not the first one he came to but a smaller one farther up the street. "I want some biscuit for small, young dogs," he said to the clerk. "Any special brand, sir?" The greatest pistol shot in the world thought a moment. "It says 'Puppies Bark for It' on the box," said Walter Mitty.

His wife would be through at the hairdresser's in fifteen minutes, Mitty saw in looking at his watch, unless they had trouble drying it; sometimes they had trouble drying it. She didn't like to get to the hotel first; she would want him to be there waiting for her as usual. He found a big leather chair in the lobby, facing a window, and he put the overshoes and the puppy biscuit on the floor beside it. He picked up an old copy of *Liberty* and sank down into the chair. "Can Germany Conquer the World Through the Air?" Walter Mitty looked at the pictures of bombing planes and of ruined streets.

. . . "The cannonading has got the wind up in young Raleigh, sir," said the sergeant. Captain Mitty looked up at him through tousled hair. "Get him to bed," he said wearily. "With the others. I'll fly alone." "But you can't, sir," said the sergeant anxiously. "It takes two men to handle that bomber and the Archies are pounding hell out of the air. Von Richtman's circus is between here and Saulier." "Somebody's got to get that ammunition dump," said Mitty. "I'm going over. Spot of brandy?" He poured a drink for the sergeant and one for himself. War thundered and whined around the dugout and battered at the door. There was a rending of wood and splinters flew through the room. "A bit of a near thing," said Captain Mitty carelessly. "The box barrage is closing in," said the sergeant. "We only live once, Sergeant," said Mitty, with his faint, fleeting smile. "Or do we?" He poured another brandy and tossed it off. "I never see a man could hold his brandy like you, sir," said the sergeant. "Begging your pardon, sir." Captain Mitty stood up and strapped on his huge Webley-Vickers automatic. "It's forty kilometers through hell, sir," said the sergeant. Mitty finished one last brandy. "After all," he said softly, "what isn't?" The pounding of the cannon increased; there was the rat-tat-tatting of machine guns, and from somewhere came the menacing pocketa-pocketa-pocketa of the new flame-throwers. Walter Mitty walked to the door of the dugout humming "Auprès de Ma Blonde." He turned and waved to the sergeant. "Cheerio!" he said. . . .

Something struck his shoulder. "I've been looking all over this hotel for you," said Mrs. Mitty. "Why do you have to hide in this old chair? How did you expect me to find you?" "Things close in," said Walter Mitty vaguely. "What?" Mrs. Mitty said. "Did you get the what's-its-name? The puppy biscuit? What's in that box?" "Overshoes," said Mitty. "Couldn't you have put them on in the store?" "I was thinking," said Walter Mitty. "Does it ever occur to you that I am sometimes thinking?" She looked at him. "I'm going to take your temperature when I get you home," she said.

They went out through the revolving doors that made a faintly derisive whistling sound when you pushed them. It was two blocks to the parking lot. At the drugstore on the corner she said, "Wait here for me. I forgot something. I won't be a minute." She was more than a minute. Walter Mitty lighted a cigarette. It began to rain, rain with sleet in it. He stood up against the wall of the drugstore, smoking. . . . He put his shoulders back and his heels together. "To hell with the handkerchief," said Walter Mitty scornfully. He took one last drag on his cigarette and snapped it away. Then, with that faint, fleeting smile playing about his lips, he faced the firing squad; erect and motionless, proud and disdainful, Walter Mitty the Undefeated, inscrutable to the last.

Richard Wright / *Black Boy*
[Discovering Books]   1945

Born into a sharecropper family in Natchez, Mississippi, in 1908, Richard Wright spent his youth in Memphis, Tennessee, with relatives and, for a while, in an orphanage. His desultory formal education ended in the eighth grade but was augmented by the young man's own fervid program of extensive reading. Determined to be a writer but limited to menial employment, Wright broke from Depression-torn Memphis, working first in Chicago for the Federal Writers Project and then in New York where he compiled the government-sponsored Guide to Harlem (1937).*

Though the five novellas comprising Uncle Tom's Children (1938) *were his first published works, Wright did not gain national prominence or financial security until the publication of his best-selling first novel,* Native Son (1940). *In the following chapter from his autobiography,* Black Boy, *Wright poignantly recounts his discovery of the freedom and influence exercised by writers and the inception of his own commitment to a literary career.*

Soon after the appearance of Black Boy, *Wright left for Paris, where he lived and wrote until his death in 1960.*

One morning I arrived early at work and went into the bank lobby where the Negro porter was mopping. I stood at a counter and picked up the Memphis *Commercial Appeal* and began my free reading of the press. I came finally to the editorial page and saw an article dealing with one H. L. Mencken. I knew by hearsay that he was the editor of the *American Mercury,* but aside from that I knew nothing about him. The article was a furious denunciation of Mencken, concluding with one, hot, short sentence: Mencken is a fool.

I wondered what on earth this Mencken had done to call down upon him the scorn of the South. The only people I had ever heard denounced in the South were Negroes, and this man was not a Negro. Then what ideas did Mencken hold that made a newspaper like the *Commercial Appeal* castigate him publicly? Undoubtedly he must be advocating ideas that the South did not like. Were there, then, people other than Negroes who criticized the South? I knew that during the Civil War the South had hated northern whites, but I had not encountered such hate during my life. Knowing no more of Mencken than I did at that moment, I felt a vague sympathy for him. Had not the South, which had assigned me the role of a non-man, cast at him its hardest words?

Now, how could I find out about this Mencken? There was a huge library near the riverfront, but I knew that Negroes were not allowed to patronize its shelves any more than they were the parks and playgrounds of the city. I had gone into the library several times to get books for the white men on the job. Which of them would now help me to get books? And how could I read them without causing concern to the white men with whom I worked? I had so far been successful in hiding my thoughts and feelings from them, but I knew that I would create hostility if I went about this business of reading in a clumsy way.

I weighed the personalities of the men on the job. There was Don, a Jew; but I distrusted him. His position was not much better than mine and I knew that he was uneasy and insecure; he had always treated me in an offhand, bantering way that barely concealed his contempt. I was afraid to ask him to help me to get books; his frantic desire to demonstrate a racial solidarity with the whites against Negroes might make him betray me.

Then how about the boss? No, he was a Baptist and I had the suspicion that he would not be quite able to comprehend why a black boy would want to read Mencken. There were other white men on the job whose attitudes showed clearly that they were Kluxers or sympathizers, and they were out of the question.

There remained only one man whose attitude did not fit into an anti-Negro category, for I had heard the white men refer to him as a "Pope lover." He was an Irish Catholic and was hated by the white Southerners. I knew that he read books, because I had got him volumes from the library several times. Since he, too, was an object of hatred, I felt that he might refuse me but would hardly betray me. I hesitated, weighing and balancing the imponderable realities.

One morning I paused before the Catholic fellow's desk.

"I want to ask you a favor," I whispered to him.

"What is it?"

"I want to read. I can't get books from the library. I wonder if you'd let me use your card?"

He looked at me suspiciously.

"My card is full most of the time," he said.

"I see," I said and waited, posing my question silently.

"You're not trying to get me into trouble, are you, boy?" he asked, staring at me.

"Oh, no, sir."

"What book do you want?"

"A book by H. L. Mencken."

"Which one?"

"I don't know. Has he written more than one?"

"He has written several."

"I didn't know that."

"What makes you want to read Mencken?"

"Oh, l just saw his name in the newspaper," I said.

"It's good of you to want to read," he said. "But you ought to read the right things."

I said nothing. Would he want to supervise my reading?

"Let me think," he said. "I'll figure out something."

I turned from him and he called me back. He stared at me quizzically.

"Richard, don't mention this to the other white men," he said.

"I understand," I said. "I won't say a word."

A few days later he called me to him.

"I've got a card in my wife's name," he said. "Here's mine."

"Thank you, sir."

"Do you think you can manage it?"

"I'll manage fine," I said.

"If they suspect you, you'll get in trouble," he said.

"I'll write the same kind of notes to the library that you wrote when you sent me for books," I told him. "I'll sign your name."

He laughed.

"Go ahead. Let me see what you get," he said.

That afternoon I addressed myself to forging a note. Now, what were the names of books written by H. L. Mencken? I did not know any of them. I finally wrote what I thought would be a foolproof note: *Dear Madam: Will you please let this nigger boy*—I used the word "nigger" to make the librarian feel that I could not possibly be the author of the note—*have some books by H. L. Mencken?* I forged the white man's name.

I entered the library as I had always done when on errands for whites, but I felt that I would somehow slip up and betray myself. I doffed my hat, stood a respectful distance from the desk, looked as unbookish as possible, and waited for the white .patrons to be taken care of. When the desk was clear of people, I still waited. The white librarian looked at me.

"What do you want, boy?"

As though I did not possess the power of speech, I stepped forward and simply handed her the forged note, not parting my lips.

"What books by Mencken does he want?" she asked.

"I don't know, ma'am," I said, avoiding her eyes.

"Who gave you this card?"

"Mr. Falk," I said.

"Where is he?"

"He's at work, at the M—— Optical Company," I said. "I've been in here for him before."

"I remember," the woman said. "But he never wrote notes like this."

Oh, God, she's suspicious. Perhaps she would not let me have the books? If she had turned her back at that moment, I would have ducked out the door and never gone back. Then I thought of a bold idea.

"You can call him up, ma'am," I said, my heart pounding.

"You're not using these books, are you?" she asked pointedly.

"Oh, no, ma'am. I can't read."

"I don't know what he wants by Mencken," she said under her breath.

I knew now that I had won; she was thinking of other things and the race question had gone out of her mind. She went to the shelves. Once or twice she looked over her shoulder at me, as though she was still doubtful. Finally she came forward with two books in her hand.

"I'm sending him two books," she said. "But tell Mr. Falk to come in next time, or send me the names of the books he wants. I don't know what he wants to read."

I said nothing. She stamped the card and handed me the books. Not daring to glance at them, I went out of the library, fearing that the woman would call me back for further questioning. A block away from the library I opened one of the books and read a title: *A Book of Prefaces*. I was nearing my nineteenth birthday and I did not know how to pronounce the word "preface." I thumbed the pages and saw strange words and strange names. I shook my head, disappointed. I looked at the other book; it was called *Prejudices*. I knew what that word meant; I had heard it all my life. And right off I was on guard against Mencken's books. Why would a man want to call a book *Prejudices?* The word was so stained with all my memories of racial hate that I could not conceive of anybody using it for a title. Perhaps I had made a mistake about Mencken? A man who had prejudices must be wrong.

When I showed the books to Mr. Falk, he looked at me and frowned.

"That librarian might telephone you," I warned him.

"That's all right," he said. "But when you're through reading those books, I want you to tell me what you get out of them."

That night in my rented room, while letting the hot water run over my can of pork and beans in the sink, I opened *A Book of Prefaces* and began to read. I was jarred and shocked by the style, the clear, clean, sweeping sentences. Why did he write like that? And how did one write like that? I pictured the man as a raging demon, slashing with his pen, consumed with hate, denouncing everything American, extolling everything European or German, laughing at the weaknesses of people, mocking God, authority. What was this? I stood up, trying to realize what reality lay behind the meaning of the words . . . Yes, this man was fighting, fighting with words. He was using words as a weapon, using them as one would use a club. Could words be weapons? Well, yes, for here they were. Then, maybe, perhaps, I could use them as a weapon? No. It frightened me. I read on and what amazed me was not what he said, but how on earth anybody had the courage to say it.

Occasionally I glanced up to reassure myself that I was alone in the room. Who were these men about whom Mencken was talking so passionately? Who was Anatole France? Joseph Conrad? Sinclair Lewis, Sherwood Anderson, Dostoevski, George Moore, Gustave Flaubert, Maupassant, Tolstoy, Frank Harris, Mark Twain, Thomas Hardy, Arnold Bennett, Stephen Crane, Zola, Norris, Gorky, Bergson, Ibsen, Balzac, Bernard Shaw, Dumas, Poe, Thomas Mann, O. Henry, Dreiser, H. G. Wells, Gogol, T. S. Eliot, Gide, Baudelaire, Edgar Lee Masters, Stendhal, Turgenev, Huneker, Nietzsche, and scores of others? Were these men real? Did they exist or had they existed? And how did one pronounce their names?

I ran across many words whose meanings I did not know, and I either looked them up in a dictionary or, before I had a chance to do that, encountered the word in a context that made its meaning clear. But what strange world was this? I concluded the book with the conviction that I had somehow overlooked something terribly important in life. I had once tried to write, had once reveled in feeling, had let my crude imagination roam, but the impulse to dream had been slowly beaten out of me by experience. Now it surged up again and I hungered for books, new ways of looking and seeing. It was not a matter of believing or disbelieving what I read, but of feeling something new, of being affected by something that made the look of the world different.

As dawn broke I ate my pork and beans, feeling dopey, sleepy. I went to work, but the mood of the book would not die; it lingered, coloring everything I saw, heard, did. I now felt that I knew what the white men were feeling. Merely because I had read a book that had spoken of how they lived and thought, I identified myself with that book. I felt vaguely guilty. Would I, filled with bookish notions, act in a manner that would make the whites dislike me?

I forged more notes and my trips to the library became frequent. Reading grew into a passion. My first serious novel was Sinclair Lewis's *Main Street*. It made me see my boss, Mr. Gerald, and identify him as an American type. I would smile when I saw him lugging his golf bags into the office. I had always felt a vast distance separating me from the boss, and now I felt closer to him, though still distant. I felt now that I knew him, that I could feel the very limits of his narrow life. And this had happened because I had read a novel about a mythical man called George F. Babbitt.

The plots and stories in the novels did not interest me so much as the point of view revealed. I gave myself over to each novel without reserve, without trying to criticize it; it was enough for me to see and feel something different. And for me, everything was something different. Reading was like a drug, a dope. The novels created moods in which I lived for days. But I could not conquer my sense of guilt, my feeling that the white men around me knew that I was changing, that I had begun to regard them differently.

Whenever I brought a book to the job, I wrapped it in newspaper—a habit that was to persist for years in other cities and under other circumstances. But some of the white men pried into my packages when I was absent and they questioned me.

"Boy, what are you reading those books for?"

"Oh, I don't know, sir."

"That's deep stuff you're reading, boy."

"I'm just killing time, sir."

"You'll addle your brains if you don't watch out."

I read Dreiser's *Jennie Gerhardt* and *Sister Carrie* and they revived in me a vivid sense of my mother's suffering; I was overwhelmed. I grew silent, wondering about the life around me. It would have been impossible for me to have told anyone what I derived from these novels, for it was nothing less than a sense of life itself. All my life had shaped me for the realism, the naturalism of the modern novel, and I could not read enough of them.

Steeped in new moods and ideas, I bought a ream of paper and tried to write; but nothing would come, or what did come was flat beyond telling. I discovered that more than desire and feeling were necessary to write and I dropped the idea. Yet I still wondered how it was possible to know people sufficiently to write about them? Could I ever learn about life and people? To me, with my vast ignorance, my Jim Crow station in life, it seemed a task impossible of achievement. I now knew what being a Negro meant. I could endure the hunger. I had learned to live with hate. But to feel that there were feelings denied me, that the very breath of life itself was beyond my reach, that more than anything else hurt, wounded me. I had a new hunger.

In buoying me up, reading also cast me down, made me see what was possible, what I had missed. My tension returned, new, terrible, bitter, surging, almost too great to be contained. I no longer *felt* that the world about me was hostile, killing; I *knew* it. A million times I asked myself what I could do to save myself, and there were no answers. I seemed forever condemned, ringed by walls.

I did not discuss my reading with Mr. Falk, who had lent me his library card; it would have meant talking about myself and that would have been too painful. I smiled each day, fighting desperately to maintain my old behavior, to keep my disposition seemingly sunny. But some of the white men discerned that I had begun to brood.

"Wake up there, boy!" Mr. Olin said one day.

"Sir!" I answered for the lack of a better word.

"You act like you've stolen something," he said.

I laughed in the way I knew he expected me to laugh, but I resolved to be more conscious of myself, to watch my every act, to guard and hide the new knowledge that was dawning within me.

If I went north, would it be possible for me to build a new life then? But how could a man build a life upon vague, unformed yearnings? I wanted to write and I did not even know the English language. I bought English grammars and found them dull. I felt that I was getting a better sense of the language from novels than from grammars. I read hard, discarding a writer as soon as I felt that I had grasped his point of view. At night the printed page stood before my eyes in sleep.

Mrs. Moss, my landlady, asked me one Sunday morning:

"Son, what is this you keep on reading?"

"Oh, nothing. Just novels."

"What you get out of 'em?"

"I'm just killing time," I said.

"I hope you know your own mind," she said in a tone which implied that she doubted if I had a mind.

I knew of no Negroes who read the books I liked and I wondered if any Negroes ever thought of them. I knew that there were Negro doctors, lawyers, newspapermen, but I never saw any of them. When I read a Negro newspaper I never caught the faintest echo of my preoccupation in its pages. I felt trapped and occasionally, for a few days, I would stop reading. But a vague hunger would come over me for books, books that opened up new avenues of feeling and seeing, and again I would forge another note to the white librarian. Again I would read and wonder as only the naïve and unlettered can read and wonder, feeling that I carried a secret, criminal burden about with me each day.

That winter my mother and brother came and we set up housekeeping, buying furniture on the installment plan, being cheated and yet knowing no way to avoid it. I began to eat warm food and to my surprise found that regular meals enabled me to read faster. I may have lived through many illnesses and survived them, never suspecting that I was ill. My brother obtained a job and we began to save toward the trip north, plotting our time, setting tentative dates for departure. I told none of the white men on the job that I was planning to go north; I knew that the moment they felt I was thinking of the North they would change toward me. It would have made them feel that I did not like the life I was living, and because my life was completely conditioned by what they said or did, it would have been tantamount to challenging them.

I could calculate my chances for life in the South as a Negro fairly clearly now.

I could fight the southern whites by organizing with other Negroes, as my grandfather had done. But I knew that I could never win that way; there were many whites and there were but few blacks. They were strong and we were weak. Outright black rebellion could never win. If I fought openly I would die and I did not want to die. News of lynchings were frequent.

I could submit and live the life of a genial slave, but that was impossible. All of my life had shaped me to live by my own feelings and thoughts. I could make up to Bess and marry her and inherit the house. But that, too, would be the life of a slave; if I did that, I would crush to death something within me, and I would hate myself as much as I knew the whites already hated those who had submitted. Neither could I ever willingly present myself to be kicked, as Shorty had done. I would rather have died than do that.

I could drain off my restlessness by fighting with Shorty and Harrison. I had seen many Negroes solve the problem of being black by transferring their hatred of themselves to others with a black skin and fighting them. I would have to be cold to do that, and I was not cold and I could never be.

I could, of course, forget what I had read, thrust the whites out of my mind, forget them; and find release from anxiety and longing in sex and alcohol. But the memory of how my father had conducted himself made that course repugnant. If I did not want others to violate my life, how could I voluntarily violate it myself?

I had no hope whatever of being a professional man. Not only had I been so conditioned that I did not desire it, but the fulfillment of such an ambition was beyond my capabilities. Well-to-do Negroes lived in a world that was almost as alien to me as the world inhabited by whites.

What, then, was there? I held my life in my mind, in my consciousness each day, feeling at times that I would stumble and drop it, spill it forever. My reading had created a vast sense of distance between me and the world in which I lived and tried to make a living, and that sense of distance was increasing each day. My days and nights were one long, quiet, continuously contained dream of terror, tension, and anxiety. I wondered how long I could bear it.

Flannery O'Connor / The Life You Save May Be Your Own   1953

Born in Savannah, Georgia, in 1925, Flannery O'Connor was educated and spent most of her adult life in the small town of Milledgeville, Georgia. Her muse, like Hawthorne's, is lovingly provincial and, also like Hawthorne's, her grotesques, eccentrics, and spooks, though insistently local, live at the heart of the human condition. "My people," she said in an interview, "could come from anywhere, but naturally since I know the South they speak with a Southern accent."

"The Life You Save May Be Your Own" was originally published in the Spring 1953 issue of The Kenyon Review, *a quarterly periodical devoted to literature and criticism. As "The Life You Save," the story appeared in 1957 as a television play, ending, however, on a more positive note.*

The old woman and her daughter were sitting on their porch when Mr. Shiftlet came up their road for the first time. The old woman slid to the edge of her chair and leaned forward, shading her eyes from the piercing sunset with her hand. The daughter could not see far in front of her and continued to play with her fingers. Although the old woman lived in this desolate spot with only her daughter and she had never seen Mr. Shiftlet before, she could tell, even from a distance, that he was a tramp and no one to be afraid of. His left coat sleeve was folded up to show there was only half an arm in it and his gaunt figure listed slightly to the side as if the breeze were pushing him. He had on a black town suit and a brown felt hat that was turned up in the front and down in the back and he carried a tin tool box by a handle. He came on, at an amble, up her road, his face turned toward the sun which appeared to be balancing itself on the peak of a small mountain.

The old woman didn't change her position until he was almost into her yard; then she rose with one hand fisted on her hip. The daughter, a large girl in a short blue organdy dress, saw him all at once and jumped up and began to stamp and point and make excited speechless sounds.

Mr. Shiftlet stopped just inside the yard and set his box on the ground and tipped his hat at her as if she were not in the least afflicted; then he turned toward the old woman and swung the hat all the way off. He had long black slick hair that hung flat from a part in the middle to beyond the tips of his ears on either side. His face descended in forehead for more than half its length and ended suddenly with his features just balanced over a jutting steel-trap jaw. He seemed to be a young man but he had a look of composed dissatisfaction as if he understood life thoroughly.

"Good evening," the old woman said. She was about the size of a cedar fence post and she had a man's gray hat pulled down low over her head.

The tramp stood looking at her and didn't answer. He turned his back and faced the sunset. He swung both his whole and his short arm up slowly so that they indicated an expanse of sky and his figure formed a crooked cross. The old woman watched him with her arms folded across her chest as if she were the owner of the sun, and the daughter watched, her head thrust forward and her fat helpless hands hanging at the wrists. She had long pink-gold hair and eyes as blue as a peacock's neck.

He held the pose for almost fifty seconds and then he picked up his box and came on to the porch and dropped down on the bottom step. "Lady," he said in a firm nasal voice, "I'd give a fortune to live where I could see me a sun do that every evening."

"Does it every evening," the old woman said and sat back down. The daughter sat down too and watched him with a cautious sly look as if he were a bird that had come up very close. He leaned to one side, rooting in his pants pocket, and in a second he brought out a package of chewing gum and offered her a piece. She took it and unpeeled it and began to chew without taking her eyes off him. He offered the old woman a piece but she only raised her upper lip to indicate she had no teeth.

Mr. Shiftlet's pale sharp glance had already passed over everything in the yard— the pump near the corner of the house and the big fig tree that three or four chickens were preparing to roost in—and had moved to a shed where he saw the square rusted back of an automobile. "You ladies drive?" he asked.

"That car ain't run in fifteen year," the old woman said. "The day my husband died, it quit running."

"Nothing is like it used to be, lady," he said. "The world is almost rotten."

"That's right," the old woman said. "You from around here?"

"Name Tom T. Shiftlet," he murmured, looking at the tires.

"I'm pleased to meet you," the old woman said. "Name Lucynell Crater and daughter Lucynell Crater. What you doing around here, Mr. Shiftlet?"

He judged the car to be about a 1928 or '29 Ford. "Lady," he said, and turned and gave her his full attention, "lemme tell you something. There's one of these doctors in Atlanta that's taken a knife and cut the human heart—the human heart," he repeated, leaning forward, "out of a man's chest and held it in his hand," and he held his hand out, palm up, as if it were slightly weighted with the human heart, "and studied it like it was a day-old chicken, and lady," he said, allowing a long significant pause in which his head slid forward and his clay-colored eyes brightened, "he don't know no more about it than you or me."

"That's right," the old woman said.

"Why, if he was to take that knife and cut into every corner of it, he still wouldn't know no more than you or me. What you want to bet?"

"Nothing," the old woman said wisely. "Where you come from, Mr. Shiftlet?"

He didn't answer. He reached into his pocket and brought out a sack of tobacco and a package of cigarette papers and rolled himself a cigarette, expertly with one hand, and attached it in a hanging position to his upper lip. Then he took a box of wooden matches from his pocket and struck one on his shoe. He held the burning match as if he were studying the mystery of flame while it traveled dangerously toward his skin. The daughter began to make loud noises and to point to his hand and shake her finger at him, but when the flame was just before touching him, he leaned down with his hand cupped over it as if he were going to set fire to his nose and lit the cigarette.

He flipped away the dead match and blew a stream of gray into the evening. A sly

look came over his face. "Lady," he said, "nowadays, people'll do anything any-
ways. I can tell you my name is Tom T. Shiftlet and I come from Tarwater, Tennessee, but you never have seen me before: how you know I ain't lying? How you
know my name ain't Aaron Sparks, lady, and I come from Singleberry, Georgia, or
how you know it's not George Speeds and I come from Lucy, Alabama, or how you
know I ain't Thompson Bright from Toolafalls, Mississippi?"

"I don't know nothing about you," the old woman muttered, irked.

"Lady," he said, "people don't care how they lie. Maybe the best I can tell you
is, I'm a man; but listen lady," he said and paused and made his tone more ominous
still, "what is a man?"

The old woman began to gum a seed. "What you carry in that tin box, Mr.
Shiftlet?" she asked.

"Tools," he said, put back. "I'm a carpenter."

"Well, if you come out here to work, I'll be able to feed you and give you a place
to sleep but I can't pay. I'll tell you that before you begin," she said.

There was no answer at once and no particular expression on his face. He leaned
back against the two-by-four that helped support the porch roof. "Lady," he said
slowly, "there's some men that some things mean more to them than money." The
old woman rocked without comment and the daughter watched the trigger that
moved up and down in his neck. He told the old woman then that all most people
were interested in was money, but he asked what a man was made for. He asked her
if a man was made for money, or what. He asked her what she thought she was
made for but she didn't answer, she only sat rocking and wondered if a one-armed
man could put a new roof on her garden house. He asked a lot of questions that she
didn't answer. He told her that he was twenty-eight years old and had lived a varied
life. He had been a gospel singer, a foreman on the railroad, an assistant in an undertaking parlor, and he come over the radio for three months with Uncle Roy and
his Red Creek Wranglers. He said he had fought and bled in the Arm Service of his
country and visited every foreign land and that everywhere he had seen people that
didn't care if they did a thing one way or another. He said he hadn't been raised
thataway.

A fat yellow moon appeared in the branches of the fig tree as if it were going to
roost there with the chickens. He said that a man had to escape to the country to see
the world whole and that he wished he lived in a desolate place like this where he
could see the sun go down every evening like God made it to do.

"Are you married or are you single?" the old woman asked.

There was a long silence. "Lady," he asked finally, "where would you find you
an innocent woman today? I wouldn't have any of this trash I could just pick up."

The daughter was leaning very far down, hanging her head almost between her
knees, watching him through a triangular door she had made in her overturned hair;
and she suddenly fell in a heap on the floor and began to whimper. Mr. Shiftlet
straightened her out and helped her get back in the chair.

"Is she your baby girl?" he asked.

"My only," the old woman said, "and she's the sweetest girl in the world. I
would give her up for nothing on earth. She's smart too. She can sweep the floor,
cook, wash, feed the chickens, and hoe. I wouldn't give her up for a casket of
jewels."

"No," he said kindly, "don't ever let any man take her away from you."

"Any man come after her," the old woman said, "he'll have to stay around the
place."

Mr. Shiftlet's eye in the darkness was focused on a part of the automobile bumper
that glittered in the distance.

"Lady," he said, jerking his short arm up as if he could point with it to her house
and yard and pump, "there ain't a broken thing on this plantation that I couldn't fix

for you, one-arm jackleg or not. I'm a man," he said with a sullen dignity, "even if I ain't a whole one. I got," he said, tapping his knuckles on the floor to emphasize the immensity of what he was going to say, "a moral intelligence!" and his face pierced out of the darkness into a shaft of doorlight and he stared at her as if he were astonished himself at this impossible truth.

The old woman was not impressed with the phrase. "I told you you could hang around and work for food," she said, "if you don't mind sleeping in that car yonder."

"Why listen, lady," he said with a grin of delight, "the monks of old slept in their coffins!"

"They wasn't as advanced as we are," the old woman said.

The next morning he began on the roof of the garden house while Lucynell, the daughter, sat on a rock and watched him work. He had not been around a week before the change he had made in the place was apparent. He had patched the front and back steps, built a new hog pen, restored a fence, and taught Lucynell, who was completely deaf and had never said a word in her life, to say the word "bird." The big rosy-faced girl followed him everywhere, saying "Burrttddt ddbirrrttdt," and clapping her hands. The old woman watched from a distance, secretly pleased. She was ravenous for a son-in-law.

Mr. Shiftlet slept on the hard narrow back seat of the car with his feet out the side window. He had his razor and a can of water on a crate that served him as a bedside table and he put up a piece of mirror against the back glass and kept his coat neatly on a hanger that he hung over one of the windows.

In the evenings he sat on the steps and talked while the old woman and Lucynell rocked violently in their chairs on either side of him. The old woman's three mountains were black against the dark blue sky and were visited off and on by various planets and by the moon after it had left the chickens. Mr. Shiftlet pointed out that the reason he had improved this plantation was because he had taken a personal interest in it. He said he was even going to make the automobile run.

He had raised the hood and studied the mechanism and he said he could tell that the car had been built in the days when cars were really built. You take now, he said, one man puts in one bolt and another man puts in another bolt and another man puts in another bolt so that it's a man for a bolt. That's why you have to pay so much for a car: you're paying all those men. Now if you didn't have to pay but one man, you could get you a cheaper car and one that had had a personal interest taken in it, and it would be a better car. The old woman agreed with him that this was so.

Mr. Shiftlet said that the trouble with the world was that nobody cared, or stopped and took any trouble. He said he never would have been able to teach Lucynell to say a word if he hadn't cared and stopped long enough.

"Teach her to say something else," the old woman said.

"What you want her to say next?" Mr. Shiftlet asked.

The old woman's smile was broad and toothless and suggestive. "Teach her to say 'sugarpie,' " she said.

Mr. Shiftlet already knew what was on her mind.

The next day he began to tinker with the automobile and that evening he told her that if she would buy a fan belt, he would be able to make the car run.

The old woman said she would give him the money. "You see that girl yonder?" she asked, pointing to Lucynell who was sitting on the floor a foot away, watching him, her eyes blue even in the dark. "If it was ever a man wanted to take her away, I would say, 'No man on earth is going to take that sweet girl of mine away from me!' but if he was to say, 'Lady, I don't want to take her away, I want her right here,' I would say, 'Mister, I don't blame you none. I wouldn't pass up a chance to live in a permanent place and get the sweetest girl in the world myself. You ain't no fool,' I would say.''

''How old is she?'' Mr. Shiftlet asked casually.

''Fifteen, sixteen,'' the old woman said. The girl was nearly thirty but because of her innocence it was impossible to guess.

''It would be a good idea to paint it too,'' Mr. Shiftlet remarked. ''You don't want it to rust out.''

''We'll see about that later,'' the old woman said.

The next day he walked into town and returned with the parts he needed and a can of gasoline. Late in the afternoon, terrible noises issued from the shed and the old woman rushed out of the house, thinking Lucynell was somewhere having a fit. Lucynell was sitting on a chicken crate, stamping her feet and screaming, ''Burrddttt! bddurrddtttt!'' but her fuss was drowned out by the car. With a volley of blasts it emerged from the shed, moving in a fierce and stately way. Mr. Shiftlet was in the driver's seat, sitting very erect. He had an expression of serious modesty on his face as if he had just raised the dead.

That night, rocking on the porch, the old woman began her business at once. ''You want you an innocent woman, don't you?'' she asked sympathetically. ''You don't want none of this trash.''

''No'm, I don't,'' Mr. Shiftlet said.

''One that can't talk,'' she continued, ''can't sass you back or use foul language. That's the kind for you to have. Right there,'' and she pointed to Lucynell sitting cross-legged in her chair, holding both feet in her hands.

''That's right,'' he admitted. ''She wouldn't give me any trouble.''

''Saturday,'' the old woman said, ''you and her and me can drive into town and get married.''

Mr. Shiftlet eased his position on the steps.

''I can't get married right now,'' he said. ''Everything you want to do takes money and I ain't got any.''

''What you need with money?'' she asked.

''It takes money,'' he said. ''Some people'll do anything anyhow these days, but the way I think, I wouldn't marry no woman that I couldn't take on a trip like she was somebody. I mean take her to a hotel and treat her. I wouldn't marry the Duchesser Windsor,'' he said firmly, ''unless I could take her to a hotel and giver something good to eat.

''I was raised thataway and there ain't a thing I can do about it. My old mother taught me how to do.''

''Lucynell don't even know what a hotel is,'' the old woman muttered. ''Listen here, Mr. Shiftlet,'' she said, sliding forward in her chair, ''you'd be getting a permanent house and a deep well and the most innocent girl in the world. You don't need no money. Lemme tell you something: there ain't any place in the world for a poor disabled friendless drifting man.''

The ugly words settled in Mr. Shiftlet's head like a group of buzzards in the top of a tree. He didn't answer at once. He rolled himself a cigarette and lit it and then he said in an even voice, ''Lady, a man is divided into two parts, body and spirit.''

The old woman clamped her gums together.

''A body and a spirit,'' he repeated. ''The body, lady, is like a house: it don't go anywhere: but the spirit, lady, is like a automobile: always on the move, always . . .''

''Listen, Mr. Shiftlet,'' she said, ''my well never goes dry and my house is always warm in the winter and there's no mortgage on a thing about this place. You can go to the courthouse and see for yourself. And yonder under that shed is a fine automobile.'' She laid the bait carefully. ''You can have it painted by Saturday. I'll pay for the paint.''

In the darkness, Mr. Shiftlet's smile stretched like a weary snake waking up by a fire. After a second he recalled himself and said, "I'm only saying a man's spirit means more to him than anything else. I would have to take my wife off for the week end without no regards at all for cost. I got to follow where my spirit says to go."

"I'll give you fifteen dollars for a week-end trip," the old woman said in a crabbed voice. "That's the best I can do."

"That wouldn't hardly pay for more than the gas and the hotel," he said. "It wouldn't feed her."

"Seventeen-fifty," the old woman said. "That's all I got so it isn't any use you trying to milk me. You can take a lunch."

Mr. Shiftlet was deeply hurt by the word "milk." He didn't doubt that she had more money sewed up in her mattress but he had already told her he was not interested in her money. "I'll make that do," he said and rose and walked off without treating with her further.

On Saturday the three of them drove into town in the car that the paint had barely dried on and Mr. Shiftlet and Lucynell were married in the Ordinary's office while the old woman witnessed. As they came out of the courthouse, Mr. Shiftlet began twisting his neck in his collar. He looked morose and bitter as if he had been insulted while someone held him. "That didn't satisfy me none," he said. "That was just something a woman in an office did, nothing but paper work and blood tests. What do they know about my blood? If they was to take my heart and cut it out," he said, "they wouldn't know a thing about me. It didn't satisfy me at all."

"It satisfied the law," the old woman said sharply.

"The law," Mr. Shiftlet said and spit. "It's the law that don't satisfy me."

He had painted the car dark green with a yellow band around it just under the windows. The three of them climbed in the front seat and the old woman said, "Don't Lucynell look pretty? Looks like a baby doll." Lucynell was dressed up in a white dress that her mother had uprooted from a trunk and there was a Panama hat on her head with a bunch of red wooden cherries on the brim. Every now and then her placid expression was changed by a sly isolated little thought like a shoot of green in the desert. "You got a prize!" the old woman said.

Mr. Shiftlet didn't even look at her.

They drove back to the house to let the old woman off and pick up the lunch. When they were ready to leave, she stood staring in the window of the car, with her fingers clenched around the glass. Tears began to seep sideways out of her eyes and run along the dirty creases in her face. "I ain't ever been parted with her for two days before," she said.

Mr. Shiftlet started the motor.

"And I wouldn't let no man have her but you because I seen you would do right. Good-by, Sugarbaby," she said, clutching at the sleeve of the white dress. Lucynell looked straight at her and didn't seem to see her there at all. Mr. Shiftlet eased the car forward so that she had to move her hands.

The early afternoon was clear and open and surrounded by pale blue sky. Although the car would go only thirty miles an hour, Mr. Shiftlet imagined a terrific climb and dip and swerve that went entirely to his head so that he forgot his morning bitterness. He had always wanted an automobile but he had never been able to afford one before. He drove very fast because he wanted to make Mobile by nightfall.

Occasionally he stopped his thoughts long enough to look at Lucynell in the seat beside him. She had eaten the lunch as soon as they were out of the yard and now she was pulling the cherries off the hat one by one and throwing them out the window. He became depressed in spite of the car. He had driven about a hundred miles when he decided that she must be hungry again and at the next small town they came to, he stopped in front of an aluminum-painted eating place called The Hot

Spot and took her in and ordered her a plate of ham and grits. The ride had made her sleepy and as soon as she got up on the stool, she rested her head on the counter and shut her eyes. There was no one in The Hot Spot but Mr. Shiftlet and the boy behind the counter, a pale youth with a greasy rag hung over his shoulder. Before he could dish up the food, she was snoring gently.

"Give it to her when she wakes up," Mr. Shiftlet said. "I'll pay for it now."

The boy bent over her and stared at the long pink-gold hair and the half-shut sleeping eyes. Then he looked up and stared at Mr. Shiftlet. "She looks like an angel of Gawd," he murmured.

"Hitch-hiker," Mr. Shiftlet explained. "I can't wait. I got to make Tuscaloosa."

The boy bent over again and very carefully touched his finger to a strand of the golden hair and Mr. Shiftlet left.

He was more depressed than ever as he drove on by himself. The late afternoon had grown hot and sultry and the country had flattened out. Deep in the sky a storm was preparing very slowly and without thunder as if it meant to drain every drop of air from the earth before it broke. There were times when Mr. Shiftlet preferred not to be alone. He felt too that a man with a car had a responsibility to others and he kept his eye out for a hitchhiker. Occasionally he saw a sign that warned: "Drive carefully. The life you save may be your own."

The narrow road dropped off on either side into dry fields and here and there a shack or a filling station stood in a clearing. The sun began to set directly in front of the automobile. It was a reddening ball that through his windshield was slightly flat on the bottom and top. He saw a boy in overalls and a gray hat standing on the edge of the road and he slowed the car down and stopped in front of him. The boy didn't have his hand raised to thumb the ride, he was only standing there, but he had a small cardboard suitcase and his hat was set on his head in a way to indicate that he had left somewhere for good. "Son," Mr. Shiftlet said, "I see you want a ride."

The boy didn't say he did or he didn't but he opened the door of the car and got in, and Mr. Shiftlet started driving again. The child held the suitcase on his lap and folded his arms on top of it. He turned his head and looked out the window away from Mr. Shiftlet. Mr. Shiftlet felt oppressed. "Son," he said after a minute, "I got the best old mother in the world so I reckon you only got the second best."

The boy gave him a quick dark glance and then turned his face back out the window.

"It's nothing so sweet," Mr. Shiftlet continued, "as a boy's mother. She taught him his first prayers at her knee, she gave him love when no other would, she told him what was right and what wasn't, and she seen that he done the right thing. Son," he said, "I never rued a day in my life like the one I rued when I left that old mother of mine."

The boy shifted in his seat but he didn't look at Mr. Shiftlet. He unfolded his arms and put one hand on the door handle.

"My mother was a angel of Gawd," Mr. Shiftlet said in a very strained voice. "He took her from heaven and giver to me and I left her." His eyes were instantly clouded over with a mist of tears. The car was barely moving.

The boy turned angrily in the seat. "You go to the devil!" he cried. "My old woman is a flea bag and yours is a stinking pole cat!" and with that he flung the door open and jumped out with his suitcase into the ditch.

Mr. Shiftlet was so shocked that for about a hundred feet he drove along slowly with the door still open. A cloud, the exact color of the boy's hat and shaped like a turnip, had descended over the sun, and another, worse looking, crouched behind the car. Mr. Shiftlet felt that the rottenness of the world was about to engulf him. He raised his arm and let it fall again to his breast. "Oh Lord!" he prayed. "Break forth and wash the slime from this earth!"

The turnip continued slowly to descend. After a few minutes there was a guffaw-
ing peal of thunder from behind and fantastic raindrops, like tin-can tops, crashed
over the rear of Mr. Shiftlet's car. Very quickly he stepped on the gas and with his
stump sticking out the window he raced the galloping shower into Mobile.

Tille Olsen / *Tell Me a Riddle*   1953–54

In Tell Me a Riddle, *Tillie Olsen "found characters who could fully embody her
vision of hope with hopelessness, of beauty in the midst of ugliness," in the
view of one critic writing for the* New Republic. *Many of the stories in that collection have been anthologized and widely acclaimed. "I Stand Here Ironing"
has been read on the radio and recorded in the Lamont Poetry Room at Harvard. Her latest book is* Silences (1979).

*Born in Omaha, Nebraska, in 1913, Olsen has worked in factories and
as a typist-transcriber. She was awarded a Stanford University Creative Writing
Fellowship (1955–56), a Ford Foundation Grant in Literature (1956), and a
fellowship to the Radcliffe Institute for Independent Study (1962–64).*

I STAND HERE IRONING

I stand here ironing, and what you asked me moves tormented back and forth with
the iron.

"I wish you would manage the time to come in and talk with me about your
daughter. I'm sure you can help me understand her. She's a youngster who needs
help and whom I'm deeply interested in helping."

"Who needs help." . . . Even if I came, what good would it do? You think
because I am her mother I have a key, or that in some way you could use me as a
key? She has lived for nineteen years. There is all that life that has happened outside of me, beyond me.

And when is there time to remember, to sift, to weigh, to estimate, to total? I
will start and there will be an interruption and I will have to gather it all together
again. Or I will become engulfed with all I did or did not do, with what should
have been and what cannot be helped.

She was a beautiful baby. The first and only one of our five that was beautiful at
birth. You do not guess how new and uneasy her tenancy in her now-loveliness.
You did not know her all those years she was thought homely, or see her poring
over her baby pictures, making me tell her over and over how beautiful she had
been—and would be, I would tell her—and was now, to the seeing eye. But the
seeing eyes were few or nonexistent. Including mine.

I nursed her. They feel that's important nowadays. I nursed all the children, but
with her, with all the fierce rigidity of first motherhood, I did like the books then
said. Though her cries battered me to trembling and my breasts ached with swol-
lenness, I waited till the clock decreed.

Why do I put that first? I do not even know if it matters, or if it explains anything.

She was a beautiful baby. She blew shining bubbles of sound. She loved motion, loved light, loved color and music and textures. She would lie on the floor in
her blue overalls patting the surface so hard in ecstasy her hands and feet would
blur. She was a miracle to me, but when she was eight months old I had to leave

her daytimes with the woman downstairs to whom she was no miracle at all, for I worked or looked for work and for Emily's father, who "could no longer endure" (he wrote in his good-bye note) "sharing want with us."

I was nineteen. It was the pre-relief, pre-WPA world of the depression. I would start running as soon as I got off the streetcar, running up the stairs, the place smelling sour, and awake or asleep to startle awake, when she saw me she would break into a clogged weeping that could not be comforted, a weeping I can hear yet.

After a while I found a job hashing at night so I could be with her days, and it was better. But it came to where I had to bring her to this family and leave her.

It took a long time to raise the money for her fare back. Then she got chicken pox and I had to wait longer. When she finally came, I hardly knew her, walking quick and nervous like her father, looking like her father, thin, and dressed in a shoddy red that yellowed her skin and glared at the pockmarks. All the baby loveliness gone.

She was two. Old enough for nursery school they said, and I did not know then what I know now—the fatigue of the long day, and the lacerations of group life in the kinds of nurseries that are only parking places for children.

Except that it would have made no difference if I had known. It was the only place there was. It was the only way we could be together, the only way I could hold a job.

And even without knowing, I knew. I knew the teacher that was evil because all these years it has curdled into my memory, the little boy hunched in the corner, her rasp, "why aren't you outside, because Alvin hits you? that's no reason, go out, scaredy." I knew Emily·hated it even if she did not clutch and implore "don't go Mommy" like the other children, mornings.

She always had a reason why we should stay home. Momma, you look sick. Momma, I feel sick. Momma, the teachers aren't there today, they're sick. Momma, we can't go, there was a fire there last night. Momma, it's a holiday today, no school, they told me.

But never a direct protest, never rebellion. I think of our others in their three-, four-year-oldness—the explosions, the tempers, the denunciations, the demands— and I feel suddenly ill. I put the iron down. What in me demanded that goodness in her? And what was the cost, the cost to her of such goodness?

The old man living in the back once said in his gentle way: "You should smile at Emily more when you look at her." What was in my face when I looked at her? I loved her. There were all the acts of love.

It was only with the others I remembered what he said, and it was the face of joy, and not of care or tightness or worry I turned to them—too late for Emily. She does not smile easily, let alone almost always as her brothers and sisters do. Her face is closed and sombre, but when she wants, how fluid. You must have seen it in her pantomimes, you spoke of her rare gift for comedy on the stage that rouses a laughter out of the audience so dear they applaud and applaud and do not want to let her go.

Where does it come from, that comedy? There was none of it in her when she came back to me that second time, after I had had to send her away again. She had a new daddy now to learn to love, and I think perhaps it was a better time.

Except when we left her alone nights, telling ourselves she was old enough.

"Can't you go some other time, Mommy, like tomorrow?" she would ask. "Will it be just a little while you'll be gone? Do you promise?"

The time we came back, the front door open, the clock on the floor in the hall. She rigid awake. "It wasn't just a little while. I didn't cry. Three times I called you, just three times, and then I ran downstairs to open the door so you could come faster. The clock talked loud. I threw it away, it scared me what it talked."

She said the clock talked loud again that night I went to the hospital to have Susan. She was delirious with the fever that comes before red measles, but she was fully conscious all the week I was gone and the week after we were home when she could not come near the new baby or me.

She did not get well. She stayed skeleton thin, not wanting to eat, and night after night she had nightmares. She would call for me, and I would rouse from exhaustion to sleepily call back: "You're all right, darling, go to sleep, it's just a dream," and if she still called, in a sterner voice, "now go to sleep, Emily, there's nothing to hurt you." Twice, only twice, when I had to get up for Susan anyhow, I went in to sit with her.

Now when it is too late (as if she would let me hold and comfort her like I do the others) I get up and go to her at once at her moan or restless stirring. "Are you awake, Emily? Can I get you something?" And the answer is always the same: "No, I'm all right, go back to sleep, Mother."

They persuaded me at the clinic to send her away to a convalescent home in the country where "she can have the kind of food and care you can't manage for her, and you'll be free to concentrate on the new baby." They still send children to that place. I see pictures on the society page of sleek young women planning affairs to raise money for it, or dancing at the affairs, or decorating Easter eggs or filling Christmas stockings for the children.

They never have a picture of the children so I do not know if the girls still wear those gigantic red bows and the ravaged looks on the every other Sunday when parents can come to visit "unless otherwise notified"—as we were notified the first six weeks.

Oh it is a handsome place, green lawns and tall trees and fluted flower beds. High up on the balconies of each cottage the children stand, the girls in their red bows and white dresses, the boys in white suits and giant red ties. The parents stand below shrieking up to be heard and the children shriek down to be heard, and between them the invisible wall "Not To Be Contaminated by Parental Germs or Physical Affection."

There was a tiny girl who always stood hand in hand with Emily. Her parents never came. One visit she was gone. "They moved her to Rose Cottage" Emily shouted in explanation. "They don't like you to love anybody here."

She wrote once a week, the labored writing of a seven-year-old. "I am fine. How is the baby. If I write my leter nicly I will have a star. Love." There never was a star. We wrote every other day, letters she could never hold or keep but only hear read—once. "We simply do not have room for children to keep any personal possessions," they patiently explained when we pieced one Sunday's shrieking together to plead how much it would mean to Emily, who loved so to keep things, to be allowed to keep her letters and cards.

Each visit she looked frailer, "She isn't eating," they told us.

(They had runny eggs for breakfast or mush with lumps, Emily said later, I'd hold it in my mouth and not swallow. Nothing ever tasted good, just when they had chicken.)

It took us eight months to get her released home, and only the fact that she gained back so little of her seven lost pounds convinced the social worker.

I used to try to hold and love her after she came back, but her body would stay stiff, and after a while she'd push away. She ate little. Food sickened her, and I think much of life too. Oh she had physical lightness and brightness, twinkling by on skates, bouncing like a ball up and down up and down over the jump rope, skimming over the hill; but these were momentary.

She fretted about her appearance, thin and dark and foreign-looking at a time when every little girl was supposed to look or thought she should look a chubby blonde replica of Shirley Temple. The doorbell sometimes rang for her, but no one seemed to come and play in the house or be a best friend. Maybe because we moved so much.

There was a boy she loved painfully through two school semesters. Months later she told me how she had taken pennies from my purse to buy him candy. "Licorice was his favorite and I brought him some every day, but he still liked Jennifer better'n me. Why, Mommy?" The kind of question for which there is no answer.

School was a worry to her. She was not glib or quick in a world where glibness and quickness were easily confused with ability to learn. To her overworked and exasperated teachers she was an overconscientious "slow learner" who kept trying to catch up and was absent entirely too often.

I let her be absent, though sometimes the illness was imaginary. How different from my now-strictness about attendance with the others. I wasn't working. We had a new baby, I was home anyhow. Sometimes, after Susan grew old enough, I would keep her home from school, too, to have them all together.

Mostly Emily had asthma, and her breathing, harsh and labored, would fill the house with a curiously tranquil sound. I would bring the two old dresser mirrors and her boxes of collections to her bed. She would select beads and single earrings, bottle tops and shells, dried flowers and pebbles, old postcards and scraps, all sorts of oddments; then she and Susan would play Kingdom, setting up landscapes and furniture, peopling them with action.

Those were the only times of peaceful companionship between her and Susan. I have edged away from it, that poisonous feeling between them, that terrible balancing of hurts and needs I had to do between the two, and did so badly, those earlier years.

Oh there are conflicts between the others too, each one human, needing, demanding, hurting, taking—but only between Emily and Susan, no, Emily toward Susan that corroding resentment. It seems so obvious on the surface, yet it is not obvious. Susan, the second child, Susan, golden- and curly-haired and chubby, quick and articulate and assured, everything in appearance and manner Emily was not; Susan, not able to resist Emily's precious things, losing or sometimes clumsily breaking them; Susan telling jokes and riddles to company for applause while Emily sat silent (to say to me later: that was *my* riddle, Mother, I told it to Susan); Susan, who for all the five years' difference in age was just a year behind Emily in developing physically.

I am glad for that slow physical development that widened the difference between her and her contemporaries, though she suffered over it. She was too vulnerable for that terrible world of youthful competition, of preening and parading, of constant measuring of yourself against every other, of envy, "If I had that copper hair," "If I had that skin. . . ." She tormented herself enough about not looking like the others, there was enough of the unsureness, the having to be conscious of words before you speak, the constant caring—what are they thinking of me? without having it all magnified by the merciless physical drives.

Ronnie is calling. He is wet and I change him. It is rare there is such a cry now. That time of motherhood is almost behind me when the ear is not one's own but must always be racked and listening for the child cry, the child call. We sit for a while and I hold him, looking out over the city spread in charcoal with its soft aisles of light. "*Shoogily*," he breathes and curls closer. I carry him back to bed, asleep. *Shoogily*. A funny word, a family word, inherited from Emily, invested by her to say: *comfort*.

In this and other ways she leaves her seal, I say aloud. And startle at my saying it. What do I mean? What did I start to gather together, to try and make coherent? I was at the terrible, growing years. War years. I do not remember them well. I was working, there were four smaller ones now, there was not time for her. She had to help be a mother, and housekeeper, and shopper. She had to set her seal. Mornings of crisis and near hysteria trying to get lunches packed, hair combed, coats and shoes found, everyone to school or Child Care on time, the baby ready for transportation. And always the paper scribbled on by a smaller one, the book looked at by Susan then mislaid, the homework not done. Running out to that huge school where she was one, she was lost, she was a drop; suffering over the unpreparedness, stammering and unsure of her classes.

There was so little time left at night after the kids were bedded down. She would struggle over books, always eating (it was in those years she developed her enormous appetite that is legendary in our family) and I would be ironing, or preparing food for the next day, or writing V-mail to Bill, or tending the baby. Sometimes, to make me laugh, or out of her despair, she would imitate happenings or types at school.

I think I said once: "Why don't you do something like this in the school amateur show?" One morning she phoned me at work, hardly understandable through the weeping: "Mother, I did it. I won, I won; they gave me first prize; they clapped and clapped and wouldn't let me go."

Now suddenly she was Somebody, and as imprisoned in her difference as she had been in anonymity.

She began to be asked to perform at other high schools, even in colleges, then at city and statewide affairs. The first one we went to, I only recognized her that first moment when thin, shy, she almost drowned herself into the curtains. Then: Was this Emily? The control, the command, the convulsing and deadly clowning, the spell, then the roaring, stamping audience, unwilling to let this rare and precious laughter out of their lives.

Afterwards: You ought to do something about her with a gift like that—but without money or knowing how, what does one do? We have left it all to her, and the gift has as often eddied inside, clogged and clotted, as been used and growing.

She is coming. She runs up the stairs two at a time with her light graceful step, and I know she is happy tonight. Whatever it was that occasioned your call did not happen today.

"Aren't you ever going to finish the ironing, Mother? Whistler painted his mother in a rocker. I'd have to paint mine standing over an ironing board." This is one of her communicative nights and she tells me everything and nothing as she fixes herself a plate of food out of the icebox.

She is so lovely. Why did you want me to come in at all? Why were you concerned? She will find her way.

She starts up the stairs to bed. "Don't get me up with the rest in the morning." "But I thought you were having midterms." "Oh, those," she comes back in, kisses me, and say quite lightly, "in a couple of years when we'll all be atom-dead they won't matter a bit."

She has said it before. She *believes* it. But because I have been dredging the past, and all that compounds a human being is so heavy and meaningful in me, I cannot endure it tonight.

I will never total it all. I will never come in to say: She was a child seldom smiled at. Her father left me before she was a year old. I had to work her first six years when there was work, or I sent her home and to his relatives. There were years she had care she hated. She was dark and thin and foreign-looking in a world where the prestige went to blondeness and curly hair and dimples, she was slow where glibness was prized. She was a child of anxious, not proud, love. We were poor and could not afford for her the soil of easy growth. I was a young mother, I was a distracted mother. There were the other children pushing up, demanding. Her younger sister seemed all that she was not. There were years she did not want me to touch her. She kept too much in herself, her life was such she had to keep too much in herself. My wisdom came too late. She has much to her and probably little will come of it. She is a child of her age, of depression, of war, of fear.

Let her be. So all that is in her will not bloom—but in how many does it? There is still enough left to live by. Only help her to know—help make it so there is cause for her to know—that she is more than this dress on the ironing board, helpless before the iron.

DISCUSSION QUESTIONS

1. Characterize the speaker in this piece. Whom is she addressing? How does she feel about her daughter? About her own life?

2. The piece ends with an appeal: "Only help her to know—help make it so there is cause for her to know—that she is more than this dress on the ironing board, helpless before the iron." Explain the significance of the image. Does the speaker seem to wish someone could have helped her to know the same thing earlier in her life? Does she still seem "helpless before the iron" herself? What do you think the author wants us to feel for the speaker? For the daughter? What specifically makes you think so?

Allen Ginsberg / A Supermarket in California   1955

The author of poetry regarded as "great," "strange," "angelic," "degenerate," "unsurpassed," and "apocalyptic," Allen Ginsberg remains one of the most celebrated and vilified literary figures of the past three decades. Born in Newark, New Jersey, in 1926, Ginsberg graduated from Columbia University in 1948 and spent several years on the road, supporting himself as a spot welder, reporter, dishwasher, porter, book reviewer, and seaman. Soon after his arrival in San Francisco, he launched an immediately successful career as a market research consultant. But a year of psychoanalysis prompted him, as he says, to "quit the job, my tie and suit, the apartment on Nob Hill . . . and do what I wanted"—write poetry. By the mid-1950s, Ginsberg was identified—along with, among others, Jack Kerouac, Lawrence Ferlinghetti, and William Burroughs—as a cofounder of the Beat Generation. Lionized for his experimentations with literary forms and unconventional life-styles, Ginsberg remains an ardent supporter of political and social causes. A late-1960s profile in The New Yorker *characterized him not only as a major American poet but also as a guru of the "amalgamated hippie-pacifist-activist-visionary-orgiastic-anarchist-Orientalist-psychedelic underground."*

Ginsberg's first volume of poetry, Howl *(1956), is also his most famous. It has gone through more than thirty printings, In a preface to the volume, William Carlos Williams cautions readers that Ginsberg's vision of contemporary America is like "going through hell" but also reminds us that Ginsberg "proves to us, in spite of the most debasing experiences that life can offer a man, the spirit of love survives to ennoble our lives if we have the wit and the courage and the faith—and the art! to persist."*

"A Supermarket in California" was included in Ginsberg's first controversial volume. The poem remains a pensive rendition of Walt Whitman's vision of America as a land of abundance.

What thoughts I have of you tonight, Walt Whitman, for
I walked down the sidestreets under the trees with a headache
self-conscious looking at the full moon.

In my hungry fatigue, and shopping for images, I went
into the neon fruit supermarket, dreaming of your enumerations!

What peaches and what penumbras! Whole families
shopping at night! Aisles full of husbands! Wives in the
avocados, babies in the tomatoes!—and you, Garcia Lorca,
what were you doing down by the watermelons?

I saw you, Walt Whitman, childless, lonely old grubber,
poking among the meats in the refrigerator and eyeing the
grocery boys.

I heard you asking questions of each: Who killed the   5
pork chops? What price bananas? Are you my Angel?

I wandered in and out of the brilliant stacks of cans
following you, and followed in my imagination by the store
detective.

We strode down the open corridors together in our
solitary fancy tasting artichokes, possessing every frozen
delicacy, and never passing the cashier.

Where are we going, Walt Whitman? The doors close in
an hour. Which way does your beard point tonight?

(I touch your book and dream of our odyssey in the
supermarket and feel absurd.)

Will we walk all night through solitary streets? The trees   10
add shade to shade, lights out in the houses, we'll both be
lonely.

Will we stroll dreaming of the lost America of love past
blue automobiles in driveways, home to our silent cottage?

Ah, dear father, graybeard, lonely old courage-teacher,
what America did you have when Charon quit poling his ferry
and you got out on a smoking bank and stood watching the
boat disappear on the black waters of Lethe?

E. B. White / The Ring of Time   1956

*Perhaps the most respected twentieth-century American essayist, E.B. White
once claimed that the essay writer is "sustained by the childish belief that
everything he thinks about, everything that happens to him, is of general interest." In other words, the writer begins by being self-centered; only then can the
writer's self imaginatively engage the centers of other selves.*

*White was born in Mt. Vernon, New York, in 1899. After graduating
from Cornell in 1921, he worked as a journalist for several years and then
landed a position with the newly formed* New Yorker *magazine, where he contributed the "Talk of the Town" column. The winner of the National Institute of
Arts and Letters gold medal in 1960, White is the author of nineteen books, including two classics for children,* Stuart Little *(1948) and* Charlotte's Web
(1952). Regarded as an eminent stylist, White revised his former teacher's brief

writing manual, The Elements of Style *(1959), and the tiny edition known as*
"Strunk and White" can probably be seen on the desks of more professional
writers than any other book of its kind.
   "The Ring of Time" is reprinted from Essays of E. B. White *(1977).*

Fiddler Bayou, March 22, 1956

After the lions had returned to their cages, creeping angrily through the chutes, a
little bunch of us drifted away and into an open doorway nearby, where we stood
for a while in semidarkness, watching a big brown circus horse go harumphing
around the practice ring. His trainer was a woman of about forty, and the two of
them, horse and woman, seemed caught up in one of those desultory treadmills of
afternoon from which there is no apparent escape. The day was hot, and we kib-
itzers were grateful to be briefly out of the sun's glare. The long rein, or tape, by
which the woman guided her charge counterclockwise in his dull career formed
the radius of their private circle, of which she was the revolving center; and she,
too, stepped a tiny circumference of her own, in order to accommodate the horse
and allow him his maximum scope. She had on a short-skirted costume and a conical straw hat. Her legs were bare and she wore high heels, which probed deep
into the loose tanbark and kept her ankles in a state of constant turmoil. The great
size and meekness of the horse, the repetitious exercise, the heat of the afternoon,
all exerted a hypnotic charm that invited boredom; we spectators were experiencing a languor—we neither expected relief nor felt entitled to any. We had paid a
dollar to get into the grounds, to be sure, but we had got our dollar's worth a few
minutes before, when the lion trainer's whiplash had got caught around a toe of
one of the lions. What more did we want for a dollar?

   Behind me I heard someone say, "Excuse me, please," in a low voice. She
was halfway into the building when I turned and saw her—a girl of sixteen or
seventeen, politely threading her way through us onlookers who blocked the entrance. As she emerged in front of us, I saw that she was barefoot, her dirty little
feet fighting the uneven ground. In most respects she was like any of two or three
dozen showgirls you encounter if you wander about the winter quarters of Mr.
John Ringling North's circus, in Sarasota—cleverly proportioned, deeply browned
by the sun, dusty, eager, and almost naked. But her grave face and the naturalness
of her manner gave her a sort of quick distinction and brought a new note into the
gloomy octagonal building where we had all cast our lot for a few moments. As
soon as she had squeezed through the crowd, she spoke a word or two to the older
woman, whom I took to be her mother, stepped to the ring, and waited while the
horse coasted to a stop in front of her. She gave the animal a couple of affectionate swipes on his enormous neck and then swung herself aboard. The horse immediately resumed his rocking canter, the woman goading him on, chanting something that sounded like "Hop! Hop!"

   In attempting to recapture this mild spectacle, I am merely acting as recording
secretary for one of the oldest of societies—the society of those who, at one time
or another, have surrendered, without even a show of resistance, to the bedazzle-
ment of a circus rider. As a writing man, or secretary, I have always felt charged
with the safekeeping of all unexpected items of worldly or unworldly enchantment, as though I might be held personally responsible if even a small one were
to be lost. But it is not easy to communicate anything of this nature. The circus
comes as close to being the world in microcosm as anything I know; in a way, it
puts all the rest of show business in the shade. Its magic is universal and complex.
Out of its wild disorder comes order; from its rank smell rises the good aroma of
courage and daring; out of its preliminary shabbiness comes the final splendor.

And buried in the familiar boasts of its advance agents lies the modesty of most of its people. For me the circus is at its best before it has been put together. It is at its best at certain moments when it comes to a point, as through a burning glass, in the activity and destiny of a single performer out of so many. One ring is always bigger than three. One rider, one aerialist, is always greater than six. In short, a man has to catch the circus unawares to experience its full impact and share its gaudy dream.

The ten-minute ride the girl took achieved—as far as I was concerned, who wasn't looking for it, and quite unbeknownst to her, who wasn't even striving for it—the thing that is sought by performers everywhere, on whatever stage, whether struggling in the tidal currents of Shakespeare or bucking the difficult motion of a horse. I somehow got the idea she was just cadging a ride, improving a shining ten minutes in the diligent way all serious artists seize free moments to hone the blade of their talent and keep themselves in trim. Her brief tour included only elementary postures and tricks, perhaps because they were all she was capable of, perhaps because her warmup at this hour was unscheduled and the ring was not rigged for a real practice session. She swung herself off and on the horse several times, gripping his mane. She did a few knee-stands—or whatever they are called—dropping to her knees and quickly bouncing back up on her feet again. Most of the time she simply rode in a standing position, well aft on the beast, her hands hanging easily at her sides, her head erect, her straw-colored ponytail lightly brushing her shoulders, the blood of exertion showing faintly through the tan of her skin. Twice she managed a one-foot stance—a sort of ballet pose, with arms outstretched. At one point the neck strap of her bathing suit broke and she went twice around the ring in the classic attitude of a woman making minor repairs to a garment. The fact that she was standing on the back of a moving horse while doing this invested the matter with a clownish significance that perfectly fitted the spirit of the circus—jocund, yet charming. She just rolled the strap into a neat ball and stowed it inside her bodice while the horse rocked and rolled beneath her in dutiful innocence. The bathing suit proved as self-reliant as its owner and stood up well enough without benefit of strap.

The richness of the scene was in its plainness, its natural condition—of horse, of ring, of girl, even to the girl's bare feet that gripped the bare back of her proud and ridiculous mount. The enchantment grew not out of anything that happened or was performed but out of something that seemed to go round and around and around with the girl, attending her, a steady gleam in the shape of a circle—a ring of ambition, of happiness, of youth. (And the positive pleasures of equilibrium under difficulties.) In a week or two, all would be changed, all (or almost all) lost: the girl would wear makeup, the horse would wear gold, the ring would be painted, the bark would be clean for the feet of the horse, the girl's feet would be clean for the slippers that she'd wear. All, all would be lost.

As I watched with the others, our jaws adroop, our eyes alight, I became painfully conscious of the element of time. Everything in the hideous old building seemed to take the shape of a circle, conforming to the course of the horse. The rider's gaze, as she peered straight ahead, seemed to be circular, as though bent by force of circumstance; then time itself began running in circles, and so the beginning was where the end was, and the two were the same, and one thing ran into the next and time went round and around and got nowhere. The girl wasn't so young that she did not know the delicious satisfaction of having a perfectly behaved body and the fun of using it to do a trick most people can't do, but she was too young to know that time does not really move in a circle at all. I thought: "She will never be as beautiful as this again"—a thought that made me acutely unhappy—and in a flash my mind (which is too much of a busybody to suit me) had projected her twenty-five years ahead, and she was now in the center of the ring, on foot, wearing a conical hat and high-heeled shoes, the image of the older woman, holding the long rein, caught in the treadmill of an afternoon long in the future. "She is at that enviable moment in life [I thought] when she believes she can go once around the ring, make one complete circuit, and at the end be exactly the same age as at the start." Everything in her movements, her expression, told you that for her the ring of time was perfectly formed, changeless, predictable, without beginning or end, like the ring in which she was traveling at this moment with the horse that wallowed under her. And then I slipped back into my trance, and time was circular again—time, pausing quietly with the rest of us, so as not to disturb the balance of a performer.

Her ride ended as casually as it had begun. The older woman stopped the horse, and the girl slid to the ground. As she walked toward us to leave, there was a quick, small burst of applause. She smiled broadly, in surprise and pleasure; then her face suddenly regained its gravity and she disappeared through the door.

It has been ambitious and plucky of me to attempt to describe what is indescribable, and I have failed, as I knew I would. But I have discharged my duty to my society; and besides, a writer, like an acrobat, must occasionally try a stunt that is too much for him. At any rate, it is worth reporting that long before the circus comes to town, its most notable performances have already been given. Under the bright lights of the finished show, a performer need only reflect the electric candle power that is directed upon him; but in the dark and dirty old training rings and in the makeshift cages, whatever light is generated, whatever excitement, whatever beauty, must come from original sources—from internal fires of professional hunger and delight, from the exuberance and gravity of youth. It is the difference between planetary light and the combustion of stars.

The South is the land of the sustained sibilant. Everywhere, for the appreciative visitor, the letter "s" insinuates itself in the scene: in the sound of sea and sand, in the singing shell, in the heat of sun and sky, in the sultriness of the gentle hours, in the siesta, in the stir of birds and insects. In contrast to the softness of its music, the South is also cruel and hard and prickly. A little striped lizard, flattened along the sharp green bayonet of a yucca, wears in its tiny face and watchful eye the pure look of death and violence. And all over the place, hidden at the bottom of their small sandy craters, the ant lions lie in wait for the ant that will stumble into their trap. (There are three kinds of lions in this region: the lions of the circus, the ant lions, and the Lions of the Tampa Lions Club, who roared their approval of segregation at a meeting the other day—all except one, a Lion named Monty Gurwit, who declined to roar and thereby got his picture in the paper.)

The day starts on a note of despair: the sorrowing dove, alone on its telephone wire, mourns the loss of night, weeps at the bright perils of the unfolding day. But soon the mockingbird wakes and begins an early rehearsal, setting the dove down by force of character, running through a few slick imitations, and trying a couple of original numbers into the bargain. The redbird takes it from there. Despair gives way to good humor. The Southern dawn is a pale affair, usually, quite different from our northern daybreak. It is a triumph of gradualism; night turns to day imperceptibly, softly, with no theatrics. It is subtle and undisturbing. As the first light seeps in through the blinds I lie in bed half awake, despairing with the dove, sounding the A for the brothers Alsop. All seems lost, all seems sorrowful. Then a mullet jumps in the bayou outside the bedroom window. It falls back into the water with a smart smack. I have asked several people why the mullet incessantly jump and I have received a variety of answers. Some say the mullet jump to shake off a parasite that annoys them. Some say they jump for the love of jumping—as the girl on the horse seemed to ride for the love of riding (although she, too, like all artists, may have been shaking off some parasite that fastens itself to the creative spirit and can be got rid of only by fifty turns around a ring while standing on a horse).

In Florida at this time of year, the sun does not take command of the day until a couple of hours after it has appeared in the east. It seems to carry no authority at first. The sun and the lizard keep the same schedule; they bide their time until the morning has advanced a good long way before they come fully forth and strike. The cold lizard waits astride his warming leaf for the perfect moment; the cold sun waits in his nest of clouds for the crucial time.

On many days, the dampness of the air pervades all life, all living. Matches refuse to strike. The towel, hung to dry, grows wetter by the hour. The newspaper, with its headlines about integration, wilts in your hand and falls limply into the coffee and the egg. Envelopes seal themselves. Postage stamps mate with one another as shamelessly as grasshoppers. But most of the time the days are models of beauty and wonder and comfort, with the kind sea stroking the back of the warm sand. At evening there are great flights of birds over the sea, where the light lingers; the gulls, the pelicans, the terns, the herons stay aloft for half an hour after land birds have gone to roost. They hold their ancient formations, wheel and fish over the Pass, enjoying the last of day like children playing outdoors after suppertime.

To a beachcomber from the North, which is my present status, the race problem has no pertinence, no immediacy. Here in Florida I am a guest in two houses—the house of the sun, the house of the State of Florida. As a guest, I mind my manners and do not criticize the customs of my hosts. It gives me a queer feeling, though, to be at the center of the greatest social crisis of my time and see hardly a sign of it. Yet the very absence of signs seems to increase one's awareness. Colored people do not come to the public beach to bathe, because they would not be made welcome there; and they don't fritter away their time visiting the circus, because they have other things to do. A few of them turn up at the ballpark, where they occupy a separate but equal section of the left-field bleachers and watch Negro players on the visiting Braves team using the same bases as the white players, instead of separate (but equal) bases. I have had only two small encounters with "color." A colored woman named Viola, who had been a friend of my wife's sister years ago, showed up one day with some laundry of ours that she had consented to do for us, and with the bundle she brought a bunch of nasturtiums, as a sort of natural accompaniment to the delivery of clean clothes. The flowers seemed a very acceptable thing and I was touched by them. We asked Viola about her daughter, and she said she was at Kentucky State College, studying voice.

The other encounter was when I was explaining to our cook, who is from Finland, the mysteries of bus travel in the American Southland. I showed her the bus stop, armed her with a timetable, and then, as a matter of duty, mentioned the customs of the Romans. "When you get on the bus," I said, "I think you'd better sit in one of the front seats—the seats in back are for colored people." A look of great weariness came into her face, as it does when we use too many dishes, and she replied, "Oh, I know—isn't it silly!"

Her remark, coming as it did all the way from Finland and landing on this sandbar with a plunk, impressed me. The Supreme Court said nothing about silliness, but I suspect it may play more of a role than one might suppose. People are, if anything, more touchy about being thought silly than they are about being thought unjust. I note that one of the arguments in the recent manifesto of Southern Congressmen in support of the doctrine of "separate but equal" was that it had been founded on "common sense." The sense that is common to one generation is uncommon to the next. Probably the first slave ship, with Negroes lying in chains on its decks, seemed commonsensical to the owners who operated it and to the planters who patronized it. But such a vessel would not be in the realm of common sense today. The only sense that is common, in the long run, is the sense of change—and we all instinctively avoid it, and object to the passage of time, and would rather have none of it.

The Supreme Court decision is like the Southern sun, laggard in its early stages, biding its time. It has been the law in Florida for two years now, and the years have been like the hours of the morning before the sun has gathered its strength. I think the decision is as incontrovertible and warming as the sun, and, like the sun, will eventually take charge.

But there is certainly a great temptation in Florida to duck the passage of time. Lying in warm comfort by the sea, you receive gratefully the gift of the sun, the gift of the South. This is true seduction. The day is a circle—morning, afternoon, and night. After a few days I was clearly enjoying the same delusion as the girl on the horse—that I could ride clear around the ring of day, guarded by wind and sun and sea and sand, and be not a moment older.

P.S. (April 1962).   When I first laid eyes on Fiddler Bayou, it was wild land, populated chiefly by the little crabs that gave it its name, visited by wading birds and by an occasional fisherman. Today, houses ring the bayou, and part of the mangrove shore has been bulkheaded with a concrete wall. Green lawns stretch from patio to water's edge, and sprinklers make rainbows in the light. But despite man's encroachment, Nature manages to hold her own and assert her authority: high tides and high winds in the gulf sometimes send the sea crashing across the sand barrier, depositing its wrack on lawns and ringing everyone's front door bell. The birds and the crabs accommodate themselves quite readily to the changes that have taken place; every day brings herons to hunt around among the roots of the mangroves, and I have discovered that I can approach to within about eight feet of a Little Blue Heron simply by entering the water and swimming slowly toward him. Apparently he has decided that when I'm in the water, I am without guile— possibly even desirable, like a fish.

The Ringling circus has quit Sarasota and gone elsewhere for its hibernation. A few circus families still own homes in the town, and every spring the students at the high school put on a circus, to let off steam, work off physical requirements, and provide a promotional spectacle for Sarasota. At the drugstore you can buy a postcard showing the bed John Ringling slept in. Time has not stood still for anybody but the dead, and even the dead must be able to hear the acceleration of little sports cars and know that things have changed.

From the all-wise *New York Times,* which has the animal kingdom ever in mind, I have learned that one of the creatures most acutely aware of the passing of time is the fiddler crab himself. Tiny spots on his body enlarge during daytime hours, giving him the same color as the mudbank he explores and thus protecting him from his enemies. At night the spots shrink, his color fades, and he is almost invisible in the light of the moon. These changes are synchronized with the tides, so that each day they occur at a different hour. A scientist who experimented with the crabs to learn more about the phenomenon discovered that even when they are removed from their natural environment and held in confinement, the rhythm of their bodily change continues uninterrupted, and they mark the passage of time in their laboratory prison, faithful to the tides in their fashion.

John Updike / A & P

1962

After graduating from Harvard in 1954, where he was president of the Lampoon, *John Updike joined* The New Yorker *magazine as a reporter. Though he officially left the staff of that magazine in 1957 to concentrate on his fiction, issue after issue of* The New Yorker *declares Updike's presence in short stories, sketches, book reviews, and occasional light verse. "A & P," a tale of adolescent sensibility and one of the most widely anthologized short stories by a contemporary American writer, shows Updike's characteristic concern for the minutiae of sensory perceptions and the achievement of individual identity.*

In walks these three girls in nothing but bathing suits. I'm in the third checkout slot, with my back to the door, so I don't see them until they're over by the bread. The one that caught my eye first was the one in the plaid green two-piece. She was a chunky kid, with a good tan and a sweet broad soft-looking can with those two crescents of white just under it, where the sun never seems to hit, at the top of the backs of her legs. I stood there with my hand on a box of HiHo crackers trying to remember if I rang it up or not. I ring it up again and the customer starts giving me hell. She's one of these cash-register-watchers, a witch about fifty with rouge on her cheekbones and no eyebrows, and I know it made her day to trip me up. She'd been watching cash registers for fifty years and probably never seen a mistake before.

By the time I got her feathers smoothed and her goodies into a bag—she gives me a little snort in passing, if she'd been born at the right time they would have burned her over in Salem—by the time I get her on her way the girls had circled around the bread and were coming back, without a pushcart, back my way along the counters, in the aisle between the checkouts and the Special bins. They didn't even have shoes on. There was this chunky one, with the two-piece—it was bright green and the seams on the bra were still sharp and her belly was still pretty pale so I guessed she just got it (the suit)—there was this one, with one of those chubby berry-faces, the lips all bunched together under her nose, this one, and a tall one, with black hair that hadn't quite frizzed right, and one of these sunburns right across under the eyes, and a chin that was too long—you know, the kind of girl other girls think is very "striking" and "attractive" but never quite makes it, as they very well know, which is why they like her so much—and then the third one, that wasn't quite so tall. She was the queen. She kind of led them, the other two peeking around and making their shoulders round. She didn't look around, not this queen, she just walked straight on slowly, on those long white prima-donna legs. She came down a little hard on her heels, as if she didn't walk in her bare feet that much, putting down her heels and then letting the weight move along to her toes as if she was testing the floor with every step, putting a little deliberate extra action into it. You never know for sure how girls' minds work (do you really think it's a mind in there or just a little buzz like a bee in a glass jar?) but you got the idea she had talked the other two into coming in here with her, and now she was showing them how to do it, walk slow and hold yourself straight.

She had on a kind of dirty-pink—beige maybe, I don't know—bathing suit with a little nubble all over it and, what got me, the straps were down. They were off her shoulders looped loose around the cool tops of her arms, and I guess as a result the suit had slipped a little on her, so all around the top of the cloth there was this shining rim. If it hadn't been there you wouldn't have known there could have been anything whiter than those shoulders. With the straps pushed off, there was nothing between the top of the suit and the top of her head except just *her*, this clean bare plane of the top of her chest down from the shoulder bones like a dented sheet of metal tilted in the light. I mean, it was more than pretty.

She had sort of oaky hair that the sun and salt had bleached, done up in a bun that was unravelling, and a kind of prim face. Walking into the A & P with your straps down, I suppose it's the only kind of face you *can* have. She held her head so high her neck, coming up out of those white shoulders, looked kind of stretched, but I didn't mind. The longer her neck was, the more of her there was.

She must have felt in the corner of her eye me and over my shoulder Stokesie in the second slot watching, but she didn't tip. Not this queen. She kept her eyes moving across the racks, and stopped, and turned so slow it made my stomach rub the inside of my apron, and buzzed to the other two, who kind of huddled against her for relief, and then they all three of them went up the cat-and-dog-food-breakfast-cereal-macaroni-rice-raisons-seasonings-spreads-spaghetti-soft-drinks-crackers-and-cookies aisle. From the third slot I look straight up this aisle to the meat counter, and I watched them all the way. The fat one with the tan sort of fumbled with the cookies, but on second thought she put the package back. The sheep pushing their carts down the aisle—the girls were walking against the usual traffic (not that we have one-way signs or anything)—were pretty hilarious. You could see them, when Queenie's white shoulders dawned on them, kind of jerk, or hop, or hiccup, but their eyes snapped back to their own baskets and on they pushed. I bet you could set off dynamite in an A & P and the people would by and large keep reaching and checking oatmeal off their lists and muttering "Let me see, there was a third thing, began with A, asparagus, no, ah, yes, applesauce!" or whatever it is they do mutter. But there was no doubt, this jiggled them. A few houseslaves in pin curlers even looked around after pushing their carts past to make sure what they had seen was correct.

You know, it's one thing to have a girl in a bathing suit down on the beach, where what with the glare nobody can look at each other much anyway, and another thing in the cool of the A & P, under the fluorescent lights, against all those stacked packages, with her feet paddling along naked over our checkerboard green-and-cream rubber-tile floor.

"Oh Daddy," Stokesie said beside me. "I feel so faint."

"Darling," I said. "Hold me tight." Stokesie's married, with two babies chalked up on his fuselage already, but as far as I can tell that's the only difference. He's twenty-two, and I was nineteen this April.

"Is it done?" he asks, the responsible married man finding his voice. I forgot to say he thinks he's going to be manager some sunny day, maybe in 1990 when it's called the Great Alexandrov and Petrooshki Tea Company or something.

What he meant was, our town is five miles from a beach, with a big summer colony out on the Point, but we're right in the middle of town, and the women generally put on a shirt or shorts or something before they get out of the car into the street. And anyway these are usually women with six children and varicose veins mapping their legs and nobody, including them, could care less. As I say, we're right in the middle of town, and if you stand at our front doors you can see two banks and the Congregational church and the newspaper store and three real-estate offices and about twenty-seven old freeloaders tearing up Central Street because the sewer broke again. It's not as if we're on the Cape; we're north of Boston and there's people in this town haven't seen the ocean for twenty years.

The girls had reached the meat counter and were asking McMahon something. He pointed, they pointed, and they shuffled out of sight behind a pyramid of Diet Delight peaches. All that was left for us to see was old McMahon patting his mouth and looking after them sizing up their joints. Poor kids, I began to feel sorry for them, they couldn't help it.

Now here comes the sad part of the story, at least my family says it's sad, but I don't think it's so sad myself. The store's pretty empty, it being Thursday afternoon, so there was nothing much to do except lean on the register and wait for the girls to show up again. The whole store was like a pinball machine and I didn't know which tunnel they'd come out of. After a while they come around out of the far aisle, around the light bulbs, records at discount of the Caribbean Six or Tony Martin Sings or some such gunk you wonder they waste the wax on, sixpacks of candy bars, and plastic toys done up in cellophane that fall apart when a kid looks at them anyway. Around they come, Queenie still leading the way, and holding a little gray jar in her hand. Slots Three through Seven are unmanned and I could see her wondering between Stokes and me, but Stokesie with his usual luck draws an old party in baggy gray pants who stumbles up with four giant cans of pineapple juice (what do these bums *do* with all that pineapple juice? I've often asked myself) so the girls come to me. Queenie puts down the jar and I take it into my fingers icy cold. Kingfish Fancy Herring Snacks in Pure Sour Cream: 49¢. Now her hands are empty, not a ring or a bracelet, bare as God made them, and I wonder where the money's coming from. Still with that prim look she lifts a folded dollar bill out of the hollow at the center of her nubbled pink top. The jar went heavy in my hand. Really, I thought that was so cute.

Then everybody's luck begins to run out. Lengel comes in from haggling with a truck full of cabbages on the lot and is about to scuttle into that door marked MANAGER behind which he hides all day when the girls touch his eye. Lengel's pretty dreary, teaches Sunday school and the rest, but he doesn't miss that much. He comes over and says, "Girls, this isn't the beach."

Queenie blushes, though maybe it's just a brush of sunburn I was noticing for the first time, now that she was so close. "My mother asked me to pick up a jar of herring snacks." Her voice kind of startled me, the way voices do when you see the people first, coming out so flat and dumb yet kind of tony, too, the way it ticked over "pick up" and "snacks." All of a sudden I slid right down her voice into her living room. Her father and the other men were standing around in ice-cream coats and bow ties and the women were in sandals picking up herring snacks on toothpicks off a big glass plate and they were all holding drinks the color of water with olives and sprigs of mint in them. When my parents have somebody over they get lemonade and if it's a real racy affair Schlitz in tall glasses with "They'll Do It Every Time" cartoons stencilled on.

"That's all right," Lengel said. "But this isn't the beach." His repeating this struck me as funny, as if it had just occurred to him, and he had been thinking all these years the A & P was a great big dune and he was the head lifeguard. He didn't like my smiling—as I say he doesn't miss much—but he concentrates on giving the girls that sad Sunday-school-superintendent stare.

Queenie's blush is no sunburn now, and the plump one in plaid, that I liked better from the back—a really sweet can—pipes up, "We weren't doing any shopping. We just came in for the one thing."

"That makes no difference," Lengel tells her, and I could see from the way his eyes went that he hadn't noticed she was wearing a two-piece before. "We want you decently dressed when you come in here."

"We *are* decent," Queenie says suddenly, her lower lip pushing, getting sore now that she remembers her place, a place from which the crowd that runs the A & P must look pretty crummy. Fancy Herring Snacks flashed in her very blue eyes.

"Girls, I don't want to argue with you. After this come in here with your shoulders covered. It's our policy." He turns his back. That's policy for you. Policy is what the kingpins want. What the others want is juvenile delinquency.

All this while, the customers had been showing up with their carts but, you know, sheep, seeing a scene, they had all bunched up on Stokesie, who shook open a paper bag as gently as peeling a peach, not wanting to miss a word. I could feel in the silence everybody getting nervous, most of all Lengel, who asks me, "Sammy, have you rung up their purchase?"

I thought and said "No" but it wasn't about that I was thinking. I go through the punches, 4, 9, GROC, TOT—it's more complicated than you think, and after you do it often enough, it begins to make a little song, that you hear words to, in my case "Hello (*bing*) there, you (*gung*) hap-py *pee*-pul (*splat*)!"—the *splat* being the drawer flying out. I uncrease the bill, tenderly as you may imagine, it just having come from between the two smoothest scoops of vanilla I had ever known were there, and pass a half and a penny into her narrow pink palm, and nestle the herrings in a bag and twist its neck and hand it over, all the time thinking.

The girls, and who'd blame them, are in a hurry to get out, so I say "I quit" to Lengel quick enough for them to hear, hoping they'll stop and watch me, their unsuspected hero. They keep right on going, into the electric eye; the door flies open and they flicker across the lot to their car, Queenie and Plaid and Big Tall Goony-Goony (not that as raw material she was so bad), leaving me with Lengel and a kink in his eyebrow.

"Did you say something, Sammy?"

"I said I quit."

"I thought you did."

"You didn't have to embarrass them."

"It was they who were embarrassing us."

I started to say something that came out "Fiddle-de-doo." It's a saying of my grandmother's, and I know she would have been pleased.

"I don't think you know what you're saying," Lengel said.

"I know you don't," I said. "But I do." I pull the bow at the back of my apron and start shrugging it off my shoulders. A couple customers that had been heading for my slot begin to knock against each other, like scared pigs in a chute.

Lengel sighs and begins to look very patient and old and gray. He's been a friend of my parents for years. "Sammy, you don't want to do this to your Mom and Dad," he tells me. It's true, I don't. But it seems to me that once you begin a gesture it's fatal not to go through with it. I fold the apron, "Sammy" stitched in red on the pocket, and put it on the counter, and drop the bow tie on top of it. The bow tie is theirs, if you've ever wondered. "You'll feel this for the rest of your life," Lengel says, and I know that's true, too, but remembering how he made that pretty girl blush makes me so scrunchy inside I punch the No Sale tab and the machine whirls "pee-pul" and the drawer splats out. One advantage to this scene taking place in summer, I can follow this up with a clean exit, there's no fumbling around getting your coat and galoshes, I just saunter into the electric eye in my white shirt that my mother ironed the night before, and the door heaves itself open, and outside the sunshine is skating around on the asphalt.

I look around for my girls, but they're gone, of course. There wasn't anybody but some young married screaming with her children about some candy they didn't get by the door of a powder-blue Falcon station wagon. Looking back in the big windows, over the bags of peat moss and aluminum lawn furniture stacked on the pavement, I could see Lengel in my place in the slot, checking the sheep through. His face was dark gray and his back stiff, as if he'd just had an injection of iron, and my stomach kind of fell as I felt how hard the world was going to be to me hereafter.

Martin Luther King, Jr. / I Have a Dream 1963

Martin Luther King, Jr., accomplished a great deal in a short time. The son of a Baptist minister, King was himself ordained at the age of eighteen. At twenty-six he became nationally prominent as a spiritual and civil-rights leader when he led a successful boycott in 1955 of the segregated bus system in Montgomery, Alabama. He became the first president of the Southern Christian Leadership Conference and was awarded the Nobel Peace Prize in 1964, largely for his policy of nonviolent resistance to racial injustice. Along the way, he studied at Morehouse College, Crozer Theological Seminary, Boston University, and Chicago Theological Seminary.

One of the most eloquent speakers and charismatic leaders of modern times, King was assassinated in Memphis, Tennessee, in 1968, shortly before his fortieth birthday. He has become an American folk hero.

His "I Have a Dream" speech epitomizes King's vision of the future. He delivered his sermon from the steps of the Lincoln Memorial to more than 200,000 people who had come to Washington, D.C., to show their support of civil rights as an issue and of King as a man.

Five score years ago, a great American, in whose symbolic shadow we stand, signed the Emancipation Proclamation. This momentous decree came as a great beacon light of hope to millions of Negro slaves who had been seared in the flames of withering injustice. It came as a joyous daybreak to end the long night of captivity.

But one hundred years later, we must face the tragic fact that the Negro is still not free. One hundred years later, the life of the Negro is still sadly crippled by the manacles of segregation and the chains of discrimination. One hundred years later, the Negro lives on a lonely island of poverty in the midst of a vast ocean of material prosperity. One hundred years later, the Negro is still languishing in the corners of American society and finds himself an exile in his own land. So we have come here today to dramatize an appalling condition.

In a sense we have come to our nation's Capitol to cash a check. When the architects of our republic wrote the magnificent words of the Constitution and the Declaration of Independence, they were signing a promissory note to which every American was to fall heir. This note was a promise that all men would be guaranteed the unalienable rights of life, liberty, and the pursuit of happiness.

It is obvious today that America has defaulted on this promissory note insofar as her citizens of color are concerned. Instead of honoring this sacred obligation, America has given the Negro people a bad check; a check which has come back marked "insufficient funds." But we refuse to believe that the bank of justice is bankrupt. We refuse to believe that there are insufficient funds in the great vaults of opportunity of this nation. So we have come to cash this check—a check that will give us upon demand the riches of freedom and the security of justice. We have also come to this hallowed spot to remind America of the fierce urgency of *now*. This is no time to engage in the luxury of cooling off or to take the tranquilizing drug of gradualism. *Now* is the time to make real the promises of Democracy. *Now* is the time to rise from the dark and desolate valley of segregation to the sunlit path of racial justice. *Now* is the time to open the doors of opportunity to all of God's children. *Now* is the time to lift our nation from the quicksands of racial injustice to the solid rock of brotherhood.

It would be fatal for the nation to overlook the urgency of the moment and to underestimate the determination of the Negro. This sweltering summer of the Negro's legitimate discontent will not pass until there is an invigorating autumn of freedom and equality. 1963 is not an end, but a beginning. Those who hope that the Negro needed to blow off steam and will now be content will have a rude awakening if the nation returns to business as usual. There will be neither rest nor tranquility in America until the Negro is granted his citizenship rights. The whirlwind of revolt will continue to shake the foundations of our nation until the bright day of justice emerges.

But there is something I must say to my people who stand on the warm threshold which leads into the palace of justice. In the process of gaining our rightful place we must not be guilty of wrongful deeds. Let us not seek to satisfy our thirst for freedom by drinking from the cup of bitterness and hatred. We must forever conduct our struggle on the high plane of dignity and discipline. We must not allow our creative protest to degenerate into physical violence. Again and again we must rise to the majestic heights of meeting physical force with soul force. The marvelous new militancy which has engulfed the Negro community must not lead us to a distrust of all white people, for many of our white brothers, as evidenced by their presence here today, have come to realize that their destiny is tied up with our destiny and their freedom is inextricably bound to our freedom. We cannot walk alone.

And as we walk, we must make the pledge that we shall march ahead. We cannot turn back. There are those who are asking the devotees of civil rights, "When will you be satisfied?" We can never be satisfied as long as the Negro is the victim of the unspeakable horrors of police brutality. We can never be satisfied as long as our bodies, heavy with the fatigue of travel, cannot gain lodging in the motels of the highways and the hotels of the cities. We cannot be satisfied as long as the Negro's basic mobility is from a smaller ghetto to a larger one. We can never be satisfied as long as a Negro in Mississippi cannot vote and a Negro in New York believes he has nothing for which to vote. No, no, we are not satisfied, and we will not be satisfied until justice rolls down like waters and righteousness like a mighty stream.

I am not unmindful that some of you have come here out of great trials and tribulations. Some of you have come fresh from narrow jail cells. Some of you have come from areas where your quest for freedom left you battered by the storms of persecution and staggered by the winds of police brutality. You have been the veterans of creative suffering. Continue to work with the faith that unearned suffering is redemptive.

Go back to Mississippi, go back to Alabama, go back to South Carolina, go back to Georgia, go back to Louisiana, go back to the slums and ghettoes of our northern cities, knowing that somehow this situation can and will be changed. Let us not wallow in the valley of despair.

I say to you today, my friends, that in spite of the difficulties and frustrations of the moment I still have a dream. It is a dream deeply rooted in the American dream.

I have a dream that one day this nation will rise up and live out the true meaning of its creed: "We hold these truths to be self-evident; that all men are created equal."

I have a dream that one day on the red hills of Georgia the sons of former slaves and the sons of former slave-owners will be able to sit down together at the table of brotherhood.

I have a dream that the state of Mississippi, a desert state sweltering with the heat of injustice and oppression, will be transformed into an oasis of freedom and justice.

I have a dream that my four little children will one day live in a nation where they will not be judged by the color of their skin but by the content of their character.

I have a dream today.

I have a dream that the state of Alabama, whose governor's lips are presently dripping with the words of interposition and nullification, will be transformed into a situation where little black boys and black girls will be able to join hands with little white boys and white girls and walk together as sisters and brothers.

I have a dream today.

I have a dream that one day every valley shall be exalted, every hill and mountain shall be made low, the rough place will be made plain, and the crooked places will be made straight, and the glory of the Lord shall be revealed, and all flesh shall see it together.

This is our hope. This is the faith with which I return to the South. With this faith we will be able to hew out of the mountain of despair a stone of hope. With this faith we will be able to transform the jangling discords of our nation into a beautiful symphony of brotherhood. With this faith we will be able to work together, to pray together, to struggle together, to go to jail together, to stand up for freedom together, knowing that we will be free one day.

This will be the day when all of God's children will be able to sing with new meaning:

> My country, 'tis of thee
> Sweet land of liberty
>   Of thee I sing:
> Land where my fathers died,
> Land of the pilgrims' pride,
> From every mountainside
>   Let freedom ring.

And if America is to be a great nation this must become true. So let freedom ring from the prodigious hilltops of New Hampshire! Let freedom ring from the heightening Alleghenies of Pennsylvania!

Let freedom ring from the snowcapped Rockies of Colorado!

Let freedom ring from the curvaceous peaks of California!

But not only that; let freedom ring from Stone Mountain of Georgia!

Let freedom ring from every hill and molehill of Mississippi. From every mountainside, let freedom ring.

When we let freedom ring, when we let it ring from every village and every hamlet, from every state and every city, we will be able to speed up that day when all of God's children, black men and white men, Jews and Gentiles, Protestants and Catholics, will be able to join hands and sing in the words of the old Negro spiritual, ''Free at last! free at last! thank God almighty, we are free at last!''

Sylvia Plath / America! America!   1963

Sylvia Plath (1932–63) was born in Boston, graduated from Smith College with honors, attended Newham College, Cambridge, on a fellowship, and lived in England during the last years of her life. While writing the stunning poetry that brought her posthumous acclaim, she longed to publish fiction in American magazines. ''Poetry,'' she once wrote, ''is an evasion from the real job of writing prose.''

Founded in 1841, the British magazine Punch *has poked fun at almost every-one during its long history. Americans seemed to be among its favorite targets. Plath sent the magazine her own very personal view of America, "America! America!" an essay later printed in a posthumous collection of her prose,* Johnny Panic and the Bible of Dreams *(1979).*

I went to public schools—genuinely public. *Everybody* went: the spry, the shy, the podge, the gangler, the future electronic scientist, the future cop who would one night kick a diabetic to death under the mistaken impression he was a drunk and needed cooling off; the poor, smelling of sour wools and the urinous baby at home and polyglot stew; the richer, with ratty fur collars, opal birthstone rings and daddies with cars ("Wot does *your* daddy do?" "He don't woik, he's a bus droiver." Laughter). There it was—Education—laid on free of charge for the lot of us, a lovely slab of depressed American public. *We* weren't depressed, of course. We left that to our parents, who eked out one child or two, and slumped dumbly after work and frugal suppers over their radios to listen to news of the "home country" and a black-moustached man named Hitler.

Above all, we did feel ourselves American in the rowdy seaside town where I picked up, like lint, my first ten years of schooling—a great, loud cats' bag of Irish Catholics, German Jews, Swedes, Negroes, Italians and that rare, pure May-flower dropping, somebody *English*.

On to this steerage of infant citizens the doctrines of Liberty and Equality were to be, through the free, communal schools, impressed. Although we could almost call ourselves Bostonian (the city airport with its beautiful hover of planes and silver blimps growled and gleamed across the bay), New York's skyscrapers were the icons on our "home room" walls, New York and the great green queen lifting a bedlamp that spelled out Freedom.

Every morning, hands on hearts, we pledged allegiance to the Stars and Stripes, a sort of aerial altarcloth over teacher's desk. And sang songs full of powder smoke and patriotics to impossible, wobbly, soprano tunes. One high, fine song, "For purple mountain majesties above the fruited plain," always made the scampi-size poet in me weep. In those days I couldn't have told a fruited plain from a mountain majesty and confused God with George Washington (whose lamblike granny-face shone down at us also from the schoolroom wall between neat blinders of white curls), yet warbled, nevertheless, with my small, snotty compatriots "America, America! God shed His grace on thee, and crown thy good with brotherhood from sea to shining sea."

The sea we knew something about. Terminus of almost every street, it buckled and swashed and tossed, out of its gray formlessness, china plates, wooden mon-keys, elegant shells and dead men's shoes. Wet salt winds raked our playgrounds endlessly—those Gothic composites of gravel, macadam, granite and bald, flailed earth wickedly designed to bark and scour the tender knee. There we traded play-ing cards (for the patterns on the backs) and sordid stories, jumped clothes rope, shot marbles, and enacted the radio and comic book dramas of our day ("Who knows what evil lurks in the hearts of men? The Shadow knows—nyah, nyah, nyah!" or "Up in the sky, look! It's a bird, it's a plane, it's Superman!"). If we were destined for any special end—grooved, doomed, limited, fated, we didn't feel it. We beamed and sloshed from our desks to the dodge-ball dell, open and hopeful as the sea itself.

After all, we could be anybody. If we worked. If we studied hard enough. Our accents, our money, our parents didn't matter. Did not lawyers rise from the loins of coalheavers, doctors from the bins of dustmen? Education was the answer, and heaven knows how it came to us. Invisibly, I think, in the early days—a mystical infra-red glow off the thumbed multiplication tables, ghastly poems extolling October's bright blue weather, and a world of history that more or less began and ended with the Boston Tea Party—Pilgrims and Indians being, like the eohippus, prehistoric.

Later, the college obsession would seize us, a subtle, terrifying virus. Everybody had to go to *some* college or other. A business college, a junior college, a state college, a secretarial college, an Ivy League college, a pig farmers' college. The book first, then the work. By the time we (future cop and electronic brain alike) exploded into our prosperous, postwar high school, full-time guidance counselors jogged our elbows at ever-diminishing intervals to discuss motives, hopes, school subjects, jobs—and colleges. Excellent teachers showered onto us like meteors: Biology teachers holding up human brains, English teachers inspiring us with a personal ideological fierceness about Tolstoy and Plato, Art teachers leading us through the slums of Boston, then back to the easel to hurl public school gouache with social awareness and fury. Eccentricities, the perils of being *too* special, were reasoned and cooed from us like sucked thumbs.

The girls' guidance counselor diagnosed my problem straight off. I was just too dangerously brainy. My high, pure string of straight A's might, without proper extracurricular tempering, snap me into the void. More and more, the colleges wanted All-Round Students. I had, by that time, studied Machiavelli in Current Events class. I grabbed my cue.

Now this guidance counselor owned, unknown to me, a white-haired identical twin I kept meeting in supermarkets and at the dentist's. To this twin, I confided my widening circle of activities—chewing orange sections at the quarters of girls' basketball games (I had made the team), painting mammoth L'il Abners and Daisy Maes for class dances, pasting up dummies of the school newspaper at midnight while my already dissipated co-editor read out the jokes at the bottom of the columns of *The New Yorker*. The blank, oddly muffled expression of my guidance counselor's twin in the street did not deter me, nor did the apparent amnesia of her whitely efficient double in the school office. I became a rabid teenage pragmatist.

"Usage is Truth, Truth, Usage," I might have muttered, leveling my bobbysocks to match those of my schoolmates. There was no uniform, but there *was* a uniform—the pageboy hairdo, squeaky clean, the skirt and sweater, the "loafers," those scuffed copies of Indian moccasins. We even, in our democratic edifice, nursed two ancient relics of snobbism—two sororities: Subdeb and Sugar 'n' Spice. At the start of each school year, invitation cards went out from old members to new girls—the pretty, the popular, the in some way rivalrous. A week of initiation preceded our smug admittance to the cherished Norm. Teachers preached against Initiation Week, boys scoffed, but couldn't stop it.

I was assigned, like each initiate, a Big Sister who systematically began to destroy my ego. For a whole week I could wear no make-up, could not wash, could not comb my hair, change clothes or speak to boys. By dawn I had walked to my Big Sister's house and was making her bed and breakfast. Then, lugging her intolerably heavy books, as well as my own, I followed her, at a dog's distance, to school. On the way she might order me to climb a tree and hang from a branch till I dropped, ask a passer-by a rude question or stalk about the shops begging for rotten grapes and moldy rice. If I smiled—showed, that is, any sense of irony at my slavishness, I had to kneel on the public pavement and wipe the smile off my face. The minute the bell rang to end school, Big Sister took over. By nightfall I ached and stank; my homework buzzed in a dulled and muzzy brain. I was being tailored to an Okay Image.

Somehow it didn't take—this initiation into the nihil of belonging. Maybe I was just too weird to begin with. What did these picked buds of American womanhood do at their sorority meetings? They ate cake; ate cake and catted about the Saturday night date. The privilege of being anybody was turning its other face—to the pressure of being everybody; ergo, no one.

Lately I peered through the plate-glass side of an American primary school: child-size desks and chairs in clean, light wood, toy stoves and minuscule drinking fountains. Sunlight everywhere. All the anarchism, discomfort and grit I so tenderly remembered had been, in a quarter century, gentled away. One class had spent the morning on a bus learning how to pay fares and ask for the proper stop. Reading (my lot did it by age four off soapbox tops) had become such a traumatic and stormy art one felt lucky to weather it by ten. But the children were smiling in their little ring. Did I glimpse, in the First Aid cabinet, a sparkle of bottles— soothers and smootheners for the embryo rebel, the artist, the odd?

David Wagoner / The Shooting of John Dillinger outside the Biograph Theater, July 22, 1934   1966

At various times a railroad section hand, a concentrated soup scooper at a steel mill, a park policeman, and a short-order cook, David Wagoner has been a professor of English at the University of Washington at Seattle since 1954. His first volume of poems, Dry Sun, Dry Wind, *appeared in 1953, when he was twenty-seven years old. Since then, he has published numerous books of poetry, served as editor of* Poetry Northwest, *and written film scripts and several novels, the most noted of which is* The Escape Artist *(1965).*

The poem printed below is from his collection Staying Alive *(1966).*

Chicago ran a fever of a hundred and one that groggy Sunday.
A reporter fried an egg on a sidewalk; the air looked shaky.
And a hundred thousand people were in the lake like shirts in a laundry.
Why was Johnny lonely?
Not because two dozen solid citizens, heat-struck, had keeled over backward.   5
Not because those lawful souls had fallen out of their sockets and melted.
But because the sun went down like a lump in a furnace or a bull in the Stock-
        yards.
Where was Johnny headed?
Under the Biograph Theater sign that said, "Our Air is Refrigerated."   10
Past seventeen FBI men and four policemen who stood in doorways and sweated.
Johnny sat down in a cold seat to watch Clark Gable get electrocuted.
Had Johnny been mistreated?
Yes, but Gable told the D. A. he'd rather fry than be shut up forever.
Two women sat by Johnny. One looked sweet, one looked like J. Edgar Hoover. 15
Polly Hamilton made him feel hot, but Anna Sage made him shiver.
Was Johnny a good lover?
Yes, but he passed out his share of squeezes and pokes like a jittery masher
While Agent Purvis sneaked up and down the aisle like an extra usher,
Trying to make sure they wouldn't slip out till the show was over.   20
Was Johnny a fourflusher?
No, not if he knew the game. He got it up or got it back.
But he liked to take snapshots of policemen with his own Kodak,
And once in a while he liked to take them with an automatic.

Why was Johnny frantic?   25
Because he couldn't take a walk or sit down in a movie
Without being afraid he'd run smack into somebody
Who'd point at his rearranged face and holler, "Johnny!"
Was Johnny ugly?
Yes, because Dr. Wilhelm Loeser had given him a new profile   30
With a baggy jawline and squint eyes and an erased dimple,
With kangaroo-tendon cheekbones and a gigolo's mustache that should've been
    illegal.
Did Johnny love a girl?
Yes, a good-looking, hard-headed Indian named Billie Frechette.   35
He wanted to marry her and lie down and try to get over it,
But she was locked in jail for giving him first-aid and comfort.
Did Johnny feel hurt?
He felt like breaking a bank or jumping over a railing
Into some panicky teller's cage to shout, "Reach for the ceiling!"   40
Or like kicking some vice president in the bum checks and smiling.
What was he really doing?
Going up the aisle with the crowd and into the lobby
With Polly saying, "Would *you* do what Clark done?" And Johnny saying,
    "Maybe."   45
And Anna saying, "If he'd been smart, he'd of acted like Bing Crosby."
Did Johnny look flashy?
Yes, his white-on-white shirt and tie were luminous.
His trousers were creased like knives to the tops of his shoes,
And his yellow straw hat came down to his dark glasses.   50
Was Johnny suspicious?
Yes, and when Agent Purvis signalled with a trembling cigar,
Johnny ducked left and ran out of the theater,
And innocent Polly and squealing Anna were left nowhere.
Was Johnny a fast runner?   55
No, but he crouched and scurried past a friendly liquor store
Under the coupled arms of double-daters, under awnings, under stars,
To the curb at the mouth of an alley. He hunched there.
Was Johnny a thinker?
No, but he was thinking more or less of Billie Frechette   60
Who was lost in prison for longer than he could possibly wait,
And then it was suddenly too hard to think around a bullet.
Did anyone shoot straight?
Yes, but Mrs. Etta Natalsky fell out from under her picture hat.
Theresa Paulus sprawled on the sidewalk, clutching her left foot.   65
And both of them groaned loud and long under the streetlight.
Did Johnny like that?
No, but he lay down with those strange women, his face in the alley,
One shoe off, cinders in his mouth, his eyelids heavy.
When they shouted questions at him, he talked back to nobody.   70
Did Johnny lie easy?
Yes, holding his gun and holding his breath as a last trick,
He waited, but when the Agents came close, his breath wouldn't work.
Clark Gable walked his last mile; Johnny ran half a block.
Did he run out of luck?   75
Yes, before he was cool, they had him spread out on dished-in marble
In the Cook County Morgue, surrounded by babbling people
With a crime reporter presiding over the head of the table.

Did Johnny have a soul?
Yes, and it was climbing his slippery wind-pipe like a trapped burglar.   80
It was beating the inside of his ribcage, hollering, "Let me out of here!"
Maybe it got out, and maybe it just stayed there.
Was Johnny a money-maker?
Yes, and thousands paid 25¢ to see him, mostly women,
And one said, "I wouldn't have come, except he's a moral lesson,"   85
And another, "I'm disappointed. He feels like a dead man."
Did Johnny have a brain?
Yes, and it always worked best through the worst of dangers,
Through flat-footed hammerlocks, through guarded doors, around corners,
But it got taken out in the morgue and sold to some doctors.   90
Could Johnny take orders?
No, but he stayed in the wicker basket carried by six men
Through the bulging crowd to the hearse and let himself be locked in,
And he stayed put as it went driving south in a driving rain.
And he didn't get stolen?   95
No, not even after his old hard-nosed dad refused to sell
The quick-drawing corpse for $10,000 to somebody in a carnival.
He figured he'd let *Johnny* decide how to get to Hell.
Did anyone wish him well?
Yes, half of Indiana camped in the family pasture,   100
And the minister said, "With luck, he could have been a minister."
And up the sleeve of his oversized gray suit, Johnny twitched a finger.
Does anyone remember?
Everyone still alive. And some dead ones. It was a new kind of holiday
With hot and cold drinks and hot and cold tears. They planted him in a
        cemetery   105
With three unknown vice presidents, Benjamin Harrison, and James
        Whitcomb Riley,
Who never held up anybody.

Maya Angelou / *I Know Why the Caged Bird Sings*   1969

Maya Angelou was born Marguerite Johnson in St. Louis in 1928. After her
turbulent youth ("from a broken family, raped at eight, unwed mother at six-
teen"), she went on to study dance with the Pearl Primus company in New
York, star in an off-Broadway show (The Blacks), *write three books of poetry,*
produce a series on Africa for PBS, serve as coordinator for the Southern
Christian Leadership Conference at the request of Martin Luther King, Jr., and
accept three honorary doctorates.

As an author, actress, singer, dancer, songwriter, teacher, editor, and film
director, Angelou has been a pioneer in furthering the role of the American
black woman in the arts.

She is best known for her autobiography, I Know Why the Caged Bird Sings
(1969), from which the following reminiscence is taken. For another memory of
Joe Louis, see Howie Evans's "Joe Louis: American Folk Hero" (in "Press").

CHAMPION OF THE WORLD

The last inch of space was filled, yet people continued to wedge themselves along
the walls of the Store. Uncle Willie had turned the radio up to its last notch so

that youngsters on the porch wouldn't miss a word. Women sat on kitchen chairs, dining-room chairs, stools and upturned wooden boxes. Small children and babies perched on every lap available and men leaned on the shelves or on each other.

The apprehensive mood was shot through with shafts of gaiety, as a black sky is streaked with lightning.

"I ain't worried 'bout this fight. Joe's gonna whip that cracker like it's open season."

"He gone whip him till that white boy call him Momma."

At last the talking was finished and the string-along songs about razor blades were over and the fight began.

"A quick jab to the head." In the Store the crowd grunted. "A left to the head and a right and another left." One of the listeners cackled like a hen and was quieted.

"They're in a clinch, Louis is trying to fight his way out."

Some bitter comedian on the porch said, "That white man don't mind hugging that niggah now, I betcha."

"The referee is moving in to break them up, but Louis finally pushed the contender away and it's an uppercut to the chin. The contender is hanging on, now he's backing away. Louis catches him with a short left to the jaw."

A tide of murmuring assent poured out the doors and into the yard.

"Another left and another left. Louis is saving that mighty right . . ." The mutter in the Store had grown into a baby roar and it was pierced by the clang of a bell and the announcer's ·"That's the bell for round three, ladies and gentlemen."

As I pushed my way into the Store I wondered if the announcer gave any thought to the fact that he was addressing as "ladies and gentlemen" all the Negroes around the world who sat sweating and praying, glued to their "master's voice."[1]

There were only a few calls for R.C. Colas, Dr. Peppers, and Hires root beer. The real festivities would begin after the fight. Then even the old Christian ladies who taught their children and tried themselves to practice turning the other cheek would buy soft drinks, and if the Brown Bomber's victory was a particularly bloody one they would order peanut patties and Baby Ruths also.

Bailey and I laid the coins on top of the cash register. Uncle Willie didn't allow us to ring up sales during a fight. It was too noisy and might shake up the atmosphere. When the gong rang for the next round we pushed through the near-sacred quiet to the herd of children outside.

"He's got Louis against the ropes and now it's a left to the body and a right to the ribs. Another right to the body, it looks like it was low. . . . Yes, ladies and gentlemen, the referee is signaling but the contender keeps raining the blows on Louis. It's another to the body, and it looks like Louis is going down."

My race groaned. It was our people falling. It was another lynching, yet another Black man hanging on a tree. One more woman ambushed and raped. A Black boy whipped and maimed. It was hounds on the trail of a man running through slimy swamps. It was a white woman slapping her maid for being forgetful.

The men in the Store stood away from the walls and at attention. Women greedily clutched the babes on their laps while on the porch the shufflings and smiles, flirtings and pinching of a few minutes before were gone. This might be the end of the world. If Joe lost we were back in slavery and beyond help. It would all be true, the accusations that we were lower types of human beings. Only a little higher than apes. True that we were stupid and ugly and lazy and dirty and, unlucky and worst of all, that God Himself hated us and ordained us to be hewers of wood and drawers of water, forever and ever, world without end.

We didn't breathe. We didn't hope. We waited.

---

1. A famous advertising slogan for RCA phonographs.

"He's off the ropes, ladies and gentlemen. He's moving towards the center of the ring." There was no time to be relieved. The worst might still happen.

"And now it looks like Joe is mad. He's caught Carnera with a left hook to the head and a right to the head. It's a left jab to the body and another left to the head. There's a left cross and a right to the head. The contender's right eye is bleeding and he can't seem to keep his block up. Louis is penetrating every block. The referee is moving in, but Louis sends a left to the body and it's an uppercut to the chin and the contender is dropping. He's on the canvas, ladies and gentlemen."

Babies slid to the floor as women stood up and men leaned toward the radio.

"Here's the referee. He's counting. One, two, three, four, five, six, seven . . . Is the contender trying to get up again?"

All the men in the store shouted, "NO."

"—eight, nine, ten." There were a few sounds from the audience, but they seemed to be holding themselves in against tremendous pressure.

"The fight is all over, ladies and gentlemen. Let's get the microphone over to the referee . . . Here he is. He's got the Brown Bomber's hand, he's holding it up . . . Here he is . . ."

Then the voice, husky and familiar, came to wash over us—"The winnah, and still heavyweight champeen of the world . . . Joe Louis."

Champion of the world. A Black boy. Some Black mother's son. He was the strongest man in the world. People drank Coca-Colas like ambrosia and ate candy bars like Christmas. Some of the men went behind the Store and poured white lightning in their soft-drink bottles, and a few of the bigger boys followed them. Those who were not chased away came back blowing their breath in front of themselves like proud smokers.

It would take an hour or more before the people would leave the Store and head for home. Those who lived too far had made arrangements to stay in town. It wouldn't do for a Black man and his family to be caught on a lonely country road on a night when Joe Louis had proved that we were the strongest people in the world.

Norman Mailer / *Of a Fire on the Moon*
[The First Moon Walk]   1970

Born in New Jersey in 1923 and brought up in Brooklyn, Norman Mailer began writing while still an undergraduate at Harvard. In his fiction, essays, and highly personal journalism, Mailer has covered many significant phases of American life since the end of World War II. Part of his account of the Apollo XI *voyage first appeared in* Life *magazine and was later expanded into a book-length study of the astronauts,* Of a Fire on the Moon, *from which the following passage is excerpted. Always attracted to the action at the center of the arena, as his reporting of political conventions* (Miami and the Siege of Chicago) *and the peace movement of the sixties* (Armies of the Night) *testifies, Mailer finds himself during his coverage of the moon walk an unwilling nonparticipant on an assignment without a location.*

They had landed, there was jubilation in Mission Control, and a moment of fraternization between Armstrong and Aldrin, but in fact they were actually at work in the next instant. No one knew what would await them—there were even theories that most of the surface of the moon was as fragile as icing on a cake. If they landed, and the moon ground began to collapse, they were ready to blast off with the ascent stage even as the descent stage was sinking beneath. But no sound of crumbling came up through the pipes of the legs, no shudder of collapse. A minute passed. They received the order to Stay. The second Stay–No Stay would be on them nine minutes later, and they rushed through a checklist, testing specific instruments to make certain they were intact from the landing. The thirty-odd seconds of fuel they still had left when they touched down was vented from the descent stage, a hissing and steaming beneath the legs like a steed loosing water on icy ground. Verbs and Nouns were punched into the DSKY. Now came the second Stay. There would not be another Stay–No Stay until the Command Module had made a complete revolution of the moon and would be coming back toward them in good position for rendezvous. So, unless some mishap were suddenly to appear, they had at least another two hours on the satellite. It was time to unscrew their gloves at the wrist and take them off, time to unscrew their helmets at the neck, lift them off.

They gave their first description of the landing, and made a few general remarks about the view through the window, the variety of rocks. But there was too much work to look for long. After a few comments on the agreeableness of lunar gravity, after a conversation with Columbia and mutual congratulations, they were back at the computer. Now, in the time before the next Stay–No Stay, they had to simulate a countdown for a planned ascent and realign the Inertial Measurement Unit, that is, determine the vertical line of moon gravity, and install its index into the Inertial Measurement Unit, then level the table and gyroscope from which all navigation was computed. Star checks were taken. Meanwhile, Armstrong was readying the cameras and snapping photographs through the window. Now Aldrin aligned the Abort Guidance Section. Armstrong laid in the data for Program 12, the Powered Ascent Guidance. The Command Module came around again. The simulated countdown was over. They had another Stay. They powered down their systems.

In the transcript the work continues minute after minute, familiar talk of stars and Nouns, acronyms, E-memory dumps, and returns to POO where Pings may idle. They are at rest on the moon, but the dialogue is not unencumbered of pads, updata link switches and noise suppression devices on the Manned Space Flight Network relay.

Then in what is virtually their first pause in better than an hour on the moon, they request permission to do their EVA early, begin in fact in the next few hours rather than take a halt to sleep. For days there had been discussion in every newspaper of the world whether the astronauts could land on the moon and a few hours later go to sleep before they even stepped out of the Lem; now the question has been answered—they are impatient to go.

CAPCOM: *We will support it.*
ALDRIN: *Roger.*
CAPCOM: *You guys are getting prime time TV there.*
ARMSTRONG: *Hope that little TV set works, but we'll see.*

Now the astronauts stopped to eat and to relax. Over the radio came the dialogue of Mission Control talking to Collins in orbit overhead. Around them, through each pinched small window, were tantalizing views of the moon. They could feel themselves in one-sixth gravity. How light were their bodies. Yet they were not weightless. There was gravity beneath them, a faint sensuous tug at their limbs. If they dropped a pencil, it did not float before drifting slowly away. Rather, it dropped. Slowly it dropped, dropped indeed at the same leisurely speed with which Apollo-Saturn had risen off its launching pad four and a half days ago. What a balm for the muscles of the eye! One-sixth of earth gravity was agreeable, it was attractive, it was, said Aldrin, "less *lonesome*" than weightlessness. He had, at last, " a distinct feeling of being somewhere." Yes, the moon was beneath them, hardly more than the height of a ten-foot diving board beneath them—they were in the domain of a presence again. How much like magnetism must lunar gravity have felt.

ALDRIN: *This is the Lem pilot. I'd like to take this opportunity to ask every person listening in, whoever and wherever they may be, to pause for a moment and contemplate the events of the past few hours, and to give thanks in his or her way.*

In the silence, Aldrin took out the bread, the wine, and the chalice he had brought in his Personal Preference Kit, and he put them on the little table in front of the Abort Guidance Section computer. Then he read some passages from the Bible and celebrated Communion.

A strange picture of religious intensity: there is of course no clue in Aldrin's immediate words—they are by now tuned to precisely what one would expect.

"I would like to have observed just how the wine poured in that environment, but, it wasn't pertinent at that particular time. It wasn't important how it got in the cup. It was important only to get it there"—and not spill, we may assume, this most special blood of the Lord. "I offered some private prayers, but I find now that thoughts, feelings, come into my memory instead of words. I was not so selfish as to include my family in those prayers at the moment, nor so spacious as to include the fate of the world. I was thinking more about our particular task, and the challenge and the opportunity that had been given us. I asked people to offer thanks in their own way, and it is my hope that people will keep this whole event in their minds and see beyond minor details and technical achievements to a deeper meaning behind it all, challenge, a quest, the human need to do these things and the need to recognize that we are all one mankind under God."

Yes, his recollections are near to comic in their banality, but one gets a picture of this strong-nosed strong-armed gymnast in his space suit, deep in prayer in the crowded closet space of the Lem, while Armstrong the mystic (with the statue of Buddha on his living room table) is next to him in who knows what partial or unwilling communion, Armstrong so private in his mind that when a stranger tried to talk to him one day on a bus, he picked up a book to read. There, before his partner, Aldrin prayed, light lunar gravity new in his limbs, eyes closed. Can we assume the brain of his inner vision expanded to the dimensions of a church, the loft of a cathedral, Aldrin, man of passions and disciplines, fatalist, all but open believer in predestination, agent of God's will, Aldrin, prodigy of effort on Gemini 12, whose pulse after hours of work in space had shot up only when he read a Veteran's Day message to the ground. Patriotism had the power of a stroke for Aldrin and invocation was his harmony. Tribal chief, first noble savage on the moon, he prayed to the powers who had brought him there, whose will he would fulfill—God, the earth, the moon and himself all for this instant part of the lofty engine of the universe, and in that eccentric giant of character, that conservative of all the roots in all the family trees, who now was ripping up the roots of the ages, that man whose mother's name was Moon, was there a single question whose lament might suggest that if the mission were ill-conceived or even a work of art designed by the Devil, then all the prayers of all good men were nothing but a burden upon the Lord, who in order to reply would be forced to work in the mills of Satan, or leave the prayers of his flock in space. Not likely. Aldrin did not seem a man for thoughts like that, but then his mind was a mystery wrapped in the winding-sheet of a computer with billions of bits.

Later, Armstrong would say, "That first hour on the moon was hardly the time for long thoughts; we had specific jobs to do. Of course the sights were simply magnificent, beyond any visual experience that I had ever been exposed to,'' and Aldrin would describe it as ''a unique, almost mystical environment.'' In fact, there is an edge of the unexplained to their reactions. Their characteristic matter-of-fact response is overcome occasonally by swoops of hyperbole. And to everyone's slight surprise, they were almost two hours late for their EVA. Their estimate of time was off by close to fifty percent. For astronauts that was an error comparable to a carpenter mistaking an eight-foot stud for a twelve-foot piece. If a carpenter can look at a piece of wood and guess its length to the nearest quarter-inch, it is because he has been working with lengths all his life. Equally, people in some occupations have a close ability to estimate time.

With astronauts, whose every day in a simulator was a day laid out on the measure of a time-line, the estimate of time elapsed had to become acute. Armstrong and Aldrin had consistently fulfilled their tasks in less time than was allotted. Now, curiously, they fell behind, then further behind. There were unexpected problems of course—it took longer to bleed the pressure out of the Lunar Module than had been anticipated, and the cooling units in the backpacks were sluggish at first in operation, but whether from natural excitement and natural anxiety, or an unconscious preoccupation with lunar phenomena so subtle that it is just at the edge of their senses, any extract from the transcript at this point where they are helping to adjust the Portable Life Support System on each others' backs shows real lack of enunciation. Nowhere else do the NASA stenographers have as much difficulty with where one voice ends and another begins.

TRANQUILITY: *Got it (garbled) prime rows in.*
TRANQUILITY: *Okay.*
TRANQUILITY: *(garbled)*
TRANQUILITY: *Let me do that for you.*
TRANQUILITY: *(Inaudible)*
TRANQUILITY: *Mark I*
TRANQUILITY: *(garbled) valves*
TRANQUILITY: *(garbled)*
TRANQUILITY: *Okay*
TRANQUILITY: *All of the (garbled)*
TRANQUILITY: *(garbled) locked and double-locked.*
TRANQUILITY: *Did you put it—*
TRANQUILITY: *Oh, wait a minute*
TRANQUILITY: *Should be (garbled)*
TRANQUILITY: (garbled)
TRANQUILITY: *Roger. (garbled)*
TRANQUILITY: *I'll try it on the middle*
TRANQUILITY: *All right, check my (garbled) valves vertical*
TRANQUILITY: *Both vertical*
TRANQUILITY: *That's two vertical*
TRANQUILITY: *Okay*
TRANQUILITY: *(garbled)*
TRANQUILITY: *Locked and double-locked*
TRANQUILITY: *Okay*
TRANQUILITY: *Miss marked*
TRANQUILITY: *Sure wish I would have shaved last night.*
PAO: *That was a Buzz Aldrin comment.*

The hint is faint enough, but the hint exists—something was conceivably interfering with their sense of order. Could it have been the lunar gravity? Clock-time was a measure which derived from pendulums and spiral springs, clock-time was anchored right into the tooth of earth gravity—so a time might yet be coming when psychologists, not geologists, would be conducting experiments on the moon. Did lunar gravity have power like a drug to shift the sense of time?

Armstrong was connected at last to his PLSS. He was drawing oxygen from the pack he carried on his back. But the hatch door would not open. The pressure would not go low enough in the Lem. Down near a level of one pound per square inch, the last bit of man-created atmosphere in Eagle seemed to cling to its constituency, reluctant to enter the vacuums of the moon. But they did not know if they could get the hatch door open with a vacuum on one side and even a small pressure on the other. It was taking longer than they thought. While it was not a large concern since there would be other means to open it—redundancies pervaded throughout—nonetheless, a concern must have intruded: how intolerably comic they would appear if they came all the way and then were blocked before a door they could not crack. That thought had to put one drop of perspiration on the back of the neck. Besides, it must have been embarrassing to begin so late. The world of television was watching, and the astronauts had exhibited as much sensitivity to an audience as any bride on her way down the aisle.

It was not until nine-forty at night, Houston time, that they got the hatch open at last. In the heat of running almost two hours late, ensconced in the armor of a man-sized spaceship, could they still have felt an instant of awe as they looked out that open hatch at a panorama of theater: the sky is black, but the ground is brightly lit, bright as footlights on the floor of a dark theater. A black and midnight sky, yet on the moon ground, "you could almost go out in your shirt-sleeves and get a suntan," Aldrin would say. "I remember thinking, 'Gee, if I didn't know where I was, I could believe that somebody had created this environment somewhere out in the West and given us another simulation to work in.' " Everywhere on that pitted flat were shadows dark as the sky above, shadows dark as mine shafts.

What a struggle to push out from that congested cabin, now twice congested in their bulky-wham suits, no feeling of obstacle against their flesh, their sense of touch dead and numb, spaceman body manipulated out into the moon world like an upright piano turned by movers on the corner of the stairs.

"You're lined up on the platform. Put your left foot to the right a little bit. Okay, that's good. Roll left."

Armstrong was finally on the porch. Could it be with any sense of an alien atmosphere receiving the fifteen-layer encapsulations of the pack and suit on his back? Slowly, he climbed down the ladder. Archetypal, he must have felt, a boy descending the rungs in the wall of an abandoned well, or was it Jack down the stalk? And there he was on the bottom, on the footpad of the leg of the Lem, a metal plate perhaps three feet across. Inches away was the soil of the moon. But first he jumped up again to the lowest rung of the ladder. A couple of hours later, at the end of the EVA, conceivably exhausted, the jump from the ground to the rung, three feet up, might be difficult in that stiff and heavy space suit, so he tested it now. "It takes," said Armstrong, "a pretty good little jump."

Now, with television working, and some fraction of the world peering at the murky image of this instant, poised between the end of one history and the beginning of another, he said quietly, "I'm at the foot of the ladder. The Lem footpads are only depressed in the surface about one or two inches, although the surface appears to be very very fine-grained as you get close to it. It's almost like a powder." One of Armstrong's rare confessions of uneasiness is focused later on this moment. "I don't recall any particular emotion or feeling other than a little caution, a desire to be sure it was safe to put my weight on that surface outside Eagle's footpad."

Did his foot tingle in the heavy lunar overshoe? "I'm going to step off the Lem now."

Did something in him shudder at the touch of the new ground? Or did he draw a sweet strength from the balls of his feet? Nobody was necessarily going ever to know.

"That's one small step for a man," said Armstrong, "one giant leap for mankind." He had joined the ranks of the forever quoted. Patrick Henry, Henry Stanley and Admiral Dewey moved over for him.

Now he was out there, one foot on the moon, then the other foot on the moon, the powder like velvet underfoot. With one hand still on the ladder, he comments, "The surface is fine and powdery. I can . . . I can pick it up loosely with my toe." And as he releases his catch, the grains fall back slowly to the soil, a fan of feathers gliding to the floor. "It does adhere in fine layers like powdered charcoal to the sole and sides of my boots. I only go in a small fraction of an inch. Maybe an eighth of an inch. But I can see the footprints of my boots and the treads in the fine sand particles."

Capcom: "Neil, this is Houston. We're copying."

Yes, they would copy. He was like a man who goes into a wrecked building to defuse a new kind of bomb. He talks into a microphone as he works, for if a mistake is made, and the bomb goes off, it will be easier for the next man if every detail of his activities has been mentioned as he performed them. Now, he released his grip on the ladder and pushed off for a few steps on the moon, odd loping steps, almost thrust into motion like a horse trotting up a steep slope. It could have been a moment equivalent to the first steps he took as an infant for there was nothing to hold onto and he did not dare to fall—the ground was too hot, the rocks might tear his suit. Yet if he stumbled, he could easily go over for he could not raise his arms above his head nor reach to his knees, his arms in the pressure bladder stood out before him like sausages; so, if he tottered, the weight of the pack could twist him around, or drop him. They had tried to shape up simulations of lunar gravity while weighted in scuba suits at the bottom of a pool, but water was not a vacuum through which to move; so they had also flown in planes carrying two hundred pounds of equipment on their backs. The pilot would take the plane through a parabolic trajectory. There would be a period of twenty-two seconds at the top of the curve when a simulation of one-sixth gravity would be present, and the two hundred pounds of equipment would weigh no more than on the moon, no more than thirty-plus pounds, and one could take loping steps down the aisle of the plane, staggering through unforeseen wobbles or turbulence. Then the parabolic trajectory was done, the plane was diving, and it would have to pull out of the dive. That created the reverse of one-sixth gravity—it multiplied gravity by two and a half times. The two hundred pounds of equipment now weighed five hundred pounds and the astronauts had to be supported by other men straining to help them bear the weight. So simulations gave them time for hardly more than a clue before heavy punishment was upon them. But now he was out in the open endless lunar gravity, his body and the reflexes of his life obliged to adopt a new rhythm and schedule of effort, a new disclosure of grace.

Still, he seemed pleased after the first few steps. "There seems to be no difficulty in moving around as we suspected. It's even perhaps easier than the simulations . . ." He would run a few steps and stop, run a few steps and stop. Perhaps it was not unlike directing the Lem when it hovered over the ground. One moved faster than on earth and with less effort, but it was harder to stop—one had to pick the place to halt from several yards ahead. Yes, it was easier once moving, but awkward at the beginning and the end because of the obdurate plastic bendings of the suit. And once standing at rest, the sense of the vertical was sly. One could be leaning further forward than one knew. Or leaning backward. Like a needle on a dial one would have to oscillate from side to side of the vertical to find position. Conceivably the sensation was not unlike skiing with a child on one's back.

It was time for Aldrin to descend the ladder from the Lem to the ground, and Armstrong's turn to give directions: "The shoes are about to come over the sill. Okay, now drop your PLSS down. There you go. You're clear. . . . About an inch clearance on top of your PLSS."

Aldrin spoke for future astronauts: "Okay, you need a little bit of arching of the back to come down . . ."

When he reached the ground, Aldrin took a big and exuberant leap up the ladder again, as if to taste the pleasures of one-sixth gravity all at once. "Beautiful, beautiful," he exclaimed.

Armstrong: "Isn't that something. Magnificent sight out here."

Aldrin: "Magnificent desolation."

They were looking at a terrain which lived in a clarity of focus unlike anything they had ever seen on earth. There was no air, of course, and so no wind, nor clouds, nor dust, nor even the finest scattering of light from the smallest dispersal of microscopic particles on a clear day on earth, no, nothing visible or invisible moved in the vacuum before them. All light was pure. No haze was present, not even the invisible haze of the finest day—therefore objects did not go out of focus as they receded into the distance. If one's eyes were good enough, an object at a hundred yards was as distinct as a rock at a few feet. And their eyes were good enough. Just as one could not determine one's altitude above the moon, not from fifty miles up nor five, so now along the ground before them no distance was real, for all distances had the faculty to appear equally near if one peered at them through blinders and could not see the intervening details. Again the sense of being on a stage or on the lighted floor of a room so large one could not see where the dark ceiling began must have come upon them, for there were no hints of gathering evanescence in ridge beyond ridge; rather each outline was as severe as the one in front of it, and since the ground was filled with small craters of every size, from antholes to potholes to empty pools, and the horizon was near, four times nearer than on earth and sharp as the line drawn by a pencil, the moon ground seemed to slope and drop in all directions "like swimming in an ocean with six-foot or eight-foot swells and waves," Armstrong said later. "In that condition, you never can see very far away from where you are." But what they could see, they could see entirely—to the depth of their field of view at any instant their focus was complete. And as they swayed from side to side, so a sense of the vertical kept eluding them, the slopes of the craters about them seeming to tilt a few degrees to one side of the horizontal, then the other. On earth, one had only to incline one's body an inch or two and a sense of the vertical was gone, but on the moon they could lean over, then further over, lean considerably further over without beginning to fall. So verticals slid and oscillated. Rolling from side to side, they could as well have been on water, indeed their sense of the vertical was probably equal to the subtle uncertainty of the body when a ship is rolling on a quiet sea. "I say," said Aldrin, "the rocks are rather slippery."

They were discovering the powder of the moon soil was curious indeed, comparable in firmness and traction to some matter between sand and snow. While the Lem looked light as a kite, for its pads hardly rested on the ground and it appeared ready to lift off and blow away, yet their own feet sometimes sank for two or three inches into the soft powder on the slope of very small craters, and their soles would slip as the powder gave way under their boots. In other places the ground was firm and harder than sand, yet all of these variations were to be found in an area not a hundred feet out from the legs of the Lem. As he explored his footing, Aldrin sent back comments to Mission Control, reporting in the rapt professional tones of a coach instructing his team on the conditions of the turf in a new plastic football field.

Meanwhile Armstrong was transporting the television camera away from the Lem to a position where it could cover most of their activities. Once properly installed, he revolved it through a full panorama of their view in order that audiences on earth might have a clue to what he saw. But in fact the transmission was too rudimentary to give any sense of what was about them, that desert sea of rocks, rubble, small boulders, and crater lips.

Aldrin was now working to set up the solar wind experiment, a sheet of aluminum foil hung on a stand. For the next hour and a half, the foil would be exposed to the solar wind, and invisible, unfelt, but high-velocity flow of noble gases from the sun like argon, krypton, neon and helium. For the astronauts, it was the simplest of procedures, no more difficult than setting up a piece of sheet music on a music stand. At the end of the EVA, however, the aluminum foil would be rolled up, inserted in the rock box, and delivered eventually to a laboratory in Switzerland uniquely equipped for the purpose. There any nobles gases which had been trapped in the atomic lattice of the aluminum would be baked out in virtuoso procedures of quantitative analysis, and a closer knowledge of the components of the solar wind would be gained. Since the solar wind, it may be recalled, was diverted by the magnetosphere away from the earth it had not hitherto been available for casual study.

That was the simplest experiment to set up; the other two would be deployed about an hour later. One was a passive seismometer to measure erratic disturbances and any periodic vibrations, as well as moonquakes, and the impact of meteors in the weeks and months to follow; it was equipped to radio this information to earth, the energy for transmission derived from solar panels which extended out to either side, and thereby gave it the look of one of those spaceships of the future with thin extended paperlike wings which one sees in science fiction drawings. In any case it was so sensitive that the steps of the astronauts were recorded as they walked by. Finally there was a Laser Ranging Retro-Reflector, an LRRR (or LRQ, for L R-cubed), and that was a mirror whose face was a hundred quartz crystals, black as coal, cut to a precision never obtained before in glass—one-third of an arch/sec. Since each quartz crystal was a corner of a rectangle, any ray of light striking one of the three faces in each crystal would bounce off the other two in such a way that the light would return in exactly the same direction it had been received. A laser beam sent up from earth would therefore reflect back to the place from which it was sent. The time it required to travel this half-million miles from earth to moon round trip, a journey of less than three seconds, could be measured so accurately that physicists might then discern whether the moon was drifting away from the earth a few centimeters a year, or (by using two lasers) whether Europe and America might be drifting apart some comparable distance, or even if the Pacific Ocean were contracting. These measurements could then be entered into the caverns of Einstein's General Theory of Relativity, and new proof or disproof of the great thesis could be obtained.

We may be certain the equipment was remarkable. Still, its packaging and its ease of deployment had probably done as much to advance its presence on the ship as any clear priority over other scientific equipment; the beauty of these items from the point of view of NASA was that the astronauts could set them up in a few minutes while working in their space suits, even set them up with inflated gloves so insensitive that special silicone pads had to be inserted at the fingertips in order to leave the astronauts not altogether numb-fingered in their manipulations. Yet these marvels of measurement would soon be installed on the moon with less effort than it takes to remove a vacuum cleaner from its carton and get it operating.

It was at this point that patriotism, the corporation, and the national taste all came to occupy the same head of a pin, for the astronauts next proceeded to set up the flag. But that operation, as always, presented its exquisite problems. There was, we remind ourselves, no atmosphere for the flag to wave in. Any flag made of cloth would droop, indeed it would dangle. Therefore a species of starched plastic flag had to be employed, a flag which would stand out, there, out to the nonexistent breeze, flat as a slab of plywood. No, that would not do either. The flag was better crinkled and curled. Waves and billows were bent into it, and a full corkscrew of a curl at the end. There it stands for posterity, photographed in the twists of a high gale on the windless moon, curled up tin flag, numb as a pickled pepper.

Aldrin would hardly agree. "Being able to salute that flag was one of the more humble yet proud experiences I've ever had. To be able to look at the American flag and know how much so many people had put of themselves and their work into getting it where it was. We sensed—we really did—this almost mystical identification of all the people in the world at that instant."

Two minutes after the flag was up, the President of the United States put in his phone call. Let us listen one more time:

"Because of what you have done," said Nixon, "the heavens have become a part of man's world. And as you talk to us from the Sea of Tranquility, it inspires us to redouble our efforts to bring peace and tranquility to earth . . ."

"Thank you, Mr. President. It's a great honor and privilege for us to be here representing not only the United States, but men of peace of all nations . . ."

In such piety is the schizophrenia of the ages.

Immediately afterward, Aldrin practiced kicking moon dust, but he was somewhat broken up. Either reception was garbled, or Aldrin was temporarily incoherent. "They seem to leave," he said to the Capcom, referring to the particles, "and most of them have about the same angle of departure and velocity. From where I stand, a large portion of them will impact at a certain distance out. Several—the percentage is, of course, that will impact . . ."

Capcom: "Buzz this is Houston. You're cutting out on the end of your transmissions. Can you speak a little more forward into your microphone. Over."

Aldrin: "Roger. I'll try that."

Capcom: "Beautiful."

Aldrin: "Now I had that one inside my mouth that time."

Capcom: "It sounded a little wet."

And on earth, a handful of young scientists were screaming, "Stop wasting time with flags and presidents—collect some rocks!"

DISCUSSION QUESTIONS

1. How does the language of the astronauts, especially Aldrin's, affect Mailer? Why does Mailer use their words and NASA terminology so frequently? How are these transcripts and codes used by O'Toole in his account of the moon landing for the *Washington Post* (see "Press")?

2. Why does Mailer concentrate on a particular spot where the transcript is garbled? Why does he speculate on the length of time it takes the astronauts to step out onto the moon? How does his description of the "clarity of focus" on the moon suggest an environment that is different from the one described by the astronauts? For example, how does Aldrin's comparison of the moon landscape to "an environment somewhere out West" affect our response to what they are seeing? What does Mailer want us to see?

Eudora Welty / The Little Store

*Eudora Welty was born in Jackson, Mississippi, in 1909 and attended Missis-
sippi State College for Women, the University of Wisconsin, and the School of
Business at Columbia University. During the Depression, while working for
newspapers, radios, and the Works Progress Administration, she traveled
throughout Mississippi taking numerous photographs which were later exhibited
in New York. Her first collection of stories,* A Curtain of Green, *appeared in
1941. Since that time, Welty has written several more story collections and novels including* The Robber Bridegroom *(1942),* The Ponder Heart *(1954),* Losing
Battles *(1970), and the Pulitzer Prize-winning* The Optimist's Daughter *(1972).
She is also regarded as a talented essayist and critic.*

*Welty still resides in Jackson, and the following sketch recalls the flavor of
her childhood years there.*

My mother considered herself pretty well prepared in her kitchen and pantry for
any emergency that, in her words, might choose to present itself. But if she should,
all of a sudden, need another lemon or find she was out of bread, all she had to
do was call out, "Quick! Who'd like to run to the Little Store for me?"

I would.

She'd count out the change into my hand, and I was away. I'll bet the nickel
that would be left over that all over the country, for those of my day, the neighborhood grocery played a similar part in our growing up.

Our store had its name—it was that of the grocer who owned it, whom I'll call
Mr. Sessions—but "the Little Store" is what we called it at home. It was a block
down our street toward the capitol and half a block further, around the corner,
toward the cemetery. I knew even the sidewalk to it as well as I knew my own
skin. I'd skipped my jumping-rope up and down it, hopped its length through mazes
of hopscotch, played jacks in its islands of shade, serpentined along it on my Princess bicycle, skated it backward and forward. In the twilight I had dragged my
steamboat by its string (this was home-made out of every new shoebox, with candle in the bottom lighted and shining through colored tissue paper pasted over
windows scissored out in the shapes of the sun, moon and stars) across every crack
of the walk without letting it bump or catch fire. I'd "played out" on that street
after supper with my brothers and friends as long as "first-dark" lasted; I'd caught
its lightning bugs. On the first Armistice Day (and this will set the time I'm speaking of) we made our own parade down that walk on a single velocipede—my brother
pedaling, our little brother riding the handlebars, and myself standing on the back,
all with arms wide, flying flags in each hand. (My father snapped that picture as
we raced by. It came out blurred.) . . .

Our Little Store rose right up from the sidewalk; standing in a street of family
houses, it alone hadn't any yard in front, any tree or flowerbed. It was a plain
frame building covered over with brick. Above the door, a little railed porch ran
across on an upstairs level and four windows with shades were looking out. But I
didn't catch on to those.

Running in out of the sun, you met what seemed total obscurity inside. There
were almost tangible smells—licorice recently sucked in a child's cheek, dill-
pickle brine that had leaked through a paper sack in a fresh trail across the wooden
floor, ammonia-loaded ice that had been hoisted from wet croker sacks and slammed
into the icebox with its sweet butter at the door, and perhaps the smell of still-
untrapped mice.

Then through the motes of cracker dust, cornmeal dust, the Gold Dust of the Gold Dust Twins that the floor had been swept out with, the realities emerged. Shelves climbed to high reach all the way around, set out with not too much of any one thing but a lot of things—lard, molasses, vinegar, starch, matches, kerosene, Octagon soap (about a year's worth of octagon-shaped coupons cut out and saved brought a signet ring addressed to you in the mail. Furthermore, when the postman arrived at your door, he blew a whistle). It was up to you to remember what you came for, while your eye traveled from cans of sardines to ice cream salt to harmonicas to flypaper (over your head, batting around on a thread beneath the blades of the ceiling fan, stuck with its testimonial catch).

Its confusion may have been in the eye of its beholder. Enchantment is cast upon you by all those things you weren't supposed to have need for, it lures you close to wooden tops you'd outgrown, boy's marbles and agates in little net pouches, small rubber balls that wouldn't bounce straight, frazzly kitestring, clay bubble-pipes that would snap off in your teeth, the stiffest scissors. You could contemplate those long narrow boxes of sparklers gathering dust while you waited for it to be the Fourth of July or Christmas, and noisemakers in the shape of tin frogs for somebody's birthday party you hadn't been invited to yet, and see that they were all marvelous.

You might not have even looked for Mr. Sessions when he came around his store cheese (as big as a doll's house) and in front of the counter looking for you. When you'd finally asked him for, and received from him in its paper bag, whatever single thing it was that you had been sent for, the nickel that was left over was yours to spend.

Down at a child's eye level, inside those glass jars with mouths in their sides through which the grocer could run his scoop or a child's hand might be invited to reach for a choice, were wineballs, all-day suckers, gumdrops, peppermints. Making a row under the glass of a counter were the Tootsie Rolls, Hershey Bars, Goo-Goo Clusters, Baby Ruths. And whatever was the name of those pastilles that came stacked in a cardboard cylinder with a cardboard lid? They were thin and dry, about the size of tiddlywinks, and in the shape of twisted rosettes. A kind of chocolate dust came out with them when you shook them out in your hand. Were they chocolate? I'd say rather they were brown. They didn't taste of anything at all, unless it was wood. Their attraction was the number you got for a nickel.

Making up your mind, you circled the store around and around, around the pickle barrel, around the tower of Cracker Jack boxes; Mr. Sessions had built it for us himself on top of a packing case, like a house of cards.

If it seemed too hot for Cracker Jacks, I might get a cold drink. Mr. Sessions might have already stationed himself by the cold-drinks barrel, like a mind reader. Deep in ice water that looked black as ink, murky shapes that would come up as Coca-Colas, Orange Crushes, and various flavors of pop, were all swimming around together. When you gave the word, Mr. Sessions plunged his bare arm in to the elbow and fished out your choice, first try. I favored a locally bottled concoction called Lake's Celery. (What else could it be called? It was made by a Mr. Lake out of celery. It was a popular drink here for years but was not known universally, as I found out when I arrived in New York and ordered one in the Astor bar.) You drank on the premises, with feet set wide apart to miss the drip, and gave him back his bottle.

But he didn't hurry you off. A standing scales was by the door, with a stack of iron weights and a brass slide on the balance arm, that would weigh you up to three hundred pounds. Mr. Sessions, whose hands were gentle and smelled of carbolic, would lift you up and set your feet on the platform, hold your loaf of bread for you, and taking his time while you stood still for him, he would make certain of what you weighed today. He could even remember what you weighed the last time, so you could subtract and announce how much you'd gained. That was goodbye.

Joan Didion / On the Mall   1975

A former associate feature editor at Vogue *and contributing editor to the* National Review, The Saturday Evening Post, *and* Esquire, *Joan Didion has written for* Mademoiselle, Holiday, The American Scholar, *and* Life *magazines. Interviews and self-assertion are not her journalistic forte:*

> *My only advantage as a reporter is that I am so physically small, so temperamentally unobtrusive, and so neurotically inarticulate that people tend to forget that my presence runs counter to their best interests. And it always does. That is one last thing to remember: writers are always selling somebody out.*

*The author of three novels—*Run River, Play It as It Lays, *and* Democracy*— Didion has also published two collections of essays,* Slouching Towards Bethlehem *(1968) and* The White Album *(1979), from which the following essay on shopping malls is taken. Her study of the politics and culture of Central America,* Salvador, *appeared in 1983.*

They float on the landscape like pyramids to the boom years, all those Plazas and Malls and Esplanades. All those Squares and Fairs. All those Towns and Dales, all those Villages, all those Forests and Parks and Lands. Stonestown. Hillsdale. Valley Fair, Mayfair, Northgate, Southgate, Eastgate, Westgate. Gulfgate. They are toy garden cities in which no one lives but everyone consumes, profound equalizers, the perfect fusion of the profit motive and the egalitarian ideal, and to hear their names is to recall words and phrases no longer quite current. Baby Boom. Consumer Explosion. Leisure Revolution. Do-It-Yourself Revolution. Backyard Revolution. Suburbia. "The Shopping Center," the Urban Land Institute could pronounce in 1957, "is today's extraordinary retail business evolvement. . . . The automobile accounts for suburbia, and suburbia accounts for the shopping center."

It was a peculiar and visionary time, those years after World War II to which all the Malls and Towns and Dales stand as climate-controlled monuments. Even the word "automobile," as in "the automobile accounts for suburbia and suburbia accounts for the shopping center," no longer carries the particular freight it once did: as a child in the late Forties in California I recall reading and believing that the "freedom of movement" afforded by the automobile was "America's fifth freedom." The trend was up. The solution was in sight. The frontier had been reinvented, and its shape was the subdivision, that new free land on which all settlers could recast their lives *tabula rasa*. For one perishable moment there the American idea seemed about to achieve itself, via F.H.A. housing and the acquisition of major appliances, and a certain enigmatic glamour attached to the architects of this newfound land. They made something of nothing. They gambled and sometimes lost. They staked the past to seize the future. I have difficulty now imagining a childhood in which a man named Jere Strizek, the developer of Town and Country Village outside Sacramento (143,000 square feet gross floor area, 68 stores, 1000 parking spaces, the Urban Land Institute's "prototype for centers using heavy timber and tile construction for informality''), could materialize as a role model, but I had such a childhood, just after World War II, in Sacramento. I never met or even saw Jere Strizek, but at the age of 12 I imagined him a kind of frontiersman, a romantic and revolutionary spirit, and in the indigenous grain he was.

I suppose James B. Douglas and David D. Bohannon were too.

I first heard of James B. Douglas and David D. Bohannon not when I was 12 but a dozen years later, when I was living in New York, working for *Vogue,* and taking, by correspondence, a University of California Extension course in shopping-center theory. This did not seem to me eccentric at the time. I remember sitting on the cool floor in Irving Penn's studio and reading, in *The Community Builders Handbook,* advice from James B. Douglas on shopping-center financing. I recall staying late in my pale-blue office on the twentieth floor of the Graybar Building to memorize David D. Bohannon's parking ratios. My "real" life was to sit in this office and describe life as it was lived in Djakarta and Caneel Bay and in the great châteaux of the Loire Valley, but my dream life was to put to-gether a Class-A regional shopping center with three full-line department stores as major tenants.

That I was perhaps the only person I knew in New York, let alone on the Condé Nast floors of the Graybar Building, to have memorized the distinctions among "A," "B," and "C" shopping centers did not occur to me (the defining distinc-tion, as long as I have your attention, is that an "A," or "regional," center has as its major tenant a full-line department store which carries major appliances; a "B," or "community," center has as its major tenant a junior department store which does not carry major appliances; and a "C," or "neighborhood," center has as its major tenant only a supermarket): my interest in shopping centers was in no way casual. I did want to build them. I wanted to build them because I had fallen into the habit of writing fiction, and I had it in my head that a couple of good centers might support this habit less taxingly than a pale-blue office at *Vogue.* I had even devised an original scheme by which I planned to gain enough capital and credibility to enter the shopping-center game: I would lease warehouses in, say, Queens, and offer Manhattan delicatessens the opportunity to sell competi-tively by buying cooperatively, from my trucks. I see a few wrinkles in this scheme now (the words "concrete overcoat" come to mind), but I did not then. In fact I planned to run it out of the pale-blue office.

James B. Douglas and David D. Bohannon. In 1950 James B. Douglas had opened Northgate, in Seattle, the first regional center to combine a pedestrian mall with an underground truck tunnel. In 1954 David D. Bohannon had opened Hillsdale, a forty-acre regional center on the peninsula south of San Francisco. That is the only solid bio I have on James B. Douglas and David D. Bohannon to this day, but many of their opinions are engraved on my memory. David D. Bohannon be-lieved in preserving the integrity of the shopping center by not cutting up the site with any dedicated roads. David D. Bohannon believed that architectural setbacks in a center looked "pretty on paper" but caused "customer resistance." James B. Douglas advised that a small-loan office could prosper in a center only if it were placed away from foot traffic, since people who want small loans do not want to be observed getting them. I do not now recall whether it was James B. Douglas or David D. Bohannon or someone else altogether who passed along this hint on how to paint the lines around the parking spaces (actually this is called "striping the lot," and the spaces are "stalls"): make each space a foot wider than it need be—ten feet, say, instead of nine—when the center first opens and business is slow. By this single stroke the developer achieves a couple of important objec-tives, the appearance of a popular center and the illusion of easy parking, and no one will really notice when business picks up and the spaces shrink.

Nor do I recall who first solved what was once a crucial center dilemma: the placement of the major tenant vis-à-vis the parking lot. The dilemma was that the major tenant—the draw, the raison d'être for the financing, the Sears, the Macy's, the May Company—wanted its customer to walk directly from car to store. The smaller tenants, on the other hand, wanted that same customer to *pass their stores* on the way from the car to, say, Macy's. The solution to this conflict of interests was actually very simple: *two major tenants,* one at each end of a mall. This is called "anchoring the mall," and represents seminal work in shopping-center theory. One thing you will note about shopping-center theory is that you could have thought of it yourself, and a course in it will go a long way toward dispelling the notion that business proceeds from mysteries too recondite for you and me.

A few aspects of shopping-center theory do in fact remain impenetrable to me. I have no idea why the Community Builders' Council ranks "Restaurant" as deserving a Number One (or "Hot Spot") location but exiles "Chinese Restaurant" to a Number Three, out there with "Power and Light Office" and "Christian Science Reading Room." Nor do I know why the Council approves of enlivening a mall with "small animals" but specifically, vehemently, and with no further explanation, excludes "monkeys." If I had a center I would have monkeys, and Chinese restaurants, and Mylar kites and bands of small girls playing tambourine.

A few years ago at a party I met a woman from Detroit who told me that the Joyce Carol Oates novel with which she identified most closely was *Wonderland.*
I asked her why.
"Because," she said, "my husband has a branch there."
I did not understand.
"In Wonderland the center," the woman said patiently. "My husband has a branch in Wonderland."
I have never visited Wonderland but imagine it to have bands of small girls playing tambourine.

A few facts about shopping centers.
The "biggest" center in the United States is generally agreed to be Woodfield, outside Chicago, a "super" regional or "leviathan" two-million-square-foot center with four major tenants.
The "first" shopping center in the United States is generally agreed to be Country Club Plaza in Kansas City, built in the twenties. There were some other early centers, notably Edward H. Bouton's 1907 Roland Park in Baltimore, Hugh Prather's 1931 Highland Park Shopping Village in Dallas, and Hugh Potter's 1937 River Oaks in Houston, but the developer of Country Club Plaza, the late J. C. Nichols, is referred to with ritual frequency in the literature of shopping centers, usually as "pioneering J. C. Nichols," "trailblazing J. C. Nichols," or "J. C. Nichols, of the center as we know it."
Those are some facts I know about shopping centers because I still want to be Jere Strizek or James B. Douglas or David D. Bohannon. Here are some facts I know about shopping centers because I never will be Jere Strizek or James B. Douglas or David D. Bohannon: a good center in which to spend the day if you wake feeling low in Honolulu, Hawaii, is Ala Moana, major tenants Liberty House and Sears. A good center in which to spend the day if you wake feeling low in Oxnard, California, is The Esplanade, major tenants the May Company and Sears. A good center in which to spend the day if you wake feeling low in Biloxi, Mississippi, is Edgewater Plaza, major tenant Godchaux's. Ala Moana in Honolulu is larger than The Esplanade in Oxnard, and The Esplanade in Oxnard is larger than Edgewater Plaza in Biloxi. Ala Moana has carp pools. The Esplanade and Edgewater Plaza do not.

These marginal distinctions to one side, Ala Moana, The Esplanade, and Edgewater Plaza are the same place, which is precisely their role not only as equalizers but in the sedation of anxiety. In each of them one moves for a while in an aqueous suspension not only of light but of judgment, not only of judgment but of "personality." One meets no acquaintances at The Esplanade. One gets no telephone calls at Edgewater Plaza. "It's a hard place to run in to for a pair of stockings," a friend complained to me recently of Ala Moana, and I knew that she was not yet ready to surrender her ego to the idea of the center. The last time I went to Ala Moana it was to buy *The New York Times*. Because *The New York Times* was not in, I sat on the mall for a while and ate caramel corn. In the end I bought not *The New York Times* at all but two straw hats at Liberty House, four bottles of nail enamel at Woolworth's, and a toaster, on sale at Sears. In the literature of shopping centers these would be described as impulse purchases, but the impulse here was obscure. I do not wear hats, nor do I like caramel corn. I do not use nail enamel. Yet flying back across the Pacific I regretted only the toaster.

DISCUSSION QUESTIONS

1. Compare Didion's "On the Mall" to Eudora Welty's "The Little Store." How do these two essays convey changes in American society? Discuss the pros and cons of both the little store and the giant mall.

2. Compare Didion's description of shopping malls to the one that forms the setting of Bob Greene's "Fifteen" (in "Magazines"). In what ways are the authors' attitudes similar? How does your own personal attitude toward malls compare to the attitude of each of these writers?

John McPhee / *Coming into the Country*   1976

The range of topics in John McPhee's nearly two dozen books and scores of magazine articles reads like the categories in a well-stocked bookstore: literature, education, military science, travel, environmental studies, history, geography, science, cooking, dining, and sports. And what makes McPhee's writing so successful is his ability to see each subject so freshly, be it a celebrated athlete or a remote stretch of frontier landscape. McPhee labors tirelessly on his writing; he regularly spends twelve-hour days transforming extensive research and interview notes into finely crafted sentences. He never overwrites, preferring to boil down a phrase before putting it into type. The result is prose at once taut, precise, and impersonal yet insistently detailed, highly figurative, and immensely energetic.

Born in 1931, McPhee was raised and educated in Princeton, New Jersey, where he has permanently settled. His writing career began in a high-school English class that required three essays (plus outlines) a week, practice that prepared him well for the carefully documented "fact pieces"—to use The New Yorker's *term—which have earned him international acclaim. A former television scriptwriter and staff reporter for* Time *magazine, where he wrote features on show business as well as film and book reviews, McPhee has been a staff writer for* The New Yorker *for more than twenty years. He also teaches a writing course ("The Literature of Fact") at Princeton University.*

In the following selection, drawn from his best-selling book Coming into the

Country *(1976), McPhee celebrates America's last frontier and recounts his first encounter with the majestic ruler of that Arctic land. For other dramatic first sightings of bears, see William Faulkner's* The Bear *(in ''Classics'') and Lew Dietz's ''The Myth of the Boss Bear'' (in ''Magazines'').*

BEAR LAND

The river was low, and Pat Pourchot had picked a site as far upstream as he judged we could be and still move in boats. We were on an island, with the transparent Salmon River on one side—hurrying, scarcely a foot deep—and a small slough on the other. Deeper pools, under bedrock ledges, were above us and below us. We built our fire on the lemon-sized gravel of what would in higher water be the riverbed, and we pitched the tents on slightly higher ground among open stands of willow, on sand that showed what Bob Fedeler called ''the old tracks of a young griz.'' We would stay two nights, according to plan, before beginning the long descent to the Kobuk; and in the intervening day we would first assemble the kayaks and then be free to disperse and explore the terrain.

There was a sixth man with us, there at the beginning. His name was Jack Hession, and he was the Sierra Club's only salaried full-time representative in Alaska. Pourchot had invited him as an observer. The news that he was absent at the end of the trip could instantly cause hopes to rise in Alaska, where the Sierra Club has long been considered a netherworld force and Hession the resident Belial. Hession, though, was not going to perish on the Salmon. Pressures from Anchorage had travelled with him, and before long would get the better of him, and in cavalier manner—in this Arctic wilderness—he would bid us goodbye and set out early for home. Meanwhile, in the morning sun, we put together the collapsible kayaks—two single Kleppers and Snake Eyes. Hession's own single was the oldest of the three, and it had thirty-six parts, hardware not included. There were dowels of mountain ash and ribs of laminated Finnish birch, which fitted, one part to another, with hooks and clips until they formed a pair of nearly identical skeletal cones—the internal structures of halves of the boat. The skin was a limp bag made of blue canvas (the deck) and hemp-reinforced vulcanized rubber (the hull). The concept was to insert the skeletal halves into the skin and then figure out how to firm them together. We had trouble doing that. Hession, who ordinarily used rigid boats of fibre glass in his engagements with white water, could not remember how to complete the assembly. Stiff toward the ends and bent in the middle, his kayak had the look of a clip on tie, and would do about as well in the river. We all crouched around and studied amidships—six men, a hundred miles up a stream, above sixty-seven degrees of latitude, with a limp kayak. No one was shy with suggestions, which were full of ingenuity but entirely failed to work. By trial and error, we finally figured it out. The last step in the assembly involved the center rib, and we set that inside the hull on a tilt and then tapped it with a rock and forced it toward the vertical. When the forcing rib reached ninety degrees to the longer axis of the craft, the rib snapped into place, and with that the entire boat became taut and yare. Clever man, Johann Klepper. He had organized his foldboat in the way that the North American Indians had developed the construction of their bark canoes. Over the years, the Klepper company had simplified its process. Our other single kayak, the more recent model, had fewer and larger skeletal parts, and it went together more easily; but it was less streamlined than the first. Snake Eyes, for its part—all eight hundred dollars' worth of Snake Eyes—was new and had an interior of broad wooden slabs, conveniently hinged. Snake Eyes had the least number of separate parts (only fifteen) and in the way it went together was efficient and simple. Its advanced design had been achieved with a certain loss of grace, however, and this was evident there on the gravel. The boat was lumpy, awkward, bulging—a kayak with elbows.

Toward noon and after an early lunch, we set off on foot for a look around. Pourchot went straight up the hills to the west, alone. Stell Newman and John Kauffmann intended lesser forays, nearer the campsite. I decided I'd go with Bob Fedeler, who, with Jack Hession, had the most ambitious plan. They were going north up the river some miles and then up the ridges to the east. I hoped my legs would hold up. I didn't want to embarrass myself, off somewhere in the hills, by snapping something, but I could not resist going along with Fedeler. After all, he was a habitat biologist, working for the state, and if the ground around here was not habitat then I would never be in country that was. The temperature had come up to seventy. The sky was blue, with moving clouds and intermittent sun. We stuffed our rain gear into day packs and started up the river.

Generally speaking, if I had a choice between hiking and peeling potatoes, I would peel the potatoes. I have always had a predilection for canoes on rivers and have avoided walking wherever possible. My experience, thus, was limited but did exist. My work had led me up the Sierra Nevada and across the North Cascades, and in various eras I had walked parts of the Long Trail, the Appalachian Trail, trails of New Hampshire, the Adirondacks. Here in the Brooks Range, of course, no one had been there clearing the path. A mile, steep or level, could demand a lot of time. You go along with only a general plan, free lance, guessing where the walking will be least difficult, making choices all the way. These are the conditions, and in ten minutes' time they present their story. The country is wild to the limits of the term. It would demean such a world to call it pre-Columbian. It is twenty times older than that, having assumed its present form ten thousand years ago, with the melting of the Wisconsin ice.

For several miles upstream, willow and alder pressed in on the river, backed by spruce and cottonwood, so the easiest path was the river itself. Gravel bars were now on one side, now the other, so we crossed and crossed again, taking off our rubber boots and wading through the fast, cold water. I had rubber bottomed leather boots (L.L. Bean's, which are much in use all over Alaska). Fedeler was wearing hiking boots, Hession low canvas sneakers. Hession had a floppy sun hat, too. He seemed to see no need to dress like Sir Edmund Hillary, or to leave the marks of waffles by the tracks of wolves. He was a brief, trim, lithe figure, who moved lightly and had seen a lot of such ground. He stopped and opened his jackknife, and stood it by a track in sand at the edge of the river. Other tracks were near. Two wolves running side by side. He took a picture of the track. We passed a deep pool where spring water came into the river, and where algae grew in response to its warmth. Grayling could winter there. Some were in the pool now— bodies stationary, fins in motion, in clear deep water as green as jade. Four mergansers swam up the river. We saw moose pellets in sand beyond the pool. I would not much want to be a moose just there, in a narrow V-shaped valley with scant protection of trees. We came, in fact, to the tree line not long thereafter. The trees simply stopped. We took a few more northward steps and were out of the boreal forest. Farther north, as far as land continued, there would be no more. I don't mean to suggest that we had stepped out of Sequoia National Park and onto an unvegetated plain. The woods behind us were spare in every sense, fingering up the river valley, reaching as far as they could go. Now the tundra, which had before been close behind the trees, came down to the banks of the river. We'd had enough of shoelaces and of bare feet crunching underwater stones, so we climbed up the west bank to walk on the tundra—which from the river had looked as smooth as a golf course. Possibly there is nothing as invitingly deceptive as a tundra-covered hillside. Distances over tundra, even when it is rising steeply, are like distances over water, seeming to be less than they are, defraying the suggestion of effort.

The tundra surface, though, consists of many kinds of plants, most of which seem to be stemmed with wire configured to ensnare the foot. For years, my conception of tundra—based, I suppose, on photographs of the Canadian north and the plains of the Alaskan Arctic slope—was of a vast northern flatness, water-flecked, running level to every horizon. Tundra is not topography, however; it is a mat of vegetation, and it runs up the sides of prodigious declivities as well as across the broad plains. There are three varying types—wet tundra, on low flatland with much standing water; moist tundra, on slightly higher ground; and alpine tundra, like carpeted heather, rising on mountains and hills. We moved on, northward, over moist tundra, and the plants were often a foot or so in height. Moving through them was more like wading than walking, except where we followed game trails. Fortunately, these were numerous enough, and comfortably negotiable. They bore signs of everything that lived there. They were highways, share and share alike, for caribou, moose, bears, wolves—whose tracks, antlers, and feces were strewn along the right-of-way like beer cans at the edge of a road. While these game trails were the best thoroughfares in many hundreds of square miles, they were also the only ones, and they had a notable defect. They tended to vanish. The trails would go along, well cut and stamped out through moss campion, reindeer moss, sedge tussocks, crowberries, prostrate willows, dwarf birch, bog blueberries, white mountain avens, low-bush cranberries, lichens, Labrador tea; then, abruptly, and for no apparent reason, the trails would disappear. Their well-worn ruts suggested hundreds of animals, heavy traffic. So where did they go when the trail vanished? Fedeler did not know. I could not think of an explanation. Maybe Noah had got there a little before us.

On the far side of the river was an isolated tree, which had made a brave bid to move north, to extend the reach of its progenitive forest. The Brooks Range, the remotest uplift in North America, was made a little less remote, fifty years ago, by the writing of Robert Marshall, a forester, who described several expeditions to these mountains in a book called "Alaska Wilderness." Marshall had a theory about the tree line, the boundary of the circumboreal world. He thought that white spruce and other species could live farther north, and that they were inching northward, dropping seeds ahead of them, a dead-slow advance under marginal conditions. Whatever it may have signified, the tree across the river was dead, and out of it now came a sparrow hawk, flying at us, shouting *"kee kee kee,"* and hovering on rapidly beating wings to study the creatures on the trail. There was not much it could do about us, and it went back to the tree.

The leaves of Labrador tea, crushed in the hand, smelled like a turpentine. The cranberries were early and sourer than they would eventually be. With the arrival of cold, they freeze on the vine, and when they thaw, six months later, they are somehow sweeter and contain more juice. Bears like overwintered berries. Blueberries, too, are sweeter after being frozen on the bush. Fried cranberries will help relieve a sore throat. Attacks in the gall bladder have been defused with boiled cranberries mixed with seal oil. The sedge tussocks were low and not as perilous as tussocks can be. They are grass that grows in bunches, more compact at the bottom than at the top—a mushroom shape that can spill a foot and turn an ankle. They were tiresome, and soon we were ready to move upward, away from the moist tundra and away from the river. Ahead we saw the configurations of the sharp small valleys of three streams meeting, forming there the principal stem of the Salmon. To the east, above the confluence, a tundra-bald hill rose a thousand feet and more. We decided to cross the river and go up the hill. Look around. Choose where to go from there.

The river was so shallow now that there was no need for removing boots. We walked across and began to climb. The going was steep. I asked Jack Hession how long he had been in Alaska, and he said seven years. He had been in Alaska longer than two-thirds of the people in the state. He was from California, and had lived more recently in western Washington, where he had begun to acquire his expertise in boats in white water. Like Fedeler—like me, for that matter—he was in good condition. Hession, though, seemed to float up the incline, while I found it hard, sweaty work. From across the river it had looked as easy as a short flight of stairs. I went up it a trudge at a time—on reindeer moss, heather, lupine. The sun had suddenly departed, and a cool rain began to fall. At the top of the hill, we sat on a rock outcropping and looked back at the river, twelve hundred feet below. Everywhere around us were mountains—steep, treeless, buff where still in the sun. One was bright silver. The rain felt good. We nibbled M&M's. They were even better than the rain. The streams far below, small and fast, came pummelling together and made the river. The land they fell through looked nude. It was all tundra, rising northward toward a pass at the range divide. Looking at so much mountain ground—this immense minute fragment of wilderness Alaska—one could wonder about the choice of words of people who say that it is fragile. "Fragile" just does not appear to be a proper term for a rugged, essentially un-invaded landscape covering tens of thousands of square miles—a place so vast and unpeopled that if anyone could figure out how to steal Italy, Alaska would be a place to hide it. Meanwhile, earnest ecologues write and speak about the "fragile" tundra, this "delicate" ocean of barren land. The words sound effete, but the terrain is nonetheless vulnerable. There is ice under the tundra, mixed with soil as permafrost, in some places two thousand feet deep. The tundra vegetation, living and dead, provides insulation that keeps the summer sun from melting the permafrost. If something pulls away the insulation and melting occurs, the soil will settle and the water may run off. The earth, in such circumstances, does not restore itself. In the nineteen-sixties, a bulldozer working for Geophysical Service, Inc., an oil-exploration company, wrote the initials G.S.I. in Arctic Alaskan tundra. The letters were two hundred feet from top to bottom, and near them the bulldozer cut an arrow—an indicator for pilots. Thermokarst (thermal erosion) followed, and slumpage. The letters and the arrow are now odd-shaped ponds, about eight feet deep. For many generations that segment of tundra will say "G.S.I." Tundra is even sensitive to snow machines. They compress snow, and cut off much of the air that would otherwise get to the vegetation. Evidence appears in summer. The snow machines have left brown trails on ground they never touched.

Both sunlight and rain were falling on us now. We had a topographic map, of the largest scale available but nonetheless of scant detail—about five miles to half a thumb. Of the three streams that met below us, the nearest was called Sheep Creek. A rainbow wicketed its steep valley. The top of the arch was below us. The name Sheep Creek was vestigial. "Historically, there were Dall sheep in these mountains," Fedeler said.

"What happened to them?"

"Who knows?" He shrugged. "Things go in cycles. They'll be back."

Alders had crept into creases in the mountainside across the Salmon valley. I remarked on the borderline conditions in evidence everywhere in this spare and beautiful country, and said, "Look at those alders over there, clinging to life."

Fedeler said, "It's hungry country, that's for sure. Drainage and exposure make *the* difference."

We ate peanuts and raisins and more M&M's—and, feeling rested, became ambitious. On a long southward loop back to camp, we would extend our walk by going around a mountain that was separated from us by what looked to be the fairly steep declivity of a tributary drainage. The terrain sloped away to the southwest toward the mouth of the tributary. We would go down for a time, and then cross the tributary and cut back around the mountain.

We passed first through stands of fireweed, and then over ground that was wine-red with the leaves of bearberries. There were curlewberries, too, which put a deep-purple stain on the hand. We kicked at some wolf scat, old as winter. It was woolly and white and filled with the hair of a snowshoe hare. Nearby was a rich inventory of caribou pellets and, in increasing quantity as we moved downhill, blueberries—an outspreading acreage of blueberries. Fedeler stopped walking. He touched my arm. He had in an instant become even more alert than he usually was, and obviously apprehensive. His gaze followed straight on down our intended course. What he saw there I saw now. It appeared to me to be a hill of fur. "Big boar grizzly," Fedeler said in a near-whisper. The bear was about a hundred steps away, in the blueberries, grazing. The head was down, the hump high. The immensity of muscle seemed to vibrate slowly—to expand and contract, with the grazing. Not berries alone but whole bushes were going into the bear. He was big for a barren-ground grizzly. The brown bears of Arctic Alaska (or grizzlies; they are no longer thought to be different) do not grow to the size they will reach on more ample diets elsewhere. The barren-ground grizzly will rarely grow larger than six hundred pounds.

"What if he got too close?" I said.

Fedeler said, "We'd be in real trouble."

"You can't outrun them," Hession said.

A grizzly, no slower than a racing horse, is about half again as fast as the fastest human being. Watching the great mound of weight in the blueberries, with a fifty-five-inch waist and a neck more than thirty inches around, I had difficulty imagining that he could move with such speed, but I believed it, and was without impulse to test the proposition. Fortunately, a light southerly wind was coming up the Salmon valley. On its way to us, it passed the bear. The wind was relieving, coming into our faces, for had it been moving the other way the bear would not have been placidly grazing. There is an old adage that when a pine needle drops in the forest the eagle will see it fall; the deer will hear it when it hits the ground; the bear will smell it. If the boar grizzly were to catch our scent, he might stand on his hind legs, the better to try to see. Although he could hear well and had an extraordinary sense of smell, his eyesight was not much better than what was required to see a blueberry inches away. For this reason, a grizzly stands and squints, attempting to bring the middle distance into focus, and the gesture is often misunderstood as a sign of anger and forthcoming attack. If the bear were getting ready to attack, he would be on four feet, head low, ears cocked, the hair above his hump muscle standing on end. As if that message were not clear enough, he would also chop his jaws. His teeth would make a sound that would carry like the ringing of an axe.

One could predict, but not with certainty, what a grizzly would do. Odds were very great that one touch of man scent would cause him to stop his activity, pause in a moment of absorbed and alert curiosity, and then move, at a not undignified pace, in a direction other than the one from which the scent was coming. That is what would happen almost every time, but there was, to be sure, no guarantee. The forest Eskimos fear and revere the grizzly. They know that certain individual bears not only will fail to avoid a person who comes into their country but will approach and even stalk the trespasser. It is potentially inaccurate to extrapolate the behavior of any one bear from the behavior of most, since they are both intelligent and independent and will do what they choose. to do according to mood, experience, whim. A grizzly that has ever been wounded by a bullet will not forget it, and will probably know that it was a human being who sent the bullet. At sight of a human, such a bear will be likely to charge. Grizzlies hide food sometimes—a caribou calf, say, under a pile of scraped-up moss—and a person the bear might otherwise ignore might suddenly not be ignored if the person were inadvertently to step into the line between the food cache and the bear. A sow grizzly with cubs, of course, will charge anything that suggests danger to the cubs, even if the cubs are nearly as big as she is. They stay with their mother two and a half years.

None of us had a gun. (None of the six of us had brought a gun on the trip.) Among nonhunters who go into the terrain of the grizzly, there are several schools of thought about guns. The preferred one is: Never go without a sufficient weapon— a high-powered rifle or a shotgun and plenty of slug-loaded shells. The option is not without its own inherent peril. A professional hunter, some years ago, spotted a grizzly from the air and—with a client, who happened to be an Anchorage barber—landed on a lake about a mile from the bear. The stalking that followed was evidently conducted not only by the hunters but by the animal as well. The professional hunter was found dead from a broken neck, and had apparently died instantly, unaware of danger, for the cause of death was a single bite, delivered from behind. The barber, noted as clumsy with a rifle, had emptied his magazine, missing the bear with every shot but one, which struck the grizzly in the foot. The damage the bear did to the barber was enough to kill him several times. After the corpses were found, the bear was tracked and killed. To shoot and merely wound is worse than not to shoot at all. A bear that might have turned and gone away will possibly attack if wounded.

Fatal encounters with bears are as rare as they are memorable. Some people reject the rifle as cumbersome extra baggage, not worth toting, given the minimal risk. And, finally, there are a few people who feel that it is wrong to carry a gun, in part because the risk is low and well worth taking, but most emphatically because they see the gun as an affront to the wild country of which the bear is sign and symbol. This, while strongly felt, is a somewhat novel attitude. When Robert Marshall explored the Brooks Range half a century ago, he and his companions fired at almost every bear they saw, without pausing for philosophical reflection. The reaction was automatic. They were expressing mankind's immemorial fear of this beast—man and rattlesnake, man and bear. Among modern environmentalists, to whom a figure like Marshall is otherwise a hero, fear of the bear has been exceeded by reverence. A notable example, in his own past and present, is Andy Russell, author of a book called "Grizzly Country." Russell was once a professional hunter, but he gave that up to become a photographer, specializing in grizzlies. He says that he has given up not only shooting bears but even carrying a gun. On rare instances when grizzlies charge toward him, he shouts at them and stands his ground. The worst thing to do, he says, is to run, because anything that runs on open tundra suggests game to a bear. Game does not tend to stand its ground in the presence of grizzlies. Therefore, when the bear comes at you, just stand there. Charging something that does not move, the bear will theoretically stop and reconsider. (Says Russell.) More important, Russell believes that the bear will *know* if you have a gun, even if the gun is concealed:

> Reviewing our experiences, we had become more and more convinced that carrying arms was not only unnecessary in most grizzly country but was certainly no good for the desired atmosphere and proper protocol in obtaining good film records. If we were to obtain such film and fraternize successfully with the big bears, it would be better to go unarmed in most places. The mere fact of having a gun within reach, cached somewhere in a pack or a hidden holster, causes a man to act with unconscious arrogance and thus maybe to smell different or to transmit some kind of signal objectionable to bears. The armed man does not assume his proper role in association with the wild ones, a fact of which they seem instantly aware at some distance. He, being wilder than they, whether he likes to admit it or not, is instantly under even more suspicion than he would encounter if unarmed.
>
> One must follow the role of an uninvited visitor—an intruder—rather than that of an aggressive hunter, and one should go unarmed to insure this attitude.

Like pictures from pages riffled with a thumb, all of these things went through my mind there on the mountainside above the grazing bear. I will confess that in one instant I asked myself, "What the hell am I doing *here?*" There was nothing more to the question, though, than a hint of panic. I knew why I had come, and therefore what I was doing there. That I was frightened was incidental. I just hoped the fright would not rise beyond a relatively decorous level. I sensed that Fedeler and Hession were somewhat frightened, too. I would have been troubled if they had not been. Meanwhile, the sight of the bear stirred me like nothing else the country could contain. What mattered was not so much the bear himself as what the bear implied. He was the predominant thing in that country, and for him to be in it at all meant that there had to be more country like it in every direction and more of the same kind of country all around that. He implied a world. He was an affirmation to the rest of the earth that his kind of place was extant. There had been a time when his race was everywhere in North America, but it had been hunted down and pushed away in favor of something else. For example, the grizzly bear is the state animal of California, whose country was once his kind of place; and in California now the grizzly is extinct.

> The animals I have encountered in my wilderness wanderings have been reluctant to reveal all the things about them I would like to know. The animal that impresses me most, the one I find myself liking more and more, is the grizzly. No sight encountered in the wilds is quite so stirring as those massive, clawed tracks pressed into mud or snow. No sight is quite so impressive as that of the great bear stalking across some mountain slope with the fur of his silvery robe rippling over his mighty muscles. His is a dignity and power matched by no other in the North American wilderness. To share a mountain with him for a while is a privilege and an adventure like no other.
>
> I have followed his tracks into an alder hell to see what he had been doing and come to the abrupt end of them, when the maker stood up thirty feet away with a sudden snort to face me.
>
> To see a mother grizzly ambling and loafing with her cubs across the broad, hospitable bosom of a flower-spangled mountain meadow is to see life in true wilderness at its best.

If a wolf kills a caribou, and a grizzly comes along while the wolf is feeding on the kill, the wolf puts its tail between its legs and hurries away. A black bear will run from a grizzly, too. Grizzlies sometimes kill and eat black bears. The grizzly takes what he happens upon. He is an opportunistic eater. The predominance of the grizzly in his terrain is challenged by nothing but men and ravens. To frustrate ravens from stealing his food, he will lie down and sleep on top of a carcass, occasionally swatting the birds as if they were big black flies. He prefers a vegetable diet. He can pulp a moosehead with a single blow, but he is not lusting always to kill, and when he moves through his country he can be something munificent, going into copses of willow among unfleeing moose and their calves, touching nothing, letting it all breathe as before. He may, though, get the head of a cow moose between his legs and rake her flanks with the five-inch knives that protrude from the ends of his paws. Opportunistic. He removes and eats her entrails. He likes porcupines, too, and when one turns and presents to him a pygal bouquet of quills, he will leap into the air, land on the other side, chuck the fretful porpentine beneath the chin, flip it over, and, with a swift ventral incision, neatly remove its body from its skin, leaving something like a sea urchin behind him on the ground. He is nothing if not athletic. Before he dens, or just after he emerges, if his mountains are covered with snow he will climb to the brink of some impossible schuss, sit down on his butt, and shove off. Thirty-two, sixty-four, ninety-six feet per second, he plummets down the mountainside, spray snow flying to either side, as he approaches collision with boulders and trees. Just short of catastrophe, still going at bonecrushing speed, he flips to his feet and walks sedately onward as if his ride had not occurred.

His population density is thin on the Arctic barren ground. He needs for his forage at least fifty and perhaps a hundred square miles that are all his own—sixty-four thousand acres, his home range. Within it, he will move, typically, eight miles a summer day, doing his travelling through the twilight hours of the dead of night. To scratch his belly he walks over a tree—where forest exists. The tree bends beneath him as he passes. He forages in the morning, generally; and he rests a great deal, particularly after he eats. He rests fourteen hours a day. If he becomes hot in the sun, he lies down in a pool in the river. He sleeps on the tundra—restlessly tossing and turning, forever changing position. What he could be worrying about I cannot imagine.

His fur blends so well into the tundra colors that sometimes it is hard to see him. Fortunately, we could see well enough the one in front of us, or we would have walked right to him. He caused a considerable revision of our travel plans. Not wholly prepared to follow the advice of Andy Russell, I asked Fedeler what one should do if a bear were to charge. He said, "Take off your pack and throw it into the bear's path, then crawl away, and hope the pack will distract the bear. But there is no good thing to do, really. It's just not a situation to be in."

We made a hundred-and-forty-degree turn from the course we had been following and went up the shoulder of the hill through ever-thickening brush, putting distance behind us in good position with the wind. For a time, we waded through hip-deep willow, always making our way uphill, and the going may have been difficult, but I didn't notice. There was adrenalin to spare in my bloodstream. I felt that I was floating, climbing with ease, like Hession. I also had expectations now that another bear, in the thick brush, might come rising up from any quarter. We broke out soon into a swale of blueberries. Hession and Fedeler, their nonchalance refreshed, sat down to eat, paused to graze. The berries were sweet and large.

"I can see why he's here," Hession said.

"These berries are so big."

"Southern exposure."

"He may not be the only one."

"They can be anywhere."

"It's amazing to me," Fedeler said. "So large an animal, living up here in this country. It's amazing what keeps that big body alive." Fedeler went on eating the blueberries with no apparent fear of growing fat. The barren-ground bear digs a lot of roots, he said—the roots of milk vetch, for example, and Eskimo potatoes. The bear, coming out of his den into the snows of May, goes down into the river bottoms, where over-wintered berries are first revealed. Wolf kills are down there, too. By the middle of June, his diet is almost wholly vegetable. He eats willow buds, sedges, cotton-grass tussocks. In the cycle of his year, roots and plants are eighty per cent of what he eats, and even when the salmon are running he does not sate himself on them alone but forages much of the time for berries. In the fall, he unearths not only roots but ground squirrels and lemmings. It is indeed remarkable how large he grows on the provender of his yearly cycle, for on this Arctic barren ground he has to work much harder than the brown bears of southern Alaska, which line up along foaming rivers—hip to hip, like fishermen in New Jersey—taking forty-pound king salmon in their jaws as if they were nibbling feed from a barnyard trough. When the caribou are in fall migration, moving down the Salmon valley toward the Kobuk, the bear finishes up his year with one of them. Then, around the first of November, he may find a cave or, more likely, digs out a cavern in a mountainside. If he finds a natural cave, it may be full of porcupines. He kicks them out, and—extending his curious relationship with this animal—will cushion his winter bed with many thousands of their turds. If, on the other hand, he digs his den, he sends earth flying out behind him and makes a shaft that goes upward into the side of the mountain. At the top of the shaft, he excavates a shelf-like cavern. When the outside entrance is plugged with debris, the shaft becomes a column of still air, insulating the upper chamber, trapping the bear's body heat. On a bed of dry vegetation, he lays himself out like a dead pharaoh in a pyramid. But he does not truly hibernate. He just lies there. His mate of the summer, in her den somewhere, will give birth during winter to a cub or two—virtually hairless, blind, weighing about a pound. But the male has nothing to do. His heart rate goes down as low as eight beats a minute. He sleeps and wakes, and sleeps again. He may decide to get up and go out. But that is rare. He may even stay out, which is rarer—to give up denning for that winter and roam his frozen range. If he does this, sooner or later he will find a patch of open water in an otherwise frozen river, and in refreshing himself he will no doubt wet his fur. Then he rolls in the snow, and the fur acquires a thick plate of ice, which is less disturbing to the animal than to the forest Eskimo, who has for ages feared—feared most of all—the "winter bear." Arrows broke against the armoring ice, and it can be heavy enough to stop a bullet.

We moved on now, in continuing retreat, and approached the steep incline of the tributary valley we'd been skirting when the bear rewrote our plans. We meant to put the valley between us and him and reschedule ourselves on the other side. It was in fact less a valley than an extremely large ravine, which plunged maybe eight hundred feet, and then rose up an even steeper incline some fifteen hundred feet on the other side, toward the top of which the bushy vegetation ceased growing. The walking looked promising on the ridge beyond.

I had hoped we might see a den site, and this might have been the place. It had all the requisites but one. It was a steep hillside with southern exposure, and was upgrown with a hell of alders and willows. Moreover, we were on the south side of the Brooks Range divide, which is where most of the dens are. But we were not high enough. We were at something under two thousand feet, and bears in this part of Alaska like to den much higher than that. They want the very best drainage. One way to become a "winter bear" is to wake up in a flooded den.

The willow-alder growth was so dense and high that as we went down the hillside we could see no farther than a few hundred yards ahead. It was wet in there from the recent rain. We broke our way forward with the help of gravity, crashing noisily, all but trapped in the thicket. It was a patch of jungle, many acres of jungle, with stems a foot apart and as thick as our arms, and canopies more than twelve feet high. This was bear habitat, the sort of place bears like better than people do. Our original choice had been wise—to skirt this ravine-valley—but now we were in it and without choice.

"This is the sort of place to come upon one of them unexpectedly," Hession said.

"And there is no going back," Fedeler said. "You can't walk uphill in this stuff."

"Good point," Hession said.

I might have been a little happier if I had been in an uninstrumented airplane in heavy mountain cloud. We thunked and crashed for fifteen minutes and finally came out at the tributary stream. Our approach flushed a ptarmigan, willow ptarmigan; and grayling—at sight of us—shot around in small, cold pools. The stream was narrow, and alders pressed over it from either side. We drank, and rested, and looked up the slope in front of us, which must have had an incline of fifty degrees. The ridge at the top looked extremely far away. Resting, I became aware of a considerable ache in my legs and a blister on one of my heels. On the way uphill we became separated, Hession angling off to the right, Fedeler and I to the left. We groped for handholds among bushes that protruded from the flaky schist, and pulled ourselves up from ledge to ledge. The adrenalin was gone, and my legs were turning to stone. I was ready to dig a den and get in it. My eyes kept addressing the ridgeline, far above. If eyes were hands they could have pulled me there. Then, suddenly, from far below, I saw Jack Hession lightly ambling along the ridge—in his tennis shoes, in his floppy cotton hat. He was looking around, killing time, waiting up for us.

Things seemed better from the ridge. The going would be level for a time. We sat down and looked back, to the north, across the deep tributary valley, and with my monocular tried to glass the grazing bear. No sight or sign of him. Above us now was a broadly conical summit, and spread around its western flank was a mile, at least, of open alpine tundra. On a contour, we headed south across it—high above, and two miles east of, the river. We saw what appeared to be a cairn on the next summit south, and decided to go to it and stand on it and see if we could guess—in relation to our campsite—where we were. Now the walking felt good again. We passed a large black pile of grizzly scat. "When it's steaming, that's when you start looking around for a tree," Hession said. This particular scat had sent up its last vapors many days before. Imagining myself there at such a time, though, I looked around idly for a tree. The nearest one behind us that was of more than dwarf or thicket stature was somewhere in Lapland. Ahead of us, however, across the broad dome of tundra, was a dark stand of white spruce, an extremity of the North American forest, extending toward us. The trees were eight hundred yards away. Black bears, frightened, sometimes climb trees. Grizzlies almost never climb trees.

At seven in the evening, after wading up a slope of medium to heavy brush, we came out onto more smooth tundra and reached the hilltop of the apparent cairn. It was a rock outcropping, and we sat on it in bright sunshine and looked at the circumvallate mountains. A great many of them had such outcroppings projecting from their ridges, and they much resembled the cairns shepherds build on bald summits in Scotland. For that matter, they suggested the cairns—closer to the Kobuk—that forest Eskimos once used in methodical slaughter of caribou. The cairns were built on the high tundra in a great V, open end to the north, and they served as a funnel for the southbound herd. To the approaching caribou, the cairns were meant to suggest Eskimos, and to reinforce the impression Eskimos spaced themselves between cairns. At the point of the V, as many caribou as were needed were killed and the rest were let through.

Before us now, lying on the tundra that stretched away toward the river we saw numerous caribou antlers. The Arctic herd cyclically chooses various passes and valleys in making its way south across the range, and of late has been favoring, among other places, the Salmon and Hunt River drainages. Bleached white, the antlers protruded from the tundra like the dead branches of buried trees. When the forest Eskimo of old went to stalk the grizzly bear, he carried in his hand a spear, the tip of which was made from bear bone or, more often, from the antler of the caribou. A bearskin was the door of an Eskimo's home if the occupant had ever killed a bear, for it symbolized the extraordinary valor of the hunter within. When the man drew close and the bear stood on its hind legs, the man ran under this cave of flesh and set the shaft of the spear firmly on the ground, then ducked out from under the swinging, explosive paws. The bear lunged forward onto the spear and died.

Eskimo knife handles were also made from caribou antlers, and icepicks to penetrate the surface of the river, and sinkers for the bottoms of willow-bark seines, and wood-splitting wedges, and arrowheads. All caribou, male and female, grow antlers. The horns of sheep, cattle, buffalo consist of extremely dense, compactly matted hair. The antler of the caribou is calcareous. It is hard bone, with the strength of wrought iron. Moving downhill and south across the tundra, we passed through groves of antlers. It was as if the long filing lines of the spring migration had for some reason paused here for shedding to occur. The antlers, like the bear, implied the country. Most were white, gaunt, chalky. I picked up a younger one, though, that was recently shed and was dark, like polished brown marble. It was about four feet along the beam and perfect in form. Hession found one like it. We set them on our shoulders and moved on down the hill, intent to take them home.

We headed for the next of the riverine mountains, where we planned to descend and—if our calculations were accurate—meet the river at the campsite. The river, far below us, now and again came into view as we walked abreast over open tundra. Fedeler, even more alert than usual, now stopped and, as before, touched my arm. He pointed toward the river. If a spruce needle had been floating on the water there, Fedeler would have seen it. We saw in an instant that we had miscalculated and were heading some miles beyond the campsite and would have come eventually to the river not knowing—upstream or downstream—which way to go. Fedeler was pointing toward a gravel bar, a thin column of smoke, minute human figures near the smoke, and the podlike whiteness of the metal canoe.

Another two miles, descending, and we were barefoot in the river, with pink hot feet turning anesthetically cold. We crossed slowly. The three others were by the campfire. On the grill were grayling and a filleted Arctic char. The air was cool now, nearing fifty, and we ate the fish, and beef stew, and strawberries, and drank hot chocolate. After a time, Hession said, "That was a good walk. That was some of the easiest hiking you will ever find in Alaska."

We drew our route on the map and figured the distance at fourteen miles. John Kauffmann, tapping his pipe on a stone, said, "That's a lot for Alaska."

We sat around the campfire for at least another hour. We talked of rain and kestrels, oil and antlers, the height and the headwaters of the river. Neither Hession nor Fedeler once mentioned the bear.

When I got into my sleeping bag, though, and closed my eyes, there he was, in color, on the side of the hill. The vision was indelible, but fear was not what put it there. More, it was a sense of sheer luck at having chosen in the first place to follow Fedeler and Hession up the river and into the hills—a memento not so much of one moment as of the entire circuit of the long afternoon. It was a vision of a whole land, with an animal in it. This was his country, clearly enough. To be there was to be incorporated, in however small a measure, into its substance—his country, and if you wanted to visit it you had better knock.

> His association with other animals is a mixture of enterprising action, almost magnanimous acceptance, and just plain willingness to ignore. There is great strength and pride combined with a strong mixture of inquisitive curiosity in the make-up of grizzly character. This curiosity is what makes trouble when men penetrate into country where they are not known to the bear. The grizzly can be brave and sometimes downright brash. He can be secretive and very retiring. He can be extremely cunning and also powerfully aggressive. Whatever he does, his actions match his surroundings and the circumstance of the moment. No wonder that meeting him on his mountain is a momentous event, imprinted on one's mind for life.

•   •   •

What had struck me most in the isolation of this wilderness was an abiding sense of paradox. In its raw, convincing emphasis on the irrelevance of the visitor, it was forcefully, importantly repellent. It was no less strongly attractive—with a beauty of nowhere else, composed in turning circles. If the wild land was indifferent, it gave a sense of difference. If at moments it was frightening, requiring an effort to put down the conflagrationary imagination, it also augmented the touch of life. This was not a dare with nature. This was nature.

The bottoms of the Kleppers were now trellised with tape. Pourchot was smoothing down a final end. Until recently, he had been an avocational parachutist, patterning the sky in star formation with others as he fell. He had fifty-one jumps, all of them in Colorado. But he had started waking up in the night with cold sweats, so—with two small sons now—he had sold his jumping gear. With the money, he bought a white-water kayak and climbing rope. "You're kind of on your own, really. You run the risk," he was saying. "I haven't seen any bear incidents, for example. I've never had any bear problems. I've never carried a gun. Talk to ten people and you get ten different bear-approach theories. Some carry flares. Ed Bailey, in Fish and Wildlife, shoots pencil flares into the ground before approaching bears. They go away. Bear attacks generally occur in road-system areas anyway. Two, maybe four people die a year. Some years more than others. Rarely will a bear attack a person in a complete wilderness like this."

Kauffmann said, "Give a grizzly half a chance and he'll avoid you."

Fedeler had picked cups of blueberries to mix into our breakfast pancakes. Finishing them, we prepared to go. The sun was coming through. The rain was gone. The morning grew bright and warm. Pourchot and I got into the canoe, which, for all its heavy load, felt light. Twenty minutes downriver, we had to stop for more repairs to the Kleppers, but afterward the patchwork held. With higher banks, longer pools, the river was running deeper. The sun began to blaze.

Rounding bends, we saw sculpins, a pair of great horned owls, mergansers, Taverner's geese. We saw ravens and a gray jay. Coming down a long, deep, green pool, we looked toward the riffle at the lower end and saw an approaching grizzly. He was young, possibly four years old, and not much over four hundred pounds. He crossed the river. He studied the salmon in the riffle. He did not see, hear, or smell us. Our three boats were close together, and down the light current on the flat water we drifted toward the fishing bear.

He picked up a salmon, roughly ten pounds of fish, and, holding it with one paw, he began to whirl it around his head. Apparently, he was not hungry, and this was a form of play. He played sling-the-salmon. With his claws embedded near the tail, he whirled the salmon and then tossed it high, end over end. As it fell, he scooped it up and slung it around his head again, lariat salmon, and again he tossed it into the air. He caught it and heaved it high once more. The fish flopped to the ground. The bear turned away, bored. He began to move upstream by the edge of the river. Behind his big head his hump projected. His brown fur rippled like a field under wind. He kept coming. The breeze was behind him. He had not yet seen us. He was romping along at an easy walk. As he came closer to us, we drifted slowly toward him. The single Klepper, with John Kauffmann in it, moved up against a snagged stick and broke it off. The snap was light, but enough to stop the bear. Instantly, he was motionless and alert, remaining on his four feet and straining his eyes to see. We drifted on toward him. At last, we arrived in his focus. If we were looking at something we had rarely seen before, God help him so was he. If he was a tenth as awed as I was, he could not have moved a muscle, which he did, now, in a hurry that was not pronounced but nonetheless seemed inappropriate to his status in the situation. He crossed low ground and went up a bank toward a copse of willow. He stopped there and faced us again. Then, breaking stems to pieces, he went into the willows.

We drifted to the rip, and down it past the mutilated salmon. Then we came to another long flat surface, spraying up the light of the sun. My bandanna, around my head, was nearly dry. I took it off, and trailed it in the river.

Tom Wolfe / *The Right Stuff* 1979

*"The me decade," "radical chic," "the right stuff"—these are a few of the
phrases that Tom Wolfe has introduced into the American vocabulary. A genius
at deciphering an attitude or an entire ideology from the slightest stylistic quirk
or idiom, Wolfe is without a doubt one of the major interpreters of contemporary American culture.*

*Born in 1931, Wolfe grew up in Richmond, Virginia. He graduated from
Washington and Lee University and then went on to receive a Ph.D. in American Studies at Yale. He spent several years as a newspaper reporter and in
1980 received the Columbia Journalism Award for distinguished service in the
field of journalism. Wolfe's first book,* The Kandy-Kolored Tangerine-Flake
Streamline Baby, *appeared in 1965 and established him at once as a leading
critic of popular culture. His other books include* The Electric Kool-Aid Acid
Test *(1968),* The Pump House Gang *(1968),* Radical Chic and Mau-Mauing the
Flak Catchers *(1970),* The Painted Word *(1975), and* From Bauhaus to Our
House *(1981).* Rolling Stone *magazine, which published portions of* The Right
Stuff, *began serializing Wolfe's first novel,* The Bonfire of the Vanities, *in 1984.*

*The following account of test pilot Chuck Yeager is an excerpt from
Wolfe's best-known book,* The Right Stuff *(1979), which won the American
Book Award for nonfiction.*

YEAGER

Anyone who travels very much on airlines in the United States soon gets to know
the voice of *the airline pilot* . . . coming over the intercom . . . with a particular
drawl, a particular folksiness, a particular down-home calmness that is so exaggerated it begins to parody itself (nevertheless!—it's reassuring) . . . the voice
that tells you, as the airliner is caught in thunderheads and goes bolting up and
down a thousand feet at a single gulp, to check your seat belts because "it might
get a little choppy" . . . the voice that tells you (on a flight from Phoenix preparing for its final approach into Kennedy Airport, New York, just after dawn):
"Now, folks, uh . . . this is the captain . . . ummmm . . . We've got a little
ol' red light up here on the control panel that's tryin' to tell us that the *land*in'
gears're not . . . uh . . . *lock*in' into position when we lower 'em . . . Now
. . . *I* don't believe that little ol' red light knows what its *talk*in' about—I believe
it's that little ol' red *light* that iddn' workin' right" . . . faint chuckle, long pause,
as if to say, *I'm not even sure all this is really worth going into—still, it may
amuse you* . . . "But . . . I guess to play it by the rules, we oughta *hum*or that
little ol' light . . . so we're gonna take her down to about, oh, two or three hundred
feet over the runway at Kennedy, and the folks down there on the ground are gonna
see if they caint give us a *vis*ual inspection of those ol' landin' gears"—with which
he is obviously on intimate ol' buddy terms, as with every other working part of
this mighty ship—"and if I'm right . . . they're gonna tell us everything is co-
pa*cet*ic all the way aroun' an' we'll jes take her on in" . . . and, after a couple
of low passes over the field, the voice returns: "Well, folks, those folks down
there on the ground—it must be too early for 'em or somethin'—I 'spect they still
got the *sleep*ers in their eyes . . . 'cause they say they caint tell if those ol' landin' gears are all the way down or not . . . But, you know, up here in the cockpit
we're convinced they're all the way down, so we're jes gonna take her on in . . .
And oh" . . . *(I almost forgot)* . . . "while we take a little swing out over the

ocean an' empty some of that surplus fuel we're not gonna be needin' anymore—
that's what you might be seein' comin' out of the wings—our lovely little ladies
. . . if they'll be so kind . . . they're gonna go up and down the aisles and show
yu how we do what we call 'assumin' the position' " . . . another faint chuckle
(*We do this often, and it's so much fun, we even have a funny little name for it*)
. . . and the stewardesses, a bit grimmer, by the looks of them, than *that voice*,
start telling the passengers to take their glasses off and take the ballpoint pens and
other sharp objects out of their pockets, and they show them *the position*, with the
head lowered . . . while down on the field at Kennedy the little yellow emergency trucks start roaring across the field—and even though in your pounding heart
and your sweating palms and your broiling brainpan you *know* this is a critical
moment in your life, you still can't quite bring yourself to be*lieve* it, because if it
were . . . how could *the captain*, the man who knows the actual situation most
intimately . . . how could he keep on drawlin' and chucklin' and driftin' and lol-
lygaggin' in that particular voice of his—

Well!—who doesn't know that voice! And who can forget it!—even after he is
proved right and the emergency is over.

That particular voice may sound vaguely Southern or Southwestern, but it is
specifically Appalachian in origin. It originated in the mountains of West Virginia,
in the coal country, in Lincoln County, so far up in the hollows that, as the saying
went, "they had to pipe in daylight." In the late 1940's and early 1950's this up-
hollow voice drifted down from on high, from over the high desert of California,
down, down, down, from the upper reaches of the Brotherhood into all phases of
American aviation. It was amazing. It was *Pygmalion* in reverse. Military pilots
and then, soon, airline pilots, from Maine and Massachusetts and the Dakotas and
Oregon and everywhere else began to talk in that poker-hollow West Virginia drawl,
or as close to it as they could bend their native accents. It was the drawl of the
most righteous of all the possessors of the right stuff: Chuck Yeager.

Yeager had started out as the equivalent, in the Second World War, of the legendary Frank Luke of the 27th Aero Squadron in the First. Which is to say, he
was the boondocker, the boy from the back country, with only a high-school education, no credentials, no cachet or polish of any sort, who took off the feed-
store overalls and put on a uniform and climbed into an airplane and lit up the
skies over Europe.

Yeager grew up in Hamlin, West Virginia, a town on the Mud River not far
from Nitro, Hurricane Whirlwind, Salt Rock, Mud, Sod, Crum, Leet, Dollie, Ruth,
and Alum Creek. His father was a gas driller (drilling for natural gas in the coal-
fields), his older brother was a gas driller, and he would have been a gas driller
had he not enlisted in the Army Air Force in 1941 at the age of eighteen. In 1943,
at twenty he became a flight officer, i.e., a non-com who was allowed to fly, and
went to England to fly fighter planes over France and Germany. Even in the tumult of the war Yeager.was somewhat puzzling to a lot of other pilots. He was a
short, wiry, but muscular little guy with dark curly hair and a tough-looking face
that seemed (to strangers) to be saying: "You best not be lookin' me in the eye,
you peckerwood, or I'll put four more holes in your nose." But that wasn't what
was puzzling. What was puzzling was the way Yeager talked. He seemed to talk
with some older forms of English elocution, syntax, and conjugation that had been
preserved uphollow in the Appalachians. There were people up there who never
said they disapproved of anything, they said: "I don't hold with it." In the present
tense they were willing to *help* out, like anyone else; but in the past tense they
only *holped*. "H'it weren't nothin' I hold with, but I holped him out with it, any-
ways."

In his first eight missions, at the age of twenty, Yeager shot down two German
fighters. On his ninth he was shot down over German-occupied French territory,

suffering flak wounds; he bailed out, was picked up by the French underground, which smuggled him across the Pyrenees into Spain disguised as a peasant. In Spain he was jailed briefly, then released, whereupon he made it back to England and returned to combat during the Allied invasion of France. On October 12, 1944, Yeager took on and shot down five German fighter planes in succession. On November 6, flying a propeller-driven P-51 Mustang, he shot down one of the new jet fighters the Germans had developed, the Messerschmitt-262, and damaged two more, and on November 20 he shot down four FW-190s. It was a true Frank Luke-style display of warrior fury and personal prowess. By the end of the war he had thirteen and a half kills. He was twenty-two years old.

In 1946 and 1947 Yeager was trained as a test pilot at Wright Field in Dayton. He amazed his instructors with his ability at stunt-team flying, not to mention the unofficial business of hassling. That plus his up-hollow drawl had everybody saying, ''He's a natural-born stick 'n' rudder man.'' Nevertheless, there was something extraordinary about it when a man so young, with so little experience 'in flight test, was selected to go to Muroc Field in California for the X-1 project'.

Muroc was up in the high elevations of the Mojave Desert. It looked like some fossil landscape that had long since been left behind by the rest of terrestrial evolution. It was full of huge dry lake beds, the biggest being Rogers Lake. Other than sagebrush the only vegetation was Joshua trees, twisted freaks of the plant world that looked like a cross between cactus and Japanese bonsai. They had a dark petrified green color and horribly crippled branches. At dusk the Joshua trees stood out in silhouette on the fossil wasteland like some arthritic nightmare. In the summer the temperature went up to 110 degrees as a matter of course, and the dry lake beds were covered in sand, and there would be windstorms and sandstorms right out of a Foreign Legion movie. At night it would drop to near freezing, and in December it would start raining, and the dry lakes would fill up with a few inches of water, and some sort of putrid prehistoric shrimps would work their way up from out of the ooze, and sea gulls would come flying in a hundred miles or more from the ocean, over the mountains, to gobble up these squirming little throwbacks. A person had to see it to believe it: flocks of sea gulls wheeling around in the air out in the middle of the high desert in the dead of winter and grazing on antediluvian crustaceans in the primordial ooze.

When the wind blew the few inches of water back and forth across the lake beds, they became absolutely smooth and level. And when the water evaporated in the spring, and the sun baked the ground hard, the lake beds became the greatest natural landing fields ever discovered, and also the biggest, with miles of room for error. That was highly desirable, given the nature of the enterprise at Muroc.

Besides the wind, sand, tumbleweed, and Joshua trees, there was nothing at Muroc except for two quonset-style hangars, side by side, a couple of gasoline pumps, a single concrete runway, a few tarpaper shacks, and some tents. The officers stayed in the shacks marked ''barracks,'' and lesser souls stayed in the tents and froze all night and fried all day. Every road into the property had a guardhouse on it manned by soldiers. The enterprise the Army had undertaken in this godforsaken place was the development of supersonic jet and rocket planes.

At the end of the war the Army had discovered that the Germans not only had the world's first jet fighter but also a rocket plane that had gone 596 miles an hour in tests. Just after the war a British jet, the Gloster Meteor, jumped the official world speed record from 469 to 606 in a single day. The next great plateau would be Mach 1, the speed of sound, and the Army Air Force considered it crucial to achieve it first.

The speed of sound, Mach 1, was known (thanks to the work of the physicist Ernst Mach) to vary at different altitudes, temperatures, and wind speeds. On a calm 60-degree day at sea level it was about 760 miles an hour, while at 40,000 feet, where the temperature would be at least sixty below, it was about 660 miles an hour. Evil and baffling things happened in the transonic zone, which began at about .7 Mach. Wind tunnels choked out at such velocities. Pilots who approached the speed of sound in dives reported that the controls would lock or "freeze" or even alter their normal functions. Pilots had crashed and died because they couldn't budge the stick. Just last year Geoffrey de Havilland, son of the famous British aircraft designer and builder, had tried to take one of his father's DH 108s to Mach 1. The ship started buffeting and then disintegrated, and he was killed. This led engineers to speculate that the g-forces became infinite at Mach 1, causing the aircraft to implode. They started talking about "the sonic wall" and "the sound barrier."

So this was the task that a handful of pilots, engineers, and mechanics had at Muroc. The place was utterly primitive, nothing but bare bones, bleached tarpaulins, and corrugated tin rippling in the heat with caloric waves; and for an ambitious young pilot it was perfect. Muroc seemed like an outpost on the dome of the world, open only to a righteous few, closed off to the rest of humanity, including even the Army Air Force brass of command control, which was at Wright Field. The commanding officer at Muroc was only a colonel, and his superiors at Wright did not relish junkets to the Muroc rat shacks in the first place. But to pilots this prehistoric throwback of an airfield became . . . shrimp heaven! the rat-shack plains of Olympus!

Low Rent Septic Tank Perfection . . . yes; and not excluding those traditional essentials for the blissful hot young pilot: Flying & Drinking and Drinking & Driving.

Just beyond the base, to the southwest, there was a rickety wind-blown 1930's style establishment called Pancho's Fly Inn, owned, run, and bartended by a woman named Pancho Barnes. Pancho Barnes wore tight white sweaters and tight pants, after the mode of Barbara Stanwyck in *Double Indemnity*. She was only forty-one when Yeager arrived at Muroc, but her face was so weatherbeaten, had so many hard miles on it, that she looked older, especially to the young pilots at the base. She also shocked the pants off them with her vulcanized tongue. Everybody she didn't like was an old bastard or a sonofabitch. People she liked were old bastards and sonsabitches, too. "I tol' 'at ol' bastard to get 'is ass on over here and I'd g'im a drink." But Pancho Barnes was anything but Low Rent. She was the granddaughter of the man who designed the old Mount Lowe cable-car system, Thaddeus S. C. Lowe. Her maiden name was Florence Leontine Lowe. She was brought up in San Marino, which adjoined Pasadena and was one of Los Angeles' wealthiest suburbs, and her first husband—she was married four times—was the pastor of the Pasadena Episcopal Church, the Rev. C. Rankin Barnes. Mrs. Barnes seemed to have few of the conventional community interests of a Pasadena matron. In the late 1920's, by boat and plane, she ran guns for Mexican revolutionaries and picked up the nickname Pancho. In 1930 she broke Amelia Earhart's airspeed record for women. Then she barnstormed around the country as the featured performer of "Pancho Barnes's Mystery Circus of the Air." She always greeted her public in jodhpurs and riding boots, a flight jacket, a white scarf, and a white sweater that showed off her terrific Barbara Stanwyck chest. Pancho's desert Fly Inn had an airstrip, a swimming pool, a dude ranch corral, plenty of acreage for horseback riding, a big old guest house for the lodgers, and a connecting building that was the bar and restaurant. In the barroom the floors, the tables, the chairs, the walls, the beams, the bar were of the sort known as extremely weather-beaten, and the screen doors kept banging. Nobody putting together such a place for a movie about flying in the old days would ever dare make it as dilapidated and generally go-to-hell as it actually was. Behind the bar were many pictures of airplanes and pilots, lavishly autographed and inscribed, badly framed and crookedly hung. There was an old piano that had been dried out and cracked to the point of hopeless desiccation. On a good night a huddle of drunken aviators could be heard trying to bang, slosh, and navigate their way through old Cole Porter tunes. On average nights the tunes were not that good to start with. When the screen door banged and a man walked through the door into the saloon, every eye in the place checked him out. If he wasn't known as somebody who had something to do with flying at Muroc, he would be eyed like some lame goddamned mouseshit sheepherder from *Shane*.

The plane the Air Force wanted to break the sound barrier with was called the X-1. The Bell Aircraft Corporation had built it under an Army contract. The core of the ship was a rocket of the type first developed by a young Navy inventor, Robert Truax, during the war. The fuselage was shaped like a 50-caliber bullet— an object that was known to go supersonic smoothly. Military pilots seldom drew major test assignments; they went to highly paid civilians working for the aircraft corporations. The prime pilot for the X-1 was a man whom Bell regarded as the best of the breed. This man looked like a movie star. He looked like a pilot from out of *Hell's Angels*. And on top of everything else there was his name: Slick Goodlin.

The idea in testing the X-1 was to nurse it carefully into the transonic zone, up to seven-tenths, eight-tenths, nine-tenths the speed of sound (.7 Mach, .8 Mach, .9 Mach) before attempting the speed of sound itself, Mach 1, even though Bell and the Army already knew the X-1 had the rocket power to go to Mach 1 and beyond, if there *was* any *beyond*. The consensus of aviators and engineers, after Geoffrey de Havilland's death, was that the speed of sound was an absolute, like the firmness of the earth. The sound barrier was a farm you could buy in the sky. So Slick Goodlin began to probe the transonic zone in the X-1, going up to .8 Mach. Every time he came down he'd have a riveting tale to tell. The buffeting, it was so fierce—and the listeners, their imaginations aflame, could practically see poor Geoffrey de Havilland disintegrating in midair. And the goddamned aero-dynamics—and the listeners got a picture of a man in balloon pumps skidding across a sheet of ice, pursued by bears. A controversy arose over just how much bonus Slick Goodlin should receive for assaulting the dread Mach 1 itself. Bonuses for contract test pilots were not unusual; but the figure of $150,000 was now bruited about. The army balked, and Yeager got the job. He took it for $283 a month, or $3,396 a year; which is to say, his regular Army captain's pay.

The only trouble they had with Yeager was in holding him back. On his first powered flight in the X-1 he immediately executed an unauthorized zero-g roll with a full load of rocket fuel, then stood the ship on its tail and went up to .85 Mach in a vertical climb, also unauthorized. On subsequent flights, at speeds between .85 Mach and .9 Mach, Yeager ran into most known airfoil problems—loss of elevator, aileron, and rudder control, heavy trim pressures, Dutch rolls, pitching and buffeting, the lot—yet was convinced, after edging over .9 Mach, that this would all get better, not worse, as you reached Mach 1. The attempt to push beyond Mach 1—"breaking the sound barrier"—was set for October 14, 1947. Not being an engineer, Yeager didn't believe the "barrier" existed.

Lewis Thomas / How to Fix the Premedical Curriculum   1979

Lewis Thomas's essays reveal a first-rate mind in motion—unassuming, alert, endlessly curious, eager to explore and know the world in its own terms. A physician, professor, and award-winning essayist, Thomas was born in Flushing, New York, in 1913. He has taught medicine at the University of Minnesota and has served as the dean of the Yale Medical School. He is currently the chancellor of the Memorial Sloan-Kettering Cancer Center in New York.

The author of several hundred scientific articles, Thomas began writing occasional essays in 1970, when he first contributed to the prestigious New England Journal of Medicine. *His first collection of essays,* The Lives of a Cell: Notes of a Biology Watcher *(1974), won the National Book Award in Arts and Letters and sold more than 300,000 hardcover copies, making it one of the most popular books of its kind. His second collection of essays,* The Medusa and the Snail *(1979), also quickly joined the best-seller lists. His most recent books are* The Youngest Science: Notes of a Medicine Watcher *(1983) and a third collection of essays,* Late Night Thoughts on Listening to Mahler's Ninth Symphony *(1983).*

Described as "quite possibly the best essayist on science now working anywhere in the world," Thomas has mastered both the art of the essay and the habit of viewing human behavior in biological terms and the world of biology in human terms. His insightful prose elegantly reaffirms his belief in the fundamental unity of life everywhere.

The influence of the modern medical school on liberal-arts education in this country over the last decade has been baleful and malign, nothing less. The admission policies of the medical schools are at the root of the trouble. If something is not done quickly to change these, all the joy of going to college will have been destroyed, not just for that growing majority of undergraduate students who draw breath only to become doctors, but for everyone else, all the students, and all the faculty as well.

The medical schools used to say they wanted applicants as broadly educated as possible, and they used to mean it. The first two years of medical school were given over entirely to the basic biomedical sciences, and almost all entering students got their first close glimpse of science in those years. Three chemistry courses, physics, and some sort of biology were all that were required from the colleges. Students were encouraged by the rhetoric of medical-school catalogues to major in such nonscience disciplines as history, English, philosophy. Not many did so; almost all premedical students in recent generations have had their majors in chemistry or biology. But anyway, they were authorized to spread around in other fields if they wished.

There is still some talk in medical deans' offices about the need for general culture, but nobody really means it, and certainly the premedical students don't believe it. They concentrate on science.

They concentrate on science with a fury, and they live for grades. If there are courses in the humanities that can be taken without risk to class standing they will line up for these, but they will not get into anything tough except science. The so-called social sciences have become extremely popular as stand-ins for traditional learning.

The atmosphere of the liberal-arts college is being poisoned by premedical students. It is not the fault of the students, who do not start out as a necessarily bad lot. They behave as they do in the firm belief that if they behave any otherwise they won't get into medical school.

I have a suggestion, requiring for its implementation the following announcement from the deans of all the medical schools: henceforth, any applicant who is self-labeled as a "premed," distinguishable by his course selection from his classmates, will have his dossier placed in the third stack of three. Membership in a "premedical society" will, by itself, be grounds for rejection. Any college possessing something called a "premedical curriculum," or maintaining offices for people called "premedical advisers," will be excluded from recognition by the medical schools.

Now as to grades and class standing. There is obviously no way of ignoring these as criteria for acceptance, but it is the grades *in general* that should be weighed. And, since so much of the medical-school curriculum is, or ought to be, narrowly concerned with biomedical science, more attention should be paid to the success of students in other, nonscience disciplines before they are admitted, in order to assure the scope of intellect needed for a physician's work.

Hence, if there are to be MCAT tests, the science part ought to be made the briefest, and weigh the least. A knowledge of literature and languages ought to be the major test, and the scariest. History should be tested, with rigor.

The best thing would be to get rid of the MCAT's, once and for all, and rely instead, wholly, on the judgment of the college faculties.

You could do this if there were some central, core discipline, universal within the curricula of all the colleges, which could be used for evaluating the free range of a student's mind, his tenacity and resolve, his innate capacity for the understanding of human beings, and his affection for the human condition. For this purpose, I propose that classical Greek be restored as the centerpiece of undergraduate education. The loss of Homeric and Attic Greek from American college life was one of this century's disasters. Putting it back where it once was would quickly make up for the dispiriting impact which generations of spotty Greek in translation have inflicted on modern thought. The capacity to read Homer's language closely enough to sense the terrifying poetry in some of the lines could serve as a shrewd test for the qualities of mind and character needed in a physician.

If everyone had to master Greek, the college students aspiring to medical school would be placed on the same footing as everyone else, and their identifiability as a separate group would be blurred, to everyone's advantage. Moreover, the currently depressing drift on some campuses toward special courses for prelaw students, and even prebusiness students, might be inhibited before more damage is done.

Latin should be put back as well, but not if it is handled, as it ought to be, by the secondary schools. If Horace has been absorbed prior to college, so much for Latin. But Greek is a proper discipline for the college mind.

English, history, the literature of at least two foreign languages, and philosophy should come near the top of the list, just below Classics, as basic requirements, and applicants for medical school should be told that their grades in these courses will count more than anything else.

Students should know that if they take summer work as volunteers in the local community hospital, as ward aides or laboratory assistants, this will not necessarily be held against them, but neither will it help.

Finally, the colleges should have much more of a say about who goes on to medical school. If they know, as they should, the students who are typically bright and also respected, this judgment should carry the heaviest weight for admission. If they elect to use criteria other than numerical class standing for recommending applicants, this evaluation should hold.

The first and most obvious beneficiaries of this new policy would be the college students themselves. There would no longer be, anywhere where they could be recognized as a coherent group, the "premeds," that most detestable of all cliques eating away at the heart of the college. Next to benefit would be the college faculties, once again in possession of the destiny of their own curriculum, for better or worse. And next in line, but perhaps benefiting the most of all, are the basic-science faculties of the medical schools, who would once again be facing classrooms of students who are ready to be startled and excited by a totally new and unfamiliar body of knowledge, eager to learn, unpreoccupied by the notions of relevance that are paralyzing the minds of today's first-year medical students already so surfeited by science that they want to start practicing psychiatry in the first trimester of the first year.

Society would be the ultimate beneficiary. We could look forward to a generation of doctors who have learned as much as anyone can learn, in our colleges and universities, about how human beings have always lived out their lives. Over the bedrock of knowledge about our civilization, the medical schools could then construct as solid a structure of medical science as can be built, but the bedrock would always be there, holding everything else upright.

DISCUSSION QUESTIONS

1. What relationship does Thomas find between the study of classics and medical performance? How does he justify this course of study? Do you agree with him that doctors should study Latin, Greek, literature, foreign languages, and philosophy? What does Thomas want future physicians to know?

2. Read Thomas's essay in connection with Perri Klass's "Who Knows This Patient?" (in "Magazines") and William Carlos Williams's "The Use of Force" (in this section). Do the doctors in these selections have anything in common with Thomas's ideal physician? Explain. How does each doctor cope with a situation that requires more than medical information?

Walker Percy / Thought Experiment: The Last Donahue Show
1983

Walker Percy's first novel, The Moviegoer *(1961), showed him to be a writer seriously interested in the effects of popular media on both the individual psyche and American society. His later books have further explored this theme, especially his use of science-fiction motifs in the companion novels* Love in the Ruins *(1971) and* The Thanatos Syndrome *(1986) and in the nonfiction work* Lost in the Cosmos: The Last Self-Help Book *(1983), in which the selection below originally appeared. Throughout his fiction and essays, Percy has proposed a disturbing message: "something has gone badly wrong with America and American life." Much of what Percy finds wrong is dramatically distilled in his version of "The Phil Donahue Show."*

Percy was born in Birmingham, Alabama, in 1916. He graduated from the University of North Carolina with a degree in chemistry and received a medical degree in 1941 from the Columbia University College of Physicians and Surgeons. A few years later, after a long recovery from tuberculosis, Percy converted to Catholicism. He has lived since 1950 in Covington, Louisiana, a small town outside of New Orleans. Besides fiction, Percy has written numerous philosophical, linguistic, and critical essays, some of which have been collected in The Message in the Bottle *(1975).*

The Donahue Show is in progress on what appears at first to be an ordinary weekday morning.

The theme of this morning's show is Donahue's favorite, sex, the extraordinary variety of sexual behavior—"sexual preference," as Donahue would call it—in the country and the embattled attitudes toward it. Although Donahue has been accused of appealing to prurient interest, with a sharp eye cocked on the ratings, he defends himself by saying that he presents these controversial matters in "a mature and tasteful manner"—which he often does. It should also be noted in Donahue's defense that the high ratings of these sex-talk shows are nothing more nor less than an index of the public's intense interest in such matters.

The guests today are:

Bill, a homosexual and habitué of Buena Vista Park in San Francisco

Allen, a heterosexual businessman, married, and a connoisseur of the lunch-hour liaison

Penny, a pregnant fourteen-year-old

Dr. Joyce Friday, a well-known talk-show sex therapist, or in media jargon: a psych jockey

BILL'S STORY: Yes, I'm gay, and yes, I cruise Buena Vista. Yes, I've probably had over five hundred encounters with lovers, though I didn't keep count. So what? Whose business is it? I'm gainfully employed by a savings-and-loan company, am a trustworthy employee, and do an honest day's work. My recreation is Buena Vista Park and the strangers I meet there. I don't molest children, rape women, snatch purses. I contribute to United Way. Such encounters that I do have are by mutual consent and therefore nobody's business—except my steady live-in friend's. Naturally he's upset, but that's our problem.

DONAHUE (*striding up and down, mike in hand, boyishly inarticulate*): C'mon, Bill. What about the kids who might see you? You know what I mean. I mean— (*Opens his free hand to the audience, soliciting their understanding*)

BILL: Kids don't see me. Nobody sees me.

DONAHUE (*coming close, on the attack but good-naturedly, spoofing himself as prosecutor*): Say, Bill. I've always been curious. Is there some sort of signal? I mean, how do you and the other guy know—help me out—

BILL: Eye contact, or we show a bit of handkerchief here. (*Demonstrates*)

STUDIO AUDIENCE: (*Laughter*)

DONAHUE (*shrugging [Don't blame me, folks], pushes up nose-bridge of glasses, swings mike over to Dr. J.F. without looking at her*): How about it, Doc?

DR. J.F. (*in her not-mincing-words voice*): I think Bill's behavior is immature and depersonalizing. (*Applause from audience*) I think he ought to return to his steady live-in friend and work out a mature, creative relationship. You might be interested to know that studies have shown that stable gay couples are more creative than straights. (*Applause again, but more tentative*)

DONAHUE (*eyes slightly rolled back, swings mike to Bill*): How about it, Bill?

BILL: Yeah, right. But I still cruise Buena Vista.

DONAHUE (*pensive, head to one side, strides backward, forward, then over to Allen*): How about you, Allen?

ALLEN'S STORY: I'm a good person, I think. I work hard, am happily married, love my wife and family, also support United Way, served in the army. I drink very little, don't do drugs, have never been to a porn movie. My idea of R & R—maybe I got it in the army—is to meet an attractive woman. What a delight it is, to see a handsome mature woman, maybe in the secretarial pool, maybe in a bar, restaurant, anywhere, exchange eye contact, speak to her in a nice way, respect her as a person, invite her to join me for lunch (no sexual harassment in the office—I hate that!), have a drink, two drinks, enjoy a nice meal, talk about matters of common interest—then simply ask her—by now, both of you know whether you like each other. What a joy to go with her up in the elevator of the downtown Holiday Inn, both of you silent, relaxed, smiling, anticipating— The door of the room closes behind you. You look at her, take her hand. There's champagne already there. You stand at the window with her, touch glasses, talk— there's nothing vulgar. No closed-circuit TV. Do you know what we did last time? We turned on *La Bohème* on the FM. She loves Puccini.

DONAHUE: C'mon, Allen. What are ya handing me? What d'ya mean you're happily married? You mean *you're* happy.

ALLEN: No, no. Vera's happy, too.

AUDIENCE (*mostly women, groaning*): Nooooooo.

DONAHUE: Okay-okay, ladies, hold it a second. What do you mean, Vera's happy? I mean, how do you manage—help me out, I'm about to get in trouble— hold the letters, folks—

ALLEN: Well, actually, Vera has a low sex drive. We've always been quite inactive, even at the beginning—

AUDIENCE (*groans, jumbled protests*): Nooooo.

DONAHUE (*backing away, holding up placating free hand, backing around to Dr. J.F.*): It's all yours, Doc.

DR. J.F.: Studies have shown that open marriages can be growth experiences for both partners. However—(*groans from audience*)—*However*: It seems to me that Vera may be getting the short end here. I mean, I don't know Vera's side of it. But could I ask you this? Have you and Vera thought about reenergizing your sex life?

ALLEN: Well, ah—

DR. J.F.: Studies have shown, for example, that more stale marriages have been revived by oral sex than any other technique—

DONAHUE: Now, Doc—

DR. J.F.: Other studies have shown that mutual masturbation—

DONAHUE (*eyes rolled back*): We're running long folks, we'll be right back after this—don't go away. Oh boy. (*Lets mike slide to the hilt through his hand, closes eyes, as camera cuts away to a Maxithins commercial*)

DONAHUE: We're back. Thank the good Lord for good sponsors. (*Turns to Penny, a thin, inattentive, moping teenager, even possibly a pre-teen*): Penny?

PENNY (*chewing something*): Yeah?

DONAHUE (*solicitous, quite effectively tender*): What's with you, sweetheart?

PENNY: Well, I liked this boy a lot and he told me there was one way I could prove it—

DONAHUE: Wait a minute, Penny. Now this, your being here, is okay with your parents, right? I mean let's establish that.

PENNY: Oh, sure. They're right over there—you can ask them. (*Camera pans over audience, settling on a couple with mild, pleasant faces. It is evident that on the whole they are not displeased with being on TV*)

DONAHUE: Okay. So you mean you didn't know about taking precautions—

DR. J.F. (*breaking in*): Now, that's what I mean, Phil.

DONAHUE: What's that, Doc?

DR. J.F.: About the crying need for sex education in our schools. Now if this child—

PENNY: Oh, I had all that stuff at Ben Franklin.

DONAHUE: You mean you knew about the pill and the other, ah—

PENNY: I had been on the pill for a year.

DONAHUE (*scratching head*): I don't get it. Oh, you mean you slipped up, got careless?

PENNY: No, I did it on purpose.

DONAHUE: Did what on purpose? You mean—

PENNY: I mean I wanted to get pregnant.

DONAHUE: Why was that, Penny?

PENNY: My best friend was pregnant.

AUDIENCE: (*Groans, laughter*)

DR. J.F.: You see, Phil, that's just what I mean. This girl is no more equipped with parenting skills than a child. She is a child. I hope she realizes she still has viable options.

DONAHUE: How about it, Penny?

PENNY: No, I want to have my baby.

DONAHUE: Why?

PENNY: I think babies are neat.

DONAHUE: Oh boy.

DR. J.F.: Studies have shown that unwanted babies suffer 85 percent more child abuse and 150 percent more neuroses later in life.

DONAHUE (*striding*): Okay, now what have we got here? Wait. What's going on?

There is an interruption. Confusion at the rear of the studio. Heads turn. Three strangers, dressed outlandishly, stride down the aisle.

DONAHUE (*smacks his forehead*): What's this? What's this? Holy smoke!

Already the audience is smiling, reassured both by Donahue's comic consternation and by the exoticness of the visitors. Clearly, the audience thinks, they are part of the act.

The three strangers are indeed outlandish.

One is a tall, thin, bearded man dressed like a sixteenth-century reformer. Indeed, he could be John Calvin, in his black cloak, black cap with short bill, and snug earflaps.

The second wears the full-dress uniform of a Confederate officer. Though he is a colonel, he is quite young, surely no more than twenty-five. Clean-shaven and extremely handsome, he looks for all the world like Colonel John Pelham, Jeb Stuart's legendary artillerist. Renowned both for his gallantry in battle and for his chivalry toward women, the beau ideal of the South, he engaged in sixty artillery duels, won them all, lost not a single piece. With a single Napoleon, he held off three of Burnside's divisions in front of Fredericksburg before being ordered by Stuart to retreat.

The third is at once the most ordinary-looking and yet the strangest of all. His dress is both modern and out-of-date. In his light-colored double-breasted suit and bow tie, his two-tone shoes of the sort known in the 1940s as "perforated wing-tips," his neat above-the-ears haircut, he looks a bit like the clean old man in the Beatles movie *A Hard Day's Night,* a bit like Lowell Thomas or perhaps Harry Truman. It is as if he were a visitor from the Cosmos, from a planet ten or so light-years distant, who had formed his notion of earthlings from belated transmissions of 1950 TV, from watching the Ed Sullivan Show, old Chester Morris movies, and Morey Amsterdam. Or, to judge from his speaking voice, he could have been an inveterate listener during the Golden Age of radio and modeled his speech on that of Harry Von Zell.

DONAHUE (*backpedaling, smacking his head again*): Holy smoke! Who are these guys? (*Beseeching the audience with a slow comic pan around*)

The audience laughs, not believing for a moment that these latecomers are not one of Donahue's surprises. And yet—

DONAHUE (*snapping his fingers*): I got it. Wait'll I get that guy. It's Steve Allen, right? Refugees from the Steve Allen show, *Great Conversations?* Famous historical figures? You know, folks, they do that show in the studio down the hall. Wait'll I get that guy.

General laughter. Everybody remembers it's been done before, an old show-biz trick, like Carson barging in on Rickles during the C.P.O. Sharkey taping.

DONAHUE: Okay already. Okay, who we got here? This is Moses? General Robert E. Lee? And who is this guy? Harry Truman? Okay, fellas, let's hear it. (*Donahue, an attractive fellow, is moving about as gracefully as a dancer*)

THE STRANGER (*speaks first, in his standard radio-announcer's voice, which is not as flat as the Chicagoans who say, Hyev a hyeppy New Year*): I don't know what these two are doing here, but I came to give you a message. We've been listening to this show.

DONAHUE (*winking at the audience*): And where were you listening to us?

STRANGER: In the green room.

DONAHUE: Where else? Okay. Then what do you think? Let's hear it first from the reverend here. What did you say your name was, Reverend?

STRANGER: John Calvin.

DONAHUE: Right. Who else? Okay, we got to break here for these messages. Don't go 'way, folks. We're coming right back and sort this out, I promise.

Cut to Miss Clairol, Land O Lakes margarine, Summer's Eve, and Alpo commercials.

But when the show returns, John Calvin, who does not understand commercial breaks, has jumped the gun and is in mid-sentence.

CALVIN (*speaking in a thick French accent, not unlike Charles Boyer*): —of his redemptive sacrifice? What I have heard is licentious talk about deeds which are an abomination before God, meriting eternal damnation unless they repent and throw themselves on God's mercy. Which they are predestined to do or not to do, so why bother to discuss it?

DONAHUE (*gravely*): That's pretty heavy, Reverend.

CALVIN: Heavy? Yes, it's heavy.

DONAHUE (*mulling, scratching*): Now wait a minute, Reverend. Let's check this out. You're entitled to your religious beliefs. But what if others disagree with you in all good faith? And aside from *that* (*prosecutory again, using mike like forefinger*) what's wrong with two consenting adults expressing their sexual preference in the privacy of their bedroom or, ah, under a bush?

CALVIN: Sexual preference? (*Puzzled, he turns for help to the Confederate officer and the Cosmic stranger. They shrug*)

DONAHUE (*holding mike to the officer*): How about you, sir? Your name is—

CONFEDERATE OFFICER: Colonel John Pelham, C.S.A., commander of the horse artillery under General Stuart.

PENNY: He's cute.

AUDIENCE: (*Laughter*)

DONAHUE: You heard it all in the green room, Colonel. What 'dya think?

COLONEL PELHAM (*in a soft Alabama accent*): What do I think of what, sir?

DONAHUE: Of what you heard in the green room.

PELHAM: Of the way these folks act and talk? Well, I don't think much of it, sir.

DONAHUE: How do you mean, Colonel?

PELHAM: That's not the way people should talk or act. Where I come from, we'd call them white trash. That's no way to talk if you're a man or a woman. A gentleman knows how to treat women. He knows because he knows himself, who he is, what his obligations are. And he discharges them. But after all, you won the war, so if that's the way you want to act, that's your affair. At least, we can be sure of one thing.

DONAHUE: What's that, Colonel?

PELHAM: We're not sorry we fought.

DONAHUE: I see. Then you agree with the reverend, I mean Reverend Calvin here.

PELHAM: Well, I respect his religious beliefs. But I never thought much about religion one way or the other. In fact, I don't think religion has much to do with whether a man does right. A West Point man is an officer and a gentleman, religion or no religion. I have nothing against religion. In fact, when we studied medieval history at West Point, I remember admiring Richard Coeur de Lion and his recapturing Acre and the holy places. I remember thinking: I would have fought for him, just as I fought for Lee and the South.

Applause from the audience. Calvin puts them off, but this handsome officer reminds them of Rhett Butler–Clark Gable, or rather Ashley Wilkes–Leslie Howard.

DONAHUE (*drifting off, frowning; something is amiss but he can't put his finger on it. What is Steve Allen up to? He shakes his head, blinks*): You said it, Colonel. Okay. Where were we? (*Turning to Cosmic stranger*) We're running a little long. Can you make it brief, Harry—Mr. President, or whoever you are? Oh boy.

THE COSMIC STRANGER (*stands stiffly, hands at his sides, and begins speaking briskly, very much in the style of the late Raymond Gram Swing*): I will be brief. I have taken this human form through a holographic technique unknown to you in order to make myself understood to you.

Hear this. I have a message. Whether you heed it or not is your affair.

I have nothing to say to you about God or the Confederacy, whatever that is— I assume it is not the G2V Confederacy in this arm of the galaxy—though I could speak about God, but it is too late for you, and I am not here to do that.

We are not interested in the varieties of your sexual behavior, except as a symptom of a more important disorder.

It is this disorder which concerns us and which we do not fully understand.

As a consequence of this disorder, you are a potential threat to all civilizations in the G2V region of the galaxy. Throughout G2V you are known variously and jokingly as the Ds or the DDs or the DLs, that is, the ding-a-lings, or the death-dealers or the death-lovers. Of all the species here and in all of G2V, you are the only one which is by nature sentimental, murderous, self-hating, and self-destructive.

You are two superpowers here. The other is hopeless, has already succumbed, and is a death society. It is a living death and an agent for the propagation of death.

You are scarcely better—there is a glimmer of hope for you—but that is of no interest to me.

If the two of you destroy each other, as appears likely, it is of no consequence to us. To tell you the truth, G2V will breathe a sigh of relief.

The danger is that you may not destroy each other and that your present crude technology may constitute a threat to G2V in the future.

I am here to tell you three things: what is going to happen, what I am going to do, and what you can do.

Here's what will happen. Within the next twenty-four hours, your last war will begin. There will occur a twenty-megaton airburst one mile above the University of Chicago, the very site where your first chain reaction was produced. Every American city and town will be hit. You will lose plus-minus 160 million immediately, plus-minus 50 million later.

Here's what I am going to do. I have been commissioned to collect a specimen of DD and return with it so that we can study it toward the end of determining the nature of your disorder. Accordingly, I propose to take this young person referred to as Penny—for two reasons. One, she is perhaps still young enough not to have become hopeless. Two, she is pregnant and so we will have a chance to rear a DD in an environment free of your noxious influence. Then perhaps we can determine whether your disorder is a result of some peculiar earth environmental factor or whether you are a malignant sport, a genetic accident, the consequence of what you would have called, quite accurately, in an earlier time an MD— *mutatio diabolica,* a diabolical mutation.

Finally, here's what you can do. It is of no consequence to us whether you do it or not, because you will no longer be a threat to anyone. This is only a small gesture of goodwill to a remnant of you who may survive and who may have the chance to start all over—though you will probably repeat the same mistake. We have been students of your climatology for years. I have here a current read-out and prediction of the prevailing wind directions and fallout patterns for the next two weeks. It so happens that the place nearest you which will escape all effects of both blast and fallout is the community of Lost Cove, Tennessee. We do not anticipate a stampede to Tennessee. Our projection is that very few of you here and you out there in radio land will attach credibility to this message. But the few of you who do may wish to use this information. There is a cave there, corn, grits, collard greens, and smoked sausage in abundance.

That is the end of my message. Penny—

DONAHUE: We're long! We're long! Heavy! Steve, I'll get you for this. Oh boy. Don't forget, folks, tomorrow we got surrogate partners and a Kinsey panel— come back—you can't win 'em all—'bye! Grits. I dunno.

AUDIENCE: (*Applause*)

Cut to station break, Secure Card 65 commercial, Alpo, Carefree Panty Shields, and Mentholatum, then *The Price Is Right.*

Question: If you heard this Donahue Show, would you head for Lost Cove, Tennessee?

(*a*) Yes

(*b*) No

(CHECK ONE)

DISCUSSION QUESTIONS

1. What characteristics of the popular ''Phil Donahue Show'' has Percy chosen to parody? Why, for example, does he use the theme of sexuality as the basis for the parody? Why does he introduce stage directions and gestures—what relation have these to Percy's parody?

2. What ''disorder'' do you think the Cosmic Stranger is referring to near the end of the selection? What has been said on the show itself to help you infer something about that ''disorder''? Would you head for Lost Cove, Tennessee? Explain.

3. Refer to the ''Scripts'' section. In what ways does Percy's selection resemble a television script or transcript? In what ways does it differ?

SCRIPTS

A story can sound so good over lunch; it's so tough to get it to come out of the typewriter the same way.

CHARLTON HESTON

THE most popular writing in America is meant to be *heard*, not read. When we watch a situation comedy on television, or go to a movie, or tune in to a radio news program, we easily forget that the language we are listening to was originally *written*. Even with today's electronic media, the written word still precedes the performance; the most visually impressive movie probably started out as an idea in a scriptwriter's head. And much of what we hear on radio and television came out of a typewriter before it went over the air.

Scripts come in a variety of shapes and sizes. A filmscript, generally called a screenplay, is defined in a leading practical manual as "a written composition designed to serve as a sort of work diagram for the motion picture director."[1] Screenplays usually contain dialogue, along with a description of action and directions for camera and lighting setups. The final working script, incorporating all the changes, is often called the shooting script. Each media industry has its own script requirements and conventions. Because of time and budget constraints, television filmscripts, usually referred to as teleplays, frequently need to be more polished and "camera-ready" than movie scripts.

All scripts have one thing in common: they are intended to be read aloud. Scripts assume the primacy of the speaking voice. If a scripted word, phrase, idion, or speech rhythm sounds unnatural, a performer or director will change it. Thus, scripts are rarely treated as finished products but are constantly revised to conform as closely as possible to the inflections of the spoken voice. Of course, the voices will be affected by the particular setting or action. A movie script portraying, for example, infantrymen in Vietnam talking about recent combat would sound very different from a television anchorperson's script reporting a similar battle. The rhythm, tone, emphasis, diction, and pacing would be dramatically different, though each script might be considered professionally well crafted with respect to its overall purpose.

Scriptwriting differs from most other kinds of writing because it is largely invisible. Movie scripts, for example, are rarely published, and when they are, they tend to be read by people who have already seen the film. A good script is so closely connected to the total effect of the film that in itself it may seem barely significant as a piece of writing. A well-crafted screenplay, in other words, should not be thought of as similar to a literary drama, which can often be rewardingly read without benefit of performance. In fact, many television and movie directors react skeptically to scripts that appear too polished, that sound too much like finished plays. Such scripts may read well but not translate easily into image and action. After all, most films consist of long stretches of action without any dialogue.

Radio scripts function differently. In radio, voice counts for everything, and any silence seems unendurably long. Radio stations select performers largely based on the quality of their voice. Most radio advertising, for example, depends almost entirely on the dramatic use of highly idiosyncratic and memorable voices. Disc jockeys, though they seldom use scripts for anything other than commercials or announcements, build reputations on unique styles of delivery. In the 1930s and 1940s—during the golden age of radio—people listened to soap operas with the same avidity with which they now watch them (the old daytime melodramas were mostly sponsored by soap products—hence their name). So identifiable were the voices on these programs that listeners could easily distinguish the good guys from the bad guys on the basis of speech char-

---

1. Lewis Herman, *A Practical Manual of Screen Playwriting for Theater and Television Films* (1952; 1974).

acteristics alone. In television, where someone can be quickly characterized by physical appearance and gesture, the individual voice plays a far less dramatic role. One has only to compare a radio and a television commercial for the same product to note how differently scripts are created for each medium.

Another way to appreciate differences in techniques between two media is to study the film adaptation of a work of literature. Though critics often praise a film that stays especially close to its original text, a literal, word-by-word translation of prose into visual image is seldom feasible and not always desirable. One author who has seen her fiction transferred to the screen, Joyce Carol Oates, wonders why there should be any "enmity" between authors and screenwriters. She argues that an adaptation is really a collaborative enterprise; it is "not only a perfectly legitimate and exciting activity, it is an artistic venture of its own." The great novelist Vladimir Nabokov, after trying to turn his own masterpiece, *Lolita,* into a screenplay, was finally forced to admire the "unfaithful" though "first-rate film with magnificent actors" that the director Stanley Kubrick managed to create: "he saw my novel in one way," said Nabokov, "I saw it in another."

This section on "Scripts" includes Robert Geller's film adaptation of Ernest Hemingway's well-known short story "Soldier's Home" (which appears in the "Classics" section). A comparison of the film adaptation with the original story provides an excellent opportunity to see how an experienced screenwriter works with material never intended for film. "Soldier's Home" seems at first to have little cinematic potential. The story is very short and lacks the full narrative development a film director might prefer. More importantly, the impact of the story occurs mainly in the narrator's voice and is not fully reflected in external activity. A film that tried to be a perfect visual enactment of the original story would certainly lack the imagery and action required for compelling drama.

As even a cursory reading shows, Geller's script differs sharply from Hemingway's story. The atmosphere, the psychological tone, and the moral nuance have been retained, but Geller has made significant changes. He has introduced new characters (the flirtatious Roselle Simmons) and developed others (Mr. Krebs, merely mentioned in the short story, is physically present in the screenplay). Geller has dramatized incidents that Hemingway only alludes to (Kreb's pool playing) and has created situations not in the original story (the scene in front of the "Greek's soda shop"). Though Geller retains nearly verbatim several crucial stretches of dialogue, most of the conversation in the script was invented expressly for the film.

Like many adaptations, Geller's version of Hemingway's story depends on the careful selection of detail. The screenwriter must be particularly alert to those parts of an original text not fully developed by the author. These implicit images, characters, locations, and incidents—elements of the literary work a reader may not always consciously attend to—frequently allow the scriptwriter to work around all of the noncinematic portions of a story. An experienced scriptwriter reads literature with a keen eye for barely noticeable descriptive details that can then be integrated into the overall visual texture of the film. In "Soldier's Home," for example, Geller turns Hemingway's brief reference to the town library into a separate scene that also helps establish character and moves the plot.

The striking contrasts between Geller's screenplay and the original short story reflect, of course, the fundamental differences between prose fiction and film. Hemingway expects a reader to *hear* silently the way the narrative voice imitates the nervous consciousness of the story's main character. To duplicate this central feature of the story, Geller resorts to the contrivance of a narrative voice-over, and he fabricates dialogue that clearly articulates in actual conversation Harold Krebs's inner thoughts. Film does not easily adapt to long stretches of private consciousness. Nor can film readily convey the complexity of the narrator's attitude toward the various characters—perhaps the essential drama of serious fiction—an attitude that can be identified from the behavior of the narrative voice as irony, sympathy, satire, parody, and so on. One of the most important critical questions to ask of Hemingway's "Soldier's Home" is, what does the narrator think of Harold Krebs? How you answer that question will most likely affect how you judge the success of Geller's adaptation.

Besides differing in basic techniques, film and literature often vary widely in their assumptions about their respective audiences. A screenwriter often makes major changes in a story's plot to satisfy popular demands or to clarify a deliberate ambiguity. When Flannery O'Connor's "The Life You Save May Be Your Own" (in the "Classics" section) was adapted for television in the 1950s, the conclusion was completely changed to end the story on a happier note. That change had nothing to do with the technical problems of translating literature to the screen but was entirely a matter of how the television network felt its audience would react to the story's original ending. In "Soldier's Home," Geller introduces no such major distortions, yet the consideration of an audience still plays a significant part in shaping the script. Why, for example, does the narrator at the end of the film repeat all of Hemingway's concluding paragraph *except* the final sentence?

Originally adapted for educational television, "Soldier's Home" was intended for a relatively small viewing audience. With scripts prepared for prime-time network television, however, audience becomes an extremely important commercial calculation. Television shows live or die according to audience ratings, and scriptwriters almost always need to shape their material with respect to elaborate guidelines and specifications so that the individual episodes of a series will follow a similar format and reflect consistent values. Networks spend small fortunes testing shows on sample audiences and using attitudinal research methods to develop the final program. For example, after assessing the preliminary audience reactions in 1976 to the pilot of the enormously popular series "Charlie's Angels," the ABC research department offered such advice as the following:

> 1. Develop the three female leading characters so that they can be made more distinctive, different, and recognizable from each other. Their motives for working for Charlie should be made clear with the emphasis on a moral desire to fight crime rather than what viewers felt was a "lust for money, clothes, or a sexual attachment to their boss." . . .
>
> 4. Improve future story lines by developing plots that are more plausible and straightforward, have greater mystery and suspense, are less corny and predictable and far less contrived.
>
> 5. Improve the dialogue in future story lines by avoiding "stock cops-and-robbers phrases" and "sexual allusions or cliches" in the talk with Charlie. . . .[1]

Scriptwriters would then be expected to adhere to such guidelines when constructing new episodes.

Prime-time television often toes a fine line between social controversy and dramatic convention. Popular new shows must appear lively and original without violating the values of mass audiences. Shows that present sharp opinions—the bigotry of an Archie Bunker, for example—are careful to neutralize those opinions by having other characters on the show tactfully express alternative ideas and attitudes. Unfortunately, the fear of offending any large group fre-

---

1. *Source:* Sally Bedell, *Up the Tube* (1981).

quently results in dramatic predictability. If an elderly person on a sitcom were to make a nasty crack about the behavior of today's teenagers, the next scene would more than likely show a teenager acting in a remarkably saintly manner. The elderly person would then be pleasantly surprised and the viewing public reassured that the show was sensitive and responsive to contemporary values. Later, if the same teenager happened to complain that old people had no energy, the audience could be fairly certain that within the next few scenes remarkably spry grandparents would bounce through several rugged sets of tennis—and, of course, thrash an exhausted teenager.

An actual example of how mass entertainment will sometimes take greater risks with an audience's presumed values can be seen in "The Blackout," Richard B. Eckhaus's award-winning script for the well-known television show "The Jeffersons." The writer chose a controversial subject: looting in a black neighborhood during a citywide power failure. The script dealt openly and even ironically with racism by having the main character, who is black, arrested as a looter while trying to protect his own store. The climax of the story occurred while a frustrated George Jefferson paced a crowded jail cell vehemently protesting his innocence:

> GEORGE: I own a chain of cleanin' stores. I made my way up BY MY-SELF, and I don't need to steal. I ain't looted from nobody, and I don't belong in this dump . . . That's all I gotta say. *(George angrily sits down on the cell floor.)*
>
> SECOND INMATE *(looking down at George):* Man . . . you're really somethin'. You DO think you're too good for us, don't you?

Though George is legally in the right (he *has* been wrongfully arrested) and is morally in the right (he *is* innocent of stealing), he is nevertheless by the script's standards dramatically and culturally *wrong*. By assuming a proud, holier-than-thou stance (always a mistake in situation comedies), he has disassociated himself from his ethnic and neighborhood roots—a worse act, the script suggests, than the looting itself. The remainder of the episode shows how George must come to terms with his momentary violation of ethnic values that not everyone in the audience would necessarily share. The spectacular success of Alex Haley's *Roots* (see "Best-sellers"), however, which reached an unprecedented television audience in January 1977, the year before "The Blackout" was aired, quite clearly helped prepare viewers for George's final—though still cautious—understanding of the importance of his cultural origins.

Radio, television, and the movies entertain and instruct us daily, even hourly, yet rarely do they confront us with a single written word. Scripts are not intended for a reading audience. When you read the screenplay of "Soldier's Home" or "The Blackout" you should keep in mind that they were written with the sole purpose of being performed. They are not finished texts in the same sense as are most of the other selections in this book. The reader needs to supply—as did the actors and directors—the missing dimensions of sound, image, and movement to bring a script to life. It is one thing to read Abbott and Costello's famous "Who's on First" routine; it is quite another to see and hear the two great comedians perform it. Reading a script is like going behind the scenes; we see what was not intended to be seen. As the audience of a print advertisement, news item, essay, or story, you are doing exactly what the writer intended—reading it. Scripts, however, require that you put yourself in the role of two different audiences: the individual reader of the actual script and the larger, intended audience of the imagined performance.

Born in Kenosha, Wisconsin, in 1915, Orson Welles had earned, by the age of twenty-six, an international reputation as an actor and director in radio, theater, and cinema. Welles's virtuosity included celebrated performances as a playwright, cartoonist, and journalist. He wrote several syndicated columns.

In 1937, Welles launched the Mercury Theatre on the Air to present a regular series of radio broadcasts of dramatic adaptations of famous novels. On October 31, 1938, Welles's "splendid purple-velvet voice" came on the radio to announce a story appropriate to a Halloween evening—H. G. Wells's The War of the Worlds, *written in 1898, depicting an invasion from Mars. Despite several reminders to the audience that they were listening to an adaptation of a novel, the authentic-sounding details and tones of the broadcast, as the following excerpts dramatize, threw much of the nation's population into mass hysteria.*

ANNOUNCER

Ladies and gentlemen, here is the latest bulletin from the Intercontinental Radio News, Toronto, Canada: Professor Morse of Macmillan University reports observing a total of three explosions on the planet Mars, between the hours of 7:45 p.m. and 9:20 p.m., eastern standard time. This confirms earlier reports received from American observatories. Now, nearer home, comes a special announcement from Trenton, New Jersey. It is reported that at 8:50 p.m. a huge, flaming object, believed to be a meteorite, fell on a farm in the neighborhood of Grovers Mill, New Jersey, twenty-two miles from Trenton. The flash in the sky was visible within a radius of several hundred miles and the noise of the impact was heard as far north as Elizabeth.

We have dispatched a special mobile unit to the scene, and we will have our commentator, Mr. Phillips, give you a word description as soon as he can reach there from Princeton. In the meantime, we take you to the Hotel Martinet in Brooklyn, where Bobby Millette and his orchestra are offering a program of dance music. (SWING BAND FOR 20 SECONDS . . . THEN CUT)

ANNOUNCER

We take you now to Grovers Mill, New Jersey.
(CROWD NOISES . . . POLICE SIRENS)

PHILLIPS

Ladies and gentlemen, this is Carl Phillips again, at the Wilmuth farm, Grovers Mill, New Jersey. Professor Pierson and myself made the eleven miles from Princeton in ten minutes. Well, I . . . I hardly know where to begin, to paint for you a word picture of the strange scene before my eyes, like something out of a modern Arabian Nights. Well, I just got here. I haven't had a chance to look around yet. I guess that's *it*. Yes, I guess that's the . . . *thing*, directly in front of me, half buried in a vast pit. Must have struck with terrific force. The ground is covered with splinters of a tree it must have struck on its way down. What I can see of the . . . object itself doesn't look very much like a meteor, at least not the meteors I've seen. It looks more like a huge cylinder. It has a diameter of . . . what would you say, Professor Pierson? . . .

ANNOUNCER

Ladies and gentlemen, I have a grave announcement to make. Incredible as it may seem, both the observations of science and the evidence of our eyes lead to the inescapable assumption that those strange beings who landed in the Jersey farmlands tonight are the vanguard of an invading army from the planet Mars. The battle which took place tonight at Grovers Mill has ended in one of the most startling defeats ever suffered by an army in modern times; seven thousand men armed with rifles and machine guns pitted against a single fighting machine of the invaders from Mars. One hundred and twenty known survivors. The rest strewn over the battle area from Grovers Mill to Plainsboro crushed and trampled to death under the metal feet of the monster, or burned to cinders by its heat-ray. The monster is now in control of the middle section of New Jersey and has effectively cut the state through its center. Communication lines are down from Pennsylvania to the Atlantic Ocean. Railroad tracks are torn and service from New York to Philadelphia discontinued except routing some of the trains through Allentown and Phoenixville. Highways to the north, south, and west are clogged with frantic human traffic. Police and army reserves are unable to control the mad flight. By morning the fugitives will have swelled Philadelphia, Camden and Trenton, it is estimated, to twice their normal population.

At this time martial law prevails throughout New Jersey and eastern Pennsylvania. We take you now to Washington for a special broadcast on the National Emergency . . . the Secretary of the Interior. . . .

ANNOUNCER

I'm speaking from the roof of Broadcasting Building, New York City. The bells you hear are ringing to warn the people to evacuate the city as the Martians approach. Estimated in last two hours three million people have moved out along the roads to the north, Hutchison River Parkway still kept open for motor traffic. Avoid bridges to Long Island . . . hopelessly jammed. All communication with Jersey shore closed ten minutes ago. No more defenses. Our army wiped out . . . artillery, air force, everything wiped out. This may be the last broadcast. We'll stay here to the end. . . . People are holding service below us . . . in the cathedral. (VOICES SINGING HYMN)

Now I look down the harbor. All manner of boats, overloaded with fleeing population, pulling out from docks. (SOUND OF BOAT WHISTLES)

Streets are all jammed. Noise in crowds like New Year's Eve in city. Wait a minute. . . . Enemy now in sight above the Palisades. Five great machines. First one is crossing river. I can see it from here, wading the Hudson like a man wading through a brook. . . . A bulletin's handed me. . . . Martian cylinders are falling all over the country. One outside Buffalo, one in Chicago, St. Louis . . . seem to be timed and spaced. . . . Now the first machine reaches the shore. He stands watching, looking over the city. His steel, cowlish head is even with the skyscrapers. He waits for the others. They rise like a line of new towers on the city's west side. . . . Now they're lifting their metal hands. This is the end now. Smoke comes out . . . black smoke, drifting over the city. People in the streets see it now. They're running towards the East River . . . thousands of them, dropping in like rats. Now the smoke's spreading faster. It's reached Times Square. People trying to run away from it, but it's no use. They're falling like flies. Now the smoke's crossing Sixth Avenue . . . Fifth Avenue . . . 100 yards away . . . it's fifty feet. . . .

The zany classic comedy routine "Who's on First," which might have been written by Samuel Beckett for the Theatre of the Absurd, had a long vaudeville history before Bud Abbott and Lou Costello gave it their special imprint. The routine—sometimes played long, sometimes short—moved with the two through radio, movies, and television. Often played live and laced with ad libs, the script clearly has no definitive text. The version printed below is a transcript from their film The Gay Nineties *(1945).*

Both comedians were born in New Jersey; Bud Abbott in Asbury Park in 1900 and Lou Costello in Paterson in 1908. They struggled through burlesque and vaudeville for nine years until 1938, when they brought their relentless corny bickering to radio and became overnight sensations.

LOU: Look, Abbott, if you're the coach, you must know all the players.

BUD: I certainly do.

LOU: Well, you know, I never met the guys, so you'll have to tell me their names and then I'll know who's playing on the team.

BUD: Oh, I'll tell you their names. But, you know, strange as it may seem, they give these ballplayers nowadays very peculiar names.

LOU: You mean funny names?

BUD: Strange names, pet names like Dizzy Dean.

LOU: And his brother Daffy.

BUD: Daffy Dean—

LOU: And their French cousin.

BUD: French?

LOU: Goofé.

BUD: Goofé Dean. Oh, I see. Well, let's see, we have on the bags, we have Who's on first, What's on second. I Don't Know is on third.

LOU: That's what I want to find out.

BUD: I say, Who's on first, What's on second, I Don't Know's on third.

LOU: Are you the manager?

BUD: Yes.

LOU: You're gonna be the coach, too?

BUD: Yes.

LOU: Do you know the fellas' names?

BUD: Well, I should.

LOU: Well, then who's on first?

BUD: Yes.

LOU: I mean the fella's name.

BUD: Who.

LOU: The guy on first.

BUD: Who!

LOU: The first baseman.

BUD: WHO!

LOU: The guy playing first.

BUD: Who is on first.

LOU: I'm asking *you* who's on first.

BUD: That's the man's name.

LOU: That's whose name?

BUD: Yes.

LOU: Well, go ahead and tell me.

BUD: That's it.

LOU: That's who?

BUD: Yes!

LOU: Look, you got a first baseman?

BUD: Certainly.

LOU: Who's playing first?

BUD: That's right.

LOU: When you pay off the first baseman every month, who gets the money?

BUD: Every dollar of it.

LOU: All I'm trying to find out is the fella's name on first base.

BUD: Who.

LOU: The guy that gets the money.

BUD: That's it.

LOU: Who gets the money?

BUD: He does, every dollar. Sometimes his wife comes down and collects it.

LOU: Whose wife?

BUD: Yes. What's wrong with that?

LOU: Look, all I wanna know is, when you sign up the first baseman, how does he sign his name to the contract?

BUD: Who.

LOU: The guy.

BUD: Who.

LOU: How does he sign his name?

BUD: That's how he signs it.

LOU: Who?

BUD: Yes.

LOU: All I'm trying to find out is what's the guy's name on first base?

BUD: No, What is on second base.

LOU: I'm not asking you who's on second.

BUD: Who's on first.

LOU: One base at a time!

BUD: Well, don't change the players around.

LOU: I'm not changing nobody.

BUD: Take it easy, buddy.

LOU: I'm only asking you, who's the guy on first base?

BUD: That's right.

LOU: Okay.

BUD: All right.

LOU: I mean, what's the guy's name on first base?

BUD: No, What is on second.

LOU: I'm not asking you who's on second.

BUD: Who's on first.

LOU: I don't know.

BUD: Oh, he's on third. We're not talking about him. Now let's get—

LOU: Now *how* did I get on third base?

BUD: Why, you mentioned his name.

LOU: If I mentioned the third baseman's name, who did I say was playing third?

BUD: No, Who's playing first.

LOU: What's on first?

BUD: What's on second.

LOU: I don't know.

BUD: *He's* on third.

LOU: There I go, back on third again.

BUD: I can't help it.

LOU: Now, will you stay on third base? And don't go off it..

BUD: All right, now what do you want to know?

LOU: Now, who's playing third base?

BUD: Why do you insist on putting Who on third base?

LOU: What am I putting on third?

BUD: No, What is on second.

LOU: You don't want *who* on second?

BUD: Who is on first.

LOU: I don't know!

BOTH: Third base!

LOU: Look, you got outfield?

BUD: Sure.

LOU: The left fielder's name?

BUD: Why.

LOU: I just thought I'd ask you.

BUD: Well, I just thought I'd tell you.

LOU: Then tell me who's playing left field.

BUD: Who is playing *first*.

LOU: I'm not—Stay out of the infield! I wanna know what's the guy's name in left field.

BUD: No, What is on second.

LOU: I'm not *asking* you who's on second.

BUD: Who's on first.

LOU: I don't know.

BOTH: Third base!

LOU: And the left fielder's name?

BUD: Why!

LOU: Because.

BUD: Oh, he's *center* field.

LOU: Bey-eeyh-echh

BUD: You know his name as well as I do.

LOU: Look, look, look you got a pitcher on the team?

BUD: Sure.

LOU: The pitcher's name?

BUD: Tomorrow.

LOU: You don't wanna tell me today?

BUD: I'm telling you today.

LOU: Then go ahead.

BUD: Tomorrow.

LOU: What time?

BUD: What time what?

LOU: What time tomorrow you going to tell me who's pitching.

BUD: Now listen, Who is not pitching. Who—

LOU: I'll break your arm you say "Who's on first." I want to know what's the pitcher's name.

BUD: What's on second.

LOU: I don't know.

BOTH: Third base!

LOU: You got a catcher?

BUD: Certainly.

LOU: The catcher's name?

BUD: Today.

LOU: Today. And tomorrow's pitching?

BUD: Now you've got it.

LOU: All we got is a couple of days of the week. You know, I'm a catcher, too.

BUD: So they tell me.

LOU: I get behind the plate, do some fancy catching, tomorrow's pitching on my team and the heavy hitter gets up.

BUD: Yes.

LOU: Now, the heavy hitter bunts the ball. When he bunts the ball, me being a good catcher, I'm going to throw the guy out at first base, so I pick up the ball and throw it to who?

BUD: Now, that's the first thing you've said right.

LOU: I don't even know what I'm *talking* about!

BUD: That's all you have to do.

LOU: Is to throw the ball to first base?

BUD: *Yes.*

LOU: Now, who's got it?

BUD: Naturally.

LOU: Look, if I throw the ball to first base, somebody's got to get it. Now, who has it?

BUD: Naturally.

LOU: Who?

BUD: Naturally.

LOU: Naturally?

BUD: Naturally.

LOU: So, I pick up the ball and I throw it to Naturally?

BUD: No, you don't. You throw the ball to Who!

LOU: Naturally.

BUD: That's different.

LOU: That's what I say.

BUD: You're not saying it—

LOU: I throw the ball to Naturally?

BUD: You throw it to Who.

LOU: Naturally.

BUD: That's it.

LOU: That's what I said.

BUD: Listen, you ask me.

LOU: I throw the ball to who?

BUD: Naturally.

LOU: Now you ask me.

BUD: You throw the ball to Who.

LOU: Naturally.

BUD: That's it.

LOU: Same as you!

BUD: Don't change them around.

LOU: Same as you!

BUD: Okay, now get it over with.

LOU: I throw the ball to who. Whoever it is drops the ball and the guy runs to second.

BUD: Yes.

LOU: Who picks up the ball and throws it to what. What throws it to I don't know. I don't know throws it back to tomorrow. Triple play.

BUD: Yes.

LOU: Another guy gets up and hits a long fly to because. Why? I don't know. He's on third and I don't *give* a darn.

BUD: —eh, what?

LOU: I said, "I don't *give* a darn."

BUD: Oh, that's our shortstop.

LOU: Ayeiiii!

Batten, Barton, Durstine, and Osborne / Ring around the Collar

ca. 1975

One of the most successful and long-running campaigns in television history, the "Ring around the Collar" commercials for Wisk were launched in 1969 by the advertising firm of Batten, Barton, Durstine, and Osborne (BBD&O). Though

GONDOLIER: Of love I sing . . . .

la-la-la-la.

ANNOUNCER: Those dirty rings . . . You tried scrubbing, even spraying, and still . . .

you've got ring-around-the-collar.

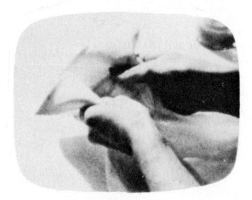

before you start to wash.

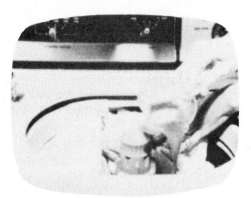

Then gets your whole wash really clean.

shoppers frequently complain about the commercials, their irritation apparently does not stand in the way of their buying the product. For more information on this commercial, see Carol Caldwell's "You Haven't Come a Long Way, Baby: Women in Television Commercials" (in "Advertising").

But you've got ring-around-the-collar-la-la.

WIFE: My powder didn't work.

Try Wisk.

Wisk sinks in and starts to clean

HUSBAND: No more ring-around-the-collar-la-la!

ANNOUNCER: Use Wisk around the collar for ring-around-the-collar.

Dick Orkin and Bert Berdis / Puffy Sleeves: A *Time* Magazine Commercial
1977

"Dick and Bert" call their brand of radio advertising humor "situation comedy commercials." Believing that advertising too often portrays ideal people in unreal situations, the team writes instead about an imperfect world:

> *People who dribble a little bit, people who get arrested for wearing their wife's housecoat to go out to buy a* Time *magazine, a guy that gets fired for reading* Time, *just the little stupid things that everyone does.*

Their radio campaign for Time *magazine aired in the mid-1970s; "Puffy Sleeves" was one of the most popular spots.*

BERT: Pardon me, sir, would you step over here to the patrol car please?

DICK: Oh, h-hello, officer.

BERT: Do you have business in this neighborhood, sir?

DICK: Yes, I live f-four blocks from here . . . It's the brick colonial with the crack in the driveway.

BERT: What are you doing out this time of night, sir?

DICK: Well, I got all ready for bed and darn it if I didn't forget to pick up a copy of *Time* magazine at the newsstand today.

BERT: What type of coat would you call that, sir?

DICK: Th-this? This is a h-housecoat. See, I spilled cocoa on mine and I just grabbed my wife's. I guess the puffy sleeves look a little silly . . . *(laugh)*. . . .

BERT: Want to get in the car, sir?

DICK: In the car . . .?

SOUND EFFECTS: *(door open)*

DICK: See, I just don't go to bed without a *Time* movie review or something from the modern living section . . .

BERT: Yes, sir. *(car pulls away)*

DICK: I tried reading something else, but there isn't anything like *Time*. Do you know, officer, how many editorial awards *Time* magazine has won?

BERT: No, sir.

DICK: And *Time* is so respected—and I'm a firm believer—along with Winston Churchill . . . that you are uh . . . what you read . . . *(pause)*. . . . Oh please don't send me up the river just for wearing puffy sleeves.

BERT: You're home, sir.

DICK: I'm home—oh . . . I thou—thank—God bless you. . . .

SOUND EFFECTS: *(door open)*

DICK: . . . Okay—bye.

ANNOUNCER: *Time* magazine makes everything more interesting, including you.

Robert Geller / Hemingway's "Soldier's Home": A Screenplay 1976

In the mid-1970s, Educational Television, with the support of the National Endowment for the Humanities, launched a series of films based on classic American short stories. Besides Ernest Hemingway's "Soldier's Home," the series offered remarkable film adaptations of such stories as John Cheever's "The Five-Forty-Eight," Sherwood Anderson's "I'm a Fool," Stephen Crane's "The Blue Hotel," and Richard Wright's "Almos' a Man." Much acclaimed, the short-story series is responsible for some of the finest television movies in the history of the medium.

Robert Geller is a scriptwriter and the author of numerous articles on film and television. He served as the executive producer of the "American Short Story" series.

1. Prologue. In sepia. Eight or ten young men are being huddled together for a fraternity picture. All dressed in high white collars. Most wear silver-rimmed glasses. Austere building in background. No laughter or chatter.

NARRATOR (*off camera*): Krebs went to the war from a Methodist college in Kansas. There is a picture which shows him among his fraternity brothers. . . .

Photographer motions them to close ranks, and sheep-like they shuffle closer. One young man, Harold Krebs, stands slightly to the side and moves just a fraction after the command "hold it."

NARRATOR (*off camera*): He enlisted in the Army in 1917. . . .

Cut to Photographer and "explosion" of his camera gun.

Cut to 2. Stock footage of WWI, expository in nature, and of returning veterans. Not meant to editorialize about the war.

NARRATOR (*off camera*): . . . and did not return to the United States until the second division returned from the Rhine in 1919.

3. Exterior. Dusk. Empty train depot in rural town. Krebs with duffle bag. Platform is deserted, with the exception of the station master and one passenger, neither of whom pays Krebs any attention.

Krebs crosses tracks deftly. Stops at depot to catch breath. Tattered signs flap in wind: "Buy U.S. Bonds," etc. At the front end of the platform a banner with "WELCOME HOME YANKS" droops limply from a worn cornice.

NARRATOR (*off camera*): By the time Krebs returned to his home town the greeting of heroes was over. He came back much too late.

4. Interior. Night. Dissolve to dining room of Krebs house. Dinner is over. Harold is still in uniform. Mr. and Mrs. Krebs and Marge hunt for words. There is no real jubilation or ease. Harold is lighting up. Faces of family watch.

MR. KREBS: Son . . . You smoke lots in battle? You seem to do it . . . naturally.

HAROLD: Not really . . . I just picked it up.

MARGE (*enthusiastic*): Did you actually smoke, in the war, Hare? Didn't they see you lighting up? The Germans?

HAROLD: Uh . . . uh. We smoked mostly when we were bored.

MRS. KREBS: Bored! Little chance you had to be bored . . .

HAROLD: We were. I was. A lot of the time.

(*Silence. Ticking of clock. It is after 11:00* P.M.)

MRS. KREBS: Harold, you must be tired . . . All that traveling. And we've asked so many questions.

HAROLD: I'm fine.

MR. KREBS: Well . . . it's gettin' late. I gotta go out in the county tomorrow. We'll get to talk . . . about what you wanna be doin'. Plenty of time.

HAROLD: Yes . . . I'll need a week or so . . .

MRS. KREBS: Of course. Let's just be thankful that you're home safe. Let us be thankful to our Dear Lord (*her eyes are raised*) that you're back home. Oh, Harold, we did pray for you. And each Sunday Reverend Nelson . . .

MR. KREBS (*interrupts with a yawn*): Folks . . . I'm goin' up. Welcome home, Harold.

(*Mr. Krebs extends his hand.*)

HAROLD: Night, Dad . . . It was a fine dinner . . . Guess I'll go up, too. (*He starts to follow Mr. Krebs out.*)

5. Interior. Hallway at foot of stairs.

MRS. KREBS (*to Harold at the foot of the stairs*): Son . . . Marjorie and I could fix up a special breakfast. Serve it to you in bed. Remember when you had those awful winter coughs and . . .

HAROLD: Not tomorrow, Mom . . . I'll want to get up early, and . . .

MRS. KREBS: Hare?

HAROLD: Mom?

MRS. KREBS (*moves to hug him*): Sleep well.

HAROLD (*stiffens, hugs her back*): I will . . . thanks . . . for everything.

Cut to 6. Interior. Night. Harold's room. Dimly lit. Flowered wallpaper. Pan to boyhood mementos, which are sparse save for some scouting medals and a trophy for track & field. Harold unpacks. Looks at photo of college fraternity at Methodist school. Considers replacing it with picture of himself and another soldier with two coarse, older German women. The military uniforms are too large.

Krebs moves around his smallish room. Picks up the trophy and buffs it. Takes out a clarinet from a book shelf and slowly assembles it. Tinkers tentatively with some scales. Begins to undress and neatly pile clothes on chair near his bed. Cranks up his phonograph. It still works. He smiles. Climbs into bed with a record playing.

Krebs lights cigarette and leans on elbow, staring out at the quiet, empty streets..

MR. KREBS (*off camera*) (*knocking at Harold's door*): Harold. Could you turn it down? It's late, and I need to be fresh and ginger tomorrow.

7. The following shots take place in one day, during which we get the feelings and rhythms of Harold being home contrasted against the rhythms of the town.

Exterior. Point of view Krebs House. Day. Harold's window. We see the shade, which is pulled half down with the tassle hanging. We hear the sound of footsteps on the porch and the rattling of bottles as the milkman puts the milk on the porch and takes the old bottles.

Cut to interior. Harold's bedroom. Day. Close-up of Harold's face. He's lying awake in bed listening to the sounds of the milkman. He's been up for a while.

Cut to interior/exterior. Harold's window. Day. Harold moves into frame, raises the shade, then looks down, out the window. Then Harold's face, close up. Then the sound of a factory whistle in the distance.

Exterior. Krebs house. Day. Harold's point of view. Looking down at the milkman walking away from the house carrying empty bottles away in a rack.

Exterior. Krebs porch and house. Day. Harold has a cup of coffee. He's wearing his army overcoat to protect him against the morning cold. Sits on the edge of the step and leans back against the pillar. Lights up a cigarette. The early morning sun comes through the trees.

Then the procession of men going to work begins. Through the bushes and through the empty spaces between the trees, Harold sees the working-class men of the town on their way to the factory. The procession begins with only a few, but builds in tempo as it gets closer to the hour to be in the factory. Then a few stragglers, and then it is quiet again.

Some of the images we see are two men walking carrying lunch pails. A third man behind them runs to catch up with them, and they then walk on together. Some of the figures are partially masked—seen through the screen of bushes—so we pan with them, seeing their lunch pails swinging and their footsteps on the pavement.

A car goes by carrying some workmen. The sounds of other cars are heard going to work and their image/presence is suggested in the movement of Harold's eyes as they go by up the street. As the procession ends, in the distance the sound of the factory whistle, which heralds the start of the day's work.

The newspaper boy throws the newspaper up the walk, and Harold picks it up.

Interior. Harold's bedroom. Day. Point of views. A series of images of Harold follow that suggest his day, to be punctuated with some activities that take place around him, such as:

A. Marge leaves for school, maybe picked up by another girl.
B. Mr. Krebs's car leaves the house. (Perhaps this could occur earlier.)
C. Two church ladies come and pick up Mrs. Krebs. We hear their voices and see them walk away from the house.

Interior. Harold's room. Day. Harold reads the sports page of the newspaper, smokes, rests, and plays his clarinet.

When Harold plays his clarinet, he plays some scales to reacquaint himself with the instrument. His playing at first is very tentative—he is feeling for the instrument and for his own voice, his own theme or melody. We would use his music as a means of expressing Harold's mood. The music creates a space for him separate from the world around him.

Exterior. Krebs house. Day. As the day grows late, the activities are reversed. The factory whistle blows late in the day, and then we see the tracking feet again, now worn, tired, the men slump-shouldered, trailing off to their homes.

8. Exterior. Bright morning. Harold walking to town. Is stopped by a prim old man.

MAN: Mornin', young Krebs. Welcome home. How long you back now?

HAROLD: It's two weeks, today.

MAN: Your folks said you had some very difficult times over there?

HAROLD: No . . . not that bad.

MAN: Anyhow, you must be glad to be home . . . Are you planning to go back to school?

HAROLD: No.

MAN: You going to be selling farm land with Dad? At the bank? It's a blessing when a man and his son can . . .

HAROLD (*edging away*): 'Scuse me.

(HAROLD *walks on down street.*)

MAN: Well, I'll be! You'd think he'd killed the Kaiser. Even as a young boy . . .

(*They exit; their voices trail.*)

9. Exterior. Day. Harold walks on to town. Nods back to few passersby who seem to remember him. Harold notices the young girls in town. He sees one through shop windows. He notices their pretty faces and the patterns that they make.

NARRATOR (*off camera*): Nothing was changed in the town except that the young girls had grown up. There were so many good-looking young girls.

10. Exterior. Day. Harold stops in front of bank where Mr. Krebs works as land agent.

NARRATOR (*off camera*): Before Krebs went away to the war he had never been allowed to drive the family motor car. The car always stood outside the First National Bank building where his father had an office. Now, after the war, it was still the same car.

Harold crosses the street, walks past the car to the window of his father's office. He looks in.

Reverse angle of Mr. Krebs amiably chatting with young customers Harold's age. Offers cigar. Laughter and clapping of each other's shoulders. Harold stares for several seconds and then turns away, crossing the street quickly.

11. Interior. Day. Signs indicate library room of YMCA. Harold is checking out books. Young male librarian, glasses, devoutly scrubbed, early 30s, is at check-out desk.

LIBRARIAN: Krebs. Are you Harold Krebs?

HAROLD (*startled*): Yes. That's me.

LIBRARIAN: Don't you remember me? I'm Mr. Phillips. I was your youth group advisor in the lower grades.

HAROLD: Sorry. I was involved with these books.

LIBRARIAN: Are you an avid reader? Have you tried the new Booth Tarkington? I try to encourage good reading. (*The* LIBRARIAN *begins to notice the books* KREBS *has checked out.*) My heavens. They're all books about the war. I should think that . . .

HAROLD: It helps to make sense out of things that happened. The maps and . . .

LIBRARIAN: But weren't you at Argonne? My Lord, the reports we received . . .

HAROLD (*eager to go*): Thanks . . . I'd like them for two weeks, or longer. All right?

LIBRARIAN (*stiffly*): Two weeks. That's all that's allowed. (*Pause.*) Krebs . . .

HAROLD (*begins to leave*): Sir?

LIBRARIAN: Krebs . . . you might want to check the social calendar on the way out of the building. We hold socials and dances so that you young vets can catch up with community activities. This Saturday . . .

HAROLD (*looks uninterested*): Thanks . . . I'll look. (HAROLD *exits.*)

Cut to 12. Interior. Late afternoon. Sitting room. Harold is absorbed in reading a book on the war. There is a map that he studies, trying to figure out the course of battle. Harold's mother comes in.

MRS. KREBS: I had a talk with your father last night, Harold, and he's willing for you to take the car out in the evenings.

HAROLD: Yeah? (*Still absorbed in his reading.*) Take the car out? Yeah?

MRS. KREBS: Yes. Your father has felt for some time you should be able to take the car out in the evenings whenever you wished but we only talked it over last night.

HAROLD: I'll bet you made him.

MRS. KREBS: No. It was your father's suggestion that we talk it over.

HAROLD: Yeah. I'll bet you made him.

MRS. KREBS: Harold . . . we'll be having dinner a little early this evening.

HAROLD: All right . . . Think I'll walk a little.

MRS. KREBS: Don't be late. I've cooked your favorite roast.

HAROLD (*mumbles*): All right. (*Looks back as he leaves.*)

13. Exterior. Day. Harold enters pool hall. (Close crop and only exterior of door is needed.)

Cut to 14. Interior. Pool hall. Cool and shaded. Proprietor is ex-pug. He and Harold shadow-box and exchange jabs. They say little. But Harold is at ease here as he picks up cue and chalks.

Harold looks relaxed and concentrates on each shot. Two younger boys admire his ease and relaxed style as he puts away each ball. He smokes casually.

FIRST BOY: Hey, Harold . . . betcha didn't get no time for pool in France . . . eh . . . didja?

(HAROLD *smiles benignly throughout their banter.*)

HAROLD: Nope, not much time for pool.

SECOND BOY: Hey . . . is it true you got home last 'cause they needed the best soldiers around to keep the Krauts in line?

(HAROLD *nods yes.* HAROLD *continues to pick off shots. Lets the ash on his cigarette grow precariously long. The younger boys edge closer, begging confidences. Smoke stings his eyes.*)

YOUNGER BOY: Hey, Harold . . . swear to the truth . . . Did you really kill Germans . . . right face to face . . . honest to God? With bayonets?

HAROLD (*nods*): That's what we went there for. Not to see the Eiffel Tower.

(*They are silent, not wanting to break his concentration.*)

PROPRIETOR (*off camera*): Gotta close up, Harold. Run 'em out—one, two, three—the way you always used ta . . .

NARRATOR (*off camera*): At first Krebs did not want to talk about the war at all. Later he felt the need to talk but no one wanted to hear about it. Krebs found that to be listened to at all he had to lie, and after he had done this twice he, too, had a reaction against the war and against talking about it.

(HAROLD *sizes up the last shot. The proprietor and the younger boys huddle close behind.* HAROLD'S *eyes open wide and . . . Cut to cue ball as it explodes into last remaining ball and pushes it deftly into far pockets. Ex-pug and younger boys nod in admiration.*)

15. Exterior. Late afternoon. Krebs walks tall and the younger boys follow as worshippers. All, as silhouettes, pass the same crisp, white houses. They pass war monument. Their questions are heard as echoes. No other sounds but their voices.

FIRST BOY: Harold, is it true that they chained Kraut women to their machine guns for GIs to . . . you know . . . to . . .

SECOND BOY: Hey, Harold, did you bring any of them pictures back . . . you know . . . the French ones . . .

FIRST BOY: Harold, are the German women all that great? Denny's brother said all they want to do is make love to Americans . . . Don't matter where they do it, or the time of day . . .

SECOND BOY: Hey, Harold, can you come to the dance at the Y Friday? Cripes . . . everybody wants to talk to you, and the girls in town are waiting for you to give them a tumble. Might even be some hard liquor if you're in the mood . . .

(*All through these questions, there are no other sounds or street noises. It is meant to be a parade, a parodied ceremony for* HAROLD KREBS'S *return. Shot almost as a dreamlike ceremony. The boys double-time like GIs to keep in step with their hero.*)

16. Same as preceding shot, but nearer to Krebs house. Harold begins to run. Close up as he feels the joy of movement. Knows he's late for dinner, too.

Harold collides abruptly with young man. They both struggle for balance. The man is Charlie Simmons, tall and bulky, dressed in prosperous attire of an older businessman.

CHARLIE SIMMONS: Ouch . . . Hey, what's goin on . . .

HAROLD: Sorry . . . I wasn't looking.

CHARLIE (*recovering*): Krebs! . . . Harold Krebs. When did you get back?

HAROLD: It's just two weeks now.

CHARLIE: You look fine, just fine.

HAROLD: Thanks.

CHARLIE: You workin' for your dad at the bank?

•HAROLD (*hedging*): Not yet.

CHARLIE: You lookin' for a permanent line of work?

HAROLD: Might be . . .

CHARLIE (*blocking HAROLD's path with his bulk*): I'm doing real well. Selling insurance. All the vets are interested and need the security. They know the future . . .

HAROLD: Makes sense.

CHARLIE: Think you'd be interested?

HAROLD: Buying some?

CHARLIE: Well . . . actually that, and maybe working with me on the selling part.

HAROLD: I'll think about it. I'm late for dinner. (*He begins to trot away.*)

CHARLIE: Hey . . . did you know I'm married now? Remember Edith Hanes? She was our class secretary and the prettiest gal in this whole town (*fishing for a compliment*).

HAROLD (*over his shoulder*): Good luck, Charlie.

17. Exterior. Night or very late afternoon. Krebs porch. Harold looks in window at his family at supper. All heads are bowed in grace. (The MOS[1] of grace exaggerates the piety.) They finally finish the prayer. Mrs. Krebs nervously eyes the clock. Harold, resigned, walks in.

18. Exterior. Greek's soda shop. Day. Car pulls up in front of soda shop with Krebs driving. Harold gets out of car and looks in window. Sees the interior, decorated with decor of period. Marge and friends are having ice-cream sodas. They are exuberant as they "recreate" some incident from school (*in pantomime*).

Harold looks in, raps on window, and beckons Marge to come outside. She signals to Harold that she'll be out in one minute.

BILL KENNER (*off camera*): Hey, Krebs . . . Harold Krebs . . .

(BILL KENNER: *early 20s. Dressed flamboyantly with bohemian dash. Sports cane with golden handle. He limps perceptibly into frame.*) Remember me? William Kenner. Your fellow sufferer in geometry and Latin. C'mere, my lovelies.

(KENNER *waves to two teenagers, who obediently follow.*)

HAROLD: Sure . . . Bill Kenner. I remember you. You all right?

BILL KENNER (*with bravura*): Sure . . . if losing a chunk of your knee on a mine is all right, then I'm just fine.

HAROLD (*embarrassed for the girls*): That's . . . that's too bad. You seem to be doin' well though.

KENNER: Well . . . with lovelies like these, *pourquoi s'en faire?* . . . Am I right?

---

1. A segment of film shot without sound.

HAROLD (*edgy*): I guess.

KENNER: You guess. Aren't we lucky to be alive? You know this little town had three killed? Lots of injured, too. In our graduating class alone . . .

HAROLD (*spots* MARGE): Here . . . Right here, Marge.

KENNER: Is that lovely mademoiselle a Krebs? (*Bows.*) May I introduce myself?

MARGE: Let's go, Hare . . .

HAROLD: Well . . . goodbye, Bill.

KENNER (*not dissuaded*): That your car?

HAROLD: My dad's.

KENNER: Splen-did work of art.

HAROLD: Thanks.

KENNER: Can you get it nights?

MARGE: (*impatient*): Har-old!

HAROLD: I guess so. Why.

KENNER: You busy this Friday?

HAROLD: Well . . . I'm not sure. Let me think about it . . .

KENNER: Think about it! About what? Let's you and I live it up, my friend. (*Girls giggle.*) There's a dance at the Y. I might even have some gen-u-ine cognac. Come by at 8:00.

HAROLD: All right . . . I'll try.

KENNER: I'll *expect* you. (*Winks.*) Bye now.

(*To* MARGE): Bye, lovely. See you on the Champs Elysées. (*Tips his hat and limps away dramatically.* HAROLD *and* MARGE *drive away.*)

19. Interior. Night. Large room of YMCA. Small crowd of fifteen to twenty is dwarfed by the place. Clusters of girls, some overly dressed and coiffed. Mr. Phillips, the librarian, and Mr. and Mrs. Charlie Simmons and chaperones are standing at punch bowl. Boys, some teenagers, busily sharing their own secrets and howling at their own jokes. Few couples are dancing.

Harold stands apart, remote from the activities, watching.

NARRATOR (*off camera*): Vaguely he wanted a girl, but he did not want to have to work to get her. He did not want to get into the intrigue and politics . . .

(*We see the usual behavior of a dance. Boys egg on one of their fellows to ask a girl to dance. A girl moves away from a boy as he approaches to ask her for a dance—as if she is too busy. Another boy approaches a girl and then veers to another girl—the first thinking he was going to ask her. All of the little intrigues of the dance.*)

NARRATOR (*off camera*): Besides, he did not really need a girl.

(KENNER *in dramatic cape and Tyrolian hat is "performing" for* ROSELLE SIMMONS, *who is flushed and heavily rouged.*)

NARRATOR (*off camera*): You did not need a girl unless you thought about them.

(*She looks toward* HAROLD, *who is obviously bored. He walks toward the door and into hallway.* ROSELLE *follows.* HAROLD *lights a cigarette.*)

NARRATOR (*off camera*): When you were really ripe for a girl you always got one. He had learned that in the army.

20. Interior. Hallway. Cases filled with trophies. Pictures of austere town philanthropist.

ROSELLE: Harold? Harold Krebs. (*For her, all conversation is a flirtation.*)

HAROLD: It's me.

ROSELLE: I'm Roselle, Roselle Simmons.

HAROLD: Charlie's sister . . . right?

ROSELLE: Why . . . heàvens . . . have I changed all that much in two years?

HAROLD: Three years . . . actually.

ROSELLE: You don't seem to be having much fun at all. . . . You haven't danced once. I've been spying on you.

HAROLD: Well, I'm not up to the steps . . . or all the chatter . . .

ROSELLE: You need to be taught. . . . Didn't your little sister Marge ever try? There are lots of new steps . . . I could teach you . . . It's my war effort . . . Trade for a smoke?

HAROLD (*doesn't offer her a cigarette*): It's a waste of time. I never could get my feet straight . . .

ROSELLE: Silly . . . the feet are the easy part . . . it's the rest of your body . . . the way you lead . . . the way you hold your partner . . . I'll bet you like to command a girl . . .

HAROLD (*surprised*): Command a girl . . . Why?

ROSELLE (*she leads to music*): Command me, Mr. Harold Krebs . . .

HAROLD (*he responds slowly*): Like this?

(*These scenes should be played slowly—moving from awkwardness to* HAROLD'S *own arousal and assertion.*)

ROSELLE (*gently circling his arms around her. Emphasize physical aspects of their dancing*): Just move one, two, three, four . . . get closer . . . Did you ever dance like this, with those foreign women?

(*Cuts to* HAROLD *dancing closer. Stroking her as he would the women he has known in Europe. The music stops, and* HAROLD *continues to caress her with sureness.*)

ROSELLE (*scared now*): Don't . . . I've got to freshen up . . . I won't be long . . . All right? Wait out here . . . Don't!

HAROLD (*confused*): Hey . . . Where're you going? C'mon back here, Roselle.

ROSELLE (*vampishly over her shoulder*): Silly . . .

(ROSELLE *leaves.* HAROLD *continues to wait. The music begins. He is filled with a crushing sadness, a new confusion, a feeling of betrayal.*)

21. Exterior. Evening. Krebs and Kenner are in the Krebs car parked out front of Kenner house.

Krebs and Kenner are getting drunk. They try to whisper, but talk loudly. Kenner is much louder in his speech and more slurred. The only real sign of drunkenness for Harold is that he's talking louder than usual and trying to tell the truth to Kenner.

KENNER: We shouldn't have left. It would've gotten better.

HAROLD: You should have stayed.

KENNER: That tart Roselle is really somethin'. Know what we'd do to girls like her in France? (*Long pause as* HAROLD *says nothing.*) Christ. What do you want to do? Just mope around forever? I can't figure you. Whenever I want to forget things, I just drink. Drink and find a woman.

HAROLD: I want to *remember*—the *good* things.

KENNER: Like being over there. Scared to death. Watching guys screamin' and bleeding to death.

HAROLD: I wasn't scared . . . not like you tell it.

KENNER: Damn . . . everybody was. Didn't you ever wake up in sweats and shivers? I used to put my blanket in my mouth and . . .

HAROLD (*shakes his head, no.*)

KENNER: Well . . . I was scared. Everybody was.

HAROLD (*softly*): That's a lie.

KENNER (*pretends not to hear*): Everybody was. Only one thing is worth remembering over there.

HAROLD: Mmm . . .

KENNER: The damned women . . . No names or faces. Those white bodies, smelling like . . . like sweet apricots in those warm hotel rooms.

HAROLD: That isn't worth remembering.

KENNER: All right . . . all right. What is worth remembering?

HAROLD: Being a good soldier. Doing what you had to . . .

KENNER: Being a good soldier? You're crazy. You really are, Krebs.

HAROLD (*softly*): And you lie, Kenner, about everything.

KENNER: Don't call me a liar.

HAROLD: It's not worth it.

KENNER: Shut up.

(*Kenner pulls the bottle from Harold, and almost falls out car door.*)

HAROLD: Hey . . . You all right?

KENNER (*getting out of car*): Bastard . . . Crazy bastard. Stay away from me. I don't need a friend like you, Krebs. You spoil things.

(HAROLD *starts to follow Kenner.*)

HAROLD: Hey . . . wait! No! Go on. Go on, Kenner.

(KENNER *stumbles up front steps of his home.*)

22. Interior. Morning. Harold's bedroom. A knock on Harold's door. Harold wakes up. He feels miserable. His mother pokes her head in the door.

MRS. KREBS (*off camera*): Will you come down to breakfast, Harold?

HAROLD: As soon as I get my clothes on.

23. Interior. Dining room. Morning.

MARGE (*bringing in folded-up newspaper*): Well, Hare, you old sleepy-head. What do you ever get up for?

(HAROLD *removes brown wrapper of newspaper and opens it to the sporting page. He folds* The Star *open and props it against the water pitcher with his cereal dish to steady it, so he can read while he eats.*)

MRS. KREBS (*standing in the kitchen doorway*): Harold, please don't muss up the paper. Your father can't read his *Star* if it's been mussed.

HAROLD: I won't muss it.

MARGE (*sitting down*): We're playing indoor over at school this afternoon. I'm going to pitch.

HAROLD: Good. How's the old wing?

MARGE: I can pitch better than lots of the boys. I tell them all you taught me. I tell them all you're my beau. Aren't you my beau, Hare?

HAROLD: You bet.

MARGE: Could your brother really be your beau if he's your brother?

HAROLD: I don't know.

MARGE: Sure you know. Couldn't you be my beau, Hare, if I was old enough and if you wanted to?

HAROLD: Sure.

MARGE: Am I really your girl?

HAROLD: Sure.

MARGE: Do you love me?

HAROLD: Uh, huh.

MARGE: Will you love me always?

HAROLD (*by now becoming impatient with* MARGE): Sure.

MARGE: Will you come over and watch me play indoor?

HAROLD: Maybe.

MARGE: Aw, Hare, you don't love me. If you loved me, you'd definitely come over and watch me play indoor.

MRS. KREBS (*entering dining room*): You run along. I want to talk to Harold. Harold . . . I wish you'd put down the paper a minute, Harold.

HAROLD (*glances at her, hard*): Mmm . . .

MRS. KREBS: You acted shamefully last night. . . . The whole neighborhood could hear you, stumbling around out there.

HAROLD (*searches for the words*): Sorry . . .

MRS. KREBS: Why? You have so much . . . our love . . . You have a fine mind and a strong body . . . Have you decided what you're going to do yet, Harold?

HAROLD: No.

MRS. KREBS: Don't you think it's about time?

HAROLD: I hadn't decided yet . . .

MRS. KREBS (*stands*): God has some work for everyone to do . . . There can be no idle hands in His Kingdom. . . .

HAROLD (*without malice*): I'm not in His Kingdom. . . .

MRS. KREBS: We are all of us in His Kingdom. . . . Harold, please . . . I've worried about you so much . . . I know the temptations you must have suffered . . . I know how weak men are . . . I have prayed for you . . . I pray for you all day long, Harold . . .

(HAROLD *stares straight at his food.*)

MRS. KREBS: Harold . . . your father is worried, too . . . He thinks you've lost your ambition, that you have no definite aim in life. The Simmons boy is just your age, and he's doing so well . . . The boys are all settling down . . . They're all determined to get somewhere. Boys like Charlie Simmons are on the way to being a credit to the community . . . all of them . . . You, too, Harold . . .

(MRS. KREBS *starts to get up. Shaken, she sits back down.*)

MRS. KREBS: Don't look that way, Harold . . . You know we love you, and I want to tell you, for your own good, how matters stand . . . Your father doesn't want to hamper your freedom . . . He thinks you should be allowed to drive the car . . . We want you to enjoy yourself . . . but you are going to have to settle down to work, Harold. . . . Your father doesn't care what you start in at . . . All work is honorable as he says . . . but you've got to make a start at something . . . He didn't like . . . what you did last night . . . He asked me to speak to you this morning, and then you can stop in and see him at his office in the bank.

HAROLD (*gets up*): Is that all, Mother?

MRS. KREBS: Yes, don't you love your mother, dear?

HAROLD (*waits, not wanting to lie, just this once*): No.

MRS. KREBS (*her eyes grow shiny. She begins to cry*): Oh . . . Harold . . .

HAROLD: I don't love anybody . . .

(MRS. KREBS *sits down.*)

HAROLD: I didn't mean it . . . I was just angry at something . . . I didn't mean I didn't love you . . . Can't you believe me? Please, Mother . . . Please believe me.

MRS. KREBS (*shakes her head, chokily*): All right . . . I believe you, Harold. I'm your mother . . . I held you next to my heart when you were a tiny baby . . .

(*She presses his hand against her bosom.*)

HAROLD (*sick and vaguely nauseated*): I know, Mom . . . I know . . . I'll try and be a good boy for you.

MRS. KREBS (*more controlled*): Would you kneel and pray with me, Harold?

(HAROLD *and* MRS. KREBS *kneel beside the table.*)

MRS. KREBS: Now, you pray, Harold . . .

HAROLD: I can't . . .

MRS. KREBS: Try, Harold . . .

HAROLD: I can't . . .

MRS. KREBS: Do you want me to pray for you? . . .

HAROLD: Yes . . .

MRS. KREBS: Our dear heavenly Father . . .

Cut to (*over continuing prayers*) (HAROLD *stares straight ahead. Dissolves of* HAROLD *packing his battered trunk. Waiting at deserted bus or train depot and riding with face against window. Looking at flat, open lands. Dusk. Tracking shots.*)

(*Clarinet music grows louder. Up with parodied version of "When Johnny Comes Marching Home Again."*)

(*Cut to reverse angle of* MRS. KREBS *monotonously droning her prayer and* HAROLD *continuing to stare into space. Music fades. Freeze on* HAROLD, *impassive.*)

NARRATOR (*off camera*): He had tried to keep his life from being complicated. He had felt sorry for his mother and she had made him lie. He would go to Kansas City and get a job and she would feel all right about it. There would be one more scene maybe before he got away. He would not go down to his father's office. He would miss that one. He wanted his life to go smoothly. Well, that was all over now, anyway.

DISCUSSION QUESTIONS

1. Read Geller's script in conjunction with Hemingway's original story (in "Classics"). Mark sections of the script that do not appear in the story. Do you think Geller's changes are substantial or trivial? Explain.

2. Discuss the nature of Geller's changes. Why were they made? What purpose do they serve? Do you think a perfectly faithful film version was possible? What would it have been like?

3. Does Geller's version of the story leave you with a different impression of its meaning? Why, for example, is the final sentence of the story omitted from the script. Point to other such changes or omissions and discuss how these affect interpretation.

Richard B. Eckhaus / *The Jeffersons:* "The Blackout"   1978

On Thursday evening, July 14, 1977, New York City was suddenly plunged into one of the worst electrical failures in recent urban history. The blackout continued through the night as thousands of looters and arsonists devastated entire neighborhoods. The New York Post *headline read, "24 Hours of Terror." More than 3,400 men and women were arrested in what the* Post *called the "worst outbreak of rioting in the city's history" and "the most expensive manmade [disaster] the nation has ever seen."*

*Though not a likely subject for television humor, the blackout nevertheless served as the situation for one comedy show—*The Jeffersons. *Written in November 1977 by Richard B. Eckhaus and produced the following year, "The Blackout" was nominated for a humanitarian award.* The Jeffersons, *which began airing in 1975, starred Sherman Hemsley as George Jefferson and Isabel Sanford as his wife, Louise. For an extended discussion of the show, see Darryl Pinckney's "Step and Fetch It: The Darker Side of the Sitcoms" (in "Magazines").*

ACT ONE

Fade in. Interior, Jefferson living room—night. (*Late evening. The drapes are closed, and the sofa is in a new position—perpendicular to the upstage wall. George and Louise are rearranging the furniture. George struggles to hold one of the chairs in the air, as Louise tries to decide its new location.*)

LOUISE (*pointing to a spot behind George*): Maybe over there . . .

(*George drops the chair with a thud and a gasp.*)

GEORGE: Weezy . . .

LOUISE (*looking at the chair*): Definitely not THERE.

GEORGE (*impatiently*): Weezy . . . that's the third time I moved that chair.

LOUISE: I know, George . . . but I want the room to look right when it's changed.

GEORGE: We've been through this before. (*lifting the chair again*) Ain't nothin' gonna' stay changed but my body.

(*Florence enters from the kitchen. She carries a coffee cup, and looks sleepy.*)

FLORENCE: Now, I'd call THAT "Urban Renewal."

GEORGE (*reacts and drops chair*): Where you been while I've been doin' your work?

FLORENCE (*yawns*): Makin' a cup of hot chocolate . . . and it ain't MY work. (*She calmly takes a sip from the cup.*)

GEORGE (*getting a bit ticked*): What do you think I'm payin' you for?

FLORENCE: Company . . . I guess.

GEORGE: You wanna' stay part of the company, you'd better help me with this chair.

(*Florence shrugs, places the cup on the dinette table, and crosses to help George.*) (*George bends over to pick up the chair, expecting Florence's help.*)

GEORGE (*grinning*): That's more like it . . .

(*Florence merely takes the cushion from the chair, and walks back to her hot chocolate.*)

GEORGE (*glaring at Florence*): You're pushin' . . .

FLORENCE: No . . . I'm drinkin' . . . (*She takes a sip from the cup.*)

SOUND EFFECTS: (*Doorbell.*)

GEORGE (*points to the door*): Florence . . . DOOR . . .

FLORENCE (*picking up the chair cushion, and pointing to it*): Mr. Jefferson . . . PILLOW . . . (*points to table*) . . . and that's a TABLE. (*George reacts, and glares at Florence.*) Ain't it amazin' what that child's learnin'?

LOUISE (*a bit impatient*): George . . . would you PLEASE get the door. I'd like to get this done TONIGHT.

(*Florence begins to exit to the kitchen.*)

GEORGE (*crossing to the door*): NOW, where do you think you're goin'?

FLORENCE: To get more cocoa. These cups are too darn small.

GEORGE (*to Florence, as he opens the door to reveal Marcus, who is carrying some cleaning*): So's your brai . . . MARCUS! (*George puts his arm around Marcus, and leads him into the apartment.*)

MARCUS: Hey, Mr. Jefferson . . . (*waving to Louise across the room, who is still studying the furniture arrangement*) . . . Mrs. Jefferson. We managed to get that gravy stain out of your suit, Mr. Jefferson.

LOUISE (*chuckling*): And he'll manage to get it back IN.

GEORGE (*forcing a laugh*): Hey, Weezy . . . you always said I needed a hobby.

LOUISE: Would you like to stay for coffee and dessert, Marcus?

MARCUS: I'd sure like to, Mrs. Jefferson, but I promised to be home early. (*He notices the half-changed furniture.*) Hey . . . you're re-doin' the living room.

GEORGE (*laughing*): Yeah . . . Mrs. Jefferson's playin' INFERIOR decorator . . . for the third time this week.

LOUISE: Funny, George. (*She starts to move one of the coffee tables.*)

MARCUS (*rushing across the room to help her*): That's too heavy for you, Mrs. Jefferson. Let me do it.

LOUISE: Oh . . . thank you, Marcus, but you'd better be going. You wanted to get home early, remember?

MARCUS: Aw, that's okay. I got a few minutes to kill . . . might as well work 'em to death. (*He lifts the table.*)

LOUISE: Marcus, you really don't have to . . .

GEORGE (*interrupting as he hangs the cleaning in the closet*): Sure he does. Marcus has got himself one good attitude . . . always ready to help people.

(*Louise points to a spot where Marcus then places the table. She turns to glare at George.*)

LOUISE: Marcus sure isn't like SOME people I know.

(*As Marcus and Louise move the other coffee table, George crosses from the hall closet, and plops into one of the armchairs.*)

GEORGE: That Florence sure is lazy . . . ain't she?

(*Louise reacts, and turns to stare at George.*)

LOUISE: And just what do you think you're doing?

GEORGE (*smiling*): Resting myself. Ain't you heard that middle-aged black men can get high blood-pressure?

LOUISE: That's ridiculous, George. In all the time we've been together, your blood pressure hasn't gone up two points.

(*Florence re-enters from the kitchen.*)

FLORENCE: If it ever does . . . SELL!!

(*Suddenly, the apartment lights begin to flicker.*)

LOUISE: What's that?

(*The lights now dim.*)

GEORGE: Just another power shortage, Weezy. The Arabs probably raised the prices again.

(*The lights go out completely. We can only hear voices.*)

LOUISE (*alarmed*): George . . . I'm scared.

GEORGE: Take it easy, Weezy. Must be a fuse. (*pause*) I'll get the flash-light . . .

(*A beat of silence, then Louise remembers something.*)

LOUISE (*urgently*): GEORGE . . . Don't forget we moved the . . .

SOUND EFFECTS: (*A crash, a thud, and a howl of pain.*)

LOUISE: . . . sofa.

(*The lights flicker on again, and we see George sprawled on the floor on the stage right side of the sofa.*)

GEORGE (*picking himself off the floor*): This all ain't REALLY happenin' . . .

LOUISE (*starting across to help George*): Are you alright, George?

(*The lights dim and go out again.*)

GEORGE (*voice in the dark*): It's happenin'. Weezy . . . you pay that damn bill?

LOUISE (*voice in the dark*): Of course, I paid it. George, I'm REALLY frightened.

(*A beat of silence.*)

GEORGE: There . . . there . . . Sugar. I've got you.

FLORENCE (*angry*): NO YOU DON'T . . . SUCKER!!

(*We hear a "thud," and George yells in pain.*)

(*Marcus lights a match, and we see Louise reach into the corner hutch. They light two candles which illuminate the room with a soft glow. George stands beside a glowering Florence. He holds his ribs in pain.*)

MARCUS: Must be some sort of bad short . . .

FLORENCE (*still frowning at poor George*): Damn right, it's a BAD SHORT!

(*Louise opens the drapes, and discovers that the entire area is dark.*)

LOUISE: Come here, George. It looks like we're not alone.

(*Still wincing, George crosses to the window, and looks out.*)

GEORGE: Just what this city needs . . . another blackout.

MARCUS: That means the subways ain't runnin'. How long you figure it'll last?

GEORGE: Long as it takes for the electric company to rook us outa' more money. Why d'ya think they're called CON Edison.

SOUND EFFECTS: (*a knock at the door.*)

(*Florence crosses, and opens the door to Harry Bentley, who carries an electric Coleman camping lantern.*)

BENTLEY: Greetings, everybody. I see you're as much in the dark about this as I am. (*He chuckles at his own pun.*)

GEORGE (*not amused*): What do you want, Bentley?

BENTLEY (*crossing into the living room*): Actually, I just popped over to borrow a few candles. I knew I'd be needing them this morning, but I forgot to stop by the store on the way home. Rather silly of me . . . wouldn't you say, Mr. J?

GEORGE: I woulda' said it, anyway. (*He thinks a beat.*) Wait a minute, Bentley. You tryin' to tell me you're psychic or somethin'?

BENTLEY (*puzzled*): How's that, Mr. J?

GEORGE: You said you knew this morning you'd be needin' candles for the blackout. Besides, you already got a lattern.

BENTLEY (*laughing*): Oh . . . I didn't know about the blackout . . . but I DID know about Susan.

GEORGE (*really puzzled*): Say what??

BENTLEY: I had already invited Susan over for a candle-light dinner. (*He looks down at his lantern.*) And as for this . . . who ever heard of a romantic FLASH-LIGHT dinner?

GEORGE (*suddenly alarmed, as he thinks of something*): OHMYGOSH!!

LOUISE: What's the matter, George?

BENTLEY: No need to get excited, Mr. J. We can use the lantern in a pinch . . . if we have to.

GEORGE: It's my mother. She's probably scared stiff in the dark.

LOUISE (*calmly*): Only if she can't find her Vodka.

GEORGE: That ain't funny, Weezy. I'd better call her. (*He crosses to the phone, and dials. Not able to get through, he hangs up, and tries again.*)

BENTLEY (*to Louise and Marcus*): You know, this reminds me of the big black-out back in 1966. There are so many similarities . . . except for Susan, of course. She doesn't look a thing like Gloria.

(*Louise listens to Bentley with an amused look.*)

MARCUS: How long did that one go for?

BENTLEY (*with a far-away look*): Gloria?

MARCUS: No, man . . . the BLACKOUT.

BENTLEY: Oh . . . that. It's hard to say. Gloria and I didn't notice for three days.

(*In the background, George has gotten through to his mother.*)

GEORGE (*on phone*): . . . that's so? Don't let it worry you, Momma. Oh you FOUND IT?! (*Embarrassed, he glances up at a smiling Louise, who has been listening to George's side of the conversation.*) Well not too much, now . . . sleep tight. (*He hangs up.*)

LOUISE: I'm sure she'll sleep tight as a drum.

GEORGE (*quickly changing the subject*): Momma heard on her radio that all of New York and part of Jersey are blacked out. (*He thinks a beat.*) We got a port-able radio?

FLORENCE (*suddenly perking up*): Hey . . . I got one. (*She exits to her bed-room.*)

GEORGE: Huh . . . FINALLY we got a reason to keep Florence around. Weezy, remind me to buy a portable radio. (*He notices Bentley.*) You still here, Bentley?

BENTLEY: Actually, I haven't had a chance to ask Mrs. J if I might borrow some candles.

(*George starts to hustle Harry to the door.*)

GEORGE: There . . . you asked . . .

LOUISE: I'm sorry, Mr. Bentley, but these are our last two.

GEORGE (*as he opens the door*): You heard her, Bentley. You'll just have to have a FLASHLIGHT dinner.

BENTLEY (*smiling licentiously*): I suppose it shan't be too bad. Susan is . . . EVEREADY. (*Bentley chuckles at his own lousy pun, but George just stares at him.*)

GEORGE: Finished, Bentley?

BENTLEY: Just one more thing, Mr. J. How come they never have a blackout during the day?

GEORGE: 'Cause then they'd call it a "WHITE-OUT." Speakin' of which . . . (*George pushes Bentley out into the hall, and slams the door.*)

(*Florence re-enters carrying a portable radio.*)

FLORENCE: This is the best idea you ever had, Mr. Jefferson. (*Florence turns on her radio. It is tuned to a soul/rock station, and she begins to dance to the music.*)

GEORGE (*grabbing the radio from her*): Gimme that!! (*He tunes the radio into a news station.*)

VOICE ON RADIO: . . . pandemonium breaking out all over the city. Police report that looters are having a field day in Bedford-Stuyvesant and the South Bronx.

(*George quickly shuts off the radio. He looks very worried.*)

LOUISE: What's the matter, George?

MARCUS: You got a store in the South Bronx . . . don't you, Mr. Jefferson?

GEORGE (*looking very upset*): I sure do . . . and it's full of customers' cleaning. (*He begins to pace the floor.*) They'll clean ME out.

LOUISE (*putting a hand on George's shoulder*): Try not to get too upset about it, dear. You can't do anything now . . . and besides, your insurance'll cover any . . .

GEORGE: WHAT insurance?

LOUISE (*shocked*): You mean you don't have insurance??!!

GEORGE: Not on the South Bronx store. They wouldn't sell me none . . . said it was a bad risk.

LOUISE: But you've been in that store for fifteen years.

GEORGE: You know that, and I know that, Weezy . . . but the insurance companies don't CARE about stuff like that. They said the neighborhood's changed, and it ain't safe for a business no more. (*He crosses to the front closet.*)

LOUISE: Does that make us liable for our customers' property?

GEORGE (*He takes an old coat from the closet.*): It sure does.

MARCUS: That's gonna' cost you a fortune, Mr. Jefferson.

GEORGE: No it ain't, Marcus.

MARCUS (*confused*): Huh??

GEORGE: Me and you are gonna' take the truck, and high-tail it up there before they get everything.

MARCUS: We are?

GEORGE: Sure . . . and we'll bring the stuff down here where it's safe.

LOUISE (*incredulous*): You WILL??

GEORGE: Sure! It'll take us no time. (*He puts on the old coat.*) This old thing'll make me look inconspicuous.

FLORENCE (*as she picks up one of the candles, and crosses to the kitchen*): You don't need a costume for that.

(*George reacts.*)

GEORGE: Common, Marcus.

(*Marcus reluctantly crosses to join George by the door.*)

LOUISE (*worried*): George . . . don't go.

GEORGE: There ain't nothin' to worry about, Weezy. We'll be home before you know it.

MARCUS (*nervous*): It sure is dark out there . . .

(*George opens the door, and they step into the hall.*)

LOUISE: George . . .

GEORGE: I told you, Weezy . . . everything's gonna' be okay. I'll take care of Marcus.

(*George and Marcus exit.*)

LOUISE (*looking very worried*): It's not Marcus I'm worried about . . .

Dissolve to:

Interior, Jefferson South Bronx store—night. (*An hour later. The store is dark, and through the front window, we can see passers-by carrying T.V. sets, stereos, etc. From the back room of the store, we can see a faint light moving about, and we hear voices.*)

FIRST VOICE: Are you crazy, man? That ain't worth a damn thing.

SECOND VOICE: Yeah . . . but it'll look good on my old lady.

FIRST VOICE: Shooot! She puts on five more pounds, an' she'll look good in commercial plates.

SECOND VOICE: Hey man . . . watch your mouth!

(*George and Marcus appear at the front door, and begin to unlock it.*)

FIRST VOICE: SSSHHH . . . somebody's comin'.

(*George and Marcus enter the store.*)

GEORGE (*relieved, as he points his flashlight around*): Whew! It looks like we ain't been hit yet.

MARCUS: The rest of the neighborhood looks like a bomb hit it.

GEORGE: Well . . . that ain't our worry. Let's get all this stuff . . .

(*There is a crash in the back room.*)

MARCUS (*stunned*): WHAAZZAATT??!!

GEORGE (*very frightened*): Who's b..b..back there?

(*Two men slowly emerge from the back room.*)

FIRST LOOTER: You ain't the cops??!!

GEORGE: No . . . we ain't . . . but . . .

SECOND LOOTER: So, split, man! (*The two looters resume picking things from the racks.*)

GEORGE: SPLIT??!! You guys'd better split.

FIRST LOOTER (*calmly turning to face George and Marcus*): You still here?

GEORGE (*indignant*): You bet I'm still here. This is MY store.

SECOND LOOTER: Wrong, brother. We was here first . . .

FIRST LOOTER: . . . and that makes it OUR store.

GEORGE: Hey, man . . . I OWN this place.

(*The two looters look at each other, then break out laughing.*)

MARCUS: Yeah . . . this here's "Jefferson Cleaners," and he's George Jefferson.

FIRST LOOTER (*still smirking*): Not THE George Jefferson??

GEORGE (*dripping with pride*): That's right . . . THE George Jefferson.

SECOND LOOTER: In that case . . . (*He takes a gun from his pocket.*). . . STICK 'EM UP!!

(*George and Marcus look at each other, and break into a nervous chuckle.*)

GEORGE: Heh . . . heh . . . you guys are funny . . .

FIRST LOOTER (*frowning*): He said "STICK 'EM UP"!! (*George and Marcus *put their hands in the air.*) Let's have your wallets. (*George and Marcus reach into their pockets, and hand over their wallets.*)

SECOND LOOTER (*examining George's wallet*): Hey . . . this cat really IS Jefferson . . . and he's loaded too.

FIRST LOOTER (*looking into the wallet*): WOW! He WAS loaded. This sure is our lucky day.

SECOND LOOTER: And you said we shoulda' hit the liquor store . . . HA!

FIRST LOOTER: Grab those leather coats, and let's split. (*The second looter exits to the back room for a beat, and returns carrying several leather garments.*) Well, Mr. Jefferson . . . it's been a pleasure doin' business with you . . . (*The two looters cross to the door.*) If you go out there tonight, be careful. This neighborhood's a jungle. (*The two looters exit.*)

GEORGE (*jumping up and down in anger*): Damn . . . damn . . . DAMN!

MARCUS: You gotta' admit . . . those guys had style.

GEORGE: Yeah . . . and now they got my wallet too.

(*Marcus steps behind the counter, and checks the register.*)

MARCUS: Empty . . .

GEORGE: It figures. (*He looks around.*) Well . . . let's get this stuff on the truck, and get outa' here.

(*George and Marcus begin to take garments from the hanging racks. Suddenly, the door bursts open, and two uniformed cops storm in with their guns drawn.*)

FIRST COP: HOLD IT . . . both of you!!

GEORGE (*stunned*): HUH??!!

SECOND COP: Drop what you're stealing, and get against the counter!

GEORGE: This ain't happenin' . . .

MARCUS (*frightened*): It's happenin', Mr. Jefferson . . . it's happenin'.

(*The cops force George and Marcus to spread-eagle against the counter, and then frisk them.*)

GEORGE: You dudes are makin' a mistake. I OWN this place.

FIRST COP: Sure, bud . . . and I'm Kojak.

GEORGE: If you guys'll just look in my wallet . . .

SECOND COP: I just frisked you, and you ain't got a wallet.

GEORGE (*remembering*): Oh yeah . . . that's right. Two guys just stole our wallets.

SECOND COP: Hey, you guys are REAL creative. The last bunch of looters just said they were takin' inventory. (*He chuckles as he handcuffs George and Marcus together.*)

GEORGE (*furious*): You guys can't do this.

(*They lead George and Marcus to the door.*)

FIRST COP: Pipe down, will ya'?

GEORGE (*as he is being dragged out the door*): I wanna' see my lawyer!!

SECOND COP: Sure . . . sure . . . good old Calhoun's out in the paddy wagon.

GEORGE (*howling*): WEEEEZZYYY. . . .

Fade out.

ACT TWO

Fade in: Interior, jail cell—night. (*A short time later. The cell is filled with surly-looking men. New York's power is still out, and the cell and hallway are only illuminated by emergency lanterns. Some of the inmates pace back and forth, others try to doze on cots or on the floor. Suddenly, the relative quiet is broken by the approaching sound of George's voice.*)

GEORGE (*off-screen*) (*angry as hell*): I'm tellin' you dudes . . . you're in BIG trouble.

FIRST COP (*off-screen*): Sure pal . . . sure.

(*George and Marcus now appear in the hallway, accompanied by the two cops.*)

GEORGE (*rubbing his hands on his old coat*): Damn ink all over my hands . . .

SECOND COP (*sarcastic, as he unlocks the cell door*): Aw, gee . . . I'm sorry. The manicurist won't be in till tomorrow.

(*George and Marcus step into the cell.*)

FIRST COP (*sarcastic, chuckling*): I do hope you find our accommodations to your liking.

GEORGE: I hope you find my lawyer to your likin'. When he gets done with you, you'll be poundin' a beat in Uganda.

SECOND COP (*slamming the cell door behind George and Marcus*): Yeah?! I could use a vacation. (*The two cops exit laughing.*)

FIRST COP: Can you believe that guy? He OWNS the place . . . the nerve of that turkey!

SECOND COP (*mocking*): YOU'LL BE POUNDING A BEAT IN UGANDA!! He probably knows Idi Amin personally.

(*Furious, George turns and looks around the cell. Upon seeing the surly inmates, who are quietly watching his performance, he panics, runs back to the bars and bellows after the cops.*)

GEORGE (*screaming*): What about my phone call??

FIRST COP (*off-screen*): Wait your turn, chump. Now . . . SHADDUP!!

MARCUS: I don't think they believed you, Mr. Jefferson.

GEORGE (*pacing the crowded floor*): They'll believe me when I sue their butts off. I'm gonna' fix Con Edison too.

MARCUS (*smiling proudly*): 'Atta' way, Mr. J! We're gonna fight City Hall.

GEORGE: No we ain't. Just the cops and Con Ed.

MARCUS: By the way . . . how come you're gonna' sue the electric company?

GEORGE (*pacing up a storm*): 'Cause if it wasn't for them turkeys, we wouldn't be here. I'll fix 'em.

(*Suddenly the cell's main lights come on. The blackout is over, and the other prisoners cheer. One of them, a raggedy-looking character, approaches George.*)

FIRST INMATE (*shaking George's hand*): Man . . . I don't know who you are, but keep talkin'. Maybe you can get us a steak dinner.

(*The other inmates now approach George and Marcus, and begin to size them up.*)

MARCUS (*aside to George*): Mr. Jefferson . . . I'm scared.

GEORGE (*trembling*): Stick close to me . . . I'll look after you.

MARCUS (*not reassured*): That's what you said right after "Let's get the truck an' go up to the Bronx."

(*A particularly tough-looking inmate stares George in the eye.*)

SECOND INMATE: What're you dudes in for? You looters?

GEORGE (*indignant*): We ain't done nothin'. It's a mistake.

SECOND INMATE (*smiling*): Sure . . . sure. We've all been framed. Don't let 'em bluff ya's. Just stick to that story . . .

GEORGE: It ain't no story. The cops picked us up in my own store.

(*The SECOND INMATE begins to laugh.*)

SECOND INMATE: Hey . . . that's rich! An' I was picked up carryin' my OWN air conditioner down the street.

FIRST INMATE (*rolling with laughter*): Yeah . . . and I wandered into that furniture factory by accident. I mean, it WAS dark.

(*All the inmates start to roar. George is frustrated and furious.*)

GEORGE (*shouting above the laughter*): I AIN'T JIVIN'!! (*The cell quiets down.*) I own a chain of cleanin' stores. I made my way up BY MYSELF, and I don't need to steal. I ain't looted from nobody, and I don't belong in this dump. (*One of the inmates, sitting on a cot, takes out a harmonica, and goes into some classic prison riff.) That's all I gotta' say. (George angrily sits down on the cell floor.)*

SECOND INMATE (*looking down at George*): Man . . . you're really somethin'. You DO think you're too good for us, don't you?

(Marcus quickly steps between George and the burly inmate.)

MARCUS (*shaking with fear*): He didn't mean nothin' by it . . . honest.

SECOND INMATE: Then what's he goin' around dumpin' that innocent jazz on us for?

MARCUS (*searching for an "out"*): Uh . . . 'cause he's a . . . he's a SMART hood, that's why. My boss always knows how to put on a front.

SECOND INMATE (*scoffing*): Boy . . . you take me for a fool?

MARCUS (*confused*): Uh . . . yeah . . . I mean . . . NO.

GEORGE: Forget it, Marcus. They ain't buyin' . . . and I ain't sellin'.

(Frustrated, Marcus slides down onto the floor next to George.)

MARCUS: I was just tryin' to help . . .

GEORGE (*patting Marcus on the back*): I know, man . . . but I ain't apologizin' 'cause I AIN'T a looter.

FIRST INMATE: Ya know . . . I think the runt is tellin' the truth. He ain't the lootin' type.

GEORGE: Damn right, I ain't.

(Another voice comes out of the crowd of inmates. Jackson is a tall, black man. He rises from one of the bunk beds, and walks over to George.)

JACKSON: Jefferson's telling the truth. He's no looter.

(George stands up to face Jackson, but still has to look way up at the man.)

GEORGE (*surprised*): You know me?

JACKSON: I've seen you around . . . with your fine clothes and your well-dressed wife.

GEORGE (*beaming*): Ha . . . see there? The man knows me.

JACKSON: Yeah . . . I've seen you. I've seen you strutting into your store to count up all the bread in your cash register. Year after year I'd see you coming by . . . getting fatter and fatter . . .

GEORGE (*self-consciously sucking in his gut*): That ain't fat . . . I slouch.

JACKSON (*looking George up and down*): Well . . . your head's sure gotten fat. Why, I bet you never REALLY noticed the change in the neighborhood . . . just the change in your pocket.

GEORGE: How could I MISS what was goin' down in that neighborhood?

JACKSON: Did you know WHY it was changing? (*George tries to answer, but can't.*) I used to be a welder at the Brooklyn Navy Yard. When I got laid-off, I found part time work for awhile . . . then nothing.

MARCUS: How'd you get in here?

JACKSON: Last night the cops caught Old Henry Jackson looting an appliance store.

GEORGE: I bet you feel like hell.

JACKSON: Sure I do . . . 'cause I got CAUGHT.

GEORGE (*puzzled*): Say what?

JACKSON: I'm not ashamed of trying to feed my family. I'm just ashamed of not being too good at it.

GEORGE: There ain't no excuse for stealin'.

SECOND INMATE: You ever been poor?

MARCUS (*jumping in to George's defense*): He was so poor . . . his folks couldn't afford a taller kid.

(George reacts.)

JACKSON: Then he doesn't REMEMBER what it's like to have to steal to eat. Man . . . that neighborhood's full of guys like me. You better believe that when the Man's pants are down, we're gonna' grab whatever we can get our hands on.

GEORGE (*not as forceful as before*): You tellin' me that nobody was lootin' just for the sake of doin' it?

JACKSON: Sure they were . . . some of them. (*He points to another man in the cell.*) Lewis over there's got a good job. He didn't have to do it. But when some guys see a crowd doing something . . .

GEORGE (*calling over to Lewis*): Hey Lewis . . . is that the truth?

LEWIS (*singing*): I LOVE A PARADE . . .

(*George reacts.*)

JACKSON: Point is . . . there is no right and wrong . . . no black and white . . .

GEORGE (*trying to make a joke*): Sure there is . . . the Willises . . . (*Nobody laughs—not even Marcus.*) Inside joke . . .

JACKSON: I don't know, Jefferson. Maybe you've just gotten out of touch . . . (*Jackson shakes his head, turns, and walks back to his cot. George leans on the bars, and looks blankly out. A weird-looking inmate now approaches George.*)

WEIRD INMATE (*in a loud whisper*): PSSST . . . Buddy . . .

(*George turns to look at the guy.*)

GEORGE: What do YOU want?

WEIRD INMATE: Just wanna' give you some advice . . . (*George listens intently.*) Keep an eye out in here . . . the place is full of crooks. (*George stares at the man in disbelief. The character rolls up his coat-sleeve, and displays a half-dozen watches to George.*) Wanna' buy an Omega watch . . .?

Dissolve to:

Interior, jail cell—night. (*Some time later. Most of the men in the cell are asleep. George dozes in a corner on the floor, his battered old coat covers him like a blanket. George tosses and turns in his sleep. Marcus is awake, and sits next to George, guarding him. The weird inmate sits by himself, wide awake and happily listening to his watches tick. We hear voices approaching off-stage. After a beat, Louise appears in the hallway outside the cell. She is accompanied by the First Cop.*)

FIRST COP (*quietly to Louise*): You see him in there?

(*She looks around the cell for a beat. As Louise's eyes search for George, Marcus happens to look up and see her. Overjoyed, he reaches over and shakes George.*)

GEORGE (*in his sleep*): Not now, Weezy . . .

MARCUS (*again shaking George*): Mr. Jefferson . . . wake up . . .

GEORGE (*turning over—still asleep*): I said not now, Weezy. I got a headache!

(*Louise spots George and Marcus, and points them out to the cop. Marcus still tries to awaken George.*)

MARCUS (*He thinks for a beat, then speaks very quietly.*): What do you mean Imperial Cleaners is cuttin' their prices again?

(*George's eyes open, and he sits up with a start. He is totally disoriented.*)

GEORGE: WHAZZAT?? Where am I? (*He looks around, sees the cell, then Marcus.*) Oh . . . yeah . . .

MARCUS (*excited*): Mrs. Jefferson's here.

(*George leaps to his feet, just as the cop unlocks the cell door.*)

FIRST COP: You sure that's him, Mrs. Jefferson??

LOUISE (*anxious*): I'm POSITIVE!

FIRST COP (*still baffled*): Gosh . . . I'm sorry for the mistake. He sure had us fooled. (*The cop unlocks the cell door.*)

LOUISE (*a bit angry*): Evidently.

(*George rushes to Louise. He is ecstatic.*)

GEORGE: WEEEEEEEZZZZZZZYYYYYYY!!!!!!!

(*They embrace, then George notices the cop standing there, and begins to glower at him.*)

FIRST COP (*nervous*): Jeez . . . I'm sorry for the mistake, Mr. Jefferson.

(*George and Marcus step into the hallway, and the cop re-locks the cell door.*)

GEORGE (*angry*): Not as sorry as you're gonna' be.

FIRST COP: We were just doing our jobs. If there were REAL looters in your store, you'd've wanted us there . . . wouldn't you?

GEORGE (*cooling down a bit*): Yeah . . . I guess so . . .

MARCUS: We were sort of askin' for it when we went up there.

GEORGE (*reluctantly*): Well, yeah . . .

LOUISE: And if they didn't let you finally make that call to me when the lines were cleared, you might have been in here all night.

FIRST COP: Next time remember, Mr. Jefferson . . . in an area like the South Bronx the only way to protect a store is steel-plated walls and iron bars. Even then there are no guarantees. The people up there are animals.

GEORGE: I dunno' . . . maybe you're right. (*yawning*) Who's got the time?

(*The weird inmate leans against the bars, and rolls up his sleeves.*)

WEIRD INMATE: What city?

GEORGE: Forget it. (*They walk down the hallway.*)

LOUISE: Let's go home and get some sleep.

GEORGE: Just a couple o' hours, Weezy. Then I gotta' go up to the South Bronx store.

MARCUS: Got some cleanin' up to do, I guess.

GEORGE (*as they exit*): No . . . I got some CLOSIN' up to do, Marcus.

Dissolve to:

Interior, Jefferson South Bronx store—morning. (*Early the next morning. The store is a disaster area. Every one of the customers' garments is missing, the shelves are empty, the windows are broken, and the floor is covered with debris. George and Louise stand sadly in the ruins.*)

GEORGE (*Looking around, he feels angry, hurt, and bitter.*): After so many years in this store, this is what I got left . . . damn!

(*Louise rummages around in the rubble.*)

LOUISE: They didn't leave much, did they?

GEORGE: The animals took EVERYTHING. I'm surprised they left the air.

LOUISE: I'm sorry Marcus had to see all this. It doesn't give him much of an outlook on things . . . does it, George? (*Louise sees something in the mess near the door.*) What's this?

GEORGE: Probably a roach . . . and the only reason they ain't stole him is 'cause they got enough of their own.

(*Louise bends down and picks up a wallet.*)

LOUISE: It's your wallet George.

GEORGE (*surprised*): You're jivin' . . .

LOUISE: No . . . it's here. (*He rushes over to look.*)

GEORGE: I'll be damned. I bet they took everything of any value.

LOUISE (*looking through the wallet*): You're right, George . . . your mother's picture's still here.

GEORGE (*He reacts, and is not amused.*): That ain't funny, Weezy.

LOUISE (*chuckling as she studies the picture*): Mother Jefferson sitting on a pony IS funny, George. (*looks through the wallet some more*) Your credit cards are still here.

GEORGE (*really surprised*): You GOTTA be kiddin'.

(*She shows him the credit cards.*)

GEORGE (*smiling*): What d'ya know . . . I got hit by dumb looters.

LOUISE: See, George? It's not all that bad.

GEORGE (*frowning*): Don't try to change my mind, Weezy. I'm not gonna' re-open this place . . . NEVER!

LOUISE: I'm not going to try . . .

GEORGE (*beginning to pace back and forth*): There's NO WAY I'm ever gonna' set foot in this neighborhood again. Give me one reason why I oughta' come back here.

LOUISE (*as she calmly resumes looking around for valuables*): I can't, George . . .

GEORGE: You heard the cop . . . they're animals up here now. We left the ghetto behind YEARS ago. (*rambling on*) I ain't got no insurance . . . I gotta' pay off all my customers for their stuff . . .

LOUISE: No question you're right, George.

GEORGE (*pacing up a storm*): . . . cop said I gotta' get steel-plated walls and iron bars to keep 'em out . . .

(*The door opens, and an elderly man enters the store.*)

LOUISE (*to the old man*): Can we help you?

OLD MAN (*sadly looking around at the damage*): They hit you pretty bad, huh?

GEORGE (*abruptly*): Yeah. Now what can we do for you?

OLD MAN: You the owners?

LOUISE: Yes . . . we're the Jeffersons.

OLD MAN: I've been a customer of yours for a long, long time. I had a suit being cleaned . . .

GEORGE (*snapping*): You'll get paid for it like everybody else . . . before we close up.

OLD MAN: No big deal. It was an old suit, anyway . . . still had pleats. (*thinks for a beat*) Did you say you're closing up?

GEORGE: You heard me. I'm shuttin' down. I got other stores to worry about.

OLD MAN (*sighing*): Can't say I blame you. You're a rich man.

(*In the background, Louise finds something.*)

GEORGE: Damn right I am . . . and I worked hard for it too.

OLD MAN: If I had what you had, I'd go too. Leave all this behind . . . that's your best bet. It's the same with all the merchants. They've gotten fat . . . (*Again George sucks in his gut, but then lets it out, thinking.*) . . . and don't need to be reminded of the old days. (*The old man looks around again.*) Well, I'll let you do your business. (*He turns and exits.*)

GEORGE (*pausing, then calling out after the man exits*): Hey . . . your suit . . .

LOUISE: George . . . look what I found. (*She holds a small, cracked picture frame.*)

GEORGE (*in thought*): Huh?

LOUISE: I found the first dollar this old store earned us. I'm surprised the looters didn't grab it.

(*George looks it over carefully.*)

GEORGE: That IS somethin', Weezy.

LOUISE: Well, at least you'll have a souvenir of your second store after we close it.

GEORGE (*stiffening his spine*): Close it? What do you mean CLOSE IT??

LOUISE (*shocked*): But George . . .

GEORGE: Ain't no "buts" about it, Weezy. I ain't no quitter. This store is more than just a business . . . it's a link to what WAS for us.

(*Louise grabs George and hugs him.*)

LOUISE: Oh, George . . . I'm so proud of you.

GEORGE (*smiling—proud of himself too*): Yeah . . . well . . . I learned a few things in the last couple o' days.

LOUISE: Like . . . ?

GEORGE: Like . . . just 'cause you're successful don't mean you ain't the same person you was.

LOUISE: And . . . ?

GEORGE: And . . . no matter what happens, you've gotta' have some trust left in people. (*She hugs him again.*) Now let's go home . . . I'm whipped. (*They walk to the door, and George turns back to look at the store again.*) Weezy . . . how much you figure steel-plated walls and iron bars'll run us?

(*Louise reacts, and stares at George, as we:*)

Fade out.

DISCUSSION QUESTIONS

1. Read the script in conjunction with Darryl Pinckney's essay on blacks in sitcoms in "Magazines." Do you think Pinckney's critical assessment of the show is correct? Explain why or why not.

2. Situation comedies require many one-liners. Identify several of the jokes in this episode and examine what they have in common. Can you state the show's central joke; that is, the joke the comedy seems to revolve around, that all the jokes grow out of? For example, is there any joke inherent in the basic situation of this series that a scriptwriter can use over and over?

3. Discuss the moral problem of this episode. What is George's dilemma? Why is *he* arrested? Does the show have a moral? If so, can you state it in one sentence?

Hill Street Blues Staff / *Hill Street Blues*: "Grace under Pressure"   1984

> *Perhaps more than any other form of writing, screenwriting is a truly collaborative effort. Nowhere is this more apparent than in a quick examination of the credits (which sometimes seem to occupy half the air time) for most television and movie scripts. The following episode of* Hill Street Blues, *"Grace under Pressure," concerning the death of Sergeant Esterhaus, was written in December 1983 by Jeffrey Lewis, Michael Wagner, Karen Hall, and Mark Frost and was based on a story by Steven Bochco, Jeffrey Lewis, and David Milch. It went through no less than six revisions before being aired during the 1984 season.*
>
> *The series itself was created by Steven Bochco and Michael Kozoll. It made its first television appearance in 1981 and since then has won more Emmies than any other dramatic series—twenty-one in its first year alone. Though now off the air, it was generally regarded as one of the best-written shows of its time.*

ACT ONE

Fade in.

1. Over black—"Roll Call—6:59 A.M."

GOLDBLUME'S VOICE: Item ten. Jailbreak.

2. Interior. Roll call—day. (*With Goldblume addressing the dayshift—*)

GOLDBLUME: Not literally, guys, but for those who don't watch TV, listen to radio, or talk to anybody—Judge Spears last night ordered two hundred forty-seven prisoners awaiting trial released o.r. from the Michigan Avenue complex, due to severe overcrowding and inhumane conditions in that facility. (*Goldblume's lack of sarcasm suggests he takes the judge's analysis seriously; but no one else does—*)

LARUE: Yeah, let's put those inhumane conditions back on the streets where they belong.

GOLDBLUME: Look, whether we agree or disagree, these alleged perpetrators are back out there. So we're probably going to be busy. Additionally—item eleven—until Division Vice is reconstituted, we're assigned ongoing prostitution enforcement for the Hill, Midtown, Washington and Jefferson Heights. Operation Pussycat commences today at 0800 hours, in sufficient time to catch the brisk breakfast hour trade. Your trained eyes may detect among us some of the personnel assigned to this operation . . . (*Bates and few other women are in hooker garb, Bates with her leather cop jacket over her shoulders.*) Additionally, Hill, Renko, Perez and Kolzicki will work back-up, Peyser and Martin will be working plain-clothes out of n.d. sedans. (*Furillo quietly slips down the roll call stairs, draws a few curious looks, waits in back, times his approach to the front to the conclusion of Goldblume's remarks.*) Item twelve, our truck hijacking problem is becoming more blatant—two more yesterday. This seems to be something of a criminal fad; the toll's up to six drivers beaten or knifed plus a couple hundred grand in merchandise boosted. Maybe catching some guys would make it less fashionable. Whattaya say? Last item, welcomes. Welcome Mike Perez back. Welcome transfer Clara Pilsky from South Ferry.

3. (*Angle—Clara, a dark-haired beauty, also dressed to go undercover as a hooker, waving off the attention a little self-consciously, mouthing ''hi's'' to a few.*)

LARUE: Hello, hello, hello.

GOLDBLUME: That's it, people. Thank you. Have a good shift.

4. (*Including Furillo, awkwardly, as though he has no idea what he's going to say, suddenly standing there—*)

FURILLO: Uh, people, uh, could you stay seated a minute, could I have your attention?

5. (*The dayshift, that had half-risen, drops down again. Sensitive to the haltingness of Furillo's diction.*)

6. (*Resume.*)

FURILLO (*cont'd*): Phil Esterhaus passed away this morning. He suffered a heart attack, that's the only detail I have at this time. (*A beat.*) Information as it comes in . . . about services . . . will be on the duty board. (*A beat.*) I don't have too many words, people. This is going to be a difficult day. I know the caution Phil would urge on you. Be careful out there. (*Another beat: Some stirrings. Some tears.*) Our friend was fifty-five years old. (*Choked.*) If people want to take a moment of silence . . .

(*He bows his head, as do others. Pan the quiet room. A couple people raise their heads too soon, put them down again. A couple, after a few seconds, just keep them up, looking around. Quite a number of seconds pass, then Furillo exits, tears in his eyes, past Hunter and Calletano. Gradually, silently, people raise their heads. A few get up, then most get up. Off the first words muttered by anyone—*)

LARUE: Sonofabitch.

Smash cut to Main Titles. Fade in.

7. Interior. Cop diner—day. (*With Coffey entering, sober, and without the sling we saw him with in roll call. Approaches the booth where Bates, Pilsky and Peyser sit quietly with their coats on, over coffees; slides in.*)

COFFEY (*mostly to Bates*): How ya doin'?

BATES (*a shrug*): How you doing?

COFFEY (*not much enthusiasm for it*): Doc gave me a clean bill. I can go back on patrol tomorrow.

BATES (*who can't muster much enthusiasm either*): Great.

BATES (*staring*): I still can't believe it. I feel like going home and crawling into bed.

COFFEY: You know it's right, what the Captain said. We gotta be careful; people could make a lot of mistakes today.

8. Include Renko.

RENKO (*subdued*): Giusepp . . .

COFFEY (*equally subdued; the minimal greetings of people sharing grief*): Hey, Renko . . . (*Follow Renko back to—*)

9. The Counter (*where he's sitting between Hill and Perez—*)

WAITRESS (*commiserative*): Poor man. Fifty-five years old. Any children? (*Hill shakes no, doesn't really want to engage in conversation.*) He must've been some wonderful guy; every one of you, you all look like ghosts.

RENKO (*dignifying her sympathy by putting some effort into a reply*): We thought he was getting better, you know? He was supposed to be getting better. (*More forthcoming with this neutral party than he could be with a lot of others just now.*) . . . He was like . . . mom and dad, you know?

WAITRESS (*commiserative*): That kind of guy. Yeah. (*Moving, next to pour Perez more coffee.*) Half a cup?

PEREZ (*raising hand to cup*): No thanks.

WAITRESS: Nice to see you back, Mike.

PEREZ (*grimace*): Thanks.

10. Angle. (*A guy, Jack, around the counter bend, a couple empty seats away—*)

JACK (*to Perez; somewhere in his voice an edge, reading the tag on Perez' jacket*): Scuze me, officer, scuze me, your name Perez?

PEREZ: That's right.

JACK: You related to that baseball player got traded back to the Reds?

PEREZ: No.

JACK: Then you must be the guy who killed the kid.

RENKO (*overhearing; moving to intervene*): Anything we can help you with, bud?

PEREZ (*calm*): Nobody needs any help here, Andy. (*To Jack.*) Yeah. What is it you want to know?

JACK: Just wonder what it feels like to be a kid-killer.

PEREZ: It feels terrible. And you try and tell yourself you were acting in the line of duty. Anything else? (*Perez is kind of shaken; the honesty of his speech leaves Jack without too much left to say.*)

JACK: No. Guess not.

RENKO: Hey, fella, you about done with your food, there? (*Half-beat; but not really permitting a reply.*) Because if you are, maybe you'd best just pay that tab and get out of here. (*Jack throws some change on the counter, gets up with an empty grin at Perez—*)

JACK: Have a nice day. (*And leaves.*)

HILL (*to Perez*): You okay?

PEREZ: Yeah (*shakes his head; sardonic*). Life goes on, huh? (*Coffey had also closed ranks with Perez. Now Renko's hand radio squawks, almost under Perez' last words.*)

RADIO DISPATCH (*filtered*): All units in vicinity, we've got a reported rape, possible robbery, 2632 Van Vuren, that's the Donut Hut.

COFFEY: Oh God . . .

RENKO (*to Coffey*): What is it?

COFFEY: My girlfriend works there. (*Off his sudden, stricken look—*)

Cut to:

11. Interior. Donut Hut. (*An SID guy dusts for prints around the rear door and adjoining window; a number of uniforms troop around trying to keep busy—camera comes to rest on—*)

12. Angle. (*At the door Washington with an SID officer, giving Washington a preliminary reading.*)

SID GUY: No signs of forced entry, no signs of struggle.

WASHINGTON: Robbery?

SID GUY: Register's rifled, he took her purse.

13. LaRue and Sandy Valpariso. (*She's seated at a small formica table, a blanket around her. Trying to tell him what happened—LaRue is being very professional, caring, taking notes—she's shaking with the effort to hold herself together—*)

SANDY: When I came in, he must've already been inside. I didn't hear anything. I just turned around and he was there—he had a knife, he said he was going to kill me . . . he made me undress and lie on the floor . . . he ran the knife over me, he put it in my mouth, his eyes were crazy, he was talking crazy, I was so frightened . . . he told me to do things . . . (*She can't continue.*)

LARUE: Can you give me a description, Sandy?

SANDY: Latin, about five eight or nine, black pants, one of those gray hooded sweatshirts . . .

(*Through a window behind her we see—*)

14. (*Joe Coffey, getting out of a unit, coming towards the shop under a head of steam—Washington moves outside to head him off—*)

WASHINGTON: Joe—

COFFEY: Where is she?

WASHINGTON: Inside.

COFFEE: It was her?

WASHINGTON: Yeah.

COFFEY (*an agonized moment, then*): She hurt?

WASHINGTON: I don't think so, no. (*Coffey starts for the door.*) Maybe you don't wanna go in there.

COFFEY: You sayin' I can't?

WASHINGTON: No. (*Coffey goes by him and enters.*)

Cut to:

15. Interior. Donut Hut. (*As Coffey moves to her—LaRue sees him first—she sees him, she starts to cry for the first time; he sits beside her, she holds his hand, clinging to him.*)

SANDY: Joe . . . I'm real glad you're here . . . (*She really lets go; needs to be hugged. He moves to her, tries to comfort her, but it's apparent his own reactions are far too complex to allow himself the unalloyed role of protector.*)

COFFEY: It's okay . . . it's okay . . . (*Washington and LaRue retreat discreetly—we move with them—Washington spots the manager, Harley, looking out at them through a window in his office—*)

WASHINGTON: Manager's here. (*They enter the office—*)

16. Donut Hut Manager's Office.

LARUE: Can you tell us which of your employees have keys to the building?

HARLEY (*surly*): No, I can't.

WASHINGTON: Why's that?

HARLEY: They trade shifts, give the keys to each other. I tell 'em not to, a lot of good it does.

WASHINGTON: What about a list of everybody's worked here the last couple years?

HARLEY (*sarcastic*): Hey, I'll take a spare morning, type it up. (*Angry; looking out his window into the shop*) So lemme ask you somethin'. Why is it the law don't apply to cops like everybody else?

WASHINGTON: How's that? (*Harley nods for Washington and LaRue to observe.*)

17. Point of view—The shop (*where a uniform's chowing down a donut, swilling coffee.*)

HARLEY: Guys come in here, it's like Attila the Hun. Close the joint down, no trade, plus you eat me out of house and home and I don't see dime one on the counter.

LARUE (*growing irritated*): We'll pay you for donuts. Give us the list.

HARLEY: What list? (*Fed up, Washington throws Harley up against some file drawers.*)

WASHINGTON: Listen up, sucker, you picked the wrong day, you understand? Now we got a rape and you're worried about donuts, but for the time being we're talking about rape, you understand? We want to know every guy's worked in here, every guy's been busted, every guy you fired for the last two years, you understand? (*Washington lets him go. Harley shakes himself for recomposure, grimaces, reaches for a creaky desk drawer.*)

HARLEY (*grumblingly concessionary, reaching for a file box*): I'll give you my file of W-4's. You can figure the rest out yourself.

(*Off Washington, still steamed, doing his best to take the file from Harley without snatching it—*)

Cut to:

18. Exterior. Street—day. (*Bates and Pilsky, on a street corner near an alley, in their hooker get-ups—Pilsky's smoking a cigarette—*)

PILSKY: I never met him, what was he like?

BATES: The Sarge? He was a piece a'work. He was like . . . he was a rock. No matter how bad it was, you saw him at the desk it took some of the edge off, you know?

PILSKY: Yeah.

BATES: I didn't think he'd ever been sick a day in his life. (*Close to tears that suddenly overtake her, gratefully seeing something.*) Got a Lincoln approaching at two o'clock.

(*A beat-up Continental is gliding their way. It stops at the curb near a hydrant, Bates sidles over to it—a black guy with a gap-toothed smile, Kelvin James, slides over to the passenger window—*)

BATES (*cont'd*): Hi there.

JAMES (*a little high*): Hi, do you recanize me? That's why I carry this credit card—(*he holds one up*)—don't leave home wid'out it.

BATES (*half a beat*): What are we talking about here?

JAMES: Somethin' 'bout me and you goin' someplace and gettin' naked somehow.

BATES: Not real impressed yet, sport.

(*James gets out of the car—he's big, muscular, more than a little menacing, even as he continues to smile—*)

JAMES: You 'be impressed—we go someplace you get this, Blondie. (*He hands her the card to look at.*)

BATES: Oh, so *you're* Virginia Kimball.

JAMES: Ac' fast you could have yourself a nice free ride, sugar. (*He smiles at her.*) So where we goin'?

BATES: Step into my office.

(*Bates gestures to Pilsky, starts leading James into the alley—Pilsky calls into a handi-talkie in background—*)

JAMES (*stopping her*): Hey, sister, I said where we goin'?

BATES: How do you feel about jail? You're under arrest, hands against the wall—	PILSKY: Back-ups, the alley off Dekker and 34th.

(*James suddenly lashes out, starts to run. Bates catches him by an ankle, trips him up—as he rises Pilsky appears in front of him—James hits her with a shoulder, knocking her down, starts to run.*)

19. (*Archie Peyser careens his n.d. sedan into the alley, blocking the mouth, cutting James off—Peyser jumps out, pulls his baton—*)

20. (*James stops, starts running back the other way—*)

21. (*Bates and Pilsky, just getting to their feet, see him coming, look at each other—*)

22. Angle. (*As James, yelling, tries to run right through them, Pilsky hits him low, Bates hits him high, James goes down—*)

23. Angle. (*They start mixing it up—James throws Pilsky off his back, grabs Bates by the throat—in background Peyser comes running up—as behind him in the street, Perez and Kolzicki pull up in a unit—*)

24. (*Bates knees James in the groin, Pilsky grabs him by the face from behind—for a moment they're all frozen in isometric opposition—sounds of their physical efforts—*)

25. (*Peyser arrives and delivers a blow to the back of James' neck with a nightstick—he yells, adrenalized, an animal—then totters, and goes over like a felled log.*)

26. (*Perez and Kolzicki just getting to them—Bates and Pilsky are winded, beat up—*)

PEREZ: Everybody okay?

BATES: Clara?

PILSKY: Just catch my breath.

BATES: Yeah . . . okay . . . nice, Archie.

PEYSER: Thanks. Same to you.

BATES (*a deep breath*): Call a dumptruck for this guy.

Cut to:

27. Interior. Squad Room—day. (*Hill and Renko entering with two diablos in tow. One is protesting loudly.*)

DIABLO #1: I told you, that was my mama's T.V. We was takin' it to be repaired.

RENKO: Tell it to the judge, son. (*As they reach booking.*) Leo, got a couple enterprisin' young T.V. thiefs for you to book.

HILL: Store owner's on his way down to I.D. them.

LEO (*upset about something*): Anybody call a P.D.?

DIABLO #1: Don't need no P.D. Just get Jesus Martinez down here, man.

28. Angle. (*Grace Gardner approaching Leo, in trenchcoat and sunglasses, having just entered the precinct house.*)

GRACE (*to Leo*): Hello, Leo. To see Captain Furillo?

LEO (*wet-eyed*): Go on, Mrs. Gardner . . . (*Grace nods by way of acknowledgment, and as Hill, Renko, Hunter, Calletano and others watch various moments of her passage, she transits the squad room to—*)

29. Furillo's office (*where Furillo is standing, waiting*).

FURILLO: Grace . . . I'm so sorry. (*He busses her lightly, gives her a small hug. She smiles distantly.*)

GRACE (*indicating a chair*): Thank you, Frank. May I?

(*Furillo nods. She sits down. Furillo shuts the door, as Grace removes her sunglasses, places them in her carrying sack, then extracts a manilla envelope from it. To judge by appearances, she'd holding herself together, though the strain of doing so is apparent in her eyes, and in the carefulness of her movements. As Furillo comes back around her, from shutting the door, she hands him the envelope.*)

GRACE: Phil asked me . . . if anything happened . . . to deliver this to you. . . . I believe he wanted you to be executor. (*Off Furillo's puzzlement.*) I was with him, Frank.

FURILLO (*spoken plainly*): I guess I didn't know how sick Phil was, or that he knew either. I saw him last week, he seemed on the mend. He said he was on the mend.

GRACE: Over the weekend, they did an angiogram. They told him his heart had weakened. Something about a "stenosis." He didn't want anyone to know. (*Furillo nods.*) The doctor told him, no this, no that . . . no sex. (*Furillo begins to wonder where Grace is going with this; but doesn't care to ask. He waits, then—*)

FURILLO: How are you, Grace?

GRACE: I'm okay . . . I'm just . . . (*remembering*) The doctor said, no this, no that, no sex, and so uh . . . I don't know why I'm telling you this, I guess it's a police station, I guess I'm coming in to confess. You see, this morning, Philip and I . . . we were together, sleeping. And he woke up . . . and we . . . were making love. And . . . that's when he died. (*Furillo nods, speechless, tears in his eyes. Grace is near tears herself.*) His great, brave heart simply exploded.

FURILLO: Grace, you can't blame yourself.

GRACE (*tears; struggling with it*): I don't, Frank. I don't. I'm proud. Phil said to me he wouldn't live the way they said he would have to. He couldn't live like a dead man in the middle of life. And this morning . . . he'd been so weak but this morning he seemed stronger. Maybe it was because we were so close to dreams. But he seemed in the darkness—this was before daybreak—to be back to himself. To be back to his magnificent self, enormous, healthy, we embraced, we made love, I held onto that man, thinking, like a miracle, the flesh is holding, it's okay, we'll go on, like always . . . (*still trying to say something definitive; something that will stop it all*). He was a beautiful, simple, honorable man, and I wanted to grow old with him, and when the wrenching spasms came . . . (*She's frightened; needs to be not alone, feels how alone she is.*) Please Frank . . . would it be too imposing of me to ask you to hold me a few seconds . . . (*Furillo takes her in his arms, holds her tightly.*) I was under him . . . just hours ago . . . we felt each other's breath . . . each other's life . . . I held his ears, God I loved his ears, his nose . . . and then . . . and then . . . ohh . . . (*She shudders lightly.*) (*low*) I miss him so. (*Grace sobs. Furillo holds her.*)

Fade out.

ACT TWO

Fade in.

30. Interior. Front desk. (*Bates, Pilsky, Peyser, Perez and Kolzicki escorting a handcuffed James into booking—*)

BATES: In there, meat.

PILSKY (*noticing for the first time*): Look at this, brand new nylons, shot to hell. (*As she stops to inspect them, raising her already heightened hem slightly, we pick up—*)

31. (*Jesus just moving past her, with one Diablo escort—*)

JESUS: Nice stems, mama.

PILSKY: In your face, punk.

JESUS (*moving on*): I wish.

Cut to:

32. Interior. Squad Room. (*As Jesus passes his two Diablo charges, seated at a desk, tended by Hill and Renko—*)

JESUS: Sit tight, we're gonna clear this up.

RENKO (*pissed; to Hill*): Walks in like he's Yes-sir Arafat.

(*Furillo meets Jesus at the door to his office—*)

JESUS: Top a' the mornin', Frankie.

FURILLO (*no patience*): Inside. (*The bodyguard stops at the door as Jesus enters—*)

33. Interior. Furillo's office. (*As Furillo closes the door—*)

FURILLO: Let's make this fast, Jesus.

JESUS: These two misguided youths you got out here—

FURILLO: Two "youths" with a half-dozen priors apiece, and they're looking at larceny, possession of stolen property, resisting—case is airtight.

JESUS: Okay, so you figure the resisting's an add-on, we're talking about a two-bit misdemeanor's hardly worth your time to do the typing. Maybe we can do some business here.

FURILLO: Let's hear it, Jesus.

JESUS: I tell you goin' in, what I'm looking for, you get this, my guys walk.

FURILLO: If it stands up . . .

JESUS: It stands up, it walks, it jogs, hey, Frankie, who are you dealin' with here?

FURILLO (*a beat*): What've you got?

JESUS: Somebody's taking down delivery trucks in the neighborhood, you heard about it? Terrible thing.

FURILLO: You have a name?

JESUS: I got the next truck they're gonna hit is what I got.

FURILLO: From where?

JESUS: All due respect, I gotta protect my sources.

FURILLO (*a beat, weary*): If it gives us a bust, we'll work it out. I'll talk to the DA's office. (*Picks up a pad and pencil.*)

JESUS (*a smile*): Reasonable men can always find a way, eh Frankie? (*Furillo stays deadpan.*) Bucky's Meat Supply, runs a delivery every afternoon. Sounds like today's the day.

FURILLO (*writing it down*): Where?

JESUS: All I got. You're gonna have to take it from there. (*He opens the door, slyly.*) So, they can go now?

FURILLO: After the bust, Jesus. (*Goes to the door, calls into the squad room.*) Mick, Ray, could you come in.

JESUS (*at the door*): Hey, sorry to hear about your loss, the sergeant, that's too bad.

FURILLO (*unprepared for that*): Thank you.

JESUS (*as Belker and Calletano arrive, quietly*): Guy had some stuff. (*Jesus tips his hat to the others and exits—we stay with him, he snaps his finger, the bodyguard joins him—stay with Jesus until we pick up and stay with—*)

34. Coffey (*At the Coffee bar, stirring up two cups. Bates approaches, solicitous. He's preoccupied, uptight.*)

BATES: Joe.

COFFEY: Luce.

BATES: How's Sandy?

COFFEY (*reluctant at first to open up*): Goin' over the books . . .

BATES: How're you doing?

COFFEY: Just tryin' to help. (*Beat; in increasing intensity.*) I don't know what I'm supposed to do. I mean, I wasn't there for her, right? And in my mind all I can see is this animal on top of her. And I want to pull him off. And I want to kill him. (*Deep breath; collecting himself.*) That's how I'm doing. (*Bates nods mute support. He moves off. Follow him to Sandy at—*)

35. A desk. (*He puts down a cup of coffee and sits behind her as LaRue moves in, puts down a mugbook and takes away the one she's been scanning. Beside her, Washington runs down a computer readout, checking against a list of W-4's they got from Harley. We can see that Coffey's manner with Sandy is increasingly distant and uncomfortable.*)

LARUE: Sandy, if you could start looking through these . . .

SANDY (*she's holding up, seems stronger*): Didn't know there were so many faces.

LARUE: Just take it one at a time.

(*A pause. Sandy starts paging through, pauses a second, takes a deep breath, a wave of fear passing through her—*)

COFFEY: You okay?

SANDY (*getting herself back*): Yeah, I'm fine, Joe. How are you? (*She looks at him with such emotional nakedness it frightens him.*)

COFFEY: Me? I'm okay. Why shouldn't I be?

SANDY (*half a beat; a little pissed*): No reason.

(*LaRue has caught this exchange, as Sandy goes back to the mugbook, opens it.*)

COFFEY (*realizing his gaffe*): I mean I'm upset.

SANDY (*nodding; not looking at him*): Good, Joe.

(*Now Coffey's pissed; he eats it. LaRue fills the silence.*)

LARUE: Can I get you some coffee or something, Sandy?

SANDY: No, thanks. Maybe later.

36. Angle. (*Washington examining a list, just out of Sandy's hearing.*)

WASHINGTON: J.D.? (*Waves him over; quietly.*) Got a match here.

LARUE: What is it?

WASHINGTON: W-4 on a Jorge Villa, stopped working at the shop thirteen months ago . . .

(*LaRue immediately takes the mugbook, lifts Villa's picture, begins putting together a small array of photos, under—*)

LARUE (*low*): What are his priors?

WASHINGTON (*from his other list*): Two b&e's, two suspicions on rape/robbery, one dismissed, other's pending.

LARUE: He should be in lock-up.

WASHINGTON (*off still another list*): Should be is right. He was released from Michigan Avenue last night, o.r.

(*They look at each other. LaRue gets the array in order, moves back to Sandy—*)

LARUE: Anyone in this bunch look familiar?

(*Sandy examines the array a few seconds, sees Jorge's picture, and it hits her like a kick in the gut; she gasps.*)

LARUE (*a beat; carefully*): That him?

(*She nods, terrorized again, tears in her eyes, unable to speak—*)

WASHINGTON (*writing it down, tearing off a sheet of paper*): Got an address.

LARUE: Let's take him.

WASHINGTON (*moving off*): I'll get back-ups.

(*LaRue gives another look at Sandy, then at Coffey, seemingly paralyzed behind her, unable to respond—LaRue hands her his handkerchief—*)

LARUE (*quietly*): If we find him, Sandy, we'll need you to ID him in a line-up. He won't be able to see you; can you do that?

SANDY: Yeah, sure.

(*LaRue pats her on the shoulder, gives a look at Coffey, starts out—Sandy uses the handkerchief, Coffey stands behind her, helplessly—*)

SANDY (*rising*): I think I wanna go to the Rape Crisis Center now, Joe. They gave me a name at the hospital.

COFFEY: Okay. I . . . you need a ride?

SANDY: Yeah.

COFFEY: Okay.

SANDY (*a beat*): Joe . . . what's wrong?

COFFEY: What do you mean?

SANDY (*a sigh*): Never mind. (*They start out; moving with them we pick up and stay with—*)

37. (*Davenport, moving down the corridor, past Leo, who's teary-eyed, blowing his nose—*)

DAVENPORT (*with a hand on his arm*): Leo, I'm so sorry. (*Leo can only nod through his tears—Davenport continues on towards—*)

38. Interior. Interrogation room. (*She enters to find the john, Kelvin James, sitting at a table. Davenport sits, opens his file.*)

DAVENPORT: Mr. James. I'm Ms. Davenport, I'll be your attorney.

JAMES (*sizing her up*): No complaints here.

DAVENPORT (*letting that pass; reading*): You were arrested two days ago on a shop-lifting charge, held for two days at the Michigan Avenue complex and released last night by order of Judge Spears.

JAMES: Correcto.

DAVENPORT (*looks at him*): And by eleven this morning you accumulated a solicitation charge, possession of stolen credit cards, possession of narcotics.

JAMES: That's the way of the world, ain't it? Guy like me, good luck's like a rumor—

(*The door opens quickly—Furillo enters brusquely with two uniforms.*)

DAVENPORT (*feeling intruded on*): Excuse me.

FURILLO: No, excuse me. I'd like to speak to you in my office. Now.

Cut to:

39. Interior. Furillo's office (*as they enter, both with an attitude—*)

DAVENPORT: Let's hear it.

FURILLO: Your client gave Bates a credit card, belonged to a Mrs. Virginia Kimball, Clearwater, Florida—she was found dead in the trunk of her car four days ago outside of Louisville.

DAVENPORT: That doesn't—

FURILLO: And a routine check on his prints gave us the name of Theotis Nickerson; escaped from Florida State Penitentiary a week ago, doing life for a double murder in a gas station hold-up—that's your client, one of the people Judge Spears released as a low-risk criminal—

DAVENPORT (*holding ground*): Then the screw-up was in Florida, Frank.

FURILLO: You don't let two hundred and forty seven criminals walk and expect to—

DAVENPORT: Why didn't this show up five days ago on the first bust?

FURILLO: My best guess is laziness—

DAVENPORT (*pissed off*): So what's the moral of the story, Frank; throw shoplifters into the hole or don't let convicted murderers escape— (*Into which comes, with a perfunctory knock, Chief Daniels, all pious gravity—*)

DANIELS: Frank, Joyce, I just got the news about Phil Esterhaus, I came as fast as I could. (*Furillo and Davenport look at each other, the pain of the loss surging up from under the anger—they both feel a little ashamed—*) (*Taking both of Frank's hands in his.*) I'm so sorry.

FURILLO: Thank you.

DANIELS: God rest him. He lived a full life. (*Davenport starts out—*) Ray tells me you picked up a murderer Judge Spears decided to exercise some selective mercy with. (*Davenport stops at the door.*)

FURILLO: Appear to have been some bureaucratic foul-ups—

DAVENPORT (*a little hot*): Not enough that you couldn't make some political hay— better they stack 'em six feet in the Tombs, like manhole covers. (*She exits.*)

DANIELS: Obviously, she's upset . . . (*sequeing to his original intention*) And I imagine the shock of Phil's passing will be with all of us for some time. But Frank, Phil would've been the first to recognize the need for an orderly transition here. (*Taking out a list.*) Now I've selected three of the department's toughest nuts, Frank, all with a lotta years behind the desk; you take your pick I'll have him at your podium tomorrow morning.

(*Furillo takes the list, stares at it in a kind of numb disbelief—*)

FURILLO: I guess I hadn't thought this far ahead just yet—

DANIELS: He was your friend, Frank, that's understandable.

FURILLO (*finding his way with this*): It had occurred to me bringing someone in from outside could be . . . somewhat disruptive.

DANIELS: You'd like to keep it in the family, then.

FURILLO: I think at least initially.

DANIELS (*taking the list back*): Alright, Frank, you tell me.

FURILLO (*half a beat*): Lucy Bates passed the exam, she was number two in line for promotion when the freeze went into effect.

DANIELS (*surprised*): You want to take her straight from patrol to turn-out responsibilities?

FURILLO: I think I'd like to give her a shot.

DANIELS: I must admit I'm skeptical, Frank, what with more qualified bodies available—

FURILLO: It'd be temporary, to start. Nobody's worked harder, nobody deserves it more.

DANIELS (*sighs*): It's your precinct. You want to put a woman in that job I guess there's nothing I can say, is there? Freeze'll come off this afternoon. (*Another gear shift.*) Funeral arrangements in place?

FURILLO: I guess I'm taking care of that.

DANIELS: Let me know. Dear Phil. Dreadful loss. Dreadful. (*Furillo nods. Daniels exits.*)

40. Interior. Coffee bar (*where Bates, alone, is pouring a cup. Coming out of Furillo's office, Daniels sees her, makes a bee-line to her—*)

DANIELS (*quietly, a pat on the back*): Just want you to know, Sergeant—you've got my every confidence.

(*And he's gone—Bates is left with a slow realization followed immediately by a sinking feeling that displaces the joy the news ordinarily would've generated—*)
Cut to:

41. Interior. Tenement hallway—day. (*LaRue and Washington facing a door open only to a latch—*)

WASHINGTON: Have to open it wider than that, ma'am. (*Whereupon it swings open to a woman in her forties, Latin, impoverished.*) We're looking to talk to your son, ma'am. Jorge Villa.

MRS. VILLA (*in Spanish*): I haven't seen him. He's locked up in the jail.

42. Point of view—through the door—a fully open window.
LARUE: Neal!

43. (*LaRue and Washington race through the apartment.*)
WASHINGTON: Kinda chilly for wide-open windows, Señora.

44. Exterior. Fire escape. (*Washington and LaRue clambering out, peering down—*)

45. Point of view. (*A Latin male in his twenties, Jorge Villa, descends break-neck towards the alley.*)

WASHINGTON'S VOICE (*to handi-talkie*): Back-ups, the alley. Suspect in the alley.

46. (*Villa drops to the alley-floor, runs.*)

47. (*LaRue and Washington clatter down the cast-iron steps.*)

48. (*A unit bursts into the alley; Perez and Kolzicki pile out.*)

49. (*Villa turns, trapped.*)

50. (*Washington drops to the ground.*)

51. (*Perez, weapon drawn, held high, moves on the retreating, confused Villa.*)

PEREZ: Hold it right there! (*Perez is breathing a little hard, but he's got it. LaRue and Washington take him, put on the cuffs.*)

WASHINGTON: Attaboy, Jorge, you're under arrest— (*Reads rights.*)

LARUE: Would you like a donut? (*Off Jorge's self-incriminating reaction—Washington reads rights under—*)

Fade to black.

ACT THREE

Fade in.

52. Exterior. Loading zone—refrigerator truck—day. (*The meat supply house named by Jesus—Bucky's. There's a couple of trucks being loaded at the ramp, others are parked here and there waiting their turn. Belker is kicking the tires of a refrigerator truck, giving it a professional once over. He wears a tanker's jacket that reads BUCKY'S MEAT SUPPLY. Parked close by is an unmarked police sedan, Hill and Renko, in plainclothes, leaning against it. They're all in a grand funk over Esterhaus; Renko, however, has felt the need to vocalize it in his own fashion.*)

RENKO: It's like a riddle in the cosmic tapestry, Bobby. That man meant as much to me as my own daddy. I wish I could tell him that. I wish I'd told him. (*Belker moves past them with an audible and directed snort of disdain. Renko glares at him.*) Now what prompted that comment from the animal world?

BELKER: People should treat people good when they're alive instead of tryin' to make up for it after they're dead.

RENKO (*boiling; swelling up*): You sayin' I am bein' less than sincere in my affections for that man?

BELKER: *Esterhaus*—his name was *Esterhaus!* And you caused him aggravation! Wisin' off in roll, duckin' assignments!

RENKO: And I suppose you never broke his nose in intramural volleyball—

BELKER: That was an accident!   HILL: Knock it off, you two!

RENKO: An exceptional police offi-   BELKER: He was my sergeant—he was
cer—That's what he called me!   my friend!

HILL (*getting between them*): I said knock it off! What is this—mom likes me best? Have some respect.

(*Bucky Nolan picks that moment to walk up to the truck with his clipboard. He's the owner and manager of Bucky's Meat Supply, a big good-natured black who's gotten where he is by working hard and taking no nonsense. He's wearing a butcher's smock and a hardhat.*)

BUCKY: What's goin' on here?

HILL: Nothin', Mr. Nolan. We're ready to roll when you are.

BUCKY (*indicates truck; eyes them*): Let's get it loaded. Which one of you's drivin'?

BELKER: Me.

(*Bucky looks him over. Isn't impressed in the slightest.*)

BUCKY: Lemme see your Class 2 license.

BELKER: You're looking at it. (*Flashes badge.*)

(*Bucky is even less impressed. He makes a face and taps the side of the truck.*)

BUCKY: And whaddaya think's goin' in the back of this thing, Mr. Police Badge?

BELKER (*not getting him*): Meat . . .

BUCKY: Uh-uh. Twelve-thousand of my hard-earned dollars is what. Now you can flash that badge at a pork roast and it's still gonna spoil if it gets above fifty-two degrees longer'n thirty minutes. You can flash it at a side of beef and it's still gonna bruise to the tune of 10¢ less a pound if it goes swinging around in the back of the truck. So you can just show me some proof you know somethin' about drivin' a refrigerator unit or I'll just take my chances with the hijackers.

RENKO (*snide*): Mr. Nolan, my partner and I can personally vouch for this man's ability to handle raw meat.

(*A strangled growl from Belker. He crushes his cigar. Climbs into the truck cab.*)

BELKER: What ramp?

BUCKY: B.

(*Belker starts up the truck. Burns rubber along the length of the loading zone and swings the truck so its tail end is pointed at the ramp like a battering ram. Throws it into reverse and burns rubber between two tightly parked trucks, stomping on the brake just in time to bring the tailgate flush with the ramp. It's a dandy piece of truckmanship. Bucky and the others stand there with their mouths open. Belker looks at them. Bucky snaps back to life. Shouts—*)

BUCKY: Okay, let's get this sucker loaded!

Cut to:

53. Interior. Furillo's office—day. (*Furillo is on the phone. Papers and documents are stacked on his desktop. He looks drained and out of his element. ADA Bernstein enters the office and they exchange nods over—*)

FURILLO (*into phone*): I understand the urgency, but my feeling is that this decision could be better made by a professional . . . I see . . . Yes . . . (*looks at watch*). Then I'll get back to you before five. Yes . . . Thanks. (*As he hangs up, he spots Bernstein in the squad room. Furillo raps on the glass and motions him into the office.*) What do you know about executing an estate?

BERNSTEIN: Enough to call Legal Referral for the name of a qualified attorney.

FURILLO: How about giving away eyes?

BERNSTEIN: Eyes?

FURILLO: Phil signed a donor's card before he died—organ transplants. (*Nods at phone.*) They've given me a list, forty people need eyes. Little girl in Tulsa, a father of five in Greenbay . . . Law says as executor I make the choice.

BERNSTEIN: Amazing, isn't it? (*Off Furillo's look.*) Part of a man can go on living like that.

(*Furillo hadn't thought of it that way. Just then, they're interrupted by Goldblume who gives Bernstein a nod.*)

GOLDBLUME: Frank, Sandy Valpariso's on her way back from the rape treatment center. We can have a line-up ready by the time she gets here.

FURILLO: Okay, put it together.

GOLDBLUME (*indicates documents*): How's it going?

FURILLO: Great. I still haven't settled with the fact he's gone and here I am parceling him out like a door prize.

BERNSTEIN (*apprehensive; funny smile*): Is it true what I heard about him?

FURILLO (*frowning*): What was that?

BERNSTEIN: I don't mean to sound cold, but I had some business at the morgue this morning, I heard a rumor that he wasn't dancing alone when the big one hit.

FURILLO (*sharply*): Irwin, I don't think we should speculate about that.

(*Bernstein shrugs and exits. Furillo and Goldblume exchange a look, off which—*)

Cut to:

54. Interior. Locker room—on Leo. (*The room is empty except for Leo. He sits on a bench in the near-darkness, shoulders hunched, face buried in his hands. He is sobbing pitifully. Just then, Calletano appears at the far end of the lockers. He sees Leo and his heart goes out to him. Leo becomes aware of his presence and tries to cover up red eyes and a runny nose. Calletano sits down beside him and puts a fatherly arm around him.*)

CALLETANO: I understand, Leo . . . We all loved him. But there's no need to hide your grief. Rather we must share it, let it strengthen us.

LEO: It isn't that.

CALLETANO (*puzzled*): No? What then?

LEO: Oh God! (*Leo sinks back into shuddering sobs.*)

CALLETANO: Leo, what is it? Please, tell me!

LEO (*reluctant*): I followed her last night . . .

CALLETANO: Who?

LEO (*oblivious*): She said she was going to aerobics class—but she hasn't been there in weeks. I know, I called. I followed her to the Computer Software Place on Ethel and Hollondorf. That's where she met him.

CALLETANO: Who met who?

LEO: My wife met Roger. Six feet. Blond hair. Sideburns. Goyim computer programmer. They're having an affair.

CALLETANO: Leo, you must confront her with this.

LEO: I did. On the spot. She got mad, she said he was the best thing that's happened to her in years. She isn't gonna give him up. (*Buries face.*) I wanted to call her names . . . I can't. I love her too much. (*Leo starts sobbing again. Calletano tries to comfort him but is at a loss for words. That's when Hunter appears. Seeing Leo in such grief, he approaches and sits opposite Calletano. It's his turn to put an arm around Leo.*)

HUNTER: I knew you'd take it hardest of all, old friend. When a warrior falls, there is no anguish more profound than that of his shield bearer.

LEO (*burning look*): It's not that! (*Hunter moves back in surprise. Calletano tries to smooth it over.*)

CALLETANO: Leo has a personal problem, Howard.

HUNTER: Nothing wrong with Mrs. Snitz, I hope.

LEO: Oh God! (*Leo takes the plunge into despair again. Goldblume attracted by the noise, joins the crowd at the bench. Puts a hand on Leo's shoulder.*)

GOLDBLUME (*sympathetically*): Leo . . .

LEO (*leaping up; a shriek*): The Sarge is dead—I'm sorry about that! He was a wonderful man! But my wife is having an affair, okay!? Satisfied!? (*With that, Leo bolts from the room leaving behind some bewildered people.*)

Cut to:

55. Interior. Line-up—day. (*Furillo, LaRue, Washington, Coffey and Sandy are present. Six men are filing in behind the glass. Sandy watches their profiles apprehensively—the day's events are beginning to take a toll on her. Washington is conducting the line-up.*)

WASHINGTON: Keep moving, all the way to your marks and face forward.

(*As they turn to face forward, Sandy recognizes the rapist and lets out a small gasp, then quickly composes herself.*)

SANDY: That's him, number two . . . second from the left.

FURILLO: You're positive?

SANDY (*her voice quivering*): Believe me, I'm not gonna forget his face any time soon. (*She is embarrassed by her sudden lack of control over her emotions; she dabs at her eyes, trying to keep from crying. Coffey silently offers a handkerchief, which she takes. Furillo nods to Washington.*)

FURILLO: Thank you, Miss Valpariso. We're done.	WASHINGTON (*to line-up*): That's it. Turn to your right, move down the steps to the door.

(*The men file out; Furillo and Washington exit. LaRue stops to give Sandy a supportive pat on the shoulder.*)

LARUE: You all right?

SANDY (re *her emotional state*): I'm sorry. It's been a long day.

LARUE: Are you kiddin'? You've been great.

SANDY: What next?

LARUE: Way things are backed up, I doubt they'll arraign before tomorrow morning. We'll call and let you know.

SANDY (*She nods.*): Thanks. Thanks a lot.

(*LaRue exits, leaving Sandy and Coffey alone. Coffey has been sitting quietly through all of this. He stands.*)

COFFEY: Come on, let's find you a ride home.

SANDY: Not yet. Just sit with me for a few minutes, okay?

COFFEY (*noncommittal*): In here?

SANDY: Why not? Are you afraid to be alone with me?

COFFEY: No, of course not.

(*Sandy goes over and closes the door. Coffey, despite his claims to the contrary, is not a bit comfortable.*)

SANDY: Joe, what's goin' on with you?

COFFEY: Nothin'. What are you talkin' about?

SANDY: All day long you've been so nice—the perfect gentleman, the perfect cop—but I feel like you're a million miles away from me.

COFFEY: I've been with you every minute!

SANDY: All the way to the rape center and back, you barely said a word to me. And you haven't said anything to me today that hasn't been straight from a manual.

COFFEY: I'm used to dealin' with it a certain way. It's my job.

SANDY: We've been sleeping together for two weeks! I'm more than just your job. (*Beat.*) I'm trying to work this out for myself, but I need my lover's help right now, not another cop.

COFFEY: I'm sorry.

SANDY: You don't *act* like you're sorry. You haven't touched me all day long.

COFFEY: I didn't know if you'd want that.

SANDY (*thinking she's breaking through*): That's exactly what I want. I want you to hold me, I want to feel like everything is going to be okay.

(*Coffey thinks about it for a beat. Doesn't make any physical response.*)

COFFEY: I've just got some things I've gotta work out.

(*Sandy becomes cooler after realizing that he refuses to touch her.*)

SANDY: What things?

COFFEY: I gotta understand it in my mind, what happened to you.

SANDY (*angry*): What do you have to understand? The guy grabbed me, pointed a knife at me, made me take off my clothes and lie down on a cold, dirty floor and—

COFFEY (*cutting her off*): Sandy, don't.

SANDY: What, it's too unpleasant for you to *hear*? I *lived through it,* you jerk!

COFFEY: I just need a little time. I have to make myself understand why it happened.

SANDY: You mean why I didn't do anything to prevent it?

COFFEY: I know you couldn't. It just needs to sink in.

SANDY: What do you think I could have done? What would *you* do, with some drugged-up crazy pointing a knife at your throat? Put up a fight?

COFFEY: No—

SANDY: What, then? Try to talk him out of it?

COFFEY: I don't know. Maybe.

SANDY: Is that it? You think I didn't try hard enough?

COFFEY (*angry*): Sandy, would you stop it! You're forcin' me to say stuff that I don't want to say—

SANDY: I'm forcing you to tell the truth! You think I could have gotten out of it! You think if it was that awful, why didn't I put up more of a fight! (*Beat.*) Come on, Joe, at least have the guts to admit it!

COFFEY (*provoked*): Okay, maybe that *is* what I think. I mean, you're always hearin' about women who got out of it by sayin' they were pregnant or had VD or somethin'. Maybe I wonder why you didn't try that!

(*Sandy stares at him for a moment; she is livid.*)

SANDY: If he'd slashed my throat or bashed my head in a little, would that make you feel better? Would that help you understand?

COFFEY (*anguished*): No! I just . . . I don't know. I don't know what I think!

SANDY (*quietly furious*): Well, why don't you just sit here for a few years and see what you can figure out.

(*She wheels and is out of the door, slamming it behind her, leaving Coffey alone in the room. He sinks into a chair and pounds his fist on the table—there are tears in his eyes.*)

56. Interior. Refrigerator truck—moving—day. (*Belker is at the wheel. He checks a schedule of deliveries on a clipboard, then looks in his sideview mirror.*)

57. Tight on mirror. (*We see Hill and Renko's unmarked sedan following about four car-lengths behind.*)

58. Interior. Sedan—moving. (*Hill is driving. Renko is going over the schedule, figuring, frowning.*)

RENKO: If he don't move that thing a little faster, we're gonna be seven minutes behind schedule next stop.

HILL: Lighten up, will you? If they're lookin' for us, they'll find us. (*Hill sees something on the truck up ahead.*)

59. His point-of-view—rear of truck. (*The latch on the back door is swinging loose.*)

60. Back to Hill.

HILL: You wanna call him up, tell him the latch on the back door's come loose.

(*Renko picks up the handi-talkie with a kind of mischievous glee and transmits—*)

RENKO: Farmer Brown, this is Meat Loaf. Your barn door's in danger of flyin' open, pal. Careful you don't let the cow get out. (*Renko snickers. Hill gives him a critical look. Belker's reply comes in loud and clear.*)

BELKER'S VOICE: You watch your mouth, Renko, or you're gonna be the fattest side of beef hanging in this truck.

(*Renko is about to retort when the radio interrupts:*)

RADIO: All units in the area of 315 S. Polk Avenue, robbery in progress, shots fired, officer needs assistance.

RENKO: Let's go. (*Hill has already begun a U-turn.*)

61. Interior. Refrigerator truck. (*Belker sees Hill slam the flasher on the roof of the sedan and rocket away. Grabs his handi-talkie.*)

BELKER: Meat Loaf where the hell you goin'?

RENKO'S VOICE: Farmer Brown, we got ourselves a robbery in progress—we're takin' it!

BELKER: No, you're not—call it in! You ain't leavin' my rear end exposed! (*No reply.*) You hear me! Get back here! (*Belker is so furious he forgets what he's doing. Sticks his head out the window to see where the sedan is. What happens next is totally his fault—*)

62. Exterior. City street. (*The refrigerator truck slams hard into the rear of a van stopped at a light. Smoke, broken glass, the rear door of the truck pops open and a ham rolls out.*)

63. Exterior. Truck cab—on Belker. (*Stunned. Trying to figure out what happened. The driver of the van, a towering moose of a blue-collar worker, jumps out of his damaged vehicle with mayhem on his mind. Goes to the truck cab—*)

VAN DRIVER: You hit my van, you stupid jerk! You got your head in your shorts or something?

BELKER: I see it. I'm sorry. (*Belker doesn't sound all that convincing.*)

64. Intercut with rear of truck. (*A pedestrian has seen the ham in the street. He picks it up, puts it under his coat and walks away. Two other bystanders have watched him do it. They go up to the truck's open door to see what's inside. All this over—*)

VAN DRIVER: You're sorry! Get out of that truck, you sawed-off little wimp. I'll make you sorry!

BELKER (*flies out of the truck*): Who you callin' sawed-off, hairbag!

VAN DRIVER: You, you pint-sized dwarf numbnut! No wonder you had an accident!

BELKER (*rips out badge*): Police, mudbrain!

(*The two bystanders, meanwhile, have walked away with massive sides of beef. The back of the truck is then besieged by a swarm of refugees from the neighboring tenements.*)

VAN DRIVER (*rearing up to Belker*): Good! 'Cause I'm suing you, I'm suing the Department and I'm suing the City!

BELKER: Don't crowd me—I'm tellin' you not to crowd me!

(*The van driver gives Belker a shove that sends him into the side of the truck. Belker springs back like a miniature cyclone, taking the van driver down. They roll in the street, punching, kicking, screaming—a badger attacking an elephant. It's then that Belker catches sight of the looting that's going on in back of the truck.*)

BELKER: Hey—stop that! Put it back! You're all under arrest!

(*But no one pays him the slightest attention. For one thing, he's too busy fighting for his life to do anything. Belker throws himself into the battle with psychotic vigor, deciding the match with a well-placed, scream-inducing bite to the van driver's thigh.*)

VAN DRIVER: Okay—I give, I give!

(*Belker slaps cuffs on him and then jumps to the back of the truck. Those with meat in their arms take off running.*)

BELKER: Get back here! Stop!

(*Belker's wasting his breath. And then he hears the sound of someone rummaging inside the truck. In a rage, he pulls his piece. Levels it at the door . . . just as a small Latino child with a chicken in either hand comes stumbling out. The child's eyes go wide as he sees the gun. Belker nearly freaks. Almost throws the gun to the pavement. The child is frozen with fright, looking at Belker with horrified eyes.*)

BELKER: Go on—get out of here!

(*The child, still holding the chickens, runs away. Camera holds on Belker, shaking, trying to get himself under control as we—*)

Fade out.

ACT FOUR

Fade in. 65.

Interior Peyser's sedan—moving. (*Peyser is tired and cold. He speaks into a handi-talkie:*)

PEYSER: I'm taking a last pass down Avenue C. I haven't seen one hooker.

(*Bates responds through the handi-talkie:*)

BATES' VOICE (*surprised*): You sure you're on Avenue C?

PEYSER: Roger. And there ain't nothin' on this road but potholes.

BATES' VOICE (*comes across in impatient elucidation*): Hard to believe. Tell me what you're seein'.

(*Peyser is trying his best. Picks up the handi-talkie in his lap.*)

PEYSER: Roger. (*Looking.*) Well, there's two winos working a trashcan fire . . . and I just passed a lady standing by a station wagon with the hood up. She waved at me . . .

BATES' VOICE: Archie, that's an old gimmick to fool patrol cars. They put up a citizen's car hood and pretend it's theirs. Turn around and check it out, okay?

(*Peyser swings his sedan around with—*)

PEYSER (*into handi-talkie*): Roger. Will do.

BATES' VOICE: We're headed home, buddy. You're on your own.

66. Exterior. City Street. (*As Peyser brakes by the side of the stranded station wagon. Our view of it is restricted. Peyser exits and steps around his vehicle toward the woman, who we descry at the last instant as Fay Furillo, flushed and grateful.*)

FAY: Thank God. The answer to a woman's prayers. (*Grabbing Peyser by the hand.*) How would you like to peek under my hood?

(*Peyser, in his enthusiasm, thinks he's being propositioned.*)

PEYSER: And then what, lady?

FAY: If you could give me a jump . . . (*indicates the flat wagon trunk*) I've got some chords and clamps back there. They hook right on.

PEYSER (*A beat as he cagily sizes her up.*): Sounds good. So how much is this sort of thing worth to you?

FAY (*Her turn to misunderstand. She flares—*): How much? You're a real sport. All right—I'll do anything to get out of the cold. Ten dollars.

PEYSER (*flashes his badge*): Police, you're under arrest—unlawful solicitation! Turn around and put your hands behind your back.

(*It's all happened too fast for Fay. She doesn't resist as he turns her around and whips out the cuffs.*)

FAY: Solicitation? What do you mean, solicitation? My battery's dead!

PEYSER: Don't make it any worse on yourself, ma'am. You stated an act and the amount. Now you have the right to remain silent. Anything you say can and will be used against you . . .

FAY (*over his Miranda*): I don't believe this! This is crazy! You can't actually believe for one second that I was asking you to . . . that I wanted to . . . (*She starts to giggle. It catches Peyser completely off guard.*)

PEYSER: What's the matter? What's so funny?

FAY: How old are you?

PEYSER: What?

FAY: Are you sure you're a police officer and not a safety patrol?

PEYSER (*getting miffed*): In the car, lady. Let's go.

FAY: Where? Hill Street?

PEYSER: Yeah.

FAY: Good. I need a ride.

(*He opens the sedan door. She climbs in. Can't suppress another giggle.*)

FAY (*directing*): Make a left up on Euclid. It's faster this time of day.
Cut to:

67. Interior. Front desk—day. (*On the cut, pick up a taciturn Bates, along with Pilsky and Perez, entering the doors and passing the desk, where the fallout from Belker's meaty misadventure is piling up under Leo's snuffly nose. Returned or impounded, a couple armloads of steaks and chops. Adding to which evidence now, a half dozen pork chops are slapped onto the desk by a uniform, whose other hand grasps a large, cuffed, carnivorous-looking perp.*)

UNIFORM: Doing a brisk sidewalk business at Dekker and 108, Leo. He tried to dump this stuff when I found him.

PERP (*shrugs; by way of lame explanation*): I'm a vegetariast.

(*Include Belker lugging his bloodied van driver up to the desk—*)

BELKER: Move it, mudball.

(*And, close on Belker's heels, the distraught butcher, Bucky Nolan, who eye-balls the stash on the desk.*)

BUCKY: This is all you retrieved? This is all? (*At a weary Belker.*) You drove me right into the slaughterhouse, you idiot. D'you hear? Seventy-five cases of New York strippers. Hundred cases o'rib-eyes. Hundred whole filets. Seventy pounds a case. Six bucks a pound. JUST WHOLESALE! You put me up on a hook, y'know that?

(*Under which rant, Jesus Martinez and bodyguard have entered. Follow to—*)

68. Interior. Furillo's office—day—Furillo and ADA Bernstein. (*A perfunctory knock and, without waiting, Martinez struts in. The guard waits outside.*)

JESUS: Yo, Frankie.

FURILLO: Jesus . . .

JESUS: Anybody call for a pickup? (*Holds up fingers.*) Dos Diablos. (*Off silence and Bernstein's frown, Jesus senses something queering his deal. He lashes out—*) Hey, your clown can't keep his meat on the road, 's not my problem.

FURILLO: Give us a minute, Jesus.

JESUS: I paid for the goods, Frankie—you deliver or your word's garbage on the street.

(*Off Furillo's silence, Jesus stares daggers at him a half beat, then saunters to the door tossing a look of contempt at Bernstein. He hovers outside, looking in through the glass.*)

BERNSTEIN: Frank . . .

FURILLO: Martinez and I had an agreement.

BERNSTEIN (*hot*): Based on information you never had a chance to verify! How'm I gonna sell that downtown?

FURILLO (*just as hot*): Irwin—it's a lousy T.V. set! What's the big deal?

BERNSTEIN (*throwing in the towel*): Okay, Frank, do what you want. The meat supplier's filed an eight-thousand-dollar claim, the driver of the van's bringing suit for abusive process and our hijackers are doing business as usual. Why not make the disaster complete?

FURILLO (*trying to calm things*): I'm sorry. (*Opens the door, motions and calls—*) Leo! (*Waves Martinez in.*) We keep our end of the bargain.

JESUS: Good decision, Frankie. (*To the stewing Bernstein.*) Gotta go by the rules, right?

(*Bernstein glowers, under which Leo has arrived.*)

FURILLO: Leo, release the two Diablos in Mr. Martinez' custody.

LEO: Right, Captain.

(*Smirking, Martinez exits along with his guard. Bernstein trails, notes Leo's puffy red eyes, turns back to Furillo.*)

BERNSTEIN: Be the executor of my will, too, okay Frank? (*Bernstein puts his arm around Leo's shoulder. As they move off—*) . . . I know how you must feel, Leo.

(*No sooner are they gone, than Bates is in the doorway.*)

FURILLO: Luce . . . you waiting to see me?

(*Bates solemnly enters Furillo's office and closes the door behind her.*)

FURILLO: What's up?

BATES: I'm not sure. While ago the Chief comes up to me, slaps me on the back and calls me "Sergeant." You know what he's talking about?

FURILLO: We had a discussion this morning about the desk sergeant vacancy, we agreed the best course would be to move someone up from inside. I recommended you.

BATES: Me? Take the Sarge's place? No way, Captain. I couldn't fill those shoes in a hundred years!

FURILLO: You shouldn't try. Just be your own person.

BATES (*still confused*): I don't know . . . I've been wanting it for so long. It's just the circumstances, it's all wrong.

FURILLO: Lucy, you've put a lot of hard work into making sergeant. It shouldn't be a punishment. Take some time and think it over. If you still feel uncomfortable, we'll try something else. Frankly, I think you're the best choice for the job.

BATES: Well . . . if you say so, Captain.

FURILLO: Keep it under wraps a couple of days, then we'll make an orderly transition.

BATES (*nods; starts for the door, then stops*): Is it appropriate to say "thanks"?

FURILLO (*nodding*): Congratulations, Sergeant Bates.

(*Bates nods, smiles tentatively and exits.*)

Cut to:

69. Interior. Booking area. (*Peyser enters the precinct and delivers his charge to the desk. Fay remains unnoticed by Leo,* who is immersed in paperwork over the Diablos release. But Jesus is standing by.*)

JESUS: Yo, mama, where'd you buy those fancy bracelets?

FAY (*kicking at his shin*): Keep away from me, guttersnipe.

JESUS (*through his laughter*): You got a prize there, officer, you know that?

PEYSER: What?

JESUS: You better get thick shoes. You standing in the dog's business.

(*Peyser looks at his shoes, convulsing Martinez.*)

PEYSER (*confused; flustered*): What?

JESUS: You got the Captain's ol' lady.

(*Just then, Leo wheels around and slaps down some release papers and a pen in front of Martinez.*)

LEO: Sign these. (*Leo's attention fixes on Fay. He reacts as if being hit by a cattle prod.*) Mrs. Furillo!

(*Peyser is horrified. He shrinks away from her.*)

PEYSER: Mrs. *Furillo?*

FAY: Fast Fay, Leo. The Strumpet of State Street. A fallen woman.

LEO: Get her out of those cuffs!

PEYSER (*scrambling; clumsy*): Aw, gee—I'm sorry—I didn't know. I'm an idiot, a moron . . .

(*Under which, in the background, we have become aware of a growing argument between a furious—*)

70. (*Belker nose to nose with Hill and Renko, heating up as well, in the middle of the squad room.*)

BELKER: You were supposed to be backin' me up—where the hell were you?

HILL: We had an all units—we radioed you—

BELKER: Somebody coulda got killed out there!

RENKO: Somebody wasn't lookin' where he was goin' is the way I hear it!

BELKER: You're around plenty with your fat mouth when I don't need you, Renko!

RENKO: Now, now—you think the sarge would approve of you talkin' like that?

(Off which, with a feral growl, Belker leaps on Renko and the two of them are into it; Hill and others immediately jump in to pull them apart, as—)

71. *(Furillo comes barrelling out of his office. He arrives just as Belker and Renko are separated.)*

FURILLO: No! *(His cold glare freezes Belker and Renko and everybody else in the squad room, including—)*

72. *(Fay, who reacts with stunned pain to—)*

FURILLO: Look, I'm not insensitive to the fact that Phil Esterhaus' death has hit all of us pretty hard . . .

73. *(Wider, as Furillo includes the entire squad room.)*

FURILLO: If you had respect for the man, honor his memory by being what he wás—a gentleman and a good cop.

(A moment more, to make sure the message has been heard, then he turns and moves off. Spotting Fay, having sunk into a chair, beginning to tear up in grief, Furillo veers over to her, hunkers down and takes her hand.)

FURILLO: I'm sorry, Fay. That was no way for you to find out.

FAY: Phil's dead? How? When?

FURILLO: At home. Early this morning. *(A beat.)*

FAY: He taught Frank, Jr. how to box . . . *(A beat, then,)* How did he die?

(Furillo and Goldblume exchange a glance, as we—)

Cut to:

74. Interior. Cop bar—night *(crowded with regulars, the atmosphere appropriately subdued, as, on the cut—)*

HILL: I hear he died in the saddle.

BELKER *(subdued in the company of Tataglia; nevertheless—)*: Hey, that's a lotta crap.

HILL *(the tiniest grin)*: Just sayin' what I heard, Mick.

LARUE: Anybody hear any rumors who's gonna replace him?

BATES: Hey, why don't we at least wait for the body to get cold, huh?

WASHINGTON: Scenario: Foster up in the Heights retired last month. Jaffe in South Ferry bit the biscuit coupla weeks ago—Mayor's office lifts the hiring freeze, you get your stripes, and just like that we got us a new Sarge.

BATES *(hot; defensive)*: Look, this is outa line—no one's said anything about anybody replacing the Sarge—so just drop it, okay?

RENKO *(semi-blitzed, raises his glass)*: I propose a toast. To the Sarge. We loved him, we're gonna miss him, God bless him.

(General agreement all around, with the exception of—)

LARUE: Tell you the truth—I respected him, but the guy wasn't exactly on my Christmas list.

BATES *(having overheard)*: Hey, J.D. Go kill yourself. *(And she pushes away from the bar, heading for the bathroom. As she exits—)*

LARUE *(philosophically)*: Lemme tell you somethin' about women, Neal. I'm all for equal rights . . . Sorta . . . But I think you gotta smack 'em when they talk to you that way.

(And we angle over to pick up—)

75. Belker and Tataglia.

TATAGLIA (*to a dour, quiet Belker*): When I was first up here . . . boy, he was such . . . you just got the feeling he *liked* you, you know? Deep down. Like he just liked people. Hey, guess he went out liking someone.

76. (*Include Renko, having listened in.*)

RENKO (*a lascivious grin*): Ba-bing, ba-bing, ba—(*He gasps, clutching at his chest.*)

BELKER: It didn't happen like that—I don't believe it.

RENKO: Why don't we call the Captain?

HILL: Great, wake him up. He'll love you for it.

RENKO: It's covered under your Freedom of Information Act, Robert—tender me a ten cent piece—(*And as he pulls a dime from Hill's collection of change on the bar—*)

Cut to:

77. Interior. Bedroom—night. (*Furillo and Davenport in bed, she doing homework and he poring over the bullshit of executorship. On the cut, the phone is ringing, and—*)

FURILLO (*grabbing it*): Furillo.

Intercut with:

78. Interior. Bar—night. (*Renko cupping his other ear against the noise.*)

RENKO: Captain Furillo, sir.

FURILLO: Who is this?

RENKO: Andy Renko, sir. How are you?

FURILLO: Fine.

RENKO: Hope we didn't wake you or the wife, sir, but a few of us're down here at Mulligan's, toastin' the Sarge. Me 'n Bobby Hill, Joe 'n Luce, Belker, J.D., Neal, Leo—now that poor guy's really tore up, sir—

FURILLO: What can I do for you, Andy?

RENKO: Well, in payin' our last respects and all, we got to talkin' about life and death, and how fleeting our moment in the sun is, and how all of us need to plant our flag on this earth, as it were, and we got to speculating about the Sarge's flag and all . . .

FURILLO (*amused with the drift*): You want to get to what this is about, Andy?

RENKO: Is it true the Sarge deceased himself whilst in the act?

FURILLO: Yes. It's true.

RENKO (*with a shit-eating grin*): Damn that's a good way to check out . . . Course, it couldn't've been no tea party for his paramour now, could it?

FURILLO: G'night, Andy.

RENKO: Yessir. Goodnight.

79. Stay with Furillo (*hanging up the phone, pinching the bridge of his nose in amusement.*)

DAVENPORT: Renko?

FURILLO (*nods*): Wanted to know was it true how Phil died.

DAVENPORT (*a chuckle*): A legend is born . . .

FURILLO: I'll miss him.

DAVENPORT: So will I.

FURILLO (*a beat*): You want to make love?

DAVENPORT (*a glint*): It could cost you your life.

FURILLO: I'll risk it.

(*And as he kisses her, and she kisses back, we:*)

Fade out.